A Political Map

(States drawn in proportion to the number of Electoral Votes)

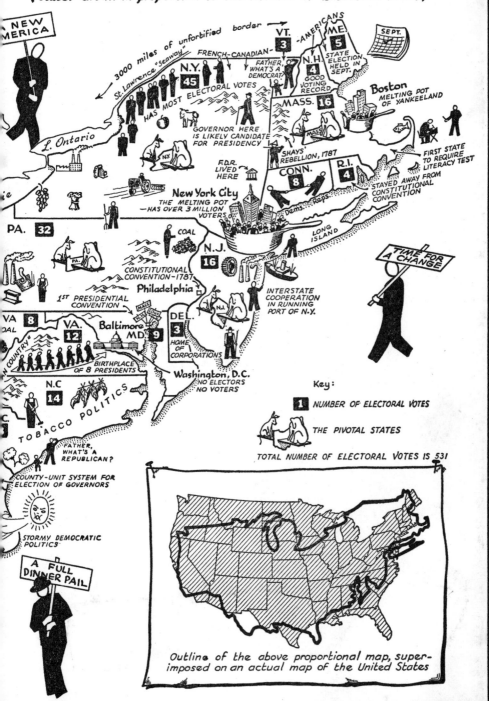

NEW AMERICA

3000 miles of unfortified border
St. Lawrence "seaway"
FRENCH-CANADIAN
AMERICANS

L. Ontario

VT. 3

ME. 5
STATE ELECTION HELD IN SEPT.

SEPT.

N.H. 4
GOOD VOTING RECORD

N.Y. 45
HAS MOST ELECTORAL VOTES
FATHER, WHAT'S A DEMOCRAT?

MASS. 16

Boston
MELTING POT OF YANKEELAND

GOVERNOR HERE IS LIKELY CANDIDATE FOR PRESIDENCY

FIRST STATE TO REQUIRE LITERACY TEST

F.D.R. LIVED HERE

SHAYS' REBELLION, 1787

CONN. 8

R.I. 4

STAYED AWAY FROM CONSTITUTIONAL CONVENTION

New York City
THE MELTING POT — HAS OVER 3 MILLION VOTERS

Dems. vs. Reps.

LONG ISLAND

PA. 32

COAL

N.J. 16

TIME FOR A CHANGE

CONSTITUTIONAL CONVENTION — 1787

Philadelphia

1ST PRESIDENTIAL CONVENTION

INTERSTATE COOPERATION IN RUNNING PORT OF N.Y.

VA. 8

VA. 12

Baltimore MD. 9

DEL. 3
HOME OF CORPORATIONS

BIRTHPLACE OF 8 PRESIDENTS

Washington, D.C.
NO ELECTORS NO VOTERS

N.C. 14

TOBACCO POLITICS

Key:

1 NUMBER OF ELECTORAL VOTES

THE PIVOTAL STATES

TOTAL NUMBER OF ELECTORAL VOTES IS 531

FATHER, WHAT'S A REPUBLICAN?

COUNTY-UNIT SYSTEM FOR ELECTION OF GOVERNORS

STORMY DEMOCRATIC POLITICS

A FULL DINNER PAIL

Outline of the above proportional map, super-imposed on an actual map of the United States

GOVERNMENT
by the
PEOPLE

The dynamics of American

national, state, and local government

GOVERNMENT

The dynamics of American
national, state, and local government

THIRD EDITION

Englewood Cliffs, N.J.   PRENTICE-HALL, INC.

by the PEOPLE

James MacGregor Burns

Williams College

Jack Walter Peltason

1957

University of Illinois

36089

To the memory of

John Calyer Ranney, 1915-1950

Teacher, scholar, friend

T HE MEANING AND CHALLENGE OF AMERICAN
government are in the spotlight. The meaning goes beyond the headlines,
and the challenge transcends the latest crises. In this third edition of *Government by the People,* the authors have tried to clarify, relate, and integrate
the facts. Information about American government and political institutions
has been organized to encourage conceptual and critical thinking. Training
for citizenship and cultivating a basic interest in liberal and general education both remain as related aims of this edition.

The chief method of trying to reach these goals continues to be an emphasis on problems. Because the problems as well as the facts of the American political system are extremely varied and wide-ranging, a special effort
has been made in this edition to organize these problems in terms of five
basic questions that the authors consider fundamental in understanding and
evaluating American democratic government. These five questions are listed
in the introductory title page to Part One, and the introductions to the remaining parts can serve as guides to places where aspects of these basic
problems are treated.

In other respects, too, this edition seeks to improve as well as to modernize the previous editions. Such improvement would be impossible without
the generous advice and criticism of users and readers of earlier editions.
For invaluable help on this edition we wish to thank Hollis W. Barber, University of Illinois (Navy Pier); Clarence A. Berdahl, University of Illinois;
Donald C. Blaisdell, City College of New York; Gordon B.
Cleveland, University of North
Carolina; Samuel J. Eldersveld, University of Michigan;
George Harvey, University of
Missouri; Robert F. Karsch,
University of Missouri; Mahmut N. Lacin, Sacramento
State; Frederic D. Ogden, University of Alabama; Thomas
Page, J. Austin Ranney, Robert E. Scott, and Clyde F.
Snider, all of University of
Ilinois; Gustave R. Serino,
Edward Sofen, and J. Ben
Stalvey, all of University of
Miami; and Pauline Yelderman, University of Houston.
We deeply appreciate the special generosity of Professor

Preface

Valentine Jobst III, of the University of Illinois, in subjecting the galleys to his careful and knowing scrutiny. Special thanks are also due to Maurine Lewis and the staff at Prentice-Hall for work "beyond the call of duty" in preparing the manuscript for publication. Any errors are the authors' responsibility.

Those who have contributed to either or both of the earlier editions ideas and criticisms meriting special appreciation are: Professors S. S. Aichele, Temple; Charles Aikin, University of California (Berkeley); Charles R. Cherington, Harvard; Thomas I. Cook, Johns Hopkins; U. G. Dubach, Lewis and Clark; Charles D. Goff, University of Wisconsin (Milwaukee Extension); Fred Greene, Williams; Cecilia Kenyon, Smith; Robert E. Lane, Yale; Donald R. Larson, University of Miami; Clay P. Malick, University of Colorado; Alpheus T. Mason, Princeton; James W. Prothro, Florida State University; Landon G. Rockwell, Hamilton; Victor G. Rosenblum, University of California (Berkeley); Wallace Sayre, City College; Carl O. Smith, Wayne University, and Joseph R. Starr, University of Maryland. Colleagues at the University of Illinois and at Williams have been most generous in their advice and assistance. Professors Charles M. Kneier, University of Illinois; Rollin B. Posey, Northwestern; and Paul N. Ylvisaker, Swarthmore, have given informed advice on the state and local chapters.

Harriet Simpson and Elizabeth Brown kindly read page proofs for a final check.

The names and dates of court decisions are given in the body of the text, but full citations of all cases mentioned can be found in the Index.

A final note: Both the National and the National-State-Local editions have been so organized that they can be adapted for use in several different types of courses. For those who want the minimum essentials of American national government, chapters 2-21, numbering about 540 pages, provide a self-contained core coverage for the standard shorter course. For courses covering the basic materials of state and local government also, Part Seven of the larger edition can be included. Governmental functions are described in Part Six. Part One and Epilogue cover materials directly related to the study of American government and permit more extended coverage, either by themselves or in conjunction with any of the excellent problem or reading texts now available. Further suggestions on use of the text are available in the teaching manual for this edition prepared by Walter S. Wilmot, Jr.

J.W.P.

J.M.B.

Contents

170,000,000 Americans

PART ONE ~ A PROBLEM GUIDE

This volume presents information about the American political system, but it also presents a number of problems and questions relating to that system. Five of the most important of these questions are as follows.

First, the problem of keeping popular government stable and orderly and yet alert and forward looking. How can we adhere to basic constitutional principles but still adapt our governmental system to changing needs and demands? How can we give our leaders, both civil and military, enough power to do their jobs well and still prevent the misuse of that power? How can we create enough teamwork in Washington, and between Washington and the state capitals?

Second, how does democratic government achieve a balance between liberty and order, between uniformity and diversity, between individual rights and collective needs? The problem has been well stated by the philosopher Bertrand Russell: "How can we combine that degree of individual initiative which is necessary for progress with the degree of social cohesion that is necessary for survival?"

PART ONE

1. Democratic
   Government
   in America

Third, how well are the American people organized for representation in a democratic manner? As an example of this problem of representation, how much influence should the majority have, as compared with the minority, on a given issue? How can we meet the demands of organized groups without sacrificing the welfare of the people as a whole?

Fourth, in what ways should our leaders be accountable to the people, and to what people? Or to turn that question around, how can the people best control their leaders? Should we make our leaders—President, senators, and so on—more responsible to the majority of the people, and if so, how can this be done?

Fifth and finally, the problem of answering the challenge of Communists and other antidemocrats. Is democracy in fact realistic, superior, effective, vital to individual dignity—a luxury which many can enjoy?

This book will return often to these and related questions as it seeks to picture the workings, the great achievements, and the serious problems of the American system of government.

The following chapters will refer back to these questions while presenting facts and concepts designed to help the student deal with them. The pages prefacing each part of the book list the chapters in that part, indicate the problems that receive special attention in those chapters, and refer by chapter or page number to the places where discussion of the important problems will be found.

THE PLACE IS ANYTOWN, U.S.A. THE TIME IS IM-
mediately before an election. The events are commonplace. Candidates for
office high and low have been for months viewing with alarm and pointing
with pride. The papers have been carrying big headlines:

SENATOR BLACK ACCUSES WHITE OF RED LINKS

WHITE SAYS NATION'S MAIN THREAT IS BLACKISM

WHITE TOOL OF LABOR BOSSES, BLACK CHARGES

BLACK AGENT OF WALL STREET, WHITE SAYS

DEFEAT WHITE TO SAVE AMERICAN WAY OF LIFE, URGES SENATOR BLACK

OPPOSITION DESPERATE, WILL GO TO ANY LENGTHS—WHITE SAYS

The day after the election, the count is White, 1,511,000; Black, 1,403,-
000. At eleven in the morning Black wires White: "YOU HAVE BEEN EN-
TRUSTED BY THE PEOPLE WITH GREAT RESPONSIBILITY STOP MY CONGRAT-
ULATIONS AND COMMISERATIONS TO YOU."

All is calm. The factories are open, people at work, stores crowded, stu-
dents in their classrooms. On Main Street there are no barricades, no angry mobs, no protesting parades. The people of a large country, after months of vigorous campaigning and bitter argument, have chosen the men who are to run their school systems, direct their cities, legislate in their state capitols, and guide the nation in Washington. These decisions will closely affect their lives and their fortunes. Yet they were made without bloodshed. When the votes were all counted, the Blackites shook their heads in disgust, but it never entered their minds not to accept the verdict of the ballot box. The "College Students

1 ★

Democratic

government

in America

for Black" did not meet to discuss whether to take up arms in defense of the American way of life—the very way of life which they had insisted before the election would be destroyed if White were elected. Nor did the Whites, now that they had power, proceed to round up their political enemies and throw them into jail.

Is this not a remarkable thing? So deeply ingrained are the habits of democracy that Americans sometimes forget that in relatively few places in the world could such an event take place. In other countries and in other times, brute force has often been the usual way of deciding who should run the country. Even where no open clash occurs, a small group of self-appointed bosses, by stifling criticism and manipulating propaganda, can make decisions without consulting anyone else. Such are the tactics of the totalitarians.

To Americans, the workings of democratic government are a common and rather dull matter. We tend to take democratic government for granted; even worse, we seem to consider it inevitable. We take pride in our ability to make it work, and rightly so, but we must remember that we inherited a going system. Its establishment was the work of others, not of ourselves. Our job is to keep it going. To keep it going we must understand it.

This introductory chapter will first discuss in a general way the nature of government: what is the study of government all about? It will then take up the essentials of *democratic* government and, next, some basic aspects of democratic government as it is affected by the *American context*. This chapter will then turn to the *threats* to democratic government, both internal and external. Finally, it will describe briefly how this book tackles the challenging job of describing the American governmental and political system.

THE STUFF OF GOVERNMENT

One freshman, after reading a book about government, laid down the volume, threw up his hands, and exclaimed, "It is just a big, buzzing confusion to me!" He was right. Government *is* immensely complex, especially in a large, industrialized society. Veteran reporters in Washington sometimes describe the nation's capital as a jungle, because they have a hard time following its highly competitive and sometimes subterranean politics. But let us see if we can find some kind of order and sense in all this complexity.

To begin with, it is well to remember that "government" is not just the national government, or city government, or British, or Russian government. Government is all around us, for in its broadest sense government is the *ordering* of human relations. Hence, it takes many forms. The most common government—in this broad use of the term—is the *family,* where rules are laid down and decisions are made by the head of the family. Other examples are student government, church government, fraternity government, the government of groups such as organizations of doctors.

Political scientists are especially concerned with *more formal government* operating amid the informal governments. They are concerned, that is, with *centralized organizations* that maintain *systems of order* over communities large and small.[1] Unlike the family or many other informal governments, these organizations usually have constitutions, legislatures, elections, bureaucracies. Such a formal government—that of the United States—is the subject of this book. But it must be kept in mind that a big formal government such as that of the United States cannot be understood as something sharply separated from the thousands of informal governments that cluster throughout our society, and with which formal government continually interacts.

THE GIRLS   By Franklin Folger

"When you say that it's all about government, do you mean it doesn't make sense?"

So much for government in general. What are the ingredients of formal government? How can we begin to make our path through the "big buzzing confusion"?

The four I's

Glance through the Table of Contents of this book and you will get a sense of the component parts of the great machine that is the American political system—parts such as the Constitution, federalism, civil liberties, political parties and groups, elections, Congress, President, and so on. These are described one by one because each is a big subject in itself. Yet there is inevitably an artificial quality in such a description. It is like describing a baseball game by picturing first the catcher, pitcher, first baseman, and so on, then the players on the other side, then the rules, the ball, the gloves, and all the rest, without describing the players in *action*. Actually it is the interaction or give-and-take among the players that make up the essence of the ball game.

So it is with government. All its component parts—constitutions, legislatures, political parties, and so on—affect one another. Are there any

[1] R. M. MacIver, *The Web of Government* (New York: The Macmillan Company, 1947).

elements that cut across all these component parts and aid us in understanding the *totality* of the political system? One way to understand the political system in its wholeness instead of piece by piece is to see it as the interaction of the "Four I's"—institutions, interests, ideas, and individuals.[2]

1. *Institutions.* An institution is any organized pattern of behavior that is well established as a continuing part of a political system: secret ballots, government agencies, courts, press conferences, congressional committees. They have a strong element of permanence; they are often embedded in law or tradition. They are somewhat predictable: we know that a presidential election will be held in 1960 and a new Congress elected, even though we do not know who the President will be or what bills the new Congress will pass.

2. *Interests.* Government operates amid a web of interests, among the pushing and hauling of millions of men striving for certain goals. Workers want more pay; farmers seek higher prices; businessmen demand less government interference; veterans ask higher pensions. Many other interests are less economic, as in the case of religious or temperance groups. Groups tend to grow out of interests and to create new interests in turn. Interest groups affect the operations of government and are affected by it. The American system would look very different without the business, labor, professional, and hundreds of other groups that exert political pressure.

3. *Ideas.* Men possess thoughts, it is said, but ideas possess men. Ideas come in all shapes and sizes. They may be strong and durable, such as the general American belief in "government by the people," or they may be superficial or short-lived. They may be rational or irrational. An example of the latter was the fervent belief of millions of Germans that the "Aryan" race was superior to others. They may relate closely to people's economic interests, as in the case of trade union support of social welfare laws, or they may run directly counter to the material welfare of those holding the belief. Ideas, in short, may be forces that in themselves have an impact on politics.

4. *Individuals.* All the above forces operate through, and are transformed by, the people and their leaders. Obviously, America would be a different kind of country if it had not been for great Presidents such as Washington and Lincoln, potent senators such as Henry Clay and Robert A. Taft, famous Supreme Court justices such as John Marshall and Oliver Wendell Holmes—and hundreds of industrialists, warriors, inventors, scholars, financiers, and writers who have left their images across American history. America would also be a much different place were it not for the millions of "plain" or "common" men and women—the Smiths, Cohens, Murphys,

---

[2] After Pendleton Herring; for an excellent example of how this method of analysis can be used to illuminate the policy-making process, see Stephen K. Bailey, *Congress Makes a Law* (New York: Columbia University Press, 1950).

Muellers, and all the rest—who elected Presidents and congressmen, fought wars, built railroads and dams, and paid taxes.

These, then, are four basic forces that interact among one another, like the players in a baseball game, and produce the political system that will be described in the following chapters.

The role of government

What is the purpose of government? Government is often damned as an evil or, at best, as a necessary evil. Some philosophers have believed that man in his most exalted state might live best without government, in a state of anarchy. But hard experience teaches that, man being what he is, the absence of government means the absence of peace and liberty. Without government, private individuals and groups would seize power and would set up a narrow "private" government of their own; injustice, chaos, and conflict would then be the order of the day. Without government, as Hobbes wrote long ago, "the life of man would be solitary, poor, nasty, brutish, and short." Because ultimately it monopolizes force, government can establish the framework within which groups and individuals can live and work together peacefully.

The most essential task of government, then, might be summed up as "insuring domestic tranquillity." This, incidentally, is one of the historic purposes of the new American government as set forth in the preamble of the Constitution. Four other purposes described in that preamble ably define the role of government, especially democratic government.

1. *"Provide for the Common Defense."* This is probably the oldest task of government, and today it is the most demanding of our resources and physical effort. In the absence of international tranquillity, nations must be ready to protect themselves through military strength and alliances with other nations. Under Jefferson, the national government spent a few millions a year for defense. In President Eisenhower's budget for the fiscal year 1958, $43,000,000,000 was requested for defense—59 per cent of the whole budget.

2. *"Establish Justice."* Another vital task of government is to regulate and order the lives of men fairly and humanely, with a quality called "justice." In a legal sense, justice calls for impartial judges and juries and for laws that are clear and explicit, that reflect the settled attitudes of the great mass of fair-minded people, that apply alike to rich and poor, white and Negro, Catholic and Protestant, and to all other human beings. In a broader sense, "justice" means that government serves as one agent that helps to distribute the good things of life as widely and fully as possible. Legal justice is an accepted function of government; to what extent government is responsible for "social justice" is one of the great questions of our time.

3. *"Promote the General Welfare."* Like "social justice," promoting the

general welfare is one of the more controversial problems of the day. Most people, of course, believe that government should protect the welfare of those who cannot take care of themselves—the infirm, aged, blind. But how much farther should government go to help farmers, workers, business-men, consumers? Lincoln's answer was that government should "do for the community of people whatever they need to have done, but cannot do so well for themselves in their separate and individual capacities."

4. *"Secure the Blessings of Liberty."* This, the last function of govern-ment listed in the Preamble, is, in a democracy, by no means the least important. To many, the noblest role of government is to enlarge the liberties and opportunities of the individual. This means in part the *limitation* of government so that the heavy hand of law and police will not stifle rightful individual activity. But it may mean—and this is another key issue of our time—the *expansion* of government so that it may be better able to protect individual liberties against other individuals or groups. The power of gov-ernment to prevent a lynching is an example of the use of government to protect an elementary right, the right to life and to a fair trial. The govern-ment's far-reaching control over highways through traffic laws and hordes of "state cops" is a way of expanding another freedom, that of travelling freely and securely.

We have been discussing government in general. But what are the dis-tinctive features of *democratic* government?

ESSENTIALS OF DEMOCRATIC GOVERNMENT

Democracy—like liberty, equality, and justice—is hard to define. Democ-racy is a way of life, a form of government, a way of governing, a type of nation, and a variety of particular programs. The term democracy is so broad and has such great appeal that even the communists have tried to take it over. It may help matters for us first to take up democracy in general and then to talk in terms of *democratic government,* which is both an essential element of democracy in general and a means of putting it into practice.

The word "democratic" is derived from two Greek roots—*demos,* the people, and *kratos,* authority—and in its political sense democracy means government by the people, the many, as contrasted with government by the one, autocracy, the dictator, or by the few, oligarchy. The word came into English usage in the seventeenth century to denote *direct* democracy, the kind of government that existed in Athens and other Greek city states, where all enfranchised citizens came together to discuss and enact laws. Today democ-racy has a broader meaning, to include representative democracy or *repub-lican government.* Until the middle of the nineteenth century democracy was a smear word for mob rule. Only in the last 100 years has it taken on a gen-erally favorable meaning.

Three basic principles of democracy

Democracy rests on a belief in the fundamental dignity and importance of the *individual,* in the essential *equality* of human beings, and in the need for *freedom.*

The emphasis on the supreme worth and central position of the individual has been an unbroken thread in democratic thought. It can be found in the writings of Thomas Jefferson, especially in the Declaration of Independence, where he eloquently proclaimed that all men have been endowed by their Creator with certain inalienable rights and that men create governments to secure these rights. This thought can be found in the speeches of present-day democrats such as David E. Lilienthal, former chairman of the T.V.A. and of the Atomic Energy Commission, who said: "all government and all private institutions must be designed to promote and protect and defend the integrity and dignity of the individual."[3]

This doctrine of *individualism* (not to be confused with the doctrine of laissez faire) is the belief that there is something of supreme worth in every human being. It is the doctrine that we should, in the words of a great philosopher, Immanuel Kant, "so act as to treat humanity, whether in thine own person or in that of any other, in every case as an end withal, never as means only." Individualism makes the individual the central point in the measure of value. The state, the union, and the corporation are tested solely in terms of their usefulness for individuals.

The doctrine of *statism,* on the other hand, makes the state the measure of value, and holds that the good is that which promotes the well-being of the state. Democratic political theory has refused to glorify the state or to shroud it in metaphysical abstractions. The state is nothing more than the organized political society that operates through government. And the government is a group of men called congressmen, members of parliament, presidents, prime ministers, judges, and bureaucrats who, as agents of society, are granted certain powers and perform certain public functions. The welfare of the state has no meaning except in terms of the welfare of the individuals in it.

The second basic premise of democracy is the right of *each* individual to be treated as a unique and inviolable person. By equality of rights the democrat does not mean, as his critics sometimes imply, that all men are equal in talents, virtues, or capabilities. He does mean that the claims of one individual to his life, liberty, and happiness must be treated equally with those of any other individual. He means that "the poorest he that is in England has a life to live as the richest he,"[4] as Colonel Rainboro said as long ago as 1647.

---

[3] David E. Lilienthal, *This I Do Believe* (New York: Harper & Brothers, 1949), p. x.
[4] Col. Thomas Rainboro, "Debates on the Putney Project, 1647," from A. T. Mason, *Free Government in the Making* (New York: Oxford University Press, 1949), p. 12.

The third cardinal principle of a democrat is the belief in the desirability of liberty, the belief that freedom is good. "Liberty" and "freedom" are slippery words, probably the most slippery in the lexicon of political science. As used here they are interchangeable and mean that each individual should have the maximum opportunity to select his own purposes in life and to choose the means to accomplish those purposes. The core of liberty is self-determination. "Positive freedom consists," writes Erich Fromm, "in the spontaneous activity of the total, integrated personality."[5] Liberty and freedom mean more than the absence of external restraint, and include the "power" to act positively toward those goals that one has chosen.

Why is freedom desirable? Briefly, and of course oversimply, it is because the freedom *to make choices* and *to act upon them* is essential to the development of those faculties that make one a human being. Denied this freedom, the individual becomes something less than a man. It is this quality of being able to make rational choices, to select the good from the bad and to decide whether to seek the good, that distinguishes men from other animals. It is only through the use of his freedom that the individual develops a sense of responsibility and self-restraint. It is only by acting as free and responsible individuals that men are able to exploit their full capacity for growth.

From the viewpoint of society, a condition of freedom is desirable because both history and logic suggest that liberty is the key to social progress. The greater the area of freedom, the greater the probability of discovering better ways of living. Where men have freedom of inquiry and expression, error more probably will be found out and truth uncovered. Progress is stifled wherever an authoritarian group or even social custom imposes an orthodoxy that none may question. Denial of freedom, moreover, causes personal frustration, which in turn may erupt in aggressive, antisocial behavior.

Democrats point out, quite rightly, that these basic principles are not new. They express ancient ideals of brotherhood, compassion, justice, and the dignity of man, that have deep roots in the religions of mankind.

Democratic government means popular government

Democratic government is a way of trying to realize these ideals in relations among men.

First, it assumes that the *people* must be the source of all political power, and that government is their *instrument*. But the idea that the government rests on the consent of the people is not the distinguishing feature of democratic government. *All* governments, dictatorial as well as democratic, can claim to rest on the consent of the people. Possibly a large number of Soviet citizens support their leaders. But this is a consent of ignorance, since the

[5] Erich Fromm, *Escape from Freedom* (New York: Farrar & Rinehart, Inc., 1941), p. 258.

ruling elite secures the people's support through a complete monopoly of all the sources of information. In a democracy, on the other hand, the consent of the governed is positive and not negative. It is "a matter of routine, rather than revolution."[6] A democratic government rests on the active and continuous consent of the people, given in regular and orderly fashion.

Second, the people choose the major policy-making agents of government at *free* and *relatively frequent* elections. Here we pass over the important question of just what proportion of the adult population must be given a voice in the political affairs of the community in order to conform to democratic principles. The proportion must be large enough, however, so that the electorate will represent, more or less effectively, the interests of all and all the interests. The elections must be free. There is no meaning to sham elections where no criticism is permitted and no opposition party is allowed to organize.

Third, under democratic government all citizens have the same voting power, and all are equal before the law. This does not mean that all citizens must or will have equal political influence. Some men by their wealth, their talents, and their positions will have much greater political power than their fellow citizens. But the rich and the poor,

Courtesy DES MOINES REGISTER & TRIBUNE *and Interlandi*

"Gad, when I think of the power the people have . . . It just isn't fair. . . ."

the educated and the ignorant have an equal vote and before the law are equally important.

Fourth, in a democracy, government by the people means government by the *majority*. There is no magic in a numerical majority, but some practical means is needed to determine the outcome of elections and to make decisions. The people do not speak with a united voice; they are divided into groups and parties that struggle with one another for the control of the government. Some people want White for Senator, others want Black. The majority is not necessarily right, but it is right to do what the majority wishes. For a majority usually means a wider basis of consent than does a minority.

Finally, before majority rule has any significance, each individual must enjoy the right to criticize, have access to the facts, participate in political deliberations, and organize for political purposes. The last is of especial

[6] Edward Dumbauld, *The Declaration of Independence and What It Means Today* (Norman: University of Oklahoma Press, 1950), p. 77.

importance in modern societies where the units of politics are organized groups. Individuals can be politically effective only when joined with others. Those who hold power can be checked only when there is freedom to form pressure groups and political parties, and to use all methods of peaceful persuasion. And the right to participate in the deliberative process by which decisions are reached is as important as being counted in the final vote. Democratic government must tolerate opposition; indeed, it must *foster* it. In Britain, the leader of the "loyal opposition" is paid by the government for doing the vital job of opposing the government.

Democratic government means limited government

In a democracy, the *source* of governmental power is the people. What are the *limits* of governmental power? Here we run into the concept of *constitutionalism*, the concept of limited government which is to be discussed at greater length in Chapter 3.

Constitutional governments are not necessarily democratic, but all representative democracies are constitutional. There are recognized and generally accepted limits to the power of those who govern as well as to the authority of the electorate itself. Officials have only the authority that the people delegate to them either directly or through their elected representatives. Any official who exceeds the scope of his authority ceases to have a claim to obedience.

A democratic government is limited by the purposes for which it is established. It is a fundamental tenet of democracy that government is but an *instrument* created by the people in order to enlarge freedom and promote the welfare of the people. And as the Declaration of Independence proclaims: "whenever any Form of Government becomes destructive" of the ends for which it was established, "it is the Right of the People to alter or to abolish it, and to institute new Government, laying its foundation on such principles and organizing its powers in such form, as to them shall seem most likely to effect their Safety and Happiness."

The primacy of the individual and the secondary importance of government limit the scope of even a government that speaks for a majority. The individual has certain basic rights which he enjoys merely because he is a human being, and not at the sufferance of the government or at the pleasure of the majority. There is no unanimity as to the concrete content of these rights, but it is agreed that there are certain things that no government may do and others that it may do only according to proper and fair procedure. At a minimum, the government may not deny to any person his life, liberty, or property except by the due and fair procedures of the law.

The democratic concept of majority rule also limits the majority. It is not *any* majority whose will is to prevail in a free government, but only one formed as the result of free and open deliberations in which all citizens can participate. The right to differ does not end with the victory of the majority. Only so long as the majority respects the right of the minority does the majority have a claim to minority acquiescence in it decisions. Majority rule and minority rights are neither antagonistic nor incompatible doctrines; both are vital parts of the democratic technique. Inherent in the idea of majority rule is the right of the minority to try to become a majority.

Democratic government, then, is *limited* or *constitutional* government. Although there have been in the past, under unusual circumstances, constitutional governments that were not democratic, it is unlikely that a limited government could be maintained in the modern world unless it were also democratic. The primary sanction for insuring that the government does not exceed the limits of its authority is the right of unfettered criticism plus the power to throw the rascals out of office at election time. Constitutionalism, with its emphasis on *limited* government, and democracy, with its emphasis on *self-government,* are not exclusive categories but mutually supporting institutions.

What democratic government is not

Democracies come in many varieties. The American variety is only one of several brands. Yet some Americans assume that only governments exactly like our own are democratic. They confuse the essentials with the nonessentials. Separation of powers, written constitutions, federalism, and judicial review—to mention just a few of the basic features of American government—are principles that Americans generally support as desirable ways of limiting government and making it responsible to the people. But these do not in themselves make our government democratic. The government of England has virtually none of these features; the Canadian, Australian, French, and Swedish governments have them only in part. But in all these countries the majority rules, and minority rights are secure. On the other hand, the Soviet Union has a written constitution and, at least formally, federalism; but the government is in the hands of a self-appointed elite, and those who differ with the rulers have the choice of silence or Siberia.

Some Americans assume also that only countries that have our kind of economy or that adopt our policies can be considered democratic. Democracy is not an economic system, though it is intimately connected with the economy. But can democratic government be maintained when the economy is controlled by the government? Democracy has in the past been closely associated with capitalism. It developed along with the rise of the middle class and the growth of the private enterprise system. Because of this historical connection, many argue that capitalism is necessary to democracy and that the end of capitalism would mean the end of democracy. Others are equally convinced, however, that democracy does not depend upon capitalism. They believe, on the contrary, that effective democracy cannot be achieved until economic power is made subject to governmental control. Political democracy, they say, is impossible without "economic democracy."

In a like manner, some believe that a planned economy is the "road to serfdom," while others consider it to be the road to freedom. Some believe that the welfare state will undermine democratic government, while to others such a program is essential for the preservation of republican government. These positions, and all those in between, are tenable. Plausible arguments can be made and evidence marshaled to support any of them.

But democracy is not capitalism, socialism, the welfare state, planning, the absence of planning, or any other particular economic system. At times our government has followed the favorite policies of business, at times those of labor. In our country the coal industry is privately owned and operated; in England it is owned and operated by the government. But we and the British both have democratic governments because in all these cases the decisions were made after free discussion and free elections, and the government did not jeopardize the right of the opposition to oppose. Within limits it is not the *content* of the economic policies that makes a government democratic as much as it is the *procedures* by which they are adopted. A free people have the right to choose socialism, laissez faire, the welfare state, or any mixture they want.

Democratic government, then, is not an economic system but a *way of governing and of being governed*. This does not mean that an economic system is unrelated to the amount of democracy in a country. The point is that democratic government allows the people to discuss different economic arrangements, to test them in terms of democratic ideals, and to change them if they are found wanting. Wise economic policies will help democratic government survive, but democratic government, in turn, enables us to develop wise economic policies.

Conditions of democracy

Why do democratic governments exist in so few places in the world? In part, because democratic government depends for success upon certain material and intellectual conditions. Though these conditions are difficult to define precisely, hard experience teaches that vigorous democratic governments flourish best in certain types of environment.

1. *Educational conditions.* Before democratic governments can operate in any nation of size, most of the people must be able to read and write. It is also desirable that there be a widespread sharing of knowledge, which depends upon a relatively efficient system of communication and transportation.

2. *Economic conditions.* A relatively prosperous nation with a general measure of economic security and widespread distribution of wealth provides the best milieu. Starving men have little energy to be concerned about

liberty. Where economic power is concentrated, political power is apt to be concentrated too.

3. *Social conditions.* If a society is divided into antagonistic groups that differ with each other on fundamental questions, government by discussion and compromise is almost impossible. Without a widespread sharing of democratic values, the community lacks an essential condition of democracy. Agreement to proceed by democratic methods is most likely where a large number of groups encourage men to have overlapping allegiances—a condition that prevents groups from solidifying and developing loyalties superior to those they feel to democratic government. Democratic government also thrives best where groups in the society proceed by discussion and compromise, so that democratic habits are developed early and strengthened by their constant use.

We have looked briefly at the nature of government generally. We have discussed the essentials and conditions of *democratic* government. But government, especially democratic government, is powerfully influenced by the nature of the society in which it is rooted.

DYNAMIC AMERICA

What are the salient aspects of American society that condition and influence the nature of American democratic government? First of all, the United States is a land of infinite diversity. Consider our climate and geography. The continental sweep of our nation embraces burning deserts, thousand-mile-long mountain ranges, humid areas drenched with rain, immense prairies, dust bowls, lake regions, vast forests, and many thousands of miles of coastline. We are a nation of regions vast enough to be called subnations, and each subnation is bound by ties of history, politics, economics, and language. Each is a nation in itself, embracing nearly as much diversity as France, Spain, or England.

Ours is a nation of nations in an even more literal sense. America is the fabled "melting pot." To its shores have come two great waves of immigrants. The first arrived mainly from northwestern Europe after the Civil War. The second, coming largely from eastern and southern Europe, started at the end of the century and reached its peak in the decade before 1914.[7] We are a nation of Italian-Americans, Irish-Americans, Polish-Americans, Swedish-Americans, German-Americans, Latin-Americans, and many other "hyphenated" groups, along with Negroes, old Yankee groups, Indians, and others. The millions of immigrants brought the old country with them; they imported not only differences in languages and customs but also clashing religious and political attitudes. They could not discard their old beliefs and languages and customs overnight; on the contrary, they often clung to

[7] F. J. Brown and J. S. Roucek, eds., *One America,* 3rd ed. (Englewood Cliffs, N.J.: Prentice-Hall, Inc., 1952), pp. 8-11.

their separate ways as long as they could. In short, the melting pot did not melt everyone into the same dull gray.

Put these two elements together—sectionalism and groups of various national origins—and the checkered, polyglot nature of America begins to emerge. Add to these the religious diversity—the scores of Protestant sects, the powerful Catholic and Jewish bodies; add also the divisive impact of political doctrines that have swept the country, some coming from Europe, some home-grown; add finally the influence of that competitiveness and individualism that Americans have long praised and practiced—combine all these forces, and the heterogeneity of America begins to take full form.

EVOLUTION

From the infinite variety of Nature to the universal pudd'nhead

David Low for *Survey Graphic.* Copyright Low all countries. Reprinted by permission of Low.

Unity is not uniformity.

Yet there are great uniformities too. Americans have a common language and together pay homage to national heroes like George Washington and Thomas Jefferson. Wherever we live we listen to the same song hits, read the same comic strips, watch the same movies. Great corporations, labor unions, farm organizations span the nation and affect the lives of people everywhere. To walk down Main Street in our home town, with its bright lights, chain stores, parking meters, traffic jams, is to walk down *any* Main Street in all America.

Our national motto, *e pluribus unum*—one from many—well sums up these two great forces. "Homogeneity and diversity—these are the stupendous rival magnets," John Gunther has said.

A third key fact about this country is its economic power. Today this economic power is a central fact in the world-wide balance of military power. Our economic strength is based upon a variety of factors. One of these is manpower. We have a labor force (all persons gainfully occupied) of over 65 million, with many more millions of potential workers in reserve. The productivity of our workers, based upon our technological advances and our skills, is very high, and our natural resources are still immense and varied. We produce half the world's steel, most of its sulfur, a third of its coal and oil, and large chunks of its iron ore, copper, lead, zinc, phosphate, and uranium.

Amid these superlatives, two cautious comments are in order. Although in the United States there is a wider sharing of wealth than in most other nations, certain groups do not benefit from the high American standard of living. Tenant farmers, migratory workers, some members of fixed-income groups, certain white-collar workers, low-paid factory workers, and members of some minority groups, for example, have little of the material goods of life. Second, there is no guarantee that our prosperity will last forever. Our economy is subject to pressures from within and without; it is in a constant process of change in almost all its aspects. These changes and trends are worth a closer look.

Economic trends

The United States, like a number of other nations, seems to be involved in a permanent industrial revolution. Five basic trends characterize the ceaseless transformation of our economy.

1. *Technological progress.* From the Stone Age and Iron Age, man has passed into the age of glass, plastic, fibers, alloys; the age of crop genetics, agrobiology, and mechanized farming; and the age of speed, when men move faster than sound. A century ago a commissioner of patents asked Congress to abolish his office because everything had been invented, but inventions come at a faster and faster rate; twice as many patents were granted between 1940 and 1950 as between 1890 and 1900. Less dramatic than the technological miracles, but perhaps as important, is the advance made in understanding the human problems of our industrial civilization, such as employer-employee relations.

Two rather recent developments indicate that more industrial revolutions lie ahead. One of these, of course, is atomic energy. Here is a source of vast power which, scientists think, can be harnessed to peacetime as well as wartime uses. The second is automation. Fantastically complicated but reliable machines can do certain kinds of work, including "thinking work," now done by skilled and white-collar people—and do that work much more cheaply.[8] And such machines, unlike a human operator, cannot be bored, unhappy, distracted, or rebellious.

2. *Mass production and consumption.* As a result of technology, resources, and skills, Americans produce and consume more goods than any other people. Physical output has increased at least fivefold in the last fifty years, while the number of employees has only doubled, and hours of work per day have dropped by a third. Output per man hour is still increasing. In 1944, at the peak of our war effort, 63 million persons working 47 hours a week produced a gross national product of $200 billion. It has been estimated that our gross product in 1960 (in terms of 1951 dollars) will be $425 billion.[9]

Our capacity to consume is equally gigantic. Our appetite for goods and services is getting bigger, changing. In the past fifty years the proportion of our income spent on food, liquor, and tobacco has decreased slightly, and the proportion spent on clothing and personal care has stayed about the same. The proportion spent on personal transportation (notably automobiles) and on medical care and insurance, however, has doubled.

3. *Interdependence.* Years ago, members of a family could make most of what they needed with their own hands; today the average urban family produces only a tiny fraction of its needs. We have become increasingly *specialized* in our work. Specialization promotes greater efficiency; it also allows economic disturbances in one sector of the economy to move quickly to other areas. We sink or swim together.

Related to this interdependence is concentration of industrial and financial strength in fewer and larger corporations. Despite antitrust laws and the like, the process of consolidation appears to go on. Today we have scores of "supermonopolies" in basic industries such as banking, railroads, automobiles, insurance, and public utilities. There has been widespread consolidation also in textiles, foods, and the distributive trades. Interdependence is growing not only in business and industry but also in other areas. Labor organizations, for example, have tended to become more and more centralized and integrated nationally.

4. *A mature or expanding economy?* Our economy is showing some signs of old age. We no longer have a western frontier offering limitless expansion and opportunities. The rate of population growth dropped sharply in the 1930's, and immigration today is small compared to that of fifty or seventy-five years ago. Certain areas of the country are declining economically and some investment outlets have dwindled sharply.

But there are also signs of youthful vigor. Our power to produce, as noted previously, continues to increase. Population and national income have soared in the last fifteen years. Some sections of the country—nota-

[8] Norbert Wiener, *The Human Use of Human Beings* (Boston: Houghton Mifflin Company, 1950).

[9] Gerhard Colm, *The American Economy in 1960* (Washington: National Planning Association, Planning Pamphlet 81, 1952), pp. 161, 166.

bly the West and Southwest—are still expanding their economies. Even older areas, such as the South and Northeast, have shown amazing powers of growth during recent years of prosperity. Instead of a western frontier, we have a sort of internal frontier that offers tremendous possibilities for the investment of money and manpower. We could use, for example, many more hospitals, schools, and parks, better houses and roads. As long as we have enormous productive power and vast needs, our economy can hardly be called old or mature.

5. *Economic instability.* Our economy continues to be unstable. For over a century our business cycle indexes have resembled a roller coaster. We had long and severe depressions in the late 1830's, the 1870's, the 1890's, and the 1930's. In between were sharp but minor slumps, as in 1884-1885, 1904, 1914, 1920, and 1937. We have had periods of sustained prosperity, such as during the 1880's and recent years.

Is there a trend toward economic stability? Nobody knows. We have acquired a good deal of economic understanding in recent years and we have established rudimentary machinery for evening out the peaks and canyons in the business cycle. Some economists, however, have grave doubts that we can yet achieve long-term stability in peacetime.

Social trends

Economic changes are important only as they affect people. Here are some social trends that are at work in America midway through the twentieth century.

1. *Population changes.* The American people numbered about 170 million by 1957. Our population has doubled in the last fifty years. Not long ago the demographers, who study vital statistics such as births, marriages, and deaths, were expecting that the population curve would soon flatten out and that the proportion of young people in the total population would decline at a rapid rate. The tremendous increase in population during recent years of prosperity, however, has led to a revision of these estimates. It has been predicted that, barring catastrophic wars or depressions, our population will reach 200 million as early as, or before, 1975.

Population is also changing in character. For many decades there has been an increase in urban population, as compared with rural, and this trend is continuing. Almost two-thirds of the people live in urban areas as defined by the Census Bureau. The suburban communities on the outskirts of cities are growing at a much faster rate than the central, built-up areas. The rise of "suburbia" is having a variety of social and political effects. Population increase is also uneven in different areas of the country. During the 1940's the population of the West grew by about 40 per cent and that of the South by almost 13 per cent. During the same period several agricultural states declined in population.

Our population is *aging* as well as growing. The median age in 1900 was 23 years; in 1960 it will probably reach 33. The proportion of people over 65 was 4 per cent in 1900 and is about twice that today. Such changes have important implications for government—for example, in the scope of old-age assistance.

2. *The class system.* In certain ways American society is stratified. Study after study of American communities has revealed a social-economic class system based largely upon wealth. People with similar incomes, occupations, or social positions tend to associate and to form relatively distinct classes. In the typical community at least three basic classes are found— upper, middle, and lower—but usually there are gradations within classes, such as the upper middle class (wealthy business and professional groups) and the lower middle class (clerical workers and highly skilled labor).

The important question is not whether classes exist but whether America is becoming more or less stratified. The period of rapid movement upward in the class system seems to be passing. The "rags to riches" feats of Horatio Alger heroes were always exaggerated, but they happen even less often today. Increasingly, people seem to follow the occupational and social paths of their parents. On the other hand, there is considerable mobility and flexibility in the largest and most dynamic strata, the middle classes.[10] Here people move "down" or "up" much more freely than in the more stratified upper or lower classes. There are *caste* tendencies, too, in American life, especially in the case of minority groups; but the caste system also is in a state of flux, owing to pressures from inside the caste and from outside. Our class system contains within itself the seeds of change.

3. *Mass culture.* The United States, as noted at the outset of this chapter, is a medley of diverse groups and subcultures. But the nation and its people need a sense of unity. There must be a mass culture that is common to all the subcultures. Our mass culture is the result of many things —common traditions, folklore, a common language, past and present wars and crises, and the like. It is produced also by our mass media of communications—films that are shown in every movie house in the land, magazines that sell millions of copies an issue, and radio and television programs that span the nation.

What happens when a mass culture exists along with many subcultures? The mass culture serves as a bridge linking one group to another. But can the mass culture go very deep? Must it be a kind of least common denominator? Is it like white icing on a fruit cake that hides the variety of ingredients within? Our mass culture, according to some sociologists, lacks roots. It consists of a shifting set of attitudes and values that tend to be simple and fleeting in nature: the fads of teen-agers, the cult of

10 J. W. Bennett and M. M. Tumin, *Social Life* (New York: Alfred A. Knopf, Inc., 1948), pp. 570-600. See also C. Wright Mills, *White Collar* (New York: Oxford University Press, 1952).

actor worshippers, food fetishes, and self-improvement procedures involving everything from hair styles to hypnosis. Such common patterns do not provide a core of common fixed meanings and values. It seems possible, however, that a deeper unity will flow from the economic and military stresses of the last decade or two.

4. *War.* Fourteen million Americans were in uniform in World War II, and countless other millions worked in the war program at home. Almost six million took part in the three-year-long Korean war, and we

THE AMERICAN CLASS SYSTEM

(Tendency toward rigidity of this UPPERstratum through hereditary wealth and social position)

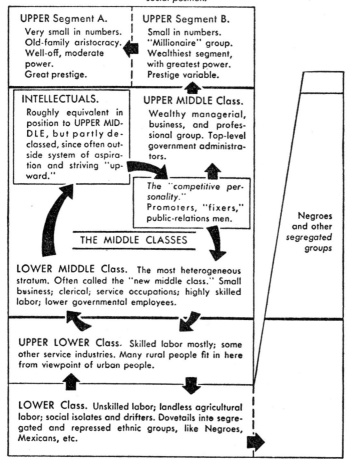

UPPER Segment A.
Very small in numbers. Old-family aristocracy. Well-off, moderate power. Great prestige.

UPPER Segment B.
Small in numbers. "Millionaire" group. Wealthiest segment, with greatest power. Prestige variable.

INTELLECTUALS.
Roughly equivalent in position to UPPER MIDDLE, but partly de-classed, since often outside system of aspiration and striving "upward."

UPPER MIDDLE Class.
Wealthy managerial, business, and professional group. Top-level government administrators.

The "competitive personality." Promoters, "fixers," public-relations men.

THE MIDDLE CLASSES

LOWER MIDDLE Class. The most heterogeneous stratum. Often called the "new middle class." Small business; clerical; service occupations; highly skilled labor; lower governmental employees.

UPPER LOWER Class. Skilled labor mostly; some other service industries. Many rural people fit in here from viewpoint of urban people.

LOWER Class. Unskilled labor; landless agricultural labor; social isolates and drifters. Dovetails into segregated and repressed ethnic groups, like Negroes, Mexicans, etc.

Negroes and other segregated groups

(Tendency toward rigidity of this LOWER class through constant economic under-privilege and unemployment)

From John W. Bennett and Melvin M. Tumin, SOCIAL LIFE, by permission of Alfred A. Knopf, Inc. Copyright 1948 by Alfred A. Knopf, Inc.

are still involved in a gigantic defense effort. In a sense, we have a whole new subculture—that of millions of men, and some women, working and training in camps and other military installations at home and abroad. It is too early to estimate the impact of continued war crises upon Americans, but surely it will leave its mark on our attitudes, customs, behavior, and way of life.

Psychological trends

These economic and social trends are of many types, but in general they reveal a common trend. This trend is toward *bigness*. Ours is becoming increasingly a civilization of big cities, big machines, big labor, big business, big bombs, and big government. In the shadow of this bigness, the individual stands as a tiny and puny figure. To be sure, he created the giants, but in doing so he may have built a Frankenstein's monster that in turn will destroy him, or at least destroy his power to fashion his life as he wishes.

Little man, big world—this is the nub of the problem. But the problem has several aspects. One is the individual's feeling of *helplessness*. The world is swept by gigantic forces over which he has little sense of control. A second is his feeling of *rootlessness* and loneliness. Millions of men, living in cities, have little of the sense of belonging and permanence that their grandfathers experienced in more stable, rural areas. A third aspect, closely related to the other two, is the feeling of *impersonality*. Our social relationships often lack depth and meaning; in the fast pace of urban life our contacts with others may be fleeting and shallow. Individual personality is ignored or perhaps crushed under such conditions.

These feelings of helplessness, rootlessness, and impersonality have burst forth in our literature and art. Think of Charlie Chaplin in the movie *Modern Times*—the little man controlled by the great machine. Or take Franz Kafka's famous novel *The Trial*, in which the hero, accused of a crime he did not commit and even the nature of which he knows not, becomes entangled in a vast nightmarish bureaucracy and is finally destroyed. Social scientists have become increasingly interested in the fate of the little man in the big society.

Psychologists have noticed three important psychological forces, all of which relate to government:

1. *The quest for security*. Man has freed himself from many old bonds, such as slavery and feudalism, and has become an individual enjoying certain rights and liberties. But in gaining freedom from the old controls man has often failed to gain freedom in the positive sense of realizing his intellectual and artistic possibilities. On the contrary, freedom has posed problems that he feels unable to meet. Living amid modern industrial civilization—with its large-scale organization, its mobility and competitiveness, its impersonality, its sheer bigness—he feels isolated, insecure,

and lonely. Gone is the old framework of custom and authority, of life in small groups and stable communities. The machine age has made man rich in material things, but he feels insecure, helpless, isolated, powerless, and lost.

What is the result? It is man's attempt, in the words of Erich Fromm, a psychoanalyst, to *escape* from freedom. Faced with impossible situations and decisions, he may turn away from freedom and individuality and try to fuse himself with some outside person or thing to gain a sense of security.[11] He may submit to some self-confident person who has all the "answers" and issues all the orders. One reason Hitler took power in the early 1930's was the feeling of millions of Germans that they were in the grip of giant economic and social forces that they could not control.

2. *The quest for conformity.* Another effect of modern industrialism, some social scientists feel, is to make people desperately eager to conform to the standards of men and women around them. In bringing up children, David Riesman has noted, the emphasis is often on their being *popular* with *other* children.[12] Mother becomes a chauffeur and a booking agent. The teen-ager's most important possession is a "popularity kit" composed of set types of clothes, a knowledge of the latest gadgets, of movie and TV stars, of popular tunes, plus an amazing storehouse of small talk on all sorts of subjects. One must conform and adjust. Being high-hat or "different" is forbidden.

Many adults show the same quest for conformity. But adjustment is not freedom. The person whose greatest need in life is the approval of his neighbors, whose aim in life is to get along with others at almost any price—such a person may always be lonely in the great crowd. There is a need for autonomy as well as for adjustment, for individuality as well as for conformity. A measure of independence is vital to the diversity that underlies initiative and progress. Democratic government cannot last in a society of automatons; civil liberties, for example, could never flourish in a society where men will not tolerate political opinions other than their own.

3. *The quest for community.* Closely related to these forces is man's desire for some sense of *direction,* of *belonging,* of *community* with his neighbors. Just as children become anxious when separated from their parents, says Sebastian de Grazia, adults show a similar anxiety when they feel separated from their political and religious "fathers"—from tribal chiefs, priests, gods, kings, and presidents.[13] People *need* such rulers, for the rulers issue the moral codes that help bind citizens together and give them a sense of purpose and direction.

Trouble may result when our moral codes conflict. Our religion, de

---

[11] Erich Fromm, *Escape from Freedom* (New York: Farrar & Rinehart, Inc., 1941).

[12] David Riesman, *The Lonely Crowd* (New Haven: Yale University Press, 1950).

[13] Sebastian de Grazia, *The Political Community* (Chicago: The University of Chicago Press, 1948), p. ix.

Grazia says, teaches us the need for brotherly love, while our economic philosophy teaches the need for competitiveness. Modern Western culture, with its stress on individual liberty, tends to leave people confused, insecure, and lacking in purpose. *Men must believe in something or somebody.* They must have leaders who can symbolize and help realize men's highest aspirations and who can give them a sense of community.

A word of caution is in order. Many social scientists disagree that the social and psychological trends outlined here are so clear or the situation so serious as some of the above views seem to indicate. Other and even contradictory generalizations could be made. It is not certain, for example, that life in rural communities of 100 years ago was idyllic or that modern urban man feels less secure than did some of his isolated and culturally poverty-stricken forefathers. Generalizations about social and psychological trends often depend upon which evidence is emphasized. Usually there are many forces working in many directions.

You may wonder what all these things about economics, population, social and psychological trends have to do with the subject of American government. But the student of government should also be something of an economist, something of a sociologist, something of a social psychologist.

Economic trends, for example, have had a direct effect on government. Think for a moment of the impact of the Great Depression of the 1930's on the growth of national governmental functions, the extension of executive authority, the political habits of voters. New transportation and communication methods, too, have confronted government with complex problems and have altered the forms of government. The internal combustion engine and the automobile, as obvious examples, have required government expenditures for roads, changed the nature of police work, led to growth of suburbs, created new strains on city governments, and have affected political techniques.

Social trends, too, have had direct effect on government. The movements of the people—first from country to the city and now from the city to the suburbs—have forced politicians to change their campaign appeals. The aging of our population has directed attention to pensions and programs for the elderly, whose numbers have increased their political power. War and fear of war have led, among other things, to huge government bureaucracies for defense and for veterans welfare. And an alleged psychological trend—the quest for security—is often cited as one of the factors lying behind the rise of "big government." What happens to Americans happens to American government.

DEMOCRACY UNDER FIRE

Today democracy is under fire from many directions. Some critics of democracy are the brutalitarians of fascism and communism who wish to discredit the American democracy and to destroy our freedom. These totalitarians question the desirability of liberty, deny the primacy of the individual, and consider human inequality inevitable and desirable. Other critics of democracy are men of good will. They accept some of the basic democratic values but maintain that democratic government, as we know it, destroys those values and that other forms of government are better designed to protect them.

It is dangerous to brush aside criticisms of democracy; they must be understood and answered. This entire volume, it is hoped, is an answer to the criticism of fascists, communists, and others who reject government by the people. The following sections, in particular, deal with the direct threats to democracy, both external and internal, and with the arguments advanced by believers in aristocracy (government by an elite) and by communist totalitarians.

The challenge from outside

A little over 100 years ago, in 1848, Karl Marx and Friedrich Engels published *The Communist Manifesto*. Today, one-third of the world's population is governed by men who claim to have answered that call to action. Modern communists attack not merely our capitalistic economy but the whole democratic system of government. They insist that behind our democratic exterior, a small group of capitalists dominate public affairs. They urge members of the working class to believe that their real interests are identical with the Soviet Union, which, they argue, speaks for workers everywhere against the capitalists who dominate nations outside the Soviet orbit.

Marxism is shot through with errors and contradictions. It grossly overestimates the power and unity of the working class; it underestimates the size and influence of the middle class under capitalism. The class structure of any modern industrial nation is far more complex than the simple capitalistic-proletarian division that Marx foresaw, as this chapter has suggested earlier. Capitalism has shown considerable adaptability and flexibility, and a modified form of capitalism, at least in the United States, has shown the capacity to distribute goods and services rather widely. Contrary to Marx, it has not been capitalistic nations where communists have taken power, but precapitalistic countries like Russia and China.

But whatever the errors of Marxism, we must recognize its powerful grip on the minds of millions who live in hunger and despair. Democracy's best answer to communism has been less in the realm of debate than in the realm of action—in raising the living standards of the mass of people, in making civil liberties and civil rights tangible things for all citizens, in acting fairly and responsibly in international affairs. In the same way, the communist philosophy is less significant than communist action. Wherever the communists have taken power they have set up an elite that felt it knew what was good for the people better than the people themselves. They have ruthlessly destroyed those who differed with them. They have crushed the individual in trying to make him conform to the totalitarian pattern. Doubtless some of these evils result from international and domestic tension as well as from communism itself. But if a doctrine is known by its works, communism can be understood best by the trail of brutal purges, slave-labor camps, fake elections, and party-line art, music, science, and thought that it has left in its wake.

The antidemocratic communists should not be confused with the democratic socialists of England, Australia, Scandinavia, the United States, or elsewhere. These socialists, although drawing many insights from Karl Marx and critical of many aspects of capitalistic economics, are democrats. They reject revolutionary tactics and are dedicated to working within the democratic framework in attempting to achieve their goals. Many Americans are critical of their programs and many fear that they would endanger or destroy democratic government, but both democratic socialists and democratic capitalists agree that democracy, not the dictatorship of workers or any other group, is the best form of government.

The challenge from within

1. *The communist threat.* The communist attack upon democracy proceeds on many fronts and in many places. Communism has developed to a high degree the tactics of infiltration and propaganda. Even so, it is very doubtful if communists could win a free election in any established democracy (see Chapter 6). Certainly in the United States democracy is not seriously threatened at the polls by communists. But communists, whose first loyalty is to the Soviet Union and who are working for the destruction of our democratic system, present a serious danger when they get into positions of influence. At critical times they can use these positions to aid our enemies. The danger from these subversives must be recognized, and, as enemies of democracy, they must be fought. But a danger no less real is that self-government will be lost in the very process of meeting the threat of foreign attack from without and subversives from within.

2. *The garrison state.* It is more than coincidence that democracy has been most firmly established in countries that did not have to maintain large standing armies and that, for one reason or another, did not live in constant fear of attack. A nation at war or in constant fear of war does not provide a very satisfactory milieu for the toleration and encouragement of difference and discussion. Concern with security matters, fear of disloyal persons, demand for swift action, and an atmosphere of fear are not conducive to free and open debate, protection of individual liberty, and careful deliberation.[14]

[14] H. D. Lasswell, *National Security and Individual Freedom* (New York: McGraw-Hill Book Company, Inc., 1950).

The internal conditions and the world position of the United States have, in the past, created an ideal environment for the development of democratic government. Wars were rare, and the nation was relatively secure. Unfortunately, these favorable ˚conditions for cultivating liberty are no longer with us. Peace did not follow World War II. For the first time, Americans must expect a long period when a large standing army will be necessary and the economy will have to be geared to defense production. Large armed forces, military training for all citizens, civilian defense preparation, sizable defense expenditures, and the military's great prominence in public affairs will be normal features of the American republic for some time to come. The security of the United States is, and will be, immediately and imminently in danger.

Modern warfare has so expanded the scope of military affairs that there is no longer a clear separation between military and civilian spheres of activity. All aspects of society—labor relations, science, the press, entertainment—affect the nation's military power. As military aspects of proble is are brought to the fore, the generals, often reluctantly, are called upon to pass judgment on issues that in the past have not been thought to be within the scope of their competence. At the same time, their civilian superiors find it more difficult to secure the information that they need to exercise control. In many cases it is the military who decide what information must remain top secret. Congressmen and the general public are at a disadvantage in exercising effective supremacy over the military.

When security matters are emphasized, there is a natural tendency to enhance the military method of doing things. The armed services are organized for fast action. Authority is concentrated at the top, and the emphasis is on unquestioning obedience to orders. Civilian government, at the other extreme, gives to the privates the constitutionally protected right of telling the generals where they get off. The major agent of democracy is the politician, the man of talk and compromise. But when people become frightened, they are apt to find the man of action more appealing. The general's prestige rises; the politician's falls.

3. *Authoritarianism.* The instability of democracy is one of the oldest themes of political science. Some writers have always insisted that if the people are given power, they will hand it over to the demagogue who makes the most appealing promises. Authoritarians of all kinds—caesars, demagogues, fascists, communists, anti-Semites—exist in all democracies. They create confusion and spread hate. Most of the time their appeals have little attraction except to the lunatic fringe. But during a crisis or period of tension when people feel emotionally insecure, when they feel caught in critical situations, those with simple authoritarian panaceas become a real threat to democracy.

The antidemocratic leader and his popularity are less the *cause* than the *result* of social maladjustments. He becomes dangerous when the democratic leaders fail to respond to the demands of the people. It is when responsible government is too weak to respond to the needs of the time, not when it is too strong, that it is most likely to be destroyed. When peaceful change is difficult, violent and revolutionary change is most likely.

Where does the demagogue find his audience? Mainly among the helpless and the hopeless, among those who have genuine and deep-seated

Courtesy THE SATURDAY REVIEW *and Mirachi*

"That's the trouble with a monarchy—they can't vote you out of office."

grievances. He plays on peoples' fears and hopes. He promises to make the sharecropper a king. He is a great simplifier. He has an answer for the confused clerk thrown out of a job, for the frustrated student, and for the underpaid worker: it is all the fault of Wall Street, the Communists, the Jews, or the international bankers. His appeal, however, is not only to the poor and downtrodden. Social crises create frustrations and lead to aggressive feelings among the wealthy as well as among the poverty-stricken.

In the Great Depression of the 1930's, millions of people were cut loose from their traditional moorings. They were at the mercy of forces that they could not understand. They were bitter because they had lost their jobs, had been forced out of their homes, had been deprived of rights to which they felt entitled. In Germany, Hitler had explanations and panaceas, and in the United States so did Gerald L. K. Smith, Father Coughlin, and Huey Long. But in the United States democratic government responded to the needs of the times, gave hope to millions, and acted to maintain their faith in democracy. By peaceful change, the threat of social revolution was met.

The case against democracy

Aside from tangible threats to democracy from outside and from within, there is an intellectual case against democracy. Democrats who are worth their salt must recognize and answer this case rather than evade it. From Plato's day to the present, men of thought and men of action have argued against democracy both in practice and in theory. Here is how a forthright antidemocrat might argue his case:

"You democrats have an overoptimistic view of human nature. You think that men are rational, inherently good, and have an infinite capacity for self-improvement. How foolish you are! Haven't you heard of Freud? Don't you know that modern psychology proves that man is a *rationalizing* as well as a rational animal? Can you deny that man sees the public interest in terms of his own *self* interest?

"You have a false concept of people and politics. Politics is not a struggle among *rational individuals.* It is a contest among a few powerful *leaders* and *groups* who compete for the support of a bored public—so bored that many people don't even vote. As for your naïve belief in the goodness of man, need I do more than point to today's paper for many examples of man's inhumanity to man?

"Most people are ignorant. They haven't had much schooling; they don't know what's going on in the world; they can't even tell you the name of their senator or congressman. They are not competent to govern themselves. Indeed, they often sell their 'birthright' by voting for the demagogue who promises the most. They become the corrupt tools of selfish leaders.

"Rule by the many—'government by the people,' as you so hopefully call it—means necessarily government by the great mass, rule by the common, the coarse, the vulgar. Culture—music, the arts, literature—is transmitted by the educated and cultivated few, or else it disappears. So democracy means a general lowering of standards; it leads to stagnation and incompetence.

"Even if you democrats could demolish all these arguments, I have one final unanswerable point. Democracy is a luxury for the few, not the necessity of the many. It exists in only a small part of the world, and some so-called democratic governments are merely masks for rule by an elite. Democracy is a luxury because it can exist only in a certain type of environment—as even some of you democrats admit."

There is the intellectual challenge to democracy, put as forcefully as possible. The authors of this book would deny most of these arguments; those that the authors would accept do not, in their opinion, necessarily prove a case against democracy. But what is your response to this intellectual challenge to democracy? Perhaps the reader, like the authors, is impatient to answer. But since this whole book is a description of the workings, problems, and accomplishments of democratic government in one great nation, the authors will provide their answers in the last chapter, after the whole terrain is surveyed. You are invited to formulate *your* own answer to the case against democracy as you study American government.

The rules and how they grew

PART TWO ~ A PROBLEM GUIDE

Part Two offers information relating to all five basic questions listed in Chapter 1 (pp. 1-2), but it particularly involves our first question—"how to keep popular government constitutional and stable and yet alert, and forward-looking."

Chapter 2 describes how and why the framers established a Constitution filled with compromises—compromises designed to make the new government responsive to popular wishes but not too responsive, designed to divide power between the national government and the state governments and to redivide it among the three branches of the national government, designed to put checks on governmental power but still allow enough power for effective governing.

Chapter 3 answers this last question. It shows how the system of checks and balances stops popular majorities from easily getting control of the national government (pp. 64-67) and contrasts this arrangement with the British system of majority rule. It shows also (pp. 71-82) how the Constitution has been changed in letter and in spirit to keep it adapted to new

PART TWO

conditions. It demonstrates that certain political and governmental changes (pp. 69-70) have strengthened the power of government to act in response to popular demands without destroying the basic system of checks and balances.

Chapter 4 describes federalism, the division of powers between the national and state governments. Here again the original system has been adapted to meet the problem of a nation going through vast economic, social and military changes (pp. 89-96).

Chapter 5 takes up problems stemming from our system of federalism. It examines the question (136-138) whether federalism is obsolete because it makes government divided and weak in facing new challenges; hence it brings us back to the basic question of how to keep popular government both constitutional and effective. American experience so far suggests that our constitutional arrangements can be satisfactorily modified to meet new problems without violating fundamental democratic and constitutional principles. Our past successes give us courage to meet even sterner challenges in the future.

O N A BRIGHT SUNDAY AFTERNOON IN MAY 1787 George Washington, escorted by three generals and a troop of light horse, arrived in Philadelphia to the sound of chiming bells and cheering citizens. After depositing his baggage at the fine house where he was to stay, Washington went around the corner to call on an old friend, Benjamin Franklin. It was not coincidence that these two world-famous Americans should meet on this day in Philadelphia. They had much to talk about. For Washington, as a delegate from Virginia, and Franklin, as delegate from Pennsylvania, were in the vanguard of a group of illustrious men who were to spend the hot summer of 1787 writing a new constitution for the thirteen American states.

A constitution that is to endure must reflect the hard experience and high hopes of the people for whom it is drawn. It cannot emerge merely from the inspiration of a few leaders. Our Constitution is no exception. Those who framed it built with the institutions and ideas that they knew. But they did build; their creative feat can hardly be exaggerated. They did not, of course, complete the job of constitution-making, for it is a process that never can be completed. It began long before the constitutional convention met and it continues today. Constitutions—even written ones—are *growing* and *evolving* organisms rather than documents that are "struck off, at a given time, by the brain and purpose of man" (as Gladstone once described our Constitution). That is why we must leave Washington and Franklin for a moment and begin by looking at the materials out of which our Constitution has grown.

TOWARD INDEPENDENCE AND SELF-GOVERNMENT

To trace the Constitution to its real sources would take us to ancient times. For our purposes it is enough to note that the first immigrants to this continent brought with them political ideas and institutions that had been shaped in England. But these ideas and institutions were soon molded to the conditions of the New World. By July 4, 1776, the American colonists, with over

2

The

birth of

a nation

a century of experience behind them, had shaped the basic framework that is still the pattern of our structure of government. Many of the institutions that will be discussed in this book—such as written constitutions, separation of powers, bicameralism, executive veto, legislative control of spending—were part of that early experience.

Thirteen schools of government

In the thirteen colonies early Americans learned something of the difficult art of government. There were three kinds of colonial governments: royal, proprietary, and charter. By the middle of the 1750's most of the colonies were royal, with charters from the King setting forth the terms of government and giving the Crown considerable supervisory authority. Proprietary colonies—Maryland, Pennsylvania and Delaware—were based on feudal concepts. The King issued patents to proprietors, giving them the right to establish colonies; the proprietors had a position within the colony similar to that of the King in England. Although Pennsylvania had achieved a considerable measure of independence from the proprietor, by the middle of the eighteenth century the Crown exerted almost the same control over proprietary colonies as it did over the royal ones.

The two charter colonies of Rhode Island and Connecticut were unique. Charters issued in 1662 and 1663 from the King confirmed the governmental compacts which the colonists had drawn up to govern themselves. These two colonies were required to conform to the laws of England and to recognize appeals from their courts to the Privy Council in London, but they did not have to send their enactments to England for review, and their legislative assemblies elected their own governors.

"The differences between the governments of royal, proprietary, and charter colonies," it has been said, "were slight in actual practice. . . . It is therefore possible to subject all colonial governments to common analysis."[1] All the colonies had written *charters* that outlined the frame of government, set forth the rights of the colonists, and were not subject, the colonists felt, to change by ordinary laws. Power was divided among the legislative, executive, and judicial branches.

All but one of the colonies had a *bicameral* (two-house) *legislature*. The upper house, composed of a dozen or so landed gentlemen and wealthy merchants, advised the governor and heard appeals from the decisions of colonial courts. These men were appointed by the Crown or the proprietor upon the recommendation of the governor. The lower house was elected by colonists who owned property. Over the years, these lower chambers gradually assumed power to legislate for the colonies, subject to veto by the governor and the upper house. Since the colonists' representatives staunchly refused to pass permanent revenue measures, they had control

[1] Alfred H. Kelly and Winfred A. Harbison, *The American Constitution: Its Origins and Development* (New York: W. W. Norton & Company, Inc., 1948), p. 28.

over colonial appropriations, often including the governor's salary. They used this weapon to gain further power. The British government had the right to veto colonial legislation; but London was more than three months away, and for a long time the colonists handled their own affairs with little interference from abroad.

In the royal colonies the *governors* were appointed by the King and served as his representatives and as agents through whom instructions from London were transmitted. In proprietary colonies, the proprietor selected the governor, but these appointments were subject to confirmation by the Crown, and the governors had to give bond to execute the laws of Parliament relating to America. Governors of Rhode Island and Connecticut owed their offices to the colonial assemblies.

The royal and proprietary governors were powerful. They had an absolute veto over legislation, they could dissolve the legislatures, they appointed the officials, they commanded the colonial militia, and they presided over religious and social activities. Despite their great authority, the governors had a difficult job. They had to please both the colonists and the British government, and often ended up by pleasing neither.

The *judicial system* grew more slowly than the other two branches, but eventually both lower and higher courts were established. The judges were appointed by the Crown, although in some colonies they depended upon the legislatures for their salaries. In most cases appeals could be taken from the decisions of colonial judges to the Privy Council in London, an important device of British control to insure that colonial legislation conformed to the laws of England.

During the Colonial period, the basic pattern of American government with which we are familiar today had been laid down. Relations between the colonies and England familiarized Americans with the division of powers between a central and constituent governments and made federalism a natural development. The role of the Privy Council in enforcing English law as superior to colonial legislation was a forerunner to the Supreme Court's task of deciding whether state acts violate the Constitution or national law. The familiar separation of powers and bicameral legislatures were developed during this time. The roots of the modern American governmental system go deep.

Early Americans became experts at operating, or at times evading, this governmental machinery, and by the latter part of the eighteenth century it was becoming clear that they might soon have further use for that expertness.

The kindling of nationalism

Despite the wealth of their governmental experience within the several colonies, the colonists had little training in *inter*colonial problems. Under a divide-and-rule policy, London tried to keep the colonies separate and dependent on England. The colonists themselves did not become especially aware of any real unity until the events leading to the Revolutionary War stirred American patriotism. Until a few years before the Revolution, the colonists considered themselves Englishmen, and their national loyalty was to the British Crown. The local loyalty of each was to his own colony, not to America. Beyond this there was some sectional feeling based on familiarity and identity of interests, so that New England, the South, and, to a lesser extent, the Middle Colonies became identifiable communities.

Yet throughout the Colonial period, the demands of war and the needs of common defense forced the colonies to think of problems beyond their own boundaries. The origins of American federalism and the roots of American patriotism reach back into this period. As early as 1643 the New England Confederation was organized to provide unified action against the threats of the Indians, Dutch, and French. The Confederation lasted as an effective organization until 1664. Not for almost 100 years was there another important proposal for intercolonial cooperation. In 1754 the British Ministry called the nine northern colonies into conference at Albany to discuss Indian affairs. Benjamin Franklin, who early became aware of an underlying cultural and political identity among the colonies, seized the opportunity to propose a scheme of continental government. Franklin's proposals, known as the Albany Plan, called for the creation of a Grand Council composed of delegates elected by the colonial assemblies and a President General appointed by the King. This central government was to be given the power to regulate trade with the Indians, make war and peace, and to *levy taxes* and collect customs duties in order to raise military and naval forces.

Meeting under the threat of attack by the French and Indians, delegates to the Albany Conference avowed that some form of union was necessary to preserve the colonies. They recommended proposals for unity to the colonial assemblies, but not a single assembly approved. Those who controlled colonial affairs saw no need to subordinate their authority to an intercolonial government. Among the people there were no common American loyalties, no consciously shared experiences, no powerful American ideas. It was to take another thirty years and two wars before a strong central government would be acceptable to the colonists.

But the groundwork was being laid. During the French and Indian War American war heroes began to emerge. In 1763 at the end of the Seven Years' War, the French were driven from the North American continent. New territories came under English control, and money was needed to administer them. The British government had gone into debt fighting the French; its ministers decided that the colonies should pay some of the cost of defending the Empire. Steps were taken to raise revenue among the colonies, to enforce the trade laws more rigorously, and to tighten English control over colonial affairs. These decisions caused trouble in America.

Businessmen wanting to develop their own industries, merchants and ship-pers wishing to trade with nations other than England, planters believing they could get better prices from the Dutch and French than from the Eng-lish, speculators wishing to buy western land—all these and others found reason to chafe under the heavier taxes and harsher restrictions.

What did these restless colonists want to do? Not very much. They had hardly a thought of independence. They merely wanted Parliament to repeal the onerous laws and to leave the colonists alone as much as pos-sible. Their protests were couched in legal and constitutional phraseology.

But to make their protests more effective, these essentially conservative-minded men stirred up the feelings of other elements in the colonies. Many of the small artisans, lesser merchants, and farmers were not directly af-fected by the tax and trade laws, and many of them did not have the right to vote; nevertheless the actions of the English government affronted their developing national feeling. They were not to be easily quieted. Leadership of the protest movement began to pass from the hands of the more re-strained group into those who were asking for more radical action, men like Sam and John Adams in Massachusetts and Patrick Henry and Thomas Jefferson in Virginia. These men gave more stress to the concepts of the natural rights of men and of government resting on the consent of the gov-erned and less emphasis to constitutional and legal arguments. They quoted Locke on individual liberty and human rights.[2]

These arguments were a double-edged sword. They could be used against the dominant groups *within* the colonies as well as against the British.[3] Gradually some of the conservatives began to lose their enthusiasm for protest. They rightly feared that the revolution might lead not merely to changes in Empire relations but also to domestic reform. Feeling against England, however, did become sharper. The colonists were forced, first for political and then for military purposes, to join together in defense of their common cause. Gradually they became aware of an *American* interest, as distinct from English or purely local interests. Colonial leaders began to get in closer touch with one another. The Committees of Correspondence, the Stamp Act Congress, and the First Continental Congress stimulated aware-ness of the common bond and gave the colonists experience in intercolonial cooperation. Finally, in 1775, the Second Continental Congress began to speak for *Americans*.

The surge toward independence

Even after minutemen began fighting with redcoats in 1775, the idea of independence was unacceptable to many Americans. They still hoped for

[2] Cf. J. F. Jameson, *The American Revolution Considered as a Social Movement* (Princeton: Princeton University Press, 1926).

[3] See Elisha P. Douglas, *Rebels and Democrats: The Struggle for Equal Political Rights and Majority Rule during the American Revolution* (Chapel Hill: University of North Carolina Press, 1955).

reconciliation with England. But as the months went on, the fighting continued and the English government refused to make concessions to American demands. In August 1775, the King issued a proclamation declaring the colonies to be in a state of rebellion, and in December 1775 Parliament forbade all trade with the colonies. These actions played into the hands of the radicals and strengthened their cause. Then in January 1776 Thomas Paine issued his pamphlet, *Common Sense,* calling on Americans to proclaim their independence. Seldom in history has a single pamphlet had so much influence. As Morison and Commager have said, "It rallied the undecided and the wavering, and proved a trumpet call to the radicals."

Those wanting independence became stronger. In Pennsylvania the struggle was especially bitter; there the radicals finally gained control, established a new government, drew up a new constitution, and instructed their delegation in Congress to work for independence. On June 7, Richard Henry Lee, pursuant to instructions from the Virginia Assembly, moved in Congress "that these United Colonies are, and of right ought to be, Free and Independent States." After bitter debate, Lee's motion was adopted on July 2. The Congress had already appointed a committee, consisting of Thomas Jefferson, John Adams, Benjamin Franklin, Roger Sherman, and Robert Livingston, to prepare a formal declaration of "the causes which impelled us to this mighty resolution." This Declaration of Independence was adopted on July 4, 1776.

The Declaration is more than a justification of rebellion. It is also a statement of the American democratic creed, "designed to justify the past and chart the future."[4] This creed is set forth in succinct and eloquent language:

We hold these truths to be self-evident, that all men are created equal, that they are endowed by their Creator with certain unalienable Rights, that among these are Life, Liberty, and the pursuit of Happiness. That to secure these rights, Governments are instituted among Men, deriving their just powers from the consent of the governed. That whenever any Form of Government becomes destructive of those ends, it is the Right of the People to alter or abolish it, and to institute new Government, laying its foundation on such principles and organizing its powers in such form, as to them shall seem most likely to effect their Safety and Happiness. . . .

Here we find the democratic beliefs in man's *natural rights,* in *popular consent* as the only just basis for political obligations, in *limited government,* and in the right of the people to *revolt* against *tyrannical government.*

Some intellectual luggage

These doctrines were part of the political common sense of most American patriots in 1776. Jefferson, who wrote the Declaration, stated, in a letter

[4] Ralph Barton Perry, *Puritanism and Democracy* (New York: Vanguard Press, 1944), pp. 124-125.

to Henry Lee, that he did not feel it his duty to set out "new principles . . . never before thought of," but to "place before mankind the common sense of the subject, in terms so plain and firm as to command their assent, and to justify ourselves in the independent stand we are compelled to take." These ideas had come to a white heat in the crucible of America. But in essence they were part of the intellectual luggage that the colonists had brought with them, or later imported, from the Old World.

The man most responsible for popularizing these doctrines was *John Locke,* who had written his famous *Second Treatise on Civil Government* a century before to justify the English Revolution of 1688. Locke's arguments were tailor-made for the defense of the American cause. He profoundly influenced the patriot leaders, and his ideas, along with some of his phraseology, found their way into the Declaration.

Prior to the establishment of organized society and government, wrote Locke, man lived in a state of nature. This was not a lawless condition, however, because the natural law was known to all men through the use of reason and was binding on all. (The real nature of natural law has been argued by philosophers for centuries; for our purposes it is enough to think of the laws of nature as inherent, inescapable rules of human behavior— laws, in Cicero's words, that are in accordance with nature, apply to all men, and are unchangeable and eternal.) According to the natural law, each individual has a basic, inalienable right to his life, liberty, and that property with which he has mixed his own labor. Whoever deprives another of his natural rights violates the natural law and can be justly punished.

Most men obeyed the natural law, but living in a state of nature was inconvenient. There were always a few lawless souls; and whenever a person's natural rights were violated, he had to enforce the law himself. Furthermore, when people had differences, there was no common impartial judge to whom they could turn for a decision. Therefore, being endowed with reason, men decided to end this inconvenience by *contracting* among themselves to form a society and to establish a government for the purpose of protecting each man's natural rights. By the terms of the social contract, each individual promised to abide by the decisions of the majority and to surrender to society his private right to enforce the law.

Government was thus limited by the purpose for which it was established. It had only the authority to enforce the natural law. *When government becomes destructive of man's inalienable rights,* it ceases to have a claim on his allegiance. The people then have the duty to revolt and to create a government better designed to promote their natural rights.

Does this sound like pretty radical doctrine? It must be remembered that while Locke's ideas would give power to the people, they also put checks on that power. In effect, depending on one's interpretation of natural rights, these theories could be used either to strengthen or to weaken the right of the people to control their relations with one another through government.

Moreover, early Americans were also influenced by other thinkers in the Old World. One of the most prominent of these was *Montesquieu*. Living under Louis XIV and Louis XV, he believed that liberty must be secured *against* government. Montesquieu's importance lies in the fact that he had a very practical scheme to keep government from violating man's natural right to liberty. This was the *separation of powers*. The way to prevent the abuse of power is to check power with power, said Montesquieu, by giving some authority to the legislative branch, some to the executive, and some to the judicial. Liberty is safe against a government with this kind of built-in mechanism.

These ideas set the intellectual tone during the period when Americans were turning to the business of replacing English authority with their own governments. Broadly speaking, our forefathers leaned more heavily on Locke in setting up government under the Articles of Confederation, more heavily on Montesquieu in framing the Constitution of 1787.

EXPERIMENT IN CONFEDERATION

The American Revolution was more than a colonial rebellion. It was also an internal revolution. Although as Daniel J. Boorstin has pointed out, "in the modern European sense of the word, it was hardly a revolution at all,"[5] important internal changes were made. Government remained in the hands of a relatively small governing class, and there were no sharp breaks with the past, but steps toward popular control were taken and the new governments that replaced royal authority were in many ways different from those existing before the Revolution.

The English had tried to regulate the colonists from London; now power was to be firmly in the hands of local state governments. The authorities had trampled on men's liberties; now bills of rights were adopted, and religious qualifications for voting were abolished, although property and tax requirements were retained.

The most glaring difference between the old colonial charters and the new state constitutions was the *concentration of power* in the *legislatures*. The legislative branches had enhanced their prestige as champions of popular causes. The current emphasis on the consent of the governed, borrowed from Locke and others, also stressed the legislature as the repository of that consent. The governorship, on the other hand, savored of royalty and stirred unpleasant memories. In most of the states the governors were made dependent on the legislature for election, their terms of office were shortened, their veto power reduced, their power to appoint officials curbed. Judges, too, carried overtones of royalty. The new state legislatures saw no reason why they should not override judicial decisions and scold judges

---

[5] Daniel J. Boorstin, *The Genius of American Politics* (Chicago: The University of Chicago Press, 1953), p. 68.

THE BIRTH OF A NATION 41

whose rulings were unpopular. The legislative branch, complained Madison later in *Federalist No. 48,* was "drawing all power into its impetuous vortex."

The Articles of Confederation

What about the central government? The Continental Congress, like the colonial legislatures, had assumed governmental powers at the outbreak of hostilities. Although the Congress appointed General Washington commander in chief of the Continental Army, carried on negotiations with foreign countries, raised and supported troops, borrowed and printed money, its powers were based only on a revolutionary act. A more permanent constitutional arrangement was needed. Accordingly the Congress created in June 1776 a committee to draft a constitution. A few days after the Declaration was adopted this committee submitted a plan for a "league of friendship and perpetual Union," but not until a year later, after months of interrupted debate, did Congress finally submit the Articles of Confederation to the states for their approval. Within two years all the states except Maryland had ratified the Articles; but since unanimous consent was required, the Articles did not go into effect until 1781, when Maryland finally signed up.

The Articles more or less constitutionalized the existing arrangements. They frankly established only a league of friendship and cooperation— not a national government. Each state retained its "sovereignty, freedom, and independence, and every power, jurisdiction, and right" that was not *expressly* delegated to "the United States, in Congress assembled." The states had jointly declared their independence of the King and had jointly fought against him, but they considered themselves free and independent sovereignties. They were loath to part with any of their newly won powers. After fighting a war against centralized authority, they did not want to create another central government, even though it would be American rather than English. Most of the patriots shared the belief that republican governments could exist only in small states. They feared that a strong central government would fall into the hands of those who would nullify the work of the Revolution.

There was, nevertheless, a universal recognition of the need for "the more convenient management of the general interests of the United States," and for this purpose a Congress was established in which each state was to be represented by not less than two nor more than seven delegates. The voting in Congress was by states, each state having one vote regardless of size or contributions to the general treasury. Delegates were chosen by the state legislatures, and their salaries were paid from their respective state treasuries. As the delegates were state representatives rather than national legislators, they were subject to recall by their state legislatures.

Congress was given the power to determine peace and war, to make treaties and alliances, to coin money, to regulate trade with the Indians, to borrow money, to emit bills of credit, to build and equip a navy, to establish a postal system, and to appoint senior officers of the United States Army (composed of state militias). In short, Congress was given substantially the same powers that the Continental Congress had already been exercising. Approval of nine of the thirteen states was required to make important decisions.

The two most important powers *denied* to Congress were those of taxation and of regulation of commerce. It was the abuse of these two powers by the British government that had precipitated the Revolutionary War. Naturally enough there was little desire to grant them to another central government. All that Congress could do was to ask the states for funds. It had to depend on the state governments to collect the taxes and turn the money over to the central treasury. And though the states promised to refrain from discriminating against one another's trade, Congress had no power to prevent such discrimination or to pass positive measures to promote national commerce. Only through treaties could Congress regulate foreign commerce, but here, too, the Congress had no enforcement powers.

Clearly Congress under the Confederation was a feeble body. It had no authority to enforce any of its laws either by the use of military force against the states or by punishing individuals. There was neither a federal executive nor a federal judiciary to enforce national laws. There was simply the promise of each state to observe the Articles and abide by the decisions of Congress. The Articles were ratified by the several state legislatures, not by the voters. The Articles could be amended, but—more like a treaty than a constitution—approval of all thirteen state legislatures was needed. In many respects the national government was like the United Nations today—although the similarity has often been exaggerated.

Nevertheless, the government created by the Articles of Confederation, however weak, was what the people in power wanted. They believed that the goals of the Revolution could be achieved only through strong local governments and that centralized authority was dangerous. A truly national government at this time could have been established only by the sword and probably would have been destroyed by the sword. The Articles reflected public sentiment and rested on political reality. A unified national government cannot be created by documents; it must have the support of diverse interests and individuals within the community.

Postwar problems

The war was over and independence won. Could the new nation survive —a nation just becoming conscious of its own nationality, "conceived in liberty and dedicated to the proposition that all men are created equal"? The practical difficulties confronting the infant America would have tested the strongest and best-entrenched government. Within the limits of its powers, the government of the Confederation did an excellent job: a program was adopted for the governing and development of western lands, diplomatic relations with other nations were established, the foundations of a central bureaucracy were set up, and the financial problems growing out of the war were being met. By the time the Constitutional Convention assembled, the postwar depression was giving way to a period of business and commercial expansion.

Yet the problems were great and the central government was unable to provide strong leadership. In the years immediately following the war, business and commerce declined after a brief boom. Newly won independence deprived Americans of some of the special trading and commercial privileges they had enjoyed as members of the British Empire. The profitable trade with the English West Indies was prohibited. Congress found it difficult to negotiate favorable trade treaties with other nations because of a general belief in Europe that the states would not comply with the treaties even if they would permit them to be ratified. The Spanish closed the mouth of the Mississippi at New Orleans to all American goods, and Barbary pirates freely looted American shipping in the Mediterranean. There was no uniform medium of exchange, because each state provided its own money, which fluctuated greatly in value. Paper money issued by Congress to finance the war was circulating at about one-thousandth of its face value. Lacking confidence in Congress' ability to redeem its pledges, creditors were reluctant to lend money to the central government except at high rates. Public securities sold at a fraction of their face value. The states themselves began to default in their payments into the federal treasury. Each state regulated commerce, some discriminating against their neighbors, and the lack of uniformity of trade regulations made it difficult to develop interstate commerce. The end of the war reduced the sense of urgency that had helped to unite the several states, and conflicts among the states were frequent.

The property laws were harsh. Delinquent debtors, primarily farmers, faced the loss of all their property and the prospect of debtor's prison. Quite naturally, they began to exact pressure on the state legislatures for relief. In several of the states they were successful, and the legislatures extended the period for the payment of mortgages, issued legal tender paper money for the payment of debts, and scaled down the taxes. Creditors resented these interferences. Throughout the nation the conflicts grew bitter between debtor and creditor, between poor and rich, between manufacturer and shipper.

To add to the difficulties, neither the English nor the states would live up to the terms of the treaty of peace. The English refused to withdraw their troops from the western frontier until American debtors paid their English creditors and until the states repaid the loyalists for confiscated property. Congress lacked the power to force either the English or the states to comply. To the English on the west and the Spanish and French in the south, the new nation, internally divided and lacking a strong central government, made a tempting prize.

Movement for revision

Was it surprising that, in the face of postwar problems of demobilization, economic changes and expansion, foreign relations, and conflicts among the various sectional and economic interests, some of the democratic ardor of the revolutionary days began to wane? The radicals, who had engineered the Revolution, began to lose power. Most of the conservatives —the property owners, the creditors, the shippers, the "better people"— had never been satisfied with the Articles of Confederation; they considered them too democratic and too feeble. The inability of the Confederation to provide a strong union, to prevent state interferences with business, to pay its creditors, added to the conviction of the conservatives that the central government must be strengthened and that checks must be placed on the state governments. They undoubtedly did, for partisan purposes, "paint dark the picture of the times and blame the supposed woes of the country on the Articles of Confederation,"[6] but they were genuinely alarmed. Their contracts were the ones that the state legislatures were interfering with, their bonds that the central government was unable to pay, their businesses that needed uniform commercial regulations and national protective tariffs, their manufacturing for which they wanted bounties. But beyond this they were concerned about the dangers of disunion, anarchy, and tyranny.

These fears were sharpened by the growth of a small but dangerous group, composed chiefly of men who had never believed in government by the people. These men began to argue publicly that republican government was a failure—that a strong monarchical government was needed to protect persons and property. Washington, who, fortunately for the nation, would have nothing to do with the persistent attempts to make him a king or dictator of the United States, wrote in alarm in August 1786 to John Jay, Director of Foreign Affairs:

What astonishing changes a few years are capable of producing! I am told that even respectable characters speak of a monarchical form of Government without horror. But how irrevocable and tremendous! What a triumph for our enemies to verify their predictions. What a triumph for the advocates of despotism to find that we are incapable of governing ourselves, and that systems founded on the basis of equal liberty are merely ideal and fallacious. Would to God that wise measures be taken in time to avert the consequences we have but too much reason to apprehend.[7]

[6] Merrill Jensen, *The Articles of Confederation* (Madison: University of Wisconsin, 1940), p. 245.

[7] John D. Fitzpatrick, ed., *The Writings of George Washington* (Washington: Government Printing Office), XXVIII, 503.

The politicians, creditors, speculators, merchants, manufacturers, army officers, and others who believed that wise measures should be taken to avert disaster, felt that the situation was so critical that it would not be enough to amend the Articles of Confederation. They wanted to alter the basic nature of the Union and to create a strong national government with coercive powers. They wanted to place checks on the state legislatures to prevent interference with property rights.

How could all this be done? The nationalists had to move carefully. Although there was growing recognition of the need to amend the Articles in order to give Congress the power to collect taxes and to regulate commerce among the states, many Americans were still suspicious of a central government with coercive powers. Many of the people did not think things were so bad. Certainly they were not so desperate that they were willing to make any basic alterations in their governmental structure. Debtor laws and paper currency were not to them abuses of republican liberty, and whatever evils existed, they felt, could not be attributed to the venality of the state legislators or to the weakness of the central government. John Fiske, noted nineteenth-century historian, stated, "At no time in this distressed period would a frank and abrupt proposal for a convention to remodel the government have found favour."

Nevertheless, knotty practical problems—problems of boundaries, navigation, tariffs, and so on—continued to arise, and often these problems were common to most or all of the states. In the fall of 1786 the Virginia legislature, guided by James Madison, invited the states to send delegates to Annapolis to discuss uniform trade regulation. This was the ostensible purpose of the convention, but as Madison wrote Jefferson, "Many gentlemen both within and without Congress wish to make this meeting subservient to a plenipotentiary Convention for amending the Confederation."[8] Only five states sent delegates. Many who wanted action lost hope. But Alexander Hamilton seized the opportunity to engineer through the Annapolis Convention a discreetly worded resolution. Congress was requested to ask the states to send commissioners to Philadelphia to "devise such further provisions as shall appear to them necessary to render the Constitution of the Federal Government adequate to the exigencies of the Union." But Congress, apathetic and perhaps suspicious that Hamilton had more in mind than amending the Articles, was loath to act. Some state legislatures appointed delegates, but throughout the states not much more than polite interest was shown. It seemed likely that little would come of the project.

Incident in Massachusetts

In the fall and winter of 1786-1787, events in western Massachusetts seemed to justify the dire predictions that the country was on the verge of

[8] Quoted by Charles Warren, *The Making of the Constitution* (Boston: Little, Brown & Company, 1937), p. 22.

anarchy. The farmers were in a desperate plight. Many faced imprisonment through inability to meet their mortgages or their taxes. They had
unsuccessfully petitioned the Massachusetts General Court legislature for
relief. Finally, the angry farmers rallied around Daniel Shays, and marching
into Northampton, they blocked the entrance to the courthouse and forcibly
restrained the judges from foreclosing mortgages on their farms.

The militia readily put down the uprising, but the revolt sent a shudder
down the spines of the more substantial citizens. The outraged General
Knox, Secretary of War, wrote to Washington:

This dreadful situation has alarmed every man of principle and property in
New England. They start as from a dream and ask what has been the cause of
our delusion? What is to afford us security against the violence of lawless men?
Our government must be braced, changed or altered to secure our lives and
property. . . .[9]

During the winter as the story of this open rebellion spread through the
nation, it took on lurid overtones and, in the minds of many, became a
threat to each person's life and fortune. Some reacted by abandoning any
pretense of support for republican principles. Madison warned that the
"turbulent scenes" in Massachusetts had done inexpressible injury to the
republican cause and even had caused a "propensity toward Monarchy" in
some leading minds.[10] A letter widely circulated throughout the states argued that it would be "preferable to distribute the United States into Three
Republics, who should enter into a perpetual league and alliance for mutual defence."[11]

What could be done? The more respectable leaders were not ready to
plunge into either monarchy or disunion. Fortunately, an instrument was
at hand that promised a better way to deal with the crisis—the proposed
Philadelphia Convention. Shays' Rebellion served as a catalyst, and the
movement toward revision of the Articles, which had been brewing for a
long time, began to boil. Throughout the states there was a quickening of
interest in the recommendation of the Annapolis Convention. Seven
states appointed delegates without waiting for Congress to act. Finally Congress jumped on the convention band wagon with a cautiously worded request to the states to appoint delegates for the "sole and express purpose
of revising the Articles of Confederation . . . to render the Federal Constitution adequate to the exigencies of Government, and the preservation of
the Union." The careful congressmen specified that no recommendation
would be effective unless approved by Congress and confirmed by all the
state legislatures as provided by the Articles.

[9] *Ibid.*, p. 31.
[10] Madison to Edmund Pendleton, February 28, 1787. Cited by Warren, *The Making of the Constitution*, p. 45.
[11] *Ibid.*, p. 29.

Eventually every state except Rhode Island appointed delegates. (The debtors and farmers who controlled the Rhode Island legislature suspected that the very purpose of the convention was to place limits on their power.) Many of the delegations were bound by instructions only to consider amendments to the Articles of Confederation. Delaware went so far as to forbid her representatives to consider any proposal that would deny any state equal representation in Congress. Few people were aware of the portentous changes that were in store.

THE PHILADELPHIA STORY

The Constitutional Convention was the third step in the birth of the new nation. The first step was the destruction of English governmental authority. The next step was the creation of new state governments to replace those destroyed. But after fighting against foreign despotism under banners of liberty and local self-government, the patriots had failed to establish systems capable of providing the order and unity in which liberty and diversity could thrive. The third step began in Philadelphia in the summer of 1787. The delegates to the convention were presented with a condition, not a theory. They had to establish a national government that had enough power to prevent the nation from degenerating into anarchy or despotism.

Although 74 delegates were appointed by the various states, only 55 put in an appearance in Philadelphia, and only 39 took real part in the work of the convention. But it was a distinguished gathering. Many of the most important men of the nation were there—successful merchants, planters, bankers, and lawyers, former and present governors and congressional representatives. As theorists, they had read Locke, Montesquieu, and other philosophers. As men of affairs, they were interested in the intensely practical job of constructing a national government. Theory played its part, but experience was to be their main guide.

The cast

Although most of the revolutionary leaders eventually supported the Constitution in the ratification debate, only 8 of the 56 signers of the Declaration of Independence were present at the Constitutional Convention. Among the revolutionary leaders absent (for various reasons) were Jefferson, Paine, Henry, Richard Henry Lee, Sam and John Adams, and John Hancock. The delegates to the convention were mainly aristocrats. There were no small farmers and working artisans among them. But in the 1780's the common men were not expected to participate in politics, and the Constitutional Convention was as representative as most meetings of the time. Of the 39 active participants, the following stand out as the prime movers of the convention.

Alexander Hamilton was, as we have already noted, one of the most impassioned proponents of a strong national government. He had been the engineer at the Annapolis Convention, and as early as 1778 he had been urging upon his wealthy and aristocratic friends the necessity for invigorating the national government. Born in the West Indies, he lacked strong local attachments and was dedicated to the vision of a unified and powerful United States. He had come to the United States when only sixteen, and while still a student at Kings College (now Columbia University) had won national attention by his brilliant pamphlets in defense of the colonial cause. He married Elizabeth Schuyler, daughter of one of New York's most important gentlemen, and soon became a member of the governing group in that state. During the war he served as General Washington's aide, and his war experiences confirmed his distaste for a Congress so weak that it could not even supply its troops with enough food or arms. Although highly influential in the movement leading to the convention and afterwards in securing ratification of the Constitution, he did not play as important a role during the deliberation as might be expected. Behind the closed doors of the convention he freely expressed his views, but they were much too nationalistic and aristocratic—his advocacy of a central government patterned after that of England was unacceptable. The two other delegates from New York, Robert Lansing and John Yates, were, ideologically, at the pole opposite from Hamilton. They had little desire to strengthen the national government. Since the voting was by states, Yates and Lansing, when present, controlled the vote of New York. They went home early and Hamilton followed. He returned only at the end of the summer, so New York was unrepresented most of the time.

From Virginia came three of the leading delegates, General George Washington, James Madison, and Edmund Randolph. *Washington* was even at that time "first in war, first in peace, and first in the hearts of his countrymen." Although active in the movement to revise the Articles of Confederation, he had been extremely reluctant to attend the convention. He accepted only when persuaded that his prestige was needed for its success. When the Virginia legislature placed his name at the top of their list of delegates, the importance of the convention was made manifest. After Franklin withdrew his name from consideration, Washington was unanimously selected to preside over the meetings. According to the records, he spoke only twice during the deliberations, but his influence was felt in the informal gatherings as well as during the sessions. His views were well known, and he was counted among those who were convinced of the necessity for a drastic revision of the Articles. The universal assumption that Washington would become the first President under the new Constitution inspired confidence in it.

James Madison, slight of build and small in voice, was only 36 at the time of the convention, but he was one of the most learned members present.

Despite his youth, he had helped frame Virginia's first constitution and had served in both the Virginia Assembly and in the Congress. Realizing the importance of the convention, Madison had spent months in preparation by studying the history of Greek confederacies and Italian republics. During the deliberations, he sat in the front of the room and kept full notes on what was said and done. These notes are the major source of information about the convention. Madison was also a member of the group who favored the establishment of a real national government.

Of less importance than either Washington or Madison, but still a man of front rank, was *Edmund Randolph,* the 34-year-old governor of Virginia, who, as such, was titular head of the Virginia delegation. His political views were ambiguous and erratic, but he usually voted with Madison. Although he refused to sign the Constitution, he later worked actively for its ratification in Virginia. *George Mason* was another influential Virginia delegate who refused to sign the Constitution. Mason, a close friend of Jefferson, was the author of the Virginia Declaration of Rights in 1776 and worked unsuccessfully to get the Constitutional Convention to include a bill of rights in the proposed Constitution.

The Pennsylvania delegation rivaled that of Virginia. Its membership included Benjamin Franklin, James Wilson, and Gouverneur Morris. *Franklin,* at 81, was the convention's oldest member and, as one of his fellow delegates said, "He is well known to be the greatest philosopher of the present age." Second only to Washington in the esteem of his countrymen, he had a world reputation unrivaled by any American. He was one of the first to hold a vision of a strong and united America. Because of his age and because his opinions were too democratic for most of the delegates, his views were usually given polite attention and then ignored. But at critical moments his sage and humorous remarks served to break the tension and prevent bitterness.

Gouverneur Morris, "a very handsome, bold, and—the ladies say—a very impudent man," was more eloquent than brilliant. He addressed the convention more often than any other person. His views were those of an aristocrat with disdain for both the rabble and the uncouth moneymakers. The elegance of the language of the Constitution is proof of his facility with the pen, for he was responsible for the final draft. Another Pennsylvanian of importance was *James Wilson,* a tall, Scottish-born and Scottish-trained lawyer. He was one of the eight men who had signed the Declaration of Independence. His keen mind was an important asset to those working for a strong central government.

Of course there were many other distinguished gentlemen present. Luther Martin of Maryland, John Dickinson of Delaware, and William Paterson of New Jersey were not in agreement with a majority of the delegates, but they ably defended the position of those insisting upon equal representation for the smaller states.

The convention was a secret affair. Delegates were forbidden to discuss any of the business of the convention with outsiders. This rule was adopted to encourage men to speak freely. It was feared that if a member publicly took a particular stand, it would be harder for him to change his mind after debate and discussion. Looking ahead to the ratification struggle, the members knew that if word of the inevitable disagreements got out it would provide ammunition for the many enemies of the convention. There were critics of this secrecy rule, but probably it was a wise move. Without it agreement might have been impossible.

Consensus

The Constitutional Convention is usually discussed in terms of the three famous compromises: the compromise between large and small states over representation in Congress; the compromise between North and South over the counting of slaves for taxation and representation; and the compromise between North and South over the regulation and taxation of foreign commerce. But this emphasis obscures the facts that there were many other important compromises and that on many of the more significant issues most of the delegates were in substantial agreement. While it is impossible to make neat generalizations about the ideas of some thirty-odd men, it is clear that certain basic ideas were part of the operating assumptions of the leading delegates. Underlying all the compromises was a general concurrence on certain basic principles.

A few delegates personally favored a limited monarchy, but almost all were convinced supporters of republican government, and this was the only form seriously considered. It was obvious that no other kind of government would be acceptable to the nation. Most important, all the delegates, including those few who favored a monarch, were *constitutionalists,* opposing arbitrary and unrestrained government, whether monarchical, aristocratic, or democratic.

All agreed that society is divided along class lines and that "the most common and durable source of factions" was "the various and unequal distribution of property," as Madison wrote in *Federalist No. 10.* The common philosophy accepted by most of the delegates was that of *balanced government.* They wanted to construct a national government in which no single interest would dominate the others. Since the men in Philadelphia represented groups alarmed by the tendencies of the agrarian interests to interfere with property, they were primarily concerned with balancing the government in the direction of protection for property and business. George Mason and Benjamin Franklin warned of the danger of going too far in this direction, but there was an almost universal concurrence in the remarks of Elbridge Gerry (delegate from Massachusetts),

"The evils we experience flow from the excess of democracy. The people do not want virtue, but are dupes of pretended patriots."

Likewise there was substantial agreement with Gouverneur Morris' statement that *property* was the *"principal object of government."* John Rutledge of South Carolina not only agreed, but went one step further and stated that "property was the sole end of government." Nor was there dissent from Madison's statement that the meddling by state legislatures with the rights of property had, more than anything else, made the convention necessary.

Benjamin Franklin favored extending the right to vote to nonproperty owners, but most of the delegates agreed in general with the sentiments expressed by John Dickinson, James Madison, and Gouverneur Morris. Dickinson argued that the property holders were the best guardians of liberty and that only they could be counted on to resist the "dangerous influence of those multitudes without property and without principle." James Madison voiced the fear that those without property would soon become the largest part of the population and, if given the right to vote, would either combine to deprive the property owners of their rights or would become the "tools of opulence and ambition." Gouverneur Morris, too, was inclined to the view that the masses would sell their votes to the rich. The delegates agreed in principle on restricted suffrage, but they differed over the kind and amount of property that one must own in order to vote. As a result, each state was left to determine the qualifications for electing members to the House of Representatives, the only branch of the national government in which the electorate was given a direct voice.

Within five days of its opening, the convention ("with more boldness than legality"), only Connecticut dissenting, voted to approve the Fourth Virginia Resolve that "a national government ought to be established consisting of a supreme legislative, executive, and judiciary." All the delegates were bound by the instructions from Congress merely to suggest amendments to the Articles of Confederation, and some were bound by even more strict instructions from their state legislatures. Yet this decision, approved by a majority of the delegates, to establish *a national government resting on and exercising power over individuals* profoundly altered the nature of the central government—it changed it from a league of states to a national government. At a later date in the convention, delegates from the smaller states contended that the convention had no authority to establish a national government operating over individuals through its own agents. But these objections were primarily tactical maneuvers to force the large states to make concessions.

At no time was there serious consideration of constructing the national government in any way except by *a distribution of powers among the three branches of government.* A strong executive would provide the energy and direction for the general government that had been lacking under the Articles, and, with an independent judiciary, would provide a practical remedy to check the excesses of democracy. Here the delegates borrowed from Montesquieu. There was little dissent from the proposal to grant the new Congress all the powers of the old Congress, and all other powers in which the separate states were incompetent or in which the harmony of the United States might be interrupted by the exercise of individual legislation. Bicameralism was also accepted without much debate, with only Franklin favoring a single-house national legislature. Almost all the states had two-chamber legislatures from colonial times, and the delegates were used to the system. Bicameralism also conformed to their belief in the need for balanced government, the upper house representing the aristocracy to offset the more democratic lower house.

Conflict

There were, too, serious differences among the various groups, especially between the representatives of the large states who favored a strong national government and the delegates from the small states who were anxious to preserve the confederate character of the Union.

The nationalists took the initiative. The Virginia delegation had caucused during the delay before the convention. As soon as the convention was organized, they were ready with fifteen resolutions. These resolutions, known as the *Virginia Plan,* contemplated a strong central government. The legislature was to be composed of two chambers. The members of the lower house were to be elected by the people, those of the upper house to be chosen by the lower chamber from nominees submitted by the state legislatures. Representation in both branches was to be on the basis of either wealth or numbers, thus giving the more populous and wealthy states-—Virginia, Massachusetts, and Pennsylvania—a majority in the legislature.

The Congress thus created was to be given all the legislative power of its predecessor under the Articles of Confederation and the right "to legislate in all cases in which the separate States are incompetent." Furthermore, it was to have the authority to disallow state legislation in conflict with the articles of Union. The Virginia Plan also called for a national executive to be chosen by the legislature and a national judiciary with rather extensive jurisdiction. The national supreme court along with the executive were to have an absolute veto over the acts of the Congress.

For the first few weeks the nationalists were in control. But by June 15 additional delegates from the small states had arrived and they began to counterattack. They rallied around William Paterson of New Jersey who presented a series of resolutions, known as the *New Jersey Plan,* which represented the views of the small-state group. This plan struck at the heart of the convention's earlier basic decision to set aside the Articles of Confederation and to establish a national government. Paterson merely proposed a series of amendments to the existing Articles. He would give Congress the right to tax and regulate commerce and to coerce recalcitrant states, but he would retain a single-house legislature in which all states would have the *same vote, regardless of size*. The New Jersey Plan called for a plural national executive with little power. A national supreme court was to hear appeals from state judges who were to have the authority to interpret the basic charter. These judges were to be instructed to treat laws of the national Congress and the treaties of the United States as superior to the laws of their own states.

For a time the convention was deadlocked. The small states argued that states should be represented in Congress, at least in the upper house. The large states were equally adamant. They wanted representation in both houses on the basis of population or wealth and election by the electorate rather than the state legislatures. Finally a Committee of Eleven was selected to devise a compromise, and on July 5 it presented its proposals. Because of the prominent role of the Connecticut delegation this plan has since been known as the *Connecticut Compromise*. It called for: a lower house in which representation would be on the basis of population, the origination in the lower house of all bills raising or appropriating money, and an upper house in which each state would have an equal vote. This was a setback to the large states. They gave way only when the small states made it clear that this was their price for union. After equality of representation for the states in the Senate was accepted, most objections to the establishment of a strong national government dissolved.

The problem of representation was complicated by the existence of slavery. Looking back today, we are apt to exaggerate the differences that existed between the North and South over slavery. At that time the question was not one that divided the nation along sectional lines. Slavery was already dying in the North, and there were signs of its demise in the South. Southerners and northerners generally agreed that it was an unfortunate system, that eventually it would have to be removed. There was neither the intense opposition to the slavery system in the North nor the impassioned defense of it in the South that later developed. States with large numbers of slaves, nevertheless, wanted them to be counted in determining representation in the House of Representatives. At the same time they did not want to count them as property for tax purposes. A compromise worked out under the Articles of Confederation was agreed on: that a slave should count as three-fifths of a free person, both in determining representation in the House of Representatives and in apportionment of direct taxes.

Perhaps more important to the southerners was the fear that the northern majority in Congress might discriminate against southern trade. They had some basis for this concern. John Jay, Director of Foreign Affairs for the Confederation, had proposed a treaty with Great Britain that gave advantages to northern merchants at the expense of the southern exporters. To protect themselves, the southern delegates insisted on requiring a two-thirds majority for Senate consent to the ratification of treaties. This sectional check on treaties was supplemented by a provision denying to Congress the power to levy taxes on exports. Another dispute involved the slave trade. To meet the demands of South Carolina and Georgia, Congress was denied until 1808 the right to prohibit the importing of slaves. By that time, it was thought, there would be enough slaves within the United States to supply all demands.

The delegates found other issues, of course, to argue about. Should the national government have lower courts or would one federal Supreme Court be enough? This was resolved by postponing the issue. The Constitution merely states that there *shall* be one Supreme Court and that Congress *may* establish inferior courts. How should the President be selected? For a long time the convention accepted the idea that the President should be elected by the Congress. But it was feared that either the Congress would dominate the President or *vice versa*. Election by the state legislatures was rejected because of distrust of these bodies. Some of the nationalistic delegates favored election by the voters, but others believed that the voters would not be sufficiently informed or dispassionate to make the selection. Finally, after much discussion, the electoral college was decided upon. This part of the Constitution is perhaps the most original contribution of the delegates, although it was patterned after procedures used by Delaware to select state senators. It is also one of the most criticized constitutional provisions (see Chapter 14).

Finally, after three months, the delegates ceased their debating. On September 17, 1787, they assembled for the impressive ceremony of placing their names on the document they were recommending to the nation. All but three of those still present signed; others who opposed the general drift of the convention had already left. Their work over, the delegates adjourned to the City Tavern to relax and celebrate a job well done.

What manner of men?

Were the delegates an inspired group of men who cast aside all thoughts of self-interest? Were they motivated by the desire to save the Union or by the desire to save themselves? Was the convention the inevitable result of the weaknesses of the Articles, and was it produced by the sweep of social forces that were reacting to the democratic dogmas of the Declaration of Independence? Was it a carefully maneuvered *coup d'état* on the part of the wealthy aristocrats?

All these interpretations—and a few others—have been put forward by students of history and government. During the early part of our history, the members of the convention were the object of uncritical adulation; the Constitution was the object of universal reverence. Early in the twentieth century a more critical attitude was inspired by the scholarship of J. Allen Smith and Charles A. Beard. Smith, in his *The Spirit of American Govern-*

ment, painted the Constitution as the outgrowth of an antidemocratic re-action, almost a conspiracy, against the rule of majorities. Beard's thesis was that the Constitution represents the platform of the propertied groups who wanted mainly to secure limitations on state legislatures and a strong national government as a means of protecting property. In his famous volume *An Economic Interpretation of the Constitution* he describes the economic interests of the delegates and demonstrates their concern to protect these interests. Recently Professor Robert E. Brown has questioned Beard's thesis that divisions over the Constitution rested primarily on an economic basis. He has written, "We would be doing a grave injustice to the political sagacity of the Founding Fathers if we assumed that property or personal gain was their only motive."[12] Moreover, Brown points out that there was no great propertyless mass in the United States, and "practically everybody was interested in the protection of property."[13]

It is doubtful that any interpretation giving an exclusive role to any one facet of human motivation can be satisfactory. Beard himself recognized this. Men are motivated by a complex of factors, conscious and unconscious. Self-interest and principle are inextricably mixed in human behavior. The Founding Fathers were neither minor gods in whom self-interest was of no importance, nor—on the other hand—men who thought only in terms of their own pocketbooks. They were concerned with the state of the Union and they wanted to protect the nation from aggression abroad and dissension at home. Fortunately, their own interests coincided with the long-run interests of the nation. Stability and strength were needed to protect property; these qualities were also needed to secure the unity and order indispensable for the operation of a democracy. The delegates were, as Woodrow Wilson wrote, "a strong and intelligent class possessed of unity and informed by a conscious solidity of interest."

Nor can the Constitutional Convention be explained as the inevitable march of history—the outcome of underlying social and economic forces beyond the control of man. Equally doubtful are theories that make mankind absolute masters of their own destiny. Men are limited by certain general movements of history but, within broad channels, are free to determine their own fate. The convention was not the product of social forces independent of the wishes of mankind. Nor did a small group of leaders mold the nation and establish the government out of whole cloth. Past events created the conditions and emotions that made it possible, but not inevitable, to create a more perfect Union. But it must be recognized that the new nation was blessed with leaders who had both the desire and the capacity to lead.

[12] Robert E. Brown, *Charles Beard and the Constitution* (Princeton: Princeton University Press, 1956), p. 198.
[13] *Ibid.,* p. 197.

TO ADOPT OR NOT TO ADOPT

The delegates had gone far. After exceeding their authority by completely setting aside the Articles of Confederation, they had not hesitated to contravene Congress' instructions about ratification, or to ignore Article XIII of the Articles of Confederation. This Article declared the Union to be *perpetual* and prohibited any alteration in the Articles unless agreed to by the Congress and by *every one* of the state *legislatures*. This veto had made it impossible to amend the Articles. The delegates were aware that there was little chance of securing approval of the new Constitution in all the state legislatures. They boldly declared that the Constitution should go into effect for those states that approved as soon as ratified by *conventions* in *nine* states.

But even this method was not going to be easy. Any political pollsters around in the fall of 1787 would probably have predicted defeat for the Constitution. Certainly the nation was not ready to adopt without a full-dress debate, and the country was soon divided into two camps. The supporters of the new government cleverly appropriated the name of Federalists and thereby took some of the sting out of the charges that they were trying to destroy the states and establish an all-powerful central government. By dubbing their opponents Anti-Federalists, they pointed up the essentially negative character of the arguments of those who opposed ratification.

The split was in part geographical. The seaboard and city regions where the propertied and wealthy classes—the businessmen and the speculators—resided were the strongholds of the Federalists. The vast back country regions from Maine through Georgia, inhabited by farmers and lesser folk, were the areas in which the Anti-Federalists were most strongly entrenched. This cleavage was not entirely due to economic influences but also to the West's suspicion of the East. Of course, there were Federalist farmers as well as Anti-Federalist merchants, but, in general, the division over the Constitution foreshadowed the pattern on which our first political parties were based.

From the vantage point of the present, many of the criticisms raised by the Anti-Federalists obviously were unfounded and many of their fears were unjustified. It used to be the fashion among historians to picture these opponents of our Constitution as small-minded, selfish men who could not see beyond their own local interests. With the introduction of a more critical attitude toward the Constitution, there was a reaction to the other extreme; the Anti-Federalists were then described as the true defenders of liberty and democracy against the economically motivated aristocracy. Quite obviously both of these characterizations are overdrawn. Each side included able and enlightened men as well as those with less admirable motives. The public was surfeited with pamphlets, papers, letters to the editors, and speeches. Interest was intense and the issue important. Nevertheless the argument was, in the main, carried on in a temperate manner. This great debate stands as an example to the world of a free people using the techniques of free discussion to determine the momentous questions of the nature of their fundamental laws.

The great debate

In general, the Anti-Federalist argument developed along these lines: There is much of merit in the proposed Constitution, but it contains many provisions that show the aristocratic bias of its authors. It lacks many guarantees of the people's fundamental rights. Present conditions are not as bad as the Federalists make out: we are at peace, and there is no danger of internal dissension. What we need is a correction of the Articles of Confederation, but a correction that preserves, as the Constitution does not, the power of the states and the freedom of the people. We should not ratify the proposed Constitution; but after it has been fully discussed and its defects made apparent, another convention should be called to revise the Articles in the light of these discussions.

This summary cannot, of course, give a complete catalogue of all the objections raised to the Constitution, for almost all its articles and provisions were criticized. The Anti-Federalists were suspicious of the intentions of the delegates to the convention—delegates who had exceeded their instructions, deliberated in secret, and presented a Constitution that established a powerful national government. Something of this suspicion can be gained from the remarks of Amos Singletary, delegate from a western town in the Massachusetts ratifying convention. Singletary was a veteran member of the Massachusetts General Court and had served in the Revolutionary army. He said:

Mr. President, if any body had proposed such a constitution as this in that day [Revolutionary period], it would have been thrown away at once. . . . These lawyers, and men of learning, and moneyed men, that talk so finely, and gloss over matters so smoothly, to make us poor illiterate people swallow down the pill, expect to get into Congress themselves; they expect to be the managers of this Constitution, and get all the power and all the money into their own hands, and then they will swallow up all of us little folks, like the great *Leviathan,* Mr. President; yes, just as the whale swallowed up *Jonah.*

The Federalists, on the other side, presented the alternatives in terms of adoption of the Constitution or disunion. They argued that the Confederation was hopelessly defective and, unless quickly altered, the Union would be lost. Arguing that union was indispensable to liberty and security, they defended the Constitution as conforming to the true principles of republican government. They admitted that it was not perfect, but held that it was the best that could be obtained, and that the way was open to correct such deficiencies as were uncovered through time and experience.

Federal Farmer versus Publius

One of the best attacks produced by the Anti-Federalists was a series of articles written by Richard Henry Lee, the man who had introduced the resolution in the Second Continental Congress calling for independence. Lee's *Letters of the Federal Farmer,* published in the fall of 1787, were widely circulated throughout the nation. *The Federalist,* on the other hand, is without doubt the best defense of the Constitution produced by the Federalists. Charles and Mary Beard have written, "From that day to this *The Federalist* has been widely regarded as the most profound single treatise on the Constitution ever written and as among the few masterly works on political science produced in all the centuries of history."[14] These papers were written by Alexander Hamilton, James Madison, and John Jay. Over the name of Publius they were published serially in the New York papers during the winter of 1787. Taking historic license, let us rearrange and paraphrase this great debate in order to get the feel of the times, and to understand better the fears and hopes of the Federal Farmer and Publius.

Lee opened the argument by admitting that the Articles of Confederation were defective, but he said, in effect:[15]

Ought we to precipitate the adoption of the proposed constitution? We are in no immediate danger of any commotion; we are in a state of perfect peace, and in no danger of invasion. We have hardly recovered from a long and distressing war, and we impute to the defects in our government many evils and embarrassments which are most clearly the result of the late war. It is natural for men who wish to hasten the adoption of a measure to tell us, "now is the crisis."

Publius spoke up:[16]

I acknowledge that I cannot entertain an equal tranquillity with those who affect to treat the dangers of a longer continuance in our present situation as imaginary. A nation without a national government is, in my view, an awful spectacle. Nothing can be more evident, to those who are able to take an enlarged view of the subject, than the alternatives of an adoption of the new Constitution or a dismemberment of the Union.

[14] Charles and Mary Beard, *A Basic History of the United States* (Philadelphia: The New Home Library, 1944), p. 136.

[15] See P. L. Ford, *Pamphlets on the Constitution of the United States* (Brooklyn, New York: 1888), pp. 260-325.

[16] *The Federalist* is available in several editions. One of the best is that edited by Max Beloff, *The Federalist* (New York: The Macmillan Company, 1948).

Lee pressed his point:

Probably not one man in ten thousand in the United States, till within these
last few days, had an idea that the old ship was to be destroyed. The states universally supposed the convention would report alterations in the confederation.
But when Virginia made a very respectable appointment, and placed at the
head of it the first man in America, Pennsylvania appointed principally those
men who are esteemed aristocratic. We shall view the convention with proper
respect—and, at the same time, we must recollect how disproportionately the
democratic and aristocratic parts of the community were represented.

Publius retorted:

A dangerous ambition more often lurks behind the specious mask of zeal
for the rights of the people than under the forbidding appearance of zeal for
the firmness and efficiency of government. While our opponents admit that the
government of the United States is destitute of energy, they contend against conferring upon it those powers which are requisite to supply that energy. They
seem still to aim at things repugnant and irreconcilable; at an augmentation of
federal authority, without a diminution of State authority; at sovereignty in the
Union, and complete independence of the members. They fail to see that the
evils we experience proceed not from minute or partial imperfections, but from
fundamental errors in the structure of the building, which cannot be amended
otherwise than by an alteration in the first principles and main pillars of the
fabric.

Still unsatisfied, Lee returned to the attack:

The plan of government now proposed is clearly designed to make us one
consolidated government. The general government will possess all essential
powers, the states a mere shadow of power. The general government, far removed from the people, will find either that its laws are neglected or that it must
use military force to execute them; either will lead to a revolution, and to the
destruction of freedom.

Publius answered:

It will always be far more easy for the state governments to encroach upon
the national authority than for the national government to encroach upon the
state authorities. The people of each state would be apt to feel a stronger bias
towards their local government than towards the government of the Union. Nor
will the government of the Union have to use the sword to execute its laws. The
great and radical vice in the construction of the existing Confederation is in the
principle of *legislation for states* or governments, in their corporate or collective
capacities, as contradistinguished from the individuals of which they consist.

Lee summed up his arguments:

An examination of the proposed constitution opens to my mind a new scene; instead of seeing powers lodged cautiously in the hands of numerous legislators, and many magistrates, we see all important powers collecting in one center, where a few men can use them almost at discretion. There are many good things in the proposed system. It is founded on elective principles, and the deposit of powers in different hands is essentially right. But the value of every feature is vastly lessened for the want of that one important feature in a free government, a representation of the people. Because we have sometimes abused democracy, I am not among those who think a democratic branch a nuisance.

Perhaps the most telling criticism of the proposed Constitution made by Lee and others was its failure to include a bill of rights.[17] The Federalists' explanations did not sound highly convincing. They argued that a bill of rights would be superfluous. The general government had only delegated powers, and there was no need to specify that Congress could not, for example, abridge freedom of the press. It had no power to regulate the press. Moreover, the Federalists argued, to guarantee *some* rights might be dangerous because it would then be thought that rights *not* listed could be denied. Contradictorily, they then pointed out that the Constitution protected some of the most important rights—trial by jury in federal criminal cases, for example. Hamilton and others also insisted that paper guarantees were false reeds upon which to depend for protection against governmental tyranny.

The Anti-Federalists, as well as many who were otherwise generally favorable to ratification, were unconvinced. If some rights were protected, what could be the objection to providing constitutional protection for others? Without a bill of rights, what was to prevent Congress from using one of its delegated powers in such a manner that free speech would be abridged? If bills of rights were needed in state constitutions to limit state governments, why was one not needed in the national constitution to limit the national government—a government more distant from the people and more likely to subvert the natural rights? The Federalists were forced to concede, and they agreed to add a bill of rights if and when the new Constitution was approved.

The politics of ratification

Despite the great debate, many people remained apathetic. The only direct voice that the electorate had in the writing and adopting of our Constitution was in choosing delegates to the state ratifying conventions. In some states suffrage requirements were liberalized, but only a fraction of

---

[17] See Robert A. Rutland, *The Birth of the Bill of Rights* (Chapel Hill: The University of North Carolina Press, 1955).

those qualified to vote actually did so.[18] This worked to the advantage of the Federalists.

The political strategy of the Federalists was to secure ratification in as many states as possible before the opposition had time to organize. The Anti-Federalists were handicapped because their main strength was in the rural areas, which were underrepresented in some state legislatures and which were the most difficult to arouse for political action. They needed time to perfect their organization and collect their strength. But the Federalists, composed of a more closely knit group of leaders throughout the colonies, moved in a hurry. "Unless the Federalists had been shrewd in manipulation as they were sound in theory, their arguments could not have prevailed."[19]

Delaware was the first state to ratify; in most of the small states, now propitiated by equal representation in the Senate, ratification was gained without difficulty. The first large state to take action was Pennsylvania. The Federalists presented the Constitution to it immediately after the Philadelphia Convention adjourned in September, 1787, urging the legislature to issue the call for the ratifying convention to consider adoption of the new Constitution. But the legislature was about to adjourn, and the Anti-Federalist minority felt that this was moving with unseemly haste (especially since Congress had not even formally transmitted the document to the legislature for its consideration!). They wanted to postpone action until after the coming state elections, when they hoped to win a legislative majority, in which event they would not call a ratifying convention. When it became clear that the Federalists were going to move ahead, the Anti-Federalists left the legislative chamber. With three short of a quorum, business was brought to a standstill. Philadelphia, the seat of the legislature, was a Federalist stronghold. The next morning three Anti-Federalists were roused from their taverns, forcibly carried into the legislative chamber, sat on, and with a quorum thus obtained, the resolution calling for election of delegates to a ratifying convention was adopted. Under the astute generalship of James Wilson, the Pennsylvania Convention ratified by a vote of 46 to 23, the opposition coming from the western districts.

By the middle of January, New Jersey, Connecticut, and Georgia had ratified. The scene of battle then shifted to Massachusetts, a key state and a doubtful one. John Hancock and Samuel Adams had not declared themselves, and these gentlemen, with their great popular following, held the balance of power. The Federalists cleverly pointed out to Hancock that Washington would be the first President, and that therefore the Vice-Presi-

[18] A. C. McLaughlin, *A Constitutional History of the United States* (New York: D. Appleton-Century Company, 1935), pp. 220-221. See also Brown, *op. cit.*, p. 197.
[19] S. E. Morison and H. S. Commager, *The Growth of the American Republic* (New York: Oxford University Press, 1936), p. 163.

dent would undoubtedly be a New Englander. What citizen of New England was more distinguished than John Hancock? Whether or not this hint was the cause, Hancock eventually came out for ratification, and Adams was persuaded to vote for approval after securing a promise that a bill of rights would be forthcoming after adoption. Even so, Massachusetts ratified by the narrow margin of 187 to 168.

By June, Maryland, South Carolina, and New Hampshire had ratified, so the nine states required to bring the Constitution into effect had been obtained. But neither Virginia nor New York had taken action, and without them the new Union had little chance of success. Virginia was the most populous state and the home of many of the nation's outstanding leaders, and New York's geographical position split the ratifying states in two.

The Virginia ratifying convention rivaled the Constitutional Convention in the caliber of its delegates. James Madison was the captain of the Federalist forces, and he had able lieutenants in Governor Randolph and young John Marshall. Patrick Henry, George Mason, and James Monroe within the convention, and Richard Henry Lee outside, led the opposition. Henry attacked the proposed government, point by point, with great eloquence; Madison turned back each attack quietly but cogently—sometimes in a voice so low that the recorder of the debates was unable to hear him. At the critical juncture Washington sent a letter to the convention urging unqualified ratification. This tipped the scale, and Virginia ratified. News was rushed to New York.

The great landowners along the Hudson, unlike their southern planter friends, were opposed to the Constitution. They feared federal taxation of their holdings, and they did not want to abolish the profitable tax that New York had been levying on the trade and commerce of the other states. When the convention assembled, the Federalists were greatly outnumbered, but through the strategy and skill of Hamilton, and aided by word of Virginia's ratification, New York approved by a margin of three votes.

Although North Carolina and Rhode Island still remained outside the Union (the former ratifying in November 1789 and the latter six months later), the new ship of state was launched. In New York, a few members of the old Congress assembled to issue the call for elections under the new Constitution, and then Congress adjourned *sine die*. Throughout the nation citizens paraded and gave toasts to the new ship, *The Constitution*.

Some people remained skeptical of the new
Constitution. After watching merchants and mechanics march side by side
in a ratification parade, a Bostonian remarked sourly that "it may serve to
please children, but freemen will not be so easily gulled out of their liberties." A Philadelphian said that the procession in his city had "made such
an impression on the minds of our young people that 'federal' and 'union'
have now become part of the household words of every family in the city."
This effect on the youth was significant, for it was on the younger generation
that hopes for the new government depended.

The new ship of state was launched in favorable seas. The adoption of
the Constitution coincided with the return of prosperity; markets for
American goods were opening in Europe, and business was coming out of
its postwar slump. The events seemed to justify the Federalists' claims
that adoption of the Constitution would correct the nation's ills. Within
a surprisingly short time the Constitution lost its partisan character. Anti-
Federalists vied with Federalists in honoring it—so much so, said one
cynic, that "whenever its eulogium is pronounced, I feel an involuntary
apprehension of mischief." Politicians less and less differed over whether
the Constitution was good. More and more they argued over what it meant.

As the Constitution won the support of Americans it began to take on
the aura of the higher natural law itself. "Here was the document," says
Max Lerner, "into which the Founding Fathers had poured their wisdom
as into a vessel; the Fathers
themselves grew ever larger in
stature as they receded from
view; the era in which they
lived and fought became a
Golden Age; in that age there
had been a fresh dawn for the
world, and its men were giants
against the sky; what they had
fought for was abstracted from
its living context and became
a set of 'principles,' eternally
true and universally applicable."[1] This adoration of
the Constitution—sometimes
called the "cult of the Constitution"—was important as a
means of bringing unity into

3 ★

The

living

Constitution

[1] Max Lerner, *Ideas for the Ice
Age* (New York: Viking Press,
1941), pp. 241-242.

the diversity of the new nation. Like the Crown in Britain, the Constitution was a symbol of national loyalty, a unifying symbol that evoked both emotional and rational support from all Americans regardless of their differences. The framers' work became part of the American creed; it stood for liberty, equality before the law, limited government—indeed, for whatever anyone wanted to build into it.

The new Constitution was thus a *symbol*. It was also an *instrument*. It is a fundamental supreme and binding law that both *grants* and *limits* powers. "In framing a government which is to be administered by men over men," wrote Madison in *The Federalist*, "the great difficulty lies in this: you must first enable the government to control the governed; and in the next place oblige it to control itself." As an instrument, the Constitution serves a dual function. It is a *positive* instrument of government enabling the governors to control the governed. It is also a *restraint* on government, a device by which the ruled check the rulers.

In what ways does the Constitution *limit* the power of the national government? In what ways does it *create* national power? How has it managed to serve both as a great symbol of national unity and at the same time as a somewhat adaptable and changing instrument?

CHECKING POWER WITH POWER

It is strange, perhaps, to begin by stressing the ways that the Constitution *limits* national power. Yet we must keep in mind the dilemma that the framers faced. They wanted a more effective national government. At the same time they were keenly aware that the voters would not accept too strong a national government. Accordingly, they allotted certain powers to the *national* government, and reserved the rest for the *states*. In short, they established a system of *federalism* (the nature and problems of which will be taken up in chapters 4 and 5). But this distribution of powers between the national and state governments, they felt, was not enough. Other ways of limiting the national government were sought.

The most important device to enforce constitutional limitations is the right of voters to go to the polls and defeat those who abuse power. Why were the framers not willing to depend solely on such *political* controls? The answer is simple. They did not fully trust the people's judgment on this matter. And perhaps even more important, the framers feared that the new central government would fall into the hands of a popular majority. "A dependence on the people is, no doubt, the primary control on the government," Madison admitted, "but experience has taught mankind the necessity of auxiliary precautions."

What were these "auxiliary precautions"? The framers hoped that two different but related arrangements—*separation of powers* and *checks and balances*—would achieve their supreme goal of preventing public officials from abusing their power and preventing any one group of people, even a majority, from capturing control of the government and tyrannizing the rest of the people.

Dividing national power

The first step was the *separation of power*—that is, dividing power among the three branches of the national government. As we have seen, the idea of parceling out power is an old one. Locke had discussed the need for separating powers, and Montesquieu had argued that liberty could last only where powers were distributed among different departments of government. American leaders were familiar with the arguments of both. In *Federalist No. 47* James Madison wrote:

> No political truth is certainly of greater intrinsic value, or is stamped with the authority of more enlightened patrons of liberty, than that . . . the accumulation of all powers, legislative, executive, and judiciary, in the same hands . . . may justly be pronounced the very definition of tyranny.

But the power of Locke's and Montesquieu's logic alone does not account for the incorporation of the doctrine of separation of powers in our basic document. It was, as we have seen, no novelty, and had been the operating practice in the colonies for over 100 years. Only during the Revolutionary period was the doctrine compromised and power concentrated in the hands of the legislature. This experience merely confirmed the belief in the merits of separation of powers. Many of the framers attributed the evils of state government and the want of energy of the central government to the lack of a strong executive who could both check legislative abuses and give energy and direction to administration.

But dividing up power in itself was not enough. For there was always the danger—from the framers' point of view—that different officials with different powers might pool their authority and act in a tyrannical way. Two modern examples may make this situation clear. In a football team, power is distributed—the quarterback has one job, the center another, the guards still another. But all players act in harmony in their efforts to score. In Britain today there are executive, legislative, and judicial officials, but they act together in response to directions from the Cabinet. How could the framers use the separation of powers principle to prevent governmental branches and officials from acting together in a tyrannical way?

Checks and balances

Their answer was to make these officials responsive to different pressures. This is the system of *checks and balances*. The framers deliberately designed a system in which President, legislators, and judges would not be dependent on one another or on the same source of popular support. The President was to be chosen by a group of *electors,* so that he would have different loyalties and interests from senators chosen by state legislators, from representatives directly elected by local constituencies, from judges holding office for life and appointed by the President with the consent of the Senate.

The framers were also careful to arrange matters so that a majority could win control over only part of the government at one time. A popular majority might take control of the House of Representatives in an off-year election, but the President, representing previous popular sentiment, would still have two years to go. That majority might win the Presidency (difficult, however, because of the electoral-college system), but other forces might still control the Senate.

Moreover, each branch of our national government is given some responsibilities in performing the functions of the other, and each is given some agency to control the operations of the other. Congress enacts laws, the President can veto them, and Congress can repass them over his veto. The Supreme Court can invalidate laws passed by Congress and signed by the President, but the Chief Executive and the Senate appoint the judges. The President administers the laws, but Congress provides the money for him and his agencies. Senate and House of Representatives have an absolute veto on each other. These are the essential features of the blending and checking of power, but the system has almost endless ramifications.

It was the legislative branch that the framers felt was most likely to take over the whole government. "In republican government," Madison wrote, "the legislative authority necessarily predominates." It was in part to meet this problem that the framers chopped the legislature in two and made the two branches responsible to different constituencies. Thus, said Madison, the two branches were rendered "by different modes of election and different principles of action, as little connected with each other as the nature of their common functions and their common dependence on the society will admit."

Finally, if this did not work, there were the judges. It was not for some years after the Constitution was in operation that the judges obtained the power of *judicial review*—the right to be the official interpreters of the Constitution and to refuse to enforce those laws of Congress which in the judges' opinion were unconstitutional (see page 71). But from the beginning, the judges were expected to check the legislature and the groups that the Congressional majority might represent. "Independent judges," wrote Alexander Hamilton in *Federalist No. 78,* would be "an essential safeguard against the effects of occasional ill humors in society. These sometimes extend no farther than to the injury of the private rights of particular classes of citizens, by unjust and partial laws." Independent judges, Hamilton pointed out, were in a monarchy "an excellent barrier to the despotism of the prince," and, in a republic, they were "no less excellent barrier to the encroachments and oppressions of the representative body."

Ambition to counteract ambition

The doctrine of separation of powers, at least as it is combined with checks and balances in American practice, is one of *interdependence* rather than *independence*. It is, as Madison pointed out, merely the principle that the accumulation of *all* powers in the *same* hands is to be avoided. Governmental power cannot be divided neatly into three separate categories, nor can the three departments be kept separate and distinct. That is not the intent of the maxim of separation of powers. What is required is a *blending* and *mingling* of powers. "The great security against a gradual concentration of the several powers in the same department," wrote Madison, "consists in giving to those who administer each department the necessary constitutional means and personal motives to resist encroachment on the others. . . . Ambition must be made to counteract ambition."

Could such a system really work? What if a majority of the people should get control of all branches of government and force through radical and impulsive measures? The framers were realists. They knew that if the great majority of the voters wanted over a period of years to take some step, nothing could stop them. Nothing, that is, except despotic government, and they did not want that. The men of 1787 reasoned that all they could do—and this was quite a lot—was to stave off, temporarily, full control by the popular majority.

It may seem surprising that the people—or at least the large number of them who were suspicious of the new Constitution—did not object to these "auxiliary precautions," which were barriers to action by a popular majority. But most early Americans, like many Americans today, had an innate distrust of government, especially a national government. They did not look on government as an instrument they could seize with their votes and use for their own purposes. And in the eighteenth century, only a small percentage of the population had the right to participate in selecting the governors. They looked on government as something to be handcuffed, hemmed in, and rendered harmless. Thus separation of powers and checks and balances have come to serve two roles: to *make it difficult for a majority to control the government,* and to *restrain all government.*

A study in contrasts

Most Americans take this system for granted. To them the separating and checking of power seem to be the very essence of constitutional government. Like Madison, they view the amassing of power in the hands of any one department as the essence of tyranny. Yet government can be constitutional without such an apparatus. Consider the British system. The voters elect members of Parliament from districts throughout the nation (much as we elect members of the House of Representatives). The members of the Commons have almost complete constitutional power. The House of Lords once could check the House of Commons, but today the Lords are almost powerless. There is no High Court with power to void acts of Parliament: the Prime Minister cannot veto them. If, tomorrow, Parliament decided to outlaw mustaches or make everyone wear green clothes, it could do so constitutionally through a majority vote. Its decisions would be carried out by the Cabinet, which constitutionally is simply the organ of Parliament (although *politically* Parliament is largely controlled by the Prime Minister and the Cabinet). And, of course, good Englishmen take their system for granted, too.

The British system is strict majority rule; that is, a majority of the voters can elect a majority of the legislators, who can put through the majority's program without hindrance, at least until the next election rolls around. Ours is something else; it usually depends for action on the agreement of many elements of the society, comprising much more than a mere majority. The British system *concentrates* control and responsibility in the legislature; ours *diffuses* control and responsibility among the several organs of government.

But both systems can be described as constitutional government. In both the rulers are subjected to regular restraints—in Britain to free elec-

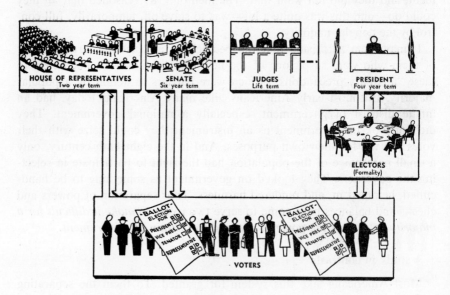

AMERICAN SYSTEM OF SEPARATION OF POWERS

tions and constant open criticism; in the United States to these *plus* the "auxiliary precautions" Madison mentioned. In both, the constitutional limitations are binding on all those who exercise governmental power—on President and Prime Minister, congressmen and members of Parliament, judges, sheriffs, the London bobby and the corner cop. Both systems are constitutional in the basic sense that the rulers are subject to regular restraints. In contrast, an arbitrary government is checked only by the rulers' fear that if the people are pushed around too much they might revolt. But revolution today is a small threat when the rulers control modern arms and communications, and the people are unarmed.

Which system is better, British or American? Each has its supporters, and some very able Americans have been among the sternest critics of our system of checks and balances. Some Englishmen have admired certain aspects of our system—or at least have believed that it well suited a nation as safe and prosperous as ours. James Bryce, writing in 1893, pointed out: "Social convulsions from within, warlike assaults from without, seem now as unlikely to try the fabric of the American Constitution, as an earthquake to rend the walls of the Capitol. This is why Americans sub-

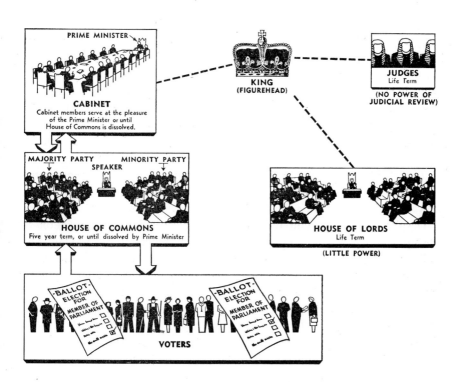

BRITISH SYSTEM OF CONCENTRATION OF RESPONSIBILITY

mit, not merely patiently but hopefully, to the defects of their government. The vessel may not be any better built, or found, or rigged than are those which carry the fortunes of the great nations of Europe. She is certainly not better navigated. But for the present at least—it may not always be so—she sails upon a summer sea."[2] Today, of course, the seas are no longer so smooth. Today the ship must be navigated with more precision; the government's responsibilities are much bigger.

The attack on our system of checks and balances, and the defense of it, will be described in Chapter 21. It is important to note here, however, that several developments have modified the system in the past 165 years.

The rise of national political parties. They have served to some extent as unifying factors, drawing together the President, senators, representatives, and even judges behind a common program. However, parties in turn have been divided and weakened by the workings of the checks and balances system.

Changes in electoral methods. The framers wanted the President to be chosen by wise, independent-minded men not too subject to popular passions and hero worship. From almost the beginning, however, the presidential electors have acted as automatons, voting for the candidate winning a plurality of the votes in their states. And senators, who were originally elected by state legislatures, are today directly chosen by the people.

The establishment of agencies exercising all three functions, legislative, executive, and judicial. When the government began to regulate the economy, it became clear that some problems had to be treated as a unit. It was difficult, if not impossible, to grant an agency only administrative powers when detailed rules had to be made and judgments rendered on highly complex matters such as policing air waves or checking the purity of food and drugs.

The rise of the President as the dominating, unifying element in national government. Drawing on his constitutional, political, and emergency powers, he has overcome some of the divisive effects of checks and balances.

Despite these important developments, however, the fragmentation of governmental power remains a basic factor in American government and politics, as almost every page of this book will testify. Other developments, of course, have had the effect of *strengthening* the checks and balances. One of the most important of these should be mentioned now because it began to take place early in our history and an aspect of it will be treated briefly in this chapter. This was the rise of the *power of judicial review* through which the judicial branch could invalidate actions of the other two branches. The judges not only had the power to protect their own inde-

[2] James Bryce, *The American Commonwealth* (New York: The Macmillan Company, 1911), I, 310. This classic study remains one of the most perceptive interpretations of American government and society.

pendence from President and congressmen. They assumed the broader power of strengthening the operations of the whole system of federalism and checks and balances. Before federal judges—ultimately before the federal judges on the Supreme Court—came case after case that enabled the judges to draw elaborate jurisdictional lines between the powers of the national and the state governments, and between the powers of the various branches of the national government. How the Supreme Court got this power will be described in Chapter 20. It is important, meantime, to remember that the Supreme Court's power to interpret the Constitution is an important part of the "living Constitution."

THE LIVING CONSTITUTION

Our formal, written Constitution is of primary importance, but it does not contain all the fundamental rules by which we govern and are governed. The actual putting down on paper of the 89 sentences of the original document was only one part of a long process. The Constitution itself is but the skeleton of our constitutional system. The framers knew that if the Constitution was to endure there must be "play within the joints"; it must be flexible and adaptable to changing conditions. They did not try to put it all down in black and white, but rather left room for the system to grow.

As a result our written Constitution is supplemented by a number of practices and procedures that have evolved over the last 165 years and are so fundamental that they must also be considered part of our Constitution in its large sense. These features can be found in basic statutes of Congress, decisions of the Supreme Court, actions of the President, and customs and usages of the nation.

Congressional elaboration of our Constitution can be seen in such fundamental legislation as the Judiciary Act of 1789, which laid the foundations of our national judicial system; in the Presidential Succession Act of 1947, which determines the succession to the Presidency in the event of the death of the President and Vice-President; and in the rules of procedure and internal organization and practices of the Congress itself.

Judicial interpretation, especially by the Supreme Court, has played an important part in the continuous process of constitution-making as we have already seen. The Supreme Court has the final power of judicial review, the power to refuse to enforce those laws and to insure judicial processes against those practices which in the opinion of a majority of the justices are unconstitutional. The power of judicial review itself furnishes the classic example of constitutional growth by judicial interpretation rather than by formal amendment. The Constitution does not specifically state that judges rather than congressmen or Presidents should have the responsibility for giving the official interpretation of the Constitution. Rather, judges acquired this important power by their own interpretation of the Constitution, an interpretation that ultimately won acceptance by the people.

Presidential practices too have had much to do with the direction in which our constitutional system has developed. Jackson, Lincoln, Wilson, and both Roosevelts have had an impact on our Constitution at least equal to that of any of the original framers. By their vigorous use of presidential power they made the presidency an office of legislative as well as executive leadership. Today most Americans expect a President to have a legislative program and to use the powers of his office to secure its enactment by Congress. In fact, we judge Presidents primarily by the policies they stand for rather than by their executive talents.

Customs and *usages* of the nation have rounded out our governmental system. The presidential cabinet, senatorial courtesy, presidential nominating conventions and other party activities, the residence requirement for congressmen—all to be described in later chapters—are examples of constitutional usages. One can search the written Constitution in vain for any specific mention of these practices, but they are essential parts of the basic framework and fundamental rules of the government of our country today.

Mainly through these informal methods of development, our Constitution has been modernized over the years and democratized. The most significant alteration in our constitutional system came about by the *extra*constitutional development of national political parties and the extension of the suffrage within the states. A broader electorate began to exercise control over the national government. The presidential office was made more responsive to the people, and the relationship between Congress and the President was altered. Through the growth of political parties some of the blocks placed in the Constitution to prevent majority rule were overcome. In like manner, the extension of the national government's functions came about through adaptation and interpretation of the broad words of the Constitution, not through formal amendment (see Chapter 4).

These rules and practices have given our constitutional system a flexibility not always realized by Americans themselves. Some people contrast the American written and rigid Constitution with the English unwritten and flexible constitution as if the distinctions were much more sharp than is the actual case. Our Constitution is not so rigid, nor is the English constitution so flexible, as is often believed. Again, as is the case in many matters of government, it is a question of degree rather than kind.

A rigid or flexible constitution?

This picture of a constantly changing Constitution disturbs many people. They would prefer a rigid Constitution which establishes certain rules that can be altered only in the prescribed manner. How, they argue, can you have a constitutional government when the Constitution is constantly being twisted by interpretation and changed by informal methods? This view fails to distinguish between the twofold aspects of the Constitution. In terms of the defense of basic and almost timeless personal liberties, it is disturbing to think that the Constitution tomorrow will mean something different than it means today. Certain fundamental truths are the essence of constitutional government. Although the manner in which personal liberties are exercised changes, and the social context of their enjoyment differs, the wisdom of denying to the government the power to deprive any person of his life without due process of law is as sound today as it was in 1787. No government can today, any more than it could yesterday or can tomorrow, abridge the right to free speech and remain a constitutional government.

Yet when we turn our attention to the Constitution as an *instrument of government* and a *positive grant of power,* we realize that if it does not grow with the nation it serves, it soon will be pushed aside. The purposes of government remain the same, to establish liberty, promote justice, ensure domestic tranquility, and provide for the common defense. But powers adequate in 1787 are not the same as those needed in the 1950's. A constitution suitable to promote justice, let us say, for a small agricultural nation may not be suitable for a large industrial nation. No constitution can long deny to the government the right to do what its people want done.

"We the people" ordain and establish the Constitution; it was not the people of 1787 who ordained and established it once and for all—for all generations. "The Constitution," wrote Jefferson, "belongs to the living and not to the dead." So firmly did he believe this that he advocated a new constitution for every generation. New constitutions have not been necessary because in a less formal way each generation has taken part in the never ending process of developing the Constitution. Because of its remarkable adaptability the Constitution has survived the rigors of democratic and industrial revolutions, the turmoil of the Civil War, the tensions of major depressions, and the dislocations of world wars.

The problem is, then, to preserve the Constitution in its role of a protector of fundamental liberties, to preserve the essentials of justice and democracy upon which our system is based, and at the same time to permit government to operate in accordance with the wishes of the people and to adapt itself to new conditions. The problem is the same today as it was in Madison's time: to enable the government to govern the people and at the same time to respond to their needs and demands.

CHANGING THE LETTER OF THE CONSTITUTION

The framers of the Constitution knew that future experience would call for changes and that some means of formal amendment would be necessary. Accordingly, they set forth two ways to *propose* amendments to the Constitution and two ways to *ratify* them. Furthermore, they carefully saw to it that amendments could not be made by simple majorities.

Proposing and ratifying

The first method of *proposing* amendments, and the only one that has ever been used, is by a two-thirds vote of both houses of Congress. The second method is by a national convention called by Congress at the request of the legislatures of two-thirds of the states. Shortly before the Civil War there was some discussion about holding a national convention, but nothing came of it. Several scholars have advocated the calling of such a

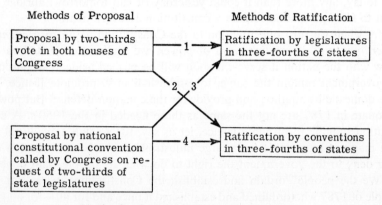

Methods of Proposal   Methods of Ratification

Methods of amending the Constitution.

convention to revise the Constitution in the light of modern conditions, and from time to time several states have petitioned Congress with respect to specific amendments. During the last decade or so over half the state legislatures asked Congress either to propose or to call a convention to propose an amendment limiting the power of the national government to tax incomes, gifts, and estates. Many of these state legislatures have, however, rescinded their previous actions. But the state legislatures by themselves, no matter how many of them act, can merely petition. There is no legal way to force Congress to call a national convention even if the necessary two-thirds of the state legislatures petition for it. In the past Congress has preferred to propose amendments itself instead of calling a convention to do so. Perhaps Congress remembers the fate of its predecessor at the hands of the convention it called into being in 1787!

After an amendment has been proposed it must be *ratified*. Again two methods are provided: by approval of *legislatures* in three-fourths of the states, or of specially called ratifying *conventions* in three-fourths of the states. Congress determines which method of ratification shall be used. Ratification by the legislature permits decision on amendments without any clear expression from the electorate. The state legislators who do the ratifying are often elected even before the proposed amendments are submitted to the states. In any case, state legislators are chosen because of their views on schools, taxation, bond issues, because they are supported by the proper political organizations—practically never because of their attitude toward proposed constitutional amendments. Yet the only amendment to be submitted to ratifying conventions was the Twenty-first (to repeal the Eighteenth or Prohibition Amendment). The "wets" rightly believed that repeal had a better chance of success with conventions than with the rural-dominated state legislatures. This political consideration, rather than any desire to submit the question to the people, was the important factor, but many commentators thought that a new precedent had been set and that in the future Congress would choose the more democratic ratification method. When Congress in 1947 proposed the Twenty-second Amendment to limit the presidential tenure, however, it reverted to previous practice and submitted the amendment to the state legislatures.

The submission of amendments to legislatures instead of to ratifying conventions has been criticized as undemocratic. Many people were surprised to hear that the Anti-third-term Amendment had been ratified. Although the subject of limiting presidential tenure had long been debated, little interest was aroused as each of the necessary 36 state legislatures approved the amendment. Within the legislatures themselves, debate was brief. However, 41 state legislatures have ratified the amendment which indicates rather widespread support for it.

The President is completely out of the amendment picture. His veto power does not extend to amendments. (Nor may governors veto legislative ratifications.) But Congress has a central role. The Supreme Court has been generally inclined to leave to Congress the interpretation and enforcement of the amendatory article. Congress thus determines the time limit within which proposed amendments may be ratified. It may do this when it proposes amendments by including within the amendment a specific time limit, or it may determine the effectiveness of ratification at a later date. For example, the child labor amendment was proposed by Congress in 1924 with nothing said about the time limit for ratifications. To date, only 28 states have ratified, the last one being Kansas in 1937. If 8 more states were ever to ratify, Congress would then have to decide if the amendment had been ratified within a "reasonable time" and whether it should be promulgated as part of the Constitution. Logically enough, a state may ratify an amendment after it has once voted against ratification, but once it approves it cannot change its mind and "unratify." If this were permitted, then a state could conceivably decide to "unratify" its ratification of the Constitution.

Are there any limits to the amendatory power? Not if Congress and enough state legislatures or conventions can agree on a change. The Constitution says that no state shall be deprived of its equal suffrage in the Senate, nor be deprived of territory, nor joined with another state except with its own consent. Theoretically, these provisions could be repealed by amendment, but this is an academic question, since such an amendment would hardly be approved by Congress or ratified by the states.

The advantages of a broad, flexible, and adaptable Constitution can be seen when it is compared with the rigid and overspecific constitutions of the states. Many state constitutions are more like legal codes than constitutions. They are long and complex and include much detail that ties the hands of the government and gives the courts unusual opportunities to declare laws unconstitutional. Hence, in order to modernize state governments, their constitutions must be often amended or replaced every generation or so. The federal Constitution, however, because of its flexibility, has not required frequent formal amendment. If one subtracts the Bill of Rights, which for all practical purposes can be considered as part of the original document, there have been only twelve amendments (and two of these, the Eighteenth and Twenty-first, cancel each other out). The twelve amendments are difficult to classify, but they can be grouped somewhat arbitrarily into the following categories: (1) those whose chief importance is to add to or subtract from the power of the national government; (2) those whose main effect is to limit the power of the states; (3) those whose chief impact has been to add to or subtract from the political power of the electorate; and (4) those that make structural improvements in governmental machinery. Each of these will be discussed in turn.

BORN TO COMMAND.

OF VETO MEMORY.

HAD I BEEN CONSULTED.

KING ANDREW THE FIRST.

Fear of executive power developed early in our history.

Changes in national power

The Eleventh Amendment. This amendment withdraws from the jurisdiction of the federal courts suits *commenced* or prosecuted by individuals against the states. When the Constitution was adopted, it was generally thought that the grant of judicial power to the United States did not affect the doctrine that a state could not be sued by private individuals without its own consent. But in 1793 the Supreme Court ruled otherwise in the case of *Chisholm* v. *Georgia.* There was immediate alarm lest citizens flood the federal courts with suits against states that were in default on their debts.

The Eleventh Amendment was proposed, and it became part of the Constitution in 1798.

The Sixteenth Amendment. This amendment was also adopted to reverse a Supreme Court decision. In 1895 the Supreme Court, overruling a long line of precedents, for all practical purposes denied to the federal government the power to levy an income tax.[3] The Sixteenth Amendment, adopted in 1913, empowers the national government to collect such taxes without the need for apportioning the tax among the states according to population (as the Supreme Court had said it must because the tax was a direct tax).

The Eighteenth Amendment. This amendment, adopted in 1919, was the culmination of a long struggle by the prohibitionists against the use of alcoholic beverages. The amendment gave Congress concurrent power with the states to enforce the prohibitions of the amendment against the manufacture, sale, or transportation of intoxicating liquors. Although the amendment was ratified by all but two state legislatures, prohibition did not have the support of large groups of people, especially in urban areas. During the 1920's public indifference made it impossible to enforce prohibition without adopting police-state methods and spending vast sums of money. A thriving bootlegging industry developed, and prohibition, instead of cutting down the consumption of alcohol, served mainly to enrich criminals and to foster a callous attitude toward the law. After thirteen years of disappointment and the arrival of the Great Depression that made new taxes desirable, the *Twenty-first Amendment* was adopted in 1933, returning control over liquor to the states.

The Thirteenth Amendment. Although this amendment by its own force freed the slaves and continues to restrict the power of the national and state governments, its chief significance today is that it gives to Congress power to prevent any attempt to hold a human being in slavery or involuntary servitude (see Chapter 7).

Formal amendments, it is clear, have not been very important in adding to or detracting from the power of the federal government. One amendment took away power that the national government was not thought to have had; one added power that it was believed to have had; one grant of power was subsequently repealed; and one gave it power which it has never chosen to exercise vigorously and which has been narrowed by judicial interpretation (see Chapter 7).

Limiting state power

The Fourteenth and Fifteenth Amendments. Along with the Thirteenth Amendment, these two were adopted following, and largely as a result of, the Civil War. As we have noted, the major purpose of the Thirteenth was to free the slaves; the major purpose of the Fourteenth was to make them

[3] *Pollock v. Farmers' Loan and Trust Co.*

citizens and to protect their civil rights, and that of the Fifteenth was to protect their right to vote. Only the objectives of freedom and citizenship were immediately accomplished. But the amendments had other consequences not generally anticipated, the most important being that the Supreme Court for a time used the Fourteenth Amendment to limit the regulatory power of the states and to give constitutional sanction to the gospel of laissez faire (see Chapter 8).

These amendments substantially increased the power of the Supreme Court to review actions of the state governments and might well be placed among those that add to the power of the national government—or at least to the judicial branch of that government.

The Nineteenth Amendment. This amendment, adopted in 1920, deprives the states (and the national government) of the right to deny any citizen the right to vote because of sex. Although women were voting in many states prior to its adoption, the amendment was the final step in providing the constitutional framework for universal suffrage (see Chapter 9).

Changing the power of the voters

The Seventeenth Amendment. This amendment, adopted in 1913, provides for direct election of United States senators instead of their selection by the state legislatures. When the Constitution came from the hands of its framers, the House of Representatives was the only branch of the national government that the electorate chose directly. The rise of political parties and the extension of the suffrage within the states brought the presidential office under the control of the voters by the 1830's. From then on it was a matter of time before the people would demand the right to choose their senatorial representatives.

As the twentieth century opened, the people in many of the states were, in effect, choosing their senators, because the legislatures were simply ratifying the results of popular referendums. But demand for constitutional change became insistent. It was charged that great sums of money were being used to bribe state legislators to choose men of wealth and conservative outlook. The Senate came to be dubbed the "Millionaires' Club," and individual senators were tagged as representatives, not of the people, but of the Steel Trust, the Sugar Trust, the Railroad Trust, and so on. Several times the House of Representatives approved an amendment calling for direct election, but the Senate resisted. Finally, in 1912, the Senate capitulated. The amendment rounded out the process by which the political branches of the national government were made more directly responsive to the voters.

The Twenty-second Amendment. This, the newest amendment, was adopted in 1951. It prevents anyone from being elected to the office of President more than twice (except the incumbent at that time, Harry S.

Truman). A man succeeding to the Presidency and serving more than two years may be elected President in his own right only once. The chief significance of the amendment, however, is that it limits the electorate. Prior to the third-term election of Franklin D. Roosevelt in 1940, one of the unwritten usages of the American Constitution was that a man should not run and the voters should not elect a man to this high office for more than two terms. In 1940 and again in 1944, a majority of the voters, aided by Roosevelt, "amended" this unwritten rule. But with the adoption of the Twenty-second Amendment, the restriction on the political majority was made absolute.

Changing the constitutional structure

The Twelfth Amendment. This amendment was adopted in 1804 to correct a deficiency in the original Constitution. The original provisions for the selection of President and Vice-President were that electors should be chosen in each state, according to the method prescribed by the state legislatures. Each elector, without consultation with others, was to vote for the two men he deemed best qualified to serve as President. The person with the most votes, provided the number of votes represented a majority of the electors, was to be President, and the person with the next highest number of votes was to be the Vice-President. It was generally expected that the electors in the several states would normally cast their votes for the leading members of their own states and that no one would receive a majority. In such cases the House of Representatives, voting by states, was to

The Twenty-second Amendment bans presidential third terms.

choose the President from among the five men with the most votes. In the event that two men received the same number of votes, each representing a majority of the number of electors, the House was to choose between them.

The rise of national political parties made this system unworkable. By the time the presidential election of 1800 took place, the electors were party functionaries pledged to vote for the candidates of their own parties. In that year the Republicans, whose candidates were Jefferson for President and Aaron Burr for Vice-President, elected a majority of the electors. Each Republican elector, as pledged, cast one of his ballots for Jefferson and one for Burr, so that each man had the same number of electoral votes. As a result, the election was thrown into the House of Representatives, still controlled by the Federalists. For a while the Federalists toyed with the idea of making Burr President, from their point of view the lesser of two evils. It was only with the greatest difficulty that Jefferson was finally installed in the White House. Immediately thereafter the Twelfth Amendment was adopted, to avoid repetition of this incident.

From PUCK, *January 23, 1889. Courtesy Roger Butterfield*

The United States Senate was called the "Millionaires Club" before adoption of the 17th Amendment.

Each elector now votes separately for President and for Vice-President, the man with the majority of the votes in each case being elected. In the event no man receives a majority of the votes for President, the House, voting by states, chooses from among the three men with the most electoral votes. If no man receives a majority of the votes cast for Vice-President, the Senate chooses between the two men with the most votes.

The Twentieth Amendment. This is popularly known as the "lame-duck amendment" and was largely inspired by the late Senator George Norris of Nebraska. Before it was adopted, a President elected in November did not take office until the following March, and congressmen chosen at the same time did not begin to legislate for thirteen months after their election. Meanwhile those congressmen defeated in the elections continued to represent—or misrepresent—their constituents in the short and ineffective December to March session. The Twentieth Amendment rearranged the schedule of congressional and presidential terms so that congressmen elected in November now begin their duties on January 3, and the President takes office on January 20. This also does away with the short December to March session of Congress which used to specialize in filibusters.

These, then, are the twelve formal amendments to the Constitution. Important though they are, the Constitution has developed mainly, as we have noted, by less formal methods. Undoubtedly one of the reasons other methods have been used is that it is difficult to secure formal amendment.

The amending procedures have been criticized because they are undemocratic and place restrictions on the majority. According to democratic theory, sovereignty—the power that is the source of all governmental authority—should be in a majority of the people, but neither a majority of the voters at large, nor even a majority of the voters in a majority of the states, can formally alter the Constitution. Some have argued that the amending procedure is a limitation on majority rule self-imposed by the majority and is therefore consistent with democratic theory. This is juggling words. Some have used a new term, "the constituent power," to refer to the ultimate underlying authority of the majority as distinguished from the amending power belonging to two-thirds of both houses of Congress and three-fourths of the state legislatures. This is an interesting question, but whatever it is called, our method of amendment gives a veto to a minority. The veto is, however, temporary and not absolute. When a majority of the people are serious in their desire to bring about a change in the Constitution, their wishes will probably prevail either by amendment or by the more subtle methods of interpretation and adaptation.

The changing Constitution: a case study

The history of the proposed child labor amendment offers an interesting example of constitutional change by a combination of all the methods previously discussed. At the beginning of the twentieth century, people were becoming alarmed over the widespread employment of children. Many of these children were working in heavy and dangerous industries at an age when they should have been in school. In some places the conditions were so deplorable, the hours so long, that young children of eight and ten were slowly dying of ill nourishment, disease, or overwork. Wages were so low that those who exploited this labor were able to undersell their competitors. To meet the competition, other employers, in turn, were forced to hire children.

Here was an admitted evil; yet, individually, the states were unable to act. If the more progressive states outlawed child labor, they could not prevent the sale within their boundaries of cheap goods produced elsewhere by children, and they could not attract industries seeking cheap labor. Finally, in 1916, after years of agitation, Congress closed the channels of interstate commerce to goods manufactured by, or with the help of, child labor. But the Supreme Court, by a close decision and—it now seems fair to say—tortured construction of the Constitution, in *Hammer* v. *Dagenhart* (1918), struck down the law as an interference with the reserved powers of the states. Congress tried to overcome the constitutional block by placing a tax on goods produced by or with the help of children. In 1922, in *Bailey* v. *Drexel Furniture Company,* the Court ruled this law unconstitutional.

Apparently nothing could be done without a constitutional amendment. In 1924 Congress proposed an amendment that would give to the national government the power to "limit, regulate, and prohibit the labor of persons under 18 years of age." The amendment specifically stated that "the power of the several States is unimpaired by this Article except that the operations of State laws shall be suspended to the extent necessary to give effect to legislation enacted by Congress," but the opponents of the measure, using the mask of states' rights, were able to prevent ratification by the necessary three-fourths of the states.

By 1937 there had been a major depression and a change in political climate. Yet the Supreme Court was still dominated by judges who represented the views of the 1920's. Congress in 1935 had enacted a law that, if upheld, would indicate that Congress could use its power over interstate commerce to limit child labor. Would the Court approve? After much agitation by the President (see Chapter 20), including a proposal to pack the Supreme Court with judges more responsive to the political majorities of the 1930's, the Supreme Court reversed its ruling as to the extent of Congress's power over interstate commerce.[4] The following year, 1938, Congress once again enacted a law closing the channels of interstate commerce to goods produced by child labor. This time the Supreme Court upheld the law, specifically overruling its decision of 1918.[5] It had taken twenty years, but by congressional and presidential action the Constitution had been brought in line with the desires of the people. Since 1937 no state has ratified the child labor amendment, for it was no longer so vitally needed. The Constitution had been "amended" by other means.

Summary

Before we leave the story of our Constitution, a summary of the chapter is in order:

1. The Constitution is a symbol of national unity.
2. The Constitution both limits and grants powers.
3. Powers are limited in order to preserve the federal system, and to protect rights reserved for the people that are necessary in order to operate a free government and to live a free life.

[4] *National Labor Relations Board* v. *Jones & Laughlin Steel Corporation.*
[5] *United States* v. *Darby* (1941).

4. These limitations upon governmental power are enforced by the ballot box, by the power of independent judges to void laws that encroach upon constitutional limitations, by a further distribution of authority between the national and the state governments, and, most important of all, by scattering power among President, House, Senate, and judges and making the different branches of government responsible to different combinations of voters.

5. At the same time the Constitution limits and restricts the power of the rulers, it also checks the power of popular majorities.

6. The Constitution is also an instrument designed to provide a government with sufficient powers to meet national problems.

7. As an instrument of government, the Constitution must grow and be adapted to changing conditions, but at the same time the basic liberties of the people must be protected.

8. The Constitution is kept alive by informal methods of interpretation and through formal amendment.

9. The problem of the Constitution is to create a government that "enables the government to control the governed," and, at the same time, one that permits the governed to control the government.

The one principal feature of our constitutional system that remains to be examined is *federalism*. Federalism is one of the most important "auxiliary precautions" to prevent abuse of power. At the same time, the framers of the Constitution mainly intended to create a strong federal union in order to provide stronger and more stable government.

The United States is not the only or even the oldest federal union, but it was the first to operate successfully a federal system of continental proportions. This has been one of America's major contributions to the science and art of government.

AMERICAN FEDERALISM HAS NOT BEEN A static affair. Since 1787 it has been molded by our dynamic society and by the thoughts and actions of thousands of men. Federalism, 1787 style, and federalism today are as different as the clothing styles of the two periods. Yet the essential purpose remains the same: to reconcile the demands of unity and diversity, of cohesion and localism.

This chapter will explore the nature of American federalism, its constitutional structure, and its dynamic qualities, but first we must define our terms. What are the essential attributes of federalism? A *federal* system of government has a *constitutional* distribution of powers among central and constituent governments (called "states" in the United States), each entrusted with substantial duties. The constituent governments have some leeway in establishing their own governments. Neither the central nor the constituent governments receives its powers from the other, but both get them from a common source, the *Constitution*. This constitutional distribution of powers cannot be altered by the ordinary process of legislation—for example, an act of Congress. Finally, *both* levels of government operate through their own agents and exercise power directly over *individuals*.[1] Among the governments that both proclaim and practice federalism are the United States, Canada, Switzerland, and Australia.

In a *unitary* system of government, on the other hand, all governmental power is *constitutionally* vested in the *central* government, and local units exercise only the authority given them by the central government. Britain and France are examples of unitary governments. The unitary form should not seem strange to Americans, however, for the relations between states and municipalities is ordinarily a unitary relation.

Some students distinguish a *confederation* from a federation by defining a confederation as a government in which there is a constitutional distribution of powers among

★ 4

Dynamics

of

federalism

[1] Based on discussion of A. W. Macmahon, ed., "The Problems of Federalism," *Federalism Mature and Emergent* (Garden City: Doubleday & Company, Inc., 1955), pp. 4-5.

central and constituent governments, but the central government has no authority over individuals and operates through the constituent governments. The thirteen states operating under the Articles of Confederation fit this definition.

Warning: American federalism is not the only kind that can or does exist. Nor does federalism refer to how power is divided among leaders and followers or among branches of the *same* government; it describes how power is divided constitutionally and geographically among central and subdivisional governments. *Note also:* Prior to 1880 the term "federal" was often used to describe what we now call "a confederate form of government." And to add to the confusion, "federal" is frequently used today as a synonym for "national," that is, the federal government in Washington. In an exact sense, of course, the state *and* the national government make up our federal system of government.

WHY FEDERALISM?

Why do we have the federal form of government? The answer is, in part, because in 1787 there was no other choice. After *con*federation had been tried and found wanting, the only choice that was in a real sense open to those working for a more closely knit union was federation. "No political dreamer was wild enough," said John Marshall in *McCulloch* v. *Maryland,* "to think of breaking down the lines which separate the States and of compounding the American people into one common mass." Perhaps Marshall's statement is too extreme. Hamilton, for one, is on record as favoring such a policy, and at least one scholar believes that the framers did intend to establish a national government with full power over affairs that affected the whole nation.[2] At any rate Hamilton knew, as did all the leaders, that the overwhelming majority of the people were too deeply attached to the state governments to permit their complete subordination to a central government. They were even reluctant, as we have seen, to substitute federation for confederation.

Whether or not a unitary state democratically operated is possible today, it is clear that in 1787 distances were too great, the methods of transportation and communication too inadequate, and the techniques of democratic government too new to have made possible the operation of a large unitary state by republican methods. In the absence of wide cohesion and nationally shared sentiments, such a union could have been held together only by force. Federalism, 1787 style, went as far in the direction of union as public opinion would support and as the technology of the time permitted. But the

[2] W. W. Crosskey, *Politics and the Constitution in the History of the United States* (Chicago: University of Chicago Press, 1953), 2 vols. Most students of constitutional history remain convinced, despite Mr. Crosskey's impressive work, that it was not the intention of the framers to create a consolidated national government.

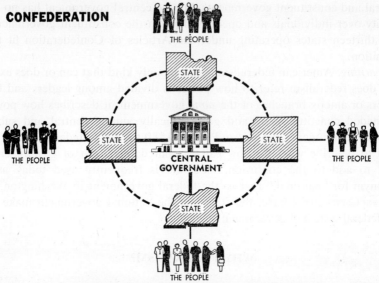

CONFEDERATION

The Confederation was a union of states. The Central Government received power from the states and had no direct authority over the people

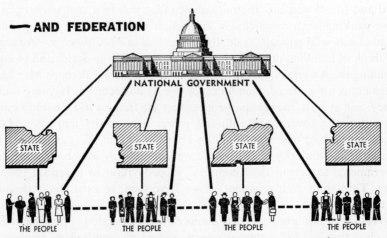

— AND FEDERATION

The Federal Union is a union of people. The National Government receives power from the people and exercises authority directly over them as well as over the states.

framework was established for time and more cohesive national sentiments to develop a national government resting upon a national community and operated by democratic procedures.

Moreover, federalism, as Professor Corwin has pointed out, was the ideal system for "the great enterprise of appropriating the North American Continent to western civilization."[3] New states were added to the Union, and

[3] Edward S. Corwin, *American Federalism—Past, Present, and Future,* Princeton University Bicentennial Address, October 7, 1946.

it was easily enlarged from thirteen to forty-eight without disrupting or causing any drastic rearrangement in governmental structure. As people moved into a new territory, they drew up state constitutions which were then approved by the Congress and the President. The new state became a member of the Union with the same powers and responsibilities as the original thirteen. When Hawaii and Alaska are added, as they probably will be, the only changes required will be the addition of new desks in the Senate and House of Representatives and new stars in the flag.

Unity without uniformity

Beyond these historical credits, and even if a unitary state had been politically possible in 1787, federalism is thought to be the most appropriate form of government for the United States. It is especially tailored to meet the needs of a country composed of relatively heterogeneous people who are spread over a large continent, who are suspicious of concentrated power, and who desire unity but not uniformity.

Federalism institutionalizes American suspicion of concentrated powers. It adds another whole dimension to the checks and balances system. By distributing governmental power on a geographical basis, another block is placed in the path of would-be dictators. Tyrannical action by the national government can be checked by those who control the state governments. And as Madison pointed out in *Federalist No. 10,* "those factious leaders who may kindle a flame within their particular states . . . will be unable to spread a general conflagration into the other states."

This diffusion of power, however, makes it difficult for a popular majority to carry into effect a national program of action. To control the three branches of the national government is not enough; power must be won in each state. Whether this is an advantage or disadvantage depends on one's political outlook. To the Founding Fathers it was an advantage. As we know, they did not favor majority rule and they feared that the mass of people "without property or principle" would seize control of the government. Federalism, they hoped, would make such a seizure of power less probable, since *national* majorities could be checked by *local* majorities. Of course—and this is a point often overlooked—the extent of the nation and the multiplicity of interests within it are the greatest obstacles to the formation of an arbitrary, single-interest majority. But even if such a majority should ever be formed, the fact that it would have to work through a federal system would serve to restrain its power.

Federalism avoids the thrusting of all problems into the national area, thereby making easier national compromise on national problems. Instead of one big struggle, there are many little struggles for power, and national politicians and parties do not have to iron out every difference on every problem between northerners and southerners, easterners and westerners,

New Englanders and midwesterners. As a result, many issues that might be irreconcilable in Congress are more readily disposed of in the state legislatures. If Congress were the nation's only legislative body, it would be forced to solve all the issues that divide people along religious, racial, and social lines. The continental dimensions of the United States, embracing many diverse cultures, make difficult the setting of national norms for ticklish local issues.

Suppose, for example, that Congress had to establish important national public policy toward morals or education. The problem of securing agreement would be infinitely complicated. Or take the control of alcoholic beverages. Many persons living in the large cities feel that the moderate use of alcohol is one of the amenities of life and that prohibition of its manufacture or sale is an infringement on their personal liberty. Many people in rural areas, on the other hand, are convinced that alcohol harms morals and health, causes many social problems, and should be outlawed. Our federal system permits these battles to be fought in the state legislatures. There is no need to try to enforce an inflexible national standard on the divergent areas and cultures.

The states as proving grounds

Federalism also encourages experimentation. The states can more safely change their constitutions and laws than can the central government. Forty-nine governments give us more latitude to try out new methods and to compare results. Legislative procedures, police and welfare administration, budgetary and personnel services are only a few of the subjects on which state experiences provide a wealth of materials from which the best can be adopted. The national government benefited from this experience, for example, when it adopted modern budgetary methods in 1921. The successful use of the item veto in 39 of the states has much to do with the growing demand that it be adopted by the national government. Unfortunately, neither the states nor the national government have taken full advantage of the opportunities of federalism's "many laboratories of political science." Lately there has been a much greater exchange of information among the states, but experimentation is still limited. The newer states followed, almost blindly, the general pattern of the older states. Little change has taken place in the basic structure of governments in the United States since the 1760's, for the federal Constitution was drawn up in large part on the basis of the state constitutions.

The states, in addition to developing new techniques of government, serve as training grounds for Presidents, congressmen, federal judges, and, to a lesser extent, federal administrators. Generally, more than half of the members of Congress have had prior service in their own state legislatures, and many of our Presidents served apprenticeships as governors of their own states.

By its constitutional decentralization of power, federalism emphasizes the importance of keeping the governed and the governors in close communion. Few people can serve the national government as President, congressmen, cabinet members, or even as administrators, but many thousands can participate in the operation of their state and local governments. By so doing they can strengthen democratic habits. Only by the use and re-use of democratic techniques to settle public problems do these techniques become functioning parts of our system. In this way the national government may be kept on a firm foundation of enlightened, trained, and democratically oriented citizenry.

This, then, is why we have federalism. Clearly, it offers many advantages. It also creates some difficult problems and exaggerates others. These we shall discuss in the following chapter. Now we turn to the constitutional basis of American federalism and to the ways it has been adapted to changing conditions.

THE CONSTITUTIONAL POSITION OF THE NATIONAL GOVERNMENT

The constitutional framework of federalism can be simply outlined: the national government, with one important exception, has only those powers *delegated* to it by the Constitution; the states have all the powers that are not delegated to the United States except those *denied* them by the Constitution; but within the scope of its operation, the national government is supreme. Furthermore, some powers are specifically denied *both* national and state governments; others are specifically denied only to the states; still others only to the national government. The chart on page 90 illustrates these constitutional arrangements.

How much national power?—the doctrines of liberal construction and implied powers

The chart of the constitutional framework of federalism is really an oversimplification and overlooks some difficult problems. Does the national government have powers that are *implied* from those granted or does it have only those *specifically* given?

The Founding Fathers had learned that weak government, incapable of governing, is as great a danger to liberty as government that is too powerful. They wished to create a national government within the framework of a federal system and endow that government with enough authority to meet the exigencies of all times. But how much power would be needed? The framers wisely did not attempt to grant detailed and specific power. They wanted the general government to endure. They knew that to endure, it must meet the needs of future generations whose problems could not be anticipated. Therefore, they made the grants of power to the national government in general terms, leaving the way open for succeeding generations to fill in the details and operate the structure in accordance with experience.

This initial wisdom was matched by the vision of those who first had to

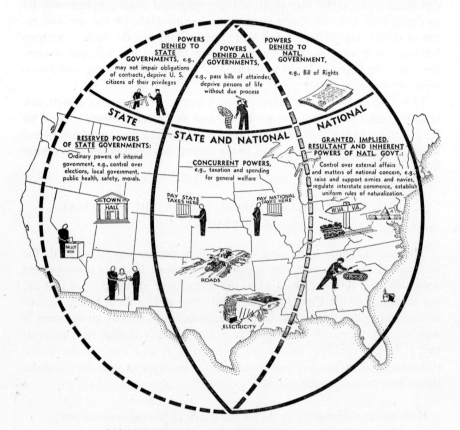

CONSTITUTIONAL DISTRIBUTION OF POWERS

deal with problems of constitutional interpretation. Foremost among these was Chief Justice John Marshall, nationalist and advocate of a liberal interpretation of the national government's constitutional authority. Marshall espoused these views in the celebrated case of *McCulloch* v. *Maryland*.

The case developed when the cashier of the Baltimore branch of the Bank of the United States, a bank chartered by the national government, refused to pay a tax levied against the bank by Maryland. Argued before the Supreme Court in 1819, the case presented two immediate questions: Does the United States have the authority to incorporate and operate a bank? May a state tax such a bank? But also involved were the questions, "Is the

American Union a union of *states* or a union of *people?*" "Is the Constitution a law emanating from the *people* or is it merely a *compact among the states?*" and "Should the powers given to the national government be narrowly or liberally construed?"

Maryland was represented before the Court by some of the most distinguished men of the bar, including Luther Martin. Martin had left the Philadelphia Convention when it became apparent that a strong national government was in the making. Martin and the other Maryland attorneys opened their arguments by pointing out that the power to incorporate a bank is not among those *specifically* delegated to the general government. Nor can it be *implied* within those delegated, they argued, because the Constitution is a compact among the states and should be interpreted as a contract. The states had created the central government as their agent, and in their organized sovereign capacities had given limited authority to it; its powers, like those of all agents, should be narrowly limited to the express terms of the contract. The Maryland lawyers further argued on the basis of this premise that Article I, Section 8 (which gives Congress the right to choose whatever means are necessary and proper to carry out its delegated powers) should also be narrowly construed. Congress has only the power to choose those means *absolutely* necessary to the execution of its powers. Since, they reasoned, a bank is not absolutely necessary to the exercise of any of its delegated powers, Congress had no authority to establish it.

In answer to the question, "Does Maryland have the right to tax the bank?" Maryland held that the power to tax is reserved to the states and could not be restricted by the general government.

Marshall's decision

Marshall, however, rejected every one of Maryland's contentions. In his usual forceful style he wrote: "We must never forget that it is a *constitution* we are expounding. . . . [A] constitution intended to endure for ages to come, and consequently, to be adapted to the various crises of human affairs." The Constitution is a supreme and binding law ordained and established by the people, not merely a contract among the states. The national government was an agent of the people, not of the states, who delegated their sovereign power to it so that it could promote the general welfare, provide for the blessings of liberty, insure domestic tranquility, and promote justice. In order to allow it to accomplish these purposes, the sovereign people intended the general government's powers to be liberally interpreted. The "necessary and proper" clause makes this clear, said Marshall, for it gives Congress the freedom to choose whatever means are appropriate, convenient, or useful in order to execute its delegated powers. The incorporation of a bank is only a means, but it is an appropriate, convenient, and useful means for Congress to employ in order to exercise its granted powers to lay and collect taxes, borrow money, and to care for the property of the United States. Marshall summarized his opinion in words that have become famous:

Let the end be legitimate, let it be within the scope of the Constitution, and all means which are appropriate, which are plainly adapted to that end, which are not prohibited, but consist with the letter and spirit of the Constitution, are constitutional.

Having thus established the constitutionality of the bank and having set forth the doctrine of implied powers, Marshall then ruled that Maryland could not tax a federal instrumentality. He conceded that Maryland had the power to tax, but no state could use its reserved powers to interfere with the general government's exercise of its granted powers. "If the right of the states to tax the means employed by the general government be conceded," he wrote, "the declaration that the Constitution, and the laws made in pursuance thereof, shall be the supreme law of the land, is empty and unmeaning declamation."

The significance of *McCulloch* v. *Maryland* can hardly be overstated. In this opinion Marshall established the doctrines that the powers of the national government should be *liberally interpreted,* that Congress has wide latitude in its choice of means, and that the national government is supreme when exercising its delegated powers.

The arguments of the Maryland attorneys overlooked the fact that the Constitution is a positive instrument of government. If Marshall had accepted the narrow and limiting view they advocated, the national government would have been strapped in a constitutional strait jacket and denied the powers needed to handle the problems of an expanding nation. In all probability, the Constitution would have been replaced many years ago as succeeding generations would be forced, once again, to render the central government adequate to the exigencies of each new age. Marshall's vision accounts in part for the longevity of our Constitution, today the oldest written constitution in the world—and truly a living constitution.

The reserved powers of the states and the doctrine of national supremacy

The Tenth Amendment reads: "The powers not delegated to the United States by the Constitution, nor prohibited by it to the States, are reserved to the States respectively, or to the people." Does this amendment mean that the national government may not use its delegated powers in such a way as to interfere with subjects normally regulated by the states under their reserved powers? John Marshall's answer was an emphatic "no," and his is now the generally accepted view. But this doctrine of national supremacy has had to contend from time to time with what Edward S. Corwin has termed "the doctrine of dual federalism."

Dual federalists argue that the national and state governments are equal sovereigns, each supreme in its own sphere, and that just as the states may not use their reserved powers to interfere with national functions, so the national government may not use any of its granted powers to regulate subjects reserved to the states. For many years, roughly from 1890 to 1937, the Supreme Court espoused dual federalism and ruled, for example, that Congress could not use its powers over interstate commerce to regulate agriculture or child labor, because the Constitution left these subjects to the States.

Since 1937, more especially since 1941, the Court has returned to the doctrine of national supremacy. As Chief Justice Stone declared in *United States* v. *Darby* (1941), "The [Tenth] Amendment states but a truism that all is retained which has not been surrendered. . . . From the beginning and for many years the Amendment has been construed as not depriving the national government of authority to resort to all means for the exercise of its granted powers which are appropriate and plainly adapted to the permitted end." Thus, as presently interpreted, the national government's use of its power is not limited in degree, manner, or purpose by the reserved powers of the states.

The existence of the states, does, however, restrict the use of national authority. The Constitution "looks in all its parts to an indestructible Union, composed of indestructible states."[4] Therefore, the national government may not employ its powers to destroy the republican character of the states or to impair seriously their ability to carry out governmental responsibilities. The national government may not, for example, tax the state governments in a way that will jeopardize their ability to govern. The extent to which the federal system limits the national government's taxing power is hard to state briefly. But within recent years, before the Supreme Court will strike down a national tax provision, it has required the demonstration of an *actual* rather than a theoretically possible serious burden on essential state functions.

National powers and foreign affairs

In domestic affairs, the national government is supreme within the scope of its operations, but it is restricted to the powers granted by the Constitution and those that may be implied from them. But in the field of foreign relations, the national government has *inherent powers* that are derived only indirectly from the Constitution. As far as the *external* relations of the United States are concerned, the central government has almost the same authority as it would if it were a unitary government. International law, not

4 *Texas* v. *White* (1869).

constitutional law, determines the limits of the national government's powers in its relations with the other members of the society of nations. For example, the government of the United States may acquire territory by discovery and occupation even though there is no specific constitutional basis for such acquisition, and may make agreements other than constitutionally defined treaties. Even if the Constitution were silent—which it is not—the national government would have as "necessary concomitants of its nationality"[5] the right to declare war, make treaties, and appoint and receive ambassadors.

Not only does the national government have inherent power as far as external relations are concerned, but this power "is not shared by the states; it is vested in the national government exclusively."[6] In short, federalism stops at the water's edge. Of course, the fact that ours is a federal system does have its impact on our foreign relations. Relations between the United States and other nations have been embarrassed by the failure of some states to prosecute persons who have injured foreign nationals, by the passage of state laws that discriminate against aliens, and by critical speeches of public officials. And national officials are often cautious in making agreements with other nations that cover subjects normally handled by states. But as far as the constitutional distribution of powers is concerned, the national government has *ample* and *exclusive* authority.

Treaties and the federal system

The national government's power to make treaties, vested in the President with the advice and consent of two-thirds of the Senate, is *not unlimited*. The national government cannot, by treaty, abridge rights specifically guaranteed by the Constitution. It could not, for example, deprive a person of his First Amendment rights by treaty or by a law to implement a treaty any more than it could do so by any other law. Treaties and laws passed to carry them into effect, like all laws, must conform to the Constitution. Furthermore, Congress may, at any time, as far as its application within the United States is concerned, abrogate a treaty.

The reserved powers of the states, however, neither set the bounds to the national government's treaty power nor measure its scope. On the contrary, self-executing treaties made under the authority of the United States and laws passed by Congress to carry treaties into effect are *superior* to state constitutions and state laws. A *self-executing treaty,* one that operates of itself and goes into effect without the need of any further action by Congress, is regarded by the courts on the same (but not higher) level as any other national law. The framers felt that the national interest was su-

[5] *United States* v. *Curtiss-Wright Export Corporation* (1936).
[6] *United States* v. *Pink* (1942).

perior to the interest of any state and that if a conflict arose between a national treaty and state policy, the *state* policy should give way.

In short, so long as treaties do not abridge a specific provision of the Constitution, the national government may make agreements with foreign countries regulating subjects, or giving Congress the power to pass laws regulating subjects, which Congress could not directly touch under the lawmaking power granted by the Constitution. This was old doctrine by 1920, but in that year the Supreme Court's decision in *Missouri* v. *Holland* made its implications clear. In 1914 Congress had passed a law dealing with the hunting of birds that migrate between the United States and Canada. Two federal district courts held that this law was unconstitutional on the ground that Congress had no authority over the subject. The Supreme Court did not pass on the rightness of these decisions, but a few years later Congress enacted an even more stringent law governing the hunting of such birds. This measure, however, was passed in order to comply with a *treaty* between the United States and Great Britain. This time the law did get to the Supreme Court. Justice Holmes, speaking for the Court, upheld its constitutionality in these words:

Acts of Congress are the supreme law of the land only when made in pursuance of the Constitution, while treaties are declared to be so when made under the authority of the United States. It is open to question whether the authority of the United States means more than the formal acts prescribed to make the convention. We do not mean to imply that there are no qualifications to the treaty-making power; but they must be ascertained in a different way. It is obvious that there may be matters of the sharpest exigency for the national well being that an act of Congress could not deal with, but that a treaty followed by such an act could, and it is not lightly to be assumed that, in matters requiring national action, "a power which must belong to and somewhere reside in every civilized government" is not to be found. . . . Here a national interest of very nearly the first magnitude is involved. It can be protected only by national action in concert with that of another power. The subject matter is only transitorily within the state. . . . We see nothing in the Constitution that compels the government to sit by while a food supply is cut off and the protectors of our forests and our crops are destroyed.[7]

Some time ago Sei Fujii, a Japanese alien, raised issues closely related to those discussed in *Missouri* v. *Holland*. Fujii argued that the provisions of the United Nations Charter in which the United States promised to promote respect for human rights without distinction as to race, sex, language, or religion were superior to and in conflict with the California law prohibiting aliens ineligible for citizenship (at that time this covered Japanese aliens) from owning real property. It has been generally assumed that the United Nations Charter is not a self-executing treaty and therefore does

[7] *Missouri* v. *Holland.*

not apply as domestic law within the United States. But a California district court of appeals ruled to the contrary and held the Charter to be a self-executing treaty.[8]

Although the Supreme Court of California reversed the lower court on this ruling, the Sei Fujii case provoked a storm of comment. Many groups continue to point to the lower court ruling as evidence of the danger to state powers growing out of our treaty commitments. (Apparently, the Constitution of the United States presents the same danger to state powers. Although the California Supreme Court ruled that the alien land law did not come into conflict with the United Nations Charter, it did hold that the law violated the Fourteenth Amendment of the Constitution.)[9]

The doctrine of *Missouri* v. *Holland* and its implications are the center of a major controversy. Some people fear that the treaty power will be used to regulate matters normally handled by state governments. They see a grave danger that the treaty power will be used to make basic alterations in our constitutional system. They have urged that we amend the Constitution to limit the national government's powers to make agreements with foreign nations and international agencies. Amendments to this effect, sponsored by Senator Bricker and Senator Dirksen and backed by the American Bar Association, have been considered by Congress and are discussed in Chapter 22.

THE CONSTITUTIONAL POSITION OF THE STATES

The power of the states, unlike that of the national government, is only indirectly derived from the Constitution; they have *inherent* governmental powers subject only to the limitations of the Constitution. Of course, within its field the national government is supreme, and the states may not use their reserved powers to frustrate national policies.

The Constitution contains certain *explicit limitations upon state power*. These are largely contained in Article I, Section 10, and in the Thirteenth, Fourteenth, Fifteenth, and Nineteenth amendments. The amendments are, as we have noted, prohibitions on state governments in behalf of individual liberties. In addition, the Constitution forbids the states to make treaties, impair the obligation of contracts, coin money, pass bills of attainder and ex post facto laws (see Chapter 8). States may not, except with the consent of Congress, collect duties on exports or imports, enter into any agreement with a foreign government, or make compacts with another state.

Does the mere vesting of power in the national government withdraw the power from the states? There is no general answer to this question. In some fields the national government has *exclusive* power—the determination of the rules of naturalization is an example. On the other hand, both the

[8] *Sei Fujii* v. *California* (1950).
[9] *Sei Fujii* v. *California* (1952).

national and state governments have *concurrent* powers to tax, and as long as a state tax measure does not conflict with a national law or treaty or unduly burden a federal function, it is constitutional.

The commerce clause illustrates the complexities of the situation. Some of the most difficult questions of constitutional law arise over the extent to which this clause, granting to Congress the power to regulate interstate and foreign commerce, limits the reserved powers of the state. Obviously, congressional regulations of this commerce take precedence over any state enactments. But what if Congress has said nothing? May the states regulate interstate commerce? May they apply their own police power regulations to it? The answer would be simpler if the Supreme Court had adopted the position that the commerce clause totally excludes any state regulation. But the Court has ruled that the states may—when Congress has not acted—regulate those local aspects of interstate commerce that do not require uniform national treatment, and they may apply their laws, designed to protect the public, to interstate commerce, if those laws do not unduly burden, obstruct, or discriminate against such commerce.

Who is to say whether a particular measure discriminates against interstate commerce or that the subject in question requires uniform national treatment? When Congress has not acted, the Supreme Court is the "arbiter of the competing demands of state and national interest." In each case, the Court must make the decision, after weighing state and national considerations. Proceeding by this method, the Court in 1946 declared that a Virginia statute requiring segregation of Negroes and whites on interstate buses was an unconstitutional attempt by a state to regulate an aspect of interstate commerce requiring uniformity of treatment.[10] State laws imposing speed limits on trains within city limits and requiring the elimination of grade crossings have been upheld, but laws requiring trains to stop at every crossing have been invalidated.[11] The Court has upheld the right of a state to refuse a permit to an interstate motor carrier because the resulting congestion on the highways would create a hazard.[12] On the other hand, it has held that a state unconstitutionally interfered with interstate commerce when it refused to grant a permit to an interstate motor carrier because of fear of excessive competition.[13]

Obligations of the national government to the states

The Constitution obliges the national government to guarantee to each state a republican form of government. It does not define what is meant by

[10] *Morgan* v. *Virginia.*

[11] *Erb* v. *Morasch* (1900); *Erie R. Co.* v. *Board of Public Utility Commissioners* (1921); *Seaboard Air Line Ry. Co.* v. *Blackwell* (1917).

[12] *Bradley* v. *Public Utilities Commission of Ohio* (1933).

[13] *Buck* v. *Kuykendall* (1925); see also *Southern Pacific* v. *Arizona* (1945) and cases mentioned therein.

a republican form—the framers undoubtedly used the term to distinguish it from a monarchy on the one hand, and a pure direct democracy on the other—and the Supreme Court has consistently held that the enforcement of this constitutional clause is a congressional obligation. The Court refused, for example, to intervene when Oregon's use of the initiative system of direct legislation some years ago was challenged on the grounds that it destroyed the republican character of the government.[14] Congress determines whether a state has a republican form of government when it decides whether or not to permit the congressional representatives of that state to take their seats in Congress.

In addition to guaranteeing to each state a republican form of government, the national government is obliged by the Constitution to protect the states against domestic insurrection. Congress has delegated to the President the authority to send troops to quell such insurrections on the request of the proper state authorities. This gives the President the power to determine which of contending factions is the proper authority in a state. President Tyler's decision was binding on the courts when he threatened to send federal troops to protect the Rhode Island government against the "domestic insurrection" of a rival government that was contending for the right to speak for the state.[15]

Horizontal federalism—interstate constitutional relations

What obligations does the Constitution impose on the states in their *dealings with one another?* Three clauses of the Constitution, taken from the Articles of Confederation, require the states to give full faith and credit to one another's public acts, records, and judicial proceedings; to extend to one another's citizens the privileges and immunities of their own citizens; and to return persons who are fleeing from justice in sister states.

Full faith and credit. This clause requires states to enforce validly obtained civil judgments of other states and to accept the public records and acts of other states as enforceable documents. The clause does not require states to enforce the *criminal laws* of other states. In fact, in most cases for a state to do so would be unconstitutional. But if Mr. A, for example, should obtain a Pennsylvania civil judgment against Mr. B, and then B moves to California, the California courts must enforce the judgment just as they would one from their own courts.

The full faith and credit clause is one of the most technical and complicated provisions of the Constitution. Some idea of the complexity can be obtained from the problems arising out of an automobile accident that took place in Illinois between two Wisconsin citizens, one of whom was killed. The victim's heirs sued in the Wisconsin state courts to recover damages for

---

[14] *Pacific States Telephone and Telegraph Co.* v. *Oregon* (1912).
[15] *Luther* v. *Borden* (1849).

wrongful death. The defendant was a citizen of Wisconsin, as was his insurance company. And the law of Illinois, where the accident occurred, permitted such damage suits for deaths occurring within Illinois. The laws of Wisconsin, however, forbade wrongful death suits in its courts for deaths occurring *outside* Wisconsin. The Wisconsin courts obeyed the mandate of their laws and refused to entertain the suit. But by a five to four decision, the United States Supreme Court decided that the full faith and credit clause required Wisconsin to give full faith and credit to the law of Illinois and to hear the suit.[16]

Privileges and immunities. States may not deny to citizens of other states the full protection of the law, the right to engage in peaceful occupations, or access to the courts. States may not tax citizens of other states at a discriminatory rate or otherwise arbitrarily interfere with the use of their property within the state. Although states must extend to citizens of other states the privileges and immunities of their own citizens, they are not required to permit out-of-state citizens to vote or serve on juries, nor to admit them to publicly supported institutions such as schools and hospitals.

Extradition. The Constitution asserts that a state shall, when requested by the governor of the state from which a fugitive has fled, deliver him to the proper officials. Congress has supplemented this provision by making the governor of the state to which the fugitive has fled responsible for returning him. Despite the use of the word "shall," the federal courts will not order governors to extradite (return) persons wanted in other states. A few years ago the Governor of New Jersey, horrified at the conditions under which men lived in a chain gang, refused to hand over a fugitive to Georgia officials. There was nothing that Georgia could do about it. An 1861 decision of the Supreme Court, *Kentucky* v. *Dennison,* held that Congress could not, even if it wanted to, establish procedures to force states to comply with the extradition clause of the Constitution. This decision rested on a theory of the federal union as a compact among sovereign states depending primarily for its enforcement on the good will of the states who were parties to the contract. The theory of federalism on which this decision is based has been rejected, but the decision itself has never been reversed. Although there are some spectacular examples of governors refusing to deliver persons wanted in other states, extradition is normally handled in a routine fashion. Furthermore, Congress has closed this "gap" in part by making it a federal crime to flee from one state to another for the purpose of avoiding prosecution for certain felonies. Trial for this federal crime is held in the state from which the fugitive has fled, thus making it possible for federal authorities to turn him over to the state officials to prosecute him for state crimes.

In addition to these three obligations, the Constitution also requires the states to settle their disputes with one another without the use of force. States may carry their legal arguments to the Supreme Court or may negoti-

[16] *Hughes* v. *Fetter* (1951).

ate *interstate compacts.* Compacts may also be used to establish interstate agencies and to solve joint problems (see Chapter 5). Before interstate compacts become effective, the approval of Congress is required, an approval that is sometimes given in advance. After a compact has been signed and approved by Congress, it becomes binding on all signatory states, and its terms are enforceable by the Supreme Court. Not all agreements among states, however, require congressional approval—only those, the Supreme Court held in 1893, "tending to increase the political power of the States, which may encroach upon or interfere with the just supremacy of the United States."[17]

The Supreme Court as umpire of the federal system

This discussion of the constitutional relations between the national and state governments shows the important role of the Supreme Court as the umpire of the federal system. The Court is not the only umpire. Congress has much to say about the distribution of functions and the extent to which state regulations will be permitted.[18] The courts, however—ultimately the Supreme Court—determine whether the national government is going to be called to task for invading the sphere left to the states or whether the states have usurped national duties.

The Supreme Court, itself a branch of the national government, has often been accused of being biased. Professor Oliver P. Field has written, "The *States* . . . have had to play against the umpire as well as against the national government itself."[19] Though the states have had their innings, over the long pull the Court's decisions have favored national powers. Especially in recent years, Congress has shown more of a tendency than the Supreme Court to respond to local pressures and to favor local regulations. And the local majorities that control the state governments have been severe in their criticism of the Court for its decisions curtailing their authority.

Despite the frequent criticism of the Supreme Court by some outraged groups who control the machinery of state government, not many would deny the Supreme Court the power to review state actions. Support for Supreme Court review of actions of state and local governments rests upon a different basis than does the argument for Supreme Court review of acts of Congress or the President. As Justice Holmes once remarked, "I do not think the United States would come to an end if we lost our power to declare an Act of Congress void. I do think the Union would be imperiled if we could not make that declaration as to the laws of the several states."[20] Or, as Justice

[17] *Virginia* v. *Tennessee* (1893).
[18] See Paul A. Freund, "Umpiring the Federal System," *Federalism Mature and Emergent, op. cit.,* p. 160.
[19] O. P. Field, "State versus Nation, and the Supreme Court," *American Political Science Review,* Vol. 00, No. 00, April 1934, p. 233.
[20] O. W. Holmes, *Collected Legal Papers* (New York: Harcourt, Brace and Co., Inc., 1920), pp. 295-296.

Story wrote many years earlier, such a review is necessary to maintain "uniformity of decisions throughout the whole United States, upon all subjects within the purview of the constitution. . . . Judges of equal learning and integrity, in different states, might differently interpret a statute, or a treaty of the United States, or even the constitution itself: If there were no revising authority to control these jarring and discordant judgments, and harmonize them into uniformity, the laws, the treaties and the constitution of the United States would be different in different states and might, perhaps, never have precisely the same construction, obligation or efficacy, in any two states."[21]

This review of the formal constitutional structure of American federalism contains little that would have startled the generation of 1787. The *structure* of our federalism is little changed; its actual *operation* has been drastically altered.

GROWTH OF THE NATIONAL GOVERNMENT

The words of the Constitution, wrote Justice Holmes in *Missouri* v. *Holland,* called into life a being whose development "could not have been foreseen completely by the most gifted of its begetters. It was enough for them to realize or to hope that they had created an organism; it has taken a century and has cost their successors much sweat and blood to prove that they created a nation." The Constitution established a framework in which a national government could develop, but it was some time in fact before a national government existed.

As we saw in the case of *McCulloch* v. *Maryland,* John Marshall argued that ours is a union of *people,* that the central government is both in theory and in fact a national government resting directly on the people. But there were many, foremost of whom was John C. Calhoun, who dissented. These dissenters argued that the central government was only a *federal,* not a national, government, created by the states and receiving all its powers from the states acting in their organized sovereign capacities. When the Constitution of the Southern Confederacy was written, its Preamble pointedly declared, "We, the People of the Confederate States, each State acting in its sovereign and independent character do ordain and establish this Constitution. . . ."

The question was ultimately decided at Appomattox Court House, but from the beginning the logic of events vindicated the nationalists. It has made no difference whether the party in power has been Federalist, Jeffersonian, Whig, Republican, or Democratic—the national government's sphere has constantly expanded. Since the platforms of both major parties reflect the wishes of the major interest groups and continue to call for programs that require greater activity by the central government, it is a safe bet that its domain will continue to grow.

[21] *Martin* v. *Hunter's Lessee* (1816).

Basis of the growth

How has this expansion taken place? Not by amendment: the formal constitutional powers of the national government are essentially the same today as they were in 1789. But the Supreme Court (building on Marshall's work in *McCulloch* v. *Maryland*), the Congress, the President, and—ultimately— the people, have taken advantage of the Constitution's flexibility to permit the federal government to exercise the powers needed to fight wars and depressions and to serve the needs of a modern industrial nation. The full scope of the central government's constitutional powers has been used to support this expansion of functions, but there are three major constitutional pillars on which the expansion has taken place.

The war power. The national government traditionally has been responsible for protecting the nation from external aggression, and, when necessary, for waging war. In a world community that knows total war, the power needed to provide for the common defense is of a scope hardly dreamed of in 1787. With the possibility of attack always present, the national government cannot wait until war is declared. It must keep the nation strong enough to prevent wars if possible and to win them if it can. Military strength no longer depends primarily upon troops in the field, but upon the ability to mobilize the nation's industrial might and to apply its scientific knowledge to the tasks of defense. Everything from the physics courses taught in the schools to the conservation of natural resources and the maintenance of a prosperous economy affects the war-making potential (see Chapter 24).

During time of war the national government has to organize, coordinate, and channel all human and natural resources to the end of destroying the war-making power of the enemy. It then becomes not only proper, but absolutely necessary, to conscript men, requisition property, control prices, encourage scientific studies, allocate resources, maintain the supporting economy, and bolster public morale. And when the fighting ceases, the government must cope with the problems of demobilization and reconversion. After disrupting the national life by converting manpower, materials, and machines to war, it is responsible for achieving the return to peacetime living as smoothly as possible. It must give aid to veterans and correct the many war-caused or war-aggravated maladjustments in the economy, such as housing shortages.

In brief, the national government has the power to wage war and to wage it successfully. In total war this means almost total power. As long as we live in a world where war is an ever present possibility, the defense activities of the government will be many and varied, and they will impinge on all aspects of our lives.

The power to regulate interstate and foreign commerce. This is the second constitutional pillar supporting the expansion of the national government's functions. Congressional authority extends to all commerce *that affects more states than one*—to those activities wherever they exist or whatever their nature, whose regulation is necessary and proper to regulate interstate and foreign commerce. The term "commerce" includes all commercial inter- course, the production, buying, selling, and transporting of goods. The power to regulate is the power to prescribe the rules by which this commerce is governed; that is, the right to foster, promote, protect, defend all com- merce that affects more states than one. Hence, the short constitutional clause giving Congress the power to regulate commerce among the states and with foreign nations carries a tremendous constitutional punch. From these few words the national government has been able to find constitutional props for regulating persons and property in the public interest. The national government, unlike the states, has no inherent police power (the power to regulate persons and property for the general welfare), but it can and does use its power to regulate interstate commerce in order to promote the general welfare. For example, it is now a federal crime to use the channels of inter- state commerce to sell adulterated goods, to steal automobiles, to rob a bank, to kidnap, and to transport women for immoral purposes. Moreover, Congress has forbidden the *production* of goods intended for the interstate market by persons who receive less than a federally established minimum wage.

Today there are few aspects of our economy that do not affect commerce in more states than one. When Farmer Filburn plants wheat in his own back yard to feed his own children and chickens, his actions affect the price of wheat in the interstate market, and therefore his activities are within the scope of congressional authority. When a large steel company fires men because they belong to a labor union, it enhances the danger of industrial strife and threatens the flow of goods in interstate commerce. Thus, national laws regulating employer-employee relations in industries that affect inter- state commerce have been upheld as necessary and proper means to protect the free flow of this commerce.

Many people have criticized the Supreme Court for what they deem strained interpretations of the Constitution. But wheat planted in people's back yards *does* today affect interstate commerce, and a strike in Pittsburgh or Detroit *does* affect commerce in California and New York. Our economy is so closely interconnected that each part affects every other part. The responsibility for this does not belong to the Supreme Court but to those many millions who contributed to the development of a mass-production, nationwide, closely interconnected economy. The Court has simply rec- ognized the obvious facts of life and has refused to make its decisions in an "intellectual vacuum."

The power to tax and spend for the general welfare. Congress may not constitutionally pass laws solely on the ground that they further the general welfare; it may *tax* and *spend* for the general welfare. For example, it would be unconstitutional for Congress to deal directly with the problems of housing, agriculture, and education, but it may spend money for these general welfare purposes. The national government directly spends large sums of money for subsidies to business and agriculture, for social security, for veterans' benefits, and for public works; moreover, it indirectly spends many more millions by granting money to the states for education, highways, slum clearance, housing, health, and old age benefits. These federal *grants-in-aid* are generally conditional on the states' matching federal funds, creating agencies to supervise the spending, and providing safeguards to see that the money is spent for the purposes for which it was granted.

Since Congress puts up a large share of the money, it has a loud voice in calling the tune. By withholding or simply by threatening to withhold funds, national agencies are able to supervise state operations. Furthermore, it may use its taxing powers for regulatory as well as for revenue purposes: for example, taxes on white phosphorus matches, on the sale of sawed-off shotguns, on sales of narcotics, and on the importation of goods from foreign nations (tariffs). The taxing power can also be used to "induce" states to adopt programs desired by the national government, as was done, for example, in the use of unemployment insurance and inheritance taxes.

These three clauses of the Constitution—the war power, the power over interstate commerce, and the power to tax and spend for the general welfare—have supported a tremendous expansion of federal functions. If all the laws Congress has passed in pursuance of these clauses were wiped off the statute books, the size of the federal government and the scope of its functions would shrink drastically.

Reason for the growth

Why has this expansion of federal functions taken place? Certainly not because of the superior logic of the affirmative side in the age-old debate: "Resolved: that the powers of the federal government should be increased." Nor has it come about because of the desire of "that man" or "those men" to consolidate power in Washington. Such glib explanations, so prevalent in political campaigns, overlook many fundamental factors. Rather, "big government" has come about as the result of the pushing and hauling of interest groups, in turn reflecting deep-seated changes in our society.

Since 1789 we have grown from a poor, sparsely populated agricultural society to a rich, densely populated industrial nation. Our meager and slow transportation and communication network has been replaced by one that is vast and rapid. The farmer who used to eat what he raised now produces for people who live thousands of miles away. The small, local businessman who owned, organized, and operated his business has been joined by large-scale business owned by thousands of persons throughout the nation and operated by a nationally organized corporation. Our labor force has grown from unorganized artisans to nationally organized mass-production workers.

The United States has grown from a weak, isolated debtor nation to a powerful creditor who plays a central role in the world community.

It is self-evident that such profound alterations in any society would have a powerful impact on the government of that society. Not least in importance is the change in people's attitudes toward the national government. While the government of the Union was viewed in the 1780's as a distant, even foreign government, today most people identify their fortunes much more closely with Washington than they do with their own state governments. The railroad, telegraph, telephone, radio, airplane, and television have done their work in making the activities of federal officials familiar to all. While most people do not even know when their state legislature is in session, what goes on in Washington is known throughout the land in a matter of minutes. The President, his family, their troubles and habits—even the President's golf score—are objects of dinner table conversations. Likewise, citizens of other states are no longer considered strange. The highway, automobile, and house on wheels have made us a nation on the move. This mobility and intermixture of people from all parts of the nation are not conducive to the building of strong local attachments and deep sectional ties. One hundred and seventy years of common experiences, especially the fighting of two major wars, have cemented the Union and made Washington the focus of attention.

An urban society, moreover, requires greater *social control* than does an agricultural one. A thousand people in the country might need only one policeman, since informal pressures can be counted on to keep them in line. The same number of people living in the city, with its impersonal and diversified make-up, might require five policemen to enforce the social sanctions. The states have also had to expand their functions, but because many of our problems have become national in scope, even greater responsibilities have been assumed by the national government. In recent decades the national government has gradually taken over a greater role in fields of business regulation, law enforcement, conservation, education, housing, and civil rights, among others. What was local in 1789, or even in 1860, is now often national. It is axiomatic that the unit of government dealing with a problem should be coextensive in area with the problem. States could most efficiently and democratically supervise the relations between a small merchant, who bought and sold his products within the local market, and his few employees. In fact, little supervision was needed, as the employer was undoubtedly well acquainted with his workers, knowing their names, their families, and their problems. But only the national government can supervise the relations between a nationally organized industry that buys and sells its materials all over the world and its thousands of employees organized into national unions.

With the industrialization of the United States there also came about concentration of economic power, first in the form of business units and later in the form of labor unions. These units, along with professional organizations, are private governments exercising *political* as well as *economic* power. Concentration of economic power required a corresponding concentration of political power; if the unit of public government that regulates is not as powerful as the thing regulated, the regulated often regulates the regulator. The activities of a John L. Lewis or an American Telephone and Telegraph Company are too far-flung and their power is too formidable to enable the states to provide the needed social control. Big business, big agriculture, big labor, all add up to big government. As can be seen from the following table, many private governments—financial corporations—are larger than the states:

	1955 gross revenue (in millions)	Employees
General Motors Corporation	$12,443	624,000
Standard Oil Company (New Jersey)	6,272	153,000
United States Steel Corporation	4,080	273,000
California	2,206	99,000
New York State	1,975	99,000
Pennsylvania Railroad System	1,065	126,000
Michigan	1,091	51,000
Illinois	796	52,000
Oregon	274	19,000
Wyoming	72	4,000
Vermont	49	5,000

Compiled from *Moody's Manual of Investments,* 1956, Moody's Investors Service, New York; *Compendium of State Government Finances in 1955,* p. 8, Bureau of Census; *State Distribution of Public Employment in 1955,* March 23, 1956, p. 11, Bureau of Census.

As industrialization progressed, various powerful interests began to make demands on the national government. First the business groups, who were largely responsible for building industrial America, called upon the government for aid in the form of tariffs, a national banking system, a uniform and stable currency, and subsidies to railroads, airplanes, and the merchant marine. After the business groups had got what they wanted and generally felt strong enough to take care of themselves, they began to oppose governmental aid to other groups. But then the farmers learned that the national government could give them much more aid in solving their economic problems than could their states, and they too began to demand help. The farm groups used their powers to secure such laws as regulation of the railroads, antitrust legislation, paper currency, parcel post, and finally government support for farm prices. Industrialization did not diminish the influence of the farmers; on the contrary, it gave them a balance of power position. By the beginning of the present century, the urban groups generally, and especially organized labor, began to press their demands. Workers found that they could not organize unions with a hostile government issuing injunctions and calling out troops. They began to work for restrictions on injunctions and for friendly administrations. Finally, with increased industrialization and urbanization, the working groups and city dwellers found that, for political reasons, they normally received more help from the national government than from the states.

How has the changed world role of the United States contributed to the growth of the national government? Until recently, the United States played a small part in maintaining order in the world community. Because of our isolated geographic position, a favorable balance of power in Europe, and a relatively stable world in Asia, we easily maintained our security without the need for a positive foreign policy. All this, of course, has changed. Today the United States has to work at the job of maintaining order and stability in the world; we no longer get a free ride. The defense of the free democratic world requires a great deal of effort and money on the part of the national government. The funds spent for direct military expenditures, aid to allies, to veterans, and for interest on a debt largely acquired fighting past wars, account for approximately 80 per cent of the central government's annual budget, and the activities of well over one-half of its employees.

Weaknesses in the states

Finally, we must turn to what might be called the *failures* of the states. Many of our 48 states were arbitrarily formed and do not correspond to any underlying geographic, social, or historical realities. With the passage of time, growing discrepancies have developed between state boundaries and those physiographic conditions that have proved to be of lasting significance. Natural regions such as river valleys are frequently divided. Many boundaries place the large cities on the fringe of a state, dividing a metropolitan region between two or three states. New York City, Kansas City, Washington, D. C. are examples. When the people of a river valley or a metropolitan region want to act through their governments to conserve human and natural resources, they often find that no state has jurisdiction to deal with the problems of the area. A few states are too large; most are too small. They vary in size from Rhode Island to Texas and in population from New York to Nevada. Regardless of size or population, however, they all support the same elaborate governmental organization.

Some states lack the resources to provide minimum public needs. Of much greater importance, many problems that affect the citizens most directly are of such scope that only the national government can handle them. Faced with the Great Depression of the 1930's, when there were over twelve million unemployed out of a labor force of fifty million, and many more millions were destitute, the states did not have the financial resources for relief nor did they have power over a wide enough area to stimulate recovery. The national government, with its much greater tax resources and almost unlimited borrowing power, was literally forced to act. It was the only government capable of dealing with a national—a world-wide—depression.

Parallel to the increased confidence in the national government has been the decreasing strength of the traditional ties of loyalty to the states. This is due in part, as we have noted, to the greater mobility of our population. Also, most states had no independent existence prior to becoming members of the Union. There developed no strong feeling of local pride, and the original settlers long looked to the central government for protection and advancement.

But the state governments themselves must share some of the blame. Even within the limits of their jurisdiction and their resources, many of our state governments, through their failure to provide desired programs, have failed to keep the loyalty of large numbers of their citizens. As long as fifty years ago Elihu Root warned, "It may be that [governmental] control would be better exercised in particular instances by the governments of the states, but the people will have the control they need, either from the states or from the national government; and if the states fail to furnish it in due measure sooner or later constructions of the constitution will be found to vest the power where it will be exercised—in the national government."[22] And more recently J. Melville Broughton, a former governor of North Carolina, wrote: "Those of us who believe in the fundamental principles of states' rights and local self-government may as well concede frankly that much of the almost terrifying expansion of federal encroachment upon the original domain of the States has come about because state governments failed to meet the challenge of the new day. Inadequate educational opportunities, archaic labor laws and regulations, unrelieved hardships and inequities suffered by the working people, low-pitched politics and unjust class and race discriminations have, all too frequently, caused the people to lift their eyes beyond the horizon of state lines and call for relief from the Federal Government. . . ."[23]

Although more attention is paid to the waste and extravagance of the national government, Washington is almost a model of perfection when compared to *some* state capitals which are graft-ridden, inefficient, and unable to provide the services that the people expect. No generalization can be made to fit all 48 states, though it is difficult to deny that "the most critically defective part of our present system is the state government."[24] Some states, of course, are doing an excellent job of providing a high level of public service. But there are others that reflect the interest, not of the majority, but of political bosses or powerful economic interests.

Even with the best state governments, the national government's functions would expand in response to national needs. But as a result of these

[22] Elihu Root, Address before the Pennsylvania Society, September 1906, quoted in The Commission on Intergovernmental Relations, *A Report to the President* (Washington, D.C.: Government Printing Office, 1956), p. 56.
[23] "The Future of the States," *State Government,* March 1943, pp. 142-143.
[24] G. C. S. Benson, *The New Centralization* (New York: Farrar & Rinehart, Inc., 1941), p. 157.

deficiencies—state officials operating inefficient governmental machines in behalf of special interest groups—the central government has acquired some functions by default. The people demand that certain things be done, and if the states cannot or do not act, the people inevitably turn to Washington.

The primary reasons, then, for the expansion of federal functions are the industrialization of the United States, the consequent concentration of economic power, the resulting national problems that require action by a national government with sufficient resources and extensive jurisdiction, and the deficiencies of the states. Governments, like men, can survive only by adapting themselves to their changing environment. It is not surprising that a central government adequate for the days of the stage coach is not suitable in an era of television and hydrogen bombs.

Up to this point we have been talking about the constitutional relations between national and state governments and have commented on the dynamic character of our federal system. This dynamic quality is also illustrated by the ability of the federal system to incorporate without interruptions new units and to grow from thirteen states to forty-eight. But what about the relations between the national government and our territories and possessions and the District of Columbia?

THE "AMERICAN EMPIRE"

To over four million people the United States is a unitary and not a federal government. These four million live in the District of Columbia or in the several territories under the control of the United States. Over these people the national government has full governmental power, though in most cases it has established local governments and has given the people a voice in their local affairs.

Hawaii and Alaska—48 or 50 states?

Alaska and Hawaii are probably destined for eventual statehood. They are *incorporated territories;* the other territories are *un*incorporated. What is the difference? Incorporated territories are part of the United States, the Constitution applies in all parts to them, and such a territory is considered to be an "inchoate state" on its way to statehood. Unincorporated territories, on the other hand, *belong to* but are not *a part* of the United States. The *fundamental* but not the *formal* parts of the Constitution apply. These fundamental parts of the Constitution have never been enumerated, but they would appear to include those provisions essential to secure a certain standard of justice—such as the provision protecting the right to free speech. The formal provisions are those safeguarding *pro-*

cedural rights that are not indispensable in order to secure justice, such as the right to trial by jury.

At the present time both Alaska and Hawaii have their own territorial legislatures and local governments, though their respective governors are appointed by the President with the consent of the Senate for a four-year term. Each territory sends to the House of Representatives a delegate who has the right to debate but no vote.

When Congress incorporated these territories it signified its intention that they should eventually become states. But Congress has full authority to determine when and under what conditions this shall be done. The traditionally accepted requirements for statehood have been:

(1) That the inhabitants of the proposed new State are imbued with and are sympathetic toward the principles of democracy as exemplified in the American form of government and have proved their political maturity by having undergone a period of "tutelage" under incorporated Territorial government status.

(2) That a majority of the electorate wish statehood.

(3) That the proposed new State has sufficient population and resources to support State Government and at the same time carry its share of the cost of the Federal Government.[25]

The politics of admission

It is argued that both Hawaii and Alaska have met these requirements. The Hawaiians have been especially active in their attempt to be admitted as a full state partner into the Union. Since 1903 the people of the Islands have petitioned Congress over seventeen times for permission to become a state. During the past fifteen years over nine separate congressional committees have held statehood hearings, testimony has been collected from 700 witnesses, and more than 35,000 pages of official documents have been compiled. Both major political parties in the United States have endorsed Hawaiian statehood in their platforms. It has been supported by presidential candidates of both parties, and has had the backing of the Governors' Conference as well as countless other organizations. Several times the House of Representatives has approved bills to admit Hawaii, the Hawaiians have drafted a constitution that meets all the requirements laid down in the house bill, and the Senate committee considering the matter has urged admission. But the Senate voted to admit Hawaii only if Alaska was admitted at the same time—a condition that proved unacceptable to the House of Representatives.

Those who favor Hawaii's admission argue that it would strengthen our military defense, that it would raise our international standing in the eyes of the peoples of the Pacific, and that the half million Hawaiians who pay more taxes than do the people of nine existing states have shown their

[25] *Senate Report 1929,* Eighty-first Congress, second session, 1950, p. 7.

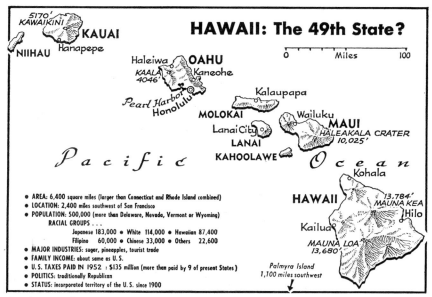

HAWAII: The 49th State?

- AREA: 6,400 square miles (larger than Connecticut and Rhode Island combined)
- LOCATION: 2,400 miles southwest of San Francisco
- POPULATION: 500,000 (more than Delaware, Nevada, Vermont or Wyoming)
  RACIAL GROUPS . . .
  Japanese 183,000 ● White 114,000 ● Hawaiian 87,400
  Filipino 60,000 ● Chinese 33,000 ● Others 22,600
- MAJOR INDUSTRIES: sugar, pineapples, tourist trade
- FAMILY INCOME: about same as U.S.
- U.S. TAXES PAID IN 1952 : $135 million (more than paid by 9 of present States)
- POLITICS: traditionally Republican
- STATUS: incorporated territory of the U. S. since 1900

Based on map from U.S. NEWS & WORLD REPORT, *an independent weekly news magazine published at Washington. Copyright 1953, United States News Publishing Corporation*

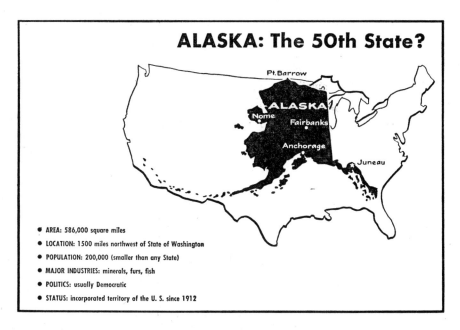

ALASKA: The 50th State?

- AREA: 586,000 square miles
- LOCATION: 1500 miles northwest of State of Washington
- POPULATION: 200,000 (smaller than any State)
- MAJOR INDUSTRIES: minerals, furs, fish
- POLITICS: usually Democratic
- STATUS: incorporated territory of the U. S. since 1912

capacity for self-government, their loyalty to the United States, and are entitled to equal political rights with other American citizens.

Heretofore no territory separated from the other states by miles of ocean has ever been added as a state, but the opposition to statehood grows mainly out of the diverse racial background of the Hawaiian people. A majority of the Hawaiians are Orientals (some are not citizens of the United States and others hold dual citizenship; that is, they are citizens both of the United States and of another nation, primarily Japan). Because of this situation, it is argued, "It will be extremely difficult to inculcate any sound concept of American ideals in a group with foreign background, dominant in its own little area, but isolated from the rest of the States." Moreover, it has been charged, "International revolutionary communism has a firm grip on the economic, political, and social life of the Territory of Hawaii." A subcommittee of the House Committee on Un-American Activities recently visited the territories and, with the help of the F.B.I. and of Naval and Military Intelligence, discovered that there were not more than ninety Communists in Hawaii; nevertheless, some senators are concerned about the alleged Communist domination of the labor unions of Hawaii. Although not a single case of sabotage by a Hawaiian civilian was reported during World War II, it is claimed that a large minority of the population is not loyal to the United States.

The issue is essentially partisan. Hawaii is usually controlled by Republicans, whereas the Democrats normally dominate in Alaska, although recent developments make these conditions less predictable. In recent years the admission of one of the territories could have upset party control of the United States Senate. Republicans have been more eager to admit Hawaii, and Democrats are more favorable to Alaska. But back of all the discussions pro and con about admission of the two territories is the issue of federal protection of civil rights. Hawaii has an enviable record of people of many diverse racial and national backgrounds living together peacefully. It can be reasonably anticipated that the addition of two senators and at least two representatives from Hawaii would strengthen the forces in Washington working for a more active federal civil rights program. And the admission of Alaska would further dilute the strength of the southern senators. For this reason, many southern senators and representatives are hesitant to support admission.

Alaskans were not as active as the Hawaiians in seeking statehood; but in the last few years they, too, have petitioned Congress and have adopted a constitution which, incidentally, incorporates features long advocated by students of state governments. Furthermore, in order to press their demands for statehood, Alaskans have adopted the "Tennessee Plan" of proceeding with the election of two "senators" and a "representative" and have sent them to Washington to lobby for admission.

The question of Alaskan statehood involves some of the same issues involved in Hawaiian statehood. Both are noncontiguous territories. Alaskan senators could probably be counted on to oppose the southern Democrats on issues of civil rights. But there are also major differences between the two situations. The problem of diversity of racial backgrounds is not so pressing. Alaska, twice as large as Texas, three and one-half times as large as

California, has an estimated population of about 200,000. The federal government owns, in behalf of all the people, about 90 per cent of the land in Alaska, but the major industry, fishing, is dominated by a relatively small number of concerns. The territory is rich in undeveloped resources, and its strategic location led General Billy Mitchell to declare, "He who holds Alaska holds the world."

Proponents of statehood claim that opposition comes primarily from the fish-packing industry which fears its special fishing privileges will be lost, but that the Alaskans desire statehood (as a popular referendum would indicate) and meet all the requirements. Opponents of statehood point out that Alaska would have the smallest population of any state in the Union, and that it would be unfair to citizens of others states to give these 200,000 people equal representation in the Senate. Furthermore, it is argued, statehood would impose financial burdens too great for Alaska to bear.

One of the most difficult issues arises over the allocation of territory and resources now chiefly owned by the federal government. If turned over to the state, 200,000 Alaskans would be given valuable property belonging to 170 million Americans. On the other hand, to deprive Alaska of control over such a vast part of its territory would place it under a handicap. Present proposals for statehood seek to work out a compromise by permitting the new state to select large land areas, but still leaving control over the major portion of federal territory in the hands of the federal government.

Admission of new states into the Union

How are new states admitted to the Union? This power is vested in Congress and the President. The procedure—though it varies—is normally for the inhabitants of a territory to petition Congress through their territorial legislature for authority to hold a constitutional convention. If Congress approves, and after the constitution has been submitted to the voters of the territory, the proposed constitution is presented to Congress with request for formal admission. The territory is then admitted into the Union as an equal partner with all other states by resolution approved by Congress and signed by the President.

Prior to admission, Congress may impose any condition it sees fit upon a territory as the price of admission. For example, Congress authorized Utah to draw up a constitution but stipulated that it contain a prohibition outlawing polygamy forever. President Taft refused to approve the admission of Arizona until the constitution was amended to abolish the provisions permitting the recall of judges. Once a state has been admitted, however, it is free to ignore those conditions which relate to its governmental authority and place it on unequal footing with other states. Thus after admission, Arizona amended its constitution to provide for recall of judges. On the other hand, conditions that are in the nature of business agreements relating to property, such as Ohio's promise not to tax certain lands for five years, are enforceable.[26]

The Commonwealth of Puerto Rico and other territories

Puerto Rico, an island only 95 by 35 miles but inhabited by over two million people, was acquired from Spain as a result of the Spanish-American War. It has many of the characteristics of an incorporated territory, but it is not one. Puerto Ricans are American citizens, governed under their own constitution and through their own elected representatives.

Independence or "dominion status" rather than statehood has been the aim of many Puerto Ricans. Most of the people have a Latin culture and lack any strong affinity for American ways. But proximity, historical attachment to the United States, and a need for help in overcoming economic problems will sustain Puerto Rico's close ties with the United States.

Its present relation to the United States is ambiguous. In 1950 Congress authorized the Puerto Ricans to draw up their own constitution. After Congress deleted a provision dealing with economic and social rights, this constitution was approved, signed by the President, and became the basic charter of the Commonwealth of Puerto Rico.[27] This constitution establishes a form of government much like that of our states. Although Puerto Ricans may amend their constitution without submitting the changes to Congress, and are considered by the United Nations to be self-governing, their constitution and laws are subordinate to the national Constitution and the applicable federal laws. Although most of our federal laws do not apply to Puerto Rico—the income tax, for example—Congress sometimes makes laws specifically applicable to the Island Commonwealth.

Many Puerto Ricans live in poverty. The death rate is high. Education is woefully below our standard. Within recent years modern sanitation and health programs have brought the death rate down, with the result that the population is growing fast and pressing against the limited resources. Despite much improvement, the economy is not diversified and depends primarily upon the sugar industry. Until the recent movement of many Puerto Ricans to the United States, the people of the mainland paid little attention to their depressed fellow citizens. Often settling in conditions as squalid as they left, their plight is now arousing increasing public concern. As these citizens begin to exercise their political power, more attention will undoubtedly be paid to attempting to solve the social and economic problems of Puerto Rican American citizens.

The United States domain also includes other territories in various categories of development. The most important of these are the Virgin Islands, Samoa, Guam, the Panama Canal Zone, and the trust territories. American

---

[26] See *Coyle* v. *Smith* (1911) where Supreme Court makes this distinction.

[27] Gordon K. Lewis, "Puerto Rico: A New Constitution in American Government," *The Journal of Politics*, Vol. 15, No. 1 (February 1953), pp. 42-66.

citizenship has been given to the residents of the Virgin Islands and Guam; residents of Samoa are American *nationals*. Nationality is a condition of less than full citizenship, but it involves allegiance to the United States and the obligation of protection by the national government. The people of the Virgin Islands and Guam have a large measure of self-government. The trust territories in the Pacific—the Marianas, Marshalls, and Carolines—are strategic trusteeships acquired by the United States by conquest. Most of these islands were formerly Japanese mandates under the League of Nations. They are now held by the United States under limited supervision of the United Nations. The United States also controls with Great Britain the Canton and Enderbury Islands in the Central Pacific.

Although the Philippine Commonwealth became a completely independent and sovereign nation on July 4, 1946, the United States still maintains close ties with its former dependency. The Commonwealth receives special tariff concessions, and the United States maintains naval bases there. Because the Philippines are important links in the American defense system and because of their former relations, the United States exercises what is tantamount to a protectorate over the Islands.

The District of Columbia

Almost all our territories have a large measure of home rule, but this is not the case with the nation's capital.

Congress itself serves as the city council of Washington, D. C., although most of the work is done by the House and Senate Committees on District Affairs. Three commissioners appointed by the President with the consent of the Senate administer the laws. Local judges are chosen by the President with approval of the Senate. In addition, there are the regular federal courts.

Except for those who maintain a legal residence elsewhere, citizens in the District of Columbia have no voice in electing either national or their local officials. It would take a constitutional amendment to give them the right to participate in federal elections, but it would require only an ordinary law to empower

"Honestly, I'd Rather Walk"

From THE HERBLOCK BOOK (*Beacon Press*)

them to run their own local affairs. Prior to 1874 Washington did have home rule, but because of corruption and inefficiency—evils not confined to Washington, especially in 1874—the present system was adopted. Since that time residents in the District have agitated for a return to home rule. Within recent years the pressures for a change have grown stronger. The Senate has twice approved.

The advocates of home rule have many complaints. In addition to the obvious injustice of being denied the right to govern themselves, they argue, most congressmen are little concerned about District affairs. Housing, hospital, and educational conditions in Washington, it is argued, are deplorable. Home rule would relieve Congress of attending to petty details and give it much needed time for more important responsibilities. But the rest of the nation has not been sufficiently aroused to press for reform. Furthermore, some people believe that since the District is the capital of all the people, it should be governed by the national legislature. Undoubtedly, Congress will always exercise more authority in Washington than in other cities, but it is questionable if this requires the denial of local self-government.

Summary

1. A federal system of government is one in which power is divided constitutionally among common (national) and constituent (state) governments, both sets of governments have substantial powers, and both exercise power directly over individuals.

2. American federalism in practice provides a compromise between excessively centralized and dangerously decentralized government, permits the states to serve as proving grounds for new ideas, and keeps leaders close to the people.

3. Simply put, the Constitution delegates certain powers to the national government and reserves the rest for the states. The Constitution places some limits on the powers of both the national and state governments. When acting within the scope of its constitutional powers, the national government is supreme. In foreign affairs, the national government is not only supreme, but it has inherent, complete, and exclusive powers. In domestic matters, there is considerable controversy over the precise division of power between the national and state governments.

4. Questions as to this division of power are decided by the Supreme Court, itself a branch of the national government and indirectly responsive to national political developments.

5. Constitutional powers that have helped create the expansion of the national government include the powers to wage war, to regulate interstate and foreign commerce, to tax and spend for the general welfare. Responding to popular needs and demands, the national government has often exercised these powers vigorously in dealing with economic and social problems,

6. Congress and the President have authority to admit new states to the Union, but recently the admission of Hawaii and Alaska has been immersed in political differences in Washington.

7. Congress has granted varying degrees of self-government to United States territories but directly legislates for the District of Columbia.

T HERE IS A "BILLIARD-BALL" CONCEPT OF FED-
eralism that abstracts the national and state governments from the social
system and talks of them as though they were things separate from America and Americans. Sometimes we forget that to talk of states' rights is but a
shorthand way to speak of the rights of *people* who live in states and the
authority of state officials. It is not Texas that has rights, but Texans. Likewise there is no such thing as the national government divorced from the
people of which it is made up and to whom it responds.

National and state governments provide arenas in which the differing
groups engage in peaceful conflict about public policies and programs. Often
congressmen and state legislators respond to the same groups and represent
the same values. But at other times, and on other issues, national and state
officials represent sharply different combinations of interests. This conflict
between the two levels of government is part of the struggle among groups
that make up our politics.

THE POLITICS OF FEDERALISM

From the day that the first colonists set foot on American soil, arguments
have arisen about the division of powers between the central and the local
governments. Throughout our history from pre-Revolutionary times to the
most recent attempt by the Commission on Intergovernmental Relations
(appointed by Congress and
the President to make a report
on the "proper" allocation of
functions between nation and
states), it has been impossible
to disentangle substantive issues of politics—slavery, labor-
management relations, government regulation of business,
civil rights—from discussions
of national-state relations. National action is favored by those
who anticipate that national
officials will be most responsive
to what they conceive to be in
the national interest. But those
who believe that state officials
will be most likely to support
their goals often become champions of states' rights.

The doctrine of states' rights

★ 5

Problems

of

federalism

illustrates how the issues of American politics are inextricably intermeshed with discussions of federalism. At one time or another, northerners, southerners, businessmen, farmers, workers, Federalists, Democrats, Whigs, and Republicans have opposed, in the name of states' rights, action by the central government.

When the Federalists controlled the central government and, in behalf of merchants and creditors, established a national bank, assumed state debts in full, proclaimed neutrality of the United States in the French-English struggles, and passed the Alien and Sedition laws, the Jeffersonian agrarians and debtors protested each move in the name of "states' rights." But when these same Jeffersonians captured the national government and placed embargoes on shipping, purchased Louisiana, and fought the War of 1812, the New England Federalists raised the cry, "states' rights." When the Republican party threatened the slave economy, the South arose to defend "states' rights." When the industrial interests used their influence with the national government to raise the tariff, secure land grants for railroads, and to tax state bank notes out of existence, the exporters and agrarians championed "states' rights." But when the Square Dealers, and especially the New Dealers, used the same national government to regulate business, protect the workers' right to bargain collectively, and grant generous subsidies to the farmers, the industrialists demanded a return to "states' rights."

The agility with which groups rush to the defense of states one year and leave them to their fate the next is demonstrated by the railroaders who protested, when the states started to regulate their activities in the 1870's, that Congress alone should regulate interstate commerce. When Congress started to move in this direction in the 1880's, these same railroad men charged that Congress was subverting the reserved power of the states. With this type of maneuvering, certain groups, helped by the Supreme Court, were able, during the period 1890-1937, to create a no man's land between the national and state governments, in which they found safety against any social control. Child labor is a case in point, as we have noted.

With the advent of the New Deal, business groups became the outstanding champions of states' rights. The national government was controlled by persons in whom many businessmen had little confidence and with whom they had less influence, while state governments were often more favorable toward the business community. More important, only the national government had broad enough jurisdiction to regulate large-scale industry effectively.

In recent years, those who favor racial segregation dominate some state governments and, naturally, they have asserted the right of the states to compel segregation in public institutions. On the other hand, those who want legal segregation abolished have urged the use of national power because they believe state governments controlled by segregationists will never do so.

So it is that the politics of federalism is involved in discussion of national-state relations. Nevertheless, almost all agree, however they differ on particular issues, that a country the size of the United States needs strong and active state governments and that a major problem of federalism is how to maintain a balance between national and state governments.

MAINTAINING THE BALANCE

The awful spectacle that disturbed Hamilton, "a nation without a national government" need frighten us no longer. As noted above, the national government's activities have greatly expanded. And it is probable that they will continue to expand. What can be done to prevent the creation of a colossus in Washington that can be neither efficiently operated nor democratically controlled?

Improvement of state and local governments

As noted in Chapter 4, one reason for the expansion of national programs has been the failure of the states to provide satisfactory services. Hence it is obvious that one of the most promising approaches is to improve, simplify, and modernize state governments. Many reforms to vitalize state governments have long been advocated—such improvements as reorganizing administration, streamlining legislative procedures, modernizing the basis of representation in state legislatures in order to represent fairly the growing urban population, shortening the ballot, and making officials respond to wider segments of the electorate. Although many recommendations for improvement have been filed and forgotten, several states—New Jersey, New York, and Virginia, for example—have made considerable progress. But much remains to be done.

We hear so much about the growth of national governmental functions that we sometimes overlook the growth of *state* activities. State and national power is not a seesaw in which one side has to be up and the other down. An increase in the authority of one does not necessarily detract from the importance of the other. On the contrary, the entrance of the national government into new fields has in many cases *strengthened* the states and helped them to improve their services. Despite the lamented condition of states and the constant cries about national interference, states are today, measured by the amount of money spent and number of functions, stronger units of government than they were in 1787. Indeed, in recent years activities of the states and their subdivisions have been increasing at a faster rate than the nondefense activities of the national government.[1]

[1] The Commission on Intergovernmental Relations, *Report to the President* (Washington, D.C.: Government Printing Office, 1955), p. 36.

Regional administration of federal functions

Even where state governments are strong, some activities can be best handled by the national government. But centralization of *policy-making* need not lead to centralization of *administration*. Policies and programs can be adopted at the national level, but their administration and implementation can be decentralized. In fact, some of the most informed and experienced political scientists believe that greater flexibility and more citizen participation can be achieved through federal decentralization than through state control. President Dodds of Princeton, however, voiced the warning: "A greater degree of administrative decentralization from Washington is required to make national administration as efficient as it may be, but to increase the efficiency of national administration without correspondingly improving state governments will contribute to further weakening of the states."[2] Be that as it may, regional administration of national programs is a reality. Only 11 per cent of federal employees work in the Washington metropolitan area. This decentralization avoids excessive centralization of administration, permits greater local participation in national programs, and encourages adjustment of policies to local conditions.

Hitherto, each agency in Washington has created its own field headquarters chiefly in accordance with the demands of its own activities and without much consideration of the regional divisions created by other federal agencies. The United States is now blanketed by approximately 110 different federal administrative regions, but there is a growing tendency for one agency to use the regional divisions created by another. Perhaps in time we shall have regional national capitals throughout the United States.

Another kind of federal decentralization is represented by the Tennessee Valley Authority. The T.V.A. was established by Congress in 1933 to develop the resources of the Tennessee Valley. Instead of having the Army Corps of Engineers deal with flood control and navigation, the Bureau of Reclamation with irrigation, the Department of Agriculture with conservation, the Federal Power Commission with power, and so on, one Federal corporation was established to deal with the problems of the valley as a unit. Working very closely with the states, cities, and private organizations in the valley, the T.V.A. has done an effective job of preventing floods, providing cheap power, controlling the soil, improving navigation, providing irrigation, preventing stream pollution, and developing recreational facilities.

Originally, many people within the Tennessee Valley and the governmental officials in the area opposed the creation of the Authority because of the fear that it would dwarf and dominate state governments. But from the outset, the T.V.A. has championed "grass-roots" administration and has cooperated closely with state and local officials. Wherever possible it even has delegated responsibility for functions to state and local agencies. The resources of the Authority and its experts help local groups to solve their

2 *State Government,* June 1943, pp. 142-143.

problems. State departments of health, conservation, education, highways, and other agencies have joined with the T.V.A. to improve the general level of government in the entire valley. The T.V.A.'s success has led to proposals for authorities for the Missouri, Columbia, and other river valleys.

Some federal administrators object to the idea of too great a parceling out of federal powers to regional authorities. If there were four or five T.V.A.'s, these administrators insist, the problems of providing political control and securing national action on national problems would be most difficult. There is also the very real difficulty of ensuring political control of river valley authorities. Despite the T.V.A.'s solicitude toward local and state governments, it is a federal agency and responsible to the people of the valley only through Congress and the President. Certainly, the T.V.A. method is not the solution to all problems, but it is one of the best examples of creative statesmanship and social innovation developed by the American people to meet some of the difficulties that grow out of our federal system.

The T.V.A. idea does not exhaust the possibilities of federal regional development. The Missouri River Valley, for example, does not have an overall regional authority, but the departments of Interior; Agriculture; Commerce; Health, Education, and Welfare; Labor; Army; and the Federal Power Commission maintain an Interagency Committee on Water Resources that, along with the governors of five of the river valley states, forms the Missouri Basin Interagency Committee. This committee, meeting in monthly session, has attempted to coordinate the efforts of the various federal and state agencies. It has met with some success, though the proponents of a regional authority insist that the committee has been unable to work out unified programs and is merely an attempt to forestall a valley authority. Unlike the T.V.A., there is no one agency with over-all authority, and each federal agency and each state is free to go on its own way. Moreover, no one agency has the authority to coordinate the operations of the various completed projects.

Thus the pattern of federalism is being altered. Throughout the nation are a variety of regional organizations, some the result of federal action, others of federal-state cooperation, and, as we shall presently note, still others result from actions of the states. These regional organizations supplement the constitutional division between the central government and the states. At present, they are mainly concerned with the administration of single programs; but perhaps in the future, as they assume more functions of national, state, and local governments, they will be given representative institutions—legislatures, executives, and courts—and a new dimension will be added to our federal union.

"Federalism without Washington"—interstate cooperation

There is no reason why the states have to wait for the national government to take the initiative in dealing with problems that require regional action. Several states together can deal with problems too large for any one to handle alone. If states would solve their own regional problems the national government might not need to step in (aside from giving financial aid).

One of the most successful interstate agencies operating under an interstate compact is the Authority of the Port of New York, established by New Jersey and New York. This authority develops, plans, and operates the harbor as a unit, and recently it has been made responsible for the coordinated operation of the airports of the area. Regional programs that offer promise are the attempts by southern and western states to pool their educational resources in order to create regional colleges. Other interstate compacts deal with abatement of water pollution, conservation of oil and gas, parole and probation, and conservation of fish.

In addition to these more formal interstate compacts, state officials often get together to handle a particular problem: for example, to establish joint operations of police radio broadcasting nets or conferences on highway safety. Some of them have created regular organizations, such as the Interstate Commission on the Delaware River Basin, composed of representatives from New York, New Jersey, Pennsylvania, and Delaware, or the Conference of Southern Governors. In addition to these regional conferences, we have nationwide organizations of state officials—the American Legislators' Association, the National Associations of Attorneys General, of Secretaries of State, of State Budget Officers, of State Purchasing Officials, and others. Each state now has a Commission on Interstate Cooperation. Most of the interstate agencies are coordinated through the Council of State Governments. The Council serves as a secretariat to the various organizations of state officials, collects data, sponsors research, and publicizes the results. This kind of cooperation is bearing fruit in bringing about greater uniformity among the states and higher standards in the administration of the laws within the states.

Through interstate cooperation, we could get more *uniform laws*. Diversity, which is one of the virtues of federalism, can also be a fault. Because of the diversity of traffic rules—even in neighboring states—it is virtually impossible to drive across the nation without violating some law along the way. The story of Harry Harper, an Iowa farmer, is not unusual. Harper "started out for St. Louis, Missouri, to sell a load of melons he had grown. During his journey he was stopped by the Iowa Highway Patrol at night and required to put three green lights on his truck. After driving across the state line into Missouri, the Missouri police stopped him and told him it was illegal in Missouri to have three green lights on his truck, so he had to take them off."[3] Worse, the lack of uniformity increases the hazards facing those on the highways.

[3] Related by Frank Bane and reported in W. Brooke Graves, *American State Government,* 3rd ed. (Boston: D. C. Heath and Company, 1946), p. 914. Used by permission of D. C. Heath and Company.

Diversity of state laws about insurance, contracts, negotiable instruments, judicial procedures—in fact on the whole scope of business transactions—increases the costs and makes it difficult to do business on a national basis. Labeling laws designed to protect consumers against fraud, for example, are so diverse that manufacturers often have to make special labels in order to sell their products in certain states.

The application and interpretation of all these laws by the 49 court systems in the United States add another dimension to the problem. Congress has the authority to integrate better our legal system so that there will be less confusion about the effect of judicial decisions in other jurisdictions, but many problems would still remain as to which of the many diverse laws applies to a particular case. What law applies to a contract signed in California, delivered in New York, between citizens of Wisconsin and Minnesota about property located in New Jersey? This is not a fanciful question, but an example of the kind of problems confronting judges in their everyday business.

To try to create uniformity and to secure adoption of the best practices members of the American Bar Association in 1892 organized a Conference of Commissioners on Uniform State Laws. Under the guidance of this conference, composed of commissioners appointed by the governors of the several states, committees have been established to recommend uniform laws to the states. All the states have adopted the Negotiable Instrument Law and the Warehouse Receipt Act, and many other uniform laws have been adopted by some of the states, including those dealing with stock transfers, narcotics, drugs, criminal extradition. The most ambitious project of the conference is the attempt to secure adoption of a Uniform Commercial Code. But even after all the states adopt a particular code, there is no guarantee of uniformity. The 48 separate state court systems are likely to interpret the codes in their 48 separate ways, and before long there are again wide differences in interpretation and application. The process must start over again. J. A. C. Grant of the University of California has suggested that a common system of interpretation would result if the states adopted federal laws. These attempts to bring about uniformity of the laws also have the desirable effect of raising standards as the best practices are spread throughout the states. But despite occasional successes, over sixty years' work has not noticeably decreased the diversity of state laws.

How successful, then, has cooperation among the states been? Without minimizing the accomplishments or underestimating the potentialities, "Federalism without Washington" has not brought about the results that its sponsors had hoped. One of the difficulties has been too much emphasis on simply forestalling centralization. Horizontal cooperation has perhaps made its best contribution "in providing central staff research and educational facilities to strengthen the competence with which the governments at a particular level do their job, so that governmental bankruptcy alone cannot justify the transference of authority to higher levels of government."[4] Horizontal federalism, then, has brought only marginal results. What about "vertical" cooperation?

COOPERATIVE FEDERALISM

Cooperative federalism is more a general approach than a particular program. It visualizes the national and state governments as *partners* in the common function of serving the people. It rejects the concept of two governments as antagonistic sovereigns jealously competing with each other for power. Cooperative federalism is the search for a middle ground between the either-or attitude typified by discussions of national government *versus* the states or the advantages of centralization *versus* decentralization. Through joint action of both federal and state governments it is hoped that gradually the advantages of a unitary state can be gained without losing the essential values of federalism.

Types of joint action

Cooperation among national and state and local governments takes many forms. When the secret service man uncovering a counterfeiter gets help from the state and local police, he is benefiting from cooperative federalism. A public health official tracking down carriers of disease will use both federal and state services. Many federal agencies, such as the United States Public Health Service, the United States Office of Education, and the Bureau of the Census, conduct surveys and gather statistics for state officials. Others train local employees and help enforce state laws. This form of cooperation avoids duplication and provides better services at less cost.

In some cases, the administration of federal programs is delegated to state and local governments. In part this is what the T.V.A. has tried to do by encouraging state and local officials to take over the administration of parts of the T.V.A. program. This is essentially what is done in the case of selective service, in which the actual administration of the draft is primarily a responsibility of state and local officials. Some people favor a broad extension of this kind of program. They believe that the national government should lay down general policies but delegate administration to state and local governments. It is doubtful, however, if this can be done except on a limited scale. As Professor Anderson has pointed out, "State administrations that are not in sympathy with the National Government will cause considerable difficulty; and it is doubtful whether United States Senators will favor administrative methods that give their potential or actual

[4] James W. Fesler, *Area and Administration* (University, Ala.: University of Alabama Press, 1949), p. 40.

rivals, the state Governors, the power of patronage over national programs in their States."[5]

In addition, when national programs are turned over to the state governments, there is the risk that they will not be administered in accordance with national purposes. Philip Selzick in his discerning study, *TVA and the Grass Roots* (1949), has presented evidence that T.V.A.'s policy of working with local governments and local groups often amounts to handing over the T.V.A. to powerful local interests. And Paul A. Appleby, an experienced administrator, also dissents: "If a program is Federal and if the responsibility is Federal, the authority should be Federal and the administering bureaucracy should almost always be Federal."[6]

Conversely, some oppose state administration of national policies on the grounds that it turns the states into administrative districts of the federal government. Nevertheless, where responsibility for programs is only partly federal, delegation of administration to the states would be feasible. But further delegation to state and local officials depends in large part on their modernizing their governmental statutes and practices so that they can more effectively handle the jobs given to them.

Grants-in-aid

More promising than turning over complete administration of federal policies to the states is the joint operation of programs through the *grant-in-aid*. There are some programs for which the states have chief constitutional responsibility, but in which the entire nation has an interest. By the accident of geography, for example, some children are deprived of an adequate education, and many people are denied good health services. The states in which they live either do not have adequate resources to provide minimum essential services or the dominant groups within the state lack the desire to do so.

These problems can no longer be considered of only local concern. Children and bacteria travel everywhere these days. Young people who have been deprived of educational opportunities or whose health has been impaired, are national liabilities. Even those who stay at home will some day help to elect men to make laws for the entire nation. Furthermore, our economy depends upon a national market, and draws its resources from all over the United States; the more prosperous states depend on the markets and raw materials of the entire nation.

Since wealth is concentrated in the industrialized areas—the northeastern, middle western, and far western states—in other areas, especially the rural South, some states find it difficult to raise funds for public services. Many

[5] Anderson, "Federalism—Then and Now," *State Government,* Vol. XVI, May 1943, pp. 107-111.
[6] Paul H. Appleby, *Big Democracy* (New York: Alfred A. Knopf, Inc., 1945), p. 87.

southern industries are owned by persons living elsewhere, so profits are drained from the South, leaving the states without funds to support adequate facilities for education, welfare, and highways, for example. This is only one reason why public services in some states are below the national level, but it is an important reason.

What can be done? The national government could take over the entire responsibility for the programs. (In some fields there are constitutional limitations that prevent federal action except by a constitutional amendment, although the number of such cases is no longer so important because of liberal interpretation of national powers by the Supreme Court.) But as an alternative to federalization, Congress, through the grant-in-aid, has tried to secure a national minimum level and to encourage the states to take action. With its broader tax base, it taxes the wealth where it is located and turns the money over to the states for programs that Congress feels should be more adequately supported. This system of federal grants-in-aid goes back at least as far as 1802, but got its real start in 1916 when Congress gave money to the states for the construction of "rural post roads." During the great depression the number of federal grants greatly increased; today the national government gives money to the states for agricultural extension work, forest preservation, land-grant colleges, wildlife restoration, highways, old age assistance, aid to dependent children, aid to the blind, maternal and child health services, and aid to crippled children, to mention only some of the more important. On the average, the states now receive from the national government about one-sixth of the money they spend.

Most of these grants are *conditional*. The states must match the federal funds, establish agencies to expend the funds, submit their plans for advance approval, permit federal inspection of the work done, and place the employees who administer the grant under a merit system.

Since most grants require the states to match the federal dollars, the poor states, even with federal assistance, are often unable to provide the same kinds of services as their richer sisters. For example, an aged indigent in recent years might receive as much as $85.10 per month in Colorado or as little as $27.69 in another state. To help correct these inequalities, formulas for the distribution of federal funds have been proposed that take the relative needs of the several states into account. Quite naturally, the wealthy states that contribute most of the money to the federal treasury are not happy when much of it goes to the less fortunate areas.

One of the dangers of federal grants is that states sometimes are tempted to match federal money for prescribed purposes even when they could better spend their limited resources for something else. States can now receive federal dollars for the dollars they spend for the construction of highways, but in many states the money could be better spent for schools or mental hospitals. The lure of federal funds tends to destroy the flexibility of state programs, and leaves the states the back seat in planning their own expenditures.

Is there any way out of this dilemma?

Some students have urged the substitution of *block* grants or broad *subsidies* for the present single-purpose ones. Such grants are made by central governments in other federal systems—Canada and Australia for example—and it is argued that under such a system the national government could use its greater tax resources to give the states funds for minimum services, but each state could use the money as it wished. Safeguards would still have to be provided so that the money did not go to feed local political organizations. But the Commission on Intergovernmental Relations recommended against such subsidies because of the fear that they would not be used to provide all the services thought necessary by Congress and there would still be pressure for grants for specific programs. Furthermore, they reported, "a policy of unconditional subsidies with no matching requirements would be likely to undermine the sense of financial responsibility. The tendency would be for states and localities to look more and more to the national government to perform the disagreeable task of extracting money from the taxpayer."[7]

The first Hoover Commission (a group of distinguished public servants headed by former President Herbert Hoover who directed an exhaustive study by experts of the national administration in 1948-1949) recommended to Congress that grants be established on the basis of broad *categories* such as highways, education, public assistance, and public health. Pointing out that under the "present system of extensive fragmentation" there are at least ten separate and distinct federal grants in the field of public health, the commission stated that grants for broader purposes would return the initiative to the states and place on the states the responsibility for working out their own programs.[8] But the Commission on Intergovernmental Relations, although agreeing that the broadening of some grants might be desirable, opposed more general grants. Since grants are almost always made in fields where states have major responsibilities, the national grants should be narrowly restricted, the commission recommended, in order to leave the largest portion of the fields to the states.[9] The commission did, however, favor allowing states to transfer funds on a limited basis from one program to another within broad fields.[10]

[7] *Report,* of Commission on Intergovernmental Relations, p. 122.

[8] Commission on Organization of the Executive Branch of the Government, *Overseas Administration, Federal-State Relations, Federal Research* (Washington, D.C.: Government Printing Office), p. 36.

[9] The Commission on Intergovernmental Relations, *op. cit.,* pp. 132-133.

[10] *Ibid.,* pp. 133-134.

Grants-in-aid: a trial balance

After a careful study of the federal grant system, V. O. Key came to the conclusion that it

strengthens the states and thereby strengthens but profoundly modifies the federal system. . . . The achievements of direct federal administration are not so striking as to make federal assumption an inviting alternative to the grant system. The governance of a nation of continental proportions is a matter for which no simple blueprint and specifications are available. The grant system builds on and utilizes existing institutions to cope with national problems. Under it the states are welded into national machinery of sorts and the establishment of costly, parallel, direct federal services is made unnecessary. A virtue of no mean importance is that the administrators in actual charge of operations remain amenable to local control. In that way the supposed formality, the regularity, and the cold-blooded efficiency of a national hierarchy are avoided.[11]

The Commission on Intergovernmental Relations confirms Key's judgment. The grant system is here to stay. Its constitutionality is beyond question in more senses than one. The Supreme Court has ruled that neither a state nor a taxpayer has the right to contest the constitutionality of a grant.[12] Today discussion centers around the more specific questions as to just what particular functions should be supported by federal money, what conditions should be tied to the grant, and how they should be administered.

The federal grant will not solve all problems. And certainly the grant system can be abused. Federal money is not "free"; all services must be paid for by the taxpayers. Nevertheless, an intelligently administered program can bring greater strength to the states and better services to the people.

By-passing the states—national-local cooperation

A more controversial example of cooperative federalism involves the relations between the national and the local governments. According to the traditional theory of American federalism, the national government should deal with local governments through the states. In a constitutional sense local governments are creatures of the states. But as Professor Swisher has pointed out: "To refer to Chicago as but an arm of Illinois or to New York City as but an arm of New York is as unrevealing as to call the General Motors Corporation an instrument of Delaware or the Southern Pacific Company an instrument of Kentucky, under whose laws it is organized."[13]

[11] V. O. Key, Jr., *The Administration of Federal Grants to States* (Chicago: Public Administration Service, 1937), pp. 375, 383.

[12] *Massachusetts* v. *Mellon* (1923).

[13] C. B. Swisher, *American National Government* (Boston: Houghton Mifflin Company, 1951), p. 908.

All that the national government does sooner or later affects the affairs of cities and other units of local government. But during the depression, and from that time on, the national government began to deal directly with local governments, extending financial aid to them, building post offices, auditoriums, high schools, and other public works for them, and providing judicial procedures through which the cities and other local units could "reorganize" their debt situations. Cities received federal aid for building streets and airports, and for slum clearance and housing projects.

This by-passing of the states has been sharply criticized. Most of the objections have come from state officials; municipal officials and associations, on the other hand, naturally favor direct federal help. This difference of opinion points to a much more important conflict between the cities and the states. Many large cities—actually city-states in many respects—fail to receive sympathetic treatment from the state legislatures, which often are dominated by rural representatives with little sympathy or understanding for city problems. In many states, the cities contribute most of the tax money to support state activities, but have a proportionately smaller voice in its allotment. Urban populations are apt to have a stronger influence with the national government than with the states. It is not surprising that the states thus sometimes get the squeeze play between national and city governments. Probably the most effective way to prevent this short circuit of the states would be to reorganize state and local governments in such a way that states could more effectively serve as intermediaries between national and local governments.[14]

Enough has been said to make it clear that intergovernmental relations can be cooperative as well as competitive, and that cooperative federalism is a going business. Cooperative federalism means all things to all men. To some it is a midway station on the road to greater power for the national government; to others it is a method to strengthen the states; but above all it is an example of what de Tocqueville noticed over a hundred years ago: "I have never been more struck by the good sense and the practical judgment of the Americans than in the manner in which they elude the numberless difficulties resulting from their Federal Constitution."[15]

TROUBLE SPOTS OF FEDERALISM

The truck driver who is stopped at the state boundary because his vehicle is six inches too long, the governor who would like to sign a new tax measure but is warned that industry may move out of the state if he does so, the consumer who finds some products that compete with local industry

---

[14] This was also recommended by the Commission on Intergovernmental Relations, *Report*, p. 40.

[15] Alexis de Tocqueville, *Democracy in America*, ed., Phillips Bradley (New York: Alfred A. Knopf, 1946), I, p. 167.

taxed so high that he cannot afford them, these people, like all of us, face problems of federalism. How can the techniques described earlier in this chapter be used to adjust these problems?

Law enforcement

Not many years ago a stranger in town was something of an event, and the local constabulary had little difficulty in dealing with crime. Whenever the need arose the sheriff could rally the law-respecting by raising the "hue and cry." Today criminals roam the entire nation in high-powered automobiles. These lawbreakers respect no jurisdictional boundaries, and the multitude of police agencies, all with overlapping responsibilities, gives the criminals an advantage that they are quick to exploit. On the national level, postal inspectors, "T" men, "G" men, and others have limited responsibility for enforcing the several categories of federal laws. The authority of state police officers is limited to their own states, and within the states power is further divided among state troopers, city policemen, county sheriffs, and township constables. All this leads to conflict, confusion, and duplication of effort.

The modern criminal soon learns what states and cities are "safe" and uses them as bases of operations. Some cities have even gone so far as to extend protection to lawbreakers who agree not to commit their crimes within the city. Even where this policy is not in effect, the police officers are primarily interested in preventing crime only within their own state, city, or county. Frequently, troublemakers are simply escorted across the state line, or judges "solve" the problem by handing out sentences of "thirty days or out of town." States have great difficulty in enforcing their own laws when neighboring states are lax.

A Senate Committee Investigating Crime in 1951 uncovered many instances where the states were failing to cooperate in the most obvious ways. The committee pointed to the case of a gambling house located right on the Missouri-Kansas border. Whenever the Missouri police staged a raid, the gamblers merely moved into the back of the house and into Kansas. Conversely, whenever the Kansas police knocked on the back door, the criminals merely moved into the front of the house and into Missouri. Apparently it never occurred to the Missouri police chief to pick up the phone and arrange a simultaneous raid with the Kansas police officers.

Although it might be more efficient to centralize police authority in the federal government, it would be dangerous. This is a field in which the wisdom of avoiding concentration of power has special importance. Centralization of police authority is, however, only a potential danger, and in general we have erred too much in the opposite direction. Within the states reorganization and rationalization of police activities are necessary to avoid duplication and overlapping of responsibilities, to adopt modern police methods, and to recruit able men. Crime anywhere must be seen as a threat to everyone's peace and security.

Here again, cooperative federalism is needed. Already much is being done. The F.B.I. Police Academy has been opened to state and local law enforcement officers, and the F.B.I. fingerprint file, with over 21 million prints, is available to all law enforcement officers who in turn record their prints with the F.B.I. Federal officers enforcing national law turn over to state officials any evidence uncovered of the violation of state laws. Congress has laid a basis of cooperation between the F.B.I. and state police. It has endeavored to help states enforce their laws by making it a federal offense to steal property valued at over $5000 by the use of the channels of interstate commerce, as well as to rob a bank, to kidnap, or to transport women for immoral purposes through the channels of interstate commerce. The states themselves have coordinated their police radio networks, and neighboring states often grant reciprocal arrest privileges to out-of-state officers who are in "hot pursuit" of offenders.

Of course, even with the best state and local police forces, the role of the national government will expand. Crime is a national problem. Criminals are organized in national syndicates and they use two-way radios, airplanes, and telegraph systems for flashing racing information. But this traditional state activity need not be abandoned if the states clean their own houses and provide, in cooperation with the national government, the protection that the people demand.

Law avoidance

Federalism also helps people who can hardly be called criminals to evade state laws. State sales taxes on cigarettes, liquor, and gasoline, for example, can often be avoided simply by crossing the state line. "Last-chance" gasoline stations that dot the highways just before one enters a state with higher taxes are evidence of this everyday tax evasion. Cigarette dealers in low-tax states did a thriving business by sending their wares to people all over the nation until 1949, when the national government required all persons who regularly shipped cigarettes by mail or through the channels of interstate commerce to report the sale to officials in the receiving state. When metropolitan cities are located near state boundaries, persons who earn their living in one state and benefit from its public services can in certain cases avoid paying city and state taxes by commuting to work from an adjoining low-tax state.

A more spectacular form of law avoidance is carried on by those who have the money and time to go to Reno for six weeks, solely to avoid their own state divorce laws. The validity of some of these divorces has been questioned, but Nevada still does a thriving divorce business and, in a sense, sets the divorce standards for the wealthy members of the entire nation. Moreover, despite the efforts of the Supreme Court to protect each state's right to control the matrimonial affairs of its own citizens and at the same time to accommodate the national interest in seeing that states respect the full faith and credit clause, there is greater confusion than ever about the validity of divorces. Some favor uniform divorce standards. Since all 48 state legislatures could probably never agree on the same standards, federal action would be required, and this would call for a constitutional amendment. Congress could, however, under the full faith and credit clause determine the type of divorce judgment that must be recognized by sister states. A suitable law could put a stop to this kind of evasion of the laws and bring some order into the confused picture. Although the Supreme Court has had no occasion to decide whether Congress has such power, Justice Jackson has said, "I should say it has been fairly ostentatious in leaving the way open to sustain such enactments without embarrassment."[16]

New Jersey, in earlier years, and Delaware today are the Renos of the world of *corporation charters*. Many corporations that do most of their business and sell most of their securities in other states have responded to advertisements such as this:

Charters—Delaware Best, Quickest, Cheapest, Most Liberal. Nothing needs to be paid in. Do business and hold meetings anywhere. Free forms. Colonial Charter Company, Wilmington, Delaware.[17]

These corporations maintain nominal one-room-one-desk headquarters in Wilmington simply to escape compliance with the charter laws of the states in which they do business. The purpose of these laws is to protect the stockholders, consumers, and the public. Periodically, it is proposed that all corporations who do an interstate business be required to incorporate under national law, but so far nothing has come of it. Congress also could require all corporations that use interstate commerce or the mails to incorporate henceforth in the state in which they maintain their real headquarters or do the bulk of their business. But until action is taken, the most lax state is permitted to set the standards for the entire nation and to profit by it.

Interstate competition

In their zeal to attract business, some states and cities offer free factory sites, tax exemptions, free water, and laws that make it difficult for labor to organize unions. Often these advantages are at the public expense. Many states hesitate to levy taxes to pay for better schools or to increase aid to

[16] Robert H. Jackson, *Full Faith and Credit* (New York: Columbia University Press, 1945), p. 37.
[17] W. Z. Ripley, *Main Street and Wall Street* (Boston: Little, Brown & Company, 1927), p. 29, cited by George C. S. Benson, *The New Centralization* (New York: Farrar & Rinehart, Inc., 1941), p. 28.

the needy because of the fear that resulting higher taxes may cause industries to go to the less progressive states. There is no conclusive evidence that the tax rate is a cause of business migrations, but the fear that higher taxes will keep business away is often strong enough to defeat needed tax measures. Similarly, states are often reluctant to establish minimum wages or to extend social security because it places their industries at a competitive disadvantage to those in states without these laws.

Interstate competition also retards the development of state conservation programs. Each state fears that if it forces conservation practices on its industries, the resulting expenses will cause them to lose the market to industries in "get-rich-quick" states. Agreements among the states, especially in the oil and gas industry, have brought about some conservation, though the purpose is also to prevent flooding the market and depressing prices.

Maintaining the national market

One of the major goals of the Constitution was a free trade area within the United States. To a large extent this goal was achieved. Certainly one of the major reasons for the remarkable economic development of this nation was the absence of artificial barriers to interstate trade and commerce. Through the years, however, the states have erected barriers that have threatened to "Balkanize" the national market. Some of these barriers result from attempts by the states to protect their citizens and to collect a fair share of taxes from those who use their roads or other tax-supported facilities. Others, however, are devices to favor the home industries and to make the "foreigner" pay. Laws passed ostensibly to protect persons from disease or fraud, or to protect animals and crops from infection, are actually designed to give home industries the advantage of the home market. Almost all states favor their own workers, contractors, or products in making their own purchases, sometimes at great expense to the taxpayer.

States may not tax interstate commerce as such, but they may levy fees for the use of their highways, require outstate trucks to secure licenses, permits, and registration tickets. As long as the fee bears some reasonable relationship to the use of the highways, it is not forbidden by the interstate commerce clause. No state has yet tried to collect fees from nonresident passenger vehicles, but they all have some form of taxation of trucks. Registration fees, mileage taxes, consumption-of-gasoline taxes, and levies on the receipts received for hauling goods are the methods most frequently used by the several states to secure revenue from outstate trucks. One survey reports that a trucker traveling from Alabama to South Carolina in a five- to six-ton truck would have to pay fees totaling several hundred dollars.

These burdens are to some extent lightened by reciprocity agreements among the states granting to each others' trucks some measure of relief, but only nine states grant complete freedom from fees by reciprocal agreement. During World War II many of the barriers were relaxed in order to help the war effort, but since the war they have been set up again. States are rightly entitled to receive some payment for the use of their highways by those who do not pay the normal state taxes. But many state highways are in part financed by federal grants which are composed of tax money paid by all persons throughout the nation, and the burdens placed on the free movement of goods are ultimately paid for by all the people of the United States.

True to the traditions of John Marshall, the Supreme Court has struck down some laws whose purpose it is to discriminate against the commerce of other states. Many cases, however, are never brought to court, and many others are not of a nature to come within the purview of the commerce clause. Other laws are not in themselves discriminatory; rather, diversity creates the problem. Despite the efforts of the Council of State Governments, state action has not materially reduced the barriers. This would appear to be a place where Congress should use its powers over interstate commerce to destroy the barriers to the free movement of goods and to protect the American free market.

Legalism and confusion

"Federalism . . . means legalism" wrote Dicey. Certainly much time and energy are spent on the "legalistic" and "constitutional" aspects of public problems. We have previously noted how issues such as "states' rights" versus "national action" can be used to confuse issues of policy. The constitutional aspects of federalism are important, but they should not be permitted to exclude or confuse considerations of the merits of issues—"Is it constitutional?" is an important question to ask, but so is the question, "Is it desirable?"

The division of powers creates opportunities for buck-passing. Early in 1950, for example, long after the need for taking action on a civil defense program was apparent, nothing had been done. The states blamed the central government, the central government blamed the states. It was not until after the Korean invasion that a jointly administered program of civil defense was established.

By way of *summary,* many of the problems of federalism are offset by corresponding advantages, many of the difficulties are unavoidable and are the price we gladly pay for federalism, but many are correctable, at least "improvable," and stem from the failure to understand that we must sink or swim together. Through the intelligent use of regional organizations, interstate compacts, grants-in-aid, and closer cooperation among federal-state-local officials, much can be done to create a "more perfect union." This optimism, however, is by no means shared by all.

THE FUTURE OF FEDERALISM

There are many who consider federalism but a midway station between confederation and a unitary state. Some federal systems of the past eventually became unitary. Basing their arguments on such historical examples,

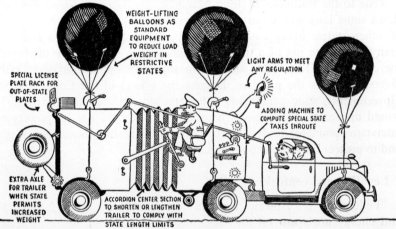

The "POSTWAR TRAILER" to fit all State Laws

Ike Doodleschmalz M.E. DDS.—Independent industrial engineer deluxe, has submitted this design to the Fruehauf Trailer Company as the answer to some of the conflicting state laws and trade barriers which prevent motor transport from properly serving the public. Maybe he has something. *Courtesy Fruehauf Trailer Company*

and pointing to the development of new methods of transportation and communication that have in part overcome the barriers of time and distance, many insist that federalism is obsolete.

Is federalism obsolete?

Harold J. Laski, the late noted British political scientist and socialist pamphleteer, was one of the foremost critics of American federalism. He said that federalism

is insufficiently positive in character; it does not provide for sufficient rapidity of action; it inhibits the emergence of necessary standards of uniformity; it relies upon compacts and compromises which take insufficient account of the urgent category of time; it leaves the backward areas a restraint, at once parasitic and poisonous, on those which seek to move forward. . . .

The crux of his argument is that

Giant capitalism has . . . concentrated the control of economic power in a small proportion of the American people. . . . For forty-eight separate units to seek to compete with the integrated power of giant capitalism is to invite defeat in every element of social life where approximate uniformity of condition is the test of the good life.

Laski charged that the national government does not have the power to control these vested interests, and the state governments cannot afford to attack them, since the industrial empires can withdraw their patronage and go elsewhere.

Laski rejected the possibility of materially improving the situation through greater cooperation among the 49 units of government, nor did he think the creation of regional governments would solve the problem. He argued that federalism is suited only to the *negative* or *limited* state:

Giant industry requires a positive state; federalism, in its American form, is geared to vital negations which contradict the implications of positivism. Giant industry requires uniformities in the field of its major influence; American federalism is the inherent foe, both in time and space, of these necessary uniformities. . . . Above all . . . giant industry, in an age of economic contraction, is able to exploit the diversities of a federal scheme, through the delays they permit in the attainment of uniformity, to reactionary ends.

On the basis of these arguments Laski concludes that federalism is obsolete.[18]

Laski was not so much predicting the end of federalism as he was arguing for its abolition. Favoring a more vigorous national regulation of business and more active government management of the economy, he believed that the federal system stood in the way of achieving these goals. Professor Karl Lowenstein, on the other hand, predicts that if our free economic system is abandoned, federalism will be undermined. He has written, "Federalism . . . thrives as long as a free economy thrives. Speaking . . . sententiously: Economic planning is the DDT of federalism."[19]

Perhaps both those who predict and those who propose the obsolescence of federalism fail to give enough credit to its dynamic character. It has been, and is being, adapted to changing conditions. In large part, Laski seemed to be criticizing in the 1930's the federalism of the 1920's, which is unquestionably obsolete. The *national government today, however, has sufficient constitutional power to dispose of virtually any problem of national*

[18] H. J. Laski, "The Obsolescence of Federalism," *The New Republic*, May 3, 1939, pp. 367-369.

[19] Karl Lowenstein, "Reflections on the Value of Constitutions in Our Revolutionary Age," *Constitutions and Constitutional Trends Since World War II*, ed. Arnold Zurcher (New York: New York University Press, 1951), pp. 211-212.

extent. At the same time, we have made progress in strengthening the states and the local governments and in overcoming the weakness of our system.

Laski, like many others, attributed to federalism difficulties for which it is only partly responsible. Many of the problems discussed above are just as troublesome in unitary countries as they are in federations. Many of our difficulties arise not from our federal system, but because we are a nation of continental proportions with a rich variety of groups and associations. Sectionalism and localism, for example, would remain even if the federal system were abolished tomorrow. There would still be a South and a New England, and the South would still object to freight differentials and New England would still favor them. The giant capitalists would remain strong, and positive action by the national government would not necessarily be forthcoming.

Constitutional forms are only part of the picture. England is a unitary state, and the English Parliament, it is often said, in contrast to Congress, has unlimited power over local governments. This observation is true, but Parliament is effectively restrained by strong English traditions in favor of local government while Congress is not wholly powerless, as we have seen, to influence the operations of local governments. Many of the advantages of a federal system, moreover, can be secured within the unitary framework—experimentation, central-local cooperation, decentralization of power are not unknown in England or France. On the other hand, many of the problems of federalism also plague unitary states—sectionalism and conflict between functional and geographic administration, for example. It is true that federalism accentuates both the positive and negative problems of the geographical distribution of governmental power, but comparisons between federal and unitary states are comparisons of degree rather than kind.

Whether or not federalism is obsolete, there is little chance that it will be replaced in the United States by the unitary form. It is the system under which we will have to solve the urgent problems that confront us. If we fail to solve those problems, little of the fault will lie with federalism. Moreover, as long as we want union without uniformity, federalism, adapted to our changing society, remains our best bet.

American federalism—world federalism

Many believe that, just as federalism served to create the United States, so it can serve to create a united world. It has been suggested that the Philadelphia Convention was "the great rehearsal" for a world constitutional convention.

The differences, however, between the North American continent in 1787 and the world community today are greater than often realized. Despite the importance of other national groups in the United States, the great bulk of the colonists, who first formed the United States under the

Articles of Confederation and then moved on to the Constitution, had lived under and been loyal to the same crown and parliament for more than 150 years. They shared some common loyalties and ideas. Prior to the Revolution, most citizens of Massachusetts might have thought of a Virginian as a strange character, but they knew that they, their father, and their father's father, and the Virginian, his father, and his father's father, were all loyal subjects of the King of England. They spoke the same language, were almost all some variety of Christian, and shared a common political heritage. The leaders from the several states who assembled to write the Constitution represented the same general outlook, they all came from the same social and economic classes, and they agreed upon the essentials. The words "justice," "property," "republican," "natural law," had approximately the same meaning for all the delegates and evoked the same emotional responses in them.

In other words, there was present what A. V. Dicey, in his famous *Law of the Constitution* called the first requirement for the formation of a federation, "A body of countries . . . so closely connected by locality, by history, by race, or the like, as to be capable of bearing, in the eyes of its inhabitants, an impress of common nationality."[20]

Unfortunately, in the world as a whole, the common heritage of membership in the human race, whose ultimate interests in survival and freedom are identical, is today lost or hidden by the more immediate conflicts and divisions.[21] National feeling and loyalties are the most obvious divisions between the peoples of the world. But the differences between "we" and "they," between friend and foe, are intensified not merely by differences in nationality, but by the thousand other ways in which man is separated from his fellow man. Christians, Buddhists, Moslems, Hindus, and the hundreds of other religious divisions; democrats, fascists, and communists; capitalists and socialists; "civilized" and "primitive"; literate and illiterate; Occidental and Oriental; white and black—these things set men apart more than their underlying common interest joins them together.

Even within the so-called western democratic community, it would be difficult to secure agreement on certain basic ideas—civil rights, the basis of representation, trial by jury, for example. Government's obligation to property—a subject on which all delegates to the Philadelphia Convention were in substantial agreement—is a question that could be "compromised" only with great difficulty by representatives of the various existing societies in the world. And it must be remembered that democracy and the possibility of using democratic techniques for the settlement of differences rest upon agreement by the overwhelming majority of the people on certain basic

[20] A. V. Dicey, *Introduction to the Study of the Law of the Constitution,* 8th ed. (London: Macmillan & Co., Ltd., 1915).
[21] The bibliography contains reference to books written by men who have argued effectively that a world federation is possible at the present time.

ideas. Without this consensus, the community can be held together and operated only by force.

Yet American federalism does have its lessons for the world. For as Dicey wrote, the second condition "absolutely essential to the founding of a federal system is the existence of a very peculiar state of sentiment among the inhabitants of the countries which it is proposed to unite. They must desire union, and must not desire unity."[22] At the present, the peoples of the world prefer independence, having no strong desire for either union or unity. Events may educate, however. A world-wide sentiment for union may some day exist; if and when it does, federalism offers the hope of union and the preservation of diversity—unity without uniformity. If and when such world sentiments exist, a world federation will be possible. In this sense federalism is, perhaps, man's last best hope.

A brief chapter summary

1. Federalism is a political issue as well as a mechanical or structural arrangement. People differ over federalism not just as an abstract issue but largely because they differ over how much power the national government should have.

2. A good balance between national and state power can be achieved best by improving state and local governments and also by regional administration of federal functions and interstate cooperation.

3. Cooperative federalism between Washington and the states through grants-in-aid is the most important method of national-state cooperation but raises difficult problems—especially that of allowing proper national supervision without too much national control.

4. Other problems of federalism are law enforcement and avoidance, interstate competition, and confusion as to which level of government is responsible for what.

5. Some believe that federalism is obsolescent on the grounds that it thwarts necessary national action, but others hold that federalism is a flexible and evolving system adaptable to changing national and state needs—and that it may even serve as a model for world organization.

[22] Dicey, op. cit., p. 137.

Civil liberties and citizenship

PART THREE ~ A PROBLEM GUIDE

This part will examine some of the most important problems of American democratic government: How do we achieve balance between the values of individual freedom and the demands of social order? How do we choose among conflicting civil liberties? How do we give concreteness to freedom?

Chapter 6 points out that certain liberties are essential in order to operate a democratic government—primarily, the rights of free conscience and expression, embodied in the guarantees of the First Amendment and the protection of the Fourteenth. The importance of these liberties is agreed upon. But under what conditions should they be curtailed in behalf of other values, in behalf of national security? Which value receives priority—and when? The assignment is an ever-challenging and unending task (pp. 147-149). The threat of communism and even the use of new techniques, television, and sound trucks (pp. 156-159) create subtle problems in protecting individual liberty.

Chapter 7 discusses the constitutional guarantees and political battles to implement the ideal that no man should suffer pains and penalties because of his race,

PART
THREE

6. The First Amendment and the First Freedoms

7. Equality Under the Law

8. Rights to Life, Liberty, and Property

9. Immigrants, Aliens, and Citizens

religion, national origin, or other attributes that are irrelevant to his in-
dividual merits. (These rights to equal treatment under and through the
law are sometimes called "civil rights," distinguished from civil liberties
dealt with in chapters 6 and 8.) Chapter 7 describes the constitutional clauses
that limit the use of governmental power to enforce private prejudices. It
also points out that civil rights can be threatened—as can all civil liberties
—by private individuals (pp. 188-190), especially when they organize as
groups, and that governmental power can be used to protect as well as
to deny these rights (191-198).

Chapter 8 emphasizes constitutional protection of life, liberty, and prop-
erty. Developed through centuries of experience to protect individuals
against arbitrary governmental deprivations, the protection of individual lib-
erty involves not only the national government and not only the Supreme
Court, but many different officials, serving national, state, and local com-
munities, and the people they represent (212-216).

Chapter 9 turns to a separate but related problem: the status and rights of
immigrants, aliens, and citizens. There is no constitutional right to be ad-
mitted to the United States, and aliens do not enjoy all the privileges of
American citizens, but important problems of individual liberty are involved.
It is well to remember that many who seek to enter the United States and to
become citizens have the same desires for liberty as Americans in general;
indeed, in many cases they have come to this country partly because it has
been the historic haven for those who love liberty.

All these chapters suggest that while the conditions of liberty change and
new problems are presented, Americans seek over the long run always to
respond in terms of our best and most basic traditions—traditions that call
for continued effort to expand the freedom of all.

CONGRESS SHALL MAKE NO LAW," DECLARES the First Amendment, "respecting an establishment of religion, or prohibiting the free exercise thereof; or abridging the freedom of speech, or of the press; or the right of the people peaceably to assemble, and to petition the Government for a redress of grievances." Here in bold and absolute terms are set forth the basic and indispensable props of a free society—freedom of conscience and of expression.

It is heartening to remind ourselves that although the framers drafted the Constitution, in a sense the *people* drafted our basic charter of liberties. The Constitution's lack of specific guarantees for freedom of religion and speech and other basic freedoms so disturbed the people that the Federalists had to promise to deliver such a charter in the very first session of the new Congress. They lived up to their promise, and by the end of 1791 the First Amendment and the other nine that make up the Bill of Rights had been ratified.

Note carefully, the first ten amendments are addressed to *Congress*. John Marshall held long ago that the Bill of Rights limits the *national* government but not the states.[1] Why not the states? In the 1790's most people were confident that they could control their own state officials. It was the new and distant central government that they feared.

Not long after the Bill of Rights was adopted, however, many people began to believe that it had been a mistake not to apply the original Bill of Rights, especially the First Amendment, to the state governments. In practice, the national government, responsive to a national majority composed of many races, creeds, and religions, had been more devoted to the ideals of the Bill of Rights than had many states. True, each state had its own bill of rights, but in some they were not being rigorously enforced by the state courts.

In 1925 the Supreme Court took an important step. The judges ruled in *Gitlow* v. *New York* that the due process clause of the *Fourteenth Amendment,* which applies to *state* and *local* officials, pro-

[1] *Barron* v. *Baltimore* (1833).

6 ★

The first

amendment

and the

first freedoms

143

tects freedom of speech. By 1937 the High Court had brought *all* the liberties of the *First* Amendment under the protection of the Fourteenth. For all practical purposes, therefore, the Fourteenth Amendment places on state and local governments the same restrictions which the First Amendment places on the national government. (However, most of the other provisions of the Bill of Rights have not been made part of the Fourteenth. See pages 212-216).

Today virtually all Americans agree that governmental power should not be used to interfere with the rights to free speech or freedom of conscience. Yet the country seems to be almost constantly involved in quarrels about the specific application of these liberties. Why? First, because no liberty is limitless. Second, because some liberties conflict with other liberties. Third, because some liberties seem to threaten other values we hold equally dear. It is all very well to venerate our liberties in general. The problem comes when we move from generalities to specifics. And in few areas are the problems more difficult to resolve than in those involving freedom of religion.

EACH MAY WORSHIP IN HIS OWN WAY

Since a society is composed of many people with conflicting needs, very few rights can be absolute. But the right to hold any religious view is one of these few. One's religious beliefs are inviolable, and democratic government has no right whatsoever to compel the acceptance of, or to censor, any creed. Furthermore, the advocacy of one's religion by speech or writing—like all speech or writing—can be curbed only when there is danger of substantial injury to others. In fact, the Supreme Court has shown greater concern for religious advocacy than for political advocacy, perhaps because Congress is specifically enjoined by the First Amendment (and the states through interpretation by the Fourteenth) to make no law "prohibiting the free exercise" of religion. Hence, the Court has struck down city ordinances that forbade ringing doorbells to distribute literature when those ordinances were applied to persons handing out religious pamphlets.

The *practice* of one's religion has less protection than its *advocacy,* and does not include actions that are "in violation of social duties or subversive of good order." As the Supreme Court has said, "It was never intended that the First Amendment . . . could be invoked as a protection against legislation for the punishment of acts inimical to the peace, good order and morals of society." One cannot claim exemption from payment of taxes because of religious scruples; and if one's religious practices interfere with the peace, health, safety, or morals of the public, they may be regulated by reasonable state laws (doorbell ringing being a possible exception).

"Establishment of religion"

The First Amendment not only forbids Congress and the states (via the Fourteenth) to prohibit the free exercise of religion, but it also forbids them to pass laws respecting an establishment of religion. But what does "the establishment of religion" mean? At the time of adoption it meant, according to James Madison, that "Congress should not establish a religion, and enforce the legal observation of it by law, nor compel men to worship God in any manner contrary to their conscience." The Supreme Court has, however, considerably expanded the scope of the clause to include the doctrine of *separation of church and state*. In an opinion that sustained the right of New Jersey to reimburse parents for their children's bus fares to Roman Catholic parochial schools (*Everson* v. *Board of Education,* 1947), the Court, speaking through Justice Black, laid down the following sweeping dicta:

Neither a state nor the Federal Government can set up a church. Neither can pass laws that aid one religion, aid all religions, or prefer one religion over another. Neither can force nor influence a person to go to or to remain away from church . . . or force him to profess a belief or a disbelief in any religion. . . . No tax in any amount, large or small, can be levied to support any religious activities or institutions, whatever they may be called, or whatever form they may adopt to teach or practice religion. Neither a state nor the Federal Government can, openly or secretly, participate in the affairs of any religious organizations or groups and vice versa. In the words of Jefferson, the clause against establishment of religion by law was intended to erect "a wall of separation between Church and State."

In view of these statements, how did the Supreme Court sustain the payment of tax money for transportation of children to church schools? A bare majority of the Court reasoned that this was state aid to *school children* and not to *religion*. Similar distinctions have been used to uphold state expenditures for school books and hot lunches for children attending parochial schools. Nor has anyone seriously challenged the constitutionality of the practice of granting tax exemptions to property owned and used by a church or of providing chaplains for Congress, the state legislatures, or the armed forces.

Does the establishment of the religion clause forbid public schools to release school children to attend religious classes? Few questions have caused more difficulty than this one. In 1947 Illinois, acting through the Champaign Board of Education, ran afoul of the clause when it allowed privately chosen religious instructors to teach religion during school hours and in public school rooms to students whose parents approved such instruction. Children who chose not to attend these religious classes were required to remain in study hall. By an eight-to-one majority the Supreme Court struck this program down, saying, "Here not only are the State's tax-supported public school buildings used for the dissemination of religious doctrines. The State also affords sectarian groups an invaluable aid in that it helps to provide pupils for their religious classes through the use of the State's compulsory school machinery. This is not separation of Church and State."[2]

The Illinois decision was received with varied feelings. People naturally have strong emotions on this kind of question, some holding that a high and strong wall must separate church and state, others that government must simply treat all religious groups equally. The dicta in the New Jersey case and the decision in the Illinois case appeared to place the Supreme Court on the side of those who believe that the Constitution forbids any form of state encouragement to religion.

Then in 1952 the Supreme Court reconsidered its position. The issue before the judges was the constitutionality of New York City's released time program. This program was essentially like that of Champaign, the only substantial difference being that in New York the religious classes took place outside the school buildings in classrooms provided by the particular religious bodies. Six justices, although refusing to overrule the Champaign decision, thought that this difference saved New York's program from unconstitutionality. The dissenting justices pointed out that New York like Champaign was helping sectarian groups secure pupils for their religious classes through the use of the state's compulsory school machinery. Justice Douglas's opinion for the majority was also at odds with the doctrines previously supported by the Court. He wrote:

The First Amendment . . . does not say that in every and all respects there shall be a separation of Church and State. . . . We are a religious people. . . . When the state encourages religious instruction or cooperates with religious authorities by adjusting the schedule of public events to sectarian needs, it follows the best of our traditions.[3]

How much of a retreat from the doctrines of the New Jersey and Illinois cases this decision foreshadows remains to be seen. One thing is sure: If the High Court continues to hold to the views expressed in the New York case it will be soundly criticized. We can be equally sure that if it changes its views, it will be soundly criticized.

FREE SPEECH AND FREE MEN

Government by the people assumes men's right to speak freely, to organize in groups, to question the decisions of the government, to campaign

[2] *Illinois ex rel McCollum* v. *Board of Education* (1948).
[3] *Zorach* v. *Clauson.*

openly against it. Only through free and uncensored expression of opinion is the government kept responsive to the electorate, or is peaceful change of governmental power possible. Elections, separation of powers, and constitutional guarantees are meaningless unless each person has the right to speak frankly and to hear and judge for himself the worth of what others have to say.

Despite its fundamental importance, some seem to believe that speech should be free only for those with whom they agree. A recent national poll indicated that one American in three did not seem truly to believe in free speech; for example, he did not think that the newspapers should be permitted to criticize the government, even in peacetime.

Why, one might well ask, should evil and ignorant men be permitted to speak falsehoods and to confuse the minds of others? Why should they be allowed to utter dangerous ideas that subvert the very foundations of our democratic society? These are challenging questions. How can they be answered?

The best test of truth

Believers in democracy insist upon free debate and the unlimited exchange of ideas because they hold that no group has a monopoly on truth; that no group has the right to establish absolute political standards of what is true and what is false which others must accept. A man may be convinced that he is right, that truth is on his side, but in the midst of debate he appeals to no philosopher-king, commissar, or oracle of wisdom, but to the power of his reason. As Justice Holmes wrote: "The best test of truth is the power of the thought to get itself accepted in the competition of the market." The insistence upon free speech for others is the recognition by men that they are not infallible, that perhaps the other person is right, or at least, "I might be wrong."

Free speech is not simply the personal right of an individual to have his say: *it is also the right of the rest of us to hear him.* When John Smith out in California is denied the right to speak, the Bill Browns all over the United States are denied the right to hear what he had to say and to judge its worth for themselves. John Stuart Mill, whose *Essay on Liberty* is still an illuminating defense of free speech, put it this way: "The peculiar evil of silencing the expression of opinion, is that it is robbing the human race: . . . If the opinion is right, they are deprived of the opportunity for exchanging error for truth; if wrong, they lose, what is almost as great a benefit, the clearer perception and livelier impression of truth, produced by the collision with error."[4]

Freedom of speech is not merely freedom for those persons and ideas that differ from us and our ideas only slightly; it is, as Justice Jackson has said,

[4] John Stuart Mill, *Essay on Liberty, The English Philosophers from Bacon to Mill,* ed. Edwin A. Burtt (New York: The Modern Library, 1939), p. 961.

"freedom to differ on things that go to the heart of the matter." There are people, however, who say that they believe in free speech, except for those ideas that they consider abhorrent or dangerous. But what is a dangerous idea? Who decides? Socrates was forced to drink the cup of hemlock for expressing dangerous ideas. Christians were once thought to hold dangerous ideas. It is a profound though sometimes disquieting truth that some of the heresies of yesterday are the orthodoxies of today. In the realm of political ideas who can find an objective, eternally valid standard of right? The search for truth is an endless one. It involves the possibility—even the inevitability—of error. The search cannot go on unless it proceeds unfettered in the minds and speech of men. This means, in the words of Justice Holmes, not only free thought for those who agree with us "but freedom for the thought that we hate."

To forbid ideas on the ground that they are dangerous, in short, is to set oneself up as the infallible judge of what speech should be permitted. It is to drive thoughts underground where they cannot be exposed by free debate. And it is to short-circuit the procedures of democratic government. It is these procedures that are guaranteed by the First Amendment.

Constitutional guarantees

Despite the fact that the First Amendment emphatically and absolutely denies to government the power to pass *any* law abridging freedom of speech, the Amendment has never been interpreted in such restrictive terms. Liberty of expression is important—but it is not absolute. Like almost all rights, the right to freedom of speech and press is limited by the fact that its free exercise "implies the existence of an organized society maintaining public order without which liberty itself would be lost in the excess of unrestrained abuses."[5] But how is the line to be drawn between permitted and prohibited governmental interference with freedom of speech?

In discussing the constitutional aspects of free speech, it is useful to distinguish among thought, speech, and nonspeech activity. Thoughts are inviolable, and no government has the right to punish a man for his beliefs or to interfere in any way with his freedom of conscience. This right is as absolute as any right can be for men who live in organized societies. In 1950, however, the Supreme Court voted three-to-three to uphold a lower court's decision that labor unions could be refused the use of national collective bargaining machinery unless their officials swore that they did not *believe* in the overthrow of the government by force or unconstitutional methods. The three justices who upheld this provision reasoned that though belief is inviolate, "beliefs are springs to action." They arrived at the conclusion that, without violating the First Amendment, Congress could encourage labor unions to get rid of persons "of great power over the national

[5] *Cox* v. *New Hampshire* (1941).

economy" who believe in the overthrow of government.[6] They pointed out that such persons were free to believe what they wished, but should not be free to be officers of unions that profited from the national collective bargaining machinery.

Justice Jackson dissented. "While the governments . . . have expansive powers," he wrote, "neither has any power on any pretext, directly or indirectly to attempt foreclosure of any thought. . . ." Calling such action "thought control of the totalitarian pattern" he concluded, "I think that under our system, it is time enough for the law to lay hold of the citizen when he acts illegally, or in some rare circumstances when his thoughts are given illegal utterance. I think we must let his mind alone."

In this case the justices differed in their interpretation of the effect of the law, but they all agreed that belief is inviolate. Action, on the other hand, is another matter. One man's action directly affects the liberty and property of others and "his right to swing his arm ends where the other fellow's nose begins." Freedom of action is constantly constrained—we may not go over twenty miles an hour in business sections, we may not construct glue factories in residential districts, we may not use our property to injure others. Almost every law is in some way a restriction on the action of some individual.

Speech stands between thought and action; it is not an absolute right like thought, but it is not so exposed to governmental restraint as is action. A certain narrowly limited class of speech government clearly may prevent or punish. These are the obscene, the profane, the libelous, and the insulting or fighting words that "by their very utterance inflict injury or tend to incite an immediate breach of the peace." But what about speech outside this narrow category?

Clear and present danger

The first test announced by the Supreme Court was contained in Justice Holmes' opinion in the *Schenck* case (1919) where he said, "The question in every case is whether the words are used in circumstances and are of such a nature as to create a clear and present danger that they will bring about the substantive evils that Congress has a right to prevent." Furthermore, "no danger flowing from speech can be deemed clear and present," wrote Justice Brandeis in 1927 (concurring in *Whitney* v. *California*), "unless the incidence of the evil is so imminent that it may befall before there is opportunity for full discussion. If there be time to expose through discussion the falsehood and facilities to avert the evil by the process of education, the remedy to be applied is more speech, not enforced silence."

But in 1925, over Holmes' and Brandeis' dissent, the Supreme Court propounded in the *Gitlow* case the "bad tendency test" and ruled that the

---

[6] *American Communications Association* v. *Douds.*

state could "suppress the threatened danger in its incipiency" and could forbid speech that merely tended to lead to a substantive evil. This test was applied in only one case, but it remained in the storehouse of verbal devices for possible later use. Eventually, however, the clear and present danger doctrine carried the day. After 1940, the Court was controlled by men who assigned first place to civil liberties in their hierarchy of constitutional values, and they developed the clear and present danger formula to translate their values into constitutional law.

Holmes and Brandeis had used this test merely to guide judges and prosecutors in *applying the laws* to particular cases, not as a test of the constitutionality of the laws themselves. If the *words of a defendant* actually constituted a clear and present danger, Holmes and Brandeis believed that the law could be applied. If not, the law in question was presumed to be inapplicable. The 1940-1950 majority, however, extended the clear and present danger doctrine to test the constitutionality of the *laws themselves*. They used it as an instrument of judicial review. Did the law deal with speech that involved a clear and present danger? If not, it was unconstitutional regardless of the defendant's words.

In effect, the usual *presumption of constitutionality* accorded to legislative acts was reversed in the case of those laws that affected the First Amendment. It is an ancient judicial canon (see Chapter 20) that laws should be presumed to be constitutional. Legislatures are the responsible agents of the electorate, and they, not the courts, are the proper organs to choose among the several means to achieve public purposes. As long as the methods chosen are not clearly unreasonable, judges are reluctant, at least openly, to interfere. But this was not so if the law affected free speech. A majority of the justices drew from their philosophy of democracy the belief that *courts* should give civil liberties preferential treatment. Therefore laws that affected the First Amendment were upheld only when the legislature and prosecutors could demonstrate that the law was necessary to avoid a clear and *extremely imminent* danger to *extremely serious* substantive interests. It was not enough that the law was a reasonable means to deal with a particular problem. The Court, not the legislature, was to have the final say whether the danger was sufficiently clear and present to justify the restriction on speech.

This was the dominant doctrine from approximately 1940 to 1950, despite strong dissents. Although the Court did not declare any congressional acts unconstitutional, it gave no reason to assume that it would accord the First Amendment any less preferential treatment when affected by congressional laws than when touched by state laws.

Retreat from clear and present danger

In 1949 Justices Rutledge and Murphy, who placed civil liberties topmost in their scale of values, were replaced by Justices Clark and Minton.

At the same time the threat of international communism became more menacing, and popular demand grew for more restrictive legislation against communistic and other disloyal speech. By 1951 only Justices Douglas and Black avowed a belief in the doctrine that the Supreme Court should give the First Amendment a preferred position. The Court appears to have made a definite retreat from the position it supported during the 1940's.

In a series of important cases, the High Court has ruled:

1. "When the effect of a statute or ordinance upon the exercise of First Amendment freedoms is relatively small and the public interest to be protected is substantial, no showing of imminent danger to the security of the nation is necessary." (*American Communications Association* v. *Douds.*)

2. When the substantive evil to be avoided is the overthrow of the government by force, advocacy of this doctrine or conspiracy to advocate it can be punished even when there is no imminent danger that it will actually lead to overthrow. The danger need only be clear and probable. (*Dennis* v. *United States.*)

3. Free speech can be invaded whenever "the gravity of the evil, discounted by its improbability, justifies such invasion . . . as is necessary to avoid the danger." (*Dennis* v. *United States.*)

In other words, the Court majority now gives greater emphasis to the *gravity of the evil* the law is attempting to prevent and less to the degree of probability that the words will ripen into action. Hence, laws designed to prevent riots or overthrow of government justify greater restrictions on speech than, say, laws designed to prevent a less serious evil, such as forbidding circularization of political pamphlets in order to keep the streets clean.

But whether the test is "clear and present danger," or "reasonable tendency," or "gravity of the evil, discounted by its improbability," these formulas do not decide cases. There is no pat rule, no easy answer. Behind the formulas stand a host of considerations. *What* is said? Obscene speech, libelous, fighting words are not in the same category as political disputations. *Where* is it said? On the street corner, in a man's living room, over the radio? *How* is it said? In an inflammatory manner? What is the *intent* of the persons who said it? To encourage people to violate the laws, to stir them to violence, to cause them to think? What are the *circumstances* in which it is said? During time of war, in front of a hostile audience? *Which* government is attempting to regulate the speech? The city council that speaks for a few people or the Congress that speaks for a wide variety of people? (No Congressional enactment has ever been struck down because of conflict with the First Amendment.) *How* is the government attempting to regulate the speech? By prior censorship, by punishment after the speech, by administrative procedures? *Why* is the government attempting to regulate the speech? To protect the national security, to keep the streets clean, to protect the rights of unpopular religious minorities, to prevent criticism of those in power? These and scores of other considerations are involved. The social interests involved must be weighed in each case. And there is the further question of how much deference judges should show to the legislature's attempt to adjust these social interests. In short, no test has been devised that will automatically weigh all the factors.

In addition to analyzing the doctrines announced by judges, it is sometimes useful to examine the cases in terms of the effect of the decisions. R. L. Sklar has done this with respect to 21 cases that have confronted the Supreme Court since 1919 involving *political* speech. His findings are thought-provoking. "First, left-wingers charged with the advocacy of illegal conduct in wartime have invariably lost in the Supreme Court. Only right-wingers have been exonerated for proposing illegal conduct while the nation was at war. Second, insofar as the Supreme Court is concerned, there is not, nor has there ever been, any right to advocate revolution. Third, with the exception of the German-American Bund, the Supreme Court has never maintained anyone's right to engage in political advocacy of illegal conduct. . . . In dealing with these cases, the Supreme Court has not followed any discernible rule . . . the results do not correspond to any legal norms, such as the clear and present danger test, but to the discretion of the Court."[7] The conclusions perhaps are not so surprising when one remembers that Supreme Court justices are men who have the awesome responsibility of making value choices, choices that in a democratic society more or less accurately reflect the values of dominant groups. The difficulties involved can readily be seen with respect to the application of the First Amendment to modern methods of communication.

Freedom of the press

"Upon what meat doth this our democracy feed?" asks Herbert Brucker, a noted newspaper editor. "It feeds upon facts brought into the minds of its citizens by the press, the radio, and the supplementary media of information."[8] So important is this information system, says Brucker, that it constitutes the indispensable "fourth branch" of the national government. Today most information is not spread in street-corner meetings or public assemblies, the classic centers of debate. It is broadcast wholesale by the press, television, radio, movies, and other media.

On the whole, the Supreme Court has guarded zealously the freedom of the press from restriction by government in peacetime. In general terms it has followed a basic rule of the English constitution described

[7] Richard L. Sklar, "The Fiction of the First Freedom," *The Western Political Quarterly*, Vol. VI, No. 2, June 1953.

[8] Herbert Brucker, *Freedom of Information* (New York: The Macmillan Company, 1949), p. 10.

almost two centuries ago by Blackstone, who said, "The liberty of the press is indeed essential to the nature of a free state; but this consists in laying no *previous* restraints upon publications, and not in freedom from censure for criminal matter when published." This is a useful general rule, since it suggests that freedom of the press while important is not absolute. But how broad is this freedom?

The case of *Near* v. *Minnesota* (1931) provided a partial answer. A Minneapolis newspaper charged, among other things, that a known gangster controlled racketeering in the city and that the chief of police was receiving graft. Under a Minnesota law authorizing injunctions against "malicious, scandalous, and defamatory" action, the newspaper was permanently enjoined from being published. The editor appealed ultimately to the Supreme Court. "The question," said Chief Justice Hughes for a closely divided court, "is whether a statute authorizing such proceedings in restraint of publication is consistent with the conception of the liberty of the press as historically conceived and guaranteed. . . . The fact that the liberty of the press may be abused by miscreant purveyors of scandal does not make any the less necessary the immunity of the press from previous restraint in dealing with official misconduct." Freedom to publish without restraint did not depend on proof of truth. The Court held the law to be an infringement of the liberty of the press. This case made clear that government may not set up advance censorship except in extraordinary circumstances.

The Court has further defined its position in later decisions. For example, when Huey Long, bitter at the opposition to him of the larger Louisiana newspapers, put through a special tax on their advertising income, the Supreme Court (*Grosjean* v. *American Press Co.,* 1936) struck down the tax law.

Sometimes freedom of the press comes into conflict with another basic right, trial by an impartial judge and jury in a calm and judicious atmosphere. When newspapers and other mass media report in vivid detail the facts of a lurid crime and secure press releases from the prosecutor, it may be impossible to hold a trial in an atmosphere free from hysteria or to secure a jury that can decide in an impartial manner. In England the weight is on the side of fair trial. British courts do not hestitate to hold in contempt newspapers that comment on pending criminal proceedings. In the United States the weight is on the side of free comment. The Supreme Court has ruled that the First and Fourteenth amendments narrowly restrict a judge's contempt authority. The Court has sustained the right of the press to criticize judges, even to the point of allowing editors to threaten judges with political reprisals unless they dealt with defendants in a certain fashion. As Justice Douglas put it, "judges are supposed to be men of fortitude, able to thrive in a hardy climate" (*Craig* v. *Harney,* 1947). When *juries* are involved, less leeway is given to hostile criticism; but rather than punish the newspapers, defendants are sometimes permitted new trials. In 1952, for example, a defendant was given a new trial because, after his indictment, a congressional investigating committee held open hearings which the judges believed so inflamed public opinion and created such a hostile atmosphere that a fair trial was impossible.[9]

Recently a new threat to freedom of the press has come to public attention. Governments have always withheld secret information, especially during time of war. But as more and more matters have involved security, there has been a growing tendency of public officials to classify information and make it a crime to divulge it. The Department of Defense, for example, ordered officials not to release information unless it would "constitute a constructive contribution to the primary mission of the Department of Defense." This censorship at the source is not unconstitutional but, as newspaper men and some congressmen have pointed out, it does seriously cut down on the flow of information and permits officials to shield themselves from criticism. We must remember, however, that threats to freedom of information do not come only from government. They may also come from timid editors, local self-constituted censors of what is fit to print, public hysteria, or apathy.

Other means of communication

Does the right of free speech and press extend to books and magazines, motion pictures, radio and television, and does it include the right to use picketing and sound trucks? No general answer can be given. Each of these media presents special problems.

Books and magazines. Through a progressive relaxation of the common law of libel, these state-administered laws no longer constitute a serious threat to freedom of information. The *fair comment* doctrine permits wide latitude of criticism of the conduct and reputation of public men, comments which might be libelous if directed toward a private citizen. More difficult problems are raised by group libel statutes which permit criminal prosecution for publishing materials that defame races, religions, and other such groups. A closely divided Supreme Court sustained an Illinois statute that makes it a crime to portray any class of citizens of any race, color, creed, or religion as depraved, criminal, or unchaste or to expose them to contempt or derision (*Beauharnais* v. *Illinois* 1952). The dissenting justices held that since there was not in this particular case any evidence of any clear and present danger of disorder arising from the publication in question, the state had exceeded its constitutional authority.

Obscene publications, like libelous ones, are not entitled to protection. However, there is inevitably the problem of standards. *Who is to say which publications are obscene?* The national government, through its control over customs, postal, and interstate commerce matters, outlaws the importation, mailing, and shipment of obscene literature. For many years James Joyce's

[9] *Delaney* v. *United States,* United States Court of Appeals (1952).

classic *Ulysses* was alleged to be obscene by customs officials, a ruling finally reversed by the courts. The Post Office has also threatened to ban the mailing of Aristophanes' *Lysistrata,* but it backed down in the face of public protest and threatened judicial action. The Postmaster General has the authority to exclude from the mails publications he judges to be obscene or seditious, or he may revoke their second-class mailing privileges, or he may cut off all *incoming* mail to a person selling obscene matter. The basic doctrine on which these laws rest is that the use of the mails is a privilege, but in the last decade judges have started to question this basic assumption and have been clamping down on the Postmaster General's discretion. tion and have been clamping down on the Postmaster General's discretion.[10] The Post Office, however, continues to exercise its authority. In addition it claims that the Foreign Agents Registration Act gives it the power to refuse to deliver to private individuals printed matter from Russia, China, and other nations. This is a contention for the courts to pass on.

States have the constitutional power to punish those who publish, sell, or distribute obscene literature. All the Constitution requires is that the statutes be precise. Interpretations of what is "obscene," however, have been given wide scope, and books by distinguished writers such as James M. Cain, Edmund Wilson, Lillian Smith, and others have in various states been so judged. There is growing agreement that books should be measured as a whole rather than by abstracting a few scattered passages, and that they should be assessed for their impact on normal adults rather than on especially susceptible groups. To be sure, obscenity statutes do not involve prior censorship, but in some cities private groups place such strong pressures on booksellers that they maintain an effective censorship on the books and publications.

Motion pictures. Does the Constitution protect motion pictures from governmental censorship? In 1915 the Supreme Court said "No" (*Mutual Film Corporation* v. *Ohio Industrial Commission*). Pictures, argued the justices, were a form of entertainment, a profit-making business, not methods of speech or press. Taking advantage of this opening, censors in seven states and over 100 cities prohibited the showing of pictures that violated their sense of propriety. Unlike laws that apply to newspapers, magazines, and books, these motion picture regulations were *prior censorship.* Then in 1951 the Supreme Court brought the movies under the protection of the national Constitution and ruled that New York officials could not prevent the showing of a film called *The Miracle* because they thought it to be "sacrilegious" (*Joseph Burstyn, Inc.* v. *Wilson*). The term "sacrilegious" lacks precise meaning. Furthermore, government has no authority to censor movies solely because they may offend some people's religious sensibilities. The Supreme Court has since then upset attempts to ban pictures on the grounds that they "tend to corrupt morals" or "on account of being

[10] *Hannegan* v. *Esquire, Inc.,* 1946 and decision of Court of Appeals, *Summerfield* v. *Sunshine Book Company,* 1954.

harmful."[11] But the Supreme Court made no attempt to explain its decisions, and whether they mean that all kinds of governmental movie censorship are unconstitutional is uncertain. In the next few years the High Court will probably be called upon to decide whether a carefully drawn statute that authorizes officials to ban "obscene pictures" is constitutional. And of course the general laws of libel and obscenity apply to motion pictures as well as to books and other publications.

Radio and television. The number of airways is limited. For technological and other reasons, the national government has used its power over interstate commerce to allocate the airways and to issue licenses for broadcasting and television. The First Amendment does not include "the right to use the facilities of a radio without a license." (*National Broadcasting Co.* v. *United States,* 1943.) Nor does the First Amendment prevent the Federal Communications Commission from refusing or canceling a license if, in its opinion, the broadcasting station is not serving the public interest, convenience, or necessity. Federal regulation of radio and television does, however, protect these media from state regulation. When Philadelphia officials tried to censor motion pictures shown on television, a United States Court of Appeals ruled that the federal regulation was exclusive (*Dumont Laboratories* v. *Carroll,* 1950).

Picketing. This is a means of speech traditionally used by workers to convey their messages to the public. At the same time it is an economic weapon in the struggle between labor and capital. In 1940 the Supreme Court ruled in *Thornhill* v. *Alabama* that picketing was a form of communication protected by the First and Fourteenth Amendments; therefore, a state law forbidding peaceful picketing carried on for any purpose was an unconstitutional invasion of freedom of speech. By 1949, however, the Supreme Court had narrowed the scope of its earlier rulings. The Court has held that even peaceful picketing can be restricted if it is conducted for a purpose that is against public policy as declared either by the state legislatures or by state judges.[12]

Sound trucks. What is more important—the right to an undisturbed Sunday afternoon nap or the right to use an amplification device in order to publicize a message? In 1948, by a five-to-four decision, the Supreme Court held in *Saia* v. *New York* that the Fourteenth Amendment was violated by a city ordinance requiring an official permit issued at the discretion of the chief of police before one could use a sound truck. Justice Douglas for the Court majority said that sound trucks are "indispensable instruments of effective public speech, and . . . such abuses as they create can be controlled only by statutes narrowly drawn." The very next year, however, the authority of this ruling was placed in doubt by another five-to-four ruling in

[11] *Commercial Pictures Corp.* v. *Regents of University of State of New York* (1954), and *Superior Films, Inc.* v. *Department of Education of Ohio* (1954).
[12] *Building Service Employees* v. *Gazzam* and cases cited therein (1950).

Kovacs v. *Cooper* upholding a municipal ordinance forbidding any sound truck that emitted "loud and raucous noises." The Court majority believed that this ordinance provided a definite enough standard to guide administrators, and that it was a justifiable exercise of the police power "to protect the well-being and tranquility of a community."

Freedom of assembly

The right to assemble peaceably extends not only to meetings in private homes and assembly places, but also to those held in public streets and parks which, said the Supreme Court, "time out of mind have been used for purposes of assembly . . . and discussing public questions" (*Hague* v. *C.I.O.*, 1939). The government has the duty to protect persons who wish to sound off on public questions. But people are not free to incite riots, to block traffic, to hold parades, or to make speeches in public places in the middle of rush hour, and the government may make reasonable regulations to preserve order. The Court, however, has struck down licensing laws that give administrative officials unfettered discretion to decide who can speak in a public park or on the street corner. Such laws involve *prior* censorship, to which the Supreme Court has been especially opposed (*Kunz* v. *New York,* 1951) although a law providing precise standards to guide officials might get by the Court.

Laws regulating uses of streets and parks but not involving prior censorship have won more judicial support. This is well illustrated by *Feiner* v. *New York* (1951), which arose out of the following situation: Feiner a university student, stood on a large box in a predominantly Negro residential section of Syracuse and spoke over a loud speaker to an audience of about 75 people, Negro and white. He was publicizing a meeting to be held that evening by the Young Progressives of America and protesting the revocation of a permit to use the public school auditorium so that the meeting had to be transferred to a local hotel. In the course of his speech he made derogatory remarks about public officials and exhorted Negroes to "rise up in arms and fight for their rights." His speech stirred up a little excitement among the crowd, and one man threatened to haul him from his platform. Two police officers were on the scene, and, in order to avoid a fight, asked Feiner to stop his speech. He refused, and finally the officers arrested him. Feiner was tried and convicted for disorderly conduct. The Supreme Court, six to three, upheld the conviction on the ground that a clear danger of disorder was threatened and the state had the right to preserve peace on the streets.

Justices Douglas, Black, and Minton dissented. They argued that the record showed only an unsympathetic audience, that there was no danger of a riot, and if the police were really interested in preserving public order they should have arrested those who would break up the meeting instead of Feiner, who was exercising his right to speak. Justice Black said, "I think this conviction makes a mockery of the free speech guarantees of the First and Fourteenth Amendments. . . . I will have no part or parcel in this holding which I view as a long step toward totalitarian authority."

Freedom of petition and association

The right to petition the government along with freedom of speech, press, and assembly is specifically protected by the First Amendment, but the amendment says nothing about freedom of *association,* one of the most important political rights. The framers of the Bill of Rights did not look kindly on political groups and political parties. They had yet to accept fully one of the most important concepts of modern political theory, the idea of "His Majesty's loyal opposition." To some, political associations were needless causes of controversy and generators of particular loyalties that jeopardized national unity. Perhaps this accounts for the First Amendment's silence on the right to organize peacefully for political purposes.

Despite the lack of specific guarantees of freedom of political association, there is substantial ground for arguing that this right grows out of the freedoms of the First Amendment and is protected by that amendment. The Supreme Court may be called upon to rule specifically on this question if the several state laws that ban the National Association for the Advancement of Colored People are brought before its bar. The NAACP, which proceeds mainly by pressing cases before the courts, is working to secure compliance with the Supreme Court's decisions against racial segregation (see pages 175-177), and those laws that attempt to make its operations illegal raise serious First and Fourteenth Amendment questions.

SUBVERSIVE CONDUCT AND SEDITIOUS SPEECH

"If there is any fixed star in our constitutional constellation," said Justice Jackson in the West Virginia flag salute case, "it is that no official, high or petty, can prescribe what shall be orthodox in politics, nationalism, religion, or other matters of opinion." Any group that abides by the basic rules of democracy can champion whatever position it wishes, whether vegetarianism, socialism, or even communism. But what about the American Communist party? Its leaders are unwilling to abide by democratic methods. They use force and deceit. Their organization is an instrument of a foreign power whose aggressive policies threaten the free world.[13] Yet they claim the right under the Constitution to carry on their propaganda and other activities.

[13] See decision of Subversive Activities Control Board, which after fourteen months of hearings concluded that the Communist Party is dominated by the Soviet Union and ordered it to register as a "communist-action organization" (see page 164). F.R. Vol. 18, No. 83, p. 2513, April 30, 1953. The Communists have appealed this decision to the courts.

Traitors, spies, saboteurs, revolutionaries

Here is a perplexing problem for American democratic government. How can the United States protect itself against Communists and other disloyal Americans and at the same time preserve the traditional American freedoms?

The weapons in the battle against disloyalty are hazardous. There is the constant risk that they will backfire. If used clumsily, they can destroy more freedom and do more to undermine the security of the United States than can the Communists themselves. The least dangerous weapons are those aimed at disloyal *actions*.

The laws that punish disloyal *nonspeech* activities raise no constitutional questions nor do they infringe on civil liberties, except as they are loosely drawn or indiscriminately administered. The framers of the Constitution—themselves considered traitors by the English government—knew that "new-fangled and artificial treasons have been the great engines by which violent factions, the natural offspring of free governments, have usually wreaked their alternate malignity on each other,"[14] so they carefully inserted a constitutional definition of the crime. *Treason* consists only of the overt acts of giving aid and comfort to the enemies of the United States or levying war against the United States. Furthermore, the government must provide the testimony of two witnesses to the overt act, or else the traitor must confess in open court.

Modern antidemocrats can, however, subvert the nation without committing treason. Though American Communists are giving aid and comfort to the Soviet Union in the cold war, that nation is not, within the meaning of the Constitution, an enemy of the United States. Only in the event of war between the United States and Russia would it be possible to bring treason charges against the communists. Constitutionally defined treason, on the other hand, is not the limit of the government's power to protect itself. The government may punish by appropriate procedures spies, saboteurs, and those who are plotting to alter or overthrow the government by violence. The fact that speech is involved in a conspiracy to overthrow the government by force does not bring the First Amendment into play any more than the fact that speech is involved in a conspiracy among bandits to rob a bank.

The United States originated in revolution, as extreme leftists constantly remind us. How, then, can the government constitutionally punish revolutionaries?

Revolution is not a constitutional right; it is not one that the government is obliged to protect. On the contrary, it is a power that any group exercises at its own peril. Furthermore, most of the American patriots talked about revolutions when there were no representative institutions. They referred to the right of a majority (though revolutions are usually instigated by a minority) to change the government whenever it becomes destructive of life and

[14] See, Harold W. Chase, *Security and Liberty: The Problem of Native Communists, 1947-1955* (Garden City, New York: Doubleday & Company, Inc., 1955).

liberty and blocks the peaceful transfer of power. They were not speaking of the right of a minority to destroy representative institutions in order to establish a dictatorship of the proletariat. The very nature of American representative systems makes revolution unnecessary so long as it guarantees to all the right to pursue their goals by peaceful methods. If democracy is to operate, the government must act against those who use undemocratic procedures of force and violence to achieve their goals.

In 1950 Congress, in the Internal Security Act, added a new kind of cold war crime which not only covers speech (discussed on pages 163-165) but makes illegal any action peaceful or not (except agitation for a constitutional amendment) that has as its purpose the knowing attempt to conspire to contribute substantially to the establishment within the United States of a totalitarian dictatorship controlled by a foreign government, organization, or individual. Unlike other statutes aimed at subversive conduct, this law is not restricted to violent acts or specific illegal acts like sabotage or espionage. Whether government has the constitutional power to cast its net so wide in a criminal statute remains to be determined.

What of conduct that is limited to speaking, writing, and publishing? May it, too, be outlawed?

Seditious speech

One of the most hazardous weapons for a free government to use is the punishment of disloyal speech. The story of the development of free government is in large measure the story of the narrowing of the crime of *sedition,* the crime that has been used for centuries to suppress political criticism of those in power. Walter Gellhorn has defined sedition as consisting of "advocacy by word of mouth, publication, or otherwise which incites discontent and contempt for the present form of government, causing people to flout its laws and tending to destroy the government itself. It includes advocacy which incites to overthrow the existing government, by force and violence, to bring into contempt the form of government, its public officers, its military forces, flags, and other symbols."[15]

The first attempt by the national government to punish seditious speech was in 1798, when the Bill of Rights was only seven years old. It was a period of alarm; war with France was imminent. The Federalists controlled Congress. Stung by criticism from their political opponents, they made it a crime to make false, scandalous, or malicious statements with the intent to bring the government or any of its officers into disrepute or "to incite against them the hatred of the good people of the United States." Federalists, of course, like all those in power, considered political criticism to be false, scandalous, or malicious and used the law to punish Jeffersonian Republicans who dared to criticize the Federalist administration.

[15] Walter Gellhorn, *States and Subversion* (Ithaca: Cornell University Press, 1952), p. 397.

The popular reaction to the Sedition Act helped defeat the Federalists at the polls. Those who passed and enforced this act had failed to grasp the core of the democratic idea. They did not understand that a man may criticize the *government of the day,* he may work for its downfall, he may oppose its policies, and still be loyal to the *nation.* If the Sedition Act had been left on the statute books and applied in its full measure, neither the "loyal opposition" nor free government would have been possible.

The Sedition Act of 1918

It was not until World War I that such a severe measure again became the law of the land. In 1918 it was made a crime to print, write, or publish any "disloyal, profane, scurrilous, or abusive language about the form of government of the United States or the Constitution . . . or any language intended to bring the form of government of the United States, or the Constitution of the United States, or the military forces . . . or the flag . . . or the uniform of the Army and Navy . . . into contempt, scorn, contumely, or disrepute."

This drastic measure was not aimed at talk that might lead to specific kinds of harmful activities, but made the speech itself illegal. Like the Sedition Act of 1798, it made it a crime not only to advocate illegal activities, but to criticize the government. It was loosely drawn and poorly administered. Though limited to a war period, it was applied when many people, emotionally aroused during the war, were willing to restrict the liberties of their fellow citizens. When supplemented by state laws against anarchy, syndicalism, and sedition, and by federal laws against interfering with drafting men for the army, it became a crime "to advocate heavier taxation instead of bond issues, to state that conscription was unconstitutional . . . to say that the sinking of merchant vessels was legal, to urge that a referendum should have preceded our declaration of war, to say that war was contrary to the teachings of Christ."[16] A twenty-one-year-old girl was sentenced to fifteen years in jail for taking part in the scattering of some pamphlets attacking President Wilson and opposing American intervention in Russia.[17] A "red scare" followed the war. Judges and juries punished hundreds of people who expressed ideas to which their neighbors objected.

The Smith Act of 1940

The next sedition law, the first to apply in peacetime since the Sedition Act of 1798, was the Smith Act of 1940. Unlike earlier sedition laws, it does not make mere criticism of the government a crime, nor does it contain such loose language as "bring into contempt" or "cause discontent." The central core of the offense is to advocate the overthrow of government by force with

[16] Zechariah Chafee, Jr., *Free Speech in the United States* (Cambridge: Harvard University Press, 1942), p. 51.
[17] *Abrams* v. *United States* (1919).

the intent to bring about this overthrow. It forbids persons to advocate forceful overthrow, to distribute, with disloyal intent, matter teaching or advising the overthrow of government by violence; to organize knowingly or help to organize any group having such propaganda as its purposes. The Act also, according to Zechariah Chafee, a leading authority on the problems of free speech, introduces for the first time into federal criminal law the concept of *guilt by association,* by making it a crime to be a member of any organization that advocates forceful overthrow when the individual *knows* that this is its purpose (even though he does not himself so advocate).

Although some anti-Soviet Trotskyites were punished under the Smith Act, its constitutionality was not tested before the Supreme Court until *Dennis* v. *United States* in 1951. This is undoubtedly one of the most significant civil liberties cases in recent years. Men will argue for some time just what its significance may be. The case arose out of the conviction of the leaders of the Communist party for violating the Smith Act by *conspiring to advocate* the overthrow of the government by force.

The attorneys for the Communist leaders pointed out that the charge was not the attempt to overthrow, conspiring to overthrow, or even advocating the overthrow, but solely of *conspiring to advocate.* They argued that unless the government could prove (which they held it had not done) a clear and present danger that the conspiracy to advocate was about to ripen into action, the First Amendment forbade conviction.

The Supreme Court rejected this contention by a six-to-two vote. Chief Justice Vinson spoke for the Court in an opinion joined by three other justices. He distinguished previous applications of the clear-and-present-danger doctrine on the grounds that in the earlier cases "the interest which the State was attempting to protect was itself too insubstantial to warrant restriction of speech." But in this case, the government was protecting its *right to existence.* Therefore the probability of success of the speech in question was not to serve as a criterion. Quoting from Circuit Judge Learned Hand, the Chief Justice said the question was "whether the gravity of the evil, discounted by its improbability," justified such invasion of free speech as was necessary to avoid the danger. The evil was grave. Moreover, the danger presented by the Communists could not be discounted. The Chief Justice, as did Justices Frankfurter and Jackson in their respective concurring opinions, gave great weight to the fact that this was not a case of an isolated socialist who might scatter a few insignificant pamphlets, or of a zealot on the street corner, but of a conspiratorial group of rigidly disciplined members in a world-wide apparatus whose purpose it was to destroy democracy. This group existed in the context of world crisis. Thus invasion of their freedom to conspire to advocate the overthrow of the government by force could be sustained.

Justices Douglas and Black dissented. Justice Douglas said that no evidence had been introduced that the Communists were teaching the techniques of sabotage, advising the desirability of assassinating the President, or giving instructions on the filching of documents from public files. "The teaching of methods of terror and seditious conduct should be beyond the pale along with obscenity and immorality." But, he argued, the only evidence presented by the government was that the Communists had organized people to teach them Marxist-Leninist doctrines. Moreover, the evidence did not show that this teaching presented any danger to the government. And the Court's ruling that the Communists were a dangerous group because they were part of a world-wide apparatus owing allegiance to the Soviet Union did not, argued Justice Douglas, meet the issues in the case. "We might as well say that the speech of petitioners is outlawed because Soviet Russia and her Red Army are a threat to world peace." Although he recognized the connection between the external and the internal threat of the Communists, Justice Douglas stated that there was no evidence that the eleven Communist leaders were any threat. The Communists in America, he wrote, are "miserable merchants of unwanted ideas; their wares remain unsold. The fact that their ideas are abhorrent does not make them powerful. . . . The invisible army of petitioners is the best known, the most beset, and the least thriving of any fifth column in history. Only those held by fear and panic could think otherwise. . . . Unless and until extreme and necessitous circumstances are shown our aim should be to keep speech unfettered and to allow the process of law to be invoked only when the provocateurs among us move from speech to action."

Following its successful conviction of the top Communists, the Department of Justice proceeded to prosecute other leaders and approximately 100 of them have been jailed. Most of the states have sedition statutes, and they also began to prosecute Communist leaders. However, in 1956 the Supreme Court sustained a decision of the Pennsylvania Supreme Court that the Smith Act had pre-empted the field and that state laws punishing sedition against the national government could not be enforced. If Congress should enact legislation to restore the state laws, the Supreme Court might be called upon to decide "whether double or multiple punishment for the same overt acts directed against the United States has constitutional sanction."[18]

Drastic as many think the Smith Act to be, it was aimed at speech designed to promote undemocratic procedures, and it left Communists and others free to secure their goals, *provided* they used democratic techniques. As the tension between the United States and the Soviet world grew, however, many pressed for more stringent restrictions on Communist political activity. Congress responded.

The Internal Security Act of 1950

The Internal Security Act of 1950, popularly known as the McCarran Act, as mentioned on page 160, makes it a crime to take any action designed

[18] *Pennsylvania* v. *Nelson* (1956).

to contribute substantially to the establishment of a totalitarian dictatorship. This applies to speeches and publications as well as to nonspeech action, although Congress stipulated that it is not to apply to those who attempt to establish such a dictatorship by constitutional amendment. The Act in this and other provisions looks in part toward suppressing Communist political agitation by denying to Communists certain privileges and imposing on them certain disabilities. But the central thrust of the Act rests upon the assumption that Communists should be allowed to engage in peaceful politics provided the veil of secrecy is stripped from their actions.

To force Communists to disclose their activity, Congress created a Subversive Activities Control Board of five members to determine, upon the application of the Attorney General, whether any organization is a Communist action, front, or infiltrated organization. Communist *action* organizations are defined as those substantially directed by the foreign government that controls the world Communist movement or those operating primarily to advance the objectives of this movement. Communist *front* organizations are those substantially dominated by a Communist action organization or operated for the purpose of giving aid to a Communist organization or foreign government. Communist *infiltrated* organizations—a category added in 1954 and aimed at Communist dominated labor unions—are those substantially dominated by persons who are giving aid or who, within three years, have given aid, actively and knowingly, to a Communist action organization or Communist foreign government or have knowingly served to impair the military or industrial capacity of the United States. Labor organizations affiliated with national unions that are opposed to communism, however, are presumed prima facie not to be Communist infiltrated.

After the Subversive Activities Control Board issues a final order that has been sustained by the courts, the following major disabilities are imposed:

1. Action and front organizations must *register* annually with the Attorney General, giving names of officers and an account of all money spent and received, including its sources.
2. Action organizations must *report* the names of all their members. Members aware that their names are not registered must inform the Attorney General on pain of criminal punishment.
3. Action and front organizations must *submit* to the Attorney General full information on printing equipment under their control.
4. Action, front, and infiltrated organizations must *identify* all their publications that are sent through the mails or across state boundaries, and all broadcasts, as those of a communist organization.
5. Infiltrated organizations *lose all rights* accorded to unions under national laws, and employers no longer have to bargain with them.
6. No member of an action, front, or infiltrated organization may apply for or use a *passport,* hold any nonelective federal *position,* or serve as an officer or employee of a labor *union.*

7. No member of an action organization may work in a *defense plant* listed by the Secretary of Defense as a defense facility, and members of front and infiltrated organizations must make known their membership.

In addition to these registration provisions, the Internal Security Act adds penalties to laws against espionage and sedition, adds to alien registration requirements, makes it more difficult for Communist aliens to get in or remain in the United States, and establishes procedures for detaining in the event of an emergency each person who can "reasonably" be expected to engage in acts of sabotage or espionage.

The Communist Control Act of 1954

The purpose of the Internal Security Act of 1950 was to bring Communists into the open, but even before this Act could be applied, Congress decided to take more drastic action. For some time there has been agitation to outlaw the Communist party and any of its successors. Partly because of doubts of the constitutionality of such a measure, partly because of doubts about its effectiveness, no action was taken until 1954.

In that year Congress declared that the open political action of the Communist party is a front behind which the party seduces individuals into the service of world communism and is an instrument to secure the violent overthrow of the government of the United States. (Such a conspiracy, of course, is illegal; and evidence to support this finding, if properly presented in court proceedings, would be sufficient under existing law to throw the conspirators in jail.) The party's existence, declared Congress, renders it a "clear, present, and continuing danger to the security of the United States." Therefore, the party and its successors are deprived of "any of the rights, privileges, and immunities attendant upon legal bodies created under the laws of the United States" or any of the states.

The act does not make it a crime to be a Communist (but members of the party are subject to the penalties that the Internal Security Act imposes upon members of Communist action organizations). The major effect of the law is to deprive the Communist party of the right to seek places on election ballots for its candidates. For the first time in our history, a political party has been outlawed by the national government, and a group has been denied the opportunity to seek the traditional instruments of democracy.

DISLOYALTY AND THE PUBLIC SERVICE

Spies, saboteurs, and those who advocate forceful overthrow may be tried and punished. What of persons who commit no crimes, but are sympathetic to the cause of communism or have joined organizations which the Attorney General believes to be subversive? Should they be permitted to work for the government, serve in the armed forces, work in defense plants, secure passports? Apparently most Americans believe not, and a whole host of disabilities are now imposed upon such persons.

J. Edgar Hoover has estimated that there are about 20,000 hard-core Communists and perhaps ten times that many who are sympathetic to their cause. In order to forestall this group from securing public employment, receiving government financed fellowships, joining the merchant marine, or working in defense plants, about twenty million Americans have been made subject to some kind of federal security check. They may be questioned about their views on foreign policy, their reading, their friends, and the organizations to which they belong. In addition, Congress and at least six state legislatures have committees to investigate un-American activities. These committees have also checked into the loyalty of public employees, newspaper men, teachers, scientists, and others and have "exposed" those whom the committee members believe to be un-American.

Employees of the executive branch of the national government are the ones most subject to investigation. Until 1939 their private political life was of no concern to the government unless it intruded on their ability to perform their jobs. In that year, however, political tests were imposed, and persons who advocated the overthrow of government or belonged to Communist, Nazi, or Fascist organizations were disqualified. During World War II, applicants for jobs were investigated, and access to classified and secret information was denied to all except those who had been cleared. Those suspected of disloyalty were fired or transferred to nonsensitive positions— positions not directly concerned with national security.

The Truman loyalty program

In 1947 President Truman, responding to disclosures of Communist espionage and to growing public concern, inaugurated a more extensive system of loyalty investigations. He ordered an investigation of all employees of the executive branch and of all future applicants. "Reasonable grounds for belief that the person was disloyal" was recast in 1951 to "reasonable doubt as to loyalty," and such doubt could deny employment or remove an employee from office. The President listed the grounds on which employees' loyalty was to be judged, one of which was membership in an organization that the Attorney General thought to be totalitarian, fascist, communistic, or subversive. To guide administrators of the loyalty program, the Attorney General compiled a list of such organizations (the Attorney General's list is not to be confused with organizations declared communistic by the Subversive Activities Control Board; see page 164). An employee charged with disloyalty had a right to a hearing before a loyalty board in his own agency, with an appeal to a central loyalty review board. Employees were entitled to counsel, to present evidence, and to be informed of the charges. However, the investigative agency did not have to disclose the names of confidential informants, not even to the boards that were judging the case.

This loyalty program applied to all members of the executive branch from grounds keepers to cabinet members. In addition there were, and are, various *security* programs for sensitive positions, those directly concerned with national security. Persons holding sensitive positions could be suspended *immediately* not only for doubts about their loyalty but for other reasons such as untrustworthiness, liability to blackmail, drunkenness, and so on.

In 1950 Congress supplemented the President's executive orders and specifically authorized the heads of eleven sensitive agencies and departments including Defense, State, and Atomic Energy Commission, to suspend immediately without pay any employee whose suspension was necessary in the interest of national security. Before final dismissal permanent employees were entitled to a hearing and a written statement of the decision. The President was authorized to apply these provisions to other agencies whenever he deemed it necessary "in the best interests of national security."

The Eisenhower security program

In 1953 President Eisenhower abolished the Truman loyalty program and, citing the 1950 Act of Congress as his authority, extended the security program to all executive employees, ordering their immediate dismissal whenever the head of an agency had reason to believe they were security risks because of disloyalty or for such things as drug addiction, refusal to testify before a congressional committee, or general untrustworthiness. Loyalty boards were abolished, but permanent employees were to be given hearings before panels drawn from outside their agencies. The head of the agency, however, was to make the final decision. As before, the government was not required to disclose the names of its informants.

Then in 1956 the Supreme Court, without ruling directly on the constitutionality of the security program, held in *Cole* v. *Young* that the President had unlawfully extended the security programs to nonsensitive agencies. A majority ruled that Congress had intended to authorize summary dismissal only for employees who held positions immediately involving the nation's safety.

It may be that Congress will revive the *status quo ante* and extend the security programs again to all employees. Even if it does not, existing civil service regulations make it unlawful for members of Communist organizations to work for the government and permit dismissal of all employees "for the good of the service," a category broad enough to cover most persons thought to be security risks. At any rate, some kind of check on the loyalty of employees will be with us for a long time.

Does the government have the constitutional power to dismiss employees because of doubts as to their loyalty? The Supreme Court has not as yet ruled directly on this question. However, the Court of Appeals for the District of Columbia sustained the Truman loyalty program on the ground that the government has authority to establish reasonable qualifications for its employees. Moreover, the court held that employees are not entitled to due process, since employment is a privilege and not a right, and a loyalty-security hearing is not a criminal proceeding.[19] The dissenting judge argued that although employees have no right to jobs, they do have a right to be treated fairly and not to be branded as disloyal by "faceless informers." In a modern context, the judge argued, loyalty hearings should be considered punitive, and a fair hearing should be required. Moreover, at least in nonsensitive positions, the judge continued, national security cannot justify punishment of employees because of their peaceful use of political rights.

Although the Supreme Court has not clearly ruled on the security-loyalty programs, it has, as we have noted, restricted the scope of summary dismissals to sensitive positions, not on constitutional but on legislative grounds. It has also ruled that the Attorney General should notify organizations and give them a hearing before listing them as subversive[20]—a ruling, however, that the Attorney General has interpreted as merely requiring a hearing before new organizations are added to his list. And the Supreme Court has ruled it unconstitutional to dismiss persons automatically solely because they claim the privilege against self-incrimination and refuse to answer questions.[21]

Are the security programs necessary? There is much difference of opinion about this question, a difference compounded by partisan claims and counterclaims. Most appear to believe that the tactics of Communists and the needs of the cold war require unusual precautions in sensitive agencies such as the Federal Bureau of Investigation, Atomic Energy Commission, military agencies, State Department, and others exposed to internal subversion and foreign influence. But opinions differ more sharply on the need to check on thousands of others. Some argue that security programs are clumsy instruments that catch not spies but only harmless people who have been careless. Others argue that no matter how fairly administered, a program that calls for a checking on the loyalty of millions of Americans will create an atmosphere of fear and suspicion that will do more harm than might be done by a few Communists in positions which do not involve national security. Among others, a distinguished committee of the Association of the Bar of the City of New York has recommended that the security program be limited to sensitive positions.[22] Others believe with Justice Clark, however,

[19] *Bailey* v. *Richardson* (1950).

[20] *Joint Anti-Fascist Refugee Committee* v. *McGrath* (1951).

[21] *Slochower* v. *Board of Higher Education* (1956).

[22] *Report* of the Special Committee on the Federal Loyalty-Security Program of the Association of the Bar of the City of New York (New York: Dodd, Mead & Company, 1956).

that "It is unrealistic to say that the Government can be protected merely by applying the act to sensitive jobs. One never knows just which job is sensitive. The janitor might prove to be in as important a spot security-wise as the top employee in the building."[23]

Are the programs being administered wisely and fairly? Here again, a difference of opinion. Congressional committees and some private organizations have cited examples of miscarriages of justice that they claim to be typical.[24] Others argue that this evidence is not representative. But there is less doubt that the morale of civil servants has suffered. A Task Force of the Second Hoover Commission reported:

The administrative aspect of the problem . . . has had depressing effects upon morale. The handling of security cases has been such as to lead to very general views within the service that determinations are not sufficiently judicial in character (spirit being as important as procedure) to make for valid decisions. There is fear that honest and loyal employees can be destroyed by unsupported or trivial derogatory charges; there is fear that security authorities can be stampeded; and there is fear that security charges are at times a means of making "political" removals.[25]

State loyalty oaths

In addition to the twenty million people subject to investigation by the national government, many state and local governments impose loyalty oaths. In various states, oaths are required of public employees, attorneys, teachers, authors and publishers of textbooks, students in the state university, public accountants, occupants of public housing projects, organizations such as churches seeking tax exemptions, persons applying for unemployment compensation, and wrestlers and fighters (this last was needed, according to the executive secretary of the state athletic commission, because "we didn't want to license a professional boxer and wrestler who might become a hero in the eyes of youthful fans, and then discover later he was a Communist."[26]

There are many kinds of loyalty oaths. Officials have for a long time been required to swear or affirm loyalty to the Constitution and the United States.

[23] Dissenting in *Cole* v. *Young* (1956).

[24] For example see, Subcommittee on Reorganization of the Senate Committee on Government Operations, *Hearings, Commission on Government Operations,* March 8-11, 14-18, 1955, 84 Cong., 1st Sess: Subcommittee on Constitutional Rights of Senate Committee on the Judiciary, *Hearings, Security and Constitutional Rights,* November 14-18, 21-23, 25, 28-29, 1955, 84 Cong., 2nd Sess; Adam Yarmolinsky, *Case Studies in Personnel Security.* (Washington, D.C.: The Bureau of National Affairs, Inc., 1955).

[25] Commission on Organization of the Executive Branch of the Government, *Task Force Report on Personnel and Civil Service* (Washington, D.C.: Government Printing Office, 1955), p. 121.

[26] See testimony before Subcommittee on Constitutional Rights of the Senate Committee on the Judiciary, *Hearings, Security and Constitutional Rights,* 84 Cong., 2 Sess., November 17, 1955, p. 350.

Few object to these. Rather, it is the *test* oaths now being imposed that have caused some controversy. The more carefully drawn oaths require a statement that one does not advocate the overthrow of government by unlawful means or belong knowingly to any organization that does. The Supreme Court has ruled that these oaths may be required as a condition of public employment, provided they are restricted to knowing membership and do not disqualify persons who innocently join such organizations without knowledge of their character.[27] Whether governments can require oaths as a condition of receiving general public benefits and services, such as public housing, has not been clearly determined.[28]

As a result of the security programs, loyalty oaths, the Smith Act, Internal Security Act, the Communist Control Act and similar state laws, Communists and those suspected of communistic sympathies are subject to many restrictions. A Communist alien may not enter the United States, may be deported if in the United States, and cannot become an American citizen. Communists cannot work for the federal and most state and local governments, or for defense industries. They cannot teach in most school systems, cannot be labor union officials, cannot travel abroad. They must identify their propaganda and account for all money spent by their party, publicize the names of all their members, and run the risk of being prosecuted for advocating the overthrow of the government by force and contributing to the establishment of totalitarian dictatorships. They are denied the right to run for elective office. These are governmental restrictions on their activities and do not include the many serious limitations that grow out of public abhorrence of their ideas and activities.

Some feel that certain of these restrictions on Communists are unjustified. Although these people would use every resource to ferret out and punish anyone guilty of espionage or conspiracy to overthrow the government by force, they would not penalize persons who have combined for political action nor deny antidemocrats the right to use the regular methods of democratic government. They would not place any restrictions on Communists except those absolutely necessary to protect national safety, not because of love for Communists, but because of the belief that democracy itself is endangered when any group is punished because of abhorrence of its ideas. As Justice Jackson stated it, "the right of every American to equal treatment before the law is wrapped up in the same constitutional bundle with those of the communists."

Others support these governmental limitations on communist activity. They argue that the Communists are not entitled to any rights, since they are at war with the basic premises of our existence. They argue that unless

[27] *Wieman* v. *Updegraff* (1952).
[28] *Lawson* v. *Housing Authority* (1955), a decision of the Wisconsin Supreme Court, and *Rudder* v. *United States* (1955), a decision of the United States Court of Appeals for the District of Columbia, both held as unconstitutional oaths for tenants living in public housing projects,

the Communists are carefully controlled, they will use their posture of legitimate political party to camouflage their underground activities. Restrictions to strip the veil of secrecy from their actions will protect innocent persons. Democratic government, it is contended, must curtail the freedom of those who would destroy freedom.

All recognize that we must act to protect ourselves against those who are conspiring to destroy our democratic system. On the other hand, all

"Fire!"

Courtesy of Herblock

recognize that we must proceed with care in order not to jeopardize the rights that we have developed to prevent the growth of tyranny. An undemocratic but relatively insignificant minority does not justify panic. It is exactly in times of national peril that the traditional liberties must be strengthened and protected.

Summary

By way of summary: The Constitution protects the rights of freedom of conscience and expression from infringement by either national or state governments. These basic liberties are threatened by enemies of democracy. But in protecting freedom from totalitarians, the resort—either from malice or ignorance—to totalitarian patterns of thought control is a danger that cannot be overlooked.

Head-on assaults on freedom are relatively rare. The real threat comes from flanking attacks. Liberty can be lost by erosion as well as by flood. A little impairment here, a little there—never enough at one time to alert the lethargic—this is the danger. Eternal vigilance as the price of liberty is more than a Fourth of July truism; it is a statement of profound truth.

IT SHOULD BE CLEAR FROM THE LAST CHAPTER that certain rights are essential to the operation of democratic government. But liberties are not merely vital *means* to the goal of self-government. They are *ends* in themselves. In its chronological as well as in its logical and moral sense, our forefathers took the precept, "Before government there is man and his natural rights." Today we no longer accept the doctrine of an artificially established social compact and its pregovernmental state of nature, but we still believe in the moral primacy of man over government and in the equality of men. We speak of human and civil rights rather than natural rights, but the essential belief is the same, the belief in the dignity and fundamental worth of *each* individual.

The Declaration of Independence proclaims in ringing terms, "We hold these truths to be self-evident, that *all* men are created equal, that they are endowed by their Creator with certain unalienable rights, that among these are life, liberty, and the pursuit of happiness. That to *secure* these rights, governments are instituted among men . . ." This creed is older than the Declaration of Independence; at least as old as the teachings of Judaism and Christianity. The implementation of this creed, bringing our practice into conformity with our principles, has long been a central preoccupation of Americans.

Today no problem is more pervasive nor has a heavier impact upon all facets of American life than the issue of securing the basic civil rights for all Americans. American Democracy, despite its many triumphs, has not granted its full privileges to all the people, especially not to Negroes. Because we know this and feel it deeply, the issue of civil rights is one of the burning questions facing Americans today. This question has been of importance in our presidential elections, and almost every year it gives rise to a battle in Congress. It is an issue of world-wide significance, for our attacks on communist totalitarianism seem to lose force in the light of obvious chinks in our own democratic armor. And colored peoples in Asia and Africa, our actual

7 ★

Equality

under

the law

and potential allies, follow our treatment of Negroes with more than casual interest.

Our denial of equal rights to Negroes stands in the face of the equality that the Declaration of Independence acknowledges and the Constitution demands. Under our Constitution each person has the right to live and work and participate in public affairs, free of laws that might discriminate against him because of his race, religion, or other irrelevant characteristics. The Constitution is concerned with protecting these civil rights in two ways—first, by seeing to it that *government* itself imposes no discriminatory barriers; second, by conferring authority on the national and state governments to act positively to protect civil rights, as well as property rights, against interference by other private *individuals*. In this chapter we shall be concerned with both these aspects, government as *threat* to civil rights and government as their *protector*.

THE LIFE—AND DEATH?—OF JIM CROW

As slaves, Negroes mixed freely with whites. Even after reconstruction, Negroes could legally ride trains and attend shows. Most Negroes did not go to schools, and there was no hint of social equality. Social custom and economic status, rather than law, kept distance between the two races. Despite arguments that laws would be ineffective to change social behavior, measures were passed to enforce segregation, so that by the end of the nineteenth century many states and cities in the South had made it a crime for whites and Negroes to ride in the same car on a train, attend the same theater, or go to the same schools. Jim Crow laws, as they came to be called, soon blanketed all phases of southern life.

Is segregation constitutional in the face of the Fourteenth Amendment, which declares: "No state [including any subdivision of the state] shall deny to any person within its jurisdiction the equal protection of the laws . . ."? (Although there is no equal protection clause limiting the national government, discrimination on its part is made unconstitutional by the due process clause of the Fifth Amendment.) Supporters of Jim Crow argue that the Constitution simply forbids arbitrary classification and discrimination and that classification on the basis of race is not arbitrary and not discriminatory as long as equal facilities are made available to Negroes. Furthermore, they insist that such laws are necessary to preserve public order.

Before turning to the constitutionality of segregation laws in particular, it may help to discuss briefly the more general problem of classification. All laws classify, but what the Constitution forbids is *unreasonable* and *discriminatory* classification. A classification is "unreasonable" when there is no relation between the classes it creates and permissible governmental goals. For example, a law prohibiting redheads from voting would be unreasonable because there is no relation between red hair and the ability to vote. On the other hand, laws denying to people under 21 the right to vote, to marry without permission of their parents, or to drive a car are not discriminatory but reasonable classifications. To most adults, at least, there is a possible relation between maturity and voting, marrying, or driving. Similarly, the following classifications have been held to be reasonable: classification of persons on the basis of income for tax purposes, classification of property according to its use for zoning purposes, classification of employers by the number of their employees for the collection of social security taxes, classification of persons by sex for purposes of regulating hours and conditions of employment.

Classifications based on religion or race, especially the latter, have caused the most controversy. The courts have been especially suspicious of such classifications, allowing them only in the most unusual cases, when the government can demonstrate some exceptional justification and show some relation between race or religion and the permissible goal. Hence, a California statute that forbade aliens ineligible for citizenship to fish off coastal waters was held to violate the equal protection clause[1] (prior to 1953 this classification included Japanese).

Is segregation discrimination?

Since the Fourteenth Amendment and the abolition of slavery, it has been unconstitutional to discriminate against Negroes or any other racial or religious groups. But in 1896 the Supreme Court in *Plessy* v. *Ferguson* endorsed the view that segregation is not discrimination and that states could by law require the separation of races in public places so long as *equal accommodations* for all were provided. Even equal accommodations were not required except in the case of services provided out of *public funds* or in a limited category of *public utilities* such as trains and busses. Under this celebrated *separate-but-equal* formula, several states, most of them in the South, have enforced segregation in transportation, places of public accommodation such as inns, restaurants, theaters, and in educational establishments.

For many years it was a notorious fact that in practice the "equal" part of the formula was meaningless. The Supreme Court itself required only a slight nod on the part of the state in the direction of equality. In 1899, for example, the Court found no denial of equal protection in the fact that a county provided a high school for white children, but none for the sixty colored children of the district.[2] Even today, despite much improvement, educational facilities available for Negroes in segregated states are frequently in fact not equal to those provided for whites. For example, a recent report of the United States Office of Education stated that to equalize Negro and white schools, 44 per cent would have to be added to Negro

---

[1] *Takahashi* v. *Fish & Game Commission* (1948).
[2] *Cumming* v. *County Board of Education.*

teachers' salaries, 80 per cent to all current expenses, and 400 per cent to plant and equipment. Until recently, at least, the states with segregation together had fourteen medical schools for whites, none for Negroes; sixteen law schools for whites, five for Negroes; over fifteen engineering schools for whites, none for Negroes; five dental schools for whites, none for Negroes.

In the late 1930's the attack against the separate-but-equal doctrine, especially as applied to education, was intensified. It was argued that the doctrine was a sham. Facts were cited to show that in practice separate-but-equal meant discrimination against Negroes. The justices were not then willing, however, to upset openly such a long line of precedents. Rather, they began to undermine the formula. They started to look closely at the facts of each situation. They were no longer satisfied by mere token moves to provide equal accommodations.

The next step came in 1950 when the Court, although specifically refusing either to affirm or reject the doctrine of *Plessy* v. *Ferguson,* ruled (*Sweatt* v. *Painter*) that Negroes must be admitted to the University of Texas Law School because the school for Negroes did not in fact afford equal facilities. But the most significant aspect of the opinion was that the Court made it clear that it would almost be impossible for a state to establish a law school for Negroes which could in fact be equal to the one provided for whites. Even if the number of faculty, variety of courses, scope of library, availability of law reviews, reputation of faculty, and standing of the Negro school were equal to that for whites, the exclusion from the Negro law school of 85 per cent of the state's population would itself make the Negro school inferior. Negroes would not have the same opportunity as whites to study with the men who in the future would be lawyers, witnesses, jurors, judges in his state.

In other cases involving higher education, especially at the professional and graduate level, the Supreme Court did not overrule the separate-but-equal doctrine, but it insisted upon equality in fact. Expenditures for Negro educational facilities were increased, but it was estimated that really equalizing facilities would cost a billion dollars. By 1952 segregation in higher education was beginning to break down, partly because of the financial strain. Eight of the fourteen southern state universities, and a number of private colleges, were admitting Negroes to graduate schools; one state university was admitting them to the undergraduate division.

The end of separate-but-equal

Finally, in 1953 the separate-but-equal doctrine was squarely challenged when five cases involving elementary and secondary schools went to the Supreme Court. In May 1954 came perhaps the most important Supreme Court decision since the Dred Scott case a century before. "Does segregation of children in public schools solely on the basis of race," asked Chief

Justice Warren, speaking for a unanimous court, "even though the physical facilities and other 'tangible' factors may be equal, deprive the children of the minority group of equal educational opportunity? We believe that it does." Citing psychological and sociological findings as well as legal sources in its footnotes, the brief opinion stated:

In these days it is doubtful that any child may reasonably be expected to succeed in life if he is denied the opportunity of an education. . . . To separate [children] from others of similar age and qualifications solely because of their race generates a feeling of inferiority as to their status in the community that may affect their hearts and minds in a way unlikely ever to be undone.[3]

This historic decision of 1954 came in the midst of charged feelings in both the North and the South. Recognizing the formidable problems, the Court provided a "breathing-space" during which discussion could take place before the Court as to the best ways of carrying out the decision.

A year later, May 1955, after hearing suggestions from state attorney generals, the High Court directed the district judges (who could best take into account the great variety of local conditions) to supervise the implementation of the segregation decree by local school authorities. The Supreme Court established a general formula which, although allowing local officials time to make adjustments, requires the school authorities to show good faith and make a prompt and reasonable start toward admitting Negroes to public schools on a racially nondiscriminatory basis "with all deliberate speed."[4] In a subsequent decision, however, the Supreme Court stated that no delay to make adjustments is to be allowed in the case of professional graduate schools. Negroes should promptly be admitted if otherwise qualified.[5]

Following the Brown case, the Court moved into other areas besides school segregation. It ruled that laws requiring segregation in the use of public recreational facilities (parks, golf courses, etc.) and in the use of public transportation facilities are unconstitutional.[6] The Interstate Commerce Commission had already held it illegal for interstate carriers to segregate interstate passengers.[7] Clearly, the separate-but-equal formula is dead, and governmentally required racial segregation is unconstitutional.

DESEGREGATION—PROBLEM AND PROMISE

The Supreme Court has spoken. But it is one thing for judges to declare segregation unconstitutional, and it is something else to abolish segrega-

[3] *Brown* v. *Board of Education* (1954).
[4] *Brown* v. *Board of Education* (1955).
[5] *Hawkins* v. *Florida Control Board* (1956).
[6] *Mayor and City Council of Baltimore* v. *Dawson* (1955); *Holmes* v. *Atlanta* (1955), and *Gayle* v. *Browder* (1956).
[7] *NAACP* v. *St. Louis-San Francisco Railway Co.* (1955).

tion. The Court has posed for the American people—for President and
Congress, for state officials, for school administrators, ultimately for all
of us—a problem and a challenge of enormous complexity and importance.
What has been the response in the few years since the Court declared
public school segregation unconstitutional?

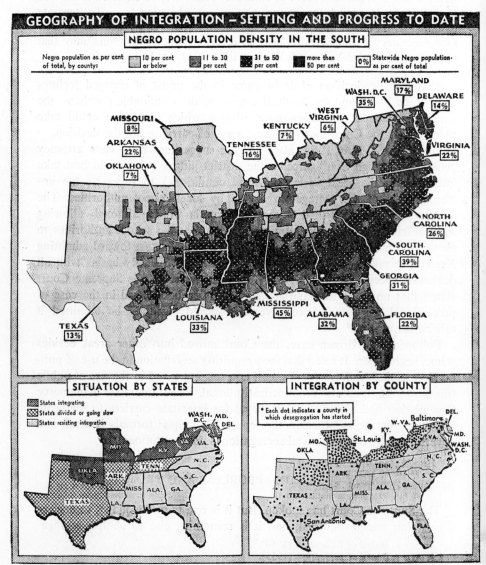

GEOGRAPHY OF INTEGRATION – SETTING AND PROGRESS TO DATE

NEGRO POPULATION DENSITY IN THE SOUTH

Negro population as per cent of total, by county:
▢ 10 per cent or below   ▢ 11 to 30 per cent   ▨ 31 to 50 per cent   ▉ more than 50 per cent   0% Statewide Negro population as per cent of total

MARYLAND 17%
WASH. D.C. 35%
DELAWARE 14%
WEST VIRGINIA 6%
MISSOURI 8%
KENTUCKY 7%
ARKANSAS 22%
TENNESSEE 16%
OKLAHOMA 7%
VIRGINIA 22%
NORTH CAROLINA 26%
SOUTH CAROLINA 39%
GEORGIA 31%
MISSISSIPPI 45%
ALABAMA 32%
FLORIDA 22%
TEXAS 13%
LOUISIANA 33%

SITUATION BY STATES

▨ States integrating
▨ States divided or going slow
▢ States resisting integration

WASH. MD.
D.C.   DEL
MO   W VA   VA.
OKLA   KY   N.C.
ARK   TENN   S.C.
TEXAS   MISS   ALA   GA.
LA   FLA.

INTEGRATION BY COUNTY

• Each dot indicates a county in which desegregation has started

DEL.
W. VA. Baltimore
St.Louis   KY.   VA.   MD.
MO.   WASH. D.C.
OKLA   TENN.   N.C.
ARK.   S.C.
TEXAS   MISS.   ALA.   GA.
LA.
San Antonio   FLA.

Courtesy THE NEW YORK TIMES. *Lower right map is based on latest data available from Southern Reporting Service in Nashville.*

Response in the South

Many white southerners are openly defiant. The Supreme Court, they argue, is ignoring strongly held racial attitudes, the relationship between the two races that has been worked out over the years, the traditional way of life in the South. According to their views, Negroes are not "ready" for integration because of failings in culture, health, and even in innate capacities. Integration, it is charged, is a step toward "race mongrelization." Many southerners also disagree strongly with the Supreme Court's interpretation of the Constitution. To them the decision is bad law and bad policy. "No decision of the Supreme Court," said former Governor Talmadge of Georgia, "is entitled to any greater moral weight than its content merits."[8]

A host of organizations have sprung up in the South to fight for continued school segregation. By 1957 the most important of these, the White Citizens Council movement, claimed a membership of half a million. Among the members are some political leaders who, either out of real beliefs or desire to survive politically, have joined with those who, although decrying force, have urged parents to barricade and boycott schools—even at the risk of creating riots—in order to prevent Negro children from attending schools formerly reserved for whites.

Other white southerners have reacted differently. They were disturbed by the Brown case and share some of the feelings described above. But they see little possibility of changing the decision or of resisting it. The decision, it is felt, simply speeds up an inevitable trend. Resignedly accepting it as the law of the land, they have set about trying to effectuate it. To these people the problem becomes one of working out methods of integrating the schools as smoothly and quietly as possible.

Some white southerners are wholeheartedly for integration. They join with many in considering the Supreme Court decision as a milestone in the long struggle to achieve equal treatment and to bring into reality the promise of the American Revolution. Outside the South the decision has been applauded by church leaders, labor organizations, newspaper editors, teachers, President Eisenhower, and by many others, including, of course, Negroes in both North and South.

Those who approve the decision differ as to how to proceed. Some of these, such as the leaders of the National Association for the Advancement of Colored People (see page 249) argue that too much delay will play into the hands of the segregationists and make integration much harder in the long run. The Supreme Court decision, they hold, calls for a drastic but necessary surgical operation, and prolonging the operation will only make matters worse. They point to incidents of violence and extremism as resulting in part from delay and obstruction. They are concerned, moreover, about the millions of Negro children now in schools, who will miss their

[8] Herman E. Talmadge, "School Systems, Segregation and the Supreme Court," *Mercer Law Review,* Vol. VI, 1954-1955.

chance to a first-class education if integration is delayed. Negro children, according to this view, do not need a good primary or high school education in ten years; they need it now.

Finally, there is a "moderate" position. In both the North and the South the moderates feel that history is on the side of eventual desegregation. They point to the fact that the South is changing economically and socially. It is becoming more industrialized and urbanized. It is attracting annually thousands of people from the North and West who are bringing with them new social and political attitudes. Many southern Negroes are still moving north; others staying in the South are winning the right to vote (see pp. 185-188). "All in all," says an Arkansas editor, "the cultural, political, and economic isolation which is necessary to the preservation of the region's special identity is breaking down—and southerners themselves are speeding the process in many ways . . ."[9] The great question is whether moderate opinion can contribute to the implementation of the desegregation decision, in view of the numberless difficulties involved.

Can the desegregation decision be carried out?

In 1954, at the time of the Brown case, segregation was required in seventeen states stretching from Texas to the Atlantic coast, from the Gulf of Mexico to Missouri, Kentucky, and West Virginia. Three years later the picture was this: full compliance had been achieved, or almost achieved, in the District of Columbia, Missouri, and Maryland. Only in the District had the schools been fully integrated. In Missouri 88 per cent of the Negro pupils were eligible to attend desegregated schools; in Maryland about 85 per cent; and in both these states, officials were moving to comply. Partial compliance is found in Arkansas, Delaware, Kentucky, Oklahoma, Tennessee, Texas, and West Virginia. In these states, moderates—in some cases over considerable opposition—had made significant strides toward desegregation. Most counties in Oklahoma and West Virginia had started desegregation. About one-third of Delaware's Negro children were eligible to attend mixed schools. In west Texas, desegregation was almost complete; but in east Texas, where live 90 per cent of the Negroes in the state, only one district had agreed to integration. In Kentucky, over 100 counties had moved to comply with the Supreme Court's orders, but here again little had been done in the fifteen counties where most Negroes live. In Arkansas and Tennessee, action was more restricted. Although in some of these states desegregation has been resisted by violent demonstrations, moderate governors supported school boards by using their executive powers, sometimes even to the point of dispatching the National Guard to back up the school authorities.

In Alabama, Florida, Georgia, Louisiana, Mississippi, North Carolina,

[9] Harry S. Ashmore, *The Negro and the Schools* (Chapel Hill: The University of North Carolina Press, 1954), pp. 138-139.

South Carolina, and Virginia, where 1,900,000 Negro children live, opposition to the Supreme Court's decision remained intense. In Virginia, North Carolina, and Louisiana, Negroes had been admitted to some of the state universities, but in all these states there were no desegregated primary or secondary schools. Outright resistance to the Supreme Court's decrees and a vigorous search for ways of getting around the decision were the chief responses of the white enfranchised majority controlling the governments of these states.

Southern state legislatures have reached back to pre-Civil War precedents and asserted the right to "interpose" and resist the Supreme Court's mandates, some even claiming the right to declare the Court's decisions null and void. They have all taken constitutional and legal measures to undermine the Court's decrees, primarily by giving officials power to abolish public schools and subsidize private education or to deny state money to local authorities who allow mixed schools. Although many of these measures may eventually be declared unconstitutional, they make possible years of delay.

In Congress, representatives from the Deep South have attacked the Supreme Court justices, and many have proposed that the Court's powers be curtailed. They took the lead in inducing 96 southern representatives and senators, including many important committee chairmen, to sign a manifesto stating that they would take all lawful means to resist the Court's mandate and reverse its decision.

In this region, moderates find it difficult to express their opinions or develop programs of action. Those favoring cautious but deliberate steps toward integration are subject to intense pressures. Public officials favoring moderate stands have often been defeated at the polls. Teachers who favor integration endanger their jobs. In some localities advocacy of integration is considered criminal. Negroes are unable to use democratic techniques of defending their rights because of the many barriers imposed between them and the ballot boxes. Some states have banned legal action by the NAACP and other groups working to enforce the Supreme Court's decisions. Such developments highlight the fact that in the Deep South the actions in the years immediately following the School Segregation Cases have served to sharpen rather than to solve the issues involved and have minimized, at least for the moment, the role and voice of the moderates.

The challenge presented by the Supreme Court is a national, not just a southern one. Many communities in the North face the same problems as those below the Mason-Dixon. Although for many years segregation has not been required by the laws in the North, residential segregation, social pressures, gerrymandering of school districts, and other devices have created in many communities a condition of school segregation. Negroes face other kinds of discrimination. In some northern cities they have had their homes bombed and their lives threatened. They face discrimination in housing, jobs, and public places. Well-meaning northerners and southerners, white and Negro, have a great deal to learn from one another as the American people face years of continuing effort to make the promise of the American Dream a reality to all its citizens.

"It's an American, not a southern problem."

Courtesy THE RICHMOND TIMES-DISPATCH *and* Seibel

THE GREAT GAME OF HOW-NOT-TO

Courtesy ST. LOUIS POST-DISPATCH
and Fitzpatrick

Two views of desegregation.

COLOR BAR AT THE POLLS

Equality in the exercise of the suffrage is in many ways one of the most important civil rights still denied many Negroes, for his social, economic, and legal rights depend largely on the Negro's success in gaining—and exercising—the right to vote. His struggle for the ballot has been more than a fight for his rights; from Civil War days to the present, it has been part of a broader struggle for political power, on the part of both Negroes and whites. (See Chapter 12 for more general discussion of the struggle for the vote and suffrage regulations.)

After the Civil War the Radical Republicans gained control, first of Congress and then of the White House. They wanted to insure the continued freedom of the newly liberated Negroes in the face of southerners who were still hostile to emancipation. Even more, they wanted to secure the supremacy of the North and of the Republican party. How to do this? A simple formula was worked out—to establish *constitutionally* the Negro's citizenship and his right to vote. To these ends the Fourteenth and Fifteenth amendments were adopted.

The Fourteenth Amendment, after making Negroes citizens (see page 230), denies states the right to deprive any person of the equal protection of the laws. Hence, a state law is unconstitutional if it gives whites the right to vote but denies it to Negroes who are otherwise qualified. The Fourteenth Amendment further declares that if, in any state, for any reason other than participation in rebellion or other crime, male citizens 21 years and over are denied the right to vote, the state is to suffer a proportionate loss of congressional representation.

Although the Fourteenth Amendment implicitly denies states the right to deprive Negroes of the suffrage because of their race, the Fifteenth Amendment makes this crystal clear. It states, "The right of citizens of the United States to vote shall not be denied or abridged by the United States or by any State on account of race, color, or previous condition of servitude."

For over a decade after the Civil War, the Fourteenth and Fifteenth amendments were backed up by federal troops. In some states Negroes in alliance with northern Radical Republicans ("carpetbaggers") and some white southerners ("scalawags") assumed full control of government. The strange new regimes passed good laws as well as bad, but uniformly they were loathed and feared by "patriotic" white southerners.

Then came the counterrevolution. Even before federal troops were withdrawn from the South in 1877, white Democrats had begun to regain power. Organizing secret societies like the Kings of the White Camelia and the dread Ku Klux Klan, the aroused southerners set out to restore southern government to white rule. Their methods were often threats, force, and fraud. Hearing stories of midnight shootings, burnings, and whippings, Negroes concluded, practically, that it would be healthier to stay away from the polls. And the carpetbaggers began to retreat North.

Circumventing the Fourteenth and Fifteenth amendments "legally"

Regaining control of the state governments, southern Democrats resolved to keep the Negro in his inferior position. They set up a battery of legal devices to bar him from the polls. It may seem strange that southerners bothered with "legal" methods when they had already regained control by force. But they had a definite purpose. The southern whites could not depend on their own side to enforce illegal restrictions on voting. They knew that some of their number, especially in localities where the Negroes were a small minority, had little fear that the ex-slaves could assume much power. They knew also that some whites could not resist the temptation to turn to Negroes for votes in fights among whites for office.

"Legal" disfranchisement did not get underway, however, until the end of the nineteenth century. For the first time since before the Civil War there were two strong parties in the South, the Democrats and the Populists, and they both started to bid for the Negroes' votes. Southerners feared that the Negro might come to have a balance-of-power role. To continue to rely on illegal means also had practical disadvantages: it undermined the moral fabric of the society, and for many years there was the possibility that a too flagrant use of force and fraud might cause a Republican President and Congress to intervene.

So the southerners turned to "legal" disfranchisement. The method was relatively simple. The Constitution forbids discrimination because of race or color. If laws could be passed that on their face seemed not to deprive people of the right to vote because of race or color but that in fact did, it would be difficult for the Negroes to challenge the laws before the courts. Some whites protested, saying that these laws could be two-sided weapons usable against both whites and blacks. But leaders in the black belt, where Negroes were a large minority and sometimes a majority, skillfully played on memories of Negro rule and northern intervention. "The disfranchisement movement of the 'nineties," says V. O. Key, "gave the southern states the most impressive systems of obstacles between the voter and the ballot box known to the democratic world."[10] By the end of the century this machinery for disfranchisement included:

Good character tests. Most southern constitutions deny the ballot to persons who have been convicted of crimes, including minor offenses such as vagrancy. These were adopted on the theory that Negroes would more often fall afoul of the law than whites.

Literacy tests. Most states in the South and some elsewhere require that citizens wishing to vote must correctly read or write sections of the state constitution. The ability to read is an important safeguard against fraud and uninformed voting, but the requirement can also be used to deprive unfairly both Negroes and whites of the right to vote.

Understanding tests. Some states require voters to demonstrate to the satisfaction of the election officials that they understand the meaning of the national and state constitutions. These tests give wide discretion to officials, who may ask Negroes impossibly difficult questions.

Poll tax. The best-known although not the most important disfranchising device is, in effect, a voluntary tax paid only by those who would vote. Thus it puts a price tag on the ballot. The price is not high—one to two dollars a year—but in some states it is cumulative (to vote one must make up for any past payments he missed). The poll tax probably keeps the ballot from more whites than Negroes. Since 1920, North Carolina, Louisiana, Florida, Georgia, South Carolina, and Tennessee have abolished the poll

10 V. O. Key, Jr., *Southern Politics* (New York: Alfred A. Knopf, Inc., 1949), p. 555.

tax as a prerequisite to voting; it remains in five other states in the South. Poll taxes are found in many other states, but they are levied whether one votes or not and are not a prerequisite for voting.

The laws are not important merely in themselves. Almost everything depends on the way that they are administered. In the South, white election officers apply these laws. White policemen stand guard at the polls. White judges hear appeals—if any—from decisions of local officials. Many southerners, convinced of the rightness of their cause, make no attempt to conceal the purpose of these laws. Asked whether a proposed state constitutional provision was intended to discriminate against the Negro, Carter Glass, later a United States senator, exclaimed: "Discrimination! Why, that is precisely what we propose; that, exactly, is what this convention was elected for—to discriminate to the very extremity of permissible action under the limitations of the Federal Constitution, with a view to the elimination of every Negro voter who can be gotten rid of, legally. . . ."[11]

This discrimination was made easy by *exemptions* designed to enable whites to vote but not Negroes. The most notorious of these was the "grandfather" clause, which exempted from literacy and property tests those who had voted before the Civil War or whose parents or grandparents had. This was a way of saying "whites only." Grandfather clauses were outlawed by the Supreme Court in 1915. Other ways of discrimination still exist, especially in the handling of literacy and understanding tests. Whites can be asked simple questions about the Constitution; Negroes can be given questions that would baffle a Supreme Court justice—perhaps while a critical crowd looks on. Or whites can be let off altogether. In Louisiana, for example, where illiterates may qualify to vote, 49,603 white voters made their marks instead of writing their names in a recent election, but only two Negroes did so. It is easy also for registration officers to seize on the smallest error in an application blank as an excuse to disqualify a hopeful voter.

The white primary

"The southern states show a kind of defense in depth against the would-be Negro voter," says Dayton McKean; "if one barrier falls before courts or legislatures there is another behind it."[12] The white primary is an excellent example of this defense in depth. It takes its importance from the fact that the decisive political contests in the South are the *primary* elections in the parties (see Chapter 14); in most sections of the South, Republicans are so scarce that the Democratic nominee is an easy winner in the fall elec-

[11] Quoted by Paul Lewinson, *Race, Class, and Party* (New York: Oxford University Press, 1932), p. 86.

[12] Dayton McKean, *Party and Pressure Politics* (Boston: Houghton Mifflin Company, 1949), p. 66.

tions. It was only natural that after the Civil War the Democratic party would become the party of whites and that Negroes would enter the Republican fold. As the Republicans lost power, however, some Negroes wanted to cast ballots in the Democratic primary, where their votes meant something. And in hot party fights some Democrats were tempted to appeal for Negro votes. To protect their party from the threat of infiltration, the Democrats passed party rules forbidding Negroes from voting in Democratic primaries.

The Fourteenth and Fifteenth amendments forbid the *states* to deprive Negroes of the right to vote. For many years the white primary seemed to be constitutional because it was argued that it was set up privately by the *party* and not by the *state*. The theory was that a political party, as a voluntary association, had as much right to exclude people as did the Elks, or the Daughters of the American Revolution, or any other social group, since the Constitution forbids only *governmental* discrimination. The problem seemed to be merely to avoid any connection between the Democratic party and the state government. For a short period in Texas, the white primary ran afoul of the Constitution when first the state legislature barred Negroes from the Democratic primary, and then the legislature authorized the executive committee of the party to prescribe the qualifications. Since in both these cases the discrimination against Negroes was authorized by *law,* the Supreme Court ruled that this was state action contrary to the Fourteenth Amendment.[13] But when the state legislature said nothing and the state convention of the Democratic party ruled that only whites could vote, the Supreme Court (in *Grovey* v. *Townsend,* 1935) decided that the exclusion rule was the work of the party itself, as a voluntary association, and that state action was not involved either directly or indirectly.

A few years later, however, a revamped Supreme Court—now the "Roosevelt" Court—looked squarely at the facts and ruled in a Louisiana case (*United States* v. *Classic,* 1941) that a primary is really an election. Soon after this, the Texas white primary finally came to an end. The Supreme Court, flatly overruling its *Grovey* decision, held in the important case of *Smith* v. *Allwright,* 1944, that the Texas primary was a basic part of the machinery for choosing officials, and that discrimination by the *party* was as unconstitutional as discrimination by the state.

Constitutionally the white primary was dead. But the white southerners did not take this decision lying down. The white primary, after all, was the simplest and most efficient of all the methods of disfranchisement. South Carolina, trying to make party primaries completely private, repealed all its laws—147 of them—that controlled nominations. But the maneuver failed. A federal district judge, an old South Carolinian himself, held that

---

[13] *Nixon* v. *Herndon* (1927) and *Nixon* v. *Condon* (1932).

this was an obvious subterfuge to circumvent the Supreme Court's rulings, that if the state turned over to the party the control of the elections in which public officials were chosen, the party was no longer a private club, and that it was "time for South Carolina to rejoin the Union."[14]

In Texas an attempt was made to set up a primary before the primary. The Jaybird Association, insisting that it was a private club, held elections from which Negroes were excluded. Only the winner of that election filed in the Democratic primary, so Negroes had no voice in selecting public officials. Again the Supreme Court struck this down as a violation of the Fifteenth Amendment.[15]

Other states, especially those in the Deep South, have tried further means of preserving the white primary or have fallen back on tried-and-true literacy and understanding tests. How successful some of these devices will be, in the face of hostility from courts and from many whites as well as Negroes, only the future will tell.[16]

Is the Negro winning his long fight for the ballot? Probably he is, although very slowly. Outside the South neither social pressure nor legal barriers stand in the way of Negroes exercising the vote. In recent decades northern Negroes have begun to use their power at the polls to insist upon better treatment for Negroes in both North and South. But Negro voting is still small in the South. It has increased sharply in recent years, although the rate of increase has slowed considerably, in some places even dropped off, in the face of intensified white hostility during recent years (see page 181). But Negroes are even winning office. At least a dozen Southern cities have Negroes serving on city councils or boards of education. The poll tax will probably go in time, and the courts may become increasingly rigorous in halting discriminatory administration of the election law.

Much depends on the attitude of southern whites. Some of them want the Negro to have the ballot, but perhaps not too soon. Hodding Carter, editor of a Mississippi newspaper, has said that Negroes must have more education before they vote, so that they will learn to vote not "by color and for color," but in terms of enlightened self-interest. He wants more schools for Negroes, decent housing, better health facilities. "We want all this too," say Negro leaders, "but how can we get it unless we can vote to get it at the polls?" Probably increased voting by Negroes and better education for Negroes must go hand in hand, the one fortifying the other. But full Negro voting will not come automatically by abolishing literacy tests and the like. Negro voters—like voters everywhere—stay away from the polls largely because of ignorance and inertia and because of a sense of inferiority and of the importance of "keeping in their places"—products of decades of deference and subordination. In the last analysis, the problem

[14] *Brown* v. *Baskin* (1948).
[15] *Terry* v. *Adams* (1953).
[16] One understanding test has already been declared unconstitutional. *Davis* v. *Schnell* (1949).

is both to give the Negro the right to vote, and also to help him see that he has a moral duty to participate in democratic politics.

GOVERNMENT AS PROTECTOR OF CIVIL RIGHTS

When the "government" does something, it frequently reflects the desires of many more people than the public officials involved. Some citizens, for example, who believe that Negroes and whites should be compelled to sit apart in buses may try to persuade the bus company managers to segregate passengers. Indeed, they may threaten them with a boycott unless they do so. Or they may try to use governmental power to achieve their goals. They might try to get the city council or state legislature to make it illegal for whites and Negroes to ride on buses except in separate sections. Opposition might be aroused. Clearly, conflicts are more than struggles between "the government" and "the people." Rather, they involve conflicts *among* people, some of whom wish to use the instruments of government to do certain things that others believe should not be done.

Hence, civil rights can be threatened not only by an abusive government but also by private action. In the United States, for example, the right to life is jeopardized more frequently by lawless individuals than by public officials. The right to pursue one's happiness without suffering disabilities because of race or religion is as often interfered with by private individuals as it is by laws or public officials.

What about the use of government to *protect* civil rights? The policeman can be a means of oppression; but to a man facing an angry mob who dislikes his religion or his race, the policeman can be a friend.

State power and private discrimination

The equal protection clause restricts only *state* governmental discrimination. Unless the denial of equal protection is sanctioned or supported by the state, the Fourteenth Amendment offers no protection. An important question, therefore, is "What is state action?" The New York Court of Appeals (that state's highest court) by a close vote decided, for example, that discrimination by a redevelopment housing corporation to which the state had given tax exemption and other privileges was not discrimination supported by the state.[17] The Supreme Court refused to review this decision, but it has held that state courts may not enforce racial restrictive covenants (provisions attached to deeds restricting the sale of property to certain groups) because this would be the use of state power to back up private discrimination.[18]

May states deny equal protection by acts of *omission* as well as com-

[17] *Dorsey* v. *Stuyvesant Town Corp.* (1950).
[18] *Shelley* v. *Kraemer* (1948) and *Barrows* v. *Jackson* (1953).

mission? Does the state deny an individual his life without due process of law when, for example, it permits private individuals to lynch him? Or is there a violation of the equal protection clause if the state permits private mobs to keep Negroes out of public schools? The Supreme Court has accepted the view that there is a denial of equal protection when state officials willfully permit others to deprive a person of civil rights. Some judges have gone farther and held that certain functions such as conducting elections and education are governmental and that a state denies equal protection if it turns these tasks over to private groups and permits them to discriminate. But the Supreme Court has refused to accept the view that the equal protection clause *requires* the states to protect individuals against discrimination by private individuals.

State civil rights powers and programs

Although private acts of discrimination are not unconstitutional, states have ample authority to make these acts *illegal*. Just as the states have the authority to protect a person's property rights against infringement by others, so it has the authority to protect civil rights. The Constitution, in fact, places the primary responsibility for protecting civil rights on the states and, as we shall shortly note, gives the national government only limited power in this respect.

Should states use their police powers to make it illegal for landlords, employers, trade unions, private schools, and others to discriminate against persons because of their race or religion? "No," say some people. Prejudice cannot be eradicated by laws. Others respond that it is not prejudice that the laws are aimed at, but protection against the *effects* of prejudice—overt discriminatory action that deprives people of their rights to be treated as human beings and American citizens.

Some see a special responsibility of state and local governments to act in this field. They have opposed national interference not because they favor discrimination but because they believe the state and local governments can do a better job than the national government. Not everyone, however, approves of governmental protection, regardless of which government acts. They believe that such laws are beyond the scope of government, that laws are ineffective, or even that discrimination is not really so bad, anyway.

In the South, as we have noted, laws *require* segregation. But in other states laws *illegalize* segregation or any other kind of racial or religious discrimination in certain areas. Eleven states outlaw discrimination in employment on public works, twenty-eight forbid discrimination in employment in civil service, eighteen prohibit unions from controlling membership on the basis of race or religion, nineteen forbid inquiries as to religious affiliations in hiring teachers. Some states have made it contrary to the law to discriminate racially or religiously against those seeking to enter colleges or universities, except, of course, religious schools. About twenty states have made it a criminal or civil offense for owners of places of recreation and public accommodation to refuse to serve patrons because of their race, religion, or place of national origin. And recently, over a dozen states have applied these civil rights statutes to *private* employment.

The weakness of many of these statutes that were passed many years ago is that no special provision is made for enforcement except by regular court action instituted by the attorney general or by local prosecutors. And many state courts have so narrowly construed the laws that they have seriously reduced their coverage. Frequently, the persons discriminated against are persons without the knowledge or the money to bring the matter to the attention of the prosecutors, who may be loaded down with other duties. And the task is one of education as well as enforcement. For these reasons, recent years have witnessed a new approach in the fight against discrimination.

A dozen states and about thirty cities have established special commissions with the single and special duty of acting in a positive manner. New York, for example, created in 1945 a five-member commission charged with the investigation and hearing of complaints in cases of alleged discrimination in employment.

The New York law forbids both employers and labor unions from excluding individuals from employment or union membership on account of race, creed, or national origin. Any person aggrieved by such discrimination may file a complaint with the commission. If, after investigation, the commission finds that the claim is justified, the commission first attempts by "conference, conciliation and persuasion" to remove the cause. If these efforts fail, a formal hearing takes place before at least three members of the commission. If, as a result of these hearings, the commission discovers evidence of violation of the law, it issues an order to cease and desist from such practices. Violation of a commission order is punishable by imprisonment for not more than one year or by a fine of not more than $500 or both. The courts may review decisions of the commission on questions of law. The commission has seldom had to rely upon its coercive powers, and through a program of education and publicity has done much to improve human relations in this most difficult of all fields.

In other states and cities the experience has been much the same. In some cases the commissions have had only advisory rather than regulatory powers and cannot punish offenders. As yet no such commissions have been established in areas where segregation has long been the customary pattern of behavior. But the efforts of these commissions are being watched with interest and each year bills are introduced in state legislatures to create new ones. More and more states seem to be concluding that civil rights are at least as worthy of legal protection as property rights.

NATIONAL PROTECTION OF CIVIL RIGHTS:
QUEST FOR A SWORD[19]

State governments have ample constitutional power, if the people wish to use it, to protect the rights of citizens against the attacks of other individuals. But what of the *national* government?

One of the most hotly debated topics of contemporary politics is whether the national government should provide positive protection for civil rights. Some believe that this is a function of state governments. They argue that federal interference would extend the scope of national government into areas that have traditionally belonged to the states, upset the federal system, and lead to dangerous centralization of power. Furthermore, federal legislation would be ineffective and would create more problems than it would solve. A national program could not be enforced contrary to local public opinion. On the other hand, the states can best protect civil rights by laws adapted to the attitudes of the local citizenry.

In answer, it is argued that the states have failed to protect civil liberties. The President's Committee on Civil Rights (see pp. 197-198) pointed out that "many of the most serious wrongs against individual rights are committed by private persons or by local public officers." Moreover, as James W. Prothro has pointed out, "not one concrete step toward full rights for the southern Negro—whether in voting or education—has been achieved without the intervention of the national government."[20] Second, rather than provide governmental support for the prejudices of local majorities, these are the very attitudes that require federal action. "It is sound policy to use the idealism and prestige of our whole people to check the wayward tendencies of a part of them." Third, violation of civil liberties is not a local matter, but has national and international implications. Finally, every person who lives under the Constitution is entitled to his freedoms, and the national government "must take the lead in safeguarding the civil rights of all Americans."

There are at least two difficulties in securing a federal civil rights program: first a constitutional problem, and second a political problem.

Does the national government have the constitutional power to guarantee civil rights? The Constitution does not grant to the central government any such specific authority, and this power is in large part reserved to the states. But the federal government has the *implied* power to protect some rights that grow out of its very existence and character, and in addition the Thirteenth, Fourteenth, and Fifteenth amendments authorize a limited federal program.

Implied powers to protect civil rights. Certain rights arise from the relationship between the individual and the federal government, and are essen-

---

[19] This is the title of an excellent volume by Robert K. Carr, published by Cornell University Press, 1947.

[20] James W. Prothro, "A Southerner's View of a Southerner's Book," *The Reporter*, September 20, 1956, p. 4f

tial for the effective operation of that government. These rights the national government can protect against encroachment by private citizens and state and local officials. The Supreme Court has not specified what these rights are, nor has Congress since the days of Reconstruction tried to use its implied powers. But the following are among those that Congress can protect against both private and governmental interference: the right of a qualified voter to vote for members of Congress, including a primary, and have that vote properly counted; the right to be free from mob violence while being held by a federal officer; the right to petition Congress about problems relating to the national government.

Although Congress has had little disposition to use its powers, several laws protect the rights mentioned above, and one criminal statute provides for a $5000 fine and not more than ten years' imprisonment if two or more persons conspire to injure any *citizen* in the enjoyment of any right or privilege secured to him by the Constitution. This conspiracy law protects only citizens, and by a 1951 decision of the Supreme Court (with the concurrence of only four justices) it was further ruled that it "applies only to interference with rights which arise from the relation of the victim and the Federal Government, and not to interference by state officers with rights which the Federal Government merely guarantees from abridgment by the States."[21] Civil action is also authorized, but the narrow construction of the statute has made it of little value to protect civil rights against private conspirators.

Thirteenth Amendment. This amendment gives the national government power to protect the basic right of personal freedom. By its own force it freed the slaves of 1865 and prevents all forms of involuntary servitude. For example, it voids state laws that force persons who have received advance wages either to work for the employer or to stand trial for fraud with the presumption of evidence against them. Further, the amendment gives Congress power to legislate against interference with the right to be free by private persons as well as public officials. If the powers of Congress under this amendment had been interpreted as liberally as its commerce powers, Congress could legislate against discrimination by private persons who refuse to permit Negroes to enter public places such as a hotel or theater. It was argued that this discrimination foisted upon Negroes a badge of slavery and inferior status contrary to the Thirteenth Amendment. But in 1883 the Supreme Court ruled otherwise in the *Civil Rights Cases.* The authority of Congress was limited to preventing coerced labor or restrictions on freedom of movement.

Congress has supplemented the Thirteenth Amendment by making it a federal crime to hold anyone in a condition of slavery or of peonage (peonage is a condition of compulsory servitude based upon the indebtedness of the slave to the master). The Anti-Slavery and Anti-Peonage Acts are archaic,

[21] *United States* v. *Williams* (1951).

ambiguous, and difficult to enforce, but they have been used to punish those who take advantage of the ignorant and the timid. Slavery is often identified with the old South, but it is not unknown in twentieth century America.

Among the more recent cases, for example, was that of Albert S. Johnson, an Arkansas plantation owner, who by threats forced fourteen persons to work for him, in some cases for as long as two and one-half years. Johnson was later convicted of violating the Anti-Peonage Act. Working with these old laws and aided by higher employment, federal officers have drastically reduced the practice of peonage during recent years.

The Fourteenth and Fifteenth amendments as grants of national power

The Fourteenth Amendment limited the states, but it also conferred upon Congress the power to enforce its prohibitions. Any hope that this amendment would serve as a grant of substantial power to Congress to protect civil rights was quickly dashed by the Supreme Court. Believing it had power to take positive action, Congress in 1875 made it a federal crime to deny anyone accommodations in public conveyances, hotels, theaters, or the like because of his race or color. When the law was applied to an innkeeper, however, the Supreme Court invalidated it in the *Civil Rights Cases* on the ground that the Fourteenth Amendment restricts only *governmental* and not private action, and that Congress may protect persons against denial of equal protection only in those instances where a state or local government in some way supports the denial.

The Fourteenth Amendment authorizes Congress also to decrease the congressional representation of any state that denies the vote to males 21 years of age and over for reasons other than crime or rebellion. This provision has become a dead letter. Many states deny adult males the right to vote for reasons other than crime or rebellion—illiteracy or failure to pay poll taxes, for example. No action has ever been or is likely to be taken under this section.

The Fifteenth Amendment, like the Fourteenth, applies only to governmental action and therefore authorizes Congress to protect persons only against abridgment of their rights by national or state officials.

Since the days of Reconstruction Congress has not used even the limited power it does have. But certain laws protect persons against deprivation of their rights by state officials, the most important being one that makes it a crime for any person acting under the *color of law* to deprive willfully any person of any rights, privileges, or immunities secured or protected by the Constitution or laws of the United States. Thus any state officer, for example, who willfully deprives any person of his right to a fair trial, or right to vote in any election because of his color, or who uses force to obtain a confession, is liable to prosecution by the federal government.[22] Federal laws also author-

[22] *Williams* v. *United States* (1951) and cases cited therein.

ize civil suits for damages, or other relief, against those who use state powers to deny or abridge federal civil rights.

To summarize, the most important national civil rights statutes are as follows: slavery and peonage are outlawed; it is a crime for any person acting under the color of law to deprive any person of a right secured to him by the Constitution or federal law; it is a crime for two or more persons to conspire to deprive any citizen of any right or privilege secured to him by the Constitution or federal law (but this statute does not protect rights secured against deprivation by states); persons denied *federal* rights by persons acting under color of *state* law may seek civil relief in *federal* courts; and citizens deprived of certain limited *federal* rights by *private* conspirators may also seek civil relief. Other statutes provided limited protection for some narrowly defined rights.

Congress could, if it so desired, expand the coverage of existing statutes and use its other powers to provide national protection for civil rights. For example, Congress might forbid any employer who is engaged in interstate commerce or whose business affects this commerce to refuse to hire any person because of his race, color, or religion. Or Congress could make as a condition of its grants of money to the states that it be used for the benefit of all persons without respect to race, color, or creed. The war power can also be used to support civil rights legislation.

In short, despite the constitutional obstacles to a federal civil rights program, Congress has all the power it might need. Whatever the constitutional obstacles, the real check is a *political* one. From 1873 to the present the national government has not been able to use the power it has. The filibuster and the determination of those who oppose such a program have been the real obstacles, not the Constitution.

Federal civil rights enforcement

Some signs indicate, however, that a more positive federal civil rights program can be anticipated. A small step was taken in 1938 by Attorney General Frank Murphy (later a justice of the Supreme Court) when he established a civil rights section in the criminal division of the Department of Justice. He instructed the section to take whatever action was legally permissible to protect civil rights. "In a democracy," he said, "an important function of the law enforcement branch of government is the aggressive protection of fundamental rights inherent in a free people."

With only a few attorneys and with inadequate congressional support, the civil rights section has struggled to work out a feasible program. The section has been forced to work with antiquated laws. These laws, relics of the Reconstruction Era, are all that remain of a civil rights program after the heart was cut out by judges who did not look with favor upon federal essays in this field. The civil rights section has to depend for enforcement of these laws on judges and juries in the state and district in which the crime was committed; in many cases this means trial by jurors who share the prejudices that led to the original deprivation of civil rights.

A revolting episode furnishes a good illustration of the difficulties involved in a federal program of protecting civil liberties. Late one night in the year 1944, a car stopped in the front of the home of Robert Hall, a citizen of the United States and of Georgia. Three men got out of the car: Screws, the county sheriff, Jones, a policeman, and Kelly, a special deputy. The men had been drinking. Screws had threatened Hall a few days before that he was going to get him, and Hall was terrified. When Screws flashed a warrant charging Hall with the theft of a tire, Hall resisted, but the three men pushed him into the waiting car. After the car pulled up in front of the courthouse square, Hall got out and immediately the three men "began beating him with their fists and with a solid-bar blackjack about eight inches long and weighing two pounds."[23] Hall was handcuffed and defenseless, and the three men continued to beat him from fifteen to thirty minutes. Then the unconscious Hall was dragged feet first through the courthouse into the jail and thrown upon the floor. He died within an hour.

Here was a clear case of murder, but as the days went by no action was taken against the three men. Hall was a Negro. The matter was brought to the attention of the civil rights section, but they waited for the state to punish the guilty men. Still no action. Finally, the civil rights section started to move. The federal criminal code provides that the penalty for willfully subjecting any inhabitant, under color of any law, to the deprivation of any rights, privileges, or immunities secured or protected by the Constitution and laws of the United States is a fine of not more than $1000 and prison sentence for not more than one year. Admittedly this was puny punishment for such a heinous crime, puny even when combined with the possible two-year imprisonment for conspiring to violate a federal law. But at least it would serve notice that the federal government was not powerless to protect rights guaranteed by the Constitution against abuse by state officers.

The federal officials had to move carefully lest they arouse local pressures against outside interference. Only southern attorneys were assigned to the case and an indictment was secured against Screws and his companions for willfully causing Hall to be deprived of rights secured or protected to him by the Fourteenth Amendment, specifically the right not to be deprived of life without due process of law; the right to be tried, upon the charge on which he was arrested, by due process, and if found guilty to be punished in accordance with the laws.

The case proceeded. In his charge to the jury, the judge said that if the jurors believed that the facts were established then the "defendants would be depriving the prisoner of certain constitutional rights guaranteed to him by

[23] *Screws* v. *United States* (1945).

the Constitution of the United States and consented to by the State of Georgia."

The jury's verdict, "Guilty." But the case was not over. An appeal was taken by Screws to the court of appeals, which affirmed the decision of the trial court. The case then went to the Supreme Court. A majority of the justices felt (there were five separate opinions) that the trial judge had erred in failing to instruct the jury that Screws and his companions could be held guilty of the crime only if they had "willfully" intended to deprive Hall of his constitutional rights, that it was not sufficient that Screws had a generally bad purpose. The justices had no doubt that Congress could have legislated more clearly to designate such activities as criminal, but they felt that unless "willfullness" was included in the interpretation to the jury of the law, it would not meet the requirement that criminal laws establish clearly what is being made criminal.

The case was returned to the district courts for a retrial. Screws and his friends were duly retried. This time they were acquitted.

The Screws decision made it difficult to secure prosecutions, but the civil rights section has been more successful in other cases. For example, in 1947 Crews, a Florida town marshall, arrested a Negro and, after beating him with a heavy whip, forced him to jump from a high bridge into a river. The Negro drowned, Crews was successfully convicted of violating the civil rights statute, and this time the conviction was sustained.[24] In another case, a private detective (but authorized by law to act as a special police officer) was convicted of extracting a confession from a prisoner by physical brutality.[25] Thus the civil rights section has been instrumental in alerting local police officers especially, but also private individuals, to the fact that they violate at their own peril rights and privileges protected by the Constitution and federal laws.

To secure these rights—the Presidents act

In recent years, the executive power of the presidency has been used with more vigor than has the legislative power of the Congress to secure equal treatment for all. In large part, this is due to the difference in nature between the President's constituency and that of the congressional majority (see Chapter 18). In 1941, President Roosevelt established a Committee on Fair Employment Practices. This order instructed all federal agencies to include in their contracts for war production a provision obliging the contractor not to discriminate, instructed the committee to investigate complaints of discrimination, conduct hearings, make findings of fact, and take appropriate steps to eliminate such discrimination. In June 1945, Congress refused to appropriate funds for the committee, and it passed out of existence.

[24] *Crews* v. *United States* (1947).
[25] *Williams* v. *United States* (1951).

After Congress failed to give its support to this venture, President Truman, by executive order, established a Committee on Government Contract Compliance composed of representatives of federal agencies. Since membership was made up of officials of the national government, no additional funds were needed for their operation. But, at the same time, the Committee had little power. After the end of the war, with the lessening urgency to use fully our manpower, the nondiscrimination clause in government contracts had little practical effect. The Committee on Government Contract Compliance reported that federal agencies had failed to establish any procedures to insure compliance and that its only weapon to enforce the clause was to terminate the contracts.

In 1953, President Eisenhower attempted to invigorate this program. He replaced the Committee on Government Contract Compliance with a Government Contract Committee composed of nine public members in addition to the representatives of six government agencies. Although responsibility for gaining compliance with the nondiscriminatory clause still rests with the head of the contracting agency, the Government Contract Committee is authorized to receive complaints and make recommendations to agencies concerned. To emphasize the importance of its functions, President Eisenhower appointed the Vice-President of the United States as chairman of the committee.

Another example of the use of executive power, and perhaps one of the most significant steps leading toward a national civil rights program, was the issuance of a report in 1947 by the President's Committee on Civil Rights. This commission, appointed by President Truman, was composed of outstanding persons from all walks of life and from both major political parties. Its report, *To Secure These Rights,* directed national attention to the whole problem of civil rights, and it stressed *positive* federal action. After directing public attention to the wholesale and daily denial of rights to many American citizens, the report recommended, among other things, abolishing segregation in the District of Columbia and in the armed forces, enlarging the civil rights section and strengthening the laws it enforced, the passage of federal antilynching and fair employment practices laws, and abolishing poll taxes. The report, of course, received a mixed reaction, and many groups were very much opposed to its recommendations.

The President submitted many of these proposals to Congress, where they met the almost united opposition of southern legislators. Opponents held that the federal government had no responsibility in this field; some opposed the report on the ground that it wanted too many changes too fast. President Truman, however, issued two executive orders in July 1948, one establishing a fair employment practices system for federal employment, and the other establishing a committee on equality of treatment and opportunity in the armed forces. The latter, after studying the problem, made a report to the President on the basis of which he, as commander in chief, ordered the armed forces to end their segregation practices as fast as practicable. Much progress has been made in this direction.

Continuing the policies of his predecessor, President Eisenhower has thrown the weight of the presidential office behind civil rights protection. Besides strengthening the Government Contract Committee, the President used his authority as commander in chief to push forward the ending of segregation in the armed forces and in military installations. The Department of Justice argued before the courts against the separate-but-equal doctrine. An old District of Columbia law illegalizing discrimination against a person in any eating place because of race or color has been enforced. The President also asked Congress to strengthen the civil rights section, to authorize the Department of Justice to seek civil remedies against violations of civil rights statutes, to increase authority of national officers to prosecute those who deny Negroes the right to vote because of their race, and to establish a commission to hear civil rights complaints. The President renewed these requests as he entered his second term early in 1957.

Summary

1. The Declaration of Independence and the Constitution assert the equal right of all men to life, liberty, property, and pursuit of their happiness.

2. The Constitution denies to both national and state governments right to discriminate against people because of race or religion and specifically deprives government of the authority to deny any person the right to vote because of race or color.

3. In the South there are still barriers in the way of Negroes voting, but the Supreme Court has been leading the other judges to scrutinize more carefully measures that in effect deprive Negroes of the right to vote. In recent years the white primary has been declared unconstitutional.

4. The Supreme Court has held public school segregation unconstitutional and has ordered school districts to take good faith action toward desegregation of public schools. The High Court has also gone very far toward the position that the Constitution is color-blind and that racial classifications are unconstitutional.

5. Considerable resistance has been aroused to the desegregation of public schools, especially in the Deep South.

6. States have the constitutional power to classify as a crime racial or religious discrimination by employers, trade unions, and operators of public places. Some states have done so.

7. The national government's constitutional authority to protect persons against discrimination is more restricted. It may legislate to protect against discrimination or denial of due process by those who act under the color of law. It also could use its other grants of power to protect civil rights, but in recent years the southern bloc in the Senate has been able to block civil rights legislation.

8. Executive power of the President has been used to protect civil rights, including a more vigorous enforcement of the civil rights statutes that were passed during Reconstruction, especially the statute making it a federal crime for persons acting under the color of state law to deprive people of equal protection or due process.

9. The struggle to achieve equality under the law is far from over.

M
AN'S STRUGGLE FOR FREEDOM HAS BEEN
chiefly a struggle against governmental tyranny. Until recent times (and even today the situation exists in many lands) government was in the hands of a few who often used their power to further their own interests; hence the emphasis in the Constitution on limiting government's power.

In the United States, governments are now elected by the majority and are, for the most part, responsive to their wishes. But most Americans still believe that constitutional restraints are necessary. Government is distinguished from other institutions in that it has the authority to use physical force. Liberty against government is no less important than it used to be, even though (as stressed in the last chapter) liberty against *private* interference is also a vital matter.

Laws in some measure infringe upon someone's freedom. The government has the authority under certain conditions to deprive people not only of their liberty of action but of the use of their property and, in extreme circumstances, of their lives. But under our Constitution, governmental authority may be used to deprive a person of his life, liberty, or property only if it is done by *reasonable laws* and through *just* and *fair procedures*. These restraints on *government* are the subject of this chapter.

LIBERTY AND PROPERTY

We frequently speak of property rights; actually we mean the right to own, use, rent, invest, or contract about property. Property has no rights; it is the *individual's* right *in* property that government, as one of its primary functions, protects. From Aristotle, through the English philosopher Harrington, to the Founding Fathers has come the emphasis on the close connection between liberty and private ownership of property, between property and power. This strain of thought has been emphasized in American political thinking and reflected in American political institutions. A major purpose of the framers of our Constitution was to establish a government strong enough to protect each person's

★ 8

Rights to

life, liberty,

and property

200

right to use and enjoy his property, and, at the same time, a government so limited that it could not interfere with men's rights in property.

The framers were, as we saw in Chapter 2, especially disturbed by the actions of some of the state legislatures in behalf of debtors and at the expense of creditors. Hence the Constitution forbids the states to make anything except gold or silver legal tender for the payment of debts or to pass any law "impairing the obligation of contracts."

Rights of the party of the first part

The *obligation of contracts clause* was aimed at state laws that extended the period during which debtors could meet their payments or that otherwise relieved them of their legal obligations. The framers had in mind an ordinary contract between private persons. But, in characteristic fashion, Chief Justice Marshall expanded the meaning of this clause to include transactions to which the state government itself was a party. So, when the Georgia legislature annulled a fraudulent grant of a large tract of land made by a previous legislature, the annulling legislation was declared to be an unconstitutional impairment of the obligation of a contract.[1]

The next step was to include *corporate* charters within the meaning of contracts so that franchises granted by a state to a corporation appeared to be irrevocable and untouchable by any subsequent law that would impair the terms of the original franchise.[2]

As a result of these developments the contract clause became for a time the protector of vested rights. In some ways the states' police power to guard the public welfare was seriously limited. Gradually, however, the Court began to restrict the scope of the contract clause. By the 1880's it was established, in the case of *Stone* v. *Mississippi,* that no state could contract away its police power and that all contracts are subject to regulations that promote the general welfare. In 1934 the Supreme Court declared that even contracts between individuals, the very ones the contract clause was intended to protect, could be reasonably modified in order to avert social and economic catastrophe resulting from the depression.[3]

But in the 1880's just as the contract clause ceased to be an important block to state regulation of property, the due process clause took over.

Without due process of law

Some of the most quoted but least understood parts of the Constitution are those clauses in the Fifth and Fourteenth amendments that forbid the national and state governments, respectively, to deny any person his life, liberty, or property without due process of law. Prior to the adoption of the Fourteenth Amendment in 1868 there was little suggestion that due

[1] *Fletcher* v. *Peck* (1810).
[2] *Dartmouth College* v. *Woodward* (1819).
[3] *Home Building and Loan Association* v. *Blaisdell.*

process had other than a *procedural* meaning. Daniel Webster had described due process as requiring "the general law; a law, which hears before it condemns, which proceeds upon inquiry, and renders judgment only after trial." This is the ancient idea that no man be deprived of his life, liberty, or property except in accordance with law and by fair and just procedures. (This *procedural* aspect of due process is discussed later in this chapter.)

Beginning in the 1870's, however, lawyers began to suggest to the Supreme Court that the due process clause prohibited not merely laws that were enforced by arbitrary *procedures,* but laws whose *purpose* was to interfere "unreasonably" and arbitrarily with a person's (including a corporation's) right to own, acquire, sell, and contract about property. At first the Supreme Court refused to broaden due process in this drastic manner, but by the end of the 1880's it finally adopted this new kind of *substantive* due process.

Substantive due process applies to the very *substance* of the law—not merely to the procedures by which a law is enforced. In effect it sets limits to the legislative power. With its adoption, the Supreme Court—not the more obviously political branches of government—became the final judge of the reasonableness of laws, especially of those affecting property rights. Along with the development of substantive due process the concept of *property* was expanded. Property came to include not merely tangible objects such as a man's home and his personal belongings, but such things as stock certificates, control over industrial combines, the right to hire and fire whomever one wished.

From 1890 to 1937 the Supreme Court was virtually the nation's economic arbiter. It was composed for the most part of conservative gentlemen to whom almost any social welfare legislation was an unreasonable interference with the rights of property. Regulation was forbidden unless the government could demonstrate that it was absolutely necessary. The Court refused to permit either the national or state governments to establish minimum wages, regulate prices charged by employment agencies, outlaw "yellow dog" contracts (to name but a few restrictions). These laws, said the justices, were arbitrary interferences with the rights of property owners. The due process clause had elevated the doctrine of laissez faire into a constitutional principle. It came to mean that no man could be deprived of his property even by the due procedures of the law unless the Supreme Court thought the *purpose* of the law was reasonable.

The question of the reasonableness of a law, especially one touching economic matters, is one upon which men differ, depending on their basic political and economic views. The Taft-Hartley Act, for instance, is unreasonable and arbitrary in the eyes of union leaders, but to most business leaders it is an entirely reasonable measure. Evaluation of the reasonableness of a law depends upon a man's economic and social views rather than on his legal training. When the Supreme Court judges laws on the basis of their social and economic merit instead of merely their legal procedures, the Court is acting virtually as a superlegislature.

In 1937 the Supreme Court began a strategic retreat from this position, which had pushed it into the middle of violent political quarrels. The doctrine of laissez faire returned to its status as an economic theory rather than a constitutional check. Today the right to use property is subject to regulation in the public interest; one has the right to use his property under and according to the law. And the law to be constitutional need only be a rational method of promoting or protecting the public welfare. Thus rights in property are, like all rights, subject to limitation when they impinge upon the liberties of others. Today most Americans apparently believe that the complexity and interdependence of society requires greater social control. But regardless of the social necessity no one can be deprived of his property by any government under any pretext except by the due procedures of the law.

The kind of regulation that we have been talking about is that incidental to general regulation. For example, when the government restricts certain areas for industrial or residential purposes, it affects rights in property, perhaps even decreasing their immediate value. The government is not required, however, to remunerate owners for such losses. But if property is taken *directly* the owner must be compensated. The power of government to take private property for public purposes is unquestioned and is known as *eminent domain*. The Constitution subjects this power to the limitation that property can be taken only for a public purpose and the government must pay the owner a fair price. In case of dispute as to what compensation is fair, the decision is made by the courts.

FREEDOM FROM ARBITRARY ARREST, QUESTIONING, AND IMPRISONMENT

James Otis' address in 1761 protesting the arbitrary searches and seizures by English customs officials was the opening salvo of the American Revolution; as John Adams later said, "American independence was then and there born." It is not surprising to find that the Fourth Amendment states:

The right of the people to be secure in their persons, houses, papers, and effects, against unreasonable searches and seizures, shall not be violated, and no Warrants shall issue, but upon probable cause, supported by Oath or affirmation, and particularly describing the place to be searched, and the persons or things to be seized.

In these historic words unreasonable searches and seizures and the general search warrant were outlawed. Today all state constitutions contain a similar clause, and in 1949 the Supreme Court ruled that the due process clause of the Fourteenth Amendment includes protection of one's liberty against unreasonable searches and seizures by state officials.[4]

Though only *unreasonable* searches and seizures are prohibited, in general searches and arrests without proper warrants are unreasonable. Certain narrowly defined exceptions, however, permit arrests to be made and certain searches and seizures undertaken without warrants. The details need not detain us here other than to note that the courts have long permitted an arrest without warrant if a crime is committed in the presence of the arresting officer. As an incident to a lawful arrest, the arrested person may be searched without a warrant, and the officers may seize not only those things on the person arrested but also those things within his immediate control. This doctrine was extended recently when the Supreme Court, over the bitter dissent of several justices, countenanced an extended search without warrant of the *rooms* belonging to a person who had been lawfully arrested.[5] Why are the courts so concerned about this problem? Mainly because experience shows that the impartial judgment of a magistrate is necessary to guard against the often overzealous actions of those engaged in the harsh job of ferreting out crime.

The Fourth Amendment is closely connected with the part of the Fifth Amendment that states, "no person shall be compelled in any criminal case to be a witness against himself." If unconstitutionally seized evidence were used in a criminal trial, it would in effect force a person to testify against himself. Therefore, the Supreme Court has ruled that such evidence may not be introduced in a *federal* court. Furthermore, federal officers may be enjoined from testifying in state courts about evidence they have obtained by illegal methods.[6] But if state officers without the help, knowledge, or connivance of a federal official, obtain evidence by unconstitutional or illegal methods and then turn it over to federal officers, it may be used in federal courts. Although the Supreme Court has held that states may not subject a person to unreasonable searches and seizures, it has ruled that evidence obtained by such methods may be used in *state* courts without violating due process of law. Most states allow the use of evidence no matter how it has been secured, except for that obtained by third-degree methods (see page 205).

The Court has refused to extend the Fourth Amendment to prevent *wire tapping,*[7] but Congress has made evidence so obtained inadmissible in federal courts. The Court, however, has narrowly construed the statute and so long as no wires are tapped or unconstitutional entries made, evi-

---

[4] *Wolf* v. *Colorado.*

[5] *Harris* v. *United States* (1947) modified by *Trupiano* v. *United States* (1948), but *Trupiano* in effect overruled by *United States* v. *Rabinowitz* (1950).

[6] *Rea* v. *United States* (1956).

[7] *Olmstead* v. *United States* (1928).

dence obtained by various listening devices such as detectaphones and concealed radio receivers can be admitted. One On Lee discovered this to his detriment when the Supreme Court permitted the use of evidence obtained by an informer who entered Lee's shop with a concealed radio in his pocket.[8] Lee, thinking he was talking only to a friend, made damaging admissions that were heard by a government agent via the concealed radio.

In interpreting the meaning of the Fourth and Fifth amendments, the justices face the difficult problem of applying the amendments in such a way as to protect individuals against arbitrary police methods without at the same time making it impossible for society to protect itself against criminals.

The third degree

Police questioning of suspects is a major technique to solve crimes. It is also at this point that constitutional rights can be easily shortcircuited. Physical torture, detention incommunicado, and long questioning to force confessions are methods of the police states. Unfortunately such tactics are not unknown in the United States.

Judges, especially those on the Supreme Court, have used their power to try to stamp out police brutalities. The High Court has ruled that any trial in which a confession secured by physical torture has been used cannot be allowed to stand. Nor are convictions based solely on confessions wrung by psychological coercion any more valid.[9] Furthermore, the Supreme Court as supervisor of federal justice has adopted a role for *federal* courts (known as the *McNabb ruling,* announced in the case of *McNabb* v. *United States,* 1943) that prevents the use of any confession obtained while a person is being illegally detained by federal officers whether given voluntarily or not. Federal police are required to take promptly all persons whom they have arrested before a United States commissioner so that the person may be informed of his constitutional rights, get in touch with friends, and seek the assistance of legal advice.

One of the rights that the commissioner will stress is that the Fifth Amendment guarantees that *no person shall be compelled to testify against himself* in criminal prosecutions. Although it directly pertains to criminal trials, it also protects those in any national governmental proceeding. What is the right to remain silent?

The right to remain silent

During the seventeenth century in England, Star Chamber and High Commission courts tried to force confessions of heresy and sedition from

[8] *On Lee* v. *United States* (1952).
[9] *Stein* v. *New York* (1953).

religious dissenters. It was out of the struggle against these practices that the British privilege against *self-incrimination* developed. As applied in federal criminal prosecutions, the accused may, if he wishes, refuse to take the stand to answer questions on the grounds of self-incrimination. If the accused does take the stand, however, he cannot claim the privilege to prevent cross-examination by the prosecution.

Before other governmental agencies, such as a congressional committee or grand jury, a witness' right to remain silent is restricted to the right to refuse to answer questions that might place him in jeopardy of legal punishment. The privilege is a personal one and is not available to protect corporations or associations from producing books and papers. Nor can the privilege be invoked in federal proceedings if the claimant fears incrimination under laws of a state. It is not enough that the answers might be embarrassing or lead to public disapproval. But if there is a reasonable ground to think that the answers would support a federal conviction or "furnish a link in the chain of evidence needed to prosecute" for a federal crime, a witness has the constitutional right to refuse to answer.[10] A witness may refuse not only to give evidence showing guilt, but also evidence that merely might lead to prosecution.

Although persons who claim the privilege against self-incrimination may not be thrown in jail for their refusal to answer, they run other risks. Teachers may lose their jobs, lawyers may face disbarment, travelers may be denied passports. The laws of several states require dismissal of employees who refuse to answer, and it is a ground justifying dismissal of federal employees as a security risk. Congress has forbidden the payment of retirement pay or annuities to employees who plead self-incrimination before any federal grand jury, court, or congressional committee. The constitutionality of some of these disabilities has recently been called into question by a Supreme Court ruling that a New York City charter provision calling for the automatic dismissal of any city employee who claims the Fifth Amendment was unconstitutional.[11] However, this decision was narrowly stated and the basic position that the Fifth Amendment protects only against criminal prosecution still stands.

Congress, anxious to force some witnesses to testify about matters involving national security, passed an *Immunity Act* in 1954 establishing a procedure by which immunity from federal and state prosecution may be conferred. Whenever a majority of either house of Congress, two-thirds of the members of a congressional committee, or a United States district attorney deem such action necessary in order to gain information concerning national security, they may petition a federal district judge to grant the witness immunity. Before the judge acts, the Attorney General has to be notified and given a chance to be heard, but the judge has no discretion and must grant

10 *Blau* v. *United States* (1950).
11 *Slochower* v. *Board of Education* (1956).

the immunity. Since witnesses who receive the immunity can no longer be prosecuted, they may be punished if they continue to remain silent.[12]

The writ of habeas corpus

Even though the framers did not think a Bill of Rights necessary, they considered certain rights important enough to include them in the original Constitution. Foremost among these provisions is the one that guarantees that the *writ of habeas corpus will be available unless suspended in time of rebellion or invasion.* The permission for suspension is found in the article setting forth the powers and organization of Congress, and presumably only Congress can suspend the writ. When President Lincoln suspended the writ during the Civil War, Congress subsequently and retroactively authorized him to do so.

There are several kinds of writs of habeas corpus and, as developed in the United States, it has several uses. Simply stated, it is a court order to any official having a person in his custody, directing that he bring forth the prisoner and explain to the court the reasons for the confinement. A person held in custody applies under oath (probably through his attorney) stating why he believes that he is being held unlawfully. The judge then issues a rule to show cause why the writ should not be issued, to which the jailer is required to answer. Testimony can be taken if there is a dispute over the facts. If the judge feels that the prisoner is being unlawfully detained, he orders the prisoner's release.

The case of Messrs. Duncan and White is a good example of one use of the writ. Duncan and White were civilians being held by military authorities in Hawaii during World War II on the basis of conviction by military tribunals. They filed petitions for writs of habeas corpus in the District Court of Hawaii. Their petitions cited both statutory and constitutional reasons to prove that the military had no right to keep them in prison. The court then asked the proper military officers to show cause why the petition should not be granted. The military replied that Hawaii had become part of an active theater of war, that the writ of habeas corpus had been suspended and martial law had been established, and that consequently the district court had no jurisdiction to issue the writs. Moreover, the military answered, assuming that the writ of habeas corpus had not been suspended, it should not be issued in this case because the trials of Duncan and White by military tribunals were valid. After hearing both sides, the district court, whose action was eventually approved by the Supreme Court, agreed with Duncan and White, and issued the writs ordering their release.[13]

State courts may not issue writs to federal officials, since the power of state courts does not reach federal officers. However, a federal judge may issue writs to *state* officers whenever it appears that a person is being held

[12] *Ullman* v. *United States* (1956).
[13] *Duncan* v. *Kahanamoku* (1946).

in violation of a federal law, treaty, or the Constitution. Although federal judges hear a sizable number of habeas corpus cases, the applicant must first show that he has exhausted his remedies at state law, and persons are released only in the most unusual circumstances. Recently, protest has been growing against the habeas corpus jurisdiction of federal district judges. Some state officials have asked that the federal district courts be denied the power to nullify state court judgments in criminal cases. On the other hand, many oppose any action to restrict the full use of this important procedure which, simple as it appears, gives to all persons within the United States easy access to the courts and protection against arbitrary arrest and imprisonment.

Bills of attainder and ex post facto laws

Neither the national nor the state government can pass any bill of attainder or ex post facto law. A bill of attainder is a legislative act that inflicts punishment on specified individuals without a judicial trial. Bills of attainder have been rare in American history, perhaps the most famous occurring quite recently and emanating from Congress.

In 1943 Representative Martin Dies, then chairman of the House Committee on Un-American Activities, denounced from the floor of Congress thirty-nine officials as "crackpot, radical bureaucrats." He singled out three of these men for special abuse. Shortly afterwards, Congress attached a rider to an appropriation bill that named these three employees and ordered that they should not receive a salary from the federal government unless the President reappointed them and the Senate confirmed their nominations. President Roosevelt refused to resubmit their names because he felt that Congress had acted unconstitutionally. The three men kept on working and sued for their salaries in the Court of Claims. The Court of Claims upheld their appeal and the Supreme Court ruled (in *United States* v. *Lovett,* 1948) that by accusing the men as disloyal and punishing them without a trial, Congress had violated the constitutional prohibition of bills of attainder.

Ex post facto laws are retroactive *criminal* laws that work to the detriment of the accused, for example, a law that makes something a crime that was legal at the time it was done. Moreover, the due process clause protects persons from laws so ambiguously worded that it is impossible for an individual to know what is made criminal. Unless a law establishes a reasonably *ascertainable standard of guilt,* it violates the first requirement of due process.

RIGHTS OF PERSONS ACCUSED OF CRIME

That the innocent will go free and that the guilty will be punished, that rich and poor, educated and ignorant will secure justice under law—these are among the ancient and honorable goals of free nations. To some, the rights of persons accused of crime do not rank in importance with other civil liberties, but as Justice Frankfurter has written, "The history of liberty has largely been the history of observance of procedural safeguards." These safeguards, moreover, have frequently "been forged in controversies involving not very nice people." Their purpose is not to "convenience the guilty but to protect the innocent."

John T. Crook* and the federal courts

Perhaps if we follow the fortunes and misfortunes of John T. Crook, a typical criminal, we can glimpse the meaning and significance of the other constitutional protections for persons accused of crime.

Crook sent circulars through the mails soliciting purchases of stock for a nonexistent gold mine. This is contrary to at least three federal laws. When postal officials uncovered these activities, they went to the district court and secured from the United States commissioner an arrest warrant for Crook and a warrant to search his house for circulars soliciting purchases of gold mine stock. They located Crook at his home, he was arrested for using the mails to defraud, and the circulars were found and seized. Shortly he was brought before a federal district judge, who ordered that Crook be held over until the convening of the next federal *grand jury* in the district and established a bail at $1500. After posting bond, Crook was permitted his freedom as long as he remained within the limits of the judicial district.

When the next grand jury was convened, the United States District Attorney brought before the 23 jurors the evidence which, he felt, showed that Crook had committed a federal crime. Since the grand jurors were not concerned with Crook's guilt or innocence but merely whether there was enough evidence to warrant his trial, Crook himself could not appear before the jury unless they invited or ordered him to do so. A majority of the grand jurors agreed that a trial was justified, so they returned a true bill.

The indictment was served on Crook and he was again ordered before a federal district judge. Crook, a poor and ignorant man, did not know that he had the constitutional right to the *assistance of counsel*, but the judge saw to it that he was informed of his rights and that a lawyer was appointed to undertake his defense. After consulting with his lawyer, Crook entered the plea of "not guilty." Since the Constitution also guarantees to the accused the right to be *informed of the nature and cause of the accusation against him* so that he can prepare his defense, the federal prosecuting officers had carefully seen to it that the indictment was drawn up to state clearly the nature of the offense, and they had given copies to Crook and his lawyer.

* Purely fictitious name.

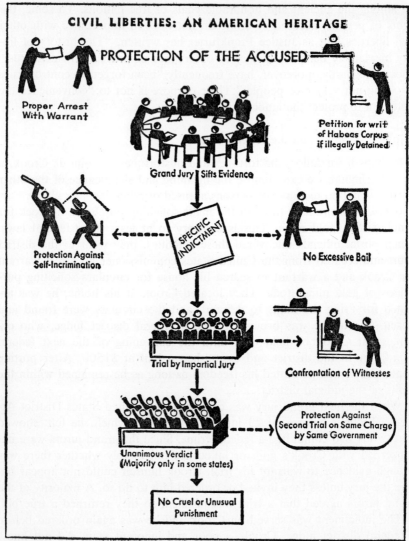

From OUR CONSTITUTIONAL FREEDOMS by Robert E. Cushman, published by the Public Affairs Committee, Inc., and the National Foundation for Education in American Citizenship

After indictment, Crook's bail was raised to $3000, and it became the obligation of the federal government to see that he was given a *speedy and public trial;* the word "speedy" should not be given a literal meaning, however, especially since Crook had to be given time to prepare his defense. His lawyer pointed out that he had the right to a *trial by an impartial jury* selected from the state and district where the crime was committed, but that this right could be waived and the trial could be held before a judge alone. After some thought, however, the attorney advised him to take a chance with the jury.

Crook told his lawyer that George X. Witness had eaten with him on the night on which he was charged with sending the damaging circulars. But when Witness was approached, he was unwilling to appear and to testify at the trial. Consequently, the attorney took advantage of Crook's constitutional right to *obtain witnesses in his favor,* and had the judge subpoena Witness to appear at the trial and testify. Although Witness could have refused to testify on the grounds that his testimony would incriminate himself, he agreed to testify. Crook, however, chose to use his constitutional right not to be a witness against himself and refused to take the witness stand. He knew that if he did so, the prosecution would have a right to cross-examination, and he was fearful of what might be uncovered. The federal judge conducting the trial cautioned the jury about drawing any conclusions from Crook's reluctance to testify—although nothing could prevent the jurors from being affected. All prosecution witnesses appeared in court and were available to defense cross-examination since the Constitution insists that the accused has the right to *be confronted with the witnesses against him.*

At the conclusion of the trial, the jury rendered a verdict of "guilty." The judge then raised the bail to $5000 and announced that he would hand down the sentence on the following Monday. The Eighth Amendment forbids *excessive bails,* the levying of *excessive fines,* and the *inflicting of cruel and unusual punishments.* But in view of Crook's past record and the nature of the offense, the bail could not be considered excessive; nor when the judge, in accordance with the law, gave Crook the maximum punishment of $5000 fine and five years in jail, could it be considered cruel and unusual punishment.

The Constitution forbids the federal government to subject anyone to being placed *twice in jeopardy for the same offense,* and Crook could not again be tried by federal courts for this crime. But double jeopardy does not apply to actions initiated by the defendant. Crook's lawyer appealed to the court of appeals on the ground that the judge had improperly instructed the jury. If the court of appeals had sustained the appeal, which it did not, and ordered a new trial, there would have been no double jeopardy. Finally, the Supreme Court refused to review the case and Crook went to jail.

In addition to the protection of the specific provisions of the Constitution, Crook is entitled to the safeguards that grow out of the more general terms of the *due process clause.* Due process requires that persons receive fair treatment and it goes beyond mere specific forms of procedures. Even if all the specific provisions of the Constitution are scrupulously followed, a trial could be unfair if, for example, the judge were in his words and manner obviously antagonistic and biased against the accused. Or suppose the jury returned a verdict of guilty on the basis of perjured testimony. Although there would be no specific procedural error in these cases, the trial would not be fair, justice would not be done, and the due process clause would be violated.

John T. Crook and the state courts

At the end of three years, Crook was paroled from the federal penitentiary. His freedom was short-lived. The next day he was arrested by *state* officers, brought before a *state* judge, and charged with violating the *state* statutes against fraud. When he protested that he had already been tried and punished by the federal government for using the mails for fraudulent purposes and that the state could not again place him in jeopardy, the judge pointed out that the double jeopardy clause prevents only two trials by the *same* government for the *same* offense,[14] and at any rate the double jeopardy provision is not a limitation on the states.[15]

What rights does Crook have in the state courts? Every state constitution has a bill of rights that binds all state officials but is enforceable only by state courts. These bills of rights contain most of the familiar guarantees for persons accused of crime found in the national Constitution. In addition, the national Constitution itself gives Crook some protection.

After the Supreme Court interpreted the due process clause of the Fourteenth Amendment to include the rights protected by the First Amendment, some began to argue that the Fourteenth Amendment should be interpreted so as to make *all* of the Bill of Rights applicable to the states, especially those provisions having to do with criminal prosecutions. Although some justices of the Supreme Court have espoused this view, the Supreme Court majority has steadfastly refused to accept it. Rather it has ruled that *some* provisions of the Bill of Rights are within the protection of the Fourteenth and *some* are not.

The Fourteenth Amendment and the Bill of Rights

This situation raises an important question: How has the Court distinguished those parts of the Bill of Rights that are thus protected against state infringement from those that are not so protected? The test as laid down by Justice Cardozo for the Court in *Palko* v. *Connecticut* (1937) is that the rights protected by the due process clause are those "implicit in the concept of ordered liberty," those that are so important that neither "liberty nor justice would exist if they were sacrificed." Freedom of thought and speech are, for example, rights so fundamental that there could be no liberty or justice if they were lost; they are "the matrix, the indispensable condition, of nearly every other form of freedom." This is why the due process clause protects these rights. On the other hand, the right to be indicted only by a grand jury, for example, or to have a trial by a jury, are not rights inherent

---

[14] *United States* v. *Lanza* (1922).
[15] *Palko* v. *Connecticut* (1937).

RELATION BETWEEN BILL OF RIGHTS AND THE FOURTEENTH AMENDMENT

DUE PROCESS CLAUSE

PROVISIONS OF NATIONAL BILL OF RIGHTS	WHICH APPLY TO STATES BECAUSE INCLUDED WITHIN THE FOURTEENTH AMENDMENT
First Amendment No law establishing a religion. Freedom of religion. Freedom of speech and press. Freedom of assembly and petition.	*Applies to states.* *Applies to states.* *Applies to states.* *Applies to states.*
Second Amendment Right to keep and bear arms not to be denied.	*Does not apply to states.*
Third Amendment No soldiers to be quartered in private homes during time of peace, and in time of war only as the law allows.	*Does not apply to states except where the taking of private property is involved (see Fifth Amendment below).*
Fourth Amendment No unreasonable searches and seizures.	*Applies to states; however, without violating the Constitution, states may use evidence obtained by an unreasonable search and seizure, provided no force was used to obtain the evidence.*
Fifth Amendment No indictments for serious offenses except by a grand jury. (Does not apply to members of armed forces.)	*Does not apply to states.*
No person shall be twice placed in jeopardy for the same offense.	*Does not apply to states. No specific Supreme Court ruling, but probably the Court would declare unconstitutional several trials of person for same offense if no errors of law were committed in the first trial.*

No person shall be compelled to be a witness against himself in criminal prosecution.	Does not apply to states; however, no state may coerce confessions by physical or mental torture or use such confessions against the defendant who made them.
No witness may be compelled to answer questions which will incriminate him (by interpretation from provisions mentioned just above).	Does not apply to states, but torture may not be used.
No person shall be denied life, liberty, or property without due process of law.	Same provision specifically applied to states by Fourteenth Amendment.
Private property may not be taken except for public use and with just compensation.	Applies to the states, the first provision of the Bill of Rights to be interpreted as within the more general words of the Fourteenth Amendment's due process clause.

Sixth Amendment

Accused persons to have speedy and public trial. Trial by impartial jury.	Applies to states. Jury trial not required; but if there is one, the jury must be impartial and states may not exclude members of defendant's race or national origin because of their race or national origin.
Trial in district where crime committed.	Does not apply.
Accused must be informed of nature and cause of accusation.	Applies to states; essential for a fair trial; criminal statutes must not be vague or ambiguous.
Accused must be confronted with witnesses against him.	No specific Supreme Court ruling, but probably necessary in order to have a fair trial.
Accused must have compulsory process for obtaining witnesses in his favor.	Does not apply to states.

To have the assistance of counsel in criminal prosecutions.	*States must permit defendants to have counsel, but not required to secure legal assistance for indigent defendants except in cases involving capital punishment or where special circumstances such as youth or ignorance make legal assistance necessary to a fair trial.*
Seventh Amendment Jury trials in suits of common law.	*Does not apply to states.*
Eighth Amendment Excessive bail shall not be required.	*Does not apply to states; however, denial of bail or imposition of excessive bail under some circumstances could result in denial of due process.*
Excessive fines shall not be imposed nor cruel and unusual punishments.	*Applies to states.*
Ninth Amendment Listing of some rights not to disparage existence of others.	*Does not apply to states.*
Tenth Amendment Powers not given to national government and not denied to states are reserved to states or to the people.	*Not applicable to states.*

NOTE: The fact that the Fourteenth Amendment may not deny a state the right to do certain things, does not automatically mean the state is free to do those things. The bill of rights in a *state* constitution frequently denies a state the power to do what the *national* Constitution would permit.

in the concept of ordered liberty; their replacement by suitable substitutes would not be "shocking to the sense of justice of the civilized world."

Using this formula, the Supreme Court has brought within the scope of the due process clause, in addition to the First Amendment, the prohibition against unreasonable searches and seizures of the Fourth, that part of the Sixth Amendment guaranteeing a public trial, and that part of the Eighth Amendment that forbids cruel and unusual punishment.[16] The Court has ruled that in no event could the following be considered due process: a conviction based solely upon a coerced confession; a trial in an atmosphere so hostile that calm deliberation is impossible; denial of assistance of counsel in cases involving possible capital punishment. On the other hand, the Court has held that indictment by other means than a grand jury, compelling a witness to testify against himself (in the absence of physical coercion), placing a man twice in jeopardy, trial without a jury, and denial of counsel in other than capital punishment cases, do not necessarily violate due process.[17] The situation is described in detail on pp. 213-215.

Thus the Constitution of the United States does not require state officials to follow in criminal prosecutions the same specific procedures that national officials must follow. But they are not free to act arbitrarily. Instead of having to abide by specific injunctions, they must treat persons accused of crime in a manner that is not "shocking to the sense of justice of the civilized world." Just what is shocking the Supreme Court finally decides as cases are brought before its bar.

The equal protection of the laws clause of the Fourteenth Amendment also protects persons accused of crime against discriminatory *state* action. Hence, in those cases where the state provides trial by jury, it must be a fair and impartial jury. A jury, either grand or petit (trial), from which Negroes have been barred because of their race would not be able constitutionally to try a Negro, for this would deny to him equal protection of the laws. (Such action would also violate the civil rights of Negroes who are denied the opportunity to serve on juries.) Nor could a state provide different punishments for persons of different races or religions.

HOW JUST IS OUR SYSTEM OF JUSTICE?

What are the major criticisms of the American system of justice? How have they been answered?

Too many loopholes. In our zeal to protect the innocent and to place the burden of proof upon the government, it is argued, we have established so many elaborate procedures that justice is delayed, disrespect for the law is

---

[16] *Wolf* v. *Colorado* (1949); *In re Oliver* (1948); *Louisiana ex rel Francis* v. *Resweber* (1947). For more detailed coverage see Richard A. Edwards, *The Fourteenth Amendment and Civil Liberty* (New York: Carrie Chapman Catt Memorial Fund, Inc., 1955).

[17] *Adamson* v. *California* (1947) and cases cited therein.

encouraged, and guilty men go unpunished. Justice should be swift and sure without being arbitrary. But under our procedures a criminal may go unpunished because (1) the police decide not to arrest him, (2) the judge decides not to hold him, (3) the prosecutor decides not to prosecute him, (4) the grand jury decides not to indict him, (5) the jury decides not to convict him, (6) the judge decides not to sentence him, (7) an appeals court decides to reverse the conviction, (8) the executive decides to pardon, reprieve, or parole him.

As a result, it is said, the public never knows whom to hold responsible if the laws are not enforced. The police can blame the prosecutor, the prosecutor can blame the police, and they can all blame the grand jury.

The step in the machinery of prosecutions that has received the most criticism is the grand jury. W. F. Willoughby has summarized the objections to the grand jury as follows:

It is in the nature of a fifth wheel; that real responsibility for the bringing of criminal charges is in fact exercised by the prosecuting attorney, the grand jury doing little or nothing more than follow his suggestions; that it complicates . . . the machinery of criminal administration; that it entails delay . . .; that it renders prosecution more difficult through important witnesses getting beyond the jurisdiction . . . or through memory of facts becoming weakened by lapse of time; that it entails unnecessary expense to the government; and that it imposes a great burden on the citizen called upon to render jury service.[18]

As the result of such criticisms the grand jury has been largely replaced in England. In 28 states indictment through *information,* an accusation by the prosecuting attorney, is permitted in most cases.

On the credit side, there is more to justice than securing prosecutions. It is better that nine guilty men go unpunished than that one innocent man be convicted. These various steps in the administration of criminal laws have been developed out of centuries of experience. Each one of them has been constructed to provide protection against particular abuses. "The awful instruments of the criminal law cannot be entrusted to a single functionary." For this reason responsibility for administration of the complicated process is vested in many officials. And as long as all these safeguards are maintained, no one need fear for his life or liberty because of overzealous or despotic action of another man.

The grand jury is necessary, it is argued, to protect innocent persons against arbitrary prosecutors. Although technically indictment is not conviction and a man is presumed to be innocent, in actual practice to be indicted hurts a person's reputation and requires him to stand the expense and effort of defending himself. On the other hand, grand juries have the power—and there are many cases where they have used it—to carry out their own independent investigations and to act when the prosecutor's

[18] W. F. Willoughby, *Principles of Judicial Administration* (Washington: Brookings Institution, 1929), p. 186.

laxity is letting crime go unpunished. The grand jury is one of the few agencies to limit the almost unfettered discretion of the prosecuting officers.

Unreliable. The chief target of the criticism of judicial administration as unreliable is the jury system. Trial by jury, it is argued, is a theatrical combat between lawyers who base their appeals on the prejudice and sentiments of the jurors. "Mr. Prejudice and Miss Sympathy are the names of witnesses whose testimony is never recorded but must nevertheless be reckoned with in trials by jury."[19] Too often cases turn upon the jurors' dislike for one of the lawyers or because they do not like the defendant's type. In addition, because of mass circulation of newspapers, jurors are influenced by the prejudices and sentiments of the community. Why do we need juries to apply community feelings or common sense to the commands of the law? This is a function of the legislature, and not of twelve men and women selected at random. No other country relies as much as does the United States on trial by jury. In short, according to this argument, the jury system is an unreliable method of sorting the guilty from the innocent.

In defense of the system, it is called an essential safeguard providing nonprofessional checks upon judges and prosecutors. Justice is too important to be left to the professionals. Twelve ordinary citizens will prevent judges from acting arbitrarily. Although juries are swayed by their feelings, the record of judges is not substantially better. Moreover, the jury system educates the citizens and provides for their participation in applying their own laws. The jury trial, said Justice Murphy, has the beneficial effect of "leavening justice with the spirit of the times." Abuses in the system call for improvement, not abolishment.

Inflexible. The elaborate and detailed procedures, it is argued, stem from the day when people wanted to limit the discretion of royal officials over whom they had no other control. But now there are better methods of preventing abuse. Modern newspapers and other means of publicity also reduce the danger that officials will act despotically. Those who administer the criminal laws are so hemmed in by detailed procedures that they do not have the discretion that modern criminology calls for. Each criminal should be dealt with as a particular case, and the findings of sociology, psychology, and criminology should be applied to protect the community and to rehabilitate the criminal. More attention should be paid to selecting better prosecutors and judges, then they should be given the discretion they need to administer justice.

In response, it is said that the day of arbitrary officials has not passed. One can cite cases in which prosecutors, judges, and juries have deprived individuals of the essentials of justice or have failed to prosecute the guilty. As long as we have to deal with men as they are, rather than as they should be, safeguards are essential to limit the discretion of those who

[19] Jerome Frank, *Courts on Trial* (Princeton: Princeton University Press, 1949), p. 122.

apply criminal law. The necessary flexibility can be achieved within the framework of the Constitution.

Undemocratic. There are two parts to this indictment. One refers to the high cost of justice, which gives an advantage to the man who can afford the best legal advice and who can pay for the appeals and other expenses connected with preparing his defense. On the other hand, those without adequate funds often lack proper legal assistance and cannot pay the cost of defending themselves. The Sixth Amendment requires federal judges to assign counsel to all impoverished persons accused of serious federal crimes. But the Fourteenth Amendment requires *state* judges to do so only in cases involving capital punishment or where there are peculiar circumstances—youth or ignorance of the defendant, for example—which make the assignment of counsel necessary for a fair trial. The second part of the indictment is that Negroes and other minorities do not get equal treatment before the law.

Undeniably there is much evidence to back up both these accusations. But a poor man or a Negro is more likely to get fair treatment before a court of justice than elsewhere in our society. The ideal of equal justice for all has a strong hold in American criminal procedures, although inevitably courts are composed of men who are part of our society and reflect the prejudices and values of that society. Poverty, like everything else in society, will affect criminal justice. Judges and juries, even when surrounded by elaborate safeguards, cannot be expected to leave behind them personal attitudes and sentiments when they come into the courtroom. Where poverty and prejudice exist in the community, they will affect all institutions of the community. Despite this, there are few places that provide as many protections as do courts, fallible as they are, in order to try to isolate prejudice and compensate for poverty.

In summary, the division between those who defend and those who criticize the American system of criminal procedures is not over the desire to secure justice. But some believe that by experimentation and adaptation the essential safeguards can be maintained and that the system can be improved. Others, however, believe along with the late Justice Rutledge that "the old time-tried 'principles and institutions of the common law' perpetuated for us in the Bill of Rights" are a "basic charter of personal liberty, and there should be no experimentation with them under the guise of improving the administration of justice."[20]

THE SUPREME COURT AND CIVIL LIBERTIES

The discussion of civil liberties in the last three chapters makes it clear that the judges, especially those on the Supreme Court, have an important part to play in enforcing the constitutional guarantees of civil liberties. This

[20] Concurring opinion, *In re Oliver* (1948).

combination of judicial enforcement and written guarantees of enumerated liberties is one of the basic features of the American system of government. The full significance of this combination as a defense of civil liberties has only recently been recognized (although at times exaggerated). Many of the framers, for example, thought of the Bill of Rights merely as a statement of general principles to guide government officials. But the Bill of Rights as a *judicially enforceable limitation* on legislative and executive powers is now an essential feature of our government.

The emphasis in the United States on constitutional limitations and judicial enforcement is an example of one of the "auxiliary precautions" Madison mentioned in order to prevent arbitrary governmental action. Other free nations give more attention to free elections and political checks to protect their rights. But in the United States we place heavy reliance on judges whom we have instructed to hear appeals in appropriate proceedings by people who believe that their freedoms are being jeopardized. All judges, not only those on the Supreme Court, have taken an oath to measure the actions of public officials against the appropriate *constitutional,* as well as legislative, provisions.

In England, judges have authority to restrain executive officials who deprive people of their legal rights, but English judges do not have the power to declare legislative acts unconstitutional. Moreover, Englishmen place primary reliance on an alert and aroused public opinion, operating through elected officials, to safeguard their liberty. The late Justice Jackson has commented: "I have been repeatedly impressed with the speed and certainty with which the slightest invasion of British individual freedom or minority rights by officials of the government is picked up in Parliament, not merely by the opposition but by the party in power, and made the subject of persistent questioning, criticism, and sometimes rebuke. There is no waiting on the theory that the judges will take care of it. . . . In Great Britain, to observe civil liberties is good politics and to transgress the rights of the individual or minority is bad politics. In the United States, I cannot say this is so."[21]

In the United States the emphasis on judicial protection of civil liberties focuses attention on the Supreme Court. The High Court gets the headlines, but it is the judges of lower courts, both national and state, policemen, prosecutors, newspaper reporters, and other citizens who are on the firing lines. Take the responsibilities of the trial judges, for example. Only a small number of controversies get to the Supreme Court. It is the inferior court judge who has to translate the doctrines of the Supreme Court and apply them to hundreds of cases. It is the police officer who, acting for his local community, has to make the on-the-spot decision whether a particular speaker is inciting people to riot or exercising his freedom of speech.

[21] Robert H. Jackson, *The Supreme Court in the American System of Government* (Cambridge: Harvard University Press, 1955), pp. 81-82.

To focus attention on constitutionality is to risk assuming that civil liberties can be protected solely by insisting upon constitutional conformity. This is not the case. There are many threats to liberty other than those that can be met by constitutional limitations. Moreover, much that may be constitutional can still be unwise. The promotion of freedom is not solely a constitutional problem. A society plagued by depression, hysteria, and fifth columnists does not provide a happy setting for the development of freedom. The problems of any of our civil liberties cannot be discussed as isolated issues; they are tied in with the whole question of preventing poverty and insecurity and maintaining order and stability and defending ourselves against totalitarians.

The role of the nine justices of the Supreme Court in defending civil liberties need not be minimized. Even aside from their decision-making power, their opinions are influential in clarifying the law and determining people's attitudes. But judges by themselves cannot guarantee anything. Neither can the First Amendment. As the late Justice Jackson asked: "Must we first maintain a system of free political government to assure a free judiciary, or can we rely on an aggressive, activist judiciary to guarantee free government? . . . [It] is my belief that the attitude of a society and of its organized political forces, rather than its legal machinery, is the controlling force in the character of free institutions. . . . [Any] court which undertakes by its legal processes to enforce civil liberties needs the support of an enlightened and vigorous public opinion. . . ."[22] In short, only so long as most groups desire liberty for themselves and are willing to restrict their own actions in order to preserve the liberty of others can freedom be maintained.

Summary

1. Property rights were built by the Supreme Court into a powerful restraint on governmental regulation of business, with the help of the doctrine of *substantive* due process. Today property rights, like all rights, are subject to regulation by the legislature, but fair procedures must be used.

2. The Bill of Rights guarantees a host of *procedural* rights against *federal* interference. All basic rights (such as freedom of speech and religion) but only *some* procedural rights are protected against *state* interference by the Fourteenth Amendment. State and local governments, however, are also restrained by their respective state constitutions which are interpreted and enforced in appropriate proceedings by state courts.

3. The American system of justice is criticized on several scores, but its defenders consider it the system best for this country to protect the innocent and punish the guilty.

4. Judges have a major responsibility to enforce the constitutional guarantees of civil liberties, but they cannot do the job without the support of most of the people. Civil liberties are everybody's business.

[22] Jackson, *op. cit.*

"REMEMBER, REMEMBER ALWAYS THAT ALL OF us, and you and I especially," President Franklin D. Roosevelt once said to a convention of the Daughters of the American Revolution, "are descended from immigrants and revolutionists." Beginning with a small trickle, rising to a flood tide, and recently subsiding to a small stream, peoples from many parts of the world made the long and arduous journey across the sea. Early arrivals generally settled the farms; later immigrants, often lacking the money and skills needed to cultivate the soil, tended to cluster in seaports and inland cities.

Once here, most of the immigrants were anxious to throw off their alien status and become full members of the body politic. This chapter describes the transformation from immigrant to citizen and the rules that determine who may come to the United States and what rights these aliens have when they get here.

THE LAND OF IMMIGRANTS

Congress has complete constitutional power to decide who shall be admitted and under what conditions. It is somewhat ironic that some Americans, who are immigrants or descendents of immigrants, have, since the days of the Alien Acts of 1798, urged Congress to use its powers to keep others from coming to the land of the free. After each generation of immigrants became integrated into American life, some of them displayed toward newer arrivals the same hostility and criticism that they, themselves, had encountered. There have always been those who have insisted that the quality of persons seeking admission is not as high as it was when they or their ancestors came. First the English looked down on the Irish, then the Irish were critical of the Germans, then the Germans were scornful of the Italians, Poles, Russians, and others from south and eastern Europe. But despite considerable agitation against the admission of the Irish, especially during the 1830's and

★ 9

Immigrants,

aliens, and

citizens

1840's, it was not until the 1880's that Congress began to impose restrictions.

In the 1880's Congress established the first of the so-called "quantitative" limitations, and the Chinese were completely excluded. Congress also imposed certain health and moral requirements—so-called "qualitative" limitations—and paupers, polygamists, persons suffering from dangerous diseases, and others were denied admittance. During the following years, additional health and moral disqualifications were added. In 1903 the first political test was established when anarchists and advocates of forceful overthrow of government were excluded. In 1917, over President Wilson's veto, Congress made illiteracy grounds for exclusion, and further racial restrictions were added to bar most Asiatics. But despite these restrictions, until World War I the land of opportunity was open to the "tired and huddled masses" of Europe. Just before that war, over a million people a year entered. Then the gates were closed.

Courtesy Library of Congress

A cartoon attacking unrestricted immigration, 1888.

Closing the gates

After the war, America became almost a closed country. Organized labor feared that European workers would undercut the American wage scale and would prevent the organization of unions. The pressures of labor were supplemented by the growing fear of un-American ideas, and by pseudo-biological claims that the population of the United States was being mongrelized. Hence, aliens ineligible for citizenship—mainly Asiatics—were barred entirely, and immigration from Europe was limited to not more than 154,000 a year. *Quotas* were allotted to each nationality in proportion to the number of people of that national background resident in the United States in 1920. The purpose of these quotas was to reduce sharply the number of people immigrating from southern and southeastern Europe. It was from this region that the greatest proportion of immigrants had come during the early years of the twentieth century. These people, primarily Catholics and Jews, aroused the prejudices of the earlier immigrants.

LEADING SOURCES OF IMMIGRATION AT DIFFERENT PERIODS
OF UNITED STATES HISTORY

Period	Country and area	Period of largest volume of immigration
Colonial 1820-60	Great Britain and Northern Ireland.	
	1. Ireland	1851-55
	2. Germany (mainly west and southwest Germany).	
	1820-30 (Palatinate—Rhine hinterland).	
	1830-40 Weser hinterland.	
	1840-50 Elbe hinterland (Westphalia, etc.).	
1861-90	1. Germany (mainly eastern Germany)	1881-85
	2. Ireland.	
	3. Scandinavia	1886-90
1891-1920	1. Italy	1906-10
	North (up to 1890).	
	South (1890-).	
	2. Austria-Hungary	1906-10
	Bohemia, Carinthia, Tyrol (up to 1900).	
	Galicia, Hungary (1900-).	
	3. Russia (chiefly non-ethnic Russians: Jews, Baltic peoples, Poles, Ukrainians).	1911-15
1921-30	1. Canada	1921-25
	2. Mexico	1921-25
	3. Italy (1921-24).	
	4. Germany.	
1931-51	1. Germany (primarily refugees).	
	2. Canada.	

Source: Report of the President's Commission on Immigration and Naturalization, *Whom We Shall Welcome* (Washington: Government Printing Office, 1952), p. 26.

Although people from other American countries could still enter the United States without quota restrictions—subject only to the general laws excluding illiterates, criminals, anarchists, and the like—the combined effect of the restrictive laws and the depression was to reduce immigration during the 1930's to the smallest number in our history. In fact, more people left the United States than came in.

The Immigration Act of 1952

During World War II Congress repealed the Chinese Exclusion Act in order, in the words of President Roosevelt, to "correct a historic mistake and silence the distorted Japanese propaganda."[1] After the war, Congress

[1] Fred W. Riggs, *Pressures on Congress* (New York: Kings Crown Press, 1950), p. 21.

passed special legislation to admit some of the millions of people uprooted from their homes by war and political upheavals (see pages 226-227). And in 1952 Congress enacted a comprehensive and controversial law to adjust immigration legislation to modern conditions.

The Immigration and Nationality Act of 1952 abolishes race as a bar to immigration, but it retains the basic national origin system, imposing an over-all annual quota of 154,657 and discriminating against Asiatics and southern and eastern Europeans. Quotas are still based on the 1920 white population; hence nationals of eastern and southern Europe received small quotas. Japan, China, and India have an allotment of only a hundred each. Furthermore, any person, no matter where born, "attributable by as much as one-half of his ancestry" to peoples native to the Asia-Pacific zones is chargeable to the limited Oriental quotas, a provision that applies to no others. Thus, a child born in England to a Chinese mother and an English father is classified as an Oriental. The act also discriminates against the colored people of the colonial regions in the Western Hemisphere by giving these dependencies an allotment within that of the mother country.

Since the largest annual allotments are given to countries whence few desire to come and the smallest to those where there are large numbers waiting, considerably less than the 154,657 quota of immigrants come to the United States each year—less, in fact, than one-fifteenth of 1 per cent of our population. The number of people actually entering is larger than this per cent indicates, however, since national-origin limitations do not apply to natives of independent countries of the Western Hemisphere; husbands, wives, and minor children of American citizens; re-entering alien residents; ministers; and a few others. (These *nonquota* immigrants, however, must meet all the other requirements of the law.) And *nonimmigrant aliens* who come to the United States just for a temporary visit do not have to secure a quota assignment.

The 1952 Act retains the "qualitative" requirements of earlier laws and adds a few new ones. Thus, all immigrants, quota and otherwise, are excluded if they are illiterate, immoral, have contagious diseases, are likely to become public charges, are subversives, are, or have been, members of totalitarian parties. A totalitarian party is defined in such a way that under present world conditions members of communist but not fascist organizations are excluded. The law also distinguishes between those who voluntarily joined a totalitarian party and those who were compelled to do so. Persons who joined these parties because of compulsion or in order to obtain the necessities of life or those whose membership terminated prior to their sixteenth birthday may be admitted. Reformed totalitarians may also be allowed to enter if they have for at least the past five years been actively opposed to the subversive organization of which they were a member, provided both the consular officials and the Attorney General believe that their admission would be in the public interest. Furthermore, Congress has given the President the power to refuse any alien entry if the President finds such entry would be detrimental to the interests of the United States, and the President's decision on this point is not subject to review by any court.

President Truman vetoed the Immigration Act of 1952 objecting especially to the retention of the discriminatory national-origin system. After Congress overrode his veto, he appointed a special commission to survey all aspects of our immigration and naturalization policy. The report of this

ANNUAL IMMIGRATION QUOTAS, BY COUNTRY, UNDER SUCCESSIVE
IMMIGRATION LAWS: 1921-1952

	1921 act 3 per cent 1910	1924 act 2 per cent 1890	1929 National Origins	1952 Immigration and Nationality Act
Total	357,803	164,667	153,714	154,657
Asia	492	1,424	1,423	2,990
Africa and Oceania	359	1,821	1,800	2,000
Europe	356,952	161,422	150,491	149,667
Northern and western Europe:				
Belgium	1,563	512	1,304	1,297
Denmark	5,619	2,789	1,181	1,175
France	5,729	3,954	3,086	3,069
Germany	67,607	51,227	25,957	25,814
Great Britain and Northern Ireland	77,342	34,007	65,721	65,361
Irish Free State	.....	28,567	17,853	17,756
Netherlands	3,607	1,648	3,153	3,136
Norway	12,202	6,453	2,377	2,364
Sweden	20,042	9,561	3,314	3,295
Switzerland	3,752	2,081	1,707	1,698
Total northern and western Europe	197,630	140,999	127,266	126,131
Southern and eastern Europe:				
Austria	7,342	785	1,413	1,405
Czechoslovakia	14,357	3,073	2,874	2,859
Greece	3,063	100	307	308
Hungary	5,747	473	869	865
Italy	42,057	3,845	5,802	5,645
Poland	30,977	5,982	6,524	6,488
Portugal	2,465	503	440	438
Rumania	7,419	603	295	289
Union of Soviet Socialist Republics	24,405	2,248	2,784	2,697
Turkey	2,654	100	226	225
Yugoslavia	6,426	671	845	933
Total southern and eastern Europe	155,585	20,423	23,235	23,536

Source: Report of the President's Commission on Immigration and Naturalization. (Washington: Government Printing Office, 1952), pp. 75, 76.

commission also was critical of the national-origins system.[2] President Eisenhower has also indicated his belief that the 1952 Act needs to be revised in order to get rid of its more obvious discriminatory provisions and has urged Congress to reconsider the matter.

Special immigration legislation

After long debate, Congress in 1948 and 1950 authorized nearly 400,000 displaced persons to enter the United States by 1951 without having to wait for a quota number. These persons, however, were charged against half of future annual quotas of the country of their national origin, so that half of the annual Greek quota, for example, is now "mortgaged" until the year 2014. After this Displaced Persons Act had expired, Congress passed the Refugee Relief Act of 1953 to admit 214,000 escapees from behind the Iron Curtain and other war refugees, without respect to quotas. But the law specifically stated that no special attempt should be made to encourage persons to come to the United States, and these refugees had to meet all the other requirements. In addition, an American citizen or organization had to assure that they would have a place to live and would not become public charges, and all had to enter by December 31, 1956. The complexities of the law combined with the rigor of its administration caused the program to get off to a slow start; but after the 1956 Hungarian uprising, President Eisenhower ordered a speed-up, and by the end of 1956 all of those permitted to enter under the 1953 act had arrived.

Admission of visitors

No quota is involved for diplomats, students, businessmen, vacationers, and other aliens who wish to visit the United States, but with certain exceptions these nonimmigrants have to comply with the same detailed requirements as do those who intend to reside permanently. Many visitors—scientists coming for a week to attend scholarly conferences; musicians, to perform; businessmen, to trade—have complained about the red tape. They tell of the days required to secure a visa (a permit to enter) and the indignity of being fingerprinted and treated with suspicion. For example, Max Beloff, a noted Oxford Don, writes, "An Englishman can travel without a visa from North Cape to Naples; it is only when he wishes to visit the United States that he becomes aware that such a thing as a visa exists, or that anyone classes him with delinquents by demanding that he have his fingerprints taken."[3] These restrictive provisions applied to temporary visitors, especially the fingerprinting requirement, have injured the world

[2] Report of the President's Commission on Immigration and Naturalization, *Whom We Shall Welcome* (Washington: Government Printing Office, 1953).

[3] Max Beloff, *Foreign Policy and the Democratic Process* (Baltimore: The Johns Hopkins Press, 1955), p. 100.

reputation of the United States.[4] Presidents Truman and Eisenhower and Secretaries of State Acheson and Dulles have asked Congress to change the procedures so that our prestige will not suffer in comparison with the practices of the Iron Curtain countries.

Administration of the immigration laws

Aliens seeking entrance have few, if any, constitutional rights. Congress has delegated to immigration officials almost unreviewable discretion and has deliberately created a system of dual administration. Applicants are screened by consular officials of the Department of State and by the Immigration and Naturalization Service of the Department of Justice, each independent of the other.

Applicants for admission must first apply for a visa at a United States consulate abroad, where they are registered, fingerprinted, and made to take a physical and mental examination. They must furnish information about past activities, present status, and future intentions. They must have a passport or a travel document and copies of birth, military, and other records. If the consular official "knows or has *reason to believe*" that the applicant is ineligible for admission to the United States, he is instructed to deny the visa, a decision that cannot be reviewed, not even by the consul's superiors in the Department.

The granting of the visa, however, is not final. When the applicant arrives at an American port of entry, Public Health Service officers make another physical and mental examination, and Immigration officials make another check of admissibility. Decisions of these officers are reviewable within the Department of Justice, but only ~ unusual circumstances by a court. Finally, when this hurdle is cleared, the alien is allowed to enter.

RIGHTS OF ALIENS

Once here, aliens remain at the sufferance of the national government. Aliens who enter illegally may be expelled without much ado. Even those who have been legally admitted may be deported for a variety of reasons, such as two convictions for crimes involving moral turpitude, joining an organization that advocates revolutionary doctrines, or if the Attorney General believes they have, or have had, a purpose to engage in activities "subversive to the national security." The Attorney General may even hold aliens without bail if he thinks necessary while he establishes whether they are to be deported. His discretion is subject only to very narrow court review.

[4] See, for example, statement of Secretary Dulles before Subcommittee on Immigration of Senate Judiciary Committee, April 25, 1956, quoted in full in *Department of State Bulletin,* Vol. XXXIV, No. 880, May 7, 1956, p. 774.

The Supreme Court has ruled that deportation, despite its drastic consequences, is a civil rather than a criminal proceeding, so that the ex post facto limitation does not apply. An alien may therefore be deported for acts which, when done, were not grounds for deportation. For example, Luigi Mascitti came to the United States in 1920 when he was sixteen. He joined the Communist party in 1923 and resigned in 1929. He testified that he did not know that the party advocated proletarian dictatorship and that he did not believe in such a policy. When he joined the party, it was a legal institution that had its name on some election ballots, and membership in the party was not then grounds for deportation. In 1940, eleven years after Mascitti had resigned, Congress changed the rules to require deportation of any alien who at "any time" after entering the United States became a member of any organization advocating unlawful overthrow. Mascitti was ordered to leave.[5] In 1950, Congress declared that it was no longer necessary in each case to show that the Communist party did, in fact, advocate violent overthrow. The mere fact of membership in the party is now enough to cause banishment.[6]

Constitutional and treaty rights of aliens

Aliens resident in the United States are subject to all general laws and, as others, must pay taxes. Congress may, if it chooses, subject them to the draft. Under present laws, if an alien raises his foreign nationality as an objection to the draft, he may be excused, but he loses all right ever to become a citizen.

Many constitutional provisions protect the rights not merely of citizens but of *persons*. For example, aliens accused of crimes enjoy the protection of the Fifth, Sixth, Eighth, and Fourteenth amendments. Moreover, government's power to regulate speech and religion is no greater when aliens are involved than when citizens are affected. Although aliens may be deported for political reasons, they have the same protection as citizens against criminal prosecution for their speech.

The United States has treaties in which Americans living abroad are given certain rights in return for rights granted to other countries' nationals living here. Like all treaties, these are the supreme law of the land and take precedence over state enactments. The states, subject to Supreme Court review, are responsible for enforcing these treaties.

The equal protection and due process clauses protect aliens against arbitrary and unreasonable deprivation of life, liberty, or property by the states. State laws interfering with an alien's right to engage in normal businesses or requiring employers to hire only citizens have been decalred unconstitutional. On the other hand, the Supreme Court has held that states

[5] *Harisiades* v. *Shaughnessy* (1952).
[6] *Galvan* v. *Press* (1954).

may constitutionally reserve certain privileges for citizens. State laws have been sustained that forbid aliens to own firearms, to enjoy the benefits of workmens' compensation, to practice law or medicine or other licensed professions, to be employed on public works, to own real estate. And there is no question that states may deny aliens the right to vote or hold public office. The Supreme Court and some state courts, however, have tended recently to look askance at state laws that discriminate against aliens, although the basic doctrine that states may exclude aliens from certain privileges still stands.

Alien registration and national control

The national government requires resident aliens to register annually, give their names, addresses, occupations, and other data, and to inform the Attorney General of any changes. During time of war, the liberty and property of resident nationals of enemy countries are further restricted. During World War II, enemy aliens were required to register, they were not permitted to move from place to place without securing official permission, they were denied the right to own short-wave radios, and to some extent they lost control over their property. (Property located in the United States and owned by *non*resident enemy aliens was taken over by the national government.)

Above all, the alien resident in the United States does not have the right to reside here. In our war-torn and dictator-ridden world, the right of an American citizen to reside in the United States takes on additional value. But how is this citizenship acquired?

CITIZENSHIP

It was not until 1868 with the adoption of the Fourteenth Amendment that the basic right to membership in the body politic was given constitutional protection. This amendment makes "all persons *born or naturalized* in the United States and subject to the jurisdiction thereof . . . citizens of the United States and of the State wherein they reside." Thus, with the minor exception of children born to foreign diplomats or to enemies in hostile occupation of the United States, all persons born in the United States are citizens of this country regardless of the citizenship status of their parents. (Congress has defined "the United States" to include Alaska, Hawaii, Puerto Rico, Guam, and the Virgin Islands.) Members of Indian tribes were not made citizens of the United States by the Fourteenth Amendment, but Congress has by law conferred citizenship on persons born in the United States to members of Indian tribes.

The Fourteenth Amendment confers citizenship according to the principle of *jus soli,* that is, by place of birth. In addition, Congress has also granted under certain conditions citizenship at birth according to the principle of *jus sanguinis,* by blood. Thus a child born of American parents living abroad becomes an American citizen at birth provided at least one of his citizen parents had been physically present in the United States or one of its possessions prior to his birth. If only one parent is an American citizen and the other an alien, the child becomes a citizen at birth provided that parent had lived in the United States or one of its possessions for at least ten years, five of which years must be after the age of fourteen. In order, however, to retain citizenship derived through only one citizen parent, a person must come to the United States before he is twenty-three and live here for at least five continuous years between his fourteenth and twenty-eighth birthday.

Citizenship can also be acquired by naturalization, collective or individual. The granting of citizenship to Puerto Ricans in 1917 is an example of collective naturalization. Individual naturalization requirements are determined by Congress.

Today any lawful permanent resident nonenemy alien over eighteen years of age (except a military deserter, draft dodger, or alien who has refused to serve in our armed forces because of allegiance to another country) can be naturalized if:

1. He has lawfully resided in the United States for at least five years and for at least six months in the state or territory in which he files his petition for naturalization. (This time is reduced for spouses and children of citizens, persons who have served in the military or maritime service, former citizens, and persons performing religious duties abroad.)

2. He can read, write, and speak words in ordinary usage in the English language provided he is physically able to do so. (This requirement is waived for persons over fifty years of age on December 24, 1952, who have lived in the United States for twenty years.)

3. He is and always has been of good moral character while a resident of the United States.

4. He understands and is attached to the fundamentals of the history, the principles, and the form of government of the United States and is well disposed toward the good order and happiness of this country.

5. He does not now (nor did he within ten years immediately prior to his application for citizenship) believe in, advocate, or belong to an organization that supports opposition to organized government, the overthrow of government by violence, the illegal destruction of property, or the doctrines of world communism or any other form of totalitarianism. If a petitioner establishes, however, that he joined a subversive organization involuntarily in order to obtain food or a job or other essentials, or that his membership occurred and terminated before he was sixteen, he may nevertheless be naturalized.

6. He takes an oath in open court to renounce all allegiance to his former

country, to support and defend the Constitution and laws of the United States against all enemies, and to bear arms in behalf of the United States when required by law. A person who is opposed to bearing arms or serving in the armed forces *because of religious belief* may, however, be naturalized if he will take an oath to serve in the armed forces as a noncombatant or perform work of national importance under civil direction.

Persons wishing to be naturalized file in the office of the clerk of a court of record—federal or state—a petition for naturalization, verified by two witnesses, which includes the assertion of all facts which are material to the applicant's naturalization. The Immigration and Naturalization Service of the Department of Justice then conducts a personal investigation and holds examinations to insure that the petitioner meets all the requirements of the law. The final step is a hearing upon the petition in open court. The judge at this time has before him the recommendation of the Immigration Service. The law now requires that all recommendations of the Service be reviewed centrally and if the Attorney General's recommendation differs from that of the original examiner both recommendations must be submitted to the judge. If the judge is satisfied that the petitioner is qualified the oath of allegiance is given and a certificate of naturalization is granted. The petitioner becomes a citizen of the United States.

What about the citizenship of minor children? As is true of most phases of the naturalization laws there are so many exceptions that it is difficult to make any blanket statements. But in general it can be said that children under sixteen years of age who are lawfully resident in the United States become citizens when both parents become citizens or if they have only one living parent and he becomes naturalized.

Until 1922 a married woman's citizenship was derived from that of her husband. Hence, an alien woman who married an American became an American citizen. On the other hand, a woman who married an alien lost her American citizenship. Today women acquire and lose citizenship on the same terms as men, and except for a shortening of the residence requirement for naturalization, a married woman's citizenship status is not affected by that of her husband. American women may marry foreigners and still retain their citizenship.

Loss of citizenship by expatriation

American citizenship can be lost by expatriation or by denaturalization. Expatriation applies of course to both natural-born and naturalized citizens. The law now specifies ten types of conduct that are considered to be inconsistent with the obligations of citizenship and that result in its loss. They include such things as being naturalized in a foreign state, taking an oath of allegiance to another country, accepting a job in a foreign state that is open only to citizens of that state, voting in the election of a foreign state, serving in the armed forces of another state unless such service is authorized by the Secretaries of State and Defense, or departing from the United States in time of war or emergency for the purpose of evading military service. Furthermore, citizenship is lost when a person is convicted of deserting the armed forces during time of war, committing treason, attempting by force to overthrow the government of the United States, advocating forceful overthrow, or conspiring to advocate forceful overthrow, of the government of the United States. It is not true as it is sometimes assumed, however, that conviction of any felony results in the loss of citizenship. Convicted felons lose some of their political rights, such as the right to vote, but unless their crime is one of those mentioned above they do not cease to be American citizens.

A person may also renounce his citizenship if he is outside the United States by making a formal declaration before an American diplomatic or consular officer. But if a person is living within the United States he may formally renounce his citizenship only during time of war and only with the approval of the Attorney General.

Although the only distinction the Constitution makes between naturalized and natural-born citizens is that the former cannot become President or Vice-President, naturalized citizens are considered to have expatriated themselves by conduct which does not deprive natural-born citizens of their citizenship. A naturalized citizen loses his citizenship by living for five continuous years in any foreign state or states or for three continuous years in the state of which he is a former national. The five-year rule does not apply to naturalized citizens who have resided in the United States for twenty-five years subsequent to naturalization and the three-year rule does not apply to citizens over sixty who have lived here for at least twenty-five years after naturalization. Exceptions are also provided for persons who are abroad working for the United States government, a United States business organization, visiting sick parents, and so on.

Loss of citizenship by denaturalization

Naturalized citizenship may be revoked at any time by a court order if the government proves that it was procured by concealment of a material fact or by willful misrepresentation. In the past the Supreme Court required the government to demonstrate by overwhelming evidence that the naturalization was illegally received before it would permit court revocation. But as the result of recent changes in the law the burden of proof for many activities has been substantially taken off the government's shoulders.

The law has long provided that a naturalized citizen who within five years after naturalization established a foreign residence would be presumed to have obtained naturalization fraudulently and unless he could overcome this presumption a court could revoke his citizenship. In 1950 and 1952

Congress added other grounds of presumptive fraud. If within five years after naturalization a person joins or affiliates with a subversive organization, it is now presumed in the absence of contrary evidence that such a person was not at the time of naturalization attached to the principles of the Constitution. If within ten years after naturalization any person is convicted of contempt of Congress for refusing to testify as a witness before a congressional committee concerning his subversive activities, this now is also held to constitute ground for revocation of naturalization.

Dual nationals

Because each nation determines for itself whom it shall consider to be its citizens, persons frequently acquire the nationality of both the United States and of a foreign state. A person born in the United States of Swiss parents, for example, is, according to the Fourteenth Amendment, an American citizen and, according to Swiss law, a Swiss citizen. Likewise, a person born of American parents abroad is an American citizen and may also acquire the nationality of the country in which he is born. A dual national who, after reaching 22, resides in the foreign state of his birth, loses his American citizenship if he voluntarily claims the benefits of his foreign nationality—in making an application for a foreign passport, for example —unless he takes an oath of allegiance to the United States before a diplomatic or consular official.

Privileges and immunities of United States citizens

States may establish residence requirements before they permit citizens to vote, attend the state university, practice law, and so on. But the Fourteenth Amendment automatically confers state citizenship upon all American citizens who reside there. (*Residence,* as used in the Fourteenth Amendment means "domicile," the place one calls "home." The legal status of domicile should not be confused with the fact of physical presence. One may be living in Washington, D.C. but be a citizen of California; that is, consider California "home." *Domicile* or *residence* as used in the Fourteenth Amendment is a question primarily of intent.)

Many American citizens are also state citizens, but some—for example, those who reside in Puerto Rico, Washington, D.C., or in England—have only national citizenship. The Fourteenth Amendment, among other things, protects this national citizenship when it denies states the right to abridge privileges and immunities of United States citizens. What are these privileges and immunities? The Supreme Court in the *Slaughter House Cases* (1873) gave them a very narrow construction. The Court carefully distinguished between privileges of *United States* citizens and of *state* citizens and held that the only privileges attaching to national citizenship are those that "owe their existence to the Federal Government, its National character, its Constitution, or its laws." Since many basic rights such as the right to engage in business or to make speeches do not depend on the Constitution, which merely protects these previously existing rights, the Supreme Court's narrow construction of the privileges and immunities clause has made it of little value as a restraint on state regulation. Nevertheless, the rights of national citizenship may be protected by national law, not merely against abridgment by the states but also against interference by *private* individuals and *groups.*

The privileges of United States citizenship have never been completely enumerated, but they include such things as the right to use the navigable waters of the United States, to assemble peaceably and petition the national government for redress of grievances, to be protected by the national government on the high seas, to travel throughout the United States, and —if qualified to do so under state laws—to vote in national elections and to have the vote counted properly.

In recent years there has been considerable discussion about the status of an American citizen's right to travel. Except for persons under legal restraint—committed to jail, subject to the draft, out on bail, etc.—American citizens may travel throughout the nation. During World War II, however, American citizens who had committed no crime, but were of Japanese ancestry, were forced to move from their homes to relocation centers. The Supreme Court reluctantly approved this denial of civil liberty. It would not call unreasonable the decision of military commanders that such measures were necessary under the circumstances. But the Supreme Court insisted that after the loyalty of these people was established, restrictions that were not legally imposed upon all other persons could not be placed on their freedom to travel.[7]

Does an American citizen have the right to travel abroad? Until World War I, American citizens could leave the country whenever they wished. No passport was required, although it could be obtained if wanted. Then other nations began to require passports before they would admit our citizens, and the Department of State was given the authority to grant them. Under present laws, it is a crime to travel abroad without a passport if an emergency has been declared, and such an emergency has existed since 1941. The Department of State has held that it has unlimited discretion to refuse passports, can do so without explanation, and that a passport is a privilege rather than a right extended by the government. The Internal Security Act of 1950 makes it a crime for Communists to seek or receive passports, and the Department of State has imposed the additional limitation that passports will not be given to persons "suspected of furthering the Communist cause" or to those whose travel the department decides "would be contrary to the best interest of the United States."

[7] *Korematsu* v. *United States* (1944) and *Ex parte Endo* (1944).

After a Nobel Prize winner, some distinguished persons, and more than three hundred Americans, had been denied passports, growing criticism and court orders resulted in the State Department's establishment of a hearings procedure to review denials of passports for all persons who would sign an affidavit denying membership, present or past, in the Communist party. Then in 1955 the Court of Appeals (the court just below the Supreme Court, see page 514) ruled that the right of an American citizen to travel abroad is a "natural right" and that the Department of State could not refuse to give a passport on grounds that do not meet the test of procedural and substantive due process. In this particular case, the judges declared that it was unreasonable and thus unconstitutional for the department to withhold a passport from an applicant solely because he belonged to an organization on the Attorney General's list.[8] The Supreme Court has not as yet, however, ruled on the matter, and the Department of State's authority to withhold passports is still a subject of controversy.

Summary

1. Immigration is restricted. Only a limited number of persons from non-American countries may enter each year for permanent residence. They must meet health, moral, and political qualifications. There is no limitation upon the number of nonimmigrant aliens who wish to enter, but they must meet other qualifications.

2. Aliens reside in the United States under terms established by Congress, and they have no constitutional right to remain. While here, however, they are entitled to certain protections of the Constitution and of treaty.

3. Citizenship may be acquired by birth in the United States, birth to American parents, and by naturalization. It may be lost by expatriation and denaturalization.

4. American citizens have certain rights denied to aliens. These rights flow directly from national citizenship and indirectly from state citizenship. The latter is acquired whenever American citizens reside in a state.

[8] *Schactman* v. *Dulles* (1955).

The people in politics

The chief problem in Part Four is that of representation—*how are the American people organized for representation in the most democratic manner? Part Four does not deal with the whole nature of this problem, because the problem of representation involves both the matter of how people are organized politically and how their leaders are organized—and the latter subject is taken up in the following part (Five).*

What this part does show is that people are organized for political expression and action in a variety of ways, most notably in interest groups (Chapter 10) and in political parties (Chapter 13). They express their opinions through many devices, and these opinions take a variety of forms (Chapter 11). They cast their votes in ways that are often unpredictable but that generally follow certain patterns (Chapter 13). The many elections (Chapter 14) themselves affect the pattern of politics and reflect—at a given point in time—peoples' interests and opinions, in all their complexity.

A key problem of representation at the popular level is this: all voters in a democracy should have, ideally at least, an actual

PART FOUR

share of political power; but in reality some have a great deal of influence, and others have virtually none. Organized interest groups (pp. 241-250) weild far more power than millions of unorganized persons. Certain political bosses and leading officeholders (pp. 258-261) have enormous influence in shaping political behavior. Some persons are not able to vote (pp. 299-300); others lack interest in voting (pp. 301-302); while still others—for example, newspaper columnists and radio commentators—can influence the voting of millions.

Sometimes this problem of representation is described as special interests versus general interests. The former are often pictured as small selfish groups "ganging up" on the rest of the people. The general interests are described as beneficial to all the people. Actually, the problem is more complex. A special interest may be selfish, or it may represent the real interest of the great majority. As used here, the term special interest *means merely the interest (goal or attitude) of less than the whole. It is special in the sense that it immediately and directly favors the part rather than the totality. The gen-eral interest simply means the interest of all, or most, of the people, as seen in the short run at least.*

Is there nothing to choose between the general and the special interest? Of course there is, if one takes into account all the circumstances of a par-ticular situation. Believers in democracy can speak of the majority interest as that which appears to be for the benefit of, or supported by, the majority. A democrat's objection to domination of government by special interests is that it is more likely to mean control by a few rather than by the many.

A believer in democracy is likely to be especially interested in a healthful two-party system (pp. 342-345) because it is—or can be—one means of dis-tilling a general interest out of the medley of more special interests. But with-out at least some protection of minority interests, the majority interest would be meaningless, as the history of dictatorships shows.

T HE UNITED STATES HAS BEEN CALLED A NA-
tion of joiners. Europeans sometimes make fun of us for setting up all
sorts of organizations, from antiprofanity leagues to zoological groups. We
ourselves are often amused by the behavior of our own groups—the noisy
conventions of a veterans' association, the solemn rites of a great fraternal
organization, the oratory of a patriotic society, the gossip of a local sewing
circle, the pomposity of a reform society. But the existence in America of
a tremendous number and variety of groups is not simply a matter for jok-
ing. Most of these groups are deadly serious in their aims, and together they
play an enormous role in politics. And joining is not simply an American
trait. It is a common trait of humans—and of many animals as well.

How many groups are there in America, and how varied are they? This
question cannot be answered with any attempt at accuracy. Families are
groups—the most basic and important groups of all—and there are at least
forty million of these in the United States. Our nation can boast of a quarter
million local religious congregations, countless athletic teams, tens of
thousands of trade unions, over two thousand trade associations—and all
these are groups. They are groups in the broadest sense of the term—in the
sense, that is, that the members of the group share some common *outlook*
or *attitude,* and *interact* with one another in some way.[1]

Nor can we measure the variety of groups in America, but we know that
our groups are fabulously complex. One student has made a list of odd
organizations that gives a hint of that complexity:[2]

The Non-Smokers Protective
   League of America
Simplified Spelling Board
American Sunbathing Associ-
   ation
Blizzard Men of 1888 (to
   commemorate a famous
   storm)
American Hackney Horse As-
   sociation

[1] D. B. Truman, *The Governmental Process* (New York: Alfred A. Knopf, 1951), Chapter 2.
The basic approach of this chapter
is drawn largely from this volume
and from the pioneer work, A. F.
Bentley, *The Process of Government* (Chicago: University of Chicago Press, 1908).
[2] From E. E. Schattschneider,
Party Government (New York:
Farrar & Rinehart, Inc., 1942), p.
26.

10 ★

The

dynamic role

of

interest groups

Soaring Society of America
Toastmasters International

Obviously one person can belong to a great variety of groups and organizations. A typical college student is a member of the college community as a whole. But he may belong to the sophomore class, the Tau Delta Tau fraternity, the basketball squad, the second floor of his dormitory, the Radio Club, the discipline committee, and classes in English, physics, French, and government. At the same time he belongs to still more groups at home—his family, neighborhood, religious congregation, and so on. This student is a member of all these groups but he is not *equally* a member of them. His loyalty to his family, his class, or his fraternity may greatly outweigh his loyalty to all the other groups.

His father may be a member of an even greater array of groups—not only his family, congregation, and neighborhood, but he belongs also—let's say—to the Rotary Club, a philatelic society, the Masons, a downtown law firm, the American Automobile Association, a taxpayer's association, the Republican party, a bowling league, the American Bar Association, the state bar association, among others. Do these group allegiances ever come into conflict with one another? Indeed yes. The A.A.A. may demand better roads, while the taxpayers' association wants less governmental spending. The neighborhood he lives in may be largely made up of Democrats, and he is not one. Even without such conflicts, belonging to a variety of groups puts a great strain on his time and his pocketbook.

The fact that groups are so numerous and varied raises a number of questions that go to the very heart of democratic politics in America. Why are some groups strong and united and organized, and others weak? What happens when competing groups overlap in membership, as in the cases just mentioned? How are groups organized, led, and governed? How do they gain influence? What is their relation to the party system, to elections, to government as a whole?

Politics is concerned with the workings of all groups, but we can simplify our effort to answer these questions by limiting ourselves to a particular type, the *interest group*. This is any group that, as a *result of sharing certain attitudes, makes claims on other groups in order to realize aims arising from these attitudes*. These interest groups are of many types. Some interest groups are formal *associations* or *organizations*. But not all interest groups are so organized. There may be, for example, in a particular place and at a particular time an "old peoples' " interest; that is, a group sharing certain attitudes and making claims on others that is nevertheless not formally organized into a particular association. Formal organizations are found *within* different interests. Thus inside the American Bar Association there may be a conflict of interest groups on a particular issue. An interest group can be either broader or narrower than a particular organization. The American Federation of Labor and Congress for Industrial Organization, for example, is opposed to the Taft-Hartley Act. But not all members of the A.F.L.-C.I.O. are opposed and some people who are not members *are* opposed. The interest group working to amend or abolish the Taft-Hartley Act then is composed of most members of the A.F.L.-C.I.O., but not all, and some people outside the formal labor organization. In this chapter we are primarily concerned with *organized* groups.

Politics is largely a conflict among competing groups with conflicting ideas of what is in the "general interest." In political arguments it is inevitable that we talk about special interests versus the general welfare. But in political analysis it is better to talk about *this* group's idea of the general welfare as compared with *that* group's idea. As political partisans we are all committed to particular ideas and values, but as social scientists we cannot pretend to set up a clearly defined national interest. For this is the question at issue—"What is the general interest?" In a democracy it is the ideas of the many rather than the ideas of the few that prevail in defining the general welfare.

UNIONS FOR ALL—OCCUPATIONAL GROUPS FOR ALL

It is only natural that men working together should combine in some sort of association. They tend to have common attitudes and interests, and directly or indirectly to deal with one another during much of their working day and after. This is true not only of factory workers, but also of businessmen, farmers, doctors, lawyers, and many others. In a sense we are all in unions, whether we are presidents of insurance companies, applegrowers, baseball umpires, professors, plumbers, or what not. Our unions come in all shapes and sizes, with all sorts of programs, memberships, and interests.

Men interact and unite on a nationwide and state-wide basis as well as in local groups. They can do so easily and effectively because of modern methods of communication and transportation. Milk producers in Vermont and Wisconsin, druggists in Boston and Seattle, garment workers in New York and Chicago can talk with one another in a matter of minutes, or meet in a matter of hours. They not only can work together but they must do so. They find added strength in unity, and they can meet common, nationwide problems only by organizing on a nationwide basis. The typical large associations comprise a mosaic of local and state bodies, heading up in the national organization. Usually they are the product of decades of slow and often painful growth. The labor movement illustrates the rise of a group of struggling separate groups to national status and influence after a period of trial-and-error organization.

Workers

The earliest trade union locals in the United States were founded during Washington's first administration. For several decades "mechanics" and other workers organized local groups in the larger cities, but often these

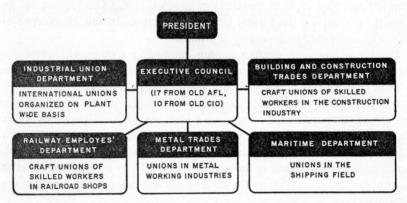

Organization of the new A.F.L.-C.I.O.

failed in the face of hard times, the hostility of employers, or the indifference of the workers. But the urge for closer union was a powerful one, and as the economy became nationally integrated, the locals in different states had to join hands with one another. Slowly taking root, the unions began to participate actively in politics. The Working Men's party, the first labor party, was born shortly before Andrew Jackson took office. An ambitious attempt to establish one big union of all types of workers came shortly after the Civil War with the founding of the Knights of Labor, which included in its membership factory workers, farmers, and others—in fact all except gamblers, stockbrokers, lawyers, or bankers! The Knights adopted a progressive platform, lobbied in state capitals, and linked arms in turn with Greenbackers, Populists, and Bryan Democrats. At one point it claimed 700,000 members. But the experiment failed. Lacking unity, the Knights lost out both in political and economic battles, and had virtually disappeared by the end of the century.

The *American Federation of Labor* was formed in 1886 by skilled workers—carpenters, machinists, and the like—who felt that their particular needs were obscured in the vastness of the Knights of Labor. Organized in tight crafts, these workers surrendered only limited power to the national A.F.L., which has continued to this day as a true confederation of strong and independent-minded national unions. Headed by Samuel Gompers, an astute ex-cigarmaker, the A.F.L. stressed the economic weapon of the strike rather than all-out political battles. When compelled to enter politics as a result of hostile governmental action, its method was to reward labor's friends and punish its enemies. Thus it followed a balance-of-power policy, steering shy of any firm party connection. The Federation was often assailed by socialists and others who felt that labor should take a more aggressive stand.

Following World War I the A.F.L. lost strength as a result of antiunion drives, unemployment, and its own failure to organize the millions of unskilled workers in the huge mass-production industries of the nation. Under the impact of the New Deal its membership soared, but only amidst internal disturbances. Failing to induce the A.F.L. craft leaders to organize the mass-production industries, a group of A.F.L. leaders, led by John L. Lewis of the miners, set up a Committee for Industrial Organization. The A.F.L. soon ejected them as "dual unionists," and the C.I.O. then continued as the *Congress of Industrial Organizations,* composed largely of workers in the steel, auto, rubber, textile, electrical, and maritime industries. Faced with vigorous competition, the A.F.L. made stronger organizing attempts, and for a short period included the miners' union again after Lewis deserted the C.I.O.

In 1955, after long negotiations, the A.F.L. and C.I.O. merged at the top levels. Since that time, various of their member unions have been combining at the national, state, and local levels. The merged national organization started life with about fifteen million members. It dominated the world of labor, but there were important groups outside the fold. The railroad brotherhoods represent over a million switchmen, Pullman porters, and other railway workers. The miners and one or two other large unions are —at the moment at least—independent. There are thousands of local unions that are not affiliated with a national union. And there are millions of workers who have no regular union at all, but who have some kind of employees' organization. But the objectives of all the different organizations are much the same—to improve wages and working conditions, to extend social security, and to stop hostile governmental action.

Farmers

Farmers, too, have their "unions." Despite their individualism and their physical separation from one another, they have long seen the need for combining to protect their interests. An early farm group—the South Carolina Agricultural Society—was founded before our Constitution was written. Since then thousands of local and state associations have sprung up. The oldest nationwide farm group today is the *National Grange* (Patrons of Husbandry). Founded in 1867 by a group of federal employees, the Grange started out as a secret society to promote social and intellectual activities, but it soon was embroiled in the political movements that swept rural areas in the 1870's. Rebelling against low farm prices, railroad monopolies, grasping middlemen, and high taxes, the Grangers turned to political action. They were pioneers in the use of lobbyists and delegations. After helping to gain certain reforms, such as railroad regulation and various direct aids to farmers, the Grange declined. Once a fighting organization with 1½ million members, the Grange today has about half that number and is the most conservative farm group. Strongest in the northeastern states, it works for price-support policies and other government protection.

The largest farm group today is the *American Farm Bureau Federation,* claiming over a million members, most of them in the corn belt. It is set up on the usual local, state, and national bases, but the Federation is some-what unique in that from the start it was organized around the system of county agents that began early in this century. As experts teaching im-proved farm methods, the county agents were in close touch with many farmers, and they became virtual organizers for the Farm Bureaus.[3] The Federation today is almost a semigovernmental agency, but it retains full freedom to fight effectively for such aims as price supports, conservation measures, and expansion of farm credit facilities.

Herblock in THE WASHINGTON POST AND TIMES HERALD

"Nah, that's not a candidate— that's a farmer."

Another important, but far smaller, organization is the *Farmers Union,* founded in 1902. This organization claims to speak largely for the family-sized farm. The Farmers Union ac-tively works for legislation that will protect the small farmer, such as aid to family-sized farms by the govern-ment, the gradual breakup of large farms, and minimum wage laws for farm labor—as well as the usual aims of price supports, rural electrification, easier loan policies, and the like. Largely based on cooperatives of various types, the Farmers Union is centered in the Missouri River Valley. It has taken a special interest in the problems of dust bowl farmers.

A great number of other farm organizations reflect the different in-terests of farmers based on the vari-ous commodities they produce. There are the National Beet Growers Association, the American Soybean Association, the American Wool Growers Association, and many others. These groups are relatively small, but they can wield power when they want. After journeying through states that maintain the sugar bloc in Congress, John Gunther wrote: "Only

[3] Wesley McCune, *The Farm Bloc* (New York: Doubleday, Doran & Company, Inc., 1943), p. 165. See also C. M. Hardin, *The Politics of Agriculture* (Glencoe, Ill.: Free Press, 1952).

3 per cent of American farmers grow sugar beet and cane; the entire processing industry employs no more than twenty-five thousand people. But sugar is spread through many states—beets grow in seventeen, cane in two—which gives it thirty-eight senators out of ninety-six, and they can certainly make a noise."[4]

Most farm organizations profess to be nonpolitical; all of them are in politics. Farmers have exerted influence on government not only through their associations; they have directly entered politics by organizing their own parties. The Greenback party in the 1870's and 1880's fought for currency inflation to ease the distress of farm debtors; at its peak it polled nearly one million votes and sent fifteen Congressmen to Washington. The Populist party did even better in the nineties, but the Democratic party under Bryan stole most of its thunder and its support. Farm votes made up much of the strength of Senator Robert La Follette's Progressive movement in 1924. Farm parties have controlled a number of state governments for long intervals.

Businessmen

Businessmen's "unions" are the most varied and numerous of all. Over 2000 trade associations and other business groups operate on a national or interstate basis, and there are at least 3000 local business groups. The nature of the hundreds of trade associations is almost as varied as the different products and services that are sold. Automobile manufacturers and pin manufacturers both have their national associations; so do canners, cotton manufacturers, retail Kosher butchers, road builders, tobacco merchants. Manufacturers of amusement tickets, clothing tickets, and transit tickets have three separate organizations. The list is almost endless. Businessmen group themselves by size and general function as well as by trade. The National Federation of Small Business, for example, is spokesman for the little businessman. The National Retail Dry Goods Association speaks for a variety of different retailers.

Two general, nationwide organizations of businessmen are especially important. One of these is the *Chamber of Commerce of the United States,* which was organized in 1912 indirectly under the sponsorship of the Taft Administration. The chamber is a federation of federations—it is composed of about 400 trade associations and over 1000 local chambers of commerce. Occupying an impressive office building a block from the White House, it calls itself "the Washington office of over 750,000 business people in America." Its members have so many different interests and attitudes that the chamber must stay aloof from many of the squabbles that divide business internally. It tries to represent business as a whole in opposing anti-business governmental measures or the demands of other groups, such as

---

[4] John Gunther, *Inside U.S.A.* (New York: Harper & Brothers, 1947), p. 221.

labor. A typical set of resolutions of the chamber might call for lower taxes, a curb on labor excesses, governmental economy, and less centralization of government. The chamber publicizes its views widely. "As a pipe line for steady, relentless, and timely opinion dissemination," one investigator says, "the Chamber of Commerce is probably unequalled."[5]

Loosely allied with the chamber on almost all issues is the *National Association of Manufacturers,* a unified organization of about 16,000 manufacturing firms and corporations. Organized in the wake of the depression of 1893, the N.A.M. today speaks for the more conservative elements of American business. Reflecting the attitudes of employers of large numbers of workers, it is more outspoken than the Chamber of Commerce in supporting restrictive labor legislation and opposing certain social legislation. The N.A.M. sponsors an annual convention of industrialists—the Congress of Business—and is run by a large part-time board of directors and by a full-time secretariat. The association uses a variety of outlets for its "public information," including motion pictures, cartoons, editorials, advertising, and radio speeches.

Professional men

Alongside the giant groups of farmers, workers, and businessmen, organizations of professional people look small, but they still are important. And they are equally varied in type. About 400 professional organizations with national membership exist in the country today, ranging from accountants to veterinarians, and including architects, beauticians, midwives, optometrists, and undertakers. Large professions are divided into many subgroups; thus teachers are organized in the National Education Association, the American Association of University Professors, and particular subject groups, like the Modern Language Association. Many professions are closely tied in with government, especially on the state level. Lawyers, for example, are licensed by the states, which set up certain standards of admission to the state bar, often as a result of pressure from lawyers themselves.

Some professions enjoy special influence because of the prestige of the members. Doctors—the "men in white"—are a case in point. Their chief organization, the American Medical Association, has had a notable role in opposing governmental intervention in the field of medicine. It has lobbied before Congress, put out literature, urged its members to talk to their patients, and assessed each of its 140,000 members $25 to build up a war chest for its fight against compulsory health insurance. The doctors are in the political battle—yet somehow they seem to be above politics; in a sense they can be both participant and referee. The professional soci-

[5] D. C. Blaisdell, "Economic Power and Political Pressures," *T.N.E.C. Monograph 26* (1941), p. 25.

eties do not claim the mass membership of an A.F.L.-C.I.O. or Farm Bureau Federation, but their prestige and expertness help make up for their lack of numbers.

THE CRISSCROSS OF INTERESTS

We have been talking about men interacting on the basis of some kind of common occupation. It would be good if we could stop here in our exploration of groups, for these occupational interests are complex enough in themselves. But we have seen only part of the picture. Man does not live by bread alone; he has other interests and attitudes beyond the essentially economic ones, and they can inspire powerful organization. One of the strongest political forces in American history—the Anti-Saloon League —was aroused not by direct economic motives but simply by a spirit of reform and religion.

Once we look on men as holding nonoccupational as well as occupational interests, the group picture becomes even more complicated and untidy. We have been discussing groups that are somewhat clear-cut and separate from one another; it is a rare person who is at once a farmer, a trade union member, and a businessman. But most men are members both of occupational and nonoccupational groupings, as in the case of a businessman who is also a Methodist. Moreover, a man can easily belong to several different nonoccupational groupings, as with a Catholic who is a Legionnaire, a trade unionist, and a member of the League to Abolish Capital Punishment. Thus we end up with a most elaborate crisscross of interests—a great scrambled collection of attitudes and loyalties working with or across one another in a thousand different ways.

Veterans

Which is the most important of the nonoccupational interest groups? The answer to this question varies according to the time and situation. In certain medieval societies the church groups were most important. In a South American country today the military organizations might be dominant. In the jumble of interest groups in the United States no single one is supreme. Since we live, however, in the wake of two world wars in which our country was heavily committed, the veterans are numerous and they are well organized. "In the next generation," said President Truman in the closing days of World War II, "the veterans of this war are going to run this country."[6]

The largest veterans' organization today is the American Legion, claiming well over two million members. Founded in Paris at the end of World War I, the Legion gradually became entrenched in thousands of local

[6] Harry S. Truman, speech in Portland, June 25, 1945.

communities. Thus it was able after World War II to attract many of the recent veterans, despite the efforts of several new outfits, including the American Veterans of World War II (Amvets) and the American Veterans' Committee. The A.V.C. attracted a good deal of attention when it based its program on the principle, "Citizens First, Veterans Second," and adopted a platform intended to benefit lower-income groups generally and not veterans alone. Its failure to attract a large membership suggested that most veterans wanted their own organizations to act essentially for their own interests. The second largest organization today is the Veterans of Foreign Wars, claiming over a million members. Like most interests the veterans are subdivided into specialized groups—for example, the Disabled American Veterans and organizations of veterans by religion or nationality.

Veterans have many reasons to organize. They share memories of common experiences in wartime. The local post is a handy place for the boys to get together. Having donned uniform for their country, many veterans feel a right and duty to speak out on governmental matters, especially on matters of patriotism and "Americanism." Above all, they have an economic interest in joining together. Veterans have demanded—and obtained —bonuses, pensions, free education, cheap loans and insurance, and a variety of other favors, even including free hunting licenses, exemptions on certain taxes, and honor guards for veterans' funerals. These favors are not new. "They saved the country, and now they want it," said an exasperated public official about the Grand Army of the Republic, the big post-Civil War veterans' organization. Veterans' lobbies are among the most influential in Washington today.

National, racial, and religious groups

Nationality groups are another important factor in American politics. In the melting-pot of the world, the American people include today over 10 million foreign-born persons and over 23 million native whites of mixed or foreign parentage. These are big numbers and they include many groups. In 1944 there were 23 German societies, 18 Slovak, 22 Polish, and many others, amounting to at least 155 nationwide organizations with 32,000 branches and 2,883,000 members. These groups have put their stamp on American politics. The Irish dominate the politics of many cities, such as Boston; Germans and Scandinavians are especially influential in the north central states; French Canadians are a cohesive group in many New England areas; New Mexico's state legislators debate in Spanish as well as English. Parties carefully balance their tickets to appeal to all national elements. It has been said that party tickets in New York, with their representatives of different nationalities, look like the line-up of the Brooklyn Dodgers.[7] Na-

[7] Warren Moscow, *Politics in the Empire State* (New York: Alfred A. Knopf, Inc., 1948), Chapter 3.

tionality groups take positions on general political issues, but they are concerned especially with such matters as easier naturalization laws and increased immigration quotas.

These nationality groups may gradually lose political leverage as their members become increasingly absorbed in the main streams of American life. Our many *racial* groups may have the same experience—but the largest racial group of all may be the last to lose its separate identity. This group consists of the sixteen million American Negroes. Decades of discrimination and segregation—political, economic, and social—forced Negroes to set up an almost separate life of their own on the less agreeable side of the color line. But colored leaders wished to share the full benefits of being Americans. In 1910 they established the National Association for the Advancement of Colored People to fight lynching and peonage, and to press for the right to vote.

Today, with 500 branches, the NAACP works for a variety of economic and social objectives. Its special concern currently is implementation of the Supreme Court's decision on public school segregation (see pages 176-177). It cooperates with the Urban League, a federation of local Negro groups, which is mainly concerned with broadening economic opportunities. In the last twenty years, Negroes have become increasingly active in politics. For decades they largely supported the Republican party, but the Depression of the 1930's and the support of New Dealers and Fair Dealers for civil rights brought large numbers of Negroes over to the Democratic party. The anticivil rights stand of southern Democrats, however, will help maintain the traditional nonpartisanship of Negro organizations. In any event Negroes, like whites, are not agreed on aims or methods. Indeed, their color is perhaps less of a unifying force than a common religious creed is to Irish Americans.

Religion plays a part in American politics. About half the people in the United States belong to some religious organization; there are more than 50,000,000 Protestants, 30,000,000 Roman Catholics, 4,500,000 Jews. Of these three groups, Protestants are the least united, for they are subdivided into large denominations, such as the Methodists and Baptists, and these denominations are in turn broken up into numerous bodies. The National Council of Churches speaks for some of these groups in its pronouncements on a wide variety of issues. As a result of its unity and discipline the Roman Catholic Church is probably at least as influential in politics as the Protestants. Some of its political activities are conducted by such Catholic groups as the Knights of Columbus (a fraternal order a half million strong), the Association of Catholic Trade Unionists, and the Catholic War Veterans. The Jews, too, are active politically;[8] they showed the influence they could muster in their fight for a national home in Palestine.

[8] See Lawrence H. Fuchs, "American Jews and the Presidential Vote," *The American Political Science Review*, Vol. XLIX, No. 2, June 1955, pp. 385-401.

Religious bodies are interested in almost every type of legislative matter —especially in education, foreign affairs (especially our relations with certain other nations, like Spain), social welfare legislation, and various social problems like gambling, child labor, divorce, birth control, euthanasia, vice. The special responsibility of the church in matters of morals gives it considerable influence in a broad sphere.

We have now seen something of the shape and size and variety of the larger interest groups in the United States. It would of course be possible to list many other types of association. There are the women's groups, like the League of Women Voters. There are the countless reform groups, such as the Woman's Christian Temperance Union, the Townsend movement, and the National Municipal League. There are groups concerned with particular problems, such as the Foreign Policy Association. A complete list would shade off into thousands of struggling groups that live for a few years, sometimes realize their objectives, and then die. It would include not only existing groups but *potential* groups that would spring into being if certain events took place, such as a new world war.

But our list is long enough. It is time to look more closely at the inner workings of organized groups, to see what makes them behave as they do.

INTEREST GROUPS IN FERMENT

Our picture of interest groups shows a cluster of organizations large and small, old and new, rising and falling, visible, invisible, and of endless number and variety. The most important thing about this picture is that it is a *moving* one. There is nothing static about group organization in America. Sometimes the changes within groups and between groups are almost imperceptible; sometimes they are sensational enough to become front-page news. Thus John L. Lewis will make headlines when he sets up the C.I.O., when he deserts it, when he joins the A.F.L., when he leaves it. On the other hand, the slow growth of religious beliefs, gradually affecting church relationships, may be less conspicuous but equally significant over a period of time.

Groups are plastic. In their internal and external relationships they are sensitive to the deep economic and social currents that flow through America and the world about it. Successive changes in industrial organization, for example, first allowed the A.F.L. to become dominant in labor organization, and then forced it to yield ground to a rival union. Improved agricultural techniques have created new patterns of life on the farm, new relationships among farm groups. The rise of big government has affected the functions of group leaders. The migration of thousands of Negroes from the South to northern cities has brought changes in their economic and social opportunities and in their role in politics.

The relation of groups to other forces is a two-way one; it is *mutually interactive*. Thus big government affects interest groups; at the same time groups help create and shape big government. Indeed, the process is more than a two-way one; it is multidirectional and many-sided. What we have is a gigantic web of interactions, flowing from interests, associations, governments, beliefs, techniques, and many other elements. A movement anywhere in this web will set the whole elastic network in motion. It is equally certain, however, that in this interrelationship some groups have much more effect than others, just as different politicians have varying influence in government.

The basis of group power

What determines the political effectiveness of an interest group? The main internal elements are two: *size* and *unity*. Obviously numbers are important. An organization with three million members will overshadow one with three thousand. But numbers do not amount to much if the group is so divided internally that the members fail to work together. Just as a small but disciplined army can rout a far larger but disorderly one, so can a compact group make its way against rival organizations, and even against the electorate as a whole.

The question then becomes: what makes a group cohesive? At least three elements are involved here.

By far the most important is the *nature of the membership*. If the members of an organization are undivided in their loyalty to it, that group will have an enormous advantage in the political arena. When the leaders can depend absolutely on the full backing of their followers, an organization is able to put its full weight into pursuing its aims. Communist groups are said to be made up of people who devote their time and energy single-mindedly to their cause; if this is true, it explains why the communists seem to have influence out of proportion to their numbers. But most Americans are not made that way. They cannot possibly give their lives over to one group— not even to their families. Most Americans, in fact, are members of many groups, as noted above. Their loyalties are divided. They cannot be depended on to go all-out for any cause.

It is this fact of *overlapping membership* that largely determines the cohesiveness of a group. It is a condition that organization leaders run up against time after time. A union official, for example, asks a dozen of his members to come to a meeting the next night. Several say they will show up. But one says that he must be with his bowling club that night. Two others have to stay home with their families. Another has a church supper. Even those who finally do show up at the union meeting are not 100 per-centers. They are asked, perhaps, to vote for a particular candidate in a coming election. Some of them will. But a union member may vote for the other candidate because they are next-door neighbors. Or because they are both Italo-Americans. Or both Republicans. Or both Legionnaires. Or perhaps he will not know what to do, and will not vote at all.

A second factor in the cohesion of a group is its *organizational structure.* Some groups have no formal organization. Many groups are loose federations of local organizations. Often the local organizations were set up first, and afterwards state and national federations were established. In such cases the local organizations retain a measure of separate power and independence, just as the states did when they entered the Union. Thus there is a form of federalism in some organizations (like the A.F.L.-C.I.O. and the A.M.A.) that may hinder unity.

A sort of separation of powers may be found as well. The national assembly of the organization establishes—or at least ratifies—policy. An executive committee meets more frequently. A president or director is elected to head up and speak for the group. And permanent paid officials form the organization's bureaucracy. Perhaps power is further divided between an organization's main headquarters and its Washington office. A structure with these characteristics would tend to be far less cohesive than a centralized, disciplined organization such as the Army or some trade unions.

Closely related to this factor is a third one—the nature of the *leadership* of the group. The heads of an organization can act in such a way as to weld the various elements together, or to sharpen their disunity. Many different attitudes and interests must be harmonized. The national business leader, for example, must tread cautiously between big business and little ones, between exporters and importers, between chain stores and corner grocery stores, between the makers and sellers of competing products. Yet he can not be a cipher—a mere punching bag for different business interests—for above all he must *lead*. He must set objectives for whatever programs can be agreed on. Thus the group leader is in the same position as a President or congressman, though his constituency is different. He must act as a diplomat patching up the differences among the subgroups. He must know when to lead his followers, when to follow them. He is at the head of the parade—but he cannot get too far ahead, or the paraders may follow someone else down a side street.

Finally, the power of a group is affected by the nature of the *political* and *governmental system* in which it operates. A system based on centralized governmental power and disciplined parties, like Britain's (see chapters 3 and 13), may be better able than the American system to withstand pressures from interest groups. Our government, with its decentralized parties, is more responsive to the appeals of well-organized minorities, as later chapters will suggest.

The group leader

Leaders of organizations use a variety of methods to hold their followers together. Directing the affairs of every group are a few insiders or old-timers who control the administrative machinery, such as admission to membership, financial affairs, correspondence, committees, and the like. This active minority actually runs the organization. It holds the strings that may make the members dance in tune. There are other methods of discipline and control. The leaders can withhold certain services (such as lobbying assistance) from rebellious members. Sometimes it can expel members who do not follow the party line; this sanction is important when the latter may lose their jobs if they lose their membership, as with the union closed shop. The leadership may control the organization's propaganda. The active minority usually puts out the newspaper or magazine that goes to the members. It arranges the meetings and works up the agenda and business.

The group leaders tend to stay in control year after year. Certain union officials such as John L. Lewis of the miners or "Big Bill" Hutcheson of the carpenters are cases in point, but actually this tendency applies to business, farm, and other organizations as well as to labor. Bossism or oligarchy exists in most groups, including parties.[9] Such leaders often contribute to the stability and adaptability of the group. Secure in its leadership, an organization may confront its enemies and pursue its program with unity and single-mindedness. On the other hand, such leadership may contribute to decay, demoralization, disunity. The active minority may stay in power by somewhat illegal means, or it may be enthusiastically re-elected or reappointed each year by a rank and file grateful for successes achieved.

Does all this mean that groups are run by little dictatorships? Not necessarily—it depends on the factors involved. *If* the members show a blind loyalty to the group, *if* the organization is centralized and compact, *if* the leaders want to be autocratic and have the means to be so—then a kind of dictatorship may result. But as we have seen, other forces within the groups, such as overlapping membership and interests, and various cross pressures, tend to work against absolutism. These internal forces are crucial. They help maintain a balance of power both *within* groups and *between* groups.

This balance of power is also upheld by external forces that operate in the whole community. One of these is democracy itself. Americans generally want to have a share in running their government—so naturally they want to have a say in the way their organizations are managed. Actually most groups are little democracies (although they may have their share of undemocratic practices). There are periodic elections; meetings are run in a parliamentary fashion; a member has the right to stand up in a meeting and say what he wants. If an organization violates democratic ways year after year, it comes into bad odor. Some of its own members may turn

[9] See Robert Michels, *Political Parties: A Sociological Study of the Oligarchical Tendencies of Modern Democracy* (London: Jarrold & Sons, 1915).

against it. Other organizations become hostile, and may refuse to play ball with it.

Probably the most powerful factors preventing one group from upsetting the balance of power are other groups. Organization invites counter-organization. The increased influence of one group forces competing groups to strengthen themselves. Decades ago nationwide corporations helped lead to the establishment of nationwide labor unions, for example, and these unions in turn stimulated the organization of business in national federations. If tomorrow people over sixty should form a powerful organization to put over a superbonus plan, people under sixty would organize against it through their existing organizations or through new ones. A sort of organizational arms race takes place, and every member feels that the devil takes the hindmost.

Groups in the political struggle

Seen in these terms, the power of organized groups does not turn only on internal factors, such as the size and unity and leadership of groups. It also turns on the nature of the environment, the attitudes of people everywhere, the strength of other groups. Adding up all these factors, what are the main advantages and disadvantages of the major groups in the American political struggle?

Numerically, businessmen are in a minority in the United States, yet they wield great power. This power has several foundations. In the first place, the business community is fairly cohesive. "To a high degree this cohesion comes from the sharing of common interests," says V. O. Key, Jr., "but not infrequently sections of the business and financial community are kept in line through pecuniary leverage. . . ." Erring businessmen can be disciplined by powerful men in the business community. But this is not a matter of deliberate conspiracy, Key notes. "Without design the system as a whole tends to produce conformity to its values. . . . A powerful discipline makes it difficult for a businessman to call his soul his own, that is, if he wants to stay in business. He must have regard for his customers, his suppliers, his bankers, his stockholders, his brokers, his lawyers, and all others with whom he deals."[10]

Second, business beliefs are shared by many Americans who are not businessmen. Business values have been stamped on American culture.[11] Many people identify themselves with business. Even after the depression and the New Deal, business leaders enjoyed higher public prestige than labor leaders, according to polls. Given this situation, it becomes easier for

[10] V. O. Key, Jr., *Politics, Parties, and Pressure Groups,* 2nd ed. (New York: The Thomas Y. Crowell Company, 1948), p. 119.

[11] The nature and extent of the domination of American thought and practice by business values was vividly described by Thorstein Veblen in a series of pioneering studies, especially in his *The Theory of the Leisure Class* (New York: The Macmillan Company, 1908).

people to accept such ideas as, "What is good for business is good for you."

Third, businessmen have money, and money means influence. It can be used to pay for propaganda, to support political parties, to finance lobbies, to influence public officials directly or indirectly. Fourth, business has important allies who share its community of interest, namely lawyers, editors, and other professional and white-collar people. Finally, businessmen have important skills, such as ability to explain their case, experience in competition, and the like.

Business has disadvantages, too. Businessmen are in a numerical minority, and in the long run votes count most in a democracy. The very concentration of business that promotes unity tends to make business a target. Americans tend to be suspicious of bigness and monopoly. Business is also a convenient scapegoat. When business falls off and jobs are scarce it is easy to blame "Wall Street."

Herblock in THE WASHINGTON POST AND TIMES HERALD

"It's terrible how the big money guys run politics."

Other groups have their own strengths and weaknesses. Industrial workers are large in numbers, and they are becoming more organizationally and politically conscious. But they are divided into organized and unorganized, white and black, skilled and unskilled. Moreover, many American workers refuse to identify themselves or their interests with an "inferior" class. In 1939—after ten years of depression—only one out of sixteen Americans identified himself as belonging to the lower classes, while about 87 per cent considered themselves as middle class. Further, it is hard for labor to make alliances with farm or business groups, because their stereotype of trade unionism is somewhat unfavorable.

The farmers' strategic situation is almost the reverse of labor's. They are declining in numerical size relative to the whole population. But their advantages are significant. The geography of American federalism gives them extra political strength, for farmers are spread through all forty-eight states. Furthermore, farmers enjoy high esteem; in the popular mind they are frugal, hard-working, independent—the backbone of the nation. Like labor, however, the farmers are divided.

These strategic factors are not static. The external factors especially tend to change over time. Business at one time may enjoy enormous prestige, as during the prosperous 1920's, when Calvin Coolidge could say that "the business of America is business." A few years later it may occupy the national doghouse because of changes in the over-all situation. Labor may be stronger during a time of ferment and reform than during a period of prosperity.

THE WEAPONS OF GROUP INFLUENCE

Groups use a wide range of political techniques in seeking to reach their goals. Their capacity to use these techniques is heavily affected by the factors we have just discussed—the size of the group, its cohesion or lack of it, its organizational structure, the skills of its leaders, the external situation. Like a good football team, every group must exploit the particular advantages that its material makes possible. Just as a team of lightweights may have to stress deception rather than power drives, so a small but well-organized group will probably rely on skillful lobbying rather than mass election tactics. In plotting their political tactics, most groups use one or more of the following:

Propaganda

All interest groups are propagandistic. They exploit the media described in the following chapter—radio, press, film, leaflets, signs, and—above all —word of mouth. As we have noted, business enjoys a special advantage in this arena of battle. Businessmen as a whole have the money to hire propaganda machinery. Being advertisers on a large scale, they have the technique of delivering their message effectively. Many of them feel that they must make up in "public information" the influence they lack in numbers. Most important, they generally have easy access to the means of propaganda, such as the press (see Chapter 11). The N.A.M. spends over $2 million a year in national advertising. It puts out four periodicals —one goes to 36,500 educators, another to 40,000 leaders of women's clubs, another to 30,000 farm leaders, another to clergymen. According to the N.A.M., during one nine-month period it "turned out 816,110 copies of 45 pamphlets, booklets, leaflets, etc." A speakers' training program, motion pictures (shown to 4620 audiences), and meetings with leaders of the main groups, such as farmers and veterans, are other features of this program of opinion molding. In any four years, says McKean, the N.A.M. "will spend more for this all-around publicity than any political party. And the material is technically excellent—very shrewdly and carefully prepared—whereas much party propaganda is crude and poorly adapted to its recipients."[12]

[12] Dayton McKean, *Party and Pressure Politics* (Boston: Houghton Mifflin Company, 1949), p. 493.

Supplementing the N.A.M.'s efforts are those of the Chamber of Commerce and of trade associations and individual corporations. An early expert in the propaganda field was the National Electric Light Association, which carried on an elaborate public relations program until it was dissolved in 1933. Its propaganda against public ownership and regulation of the electric utilities reached into churches, schools, clubs, and to the companies' own employees. This campaign cost the companies—and ultimately the public—at least $20 million a year. The electrical industries were especially vigilant in examining textbooks, and even "correcting" them.

Other groups have become increasingly aware of the uses of propaganda. Organized labor is a notable example. When a business organization places full-page messages in newspapers across the nation, unions will often find the funds to hire similar space for their answer. Recently the A.F.L. bought time on national radio networks to present its views. The C.I.O. put out highly effective pamphlets, especially on political and legislative matters. While labor has not yet matched the skill of business in the general field of propaganda, it is devoting more money and attention to this political technique. Other interest groups such as doctors and teachers are making effective use of publicity methods. The American Medical Association spent at least one million dollars in 1950 in a highly successful campaign against compulsory health insurance.

Electioneering

Almost all large organizations avow that they are "nonpolitical." The American Legion's constitution flatly bars political activity. Actually practically all organized groups are involved in politics in one way or another. What group leaders really mean when they say that they are nonpolitical is that they are *nonpartisan*. For a distinguishing feature of organized interest groups is that they try to keep their feet in both camps by working through both parties. Usually this means working for individual candidates in elections. The policy that labor has followed for years—helping our friends and defeating our enemies—is the policy of almost all organized interest groups.

The application of this method varies considerably. Occasionally organizations as organizations openly endorse a candidate and actively work for his election. Thus in 1924 many labor unions endorsed "Fighting Bob" La Follette for President; the C.I.O. officially backed President Roosevelt in 1944 and Adlai E. Stevenson in 1952. More often the organization formally stays neutral, but prominent officials take a public stand. In 1944, eleven members of the A.F.L.'s executive council worked actively for Roosevelt. Because of such factors as overlapping membership, an organization may set up a front organization to carry on its political activities, as in the case of Labor's Educational and Political League, formed by the A.F.L.

Individual labor unions, having somewhat homogeneous memberships, sometimes can afford to take a rather firm position on candidates. Other organizations often are more handicapped by the diversity of their members. A local retailers' group, for example, might be composed equally of Republicans and Democrats, and many of its members would fear to take an open position on a candidate because their business might suffer. In such cases more subtle means may be equally effective. At meetings word is passed around that Candidate X is sound from the organization's point of view. Perhaps the hat is passed around, too, and a contribution made to the cause. Members of the organization may serve as local opinion leaders in drumming up support for him. A local organization such as a Legion post may be strong enough to serve as a sort of secret caucus. Nationality groups gain much of their effectiveness from using word-of-mouth tactics.

Another method of trying to win elections is to form a separate party. Again and again some groups have decided that keeping a foot in the camps of both regular parties often leads to a choice—from their point of view—between Tweedledee and Tweedledum on election day. Third parties in the United States, however, have tended to be self-defeating (see Chapter 13). The strength of interest groups has been siphoned off into minority party politics, while the two old parties have continued to control government.

Some groups have tried a third method—trying to infiltrate the organization and machinery of *major parties*. They have placed their members on local, state, and national party committees and have helped send their members to party conventions as delegates. For years, one vice-president of the A.F.L. was prominent in Republican activities, and another was equally active for the Democrats.

Obviously, boring from within is not a new tactic; its significance today is its use on a much more intensive scale. The A.F.L.-C.I.O.'s Committee on Political Education is a case in point. Technically, C.O.P.E. is nonpartisan, assisting prolabor candidates in both parties. Actually, C.O.P.E. has come to concentrate most of its effort in the Democratic party. Not only does it endorse party candidates, like any organized interest, but in many states it has gone on to exercise electioneering functions that the parties ordinarily monopolize. C.O.P.E. pays much attention to registration (see Chapter 14) in order to insure a large vote. It takes part in primary campaigns as well as in the later election contests. It puts out posters and leaflets, holds schools on political action techniques, provides automobiles to carry voters to the polls.

Lobbying

Lobbying is a well-known weapon of interest groups. Generations of Americans have been stirred by exposés of the "social lobby" and "invisible government," of bribery and corruption and midnight revels, of invisible agents holding the strings that made politicians dance. Some of this feeling is based on folklore, but much of it on fact. From the time of the Yazoo land frauds 150 years ago, when a whole legislature was bribed and the Postmaster General put on a private payroll as a lobbyist, to the latest logrolling activity in Congress, Americans have enjoyed denouncing the "unscrupulous" lobbyists.

Over 1000 lobbyists are active in Washington today, but few of them are glamorous, unscrupulous, or very powerful. Most of the organizations maintaining lobbyists are highly specialized outfits such as the National Fertilizer Association, Retired Officers Association, Institute of Shortening and Edible Oils, Associated Tobacco Manufacturers, Texas Water Conservation Association, and a host of others. Lobbyists for these associations are usually hard-working attorneys, with long experience in Washington ways; their job is to watch a handful of bills and to keep in touch with a few administrative officials. Lawmaking today being a highly technical matter, these lobbyists—or legislative counsel, as they like to be called— play a useful part in modern government. The harried congressman or administrator, threading his way through mountains of paper and seeking to appease conflicting interests, gladly turns to them for their views and information.

Lobbyists for the big groups, such as farmers, labor, or business, operate on a loftier scale. Their specialty is knowing just how to throw their political weight around. These lobbyists are better known throughout the country than some senators, better paid, better staffed, and more secure in their positions. The groups they represent have such broad interests that these lobbyists must watch a wide variety of bills touching every phase of government. They are expert in raising such a clamor that they seem to be speaking for vast numbers of people. They exert pressure in Congress wherever they can find vulnerable points—regular committees, appropriations committees, individual legislators, even on the floor of the House or Senate (see Chapter 15). They know how to mobilize their organizations back home so that a storm of letters, telegrams, and petitions descend on Washington. They know how to draw up laws, to testify before committees, to help speed a bill through its long legislative journey, or to slow it down. They are experts in the art of influence.

Sometimes lobbyists stay in the background in order to make use of the legislator's own constituents. The following "Hints on Lobbying" sent by one organization to its members indicates the kind of methods used:

1. Interview the legislator at home if you are a constituent. If seeing him at the Capitol, impress on him that you live and vote in his district.
2. Be sure to have read the bill and to know the question with which it deals.
3. Find out main facts about legislator before interviewing him—his party, committee membership, business or profession, etc.
4. Be nonpartisan with legislator of opposite party from your own. In any case make clear our organization's nonpartisanship.

5. Don't pin legislator down to position for or against. Establish friendly relations. We will have to continue working with him in the future.
6. Use good salesmanship techniques. Our organization will be judged by the kind of interview you have.
7. Don't be "superior" even if you know far more about the question than he does. You are not there to score a point but to help get the measure passed!
8. Be patient and keep your temper.
9. Attend House and Senate galleries when bill comes up on the floor.
10. If possible, establish friendly relations with chairman and key members of at least one committee.

Bureaucrats are by no means free of the lobbyist's attentions. Many important decisions are made in the executive offices, and these decisions inevitably affect the lobbyist's "constituents." In dealing with administrators

HOW THE INTEREST GROUPS WORK

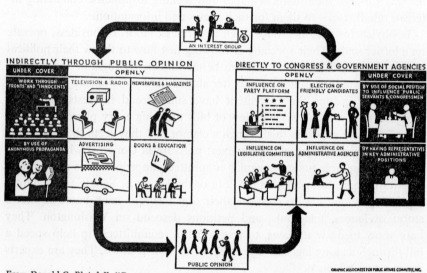

From Donald C. Blaisdell, "Government under Pressure," PUBLIC AFFAIRS PAMPHLET NO. 67

the lobbyist will often enlist the backing of a senator or representative. Interest groups claim certain departments as their own, as in the case of farmers and the Department of Agriculture, veterans and the Veterans Administration, businessmen and the Department of Commerce. In some agencies, especially at the state level, the strength of a single interest group is so great that it controls important administrative actions such as licensing of professions, control of examinations, and policing.

How many voters does a particular lobbyist represent? Nobody really knows. For one thing, their strength varies with the issue; on one matter an organization will be united, on another it will not be. Moreover, polls and voting studies indicate that the strength that an interest group can muster on election day is often exaggerated. But the real question is what the congressman *thinks* the group can do at the polls. Here he is at a disadvantage. The congressman is always feeling in the dark. As later chapters suggest, he is highly vulnerable to anything that hints of organized power, of purposeful and united action. The administrator, too, is always uncertain of the strength that a bloc in Congress can muster to deprive his agency of funds or even abolish it forever. The great weapon of the lobbyist is the appearance he gives of representing unseen millions of voters. He must remember the old maxim, "Never admit that it is only you who are talking."

Other group weapons

Force. We think of force as a weapon of nation-states (national groups) rather than internal groups. So it is, for the most part. But force has had its place in the clashes among groups at home. Revolutions and civil wars have taken place in virtually every nation. In our own, the Whisky Rebellion of 1794 occurred when Pennsylvanians refused to pay excise taxes and took up arms against troops directed by President Washington himself. Today race riots and lynchings are usually the action of one racial group attempting to coerce another. In depression years American farmers sometimes used force —or threats of force—to prevent the banks from foreclosing their mortgages. Intimidation is a close cousin to force. In 1941 Negro leaders threatened a march on Washington in protest against discrimination in employment; President Roosevelt headed off the plan by setting up a Committee on Fair Employment Practice.[13] Years ago Mary E. Lease urged farmers to "raise less corn and more hell"; this kind of advice has been followed by a variety of groups.

Strike. We usually think of the strike as a labor weapon. Certainly it is one of the trade union's chief economic methods; strikes have averaged hundreds a year over the past decade. Other groups, however, know how to make strategic use of the withdrawal of labor services. Teachers' strikes take place from time to time. During the depression years, dairymen refused to deliver milk to the retailers because of low prices; when some dairymen tried to send milk to the cities, their trucks were forced to a halt and the milk spilled into the gutters. Businessmen, too, have withheld their goods for various purposes. Professional people have used an allied weapon, the boycott—when the University of Georgia during Governor Eugene Talmadge's regime failed to meet certain standards of academic freedom some graduate schools refused to admit graduates of the university. In Britain the doctors threatened to go on strike if the Labor government's health scheme was adopted.

[13] L. C. Kesselman, *The Social Politics of FEPC* (Chapel Hill: University of North Carolina Press, 1948), pp. 13 ff.

INTEREST GROUPS AND DEMOCRATIC GOVERNMENT

Almost everyone likes to denounce the pressure groups—especially somebody else's pressure group. Editorial columns are filled with protests that big business, or big labor, or the farm bloc, is taking over the country. This viewing with alarm has put organized interest groups as a whole under a cloud. Some people even look on them as a perversion of democracy—as a blot on the otherwise fair system of representing people in a democracy. Various proposals are advanced to do away with the evil interests, at least to clip their wings.

It is easy enough to answer these gloomy observers. Obviously organized groups are here to stay. As long as there is a modicum of freedom left in America, men will associate on some basis or another. Life without group activity would be unthinkable. Actually we owe a great deal to the richness and fullness of group life in America. Our progress in many areas, technological, cultural, political and the like would have been impossible without it. Yet there are two criticisms of organized interests in America that must be examined:

Interest groups: attack and defense

Certain organizations, it is said, are becoming *too strong*. The names of these groups depend on the group allegiance of the accuser. Once upon a time big business was the chief target, but more recently farmers and unions have been pictured as the new Goliath. Are these fears justified? Our discussion above suggests that at least they are grossly exaggerated. The larger an association becomes, we noticed, the more it includes members of other groups who will have other allegiances. The stronger a group becomes, the more stimulus there will be for other groups to counterorganize. The real defense against group tyranny in America lies in the groups themselves.[14] As long as we have our great number and rich diversity of groups, and as long as we keep our liberties, no single interest or combination of interests can take America over. The competition would be too great.

A second criticism is that organizations are *unrepresentative*. There is a good deal of truth to this. In the first place, organization leaders often fail to speak fairly even for their own members. In the second place, organization leaders may ignore the many people with related interests outside their organizations, as in the case of agricultural associations that act for a narrow segment of the farm population. In the third place—and most important of all—many elements of the population are not represented in formal organizations at all, or are badly underrepresented. Not all groups receive the consideration they deserve in the collision of organized interests. Notable examples of unorganized or underorganized interests are consum-

[14] D. B. Truman, *op. cit.,* Chapter 16.

ers, nonunion labor, farm workers, certain professional and white-collar groups. Something happens to representative government under these conditions.

This criticism should not, however, be carried too far. Our government is still organized on a *territorial* or *geographical* basis; we have not built occu-

HOW TO CURB INFLATION
From the ST. LOUIS POST DISPATCH

pational representation right into the structure of government. Furthermore, Americans who are underorganized can always resort to the polls, or ultimately they can organize their own associations. They can take advantage of their democratic rights to make up for whatever defects exist in group representation. Admittedly this is a slow process, but it is a process that has occurred again and again in American history as less organized elements have striven to make up for their weakness by political and economic counterorganization. The result is a system of rough justice in the representation of groups—but admittedly a system that could be improved.

Control of lobbying: a case study

However exaggerated, these criticisms of the activities of organized interest groups cannot be ignored. And they have not been. For years Americans have been trying to curb the excesses of the "pressure groups." The attempt to control lobbying—which, as noted, is a primary weapon of the interests—is an interesting example of the difficulties in regulating the activities of dynamic groups in a democracy.

Attempts to control lobbying are at least a century old. In 1877 Georgia wrote into its constitution the simple provision that "lobbying is a crime." Early in this century a number of states passed acts to regulate lobbyists. Many of these measures require that legislative counsel or agents officially register as such, and that they file statements of expenses paid or promised in connection with promoting legislation. The Federal Regulation of Lobbying Act in 1946 (Title III of the Legislative Reorganization Act of 1946) followed this pattern. Under the national law, every person hired to influence or defeat bills in Congress must register and disclose the name and address of his employer, how much he is paid, who pays him, and the like. Every three months he must file a further statement listing the names of publications that have carried his publicity, and the nature of the bills he supports or opposes. Organizations whose main purpose is to influence legislation also must furnish information which is printed regularly in the *Congressional Record*. It seems clear, however, that the act has hardly diminished the extent of lobbying. And the registration provisions have aroused serious questions of constitutionality in federal courts.

The aim of such legislation is to turn the spotlight of publicity on the spending and activities of lobbying. How successful has the attempt been? The national lobby law has furnished a vast amount of detailed information about lobbyists—who they are, who sponsors and finances them, what bills they seek to pass or block. Some idea has been gained of the amount of money involved; in the first four years the act was in effect, lobbyists collected about $60 million and spent approximately $30 million. About 500 persons and organizations had filed, but many hundred others had not, on one pretext or another.

Some hold that publicity is not enough, that *actual regulation* of lobbying is needed. Most lobbyists, they argue, have no fear of publicity, but on the contrary actually welcome it. There is much doubt, however, that Congress will try to restrict lobbyists. For one thing, such an attempt might drive the lobbyists underground where their influence might be more insidious and just as effective. Regulation might run into serious constitutional objections based on the rights guaranteed by the First Amendment. But more important, most students of the problem feel that lobbyists serve an important and desirable function, and that nothing more than publicity is needed.

The argument goes like this: lobbyists are a sort of third house of Congress. While Senate and House are set up on a *geographical* basis, lobbyists represent people directly in terms of their *economic* or other interests. The Representative speaks for voters as members of, say, the third district of Ohio; the lobbyist speaks for people as manufacturers or steelworkers or veterans or fruitgrowers. Small but important groups, such as bankers, can get representation in this third house where they might not in the other two. In a nation of large and important interests this kind of *functional* representation, if not abused, is highly necessary as a supplement to geographical representation. The lobbyists supply vitally needed information and ideas for the legislative mill. Some European nations have gone so far as to set up formal economic organs to provide functional representation; our informal "third house" is a welcome compromise between such extreme measures and no functional representation at all.

The real problem

Another problem of interest group activity in America is perhaps more serious than those already described. This is the frequent failure of interest groups to represent broader segments of the community, organized or not. This problem in turn involves the broader question of *national unity* that we discussed in Part One and that crops up again and again in this book. Somehow Americans must live and work together. To do so they must rise above some of their differences and join hands to realize more broadly representative goals. To some extent interest groups perform this very function. Especially the great national organizations of farmers, workers, and businessmen tend to reflect broad rather than narrow interests because of the diversity of their members.

But the process of finding general areas of agreement does not go far enough. Even the strongest organized interests are still minorities—they are not big enough to embrace all the people, or even most of them. Yet they dominate national legislation. A few years ago an influential congressman was quoted as saying, after the late President William Green of the American Federation of Labor had asked him to vote for a food subsidy bill, "I have always followed Mr. Green on labor bills. But this is not a labor bill. This is a farm bill. On this bill I follow the farm leaders." Undoubtedly such a course is good pressure-group politics. But is it good *majority-welfare* politics?

Groups tend to be competitive. In the noisy clash of their interests the welfare of the great mass of Americans is sometimes drowned out. The dynamic elements of group life that contribute so much to a healthy America give rise at the same time to dangerous stresses and strains. Groups can cement individual *fragments* of the American people; what will pull together the *people as a whole,* including the organized and unorganized? Many agencies fulfill this need—our common traditions and ideas, the role of national leaders like the President, and the overlapping character of the groups themselves. On the organizational level, the political party fills this great function, but it too is divided and weakened by internal disunities (see Chapter 13). The problem of maintaining internal unity is especially acute in a day when government may need broad and firm support from the people in handling critical problems at home and abroad. We will return to this problem in Chapter 21—but first we must examine the political forces that play upon our government and the governmental machinery that both reflects and in turn affects these forces.

GOVERNMENT BY THE PEOPLE IS SUPPOSED TO be government in accordance with the will of the people. So it is, but difficulties immediately arise. What *is* the will of the people? What does government do when people disagree? What does it do when opinions change? What does it do when most of the people are indifferent about some issue, while a minority is active and noisy? Should government itself try to influence opinion? If so, how far should it go?

Let us look at these questions from the vantage point of, say, a senator in Washington. He wants to be the servant of the people. But he's not sure what people want. He cannot really tell from his mail, because he is not sure that the letter writers actually reflect opinion back home. He is suspicious of public opinion polls. He is not sure just what issues he was elected on, since he argued for and against so many propositions in his last campaign. Besides, it is five years since he was elected, and many important events have taken place in that time. He listens for the voice of the people, but the people do not speak with a single voice. No wonder he straddles the fence. From his point of view, the *people* are straddling the fence.

But governments must act. Decisions must be made. Somehow, out of the confusion of raucous voices and dead silences, politicians must shape fairly precise and positive policies. To see the relation between political opinons and governmental actions, first we must look at the variety of people involved.

MILLIONS OF PUBLICS

Imagine that the following incident takes place:

A group of college students decide—all in a spirit of frivolity—to announce to the press that they are forming a local chapter of the League of the Militant Godless. The story appears in a newspaper. Immediately a variety of responses takes place. The other students merely smile. They know a joke when they see one. The president and dean of the college do not smile. They know that this is meant as a joke, but they are afraid of

11 ★

Public

opinion:

the voices of

the people

267

the effect it might have on the "public." Local church groups are indignant. Religion is not a matter for pranks, says one minister in a sermon. Local townspeople are divided; some see the incident as a joke, but others feel that the students went too far. Several legislators at the state capital denounce the affair as another sign of communist influence in the colleges. Some people read about the incident in the newspapers, shake their heads, and forget about it. Others hear about it indirectly, and perhaps complain that there are too many reds at the state college. A few parents of undergraduates write letters of protest to the college president. But most people, even in the state, never hear about the incident at all. At any rate, a few weeks go by, and the incident is all but forgotten.

No mass mind

Now it would be wrong to say that one general public opinion, or a single mass mind, was involved here. Actually there were a number of *different public opinions* simply because there were a number of *different publics*. These publics reacted in several ways, largely in terms of their physical nearness to the incident, the extent of their understanding of the incident, their own occupational position or social group, their stake or interest in the incident, and above all, their basic attitudes. The other students, for example, were close to the incident, understood its basically frivolous nature, and considered the culprits some of their own. The college administration, the ministers, the legislators had an actual or assumed stake in the incident. The townspeople reacted largely as a close-knit group with set attitudes toward student activities. Most people elsewhere were remote from the incident, uninformed, and uninterested.

Translate all this into a real live national issue, and one sees the tremendous complexity of public opinion and the many publics involved. The President makes a speech about labor legislation, and his words fall differently on the ears of union members, businessmen, union leaders, farmers, Democrats, Republicans, and so on. The Secretary of Agriculture announces a new farm program, and he gets mixed reactions not only from the large nonfarming public, but also from the farm public itself—that is, from cotton farmers as against wheat farmers, from large farmers as compared with small farmers. A senator calls for the end of government subsidies; many businessmen applaud because they want lower taxes, but businessmen receiving subsidies, as in the case of ship operators, do not applaud. These are examples merely of different *interests*—but in fact the whole process is immensely complicated by different attitudes that people have, their economic and social status, their group loyalties, type of occupation, degree of understanding or information.

What, then, are some of the more important features of public opinions —and of the various publics that hold them?

Some qualities of public opinions

In the first place, *public opinions are often extremely fluid and changeable*. This is true even of some of the most basic, deep-seated attitudes. An example is opinion in the field of foreign policy. During the past 15 years Gallup poll-takers have asked a sample of the public: "What do you regard as the most important problem before the American people today?" Over the years the response has varied widely. In 1935 only 11 per cent of the respondents answered, "Foreign policy issues." By 1941, that answer was given by 81 per cent of them. In 1945 the figure was down to 7 per cent, but by April 1948 it had risen to 73 per cent. The public seems to have moods which shift quickly and strongly as events take place.[1]

The interested public is always changing. This is one reason for instability of opinions. Different issues attract different publics; even the same issue over a period of time may attract a changing public. People get bored with causes or issues just as they get tired of clothes or movie stars. Or the objective situation may change. For example, when they are cut out of office, Democrats may view the issue of governmental economy in a manner different from the way they view it when they are in.

People holding an opinion vary greatly in intensity of belief. Some people passively hold a belief; others are fanatics on the matter. Such variations in intensity have important results in politics. The attitudes of the passive can probably be changed more easily than the attitudes of those who have strong feelings. And the latter can be expected to act more positively on their beliefs. They may try to convert others to their cause, to organize in groups, to win votes for a politician.

Public opinion may be latent. People's attitudes may not have crystallized on some issue; still, their attitudes may be important, for those attitudes can be evoked and converted into action if certain things are done. Indeed, one can often predict how certain persons will react to an incident even though they have never indicated their views on the matter. In the incident described above, for example, the ministers and state legislators had never expressed attitudes toward the League of the Militant Godless, but anyone could have predicted what their views would be. A good politician must be able to assess latent or potential public opinion, so that he can face (or evade) new issues with some knowledge of how public opinion will line up.[2]

Finally, *the public is made up of numberless subpublics, differentiated in many ways.* This is simply another way of stating what we found in the

[1] Gabriel Almond, *The American People and Foreign Policy* (New York: Harcourt, Brace and Company, Inc., 1950), p. 66.

[2] L. W. Doob, *Public Opinion and Propaganda* (New York: Henry Holt and Company, Inc., 1948), p. 40. For a study stressing political aspects of public opinion, see M. B. Ogle, Jr., *Public Opinion and Political Dynamics* (Boston: Houghton Mifflin Company, 1950).

reaction to our college boys' prank—that different publics were encountered, or created. These subpublics vary in terms of the degree to which they are attentive to various issues, their understanding, their basic attitudes, their religion, their section or locality, their economic or social position, their national origin, their cultural inheritance, their education, and in a host of other ways. Moreover, these thousands of subpublics cut across one another in a thousand different ways, in turn creating literally millions of subpublics.

No wonder public opinion seems so illusive and intangible, that the politician treads warily, that opinion polls go wrong. The picture becomes even more complicated when we consider that there can be a difference between opinions privately held and opinions publicly expressed, and that some opinions have high "competence"—that is, are directly related to the person's factual knowledge—while other opinions are uninformed and superficial. But the picture is not one of complete confusion. There is some order, some pattern in the infinite variety of political opinions in our democracy. In part, this semblance of order stems from certain basic ideas held by a great number of Americans.

The American idea-system

What is basic in our own political idea-system? One eminent sociologist has found that the American people, despite their diversity, have a common set of beliefs. This American creed he calls "the cement in the structure of this great and disparate nation."[3] This creed, says Myrdal, has its roots in the era of "Enlightenment" when early Americans were absorbing the new philosophy of liberty, equality, and fraternity. It also has roots in Christianity—in the biblical teachings about man's need for freedom and equality, for justice and dignity. Americans, in short, believe in democracy.

Americans actually order their lives, however, according to a more specific set of beliefs which somehow they square with the basic creed. These particular beliefs are so numerous and so complex as to fill many volumes. A few of them would be worth listing here. After making an exhaustive study of a typical American city (Muncie, Indiana) in the 1930's, the investigators found that most of the citizens of "Middletown," as they called it, shared such beliefs as the following:[4]

That, when in doubt, people should act like other people.

That America is a land of progress, and that increasing size is a sign of progress.

That progress should not be speeded up artificially.

[3] Gunnar Myrdal, *An American Dilemma* (New York: Harper & Brothers, 1944), Vol. I, p. 3.

[4] R. S. Lynd and H. M. Lynd, *Middletown in Transition* (New York: Harcourt, Brace and Company, 1937), pp. 402-486.

That the middle way is the best way.

That good will and sincerity will solve most problems.

That a man should try to get ahead of his fellows, but not in an unfair way.

That if a man does not get on, it is his own fault.

That people should place *their* family, *their* community, *their* state, *their* nation first.

That American ways are better than foreign ways, and Americans superior to foreigners.

That the small businessman is the backbone of the American economic system.

That capital and labor have basically the same interests.

That such problems as corruption in government can be solved mainly by electing better men to office.

Many of the ideas by which Americans live contradict one another. The reason is partly that ideas arising in one era are carried over uncritically into new situations. "Men's ideas, beliefs, and loyalties—their nonmaterial culture—are frequently slower to be changed than are their material tools," says Professor Lynd. "It is precisely in this matter of trying to live by contrasting rules of the game that one of the most characteristic aspects of our American culture is to be seen."[5]

Here are some of our contrasting rules:

Everyone should try to be successful. *But:* The kind of person you are is more important than how successful you are.

The family is our basic institution and the sacred core of our national life. *But:* Business is our most important institution, and, since national welfare depends upon it, other institutions must conform to its needs.

Religion and the finer things of life are our ultimate values and the things all of us are really working for. *But:* A man owes it to himself and his family to make as much money as he can.

Life would not be tolerable if we did not believe in progress and know that things are getting better. We should, therefore, welcome new things. *But:* The old, tried fundamentals are best; and it is a mistake for busybodies to try to change things too fast or to upset the fundamentals.

Honesty is the best policy. *But:* Business is business, and a businessman would be a fool if he didn't cover his hand.

Education is a fine thing. *But:* It is the practical man who gets things done.

The American judicial system insures justice to every man, rich or poor. *But:* A man is a fool not to hire the best lawyer he can afford.

No man deserves to have what he hasn't worked for. It demoralizes him to do so. *But:* You can't let people starve.[6]

[5] R. S. Lynd, *Knowledge for What?* (Princeton: Princeton University Press, 1939), p. 59.

[6] From Lynd, *Knowledge for What?*, pp. 60-61. For a more recent analysis of the American system of values, see R. M. Williams, *American Society* (New York: Alfred A. Knopf, 1951).

WHERE DO OUR OPINIONS COME FROM?

Living in a democracy can be a pretty confusing business. Everyone seems to be trying to get our ear or to catch our eye so that he can press on us his point of view. Under a dictatorship life is much simpler. There is officially one public opinion—the Word that comes down from the head man. Some of the lesser citizenry growl and mutter under their breath, but they are in no position to take a public stand. In a democracy we sometimes complain about the babel of voices that shriek at us in the newspaper and over the air waves, but we sense, too, that this babel is a sign of a free society, and one of its foundation posts.

If we look sharply, however, we can see a pattern even in the complex workings of public opinion in a democracy. Along with basic ideas described above, there are certain forces that bulk large in the shaping of men's ideas. There are certain methods of persuasion and propaganda common to all opinion molders.

Opinion shapers

First of all, our opinions are molded by the *culture* we live in—by the over-all beliefs and behavior that characterize American society. Chapter 1 describes certain aspects of our society, including the shifting economic and social foundations of our society, the impact of these changes on individual and group attitudes and behavior, and some psychological factors. It will be useful to keep these factors in mind in considering the nature of public opinion. Our common membership in the same society is a source of some uniformity in our opinions. But our society is vast and highly diverse. What produces some pattern of opinion within our complex culture?

Probably the most important opinion molder of all is the *family*. We begin to form our picture of the world at our Mother's knee, or listening to Father talk at breakfast, or hearing the tales that our older brothers and sisters bring back from school. These are probably not political opinions, but the basic attitudes that will shape our future opinions—attitudes toward our neighbors, toward other classes or types of people, toward local rules or customs, toward society in general. "The family is bound up with all the great crises and transitions of life," says MacIver. "It is the primary agent in the molding of the life-habits and the life-attitudes of human beings."[7] Some of us rebel against the ways of the close little group that we live with, perhaps, but most of us conform. Thus the family is a sort of link with the past and the present. It translates the world to us, but it does so in its own terms.

We are scarcely out of the diaper age when our world is beginning to ex-

[7] R. M. MacIver, *The Web of Government* (New York: The Macmillan Company, 1947), p. 23.

pand rapidly. We go to school, we associate with different types of people, we get a more general picture of the world we live in. At school we probably learn as much outside the classroom as in it, because we are reacting not merely to teachers and books but also to behavior—the manners, dress, talk, attitudes—of other children. The same is true of our church, another opinion-making institution. We are influenced by sermons and symbols, and also by the behavior of other members of the congregation. The attitudes we develop from living in our community, through association with family, friends, school, church, are attitudes that will influence us the rest of our lives, because they are gained from *direct personal contact* with other people.

But other influences are coming to bear. We begin to look at the newspaper—perhaps only at the comics, sports, headlines, and pictures at first, but later we read news stories and possibly the editorial page. Indeed, we can hardly avoid some contact with the newspaper, for it has been estimated that only one out of every twenty families in urban areas reads no daily newspaper. The total circulation of American newspapers is over 55 million copies a day. There are countless foreign-language newspapers, and there are thousands of weeklies, ranging from mass-circulation magazines we are all familiar with, such as *Newsweek, Life,* and *The Saturday Evening Post,* to more specialized journals, and not forgetting the multitude of slicks and pulps that are sold every day. Walter Lippmann has called the newspaper the "bible of democracy, the book out of which a people determines its conduct."[8]

We begin to watch television, another key instrument of mass communication and persuasion. Studies show that pictures are often the most effective means of communication and persuasion. Television, by bringing into the home moving pictures combined with sound is probably becoming, politically, the most effective mass medium of influence.[9]

And we begin to go to the movies. Most weeks there are at least 55 million paid admissions to motion pictures. (Television may cut permanently into this figure.) They see not only one or two feature films, but short subjects, newsreels, and perhaps even documentary films. Seventy per cent of the people able to go to the movies attend at least once every three weeks, and many of them go much more often. It is estimated that two-thirds of these movie goers are under thirty years of age. Thus we tend to be most exposed to the movies at an age when our attitudes are most malleable. The movies, with an eye on the box office, may tend overly to stress the exceptional rather than the typical, the sensational rather than the significant, but they are probably no more prone to this than radio or television.

[8] Walter Lippmann, *Liberty and the News* (New York: Harcourt, Brace, and Howe, 1920), p. 47.

[9] Angus Campbell, Gerald Gurin, and Warren E. Miller, "Television and the Election," *Scientific American,* 1953, Vol. 188, pp. 46-48.

To name these major opinion-forming agencies is not to exhaust the list of influences that focus on us as we grow into citizenhood. Books, for example, play an important though often intangible role. Nor is it to do justice to the many groups or persons, such as parties, interest groups, governments, politicians, businessmen, bureaucrats, and corporations, that seek to use the media of communication and persuasion for their own ends. But first we must ask the question: How much influence do these forces have in molding opinion? Are they as formidable as they seem?

How influential are the editors?

Consider the press. It can be argued that the newspapers really do not influence opinion very much because the editors often think one way and the people vote the opposite way. The four elections of Franklin D. Roosevelt to the Presidency are often cited to support this view. It has been estimated that Roosevelt was backed by 40 per cent of the press (in terms of total circulation) in 1932, by 36 per cent in 1936, by 20 per cent in 1940, and by 17 per cent in 1944. Yet he won all these elections decisively, and he swept some urban areas overwhelmingly where he had little or no newspaper support. Harry Truman's victory in 1948 is another case in point, and bosses have flourished for years in many cities in the face of continued denunciation by the local newspapers. It is also pointed out that the vast majority of newspaper readers do not bother to look at the editorial page.

These arguments, however, do not wholly meet the issue. The real question is not whether the press directly influences our choices at the polls, but whether it gives us a conception of the world about us that indirectly influences our political behavior. Our views are shaped, in Lippman's words, by the "pictures inside our heads." The newspaper, in its front-page make-up, its headlines, its use of pictures, its playing up of some news and playing down of other, its distortion or suppression of important information (in the case of some journals), helps form those "pictures inside our heads." Thus, while it is significant that Roosevelt won out against the bulk of the press, the really central question is the extent to which he had to modify his program and actions in the face of public opinion even before he began campaigning. The press has a long-run, continuous influence on opinions that may not be obvious in a particular election.

This invisible influence is important, because it means that other media, such as radio, television, or movies, can also be effective in molding political attitudes. It is sometimes thought that radio, being ostensibly neutral in politics, and the movies, having no political views as such, cannot be viewed in the same light as the press, which often bears an obvious party label (the *New York Herald Tribune,* for example, identifies itself as an independent Republican newspaper). On the contrary, the radio, television and movies, as part of our eyes and ears, help mold our underlying attitudes and thus our decisions at the polls, just as the daily newspaper does. Indeed, their effect may be all the greater if they have no obvious party ties or open intentions of influencing voters. An Edward R. Murrow or a Walter Winchell, speaking over the radio and television to millions, may tell a story about Washington doings that will influence the votes of many more people than the speech of a leading party politician over another major network. A movie depicting Soviet brutality in dramatic and grisly terms may affect attitudes toward American foreign policy more decisively than a statement by the Secretary of State.

Mass media and local leaders

It seems clear, then, that the combined weight of mass media—the press, movies, radio, and television—in opinion making in America is very large. Some social scientists believe that these agencies are coming to have more influence than the family itself in shaping attitudes. It is difficult to prove this contention, however, because the particular influence of the home or the press cannot easily be separated out and isolated for study. For example, if reading a Democratic newspaper for many years influences a father, and he influences his son, which is the dominant factor, home or newspaper?

We do have a little evidence, however, on the relative roles of newspapers and radio in a particular campaign. In a study of Erie County, Ohio, voters indicated that radio and newspapers had helped them equally in making their final decisions on the presidential choices. But when asked for the most important single source, radio was mentioned half again as frequently as the newspaper. The investigators concluded that "to the extent that the formal media exerted any influence at all on vote intention or actual vote, radio proved more effective than the newspaper."[10] The explanation may be that the radio gives the listener a greater sense of participation than the newspaper. Perhaps the importance of radio helps account for Franklin D. Roosevelt's success in electioneering, for he was master of the art of radio speaking. (Or perhaps the situation is quite the reverse— perhaps the radio was especially significant because Roosevelt made such expert use of it, in which case it would not play such a role in the campaign ordinarily.)

But whatever the role of press and radio and other media may be, we must not lose sight of the fact, as will be noted in the next chapter, that it is above all *direct, face-to-face* contacts that influence people, whether in family, neighborhood, or group. Studies have shown that the more *personal* the means of communication, the more effective it is in changing opinions. For example, it seems clear that (other things being equal) face-

[10] P. F. Lazarsfeld, *The People's Choice* (New York: Duell, Sloan, and Pearce, 1944), p. 128.

to-face conversation has more effect than a radio talk, and a radio speech is more effective than a newspaper account of it.[11] Radio singer Kate Smith once sold almost $40 million of bonds in one day. Her phenomenal success was undoubtedly due to the fact that her listeners felt she was talking directly to each of them. Over a period of time they had gained a sense of her personality.

Does this mean that personal methods of communication have more effect on opinions than institutional methods, such as newspapers? Possibly, but the problem is not that simple. For the local opinion leaders, who influence their friends through face-to-face conversations, may have got their ideas from a newspaper or magazine and may pass those ideas on to other people virtually unchanged. If a friend drops in and sells me on the need for a sales tax, and if he in turn got the idea from a popular magazine, what is the source of the influence on me? The shaping of opinions is not a one-way or even a two-way affair. Opinions are the product of many interrelated forces, each acting on others. It seems safe to say, however, that the mass media of communication, while they may influence local opinion leaders, will never substitute for them.

"HOW TO WIN FRIENDS AND . . ."

It has been said that we live in the Propaganda Age. Propaganda is, of course, nothing new, but in the twentieth century it has truly come into its own. The reasons for this development are not hard to find. The mass media described above have become enormous enterprises, such as newspapers with circulations in the millions, air waves spanning the continent, movies showing in almost every city and town in the nation. Behind all this is the fact that techniques of communication have been vastly improved in a few decades. Then again, the art of propaganda has been refined in our century. Harold Lasswell has said that "A new skill group has come into existence in modern civilization . . . skill in propaganda has become one of the most effective roads to power in modern states." We need think only of Joseph Goebbels, the master Nazi propagandist, to realize the truth of this statement.

What is propaganda?

Is propaganda bad? Not necessarily. Indeed, it is difficult to say just where propaganda leaves off and education starts. Effective education may include some propaganda (in favor, let's say, of basic democratic values, the virtues of which must in part be taken on faith). And if propaganda is defined as a "method used for influencing the conduct of others on behalf

[11] See Wilbur L. Schramm, ed., *Communications in Modern Society* (Urbana: University of Illinois Press, 1948), esp. pp. 171-185.

of predetermined ends," then almost every person who writes or talks with a purpose becomes a propagandist. Lasswell has described propaganda as a technique of social control—"the manipulation of collective attitudes by the use of significant symbols (words, pictures, and tunes) rather than violence, bribery, or boycott." Obviously propaganda in these terms can be used for good causes as well as evil ones.

More than any other people Americans should be familiar with propaganda techniques, because we are almost constantly exposed to commercial advertising, and advertisers exploit these techniques in full. (It is said that Adolf Hitler borrowed some of his propaganda methods from American publicity experts.) Advertisements are cunningly designed by "practical psychologists" to appeal to our basic attitudes, and especially to our desire for *recognition* by others (above all, by members of our own group), for *prestige,* and for *security.* Constant repetition is the hallmark of effective propaganda. Malcolm M. Willey writes: "In straight advertising, for example, the morning newspaper will carry the [advertising] copy; it will appear again in the street car (or even in the flip device in the taxicab); at the office a letter or a telegram may supplement what already has been said; the menu and the matches of the restaurant will serve as another medium of transmission; the afternoon paper repeats what the morning issue has already said; billboards are employed to catch a wandering eye; the radio program has its sponsor; the motion picture has not been free of advertising influence; and more recently the neon sign takes the 'message' far into the night."[12] This bombardment of potential buyers from all directions seems to get results.

As with the advertiser, so with the politician. The latter, seeking votes instead of sales, makes use of every agency of communication—ranging from skywriting to automobile stickers—that will influence men's attitudes and actions. Despite the variety of channels employed, however, certain methods are characteristic of propaganda, especially political propaganda.

Some propaganda techniques

Name calling—giving an idea a bad label—is used to make us reject and condemn the idea without examining the evidence.

Glittering generality—associating something with a "virtue word"—is used to make us accept and approve the thing without examining the evidence.

Transfer carries the authority, sanction, and prestige of something respected and revered over to something else in order to make the latter acceptable.

Testimonial consists in having some respected or hated person say that a given idea or program or product or person is good or bad.

12 M. M. Willey, "Communications Agencies and the Volume of Propaganda," *Annals* of the American Academy of Political and Social Sciences, 1935, p. 197.

Plain folks is the method by which a speaker tries to convince his audience that he and his ideas are good because they are "of the people," the "plain folks."

Card stacking involves the selection of truths or falsehoods, logic or illogic, to give the best or the worst possible case for an idea, program, person, or product.

Band wagon—with this, the propagandist tries to convince us that all members of a group to which we belong accept his program and that we must *therefore* follow our crowd and "jump on the band wagon."[13]

A speech delivered in 1939 was analyzed in the above terms, with the names of the various devices italicized in parentheses:

Ours (*Plain folks*) must be a moral (*Glittering generality*) platform from which there is preached (*Transfer*) a positive (*Glittering generality*) policy based upon the principles of religion (*Glittering generality, Transfer*) and of patriotism (*Glittering generality*). For God (*Transfer*) and country (*Transfer, Glittering generality*). For Christ (*Transfer*) and the flag (*Transfer, Glittering generality*)—that is our motto as we prepare for action, for Christian American (*Transfer, Glittering generality*) action. . . .

Limitations of propaganda

These propaganda devices by no means make up an exhaustive list. Many others could be cited, such as the use of music, color, and pageantry in staging political rallies or the expert manipulation of "plus" or "minus" symbols in radio speeches. Some of the devices have been greatly developed in sheer Machiavellianism. For example, "card stacking" looks rather harmless compared to Hitler's technique of the "big lie"—the Nazi leader said in *Mein Kampf* that the "primitive" masses will "more easily fall victims to a great lie than to a small one, since they themselves perhaps also lie sometimes in little things, but would certainly still be too much ashamed of too great lies."

Far more important than the techniques of propaganda is the nature of the propagandist and of the person being propagandized, the "propagandee." What is the intention of the propagandist? What is his social or occupational position? How effective is his organization for dispensing propaganda—does he have a soapbox or a nationwide chain of newspapers?[14] What about the propagandee? How much education has he had? How firmly fixed are his ideas? What class or group position does he oc-

[13] Slightly paraphrased from A. M. Lee and E. B. Lee, eds., *The Fine Art of Propaganda* (New York: Harcourt, Brace and Co., 1939), pp. 23-24. The speech analysis was also taken from this source. For a somewhat different treatment of propaganda techniques, see L. I. Pearlin and Morris Rosenberg, "Propaganda Techniques in Institutional Advertising," *Public Opinion Quarterly*, Vol. 16, 1952, pp. 5-26.

[14] Doob, *Public Opinion and Propaganda*, pp. 287 ff; see also Ogle, *Public Opinion and Political Dynamics*, pp. 233 ff.

cupy? How strong is his resistance or skepticism—is he hard to "sell"? Clearly propaganda involves more than technique; it involves the study of *personality*. (This is an excellent example of an area where politics and psychology meet.) And because of the infinite variety of personality no propaganda "gimmick," however slickly manipulated, will always succeed in persuading people.

Thus propaganda is not an invincible weapon. Moreover, after a time the people—in a democracy, at least—somehow seem to get a picture of things as they are, if only through ordinary, day-to-day experience. Against the propaganda of the *word* is the propaganda of the *deed*. Facts to some extent speak for themselves. But if they are backed up by propaganda, they become doubly potent in shaping men's attitudes and behavior. In the long run, well-publicized *truth* is the most telling propaganda.

How, then, can we get at the truth?

A FREE MARKET PLACE FOR IDEAS?

In Justice Holmes' classic sentence, "the best test of truth is the power of the thought to get itself accepted in the competition of the market." This is a doctrine that most Americans would heartily endorse. Yet it immediately raises vital questions. In the United States do we have a free market place for ideas? Or do monopolistic practices exist in the market of opinion just as they do to some extent in the economic market place? Certainly we have a free market in the sense that the government does not control the main agencies of opinion. But the absence of governmental control does not in itself guarantee an open and competitive market.

Trends in the opinion industries

Even in the case of our own justly famed free press there are at least three disturbing tendencies:

Concentration. It has been said that we live in an era of dying dailies. Newspaper circulation keeps rising, but the number of newspapers keeps decreasing. In the 3 decades between 1920 and 1950 the number of dailies in our 25 largest cities dropped from 126 to 86, while the circulation of these dailies increased by almost 10 million. In that period, the number of cities with only one daily newspaper climbed from 724 to 1124. What is the result? "Ten states have not a single city with competing daily papers," Morris Ernst has pointed out. "Twenty-two states are without Sunday newspaper competition. Fourteen companies owning eighteen papers control about one quarter of our total daily circulation. . . . One company dominates more than 3000 weeklies."[15]

The problem is not simply one of concentration of ownership and control. It also involves the *standardizing* of news and editorial opinion. News-

[15] Morris L. Ernst, *The First Freedom* (New York: The Macmillan Company, 1946), p. xii.

papers get the bulk of their out-of-town news from great news gathering organizations like the Associated Press and the United Press. The AP, for example, sells news to papers controlling over 95 per cent of the total circulation in the United States. The country newspaper—once considered the citadel of rugged independent journalism—has come in many cases to be merely the local distributor of opinion "canned" in New York or Chicago. One great newspaper syndicate, for example, supplies boilerplate—features, editorials, and columns—to thousands of local journals. To 3000 country newspapers it sells an eight-page newspaper ready to go to press, with a few pages left blank for the local editor's news and advertising. For fear of offending someone, the boilerplate plays down controversial issues and unorthodox views, resulting in a sterile uniformity in many country newspapers from Maine to California.

Commercialism. A newspaper is a business. To survive it must sell copies, for its income depends on sales and advertising. Many publishers feel, perhaps quite rightly, that they must give the public what it wants. If the readers like screaming headlines, comics, scandal, sex, crime, features, and fiction at the expense of full and balanced news stories and editorial discussion, a newspaper can hardly hold out against its customers. Such a policy, however, means that an editor may cater to the political prejudices of his readers. By giving them what they want, he may deny them the chance to break out of their political bias and apathy. And he may block off the expression of controversial views in his columns for fear of alienating influential sections of his public.

Conservatism. Newspaper publishers are businessmen. They are worried by the things that worry every businessman, such as labor demands, costs, sales, taxes, dividends, profits. As businessmen they tend to take a conservative point of view. It is not surprising that their business attitudes are reflected in their editorial columns, and sometimes in the slanting of news. Nor is it surprising that liberal candidates and proposals so often meet stout resistance from the press. Such a situation fosters a pall of orthodoxy in the expression of viewpoints. Yet democracy demands the airing of *competing* views.

Occasionally, too, advertisers bring pressure to bear on publishers. For example, the story of a strike in a local plant may be suppressed, or the news of the indictment of a large corporation for unfair practices may be buried in the back pages. The real problem, however, is not outright pressure or conspiracy but a *community of interest* between the big businessman who is a publisher and the other big businessmen who advertise. An English poet put this in a satirical vein when he wrote:

> You cannot hope to bribe or twist,
> Thank God, the British journalist;
> But seeing what the man will do
> Unbribed, there's no occasion to.

"If modern journalism tends to speak the language of corporate business instead of that of the little fellow," says Herbert Brucker, well-known editor, "it does so not because it is corrupt and venal but because it is itself a big business, a powerful institution with its interest vested in conservative economics."[16]

Such criticism of the press is, of course, overdrawn in some instances. Certain newspapers, such as *The New York Times* and the *Christian Science Monitor,* are noted for their fair and full coverage of controversial events, and for their ability to confine their own opinions to the editorial page. Some editors print columns and features presenting different points of view; it is not unusual to see David Lawrence's conservative views next to Marquis Child's liberal ones. And most editors and reporters have an honest respect for facts, however they may wish to interpret them.

Proposals for reform

Nevertheless, the problem of monopolistic tendencies—or at least of imperfect competition—in the market place of ideas remains a serious one. Certain solutions have been put forward. One of these would be to call on editors and publishers to clean their own houses, to police their own industry. It is urged that the press draw up *codes* of fair conduct binding on all. It is suggested that the working newspaperman should be given a greater voice in the management and editorial policy of the newspaper. The difficulty is that such codes would not be enforceable, and the worst offenders would be those least likely to conform to them.

Another proposal calls for the establishment of *competing newspapers* wherever possible. Unfortunately, starting a new journal becomes increasingly difficult as the years go by. Some time ago it was possible for William Allen White to establish a famous newspaper—the Emporia (Kansas) *Gazette*—with a few hundred dollars and a lot of determination. To set up a newspaper today in a middle-sized or large city takes hundreds of thousands, perhaps millions, of dollars. Once established, the fledgling newspaper faces all the difficulties that confront any newspaper, only in intensified form.

Finally, *government intervention* has been urged as a means of promoting full competition. In 1947 a Commission on Freedom of the Press, headed by Chancellor Robert M. Hutchins of the University of Chicago, recommended that the federal government should set up its own communications agencies—a government-owned newspaper, perhaps—to tell the people of its plans and policies, if private agencies did not do the job. To encourage criticism of the press from within and from outside, it proposed the creation of a "new and independent agency" to "appraise and report annually upon the performance of the press." And the commission

[16] Herbert Brucker, *Freedom of Information* (New York: The Macmillan Company, 1949), p. 68.

called for the maintenance of competition among the larger newspapers by means of the antitrust laws. The commission concluded:

The urgent and perplexing issues which confront our country, the new dangers which encompass our free society, the new fatefulness attaching to every step in foreign policy and to what the press publishes about it, mean that the preservation of democracy and perhaps of civilization may now depend upon a free and responsible press.[17]

Thus the commission posed the vital question: Can government take steps to make the press more competitive and more responsible without imperiling our basic freedoms? There is no easy answer to this question. Yet experience with another great agency of opinion—radio—throws some light on the problem.

Lessons from radio?

Since its early infancy, radio has been under some government regulation. During the early 1920's, hundreds of radio stations were established in the United States. At this time radio was virtually a free-for-all. Broadcasters sometimes used the same wave lengths at the same time, resulting in a chaos of raucous and muffled sounds for the listener. Protests by all concerned brought government action by 1927. Today, by law, a broadcaster must conduct his station in the public interest. He cannot operate without a license from the Federal Communications Commission, a federal regulatory agency (see Chapter 25). In granting licenses, and in renewing them periodically, the F.C.C. has the power to determine whether the public interest is being met.

In practice, the radio industry operates largely under a code set up by the broadcasters themselves and under a set of model regulations issued by the F.C.C. in 1945. To prevent monopoly, the commission discourages newspaper control of radio, and it forbids one person from owning more than one station in the same area. A few years ago the F.C.C. ordered two large networks of the National Broadcasting Company to separate. The F.C.C. also enforces a measure of political neutrality, or at least equality. Station owners may speak their own minds politically, but they must make time available on the air to persons or parties on opposite sides of a question.

Radio in America thus represents a halfway house between private control and state regulation. What have been the results? Few people seem to believe that freedom of speech has been impaired in the world of radio. The F.C.C. is strictly forbidden from interfering with the content of radio programs. At the same time, there is complaint that the cooperation of

[17] *A Free and Responsible Press* (Chicago: University of Chicago Press, 1947), pp. 105-106.

the government and the radio industry has been a sterile and unfruitful relationship. Radio is criticized for its commercialism, its devotion to amusement and trivia, its failure to present controversial and competitive ideas over the air waves. It is said that the government's heavy hand is purely negative and restrictive. On the other hand, radio has engineered some magnificent reporting as in its on-the-spot coverage of political party conventions, the United Nations, and events abroad.

Great Britain has tried an entirely different approach. In that country radio has been a government monopoly for over twenty years, administered by a semi-independent government agency, the British Broadcasting Corporation. Over three main channels the B.B.C. offers a variety of programs, with considerable stress on culture, education, and broad public questions. There are no commercials. (Recently, however, England has undertaken commercially sponsored television.) The B.B.C. is financed by an annual tax on radio sets. Very rarely is the B.B.C. accused of partisanship; more often it is charged with cautiousness and timidity as a result of its efforts to avoid being partisan. Canada enjoys a mixed system. There is a government enterprise, the Canadian Broadcasting Corporation, but a good many private stations operate in local areas, carrying programs broadcast from both Canada and the United States.

It seems, then, that the main faults of democratic governments have been those of excessive caution in dealing with the market of ideas, rather than undue interference. But these faults are the reflection of great virtues. Dictators have shown that the free market becomes an absurdity when the government clamps down a rigid censorship and establishes its own monopoly over ideas. At the same time, there is the problem of private censorship, as in the case of some newspapers, or of local organizations that in some cities have power to censor movies and stage shows. A great and ticklish task of democratic government is to keep the channels of communication clear of obstruction without itself becoming the most perilous obstruction of all.

TAKING THE PULSE OF THE PEOPLE

"What I want," Abraham Lincoln once said, "is to get done what the people desire to have done, and the question for me is how to find that out exactly." This is the question that faces every politician, in office or out. And it is one of the most perplexing ones they face. Another President, Woodrow Wilson, described the problem once when he complained to some newspapermen that they had no business to say, as they often did, that all the people out their way thought so and so. Wilson said, "You do not know, and the worst of it is, since the responsibility is mine, I do not know, what they are thinking about. I have the most imperfect means of finding out, and yet I have got to act as if I knew. . . ."

What do people want?

How can the politician find out what the people are thinking? The usual way, of course, is the election itself. If John Brown wins over James Smith, presumably the people want what John Brown stands for. Thus if Brown is an out-and-out prohibitionist, and Smith is a 100 per cent wet, evidently the people support some kind of prohibition.

But we know that in practice things do not work out this way. Elections are rarely fought out on single issues like prohibition, and candidates rarely take clear-cut stands. Elections actually turn on many diverse issues, and candidates are often deliberately vague. It is impossible, moreover, to separate issues from candidates. Take the Presidential election of 1956, for example. Was President Eisenhower elected because he stood for tax reduction at home? Or because of his farm and labor policies? Or because of his strong support of the new Republicanism? Or because businessmen generally supported him? Or because he was a popular general during World War II? Or because people liked his platform manner and his wife Mamie? Or because of campaign errors of his opponents? The answer, of course, is that he won for some of these reasons, in different degree, and for others not mentioned. Which brings us right back to the basic question—what do the people want?

This is where straw votes and public opinion polls come in. It is only natural that people should try to measure the popular mind with tools more exact than election results. In this country public opinion polls are over a century old, but their main development has taken place in the last two or three decades. Some of the techniques were worked out by market research analysts who were hired by businessmen to estimate potential sales for their products. The techniques were then adapted to measuring opinions on general issues. Today there are a number of polling organizations, the most famous of which are the American Institute of Public Opinion, which puts out the Gallup poll, and the *Fortune* survey directed by Elmo Roper. Many newspapers conduct local straw votes, and parties, private associations, and governments have been polling people for many years.

Problems of polling

The most exact way to measure opinions on issues would be to poll every adult—or at least every voter—in the country. Such a procedure would of course be prohibitively expensive. Instead the pollsters interview a sample of the population. The accuracy of their final results turns largely on how *representative* this sample is. It must be drawn from a cross section of the people, and this cross section must be carefully based on the distribution of the population according to locality, sex, age, education, occupation, social or economic level, and so on. One polling organization, in testing opinion which would be affected by people's income status (for example, views on the income tax) makes up a sample based on 2 wealthy persons, 14 members of the upper class, 52 from the middle class, and 32 from the poor. Samples can be amazingly small and still be relatively accurate. In one case, the percentage of the first 500 persons answering "no" to a question was 54.9, while the percentage of all 30,000 answering "no" was 55.5 —a difference of less than 1 per cent. The Gallup poll uses a sample of from 1500 to 60,000, depending on the type of question.

Courtesy COLLIER's *and David Huffine*

"Do you, or do you not, favor U.S. participation in some form of world government, under which each nation would forfeit a certain amount of its sovereignty?"

Another difficulty in polling is the question itself. As everyone knows, there are all sorts of ways to ask questions in order to get different answers. Ask a man if he favors labor unions and he may say "no." Ask him if he favors organized efforts by workers to improve their well-being, and more likely he will answer "yes." Or trouble may arise in the alternatives that a question presents. Clearly, asking a person "Do you favor the United States entering a world government, or do you prefer our traditional independence in determining our own affairs?" is to load the dice ahead of time. To take an actual case, when people were asked late in June 1941, "So far as you, personally, are concerned, do you think the United States has gone too far in helping Britain, or not far enough?" the answers were:

Too far................15%   About right............46%
Not far enough ....32%   No opinion.............. 7%

But when the words "President Roosevelt" were substituted for the words "United States" in this question in a poll at the same time, the answers were:

Too far	20%	About right	57%
Not far enough	17%	No opinion	6%

Polling organizations go to great efforts to make their questions fair; some of them conduct trial runs with differently worded questions.

One way to meet this problem is by the multiple-choice—or "cafeteria" —type of question. Here the respondent has his choice of several answers. For example, a Gallup poll asked "How far do you, yourself, think the federal government should go in requiring employers to hire people without regard to race, religion, color, or nationality?" The choice of answers was five in number: *All the way; None of the way; Depends on type of work; Should be left to state governments; Don't know.* A variation of this type— the "open-end question"—is to allow the respondent to supply his own answer. He may be asked simply, "How do you think we should deal with the problem of disloyalty in the government?" The answers to this type of question are, of course, hard to tabulate accurately.

Interviewing itself is a delicate and difficult task. Tests show that the interviewer's appearance, clothes, language, and way of asking questions can influence the replies. Inaccurate findings can result from the bias of the interviewer, or from his failure to do his job fully and carefully. And the persons interviewed may be the source of some error. Respondents may be suspicious of the interviewer's motives, and they may give false or confused answers. To cover up ignorance they may give neutral answers, or appear to be undecided. Or they may give the answers that they think the interviewer would like them to give.

Despite these difficulties, polling is so useful a device for sounding out opinion that it is employed by a variety of organizations other than the commercial ones. During elections parties conduct polls to discover their strong sectors and weak points. Interest groups run polls to back up their claims that the people—or at least their own members—favor or oppose some bill. Advertisers and sales executives have an obvious use for them. And governments themselves poll the people. For example, the Department of Agriculture for years has conducted referendums on such questions as whether farmers want particular agricultural programs or policies maintained, or certain marketing quotas established. Some such referendums attract a large turnout of voters—more, in some states, than vote in gubernatorial elections. The most important governmental use of the referendum is found in a number of states, where voters may require by petition that a bill passed by the state legislature be referred to the whole electorate for approval or disapproval.

Forecasting elections

What about the pre-election forecast? To the average American this is the most intriguing form of public opinion polling. Everyone likes to know in advance how an election will turn out, whether it's Uncle Charlie who is laying an election bet, or a national party chairman, or a stockbroker watching the market. During election races the pollsters submit regular "returns" on the position of the candidates. The reports are compiled from interviewing conducted throughout the nation, usually on a state-by-state or regional basis. On the whole, the record of the leading forecasters has been good, as the following table shows.

SOME RECENT PRESIDENTIAL POLLS

Year	Actual Dem. Vote	Roper Poll	Gallup Poll	Crossley Poll
1936	60.2	61.7	53.8	53.8
1940	54.7	55.2	55.0	...
1944	53.8	53.6	53.3	52.0
1948	49.4	37.1	44.5	44.8
1952	45.+	43.0	46.0	47.0
1956	42.0	40.0	40.5	...

But forecasts can—and do—go wrong. In 1936 a highly unscientific poll, that of the *Literary Digest,* using mail ballots, underestimated Franklin D. Roosevelt's percentage by almost 20 per cent. Shortly after the election the magazine closed up shop. The most sensational slip came in 1948. During the Presidential battle between President Truman and Governor Dewey, the polls repeatedly indicated that Mr. Truman was far behind his opponent. When the President denounced these "sleeping polls," the pollsters stood pat on their statistics. One of them early in September announced that the race was over. Gallup gave the President 44.5 of the popular vote in his final forecast, and Roper's prediction was 37.1 per cent. Actually, Mr. Truman won 49 per cent of the popular vote, amid much ridiculing of the pollsters. In 1952 and 1956 the leading pollsters were most cautious in their predictions.

Why do polls go wrong? Part of the reason lies in the subjective factors, as noted above, that distort the results of all types of polls. Part of the trouble may lie in methods used, such as the construction of the sample. The *Literary Digest* made the mistake of polling mainly persons listed in the telephone directory, who in 1936 turned out to be a poor cross section of American voters. But forecasters face some especially difficult problems. Actually they are not polling results—only elections do that—but *intentions.* Some of the respondents may change their plans at the last minute. Following the election of 1948 a committee of experts decided that probably a last-minute swing to Truman had taken place but had not been reflected in the polls.[18] Some voters may vote contrary to how they say they will vote, or they may simply fail to go to the polls. For the forecasts must estimate *which* and *how many* of the people will vote, as well as *how* they will vote.

[18] *The Pre-Election Polls of 1948* (New York: Social Science Research Council, 1949), pp. 251 ff.

In 1948 voting turned out to be lighter than expected, and an unusually large number of people cast ballots for state and local candidates but not for the national ones. The "don't-knows"—the people who are undecided about their voting intentions—are another source of error.

Probably the pollsters learned some lessons in 1948 that will make their forecasts more exact in the future. In any event, polls are here to stay. But they will continue to be the subject of searching observation and criticism. Some objections to opinion polls have been largely overcome. For example, despite charges to the contrary, polls probably do not have a significant band-wagon effect on voting; the 1948 results would indicate quite the reverse, if anything. And the main pollsters cannot rightly be accused of dishonesty and partisanship.

But major questions remain. Polls are *quantitative,* not *qualitative.* They give equal weight to a follower and to an opinion leader who may in the end influence other votes. Polls may give a false impression of the firmness and intensity of opinion. As we have seen, opinions can be fleeting and volatile. Sixty per cent of the respondents may answer "yes" to some question, but half of them may merely lean that way, and others may have no real opinion on the subject. It is far easier to measure the surface waves and eddies of public opinion than its depth and density.

Surely the polls at best cannot substitute for elections. Faced with his ballot the voter must embody his diverse feelings in a few decisions in terms of personalities and parties. He must decide what is important, and what is less important. Out of the welter of views of all voters a decision is made for some candidate who will act in terms of some program, however vague. For democracy is more than the expression of views, more than a simple mirror of public opinion. It is also the *choosing* among issues— and the governmental action that must follow. And democracy is the thoughtful participation of people in the political process; as Lasswell says, it means *using* heads as well as *counting* them. Elections, with all their failings, at least establish the link between the many voices of the people and the decisions of their leaders.

POLITICS AND PUBLIC OPINION

We can sum up our discussion of public opinion by suggesting a few thumbnail conclusions:

1. Public opinion has many characteristics. In some respects it tends to be compact and stable; in others fluid and varied. One must speak not merely of public opinion, but of many public opinions.

2. The public, too, is many sided in its make-up. Some people are fickle in their views; others are steady and unmoving. Actually there are millions of publics, divided in a thousand different ways.

3. Despite its many shapes, public opinion shows some pattern. This

pattern is caused in part by the fact that most Americans are subjected to common influences—family, schools, press, radio, television, and so on.

4. Much public opinion is formed by deliberate manipulation of attitudes by people with all sorts of purposes, good and bad. Development of highly efficient means of communication and persuasion has enlarged the role of the propagandist, but his influence is by no means unlimited.

5. In the offering of ideas we do not have a wholly free market. In the dissemination of attitudes we find tendencies toward concentration, commercialization, and conservatism. Most Americans probably want a free market, but there is no easy way to get it. The relation of government to the market is the most difficult problem of all.

6. At the same time we have worked out fairly reliable methods of taking rough measurements of people's attitudes at a given time. But these methods cannot take the place of elections.

What is the relation of government to all this? Obviously government is not an innocent bystander in the constant play and interplay of political attitudes. It is deeply involved in the whole process. It has a stake in the way attitudes are formed, in the methods used to form them, such as the radio, and in the uses to which propaganda is put. A democratic government is especially interested in the degree of competition in the market place of ideas, and in the ways that polling organizations try to measure public opinion.

The case of television

Television, the young giant of the opinion industry, in its short history has already confronted government and politicians with a series of such problems. These problems indicate that government cannot pursue a simple hands-off attitude toward television. The development of television also illustrates how technological development continually faces government with new and baffling issues. Three brief examples are in order:

A channel for education? Television potentially is a superb vehicle for education. Its roving cameras can spotlight meetings of the United Nations, forums, debates, round tables, and of course good plays, music, painting, and the like. In the classroom television can effectively supplement (but not substitute for) the teacher, the blackboard, and the textbook. But television channels are limited, and they are greatly in demand for military, police, air and sea communications, aside from regular commercial televisers. Should certain channels be reserved for education? If so, who will sponsor educational programs? The government? This raises the problem of governmental interference. Advertisers? It is doubtful that they should be allowed to influence the content of education. Universities and foundations? They may lack the large sums needed. The federal government is in the middle of this problem because the Federal Communications Commission allots the channels. Whatever it does, it cannot duck the issue.

Probes and privacy. A Senate committee investigating crime had a sensational impact on public opinion in 1951 when it allowed the hearings to be televised. A succession of shady characters—suspected gamblers, racketeers, gangsters, and the like—appeared on television screens throughout the nation. So fascinating were the proceedings that millions of viewers sat glued to their chairs, and taxi drivers and merchants complained of a drop in business. The proceedings raised a number of questions. On the one hand, here was a window on government that could bring the citizen into intimate contact with public affairs. On the other hand, television intensified a hundredfold the problem of fairness in dealing with witnesses before investigating committees. If the hearings become a Roman holiday, if the witness wilts amid the noise, heat, and light, if the proceedings are edited so that only one side of the case gets through to the television audience— then a man may be unjustly suspect in the eyes of millions of people. At the very least his right to privacy will be almost lost.

New test for politicians. In a somewhat different area, television undoubtedly will affect the way campaigns are conducted. Franklin D. Roosevelt was a master of the use of radio; his famous fireside chats brought him directly in touch with tens of millions. Who will be the F.D.R. of television? John Crosby has stated that Thomas E. Dewey of New York "is the first political candidate to understand how to use television properly." Instead of merely giving staid speeches, in his quest for re-election as governor in 1950, according to Crosby, "Dewey threw the script away. He answered questions from the floor, as it were—the floor being a dozen street corners all over the state. He spoke extemporaneously; he moved from spot to spot, picking up reports and documents; he sat on the edge of his desk (never once did he sit behind the desk); he scratched his head, put his glasses on, took them off, wiped them; he introduced his wife when someone wanted a look at her."[19] One student of the problem points out that television has already forced the parties to alter convention rules and that it may speed up the creation of new political personalities, although "the capacity of television as candidate-maker [has] as yet produced no surprises."[20]

Government and its publics

Above all, government is concerned with the make-up of public opinion itself. To stay in office politicians must respond—or at least seem to respond—to changing opinions. They must have some sense of the scope of popular attitudes, their intensity, their stability or instability. Measuring public opinion in its many forms—often by a sort of sixth sense—is the

[19] John Crosby, *New York Herald Tribune*, November 9, 1950.
[20] Charles A. H. Thomson, *Television and Presidential Politics* (Washington, D.C.: The Brookings Institution, 1956), p. 78.

essence of the politician's job. To be successful he must have the knack of going behind propaganda fronts and gauging the real public opinion, of seeing the areas of ignorance, the areas of apathy, the areas of understanding, the areas of action.

But government does not respond to public opinion as a single solid block. Government is made up of thousands of different men, with varying attitudes, ambitions, and loyalties. Obviously, a President responsible to the whole nation and a senator elected by a state will often react differently to public opinion. And the senator will react differently from a member of the House of Representatives. And perhaps an administrative official will take still another view. Many factors lie behind the diverse attitudes of officials—their position in the government, the people by whom they are elected or appointed, the amount of security they enjoy, the date of the next election or selection, the balance of forces in their home district or in the office of their superior, their own basic attitudes and expectations. In responding differently to public opinion politicians make it even more complex and elusive.

Nor does government merely *respond* to public opinion; it also *creates* it. Government should not be seen merely as the broker of outside forces, or as putty in the hands of mighty groups. The job of the political leader is to guide political attitudes and mediate among them as well as to follow them. Hence there is a reciprocal relationship. Where leadership leaves off and followership starts the political leader cannot say, nor is it important. The important thing is that these two roles of the politician enable him to provide the great need of modern democracies—responsible leadership. Knowing how to respond to public opinion and to help shape it is much of the art of democratic leadership, as our great Presidents have shown.

Ｐolitics is sometimes called "the great American game." Thousands of politicians take part in it; millions of people follow the election fights, and they decide the winners and losers. Yet the real nature of the game remains a mystery. Why does one candidate win and another lose? What causes some people to go to the polls and vote when others do not? How do we decide to vote the way we do? Why do the voting returns from some areas shift crazily from year to year, while other areas seem to be stable? Man is a political animal, yet man knows very little of his own political behavior—or misbehavior.

Of course, there are a lot of pet theories. These are resurrected in every election by the newspapers and by the politicians themselves. Experience often deals harshly with many of these theories, but they live on. Take the old saying, "As Maine goes, so goes the nation." This has been disproved in election after election. (In 1936, Jim Farley said, "As goes Maine so goes Vermont.") But it was years before the old adage died. Again, it has long been political gospel that mid-term congressional elections foreshadow the results of the next presidential election, but the 1948 and 1956 results upset this theory—at least for a while.

We are still groping for some understanding of our own behavior. Recent years, however, have seen a more systematic approach to the study of political behavior. Political scientists, social psychologists, cultural anthropologists, sociologists, and others have been making new studies that in time may throw a flood of light on the political process. Their tools—questionnaires, voting statistics, polls, interviews, intensive studies of particular campaigns, and so on —are still crude, but they are slowly being improved. We are getting new insights into the relations among members of groups, between leaders and followers, and inside the family, as they affect political activity. We are probing into the dark forces that fight for supremacy within the individual.

One crucial fact, however, is crystal clear—one that touches every aspect of our political system. This is the

★ 12

Political

behavior

fact that political power in the American democracy is not spread evenly among all the voters. We talk about one man, one vote—but in practice millions of Americans have no part in the political game, sometimes not even as spectators, while a few Americans may call the signals. First we will look at those who do and those who do not take part in the great American game of politics.

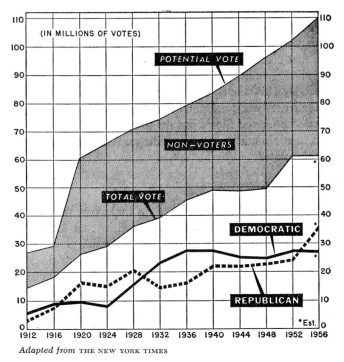

(IN MILLIONS OF VOTES)

POTENTIAL VOTE

NON-VOTERS

TOTAL VOTE

DEMOCRATIC

REPUBLICAN

*Est.

1912 1916 1920 1924 1928 1932 1936 1940 1944 1948 1952 1956

Adapted from THE NEW YORK TIMES

The presidential vote since 1912.

WHO SHALL VOTE?—THE FIGHT FOR THE BALLOT

Government by the people in the context of modern society means government elected by and responsive to the wishes of the voters. Today we have universal adult suffrage in *form,* though the struggle to extend the right to all men in *fact* is not over (as noted in Chapter 7). The history of the suffrage in the United States is one of a continuing struggle to extend the right to vote from a small group of property-owning white males to the great bulk of adults. The issue of Negro suffrage, as described in Chapter 7, is only one phase—though an important one—of this struggle.

The Declaration of Independence said that all men were created equal, but it said nothing about the right to vote. Evidently our Revolutionary forefathers were not mainly concerned about this right. They would not have dreamed of giving the ballot to Negro slaves, or women, or people under 21. They were acting in accordance with custom, for the colonies had restrictions based on property. A few of the framers of the Constitution in 1787 argued for easing up on the property requirement for voting, but as we saw in Chapter 2, most of them stood firm for it. "Give the votes to people who have no property," Gouverneur Morris warned, "and they will sell them to the rich. . . ." The safest procedure, the Founding Fathers decided, was to leave it to the *states* to set the requirements in both national and state elections.

Surely this was a faltering start. About one American in every thirty voted in the first election held under the new Constitution. But the situation was to change radically. By the 1850's the property restriction was almost extinct. By 1870 the right of the states to deprive Negroes of the vote because of their race was terminated. And by 1920 women were given the ballot. Indeed, the United States has the distinction of being the first of the great nations to attain universal adult suffrage. What caused this vast widening of the right to vote?

One man, one vote

Economic and social changes played an important part here. Property restrictions had come to be accepted in the cities and towns of the East, where most people had a sense of position and rank. Such discrimination did not mean so much along the western frontier. There the settlers were on a more equal basis; they tended to share and share alike. Why should one man have the vote and another not? State after state joined the Union with no property restrictions at all.

The impact of this kind of democracy was felt also in the East. Most of the states there had their own "western" counties where the settlers often looked on property restrictions as protection for eastern commercial interests. In urban areas, too, new ideas were taking root. In the great cities "mechanics" and other workingmen were eager to express themselves politically, and immigrants were already flowing in from abroad at an increasing rate. Here was a tremendous pool of votes that competing parties wanted to draw from. Shrewd politicians figured that they could tighten their hold on office by giving the ballot to groups likely to vote "right."

Conservatives like Chancellor Kent of New York could argue—as he did at the New York constitutional convention of 1821—that universal male suffrage would "jeopardize the rights of property and the principles of liberty." But the rising groups could not be held down. They appealed to the names of Thomas Jefferson and other popular heroes to back up their demands. A delegate to the Massachusetts convention of 1853 ridiculed property qualifications with a story that Tom Paine, the great pamphleteer of the Revolution, used to tell:

You require that a man shall have sixty dollars' worth of property, or he shall not vote. Very well, take an illustration. Here is a man who today owns a jackass, and the jackass is worth sixty dollars. Today the man is a voter and goes to the polls and deposits his vote. Tomorrow the jackass dies. The next day the man comes to vote without his jackass and he cannot vote at all. Now tell me, which was the voter, the man or the jackass?

If such common sense was not enough, men were ready to fight for the right to vote. The Rhode Islanders made this clear. For years they had protested against control of their government by a small landed oligarchy. In 1841 a convention representing the voteless met and drew up a "People's Constitution" that greatly broadened the right to vote. The old-time leaders were uneasy; they offered a new constitution that was almost equally liberal on voting. But the rebels, headed by Thomas Dorr, were too aroused to compromise. After a struggle the landowners won out and Dorr fled the state, but they were wise enough to provide broadened suffrage provisions in the new constitution of 1843.

The forces of unrest and protest worked slowly but surely. States tended first to substitute a taxpaying requirement for the property-owning requirement. Then they did away with the taxpaying provision too. By the turn of the century manhood suffrage had been established almost everywhere. North Carolina—the last of the states to yield—finally abandoned its property test for voting in 1865.

Thus one phase of a long struggle came to a happy end. But only one phase. While men were still fighting for their right to vote, women were beginning to fight for theirs. The agitation over slavery during the mid-nineteenth century gave a great impetus to the idea of woman's suffrage. Why agitate over the Negro's wrongs, some women asked their husbands, and ignore those of your own mothers, wives, and sisters? Indeed, in their legal rights women were little more than a step or two above slaves, as far as the common law was concerned. What was the men's reply? They argued loftily that woman's sacred duty was in the bosom of the family and that she could leave the stern and exacting job of politics to the males. But the argument had a hollow ring.

Suffragettes in action

Only very grudgingly did men give in to the protests of the opposite sex. As early as 1838 Kentucky allowed widows and unmarried women to vote in school elections, provided they held property taxable for school purposes; by 1890 all women in fourteen states and territories had gained the right to vote on school matters. Naturally women were not content with this; many of them were doing men's work in professions, in factories and field, and they pressed for full suffrage. Oddly enough, their first victories came in western states popularly known for their high percentage

An anti-woman's suffrage cartoon of the 1870's.

of tough hombres. Wyoming led the way. As a territory Wyoming had given women equal rights with men; it is said that when congressmen in Washington grumbled about this "petticoat provision," the Wyoming legislators replied that they would stay out of the Union 100 years rather than come in without women's suffrage. Congress gave in. By the end of World War I, over half the states had granted women the right to vote in some or all elections.

To many suffragettes, however, this state-by-state approach seemed very slow and uncertain. Some of them set their hearts on one decisive victory —a constitutional amendment that would at one blow force all states to allow women to vote. In fighting for this amendment the women gave their fathers and husbands some lessons in dynamic political tactics. Under the leadership of Miss Alice Paul, Mrs. Carrie Chapman Catt, and others, they organized pressure groups, Washington lobbies, and even a National Woman's party. They held noisy parades, drew up petitions, printed militant propaganda, put mass pressure on Congress. Where women had the vote they stole a leaf from labor's book by trying to help their friends and defeat their enemies.

The struggle came to a head during the war years when President Wilson and congressional leaders were trying—like good politicians—to dodge the issue. Women did not want any straddling. They began to picket the White House. Carrying banners and singing lustily, the suffragettes marched month after month around the executive mansion. Then the au-

Check your state:

QUALIFICATIONS FOR VOTING

State	Minimum age	U.S. citizen	Residence in State	County	District	Property	Literacy test
Alabama	21	★	2 yrs.	1 yr.	3 mo.	....	....
Arizona	21	★	1 yr.	30 da.	30 da.	....	★
Arkansas	21	★	12 mo.	6 mo.	1 mo.	....	....
California	21	(a)	1 yr.	90 da.	54 da.	....	★
Colorado	21	★	1 yr.	90 da.	15 da. (f)	....	....
Connecticut	21	(i)(b)	1 yr.	.....	6 mo.	....	★
Delaware	21	★	1 yr.	3 mo.	30 da.	....	★
Florida	21	★	1 yr.	6 mo.	.....	....	....
Georgia	18	★	1 yr.	6 mo.	.....	....	(j)
Idaho	21	★	6 mo.	30 da.	.....	....	....
Illinois	21	★	1 yr.	90 da.	30 da.	....	....
Indiana	21	★	6 mo.	60 da. (e)	30 da.	....	....
Iowa	21	★	6 mo.	60 da.	10 da.	....	....
Kansas	21	★	6 mo.	30 da. (e)	30 da.	....	....
Kentucky	18	★	1 yr.	6 mo.	60 da.	....	....
Louisiana	21	★	2 yrs.	1 yr.	3 mo. (g)	....	(k)
Maine	21	★	6 mo.	3 mo.	3 mo.	....	★
Maryland	21	★	1 yr.	6 mo.	6 mo.	....	....
Massachusetts	21	★	1 yr.	.....	6 mo. (h)	....	★
Michigan	21	★	6 mo.	.....	30 da.	(i)	....
Minnesota	21	(a)	6 mo.	.....	30 da.	....	....
Mississippi	21	★	2 yrs.	.....	1 yr. (d)	....	★
Missouri	21	★	1 yr.	60 da.	60 da.	....	....
Montana	21	★	1 yr.	30 da.	.....	(i)	....
Nebraska	21	★	6 mo.	40 da.	10 da.	....	....
Nevada	21	★	6 mo.	30 da.	10 da.	(i)	....
New Hampshire	21	★	6 mo.	.....	6 mo.	....	★
New Jersey	21	★	1 yr.	5 mo.	.....	....	....
New Mexico	21	★	12 mo.	90 da.	30 da.	(i)	....
New York	21	(a)	1 yr.	4 mo.	30 da.	....	(l)
North Carolina	21	★	1 yr.	.....	4 mo.	....	★
North Dakota	21	★	1 yr.	90 da.	30 da.	....	....
Ohio	21	★	1 yr.	40 da.	40 da.	....	....
Oklahoma	21	★	1 yr.	6 mo.	30 da.	....	....
Oregon	21	★	6 mo.	.....	30 da.	....	★
Pennsylvania	21	★	1 yr. (c)	.....	2 mo.	....	....
Rhode Island	21	★	1 yr.	.....	6 mo.	(m)	(m)
South Carolina	21	★	2 yrs. (d)	1 yr.	4 mo.	....	....
South Dakota	21	★	1 yr.	90 da.	30 da.	....	....
Tennessee	21	★	12 mo.	6 mo.	.....	....	....
Texas	21	★	1 yr.	6 mo.	6 mo.	(i)	....
Utah	21	(a)	1 yr.	4 mo.	60 da.	(i)	....
Vermont	21	★	1 yr.	.....	3 mo.	....	....
Virginia	21	★	1 yr.	6 mo.	30 da.	....	★
Washington	21	★	1 yr.	90 da.	30 da.	....	★
West Virginia	21	★	1 yr.	60 da.	.....	....	....
Wisconsin	21	★	1 yr.	.....	10 da.	....	....
Wyoming	21	★	1 yr.	60 da.	10 da.	....	★

(a) Must have been citizen ninety days.
(b) Must have been citizen five years.
(c) Six months if previously an elector or native of U.S.
(d) Ministers of the Gospel and teachers in public schools may vote after six months' residence.
(e) Township.
(f) City or town thirty days.
(g) Municipality, four months.
(h) In city or town.
(i) For vote on bond issues or special assessments only.

(j) Under 1949 act, all voters must re-register and pass literacy test. Those failing test may qualify by answering 10 of 30 oral questions prescribed by law.
(k) Literacy test required but exception allowed if person can pass certain specified requirements.
(l) A person who became entitled to vote after January 1, 1922, must be able except for physical disability, to read and write English.
(m) Ownership of property is an alternative to literacy.

Adapted from THE BOOK OF THE STATES, 1956-57.
Courtesy, Council of State Governments.

thorities made the mistake of using force. Police arrested some demonstrators for "obstructing traffic." This was just the kind of heavy-handed treatment on which agitators thrive. New picketers took up the banners; when patrol wagons carted them off, more took over. In jail, treated like common criminals, the women went on hunger strikes. Some of them—including prominent women of wealth and high social standing—had to be forcibly fed. By this time the whole nation was aroused. Protests poured in on Washington. The militant suffragettes were looked on as martyrs.

Many women, including supporters of suffrage, scorned the hot-headed tactics of their sisters. But the agitators retorted that lacking the *legal* right to vote, they had the *moral* right to resort to direct action, even violence, just as their forefathers had. In any event, their hard-hitting tactics, along with organization and propaganda, turned the trick. In 1919 an amendment passed Congress by the needed two-thirds vote in each chamber. So well were the women organized in the states that by August 1920 the amendment had been passed by the necessary three-fourths of the state legislatures.

The battle of the sexes was over—and women had written a notable chapter in the struggle to extend the suffrage. Although—as noted in Chapter 7—Negroes are still seeking full access to the ballot, in constitutional form, at least, we have universal adult suffrage. This does not mean that all adults have the right to vote. Some are not likely ever to be given the ballot: criminals and the insane, for example.

Subject to the limitations set by the Fourteenth, Fifteenth, and Nineteenth amendments, each state determines the qualifications for voting, not only for state officials but also for congressmen and President. The Constitution merely stipulates that those who are qualified under state law to vote for the most numerous branch of the state legislature are qualified to vote for congressmen and leaves it up to the state legislatures to set qualifications for voting for presidential electors. Thus the suffrage requirements—citizenship, age, residence, literacy, and so on—vary from state to state as indicated on the chart on page 297.

WHO VOTES

On the average, the proportion of Americans who vote is smaller than that of the Britishers, French, Italians—or Russians. Talk as we will about the right to vote, the hard fact remains that millions of Americans do not want to vote or somehow fail to get around to the polls on election day. They disfranchise themselves. In the most democratic of nations, of course, there will always be nonvoters. The startling feature of nonvoting in America is its extent. In recent presidential elections only about three-fifths of the potential voters showed up at the polls. Participation in state and local elections is usually even less than that. Voting for President in the 1952 and 1956 presidential elections rose to between 60 and 65 per cent of the potential vote, but this figure is still not very impressive.

Millions of nonvoters

Why do people fail to vote? Some years ago investigators interviewed several thousand Chicagoans as to their reasons for not voting in a mayoralty election.[1] The answers were illuminating. About one in every eight said that they were ill at the time; about the same number said that they were away from their voting district. Only 10 per cent simply disbelieved in voting; for one reason or another they were "disgusted with politics," or they thought that women should not vote. Some found it inconvenient to vote; a few—mostly women—feared to disclose their ages. Some persons were afraid that they would lose business or wages while they went to the polls. But one factor stood out above all others—simple lack of interest in elections. Over one-third of the nonvoters gave this as their reason. A salesman said that he was more concerned with his business than with politics. A housewife said that she did her washing that day. A mother explained simply, "Got a lot of children." A young musician confessed that he had had one of his temperamental spells on election day. Some nonvoters said that they had intended to vote, but had forgotten all about it until too late.

This high rate of indifference, ignorance, and even downright opposition to voting shows that much nonvoting is deliberate and intentional, not a result of chance factors like illness or absence. Other studies of voting underline the situation even more sharply: almost two-thirds of those who failed to vote stated to interviewers shortly before a presidential election that they did not intend to vote.[2] One conclusion is clear. An important reason for nonvoting—perhaps the most important reason—lies in peoples' *attitudes,* not in external factors beyond their control.

The extent of nonvoting in America has an enormous effect on politics. The big job for a politician is not merely to induce people to vote for him or his party; it is to get the vote out in the first place. Often the outcome of elections will turn largely on this factor. Both parties work hard to register their supporters—that is, to see that the voters get their names on registration lists (see Chapter 14) at the required time before election. The campaign itself not only influences the decisions of potential voters. It serves another purpose in that the hullabaloo of the campaign—the parades and posters, the politicians' grim warnings and bright promises—

[1] C. E. Merriam and H. F. Gosnell, *Non-Voting* (Chicago: University of Chicago Press, 1924).
[2] P. F. Lazarsfeld and Associates, *The People's Choice* (New York: Duell, Sloan, and Pearce, Inc., 1944), pp. 45-46.

helps activate people so that they will vote on election day. Nevertheless, in most elections turnout is relatively small. A study of voting in Ann Arbor, Michigan, for example, revealed that, on the average, barely more than one-fourth of eligible voters actually went to the polls in a series of elections, national, state, and local.[3] Politicians know that this low turnout plays into the hands of party or interest group machines, for it gives the organization vote much more weight in the final count.

Who fails to vote?

The discerning politician knows something even more important—that the extent of voting varies with different types of persons, different areas,[4] different elections. Observation of voting habits suggests the following:

1. *Men tend to vote more than women.* This variation between the sexes—not very great in most elections—exists in many foreign countries as well as in the United States. In recent presidential elections about 61 in every 100 women have voted, about 75 in every 100 men. Women seem to feel less social pressure to vote than men.[5] Perhaps the difference will lessen as women become more used to voting.

2. *The higher a person's income and educational level, the more likely that he will vote.* In the 1940 presidential election, according to the National Opinion Research Center, 85 per cent of the top fourth of the income scale went to the polls, 69 per cent of the middle half, and only 54 per cent of the lowest quarter. A study of the 1952 election by the Survey Research Center of the University of Michigan showed that of those earning less than $2000 a year, only 53 per cent voted; of those earning between $2000 and $3000 a year, 68 per cent voted; of those earning over $5000 a year, 88 per cent voted.[6]

3. *Younger people tend to vote less than old.* Voting seems to be highest in the middle-age groups, only to fall off in the sixties and seventies owing partly to the infirmities of old age. In Ann Arbor voting by persons in their twenties was about half that by persons in their fifties. Why do so many younger people fail to vote? And does that failure cause American politics to lack a measure of vitality?

4. *Republicans tend to vote in larger proportion than Democrats.* Of the people who show a marked preference for one or the other of our major parties, those who prefer the Republicans turn out in larger proportions than do those who prefer the Democrats. The Michigan study of the 1952 election,

[3] J. K. Pollock, *Voting Behavior: A Case Study* (Ann Arbor: University of Michigan Press, 1939).

[4] For a useful tabular summary of conclusions about voting behavior produced by recent studies, see Bernard R. Berelson, Paul F. Lazarsfeld, and William N. McPhee, *Voting* (Chicago: University of Chicago Press, 1954), pp. 331-347.

[5] Lazarsfeld, *The People's Choice,* pp. 48-49.

[6] Angus Campbell, Gerald Gurin, and Warren E. Miller, *The Voter Decides* (Evanston, Ill.: Row, Peterson and Company, 1954), pp. 70-73.

for example, showed that only 8 per cent of the people who regarded themselves as "strong Republicans" did not vote, while 24 per cent of those who
regarded themselves as "strong Democrats" stayed at home. This is probably
a result of the fact that, as we shall see in a moment, the Republicans tend to
draw their strength from the higher education and income groups (the groups
with the largest turnout), and the Democrats draw from the lower education
and income brackets (the groups with the smallest turnout).

5. *More people vote in national elections than in state or local.* In most
states presidential elections attract the greatest number of voters. Off-
year congressional elections almost invariably draw fewer persons to the
polls. City elections tend to attract the fewest voters. Participation is
lowest, of course, in party primaries. Even when voters are marking a
ballot that offers a variety of national and local contests, many voters will
check their presidential choice but not bother with the others. This is one
reason that our governmental officials are chosen by somewhat different
electorates. Does this fact intensify disunity in government?

6. *Voting varies according to party competition.* Voting turnout is lowest
in the areas in which there is little two-party competition and is highest
where such competition exists. Thus the lowest voting figures are to be found
in states such as Vermont and Mississippi, and the highest figures in states
such as New York and Pennsylvania. Voting in the "modified one-party
states," such as Oklahoma, the Dakotas, and Nebraska, is usually somewhere in between the one-party and two-party states. The number of Southern nonvoters is a crucial factor in southern politics. V. O. Key, Jr. estimates
that if southerners had voted in 1940 to the same degree as Americans as a
whole voted in the presidential election of that year, over *six million* more
ballots would have been cast in the South.[7]

To sum up, if you are a southern woman, poor, in your twenties, and
faced with a local election, the chances, *on the average,* of your going to
the polls are far less than if you are a wealthy man, in your fifties, voting
for a presidential candidate in the North.

Nonvoting is a sign of basic political apathy. To be sure, it is only one
sign, and a person can have a significant effect on politics even when he
fails to vote. There are other ways of "voting" besides formally casting a
ballot. "Citizens . . . vote by adding their names and energies to membership rolls," says Paul H. Appleby. "They vote by swelling, or failing to
swell, the circulations of particular newspapers or periodicals. They vote
by contributing to the popularity of particular radio or newspaper commentators. They vote by writing 'letters to the editor.' . . ."[8] However,
nonvoting and nonparticipation generally go hand in hand. Political poll-

[7] V. O. Key, Jr., *Southern Politics* (New York: Alfred A. Knopf, 1949), p. 506.
Southern voting figures are based on voting in primaries.
[8] Paul H. Appleby, *Policy and Administration* (University, Ala.: University of
Alabama Press, 1949), p. 168.

sters regularly discover the existence of a "hard core of chronic know-nothings"—people who know almost nothing about public affairs. These "know-nothings" do not read the newspapers, do not join organizations, do not write to the editor, and they do not vote.[9]

What causes such basic political apathy or inactivity? Some of the causes have been described as feelings that political activity may alienate one's friends or employer, that political activity is futile because "the politicians run everything anyway," that the "little man" does not know enough to act intelligently, that politics is remote and does not affect people very much. Lack of strong leadership that can arouse people is also a factor.

Should we make people vote?

Uneven voting has serious implications. It suggests that many Americans have no interest in taking part in our system of self-government. Somehow our democracy has failed to kindle their sense of participation. Moreover, it indicates that the *less protected* groups economically and socially tend to be the very group that are politically less active. In other words, the people who most need to enlist governmental protection in their support are the very ones who have least weight in the making of governmental decisions. Failure to vote may mean less public housing, fewer roads, even less police protection, for the nonvoters.

Concerned about this situation, some Americans would solve the problem of nonvoting through a drastic step. They would make voting compulsory for all those eligible. This idea has been tried in several foreign countries with mixed results. Australia makes registration (see Chapter 14) compulsory as well as voting. Thus the government takes the responsibility of mobilizing the voters at the polls, and voting becomes a legal duty as well as a legal right. The delinquent voter is fined or reprimanded.

What about compulsory voting for the United States? There are obvious practical difficulties, but probably these could be overcome through a simplifying and standardizing of election laws. A big question is whether we can expect enlightened voting from people who have to be herded to the polls, perhaps against their will. And indeed, some students of politics feel that a measure of nonvoting is a sign of a healthy society, an indication of widespread satisfaction with the existing state of affairs. They look on nonvoters as a sort of cushion or shock absorber; when tensions increase in society and political rivalries become sharp, the result is simply to draw more voters to the polls, rather than to set off a revolution or civil war.

Perhaps so. Perhaps, on the other hand, excess political steam can always be blown off through participating in political campaigns or even by running for office or starting a new political party or cause. At any rate, Americans are in the happy position where they can do much about

[9] See Morris Rosenberg, "Some Determinants of Political Apathy," *Public Opinion Quarterly*, Vol. 18, Winter 1954, pp. 349-366.

the problem of nonvoting without resorting to methods of compulsion, or, on the other hand, without worrying about the possible dangers of total voting. We can open the polls to every adult willing and able to vote. We can shorten the ballot, cutting down the number of unimportant elective positions, so that the bewildered voter does not face quite so many meaningless choices at the polls. We can simplify burdensome registration and residence requirements. (One study showed that six million Americans did not vote in 1956 because they had moved across state or county lines and were therefore unable to meet residence requirements.) Above all, we can try to strengthen our political processes—especially in the areas where one party seems to have a monopoly of power—so that more Americans would see the polling booth as a place where they could help shape their future.

So much for the nonvoters. What about the people who *do* vote?

HOW WE VOTE

Sometimes Americans are called fickle voters. It is said that the average man switches from party to party as blithely and as often as women change fashions. Actually, however, this fickleness seems to exist only in small degree. The great majority of Americans stick to one party year after year, and their sons and grandsons carry on a sort of traditional voting long after that. Politically these voters are "set in their ways." As a result both parties can count on the support of an almost irreducible minimum of voters who will go Republican or Democratic almost by habit.

Of course, there are still millions of so-called independent voters who tack back and forth from party to party. They help make our elections the unpredictable and breathless affairs that they so often are. Still, even in the variations from year to year one finds certain persistent elements. Looking closely at the complex mosaic of American politics we can see *patterns* of voting habits that help us understand *how* we vote, and a little as to *why* we vote as we do.

Patterns of voting

We find:

1. A pattern of *state* voting. Since the Civil War, Vermont has never given its electoral votes to the Democrats, and Maine has done so only once since 1912. Mississippians and South Carolinians, on the other hand, have given a fifth of their popular votes to Republicans only once, and usually much less. Between these extremes some states over the years have tended to be Republican in national elections, as in the case of Oregon, Kansas, Pennsylvania, and New Hampshire, or to be Democratic, as with several Rocky Mountain states, some border states, and of course the Solid South. Most states, however, are doubtful; they cannot be considered safe by either

party. Indeed, some doubtful states are consistent only in their inconsistency.

2. A pattern of *sectional* voting. The South is the most famous example. The Democratic solidarity of the states that formed the Confederacy has been breached in only four presidential races: in 1928, when Al Smith, a Catholic, headed the Democratic national ticket; in 1948, when President Truman was campaigning on a civil rights platform; in 1952, when Stevenson lost some southern states; and in 1956, when Eisenhower carried all but seven states. North of the Solid South lies a band of border states that lean toward the Democrats, as noted above. Republican sectionalism is not so clear-cut. New England was firmly Republican for many years, but recently Massachusetts and Rhode Island have tended to go Democratic in presidential elections. The states of the upper Midwest, and those of the Far West, had seemed to be normally Republican, but after the Democratic victories of the 1930's and 1940's they cannot be considered safe territory for that party.

3. A pattern of *national voting*. In most states party popularity rises and falls in close tune with the popularity of the party nationally. National trends, in other words, are reflected in trends in most of the states. States and sections are subject to a variety of local influences, but they cannot resist the great tides that sweep the nation. This is especially true of changes in economic conditions. Our national economy is so integrated that people in every state tend to feel the effects of zigzags in the business cycle. As a result, the percentage of the vote for a party in many states is a gauge of national voting behavior. "As the nation goes," says Louis H. Bean, "so goes Massachusetts . . . New York . . . Pennsylvania . . . Illinois . . . Ohio . . . Michigan . . . Wisconsin . . . Minnesota . . . California . . . and so goes almost any state outside the South."[10] In other words, the relation between the Democratic vote in these states and the national Democratic vote tends to remain constant. In the case of Illinois, for example, one need only add 3 or 4 percentage points to its Democratic percentage if he wants a rough gauge of the national Democratic percentage. Iowa usually stays about 7 percentage points below the national Democratic level.

4. A pattern of voting for candidates for *different offices* in the same election. Well over half the voters usually vote a straight ticket—that is, they throw their support to every one of their party's candidates. If one candidate is an especially able vote getter—as Roosevelt was in 1936, for example—the party's whole slate may gain. Thus it is said that candidates ride into office on the coattails of stronger ones. The pulling power of a presidential candidate's coattails seems to help elect members of his own party to office during presidential election years; Democrats, for example, won many more seats in Congress in 1936, 1940, and 1944 than in the off-year elections in between. It is often not easy to tell, however, which candi-

[10] Louis H. Bean, *How to Predict Elections* (New York: Alfred A. Knopf, Inc., 1948), pp. 105-106.

SIX PRESIDENTIAL ELECTIONS, 1928-1956

☐ Democratic   ■ Republican

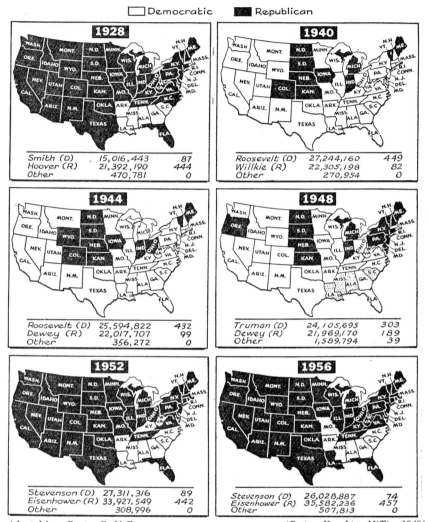

1928		
Smith (D)	15,016,443	87
Hoover (R)	21,392,190	444
Other	470,781	0

1940		
Roosevelt (D)	27,244,160	449
Willkie (R)	22,305,198	82
Other	270,954	0

1944		
Roosevelt (D)	25,594,822	432
Dewey (R)	22,017,707	99
Other	356,272	0

1948		
Truman (D)	24,105,695	303
Dewey (R)	21,969,170	189
Other	1,589,794	39

1952		
Stevenson (D)	27,311,316	89
Eisenhower (R)	33,927,549	442
Other	308,996	0

1956		
Stevenson (D)	26,028,887	74
Eisenhower (R)	35,582,236	457
Other	507,813	0

Adapted from Dayton D. McKean, PARTY AND PRESSURE POLITICS *(Boston: Houghton Mifflin, 1949)*

Patterns of voting.

date rides on whose coattails, or just how important the relation may be.[11]

5. Finally, a pattern of voting *over time*. This pattern takes the form of great political tides that seem to flow back and forth as decade follows decade. The working of the political pendulum takes at least two forms. The

[11] D. B. Truman, "Political Behavior and Voting," *The Pre-Election Polls of 1948* (New York: Social Science Research Council, 1949), pp. 239-244. See also, Malcolm Moos, *Politics, Presidents, and Coattails* (Baltimore: The Johns Hopkins Press, 1952).

general mood of the nation for the past century has seemed to alternate broadly between liberalism and conservatism; it has been suggested by one historian, for example, that the periods of 1841-1861, 1869-1901, and 1918-1931 were marked by a general emphasis on property rights, and the other periods by a stress on human rights.[12] Another type of cycle seems to be a *party* cycle. Republicans and Democrats have alternated in power (especially in their control of the House of Representatives) with a fair degree of regularity.

Behind the pendulum

What causes the political pendulum to swing back and forth? Many complex elements are involved, but one factor seems especially important. This is the business cycle. A drop in business activity has often preceded a loss of congressional seats by the party in power. But we cannot be sure that business cycles *cause* political cycles. Sometimes the two cycles shoot off from each other in erratic fashion. Psychological, political, traditional, sectional, international, and other forces may cut across the economic relationship.

Clearly, then, there are patterns in American politics. Yet these patterns are rough, and they are often blurred in the actual workings of America's motley and untidy politics by capricious and unexplainable variations. Indeed, the patterns may exist for many years and then disappear. For example, as noted above, before the election of 1948 a change in party control of Congress in an off-year election had regularly preceded a change in party fortunes in the following presidential election. But the Democrats, who lost control of Congress in 1946, won both houses of Congress and the Presidency in 1948; and despite 1954 Democratic congressional victories, the Republicans captured the White House, though not Congress, in 1956. So perhaps we will hear less of this "pattern" in the future. And the cycle theories, useful though they may be in some respects, are often not of much help in forecasting political trends because a particular phase of a cycle may last a few years or a great many.

Perhaps this murkiness in American politics is a good thing. Perhaps it shows that we are not caught up in inevitable and relentless forces beyond our control. Unfathomable factors of chance and human nature still have their place. Even the opinion polls, with all their careful scientific techniques, must reckon with these factors. As someone said following Truman's startling victory in 1948, no one can expect to deliver the American people, neatly packaged, tied, and ticketed. Men of determination in either party, campaigning skillfully and energetically, can overcome "inevitable" political trends.

[12] A. M. Schlesinger, "Tides of American Politics," *Yale Review*, Vol. 29 (1939), pp. 217-230.

WHY WE VOTE AS WE DO

Suppose we were able somehow to find ten voters who represented a tiny but fairly accurate cross section of the American electorate. Suppose—shortly after an exciting and close presidential election—we asked them to tell us in a few words why they voted as they did. And suppose they gave us the *real* reason they voted as they did. What kind of answers would we get? Studies of voting indicate that their answers might go something like this:

MR. ANDERSON (*a fruitgrower*): "I voted Republican. I always do. I'm a businessman, you see, and the Republicans have a sound, businesslike point of view. All the fruitgrowers around here voted that way."

MRS. SMITH (a *housewife*): "I supported the Democratic candidate. My husband said he was going to vote that way. He doesn't tell me how to vote, but I leave the politics to him. He always seems to vote Democratic anyway."

MARY BROWN (*a stenographer*): "Well, I didn't know what to do. I wasn't much interested, frankly, but all the girls at the office seemed to think the Democrats are doing a good job, so that's the way I decided to go."

JOE VENUTI (*a young barber*): "Me? Democratic. The Venutis always vote Democratic. We go along with Tom Murphy—he's a big wheel in the party here, and he's a nice fellow too. He's done us some good turns."

DR. WHITE (*local surgeon*): "I voted Republican. I don't like these medical programs the Democrats keep talking about. They'll hurt all us doctors if they go through."

JOHNNY BLACK (*factory worker*): "Democratic. That's the way the boys in the plant were talking. Besides, one of the boys on the union committee gave us a pep talk about supporting the Democrats."

MRS. MURPHY (*housewife*): "I was on the fence a long time. I read the speeches in the paper, and listened to the radio, and finally I went Democratic."

MR. GREEN (*industrialist*): "Republican, of course. We can't take these high taxes much longer."

BILL JOHNSON (*unemployed*): "I didn't know what to do. The family's Republican, but the Democrats seem to want to do something to get more jobs. Well, the paper we get seemed to think the Democratic candidate is on the wrong track, so I voted Republican."

SALLY GREY (*salesgirl*): "Well, I didn't even plan to vote. I'm not much interested in politics. But I was so mad after some people booed the Republican candidate at the movies the night before that I went out and voted for him."

Voting behavior

In what ways are these ten persons representative of Americans as a whole in the manner that they made up their minds? For one thing, at least half of the ten supported their party almost automatically, and this voting by *habit* is true of most American voters. No matter what the candidates or issues, no matter what tremendous events are taking place such as wars or depressions, millions of voters in both parties can be relied on to put their X's in the same party column election after election. This traditional voting is not necessarily blind or irrational. In many cases voting for the same party over the years may represent a person's rational view of his self-interest, as in the case of Mr. Anderson above, or Joe Venuti. In any case, habitual party voting is one of the decisive facts that a politician must accept in laying his campaign plans.

In the second place, most of the ten voted the same way as their *families* or *friends* or *workmates* were going to vote. On election day Americans mark their ballots in private, yet voting is essentially a *group* experience. We tend to vote as applegrowers, union members, Legionnaires, prohibitionists, Catholics, Constitution reverers, isolationists, or as members of other existing or potential groups. The most homogeneous of all groups in molding the opinions of its members probably is the family. In Erie County it was discovered that among husbands and wives, both of whom planned to vote, twenty-one couples out of every twenty-two agreed on their choice. Parents and children tended to vote the same way too; only one pair in twelve divided. As might be expected, in-laws were less in agreement, but even here four out of five agreed in their party choice.[13] The reasons for this uniformity are twofold: members of the family shape one another's attitudes (often unintentionally); and members of the same family are usually exposed to similar economic, religious, class, and geographical influences. The husband seems to be head of the house politically as well as otherwise. Most wives talk the election over with their husbands. Men, on the other hand, "do not feel that they are discussing politics with their wives; they feel they are telling them."[14]

A third influence of great importance is *economic*. When people break away from their traditional party ties, the reason may be that they have come to look on another party as more responsive to their material needs. Doubtless this factor was central in the swing away from the Republicans in 1932. As we suggested earlier, there seems to be a relationship—albeit a rough one—between income status and voting. Most recent studies of voting behavior confirm what everyday observation has already indicated to most of us: the highest proportions of persons who prefer the Republican party are in the upper income brackets, especially those with incomes of over $5000 a year.[15]

But we cannot make too much of the economic factor, or of any other single motivation. For although we can isolate economic influences that affect voting, we cannot tell just how they affect it, or to what extent. Voting

[13] Lazarsfeld, *The People's Choice*, p. 141. See also T. M. Newcomb, *Social Psychology* (New York: The Dryden Press, Inc., 1950), pp. 531-534.
[14] Lazarsfeld, *The People's Choice*, p. 141.
[15] See Berelson, Lazarsfeld, and McPhee, *op. cit.*, p. 333.

is the product of many factors besides the economic. Religion, for example, or geographical location, may cut through the lines of economic interest. Or voters of all types may respond in like fashion to national or international developments. Studies suggest, for example, that the shift from Republicans to Democrats between 1928 and 1932 and from Democrats to Republicans between 1948 and 1952 was not peculiar to one or two particular groups, but was in fact common to all economic classes.

To generalize briefly, if Mr. Jones is a wealthy businessman, Protestant, living in rural Ohio, married to a Protestant, and the son of a Republican, the chances are very good that Jones will vote Republican. Unless radical alterations occur in our party structure or in our society generally, we can predict that such a person as Jones will vote Republican in a future election before we know the candidates or the issues. Does this mean that people's political behavior can be predicted with certainty or that voting is a simple mechanical addition of set factors? Not at all. There are men like Jones who vote Democratic—or even Communist. It merely means that voting behavior, like all other behavior, is the outcome of a complex interrelationship of a number of significant factors. *On the average* the Joneses will vote as indicated.

All kinds of independents

Then there are the independent voters. Some of these are probably like our Mrs. Murphy, who made a conscientious effort to hear all sides of the argument before voting. Other independents may resemble Sally Grey, who voted almost by whim. Unable to identify themselves consistently with one party or candidate, some independents cross and recross party lines from election to election. Some "split" their ticket and vote for some candidates from one party and other candidates from another party. Some people call themselves independents because they think it is socially more respectable, but actually they vote with the same degree of regularity for one party as do others who are not so hesitant to admit party loyalty.[16] There are then all kinds of independent voters. A recent study indicates that younger voters, those who live in middle-

Copyright 1956, Crowell Collier Publishing Company by Bill Mauldin

"Me, I vote the man, not the party. Harding, Coolidge, Hoover, Landon, Dewey . . ."

size cities, those with over $3000 income, and those with a college education tend to be more independent than other groups, but that the indepen-

[16] Samuel J. Eldersveld, "The Independent Vote: Measurement, Characteristics, and Implications for Party Strategy," *American Political Science Review*, Vol. XLVI (September 1952), p. 737. In one study reported by Eldersveld one-half of those who claimed to be independents were *not*, by objective criteria.

dent vote is rather evenly distributed throughout the population.[17] On the average about one out of every five voters calls himself independent, and twelve million independent-minded voters are a fact for any politician or party to reckon with.

Variations in party strength may be due less to voters shifting from one party to another than to the acquisition of new voters from the ranks of previous nonvoters or of younger people voting for the first time. In 1952, however, voters shifting their allegiance from one party to another were of crucial importance. According to a careful study, former Democrats who voted for Dwight D. Eisenhower held the balance of power in the 1952 election.[18] "While sizable numbers of 1948 nonvoters were coming into the ranks of 1952 voters, dividing their favors rather equally between the two presidential aspirants, smaller numbers of people who had voted in 1948 were withdrawing from the political arena to become nonvoters in 1952. The net result of these additions and subtractions left the Republicans with an added 6 per cent of the population supporting their cause. In the same way, the Democrats picked up slightly more than 2 per cent of the population. As these sizable, but to some extent compensating, shifts were occurring, some 11 per cent of the citizens were deciding to change their votes from 1948 Democratic to 1952 Republican. . . ."[19] All told, the study concludes, some 25 per cent of the final Republican vote came from 1948 Democrats.

Does campaigning change votes?

What about the campaign? Does it change any votes? One might judge from our discussion of voting behavior that all the speeches of vote seekers, the hullabaloo of the campaign, had little effect compared to the other basic forces. In part this conclusion would be true. A campaign usually *converts* only a small fraction of the electorate. But it has other important effects. It *reinforces* the convictions of those already tending one way or another. And it *activates* people—that is, it arouses their interest, exposes them to particular candidates and ideas, shapes their attitudes, and stimulates them to vote on election day.[20]

Still, events between elections, and underlying attitudes, traditions, and pressures, are far more important than the campaign. Does this situation discourage the vote-seeking politician? Not at all. He knows that he is dealing in margins, often in close margins. He knows that a hundred unknown intangibles will shape the final outcome. Great political forces are balanced—

---

[17] Eldersveld, *op. cit.*, pp. 743, 751.

[18] Angus Campbell, Gerald Gurin, and Warren E. Miller, "Political Issues and the Vote: November, 1952," *The American Political Science Review*, Vol. XLVII, No. 2 (June 1953), p. 369. This study was based on data gathered through nationwide sample surveys (conducted in October and November, 1952) of over 2000 persons.

[19] *Ibid.*

[20] Lazarsfeld, *The People's Choice*, chapters 7-11.

perhaps a hard push by his party and himself will move them in the direction he wants.

To summarize briefly this discussion of voting behavior:

1. The rate of nonvoting is very high in the United States. The main cause is apathy. A number of remedies for nonvoting have been proposed, including compulsory voting.

2. Voting falls into rough patterns, mainly geographical. The somewhat

WHO PLAYS POLITICS?*

POLITICAL ACTIVITY SCORE OF THE AMERICAN PEOPLE		AFFILIATIONS OF POLITICALLY ACTIVE		
	Per cent		*Politically Very Active*	*Population as a Whole*
Very active	10		*100%*	*100%*
Active	17	Democrats	39.8	48.9
Inactive	35	Republicans	43.8	32.7
Very inactive	38	Independents	16.4	18.4

PER CENT OF VOTERS WHO VOTED ONCE IN THE PAST FOUR YEARS

	Per cent		*Per cent*
Total Population	52	By Economic Status	
		Prosperous	77
By Occupation		Upper middle income	63
Housewife	44	Lower middle income	56
Professional	74	Poor	37
Executive	75		
White-collar	63	By Education	
Labor	47	Grade school or less	43
Farmer	52	High school	52
		College	66
By Sex			
Men	57	By Size of Place	
Women	45	Over 100,000	52
		2,500 to 100,000	57
By Age		Under 2,500	48
21-34 years old	40		
35-49	59	By Region	
50 and over	60	Northwest	62
		Midwest	56
		South	39
		Far West	48

VOTING TURNOUT OF SOURCES OF REPUBLICAN PARTY STRENGTH		VOTING TURNOUT OF SOURCES OF DEMOCRATIC PARTY STRENGTH	
	Per cent		*Per cent*
Prosperous	77	Far West	48
Executive	75	Labor	47
Professionals	74	Women	45
College educated	66	Housewives	44
Upper middle income	63	Grade school or less educated	43
Northeast	62	21-34 years old	40
50 and over	60	South	39
2500-100,000 (size of place)	57	Poor	37

* Elmo Roper and Louis Harris, "Crime, Reform & the Voter," *The Saturday Review of Literature,* April 7, 1951, pp. 8, 9, 34, 35. By permission.

regular swing of the political pendulum over time is caused by a variety of economic and other factors.

3. The way we vote stems in large part from tradition, the groups we belong to (including family groups), our economic and social status. Independent voting also results from a variety of factors.

TWO-PARTY DIVISION OF ENTIRE POPULATION

vs.

DIVISION OF THE VOTING POPULATION

	Among the Population Over 21 Claiming to Be		Among Those Who Turn Out to Vote	
	Democratic per cent	Republican per cent	Democratic per cent	Republican per cent
Total	60	40	53	47
By Occupation				
Housewife	60	40	51	49
Professional	53	47	49	51
Executive	36	64	32	68
White-collar	52	48	47	53
Labor	70	30	66	34
Farmer	67	33	64	36
By Sex				
Men	59	41	55	45
Women	60	40	51	49
By Age				
21-34	66	34	61	39
35-49	59	41	51	46
50 and over	54	46	45	55
By Economic Status				
Prosperous	31	69	27	73
Upper middle income	47	53	41	59
Lower middle	60	40	55	45
Poor	70	30	64	36
By Education				
Grade school	66	34	60	40
High school	61	39	54	46
College	46	54	43	57
By Size of Place				
Over 100,000	63	37	55	45
2,500 to 100,000	58	42	49	51
Under 2,500	62	38	55	45
By Region				
Northeast	46	54	40	60
Midwest	52	48	46	54
South	80	20	80	20
Far West	64	36	61	39

As a statistical summary the data on pp. 311-312, gathered in a 1950 study, underscore some of the major points in this chapter.

CHANGING PATTERNS OF POLITICS

A century ago, American politics was still essentially a "rustic" politics. Then, as people crowded into the great cities, rustic politics came to be over-shadowed by the rise of an urban politics. Currently we are witnessing the development of a suburban politics. Of course no phase of this series of transitions has wholly obliterated the previous one. Today, in the fabulous breadth and diversity of American political life, rural, urban, and suburban politics exist comfortably side by side. Each deserves attention.

Jonesville: a case study

Jonesville is a prairie town of several thousand people located in the Middle West. It is of interest to us because it is a rather "typical" small town in an agricultural area, and because a group of sociologists made a careful study of the town and its people following World War II.[21] What did they discover about the political life of Jonesville?

In the first place, Jonesville, like so many country towns in the United States, is strongly Republican. For half a century, no Democratic President had carried the county in which Jonesville is located, except Franklin D. Roosevelt by a narrow margin in 1932. Social pressure seems to keep the town Republican, even during "Democratic" years nationally. "People around here," says a leading Democrat, "are scared to admit they're Democrats." Even voters with definite Democratic tendencies dislike to vote in the Democratic primaries, where they must openly display their party allegiance: they prefer to vote Democratic in the privacy of the polling booth at the general election.

The fact that Jonesville is a Republican stronghold does not mean that it is a bustle of partisan activity. Less than 20 per cent of the people voted Republican faithfully enough in a number of primary and general elections to be classified as "solid Republican voters." (The proportion of Democratic voters was much less—barely 2 per cent.) Significantly, voting in Jonesville tends to follow class lines—at least on the Republican side—much as it does in the country as a whole. The percentage of persons who are "solid Republican voters" is 24 per cent in the upper-middle class and 7 per cent in the lower-lower class.[22] The Republican strength in Jonesville is important for our two-party system; it indicates how a major party can survive with strength at the grass roots during long years of being in the minority nationally.

The Republicans are relatively well organized in Jonesville. There are six precinct committeemen and a number of other party workers and mis-

[21] W. L. Warner and Associates, *Democracy in Jonesville* (New York: Harper & Brothers, 1949). All the material in this section is drawn from this provocative and significant study.
[22] *Ibid.*, p. 219.

cellaneous hangers-on. Their main job is to get the vote out in primary and general elections. To do this they rely chiefly on the most important means of influence in grass-roots democracy: face-to-face contact with voters. Some of the party wheel-horses work at politics throughout the year; others are active only at election time. For the most part, the precinct committeemen deal in small political currency: "fixing" traffic tickets, arranging tax adjustments, and the like. By way of reward, the committeeman can expect an invitation to a governor's inaugural, some control of patronage, and perhaps a state job for himself.

Behind these minor politicos in Jonesville are a few "big shots" who have considerable influence over the Republican organization. Their power turns on their ability to maintain two sets of relationships, "outward" and "local." The party chiefs in Jonesville must deal outwardly with county and state politicians, the governor of the state, and leaders of interest groups; and locally with the party workers and town officials; the traffic consists of patronage, favors, legislative influence, campaign funds—and votes on election day. An important factor in maintaining both sets of relationships is "the class position of the individuals involved: the ability to circulate socially in 'important' circles at the state capital, the educational requirements of certain positions, practice in management and the exercise of initiative demand a middle-class social position as a sort of minimum if the outward connections are to be established and maintained.[23] Such connections are important also in raising campaign funds.

The Democratic party in Jonesville is a feeble organization. It lacks money, patronage, party workers, and voting support. It is split by petty factionalism. The basic fact is that Jonesville is Republican by tradition, ideology, and perhaps interest. In Jonesville, "Democrats are made, not born." In big city politics, the reverse is generally true.

Street corner politics

American politics, big-city style, traditionally involved powerful bosses, elaborate organization, myriad party workers, patronage used systematically on the grand scale, considerable party discipline over national, state, and local legislators, and hundreds of thousands of Democratic votes for national, state, and local candidates (except in Philadelphia and a few other cities that have traditionally been Republican).

It is important to remember that inside these large organizations, there is a pattern of political organization and influence on a block and street corner basis. Here one finds the "wheels within wheels" of urban political life, the crisscrossing relationships among families, neighborhoods, religious and ethnic groups, places of business, criminal groups, athletic clubs, and the like. An important "buildingblock" of political organization is the street

[23] *Ibid.*, p. 230.

corner gang of young men. Some years ago, a young social scientist, William F. Whyte, spent many months with such a gang in a slum district, inhabited mainly by Italian immigrant families, in the heart of a large city, and later reported on his observations.[24]

In "Cornerville," as Whyte calls it, there are a number of political clubs started by politicians and organized around them. These clubs supply votes to the politician that he can use to elect himself to local office or to deliver to bosses farther up in the machine hierarchy. Corner gangs usually make up an important part of these clubs. The boss who runs the club maintains close working relationships with the gang leader, consulting him on policy questions and doing favors for him. Corner-boy leaders learn the political trade by serving as apprentices to the politician. The gangs are perhaps even more important in Cornerville politics than families, for the latter have tended to be weakened by divisions between first and second generations.

Economic and social stresses of the 1930's tended to undermine some of the organizations. A former boss said nostalgically about earlier times,[25] "In those days we really controlled. We could tell within fifty votes how the ward would go in any election. One time we changed the ward from Democratic to Republican overnight. That was in the mayoralty contest of 1905. There was a meeting in the club till three in the morning right before the election. We printed the slate we were backing and circulated it around as much as we had time for. When the people came to the polls, the captain would ask them, 'Do you have the slate?' If they didn't he would give it to them, and they would go in and vote it. . . .

"Today everything has changed. We've got a floating population in the South Side now. People are moving out all the time. You can't expect a precinct captain to know everybody any more. . . ."

Cornerville political organization can best be described, according to Whyte, as a "system of reciprocal personal obligations." People do favors for one another, and mutual loyalty is an indispensable part of the political code. Affecting all these interpersonal relationships, however, are two broader influences. One is the role of national origin. In an area heavily populated by foreign-born Americans, the politician must know how to play on their national sympathies, their sense of being the "underdog," their feelings against other groups. The other is the role of class appeal. While the Cornerville politician talks little about specific national or state policy questions, he speaks often of "God's own poor" and of the lot of working people. "The most important qualification a politician can claim is that he has been and will always be loyal to his old friends, to his class, and to his race." While this is the hallmark of politicians everywhere, it takes on special importance in the politics of the melting pot.

[24] W. F. Whyte, *Street Corner Society* (Chicago: University of Chicago Press, 1943).

[25] *Ibid.,* p. 195.

The new politics of Suburbia

The old boss quoted above complained about people moving out all the time. Where are they moving to? Many of them to suburban areas outside the large and medium-sized cities. In the past decade, Americans have been flooding into Suburbia. City growth since 1940 has averaged less than 10 per cent, and the relative number of people on farms is declining. But the suburban population has shot up by 50 to 100 per cent throughout the country. New York's Nassau County alone, for example, showed a gain of over 60 per cent. Suburbs of Boston, Chicago, Philadelphia, Los Angeles, and other metropolises—along with those of middle-sized cities—have shown startling increases.

Are we finding a new suburban complexion in the pattern of American politics? Who will reap the millions of votes in Suburbia? What role will the suburban masses have in national politics? How will they line up on issues? Will they mark the supremacy of the middle classes in American politics? What, in short, will be the impact of Suburbia on American political life?

When city Democrats settle down next to suburban Republicans, the newcomer must adjust to a different political world as well as to a different social one. He often finds that the Republicans have as tight a grip on local government as the Democrats had on the politics of his former neighborhood. From the standpoint of business contacts, it may seem expedient to register Republican. Often people moving into the suburbs are also moving into higher income brackets, and changing parties seems all the more logical. But the influence is by no means all in one direction. The "immigrants" from the city have some impact too. They bring with them different ideas and often a flair for political action. They speak up at the meetings of the League of Women Voters and the Legion. Many of them vote Democratic as they have in the past.

Nevertheless, the Republicans are dominant in Suburbia, and they probably will continue to be so for some time. Here they will harvest the hundreds of thousands of votes they badly need to offset the two or three million vote edge that the Democrats have gained over them in the nation as a whole. Election night in most large states has usually seen huge urban majorities washing out the Republican votes from small towns and rural areas. In the elections lying ahead, we may see suburban majorities tipping the balance back toward the Republicans.[26]

It is easy to conclude that Suburbia will be a conservative force in American politics. But the situation is a bit more complicated than this. There is reason to expect that Suburbia will be a liberalizing and broad-

[26] Louis Harris, *Is There a Republican Majority?* (New York: Harper & Brothers, 1954), Chapter 8; and Samuel Lubell, *Revolt of the Moderates* (New York: Harper & Brothers, 1956), Chapter 5.

ening force in both parties. The economic make-up of the suburban groups is significant in this respect. Engaged as they are in hundreds of different sectors of the economy, the new suburban masses have a variety of economic interests. The suburban commuter may work in a great insurance firm; his neighbor next door is in the steel fabricating business; Mr. Jones across the street plans advertising campaigns in the headquarters of a giant food chain. Their political attitudes tend to reflect these diverse economic interests.

This situation is a far cry from the style of political life of areas dominated by a single economic interest, as in one-crop sections of the South or mining areas in Pennsylvania or cattle districts of the West. Involved in the economics of the whole nation, Suburbia is concerned more with a politics of broad national and international programs than with a politics of narrow sectional interest. It is not surprising that polls show a marked support for internationalist foreign policies in many middle-class, suburban areas. Suburbia will be more cosmopolitan and sophisticated in political outlook than rural or urban areas have been. Its representatives in Washington and the state capitals will not get far on the easy formula of "Everything for the folks back home." To act for his suburban constituents, each legislator must mediate among interests almost as diverse as those of the whole nation.

Suburbia, in short, may tend to be less concerned with pork-barrel politics, trivial favors, patronage, and errand-running, and more concerned with matters of broad policy, such as taxes, labor, foreign affairs, Cold War strategy, farm subsidies, prices. This can have a wholesome influence on American politics.

LEADERS AND FOLLOWERS

The question of who plays politics is not simply a matter of voters and nonvoters. It is also a matter of what we might call multivoters—persons whose influence over other voters is so great that they in effect control more than one voter. This influence may or may not be intended. The head of a family may be a multivoter without any effort on his part simply because he has the respect and confidence of his wife and children. The party worker, on the other hand, deliberately sets out to win votes from friends and neighbors in his ward. In either case the personal, face-to-face contact is highly effective.

We hear much of the nationally known leaders who are said to influence millions of votes through their speeches and actions. The role of such leadership should not be minimized, as the following chapters will suggest. But neither should we underestimate the importance of local "grassroots" leadership. If our country were made up of a few leaders at the top and a hundred million followers at the bottom, our democracy might not be as solid and resilient as we like to think it is. Actually leaders are found at all levels. The leader in the local community may be a follower in the county or state. The head of a local labor or business organization is perhaps a follower of a state or national labor or business leader. Thus there are *overlapping hierarchies* of leaders and followers.

Local leaders

Through their face-to-face contacts local opinion leaders, as they have been called, have an influence that national leaders, with their less personal relationship, cannot match. Many voters, moreover, pay more attention to local opinion leaders than to the radio or newspaper. "In comparison with the formal media of communication," says Lazarsfeld, "personal relationships are potentially more influential for two reasons: their coverage is greater and they have certain psychological advantages over the formal media," such as the newspaper.[27] Opinion leaders can get to some persons who rarely expose themselves to the radio or printed page. And their technique—consciously or not—is far more effective. Listening to a candidate or reading a campaign poster, the follower may suspect that someone is trying to sell him a bill of goods. But the seemingly casual remarks of the opinion leader may catch him off his guard. The leader can talk in terms that the follower understands, can find the right time to deliver his opinions, can tailor his argument to suit the follower's personality or beliefs. In politics, just as in business, face-to-face contact lowers sales resistance.

Successful political leaders understand all this. Half a century ago Boss Plunkitt, a Tammany district leader, was quoted as saying:

There's only one way to hold a district; you must study human nature and act accordin'. You can't study human nature in books. Books is a hindrance more than anything else. If you have been to college, so much the worse for you. You'll have to unlearn all you learned before you can get right down to human nature, and unlearnin' takes a lot of time. Some men can never forget what they learned at college. Such men may get to be district leaders by a fluke, but they never last.

To learn real human nature you have to go among the people, see them and be seen. I know every man, woman, and child in the Fifteenth District, except them that's been born this summer—and I know some of them, too. I know what they like and what they don't like, what they are strong at and what they are weak in, and I reach them by approachin' at the right side.

For instance, here's how I gather in the young men. I hear of a young feller that's proud of his voice, thinks that he can sing fine. I ask him to come around to Washington Hall and join our Glee Club. He comes and sings, and he's a follower of Plunkitt for life. Another young feller gains a reputation as a baseball player in a vacant lot. I bring him into our baseball club. That fixes him.

[27] Lazarsfeld, *The People's Choice*, p. 150.

. . . I don't trouble them with political arguments. I just study human nature and act accordin'. . . .

As to the older voters, I reach them, too. No, I don't send campaign literature. That's rot. People can get all the political stuff they want to read—and a good deal more, too—in the papers. Who reads speeches, nowadays, anyhow? It's bad enough to listen to them. You ain't goin' to gain any votes by stuffin' the letter boxes with campaign documents. . . .[28]

We do not need to accept all Boss Plunkitt's arguments to see the role of direct personal leadership.

All kinds of leaders

Do certain people have innate qualities of leadership and others not? Some social scientists used to believe that leadership was restricted to people possessing certain traits, such as imagination, foresight, versatility, good health, courage—or even well-functioning endocrine glands! Elaborate lists were drawn up of so-called leadership qualities.[29] Investigators had trouble, however, in agreeing what were the key, universal qualities of leadership. More recently expert opinion has shifted somewhat. Careful experiments indicate that leadership is *specific to a given situation*. A baseball team, a religious club, and a corrupt political machine will produce different types of leaders. Since America, as we noted in Chapter 1, is composed of a fabulous diversity of groups, inevitably there will be a variety of leaders.[30] A person who is a follower in one group or situation may be a leader in the next. We all know of the football captain who inspires his team on the field but who is a wallflower at the school dance, or the manager of a store who never opens his mouth at town meeting.

All this is significant. It means that political leadership is not restricted to a chosen few but can be—and is—exercised by millions of average citizens throughout the land. It means that anyone can wield influence in his own circle, for investigations show that opinion leaders are found at all economic levels and in all social groups. It means, above all, that the right to vote is only the simplest, most elementary privilege available to a citizen of a democracy. He has the further right to seek to influence other voters, and if he exercises that right he can multiply his strength manyfold. One of the hallmarks of a vigorous democracy is that *everyone* can play politics.

[28] W. L. Riordan, *Plunkitt of Tammany Hall* (New York: McClure, Phillips, 1905), pp. 33-34.
[29] See E. S. Bogardus, *Fundamentals of Social Psychology* (New York: Appleton-Century, 1942), Chapter 12.
[30] See A. W. Gouldner, ed., *Studies in Leadership* (New York: Harper & Brothers, 1950), pp. 14-44.

T HE VITAL FEATURE OF OUR NATIONAL PARTY
system is that it is essentially a two-party system. If we had three or more
parties seriously competing for power, our politics would be far different
from what it is. If we had a one-party system like the fascist or communist
type, our democracy would be far different from what it is—indeed it
would doubtless be non-existent. This does not mean that we have only
two parties. No less than 135 parties have been able to elect members to
Congress in the last 160 years, and there have been countless other local
parties. On the other hand, in many areas of the United States only one
major party dominates local affairs. Recently, in Alabama one lone Republican representative was pitted against 105 Democrats; this state has not
elected a Republican governor since Reconstruction. In North Dakota the
Senate was composed of one Democrat and 48 Republicans. Even within a
state where the two major parties are fairly evenly balanced, some precincts
are dominated by a single party.

Actually we have a series of party systems.[1] In some places one of the
major parties may dominate the state government and the state's congressional delegation, but in presidential elections both parties may be
strong. Since 1932, for example, Oregon has voted for the Democratic
candidate for President four times, but has normally sent Republican delegations to Congress and the Democrats did not control the Oregon legislature for 78 years. Texas voted for President Eisenhower in 1956, but there
is only one Republican con-
gressman from that state, and
in the state legislature the
Democrats have overwhelming
dominance.

Yet when all the qualifications are made, our national
party system meets the criterion of a two party system—
only the Democrats or the
Republicans have any real
chance to gain power, one of

★ 13

Party politics

and party

problems

[1] Austin Ranney and Willmoore
Kendall, "The American Party Systems," *The American Political Science Review*, Vol. XLVIII, No. 2
(June 1954), pp. 477-485. Also Joseph A. Schlesinger, "A Two-Di-
mensional Scheme for Classifying
the States According to Degree of
Inter-Party Competition," *The
American Political Science Review*,
Vol. XLIX, No. 4 (December
1955), pp. 1120-1128.

these parties normally can muster the majority to enable it to control the Congress or to elect the President without any help from a third party, and over a period of time the two parties alternate in power.

Why do we have a two-party system? Nobody knows for sure. Jefferson thought that men naturally divided into whigs and tories. Lord Bryce said they inevitably split into nationalists and states-righters. Some have said that "advanced Anglo-Saxon peoples" sensibly adopted tidy political systems; perhaps the sentry in *Iolanthe* was mocking them when he sang:

> Now let's rejoice
>   That Nature wisely does contrive
> That every boy and every gal
>   That's born into the world alive
> Is either a little Liberal
>   Or else a little Conservative.

Probably the explanation lies largely in the nature of our electoral system. Most of our elections are set up on the basis of single-member districts in which the candidate with the most votes wins.[2] Since only one candidate can win, the largest and next largest parties monopolize the victories, and the third party, being deprived of the rewards of office, eventually gives up the fight. The system of electing the President, the great prize of American politics, operates in this fashion on a national scale. In order to win the Presidency it is necessary for a party to win a majority of the electoral votes which requires a national organization and party support in more than one region. The two major parties alternate in their possession of the presidency; deprived of patronage and power, third parties tend to wither away. The ability of some third parties to last for two or three decades has been due largely to their hold on congressional and state offices in certain sections of the country, as in the case of the Progressives in Wisconsin.

Two important results stem from our two-party system. First, such a system requires that both parties must be broad alliances of many different interests. Parties are the means whereby groups pool their efforts to reach at least some of their goals. Successful party leaders must be group diplomats —they must know how to mediate among more or less hostile groups so that agreement can be reached on general principles. The implications of this tendency for national unity are obvious. National unity is not simply a mystical thing—it is the capacity to rise above differences (at least for a while) and pull together. Parties want to *win elections*. In order to win, each of them finds the *common beliefs* that *unite* men, and plays down the issues that divide them. Parties help reconcile unity and diversity.

[2] Maurice Klain, "A New Look At The Constituencies: The Need for A Recount and A Reappraisal," *The American Political Science Review*, Vol. XLIX, No. 4 (December 1955), p. 1105. Klain points out that in many states some state legislators are not chosen in single-member elections.

A second important result of the two-party system is the tendency of both parties to be moderate in their platforms.[3] Under a multiparty system the parties range all the way from an extremely conservative party to an extremely radical one. With two big parties, this extremism is normally avoided. Each party must embrace a variety of groups, and above all each must try to attract the crucial middle-of-the-road vote that easily switches from one side to the other. Not only do parties seek wide support, but the different interest groups try not to become alienated from either side. They keep friendly contacts with both parties. This moderating tendency helps unite the country.

How these two tendencies—toward unity and toward moderation—have worked out in practice over a century and a half of party development can be seen in a brief look at the growth of the American party sysem.

THE GRAND COALITIONS

The story of American parties is closely bound up with the economic, political, and social history of the whole nation. The full telling of that story would take a four-foot shelf in itself. Here we must oversimplify. Looking at American parties as alliances of interests, we can see three great phases. The first, lasting until the Civil War, is the Age of the Democrats; the second, stretching through the first decade of this century, is the Age of the Republicans.[4] The third, beginning in 1930, might be called a New Age of the Democrats. Whether this phase has now ended and a New Age of the Republicans has begun depends on the ability of the G.O.P. to broaden the power it won in 1952 and 1956.

The peculiar American brand of rough-and-tumble politics did not begin in Revolutionary days. Well before the Revolution there were divisions of interest between economic and sectional groups; there were political clubs and committees; there were meetings, parades, songs, oratory, and fisticuffs, just as today. But the effect of the Revolution and the post-Revolutionary struggles was to crystallize political interests and allegiances in more coherent and lasting form. The great service of George Washington was to give the fledgling government a sense of unity by his ability to rise above faction and party. He had hardly taken the oath of office, however, before there were signs of an emerging party split. On one side was Alexander Hamilton, who was not only Washington's Secretary of the Treasury but the leader of the Federalists. As a supporter of the Constitution, strong central government, and "sound" financial policies, Hamilton was spokesman for the bankers, traders, and manufacturers of the day.

[3] E. E. Schattschneider, *Party Government* (New York: Farrar & Rinehart, Inc., 1942), pp. 85 ff.
[4] See D. W. Brogan, *Government of the People* (New York: Harper & Brothers, 1933), Part Two.

Rise of the Democrats

On the other side was Thomas Jefferson and a motley collection of small farmers, frontiersmen, laborers, debtors, small proprietors, slaveowners—in general, an agrarian group.[5] Jefferson was the first national party leader. He resigned as Secretary of State in Washington's second administration to devote full time to the job of welding together a great party following. He accomplished this task by negotiating with local party leaders in New England, New York, Virginia, and other sections, and by expounding a philosophy of equality, agrarianism, and limited government that appealed alike to northern farmer, southern planter, and western frontiersman. By the turn of the century this combination overcame the Federalists. As President, Jefferson continued to serve as party chief, and he used the party to put his program through Congress.

Here was the first of the grand coalitions. It started out as the Democratic-Republican party, but soon dropped the "Democratic," later split into Republican and Democratic elements, and ended up as the Democratic party. During this sixty-year period, ending with Lincoln's election, the party changed in many ways. Millions of new voters were casting ballots. Americans were moving westward, and the party had to move with them. Republican leaders in office, like John Quincy Adams, seemed to drift away from some of the leveling sentiments of Jefferson. The rising democratic elements, led by Andrew Jackson, gave the party a southern and westward cast. Nevertheless, the party retained two of its main features. First, it won elections. The Whigs—who came to be the main opposition party—were able to elect only two Presidents, and only then by nominating war heroes. Second, it continued to play coalition politics. Its following embraced sizable numbers of cotton planters, slaveowners, small farmers in the West, workmen in eastern mills.

How does a major party lose power? In the case of the Democrats, two things happened. The party itself split in the face of the irrepressible conflict over slavery, and the opposition hammered out a superior combination of voting groups. The Whigs' coalition, composed of large sections of the propertied class, big slaveowners and planters, nativists, and anti-slavery people, had never been stable enough or large enough to turn the tide against the Democrats. The 1850's were a time of party upheaval. The conservative elements of the Whig party, especially in the South, went over to the Democrats. Other Whigs looked around for a new party. The Democrats, deeply split between northerners and southerners, broke into fragments.

Era of the Republicans

The new winning alliance—the Republican party—was founded in 1854 (not by Abraham Lincoln, who was still a Whig). Initially the party was

[5] W. E. Binkley, *American Political Parties* (New York: Alfred A. Knopf, Inc., 1947), pp. 72-78.

radical in many respects, appealing to farmers, workers, and small businessmen. To the revolutionary air of the Marseillaise the Republicans sang:

> Arise, arise, ye brave,
> And let your war-cry be
> Free speech, free press, free soil, free men,
> Frémont and victory.

The Republicans lost with Frémont in 1856 to a Democratic coalition still strong enough to win, but four years later Lincoln was the ideal politician to gain victory on a Republican platform that opposed further extension of slavery and favored internal improvements, including a "satisfactory homestead measure" for farmers and "liberal wages for workingmen and mechanics." Lincoln received 40 per cent of the popular vote in 1860, but his common appeal to North and West won him the electoral votes of every northern state.

The postwar Republican party consolidated and broadened its group coalition. Its liberal homestead policies helped solidify the support of farmers, especially in the Midwest, and of immigrants eager for land. Its humanitarian appeal and its high-tariff stand continued to attract many eastern workers. Its aids to business, such as sound money policies and railroad land grants, won the support of financiers, industrialists, and merchants. As the party of Lincoln it had a hold on the newly freed Negroes that was long to remain secure. Veterans of the northern armies were part of this coalition; for decades units of the Grand Army of the Republic worked closely with the party machine and reaped their reward in the form of pensions. Above all the Republicans were the "party of the Union," with a national appeal that seemed to transcend the lines of class, group, or section.

For five decades after 1860 this coalition was to give every presidential race to the Republicans, except for Cleveland's victories in 1884 and 1892. Not that all was smooth sailing for the Grand Old Party. It suffered from the exposure of the corruption that accompanied Grant's administrations. It was shaken by internal divisions between East and West, between conservative businessmen and not-so-conservative farmers and workers, between reform-minded Liberal Republicans and stand-patters, between party regulars (Stalwarts) and party independents (Halfbreeds), and between many different combinations of these. Yet the G.O.P. remained a grand coalition. The secret of its success lay in finding, by design or by chance, leaders who could assuage the different elements. For example, when important labor and rural elements were on the verge of deserting the party toward the end of the century, it was a group diplomat, William McKinley, who reasserted the party's broad appeal. When the upsurge of reformism and muckraking in the following years presaged a change in political moods, it was a progressive Republican, Theodore Roosevelt, who re-oriented the party's appeal.

The loyal opposition

Meanwhile, what of the Democrats? Discredited—in the minds of many —by the Civil War, this party survived with its hard core in the South. As the loyal opposition after the Civil War, the Democrats capitalized on the mistakes and excesses of the party in power. Along with winning the Presidency twice, and nearly winning it several times, the party occasionally took control of Congress and frequently of state governments. Its platforms championed the principles of low tariffs, states' rights, civil service, currency reform. But the Democrats were not able to secure power. Part of the trouble was their failure to win over dissident groups, like the Greenbackers, that spent their energies in third-party movements in behalf of such "radical" changes as bimetallism and regulation of business. But the main difficulty was that the Republicans, riding the wave of a long-term economic boom, were in accord with the main temper of the times. For even in 1896, when the Democrats under William Jennings Bryan finally formed an alliance with the Populists, the G.O.P. re-established control of the White House after one of the most turbulent election fights in American history.

For all their noisy battles during the century, the two parties had been true to the rule that under a biparty system neither side can afford to be extremist. Both parties embraced liberal and conservative elements, both reached out for the support of members of the major interest groups, especially of the dominant business groups. Democrats Tilden and Cleveland shared the major political and economic assumptions of Republicans Hayes and Harrison. Indeed, one of the main complaints of the third parties of the day—as with all third parties—was that both major parties were in a conspiracy of agreement over policy, dividing only over the distribution of the immediate spoils of office.[6] Both parties, moreover, tended to move in tune with shifting public sentiment. Thus during 1896-1912, a period of unrest and protest, the progressive wings of both parties were dominant much of the time.

In 1912 the Republican coalition split as cleanly as the Democratic one had in 1860. The conservative wing under President Taft kept a tight grip on the party machinery; the disgruntled progressives deserted the G.O.P. and nominated Theodore Roosevelt on the ticket of a new Progressive party. The Democratic party, led by Woodrow Wilson and pledged to the New Freedom, won fewer popular votes than the Republicans and Progressives combined, but it swept the electoral college. As President, Wilson used Jeffersonian precedents in putting through Congress a series of notable

[6] See Matthew Josephson, *The Politicos* (New York: Harcourt, Brace and Company, 1938).

measures including a new income tax law, a revised banking system, fair-trade and antimonopoly legislation, and lower tariffs. As party chief Wilson aimed his program at the "common man"—labor, farmers, small businessmen—and at the Solid South.

Courtesy HARPER'S WEEKLY *and Thomas Nast*

1874—The Republican Elephant appears; the party symbol is introduced by Thomas Nast in Harper's Weekly.

Gillam in JUDGE

1900—Bryan was bowled over like Don Quixote by McKinley's promise to keep the workman's dinner pail full.

Little in THE NASHVILLE TENNESSEAN

1940—Willkie's new ideas rejuvenated the G.O.P., but a dynamic challenger succumbed to F.D.R.'s old mastery.

Barrow in THE JACKSONVILLE TIMES-UNION

1948—After victory in 1946, Republicans suffered an unexpected and stunning defeat in Mr. Truman's election.

A short cartoon history

Wilson's coalition was not broad or firm enough, however, to stay in power for long. The Democrats barely won the Presidency in 1916 over a reunited Republican party, with Roosevelt back in the G.O.P. fold. And the 1920's, in the wake of World War I, were years of supremacy for the

Hutton in THE PHILADELPHIA INQUIRER

1936—Republicans lost all but Maine and Vermont in the debacle of Landon's appeal to turn back the clock.

Republicans as the "party of prosperity." To be sure, the Republicans had during this period no specialist in group diplomacy like McKinley or Roosevelt. Yet Harding, Coolidge, and Hoover triumphed easily over their Democratic opponents, perhaps because the business philosophy of the Republicans was in direct accord with the business mood of the era. The Democrats were an uneasy alliance of urban, Catholic, and "wet" groups with rural, Protestant, and "dry" elements. No matter whether they presented a liberal or a conservative candidate, they could not break the G.O.P.'s hold on masses of farmers, businessmen, and even workers.

Shanks in THE BUFFALO EVENING NEWS

1952—After 5 presidential campaigns, the Republicans break through.

Herblock in THE WASHINGTON POST AND TIMES HERALD

1956—Eisenhower scores another great triumph but cannot pull his party to victory.

of political parties.

The Great Depression changed all this. The bleak years of job hunting and breadlines brought a new political temper and new political alignments. People in all classes and groups turned away from the G.O.P. The Democrats, under Franklin D. Roosevelt, offered some kind of New Deal to the "forgotten man," and plenty of voters considered themselves forgotten. Roosevelt not only strengthened the farmer-labor-southern alliance that Wilson had led; he put together a grand coalition of these groups plus Negroes, unemployed, middle-class people, national and racial minorities— a coalition that in 1936 gave the Democrats the electoral votes of every state except two. Roosevelt was chief legislator as well as chief executive. Under his generalship Congress enacted a series of laws to provide a new deal for American labor, farmers, small businessmen, old people, and other groups. This grand coalition was strong enough to re-elect Roosevelt three times. That it was not simply F.D.R.'s personal following was indicated when Harry Truman, who lacked some of Roosevelt's superb political skills, led the Democrats to a nationwide triumph in 1948.

A new age of the Republicans?

The election of 1952 was a sweeping victory for the Republican candidate, Dwight D. Eisenhower, and the Republicans won control of the national House and Senate. Was this the start of a new era of Republican supremacy? Some observers were doubtful. It was an *Eisenhower* victory, they said, resulting from his wartime record and his great popularity.

The 1956 election was both a test of President Eisenhower's personal popularity and a test of the strength of the Republican party. On the first test the results were crystal clear. Running against Adlai E. Stevenson— the same man he had defeated in 1952—Eisenhower boosted his electoral vote margin to 383 and his popular vote margin to over nine million, compared with margins of 353 electoral votes and less than seven million popular votes over Stevenson four years before. Moreover, the President unexpectedly won large support in places where the Democrats had been clearly dominant—in northern cities, in the South, among Negroes and many national-origin groups.

The Republicans did not fare so well as a *party*. They had lost control of both houses of Congress in the 1954 midterm elections, and they failed to regain congressional majorities in 1956. They won three governorships from the Democrats but lost five others to them. East of the Mississippi all Republican members of the House of Representatives held their seats, but west of that river no Republican unseated a Democratic incumbent. Picking up scattered House seats in the Midwest and West, the Democrats actually increased their majority in the lower house by several seats.

As President Eisenhower entered his second term, the Republicans faced serious problems as a party. Their weakness was measured by the fact that not for over a century had a party won the Presidency and failed to win at least one house of Congress. Since the antithird term amendment prevented Eisenhower from running again even if his health permitted, the party faced the prospect (unless the amendment was repealed) of fighting future battles without its popular chief. Many registration and election figures, moreover, indicated that the Democratic party and its position on major issues were somewhat more popular than the Republican party and its stand. Finally, the Republicans had to face the prospect of losing more congressional seats and state and local offices in the 1958 midterm elections if the 1954 pattern prevailed.

But the Democrats faced perhaps more serious problems. With Stevenson defeated twice in a row, they lacked a party leader who could conduct an energetic and well-publicized opposition. Power in the party shifted to southern Democratic committee leaders in the House and Senate who, as conservatives, might show little interest in carrying out the Democratic national platform of 1956. More important, the voting returns concealed as much as they revealed about the strength of the Democratic party. *Outside the South,* the Republicans held more governorships and many more congressional seats after the 1956 elections than did the Democrats. Since the southern and northern wings of the Democratic party had sharply differing views on most policy issues, the Democrats were a minority party when it came to mustering enough votes in Congress to put across a Democratic program. Clearly, 1960 would be a test of how each of the major parties would meet the various problems facing it.

The mid-twentieth century revealed that each party would have to grasp a basic factor that had transformed the electorate during the previous century. American politics, in Arthur N. Holcombe's term, was no longer "rustic."[7] Parties were no longer alliances mainly of *sections,* based in turn on agrarian interests. They were coming to be increasingly centered in the urban areas. The new politics, predicted Holcombe, would be "less rustic than the old and more urbane." There would be "less sectional politics and more class politics." Unless another world war should totally change the pattern of American politics, it seems likely that both parties will base their coalitions more directly on voters living in urban and suburban areas.

FUNCTIONS OF POLITICAL PARTIES

The foregoing history of the party system, brief though it is, shows that our parties have indeed shouldered the vital job of pulling America's warring interest groups into some kind of rough unity. The *unifying* role of the parties was well shown in the years before the Civil War. Most of

[7] A. N. Holcombe, *The New Party Politics* (New York: W. W. Norton & Company, 1933), p. 11. See also Samuel Lubell, *The Future of American Politics* (New York: Harper & Brothers, 1951).

the other bonds between North and South—for example, between northern and southern members of the same religious denominations, business organizations, reform groups—snapped before the parties broke apart, and the final rending of the parties was the signal for civil war. The *moderating* role of the parties has been demonstrated recently by the Republican party, which in the past two decades has moved from its extreme Old Guard philosophy to a platform only moderately right of center.

The party in power has the formal responsibility of *governing*. It was put into power after presenting its candidates and its platform to the people; once in power it has both the duty and the authority to accept responsibility for the conduct of government. This, at least, is the theory of party government; but in the United States the parties that win elections do not necessarily govern *as parties;* why this is so will be discussed at the end of this chapter and in later chapters.

The party out of power has the job of *opposing* the ins. "The business of the opposition is to oppose" according to an old political phrase; while no party is foolish enough to denounce the party in power for every action it takes, in general the "outs" are supposed to keep before the people an alternative line of action. Our parties usually perform faithfully the basic "watchdog" function of the opposition; the harder task is to present an agreed-on alternative program.

Closely related to these functions are a number of others. In trying to gain votes parties must *simplify the alternatives*.[8] Usually they present the public with a choice between two relatively understandable solutions to a question, although most controversial matters admit of a variety of solutions. The two main parties have the equally important job of limiting the choice of candidates to two. In framing platforms and choosing candidates, the parties perform a mammoth function of sifting hundreds of issues to find the right formula. As a result, they make elections meaningful and even exciting to millions of voters who know how to choose between a few alternatives but not among a bewildering variety of men and platforms.

Parties, moreover, play a part in the *shaping of public opinion,* especially at election time. They use all the media—radio, television, press, posters, leaflets, meetings, and the like—in order to saturate the voters with their arguments. After a polite interval following the election, the opposition party maintains a drumfire of faultfinding against the party in power. Sometimes the opposition party, eager for office, has been the most effective source of criticism of an administration. In 1929 the Democrats hired a newspaperman, Charles Michelson, who set about systematically to attack President Hoover almost daily. His increasing attacks, usually issued through the mouths of Democratic congressmen, helped elect Roosevelt in 1932. Today both major parties maintain full-time publicity divisions.

Local party organizations have found more direct ways to pick up votes.

[8] Schattschneider, *Party Government,* pp. 50 ff.

Almost every political machine has been a *charitable organization,* giving the needy jobs, loans, free coal, picnics, Christmas baskets, and the like. William S. Vare, leader of the Republican machine in Philadelphia, bragged that his organization was "one of the greatest welfare organizations in the United States." In every election precinct, he said, his committeemen were at the beck and call of the people day and night, and service was rendered "without red tape, without class, religion, or color distinction." Parties also have played a notable role in helping citizens deal with an often impersonal government on such matters as pensions, unemployment benefits, taxes, and licenses. It has been predicted that the creation of the "welfare state" would make the parties give up their charitable activities. Perhaps that is true, but the chance to serve as a bridge between big government and the little man may help the machines to carry on operations for a long time to come.

Choosing candidates

Above all, parties are directly concerned with primaries and elections. Their function of selecting candidates, whom they try in turn to elect to office, makes the parties virtually semiofficial organs of the government; without parties our election system would be much different, if it existed at all.

Parties have had this task from their beginning. The earliest method of selecting party candidates was the *caucus,* a closed meeting of party leaders. The caucus was used in Massachusetts only a few years after the *Mayflower* landed, and played an important part in pre-Revolutionary politics. John Adams in 1763 described with some distaste a caucus in Tom Dawes' garret:

> There they smoke tobacco till you cannot see from one end of the garret to the other. There they drink flip, I suppose, and there they choose a moderator, who puts questions to the vote regularly; and selectmen, assessors, collectors, wardens, firewards, and representatives are regularly chosen before they are chosen by the town. . . .

After the Union was established, the national or state legislatures served for several decades as the caucus. The legislators in each party simply met separately to nominate candidates. Our first presidential candidates were chosen by senators and representatives meeting as party delegations.

"King Caucus," however, soon fell into ill repute. Its meetings smacked of secret deals and logrolling; moreover, the caucus could not be fairly representative of the people where the party was in a minority, since only officeholders were members. Andrew Jackson's supporters boycotted the Republican caucus of 1824 in the face of opposition from the congressional insiders. Although there were efforts to make the caucus more representative, gradually a system of *party conventions* took its place. The convention was made up of delegates usually chosen directly by party members in towns and cities. The conventions served several purposes. They chose the party standard-bearers. They debated and adopted a platform. And they were occasions for whipping up party spirit and perhaps painting the town red.

But the convention method in turn came in for grave criticism. It was charged—and often quite rightly—that the convention was subject to control by the party bosses and their machines. At times delegates were freely bought and sold, instructions from party members were ignored, meetings got completely out of control. To "democratize" party selections, the *direct primary* was adopted by state after state. The primary system simply gives every member of the party the right to vote on party candidates in a primary election. The state usually supplies the ballots and supervises the primary election, which takes place some time before the general election in November. The direct primary was hailed by many Americans as a major cure for party corruption but, as we shall see, it did not cure all the existing evils, and it led to new ones.

Today the primary is the main method of making party choices, but the nominating convention remains in one or two states and—grandly—in picking presidential candidates. In either case, the party carries the main burden of activity, although many of its electoral activities are closely regulated by law. In the general election, too, the party has a central role. It campaigns for its candidates, mobilizes its machinery in their behalf, helps finance them, and on election day it produces cars, advice for the voters, and workers at the polls to watch the counting of the ballots.

The role of third parties

These are the main functions of the two major parties. What about the minor parties? Obviously they have many of the same electoral and propaganda functions as the big parties, except that they cannot perform the crucial feat of mobilizing a majority of voters at the polls. In one respect, however, minor parties have a special role. This is in their handling of controversial issues that the major parties either ignore or straddle. Such notable minor parties as the Locofocos, the Greenbackers, the Socialists, the Prohibitionists, and the Progressives of 1912 and 1924 have performed this function. In taking up touchy issues the minor parties have acted as "vehicles for the expression of political discontent."[9]

Disgusted with the conservative policies of both Republicans and Democrats, farmers in the last century organized parties of their own. These parties were short-lived, but they compelled the major parties to modify their programs. In this century some labor groups have repeatedly turned

[9] M. S. Stedman and S. W. Stedman, *Discontent at the Polls* (New York: Columbia University Press, 1950), p. 168.

to the third-party technique. In 1912 and 1920 the Socialist party polled over 900,000 votes, but these were its high-water marks. The Liberal Party in New York City occasionally has enjoyed some balance-of-power influence. Over the years third parties have been organized by specialized interest groups, such as antislavery people, Prohibitionists, Christian Nationalists, Vegetarians (who nominated a candidate for President but never got on the ballot), and many others.

In many cases, however, the minor parties have won wide support for their ideas, only to see a major party filch their best planks to adorn its own platform. The Grangers campaigned for regulation of unfair railroad rates. The Greenbackers demanded a graduated income tax. The Populists proposed a constitutional amendment providing for the direct election of United States senators. The Socialists called for an end to child labor, for public works systems, old age and unemployment insurance, the adoption of the initiative and referendum. In these and many other cases such proposals, once they had gained significant popular support, were taken over by the major parties and enacted into law. Minor parties, however, deserve much of the credit for popularizing the ideas.

The failure of third parties has not been due simply to the ability of major parties to steal their thunder. That failure is due in part to the extremism of third parties, their tendency to be disrupted over issues of party dogma, their concentration on propaganda rather than political action at the grass roots. Moreover, the major parties have erected legal barriers against third party action. For example, in some states the number of signatures on petitions needed to place a third party on the ballot is very high. All these factors, plus the primary role of the single-member district system noted above, explain the fact that no minor party has succeeded in dislodging a major party in national politics at least since the Civil War.

PARTY MACHINERY AND HOW IT RUNS

On paper our parties look like armies. They have the form of a pyramid, with millions of party members and thousands of local party officials at the base, and national party heads at the top. Like the army, they have a hierarchy of leaders and followers, running from the national committee at the top down to town and precinct committees at the bottom. Actually, the analogy is a false one. The essence of an army is discipline from the top down. This sort of central discipline is precisely what our parties lack. They have been well described as "loose associations of state and local organizations, with very little national machinery and very little national cohesion."[10]

[10] "Toward a More Responsible Two-Party System," A Report of the Committee on Political Parties of the American Political Science Association, *Supplement, American Political Science Review*, Vol. XLIV, No. 3, Part 2 (September 1950), p. v.

Why are our parties decentralized and undisciplined? Many factors are involved, but perhaps the most important is the *federal* basis of our government. Earlier in the book it was suggested that the Constitution has shaped our political system, just as politics in turn has affected the structure of government. Here is an excellent example of this circular relationship. Parties tend to organize around *elections* and *officeholders*. Since our federal system sets up elections and offices on a national-state-local basis, our parties are organized on a similar basis. Just as state and local governments are largely independent of the national government, so the state and local parties are somewhat independent of the national party organizations. Thus the Constitution has given us federalism in our *parties* as well as in our *government*. The nature of our party organization in turn has had a vital impact on the workings of our government, as Part Five will show.

National party organization

The supreme authority within both major political parties is the national convention. The convention meets every four years and has four major duties; to nominate the party's candidates for President and Vice-President; to write the party's national platform; to adopt the rules of the party; and to elect formally the national committee. (In Chapter 14 we shall look more closely at the convention.) But the convention is only briefly in session, and during the interval party business is in the hands of the party executives.

National party executives

The Democratic National Committee is composed of something over 100 members—one man and one woman from every state and a few members representing territories like Alaska. The Republican National Committee is also composed of one man and one woman from each state and territorial representatives. In addition the Republicans make the Republican state chairman a member of their National Committee if that state casts its electoral vote for the Republican candidate for President in the preceding election, if a majority of the state's congressional delegation (House and Senate counted together) are Republican, or if the state has a Republican governor. In form, committeemen of both parties are elected every four years by their respective national party conventions. Actually they are chosen by party leaders in the states or by party primaries. The national committeemen often are influential in their states, but the committee itself is not very important. In fact, it rarely meets. (One of its main jobs is to choose the city where the national convention will meet, a choice usually dictated by the nature of the convention hall and facilities and by the amount of cash offered by cities for the privilege of acting as host to the convention.) The party organization is usually run by the chairman of the committee and by appointed, full-time officials.

The main job of the *chairman* is to manage the presidential campaign. Although in form he is elected by the national committee, actually he is chosen by the party's presidential candidate at the close of the quadrennial convention. It is through him that the presidential candidate—and perhaps later the President—runs the party nationally. By the same token, a defeated presidential candidate may have little control of the national chairman, or

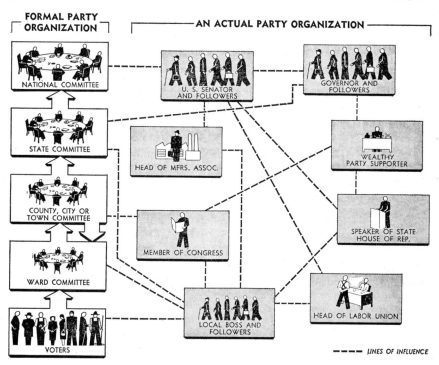

FORMAL AND ACTUAL PARTY ORGANIZATION

the national committeemen may elect a new head who responds to the balance of forces within the committee. Usually the national chairman is the chief dispenser of patronage for the President, using his control of the relatively few but politically important federal jobs that are not covered by civil service to promote harmony and some discipline in the party. If a President and a chairman cannot get along with each other, it is the chairman who must go, as in the case of President Franklin D. Roosevelt and Democratic chairman James A. Farley in 1940. Thus the chairman becomes, in V. O. Key's words, "a technician, a specialist in campaign management and machine tending, who exercises his power only so long as he enjoys the confidence of the presidential nominee."[11]

[11] V. O. Key, Jr., *Politics, Parties, and Pressure Groups*, p. 285.

It is the national chairman, backed by the President, who gives the party a measure of unity and direction when the party is in power. When a party loses the presidential race it often has no real central leadership. The defeated nominee is called the titular leader, but he usually has little real power over the organization, partly because he has no jobs to hand out. As a result, the party out of power nationally may come under the control of influential national committeemen, leading senators and representatives, and powerful state and local bosses.

Courtesy THE NEW YORK TIMES MAGAZINE and Tom Little

One failing of our party system is that the party out of power nationally does not have the kind of leadership that the President can provide for the party in power.

The *Congressional and Senatorial Campaign Committees* round out the national party structure. Their chief job is to aid congressmen in their election campaigns for re-election. Today the Republican Senatorial Campaign Committee is composed of seven senators chosen for two-year terms by the Republican senators. The Democrats through their party leader in the Senate normally choose five men for a two-year term. The men selected are usually from states in which there will be no senatorial election. The congressional campaign committees, composed of members of the House of Representatives, are more elaborately organized. In both parties the state delegations of each party choose one of their number to serve for two years in their respective congressional campaign committees. Chairman, vice-chairman, executive committee, finance committee, speaker's bureau, and other divisions are created in each campaign committee.

The congressional and senatorial campaign committees work independently of each other and of their respective party's national committee. After primaries are over they help their candidates by sending money, providing speakers, supplying campaign material, and the like. Normally they concentrate their efforts in doubtful districts and states where an expenditure of money and time can do the most good. During presidential election years, the activities of the national committee tend to overshadow the work of the congressional and senatorial campaign committees. But during off-year elections, these committees often provide the only campaign that is nationally directed.

STATE PARTY ORGANIZATION

At the next level down the party hierarchy is the *state committee*. Although these committees vary from state to state, in general they resemble the national committees. They are manned by committeemen locally chosen in counties or other areas. Like the national committee, most state committees are not powerful; they are often dominated by the governor, a United States senator, or a coalition of strong local leaders. The state chairman is sometimes the creature of the governor or senator; occasionally, however, he is really the party's boss on the state level and is able·to pick —and control—governors, senators, and other key officials. Many state parties are as undisciplined and decentralized as the national party.

Below the 48 state committees the party hierarchy broadens out into countless district and county committees. These, too, vary tremendously in their functions and power. The New York county chairmen are often powerful bosses like the late Ed Flynn of the Bronx, and many county chairmen elsewhere make up the party slates for a host of offices such as county commissioner, sheriff, treasurer, and the like. Some county chairmen, however, are mere figureheads.

It is at the base of the party pyramid—at the city, town, ward, and precinct level—that we find the grass roots of the party in all its richness and profusion. This level is where party politics in big cities is conducted by thousands of local leaders, often not as part-time diversion but as a round-the-clock, round-the-year occupation. This is where party politics, to quote Mr. Dooley, "ain't bean-bag," but a "professional spoort, like playin' baseball f'r a livin' or wheelin' a truck." Here the party's sergeants and corporals —the local ward and precinct leaders—are part of the city-wide machine run by the local leader or "boss" who is usually the chairman of the city committee. Their responsibilites are heavy and numerous. Year round they do countless favors for their constituents, from fixing parking tickets and patching up a family quarrel to organizing a clambake and supplying free legal help. At election time, the local leaders capitalize on this activity when their families and friends flock to the polls. In country areas, the party machinery is usually less tightly organized and disciplined than in the city, yet some rural machines are formidable organizations such as that run by Sheriff Birch Biggs of Polk County, Tennessee.

Parties in the United States, as we have noted, are organized around layers of government. Since we have many layers of government, we have an elaborate party system as well. To take one state as an example, Kansas party organization embraces a state committee, congressional district committees, county committees, state senatorial district committees, state judicial district committees, and precinct committees. Illinois party organization (see chart) is hardly less elaborate.

Why such complexity? As we have seen in previous chapters, our party politics tends to be highly individualistic and personalized. It would be more nearly correct to say that we have *candidate* politics or *office-holder* politics rather than party politics. That is to say, political activity tends to focus on men seeking or holding political power and the groups around them, rather than in a unified, hierarchical party system. Since our constitutional

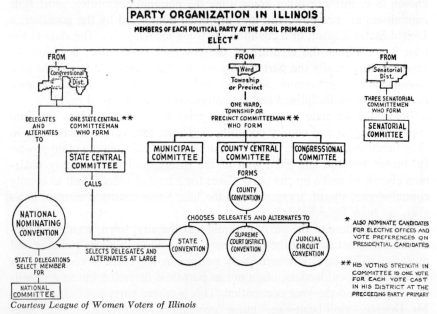

Courtesy League of Women Voters of Illinois

arrangements provide for a multiplicity of office-holders at a number of levels of government, our parties are bound to be complicated.

Party systems, as we have noted, also vary a good deal from state to state. The reasons for this stem both from the diversity of our country and the absence of strong direction and control by the national party head-quarters. In Great Britain, one would find about the same party organiza-tion and party ideology in Yorkshire, London, Glasgow, and Wales. In our country, the differences between the Democratic party in New York and in Alabama, and between the Republican organizations in Pennsyl-vania and in California, are almost polar in their extremes.

This situation inevitably causes gulfs between national party head-quarters and state and local parties. Other factors are both cause and con-sequence of these gulfs. For one thing, most election law is state election law, not national. "Political parties, as legal entities," says V. O. Key, Jr., "are by and large state parties . . . The national superstructure over the state party organizations, in a sense, derives its power from their consent."[12] Secondly, some states hold their state and local elections in different years from national elections. New York, for example, elects its governors for

12 *Politics, Parties, and Pressure Groups,* 3rd ed. (New York: Thomas Y. Crowell Co., 1952), p. 306.

REPUBLICAN PARTY IN PENNSYLVANIA
FORMAL AND INFORMAL ORGANIZATION

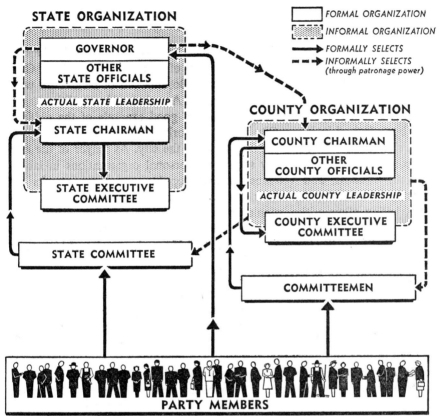

STATE ORGANIZATION

☐ FORMAL ORGANIZATION
▣ INFORMAL ORGANIZATION
→ FORMALLY SELECTS
⇢ INFORMALLY SELECTS
(through patronage power)

GOVERNOR

OTHER STATE OFFICIALS

ACTUAL STATE LEADERSHIP

STATE CHAIRMAN

STATE EXECUTIVE COMMITTEE

STATE COMMITTEE

COUNTY ORGANIZATION

COUNTY CHAIRMAN

OTHER COUNTY OFFICIALS

ACTUAL COUNTY LEADERSHIP

COUNTY EXECUTIVE COMMITTEE

COMMITTEEMEN

PARTY MEMBERS

Courtesy Samuel Humes

four-year terms on even-numbered years between presidential elections, and New York City elects its mayors on odd-numbered years.

The gulfs between national and state parties vary from state to state and from year to year. One factor tending to link national and local parties is mutual self-interest; each has a stake in the other's victory. Perhaps more important, most states—especially the more urban ones—are affected by political trends affecting the nation as a whole, as we saw in Chapter 12.

POLITICAL PARTY TRENDS

In its present form, our two-party system is well over a century old. Attempts have been made to change it: third parties have been formed; the primary system has replaced the convention system in many states; and the early end of one or the other of the major parties is often predicted. Yet, the two parties seem to survive substantially unchanged.

Despite this durability, certain basic forces seem to be at work that may powerfully influence the future shape of our party system.

Decline of the boss?

During the past century the local or state boss has thrived in the American political climate. Men like Boss Crump of Memphis, Ed Kelly of Chicago, Big Bill Thompson of Chicago, and Boss Tweed of New York won nationwide notoriety and put their stamp on American urban politics.

Boss Frank Hague of Jersey City was a good example of the oldtime city boss. Raised in Jersey City slums, he worked his way up in local politics, slowly extending his influence through the city. As mayor of the city he consolidated his power by setting up personal organizations in labor, church, business, and veterans groups, stopping newspaper attacks by drastically increasing the hostile newspaper's property assessments for taxation, jailing other critics, running a huge patronage machine, distributing favors and largesse to the voters, and extending his influence throughout the state. "I am the law," he proclaimed.[13] Hague kept most of his power until his retirement.

A different kind of boss was Edward J. Flynn of the Bronx. An educated and cultivated man, Flynn ran an efficient organization that in certain ways resembled a large business corporation. His machine supported liberal and labor legislation in exchange for union support. While the Bronx organization was relatively honest, it had the features of most political machines: it dealt in jobs and party spoils; it expected jobholders to contribute; and it delivered huge Democratic pluralities on election day. Another influential boss was J. Russell Sprague, a Republican leader in Nassau County on Long Island. Disciplined and centralized, his machine ran the county government and helped the Republicans run up a five-to-two plurality over the Democrats in the 1952 presidential election.

Are such bosses and machines on the way out? Such seems to be the case in certain respects. Few of the old-time city machines have been able to deliver the vote as they did in the past. In a recent hard-fought mayoralty contest in New York City, for example, all the Democratic bosses combined could bring hardly a quarter of the registered Democrats to the polls. The boss has far less party patronage today than in the old days. With less immigration he lacks a reservoir of newly-created citizens. Elections are more closely supervised to prevent old-fashioned ballot box stuffing. Most important, the welfare functions of modern national, state, and city government have to a large degree superseded the old charitable activities of the machine.[14]

[13] For a full treatment of the Hague machine, see D. D. McKean, *The Boss: The Hague Machine in Action* (Boston: Houghton Mifflin Co., 1940).

[14] For a poignant and amusing picture of an old-fashioned city boss, see the novel *The Last Hurrah* by Edwin O'Connor.

Yet a funeral service for machine politics would be premature. Bosses may go—but leaders remain. The old-time machine head controlling a whole city or state has given way in large part to the leader who has wide influence as governor, senator, sheriff, or other office-holder. They dominate their parties not as formal *party* leaders but as holders of important offices. For years Governor Dewey was supreme in New York State, Senator Byrd in Virginia, Governor Warren in California, Senator Taft in Ohio. A governor's or senator's office is today a far more respectable and efficient place from which to run an organization than the old "back room behind the bar," and today it is more effective in delivering votes and influencing policy.

Rise of the independent?

Some close observers of American politics report a growing disdain for party labels. Most recent presidential elections, it has been estimated, were decided by voters not claiming membership in either of the major parties. Switching back and forth, these voters are said to serve as a balance of power keeping both parties on their toes and preventing either party from gaining a monopoly.

How valid is this view? As noted in Chapter 12, much depends on how one defines the independent. The trend in independent voting is unclear also because we lack reliable comparative figures for earlier periods. What seems most likely is that there has been a trend in the past two decades to more independent voting, however defined, but this trend may be reversed as we move into new political conditions and eras. In short, there is nothing inexorable about the trend. It depends on the voters' wishes.

Is more independent voting desirable? Some argue that it keeps the parties on their toes and prevents either party from holding a monopoly. Others argue that too much independent voting can hurt the major parties, because it would drain away from the parties the talent and energy they need to operate efficiently and responsibly. It would be a pyrrhic victory for the independents themselves, according to this view, if they gained in their power to decide elections, only to discover that they were throwing their weight back and forth between less and less attractive candidates.

In any event, independence and party loyalty are not mutually exclusive. The most valuable partisan may be the man who is independent *within* his party—the man who sits in party councils and presents party regulars with fresh ideas on policies, methods, and candidates. The most valuable independent may be the man who has done what he can within his party and then follows his conscience on election day.

A nationwide two-party system?

In the past, most of our states have been dominated by one party. Democratic party control of southern states and Republican party control of northern New England were but extreme examples of the prevailing system. The basic party pattern was a sectional one—Democrats strong in certain states versus Republicans strong in other states—rather than real party competition within the states. In the past fifty years competitive two-party systems have developed within most states. Oregon and Maine, for example, are no longer guaranteed for the Republicans, nor are many southern states assured for the Democrats.

Political trends in the South are especially interesting in this regard. As a result of industrialization, urbanization, migration of northern whites into the South and of Negroes out of it, increased Negro voting, and other economic, social, and political developments, a more competitive two-party system is slowly rising in the South.[15] One southern student of this area's politics distinguishes between the "Inner South" comprising the "black belt" from Georgia to Mississippi, and the "Outer South," composed of the encircling states.[16] The latter has fewer Negroes and more urbanism and is moving faster toward a two-party alignment like that in the rest of the nation. The former will change more slowly but is headed in the same direction.

What are the implications of more nationalized parties? Some believe that such a change means a stronger national party organization than we have had in the past, with less power in the hands of state and local party leaders. Interest groups such as labor and farmers may become even more directly involved in national party politics.[17] Others believe that such a trend might lead to too much centralized party power and to a grave weakening of local and state organizations. They feel that party politics is already becoming too "professionalized," with too much tendency toward campaign mangement and even party policy being put in the hands of public relations counselors and other experts in the management of modern communications media.[18] This problem of the role of parties is discussed more fully in Chapter 21.

AMERICAN PARTIES AND AMERICAN DEMOCRACY

American parties are directly linked with American democracy. They do the jobs that have to be done in any healthy system of representative

[15] Alexander Heard, *A Two Party South?* (Chapel Hill: The University of North Carolina Press, 1952).
[16] William Buchanan, "Cracks in Southern Solidarity," *The Antioch Review,* Fall 1956, pp. 351-364.
[17] See the excellent symposium, Sigmund Neumann, ed., *Modern Political Parties* (Chicago: The University of Chicago Press, 1956), section on United States parties by E. E. Schattschneider, pp. 194-215.
[18] For a vivid treatment of this interesting recent trend, see Stanley Kelley, Jr., *Professional Public Relations and Political Power* (Baltimore: Johns Hopkins Press, 1956).

government. The parties build a bridge between people and their government. They shore up national unity by bringing warring interests into harmony. They soften the impact of the extremists on both sides. They stimulate and channel public discussion. They find candidates for the voters, and they find voters for candidates. They help run elections. Parties shoulder much of the hard, day-to-day work of democracy.

Yet today our party system is under attack. The indictment runs somewhat as follows:[19]

Parties are not responsible to their own members. It is pointed out that democracy is often conspicuously lacking *within* the party. Bosses control many local parties, urban, suburban, and rural. If there is no single boss, power often gets into the hands of a small oligarchy. The organization of the party—committee piled on committee—is such that the voice of the rank and file is obscured. Party committees and conventions, it is added, often are not fairly representative of the party members. Party platforms are drawn up secretly in "smoked-filled rooms." And what does membership mean? Anyone can join a party, no matter where his real sympathies may lie, and can outvote an old party regular who has put in years of service.

Parties have failed to keep their machinery and organization up to date. It is pointed out that formal party organization has changed little in the past century. The parties still have cumbersome committee systems. They fail to make use of modern methods of research and political analysis. The national convention is unwieldy and unrepresentative; it meets only once in four years, and sober discussion is drowned in the uproar and ballyhoo. The parties, it is said, are disorganized. Not only do the national and state organizations operate independently of one another, but even the national organization is divided into a presidential party and a congressional party. Common strategy and common program are lacking.

The parties do not take honest and clear-cut positions. It is common knowledge that platforms are evasive and obscure. Every four years national platforms are drafted hastily after spokesmen of interest groups have made appearances before a bored committee on resolutions. Platforms seem to be designed to pick up every stray vote rather than to speak out in a forthright manner on the vital questions of the day. The voter often has little choice between party platforms. And they are so vague that candidates can run on the same platform and then carry out conflicting policies when in office. According to an old saying, party platforms are like train platforms—something to get in on, not to stand on.

Parties are irresponsible; they do not deliver on their promises. This is the most important criticism of all. The party in power often shows little

[19] The following material is drawn in part from "Toward a More Responsible Two-Party System," A Report of the Committee on Political Parties of the American Political Science Association, September 1950, as cited above.

responsibility to the majority of voters who put it into power. The President goes in one direction, members of Congress go in others, and state and local organizations act on their own. The party as such is unable to carry out the program on which it was elected. A majority of voters agrees to a party platform at the election; but the party's own members will not agree to that platform when they are in office and presumably able to enact it. "The party in power has a responsibility, broadly defined, for the general management of the government, for its manner of getting results, for the results achieved, for the consequences of inaction as well as action, for the intended and unintended outcome of its conduct of public affairs, for all that it plans to do, for all that it might have foreseen, for the leadership it provides, for the acts of all of its agents, and for what it says as well as for what it does."[20] The party in power simply does not live up to these responsibilities. It is unable to hold its members in line, or to discipline those who fail to live up to party pledges. As for the opposition party, it often fails to criticize the government responsibly or to offer clear alternative policies to the voters.

Yet the failures in our parties must be viewed in proper perspective. Consider the accusation that our parties lack internal democracy. However true this charge may be, it must be remembered that the parties are under intense pressure to be responsive to public opinion as a whole. The party rulers—whether they be local bosses or national leaders—know that the parties will either remain abreast of the times or they will lose out to the opposition party or even be displaced by a minor party. Thus the *competition among parties* in a democratic political system in part offsets the lack of democracy *within* them. As for the accusation that our parties straddle issues, it can be said that fence sitting is part of the *moderating* function of a two-party system, and that some vagueness is inevitable in a country with the economic and geographical variety of the United States.

Two basic party weaknesses

When all is said and done, two major criticisms of our party system remain. One is that of the unwieldy, out-of-date party machinery that exists in virtually all the states. It is true that the *informal* party structure—for example, the party leadership of the President—in part makes up for the ramshackle nature of the formal organization. But powerful forces are constantly at work dividing and weakening party unity and effectiveness. The national committee, which should do the job of month-to-month governing of the party, is almost powerless. Financially the national party usually exists from hand to mouth. It is often heavily in debt, especially in the years directly following a presidential campaign, and recovers mainly by raising funds from party "fat cats."

[20] "Toward a More Responsible Two-Party System," p. 22.

A situation that both causes and reflects this party weakness is indeed curious: *the party has no real rank-and-file membership*. To be sure, individuals may "join" a party by voting in a primary or registering as a party member. But they assume no obligations; they pay no dues; they rarely take part in party discussions of candidates or platforms. A person is usually far more active in his favorite lodge or hobby club than he is in the organization that assumes responsibility for governing the nation—the Democratic or Republican party. Our national parties, in short, have plenty of generals, lieutenants, and sergeants, but practically no privates who are really enlisted in the party cause.[21]

The other major criticism is that of party irresponsibility. Indeed, this criticism takes on all the more importance today because of the vital role that parties *could* play in the challenging era in which we live. Today, more than ever before, governmental policies must be coordinated and coherent. One part of the government cannot pursue an inflationary policy, for example, while another is following an anti-inflationary program. Today policies must be *programmatic*—that is, they must fit into a comprehensive and self-consistent plan. The party—simply because it nominates and elects our chief policy-making officials—is the ideal agency to force these officials in every branch of government to pull together.

But the party does not do this job. It does not even perform the much more elementary task of making politicians live up to whatever hazy and inconsistent promises they make. This basic party weakness affects our whole government. We shall look again at the implications of this weakness (in Chapter 21) after considering how our politicians get into office and how they try to stay in office once they have come to hold power in Washington.

[21] See Schattschneider, *Party Government*.

THE PRECEDING FOUR CHAPTERS HAVE DEALT with some of the main aspects of political behavior. We have seen something of the role of *interest groups*—their number and complexity, the way they cut across one another and form subgroups, their internal government and external relations, their methods of gaining and wielding influence. We have looked at several factors affecting voting—the matter of who vote and fail to vote, how they vote, and why. We have noticed the ways that *opinions* are born and shaped, the various subpublics that hold these opinions, the way opinions can be measured. We have considered *parties* as grand coalitions of interest groups, doing a variety of important jobs and not always doing them well, powerful in some of their local activities but poorly coordinated as national agencies.

We have had to consider these factors in somewhat separate order, but let us not deceive ourselves into seeing them as separate entities. They are not. Parties, groups, voting behavior, public opinion—all these affect one another intimately. The forming of political opinions, for example, and the way people vote are largely matters of *group* allegiance and activity, as we have seen. Parties are inseparable from groups, and their role and effectiveness are deeply affected by voting behavior. The close relation between public opinion and voting is obvious. We must see these political processes as a vast network of interrelationships, each process affecting others and in turn being affected by them, all part of a moving balance of action and counteraction.

★ 14

Appeal

to the

voters

The workings of politics are all the more complex because of the *invisibility* of much of the political process. We cannot actually see Mr. Smith's mind at work as he decides whether or not to vote, or how to vote; we cannot possibly grasp the thousands of interrelationships among a number of groups, several political parties, and a maze of political attitudes. But there is one occasion, at least, when some of the labyrinthine attitudes and actions are brought to the surface and exposed to the public view. This occasion is an *election*. In the election campaign we get some feel for the dominant attitudes of the community, the activities of groups, the role of the party. In the election results we get some idea of the extent of certain attitudes, the power of certain parties and groups, the tendencies of voters, and the number of nonvoters. In the election, the vast subterranean elements of the political process come into some sort of focus. The people— who often find it hard to keep their eyes on the many players and the many balls in the great game of politics—finally get the score.

Elections are not merely the showdown for the restless political forces described in the last four chapters. They are also vitally affected by the constitutional and legal factors described earlier in this book. For example, a striking aspect of American elections is that they occur on several levels, local, state, and national. The "federalism" of our elections has an important effect on their outcome and meaning, as we shall see. Again, presidential elections would be different without the electoral college. Also influencing the outcome of elections are constitutional provisions allowing the states to administer voting, and state arrangements such as those making necessary the long ballot. Thus we see again the indivisibility not only of politics in the narrow sense, but of the whole political, legal, and institutional system.

WHAT EVERY VOTER SHOULD KNOW

It would be pleasant if election arrangements were simple. The fact is that they are not. They differ widely from state to state. Their sheer number is amazing—well over a hundred thousand elections a year in all states for all offices, according to the Census Bureau. Voting is a chore as well as a privilege. The Constitution authorizes the state legislatures to regulate the time, place, and manner of congressional elections, but Congress may alter these regulations and may also stipulate the day on which presidential electors shall be chosen and the day on which they should cast their votes. Other than setting the day for electing presidential electors and for the casting of their votes and prescribing the date on which congressional elections should be held (Congress permits states to elect congressmen on a different day if their constitution so prescribes, which accounts for the early Maine elections), Congress has left the regulation of elections almost entirely up to the states. And, of course, each state has control over the election of its own and local officials. The voter who wants to know the intricacies of voting and registering can see election authorities at the local city hall or town office, or consult election law.

Knowing election angles has long been a specialty of political insiders and bosses, but by a little research the interested citizen can also equip himself with the weapon of knowledge. For in elections, too, knowledge is power. Following are merely the ABC's of voting.

Registration

Almost every state requires that a person must be *registered* if he wants to vote. A registered voter is one who has appeared before election officials during a set period and has established his right to vote. In most states an otherwise qualified voter may register to vote if he has lived in the state for one year; in some states this residence requirement is shorter and in some states (mostly in the South) longer. The would-be voter also must have lived in the election district for a period, often for six months. Once registered, a person's name appears on registration lists and can be checked off when he votes. Residence requirements are designed to give the voter a chance to inform himself about state and local conditions before he votes. Some such requirements, however, are used to deny the ballot to migratory workers or to minority groups, such as Negroes.

Registration is of two types, *permanent* and *periodic*. Under the former system, now used by most states, once the voter is on the list he stays on it as long as he remains in the election district and meets any other requirements established. In a few states a person is dropped from the list if he fails to vote in two successive elections, in which case he must re-register.

DO YOUR PART...

REGISTER NOW!

Al Capp on the importance of registering.

Permanent registration is easy on the voter, but hard to administer, for elections officials must see to it that those who have left the district, have died, or have been committed to an institution, are removed from the list. The system of periodical registration requires voters to re-register from time to time. This system keeps the registration lists up to date, but it is inconvenient for the voters, expensive, and a hindrance to a large vote. Some states allow absentee registration by persons who must be absent from the state for certain reasons.

Primaries

Taking part in the selection of party candidates is often as important as voting in the election itself. As noted above, in almost all the states candidates are chosen in *direct primary elections* rather than in conventions. In almost all states, primaries are financed out of the public treasury, run by the regular election officials, and held in the same polling places as the regular election and the voters are protected by the same legal safeguards. To get on the primary ballot a candidate usually must file a petition signed by a required number of voters. In practice this means that almost anyone can get on the ballot if he does enough leg work, and the voter may find a large number of names listed on the primary ballot.

Who can vote in a party primary? In most states voters must publicly acknowledge membership in the party in order to help choose party nominees. Of course, party membership in the United States is a rather ambiguous matter, and the tests are not very severe. In some states a voter may declare his party allegiance when he registers to vote; in others the voter enrolls as a party member simply by showing up at the party primary to vote. In some states, mainly in the South, voters appearing at the primary must pledge, before receiving the ballot, that they supported the party's nominee at the last election, or will at the next, or both. In any case a voter may change party affiliation between elections by following prescribed procedures.

All this is the *closed* primary—that is, the party seeks to close the door of the polling place in the primary to all but those who are, in one way or another, party adherents. A number of states—thirteen by latest count—have the *open* primary system, under which any qualified voter may participate in the primary of any party that he pleases; but except for the State of Washington, a voter can participate in only one party's primary. In some open systems the voter is given the ballots of all the parties and he fills out the party ballot he prefers; in others he receives one ballot that lists candidates of all parties for all offices. All primary systems allow supporters of one party to enter—or "raid"—the primary of another. The aim may be to nominate the weakest candidate in a rival party's camp. But the *open* primary, exposed to the depredations of one-day Republicans and one-day

Democrats, greatly facilitates raiding. For this reason the open primary is the despair of party officials and of advocates of more strongly disciplined parties, while it is supported by those who do not like to reveal their party affiliation or who like to have an open choice on primary day as to the party contest in which they vote.

Several states use a combination convention-primary system. Party conventions—usually called *preprimary conventions*—or committees propose for each office a candidate who then runs in the ensuing primaries along with any other aspirants who may wish to compete without the convention endorsement. This procedure informs the voter as to the choice of his party's representatives in convention while leaving him free to support any other candidate who may enter the race. Two states have *postprimary conventions,* which select party nominees in the event that no candidate polled at least 35 per cent of the vote in the primary.

The *runoff primary* is used in about ten states, all southern or border. In most of these states the Democratic nomination has been virtually equivalent to election because of the weakness of the Republican opposition. Sometimes so many candidates file in the Democratic primary that the leader may have only 20 or 30 per cent of the vote. Under the runoff, if no candidate wins a majority in the first election, the two highest candidates run against each other in a second primary.

The so-called *nonpartisan primary* is a method of nominating candidates which is used in some states. No party designations are permitted; candidates who can qualify simply file and the two candidates who receive the most votes run against each other in the general election. *Cross-filing* also has a nonpartisan or at least a bipartisan tinge. Used most notably in California, it allows a candidate to enter the primaries of more than one party. A candidate may win *both* major party primaries and thus in effect the election. Former Governor Earl Warren accomplished this feat in California in 1946.

Obviously, party primaries vary widely from state to state in type and in the day when they are held. The voter would do well to inquire at city hall or town clerk's office as to the laws and arrangements of his particular state.

Administering elections

Nowhere are fairness and accuracy more important than in the handling of election day arrangements. In balloting, the *Australian ballot system* has long been accepted as a model arrangement. Under this system—used in Queensland as early as 1857—uniform ballots, printed by the government (rather than by the parties or candidates, as had been an earlier practice) on good paper, contain the names of all candidates. Ballots are given to voters only on election day, only at the official polling place, and only by public officials. They are marked secretly, folded, and deposited unopened in a ballot box. Such arrangements may seem rather obvious today, but each one has been adopted as a result of hard experience. For example, the use of good paper for ballots balks the old trick of issuing tissue-paper ballots that enabled sharp-eyed party workers to see where a voter put his mark.

Different types of ballots and voting are worth noting.

The *office-group ballot*. In some states the names and party designations of candidates for the same *office* are listed together in groups. Usually candidates for the highest offices come first, such as President and governor, and then state and local candidates. This type of ballot, on which it is usually impossible to vote a straight ticket with a single mark, encourages independent voting and split party tickets, because the voter has to read through many names to find his choices. It also leads to voters' fatigue and to failures to vote for the offices at the bottom of the ballot.

The party-column ballot. This type groups candidates by *party* in columns. One can vote for all candidates of a party, from President to sheriff, simply by making his mark in a large circle or box next to the party's name and emblem. A voter may also "scratch his ticket" by going from column to column in marking his choices for individual offices. The party-column ballot is believed to encourage straight party voting.

Stickers and write-ins. This is a device to make last-minute changes in the ballot if, for example, a candidate withdraws or dies after the ballots have been printed. Blank spaces can be filled in by the voter, or gummed labels pasted in. These devices are allowed in some states as a means of voting for some candidate other than the offerings of the parties on the ballot, but write-in or sticker campaigns are rarely successful.

Absentee voting. Almost all the states allow certain persons, such as servicemen, to vote away from home. In order to prevent fraud absentee voting has been made difficult and cumbersome—so much so that often only the most zealous citizen will go to the trouble of sending in an absentee ballot.

Stuffing the ballot box. This is a type of ballot fraud, but the term often is used to denote all methods. There have been—and still are—so many of these as to defy description; they involve frauds in marking ballots, in collecting them, and in counting them. The "endless chain" or "Tasmanian Dodge" indicates the ingenuity of the corruptionists. A person buying votes will manage somehow (there are various ways) to secure an unmarked ballot. He fills this out, gives it to the bought voter, who enters the polling place, receives a ballot, deposits the *previously* marked one, and brings out the unmarked one for the vote buyer to fill out and hand to his next man. By this method the corruptionist knows that the ballots are being cast just as he wishes.

Voting machines. Originally patented in the United States by none other than Thomas A. Edison, the voting machine is designed to stop ballot frauds and to make counting accurate and fast. The machines are expensive, and some voters seem to find them difficult to manipulate, but their advantages have led to their use or authorization in over half the states.

The long ballot and the short

The "long ballot" represents reality, the "short" ballot mainly a hope. They refer simply to the number of offices that the voter must check on his ballot. Most states have the long ballot: in filling this out the baffled voter must decide among a fantastic array of legislative and administrative offices. In one case a ballot was twelve feet long and contained almost five hundred names. Tree warden, coroner, secretary of state, county treasurer, highway inspector—candidates for these and many more offices crowd onto the ballot, along with lengthy questions or propositions to be presented to the voters. The more insignificant the office, the fewer the voters who know the qualifications of the candidates, and the greater the likelihood that party organizations or interested groups can elect their favorites, good or bad.

Herblock in THE WASHINGTON POST

There has long been a movement to shorten the ballot by restricting officials popularly elected to those concerned with broad policy determination. But progress has been slow, and the "tablecloth" or "bedsheet" ballot is still common. Many states have, however, adopted the *presidential short ballot* and instead of listing the names of all the electors, the ballot carries only the names of the presidential and vice-presidential candidates to whom the electors are pledged. The voters still choose electors rather than vote directly for President, but by casting one vote for President and Vice-President they in effect vote for the entire party slate of electors.

MONEY AND ELECTIONS

Elections cost money—often a great deal of it. Expenditures in the 1952 presidential and congressional campaigns totaled $23 million—$13.8 by Republican national and special committees and congressional candidates,

$6.2 by Democratic groups and candidates, and $3 million by labor organizations and other groups. In the 1954 congressional elections, Republicans reported spending $7.3 million and Democrats $3.8 million. In one state, Oregon, the two major party candidates for United States senator spent, combined, almost a quarter of a million dollars.

Where does the money go? A coast-to-coast television network costs (depending on the coverage) from $50,000 to $100,000 for half an hour. A one-minute television spot in a medium-sized city may cost $50. A full-page ad in a big-city newspaper costs $2500. Campaign buttons cost three cents each, and candidates distribute tens of thousands of them. One mailing to every voter in a medium-sized state might cost $20,000.[1] Gasoline, telephone, printing, posters, rental of headquarters, hiring paid help—all these and many other items send expenses soaring.

Where the money comes from

Donations to the party treasurer come from many sources. In presidential campaigns the national headquarters of the parties take in millions of dollars. Those who have given most to the Republicans in recent presidential elections have been bankers, brokers, manufacturers, utilities, insurance, mining, and oil interests; to the Democrats, brewers, distillers, contractors, builders, professions, merchants, amusement, and related interests.[2] Wealthy family groups often make big donations. In 1952, the duPonts gave over $75,000 to the Republicans, the Pews $70,000, the Rockefellers $93,-000. Enjoying less support from such big givers, the Democrats run a series of Jackson Day dinners throughout the country, charging from $5 to $100 per plate. Some money comes to both parties from thousands of small givers, but most of the campaign chest is based on large contributions. In 1952, for example, both parties together received over $23 million, and well over half of this came in donations of over $1000.

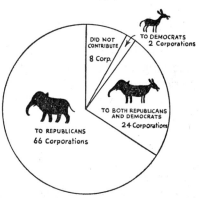

From Alexander Heard, MONEY AND POLITICS, *Public Affairs Pamphlet No. 242, Oct. 1956*

How 100 corporations' officers and directors contributed to campaign funds.

State and local parties also receive direct gifts, but much of their money comes from candidates and especially from officeholders. Sometimes candi-

[1] From Ivan Hinderaker, *Party Politics* (New York: Henry Holt and Co., 1956), pp. 579-581.
[2] See analyses by Louise Overacker, *American Political Science Review*, Vol. 35 (1941), p. 723, and Vol. 39 (1945), p. 916.

dates in effect buy the support of the local party by making a contribution. Assessing appointed officeholders frequently is a lucrative source of income. Although often kept under cover, the shakedown may be very important. It was revealed in Philadelphia, for example, that 3 to 5 per cent of city workers' salaries was collected by the Republican city committee, and 1 to 2 per cent by the ward committees where the employees lived. The Democrats in Indiana ran a notorious "Two Per Cent Club" on the same model.

Why do people give? The main reason is simply that they want something, usually for themselves. City jobholders want to stay in office. Candidates want the party's good will and support. Big donors often want the party's men in office to follow certain policies. Businessmen, for example, are concerned about taxes, tariffs, and subsidies. Labor may want the repeal of antiunion legislation. Distillers may hope to stop dry laws. Builders want government contracts; suppliers want to sell to government agencies; insurance companies want to write policies covering government property. Some big donors hope to gain prized positions, such as ambassadorships. Often what contributors want is nothing tangible but simply an "entree" or access to those in power in case the need arises.[3] The motive for giving is not always direct self-interest. Thousands of contributors simply believe that their parties will govern best for the whole people. Minor parties on the left have often received sizable gifts from wealthy persons.

Regulations of campaign finance

The national and state governments have made frequent but none too successful attempts to publicize party finance, and to limit it through *corrupt practices legislation* and other laws. Organizations receiving or spending money to influence the election of national officials under certain conditions must file statements with the clerk of the House of Representatives giving the names of all persons contributing over $100, of all persons to whom payments of more than $10 have been made, and the total of all receipts and all expenditures. The national government and most of the states have long prohibited contributions from certain types of corporations, and in 1947 the Taft-Hartley Act barred *any* corporation or labor organization from giving or spending money in connection with elections to national offices or in conventions or primaries choosing candidates for such offices.

Campaign spending is sharply limited. Under federal law, a candidate for representative may not spend more than $2500, a candidate for senator more than $10,000, or 3¢ per vote cast, up to $25,000 for a senator and

---

[3] Alexander Heard, *Money and Politics* (New York: Public Affairs Committee, 1956). For excellent material on this general problem, including recommendations from political scientists and others, see "Federal Elections Act of 1955," *Hearings Before the Subcommittee on Privileges and Elections, Committee on Rules and Elections, United States Senate 84th Congress, 1st Sess., on S. 636* (Washington, D.C.: Government Printing Office, 1955).

$5000 for a representative. The Hatch Act of 1939 and later amendments limited spending by any single political committee in presidential elections to $3 million and contributions by individuals to $5000, and it forbade forced contributions from government officeholders to candidates or parties. This Act also made it "unlawful for any person employed in the executive branch of the federal government, or any agency or department thereof, to use his official authority or influence for the purpose of interfering with an election or affecting the result thereof." Such federal employees can vote but cannot take an active part in party affairs or political campaigns.

How effective is regulation of campaign finance? The consensus is: not very effective. Much of the legislation is filled with loopholes and poorly enforced. Full publicity is often evaded by filing reports after the election is over or by submitting inadequate or even false reports. Corporations make campaign contributions through personal offerings of executives and their families, labor unions through more or less voluntary offerings by their members. The lawmakers, politicians themselves, have made no attempt to pass really rigorous or airtight laws in this field, and it is not certain that such an attempt would be successful, given traditional American attitudes toward such laws.

Senators studying the problem have recently recommended a number of steps to strengthen the regulation of party finance, including: 1. Require *all* committees working for a candidate to report contributions and expenditures; 2. Bring *primary* elections (see p. 349) under the law; 3. Prohibit political committees from receiving or spending funds for the candidate without his authorization; 4. Require every person who spends more than $1000 for candidates seeking national office to file a report; 5. Open all reports to public inspection; 6. Raise maximum spending limits to $250,000 for senators and $25,000 for representatives; 7. Limit maximum spending for committees operating in more than one state to $10 million instead of the present $3 million; 8. Restrict individual contributions to candidates or political committees to a total of $10,000, and forbid present practice whereby one person may give $5000 contributions to any number of candidates. One senator has warned that unless regulation of party finance is strengthened, drastic steps must be taken, such as financial aid to candidates from the government.

MR. SMITH RUNS FOR CONGRESS

When we think about elections, we tend to think of exciting national campaigns, of fighting speeches heard by millions of radio listeners, of political caravans crossing the nation in a blaze of publicity. It is well to remember that not all campaigns for national office are like this. A candidate for Congress often finds that a campaign means a lot of dull leg work and exhausting rounds of speeches to small audiences. "When you get away from the national arena," Pearson and Allen have written, "political campaigning gets right back to the old horse-and-buggy days. . . . What really counts is the all-important ingredient of personal contact." How a member of Congress wins office is important; watching him as a campaigner helps us understand him as a congressman. Let us look at the mythical—but rather typical—case of John Smith, aspirant to Congress.[4]

Why does Mr. Smith run for Congress? Obviously he wants to be a congressman—but so do many other people. In Mr. Smith's case, his decision is not easy. The incumbent, he knows, will be hard to beat. He's not sure that this will be a good year for his party. A campaign will mean practically deserting his law practice for three or four months. It will cost money. On the other hand, he thinks he can win. He has served as district attorney and state senator, and he feels ready for bigger things. And, he reflects, a little campaigning might help advertise his law practice even if he shouldn't win. So Mr. Smith throws his hat into the ring.

First, Mr. Smith must win the party nomination. The party's candidate of two years ago lost so badly at that time that he is not making the attempt again, but there are several other candidates in the field. Mr. Smith knows that primary contests usually do not arouse much public attention, involve important public issues, or attract a large vote. He decides on the following strategy: First, make a special appeal to party officials in the towns and cities throughout the district. While the party chairmen and committeemen are supposed to stay neutral in the primary contest, actually they are willing to help their friends in an informal way. Second, establish close relations with organizations that try to induce their members to vote on primary day. So Mr. Smith spends some time talking with leaders of farm and labor organizations in the district. Third, stress his name and personality rather than issues.

In his public talks Mr. Smith must speak cautiously. He must answer the arguments or criticisms of his fellow partisans who are opposing him within his own party primary, but he must treat them none too harshly, because if he wins he will need their support and that of their followers in the general election. He must identify himself with the party in order to gain the backing of the party organization—but not too closely if he hopes to win over support from the opposition party or from independents in the general election. But his main job is to stir up interest. Most people are indifferent toward primary elections. Only a third of the registered voters cast ballots on primary day. But Mr. Smith receives more votes than any of his opponents. While he lacks a majority of the votes, no runoff election is required in Mr. Smith's state (as it is in some) between the two highest candidates. So Mr. Smith becomes the official candidate of his party.

[4] For excellent case studies, presented in detail, of the actual campaigns of two candidates for representative, see S. K. Bailey and H. D. Samuel, *Congress at Work* (New York: Henry Holt and Co., 1952), pp. 112-135.

Planning tactics

Right away Mr. Smith begins to face a host of new questions. On what issues should he take a stand? Should he adopt the national platform and try to wage his fight on the basis of broad issues such as foreign policy, taxes, labor legislation, housing, and the like? Or should he slant his appeals to the local concerns of the people in the district? Probably Mr. Smith will compromise between the two approaches. What about campaign tactics? Should he devote his time to making party speeches at rallies, touring the district with a public-address system on his car, making as many personal appearances as possible? Or should he operate more behind the scenes by building up a personal machine throughout the area, talking with leaders of interest groups, sending out quantities of written material?

There's the problem of publicity. Many media are available—radio, newspaper advertisements, outdoor posters, lapel buttons, automobile stickers, booklets with full stories of Mr. Smith and his platform, leaflets that simply play up a few slogans, matchbooks with a thumbnail sketch, comic books that present Mr. Smith's life dramatically in many colors. And what about the theme of his publicity? Should he play up the fact that he's a family man, with pictures of himself with his wife and three children, or would this seem undignified to the voters?

Then there's the problem of money. An all-out campaign could easily cost $10,000. Of course the federal law is supposed to limit his spending. But Mr. Smith is not worried by this law. He knows that it is easy enough to arrange for persons or organizations supporting him to pay for their pro-Smith activities without turning the money over to him. What really worries him is where the money will come from. He has only $1500 of his own to put into the fight. Contributions to his cause are limited by law but, again, he knows that such laws are easily evaded. As it turns out, Mr. Smith gets contributions from a variety of sources. His friends chip in with donations. He receives a few hundred dollars from national and state party headquarters. Being friendly with union labor, he gets a sizable contribution from that source. Some money comes from people who also contribute to Mr. Smith's opponent, on the theory that it is well to have a foot in the door no matter who wins.

By midsummer—three months before election day—Mr. Smith is running hard. He puts sound equipment and a large sign, "VOTE FOR SMITH for Congress" on his sedan. A typical day goes like this:

> 6:00 A.M. Up early to finish some letters he is sending to local party leaders.
>
> 9:00 A.M. Meets at his house with some candidates for local office who want his support.
>
> 10:00 A.M. Off in his car for a series of open-air talks. First stop is at crowded street intersection in his home city.

12:00-1:00 P.M. Talks to workers at gates of factories in district's largest industrial area.
1:30 P.M. Lunch with local Smith workers.
2:00-4:00 P.M. Visits party headquarters in the towns; arranges for distribution of leaflets by canvassers.
4:00-6:00 P.M. More talks over the loud-speaker, concentrating on people returning home from work.
6:30 P.M. Ten-minute radio talk from local station.
7:00 P.M. Hurried dinner alone in restaurant. Works on notes for evening rally.
8:00 P.M. Big party rally in city auditorium. Candidates for governor and senator also attend. Mr. Smith is given 15 minutes to explain his platform, but is interrupted halfway through by arrival of gubernatorial candidate, and surrenders floor to him.
11:00 P.M. Home again, and works on some mail before getting to bed.

Reaching the man in the street

Mr. Smith's biggest problem is simply *getting* to the voters. The crowds on the street seem more curious than really interested. The people who come to party rallies seem to be already committed. How can he establish contact with the thousands of voters who do not go to party rallies or listen to speeches over the radio or pay much attention to elections at all? Mr. Smith finds that one way to reach such voters is through the leaders of organized interest groups in his district, which, like most congressional districts, is a complex of economic, religious, nationality, racial, and occupational groups. He makes every effort to gain the support of organization leaders and to induce them to introduce him formally or informally to their members. He speaks before countless groups of veterans, union members, farmers, Polish-Americans, Italo-Americans, and the like.

In appealing for the support of leaders and rank and file, he makes promises as to his future actions as a congressman. To labor he promises repeal of the Taft-Hartley Act, to farmers the continuation of price supports, to businessmen the protection by government of little business, to veterans the safeguarding of ex-servicemen's rights. Yet he never feels sure whether these appeals are striking home. The questions from the audience make him wonder whether his labor audience is concerned more about Taft-Hartley or about taxes, the veterans more about bonuses or foreign policy. In short, he comes up hard against the problem of overlapping membership of groups (see Chapter 10). He finds it difficult to thread his way through the maze of crisscrossing group interest. In any event, the groups and group leaders give him a sense of contact with the voters, and for that he is grateful.

Mr. Smith discovers that the local party organization can do little for him. Much of the drudgery falls on him; little of it is shouldered by city and town committees. Mr. Smith himself must supervise much of the work of getting people to register—the checking of lists and the mailing of letters reminding people that they must register to vote. He gets most of his help not from the party but from personal friends and leaders of interest groups. He finds that the party organization does not function as a unit but as a collection of people who attach themselves to the fortunes of particular candidates, and that often he himself must activate local party organizations to get them into motion. In effect, Mr. Smith must *build his own machine.* Naturally he develops little sense of obligation to the party, but a great deal to a number of leaders of other organizations who work zealously in his cause.

Nor does Mr. Smith run on the party platform as such. Rather he feels his way on issues, trying to gauge the interests and opinions of his audiences as he goes along. Some voters are mainly concerned with local matters, such as a proposed new highway or hospital. Others are more interested in the big issues, but their opinions often show little consistency. In the end he decides that issues as such have not played the most important role in the campaign, but rather his ability to establish personal contact with as many voters as possible. Most of the people, he discovers, are not only ignorant of the record in office of the incumbent congressman; they do not even know his name. Mr. Smith's biggest job is to drive his own name into the consciousness of the voters so that they will have at least a faint glimmer of recognition when they see "John Smith" among the many names on the ballot.

Election day finds Mr. Smith tired but hopeful. He tours the polling places, where his helpers are bringing people to the polls. By early evening the election returns start to come in over the radio. With pad and pencil Mr. Smith checks his votes against the returns of previous years. It is a seesaw battle, and more than once Mr. Smith thinks the battle is lost. But he is ahead when the final returns come in the next morning. Only then does he really start to think about being a congressman.

MR. DOUGLAS RUNS FOR SENATOR

So much for the mythical, but fairly typical, campaign of Mr. Smith for Congress. It is harder to generalize about campaigns for the United States Senate if only because of the sharp differences in the size of state populations. But the following true-life tale of his race for the Senate in 1948 by Senator Paul H. Douglas, written in the middle of the campaign, illustrates some of the more basic problems involved.[5]

[5] *The New York Times Magazine,* September 5, 1948, p. 5 ff.; reprinted by permission of *The New York Times Magazine* and of Senator Douglas.

A sore throat and temperature of 102 cannot keep him from the hustings . . .

Once the candidate has entered the race he must please everyone . . .

A few ill-chosen words on the golf course can kill the church vote . . .

He must be against the Taft-Hartley Law and a champion of labor . . .

and a moment of absent-mindedness will cost him the support of the vets . . .

and at the same time finance his campaign with management's contributions . . .

Roy Doty in THE NEW YORK TIMES

The candidate runs

Running for office means just that

The contrast between American and British campaign practices is summed up in the verbs used to describe the activities of candidates. In Great Britain one "stands" for office. In the United States we "run" for it.

As a candidate for the United States Senate from Illinois, I have a vivid sense of that word "run"—and for this reason:

Illinois holds some 8,300,000 people, divided evenly between Chicago and its suburbs on the one hand, and "down-state" on the other. And in both areas the people come from all the world's racial and religious stocks, settled in massive blocks of tens of thousands. The ways in which they make their living are as varied as the people themselves.

In industry—and moving from north to south—there are giant railroad yards, meat packing plants, steel mills and machine shops, oil fields and coal mines. Farming, on the other hand, and moving from south to north, includes cotton planting in "Little Egypt," where the soil shows signs of exhaustion; the superb corn fields of mid-Illinois, and pedigreed dairy cattle in the northern regions.

Add together the natural variety of interests which comes from such a setting and the task facing a candidate in Illinois can be seen. I have been "running" for office in every corner of the state almost incessantly ever since I was recommended by the state committee for nomination in January. And I have been "sprinting" since I was formally nominated by the Democratic party in April.

Following the state committee's action in January of this year I got hold of a jeep station wagon, had it equipped for sound and took to the road. In the primary campaign during the three months that followed I made 250 speeches and visited eighty out of our 102 counties. Since the primaries last May, I have made approximately 700 speeches in over 300 towns and cities in every county in the state. And the formal campaign doesn't open until Labor Day. A word hasn't been invented yet to describe the form of running that takes place between then and November.

My style of campaigning follows this pattern:

I pull up my sound-equipped jeep wagon at a factory gate during a change in shifts, or on a village street, or some-

He can lose the election by being seen in a non-union barber shop.

Is it all worth it? Only the returns on election day can tell.

for office,

where else near the main flow of people. I introduce myself to whatever crowd gathers, and then summarize the main themes of the campaign. Afterward I move among the clusters of people to shake hands and to distribute campaign literature which they can read at leisure. In this way I've spoken to about 225,000 people and have shaken hands with over 100,000 of them. . . .

There is a reason for this direct work. The average voter wants to see the candidates for office and form a visual as well as auditory judgment of them. But the voter is either too busy to go to formal political meetings, or he discounts them as being long winded, hot and blatantly partisan. It becomes necessary, therefore, for the candidate to go direct to the voters.

On being the object of abuse

Physical exertion is, however, the least of the burdens a candidate must bear. He must expect in advance to be abused and misrepresented. Indeed, the way the courts have interpreted the libel laws of the nation, political leaders are set

"The big guy in front is Joseph T. Cochrane. Call him Joe. You met him in Marysville three weeks ago. Talk about hunting. He goes after deer every fall. Man on left is Leo Brown. Sixteenth District in his pocket. Don't ask about his wife. She's ditched him. Fellow with mustache is Jim Cronin. Watch your step with him. He's Cochrane's brother-in-law, and . . ."

up as fair game for any attack short of murder. The whole spirit of those laws says to the candidate for elective office: "Brother, whatever happens to you— you asked for it!" It is only human, of course, for a candidate to be nettled now and then by the bare-faced lies that are spread about him. And in my own case, on being subjected to them, I at first shared the thoughts of young Count Rostov in "War and Peace." As he saw the French lancer come at him in his first engagement, young Rostov asked: "Is it really true that this man wants my life—I whom my mother loves?"

It was a source of dismay—and also the beginning of wisdom—to discover that not everyone loved me!

Since I aim to be a liberal progressive, I find myself being attacked by both the extreme left and the extreme right. The Communists whisper that I am anti-Semitic, anti-Negro, an advocate of a preventive war against Russia and the tool of bankers and industrialists. The extreme right, on the other hand, calls me a Socialist and a crafty fellow-traveler. It might seem that such mutually contradictory attacks would largely cancel themselves out, but in practice each group aims its propaganda at the circles which are closest to it, with the result that various sections of the population can at the same time believe in conflicting and slanderous reports.

It is this personal abuse which deters most competent men from running for public office. It is as though certain types of politicians tried to make the going so rough that they would shut off competition from all except their own kind, who are protected by the proverbial rhinoceros hide.

In the campaigns I've waged for elective office, I've never attacked the character of my opponents and have restrained my supporters from doing so. I've tried to address myself to issues of community importance rather than to the private habits of my opponents. But in hewing to this line I've glimpsed another danger. In waging campaigns for policies one believes to be right there is a strong temptation to become self-righteous. If this is minor compared with character assassination, it nevertheless often turns social crusaders into humorless prigs who take a dim view of the sincerity of any persons who dare to differ from them.

Pressures on the candidate

In my campaigns I've also been brought face to face with the forces which make politicians "crooked." Though I have no wealth, I have been able to earn enough in private pursuits to support my family. Yet not every politician is so situated. If he has no private means and is not skilled in a trade or profession, then the expenses of campaigning and the demands that are made upon him when he is elected exert a tremendous pressure on him to cut a few corners. . . .

With respect to the "crooked" politician, many voters who are the first to denounce him are also the first to stake out a claim to the fruits of his corruption. The way they do this is an unwitting one. Hundreds of individuals and organizations in a city or state—devoted to the very best of causes—expect the elected politician to contribute to those causes, to buy tickets to their functions or political advertisements in their fund-raising programs. The politician who balks at these demands is met with a veiled or open threat that the voting strength of the organization will be turned against him at election time.

It could be said that the politician should gladly suffer defeat and remain honest. But being human, most politicians want to stay in office, and so some make "deals" with unlawful sources of income in order to meet the demands of lawful organizations performing fine community activities—including the waging of campaigns against "crooked" politicians.

And yet, as between the politicians on the one hand with their genuine "liking for people," and the class of reformers on the other hand who think of good government as being merely a good bookkeeping process, my personal preference, like Lincoln Steffens', runs to the former type—with all their lamentable faults.

On taking an honest stand

The greatest danger to the functioning of the democratic process comes in the area of ideas and social policies. There is a subtle temptation, which operates on every candidate, to say things he doesn't believe in order to get votes, or for the same reason, to urge contradictory policies before different groups. It is this aspect of political activity which I would call most "crooked."

I do not believe it is necessary for a politician to discuss the same topics before every group he addresses—though it would be a happy state of things if every human being viewed his own welfare as indivisible with the prosperity of his neighbor. The truth is, however, that the interest of a given group in one aspect of an over-all program is much more immediate than that of a second group. And I do believe it correct for a politician to address himself to his audience's particular interests. But it is quite another thing for a politician in talking about the same subject to say one thing before a consumers' group and its opposite before a farmers' group, or to say one thing to employers and another thing to an audience of trade unionists.

Herblock in THE WASHINGTON POST AND TIMES HERALD

"I have the same trouble!"

By the most pragmatic of tests, I have found that a straightforward and consistent approach to any problem brings higher personal rewards than a policy of doubletalk. For instance, I have been a lifelong advocate of unionism and collective bargaining. Yet in this campaign I've reminded union audiences many times about the ways in which their movements could be improved. In every case I found the response of labor to be an approving and hearty one.

Closely related to this danger of being all things to all men is the added danger of treating people as votes and not as persons—as means to the end of winning an election rather than as ends in themselves. As a college student I was thrilled by Immanuel Kant's rule that one "should treat humanity, whether in one's self or in another, always as an end, never as a means." This imperative means that one should really care for people, whether they are partisans for or against you, or in the "no opinion" group. It means a constant view of politics as having one aim—the promotion of justice—justice for all men—and not the mere acquisition of power for one man.

I have dwelt at length on the trials of a campaign without mentioning its rewards. There are many of these rewards—which are independent of how things turn out at the polls. In talking face to face with people you get a renewed personal assurance of the essential decency and fairness of the human race. Most men in fact try to do good and avoid evil. Abundant proofs can be offered, of course, of the many times when community passions have twisted matters so that men in the mass act contrary to their own ultimate interests. Yet the search for truth is not killed off. It reasserts itself as the stronger force in our life and in time bears its fruits.

A second gain from these campaigns is a better appreciation of how vital our democratic process actually is. It is an unending source of joy to see thousands upon thousands ·of men and women of all ages and in all stations of life lend their efforts to the advancement of political causes. These people are not paid workers. They do not stand to benefit directly from a political victory for their candidate. But they do appreciate the indirect benefits of victory—the creation of an America which better fits their own dreams. . . .

For all its demands, a vigorous "politics" in which every one takes sides is, paradoxically, the best way to bring about a fuller sense of the community of interest. But underneath all this is needed a sense of the basic unity which should bind men together and should provide a feeling of good-will to all.

Fundamentally men are brothers and the heat and passion of political struggle should not make us forget that fact.

HOW TO BE NOMINATED FOR PRESIDENT

To attain the Presidency a man has to run two races and win them both. First he must be nominated at his party's national convention, and this is sometimes the harder of the two jobs. Then he must get a majority of the nation's electoral votes.

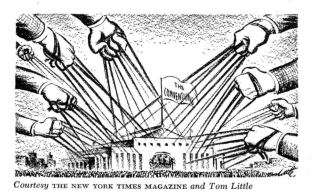

Courtesy THE NEW YORK TIMES MAGAZINE and Tom Little

Convention delegates respond to many pressures.

The first "national" convention was probably held in 1808, when a few Federalist leaders met secretly in New York to nominate candidates for President and Vice-President. In 1831, under Jackson's leadership, the first real national convention was held by a major party. Today the national convention is a famous and unique political institution. Every four years each party convention enjoys—usually for about a week—world attention; covered by batteries of cameras and microphones and by hundreds of newsmen, every incident in the great convention hall is carried to millions in this country and abroad.

Make-up: Each major party has the double task of giving representation to the states roughly in proportion to their size, and of giving a "bonus" to states that have a heavier concentration of party strength. The *apportionment* of delegates among the states reflects the attempt to do both these things.

The 1956 Democratic rules were:

1. Each state to have at least as many votes as it had in the 1952 convention. (In the 1952 convention each state had twice as many votes as the size of its delegation in Congress, plus a bonus of four extra votes if the state had cast its electoral votes for the Democratic presidential candidate.)

2. Four extra votes for each state that had voted Democratic in a presidential, gubernatorial, or senatorial election in 1952 or since.

The 1956 Republican rules were:

1. Two delegates for each of the state's senators and two for each representative at large if the state had any such representatives.

2. Six additional delegates for every state that went Republican in a presidential, gubernatorial, or senatorial election in 1952 or since.

3. One delegate for each congressional district that cast at least 2000 Republican votes in the last presidential or congressional election.

4. One *additional* delegate for each congressional district that cast at least 10,000 Republican votes in the last presidential or congressional election.

Each party also gives the District of Columbia and the territories some delegate representation even though they cast no electoral votes for President.

Certain aspects of apportionment arrangements may be confusing. For one thing, in the Democratic convention there are usually more *delegates* than delegate *votes;* to make room for all the party leaders who wish to take part in the convention, some Democratic state parties allow extra-large delegations, each member as a result having one-half of a vote. *Alternate* delegates also attend both conventions and get into the show, if only from a back seat. Second, the rules may change from convention to convention; some of the arrangements for 1956 described above are different from earlier conventions. Third, some delegates are elected for the whole state and are called "delegates at large" and others by congressional districts, called "district delegates."

Choosing delegates: The method of selecting delegates is set by *state* law and thus varies considerably from state to state. In about two-thirds of the states, delegates are chosen by party *conventions* or committees. In about one-third, which includes most of the populous states, delegates are picked in state *presidential primaries,* and a few states have a combination of the two methods. The *convention* system tends to put selection of the delegation into the hands of a party "inner circle." This may be no problem where the party is vigorous and the leadership representative, but this is often not the case. Most Republican party organizations in the South, for example, have tended to be little "closed corporations" controlled by a few Republican officeholders in Washington with the help of patronage. In such situations rival factions may spring up from the ranks of the "outs," and the question of who has the right to speak for the rank-and-file of the party becomes very obscure. This was a main cause of the fierce fight between the Taft and Eisenhower forces in the 1952 Republican convention, culminating in the unseating of the Taft delegations from Georgia, Louisiana, and Texas, and the seating of the Eisenhower forces.

Presidential primaries, the other chief method of choosing delegates, come in many forms. In all cases the basic system is the election of delegates directly by persons voting in state presidential primaries, which take place variously from March through June of election year. But the arrangements vary widely in the extent to which they enable the voter to indicate his preference for the party's presidential nominee by his vote for a candidate for delegate. At one extreme a voter may choose between rival delegate aspirants definitely pledged to specific candidates, and the voter may also indicate his *personal preference* for President by checking or listing the name of his favorite. At the other extreme a voter may have only the choice of approving a delegation slate made up of the party faithful whose qualifications and preferences for the presidential nomination are completely unknown to him. Most systems fall between these extremes.

Following are examples of the main types of presidential primaries:[6]

1. *Direct* election of delegates; no indication of delegate preference on ballot. No presidential preference poll, or inconsequential if held. Examples: West Virginia, Nebraska. This system exists in New York, Pennsylvania, and Illinois, except that the delegates at large are chosen by the party organization.
2. *Direct* election of delegates; presidential preference *poll;* and the presidential *preferences* of *delegates* may appear on the ballot. Examples: New Hampshire, Massachusetts, New Jersey.
3. Combined ballot offering a single-mark opportunity to express a presidential *preference* and to *vote* for a slate of delegates *committed* to the preferred candidate. Examples: California, Minnesota, South Dakota, Wisconsin.

This variety of methods of choosing delegates, combined with the variety of power patterns in state parties, make it impossible to generalize about the nature of the final delegations. Some may be under the thumb of a powerful state party leader. Others may be "split wide open." Some may be

[6] Drawn from an analysis by Paul T. David, director of the Cooperative Research Project on Convention Delegations, which, through the participation of political scientists in each state, has made the fullest study ever conducted of the actual methods used to select convention delegates.

willing to "go down the line" for some presidential candidate. Others may veer from candidate to candidate. Most state delegations mirror the factions in the state party, but sometimes a strong and well-organized group will gain control of the whole delegation.[7]

One thing is clear. The mere adoption of a presidential primary system does not guarantee a delegation that will reflect rank-and-file wishes. Turn-

Herblock in THE WASHINGTON POST AND TIMES HERALD

"Let's see—four oranges plus three apples, minus one monkey wrench, times two bushels—"

out in presidential primaries, as in most primaries, tends to be low. Often presidential candidates simply ignore state primaries, as Adlai E. Stevenson did in 1952, and still win the nomination. Herbert Hoover fared badly in state primaries in 1928 but won both the nomination and election. Sometimes, on the other hand, success in presidential primaries is decisive, as in the case of Adlai Stevenson's string of state victories in the spring of 1956.

The system is undermined by the tendency of many state delegations, no matter how chosen, to support a "favorite son"—a prominent state leader but often not of "presidential timber" —who is a convenient person to ballot for while the delegation leaders bargain with the main candidates. It can be said for presidential primaries, though, that they have stimulated interest in the

early stages of presidential nominations, have opened up the machinery to rank-and-file participation where the voters have been interested enough to use it, and have enabled the country to get some idea—although not a very accurate one—of the popularity of rival candidates in some of the states.

Convention organization: At meetings of the national convention the chairman of the national committee presides until temporary officers are chosen; these in turn officiate until the convention elects permanent officers. Committee organization includes: *credentials,* which in the case of disputed seats has the power to make recommendations to the convention; *permanent organization,* which recommends permanent officers for the convention; *rules,* which reports out the rules governing the convention proceedings; *resolutions,* which draws up the party platform and recommends its

[7] For a carefully prepared proposal for state presidential primary improvement, see Manning J. Dauer, William A. F. Stephenson, Harry Macy, and David Temple, "Toward a Model State Presidential Primary Law," *The American Political Science Review,* Vol. L, No. 1, March 1956, pp. 138-153.

adoption by the convention. The actions of any of these committees may be —or at least seem to be—of crucial importance to some contestant. For example, the credentials committee may recommend unseating delegates friendly to some candidate and seating his rival's, as in the Republican convention in 1952.

Voting in the national conventions is by simple majority. During most of its existence the Democratic party had the "two-thirds rule," requiring nomination of presidential and vice-presidential candidates by that fraction of the vote. This rule, supported mainly by southern Democrats who feared being outvoted by the northern majority in the party, led to endless deadlocks—in one case a candidate was nominated only after 103 ballots—and in 1936 Democrats under President Roosevelt's leadership succeeded in abolishing the rule. Democratic conventions authorize under certain circumstances the *unit rule,* under which the entire vote of a state delegation is cast as the majority of the delegation wishes. Since few state parties now instruct their delegations to act as a unit, the unit rule has become of limited importance. The Republican national convention does not accept such instructions as valid.

Preconvention campaigns

The preconvention campaign usually starts at least a year or two before the convention. The candidate—who may be a well-known governor, Cabinet member, senator, or perhaps an eminent general—is likely to act the part of the coy maiden for a time, but doubtless his scouts are busy sounding out sentiment in the party from Maine to California. The candidate has his choice of several preconvention strategies, depending on his political position. He can announce his candidacy months before the convention and try openly to capture state delegations, as the late Senator Taft did in 1951. He can keep silent if he prefers not to show his hand early, especially if it is not a strong one. He can concentrate on gaining a following among the party rank-and-file and the voters at large through public appearances, television speeches, and the like. He can try to build his strength mainly by lining up delegates through various arrangements or deals. The chances are that he will use more than one approach because of the different ways that convention delegates are chosen in different states.

As the convention nears, the hunting for delegate support becomes more and more intense. In each convention the grand object is to win the support of a simple majority of the votes cast. The job is made all the harder because the delegates leave for the conventions in all stages of definite commitment to some candidate, of noncommitment, and of semi-commitment. Some delegates are pledged to a candidate only on the first ballot; others have pledged themselves to someone until "the crack of doom." Some state delegations go by the unit rule; others split their vote according to the position of individual delegates.

As the convention opens the air is filled with talk of favorite sons; of stalking-horses, who are used as fronts for strong candidates wishing to keep some strength in reserve; and of dark horses, who "stand restively and fully accoutered in their paddocks waiting, watching, and hoping that the favorites will kill each other off, and that the convention in desperation will lead them to the starting post."[8] The big test of a candidate is his *availability*, which turns on whether he has demonstrated vote-getting power, whether he seems to have presidential stature, whether he is not closely tied to a narrow faction in the party, whether he comes from a politically strategic state or section, and—above all—whether he has not alienated some vital religious, ethnic, or economic group.

The workings of the doctrine of availability are well illustrated by the choosing of a Democratic nominee for Vice-President in 1944. It was generally known that the convention's choice might well succeed President Roosevelt in the White House. According to Bronx leader Edward J. Flynn, he and a number of other Democratic bosses canvassed the field. Vice-President Wallace was too liberal, and old-line Democrats did not like him. Speaker Rayburn of Texas would antagonize the crucial Negro vote. "Byrnes, who was the strongest candidate," says Flynn, "wouldn't do because he had been raised a Catholic and had left the church when he married, and the Catholics wouldn't stand for that." Truman, on the other hand, was known to the public but had made few enemies, "he came from a border state, and he had never made any 'racial' remarks. He just dropped into the slot."[9]

Convention battles

Both party conventions follow the same ritual. There is the keynote speech, which lauds the party and bombards the enemy in equally flamboyant words. Then come the election of convention officials, the reports of committees, the adoption of a platform. Some of these activities, such as the election of the permanent chairman and the seating of contested delegations, are occasions for tests of strength among leading candidates. After hearing statements from representatives of interested groups, a resolutions committee presents a proposed platform to the convention. Usually the planks are debated by the delegates, although sometimes they are accepted perfunctorily. Though drawn in generalities, negative in tone, and sometimes meaningless in many details, the platform indicates the way the wind is blowing. And on some issues, such as prohibition in the Democrats' 1928 and 1932 conventions and civil rights in their 1948 and 1956 conventions, stormy debate may ensue and planks may be accepted or defeated by close votes.

[8] P. H. Odegard and E. A. Helms, *American Politics,* 2nd ed. (New York: Harper & Brothers, 1947), p. 532.
[9] Flynn, *You're the Boss,* pp. 180-181.

By the third or fourth day the convention is ready for the main business. Candidates are nominated in fulsome speeches that make them out as angels blessed with every virtue, and above all with the ability to win elections. In nominating Dewey for President in 1944 a delegate orated:

We are here to restore the Presidency of the United States to the American people. (Applause). We are here to bring Washington, D.C., back into the United States. (Applause). We are here to make the American people masters in their own household. (Applause). For that job we have the means and we have the man. (Applause). I give to you the nominee of the Republican party, the spokesman of the future, Thomas E. Dewey!

In the same year Senator Alben W. Barkley nominated Roosevelt in the Democratic convention with the words:

I present to this Convention for the office of President of these United States the name of one who is endowed with the intellectual boldness of Thomas Jefferson, the indomitable courage of Andrew Jackson, the faith and patience of Abraham Lincoln, the rugged integrity of Grover Cleveland, and the scholarly vision of Woodrow Wilson—Franklin D. Roosevelt.

Pandemonium breaks forth when the name of the candidate is mentioned. Delegates march about singing and cheering in demonstrations that may last half an hour or so. Short seconding speeches come next. Then the balloting begins.

Meantime the candidates have been maneuvering for position. From their headquarters in nearby hotel rooms has emerged a stream of claims of delegate strength, counterclaims, denials, rumors, charges, and counter-charges. If one candidate comes to the convention with a big lead in delegate strength, the other delegates will attempt to head him off by combining their forces where possible. For if the convention can be deadlocked, a stampede may start toward even a weak candidate. Anyone controlling delegate votes must make the crucial decision of when to throw his strength to a candidate. If he throws his votes too soon, he may give them to a candidate who loses out in the end. If he waits too long, some candidate may acquire enough strength elsewhere. The trick is to deliver at the right time to the winning man; the reward may be the vice-presidency or some other prize.

The task of the leading contenders is even more delicate. They must mobilize enough strength in early balloting to prove their power. They must also increase their votes with every new balloting to show that they are gaining. If their total drops on any one ballot, their cause may be lost. Franklin Roosevelt's capture of the Democratic nomination in 1932 shows the intricacies of the process. With Jim Farley's invaluable help, F.D.R. received 666¼ votes in the first balloting (more than a majority, but in

1932 the Democrats still had a rule requiring nomination by a two-thirds vote). He gained 11½ votes in the next balloting, but only 5 more in the third. Some observers thought he had reached his peak. But in the next few hours while the weary convention was in adjournment, Farley managed to bring over the Texas and California delegations controlled by John Garner—an objective he had been working toward for months by holding out the vice-presidency to Garner as bait. This switch brought a break in the opponents' ranks, and a stampede to Roosevelt followed on the next ballot. Farley said later that if Illinois had come over to Roosevelt after the first or second ballot, the vice-presidency would have gone to that state.[10]

Once a candidate wins a majority, a delegate who had voted against him normally moves that his nomination be made unanimous. This is done, and then another long ovation breaks out. The victorious candidate, who usually has been directing his forces from a nearby hotel suite, may appear before the convention a short while later. Smiling wife by his side, spotlighted by movie and television cameras, the happy candidate thanks the delegates for their vote of confidence and promises a winning fight.

Nominating a vice-presidential candidate usually comes as an anticlimax. The delegates are tired, broke, and anxious to get home. While the vice-presidential nominee is formally chosen in a rollcall vote, in almost all cases the newly picked presidential nominee and his backers actually make the selection, and the convention is glad to endorse it. An effort is ordinarily made to "balance the ticket" by selecting for Vice-President a man who represents a different wing of the party, geographical area, and party faction from the presidential nominee. Sometimes the selection is partly a result of a trade by which a party faction gives its ballots to the man who wins the presidential nomination in exchange for the "consolation prize."

Should the national convention be reformed?

One of the most criticized party institutions is the national convention. The arguments against it are multifold. It is charged that party bosses actually pick the candidate in a series of unprincipled deals, in "smoke-filled rooms," and that the usual result of this is a compromise candidate who represents only the dead level of party mediocrity. The manner of choosing the delegates is also under attack. Both conventions and primaries are rigged and run by state bosses, it is said, and presidential primaries are so complicated that they baffle the voter and discourage him from taking part. Supporters of Dwight D. Eisenhower and of Robert A. Taft in the early months of 1952, it is pointed out, had to spend much of their time not in

---

[10] J. A. Farley, *Behind the Ballots* (New York: Harcourt, Brace and Company, 1938), p. 142.

championing their candidate but in explaining the intricacies and pitfalls of the ballot.

The main defense of the convention system is simple: it works. During the last century, it is argued, the convention system has brought before the country men of the caliber of Lincoln, Cleveland, McKinley, Wilson, Smith, Willkie, both Roosevelts, Stevenson, Eisenhower, and others.[11] The genius of the convention system is that it produces a candidate who represents party consensus instead of merely some wing of the party. This is important, it is said, for only such a man can enjoy the united support of the party in the campaign and in the White House. Those who look aghast at convention horse-trades and hijinks often forget that compromise is the very essence of democratic politics.

Some opponents of the convention favor a *nationwide direct presidential primary system.* President Woodrow Wilson in 1913 advocated legislation providing for primary elections to take place simultaneously throughout the country, where the voters in each party would vote directly for their favorite without the intervention of nominating conventions. The advantage of the system is that it would do away with much of the confusion and inefficiencies of the present system. The proposal, which might require a constitutional amendment, has been criticized, however, by those who feel that one nationwide direct primary would disrupt party solidarity and effectiveness. We need consensus *within* the party, they say, so that all major elements —geographical, economic, ideological—can take part in its affairs. We need division *between* the major parties so that the people will have a more meaningful choice at the polls. The primary system, critics assert, often gives us the reverse.

Both convention critics and supporters agree on at least one thing: that methods of *selecting convention delegates* should be improved. The whole system needs to be simplified, and eligibility requirements for voters clarified. Reform does not necessarily mean that the method of selecting delegates in state party *conventions* must be dropped. Both the primary system and the state convention system can be democratic methods of choosing delegates. Both can become "boss-controlled." Whether they become one or the other depends on whether or how the voters use them. The most democratic appearing methods will not do the job if they lack the propulsive power of wide participation by the people.

HOW TO BE ELECTED PRESIDENT

Immediately after nominating the vice-presidential candidate the convention adjourns. The presidential candidate may choose a new party chairman, who usually is his campaign manager. The rest of the summer is spent plan-

[11] For a foreigner's view, see H. J. Laski, "The Conventions and the Presidency," *Harper's Magazine* (July 1940), pp. 166-171.

ning electioneering tactics and arrangements. Campaign headquarters are geared for action. By early fall the presidential race is on.

Campaign strategy

Grand strategy varies in different elections, but a campaign usually has standard ingredients, such as the following:

The build-up. The personality of the candidate may be as important as the platform he runs on. If a candidate has any defects, these must be

Relax—They Only Think About Us at Election Time

Herblock in THE WASHINGTON POST

played down. The dour Calvin Coolidge had to be humanized before the presidential campaign of 1924. Franklin Roosevelt in 1936 had been pictured by the opposition as an arrogant dictator; his campaign tour was designed in part to show him as a warm and pleasing personality close to the people. The candidate's desirable features are also played up. In 1944 Dewey was presented as an aggressive young executive, in contrast with the old and tired group in power; in 1952 Eisenhower was presented as a man who could unite the American people behind a middle-of-the-road program. In the end, the man offered to the people is almost a myth. As Boss Penrose once said, "Always after a man is nominated they bring out the royal robe and put it on him, and that covers up all the cracks and nail-holes."

Taking the stump. By the end of September both candidates are usually touring the country by train, plane, and automobile. There was a time when candidates conducted front-porch campaigns, receiving friendly delegations at their homes, but that day seems gone forever. It is necessary today to carry the campaign straight to the voters. Presidents Hoover, Franklin Roosevelt, and Eisenhower stayed in the White House until late in the campaign to show their devotion to duty, but took the stump before the end. The candidates' campaign trains and caravans have been seen by too many Americans to need description here. Often overlooked, however, is the planning that goes into the choice of itinerary. Candidates sometimes try to steer clear of areas where they might be embarrassed by a local issue or an intra-party fight.

Where to stump. The electoral college system closely affects campaign strategy. Under this system, as we have seen, the presidential contest is not decided by the pooled votes of all those casting ballots throughout the nation, but by the ballots of presidential electors (see pp. 378-379). *All* the electoral votes of a state go to the candidate who gains the most popular votes in that state. As a consequence, candidates concentrate attention on big, closely divided states. This means that the Democratic candidate writes off Maine and Vermont and his Republican foe probably does the same with much of the South. Candidates will make most of their appearances in the big, doubtful states like New York, Pennsylvania, Massachusetts, Illinois, Ohio. The election outcome may easily be decided by the large block of electoral votes from such states as these.

Building group support. The essential strategy of the campaign is to build up a winning alliance of interests. These interests will be mainly sectional, economic, ideological, national-origin, racial, religious. Some of these groups will be antagonistic to one another—for example, a Democratic candidate must seek to win the support of northern Negroes without alienating too many southern whites. Most large organizations, such as the American Legion or the National Grange, will not commit themselves as organizations. The trick is to induce prominent leaders of the organizations to take part in special election groups, such as Veterans for Eisenhower or United Farmers for Truman. Each party headquarters maintains special bureaus directed at mobilizing support from organized groups. Campaign literature is slanted to appeal to housewives, businessmen, farmers, veterans, workers, and so on. The candidate himself must play the main part in pitching his appeals so that they attract the support of divergent and overlapping groups.

Choosing issues. This is one of the basic arts of campaigning. Issues may not be more important than personalities—but actually the two are inseparable. The candidate has a wide choice of alternatives, for he is not bound by his party's platform; indeed he can openly repudiate or modify planks of the platform if he wishes, as Landon did in 1936. One basic question arises: Should the candidate take a stand on specific issues, or should he speak in generalities as far as possible? Either way, he is bound both to win and to lose some votes. Traditionally, evasion of issues has been considered a generally effective tactic, but the success of Roosevelt and Truman in taking fairly definite stands in recent elections may presage a change in this respect. Usually the campaign tries to develop a basic theme, which is repeatedly played on, with variations to suit the place and hour. But there is a good deal of improvisation as candidates and campaign managers sense last-minute changes in public feeling from their audiences and from opinion polls. Sometimes developments during campaigns will affect the importance of issues and the outcome of the election, as in 1944, when Dewey's stress on postwar matters lost its appeal in the face of military events that indicated prolonged enemy resistance.

Offensive and defensive tactics. Is it better to concentrate on attacking the enemy and ignoring his charges? Or should the opposition be answered charge for charge? Is it possible to put the opposition on the defensive—and how? Do Americans really vote *for* candidates or *against* them? These questions plague any campaign strategist. Of course, a candidate for re-election is often on the defensive in the sense that his public record is up before the voters. But it is always possible to ignore the opposition's attacks and concentrate on one's own achievements. An effective tactic is to ignore the opposition's most damaging charges and to answer his weakest and wildest ones. In 1940, for example, Roosevelt said nothing about the third-term issue, but he answered at length the reckless statement of a minor Republican official that the President's only supporters were "paupers, those who earn less than $1200 a year and aren't worth that, and the Roosevelt family."

Splitting the opposition. A candidate, according to an old political maxim, should always try to separate his opponent from the party rank and file. Willkie in 1940 tried to make a distinction between New Dealers and Democrats. Stevenson in 1952 fired away at Republican "reactionaries" and "isolationists." Campaigners also try to divide the groups that seem to be united behind their opponent; thus Dewey made a point of his support from organized labor, and Roosevelt made use of businessmen's organizations set up to back him. Another splitting device is to focus the attack on a minor figure in the opposition camp, or on the sinister forces that are actually said to be in command. Republicans play up city bosses, Reds, brain trusters, arrogant bureaucrats; Democrats concentrate on big business, special interests, utilities, Hooverites, and the like. The great weakness of this device is that too much fire on minor figures may leave the candidate himself unscathed.

Auxiliary organizations. While the candidate is on display he must rely on his national, state, and local party organizations to carry the heavy burden of routine work. His own campaign headquarters will be raising money, issuing propaganda, coordinating party efforts throughout the nation, and operating special divisions that seek the vote of large groups, such as Negroes, labor, farmers, and others. An important organizational question involves the use of auxiliary organizations independent of the party. In 1940, for example, thousands of Willkie Clubs were formed, and many of these had somewhat distant relations with the Republican organization. The advantage of auxiliaries is that they can appeal more effectively to nonparty groups. Their disadvantage lies in the likelihood

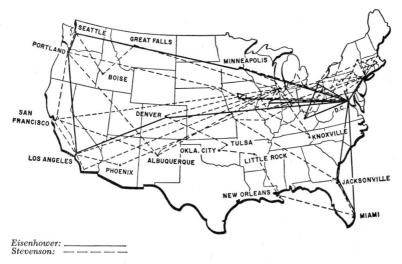

Eisenhower: _____
Stevenson: — — — — —

Routes of Eisenhower's and Stevenson's campaign trips, 1956.

of duplication of effort and even friction with the party regulars. In general, a presidential candidate must rely heavily on the party machinery throughout the nation; he could never rival such a network of organizations with a personal following. The Eisenhower clubs in 1952 and 1956, however, were probably more effective than most such organizations.

Timing. This is one of the most important and mysterious techniques of all. Candidates try to pace their campaigns so that the climax comes just before the election. Eisenhower's promise late in October 1952 to make a personal trip to Korea if elected probably was perfectly timed for maximum appeal. Some campaigns have tended to reach a peak too early. While it is doubtful that election climaxes can be planned, both candidates usually converge on the populous areas in the East shortly before election day. The final campaign speech usually takes place on the Saturday before the Tuesday election; on election eve, however, the candidates make a sober and restrained appeal to the people to do their duty at the polls next day.

An American politician can face no ordeal more exhausting or exacting than a presidential campaign. Adlai E. Stevenson, the unsuccessful Democratic candidate in 1952 and 1956, has well described the campaign from the nominee's point of view:

You must emerge, bright and bubbling with wisdom and well-being, every morning at 8 o'clock, just in time for a charming and profound breakfast talk, shake hands with hundreds, often literally thousands, of people, make several inspiring, "newsworthy" speeches during the day, confer with political leaders along the way and with your staff all the time, write at every chance, think if possible, read mail and newspapers, talk on the telephone, talk to everybody, dictate, receive delegations, eat, with decorum—and discretion!—and ride through city after city on the back of an open car, smiling until your mouth is dehydrated by the wind, waving until the blood runs out of your arms, and then bounce gaily, confidently, masterfully into great howling halls, shaved and all made up for television with the right color shirt and tie—I always forgot—and a manuscript so defaced with chicken tracks and last-minute jottings that you couldn't follow it, even if the spotlights weren't blinding and even if the still photographers didn't shoot you in the eye every time you looked at them. (I've often wondered what happened to all those pictures.) Then all you have to do is make a great, imperishable speech, get out through the pressing crowds with a few score autographs, your clothes intact, your hands bruised, and back to the hotel—in time to see a few important people.

But the real work has just commenced—two or three, sometimes four hours of frenzied writing and editing of the next day's immortal mouthings so you can get something to the stenographers, so they can get something to the mimeograph machines, so they can get something to the reporters, so they can get something to their papers by deadline time. (And I quickly concluded that all deadlines were yesterday!) Finally sleep, sweet sleep, steals you away, unless you worry—which I do.

The next day is the same.

But I gained weight on it. Somehow the people sustain you, the people and a constant, sobering reminder that you are asking them to entrust to you the most awesome responsibility on earth. It was a glorious, heart-filling, head-filling odyssey for which I shall be forever grateful to my party, to my staff and to my fellow Americans. Their faces are a friendly, smiling sea of memory stretching from coast to coast.[12]

The electoral college—mechanics

To win the Presidency, a candidate must put together a combination of electoral votes that will give him a majority in the electoral college. This unique institution has no professors or football team, never meets, and serves only a limited electoral function. Yet it has an importance of its

[12] Adlai E. Stevenson, *Major Campaign Speeches* (New York: Random House, 1953), pp. xxi-xxiii. Reprinted by permission of Random House, Inc. Copyright 1953 by Random House, Inc.

own. As noted, the framers of the Constitution devised the electoral college system because they wanted the President chosen by *electors* exercising independent judgment, but as a result of political changes electors are now straight party representatives who simply register the electorate's decision.

The system today works as follows: in picking his presidential choice on election day, the voter technically does not vote directly for a candidate but chooses between slates of *presidential electors*. Each slate is made up of men selected by the state party (in most states in party conventions) to serve this essentially honorary role. The actual names of the electors do not appear on the ballots or voting machines in many states, but in any case it is made clear that the slate is pledged to a particular candidate and that by voting for that slate the voter in effect is voting for that candidate. The entire slate that wins the most *popular* votes throughout the *state* wins, and gets to cast, *all* the *electoral* votes for the state (a state has one electoral vote for every senator and representative).

As a formality, the electors on the winning slate in the state travel to the state capital a few weeks after the election, go through the ceremony of casting their ballots for their party's candidates, perhaps hear some speeches, and go home. The ballots are sent from the state capitals to Washington, where early in January they are formally "counted" and—to the amazement of nobody—the name of the next President is announced.

The counting of the electoral votes by the House and Senate could in some cases, however, be more than a formality. In 1876 for example, there was a serious dispute as to which slate of electoral votes from several southern states should be counted. The election was so close that the outcome depended upon the choice. The Senate was Republican, the House Democratic. Finally a Commission of Fifteen was elected composed of eight Republicans and seven Democrats and by a vote of eight to seven the Commission ruled that the Republican electors in the disputed states had been properly elected; so Hayes became President over Tilden.

The House and Senate also have important roles to play in the event no candidate secures a *majority* of the electoral votes. This is not likely as long as there are only two serious contending parties, but it has happened twice in the case of President and once in the case of Vice-President. The House chooses the President from among the top three candidates, each state delegation having one vote, with a majority being necessary for election. In the vice-presidential contest if no man receives a majority of the electoral vote for Vice-President, the Senate picks from among the top two candidates, each senator has one vote, and again a majority is required.

The electoral college—politics

The operation of the electoral college, with its statewide electoral slates, has major impact upon the nature of the Presidency and presidential politics.

In order to win a presidential election a candidate must appeal successfully to urban and suburban groups in populous states such as New York, California, Pennsylvania, Illinois, and perhaps a dozen others. A Republican candidate usually enters the fray sure of the backing of rural states such as Vermont, Kansas, Oregon, and the Dakotas. Under ordinary circumstances the Democratic candidate knows that he can depend on the support of the "Solid South" and some of the border states. Under the electoral college system, as we have seen, a candidate wins *all* a state's electoral votes or *none;* hence the presidential candidate ordinarily will not waste his time campaigning in states unless he has at least a fighting chance of carrying them; nor will he waste time in states that are assuredly on his side. Consequently, the fight usually narrows down to the big states where the balance between the parties tends to be fairly even.

One result of this situation is that the presidential candidate must win over—or at least not unduly antagonize—the masses of voters in industrial centers. He must show sensitivity to the problems that worry them—problems such as working conditions, housing, wages, social security, and relations with foreign nations, especially nations whose sons and daughters have come by the million to our shores. Another result is that the candidate's appeals must transcend local and petty matters and dramatize the great national issues. He will, of course, address himself to groups such as farmers, workers, veterans, and the like, but he will probably seize on the issues that unify these groups on a nationwide basis. The candidate, in short, strikes out for a *national majority* rooted in the larger states and sacrifices many narrow issues in order to exploit the broader ones. Candidates for Congress, on the other hand, often win votes by pressing local and sectional claims against those of the rest of the nation.

Presidential elections, with the tremendous publicity, dramatic personalities, and spotlighting of great national issues, draw out a big vote. As noted, off-year congressional elections tend to attract fewer voters than presidential elections, and even in a presidential election more voters at the polls ordinarily will mark their "X" in the box for the presidential race than in those for the House and Senate races. As a result of all this, the President is usually responsible to a broader constituency than the sum of the constituencies voting for members of Congress.

How this situation may work out in practice is seen in the story of veterans' legislation in the House of Representatives. Six times during the 1920's and 1930's Presidents vetoed bills desired by the American Legion. Six times Congress overrode these vetoes. Apparently President and Congress were responding to different alignments of voters. The President did not seem to fear retaliation from the Legion at the polls; both Coolidge and Roosevelt won re-election after vetoing these bills. And the overwhelming majority of congressmen who voted as the Legion wished were also successful in the subsequent elections.[13] In short, it may often be politically expedient to *follow one path of action as President and a contrary one as congressman.*

Reform of the electoral college

Almost everyone agrees that the present electoral college method of electing Presidents is defective. Because of the unit-vote system the electoral college is inherently unable to give accurate results. For example, Roosevelt won 98 per cent of the electoral vote in 1936 with only 60 per cent of the popular vote. The system is especially unfair to minorities in the various states. No Republican in Georgia, no Democrat in Vermont, is able to make his vote count for President. Far worse, minority party members actually aid the opposition, since the size of a state's electoral vote is related to the size of its population. Although almost three million popular votes were cast for Dewey in New York in 1944, Roosevelt received even more and received all that state's electoral votes. In effect, the Dewey popular votes were converted in the electoral college to votes for Roosevelt. This situation helps maintain essentially one-party areas such as the Solid South. Finally, the system could easily break down as a result of mischance or fraud, and lead to violence if people

"Don't Expect Me To Get This Real Accurate, Bub"

Herblock in THE WASHINGTON POST

felt that they had been cheated out of a victory by this faulty machinery. Like the human appendix, the electoral college is useless, unpredictable, and a possible center of inflammation.

Many reforms have been suggested. One is to abolish the whole electoral college arrangement and to elect the President by direct popular vote. But this plan is utopian. It would be opposed by the South and by small states, who could easily muster enough strength to stop a constitutional amendment. Another proposal is more modest. It would abolish the electors but would keep the present distribution of electoral votes among the states. Each candidate would receive the same proportion of the *electoral* votes of a state as he won of its popular vote. For example, if a candidate gained one-third of

[13] See V. O. Key, "The Veterans and the House of Representatives: A Study of a Pressure Group and Electoral Mortality," *Journal of Politics,* 5 (1943), pp. 27-40; which concludes that party affiliation had a more important bearing on a Representative's chances for re-election than did his stand on veterans' bills.

the popular vote in a state holding twelve electoral votes, he would win four of the electoral votes. Minority party votes would have due weight in each state. The electoral and the popular vote would be closely—although not exactly—correlated. Minority parties and candidates would have more incentive to campaign in one-party areas.

It might seem that such a modest proposal, compromising as it does with sectional and state interests, might be quickly adopted. But the plan has not got far. An amendment embodying the proposal passed the Senate by the necessary two-thirds majority in the Eighty-first Congress, but it failed in the House. Why? Some Republicans in the House feared that the plan would bring a fairly even division between the two parties in most states in the North, but a strong Democratic electoral vote in the South that would elect the Democratic candidate in a close election. Some southerners feared that the amendment would increase the Republican vote in the South.

Many northern Democrats opposed electoral college reform, and their reasoning is significant. They argued that the present system compels presidential candidates to fight especially hard to win the support of the big pivotal states such as New York, Illinois, and California, since candidates face the prospect of winning or losing *all* the huge electoral votes in such big states. As a result, presidential candidates will pitch their appeals in these states to the great balance-of-power groups that tend to be composed largely of urban voters, including organized labor, Catholics, nationality groups, Negroes, and other groups that usually give majorities to Democratic candidates. The electoral college therefore forces presidential candidates—and ultimately the President—to be especially responsive to the problems and interests of these groups.

Thus the electoral college, even aside from its archaic and unpredictable machinery, involves ultimately the problem of *representation,* which is one of the central problems discussed in Part Five.

WHO WON THE ELECTION?

The election is over. The victors and the losers exchange gracious messages. Placards and posters blow away in the autumn storms. Soon the successful candidates are taking office in White House, Congress, statehouse, and city hall. These are the winners. But aside from the victorious candidates, can we say who really won the election?

No total victors

Did a *party* win it? Only to a limited extent, at best. No party (fortunately) ever sweeps all the national, state, and local elections, nor does any party ever elect all the members of one chamber, like the House of Representatives. And sometimes one party captures one or both chambers of Congress at the same time that the opposition party wins or retains the Presidency, leading to divided party rule. Never in the United States does one party seize control of the legislative and executive branches of the national government to the extent that the winning party in Britain takes command in Parliament and Cabinet. Indeed, we cannot speak of party control in any real sense. At most we can speak of control or influence by various factions or individuals in the party. The point is that the elected candidates are not elected by or responsible to a single monolithic party but rather to groups in and outside the party. The party as such did not win the election.

Can we say, then, that any particular *group* won the election? Of course, certain groups will say that they were the ones that elected the winning candidates. But these claims will be exaggerated. Few organized groups are big enough by themselves to muster enough votes for a majority. And big groups, whether economic, religious, or any other, do not vote as a bloc. The most we can say is that the election was won by a combination of *segments* of groups, or of *subgroups.*

Was the election a victory for a particular *principle* or set of ideas? Here again the answer must be "no." Certainly many persons will make this claim. We will hear over the radio or read in the paper that the election results were a victory for civil rights or for anti-union laws or a repudiation of the bureaucrats or of Wall Street. But an election is rarely if ever a mandate for particular policies. The party platforms are vague catchalls, and the candidates' promises are often obscure and inconsistent. An electoral majority is made up of many different elements with a variety of views. At best the election reflects general attitudes of important segments of the voters.

Who, then, did win the election? What do the election results mean? Of course the winners of the election may have been—at least in the long run—the whole nation, all the people. In a narrower and more immediate sense, the winners were the elected candidates and the voters supporting those candidates—*to the extent that the candidates can follow through on their followers' expectations.* The election results mean simply that the voters have made choices among candidates—choices that give only a rough idea of what the voters are thinking. Election results are not blueprints for future action, but crude guidelines to the general drift of popular feeling. "A vote," says Lippmann, "is a promise of support. It is a way of saying: I am lined up with these men, on this side."[14]

What elections are

To understand election results then, we must remember what elections are and what they are not. Elections are not simply a grand rally of the

[14] Walter Lippmann, *The Phantom Public* (New York: Harcourt, Brace and Company, Inc., 1925), pp. 56-57.

people, who on their own initiative debate issues, produce candidates, and decide among them. Elections are struggles among party and group leaders who go to the voters for support. The voters are of all types, organized and unorganized, active and passive, concerned with world-wide issues and with petty ones. Elections are not the spontaneous acts of a mass of people but the periodic mobilization of voters by leaders at many levels.

Elections are only one way in which the voters can have a say in their government. The people intervene in other ways between elections—by writing to their congressmen and to the editor, by signing petitions, by arguing and griping, by organizing in groups. This does not mean that elections are unimportant or uninspiring. Quite the contrary. "A presidential election," William B. Munro once said, "is merely our modern and highly refined substitute for the ancient revolution; a mobilization of opposing forces, a battle of the ins against the outs; with leaders and strategy and campaign chests and all the other paraphernalia of civil war, but without bodily violence to the warriors. This refinement of the struggle for political control, this transition from bullets to ballots, is perhaps the greatest contribution of modern times to the progress of civilization."[15] This observation applies to all elections.

Elections set the course of government only in part. Elected office holders share power with appointed ones, such as judges and administrative officials. All these officials, elected and appointed alike, do not exercise power freely but only within channels set by the forces discussed earlier in this book— the forces of tradition and practice, of laws and institutions, of popular wants and expectations. In the following chapters we turn to our national policy makers and see how they share and exercise power in the never-ending ferment of ideas, interests, individuals, and institutions.

[15] William B. Munro, *The Invisible Government* (New York: The Macmillan Company, 1928), p. 17. For an interesting development of the view that politics is simply the manipulation of rather passive voting groups by elites vying for power, see J. A. Schumpeter, *Capitalism, Socialism, and Democracy* (New York: Harper & Brothers, 1942), chapters 21-23.

Policy makers for the people

PART FIVE ~ A PROBLEM GUIDE

*We are about to inspect two of our funda-
mental problems. The first involves* representation *and the second* responsibility:
*(1) what powers should what officials
exercise on behalf of what people? and (2)
in what ways should our leaders be accountable to people—and to what people?
A third basic problem, that of the necessary teamwork among officials to do the
job efficiently, is involved in both these
questions but will be dealt with mainly in
Part Six.*

*We noted in Part Four that the elec-
torate itself is a complex array of people
holding a variety of attitudes and ideas,
exhibiting all conditions of interest and
apathy, organization and disorganization,
voting influence and lack of it, and operating through parties, interest groups, press,
TV, and other sources of power to bring
about the final result on election day. That
result—considering only the national level
—is the election of a President and members of Congress who, by the operations of
the elective system itself, are virtually
guaranteed to have divergent policies. Part
Five shows that the powers and organization of President, Congress, bureaucrats,
and courts may result in a deeply divided*

PART
FIVE

government unless policy makers are able to make many compromises with one another. Let us note why this is so.

By their internal makeup, both the House and the Senate tend to over-represent rural people (pp. 392-393, 401-407). The President tends to overrepresent the urban masses (Chapter 14); but beyond this, he also tends to act at times for a united people (pp. 454-458) or for a nationwide majority as reflected in his party (pp. 445-449). The federal courts (Chapter 20) tend to lag behind majority opinion because, among other reasons, federal judges are appointed for life. The bureaucrats, controlled by both the President and Congress (pp. 443-444, 502-509), are often caught politically between cross currents from the White House and Capitol Hill. The majority is represented, in short, not by a host of officials working together as a smooth-running machine, but by officials who are often at odds, just as the framers of the Constitution planned.

This situation also raises the problem of responsibility. If many officials have a finger in the governmental pie, if they can often stop one another from acting, who is to get the credit at election time for the policies that voters like, and who for the policies they dislike? Or to turn the problem the other way around, how are the voters to control the officeholders in Washington when there are so many officeholders and so many lines of influence? Chapter 21 tries to tackle this problem of responsibility and popular control by presenting two different approaches to it, one favoring better organized parties to serve as means of crystallizing and focusing national sentiment (pp. 560-561) and one favoring more diffused and decentralized parties such as our present ones (pp. 556-558).

Perhaps the chief implication of these problems in Part Five involves the Presidency. This office, given an incumbent willing to exert leadership, can supply the very qualities that neither our party system (Chapter 13) nor Congress (chapters 15-16) can supply: representation for the majority of the people and a focal point of responsibility and accountability. As a result of this situation, the Presidency has become an increasingly powerful office. Two vital questions remain as to whether the office is becoming too powerful (pp. 468-472) and whether other means can be found for reaching our goals of fair representation and clear responsibility to the people.

O N JANUARY 3 EVERY YEAR, 531 MEN AND women meet in the chambers of the Capitol in Washington to inaugurate a new session of Congress. These legislators—435 representatives and 96 senators—are members of one of the oldest parliaments in the world. They are the symbols of the vigor of representative government in twentieth century America. They debate and enact laws in the tradition of a legislature that has met every year for almost 170 years despite revolutionary changes in our economic and political life, depressions, and wars at home and abroad.[1]

The first important fact about Congress is its *bicameral* structure, its organization as a separate Senate and House of Representatives. As we saw in chapters 2 and 3, the framers of the Constitution set up two separate houses, partly to settle the fight between the small states and the large, and partly to make the legislators responsible to different groups of voters. The framers planned well and lastingly. Today each house has an *absolute veto* over the other in legislation, and each house responds to *different interests*.

Since the two houses of Congress resemble each other in certain ways, this chapter will first take up the basic powers and structure common to both. Since the two houses are different in certain ways, each will then be described separately. Finally, the way that the two chambers work out their differences will be explained. The next chapter will stress the personalities, processes, and problems of Congress. Both chapters will stress the *political context* in which the institutions and procedures of Congress take on special meaning.

THE POWERS OF CONGRESS

The paramount power of Congress is *legislative*. The first article of the Constitution gives Congress the authority to

[1] Every two years a new Congress comes into being. For example, the Congress that convened in January 1957, the same month President Eisenhower resumed office, was the Eighty-fifth. In each two-year Congress there are two regular sessions, beginning in January of each year, and such other special sessions as may be called by the President.

15 ★

The

houses

of Congress

levy taxes, borrow money, regulate commerce with other nations and among the states, coin money, declare war, and a host of other important matters, including passing all laws necessary and proper to execute these powers. Unquestionably the lawmaking function is the main job of Congress. But the legislators have other duties.

Congress has *amendatory powers*. Congress proposes amendments to the Constitution or calls into being a convention to propose amendments as described in Chapter 3. Moreover, Congress determines which *method* of ratification shall be used to approve the amendments it proposes and sets the time during which they may be ratified.

Congress has *electoral powers,* as described in the preceding chapter. Congress by law determines, moreover, who shall be President in the event of the death or disability of the President and Vice-President.

Each house is also the judge of the *elections* and *qualifications* of its own members. When a contest develops or irregularities are charged, each House determines the right of the member-elect to take his seat. Questions about qualifications are also resolved by each chamber. The Constitution stipulates that a member of the House must be twenty-five years old, an inhabitant of his state (American political attitudes dictate that he also be a resident of his district), and an American citizen for at least seven years. Senators must be thirty, inhabitants of their states, and citizens for at least nine years. Each House, moreover, may disqualify persons because of conduct of which a majority of the members disapprove. Although the constitutionality of this practice has been questioned, ample precedents support it. In 1926, for example, the Senate refused to seat William S. Vare because of excessive campaign expenditures.

The House has the power to *impeach* and the Senate the power to *try* any civil officer of the United States, including the President. If two-thirds of the senators uphold the lower body's impeachment charges, the officer may be removed from his position and disqualified from ever holding an office of profit or trust under the United States.

Each chamber has *disciplinary powers* over both its own members and to a limited extent over private persons. Congressmen are not subject to impeachment (they are not, the Supreme Court has said, civil officers of the United States), and it is up to each chamber to discipline its own members. Once a Congressman has been seated, he may be expelled by a two-thirds vote of his own house, a most uncommon proceeding. Each house has inherent power to punish *private* persons whose conduct directly interferes with the exercise of congressional business. If, for example, a witness before a committee refuses to answer a proper question, the chamber could sit as a court, convict him of contempt, and order the sergeant-at-arms to hold him in custody. He could not be held, however, longer than the time Congress remained in session. This inherent power to punish for contempt is not normally used. Rather Congress turns the matter over to the United States attorney for punishment under the law that makes refusal to answer appropriate questions or other interference with congressional operations a misdemeanor.

Congress has *investigatory powers*. Congress may look into any subjects whenever necessary in order to carry out its lawmaking, amendatory, electoral, or other duties. It may subpoena witnesses and documents, subject of course to constitutional limitations.

Congress *admits new states* into the Union.

Congress has *housekeeping* and *rule-making powers*. The Constitution provides for the presiding officers, determines that a majority of each house shall be a quorum (a *quorum* is the number necessary for the house to do business), requires each chamber to keep a journal of its proceedings and to record votes in the journal on the request of one-fifth of the members present, and sets forth a few other rules. The Constitution authorizes Congress to enact the necessary laws to provide for its own maintenance and gives to each house the power to make its own procedural rules.

The Senate *advises* and *consents to treaties* and *confirms most nominations* to offices of the United States (see page 404).

Great as the powers of Congress are, the framers had, of course, no intention of making it all powerful. As we have seen, they reserved a great deal of authority to the states, and they gave certain powers to the executive and judicial branches of the national government. As time passed, Congress gained power in some respects and lost it in others. As the authority of the national government has expanded, the scope of the lawmaking power of Congress has expanded with it. On the other hand, in its actual exercise of power Congress has lost out to its great rival, the President, who in many respects holds today the commanding place in our national government that the Founding Fathers wanted Congress to have.

CONGRESS: ORGANIZATION AND POLITICS

One of the first things most tourists do in Washington is to watch Congress in session. It is often a disappointing experience. A congressman is shouting into a microphone in the "well" of the House about the needs, say, of the Morumbian valley, but nobody seems to be listening to him. Representatives rush in and out, read newspapers, take catnaps, or talk in small groups in the corridors. When the congressman stops speaking, another is recognized. Does he debate the problems of Morumbians? No, he makes startling revelations about communists in the executive department. The visitor in the gallery, hoping to witness a great forensic battle between two mighty debaters, hears a disconnected string of speeches and questions, partly lost in the buzz and shuffle of the floor. Over in the Senate, the debate may be more coherent, but there, too, only a handful of members may be on the floor.

Committees—The Little Legislatures

Congress puts its worst foot forward. Formal sessions of Congress, however important, are only a small phase of congressional activities. The main legislative work is done in committees. Deluged under several thousand bills a year, Congress could not do its job unless it delegated work to these "little legislatures." The several different types of congressional committees are *standing, special, joint,* and *conference.*

There are nineteen standing committees in the House of Representatives, with an average membership of about thirty. Among the most important of these committees are the great spending and taxing committees, namely Appropriations and Ways and Means, and—for a special reason described below—the Rules Committee. Standing committees are divided into subcommittees with jurisdiction over particular subject matters. Standing committees have great powers. To them are referred all bills introduced in the House. They can kill bills, pigeonhole them for weeks, amend them beyond recognition, or speed them on their way. They are, as Speaker Reed once said, "the eye, the ear, the hand, and very often the brain of the House."

The Senate has fifteen standing committees composed of nine to twenty-three members, each senator normally serving on only two committees. Among the most important Senate committees are Foreign Relations, Finance, and Government Operations; the last supervises and investigates the executive agencies. Senate committees have the same great powers as those of the House.

Committees frequently hold open hearings, where spokesmen from executive departments, representatives of interest group organizations, experts of various sorts, and mere private citizens testify formally on pending legislation. These hearings may be far more interesting to the visitor than sessions of House or Senate, and the committee proceedings published verbatim by the government often afford rich material on the operations of government. The most important work of the committees, however, is done in *executive session,* where visitors are barred. These sessions are centers of vital decision-making, as an expert has pointed out. Their nonpublic character "promotes the free interplay of ideas among committee members. Compromises and alternatives can be shaped in a fluid environment."[2] Committee decisions are taken by majority vote.

Standing committees are bipartisan. The chairman and a majority of the members are elected from the majority party. The minority party is represented roughly in relation to the proportion of minority members in the entire chamber. Getting on a politically advantageous committee is

[2] Bertram M. Gross, *The Legislative Struggle* (New York: McGraw-Hill Book Company, Inc., 1953), pp. 309-310. See also the penetrating analysis, Ralph K. Huitt, "The Congressional Committee: A Case Study," *The American Political Science Review,* Vol. XLVIII, No. 2, June 1954, pp. 340-365.

important to members of Congress. A Representative from Nebraska, for example, would much rather be on the Agriculture or Public Works committees than on the District of Columbia committee. Members usually stay on the same committee from Congress to Congress, but on occasion they jump from one committee to what seems to them a more important one.

How are committee members chosen? At the opening of each Congress, Republican freshmen in the House are given committee assignments by a Committee on Committees of the Republican conference. The Democratic members of the Committee on Ways and Means handle this job for the Democrats. In the Senate too, committee appointments are decided by small groups of leaders in each party. Committee assignments in both chambers in effect are handled by congressional veterans; this fact is one of the reasons the veterans have more power than the newcomers. Each chamber then formally ratifies the decisions that have been made by the party leaders.

To supplement the work of standing committees the House or the Senate occasionally create *special committees*. Normally the task of these committees is to make a specific investigation and after submitting a report they come to an end. In contrast to standing committees, the speaker appoints members of special committees. Such committees are normally not authorized to introduce legislation. Very occasionally House and Senate create *joint committees* composed of members of both chambers, when problems arise that particularly need joint consideration. Some of these joint committees are permanent; the most important of these today is probably the Joint Committee on Atomic Energy. Others are temporary; one of the best known in the past was the Temporary National Economic Committee, which in the late 1930's conducted an elaborate investigation of economic problems and which included in its membership representatives from several executive agencies. *Conference committees,* a special kind of joint committee, are appointed by the presiding officers of the House and Senate when they disagree over legislation; their functions are discussed on page 407.

The House especially puts a good deal of confidence in the work of its committees. They are important also because of their power to kill a bill merely through inaction. If a committee fails to report a bill, the only way it can be brought to the floor of the House is through a *discharge petition* signed by a majority (that is, 218) of the House membership. Many petitions are filed; few gain the necessary number of signatures. Indirectly, however, the threat of a petition sometimes helps move bills out of committee.

Committee leaders—the rule of seniority

Committee leaders are important. While every member of a committee has one vote, the chairman is almost always the most influential member, for he has certain formal as well as informal powers. "The chairman is powerful," Roland Young has written, "because he can call committee meetings whenever he wishes, because he has a large amount of freedom in preparing the legislative agenda for the committee, and because he is officially consulted on questions relating to his committee. A chairmanship . . . gives the member a status with Congress, with the bureaucracy, and with the general public."[3] Like the chairman, the other ranking committee members of both parties have the advantage of experience in the committee field, legislative and parliamentary know-how, and wide contacts in Congress and outside.

Chairmanships are awarded by the rule of *seniority*. The member of the *majority* party who has had the longest continuous service on the committee becomes chairman. (The member of the minority party with the longest continuous service on the committee is the *ranking minority member*.) The chairman may be at swords' points with his fellow partisans in Congress, he may oppose his party's national program, he may even be incompetent— still, he has the right to the chairmanship under the workings of seniority.

The rule of seniority means that chairmen are not chosen by their own committees, their party, or the House or Senate as a whole. They are really picked by the voters in their districts who give them seniority by sending them back to Congress in election after election. Thus the key makers of national policy in Congress are "locally chosen and locally responsible."[4] The seniority rule puts a premium on careful cultivation of the district. It gives the most influence in Congress to those constituencies that are politically stable or even stagnant—where party competition is low, where a particular interest group or city or rural machine may dominate. It stacks the cards against areas where the two parties are more evenly matched, where the interest in politics is high, the number of votes large, and competition between groups keen. These are the very areas most likely to reflect quickly and typically the political tides that sweep the nation.

The effects of the seniority system on party operations are especially devastating. In the words of one student, it "divides the authority of the party leaders and impairs their practical capacity to carry out consistently a general program of party legislation. It may even defeat the projects to which the majority of a party have been publicly pledged. . . . It makes the party system a less effective instrument than it might and should be in organizing majorities within the House for serving the manifest needs of the people of the country."[5]

[3] Roland Young, *This Is Congress* (New York: Alfred A. Knopf, Inc., 1943), p. 108.

[4] *The Reorganization of Congress,* A Report of the Committee on Congress of the American Political Science Association (Washington: Public Affairs Press, 1945), p. 69.

[5] A. N. Holcombe, *Our More Perfect Union* (Cambridge: Harvard University Press, 1950), p. 185. For a defense of the seniority rule largely on the grounds that most committee chairmen are not so powerful as commonly supposed, see the article by a member of Congress, Stewart L. Udall, "A Defense of the Seniority System," *The New York Times Magazine,* January 13, 1957.

The politics of the seniority rule

What groups does the seniority system benefit? When Democrats control Congress, committee chairmen tend to be mainly southerners from rural areas, along with a few products of city machines. (A recent study by Professors Austin Ranney and Willmoore Kendall indicates that while the extent of control of committee chairmanships by southern Democrats has often been exaggerated, they do hold a definite edge in proportion to their numbers.) When Republicans are in control, the northern rural areas gain a disproportionate number of chairmanships. President Eisenhower, for example, has had to deal with committee chairmen who have been accumulating seniority during the years of Democratic supremacy and who generally represent different groups in the party than does the Administration. The struggle between Chairman Reed of the Ways and Means committee and the Administration soon after Mr. Eisenhower took office (see pp. 474-476) was a case in point.

Seniority is defended on the grounds that it prevents disputes among congressmen and elevates the most experienced members to committee leadership. It is attacked on the ground that it puts power into the hands of veteran members who may be out of touch with new needs and new problems of the nation. Basically the argument involves political rather than logical matters. Rural interests naturally tend to favor the system. It is opposed by groups, such as organized labor, supporters of civil rights legislation, and other urban-based interests, who feel that it gives the farmers and their conservative representatives too much power in Congress.

The power of the committees and their chairmen and the workings of the seniority rule have an important effect on Congress itself. *They scatter and disintegrate leadership.* Control of policy is divided among a score of little legislatures and powerful chairmen. There is little coordination among them. On the other hand, every parliamentary assembly must have some leadership and coordination. This function is served to some extent by the *party* leaders and organizations in the House and Senate.

Another result of the seniority rule is to intensify the contrast between presidential and congressional representation. Committee chairmen and other ranking members of committees have far more influence on legislation than the freshman legislator, no matter how capable the latter may be. The seniority rule in choosing chairmen automatically elevates the veterans to power regardless of their ability. At the same time this rule gives added influence to those states and districts that re-elect the same legislators time after time. Such states and districts, as noted above, are often politically immune to new ideas and fresh thinking. In many cases they are controlled by one party, as in the South, or by a city boss. The two-party areas where competition for votes is keen are likely to change representation often, and hence they do not have in Congress the weight they deserve.

THE HOUSE OF REPRESENTATIVES

The framers intended the Senate to be grossly unrepresentative of numbers, but this was to be offset by making the House of Representatives roughly reflect population. But even the lower chamber embodies serious distortions in the representative process. How can this be? The explanation is found in the way congressional districts are set up.

By act of Congress the membership of the House is set at 435. After each decennial census the Census Bureau submits a report showing the number of representatives each state is entitled to have in the House. (After the 1950 census, for example, California gained seven new Representatives and Pennsylvania lost three.) If a state gains or loses one or more representatives as a result of relative population changes, alterations in districts must ordinarily be made accordingly. The job of laying out the actual boundaries of the new districts falls to the *state legislatures*. At best, districting is a difficult job; districts should be as nearly equal in population as practicable, they should be fairly compact, and boundaries where possible should not cut across unified areas such as cities. In practice districting is immensely complicated because it is conducted in a *political* atmosphere, influenced by a variety of personal, group, and party forces who try to gain advantage by the districting process.

The gerrymander

One result of this political situation is *gerrymandering*. The term was coined a century and a half ago when Elbridge Gerry of Massachusetts carved out a district that had the shape of a salamander and was quickly dubbed a "Gerrymander." The term now means any attempt by a party or faction controlling a state legislature to draw the boundaries of districts in such a way that that party or group enjoys a *close but safe margin of support in many districts,* while the opposition's votes are *concentrated* in a *few districts* and thus wasted. Both parties freely indulge in this practice, one result being some fantastically shaped districts. "If you let your imagination go while thumbing through the maps of Congressional districts," Volta Torrey says, "you may readily fancy that you have seen a dumbbell, a tomahawk, a skull, a worm, the M.G.M. lion, and characters from the comic strips."[6]

Another result of the politics of districting is sometimes called the "silent gerrymander." A state legislature may perpetuate an existing inequitable arrangement simply by refusing to redistrict at all. A state gaining an increase in its quota of representatives may stand pat by electing its new representative "at large"—that is, the whole state becomes his dis-

[6] Volta Torrey, *You and Your Congress* (New York: William Morrow & Company, Inc., 1944), p. 31.

trict—hence keeping its existing districts intact. Also, a legislature may make no effort to adjust its districts to population shifts *within* the state. A city may double in population and still have only one representative, while rural

GEOGRAPHY IN POLITICS

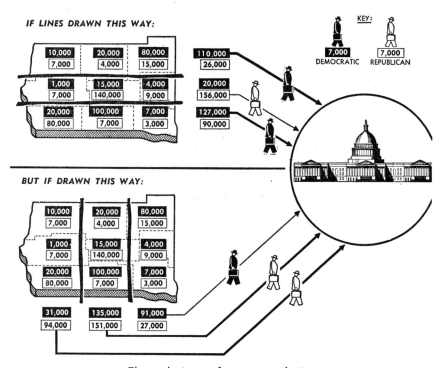

The technique of gerrymandering

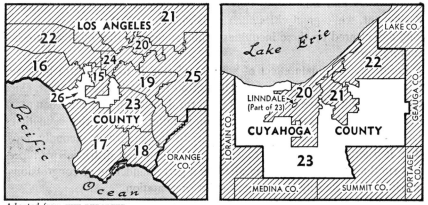

Adapted from THE REPORTER

—and a couple of results.

"It's A Crime How Those Big City Machines Operate"

From THE HERBLOCK BOOK (*Beacon Press*)

areas that have declined relatively in population may keep their past representation. Michigan's biggest district, for example, has 525,334 persons, its smallest only 178,251. To be sure, we have nothing as unrepresentative as the famous "rotten boroughs" of England, where one town, half submerged under water and numbering only fourteen voters, had two members in Parliament, while great cities such as Birmingham had none—but Britain long ago cleared up these inequities, while some fear that our own are becoming worse.

Politically, the main effect of gerrymandering is to give extra influence to representatives of *rural* areas. The reason for this is twofold: first, since population shifts have been mainly from rural to urban and suburban areas in recent decades (see Chapter 1), simple failure to redistrict strengthens rural representation at the expense of urban and suburban; secondly, most state legislatures, themselves reflecting gerrymandered districts, overrepresent rural areas, and hence any attempted gerrymandering of congressional districts will ordinarily exaggerate rural representation.

Another feature of the House of Representatives that has important political repercussions is the Rules Committee.

The Rules Committee—traffic cop or roadblock?

To get onto the floor of the House, most public bills must have a special rule or order from the Rules Committee. Every large assembly needs a traffic cop to direct the heavy stream of bills and resolutions. The members of the Rules Committee have this job—and much more. They can practically kill a bill by sitting on it indefinitely. They have power to amend measures as the price of permitting them on the floor. They can substitute a wholly new bill for the one framed by another legislative committee. They receive—and can smother—all proposals for amending the rules of the House. They provide most of the important bills with a rule that determines the procedure for handling each of the bills on the floor, and the nature of the rule greatly affects the prospects of the bill. As an example of the last power, the Rules Committee can give a bill a rule—sometimes called a "wide-open rule"—that opens the bill to crippling amendments from the floor, or it can provide a "gag rule" and prohibit such amendments.

In the words of an authority on Congress, the Rules Committee is "to a large degree the governing committee of the House . . . able to advance directly, or to retard indirectly, any measure which it selects for passage or slaughter."[7] If the committee were representative of the make-up of the House, such power might be safe in its hands. But it is not. Of recent years, at least, it has been dominated by veteran congressmen who have been re-elected time and time again regardless of the ebb and flow of national politics. After the 1936 election, for example, five anti-New Deal Democrats, representing rural constituencies, held the balance of power on the committee, and they were able to spike many of the measures of an Administration that had just won a sweeping popular victory. On the other hand, defenders of the Rules Committee argue that it does just what the framers of the Constitution wanted our system to do—it prevents the House from responding too readily to new popular majorities as represented by the President. They also point to the fact that a *discharge petition* can be used against the Rules Committee just as it can be against regular House committees, as noted above.

House procedure on the floor

Once a bill has passed through the committee stage, how is it handled on the floor of the House of Representatives? In contrast to the Senate, the large membership of the House makes imperative quick and orderly methods. Some of the important procedures are:

Calendars. Bills reported out of committee to the floor of the House are assigned to one of three main calendars. Finance measures—tax or appro-

---

[7] George B. Galloway, *Congress at the Crossroads* (New York: The Thomas Y. Crowell Company, 1946), p. 61.

priations, for example—are put on the *Union* calendar. All bills that are nonfiscal but still of a public character are placed on the *House* calendar. Private bills go on a *Private* calendar. These and other calendars serve as a traffic-directing system designed to give each bill its fair turn. But there are also various means for taking up bills out of their calendar order. For example, the rules may be suspended by a two-thirds vote on certain days; or important bills may be brought up at any time by the Rules Committee; or immediate action on a measure can be won by unanimous consent.

Committee of the Whole. This committee, made up of all 435 members of the House, is another means of expediting business. By sitting as the Committee of the Whole, members are able to operate with quicker procedures than are possible under the regular House rules. For example, a quorum in the Committee of the Whole is 100, compared with a majority of all the members (that is, 218) under the House rules. Very rarely does the whole House reject the recommendations of this committee, though it has the power to do so.

House cloture. In contrast to the smaller upper chamber, the House is too large to let everyone have his full say. Debate can be cut off simply by majority vote calling for the previous question. This ready method of closure makes filibusters impossible. Most speakers are allowed only a few minutes. Usually time is allotted to them by prior agreement between party leaders on both sides.

Voting. Ordinarily voting can be conducted quickly in the House by a viva-voce (voice) vote, or by a standing vote. Occasionally, though, some faction may want to put members on record as to how they stand on a controversial measure; in this case voting is conducted by the slower method of a vote by tellers (the members are checked off as they file past the Speaker's desk), or, upon demand of one-fifth of members present, by the still slower method of a roll call (the clerk calls each member by name).

The Speaker

The most important single leader in the House is the Speaker, who presides over its meetings. His formal authority is not what it was fifty years ago, when such Speakers as Thomas B. (Czar) Reed or Joe Cannon controlled committee assignments and wielded other important powers. Revolts of the rank and file stripped the Speaker of much of his old-time authority. Still, he is important in the work of the House. Without his recognition no person can speak on the House floor. He settles parliamentary disputes (with the help of an expert on parliamentary rules). He appoints members of select and conference committees (but not of standing committees), and in general directs the business of the House.

The Speaker's *informal* powers are greater than his formal powers—although much depends on his political talents. As leader of the majority party in the House, he deals with other national leaders in Congress and outside.

Unlike the Speaker of the British House of Commons, who is nonpartisan, the Speaker of the House of Representatives is openly a party leader. He is expected, subject to the rules of the game, to use the powers of his office to support the policies of his party. His decisions can be overruled by the House, whose agent he is, but such action is unlikely as long as he keeps the support of his own party. Formally elected by the whole House, the Speaker is actually chosen by the majority party, and he serves as liaison between his partisans and the President.

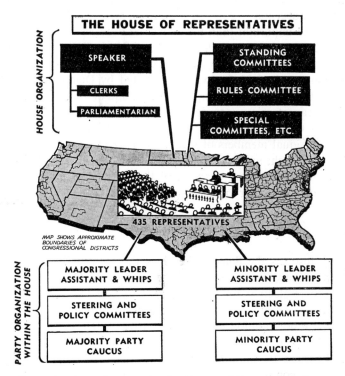

Organization of power in the House of Representatives.

Party officers and meetings

Next to the Speaker the most important *party* officer is the *majority floor leader,* who is chosen by the party caucus. He helps plan party strategy, confers with other party leaders, and tries to keep members of his party in line. The minority party elects a *minority floor leader,* who usually steps into the speakership when his party gains a majority of Representatives. Assisting each floor leader are the party *whips,* who serve as liaison between the leadership and the rank and file.

At the beginning of the session and occasionally thereafter, each party holds a *caucus* (or conference, as the Republicans call it). The caucus, composed of all the party's members in the House, meets privately to elect party officers, approve committee assignments, discuss important legislation, and perhaps try to agree on party policy. In theory, the caucus is the basic and directing party agency. In fact, the House caucus plays a small part in law-making. A decision of the Democratic caucus binds its members only when approved by two-thirds of the Democrats in the House. When it involves a matter of constitutional interpretation (as do most measures), or when different promises have been made back home (and all sorts of promises have been made), the decision is not binding at all. Republicans are not bound by any conference decision.

Hardly more important than the caucus are the *steering* or *policy committees,* made up of the party leadership, which do little steering but have some influence on party policy and tactics. The Democratic steering committee is composed of fifteen members elected by Democratic representatives from fifteen different geographical areas, and of six ex officio members. The Republican steering committee is composed of Republican members of the Rules Committee and of other top party and committee leaders. Although individual members of the steering committees are powerful, the committees, as such, are not. It has been observed that they rarely meet and never steer—one more example of the absence of *unified party* control in the House, a matter to which we will return.

THE SENATE

In many respects the Senate resembles the House. But it is a smaller body of only ninety-six members with six-year terms. Only one-third of the senators face re-election for any Congress so that the Senate, unlike the House, is always organized. It is an ever-continuing body.

The equal representation of the states in the Senate means that Nevada, with 160,000 inhabitants, has the same senatorial strength as New York, with ninety times that population. Regionally, it means that the Middle Atlantic states, comprising about one-fifth of the nation's population, hold one-sixteenth of the Senate's seats, while northern New England and the Rocky Mountain states gain at the expense of other sections. Since the sparsely settled areas are largely agricultural, the Senate tends to give special weight to the claims of the nation's farmers. In recent decades, however, the spread of urbanism in many hitherto rural areas has had the effect of making the Senate more reflective of urban opinion.

The President of the Senate is the Vice-President of the United States. Despite his exalted position, he has much less control over the Senate than the Speaker has over the House. He is not a member of the Senate—not quite a member of the exclusive senatorial club—and can vote only in case of a tie. He must recognize members in the order in which they rise. The Senate also elects from among its own membership a *president pro tempore* who presides in the absence of the Vice-President. He is of course really chosen by the majority party. As a member of the Senate, he can vote on all issues.

Party machinery in the Senate is somewhat similar to the House. There are party conferences (in the Senate both parties have given up the term "caucus"), majority and minority floor leaders, and party whips. In the Senate each party has a *policy committee* composed of the leaders of the party and theoretically responsible for the party's over-all legislative program. The Democratic policy committeemen are appointed by the Democratic floor leader and serve indefinitely, while Republican counterparts are

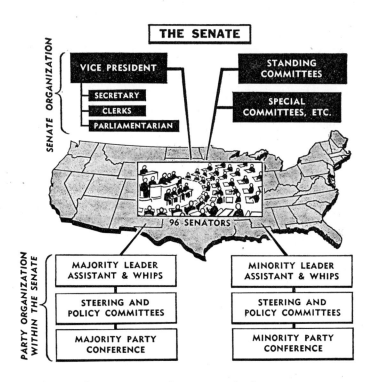

Organization of power in the Senate.

elected by the party conference for two-year terms. Unlike the House steering committees, the Senate's policy committees are formally provided for by law and each of them has a regular staff and a significant budget. While the Senate policy committees have some influence, they have not asserted strong legislative leadership or integrated party policy in the upper chamber.[8]

[8] Hugh A. Bone, "An Introduction to the Senate Policy Committees," *The American Political Science Review*, Vol. L, No. 2, June 1956, pp. 339-359.

Bills are reported to the Senate floor from standing committees in much the same fashion as in the House, but there are important differences in procedure on the two floors. The Senate has no powerful Rules Committee to expedite (or sometimes block) action. It has only two calendars, and these are usually followed rather closely. It uses its Committee of the Whole only for considering treaties. It has more time for debate and can carry on its business in a more informal manner. Measures in the Senate are normally debated in the order they are reported by committees or taken up for discussion by unanimous consent.

The filibuster

Another major difference between the two chambers is that debate is sharply limited in the House, and is almost unlimited in the Senate. Once a senator gains the floor, he has the right to it until he relinquishes it voluntarily or by exhaustion. This right to unlimited debate can be used by a small group of senators to *filibuster;* that is, *to delay the proceedings of the Senate in order to prevent a vote.* Debate in the Senate does not have to be germane. A senator may, if he wishes, read the *Congressional Record* at great length or, as the late Senator Long once did, entertain his colleagues with recipes for "Louisiana potlikker."

How can a filibuster be defeated? The majority can keep the Senate in continuous session in the hope that the filibustering senators will have to give up the floor. But if three or four senators cooperate, they can keep debate going almost indefinitely. They merely ask one another long questions that will permit their partners to take lengthy rests. As long as they keep on their feet, debate can be terminated only by *cloture* (sometimes called *closure*). Under the rule of cloture if sixteen members sign a petition, a day later the question of curtailing debate is put to a vote. If two-thirds of all the ninety-six senators (not merely of a quorum) vote for cloture, no senator may speak for more than one hour; then the motion before the Senate must be brought to a vote. Cloture can be applied to all motions except those calling for a change in the Senate rules. The exception is important, for it means that a filibuster to prevent a vote on a motion to change Senate rules curtailing filibusters could not be terminated by cloture.

The Senate has acted favorably on cloture petitions only four times since such a procedure was adopted in 1917. The mere threat of a filibuster is normally sufficient to secure the concessions demanded by dissident senators. Filibusters are especially effective near the closing days of a session when delay can be most injurious. The most spectacular filibusters and threats of them have been those of southern senators in order to block civil rights legislation. But northerners, liberals, and conservatives have used this device when it has suited their purpose. The all-time record for continuously holding the floor was achieved in 1953 by Senator Wayne

Morse of Oregon, who, with little help from "questioners," talked for 22 hours and 26 minutes.

Political role of the senators

The two houses of Congress are much alike in their concern with local and special-interest legislation, their intricate legislative and parliamentary procedure, their tendency toward voting by blocks and interest groups in defiance of party ties. Yet the upper chamber has a character all its own.

Senators are a somewhat different breed of political animal from the average representative. Most of the members of the upper house represent larger and more populous areas than do representatives. They have much more political elbow room. A representative, elected by a smaller constituency both geographically and numerically (in most cases), may feel somewhat cramped by the necessity of devoting himself to the needs of a few interest groups and a handful of local party bosses. A senator, on the other hand, can often find more chance to maneuver in representing a broader and more varied constituency. He is less exposed to the consequences of minute shifts in opinion among smaller groups.

Senators tend also to have important places in their state political parties. Sometimes they virtually dominate those parties, as in the case of Huey Long of Louisiana, Joseph Guffey of Pennsylvania, Nelson Aldrich of Rhode Island, or, more recently, Robert A. Taft of Ohio and Harry Byrd of Virginia. Their party position often rests partially on their control of federal patronage dispensed to the state, and their patronage power largely rests in turn on the constitutional provision requiring Senate confirmation of major presidential appointments.

This power of the Senate to confirm nominations is important *constitutionally* as a part of our checks and balances system. It is even more important *politically.* For under the system of *senatorial courtesy,* the individual senator has virtually a veto power over major appointments in his state (provided the President belongs to his party). The arrangement is a simple one. When presidential nominations are received in the Senate, they are referred openly to the committee having jurisdiction, and more quietly to the senator or senators from the state involved. The senator may, if he wishes, declare that the nominee is "personally obnoxious" to him, and the Senate almost always respects this declaration and rejects the appointment. Being personally obnoxious does not necessarily mean that the nominee is dishonest, or has insulted the senator on some occasion. It usually means that the nominee has not played ball with the senator *politically,* has been a member of a different personal organization in the state—perhaps that of the President. In any event, the upshot is that the President usually makes sure before submitting a nomination to the Senate (especially nominations for appointments located in the state, such as federal judgeships) that the nominee would not be *persona non grata* to his party's Senator or Senators from the state involved. The results are to give the Senators a greater role both in national administration and in state politics and to weaken national party leadership and discipline.

In 1938 President Roosevelt tried to by-pass this form of senatorial courtesy in nominating a federal judge in western Virginia. At the time, Carter Glass, a venerable member of the Senate, and his fellow Virginian, Harry Byrd, were involved in a political battle with Governor Price of Virginia. The governor and his political organization were supporting the President, while both Virginia Senators, although Democrats, were hostile to the President's New Deal policies, and maintained a political organization of their own. The President nominated a man who was believed to be in the governor's camp. Senator Byrd called the nomination personally obnoxious to both senators, and the Senate rejected it by a vote of 72 to 9. Mr. Roosevelt angrily charged that the Constitution gave only the Senate as a whole, not individual senators, the power of rejecting nominees. Senator Glass, equally aroused, replied that neither did the Constitution give the power over nominations to a state governor. At any rate, when the smoke of battle cleared away, senatorial courtesy remained supreme.

Another source of the senators' unique position is the fact that *two-thirds of the senators present* must give their consent before the President may ratify a treaty.

The Senate's power over treaties

The framers of the Constitution probably wanted the President and senators to sit down together and jointly work out a treaty. At any rate, Washington tried this experiment. The story goes that he visited the Senate to discuss a treaty with the southern Indians; when an obstreperous senator moved to commit the President's proposals to committee, Washington "started up in a violent fret" and said that, "this defeats every purpose of my coming here." No President since has conferred directly with the Senate as such—nonetheless, the senators are important in making treaties as well as ratifying them. The voices of influential senators are heard in foreign capitals as well as at home. Some of them can bring a good deal of wisdom and experience to bear in foreign policy making. Above all, the threat of Senate repudiation of a treaty makes it desirable for the President to solicit their views in advance. As a result, the Secretary of State usually works closely with the Foreign Relations Committee of the Senate and occasionally with the Foreign Affairs Committee of the House. Influential senators often undertake personal missions abroad and serve on delegations to the United Nations and other international bodies.

How important is the Senate's power over treaties? Secretary of State John Hay once complained that "a treaty entering the Senate is like a bull going into the arena; no one can say just how or when the final blow will fall—but one thing is certain—it will never leave the arena alive." The statistics suggest that Mr. Hay's remark was too severe. Despite the required two-thirds majority, the Senate has unconditionally approved about 900 of the approximately 1100 or more submitted to it; many of the remainder were passed with amendment or reservations. On the other hand, some of the rejected treaties were of supreme importance; for example, Senate disapproval of the Taft-Knox arbitration treaties of 1911-1912, the Treaty of Versailles (involving United States membership in the League of Nations), and the protocol for participating in the World Court, had a decided effect on the world role of the United States. And the *rejection* of treaties is not the whole issue.[9] On many occasions Presidents have failed to negotiate treaties, have modified treaty provisions in advance of Senate consideration, or have even recalled treaties already submitted, in the face of opposition from various Senators.

The Senate—and to a lesser degree the House—also influences foreign policy through investigations. A much publicized investigation of munitions makers by the Nye committee in 1930 undoubtedly intensified isolationist and pacifist feeling and helped pave the way for neutrality legislation in the 1930's. In 1951 a Senate investigation of the dismissal of General Douglas MacArthur by President Truman raised the whole question of American foreign policy in the Far East and forced the Administration to clarify its position. Occasionally congressional committees or subcommittees make junkets overseas to look into the operations of American agencies.

Until recently, at least, the Senate has been the congressional spokesman on foreign policy, and the House has been decidedly a junior partner. This situation was a result of both the Senate's treaty-ratifying authority and its veto power over presidential appointments of ambassadors, ministers, and other important officials. Partly because of the difficulty and unpredictability of the two-thirds treaty rule, partly because of pressure from the House, there has been growing resort to joint action by Senate and House. The Greek-Turkish aid program, the European recovery program, Point Four, the Indian grain program—to mention but a few—were undertaken by legislation rather than treaty. Some senators resent this "encroachment," as well as the President's frequent use of *executive agreements* (see Chapter 17), and periodically demands are heard in the Senate that no obligations be made except by formal treaty procedure.

The Senate as a court. Far less important than the treaty-making power, but still a factor in the Senate's unique role, is its function of sitting as a *court* in judgment upon officials who have been impeached. The initiative in impeachment proceedings is taken by the House of Representatives, which

[9] For contrasting views of the Senate treaty power see R. J. Dangerfield, *In Defense of the Senate* (Norman, Okla.: University of Oklahoma Press, 1933) and Kenneth Colegrove, *The American Senate and World Peace* (New York: Vanguard Press, 1944).

passes a resolution charging a civil officer (any federal official, including judges but not military officers or members of Congress) with "treason, bribery, or other high crimes and misdemeanors." A committee of representatives prosecutes the impeached official before the upper chamber. On such an occasion the Senate takes on a judicial mien—it issues writs, subpoenas witnesses, and administers oaths. (When a President is on trial, the Chief Justice of the United States presides.) A two-thirds vote is required for conviction; the penalty is removal from office and possible ineligibility for any other office. The Senate has sat as a court of impeachment on twelve occasions and has given a verdict of "Guilty" four times. The most dramatic trial —and the only one involving the Chief Executive—was that of President Andrew Johnson, who in 1868 escaped conviction by only one vote after a three-month sitting of the upper chamber.

Senate solidarity

In view of the Senate's political and constitutional powers, it is no wonder that the individual member is a person to be reckoned with. Even Presidents at times have had to defer to the wishes of some veteran senator who may be entrenched in a state political organization and at the same time be the chairman of a powerful legislative committee. Such a man looms large on the Washington scene. His speeches receive nationwide attention, his name comes to stand for a particular public policy, such as economy, military preparedness, social legislation, or a big air force.

The power of the individual senator is bolstered by arrangements in the upper chamber. In a sense the Senate is a mutual protection society. Each member tends to guard the rights and perquisites of his fellow senators—so that his own rights and perquisites will be protected in turn. Any legislative body is a close-knit social and occupational group, the members of which must learn to live with one another. This group feeling is especially strong in the Senate, with its small size and hallowed traditions. Senatorial solidarity often cuts across lines of party and issue. Washington correspondents have frequently reported that two senators may attack each other in vehement language on the floor, only to be seen a short time later strolling arm in arm in the corridors outside. Such a sense of solidarity means that the Senate may show a united face against some outside force, such as the President, that seems to be challenging its privileges and powers.

Two other factors lie behind a senator's sense of authority and independence. One is his six-year term of office. Members who win election four times—and many of them accomplish this feat—see six presidential terms come and go. No wonder such senators gain a sense of permanence and position even when dealing with the President. Perhaps more important is the right of unlimited debate. The *filibuster* not only symbolizes the power of the individual senator—it also provides a basis of that power. One senator, moreover, can easily disrupt the bills and business of his fellow members by spiking efforts to expedite action, by the simple means of shouting "I object" every time the presiding officer calls for unanimous consent to a particular motion. "Live and let live" might be the Senate's motto—and one that would help explain why it has become one of the most powerful and yet unpredictable assemblies in the world.

WHEN SENATE AND HOUSE DISAGREE

As we have seen, the Senate and House were originally set up to represent sharply different interests and attitudes. The upper house was to be a small chamber of men elected indirectly by the people and holding long, overlapping terms. The House of Representatives, elected *in toto* every two years, was to be the direct, strong organ of the people. Three important changes have brought the two bodies closer together. Senators are now directly elected by the voters. Gerrymandering and other factors have made the House unduly representative of rural and conservative interests. And the spread of urbanism has made the Senate more representative of urban interests. Originally, the framers thought of the Senate as a conservative check on the radical House. It would be hard to say today that the upper chamber tends to be more conservative or more liberal than the lower.

On the other hand, the framers' hope that the two houses would speak for *different* interests has been realized. The differences between the size and nature of the electoral districts in each house, between the length of terms of senators and representatives, between the internal mechanisms in each chamber, between the political contexts in which they operate, inevitably bring about sharp disagreements between Senate and House over policy. Such differences, moreover, can create an acute problem because each chamber has a veto on the other. Only if both houses pass an absolutely identical measure can it become law. How do the legislators solve this problem?

The answer is the *conference committee*. If neither house will accept the other's bill, a special committee is appointed, usually composed of three to five members from each chamber, to settle the differences. The proceedings of this committee—not open to the public—are usually a shrewd and elaborate bargaining process. Concessions must be made not only to each chamber but to the more powerful groups within the chambers. Brought back to the respective chambers, the conference report can be accepted or it can be rejected (often with further negotiations ordered), but it cannot be *amended*. Each set of conferees must convince its colleagues that any concessions made to the other house were on trivialities and nothing basic in their own version of the bill was surrendered.

How much leeway should the conference committee have? Ordinarily the conferees are expected to stay somewhere between the alternatives set by the different versions; for example, if the House should set a penalty of ten years in prison for some offense, and the Senate five years, the conference committee would hardly come up with life imprisonment. But on many matters there is no clear middle ground and conferees are sometimes accused of "exceeding their instructions" and producing a new measure. Indeed, the conference committee has even been called a "third house of Congress" that arbitrarily revises Senate and House policy in secret session. Despite such criticism, however, some kind of conference committee is indispensable to the workings of a bicameral legislature such as Congress.

Summary

1. The main power of Congress is legislative, but it has a number of other functions.

2. The main work of Congress is conducted in committees. Election of committee chairmen by the seniority rule puts power in the hands of veteran members of Congress.

3. The two chambers are much the same in general structure and function. Strong central party leadership is lacking in both.

4. Important differences between the two chambers involve their size, electoral districts, length of members' terms, the Rules Committee in the House and the filibuster in the Senate.

5. Differences between the two houses in law-making are ironed out by conference committees.

CONGRESS IS COMPOSED OF POLITICIANS, ALL of whom were successful in winning office. As politicians, the senators and representatives live amid the pulls and pressures of their constituents, powerful interest groups, party leaders in and out of Congress, the President, the opinions of the people everywhere, and many other forces. To understand Congress, we must see its institutions and procedures as part of what has well been called the "legislative struggle." Let us look at this struggle in terms of the pressures, powers, and problems that affect a typical congressman—Representative Smith—in his work on Capitol Hill.

MR. SMITH GOES TO WASHINGTON

When Mr. Smith leaves his home for Washington, he carries with him political debts and political hopes. In a way, his biggest debt is to the majority of voters in his district who elected him to office. His chief hope is to keep the support of a majority of the voters and thus to stay in office. How can he do this? It is not a simple matter of living up to the platform for which his supporters presumably voted. He does not really know just who his supporters are, or just what policies they favored. He does not really know how to keep their backing. Conditions will change. Some of his supporters will turn against him; others will return to the great ranks of the nonvoters.

Represent whom?

The chances are that Mr. Smith will work most actively for those who most directly helped him win the election. As we have seen (Chapter 14), his victory in that election did not seem to hinge chiefly on his attitude toward broad national issues, for the voters were not occupied with such issues, or their views were amorphous and diffused. If they had been interested in national problems, Mr. Smith's job of staying in office might be easier, for he could simply vote "right" on bills as they came up. As it is, Mr. Smith, like most of his fellow legislators, decides that

16

Congressmen

at

work

one way to stay in office is to maintain close and friendly contacts with the leaders of the personal organization that he set up in his campaign.

Some of his most effective support came from *leaders* of *organized groups* in his district—especially of occupational interest groups. He owes a debt to these persons, and he finds in Washington that he is expected to pay that debt. The associations that he dealt with locally—the labor organizations, or the Farm Bureau Federation, or the American Legion—are well represented in Washington, as we know, and their legislative agents are quick to arrange a meeting with Mr. Smith and acquaint him with the interest group's program.

9:00—"Congressman arrives at office."

While the organization may have taken positions on broad national issues, such as foreign policy or taxation, it is mainly concerned with specific bills conferring benefits on its members. On these bills—which are little known to his constituents as a whole—Mr. Smith is expected to vote favorably. His support of such bills is his means of paying a political debt, and he knows that his actions will be reported to the organization's members back home.

9:01—"Telephone rings. Talks, signs mail."

Then there are the *local party leaders*. Mr. Smith probably does not have a great sense of obligation to the party organization in his district, for a united organization hardly exists. But he does owe a debt to a number of individual party leaders back home who personally worked for him and used their party contacts in his behalf. These local party leaders are not, for the most part, concerned with national legislation, but they are greatly interested in patronage and favors. They look to Mr. Smith for both. As a freshman Representative, he does not control much patronage in Washington, but he is allotted certain jobs in the congressional establishment—an elevator operator, perhaps, or messenger—and he probably can find other jobs in the administrative departments. More important are the federal positions held in his district: postmasters, tax collectors, United States marshals, federal attorneys, and other positions not fully covered by

9:58—"Rushes off to committee meeting."

10 to 12—"Hearing. At noon goes to floor."

1:00—"Starts lunch. Call-bell rings."

A day in the life

nonpartisan civil service laws. Of course, Mr. Smith has little or no patronage if the President belongs to the opposition party. And he may have to share the patronage with one or two Senators. As it turns out, the scramble for jobs is one of the most trying aspects of his work. Every time he gives out a position, he suspects glumly that he is making nine enemies and one ingrate.

Mr. Smith's loyalty to some of the local party officials is not necessarily a loyalty to the national party organization. To be sure, he keeps in touch with party leaders *in* Congress, as noted below. And he must clear his patronage through the national chairman of his party, but such clearance is almost routine. Aside from the national party chairman, he sees very little of the party organization in Washington, for the national committee rarely meets or tries to set policy. Occasionally, Mr. Smith hears from the national chairman on a legislative matter that the party considers important. But he feels small sense of obligation. The national party gave him little if any help in the campaign, and he knows that voting as his district seems to want him to vote will probably win him more friends than following the national party line.

As a congressman, Mr. Smith keeps all these considerations in mind. This does not mean, however, that he is merely a calculating machine, the keys of which are punched by various forces. For Mr. Smith brings to Congress certain political convictions of his own. He may feel that labor has too much power,

3:00—"Page brings note. Lady outside."

4:00—"At office, sees home-state students."

4:15—"Call to floor again."

7 to 12—"Does homework."

6:30—"Dinner with wife." " 12:00—"And so to bed."
Roy Doty *in* THE NEW YORK TIMES

of a Congressman.

that big business should be curbed, that the cost of government should be less. He is swayed by certain ideas. No matter what pressures converge on him in Washington, Mr. Smith neither can nor wishes to shake off the ideas that have been part of his environment since birth. In short, Mr. Smith's official acts are not simply a result of the pressures *on* him. They are also a result of the pressures *in* him.[1]

Errand running

Mr. Smith knows also that one way to win the support of his constituents is by doing countless individual favors. His office is well set up for this task. He has the services of several secretaries and stenographers, as well as a full-time legislative aide. Most important, government agencies are eager to respond to Mr. Smith's requests. Often the people who ask his help are constituents who are dealing with some agency. Perhaps a businessman wants to know how to apply for a government contract, or a veteran wants to straighten out his pension situation. Mr. Smith is glad to help out. In order to serve as a sort of Washington representative for his constituents he must know how to get cooperation from administrative officials. Usually such cooperation is quickly forthcoming, however, for the administrators know that they depend on the good will of congressmen for annual appropriations.

Mr. Smith finds that he himself must do much of the errand running. One Representative has complained that:

A congressman has become an expanded messenger boy, an employment agency, getter-out of the Navy, Army, marines, ward heeler, wound healer, trouble shooter, law explainer, bill finder, issue translator, resolution interpreter, controversy oil pourer, gladhand extender, business promoter, convention goer, civic ills skirmisher, veterans' affairs adjuster, ex-serviceman's champion, watchdog for the underdog, sympathizer with the upper dog, namer and kisser of babies, recoverer of lost baggage, soberer of delegates, adjuster for traffic violators, voters straying into Washington and into toils of the law, binder up of broken hearts, financial wet nurse, good samaritan, contributor to good causes —there are so many good causes—cornerstone layer, public building and bridge dedicator, ship christener—to be sure he does get in a little flag waving—and a little constitutional hoisting and spread-eagle work, but it is getting harder every day to find time to properly study legislation—the very business we are primarily here to discharge, and that must be done above all things.[2]

There is, of course, a brighter side to the picture. In the era of big government, which often seems cold and impersonal, the congressman can play a

[1] See S. K. Bailey, *Congress Makes a Law* (New York: Columbia University Press, 1950), pp. 192-193.

[2] Quoted in Galloway, *Congress at the Crossroads*, p. 61.

vital humanizing role. He can be the mediator between the citizen and the bureaucrats. "One of the things that hold the vast area of the United States together," an English observer has said, "is the belief that the political machinery provides a means whereby local and personal interests and sentiments are really taken into account in Washington."[3] But it is not easy for Mr. Smith to be so philosophical. He has come to Washington to *legislate*— and sometimes he feels that lawmaking is one of the least of his duties.

Congressional prerogatives

Despite these difficulties Mr. Smith probably finds his job a congenial one. He is an important person in his district and an influential politician in his party. The newspapers pay him some attention, although it may often be critical. In Washington he is only one among many legislators, but there are compensations.

Representatives and senators are paid $22,500 a year. (The Speaker and Vice-President receive $35,000 and the use of a fancy automobile.) In addition each member gets an allowance for travel, for stationery, and for help to staff the office which the government also provides. This is not to say that most congressmen have no financial worries. On the contrary the financial obligations of maintaining two residences and the expenses incurred in doing his job often exceed what he gets from the government. When these expenses are added to those of campaigning and of meeting all the "touches" to which congressmen are exposed, it is a rare member of the legislature who can live on his salary. Congressmen by law determine their own salaries. They have been reluctant to increase their pay; but on the basis of the recommendations of a presidential commission, an increase was recently voted to the amount stated above. Congress also has in recent years established a contributing retirement system which gives some measure of security to congressmen who retire either voluntarily or as a result of the compulsion of the polls.

Congressmen also enjoy the *postal frank*. They may use the mails without charge in order to write to their constituents and to send out literature. This privilege can be a decided advantage to incumbent congressmen in their campaigns.

Congressmen have absolute *immunity* for whatever they say on the floor of the Congress, before a congressional committee, or in connection with congressional business. They may not be sued for libel or slander nor in any way called to question before any court. Here is absolute freedom of speech. Each chamber may, however, discipline its own members who abuse this privilege. And the voters can always make known their disapproval.

Congressmen are *privileged from arrest* during attendance at Congress and in going to and from Congress except in cases of treason, felony, and

[3] D. W. Brogan, *The American Character* (New York: Alfred A. Knopf, Inc., 1944), p. 123.

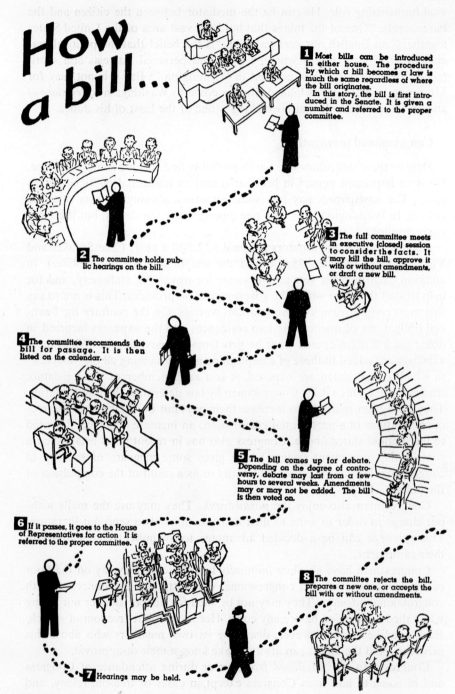

How a bill...

1 Most bills can be introduced in either house. The procedure by which a bill becomes a law is much the same regardless of where the bill originates.

In this story, the bill is first introduced in the Senate. It is given a number and referred to the proper committee.

2 The committee holds public hearings on the bill.

3 The full committee meets in executive (closed) session to consider the facts. It may kill the bill, approve it with or without amendments, or draft a new bill.

4 The committee recommends the bill for passage. It is then listed on the calendar.

5 The bill comes up for debate. Depending on the degree of controversy, debate may last from a few hours to several weeks. Amendments may or may not be added. The bill is then voted on.

6 If it passes, it goes to the House of Representatives for action. It is referred to the proper committee.

7 Hearings may be held.

8 The committee rejects the bill, prepares a new one, or accepts the bill with or without amendments.

Adapted from JOURNAL *of the National Education Association*

12 If the bill is passed by the second body but contains major differences, either house may request a conference committee The conferees meet and try to reconcile their differences. Representing both parties, five conferees are usually appointed from each house.

SENATE

HOUSE

11 It goes before the entire body, is debated and voted on.

13 Generally, they reach an agreement. They report back to their respective houses. The report is accepted or rejected.

10 The Rules Committee is one of the most powerful of the committees in the House of Representatives. After a bill has been recommended for passage by the committee to which it was referred, the Rules Committee can block it or clear it for debate before the entire House.

RULES COMMITTEE

14 If the report is accepted by both houses, the bill is signed by the Speaker of the House, the President of the Senate, and is sent to the President of the United States.

9 The committee recommends the bill for passage. It is listed on the calendar and is sent to the Rules Committee.

...Becomes a law.

15 The President may sign or veto the bill within 10 days. If he doesn't sign within 10 days and Congress is still in session, the bill automatically becomes law. If Congress has adjourned before the 10 days have elapsed and the President has not signed the bill, it does not become law. This is known as a "pocket veto." If the President returns the bill with a veto message, it may still become law if passed by a two-thirds majority in each house.

breach of the peace. This privilege does not cover a summons in a civil suit and, since the abolition of imprisonment for debt, has lost most of its significance. Congressmen are subject to criminal laws in the same manner as other individuals.

Congressmen enjoy a good deal of *legislative assistance*. The Legislative Reference Service, consisting of recognized experts in a variety of national problem areas, can supply data to congressmen quickly and authoritatively. Over 50,000 inquiries are handled by the service every year. The Office of Legislative Counsel provides bill-drafting services to senators and representatives who need such help.

THE SMITH BILL RUNS THE GANTLET

The diagram on pp. 414-415 indicates the formal stages a bill must go through to become law. But the *political* as well as the procedural aspects of lawmaking must be kept in view. Let us suppose that Representative Smith decided to sponsor a bill.

It was not until his third term of office that Mr. Smith was able to sponsor legislation on which he had set his heart from the beginning. This was a bill raising and broadening minimum wage standards. Usually even a third-termer would not have the chance to sponsor an important piece of legislation requested by the President and party leaders. Mr. Smith, a member of the Education and Labor Committee, got the chance because the chairman of the committee was a southerner opposed to the bill, the next ranking member was ill, and two other senior members did not want to commit themselves to specific changes in minimum-wage standards until a later time.[4]

The first step was a meeting with the President. Mr. Smith and several other members of the committee had a 15-minute interview with him in the White House. The President, who did most of the talking, offered no suggestions on the details of the proposed legislation; he simply asked that the coverage of the bill be as broad as possible. He also requested that the committee work closely with the Secretary of Labor and with the chief of the Wage and Hours and Public Contracts Division, so that smooth relations might exist between Congress and the executive on this matter. After the exchange of a few pleasantries, the congressmen left.

Drumming up support

Mr. Smith was glad to sponsor the bill because one of his campaign issues had been minimum wages. But now that he was ready to champion it, he

---

[4] This description is drawn chiefly from Stephen K. Bailey, *Congress Makes a Law* (New York: Columbia University Press, 1950), and J. M. Burns, *Congress on Trial*, Chapter 5, "The Story of Three Bills." Descriptions of the handling of actual bills will be found in chapters *17, 25, 26, and* below.

found little interest in the matter back home. Local labor leaders and liberal groups endorsed the proposed legislation, of course, but without creating much of a stir. Mr. Smith wanted publicity. He saw that he himself would have to create it. At his suggestion, a committee of liberals, union leaders, and small businessmen began a campaign for the bill in his district. Letters appeared in newspapers. Resolutions were adopted calling on Mr. Smith for action. Hundreds of people signed petitions demanding a raise in minimum standards. At the height of the campaign Mr. Smith appeared at a mass meeting and promised to fight for the bill. He returned to Washington with their cheers still ringing in his ears.

The next step was the difficult one of writing the bill. Mr. Smith showed a rough draft to representatives from the Department of Labor—and found that they had already drawn up their own bill, complete with preamble and a dozen clauses. Mr. Smith was disturbed to find that the Administration bill, as the Labor Department people called it, went much further than his. For example, Mr. Smith wanted to exempt from the bill businesses employing less than seven people; the Administration bill made it five. An inconclusive argument ensued. It was agreed to hold another meeting in a week.

During the next few days Mr. Smith got some telegrams from the union leaders in his district in support of the Administration bill. Surprised and disturbed, Mr. Smith telephoned them to ask why they had changed their positions. They answered that they had talked the matter over with their national headquarters. At the next meeting the Labor Department officials brought with them two national union leaders and a representative from the White House. Mr. Smith was assured by his visitors that the Administration draft was supported by the President and by the national A.F.L.-C.I.O. He soon gave in on some of the major points. He insisted, however, that the new compromise draft retain one of his provisions exempting fruit canners (who were fairly strong in his district) from any change in hours standards. He warned that unless this provision was kept in, he would not sponsor the bill. He got his way on this matter. After enlisting the help of the Office of the Legislative Counsel in giving the bill its parliamentary polish, Mr. Smith introduced the measure into the lower chamber by placing it in the hopper on the clerk's desk near the Speaker's rostrum.

The clerk, acting for the Speaker, promptly gave the bill a number—H.R. 2102—and referred it to the Committee on Education and Labor. Then ensued a delay of six weeks that considerably irritated Mr. Smith. The trouble was—and Mr. Smith knew it—that the chairman did not want to act on the bill. First the bill got lost somewhere in the chairman's office. When finally found, the bill had to wait while the chairman held hearings on some minor measures. It was only after Mr. Smith appealed to the Speaker and majority leader, and after the Labor Department asked help from the President, that the chairman finally announced that hearings on the bill would commence.

Running interference

Meanwhile Mr. Smith was busy making plans for presenting the case for his bill. (He knew that the chairman would see to it that the bill's opponents had a chance to speak.) To lead his parade of witnesses he enlisted the Secretary of Labor, the head of the A.F.L.-C.I.O., and the senator who had introduced a companion bill to H.R. 2102 in the upper chamber. As a good strategist, Mr. Smith knew that the hearings should not give the impression that labor was for the bill and business and agriculture opposed. So he tried to split the opposition. Fearing that the big organizations of farmers employing hired hands might oppose the bill, he got a promise from the National Farmers Union that it would send an official to endorse H.R. 2102. He wanted also to enlist business support. Knowing that some small manufacturers in his district feared low-wage competition in the South, he asked them to urge their national association of small businessmen to take sides. But the national association had a number of influential members from the South in its ranks, so Mr. Smith was unable to get its support. Instead some representatives of northern industry agreed to testify.

At first the hearings went splendidly for Mr. Smith and his bill. The "big names" spoke briefly for H.R. 2102, and committee members did not dare to cross-examine them too vigorously. Then trouble developed. After the Farmers Union spokesman endorsed the bill, the chairman called on representatives of the other major farm organizations, who stated that the great majority of farmers did not want an increase in minimum wages because it would raise their labor costs. By asking leading questions, the chairman brought out the fact that his witnesses spoke for many more farmers than did Mr. Smith's. That was bad enough—but then another committee member attacked one of Mr. Smith's liberal businessmen as a former member of two Communist-dominated organizations. Mr. Smith was glad that he was able immediately afterwards to present the president of a World War II veterans' organization in favor of the bill. His hope of gaining business support was further dashed, however, when the National Association of Manufacturers advanced some amendments that—in Mr. Smith's mind at least—would cripple the bill.

The hearings lasted six days. Despite frequent clashes between committeemen and witnesses—and sometimes among committeemen themselves—the hearings played a valuable role. Many useful suggestions were made. A great deal of important economic and statistical material was put into the record. And virtually every interest group involved was able to offer views orally or in writing. True, over half the committee members were not present most of the time, but they could consult later the voluminous printed record.

Following the open hearings the committee met in secret *executive session*. Mr. Smith had already begun to count noses. He knew that of the thirteen committeemen of his own (majority) party, eight favored the bill, three opposed it, and two were doubtful. Of the eight members of the minority party, five seemed hostile to the bill, one friendly, and two on the fence. Mr. Smith knew that he needed a majority of at least eleven—and twelve or thirteen would be safer—in reporting out the bill, for Congress rarely approves a bill without a favorable committee report. The first executive session, where the bill was discussed section by section, gave him a chance to see just where his fellow committeemen stood. Soon afterwards he conferred with the majority leader, who then induced the President to invite to lunch two of the doubtful members of the majority party and two of the straddlers—but not the chairman, who was considered beyond hope. At this luncheon the President did not try to pressure his guests, but he made his own position clear, described the need for party unity, and incidentally agreed to straighten out some patronage matters that were troubling one or two of the Representatives.

Mr. Smith also saw to it—with the help of labor and liberal organizations —that the erring members were deluged with letters and telegrams in behalf of the bill. Most of these communications came from within the members' districts. The combined approach worked. At the next executive session three of the President's four guests were generally in favor of the measure. The real danger now was the adoption of crippling amendments. While announcing their support of the general principles of the bill, member after member demanded amendments that would exempt certain areas, occupations, or classes of workers. Helplessly Mr. Smith watched while his colleagues logrolled with one another, each supporting another's amendment so that his own amendment would go through in turn. By the end of three such meetings the bill was a tattered remnant of what it had been. Indeed, it had been so watered down that in the final committee vote the bill received the support of half the opposition party members and of all Mr. Smith's fellow party members, including even the chairman.

Into the House

For a time Mr. Smith considered dropping the whole matter. He was reminded, however, that the bill might be strengthened on the floor of the House, and perhaps in the Senate too. He already had a favorable committee report before the House. He decided that the next step was to try to get favorable action from the Rules Committee.

Here Mr. Smith's bill came up against one of its biggest hurdles. The Rules Committee was composed of veteran Representatives, a majority of whom were members of the majority party but often sided with the minority. Not only did Mr. Smith need a go-ahead sign from Rules, but he also wanted a rule that would prevent his bill from getting loaded down with amendments during House debate. For three weeks Rules refused to act at all, but when Mr. Smith and other representatives began to talk about prying a rule out by a *discharge petition* (requiring signatures of a majority of the members), the Rules Committee granted a rule. Under the terms of the rule, debate was to take four hours, with time divided between proponents and opponents of H.R. 2102. The rule also provided, however, that anyone on the floor could offer amendments.

Mr. Smith was floor manager of the bill; with the majority leader he worked out a schedule that allotted thirty minutes to himself and brief five-minute speeches to other supporters of H.R. 2102. The rest of the time was parceled out by minority party leaders to opponents of the bill. The Speaker was to use these two lists in recognizing Representatives wishing to speak on the bill. Meanwhile Mr. Smith was busy lining up support. He arranged with a White House official for a formal message from the President endorsing the objectives of the bill and asking for stronger provisions. Labor organizations set up a nationwide Committee on Social Rights which issued propaganda for the bill. Lobbyists visited Representatives in their offices and buttonholed them in the corridors. Delegations of businessmen and workers arrived in Washington from the lawmakers' districts. A torrent of mail descended on Capitol Hill. The opposition was equally active.

By the day of the debate almost all the representatives had made up their minds; the real question was whether the bill would be amended to death and abandoned. The worst threat was an amendment that would have excluded from H.R. 2102 all employees involved in the raising, processing, or delivering of farm or related products. This catchall, which Mr. Smith knew would cut out the essence of the bill, had the backing of a formidable group of representatives from farm states, the opposition party, and low-wage areas. Only by inducing the Speaker to leave the rostrum and make a personal appeal on the floor, and by warning the farm Representatives that labor would vote down agricultural legislation unless they supported H.R. 2102, was Mr. Smith able to save the bill. The final threat came on a motion to *recommit* the bill to committee—in effect a motion to kill it. When this attempt narrowly failed, the members voted overwhelmingly in favor of the measure.

Mr. Smith's long battle was over—or perhaps half over, for H.R. 2102 would still have to clear the Senate. The sponsor of the bill in the Senate would be fortunate, in view of the minority devices in that chamber discussed above, if he encountered no more hurdles than had Mr. Smith in the House.

CONGRESSMEN AS INVESTIGATORS

Both senators and representatives are on a constant quest for facts, ideas, and advice. They need information and opinion in making laws, in publicizing governmental activities, in attacking the other party or other political officials, in overseeing the administrative agencies. They obtain their information from committee hearings, the President, administrative agencies, or other congressmen, interest groups, letters written by constituents, their own Library of Congress and its Legislative Reference Service, and from many other sources.

Why Congress investigates

Hearings by standing committees or by their subcommittees are probably the most important source of information and opinion. Such inquiries provide an arena where experts can submit their views and data, statements and statistics can be entered into the record, and congressmen can quiz a wide variety of witnesses. When an important and controversial bill is under consideration, hearings will last for weeks, and a host of administrative officials, lobbyists, technical experts, interested citizens, and members of Congress will testify. Sometimes the hearings receive front-page billing in newspapers throughout the land; more often they are little publicized unless a well-known person is testifying. Congressmen cannot go to all the hearings, of course, but by means of verbatim records of the hearings they can follow the proceedings as they wish.

Committees investigate not only to collect facts and opinions. Many inquiries are largely *political* in nature—they are designed to help or hinder some bill or party or official. Members of Congress may have information already at hand, but they know that the effective publicizing of those facts before reporters and fellow congressmen may dramatize existing evils and the need for reform. For example, many of the bad social conditions "revealed" by Congress in the 1930's were well documented in studies and reports; but the "exposés" in Washington helped create the right political climate to allow Congress to act. Hearings, in short, are often directed toward the people in order that public opinion can be mobilized.

Investigations by regular committees have another purpose—the *overseeing* of administration. A committee can summon any administrative official, from Cabinet officer to stenographer, to testify in public or private hearings. Some officials greatly fear these inquiries; they dread the loaded questions of hostile congressmen; they know the likelihood that some administrative error in their agency may be uncovered and publicized. Both the congressman and the administrator suffer from certain handicaps. The congressman is usually not expert in the field (although some members become highly expert from years of service on a particular committee), and he has a thousand other problems on his mind. The official knows his field, but he may not see the broader problems, and he feels ill at ease among unsympathetic legislators.[5] Despite the misunderstandings and abuses that often arise, the routine investigations of administration are an important means of checking administrative action. In this sense investigations are an important part of the system of checks and balances.

Under the Constitution Congress has major investigatory powers. Private

[5] Young, *This Is Congress,* pp. 228-229.

witnesses can be subpoenaed and required to testify. If the investigation is reasonably connected with matters over which Congress has power, and the questions are pertinent to the purposes of the investigation, failure of witnesses to answer questions may result in punishment for contempt of Congress. Procedures are more flexible, however, than in a court of law. Counsel, cross-examination of witnesses, presentation of the accuser are privileges and not rights. Since the purpose of an investigation is to gain information, not to prosecute, persons before such committees are not, legally speaking, in jeopardy of life or limb. The elaborate safeguards of the judicial process are not always needed, and if required they might deny essential information to Congress and country.

"Grand Inquisitions"?

We have been talking about the day-to-day inquiries conducted by regular standing committees or their subcommittees. Special investigations made by standing, special or select committees to probe particular questions present many of the same problems as the more routine inquiries, but in exaggerated form. Such special investigations have long been undertaken by Congress. The first one took place in 1793, after General St. Clair's military expedition against the Indians had ended in disaster. Some representatives wanted to let President Washington look into the causes of the failure. But the House, taking matters into its own hands, set up a special investigating committee to act for Congress.

Since that occasion, many famous investigations have taken place. Through them, corruption in public office has been repeatedly exposed, infringements of civil liberties uncovered, harmful banking, stock exchange, and utility practices publicized, bureaucratic practices checked, "un-American" practices denounced. A famous recent investigating committee was the Truman Committee, which, during World War II, probed into waste and inefficiency, made many constructive suggestions, and helped put its chairman into the White House. Special investigating committees have all the powers of standing committees except that they normally may not introduce legislation. At the same time, they usually enjoy far greater publicity—and investigations thrive on publicity. Such committees operate directly in the spotlight; often proceedings are covered by newsreel and television cameras and reported by a host of newsmen.

Yet right here is where the danger lies. So eager are the investigators for sensational results that they often permit abuses that bring the congressional power of investigation into disrepute. This is nothing new. As far back as the Seventeenth Congress, a committee was criticized for excessive zeal—probing the executive, it "pointed out little items, sniffed about dark corners, peeped behind curtains and under beds, and exploited every cupboard of the Executive household with a mousing alacrity, not so eager to correct abuses as to collect campaign material for damaging some candidate."[6] Recently some investigators have so zealously sought publicity that they have indulged in defamation of character, bullying and mistreatment of witnesses, and outright partisanship. Some of them have conducted mere fishing expeditions in the hope that something might turn up.

Members of Congress themselves are disturbed about the situation. One senator has warned that "unless Congress reforms its methods of conducting investigations, unless it puts some limits of responsibility both upon the interrogation of witnesses and upon the type of testimony which witnesses are allowed to give—unless, indeed, it adopts a wholly new and more judicious attitude—one of the great and important instruments of the legislative process will be destroyed."[7] Another senator has reminded his colleagues that the investigative function is valuable but also a "delicate instrument which cannot withstand the jolts and jars, the stress and strain of rude partisan handling."[8]

An end to "Congressional Circuses"?

Quite naturally, certain reforms have been suggested. Some of these involve internal procedure. It has been proposed that persons attacked be given the right to appear personally before the committee involved, that the committee be compelled to subpoena witnesses when requested, that accused individuals be allowed to cross-examine witnesses personally or through counsel. Some time ago, Representative Bender of Ohio proposed new rules that would regulate the conduct of investigating committees. But Congress has failed to act. Its hesitation is due in part to its fear that investigations might become hedged around by so many rigid restrictions that they would lose their usefulness.

Another proposal would delegate the handling of investigations to bodies outside Congress. It is argued that congressmen are overburdened as it is, and that investigations outside Congress might be more objective and less likely to lead to criticism of the lawmakers. Some Americans have looked enviously on the British royal commissions which, composed both of members of Parliament and outside experts, have led to many governmental reforms and continue to enjoy tremendous prestige in Great Britain. Many congressmen, however, would fear to give the President the power to appoint members of commissions, for

Courtesy THE NEW YORK TIMES and Tom Little

---

[6] Quoted in Irving M. Ives, "In Place of Congressional 'Circuses,'" *The New York Times Magazine*, August 27, 1950.

[7] Scott W. Lucas, "Congressional Hearing: a Plea for Reform," *The New York Times Magazine*, March 19, 1950.

[8] Ives, *loc. cit.*

they regard their investigative power jealously and want to keep it independent of the executive.

Fortunately, we may be slowly perfecting a method of investigation that embodies the best features of royal commissions and congressional inquiries. This is the *mixed* commission or committee, composed both of congressmen and outsiders. The Temporary National Economic Committee, an outstanding investigatory body of the 1930's, was made up of six congressmen and six representatives of departments and agencies: its chairman was a senator and its vice-chairman a representative. Equally successful were the two Commissions on Organization of the Executive Branch of the Government, under the chairmanship of former President Herbert Hoover. Each commission had twelve members: four persons (including two representatives) chosen by the Speaker of the House, four (including two senators) chosen by the president of the Senate, and four (including two members of the executive department) chosen by the President of the United States.

Such a procedure may come into wider use as the years go by. It provides a balanced group, fairly equally divided between parties, aware of the problems of both Congress and President but wholly responsible to neither branch of government, and enjoying great prestige in the nation. It must not be concluded, however, that investigating bodies can ever be taken wholly out of politics. Politicians in all parties will always make capital out of information that is unearthed. This is the way it should be in a free society. The most we can do is surround the investigatory process with proper safeguards to protect the rights of individuals, to cut down as much as possible on abuses and unfairness. In this way the power of vigorous investigation—so indispensable in a democracy—can be given its best expression.

WHAT'S THE MATTER WITH CONGRESS?

Congress is the nation's whipping boy. Newspaper editors, radio commentators, politicians, and plain citizens seem never to tire of berating individual legislators, blocs, or Congress as a whole. Cartoonists delight in portraying congressmen as timid, ignorant, selfish, and narrow-minded.

Much of this abuse is unjustified. Critics of Congress often seem to forget that our national legislature is particularly exposed to unfair attacks. In the first place, Congress does its work directly under the public eye. Unfortunate incidents—quarrels, name calling, evasive actions, inaccurate statements—that might be hushed up in the executive branch are almost always observed by the alert journalists covering Congress and reported to the whole nation. In the second place, Congress by its nature is controversial and argumentative. Its members are found on both sides—sometimes on half a dozen sides—of every important question, and the average citizen holding one opinion is likely to be intolerant of other views and the law-makers holding them.

Some of the abuse, moreover, stems from confusion *about* Congress and from confusion *in* Congress. There is lack of agreement as to what the primary functions of Congress should be. Should it concentrate on making policies, debating them, investigating problems, or curbing the President and bureau-crats—or something else? Actually Congress can and does do all these things, but not without much waste motion and unnecessary effort. Confu-sion *in* Congress arises from the different jobs that it does, the complexity of the procedure, the sheer number of legislators, the variety of viewpoints, the maze of party and group conflicts. At a baseball game almost anyone can understand the duel between pitcher and batter. In Congress a dozen pitchers throw a dozen balls to a dozen batters. Such confusion, however, is basically not the doing of Congress but the result of a constitutional system that divides up authority and checks power with power.

Granting all this, however, we must admit that some criticism of Con-gress is justified. Senators and representatives themselves have on many occasions complained about certain features of the legislature and they have demanded improvements.

"Congress is inefficient"

Critics can cite many facts to support this charge. Procedure in both chambers—especially in the Senate—is often very slow and cumbersome. The many committees, with their scores of subcommittees, operate ponder-ously. Congressmen spend much of their time on time-wasting activities, such as running errands for individual constituents or making speeches to an almost empty chamber. To take a specific example of inefficiency, calling the roll in the House uses three-quarters of an hour of valuable time.

There is, however, another side to the story. The main reason for slow, cumbersome procedure is the congressional tradition of protecting the rights of minorities and individual legislators. This tradition is an important one. Somewhere in government we must permit opposing and unorthodox views to be presented. By enabling bills to be reconsidered under certain circum-stances, by requiring them to be openly read by the clerk, by allowing roll-call votes when the decision is in doubt—to name only a few examples—Congress protects minority rights inside its two houses and outside. To be sure, this protection of minority and individual rights is abused. But abused or not, these rights are basic to the democratic, parliamentary process.

Of course, some of the inefficiencies in Congress have nothing to do with democracy. And some of these inefficiencies Congress has often at-tempted to correct. To take an important recent case, in 1945 Congress created a Joint Committee on the Organization of Congress, to make recom-mendations for improvement of its procedures. After consultation with outstanding authorities and months of study, the committee made its recommendations, some of which were enacted in the Legislative Reorganization Act of 1946. This act "streamlined" the committee system by reducing the number of committees in the House from 48 to 19, in the Senate from 33 to 15, and thus enabled members of Congress to concentrate in a smaller number of policy areas. It strengthened the professional assistance of the committees. Under the act, the jurisdiction of committees was clarified, and they were required to hold regular meetings and to keep a record of votes and proceedings. To prevent delay and obstruction, committee chairmen were required to report promptly any measures approved by their committees.

The 1946 act also tried to streamline legislative procedures by reducing the number of private bills that have taken up much of Congress's time. To strengthen the budgetary process, elaborate provisions were made to supply Congress with an over-all picture of fiscal and budgetary policy. The House Committees on Ways and Means and Appropriations and the Senate Committees on Finance and Appropriations were instructed to hold a joint meeting at the beginning of each session of Congress and, after considering the President's budgetary proposals, to make recommendations for the maximum amount Congress was to appropriate.

Further provisions of the act increased congressmen's salaries, established a retirement system for them, provided for administrative assistants for the Speaker and for the majority and minority leaders of the House, and clarified the powers and responsibilities of conference committees. The Senate amended its rules to make it more difficult to attach *riders* to appropriation bills. A rider is a provision not germane to the rest of the bill. Since the President must sign or veto an entire bill, he cannot veto the rider without losing a whole appropriation measure—a situation that facilitates "raids" on the Treasury.

How well has the Reorganization Act worked out? Some feel that it has been largely a failure. It streamlined committees, they point out, but the committees simply spawned scores of subcommittees. Some of the professional staff positions were filled by unqualified persons. The legislative budget provisions completely failed (see Chapter 27). And, critics conclude, nothing was done about the really vital problems of the Rules Committee, seniority, and the filibuster. Others feel happier about the situation. They point to the progress in clarifying committee duties and jurisdiction, regularizing and publicizing committee procedures, improving staff aids, and raising congressional salaries.[9] But both sides agree that further steps are needed.

What are the next steps? Many observers believe that committees need far better coordination. Some form of electric voting, which has been adopted

[9] G. B. Galloway, "Next Steps in Congressional Reform," *University of Illinois Bulletin,* Vol. 50, No. 31 (December 1952), p. 5.

successfully in a number of states, would save much time. Too, Congress might delegate such time-consuming functions as running the affairs of the District of Columbia. More use could be made of joint hearings by House and Senate committees. All these would save time. But the basic problem of efficiency "is the integration of Congress itself so that its autonomous and scattered units will act in harmony."[10] This goal, some feel, can best be realized by increased party solidarity and strengthened party machinery in the two houses.

Despite the disappointing results of the 1946 reforms, Congress on the whole must be acquitted of the charge of gross inefficiency. In terms of sheer output alone, its work is immense. A recent Congress passed 1625 acts, of which 733 were public and the rest private. In one session alone of that Congress 5995 bills and resolutions were introduced into the House and 2118 in the Senate. Perhaps the quality of all these acts was not what it might be—but considering the time and effort involved in passing legislation, the amount of work done is remarkable.

In this sense, then, Congress is not inefficient. If it gives the impression of inadequacy and confusion, the trouble must lie deeper.

"Congress is unrepresentative"

How *representative* Congress is depends on the definition of the word. Certainly Congress is not a microcosm of the community. It is not an accurate sample of 170 million Americans, since it is subject to the distortions mentioned above. And occupationally it notoriously overrepresents the "talking" classes such as lawyers, businessmen, and teachers (four-fifths of the members of a recent typical Congress had one of these three occupational backgrounds) at the expense of other groups such as factory workers and domestic servants.

On the other hand, Congress is highly representative of America in the sense that virtually every important minority group or opinion finds expression there. Just as America is made up of Catholics, Jews, and Protestants, of rich men and poor men, of easterners, westerners, and southerners, of radicals, liberals, middle-of-the-roaders, conservatives, and reactionaries, of prohibitionists, veterans, trade unionists, farmers, and of many other groups, so Congress is composed of a similar variety of members. The fact that certain groups are underrepresented in its members' previous occupations is perhaps not vital; many a congressman who has never worked in a factory speaks eloquently for the millions of Americans who have. The really crucial fact is that Congress provides a forum where scores of groups and ideas can find expression.

Such a situation, indeed, raises a further question: *"Should* Congress be representative of the opinions of the people, no matter how faulty or un-

[10] *Ibid.,* p. 10.

informed those opinions may be?" There is a school of thought that the representative should use his best judgment, not slavishly follow the wishes of his constituents. Over a century and a half ago the great English legislator, Edmund Burke, defended this view. Speaking to his constituents in Bristol he admitted that a representative should keep in close touch with his constituents, should look after their needs even at the expense of his own. But then he added:

> But his unbiased opinion, his mature judgment, his enlightened conscience, he ought not to sacrifice to you, to any man. . . . Your representative owes you, not his industry only, but his judgment; and he betrays, instead of serving you, if he sacrifices it to your opinion.

Most American congessmen, however, seem to follow the theory that the representative must vote according to the dominant interests in his state or district. We have farm senators, silver senators, cotton representatives, textile representatives, and so on. The result is that Congress tends to respond to local pressures, sectional forces, and organized interests. We will return to this problem of representation in Chapter 18 after we have seen how the Presidency and other national offices are also involved in the matter.

"Congress is irresponsible"

A charge against Congress graver than inefficiency is that it truckles to organized minorities and ignores the needs and aspirations of the people as a whole. There is much evidence to support this charge. The Senate knuckles under to minorities again and again, partly because of two devices for minority rule: the *filibuster* and the *two-thirds vote* required for ratifying treaties. The Senate has not been able to abolish the filibuster; on the contrary, an attempt in 1949 in that direction only strengthened this minority weapon. Before 1949 cloture could be invoked by a two-thirds vote of the senators *on the floor*. In that year cloture was weakened by a new provision that it could be invoked only by two-thirds of the *whole* Senate membership, that is, by 64 senators. The two-thirds treaty-ratifying requirement in the Senate, which allows a minority to block treaties, is not of crucial importance, as we have seen, but it can be troublesome. Finally, both houses of Congress allow minorities to raise havoc with legislation by means of parliamentary gimmicks, such as making frequent points of order and time-consuming motions, introducing irrelevant business, and repeatedly demanding quorum calls.

It may be that Congress will rid itself of some of these obstructionist weapons in time. Thus in 1949 the House of Representatives clipped the wings of its Rules Committee. Under a new arrangement the committee was left power to bottle up a bill for only a limited period, after which the chairman of the committee reporting the bill might call it up before the House. To be sure, the House restored the old power of the Rules Committee in 1951, but the 1949 change showed that the representatives could reform their methods when so minded. At the start of the 1957 session of Congress, a large minority of senators from both parties were pressing for a weakening of the power to filibuster. They wanted at least to return to the old rule that a filibuster could be ended by two-thirds of those voting, and it seemed likely that their efforts would continue. Many congressmen have also shown concern over the cumbersome procedure in both houses, and simplified methods may be adopted in time.

Nevertheless, the problem of irresponsibility remains. Some students of Congress feel that minority devices such as the filibuster are mere surface manifestations of political forces that run deep. Even if these obstructionist methods were abolished, they warn, minorities could still raise havoc with majority rule because the majority has no cohesiveness or staying power. It is constantly giving way to minorities because its own members desert. For example, most congressmen may be pledged to social reform—but some will renege on their campaign promises in the face of organized opposition in their district. Or most of them may be in favor of governmental economy, but will still vote for pork-barrel bills in order to get public projects for the home folks.

The trouble does not lie simply with Congress. It lies in part with the residence or locality rule. The Constitution merely requires congressmen to be inhabitants of the state in which they are elected. With few exceptions, however, it is politically impossible because of popular attitudes for a candidate for the House to live anywhere in the state outside his district. (Here is an excellent example of the dovetailing of the written with the "unwritten" Constitution.) This locality rule contrasts with the practice in Britain where members of Commons often are elected by districts that they have never lived in, and may have visited only a few times. The American system results from the prevailing belief here that congressmen are primarily representatives of their own districts, and only secondarily—if at all—representatives of the entire nation. It reinforces the tendency of congressmen to think in local rather than national terms.

What is lacking is a strong party system that could hold together a congressional majority—whether Republican or Democratic—in the face of minorities. Congress, in short, *lacks party responsibility*. Britain, by way of contrast, has parties that manage both to discipline their members in Parliament and to help them win elections in their districts. Our parties, as we have seen, give little aid to their members running for office, and they have little control of their members once in office. A close look at Congress reveals not only the Democratic and Republican parties, but a farmers' party, labor party, southern party, veterans' party, and others all cutting across one another and producing vast confusion.

This situation has crucial consequences. It creates friction between Congress and the President, who is national party leader. It helps produce a confused network of relationships between Congress and the bureaucracy. It even affects the role of judges in our national government. Finally, it raises the problem of the suitability of divided government, responsible to shifting and conflicting forces, in a time of domestic and world-wide tension. The next four chapters will consider these and related problems.

THE FRAMERS OF THE CONSTITUTION HAD A HARD
time deciding how to set up the executive branch. Not that they questioned
the need for an executive. As we have seen, most of the delegates to the
Philadelphia convention were tired of the system of the Articles of Confederation under which government was carried out by Congress through committees and special agents. It was agreed that this system had not worked
very well. The framers wanted a national executive who could enforce the
law and help the states put down disorder such as Shays' Rebellion. But
how strong was the new executive to be? And what was its relation to be to
the new Congress?

Day after day the delegates argued. Some, like James Wilson of Pennsylvania, wanted a strong executive, independent of the legislature—an
executive who would give "energy, dispatch, and responsibility" to the
government. Others, like Sherman of Connecticut, wished to have the "executive magistracy" appointed by Congress and wholly subject to the legislative will. Some delegates favored a one-man executive; others preferred
a plural executive composed of two or three men of equal power. Some
delegates wanted the executive to be eligible for re-election; others felt that
one term was enough.

Two basic considerations dominated the discussion of the Presidency.
The first was the need for an energetic yet dignified executive who would
enforce the national laws firmly, and who would lend a note of stability to
the new government. The other
was a general fear that the public would be critical if the executive was made too strong. The
people had rebelled against the
King—clearly they would not
want a new American mon-
arch.[1] So concerned were the
framers with popular reaction
that on five separate occasions
they voted for *appointment of
the chief executive by the legislature*—a move that would
have made the President the
tool of Congress and probably
would have given us a form
of parliamentary government

17 ★

The

President

[1] E. S. Corwin, *The President:
Office and Powers,* 3rd ed. (New
York: New York University Press,
1948), p. 10.

something like that in France today. But in the end the men of 1787 decided to set up an executive separate from Congress.

The final decision on the President was a compromise, as with so many other features of the Constitution (see Chapter 2). On the one hand, the President would be single instead of plural, eligible for re-election, and independent of the legislature. He was to have considerable power over the executive branch. On the other hand, he was hemmed in by the system of checks and balances. His appointments of major officials had to be approved by the Senate. He was given a veto over congressional acts, but Congress could override his veto by a two-thirds vote. His power to appeal directly to the voters was muzzled by an elaborate system of electors, who in choosing a President would act as a sort of screen through which popular passions would be refined and tempered. He could make treaties, but only if two-thirds of the senators present concurred.

As it turned out, the framers accomplished both their objectives. They sufficiently checked presidential power so that the new single chief executive seemed safe to the necessary number of voters in 1787-1788. At the same time, they set up an office that was to be a continuing source of energy and power in the new republic. Perhaps they built better than they knew. So powerful has the President become that thoughtful Americans today face precisely the same questions that confronted the framers 170 years ago. How strong should the executive be? And what should be its relation to Congress? Today we ask also: Why has the President become so powerful? Is this a dangerous trend?

To tackle these questions we must consider the President's vital and many-sided roles—administrative, legislative, political, military, ceremonial, and symbolic. But first let us look at the man himself.

A DAY WITH THE PRESIDENT

The President operates at the center of a vast and complex network of governmental and political activity. He has his fingers on countless levers that shape the making of public and private policies throughout the land. At the same time he in turn is surrounded by innumerable checks and balances that are inherent in our political as well as our governmental system. To him come men of all kinds, with motives of all types—to advise, beg, urge, consult, exhort, warn, dissuade, even dictate. Watching the President in action for a typical day may suggest the complexity of the job, its scope, and its frustrations. A typical day of a President in recent years might go somewhat as follows:[2]

[2] This "typical day" is based on a study of biographical material, journalistic accounts, and documents.

9:00 A.M. *President arrives at his office.*—He has already looked over several Washington and New York newspapers. He discusses the day's agenda with his staff. He reviews an important announcement with his press secretary. He reads some of his mail. (Necessarily he can see only a tiny fraction of the 5000 to 25,000 letters that flood into the White House in a single day.) He signs orders and other documents. He is given a top-secret briefing on the world situation by diplomatic and military assistants.

At ten a round of appointments with visitors gets under way.

10:00 A.M. *Farm senators.*—Five of these gentlemen, members of both parties, arrive to protest an act of the Secretary of Agriculture involving farm commodities. They indicate that if the Secretary does not rescind or modify his action, they will propose an amendment to new farm legislation that will limit the Secretary's powers. The President listens sympathetically, but makes no promises.

10:15 A.M. *The Secretary of State.*—He tells the President that reports from the United Nations and from our embassies abroad indicate that several neutral countries are planning an action that may leave the United States isolated diplomatically. He has a statement designed to clarify this nation's position. After some discussion the President signs it.

10:40 A.M. *Press conference.*—Over 100 reporters attend. They shower the President with questions. What did the farm senators want? Who will be the new Assistant Secretary of State? What is the President's reaction to yesterday's statement in *Pravda?* Will he veto the pension bill passed by Congress? What will be the government's policy if the United Nations fails to act? The President has to think fast. Some of the questions, he knows, are loaded—he will be embarrassed no matter how he answers them. Others are "iffy"—they are purely speculative in nature, and if he answers them he may unknowingly commit the Administration to a certain policy. Some questions, on the other hand, are planted by the White House itself, so that friendly reporters will ask the President questions he wishes to answer. Sometimes the President takes refuge in the answer, "No comment."

11:00 A.M. *American Legion officials.*—They have come to invite the President to address their next national convention and to put in a word for some pending veterans' legislation. White House photographers take pictures of a smiling President in the midst of the group.

11:10 A.M. *Legislative assistant.*—The President looks over the draft of a veto message, decides it is too severe in its criticism of Congress, asks his assistant to soften it.

11:30 A.M. *Cabinet meeting.*—This is the regular weekly meeting (occasionally the President calls special ones). The President makes a general statement prepared by the Budget Director on the need for economizing in departmental administration, and asks the members to submit reports on economies made. There follow brief reports and comments by the Secretaries of the Treasury, Labor, and Commerce on several different matters. The meeting is informal. Most of the business consists of reporting on departmental problems; there is little discussion of general policy. Several cabinet members stay on after the meetings to discuss privately with the President matters that they feared to bring up in the meeting because of possible opposition or leaks to the press.

12:30 P.M. *Lunch with members of the National Committee of the President's party.*—General talk—no discussion of party or governmental problems.

1:30 P.M. *Key members of the National Committee.*—A few members stay on. They comprise three city bosses, two senators who dominate their state parties, the party chairman, and several others. The President asks their help in keeping a number of congressmen friendly to the Administration. Campaign plans are discussed—also the handling of appointments to a number of federal judgeships that are vacant.

2:30 P.M. *Relaxation.*—Attends baseball game with a delegation of Eagle Scouts. Quietly leaves game at end of sixth inning.

3:45 P.M. *A.F.L.-C.I.O. leaders.*—The labor chiefs, accompanied by the Secretary of Labor, raise the question of several appointments that are to be made in the Labor Department and in two other agencies.

3:55 P.M. *Ceremony.*—President presses button starting the generators in a new dam in Colorado. Picture taken.

4:00 P.M. *Budget Director.*—He reports that there is trouble in the House of Representatives. A group of western congressmen are trying to boost appropriations for a bureau in the Interior Department. The President and the Secretary of the Interior are both opposed to the increase, but the bureau chief is working closely with the congressmen. The President telephones the Speaker of the House and asks him to look into the situation.

4:30 P.M. *I.C.A. chief.*—Just back from Europe, the director of the International Cooperation Administration is worried about appropriations and a pending amendment that might hurt the program. The President says that he thinks the amendment will be defeated, but certain cuts cannot be averted.

5:00 P.M. *Ceremony.*—Makes contribution to Red Cross, inaugurating drive for funds. Picture taken.

5:05 P.M. *Meeting with National Security Council.*—President discusses a broad range of political, military, and diplomatic problems with other members

Courtesy THE NEW YORK TIMES MAGAZINE *and Tom Little*

of the Council. The agenda is carefully prepared. A key decision is made in principle on defensive arrangements with an important ally. A secretariat, which has carefully briefed all members on major problems, records this and other decisions.

6:00 P.M. *Signing of an important act.*—Picture taken with eight senators and representatives who sponsored or supported the act. Signs a score of letters and Army and Navy commissions, looks over reports.

7:00 P.M. *Dinner with family and personal friends.*

9:00 P.M. *Brief talk to a patriotic organization.*

10:00 P.M. *Back in the White House.*—Late reports, then bed.

Looking over this full day, we note a number of facts about the President and his job.

1. The President faces a ceaseless tide of tough decisions. His staff helps him to decide many questions, but sometimes he alone must make a decision of vital importance.

2. Today diplomatic and military problems occupy much of his time.

3. Domestically, he must deal with many legislative and political matters. His greatest concern here is the unpredictable action of Congress. He spends much time dealing with individuals and factions in Congress that are holding up bills and appropriations.

4. The ceremonial job takes time—perhaps an hour or two a day.

5. His purely administrative job (in the sense of management) must be largely delegated to others. The main administrative decisions are made in the Budget Bureau and other staff agencies and in the departments. He must, however, frequently step in when administrative decisions involve important political and legislative relationships.

6. The President has little time for reflection. He must delegate this job, too. Agencies like the Bureau of the Budget, the Council of Economic Advisers, and the National Security Council do most of the long-range planning.

7. The President is an essentially lonely figure. This is paradoxical, for he sees so many people. But his visitors are usually trying to get something from the President. His staff members are his closest associates, but they are also his subordinates. He cannot always turn to the Vice-President or cabinet members, for they have their own responsibilities—and ambitions. The toughest decisions—those that divide the country, his party, and even his own Administration—he must make almost alone.

The size and complexity of the President's job we can grasp more fully by considering the chief executive in each of his five great roles—as chief administrator, party chief, chief legislator, chief foreign policy maker, commander in chief, and chief of state. Here each of these roles will be discussed in turn. But they must not be viewed as separate or compartmentalized activities. On the contrary, only in the *interweaving* of these roles can we see the full tapestry of presidential power.

THE PRESIDENT AS CHIEF ADMINISTRATOR

A century and a half ago, when Jefferson became President, the federal government employed 2120 persons—Indian commissioners, postmasters, collectors of customs, clerks, tax collectors, marshals, lighthouse keepers, and the like.[3] Today, by latest count, the President heads a colossal establishment of about 2⅓ million federal civilian employees. These employees work in 2099 component units of federal administration—2099 departments, services, bureaus, commissions, boards, governmental corporations, and other types of agencies. They work not only in Washington but throughout the world. Their salaries and wages alone amount to over $8 billion a year.

All this is big government. It is a result, as we have seen, of decades of sporadic expansion of government activities—an expansion resulting in turn from the attempts of Americans to cope with big problems, such as armed threats at home and abroad, gigantic increases in population, technological changes, depressions, social unrest, and the interdependence and complexity of our national life.

The Constitution charges the President to "take care that the laws be faithfully executed," but because of the immensity of the job, the President is only a part-time administrator. His other tasks demand most of his attention. But even if he could devote all his time to running the executive departments he could not do the job unless the administrative establishment were organized for leadership and control. It is, of course, so organized. These 2099 agencies are set up in great pyramids, each with its own hierarchical structure. Orders —theoretically at least—flow from President to department head to bureau chief down to the offices, services, and smaller units where they are carried out (see Chapter 19). This is the "line," so-called. The President, like all the top brass, is also assisted by a staff, whose job it is to advise and assist him in managing the administration. This *line* and *staff* organization—inherent in any large administrative unit, whether the Army, the General Motors Corporation, or the Veterans Administration—is worth a closer look in following the President's activities as chief administrator.

The President and his Cabinet

Directly in line under the President are the executive departments. These are the departments of: State; Treasury; Defense; Interior; Agriculture; Justice; Post Office; Commerce; Labor; Health, Education, and Welfare. The State and Treasury departments were established in 1789, the government's first year. The War Department was also set up that year, but this agency, along with the Navy Department, was reorganized into the Defense

---

[3] L. D. White, *The Federalists* (New York: The Macmillan Company, 1948), pp. 255-256.

Department in 1947. Health, Education, and Welfare was created in 1953 out of a number of previously existing agencies.

The heads of these ten executive departments comprise the Cabinet. It would be hard to find a more unusual or nondescript institution than this one. The Cabinet has existed since early in Washington's administration; yet it is not mentioned in the Constitution. It is composed—aside from the Vice-President—solely of department heads; yet the chiefs of several great agencies, such as the Veterans Administration, are not members. However, Presidents often invite high officials—for example, the Budget Director or the chairman of the Civil Service Commission—to attend Cabinet meetings. Cabinet Secretaries are often leading members of the President's party; yet several Presidents have appointed prominent members of the opposition party to their Cabinets, a notable recent example being Roosevelt's choice of two prominent Republicans for the secretaryships of War and Navy in 1940. Cabinet membership has high prestige value, and most Presidents meet regularly with their Cabinets; yet the discussions are often casual, perfunctory, and even listless. Presidents turn to their Cabinets for advice on a variety of matters; yet votes are rarely taken and the President could ignore Cabinet sentiment if he wished. (Lincoln, finding the whole Cabinet opposed to him, could say with impunity, "Seven nays, one aye—the ayes have it.") The President handpicks his Cabinets virtually free from senatorial interference; yet it has been fairly said that the President's Cabinet members are often his worst enemies.

It is also difficult to generalize as to the basis of presidential selections of Cabinet members. Political considerations are paramount. The President usually tries to give representation to various factions of his party—to its liberal and conservative wings, to different sections of the country, to major racial and religious groups. Business, farm, and labor groups must be appeased in the appointment of the Secretaries of Commerce, Agriculture, and Labor, respectively. Most Presidents face a basic dilemma in Cabinet making. To choose a weak group may put the whole Administration in disrepute. To put strong men with powerful political backing in the Cabinet may lead to quarrels within the President's official family and possibly to friction between the President and his Cabinet chiefs. President Eisenhower tried the experiment of appointing a Democratic labor leader to his Cabinet, as Secretary of Labor; the experiment came to an end nine months later, when the Secretary of Labor resigned because of differences with the Administration over policy.

Nevertheless, the Cabinet has a character and importance of its own. Membership in it continues to be the ambition of many politicians. On occasion the meetings are devoted to matters of top policy. And the discussions gain from the fact that Cabinet members usually bring lengthy political and policy-making experience to bear on the problems at hand. Most administrative problems—at the White House level—are really legislative and political problems. The Cabinet may in time, given certain over-all changes (see Chapter 17), become a team that both sustains the President and renders him more responsible to the people. But at present the American Cabinet bears little resemblance to the ideal Cabinet described by Harold J. Laski as a "place where the large outlines of policy can be hammered out in common, where the essential strategy is decided upon, where the President knows that he will hear, both in affirmation and in doubt, even in negation, most of what can be said about the direction he proposes to follow."

If the Cabinet's role is so limited, how does the President exercise direction of his far-flung administrative machine?[4] He does, of course, meet frequently with individual department and agency chiefs. Crucial decisions are sometimes reached in small, informal conferences of the President with the heads of two or three major departments and agencies and with his staff. Another factor in the President's control of administration is his ultimate power —despite certain limitations, as noted below—to hire and fire his main lieutenants as he may deem fit. The Senate must ratify major appointments, but by tradition the President is allowed to pick his immediate subordinates as he chooses—and to get rid of them.

Of a total federal civil personnel of about $2\frac{1}{3}$ million, the President, with the concurrence of the Senate, hires about 16,000. He can appoint a limited number without Senate assent. He chooses the department and agency heads who in turn employ other thousands of civil servants. Aside from his power to hire and fire, the President directly or indirectly controls promotions, demotions, and transfers, especially at the top levels. The Supreme Court has upheld (in *Myers* v. *United States,* 1926) the power of the President to remove executive officers at will but has sustained the power of Congress to limit the President's authority (see p. 484) to discharge certain officials with part judicial and part legislative responsibilities.

The single most important means of presidential control, however, is the White House staff.

The kitchen cabinet

Americans hear much about secret, invisible men who are said to control the President. Stories of a palace guard or a White House gang make good feature material for any newspaper columnist, TV or radio commentator. Such stories stem from a basic fact about the President. He needs help. He must have advisers who can assist him in handling the momentous questions that crowd into the White House for decision. Much of his effectiveness turns on their loyal, disinterested, expert services. So the Washington commentators are right in emphasizing the importance of the men who advise the President. But they are wrong when they imply that there is anything

[4] See Paul H. Appleby, *Policy and Administration* (University, Ala.: University of Alabama Press, 1949).

sinister or un-American in this situation. Andrew Jackson had his kitchen cabinet; Abraham Lincoln had his personal advisers; Woodrow Wilson had his Colonel House; Franklin Roosevelt had his Harry Hopkins. President Eisenhower, accustomed to the elaborate and powerful staffs found in military organizations, has established a large staff headed by a "staff chief" who works directly under the President. Without a large staff the President today could not possibly do the job that the Constitution—and the people—demand of him.

In recent years the kitchen cabinet has grown in numbers and in importance. Today it comprises a group of perhaps twenty close advisers, assisted by 100 or more experts of all kinds, plus another 1000 clerks, secretaries, and the like. They aid the President in all his roles, administrative, legislative, political, military. They are grouped in a complex agency called the Executive Office of the President. Physically, they work in both the east and west wings of the White House and in an ugly old building near the White House that used to house the State Department.

The President's immediate staff, the *White House Office,* does not have fixed form; indeed, part of its value is its flexibility and adaptability. Most Presidents, however, have an appointments secretary, who lets the right people see the President and keeps the others away; a press secretary, who handles presidential publicity and deals with the scores of newsmen and photographers assigned to the White House; a correspondence secretary, who watches the President's mail and often drafts important letters for his chief; a legal counsel, who advises the President on a variety of matters of broad policy (not merely on legal matters); a diplomatic aide, who is the President's eyes and ears on the many-sided diplomatic front; military aides, who often have policy as well as ceremonial functions; and several other key legislative, administrative, and political assistants. Often these assistants may have far more influence than the equivalent Cabinet member; for example, the President may lean on his legal counsel for urgent advice to a greater extent than on his Attorney General.

Outside this inner circle are the heads of a number of staff agencies who advise the President on policy and help him run the administrative leviathan. The most important of these is the Director of the *Bureau of the Budget.* This gentleman is not simply a glorified bookkeeper. He is the person who advises the President almost daily on the real needs of the hundreds of government agencies, how much money they should be allotted in the budget, and what kind of job they are doing. He and his assistants pare down requested appropriations of the agencies to fit the President's budgetary program. They also try to improve the planning, management, and statistical work of all the bureaucrats. Working under the President, they are able to survey the administration from his broader perspective and to mediate the claims and quarrels of administrators big and small. Seeking to maintain a uniform legislative program for the chief executive, budget officials review legislative proposals of the departments and advise the President on bills he should sign or veto.

Several other presidential agencies also have vital functions, especially in the making of economic and military policies. The *Council of Economic Advisers,* a three-man board with a small staff, supplies the President with a broad range of economic information and advice and each year helps him draw up a report on the nation's economic position and prospect. The *National Security Council,* composed of the President, Vice-President, Secretaries of State and Defense, and a few others, embraces a small permanent staff of military and diplomatic experts. The *Office of Defense Mobilization* advises the chief executive on the coordination of military, industrial, and civilian mobilization, and employs a staff of several hundred to assess the nation's resources of raw materials and manpower in the event of war. The work of these agencies, all of which are located in the Executive Office, will be described more fully in Part Five.

Why does the President lean so heavily on his staff? Why does he not lean more heavily, for example, on his Cabinet or on heads of vital departments? The answer is simple. The staff can give the President the help he wants. It can do so because the President can, for the most part, juggle his staff membership and organization in a way that will be most helpful to him. He chooses the men he wants; he chooses them for their experience, their ability to work as part of a team, and above all for their loyalty to himself. Nowhere else—not in Congress, not in his Cabinet, not in his party associates—can he find the loyalty, the single-mindedness, and the team spirit that he can build, if he is a leader, among his close aides. Such a staff is important to him and to the country—so important that the Hoover Commission urged that the President be given the utmost freedom in organizing his staff as he wishes.[5]

THE PRESIDENT AS CHIEF LEGISLATOR

The national government is divided into the executive, legislative, and judicial branches. This fact leads some to think that the President has only administrative functions, the Senate and House only legislative, and the judiciary only judicial. Actually, as we have seen, the keynote of the system is an *intermingling* of powers. The President is a prime example. The Constitution, as noted above, grants him certain policy-making power. A century and a half of national growth and recurrent crises have vastly increased that legislative power. Today he and his aides ordinarily have more influence

[5] Commission on Organization of the Executive Branch of the Government, *General Management of the Executive Branch* (Washington: Government Printing Office, 1949), p. 15; see also H. M. Somers, "The President as Administrator," *The Annals,* Sept. 1952, pp. 104 ff.

over national policy than any single Congressman or group of Congress-men; truly he is chief legislator.[6]

The Constitution ordains that the President "shall from time to time give to the Congress Information of the State of the Union, and recommend to their Consideration such Measures as he shall judge necessary and expedient." From the start strong Presidents have exploited this power. Washington and Adams came in person to Congress to deliver information and recom-mendations. Jefferson and many Presidents after him sent written messages, but Wilson restored the practice of a personal, and often dramatic, message. Franklin Roosevelt in particular used the personal appearance as a means of drawing the attention of the whole nation to his program—with the in-valuable help of radio and camera. The President can also dramatize his policies by calling Congress or one house separately into special session, although the legislators need not act if they do not wish.

Less obvious but perhaps equally important are the frequent written messages dispatched from the White House to Capitol Hill on a vast range of public problems. Often read aloud indistinctly by a clerk, these messages may not create much stir at the moment, but they are important in de-fining the Administration's position and giving a lead to friendly legislators. Moreover, these messages are often accompanied by detailed drafts of legislation that may be put into the hoppers by such legislators with hardly a change. These Administration bills are the products of the President's bill-drafting experts on his own staff or in the departments and agencies. Such bills may be mauled and mutilated by Congress—but many of the original provisions may survive unscathed.

The power to say "No"

The President can *veto* a bill by returning it with a statement of his ob-jections to the house in which it originated. Congress, by a two-thirds vote in each chamber, may then pass it over his veto. If the President does not sign or veto the bill within ten weekdays after he receives it, the bill becomes law without his signature. If Congress adjourns within the ten weekdays, however, the President, by taking no action, can kill the bill. This is known as the *pocket veto.*

The veto is a many-sided—and sometimes feeble—weapon. Its essential strength lies in the ordinary failure of Congress to muster a two-thirds majority of both houses in favor of a policy that the President has told the people he dislikes. Yet when Congress can repeatedly mobilize such a majority against a President, it can virtually take command of the govern-ment. Such was the fate of President Andrew Johnson. Faced after 1866

---

[6] For description of the institutionalization of the President's legislative role see, Richard E. Neustadt, "Presidency and Legislation: Planning the President's Program," *The American Political Science Review,* Vol. XLIX, No. 4 (December 1955), pp. 980-1021.

with a House of Representatives almost three to one against his reconstruc-tion policies, he was virtually helpless as bill after bill was passed stripping him of his powers, and he barely escaped being ousted from office.[7]

Even in ordinary times, when Congress cannot overcome a veto, it can maneuver so as to make a veto less likely. It can attach irrelevant but con-troversial bills, called *riders,* to vitally needed legislation; the President must either accept or reject the whole bill, for he does not have the power to strike out individual items in the bill; that is, the *item veto.* Appropriations are a special case in point. The lawmakers may combine in one appropria-tions bill badly needed funds for the armed forces and a host of costly pork-barrel items, but the President must take or reject the whole bill. Governors of most states do have the power of item veto, and it has long been urged that the President should too. It is not certain whether a constitutional amendment would be needed or not. Some argue that if the framers had foreseen the legislative use of omnibus bills and riders, they would have specifically given the President power to veto items not germane to the main bill.[8]

For his part, the President can use the veto power in a positive as well as a negative way. He can announce openly, or let it be known quietly, that a bill under consideration by Congress will be turned back at the White House door unless certain changes have been made. He can use the *threat* of a veto against some bill Congress badly wants in exchange for another bill that he badly wants. In all his dealings with Capitol Hill, the veto power is a factor in the maneuver for power. But the veto is essentially a negative weapon, of limited use to a President who has a positive pro-gram. For it is the President who usually is pressing for action. It is Con-gress that has the real power to say "no."

Filling in the details

Most federal legislation today deals with highly complex situations. A labor law, for example, may involve a great variety of industries, a number of different unions, all kinds of labor-management relationships, and diverse attitudes and traditions in different parts of the country. Agricultural legis-lation may deal with certain farm problems in general, but in practice the law involves big farmers and small ones, prosperous ones and marginal ones, cotton farmers, wheat farmers, applegrowers, and so on. No matter how wise Congress might be, it could not write a law that would automatically adapt itself to such different situations. Indeed, to try to do so would be to put the administrator into a strait jacket and to make the law unworkable.

[7] W. E. Binkley, *President and Congress* (New York: Alfred A. Knopf, Inc., 1947), pp. 128-144.

[8] See C. J. Zinn, *The Veto Power of the President,* Committee Print, Committee on the Judiciary, House of Representatives (Washington: Government Printing Office, 1951).

Consequently Congress often must content itself with prescribing general standards and delegating to the President and administrators the job of *filling in the details of the laws*. Such subordinate legislation is usually issued in the President's executive orders and in circulars, orders, rules, regulations, directives, and so on, issued by departments, regulatory boards, and other agencies.

Much of this delegation of legislative power involves making decisions within rather narrow limits. For example, a law may permit the President to vary tariff or minimum wage standards to some extent, but only in terms of a standard laid down by Congress. Yet such standards vary greatly in precision. The Trade Agreement Act of 1934 and its extensions empower the President to make trade agreements with foreign nations lowering existing tariff rates by as much as 50 per cent. Other acts authorize him to suspend the eight-hour day for federal employees, to issue civil service rules, to prevent the export of certain raw materials.

An even more radical kind of delegation was contained in the Reorganization Act of 1939. By its terms the President could reduce and rearrange certain federal agencies through plans that would come into effect sixty days after being sent to Congress unless turned down by both chambers before that time. Here was a delegation of power that amounted almost to a reversal of the usual relation of Congress and the chief executive. Subsequent reorganization acts have delegated somewhat similar power to the President (see page 508).

Thus Congress, while setting objectives and standards, in practice allows the President not only to fill in the details but even to decide when the action shall be taken. It is one thing to delegate the carrying out of specific provisions; it is something else to delegate the power to say when and whether a law will be invoked or applied. Why has Congress seen fit to delegate such sweeping powers? The reason is partly the willingness of the legislators to face the facts of modern life and to allow the President to do quickly and effectively what they could do, at best, haltingly and ineffectively. The reason is also that Congress is often so dominated by warring factions that it cannot find common ground on which to act. It defers to the President because he can act. The Constitution, it is true, prevents Congress from giving away its "essential" legislative powers. This is one of the reasons why the Supreme Court invalidated the National Industrial Recovery Act (*Schechter v. United States,* 1935). But so long as Congress lays down some kind of standard, the Supreme Court has been willing to approve extensive delegation of power.

Thousands of legislators

It should be clear by now that policy-making power is not monopolized by Congress. Nor is it monopolized jointly by Congress and President. Just as

Congress must delegate legislative power to the President, so he must *re-*delegate policy making powers to hosts of administrators down the line. Obviously the Secretary of State has a decided influence on policy, as do other department heads, along with bureau, division, and section chiefs. In a sense, there is no level in the administrative hierarchy at which discretion really ends. Even a secretary may make policy decisions as to what matters or visitors his superior should turn to first—or at all. A sort of settling-down process takes place. Routine, non-controversial decisions are made at the lower levels, vital and difficult ones at the top echelons. But at any time the most routine matter can be called to the public's attention, perhaps by a newspaper columnist or a congressman. Then the matter will be pulled out of the lower echelon and given consideration by a bureau or department chief—perhaps it will even go to the White House.[9]

Thus there are thousands of legislators throughout the government—and millions more outside, such as editors, lobbyists, and ordinary citizens, who exert pressure on a democratic government. Control of legislation cannot be pictured as Congress on top, the President in the middle, and a pyramid of department, bureau, and division heads below. It is rather a *circular* system, with President and congressmen cooperating on some matters, fighting over others, and both influencing—and being influenced by—the administrators throughout the administration and by political forces outside.

Certain agencies, moreover, have a degree of independence from the White House because of historical and political reasons. The Federal Bureau of Investigation in the Department of Justice, the Bureau of Reclamation in the Interior Department, and the Corps of Engineers in the Department of the Army are agencies somewhat insulated from the White House because of the prestige of their chiefs or the closeness of the agencies to blocs in Congress and to interest groups outside. The independent regulatory commissions (see Chapter 19) are a special case. Congress has delegated legislative (and judicial) powers to agencies like the Interstate Commerce Commission, the Federal Trade Commission, and the National Labor Relations Board in an attempt to keep partisan Presidents from interfering with their decisions. The President hires the commissioners, with the consent of the Senate, but his power to discharge them is usually limited. Hence they are often at liberty to make policies at variance with those of the Administration if they see fit. Here is one more set of little legislators in the Washington scene.

Thus the President shares his legislative power not only with Congress but also with administrators in the executive branch that he himself heads. The extent to which he wields legislative power turns not only on his formal, constitutional position and powers, but also on his political position and powers. His political powers turn on many factors. How effective is

[9] Appleby, *Policy and Administration,* p. 82.

he in appealing to the public? To what extent can he dramatize official business? How magnetic is he on radio or television? How good is his timing? How active and articulate are his lieutenants—his cabinet members and key agency heads? How close are his relations with congressional leaders? Can he mobilize public opinion on crucial issues? Does his influence reach into states and districts throughout the country so that he can "build fires" under recalcitrant legislators?

A President's power turns on factors like these as well as on constitutional grants of authority. Even more, his power rests on the extent to which he commands organized, durable, and dependable support in his political party—in short, on his effectiveness as party chief.

THE PRESIDENT AS PARTY CHIEF

The Constitution says nothing about parties or about the President as party chief. Indeed, little did the framers fear more than a chief executive acting as leader of a party or faction. They planned for a President who would rise above political divisions, who would stand for the nation as a whole, who as chief magistrate would mediate between Senate and House, between rich and poor, between North and South. They planned a system of electing Presidents—the electoral college (see pp. 378-381)—that would elevate statesmen to the office, not politicians.

Washington fitted this picture perfectly. He gave the country a form of nonpartisan government, and in his famous Farewell Address he warned the people against the spirit of party. But in a democracy some kind of factional or party politics is inevitable. Even during Washington's administration party leaders and party politics began to emerge. Thomas Jefferson symbolized this shift. He resigned from Washington's Cabinet as Secretary of State in 1793 in order to travel the country visiting local politicians and laying the groundwork for a national party.

Jefferson himself became the boss of his new Republican party. While President he showed his power by using party machinery to dominate Congress: he and his aides pushed legislation through House and Senate, stopped bills they disliked, and even influenced committee actions. Clearly, the antiparty plans of the Founding Fathers were not working out. Moreover, the provision for a nonpartisan method of picking Presidents also came to naught. Washington's own successor, John Adams, was nominated in a party caucus made up of Federalist members of the national House and Senate. Jefferson and the next three Presidents were nominated by the Republican members of Congress meeting in a similiar legislative caucus. Andrew Jackson's followers attacked "King Caucus" as being undemocratic; they replaced it with the national convention as an even more partisan method of nominating the President. Meanwhile the electoral college, as we have seen, was radically transformed. Instead of exercising independent judgment, the presidential electors became merely automatic (although in-accurate) ratifiers of the popular, partisan will.

All Presidents since Washington have been party leaders, and the stronger the President, the greater his power over party has been. Men like McKinley, Wilson, and the two Roosevelts have fortified their execu-tive and legislative influence by resort to their supremacy in the party. Yet no President has fully dominated his party, and the story of all Presidents, including the most famous, revolves largely around their party failures as well as their party triumphs.

The President and his party

How does the President direct his party? Where does his influence stop —and why?

The President is master of the party organization at the national level. Oddly, he has no position in the party structure. He stands above the party, and the national organization revolves around him. His vast in-fluence as President over vital national policies and over thousands of appointments commands respect from politicians throughout the party ma-chinery, and especially at the national level. Even aside from this, he is the party's national leader and spokesman, formally chosen at the party convention. President and party need each other. He needs the party's backing throughout the government in order to enact his program. The party needs his direction, his prestige, and the political "gravy" that flows from the White House.

The strings of the national organization are all in the President's hands. Formally, the national committee picks the national chairman; actually the President tells the committeemen whom to pick. He hires and fires national party chairmen much as he shifts department heads or, indeed, his own staff. Ordinarily his pronouncements as to national party policy are more authoritative than any other party member's, even more signifi-cant than the party program itself. The great test of the President's influ-ence in the party is his power to gain renomination if he wishes it, and all recent Presidents have met this test. Taft won renomination in 1912 despite the opposition of Theodore Roosevelt and the Progressives, as did Hoover in 1932 despite the Depression, and Truman in 1948 despite deep divisions in his party.

The President also has some influence over his party's state and local organizations. Two factors, aside from the prestige and power of his office, stand back of this influence. One is patronage. As we have seen, many party machines live off the jobs that are thrown their way, including judgeships, postmasterships, and the like. The second is the President's power over the Department of Justice and the enforcement of federal criminal law. Some machine practices are illegal; others are questionable;

and any political boss at best would prefer not to have the G-men or T-men poking into his affairs. The President can disrupt a machine whose members are vulnerable under income-tax laws, laws concerning the proper use of the mails, financial regulations, and the like. It was by this means that Huey Long's machine was attacked.[10]

Yet the President's hold on his party has limits. He *controls* the national organization; he *influences* the state and local organizations—but his power comes to an end precisely where he has the most need of it. He has little control of the selection of party candidates for Congress and for state and local office, and even less control of their actions once they gain power. The reason lies in part in his *limited control of state and local organizations;* even more, it lies in the fact that the *party organizations themselves do not control their candidates.* They do not control them because most candidates, as we have seen, win office not as a result of party action but because of their own individual campaigning in both the primary and general elections.

The situation of course varies from place to place. In a boss-controlled center like Chicago or Brooklyn the President may have great influence over the choice of candidates for Congress because (1) he has power over the machine, and (2) the machine picks faithful men, elects them to office, and holds them responsible. But most party organizations are not of this type. Because they are largely dominated by state and local leaders, because they may receive patronage from state and local governments (or from congressmen) even if the President cuts them off, they can operate independently of the national party leadership. And most local party organizations are not strong enough to put their own men into office or control them when they get there, because these organizations lack the leadership and discipline of boss-controlled machines.

Thus the President cannot use his party leadership to strengthen his legislative leadership decisively, much though he might want to. How powerless even a strong President may be to control his party's choices was dramatically shown in Franklin Roosevelt's attempt to discipline the Democratic party in 1938.

F.D.R.'s purge

Despite his own victory in the 1936 election and the lopsided Democratic majorities in Congress, President Roosevelt ran into heavy opposition from many Democratic senators and representatives in 1937 and 1938. Aroused and angry at this opposition within his own party, Mr. Roosevelt decided to take a hand in the selection of Democratic candidates in the 1938 congressional primaries. He announced that not as a President but as "head of the Democratic party, charged with the responsibility of carrying

[10] D. D. McKean, *Party and Pressure Politics* (Boston: Houghton Mifflin Company, 1949), p. 35.

out the definitely liberal declaration of principles set forth in the 1936 Democratic platform," he felt that he had "every right to speak in those few instances where there may be a clear issue between candidates for a Democratic nomination involving principles or involving a clear misuse of my own name."

In New York City, Mr. Roosevelt was successful. There he openly repudiated the Democratic chairman of the House Rules Committee, and helped a pro-Administration Democrat win the nomination against the incumbent. The President also bestowed his blessings on a number of incumbent Democratic senators, who gained renomination (as they might have done in any event). But in Maryland and the South Mr. Roosevelt met his Waterloo. Speaking in Georgia, he said in the presence of Senator Walter George, who was seeking renomination for United States senator in the Democratic primary in that state:

> To carry out my responsibility as President, it is clear that if there is to be success in our Government there ought to be cooperation between members of my own party and myself—cooperation, in other words, within the majority party, between one branch of Government, the Legislative branch, and the head of the other branch, the Executive. That is one of the essentials of a party form of government. . . . The test is not measured, in the case of an individual, by his every vote on every bill—of course not. The test lies rather in the answers to two questions: first, has the record of the candidate shown, while differing perhaps in details, a constant active fighting attitude in favor of the broad objectives of the party and of the Government as they are constituted today; and, secondly, does the candidate really, in his heart, deep down in his heart, believe in those objectives? I regret that in the case of my friend, Senator George, I cannot honestly answer either of these questions in the affirmative."[11]

Senator George replied that he "accepted the challenge," and he easily won renomination against the candidate backed by the President. Mr. Roosevelt was no more successful in efforts to oust conservative Democratic senators elsewhere.

The moral is plain. The party control of even the strongest and most skillful of Presidents has its limits. He cannot, under most circumstances, reach into the local party organizations and control their nominations or the policies of their nominees or officeholders. It has been said that Mr. Roosevelt might have dislodged Senator George & Co. had he carefully fostered a rival Democratic party organization. But such an effort would have run head on into local pride, personal followings, conservatism, and fear of outside control. In practice, the President must negotiate with state and local party chiefs, just as he negotiates with envoys from foreign nations. He cannot dictate.

[11] *The Public Papers and Addresses of Franklin D. Roosevelt,* 1938 Volume (New York: The Macmillan Company, 1941), pp. 469-470.

This weakness of the party affects the President's power not only as chief legislator but also as chief executive. If the President had a tight rein on his whole party, it might be easier for him to control the vast and sprawling executive establishment. In other countries unified parties help provide unified administration. Britain is a case in point. There a minister is ordinarily subject to party authority and discipline to the same degree as rank-and-file members of Parliament, and he is kept in line by party pressures as well as administrative ones. In the United States an important agency head can use his own backing in a section of the party —or even outside the party—to undertake veiled opposition to the President, provided that opposition does not go too far.

CHIEF FOREIGN POLICY MAKER

The framers of the Constitution foresaw a special need for speed and single-mindedness in our dealings with other nations. The Constitution makes the President the exclusive spokesman for the United States. It gives him control over relations with foreign powers. It vests in him command of the two major instruments of foreign policy, the diplomatic corps and the armed services. It gives him responsibility for negotiating with foreign powers. It permits him to make commitments in behalf of the United States. The Constitution specifically assigns to the President the authority to appoint with the consent of the Senate all United States representatives to foreign nations, and to "receive ambassadors and other public ministers."

The power to appoint ambassadors and to receive them is important and involves the vital power of *recognition*. The President has *complete discretion* to recognize or not to recognize new governments or states. In 1902 Theodore Roosevelt recognized the new state of Panama a few hours after a revolt had been staged with the help of United States forces. President Wilson withheld recognition from Mexican governments of which he disapproved, and President Hoover tried to restrain Japan by refusing to recognize its puppet Manchukuo. In 1933 President Roosevelt recognized the government of the Soviet Union whose existence the United States officially had ignored for sixteen years.

Executive agreements

The chief executive shares his treaty-making power with the Senate, as noted in Chapter 16. Presidents have found an easy way, however, to bypass the Senate under certain conditions. This is the *executive agreement*. Well over half the international agreements signed by the United States have been achieved by this procedure, which involves simply an act by the President without any participation whatsoever by Senate or House. Some executive agreements have marked famous events, such as the Boxer Protocol of 1901, the Atlantic Charter, and the "destroyer-bases" agree-

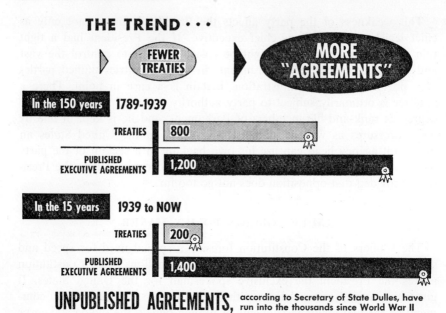

THE TREND · · ·

▷ FEWER TREATIES   ▷ MORE "AGREEMENTS"

In the 150 years   1789-1939

TREATIES | 800

PUBLISHED EXECUTIVE AGREEMENTS | 1,200

In the 15 years   1939 to NOW

TREATIES | 200

PUBLISHED EXECUTIVE AGREEMENTS | 1,400

UNPUBLISHED AGREEMENTS, according to Secretary of State Dulles, have run into the thousands since World War II

ment. In addition to the executive agreements that the President makes on the basis of his own constitutional powers, Congress often confers authority on the Chief Executive to make agreements with other nations. The reciprocal trade program is an important example. Of course executive agreements, like treaties, may be abrogated by the legislature. But as long as they are not repudiated by Congress, they seem to have much the same legal validity as treaties in the eyes of the courts. To be sure, treaties possess a "constitutional and moral control over the conscience and conduct of the American people,"[12] but agreements made by Presidents with the prestige of a Woodrow Wilson or Theodore or Franklin Roosevelt have an authority all their own.

The famous destroyer deal with Britain is an example of the uses of executive agreements. In 1940 Britain urgently needed destroyers to protect her shores and convoys. President Roosevelt and his advisers believed that prompt action was vital. They feared that the Senate might not act fast enough in ratifying a treaty, or might not act at all. By executive agreement the President traded fifty overage American destroyers to the British in return for long-term leases on military and naval bases in the Western Hemisphere. The move won a good deal of popular support; presented with a *fait accompli,* Congress made no attempt to repudiate the agreement.

[12] George B. Galloway, *Congress at the Crossroads* (New York: The Thomas Y. Crowell Company, 1946), p. 269.

POWERS OF THE PRESIDENT

GRAPHIC ASSOCIATES .

From Blair Bolles, WHO MAKES FOREIGN POLICY.
By permission of the Foreign Policy Association

Powers of the President as chief foreign policy maker.

How much power does the Chief Executive have over foreign relations? The Supreme Court has repeatedly upheld a broad exercise of presidential authority in this area. In the *Curtiss-Wright* case in 1936 the Court referred to the "exclusive power of the President as the sole organ of the Federal Government in the field of international relations—a power which does not require as a basis for its exercise an act of Congress, but which of course, like every other governmental power, must be exercised in subordination to the applicable provisions of the Constitution." These are sweeping words. Yet Congress has significant power in foreign relations. It controls the funds to back up foreign programs. It is a center of debate and criticism. And it can "take back" powers that it has delegated the President in the realm of foreign affairs.[13]

[13] For a penetrating analysis of presidential-congressional relations in this field see D. S. Cheever and H. F. Haviland, Jr., *American Foreign Policy and the Separation of Powers* (Cambridge: Harvard University Press, 1952).

The President has not only the authority but the *capacity* to act. For example, he has at his command unmatched sources of information. To his desk facts are channeled from all over the world. Diplomatic missions, military observers, undercover agents, personal agents, technical experts gather tons of material which are analyzed by experts in the State Department and elsewhere. The President has the help of the informed thinking of hundreds of specialists. When he speaks he does so on the basis of the best available information that gives his pronouncements a tone of authority. The President and his experts are sometimes wrong, many gaps appear in their information, but his sources of knowledge give him an advantage over Congress.

Diplomacy, moreover, frequently requires quick action; usually the President can act fast. Diplomacy often has to be secret; as Harold Laski has said, diplomatic negotiations, like a proposal of marriage, must be made in private even if the engagement is later discussed in public. The President can act secretly; Congress cannot. For these and other reasons Congress has granted the President wide discretion on matters affecting foreign policy and military security. Today the President has wide leeway in such matters as controlling foreign trade and exchange, in restricting imports and exports, in barring the transfer of ships to foreign registry, in buying military supplies without bids, in restricting immigration—not to mention his vast constitutional powers as commander in chief in time of crisis (see next section). Congress thus has given up foreign policy making power by wholesale quantities. It has done so not only because of the advantages of the Presidency in this sphere that have been noted above and that John Jay described in *The Federalist*—the *unity* of the office, its capacity for *secrecy* and *dispatch,* and its superior sources of *information.* It has done so also because it has recognized that the United States must present a united front in dealing with other powers.

In view of all these factors, is it surprising that the President's figure looms large in world politics? A foreign observer has said that, in the capitals of other nations, "What is the United States going to do?" usually means "What is the President going to do?" The President's words are searched for meaning in foreign offices throughout the world. But the limits to the presidential power should not be overlooked. Much depends on his ability to persuade Congress to approve—or at least to finance—his program. Checks and balances operate in foreign policy making and cannot be ignored.

THE PRESIDENT AS COMMANDER IN CHIEF

"The President shall be Commander-in-Chief of the Army and Navy of the United States," reads Section 2 of Article II of the Constitution. This is the first of the President's powers listed in the Constitution, but the framers saw his military role as a limited one. As Hamilton pointed out in *The Federalist,* the President as commander in chief would be far less powerful than the King. The President's authority, Hamilton said, "would amount to nothing more than the supreme command and direction of the military and naval forces"; he would be a sort of first general and first admiral of the new nation. As things have turned out, however, the President has become far more powerful, as both the custodian and wielder of the nation's physical forces, than Hamilton foresaw.[14]

Today the President has wide powers as commander in chief during peacetime; in wartime his authority is multiplied under emergency conditions.

In peacetime

The President is supreme military commander. He appoints, with the consent of the Senate, all officers of the armed forces, from ensigns and second lieutenants to five-star generals. This is a vitally important function; it means that largely on the President's shoulders rests the job of determining whether the Marshalls, Bradleys, and Radfords will boss our military forces and plan the over-all strategy, or whether mediocre men will rise to the top. The President has charge also of such matters as defense plans and the disposition of forces, but these military decisions he generally leaves to the chiefs of staff and other commanders.

The President's peacetime powers are limited by the same factors that restrict him as chief administrator and chief legislator—the checks and balances within government and the strength of the opposition. Congress has the power to raise armies, to enact military regulations, and to appropriate money. In practice Congress delegates a good deal of military rule-making to the commander in chief, but the legislators can revoke such grants if they wish. Congressmen also make full use of their right to investigate, to question, and to criticize, especially when the military chiefs come around hat in hand to request funds. Occasionally members of Congress attempt to take a hand in strategic and diplomatic activities, often with unhappy results.

The Constitution reserves to Congress the authority to *declare* war (with the consent of the President), but the commander in chief in practice *precipitates* war. This supreme power of war*making* has been used by the chief executives time and time again. President Polk in 1846 ordered American forces to advance into disputed territory; when Mexico resisted, Polk informed Congress that war existed by act of Mexico, and a formal declaration of war was soon forthcoming. President McKinley's dispatch of a battleship to Havana, where it was blown up, helped precipitate war with Spain. In 1918, when no state of war existed between

[14] E. S. Corwin, *The President: Office and Powers,* p. 283.

the United States and Russia, President Wilson sent American forces to Siberia to join Allied troops fighting the Bolsheviks. The United States was not formally at war with Germany until late 1941, but prior to Pearl Harbor President Roosevelt ordered the Navy to guard convoys to Great Britain and to open fire on submarines threatening the convoys. President Truman had no formal authorization from Congress in 1950 when he ordered American forces to resist aggression in Korea.

Thus the President is able to engage the country in war, given a tense situation. And an all-out war in turn means a tremendous enhancement in presidential power.

The President's war power

When war comes, the central need in a democracy is unity, teamwork, discipline—plus the preservation of our basic liberties. The people want leadership. Instinctively they turn to the President. He can tap a vast reservoir of power in planning broad strategy, raising military and industrial manpower, mobilizing the nation's economy for war.

In wartime the White House becomes G.H.Q. for *governmental* as well as for military and industrial mobilization. Political power, which is ordinarily dispersed throughout the national government, is largely centered in the President. He becomes a sort of constitutional dictator. For example, he makes secret diplomatic agreements with foreign powers, far surpassing ʹin importance many treaties that in peacetime would require senatorial consent. He authorizes the allotment of billions of dollars of funds at home and abroad. He takes final responsibility for crucial military decisions—as in the case of Roosevelt's decision in World War II to concentrate our armed might against Hitler before finishing off Japan. All this does not mean that constitutional forms are abandoned. They still exist—at least on paper. But in wartime the people become unified behind one goal—victory—and the solidarity of the people compels a unity in the government behind the President. Opposition congressmen may snipe at the commander in chief because of some of his nonmilitary plans or policies, such as domestic economic policy or postwar peace goals, but they will not ordinarily obstruct his war program, even though they may lack confidence in it.

These vast powers of the President in wartime are not a recent development. It was Lincoln himself, struggling to overcome the crisis of Civil War, who set the vital precedents for presidential quasi-dictatorship. Congress was not in session when Lincoln was inaugurated in March 1861; despite the emergency (or perhaps because of it?) the new President did not even call Congress into session for four months. Meanwhile Lincoln raised and spent money, built up the armed forces beyond the limits set by law, blockaded southern ports—all without the consent of Congress, all without clear authority under the Constitution. Lincoln had a simple defense for his assumption of dictatorial powers. "Was it possible," he asked later, "to lose the nation and yet preserve the Constitution? By general law, life and limb must be protected, yet often a limb must be amputated to save a life, but a life is never wisely given to save a limb."

Congress in wartime has handed the President great chunks of authority. In World War I, President Wilson was given power to control the production, purchase, and sale of various fuels and foods, which he could requisition if he wished. He had power to take over factories, mines, pipe lines, and the like, and he had a number of blanket controls under the Selective Service Act and the Espionage Act. In World War II, Congress again delegated vast authority to the President, who redelegated it to price, production, man power, and transportation czars, who in turn were coordinated by super czars. Mr. Roosevelt used Lincolnian as well as Wilsonian precedents. In 1942, when Congress refused to repeal a provision in the price control act that protected the farmers, the President demanded that Congress act within a month—or he would. This action of Roosevelt's has been called "a claim of power on the part of the President to suspend the Constitution in a situation deemed by him to make such a step necessary."[15] In any event Mr. Roosevelt's maneuver worked; Congress meekly repealed the provision.

Clearly, the President has vast powers in wartime. Under the Constitution he can direct military operations (taking the field himself if he wishes), establish military government in conquered lands, and end hostilities by means of an armistice. Under authority likely to be granted by Congress he can raise armies, lend or give money or goods to other countries, take over strikebound plants, requisition property needed for defense, ration goods and set prices, shift military functions from one agency to another, censor mail and radio, control vital imports and exports, and so on. The list is long—and a compliant Congress will delegate more powers if the President requests them to meet the emergency.

Certain forms of the Constitution may seem to be suspended. But two basic constitutional rights remain—or at least have remained in all our wars so far. One is the ultimate control of the President by the people. In no war so far—not in the Civil War when Lincoln had to campaign for re-election, nor in World War II, when Roosevelt had to do the same—have elections been suspended. And so far, despite certain restrictions, our basic liberties of free speech and free press have survived the hard test of war.

THE PRESIDENT AS CHIEF OF STATE

As commander in chief the President represents the whole nation. He is not directing the war for the benefit of Republicans or Democrats, of busi-

[15] E. S. Corwin, *Total War and the Constitution* (New York: Alfred A. Knopf, Inc., 1947), p. 64.

nessmen, farmers, or workers, of easterners, northerners, or southerners. He is acting for all the people. This is only one of several ways that the President serves as national leader. His military role, his ceremonial function, and his national responsibilities combine to make him a powerful chief of state representing the *whole nation* and *rising above* the *claims* of *majority* or *minority groups.*

Such was the role the framers of the Constitution hoped the President would fulfill. Looking on him as a sort of chief magistrate, they gave him judicial duties as well. These duties stem from the "power to grant reprieves and pardons for offenses against the United States, except in cases of impeachment." This *pardoning power* leaves the President a good deal of discretion. He can withhold a pardon altogether, or simply grant a reprieve (a delay in executing sentence), or lighten the sentence, such as by substituting life imprisonment for the death penalty, or grant a pardon subject to certain qualifications, or give a full pardon, which makes the offender, in the eyes of the law, as innocent as if he had never committed the offense. In any event, his power in this respect is complete; neither Congress nor courts can overrule a pardon. Since a President receives about 1600 applications for pardons a year, he must lean heavily on advice from the Department of Justice. The pardoning power includes *amnesty,* which is a device for pardoning a specific group of persons at one stroke. In the 1860's Presidents Lincoln and Johnson granted amnesties to southerners who had taken part in secession.

Even the Founding Fathers could hardly have foreseen the extent to which the President would become the *ceremonial* head of the nation. No doubt they expected him to receive ambassadors in the manner of a king, and to issue proclamations on matters of national, nonpartisan concern. But today his ritualistic role surpasses all this. He pitches out the first baseball of the season, buys Christmas seals, gets his Red Cross membership card, presses buttons that start big power projects, attends the Army-Navy football game, hurries to the scenes of national catastrophes, speaks on the Fourth of July and other patriotic occasions, reviews parades, and receives delegations of Boy Scouts, veterans, 4-H members, students, and the like.

Often these actions may be part of a deliberate effort to humanize the man and the job. But it is not a case simply of the President reaching for popular support. Also involved here is the tendency of people to turn to him. Even in a democracy—perhaps especially in a democracy—the people need a leader. They need someone who will personalize government and authority, who will simplify politics, who will symbolize the protective role of the state, who will seem to be concerned with them. How else explain the gifts they shower on him, the tens of thousands of letters that pour into the White House, especially in time of crisis, the sense of private grief felt by masses of people when a President dies? The President is head of the political family; as a sort of father image he sustains a deep-seated longing for a leader and protector (see Chapter 1).

The role of the *national* leader is pronounced in the United States. American acceptance of leadership does not rest essentially on blind worship, as in the case of fascists or communists, but partly at least on a recognition of the fact that in a competitive society the exceptional leader should be allowed to emerge from the mass, take a commanding position, and receive a vote of confidence (at least at the outset). Gunnar Myrdal, a brilliant Swedish social scientist who studied American society, has remarked on the "patterns of strong and competitive personal leadership and weak followership" in the United States. He sees our type of "individual leadership as a great strength of this nation, but the passivity of the masses as a weakness."[16]

All these factors, constitutional, political, and psychological, serve to accentuate the President's role as chief of state, or national leader. Yet under ordinary conditions the President as leader of *all* the people keeps running headlong into the President trying to act for *part* of the people.

The double role

The point is that the President's functions are fundamentally inconsistent with one another. To sum up, on the one hand he is party leader, the spokesman and representative of a popular majority more or less organized in the party that he heads. As party chief he not only directs the national party organization; he also uses his powers as chief legislator to put through the party's program. As chief administrator he must faithfully administer the laws, whether these laws were passed by Democratic or Republican majorities in Congress; yet in choosing his subordinates and in applying the law he tends to think first of the interests of his popular majority. At the same time, as commander in chief and chief of state he tends to act for *all* the people, regardless of group or faction.

How do the two Presidents live with each other? Sometimes the relationship is an uneasy one. For example, the President may wish to address the nation on an important problem. As *President* he is entitled to free time on the radio and TV networks. But if an election is in the offing, the opposition often charges that the President is really acting in his capacity as *party chief* and that his party should pay for the radio or TV time. The same question comes up in connection with the President's inspection trips, especially when he uses such trips as an occasion for political talks and general politicking. The President is often accused, too, of executing laws in a partisan manner, of putting party regulars into administrative offices, of issuing executive orders favorable to the interests of the majority he leads.

[16] Gunnar Myrdal, *An American Dilemma* (New York: Harper & Brothers, 1944), pp. 709-719. See also Eric Hoffer, *The True Believer* (New York: Harper & Brothers, 1951).

During normal times, however, the President manages to combine his roles of chief of state and party leader without too much difficulty. The people expect him to hold both roles, and he moves from one to the other as conditions demand. We grow accustomed to seeing the President operate as national leader in conferring with a foreign envoy, only to don partisan clothing an hour later in conferring with party leaders.

During emergency times such as war the problem to some extent solves itself. A crisis at home or abroad demands leadership. People in both parties instinctively turn to the White House for decision and action. The President doffs his party robes and emerges as national leader or chief of state. Two basic changes take place. The first, as we have seen, is the assumption of extraordinary powers by the President. A serious crisis invariably results in an "increase in the prestige and competence of the President."[17] The President's hold on the people is so strong, his responsibility for action is so great, that Congress almost always follows where he wishes to lead. To meet the crisis he is given wide freedom of action. The normal checks and balances in government are suspended.

Along with this shift occurs another that may have even more significance. As representative of the people as a whole, the President is likely to find that the regular operations of the two-party system are suspended. His normal opposition vanishes—or at least breaks into fragments. To be sure, critics remain. But most of the criticism involves relatively petty matters—problems of mechanics, of methods, of procedures. There remains little organized opposition to the broad goals and programs that the chief of state champions. If any party or group submits a set of alternatives, it may be suspected of seeking to sap the solidarity of the great majority. Such an opposition element may even be accused of lacking in Americanism. Under such conditions the opposition is likely to vanish.

All this may be inevitable. But is it healthy in a democracy? As chief of state, the President is responsible to the nation as a whole. Consequently, he has wide latitude in making his decisions and shaping his program. In a sense, his freedom is so great that it embarrasses him. He lacks the guidelines that serve to help chart the course of the "party President." Some decisions he must make virtually alone. Being responsible to his majority is one thing. Being responsible to the whole people as chief of state is something else. This plight leads us straight into the general problems and prospects of the Presidency.

[17] C. L. Rossiter, *Constitutional Dictatorship* (Princeton: Princeton University Press. 1948), p. 217.

Å̲S WE LOOK AT THE PRESIDENT'S MANY ROLES, we do not wonder that the Presidency has been called the toughest job in the world. This relentlessly exacting office takes the best a man can offer. Personal qualifications for the job have been well described by a leading student of the Presidency:[1]

Bounce. The President must have that "extra elasticity" that enables him to thrive on a harsh diet of work and responsibility.

Affability. "The President's heart must be not only stout but warm. . . . The Presidency is a people's office. . . ."

Political skill. The President must be able to win popular support for his programs, to deal with powerful rivals in Congress, with party and interest group leaders.

Cunning. The President must know the arts of politics—how to dodge and maneuver, when to be silent and when to speak out, when to lead the people and when to follow them.

Sense of history. The President must feel responsible to the generations who bequeathed us a great nation and to the generations still to come.

The newspaper habit. If the President does not want to be hemmed off from the outside world, he must have direct lines to information and ideas beyond his immediate staff. A secretary's briefing is no substitute for reading several newspapers of various outlooks and even glancing at columns and cartoons.

A sense of humor. At least two recent Presidents have said that they "could not have survived in office if they had been unable to laugh at the world and themselves."

The President needs these qualities to handle the problems that flood his office daily. He also needs them because of the much disputed question of the role of the Presidency itself. This chapter will take up three central problems of presi-

[1] Clinton Rossiter, *The American Presidency* (New York: Harcourt, Brace and Co., 1956), pp. 135-137. The quoted material is taken direct from this excellent volume, the other comment is condensed or adapted from it.

18 ★

The

presidency:

powers and

problems

dential power: (1) the problem of the Vice-Presidency and presidential succession; (2) the problem of the President's relation with Congress; (3) the question whether the President has the proper amount of authority in comparison with his heavy responsibilities. The chapter will conclude with an account of how the Eisenhower Administration has dealt with these and other problems.

Presidential disability and succession: the Vice-Presidency

The Constitution provides that in the event of the removal of the President from office, or his death, resignation, or inability to discharge the powers and duties of his office, the same shall devolve upon the Vice-President, and it gives Congress the power to determine who shall fill the office if there is no Vice-President. The framers were wise to provide for a Vice-President, for seven Presidents have died or have been assassinated. Never yet have both a President and a Vice-President left office, but Congress has taken precautionary steps. For a long time the law provided that the Vice-President would be succeeded by the Secretary of State—and he by other Cabinet officers in a prescribed order. In 1947, however, Congress provided that the Vice-President would be succeeded first by the Speaker of the House, then by the president pro tempore of the Senate, and only then by the Cabinet members. In no event would persons not possessing the constitutional qualifications be eligible to serve, and before assuming office as Acting President they would first have to resign from their respective offices. Moreover, a Cabinet member is to serve only until a Speaker of the House or president pro tempore of the Senate is available and qualifies to supersede him.

In the event of the President's death, the Vice-President becomes not merely Acting President but President. What about the situation when the President is too ill to discharge his duties? Should the Vice-President take over? This is not an academic question, for Garfield was disabled several weeks before he died, Wilson for several months before finishing his second term, and Eisenhower for long stretches on two separate occasions. But in no case did the Vice-President take over.

Although a Vice-President never has assumed the powers of the office because of a President's illness, most students of the Constitution agree that the Vice-President in such a situation would become merely Acting President and that the ailing President would resume the duties if and when he recovered. But there are other important unanswered questions. Who is to judge whether or not the Chief Executive can discharge his duties? The Vice-President? The Congress? The courts? Congress has recently studied the question and considered several suggestions; for example, that a group of Cabinet members and congressional leaders be authorized by law to settle these questions after consulting with a panel of doctors, but no procedure has yet been determined on.

Under the Constitution, the Vice-President serves as President of the Senate, voting only when the senators are tied. He often delegates the job of presiding temporarily to some senator, however, so that his legislative duties are not very arduous. Hence at first sight the Vice-President might seem to be an ideal officer both to take some of the burdens off the President's shoulders and to serve as liaison with Congress, or at least with the Senate.

TO INSURE HAPPY LANDINGS

Holland in the CHICAGO TRIBUNE

In practice, however, the office has been something of a joke— and the occupants themselves have often ridiculed it. One of them described his condition as that of "a man in a cataleptic fit. He is conscious of all that goes on but has no part in it."[2] At best the Vice-President is a sort of Administration handyman; at worst he is an intriguer who undermines the President's position. The trouble is that a party's candidate for Vice-President is usually chosen to balance the ticket—if the presidential candidate is a party conservative, he is a party liberal; if the head of the ticket has a special appeal to labor, he will have to possess strong farm support. Hence, in office he usually represents a wing of the party not too friendly to the President. In the face of this political fact the attempts to make the Vice-President something else than a Throttlebottom (for example, by making him a kind of general manager) have usually come to naught.

Recently, however, the Vice-President has taken on important duties, especially in the case of Vice-President Richard Nixon. President Eisenhower's illnesses dramatized the importance of the office, and the people have become far more conscious of its role in recent years. In the 1956 Democratic convention Adlai Stevenson highlighted its role further by allowing the delegates to choose the vice-presidential nominee rather than making the choice himself. The office seems destined to become more influential, but a grave question remains as to whether it is used to strengthen the President's hand or to weaken it.

PRESIDENT AND CONGRESS: TEAMWORK OR DEADLOCK?

There is a story that Theodore Roosevelt, vexed by opposition in the Senate, exclaimed that he would like to turn sixteen lions loose among that

[2] Corwin, *The President: Office and Powers*, p. 73.

body. What if the lions ate the wrong senator, he was asked. "They couldn't if they stayed long enough," Roosevelt snorted.

Many another President would have echoed Roosevelt—and thrown in a few representatives to boot. Many a member of Congress has turned a cold and bitter face toward the White House. Physically the Executive Mansion and the Capitol Building are located on the same avenue, hardly more than a dozen long blocks from each other. Yet relations between President and Congress often seem to be marked by misunderstanding, deadlock, and open warfare.

Is this hostility a recent development? Why does it exist? Should anything be done about it? Can anything be done about it?

The first question can be answered easily. To varying degrees stress and strain have marked presidential-congressional relations from the outset. The new government had hardly got under way in 1789 when Hamilton, Jefferson, and other members of Washington's Cabinet were antagonizing some members of Congress by drafting bills in their own offices and sending them to Congress to be passed. In his earlier years Jefferson had feared that the President would be too powerful; after he became President he found that he had to take firm command of Congress if he wanted his program to go through. Faced with opposition in Congress, Jefferson used his party leaders to block bills, to oust committee chairmen, to steer measures through Congress.

The first serious split between President and Congress came a generation later with Andrew Jackson's Administration. In trying to make the Presidency the "people's office," a rallying point for the popular movements of the time, Jackson ran head on into powerful men in the Senate like Daniel Webster and Henry Clay. In his famous struggle with Nicholas Biddle and Biddle's supporters in Congress over the United States Bank, the President freely used patronage, the veto power, and appeals to the people. Jackson, complained Clay, "swept over the Government like a tropical tornado."

Presidential-congressional harmony has ebbed and flowed.[3] During Andrew

—*Burck in* The Chicago Sun-Times.

"Middle of the Road."

Johnson's Presidency following the Civil War, Congress virtually took over the government by repassing bills over Johnson's vetoes, and in the end

---

[3] For an excellent history of presidential-congressional relations, see W. E. Binkley, *President and Congress* (New York: Alfred A. Knopf, 1947).

impeached and almost convicted him. Grant maintained close relations with the legislators, but at the expense of traditional presidential power. Cleveland at the start was willing to let Congress exert full legislative authority in order to maintain harmony. "I did not come here to legislate," he said bluntly, but in the end he was forced to change his mind and use patronage and other methods to enact his policies. Both Woodrow Wilson and Franklin D. Roosevelt had dramatic differences with Congress; both used the power and prestige of their high office to guide legislative programs.

Reasons for the conflict

The causes of congressional-presidential conflict are multifold. Inevitably a kind of jealousy will spring up among politicians seeking the national limelight. Sometimes trouble results from a simple lack of understanding or failure of communication between White House and Capitol Hill. Occasionally a member of Congress is congenitally unable to play as a member of a team, or a President may be unwilling to make the necessary compromises. Then, too, power is so dispersed throughout the legislative branch, and to some extent throughout the executive branch, that a great deal of confusion arises over the question of who has power to do what.

The main reason for conflict, however, goes far deeper. It lies in the fact that *President and Congress are elected by different alignments of voters and thus have differing loyalties and respond to different pressures.*

As we have seen, Congress tends to reflect sectional, local, and special interests and to overrepresent rural areas and minority groups in general, because of the size and nature of senators' and representatives' districts, gerrymandering, and various arrangements within Congress such as the seniority rule. The President, on the other hand, tends to reflect different groups, because his constituency is the whole nation, and to overrepresent urban groups, because of the electoral college. To gain and keep office, President and congressmen must simply play a different kind of politics. The resulting gap between them goes right back to Madison's old idea that "ambition must be made to counteract ambition."

Can the gap be bridged?

Some Americans are not disturbed by the conflict between President and Congress. Their reasoning is as follows: The nation has successfully survived this situation for over a century and a half. Lack of harmony between the executive and legislative branches, while troublesome and tending toward inefficiency, has not seriously endangered effective government. In moments of peril—for example, during war and depression—Congress and the President have pulled together for the nation's good. Occasional deadlock, the argument continues, is a good thing. By subjecting bills to the scrutiny of both President and Congress, our system prevents foolish legislation. It may, unfortunately, prevent good legislation but in the last analysis, national progress is based not on governmental statutes but on the free and unhampered actions of businessmen, farmers, workers, and others. If the system leads to negative government, in short, the advantages outweigh the disadvantages.

Justice Brandeis once put the point well. "The doctrine of separation of powers was adopted," he said, "not to promote efficiency but to preclude the exercise of arbitrary power . . . not to prevent friction, but, by means of the inevitable friction . . . to save the people from autocracy."[4]

Other Americans have different opinions on the matter. They point to the eternal confusion, the wasted time and effort, the irresponsibility, and the frequent deadlock that are inherent in the semi-independence of the executive and legislative branches from each other. The price is often bad legislation, or no legislation at all. Government inaction might have been endurable during most of our history, it is conceded. But with the United States acting as leader of the free world, and with the national government committed to maintaining economic stability and well-being at home (see Chapter 27), the gap between the executive and legislative branches must be closed.

Linking Capitol and White House

What can be done? Some of those who would bring the legislature and executive closer to each other propose that we forge some permanent link between the two branches. They recognize, of course, that many informal methods of liaison exist—for example, the President's meetings with the congressional Big Four (Vice-President, Speaker, and majority leaders of House and Senate), and the thousands of contacts that occur daily between legislators and administrators at conferences, over the telephone, in committee sessions, and even at cocktail parties. But these are highly informal arrangements, much dependent on the personal relations between President and congressional leaders, between rank and file legislators and bureaucrats. Proposals have been made for more permanent, institutionalized ties between the two branches.

One plan involves a *joint cabinet* or council. Advocated by the late Senator Robert M. La Follette, Jr., among others, this plan calls for a permanent group composed of congressional leaders and key cabinet officers who together would rough out the broad outlines of national policy. Meeting regularly, the members would come to know one another well and to build a team spirit. Doubtless the President would preside over the meetings. This plan has received wide support. It was recommended in 1946 by the Joint Committee on the Organization of Congress, but Congress did not adopt the proposal.

[4] *Myers* v. *United States* (1926).

Another plan, at least a century old, is to *give cabinet members seats in Congress.* The Secretaries—originally appointed, of course, by the President—could debate matters and answer questions, but they would not vote. Such a proposal would not require a change in the Constitution. Indeed, in the early years of the government certain Cabinet members did speak in Congress, but the arrangement soon fell into disuse. Today its sponsors feel that such an arrangement would create more understanding—or at least better communication—between Cabinet and Congress. As a variation of this plan, Senator Estes Kefauver of Tennessee has called for a *question and answer* period during which Cabinet members and other key administrators could report in person to House and Senate, afterward answering questions from any and all members.[5]

A final proposal would require that the President choose his advisers from *leading members of Congress,* possibly along with the more important members of the present Cabinet. Such a body would be something of an extension of the present Big Four system, but it would be larger, stronger, and more institutionalized. Here again, no constitutional problems need arise if members of Congress are not made heads of departments. To be sure, the new Cabinet would still be a body of advisers. But as Professor Corwin, a supporter of the plan, has said, there are advisers *and* advisers. Such a Cabinet, in his view, "would comprise men whose daily political salt did not come from the presidential table, whose political fortunes were not identical with his, who could bring presidential whim under an independent scrutiny which today is lacking."[6]

Criticisms of proposals

How feasible are these proposals to bring Congress and the President together through some sort of joint cabinet or council? Some observers are highly skeptical. If a joint cabinet is designed simply to acquaint President and Congress with one another's views, they argue, it is completely unnecessary. Each side knows the other's views only too well. The problem, critics of the proposal emphasize, is not one of simple communication or exchange of views, but of *differing representation.* No council or cabinet would change the basic power situation.

If a joint cabinet had real power, the critics continue, it might be effective. But would Congress ever give real power to such a body? They fear not. A central fact of Congress is the *dispersion of power* among dozens of committee chairmen and other influential party and bloc leaders. The joint council might work out satisfactory agreements with the President only to fail to get backing from other leaders and from the rank and file.

[5] Estes Kefauver and Jack Levin, *A Twentieth-Century Congress* (New York: Duell, Sloan & Pearce, Inc., 1947), pp. 65-79.
[6] E. S. Corwin, *The President: Office and Powers,* 3rd ed. (New York: New York University Press, 1948), p. 362.

Advocates of reforms believe that improvements in the relations *between* the executive and legislative branches can come about only with reforms *within* the two branches. For example, they urge that Congress abandon such devices as the seniority rule, archaic procedure, and the filibuster. They want the executive branch to be better organized, better staffed, and better led. Given such a combination of reforms (see Chapters 16 and 19), they believe that our government will be more efficient, effective, and responsible. But as we have seen, changes within Congress and the executive branch are hard to bring about.

Reforming the Constitution

Some reformers believe that all these efforts to build a bridge between Congress and the President, even if achievable, do not go far or deep enough. Tinkering with the machinery is not enough, these critics say; what we need is a *basic remodeling* of the governmental system. Such a remodeling, they grant, would call for sweeping changes in our Constitution. Many plans have been suggested, but generally they fall into two types.

One type of plan for constitutional reform would make the President and his Cabinet *responsible to Congress* by giving Congress the power to oust the chief executive and to elect a new one. This plan is precisely the one considered on several occasions by the framers in 1787, and finally rejected. It would make the President almost wholly dependent on Congress. Because most Americans do not want to reduce the President to the role of a mere agent of the legislature, this plan has won little support. It smacks too much of the rickety parliamentary regimes that are believed to have weakened democracy in Europe. A faction-ridden Congress, it is felt, would continually want to hire and fire Presidents, giving us hair-trigger government.

A second plan cuts much deeper. It provides that whenever Congress voted lack of confidence in the President (or turned down an important Administration bill), the chief executive could *dissolve Congress.* The legislators (and, under some plans, the President too) would thereupon run for re-election. Since an election would occur only when Congress and the chief executive were at odds over some vital issue or program, the results of the election could be considered a mandate for the government to follow. If the President's opponents won out, he would resign, and Congress could choose his successor. If the President was upheld by the people, his program would go through. The two plans differ—but the essential idea is the *power of dissolution of Congress,* enabling elections to revolve around great issues instead of being held at prescribed intervals.[7]

[7] For three important examples of the general plan, see W. Y. Elliott, *The Need for Constitutional Reform* (New York: Whittlesey House, 1935), pp. 27-40; Henry Hazlitt, *A New Constitution Now* (New York: Whittlesey House, 1942); and T. K. Finletter, *Can Representative Government Do the Job?* (New York: Reynal & Hitchcock, Inc., 1945).

Clearly this type of proposal bears the earmarks of parliamentary govern-ment—especially of that in Great Britain. There the Prime Minister and his cabinet members hold seats in Parliament: if they lose a vote of confidence on some issue, all the members of the House of Commons run for re-election in their constituencies, and the next government is composed of the leaders of the party that wins most of the seats in the election. In Britain this system has produced strong and stable government—yet one that is sensitive to deep shifts in public opinion. To import such a system Americans would need to adopt electoral changes and probably to reduce the power of the Senate, but supporters of the plan are willing to make the necessary changes in the Constitution.

The advocates of such a system—which is usually called "cabinet" or "parliamentary government"—believe that their plan meets the basic prob-lem of popular control of government. Cabinet government, they say, forces the rulers to keep a sharp eye cocked for changes in popular feeling. Thus the *people*—not the leaders—reign supreme. Government, moreover, is no longer divided internally. If President and Congress differ, an election is called and the people make the decision on the matter in dispute. This does not mean, it is said, that elections would take place too often. Politicians do not like to run for office, and both the chief executive and the congressmen would make every effort to compromise. Only on the most vital issues would the voters intervene. Government perforce would become alert and united without losing strength and stability.

Could cabinet government do the job?

The advocates of these constitutional changes admit that pushing through the necessary amendments would be a herculean task. A vast campaign of education would be needed, and even if most Americans were won over to the cause, thousands of politicians and groups with vested interests in the present system would stand in the way. Ratification of sweeping changes by legislatures or conventions in three-quarters of the states would be most unlikely. Nevertheless, the suggestions must be examined on their merits, regardless of their chances of adoption. They must be tested in terms of their own goals of effective, responsible, and democratic government.

Critics of cabinet government say this: To be sure, the plan would bring President and Congress into closer relationship. But at what price? Let us suppose, they argue, that a newly elected President and Congress clashed on some important issue or program. The President would let it be known that he would dissolve Congress and force another election unless the legislators went along with the White House. One of two things might then happen. Congress might give in to the President, in which case the price would be letting the chief executive have his way against the wishes of the other elected branch of government. Or—more likely—Congress might accept the challenge and an election would be called. If the President's opponents gained a majority of the seats in the election, he would resign and Congress would appoint a new chief executive. If his supporters won a majority, the new Congress and the old President could go ahead on the basis of his original program.

Everything turns, say the critics of cabinet government, on the outcome of these elections. And they feel that the outcome in every case would be predetermined. It would be a defeat for the President. Why? The reason, they say, is that Congress would accept the gauge of battle only when it was sure of its support back home. Most congressmen are well entrenched in their districts; those who are not would have time to campaign throughout their districts, while the President would have the whole nation to cover. Nor would the outcome depend simply on the national issue that touched off the battle. Many congressmen would be re-elected on the same basis that they are now—on the basis of personality, past favors to constituents, relations with local group and party leaders, and the like. The President (depending on the kind of plan adopted) might win his election only to find the opposition still in control of Congress.

If the critics are right on this count, the implications of the proposed change for our national government are clear. Such a system unquestionably would be weak and unstable. For if a majority of congressmen hostile to the President won the election, they would return to Washington eager to select a new chief executive more responsive to their views. Minority blocs would virtually take over the government. The new President necessarily would be a mediator, a compromiser, a straddler—perhaps only a political cipher. Whatever way the wind blew, he would have to trim sail accordingly if he wanted to keep his job. He would be a follower, not a leader.

Yet the times seem to call for vigorous leadership, for strong executive control, not for instability, intrigue, and balance-of-power bargaining. Cabinet government would establish a link between White House and Capitol Hill, but the price—government impotence—seems too high. Is there any other way to unify our government and to make it both effective and responsible? We will return to this basic question in Chapter 21.

IS THE PRESIDENT BECOMING TOO POWERFUL?

How much power *should* the President have? This question is hard to answer because one cannot be sure what powers the President *does* have. The Constitution, as we have seen, is somewhat vague on the matter. It seems to grant the President a broad executive power without defining that power. Some scholars see significance in the fact that the Constitution vests "the executive power of the United States" in the President but gives Congress only the legislative power "herein granted." They argue that the President has wide powers to protect the public interest in emergencies without specific legal authority or even at the cost of overriding existing laws. Despite considerable controversy over the matter, and the Supreme Court's recent rebuff of President Truman's attempt to exert "inherent powers" (see pp. 552-553), there seems to be a kind of "inherent power" of the President, vast but undefined, that an aggressive President could exploit in time of crisis. The President also has a good deal of undefined power as the chief foreign policy maker—a situation that has advantages in an era of crisis, but that makes defining presidential power difficult.

Theories of presidential power

It is not surprising that different Presidents have had different ideas of their job. Two of them have given their views with great frankness. Theodore Roosevelt wrote in his *Autobiography:*

The most important factor in getting the right spirit in my Administration, next to the insistence upon courage, honesty, and a genuine democracy of desire to serve the plain people was my insistence upon the theory that the executive power was limited only by specific restrictions and prohibitions appearing in the Constitution or imposed by the Congress under its Constitutional powers. My view was that every executive officer, and above all every executive officer in high position, was a steward of the people bound actively and affirmatively to do all he could for the people, and not to content himself with the negative merit of keeping his talents undamaged in a napkin. I declined to adopt the view that what was imperatively necessary for the Nation could not be done by the President unless he could find some specific authorization to do it. . . . Under this interpretation of executive power I did and caused to be done many things not previously done by the President and the heads of the Departments. I did not usurp power, but I did greatly broaden the use of executive power.[8]

This has been called the *stewardship* theory of presidential power. William Howard Taft, on the other hand, took a rather narrowly *constitutional* view of presidential power. He wrote in 1916:

The true view of the Executive functions is, as I conceive it, that the President can exercise no power which cannot be fairly and reasonably traced to some specific grant of power or justly implied and included within such express grant as proper and necessary to its exercise. Such specific grant must be either in the Federal Constitution or in an act of Congress passed in pursuance thereof. There is no undefined residuum of power which he can exercise because it seems to him to be in the public interest. . . .[9]

[8] T. R. Roosevelt, *An Autobiography* (New York: The Macmillan Company, 1913), pp. 388-389.
[9] W. H. Taft, *Our Chief Magistrate and His Powers* (New York: Columbia University Press. 1916), p. 139.

Franklin D. Roosevelt's conception of his powers—sometimes called the *prerogative theory*—followed more closely the view that the President in the face of emergencies had the same power that John Locke once argued that kings had—the power, in Locke's words, "to act according to discretion for the public good, without the prescription of the law and sometimes even against it."[10] The destroyer deal, for example, violated several laws.

Is the President powerful enough?

Now for the other side of the ledger. The President's power is so great that it is easy to forget the many factors limiting his freedom of action. Yet in normal times these checks are considerable. We have seen that as chief administrator and as chief legislator:

The President must, of course, share *policy-making* power with congressmen, administrators, and others.

He shares his *treaty-making* power with the Senate.

He shares his *appointing* power with congressmen, especially Senators.

His power to *dismiss* agency heads is limited.

He is powerful in his *party*, but by no means all-powerful. He has limited influence over the lower echelons of the party.

Above all, the President is held in leash by the political situation in which he operates. No matter how strong a leader he may be, he is not a free agent. Not only must he deal with key congressmen, cabinet members, important bureaucrats, the Vice-President, party chiefs, and perhaps even leaders of the opposition party. He also must cope with the great political forces operating around the White House—public opinion in all its complexity, pressures from organized interests, demands from his own party. He has the job of negotiating endlessly among individuals and among interests. Always he must act—but without stepping on too many toes. Always the fierce light of public opinion, magnified by press, radio and television, beats on the White House. It is in this respect, above all, that the President has the toughest job on earth.

In recent years the President's power has been curbed in an important respect: in his eligibility for a third term. The framers allowed the indefinite re-eligibility of the President. Washington, however, quit after two terms and set a two-term custom that Presidents followed for a century and a half. By the time Coolidge turned down a chance to run again in 1928, the tradition against a consecutive third term had acquired virtually the force of a constitutional provision. In 1940, however, Franklin Roosevelt challenged this unwritten law in seeking a third term. His victory in effect "repealed" the tradition, but the repeal was not to last long. In 1951 the thirty-sixth state

[10] E. S. Corwin, *The Constitution and What It Means Today,* 10th ed. (Princeton: Princeton University Press, 1948), pp. 84-85.

ratified the Twenty-second Amendment, which now bars President Eisenhower today or any person in the future from being elected President more than twice. It will be interesting to see if this change will survive should an immensely popular President want a third term some day. But in any event, the amendment will probably weaken Presidents during their second term, because powerful political leaders in Congress and in the Administration will feel less obliged to support a man who they know will be out of power within a given period of time.

Problem and prospects

We seem to have come to the point where we are willing to accept the President as master of our fate and fortunes in time of crisis. We have moved a long way from the idea of checks and balances that set some limit to the chief executive's role even under emergency conditions. A striking example of this situation occurred in June 1950, a few days after North Korean troops invaded South Korea. President Truman, acting on his own, ordered American forces to resist aggression. Equally significant, the few senators who criticized him for not going first to Congress found no support except in the extreme isolationist press. Today more than ever before, the President, as Woodrow Wilson once said, "is at liberty, both in law and conscience, to be as big a man as he can."

The growth of presidential power has not resulted from conspiracies of scheming men in the White House. That growth stems from many factors, including social changes, economic crises, wars, the rise of political parties, the frequent failure of Congress to act effectively in the face of national problems, the deep popular demand for leadership and action. The problem is acute today, largely because this is a time of continually recurring and deepening crises. Wars and economic dislocations inevitably demand drastic and far-reaching action on the part of the man in the White House.

How dangerous is the tendency toward "one-man rule" in time of crisis? So far it has not been a serious problem. Perhaps we have been lucky. The great wartime leaders of the United States—Lincoln, Wilson, F.D.R.—were democrats in the best sense. They did not want power for power's sake, but simply as a means of overcoming national peril. Aside from one or two lapses they maintained the basic democratic institutions of civil liberties and free elections. We may not always be so lucky. Some day we may elect a President who in time of crisis would find some pretext to postpone elections or stifle free speech. Indeed, we may elect a man who would deliberately create an emergency for the very purpose of suppressing the opposition.

The problem will become all the more serious if the twentieth century continues to be a time of endless emergencies, as seems likely from the perspective of the mid-century. But one thing seems sure. We cannot solve the problem by trying to cut the President down to size. To do this would be to blunt the very weapon—presidential power—that has served us so well in past emergencies. Nor should we try to raise Congress into full rivalry with the President, for that would give us divided government, a condition that crisis cannot tolerate. A thoughtful student of the problem has well advised us, "Leave Your Presidency Alone!"[11]

The problem is a double one. On the one hand we must see to it that the President is our servant, not our master, that he leads us only in the direction we wish to go. On the other hand we need to help the President. He must have enough authority to do his job.[12] He must be free of some of the obstacles that now confront him. Above all, he needs the wise counsel of men who, like him, take a broad, national point of view, and who can both guide him and sustain him. He cannot always find such associates in the Cabinet, for the members, though men of his choosing, seldom have national prestige of their own. He cannot often find them in Congress, because even congressmen of the same party have their own political loyalties and responsibilities. He cannot easily find such allies in his own party because our parties tend not to create national leaders.

The need, in essence, is *responsible leadership*. The Presidency can be a vast reservoir of leadership. No one saw this better than Franklin D. Roosevelt. "The Presidency is not merely an administrative office," he said. "That is the least of it. It is more than an engineering job, efficient or inefficient. It is pre-eminently a place of moral leadership. All our great Presidents were leaders of thought at times when certain historic ideas in the life of the nation had to be clarified. . . . That is what the office is—a superb opportunity for reapplying, applying in new conditions, the simple rules of human conduct to which we always go back. Without leadership alert and sensitive to change, we are all bogged up or lose our way."

How can we make such leadership responsible? Perhaps we can come to grips with this question after we have looked in the next two chapters at our other national policy makers.

EISENHOWER AND THE PRESIDENCY

When Dwight D. Eisenhower took office in January 1953, he brought to the White House a fresh approach to the Presidency after a generation of New Deal-Fair Deal leadership. He had ideas about changing the administrative organization of the Presidency. Feeling that Roosevelt and Truman had interfered too much in Congress, he hoped to close the gap between the executive and legislative branches. On the other hand, he was less interested than his two predecessors in being a strong party leader. The new

---

[11] Rossiter, *op. cit.*, p. 161.

[12] Louis Brownlow, *The President and the Presidency* (Chicago: Public Administration Service, 1949), pp. 114-115.

President was well trained to serve as commander in chief, and his middle-of-the-road policies and pleasing personality seemed ideal for his future role as chief of state.

The Presidency itself is a great institution and a great tradition; it cannot easily be changed. In some respects Eisenhower changed the office to his liking. But, as the following recapitulation shows, in other respects the office changed *him*.[13]

Eisenhower as chief administrator

In his capacity as chief administrator, the President brought about some well-received changes. Feeling that his predecessors' methods had been disorderly and hit-or-miss, he installed the military form of staff, in which directions are supposed to flow in an orderly manner from the chief executive on down, and a chief of staff (or operations officer) sees to it that the directions are carried out. Eisenhower appointed Sherman Adams, a former governor of New Hampshire, as the Assistant to the President—in effect, a powerful chief of staff overseeing the White House and top government operations.

The President tried two other innovations. He resolved to make his Cabinet a real "team" that would work together harmoniously and take some of the burdens off the President. He also asked Vice-President Nixon to serve as a leader of the executive branch, taking on important assignments and helping to smooth the Administration's relations with Congress.

In many respects the changes worked well. Adams took an immense burden off the President's shoulders, allowing him more time for reflection and relaxation. Vice-President Nixon was widely credited with able handling of a great variety of administrative, diplomatic, and legislative tasks. The Cabinet performed, at least outwardly, with more harmony than under the Roosevelt administrations (when Cabinet officers sometimes attacked one another openly in the newspapers). Agendas for meetings were more carefully prepared than in the past. These changes were especially valuable during the President's illnesses, when the top direction of government seemed to continue without major difficulty.

There was another side to the ledger. Democrats, and even some Republicans, complained that Adams was taking over too much power, making too many decisions, becoming practically the real President. Some agency chiefs complained that they could not get to the President; they felt the lack of direct and vigorous presidential support. The Cabinet never came to serve as an important policy-making body, nor was Nixon able to serve as a real substitute when his chief was ill.

[13] This section is based largely on Robert J. Donovan, *Eisenhower: The Inside Story* (New York: Harper & Brothers, 1956), a revealing and "semi-official" treatment based on interviews with Administration leaders.

Eisenhower as chief legislator

The new President brought to his office in 1953 a genuine regard for Congress and a respect for the tradition of governmental checks and balances. At his first Cabinet meeting in the White House he urged Administration leaders to cooperate with Congress. He even invited all 531 members of Senate and House to a series of luncheons. He made overtures to Senator Robert A. Taft and Taft's strong supporters on the "Hill." For a time Eisenhower seemed to feel that this friendly approach would be enough to bring cooperation between the executive and legislative branches.

But soon disillusionment set in. Although Republican-controlled, Congress was soon opposing the Administration in many time-honored ways—investigating it, holding up presidential appointments (in the Senate), cutting down requested appropriations, voting down White House measures. Even worse for the President, Senator Joseph R. McCarthy attacked him for breaking his promises to "clean up the mess in Washington" and made headlines with his probes of alleged Communists or security risks in the executive branch.

The President also had to deal with the proposed Bricker amendment (see pages 588-590) which would have limited presidential power over foreign relations. Secretary of State John Foster Dulles and other Administration leaders flatly opposed it. At first Eisenhower tried to compromise on the matter, but compromise did not work. Then he tried to exert gentle pressure through his conferences with legislative leaders. But this did little good, either. Nobody can "deliver" the Senate, warned Vice-President Nixon.

Perhaps the most revealing example of the Administration's early difficulties involved Representative Daniel Reed and excess profits legislation.

Eisenhower and Reed: a case study

As chairman of the Ways and Means Committee of the House of Representatives, Reed had charge of the committee that was responsible for framing national tax policy. He had become chairman of the committee not because his tax views necessarily represented those of the Administration, of Congress, or of his committee, but because he had been in the House for 34 consecutive years and had steadily climbed the seniority ladder. Representing a conservative Republican district in rural upstate New York, he had views on tax policy that differed sharply from those of the Republican President who had won sweeping nationwide support in his first bid for office. Thus the dispute typified many of the historic aspects of presidential-congressional conflict.

The immediate situation in the spring of 1953 was this: Reed wanted to see the federal excess profits tax expire on June 30, 1953, as had previously been scheduled by Congress. This tax, he argued, hurt business—especially small business—and the Republicans had been promising the voters for years to cut taxes when they took office. President Eisenhower and other Administration leaders agreed that the tax was "bad," but they did not want the tax to expire until December 31, 1953. Their reasons were threefold: (1) the Republicans had promised to balance the budget as well as cut taxes, and a deficit was looming; (2) Administration leaders feared it would be politically unwise to drop a tax on corporations before taxes on individuals could be cut; and (3) the government could not afford the loss in revenue—about $800 million—if EPT were not extended.

Accordingly the Administration asked Congress for legislation extending EPT by six months. Representative Reed said "no." Deciding that they could get nowhere with Reed, Administration leaders decided on a new tack. The Rules Committee of the House (see pp. 397-398) not only controlled the right of way for bills but could send its own measures to the floor of the House. Would the Rules Committee be willing to ignore the Ways and Means Committee and send its own EPT extension bill into the House? Speaker Martin quickly investigated and discovered that all the Republican members except one or two would go along with a new bill. By the skillful use of patronage, one more member was won over to the Administration's cause.

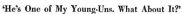

'He's One of My Young-Uns. What About It?'

Herblock in THE WASHINGTON POST

A one-time All American football player and wrestling champion, who looked the part, Reed was furious when he heard of Martin's plans. He resolved to fight to the end. Appearing before the Rules Committee, he shouted that the committee's action would destroy the "foundations of our legislative system." But a majority of the Rules Committee, anxious to support the President and the Speaker, voted to report their own EPT extension to the House.

Seemingly, the Eisenhower Administration had won the battle. Many representatives, however, were disturbed by the fact that the Ways and Means Committee had been bypassed. Moreover, an acrimonious fight over the Rules Committee's powers seemed likely on the floor. Seeking to avoid such a fight, Martin sought and gained assurances from members of the Ways and Means Committee that if no further action was taken on the Rules Committee bill, these members would sign a discharge petition, if necessary (see p. 391) to bring the EPT bill out of Reed's committee. When he heard of this move, Reed knew his battle was lost. Grudgingly, he called a meeting of Ways and Means. When a member moved for consideration of EPT, the chairman, dogged to the end, ruled him out of order. The committee by a majority vote then overruled Reed and promptly reported out the Administration's EPT extension bill.

The fight illustrated several important aspects of congressional-presidential relations: (1) the power of a committee chairman; (2) the tendency of the seniority system to put men into chairmanships who stand for different policies from the national leaders of the party; (3) the extent and limitations of presidential influence; (4) the crucial role of party leaders in Congress, like Speaker Martin.

Eisenhower takes the offensive

His experience with congressional leaders like Bricker and Reed and the failure of much of his program in Congress convinced the President that he must exert stronger leadership over legislation. At the start of the 1954 session of Congress, he announced that he was "unalterably opposed" to the Bricker amendment. He vigorously defended Administration officials against Senator McCarthy's accusations (although he did not attack the senator openly by name). Most important, the President told Republican congressional leaders that the time had come when the Republicans must face up to their responsibilities to act on their pledges during the election. He put pressure on the leaders. When one of them suggested that an independent Congress should not be pushed too far, the President shot back that he would carry the fight into the open if he had to.

Eisenhower continued to press for his program during the rest of his first term, but two things intervened. One was the Democratic capture of Congress in the fall of 1954, and the other was his health breakdowns. Paradoxically, however, the President got along better with the Democratic Congress of 1955-56 than he had with the previous Republican Congress. Democratic control to some extent isolated Republicans who had thwarted the President, and McCarthy and other committee chiefs lost their chairmanships. But the cooperation between Eisenhower and the Democrats had its complications too, for in the 1956 elections both the Administration and the Democrats claimed credit for the same bills or blamed the other side for the mistakes, so that the average voter had trouble discovering who was responsible for what.

Even so, the President had discovered what all Presidents today must discover—that they either take the reins of legislative leadership or they allow government to become bogged down in confusion and inaction. His experience well illustrates the question, as noted above, that a President may not have *enough* power to live up to his heavy responsibilities.

Eisenhower as party chief

When the new President took his oath of office, Senator Robert A. Taft was still leader of the more conservative and isolationist wing of the Republican party. The senator from Ohio had many loyal followers on the Hill, including many of the Republican committee chiefs. Taft and his supporters pledged cooperation with the President, but they became extremely disturbed by some of Eisenhower's early actions; for example, by his appointment of a labor union chief as Secretary of Labor.

For his part, the President was upset by the failure of the Taft wing to support his program. The division within the Republican party so worried him during 1953 that he began thinking of the possibility of a third party—one that would be essentially "his" party, representing his brand of middle-of-the-road domestic policy and internationlist policy abroad.[14] But then his mind turned to the failure of previous third party movements, such as the Progressives led by Theodore Roosevelt. He decided that his best hope was to keep trying to give the Republican party "a new viewpoint and a new complexion."

Accordingly the President resumed his role as party chief with new vigor. He had remarked earlier that the White House occupant was "President of all the people" and that he did not intend to use his office as an agency in partisan elections. Faced with the congressional elections of 1954, he changed his mind. He put aside his earlier wish to keep his office out of political battles and plunged into probably the most active political campaign that any President has ever waged in a midterm election. He called openly for a Republican Congress and traveled the country speaking for Republican candidates. While the Democrats nonetheless won control of Congress, some observers felt that their margin would have been larger without the President's intervention. In 1956 the President again "lent his coattails" (as far as his health permitted) to Republican candidates seeking his backing in their national and state campaigns.

The lesson Eisenhower had learned was the one that other Presidents have had to learn—that the President must be party leader as well as administrative and legislative leader. Otherwise the government would lack the needed propulsive, coordinating force to make it produce results. And somehow the President had to combine his party leadership with his leadership of all the people as commander in chief and chief of state. Faced with a Demo-

---

[14] Donovan, *op. cit.,* pp. 151-153.

cratic Congress after the 1954 and 1956 elections, Eisenhower showed his willingness to deal with the Democrats while continuing to serve as Republican chief. But the task of party leadership, difficult enough with his own party in power, was bound to be one of the most galling and perplexing problems of the President's second term with Congress controlled by the opposite party.

GOVERNMENT OFFICIALS ARE PEOPLE. WE hear so much of arrogant bureaucrats and red tape artists these days that it is well to keep this fact in mind. The bureaucrat is the postman who just stuck your mail in the door, Miss Green who teaches sixth grade at the grammar school, the cop directing traffic on Elm Street, and the judge who lives down the way. He is also a man fighting a forest fire in Wyoming, a diplomat negotiating a treaty in Argentina, a tax collector adding some figures in New Orleans, a bureau chief hurrying to the White House, a scientist studying a rare disease at a great medical center. These are people with hopes and worries, ambitions and frustrations, abilities and failings—just like all the rest of us.

Flaying the bureaucrats is an old American custom, and to an extent is a wholesome one. It is well to remember, however, that all large organizations, whether governmental or not, are run by bureaucrats. Bureaucracy is a characteristic form of modern organization. We hear much of the dead hand of bureaucracy, but bureaucracy as a type is neutral. It can be efficient or inefficient, democratic or autocratic, alert or stagnant.[1] *Some* governmental bureaucracies—like *some* private ones—are on balance inefficient (although inefficiency is very hard to measure). The sheer volume of the criticism of bureaucrats in government arises in part from a deep-seated fear of big government, in part from the fact that public officials work in a goldfish bowl under the sharp eyes of congressmen, columnists, radio commentators, lobbyists, and others.

In this chapter we are mainly interested in the 2⅓ million people who make up the executive branch of the federal government. Certain facts about these 2⅓ million people need to be emphasized at the outset:

1. Only a small part of the 2⅓ million work in Washington. The great majority are employed in regional, field, and local offices scattered throughout the country. The picture of a huge bureaucratic horde concentrated in Washington is a false one.

2. More than half of these

19 ★

The

bureaucrats

[1] John Dickinson, "The Perennial Cry of Bureaucracy," *The Yale Review*, March 1935, pp. 448-463.

2⅓ million civilian employees work for the Army, Navy, or some other war agency. Perhaps three-quarters of them are connected with the fighting of past, present, or future wars. The continuing world crisis has put its stamp on our bureaucracy.

3. Only a small part of the bureaucrats—perhaps 10 per cent—work for so-called welfare agencies, such as the Social Security Administration or the Rural Electrification Administration. The welfare state may be a major point of controversy in our party battles, but it has a minor place in today's big government. A much smaller proportion of government employees work in regulatory agencies such as the Interstate Commerce Commission.

4. Federal officials do not run to any one type. They are not all Democrats, or all Republicans. They are not all college-educated. They are not all conservatives, or all liberals. They are as varied as the American people themselves. They come from all parts of the country, have a variety of religious faiths and political views, represent a great range of national origins.

5. Their work in government is equally varied. Not all these officials pound typewriters or stamp forms or issue regulations, as the newspaper cartoons would have us think. Over 15,000 different personnel skills—about two-thirds as many as are found in all private business—are represented in the federal government. Like Americans generally, most government workers are specialists in some occupation or profession. Unlike Americans as a whole, however, most federal employees are white-collar workers—stenographers, clerks, lawyers, office heads, inspectors, and the like.

How important are the bureaucrats? In a sense, of course, they are all-important. They are the core of big government. Without officials and employees government would be a collection of politicians and lawmakers —generals without armies. Government without a bureaucracy is unthinkable. So influential are the officials that sometimes the political heads seem insignificant. Alexander Pope said over 200 years ago:

> For forms of government let fools contest
> Whate'er is best administer'd is best.

But this sentiment goes too far. *Forms of government* help shape the political world in which the administrator lives; they influence the kind of decisions made, and the way they are carried out. Administration in the United States is different from administration in Russia, Spain, or Borneo.

Actually we cannot separate administration from politics. The two are inextricably linked. Our job is not to put each in a separate sphere, but to see the interrelationship between the two. Our job is to ask questions: How is administration carried on? What kinds of problems do administrators face? What are their powers? How are they made responsible and accountable to the people? In short, how can the bureaucrats do their jobs and yet remain our servants and not our masters?

THE SHAPE OF ADMINISTRATION

Our big government is complex. The executive branch is a cluster of ten departments, twenty government corporations, and fifty or more independent agencies, together embracing over 2000 bureaus, divisions, branches, offices, services, and other subunits. Five big agencies, the Departments of Army, Navy, and Air Force, the Post Office, and the Veterans Administration, tower over all the other agencies in sheer bulk. Most of the agencies are responsible to the President, but some are partly independent of him. Virtually all the agencies exist by act of Congress; the legislators could abolish them either by passing a new law or by withholding funds. The power of Congress to set up departments and agencies stems from the Constitution. The framers simply assumed—without actually specifying—that Congress might establish such functions and organizations as it saw fit.

In its first session in 1789, Congress created the Departments of Foreign Affairs (later changed to State), War, and Treasury. During the next 100 years the government grew slowly but fairly steadily. World War I caused a mushrooming of federal agencies, and many of these remained during the postwar years. World War II brought an even greater expansion, as the government mobilized armed forces of fifteen million men, fought a war on many fronts, and controlled large areas of the nation's economy. The executive branch shrank after World War II, but not back to its prewar size, and again increased sharply during the Korean war.

Formal organization

A soldier writes to his mother that he is a member of the first squad of the second platoon of Company B of the 1st Battalion of the 426th Regiment of the 95th Division of the III Corps of the Ninth Army. A friend might work in the personnel office of the parts section of the Flint Division of the Buick Department of General Motors. Similarly a "government girl" in Washington could tell her father that she is in the stenographic section of the administrative service of the Budget and Finance Division of the Bureau of Supplies and Accounts of the Department of the Navy in the Department of Defense.

Bigness means organization. The larger the number of people and the more complex the job, the more highly organized an agency will be. Much of this organization will be carefully planned. In establishing a new agency, Congress may lay down a general structural plan in legislation, the President may give further shape to it in executive orders and in private instructions, and the head of the agency and his assistants will extend the organizational skeleton of the new agency down to small units.

The executive branch, it has been said, grew up "without plan or design like the barns, shacks, silos, tool sheds, and garages of an old farm." Different functions also will result in varying organizations. In general, however, the main agencies of government are composed of departments, corporations, independent agencies, and their subunits—bureaus, divisions, offices, and so on down the line—together with a network of regional and local offices.

The *departments,* as we noted in the previous chapter, are headed by Secretaries (except Post Office which is headed by the Postmaster General and Justice which is headed by the Attorney General). These Secretaries

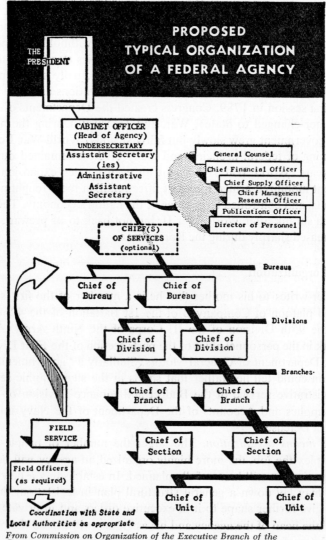

From *Commission on Organization of the Executive Branch of the Government,* CONCLUDING REPORT, *1949, p. 10*

Hoover Commission recommendation for departmental organization.

also are Cabinet members (except for the Secretaries of the Army, Navy, and Air Force, who report to the President through their chief, the Secretary of Defense) and thus directly responsible to the President. While the departments vary greatly in size, they show some common features. Often an undersecretary takes part of the administrative load off the Secretary's shoulders. One or more assistant secretaries direct major fields of action. Like the President, the Secretaries have personal assistants who help them in planning, budget, personnel, legal, public relations, and other staff functions. The departments are, of course, subdivided into bureaus and smaller units, but the basis of division may differ. The most common basis of subdivision is *function;* for example, the Commerce Department is divided into the Census Bureau, the Patent Office, the Weather Bureau, and so on. Or the basis may be *clientele* (for example the Bureau of Indian Affairs of the Interior Department), or *work processes* (for example the Bureau of Agricultural and Industrial Chemistry of the Agriculture Department), or *area* (for example, the Alaskan Air Command of the Department of the Air Force).[2] The basis of organization of most departmental units—and indeed of the departments themselves—is mixed.

The score or more of *government corporations* are "mongrel" organizations. A sort of cross between a business corporation and a regular government agency, the government corporation was designed to make possible a freedom of action and flexibility not always found in the regular federal agencies. For example, corporations have been free from control by annual appropriations by Congress and from certain regulations of the Budget Bureau and the Comptroller General. They also have had more leeway in using their own earnings as they pleased. At the same time government has basic control through its ownership of the corporations. The Tennessee Valley Authority and the Federal Deposit Insurance Corporation are two examples of this form of organization. More recently Congress has deprived the corporations of much of their freedom, and they have taken on some of the character of regular departments. Corporations are no longer free from annual congressional appropriations. They remain, however, useful means of keeping certain government activities (especially financial) somewhat apart from the routine, congested, and centralized federal agencies and from excessive congressional and presidential control, particularly in time of emergency.

The *independent agencies* embrace many types of organization and many degrees of independence. Broadly speaking, all agencies that are not corporations and are not in the executive departments (such as Treasury or Interior) are called independent agencies. Many of these agencies, however, are no more independent of the President and Congress than the regular line departments. The huge Veterans Administration is not represented in

[2] S. C. Wallace, *Federal Departmentalization* (New York: Columbia University Press, 1941), pp. 91 ff.

the Cabinet, for example, but its chief is directly responsible to the President. Their independence consists mainly in being outside the formal executive departments.

Another type of independent agency, however, really deserves the adjective. This agency is the *independent regulatory board* or *commission*. Examples are the Securities and Exchange Commission, the National Labor Relations Board, the Interstate Commerce Commission. Congress established a number of agencies somewhat independent of the President mainly in order that these agencies might be somewhat free from White House influence in exercising their quasi-*legislative* and quasi-*judicial* functions. Congress did not want the President, for example, to interfere in the I.C.C.'s setting of railroad rates or in its decisions as to whether its rules had been violated by railroad companies. Congress protected this independence in several ways. The boards are headed by three or more commissioners with overlapping terms, they often have to be bipartisan in membership, and the President's power of removal is curbed. But this independence is limited. No agency can be completely separate from its governmental and political surroundings (nor should it be). And many of the boards have found that the more independence they have of the President, the more dependent they are on Congress.[3]

Within the departments, corporations, and independent agencies are a host of subordinate units. The standard name for the largest subunit is the *bureau,* although sometimes this unit is called an office, administration, service, or what not. Bureaus are the working agencies of the federal government. In contrast to the big departments, which are often mere holding companies for a variety of agencies, the bureaus usually have fairly definite and clear-cut responsibilities, as in the case of the Bureau of Customs and Bureau of Narcotics of the Treasury Department, the Bureau of Indian Affairs of the Interior Department, the Bureau of Motor Carriers of the I.C.C. Most bureaus are overshadowed by their mother agencies, but some of them, like the Federal Bureau of Investigation and the Bureau of Reclamation, have a governmental prestige and political position of their own. Below the bureaus are the hundreds of branches, services, sections, and other units that perform even more specialized operations.

The *field service* of the federal government embraces a vast number of regional, state, county, and local units. The local post office is part of the field service; so also is the local recruiting center or veterans office. As the action end of government, the field service runs into many vitally important problems. Ticklish questions of coordination constantly arise. How to get cooperation between several federal offices with overlapping duties in the region but responsible to different departments in Washington? How far is it possible and desirable to depart from national regulations in meeting

[3] See R. E. Cushman, *The Independent Regulatory Commissions* (New York: Oxford University Press, 1941), esp. Chapter 10.

local variations? Which decisions should be made on the spot, and which should be referred to Washington? How much collaboration should be tried with state and local governments? Washington administrators face problems, too: how far to decentralize, what decisions should be delegated to the field, what type of field organization is best suited to their needs (there are many types), how to combine local flexibility with national direction and responsibility.[4]

Informal organization

All this elaborate organization is important because it gives some order and system to administration. It assigns certain functions to certain units, places one official (or sometimes more) at the head of each unit and makes him responsible for its performance, allows both specialization and coordination, permits ready communication, and in general makes our far-flung administration somewhat controllable and manageable. But this formal organization is not all-important. Indeed, it can be highly misleading if taken too seriously. The elaborate organization chart on the office wall of some administrator may represent hope and intention more than reality.

The point is that men are not standardized units. They differ in attitude, motive, ability, experience. To be useful, an organization chart must give a sense of uniformity and pattern, but men do not easily fall into uniformities and patterns. This situation leads to all sorts of complications. Relationships among officials in an agency may be based on *influence* rather than legal authority. Leadership may be lodged not at the top but in a variety of places. A certain group of officials may have considerable power, while another group, with the same *formal* status, may have much less. The loyalties of some officials may cut across the formal aims of the agency.

Consider an imaginary but typical bureau in these terms. The bureau chief is an old-line administrator who has served through four presidential administrations. He is cautious and unimaginative. He has a rival in the person of an assistant to the Secretary who heads the whole department. Some officials in the bureau look to this assistant for leadership; they share his enthusiasm and support his plans, and they hope that he may take over some day and give them the power and position they feel they deserve. But the bureau chief has his own set of motives and attitudes; moreover, he enjoys the backing of a powerful bloc in Congress that will defend him if he is attacked. Too, he has built a personal organization, made up of two or three division chiefs, an attorney, the personnel officer, and his own staff, and this personal following is intensely loyal to him.

This, perhaps, is an extreme case; there are many other types of informal organization that individually may be less significant than the example above but that together have a major effect on administration. A subordinate

<hr/>

[4] D. B. Truman, *Administrative Decentralization* (Chicago: University of Chicago Press, 1940).

official in an agency, for example, might be especially close to his chief, simply because the two men went to the same college or play poker together, or because the subordinate knows how to ingratiate himself with his chief. A staff official may have tremendous influence, not because of his formal authority, but because his qualities of experience, fairness, common sense, and general attractiveness lead men to turn to him for advice. The agency chief may be personally weak, unimaginative, phlegmatic, and incompetent; such a situation creates a vacuum in which other leaders try to take over. The private secretary of an official through her charm, tact, and understanding of the job of her boss and the politics of the agency, may gain great influence in an organization. The elevator man has no formal power at all, but he is a vital link in the informal communications network in the agency, and his rumor mongering distinctly affects the morale of the employees.

Such informal organization and communication is inevitable to some degree in any organization, public or private. Even the Army, with all its hierarchy and regimentation, abounds with these elements. Is informal organization nevertheless an evil that has been allowed to develop too far?

Certainly it has its disadvantages. It can be a *disorganizing* force, in the sense that employees may not know who is really running the agency, what orders are to be followed, where the agency is trying to go. It may be a *demoralizing* factor. Officials may come to feel that a group of "king's men" in the inner circle have a privileged position and will get quick promotions and other favors. Administrative decisions may turn too much on personal factors and not enough on written rules and tradition. Different officials and subunits may work at cross purposes, responding to different instructions or loyalties. The result may be friction and waste.

On the other hand, informal organization may be as beneficial as it is inevitable. In an agency that is unduly rigid in structure, it permits flexibility and vitality. It may give recognition to outstanding young administrators who have not yet risen very far in the formal hierarchy. It may allow more people to contribute to the agency's policies and planning, and thus it may raise agency morale. It may allow an astute administrator to put bridges across the artificial divisions, formal and informal, that always arise in an organization.[5] The wise agency chief tries not to suppress informal organization, but simply to turn it to good account.

Some administrative concepts

Administration is relatively young as a systematic technique, and still unscientific in many respects. As a body of theory and experience, however, it has evolved a number of working concepts that throw light on the accomplishments and problems of administration.

[5] F. M. Marx, ed., *Elements of Public Administration* (Englewood Cliffs, N. J.: Prentice-Hall, Inc., 1946), pp. 294-313.

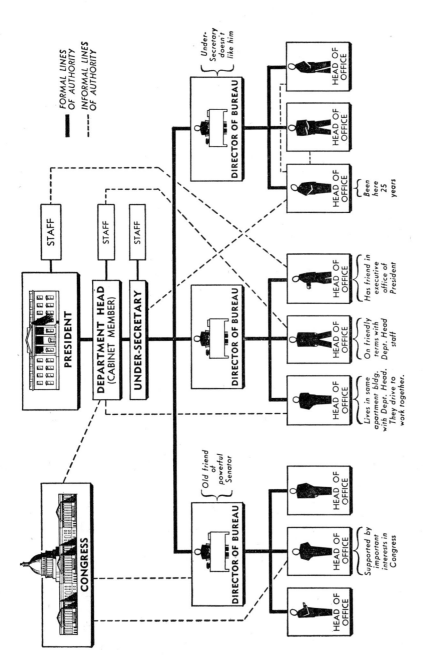

FORMAL AND INFORMAL LINES OF A BUREAUCRATIC ORGANIZATION

Unity of command. Every official should have a superior to whom he reports and from whom he takes orders. This principle of administration aims at bringing some order and unity into the actions of thousands of government employees. It is related to another concept, the *chain of command,* which suggests a firm structure of authority running from the top down, and of responsibility, running from the bottom up. But as the practical workings of informal organization show, these principles are not—and cannot be— hard and fast. A subordinate cannot get all his instructions from his chief; he is influenced by other leaders, by his associates, by experts outside the agency, by his own background and personality. Nevertheless, unity of command is an important basic principle in assigning authority and responsibility.

Line and staff. Line, as we have seen in discussing the Presidency, means the pyramid of operating agencies. These agencies directly carry out their jobs, such as preventing soil erosion or inspecting coal mines. The staff is the *advisory* agency, which does not issue orders on its own but acts *through the operating chiefs* and down the chain of command. In the Army, the staff might do intelligence work; in the Department of Agriculture it might be responsible for personnel. Standard staff work involves helping the executive in his functions of planning, organizing, staffing, directing, coordinating, reporting, and budgeting (often described as POSDCORB). Once again, no easy distinction between line and staff is possible. Often staff units actually do control and command instead of merely advising. Some staff agencies, like the Budget Bureau, employ hundreds of persons and have operating as well as advisory tasks. Many line chiefs hold important advisory functions; a bureau chief may be the main adviser to a department head. Still, the line and staff concept is useful in understanding administrative organization, especially on a large scale, as in the Army.

Span of control. How many persons can one man supervise effectively? A rule-of-thumb answer is three to fifteen. Much depends on the personality of the chief, the nature of the work, the size of the organization, the location of the subordinates (as in field offices), and many other factors. No matter how able a chief may be, a breaking point ultimately will be reached if he must supervise more and more subordinates. In practice, this principle is often violated. The Hoover Commission found that far too many officials report to the President, with the result that he could not effectively direct them.[6]

Decentralization. An administrator cannot make all the decisions himself. He must delegate decisions and responsibilities, as well as action itself, to lower levels. One sign of an able administrator is the ability to prevent

---

[6] Commission on Organization of the Executive Branch of the Government, *General Management of the Executive Branch* (Washington: Government Printing Office, 1949), p. 3.

his own desk from becoming a bottleneck. But decentralization is difficult —it may lead to problems of unity of command and the span of control.

Professionalism. Many of the most influential government people are experts in some field of study, such as law or accounting, or in some field of administration, such as sanitation, building army camps, or operating new machines. Such professionals are indispensable to modern government, but their role poses certain questions. What should be the relation between the chief, holding broad responsibilities, and the expert? How can the professionals be geared into the operating program? How can their advice be evaluated? What if their suggestions clash with those of operating heads?

LEADING THE TEAM

These concepts suggest one of the chief problems of public administration. This problem is the *effective performance of governmental services that require smooth and coordinated relations among all types of people and agencies.* Unity of command and the other concepts are simply different features of this problem. The administrator, in short, is facing the question that is central to democracy and central to this book: how to reconcile the demands of unity and diversity. He must lead a team made up of people with all sorts of skills, attitudes, and backgrounds; he must reach his goals without stifling the diversity and freedom that we prize in a democracy. Watching the administrator forming and leading the team, we see that he is both helped and handicapped by the ancient traditions and present practices of American administration.

Building the team

The government administrator is not nearly so free in building his team as is the private businessman. Government has long followed prescribed methods of recruiting, examining, classifying, promoting, and dismissing personnel. These methods are largely a result of painful experience. For many years America had a notorious appointment system that was summed up in the slogan, "To the victor belong the spoils." The underlying philosophy was simple. If a new party came to power, its leaders and followers should take over desirable government jobs. The excuse was a double one. Parties should have patronage, it was said, so that the members would work for the party, and because the people wanted the new broom in Washington to sweep clean. Men like Andrew Jackson argued, moreover, that a frequent turnover of officials would keep government democratic. Besides, they said, the duties of public officials were so plain and simple that any intelligent person could perform them.

Later in the century a sharp reaction set in to the spoils system. The job of government was becoming increasingly complex, and interested citizens, some of them organized in the National Civil Service Reform League, were agitating for reform. Presidents, too, were chafing under the pressures of hordes of job seekers. Public opinion crystallized when President James A. Garfield was shot to death in 1881 by a disappointed office seeker. Two years later Congress passed the Pendleton Act, which set up the beginnings of a merit system under a three-man bipartisan board, the Civil Service Commission. The act placed certain types of employees under a new classified service, which could be entered only by passing a competitive examination. Congress in this act put relatively few employees under the new merit system, but fortunately the President was given power to expand the classified service. As a result of a series of executive orders over the years about three-quarters of the federal employees today hold jobs that are free from patronage considerations.

Today the administrator must work closely with the Civil Service Commission in staffing his agency. With about 4000 employees, the commission acts as a central agency in recruiting, examining, and appointing government workers. It advertises for new employees, prepares oral and written examinations which it gives throughout the country, and makes up a register of names of those who passed the tests. When the hiring agency wishes to employ a person, the commission certifies to it three names taken from the top of the appropriate register. The administrator has some voice in the type of examination given, and he has some freedom of choice under the rule of three, but obviously his discretion is greatly limited.

The centralization of personnel direction in the Civil Service Commission has long disturbed administrators eager for freedom and flexibility in their agency operations. They charge that the commission has tended to entangle itself in red tape, to use old-fashioned personnel methods, and to lack initiative and imagination. Whatever its defects, the Civil Service Commission over the years has effectively helped to keep most federal jobs out of the spoils system.

This is not to say, however, that appointment to the classified service is based on merit considerations alone. There is still a strong feeling in the United States that government jobs are a form of reward.[7] The best example of this feeling is *veterans' preference*. Today five points are automatically added to the examination grades of all veterans, and they receive other special considerations. Disabled veterans, their wives, and their widows, are given favorable treatment. These provisions, supported by powerful veterans' groups in and out of Congress, have aroused much controversy. Some have charged that veterans' preference is a racket; others say that the government owes a debt to the ex-servicemen and that it can easily find able recruits from the large numbers of them. The Hoover Commission did not oppose veterans' preference, but it did favor a compromise policy that

---

[7] H. A. Simon, D. W. Smithburg, V. A. Thompson, *Public Administration* (New York: Alfred A. Knopf, Inc., 1950), pp. 323-324.

would give the administrator somewhat more leeway in making appointments. At any rate, veterans' preference is probably here to stay. It is not surprising that about half the federal employees today are veterans.

Hiring is only the first step in building the administrative team. The administrator must see that appointees get into the right positions, that they are trained effectively, that their jobs are classified properly in terms of the nature and responsibility of the work. Here, too, the administrator shares his power with the Civil Service Commission. Around each of these fields, such as job classification, an elaborate procedure—indeed, virtually an administrative science—has grown up.

Managing the team

In directing his agency the good administrator is always conscious that he is directing people. As a practical psychologist he must remember that people's actions are influenced not merely by instructions from the top. For example, he must remember that:

People are moved by many incentives. Chester I. Barnard, an outstanding businessman and author of a classic volume on administration, has listed some of these as material rewards (money), the chance for prestige or power, agreeable working conditions, pride of workmanship, happy relations with workmates, conformity to habitual practices, sense of taking part in something big, and patriotic or religious feeling.[8]

People are moved by influences from outside the agency as well as from within. Government employees do not identify themselves wholly with the administrative unit to which they belong. They come to work as members of many groups—as southerners, veterans, Negroes, taxpayers, Catholics, and so on. The administrator faces the same problem of overlapping membership as the leader of a party or interest group.

People in administrative units tend to have a powerful feeling of solidarity and defensiveness. Most government workers are members of cohesive groups. These groups are often marked by excellent communication (that is, employees see one another throughout the working day), a sense of oneness, and a feeling of mutual protection. This in-group feeling has important practical effects. For example, the group may react in a hostile way to interferences from outside the organization. It may in particular resist reorganization from outside. At the same time, the desire of each person to have the respect and affection of his fellow workers is a big factor in promoting harmony, good morale, and efficiency.

People—in the United States especially—have a mixed attitude toward authority. Generally government employees, like employees everywhere, will accept the orders of their superiors. But there are limits. Americans are individualists—they have their own opinions and they do not like to be

[8] C. I. Barnard, *The Functions of the Executive* (Cambridge: Harvard University Press, 1938), pp. 142-148.

pushed around. Much depends on the manner in which authority is exercised, and on the relations between administrator and the employees.[9]

To put the whole matter another way, the administrator finds that the morale and efficiency of his unit is affected by *informal* as well as *formal* organization. He must be *people*-minded, not simply *stereotype*-minded.[10] In directing his agency he must operate through informal channels of communication and organization as well as formal channels. He will ignore people's personalities—including their quirks and "bugs"—only at his peril.

On the other hand, the administrator has the benefit of certain powers or tools in running his unit. Much of his authority stems simply from his position as boss of the agency; his instructions are usually followed without question, and the agency is set up so that a stream of directions runs from the top to subordinate units. The administrator also has some power over promotions within the agency. Through this power he can reward able service and raise the ablest men and women to more responsible positions. Here, too, set procedures must be followed. Agencies are under pressure from the Civil Service Commission to give promotions only after examinations, and the commission itself conducts some of these. Promotions are based also on an elaborate system of efficiency ratings which are given employees by their supervisors and which can be appealed to boards of review if employees question the fairness of their ratings. Administrators also gain some flexibility through transfers of personnel to and from their agencies, although transfers often must be handled carefully because of their relation to morale.

Finally, the administrator can discharge unsatisfactory employees. Despite a popular notion to the contrary, government workers *can* be fired. The process, however, is hedged in by many rules to prevent arbitrary dismissals. During their first six months of employment, new appointees are on probation, and they can easily be dropped at the end of the period (although very few are). After the probationary period, however, an employee can be removed only "for such cause as will promote the efficiency of the service." He must be furnished with a written statement of the charges against him and be given time to reply. Some inefficient employees have used cumbersome appeal procedures to protect their jobs. The Hoover Commission unearthed one case where a stenographer appealed to four separate boards, meanwhile hanging on to her job for seventeen months before she finally quit. But such cases are exceptional; more employees are removed for cause than is generally realized.

ADMINISTRATORS AS DECISION MAKERS

A policeman stops a student who fails to bring his car to a full halt before crossing a highway. The student admits that he did not come to a

---

[9] Simon, Smithburg, and Thompson, *Public Administration*, pp. 70-71, 180-217.

[10] A. H. Leighton, *The Governing of Men* (Princeton: Princeton University Press, 1946), Chapter 3.

full halt, but he argues that he did look both ways before entering the highway, and he did slow down enough so that he had to shift into second gear. The officer lets him off with a lecture and a warning. Why? The law requires that the student be arrested and pay a fine. But the officer knows that a full halt is not necessary at this particular corner, as long as the driver is reasonably careful.

Here is a simple example of administrative discretion and decision making. The officer is not an automaton. He is an experienced man of good sense. In this case he exercised two functions basic in the administrative process: he established his own rule and he made a judicial decision. In his own way he was participating in *administrative legislation* and *administrative adjudication*.

The Constitution gives legislative powers to President and Congress, and judicial powers to the courts. Under today's big government these powers must be delegated to officials throughout the executive branch. Some officials have tremendous discretion, some have very little. Democratic government permits delegation of broad powers, but seeks to safeguard the manner in which those powers are exercised.

Big decisions

Every day in hundreds of ways federal bureaucrats make decisions that affect our jobs, our pocketbooks, our whole lives. We may or may not know of these decisions. The Board of Governors of the Federal Reserve Board issues a ruling that affects the size of the down payment we must make on a new car. The Rural Electrification Administration decides to bring electricity to farmers in one valley but not in another. The director of the Bureau of Labor Statistics formulates a new method of computing price indexes— one that may affect the government's anti-inflation policies. The Attorney General decides to prosecute a large corporation under the antitrust act. Officials in charge of civil service examinations change their methods of testing. Safety officials in the Civil Aeronautics Board issue a new and more stringent set of air safety regulations.

Wars and near wars have vastly broadened the decision-making powers of administrative officials, especially in agencies involved in making war and peace. Obviously, the Secretary of State in dealing with foreign powers makes decisions that gravely affect the chances of peace or war. The Atomic Energy Commission and the Defense Department jointly or separately decide on crucial policies that bear on our capacity to win a war. If war comes, the fate of the nation hangs on decisions of commanders in the field. Many military decisions are secret, but some are public and become subjects of wide discussion.

To say that bureaucrats make important decisions, however, is not to say that they have a wide number of alternatives to choose from. An administrator may have been given broad discretion by both Congress and the President, and yet feel constricted by other forces. For an administrator, like a congressman or a President, works amid a complex set of political pressures. In making a key decision he must try to anticipate the attitudes of his own agency, of experts inside and outside the agency, of other agencies involved in the decision, of interest groups affected by the decision, of the press, of the attentive public as a whole,[11] of the party in power and the opposition party, of Congress and the President, perhaps even of foreign governments. He must take into account all kinds of organizational and psychological relationships too numerous and complex to deal with here.[12] To make things even more difficult, he often must act in a hurry and on the basis of incomplete knowledge.

Administrative lawmakers

Given these many influences and pressures, there is always the chance that bureaucrats may act irresponsibly, or at least may ignore the interests of the many for the benefit of the few. Congress has long realized that as governmental problems have become numerous and complex, administrators have had more and more to make important decisions. The lawmakers also know—or at least most of them do—that there is no easy way to reverse this trend. However, Congress has sought to surround the decision-making process with safeguards, both because the national legislature is jealous of its own control of lawmaking and because it wants to prevent abuse of delegated power. There is not much Congress can do in a formal and systematic way to regulate the decisions made by key officials who must face new and unprecedented problems—especially when those officials are acting under broad powers granted the President. But in the cases of agencies that have functions of regulation and control on a regular and long-term basis, closely affecting private interests, an effort has been made to set up certain safeguards.

Well over 100 agencies have the power to issue rules and regulations affecting the public. Most of these agencies are *regulatory agencies,* like the Interstate Commerce Commission, which has powers over the nation's railroads, or the Federal Communications Commission, which polices the nation's radio and television waves. The most important regulatory functions have been placed in independent boards and commissions, but on occasion Congress has put these functions in line agencies such as the Department of Agriculture. Congress has a special interest in the regulatory agencies, for these agencies must interpret the broad acts of Congress and fill them

[11] G. A. Almond, *The American People and Foreign Policy* (New York: Harcourt, Brace and Company, 1950), Chapter 7.

[12] See H. A. Simon, *Administrative Behavior* (New York: The Macmillan Company, 1949).

out to meet specific problems. For example, Congress has recognized the right of employees to "organize and bargain collectively through representatives of their own choosing." Such a general provision leads to a hundred new questions and definitions, such as the nature of unions, the rights of employers, the definition of unfair labor practices, the rights of nonunion employees, the scope of collective bargaining, and so on. It is a *regulatory agency*—in this case the National Labor Relations Board—that must make the all-important interpretations.

Safeguards are of several types:

1. The agencies interpret and enforce *laws of Congress*. If they misinterpret a statute, the national legislature can always amend the act to make more plain the intent of Congress. The basic legislative power of House and Senate compels the agencies to seek to find the will of Congress and interpret and apply laws as the congressmen would wish. Congress can exercise this control also through its powers of investigating and appropriating.

2. Congress has closely regulated the *procedure* to be followed by regulatory agencies. Under the Administrative Procedure Act of 1946, agencies must publicize their machinery and organization, must give advance information of proposed rules to interested persons, must allow such persons to present their information and arguments, must allow parties appearing before the agency to be accompanied by counsel and to cross-examine witnesses.

3. Under certain conditions rules made by regulatory agencies can be appealed to the courts.

4. Administrators in regulatory agencies, as in all agencies, are surrounded by informal political checks as well as formal ones. They must keep in mind the demands of professional ethics, the advice of experts, the attitudes of congressmen, President, interest groups, political parties, interested elements of the public, and so on. In the long run, these safeguards are the most important of all.

Administrators as judges

The hardest problems facing some administrators are sometimes not ones of basic policy but those calling for judgment and judiciousness in settling disputes or mediating among conflicting claims. The Secretary of Defense, for example, might have to reconcile the demands of two rival services, such as the Navy and Air Force. The Secretary of Agriculture might need to intervene in a conflict between two interest groups, such as growers and wholesalers of grain. A bureau chief might have to referee a jurisdictional squabble between two division heads. To umpire such disputes may call for the wisdom of Solomon, and at the very least for qualities of fairness and understanding.

Here again the regulatory agencies, holding a close and continuing relation to private groups, have a special responsibility for making judicial decisions when disputes arise between two or more private interests, such as business groups, or between private interests and the government. Congress has delegated to the regulatory agencies power to make such decisions in their particular areas of regulation. In this respect, the agencies act as courts, and the administrators as judges. They receive complaints, hold hearings, listen to witnesses and lawyers, study briefs, and make decisions, much like any other court. Formal adjudicative functions have been placed mainly in independent regulatory commissions, but also in line agencies and in special courts.

. Administrative adjudication, however, is largely a matter of informal action. Much of the judicial function consists of informal, voluntary settlement of cases at lower levels in an agency. The Interstate Commerce Commission, for example, arranged voluntary settlements of all but five out of 3500 complaint cases in one year. The National Labor Relations Board, which administers a most controversial act, made formal decisions in only 4 per cent of more than 12,000 cases involving unfair labor practices during the first four years of its existence.[13]

These informal settlements illustrate the two main arguments in favor of delegation of judicial power, for these actions represent relatively quick and inexpensive settlement of disputes, taking an immense burden off the courts, and they are accomplished by men who are experts in technical fields, such as transportation, labor relations, or radio communication. Despite these advantages, many persons—especially lawyers pleading cases before the regulatory agencies—have expressed concern over the extent of the adjudicative power vested in the agencies. They complain also that the administrators violate due process of law in holding private and informal sessions, in failing to give the parties enough of a hearing, in providing the parties with insufficient information and evidence to support the decisions.

Partly as a result of these complaints the Administrative Procedures Act of 1946 provided for broader judicial review of administrative decisions. The courts have always had the power to overturn administrative judgments on points of *law*, as in cases where an agency had exceeded its authority, or misinterpreted the law, or had simply been unfair. Under the 1946 act the courts seem to have more authority to examine questions of *fact*—that is, to go over the mass of technical evidence examined by the agency. While this tendency has not gone very far, it points up the problem of maintaining the balance between judicial control and administrative efficiency and expertness. The new law also provides for procedural safeguards, such as more formalized hearings and proper notice of action.

[13] Attorney General's Committee on Administrative Procedure, *Final Report, Senate Document* 8, Seventy-seventh Congress, First Session (Washington, 1941), p. 35. For an admirable recent treatment of administrative action, see Emmette S. Redford, *Administration of National Economic Control* (New York: The Macmillan Company, 1952).

Finally, the act tackled another long-debated problem of the regulatory agencies—the concentration in these agencies of both legislative and judicial power. This administrative absolutism, as some have called it, seems to run counter to the great doctrine of the separation of powers. The act provides that there should be a greater separation *within* regulatory agencies so that the same officials would not act as both judges and prosecutors. Thus officials who investigate cases and present them for action are not to have any part in deciding them. The act did not, however, provide that the agencies be divested of legislative or judicial duties. It could not. In an era of big government and big problems, Congress and the courts must delegate much of this job to the administrators—or else the job will not be done at all. Administrators will act as lawmakers and judges as long as the functions of government are technical, complex, many-sided, and voluminous. And this means for a long time.

Those worried about the extent of the judicial power of administrators usually express the fear that these administrators will do too much *prosecuting* and not enough impartial *judging*. It is well to remember that the very opposite can happen. In some cases regulatory agencies become so occupied with umpiring disputes impartially that they may pay insufficient attention to their prosecuting functions. They tend to sit back passively and wait for complaints to be filed instead of taking the initiative in ferreting out violations of the law. They become "judicialized." Such a course may seem to be the safe thing to do; to some extent the regular courts have forced regulatory agencies to organize themselves mainly as judicial bodies. The result of this tendency may be inadequate protection of the very groups that the regulatory agencies were set up to safeguard.

ADMINISTRATORS IN ACTION: TWO CASES

We have seen something of the complex of pressures and loyalties amid which a bureaucrat must work. We have seen that the good administrator must have some of the qualities of the politician, the lawmaker, the judge, the expert, the team quarterback. Day after day he must make decisions that involve issues of policy, problems of organization, matters of law— and above all *people*. The following two cases, based on actual administrative experience, illustrate some of the painful choices that a bureaucrat may have to make, whether he is in Washington or in the field.

Mr. Brown's dilemma

George Brown is chief of the Bureau of Erosion of the Department of Conservation.[14] He is still in his early forties; his appointment to the post

[14] The persons and agencies (except for the Budget Bureau) in this case are fictitious, but the facts of the case are drawn from actual happenings in Washington.

was a result both of his ability and of luck. When the old bureau chief retired, the President wanted to bring in a new chief from outside the agency, but influential members of Congress were pressing for the selection of an ex-senator who had represented a farm state. As a compromise Brown, then a division head, was promoted to bureau chief. A graduate of a midwestern agricultural college, Brown is a career official in the federal service.

Early in March of the second year that Brown had held the new post, his boss, the Secretary of Conservation, summoned him and the other bureau heads to an important conference. The Secretary informed the group that he had just attended a Cabinet meeting, that the President had called for drastic economies wherever possible, and had specifically asked each department to effect at least a 10 per cent cut in spending in the coming fiscal year. The President, the Secretary reported, was convinced that there was a great popular demand for retrenchment.

Brown quickly calculated what this cutback would mean for his agency. For several years, the Bureau of Erosion had been spending about $45 million a year to help farmers protect their farmland. Could it get along on about $40 million, and where could savings be made? Returning to his office Brown called a meeting of his personnel, budget, and management officials, together with his four division chiefs. It was agreed after several hours of discussion that savings could be effected only by decreasing the scope of the program—which would involve ending the jobs of about 1200 of the Bureau's employees.

A few weeks later Mr. Brown presented a $40 million budget to Secretary Jones, who approved it and passed it on to the White House. The President went over the figures in a conference with the Director of the Budget, and a few weeks later the budget for the whole executive department, incorporating the Erosion Bureau's $40 million, was transmitted to Congress.

Meanwhile Brown was running into trouble. News of the proposed budget cut had leaked immediately to the personnel in the field. Nobody knew who would be dropped if the cut went through, and some of the abler officials were already looking around for other positions. Morale fell. Hearing of the cut, farmers' representatives in Washington notified local farm organizations throughout the country. Soon Brown began to receive letters asking that certain services be maintained. Members of the farm bloc in Congress were also becoming restless.

Shortly after the President's budget went to Congress, Representative Smith of Colorado asked Brown to see him. Smith was Chairman of the Agriculture Subcommittee of the House Appropriations Committee, and thus was a potent factor in congressional treatment of the budget. Brown immediately went up to the Hill. Smith began talking in an urgent tone. He said that he had consulted his fellow subcommittee members, both Democratic and Republican, and they all agreed that the Erosion Bureau's cut must not go through. The farmers needed the usual $45 million and even

more. They would practically rise up in arms if the program should be reduced. Members of Congress from agricultural areas, Smith went on, were
under tremendous pressure. Leaders of farm groups in Washington were
mobilizing the farmers everywhere. Besides, Smith said, the President was
unfair in cracking down on the farm program; he didn't understand agricultural problems, and he was not cutting other expenses.

Then Smith came to the point. Brown, he said, must vigorously oppose
the budget cut. Hearings on appropriations would commence in a few days
and Brown as bureau chief would of course testify. At that time he must
state that the cut would badly hurt the bureau and would undermine the
whole program. Brown would not need to volunteer the statement, Smith
said, but his views could be given in response to leading questions by the
congressmen. Brown's testimony, he felt sure, would help clinch the argument against the cut because congressmen would respect the judgment of
the administrator closest to the problem.

Mr. Brown's decision

Brown returned to his office in a state of indecision. He saw his own
position as a most embarrassing one. He had submitted his estimates to the
Secretary of Conservation and to the President, and it was his duty to back
them up. An unwritten rule provided, moreover, that agency heads defended
budget estimates submitted to Congress, whatever their personal feelings
might be. The President had appointed him to his position, he reflected, and
had a right to expect loyalty. On the other hand, he was on the spot with
his own agency. The employees all expected their chief to look out for them.
Brown had developed happy relations with "the field," and he squirmed at
the thought of having to let over 1000 employees go. What would they think
when they heard him defend the cut? Even more important, he wanted to
maintain friendly relations with the farmers, the farm organizations, and
the farm bloc in Congress.

In his quandary Brown sought the advice of an old friend in the Bureau
of the Budget. This friend urged him to defend the President's budget. He
appealed to Brown's professional pride as an administrator and career servant, reminding him that every student of administration agreed that the
chief executive must have central control of the budget, and that agency
heads must subordinate their own interests to the executive program. As for
the employees to be dropped—well, that was part of the game. A lot of
them could get jobs in defense agencies; civil service would protect their
status. Anyway, they would understand Brown's position. In a parting shot
his friend told Brown that the President had Brown in mind for bigger things.

The next day Brown had lunch with a senator, wise and experienced in
Washington ways, who helped him to get his start in the government. The
senator was sympathetic. He understood Brown's perplexity, for many simi-

lar cases had arisen in the past. But there was no doubt as to what Brown should do, the senator said. He should follow Representative Smith's plan, of course being as diplomatic as possible about it. This way he would protect his position with those who would be most important in the long run.

"After all," the senator said, "Presidents come and go, parties rise and fall, but Smith and those other congressmen will be here a long time, and so will these farm organizations. They can do a lot for you in future years. And remember one other thing—these people are elected representatives of the people. Constitutionally, Congress has the power to spend money as it sees fit. Why should you object if they want to spend an extra few million?"

Leaving the Senate Office Building, Brown realized that his dilemma was deeper than ever. The arguments on both sides were persuasive. He felt hopelessly divided in his loyalties and responsibilities. The President expected one thing of him. Congress (he was sure Smith reflected widespread feeling on Capitol Hill) expected another. As a career man and professional administrator he sided with the President; as head of an agency, however, he wanted to protect his team. His future? Whatever decision he made, he was bound to alienate important people and interests. There was no way to compromise, because he would have to face a group of astute congressmen.

It was Brown's realization that the arguments in a sense canceled one another out, however, that in the end helped him make his decision. For he decided finally that the issue was not merely one involving loyalties, ambitions, and programs. Ultimately it boiled down to two questions. First, to whom was he, Brown, legally and administratively responsible? Obviously to the chief executive who appointed him and who was accountable to the people for the actions of the Administration. And secondly, which course of action did he, Brown, feel was better for the welfare of all the people? Looking at the question this way, he felt the President was right in asking for economy. As a taxpayer himself, Brown knew of the strong sentiment for retrenchment. To be sure, Congress must make the final decision. But to make the decision, Brown reflected, Congress had to know the attitude of the Administration, and the Administration must speak with one voice for the majority of the people or it could hardly speak at all. Despite continued pressures and mixed feelings, Brown stuck to this decision.

Assignment in Indonesia

In August 1945, shortly after the Japanese surrender, the Republic of Indonesia declared its independence from the Netherlands.[15] A difficult political situation immediately arose. The Dutch wished to keep possession of their rich islands in southeast Asia. The Indonesians wanted their freedom as strongly as did Americans in 1776. For several months skirmishes took

[15] This case is drawn from an actual autobiographical account by the vice-consul involved, prepared for, and published by, the Committee on Public Administration Cases (Washington, 1950), under the title *Indonesian Assignment*.

place between Dutch and Indonesian forces, especially in Batavia, the capital. The United States, deeply interested in the area for economic and strategic reasons, followed a policy of neutrality.

Representing the United States in Batavia during this period was a consul general who had served in the Indies for twelve years before the war. Sixty years old, he had enjoyed pleasant relations with Dutch officials before the war and tended to feel sympathetic toward their position. As an old hand he was experienced in Indonesian affairs but he tended to be somewhat prejudiced and set in his ways. In February 1946, the consul general was joined by a vice-consul, William Jones, who was sent out by the State Department to undertake economic analysis and reporting. At this time Washington had a particular need for full and accurate information of the economic situation in Indonesia to help in developing important foreign policies.

Jones was of a different stamp from his chief. A young economist, trained in American universities and in the State Department, he had studied the prewar pattern of colonialism and had developed strong sympathies for the nationalist cause. He had no established ties with the Foreign Service; indeed, his actual appointment was in the Foreign Service Reserve (see Chapter 23). While at the State Department, moreover, Jones had learned that there was some concern in the department over the consul general's pro-Dutch views.

Within a few months of his arrival, the new vice-consul was busy preparing economic reports on Indonesian islands. His relations with his chief were most cordial. But soon a difficult situation began to develop. To get complete information Jones saw the need of approaching Indonesian as well as Dutch officials. But the consul general wanted him to see only the latter. He stressed the ticklish political situation that existed and warned Jones to move slowly. Eager to maintain friendly relations with his superior, Jones followed instructions, but he had an uneasy feeling that he was not doing a full job of reporting to Washington.

Sometime later a confidential airgram arrived from the State Department requesting an extensive economic report on Indonesia, adding that "if possible, and with the utmost discretion, Dutch, Indonesian, and British sources should be consulted as far as feasible." Jones was elated to have the assignment, but puzzled as to procedure. Should he consult the Indonesian authorities? Clearly the department had left the matter in the hands of the consulate.

Reflecting on the situation Jones realized he had several alternatives. He could consult the consul general, who would surely say "no"; this course would protect his position in the department and his friendly relations with his chief, but it would lessen the value of the report. Or he could go ahead with the report, inform the department that he had not consulted the Indonesians, and let Washington specifically request such consultation if it was still desired. This was the safest course all around, but it would have meant a long delay in the final report and perhaps a less satisfactory one. Finally,

Jones could use the airgram as justifying consultation with Indonesians, at whatever risk to his relations with his chief and to Dutch-American relations.

Jones decided on the third course. Before doing so he spoke to a high Indonesian official who assured him that he would receive useful material from the Republic and in confidence. The results of the decision were happy. His talks with the Indonesians (as well as with the Dutch and British) were fruitful, and he was later commended by the State Department for the report he submitted. Yet he had to pay the price. His relations with the consul general cooled markedly—not a trivial matter in a small office thousands of miles from home. Nevertheless, Jones was happy in his decision. He felt that he had been loyal to his profession and to the interests of his country, at the expense of loyalty to his superior. It is clear, however, that had Jones been a veteran career man, with family responsibilities, and with no particular sympathy for the Indonesians, his decision might have been very different from what it was.

CAN WE CONTROL THE BUREAUCRATS?

The foregoing case histories lead to three important generalizations:

1. Bureaucrats are people, not robots, and as people they are subject to many influences.

2. Bureaucrats do not respond merely to orders from the top but to a variety of motives stemming from their own personalities, formal and informal organization and communication, their political attitudes, their educational and professional background, and others.

3. Bureaucrats are important in government. Some of them have tremendous discretion and make decisions of great significance—and the cumulative effect of all their policies and actions on our daily lives is enormous.

Put these three factors together and a crucial question arises. How can we keep this powerful bureaucracy responsible and responsive to the people? Bureaucrats are our servants—or should be—yet our picture of the bureaucrats implies that the people's wishes are by no means the only factor in giving marching orders to the bureaucracy. Let us look more closely at the problem of maintaining democratic control of administration.

Breaks in the chain of command

Of all the 2⅓ million bureaucrats the American people hire and fire only one—the President. The chief executive must be a firm link between the people and the bureaucracy. His office is a central channel through which popular needs and expectations are converted into administrative action. Much depends on the sensitiveness of the bureaucracy to the President's—and hence to the people's—direction. Unfortunately, the chief executive does not fully control his own establishment. As the Hoover Commission discovered, lines of control are tangled and broken.

The formal organization of the agencies has not met the demands of clear-cut control. Harry Truman once showed visitors a huge chart on his office wall picturing well over 100 officials required by law to report to the chief executive alone; he complained that "I cannot even see all these men, let alone actually study what they are doing." Because of its lack of unity the Cabinet is not able to direct and coordinate the sprawling executive branch. Even the President's staff cannot help him adequately in certain areas, such as control of personnel.

The chain of command is broken also at lower levels. Some subordinate officials have been given power by Congress to act independently of the White House. For example, the Army chief of engineers can plan public works without referring to the President. Some departments are simply holding companies for independent-minded bureaus that act on their own. Such a situation breeds all sorts of difficulties, including what Pendleton Herring has called "quiet sabotage by unsympathetic technicians and genteel blackmail by high policy officials." Simple communication and action become difficult. Harry Hopkins, who served as the President's "chief of staff" during World War II, once complained that after Mr. Roosevelt and Mr. Churchill and the high command made crucial decisions, months-long delays would ensue—"and then you start investigating and it takes you weeks to find out that the orders have been deliberately stalled on the desk of some commander or lieutenant colonel."

Failures of top control are especially serious in the military agencies. Americans have always feared the man on horseback; the Founding Fathers carefully put the Army and Navy under civilian control. Under conditions of modern war—whether of the atomic, bacteriological, or push-button type—the problem becomes even more urgent. On this score the Hoover Commission found that centralized civilian control of the military "scarcely exists." The weakest link, it reported, was between the Secretary of Defense and the service departments, the Army, Navy, and Air Force.

Another weak point in the chain of command involves the independent boards and commissions. Congress made these agencies semi-independent of the President so that they could pursue their regulatory activities without undue interference from the White House. Since the members have long staggered terms, a new President must wait some time before he can install men of his own choice. For his power to fire commission members is usually limited. When President Roosevelt sought to remove William Humphrey, a conservative member of the Federal Trade Commission who hotly opposed the New Deal, the Supreme Court ruled in *Rathbun* v. *United States* that, by the terms of the act setting up the F.T.C., commissioners could be removed only for "inefficiency, neglect of duty, or malfeasance in office," not because of difference with the President over

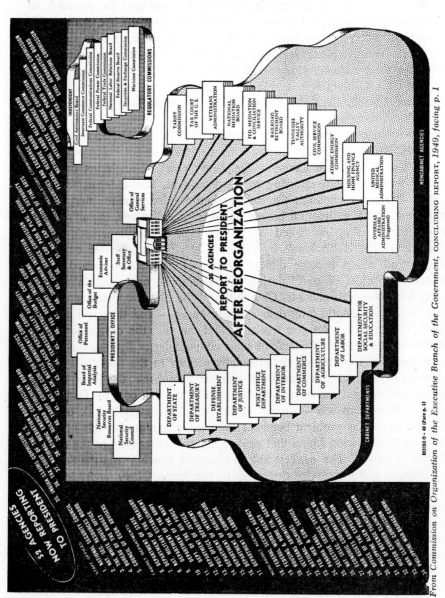

From Commission on Organization of the Executive Branch of the Government, CONCLUDING REPORT, *1949, facing p. 1*

Hoover Commission recommendation for strengthening the President's control over the bureaucracy.

policy. There might be no serious problem if the independent boards had merely *adjudicative* functions, but as we have seen they have important *lawmaking* and *administrative* powers.

Finally, central direction by the President runs into the basic political problem of pressures on administration from *interest groups*. Some *bureaus* are known as *clientele agencies* because they perform services directly for certain group interests; examples might be the Bureau of Reclamation, the Army Engineers, Rural Electrification Administration, Veterans Administration, United States Maritime Administration. Close relations develop between interest group and agency. When the President, trying to enforce his idea of the general interest, seeks to control the agency, he comes into conflict with an organized interest and its narrower conception of the general interest. Agents for the group may appeal to members of Congress—especially those who represent districts where the organized interest is strong. Then a pitched battle may occur not only between President and interest group but between President and members of Congress. Armed with various weapons, including control of appropriations, the legislators often can hold their ground against the chief executive.

Is the bureaucrat an innocent bystander in these melées? Usually not. He often will line up with the White House or Capitol Hill, choosing sides according to his own interests—and his own idea of the general interest—as he sees them. For the bureaucracy is not a static force; it has political influence of its own. This influence is built on the public relations skills of the administrator and his staff, the nature and extent of the bureau's information program, relations with legislative and executive officials, and ultimately on the amount of support that the interest groups involved and the attentive public will give to the bureau. The government executive's concern over his agency's public relations, says F. M. Marx, "requires special internal organization, technical assistance within his own office, and much hard labor on his part in mingling socially with the right crowd, in building good will at his press conferences, and in cultivating his legislative contacts."[16] This does not mean that publicity activities of the agencies are merely self-serving propaganda; despite charges to the contrary, most of the publicity is factual information about the agencies' work. It does mean that the large bureau finds public acceptance, interest-group backing, and a place in the web of government that give it a measure of political power of its own.[17]

Repairing the breaks

After studying the executive branch, the Hoover Commission concluded that the President did not have sufficient control of his own establishment.

[16] F. M. Marx, *Elements of Public Administration,* p. 200.
[17] For a discerning study of this problem and related questions, see Simon, Smithburg, and Thompson, *op. cit.,* especially chapters 18 and 19.

"Definite authority at the top, a clear line of authority from top to bottom, and adequate staff aids . . . do not exist," said the Commission. "Authority is diffused, lines of authority are confused, staff services are insufficient. Consequently, responsibility and accountability are impaired." It warned that the critical state of world affairs required the government to speak and act with unity of purpose, and that if the executive branch worked at cross purposes within itself, the whole nation would suffer from disunity and from waste of funds.

To repair and strengthen the chain of command the Commission made many recommendations, including:

1. Regrouping functions into major departments and agencies for the sake of more coherence and responsibility.

2. Giving the President and department heads better staff services to help in controlling subordinate agencies. For example, as noted above, the Commission favored setting up in the White House an Office of Personnel, headed by a director who would also be chairman of the Civil Service Commission, along with the strengthening of the Budget Bureau and other staff services.

3. In regulatory commissions, vesting all administrative responsibility in the chairmen of the commissions.[18] While this recommendation would not necessarily have extended the President's control over the commissions it would have established a clearer link between chief executive and commissions. The Hoover Commission urged also that a number of *executive* functions be transferred from the commissions to regular departments.

4. Granting the President power to propose plans for reorganization, which would go into effect unless both Senate and House disapproved them within a set period of time. And department heads, the Commission urged, should have broad authority to reorganize their own agencies internally as they saw fit.

Many of these proposals were not new. For years—in some cases decades—suggestions had been made that presidential control be strengthened. Indeed, a Committee on Administrative Management, set up by President Roosevelt in 1936, went further in some respects than the Hoover Commission. For example, it proposed placing all personnel functions, including those held by the Civil Service Commission, under a civil service administrator responsible to the President, and it favored putting the nonjudicial activities of regulatory commissions into the executive departments.[19] Presidents Taft, Wilson, and Harding had also tried to achieve better organization and control in the executive branch.

---

[18] Commission on Organization of the Executive Branch of the Government, *Regulatory Commissions* (Washington: Government Printing Office, 1949).

[19] *Administrative Management in the Government of the United States* (Washington: Government Printing Office, 1937).

What action has been taken in regard to the Hoover Commission proposals in strengthening presidential and departmental control? Decided progress has been made in certain respects. Creation of the Department of Health, Education, and Welfare in April 1953 was a milestone in the attempt to group separate agencies in departments under a Cabinet member directly responsible to the President. Rules and procedures were adopted to grant department executives more authority to control and reorganize their own departments. Grouping of bureaus within departments has been somewhat improved. More administrative responsibility has been vested in chairmen of some of the regulatory commissions. Yet in other respects progress has been very slow. One of the major recommendations of the Hoover Commission was the consolidation of 65 agencies under the direct supervision of the President into one-third of that number; aside from the one new Cabinet agency, little has been done. The President still does not have full power to reorganize his own office. Department heads, in the judgment of some observers, do not yet possess enough control over personnel policies and administration in their own organizations.

If the problem is so old, if there is wide agreement on general solutions, why are we still trying to apply first principles to the running of our administrative machinery? The answer lies in our system of *checks and balances*. The President is chief of the executive branch, but he is not its undisputed master. For Congress too has control of the executive branch. It usually sets up the agencies. It usually determines, broadly, their organization (that is, whether a job shall be done by an independent commission or by a line agency). It tells them what their job will be. It provides the money. It establishes rules to guide bureaucrats in their work. It often reviews, formally (as in hearings) or informally, the actions bureaucrats take. And, as we have seen, it helps choose men for the jobs.[20]

To be sure, Congress shares these powers with the President, but the mere sharing implies divided control at the top. Moreover, it is not really *Congress* that helps run the bureaucracy but *individual members* of Congress and of committees. Since power in Congress is scattered and diffuse, administrative control is split not between President and Congress but between President (and his staff and immediate subordinates) on the one hand and a few dozen committees and a few hundred legislators on the other.

Congress *as a whole* might have every reason to strengthen the President's administrative control, for then it could pin responsibility squarely on him. But congressmen *as individuals* often resist greater central control. They wish to maintain their own influence over an agency, perhaps because that agency serves their constituents, or because they feel that they know its functions better than the President does (which often they

[20] Charles S. Hyneman, *Bureaucracy in a Democracy* (New York: Harper & Brothers, 1950), pp. 77-203.

do), or because of a general fear of presidential power. They can use their control over funds, investigations, appointments, and lawmaking to back up their wishes.

Largely because of this situation the congressmen often have failed to grant to the President power to reorganize the executive branch, or have granted that power grudgingly and in small doses. Indeed, a bill to give President Roosevelt broad reorganization powers in 1937 was dubbed the "dictator bill" and killed. And congressmen often try to make their pet agencies exempt from reorganizations. Nevertheless, Congress has given the President power to "reduce, coordinate, consolidate, and reorganize" —and even to abolish—a large number of agencies, subject, however, to congressional veto. Under the most recent reorganization act, the President submits plans to Congress, where they may be debated but not amended. The plan may be killed by either house if a majority of the entire membership (not simply a majority of those on the floor) vote adversely. Shortly after taking office President Eisenhower asked Congress to continue the act and Congress complied.

Under the several reorganization plans that have been passed in the last two decades, the President has considerably extended his control of administration. But no reorganization act can, of course, resolve the problem that the chain of command ends up not just in the White House, but in a variety of places on Capitol Hill as well.

Loyalty to whom?

Reorganization is essentially a matter of *formal structure*. It tries to put the right men and the right jobs in the right place under presidential supervision. This is important, but it is not the whole problem. Bureaucrats have many loyalties, sometimes conflicting ones. The big job is to strengthen their loyalty to broad popular goals, to responsible leaders, to their own sense of integrity and workmanship. The problem has several important aspects.

One aspect involves *party loyalty*. That the bureaucrats, at least those at the lower levels, should be politically neutral has long been accepted policy in this country. Not only has civil service largely overcome the patronage system, but the Hatch Acts of 1939 and 1940 extended the idea of neutrality by forbidding the bureaucrats to "take any active part in political management or in political campaigns." The aim has been both to prevent the building of a gigantic machine of federal officeholders and to protect the bureaucrats against having to donate money to parties or candidates. The laws allow them to discuss politics in private and to vote, but little else.

Such an arrangement raises a number of difficult questions. At a time when we are trying to broaden interest in democratic discussion and action, is it wise to try to isolate $2\frac{1}{3}$ million people in a political vacuum, insulated against the rough and tumble of political agitation and participation? Which officials, moreover, should be "political" and which neutral? Department heads, of course, are expected to change as Presidents and parties rise and fall, but what about chiefs of bureaus, divisions, and other units? A study in 1938 revealed that of 25 bureau chiefs who had not been chosen formally under the merit system, only 6 had been selected on a political party basis.[21]

What about the conflict of loyalties between *President* and *Congress?* As we have seen in the case of Mr. Brown, this conflict is a perplexing one. The President is chief of the executive branch; Congress has the fundamental lawmaking power. Inevitably the bureaucrat must be responsible to both. The situation is immensely complicated by the fact that it is not Congress as a whole but powerful individual congressmen with whom the bureaucrat must deal, and these congressmen often differ with one another as to proper administrative policy.

What about the bureaucrat's loyalties and responsibilities to *interest groups?* His activities impinge on all sorts of groups, some in a favorable, others perhaps in an unfavorable, way. These groups have many interests; it is hard to discover just at what point the bureaucrat's help to one group, like veterans or farmers, becomes harmful to another group, like taxpayers or consumers. Obviously, a bureaucrat is confronted in acute form with the question that borders on a theme problem of this book— what is the general interest in a pluralistic society embracing many interests? And what is the relation of that interest to the interest of the popular majority that won the last election and claims the right through newly elected leaders to tell the bureaucrats what to do?

Finally, what about loyalty to the highest traditions of government service —traditions of responsibility, initiative, efficiency? Perhaps the most serious loyalty problem is right here. Bureaucracies, whether governmental or business, tend to be routinized, cautious, and heavy-handed. They are often marked by inertia and red tape. A vast amount of shuffling papers takes the place of direct dealing with real people. Procedures become clumsy and burdensome. Some bureaucrats stake out private preserves for themselves and resist change. Even their language—as revealed in instructions to the public and to employees—becomes impersonal and obscure. As a result of this "gobbledygook," as one observer has remarked, a simple sentence like "I love you" becomes "Complete assurance of maximum affection is hereby implied."[22] Of all the problems of loyalty, this may be the hardest to solve. Big government inevitably means big bureaucracies and some of the faults that are summed up in the words "red tape."[23]

[21] A. W. MacMahon and J. D. Millett, *Federal Administrators* (New York: Columbia University Press, 1939), chapters 21-24.

[22] Rudolf Flesch, "More About Gobbledygook," *Public Administration Review,* Vol. 5 (1945), pp. 240-245.

[23] For another type of loyalty required of the bureaucrat—loyalty to country and Constitution—see Chapter 6.

This last question can be turned right around—what are we the people doing to make bureaucrats feel loyal to ideals of public service and to the public interest? Any bureaucrat could make a case for the view that we are not doing much. Consider governmental salaries. The pay at lower levels compares favorably with that of private industry, but many a governmental executive with thousands of employees and the most exacting duties receives a third or half what he could get in business. Or think of the brickbats that are showered on the government official. Able bureaucrats have left Washington because they could not stand the intemperate attacks (many of them emanating from Congress) directed against both their public and private life.

Herblock in THE WASHINGTON POST

"What do you suppose keeps them away?"

The bureaucrat has very little "job security." If he fails to please the many political leaders and groups to whom he is responsible, or if there is a change of President or party, his usefulness in his agency may come to an end.

Valiant efforts have been made to raise initiative, vigor, imagination, professional standards, and *esprit de corps* in the federal service, and the efforts are continuing. Recently, the Second Hoover Commission recommended the establishment of a senior civil service group that would have special and separate status, with high rank and pay. They would be politically neutral, in order not to be exposed to cross fire from politicians inside and outside the government. This idea of a senior civil service has been hailed as a means of providing a pool of topflight men with high morale who would be able to work effectively in any agency and under any President. The idea of a senior civil service has been criticized because it sets up a special class with special privileges, because political or administrative neutrality is neither possible nor desirable, and because it would not fit well with the American tradition or practice of public administration.

In any event, the problem is clearly an important one, involving better working conditions, higher salaries (there has been a notable improvement in this respect in the last decade or two), more recognition of services beyond the call of ordinary duty, and a higher status for the government employee.

FOREIGN OBSERVERS OF THE AMERICAN SCENE ARE often amazed at the great power that Americans give to their judges, especially those who serve on the federal bench. Two of the most penetrating of these observers were the French aristocrat, Alexis de Tocqueville, and the English laborite and political scientist, Harold Laski. In 1848 Tocqueville wrote, "If I were asked where I place the American aristocracy, I should reply without hestitation . . . that it occupies the judicial bench and bar. . . . Scarcely any political question arises in the United States that is not resolved sooner or later into a judicial question."[1] A century later Laski wrote, "The respect in which the federal courts and, above all, the Supreme Court are held is hardly surpassed by the influence they exert on the life of the United States."[2]

What accounts for the great influence and prestige of American judges? In large part, it is their power to interpret the basic instrument of government, the Constitution. Only a constitutional amendment—and the judges would interpret the amendment—or the Supreme Court itself can modify the Court's constitutional doctrine. Mr. Justice Frankfurter put it tersely some years ago, "The Supreme Court is the Constitution."

When the judges interpret the Constitution, they make policy decisions. Though the arguments will be clothed in constitutional terminology, the judges must resolve important social and economic issues. Should the government regulate the economic market place? Should the activities of totalitarian political parties be restricted? Defeated at the polls or in the legislative halls, individuals may carry this kind of issue to the judicial chambers through the device of the lawsuit. "We are very quiet there," said Justice Holmes of the Supreme Court, "but it is the quiet of a storm centre."

The significance of judicial review, however, should not cause us to overlook the other important functions of judges.

[1] Alexis de Tocqueville, *Democracy in America*, 2 vols., ed. Phillips Bradley (New York: Alfred A. Knopf, Inc., 1946), I, 278, 180.

[2] Harold J. Laski, *The American Democracy* (New York: The Viking Press, Inc., 1948), p. 110.

20 ★

The

judges

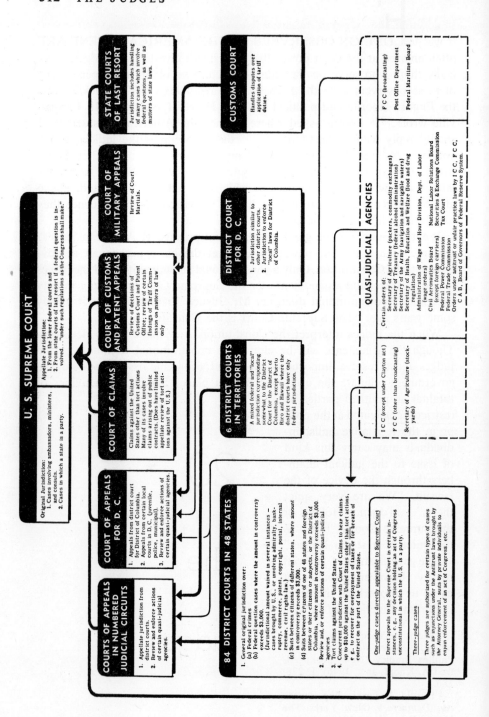

U. S. SUPREME COURT

Original Jurisdiction:
1. Cases involving ambassadors, ministers, and consuls.
2. Cases in which a state is a party.

Appellate Jurisdiction:
1. From the lower federal courts and
2. From state courts of last resort if a federal question is involved. . ."under such regulations as the Congress shall make."

STATE COURTS OF LAST RESORT

Jurisdiction includes handling of many cases which involve federal questions, as well as matters of state laws.

CUSTOMS COURT

Handles disputes over application of tariff duties.

COURT OF MILITARY APPEALS

Review of Court Martials.

COURT OF CUSTOMS AND PATENT APPEALS

Review of decisions of Customs Court and Patent Office; review of certain findings of Tariff Commission on matters of law only

DISTRICT COURT FOR D. C.

1. Jurisdiction similar to other district courts.
2. Jurisdiction to enforce "local" laws for District of Columbia.

COURT OF CLAIMS

Claims against the United States other than tort actions. Many of its cases involve claims arising out of public contracts. (Does have limited appellate review of tort actions against the U.S.)

6 DISTRICT COURTS IN TERRITORIES

A mixed federal and "local" jurisdiction corresponding somewhat to the District Court for the District of Columbia, except Puerto Rico and Hawaii where the district courts have only federal jurisdiction.

COURT OF APPEALS FOR D. C.

1. Appeals from district court for District of Columbia.
2. Appeals from certain local courts in D. C. (juvenile, police, municipal).
3. Review and enforce actions of certain quasi-judicial agencies.

COURTS OF APPEALS IN NUMBERED JUDICIAL CIRCUITS

1. Appellate jurisdiction from district courts.
2. Review and enforce actions of certain quasi-judicial agencies.

84 DISTRICT COURTS IN 48 STATES

1. General original jurisdiction over:
   (a) Federal crimes
   (b) Federal question cases where the amount in controversy exceeds $3,000.
   (Jurisdictional amount waived in several instances – cases brought by U. S., or involving admiralty, bankruptcy, commerce, patent, copyright, postal, internal revenue, civil rights law.)
   (c) Suits between citizens of different states, where amount in controversy exceeds $3,000.
   (d) Suits between citizens of one of 48 states and foreign states or their citizens or subjects, or the District of Columbia, where amount in controversy exceeds $3,000.
2. Review and/or enforce actions of certain quasi-judicial agencies.
3. Tort claims against the United States.
4. Concurrent jurisdiction with Court of Claims to hear claims up to $10,000 against the United States other than tort actions, e. g., to recover for overpayment of taxes or for breach of contract on the part of the United States.

One-judge cases directly appealable to Supreme Court

Direct appeals to the Supreme Court in certain instances, e. g., any decision holding an act of Congress unconstitutional in which the U. S. is a party.

Three-judge cases

Three judges are authorized for certain types of cases such as injunctions under the Antitrust laws brought by the Attorney General, suits by private individuals to enjoin enforcement of an act of Congress, etc.

QUASI-JUDICIAL AGENCIES

Certain orders of:
Secretary of Agriculture (packers, commodity exchanges)
Secretary of Treasury (federal alcohol administration)
Secretary of the Army (navigation and navigable waters)
Secretary of Health, Education and Welfare (food and drug wage orders)
Administration of Wage and Hour Division, Dept. of Labor (wage orders)
Civil Aeronautics Board
(except foreign carriers)
Federal Power Commission
Federal Trade Commission
Orders under antitrust or unfair practice laws by I C C, F C C, C A B, Board of Governors of Federal Reserve System.

National Labor Relations Board
Securities & Exchange Commission
Tax Court

I C C (except under Clayton act)

F C C (other than broadcasting)

Secretary of Agriculture (stockyards)

F C C (broadcasting)
Post Office Department
Federal Maritime Board

In addition, they serve as impartial tribunals for the settlement of legal controversies. They interpret the laws, determine the facts, apply the law to the facts, and see to it that the laws are enforced. Did Jones have a fair trial? Did Smith violate the terms of his contract with Brown? Is an elevator operator in a New York office building entitled to the minimum wages established by the Fair Labor Standards Act? Did the Ajax Corporation violate the anti-trust laws? Must a bus company pay the hospital bills for one of its passengers who was assaulted by a fellow passenger? Answering these questions is the daily business of judges. Their importance in settling peacefully the innumerable controversies between individuals and between individuals and the government is as notable as their role in helping to shape the grand outlines of American politics.

THE SHAPE OF FEDERAL JUSTICE

The authority of federal judges, like that of congressmen and Presidents, rests upon the Constitution. But unlike congressmen and Presidents, federal judges receive very little power directly from that document. All the authority of federal judges except the original jurisdiction of the Supreme Court (see page 514) is given to them by Congress. The Constitution merely sets the outside limits. Congress determines which, if any, federal court is to exercise some or all of the judicial authority of the United States.

The purpose of the framers of the Constitution in delegating judicial power to the national government was to enable the central government to maintain its supremacy, to meet its national responsibilities, and to provide tribunals for cases where state judges might not be appropriate. Therefore, they gave to the United States the power to hear and decide cases in law and equity if:

1. They arise under the Constitution, a federal law, or a treaty.
2. They arise under admiralty and maritime jurisdiction.
3. They arise because of a dispute involving land claimed under titles granted by two or more states.
4. The United States is a party to the case.
5. A state is a party to the case (but not including suits commenced or prosecuted against a state by an individual or a foreign nation).
6. They are between citizens of different states.
7. They affect the accredited representatives of a foreign nation.

The organization of federal courts

The Constitution provides but one Supreme Court and leaves it up to Congress to ordain and establish inferior federal courts. A Supreme Court is a logical necessity if the national government is to have the power to frame laws regulating the conduct of individuals—laws superior to those of the states. The lack of such a tribunal to maintain federal supremacy, to insure uniform interpretation of federal legislation, and to resolve conflicts among the states was one of the glaring deficiencies of the central government under the Articles of Confederation. The Constitution also allows Congress to determine the size of the Supreme Court as well as of lower courts.

A complete system of *lower* federal courts, however, did not appear to be indispensable to an effective federal system. The framers, therefore, avoided a controversial issue, and left the decision up to Congress. As a result the structure as well as the authority of the federal judiciary is in large part controlled by Congress. The First Congress divided the nation into districts and created lower federal courts for each district. That decision, although supplemented, has never been seriously questioned. Today the judicial hierarchy of the federal constitutional courts consists of the *district courts, courts of appeals,* and one *Supreme Court.*

The Supreme Court is the most glamorous and venerated federal court and the symbol of Justice. Its members are known to the public, and its decisions are often reported in the press. It has the final judicial interpretation of the meaning of the Constitution and federal laws; it serves as the court of ultimate appeal; it supervises the administration of justice by the federal courts. But the work horses of the federal judiciary are the 84 district courts within the states, the district court in the District of Columbia, and the territorial district courts in Hawaii and Puerto Rico. Each state has at least one district court, and the larger and more populous states have as many as the demands of judicial business and the pressure of politics require (no state has more than four). Each district court is composed of at least one judge, but there may be up to eighteen. District judges normally sit separately and hold court by themselves. There are 246 district judgeships, all filled by the President with the consent of the Senate, and all except those of the territorial courts holding office during good behavior.

District courts have *original jurisdiction,* that is, the power to hear and decide cases in the first instance. They are the only federal courts that regularly employ grand and petit (trial) juries. Many of the cases tried before district judges involve citizens of different states, and the judges apply the appropriate state laws. Otherwise, district judges are concerned with federal laws. For example, they hear and decide cases involving crimes against the United States, suits under the revenue, postal, patent, copyright, and trademark laws, suits to vindicate civil rights. The federal bankruptcy laws often place these judges in business, as they are responsible for the management of bankrupt concerns.

District judges are assisted by clerks, bailiffs, stenographers, law clerks, court reporters, probation officers, and United States commissioners. All these persons are appointed by the judges. The commissioners, who serve for four-year terms and are paid from fees, handle some of the preliminaries. For example, they issue warrants for arrests, and often hear the evidence to determine whether an arrested person should be held for action by the grand jury. If so, the commissioner may set the bail. A United States marshal, appointed by the President, and his deputies are assigned to each district court to maintain order in the courtroom, guard prisoners, make arrests, and carry out court orders, such as summonses for witnesses. Although not administratively responsible to the judges, a district attorney is assigned to each district court to represent the United States.

Although some important decisions of the district court judges may be appealed directly to the Supreme Court, most decisions may be carried only to the *court of appeals*. There are ten numbered courts of appeals and one for the District of Columbia, each of which is composed of three to nine circuit judges. Like all judges of federal constitutional courts, circuit judges are appointed by the President with the consent of the Senate for terms of good behavior. Circuit judges have only *appellate jurisdiction;* they review decisions of the district courts within their judicial district and also some of the actions of certain of the independent regulatory agencies such as the Interstate Commerce Commission. Each court of appeals usually hears cases in divisions of three judges, but they may sit *en banc,* that is, all the judges of the court may hear a case. The judge senior in commission is the chief judge of the court. One of the Supreme Court justices is assigned as a circuit justice for each circuit, but today his duties as circuit justice are nominal.

A sovereign nation cannot be sued without its own consent. But rather than giving consent in each individual case or in passing special legislation to indemnify those who suffer a property loss arising out of the fault of the government, Congress has created the *United States Court of Claims.* The court, consisting of a chief and four associate judges, has jurisdiction over property and contract damage suits against the United States. Until 1953 the Court of Claims was considered a legislative court (see page 516) created by Congress as a means of settling the debts of the United States. But in 1953 Congress specified that this court is to be treated as a constitutional court created under Article III to hear cases in which the United States is a party. The court sits in Washington, but commissioners of the court travel throughout the United States taking evidence. Detailed information on district courts, courts of appeals, and the Court of Claims can be found in the chart on page 512.

State and federal courts

What is the relation between the federal and state courts? Federal courts do *not* replace state courts. All cases except those encompassed by the constitutional grant of judicial power to the United States are within the *sole* jurisdiction of state courts. An ordinary lawsuit, for example, over a contract of sale between two citizens of the same state could be tried only before judges of that state.

Furthermore, state and federal courts have *concurrent* jurisdiction over some cases. Unless Congress excludes the state courts, the constitutional grant of jurisdiction to the United States does not by itself prevent state judges from exercising jurisdiction over cases within the judicial power of the United States. The most important cases in which Congress has seen fit to permit state and federal courts to exercise concurrent jurisdiction are disputes between citizens of two or more states. Congress has excluded such cases from the federal courts unless the amount in controversy exceeds $3000. But if the amount is over $3000, and the controversy is between citizens of two or more states, the parties to the controversy have some choice as to the forum in which the case shall be tried.

Congress may, however, exclude state courts from exercising the judicial power of the United States and give federal judges *exclusive* jurisdiction. Examples of cases which may be tried only in federal courts are: crimes against the United States, suits for penalties authorized by federal laws, and cases involving foreign ambassadors.

The common impression that *all* federal courts are superior to *any* state court is wrong. The two court systems are related, but they do not exist in a superior-inferior relationship. Over some cases only state courts have jurisdiction, over others both courts have jurisdiction, and over others only federal courts have jurisdiction. Except for the limited, technical, and controversial habeas corpus jurisdiction of district courts, the Supreme Court is the only federal court which may review state court decisions, and it may do so only under special conditions (see page 520).

Legislative courts and administrative tribunals

The district, appeals, Claims, and Supreme courts exercise the judicial power granted to the United States by Article III of the Constitution and are therefore known as *constitutional courts*. Congress has created other federal courts and delegated to them power derived from other constitutional provisions. These *legislative courts* have, in other words, been established as necessary and proper means to carry out other powers granted to the national government. The most important practical difference between constitutional and legislative courts is that the judges of the latter are not judges within the meaning of Article III and need not be appointed in the manner or for the term prescribed by the Constitution. In addition, Congress may bestow upon the legislative courts nonjudicial powers that would be inappropriate in the case of constitutional courts.

The most important *legislative* courts are the Court of Military Appeals, the Customs Court, the Court of Customs and Patent Appeals, and the territorial courts. Except for the territorial courts and the Court of Military Appeals, the judges of these courts are appointed by the President with the consent of the Senate for terms of good behavior. The Court of Military Appeals and the territorial courts in Alaska, the Virgin Islands, and in the Canal Zone are not classified as "courts of the United States" as are the other legislative courts. Some of these legislative courts have certain administrative duties in addition to judicial functions. The Court of Customs and Patent Appeals, for example, reviews the advisory findings of the United States Tariff Commission. Decisions of these courts on questions of law may be taken to the Supreme Court for review.

Territorial judges have varying degrees of authority. Although the national government has exclusive jurisdiction in the territories, there are local courts similar to state courts. In Puerto Rico and Hawaii the district judges are limited to questions of general national jurisdiction and have the same jurisdiction as the eighty-four district courts in the states. The other territorial judges have jurisdiction not only of matters normally within the purview of national judges but also of many local matters which within the states are decided by state courts. Territorial judges are appointed by the President and Senate for four-year terms, except in Hawaii where they serve for six years, and in Puerto Rico where they serve for eight years.

The *United States Court of Military Appeals* is the "GI Supreme Court."[3] It is composed of three civilian judges appointed by the President with the consent of the Senate for fifteen years. This Court applies *military law,* which exists separately from the body of law that governs the rest of the federal courts. Congress develops the rules and judicial organization to protect rights of persons in the military forces. The Constitution specifically denies to such persons the constitutional right to grand jury indictment, and the weight of opinion, though there is considerable dissent, appears to be that the other rights of persons accused of crime listed in the Fifth and Sixth amendments do not apply to persons in the armed forces.

During World War II there was a mounting volume of criticism of military justice. The old courts-martial system was chiefly concerned with military efficiency and vested autocratic powers in the hands of the commanding officers. With the prospect that a considerable number of Americans would be subject for some period of their lives to military justice, Congress in 1951 passed a comprehensive revision of the military judicial system and established a Uniform Code of Military Justice.

The Uniform Code attempts to balance both the needs of the military and the demands of justice. Rights of persons brought before courts-martials were considerably strengthened. Within each of the services, boards of review composed of three lawyers review major court-martial decisions. The Court of Military Appeals sits at the top of the military court hierarchy. It must review all decisions involving a flag officer, a general, imposition of

3 "A Symposium on Military Justice," *Vanderbilt Law Review,* Vol. 6, No. 2, February, 1953.

the death penalty, and questions certified to it by one of the judge-advocate generals. It has discretionary power to review decisions involving bad conduct discharges or more than one year's imprisonment when petitioned for review by the accused. The Supreme Court has not yet made clear the exact scope of its authority to review decisions of the Court of Military Appeals, but it has indicated that its authority is exceedingly limited—probably no more than to determine whether the military courts had jurisdiction, and have given fair consideration to claims of justice.[4]

Although ranking as neither constitutional nor legislative courts, many administrators and administrative agencies hear and decide cases and exercise what amounts to judicial power, though termed quasi-judicial. For example, a person or company injured by the unfair competitive practices of a business engaged in interstate commerce may file a complaint before the Federal Trade Commission. Attorneys appear, present briefs, and introduce evidence; eventually the commissioners hand down a decision. Appeals on questions of law and fairness of procedure may be taken to the court of appeals and in the regular manner to the Supreme Court.

The administration of the federal judicial system

Although federal judges have always been supposed to follow the judicial leads of the Supreme Court, until recently there was little administrative integration. Today, the *Judicial Conference of the United States,* consisting of the chief judge of each court of appeals and the Chief Justice, is the administrative head of the federal system. It meets at least once a year and establishes policies for the Administrative Office of the United States Courts which carries out the day-to-day administrative chores.

The Administrative Office is headed by a director who is appointed by the Supreme Court. His office supervises subordinate personnel of federal courts, the administration of the bankruptcy act, and the federal probation program. It prepares reports on the state of judicial business and submits to Congress the budget of all courts except the Supreme Court.

Within each of the circuits, the judges of the court of appeals and the circuit justice (the Supreme Court justice assigned to the circuit) constitute the judicial council which meets at least twice a year to discuss common problems. The chief judge of each court of appeals also summons annually a judicial conference of all circuit and district judges within the circuit. Sometimes members of the bar are invited to talk over problems.

One of the central purposes of the integration of the federal judicial system is a more efficient use of "judgepower." Each federal judge is appointed to a specific judgeship. But frequently one court is busy while another has little to do. Provisions have now been made to permit the temporary assignment of judges to other courts. For example, the chief judge

[4] *Burns* v. *Wilson* (1953).

of each court of appeals may send a district judge to another district or to serve on the court of appeals, or he may request a circuit judge to hold district court. The Chief Justice may make temporary transfers between circuits, some transfers requiring the approval of the chief judge of the court of appeals, approval that is routinely given.

Federal prosecutions

Judges decide cases; they do not prosecute persons. That job, on the federal level, falls to the Department of Justice and, more specifically, to the Attorney General, to the Solicitor General, and to the hundreds of United States attorneys and assistant attorneys throughout the country. A United States attorney is appointed by the President with the consent of the Senate for a four-year term but may be dismissed by the President at any time. There is an attorney for each district court, and these appointments are of much interest to senators who, by senatorial courtesy (see p. 403), have much to say about their selection. Assistant attorneys are appointed by the Attorney General. Assisted by the Federal Bureau of Investigation, the district attorneys start criminal proceedings against persons who break federal laws, and they may help initiate civil actions for the government. In a criminal case, the attorney presents to a grand jury evidence that a national law has been violated. If the jury brings an indictment, the attorney conducts the government's case against the accused.

Within the Department of Justice, special divisions—Criminal Division, Civil Division, Antitrust Division, for example—coordinate the work of the attorneys in the field, develop cases, and send out specialists to assist the attorneys. Of special importance is the Solicitor General, who appears for and represents the government before the Supreme Court. Moreover, no appeal may be taken by the United States to any appellate court without his approval.

Contrary to most states, prosecutions in the United States are centralized under the supervision of the Chief Executive. It is noteworthy, however, that the attorneys are lodged in the executive branch and the judges, of course, in the judicial, thus preserving the principle of separation of powers. In many European countries, both judges and prosecutors are part of the same organization, the ministry of justice. While there is no formal connection between the Justice Department and the federal courts, the attorney generalship is often a stepping stone to appointment to the Supreme Court.

What cases reach the Supreme Court?

When an irate citizen insists that he will take his case to the highest court of the land even if it costs him his last penny, he probably overestimates the cost of justice and underestimates the difficulty of securing Supreme

Court review. The Supreme Court has both original and appellate jurisdiction. Its original jurisdiction stems directly from the Constitution, and is limited to cases in which a state is a party or cases which affect foreign ambassadors, consuls, and other public ministers. Its appellate jurisdiction, like that of all federal courts, is given to it by Congress. Congress has authorized the High Court to review some decisions of both state and lower federal courts.

Cases may be carried from the state courts to the Supreme Court only if a *federal question* (the interpretation of the Constitution, or a federal law or treaty) is involved, provided the answer to that question is necessary in order to dispose of the case. And before the Supreme Court will accept jurisdiction, the litigant must have taken the case to the highest *state* court wherein a decision under *state* law can be had in that particular case. If the state court declares a federal law or treaty *un*constitutional or upholds a state law *against* a substantial challenge that it conflicts with a federal law, treaty, or the Constitution, the Supreme Court must review the case when asked to do so by the disappointed litigant. Cases of this kind are said to go to the Supreme Court *on appeal*. In all other state cases involving federal questions, however, the person disappointed by the state decision has only the right to petition the Supreme Court to issue *a writ of certiorari* (pronounced ser-shee-o-rar'-e), a writ ordering the state court to hand up the records of the case. But the Court does not have to grant the writ unless at least four justices feel that the case is of sufficient public importance to require their attention.

The Supreme Court has the same discretion in determining which cases coming up from the federal courts of appeals it shall review. Only if a court of appeals strikes down a state law because it is contrary to a federal law, treaty, or the Constitution, does a person disappointed by a decision of the court of appeals have a *right* to a Supreme Court review. Of course any disappointed litigant may petition the High Court for a writ of certiorari, but in most cases his petition will be rejected. The Supreme Court turns down about 80 per cent of the petitions, selecting for review only those cases that involve issues of significant public interest. Thus it is not enough that Jones thinks he should have won the case against Smith.

The Supreme Court usually selects for review cases where it appears that there is a conflict between the rulings of the courts of appeals or where it seems that the lower courts have departed from sound methods of judicial proceeding, thereby calling for an exercise of the Supreme Court's power of supervision over federal courts. If the High Court had to review all cases from the courts of appeals and those involving federal questions from the highest state courts, it would still be deciding cases today that originated in the 1920's. The discretion in choosing their cases also enables the justices to select those issues that they feel are most significant and timely. It also permits them to duck the issues they do not wish to meet.

How the Supreme Court operates

At high noon on the days in which the Supreme Court is in session, the eight associate justices and the Chief Justice, dressed in their judicial robes, file into the Court. As they are taking their seats—arranged according to seniority, with the Chief Justice in the center—the clerk of the Court introduces them as "the Honorable Chief Justice and Associate Justices of the Supreme Court of the United States." Though he concludes "May God save the United States," this is traditional—not editorial. Those present in the chambers then sit down, the counsel taking their places along tables in front of the bench, the attorneys for the Department of Justice, dressed in morning clothes, at the right. Counsel for each side is limited to one hour argument—in some cases even less—and the Court scrupulously enforces the time limits. The justices freely interrupt the lawyers to ask questions, to inquire for more information. Sometimes, to the annoyance of the attorneys, the justices talk among themselves. The entire procedure is formally informal and designed to bring out the facts and issues in the case as quickly as possible. Although forensic flourishes are not unknown, oratory is discouraged and arguments before the High Court are usually matter-of-fact and direct. Eloquence is less important than soundness. After two hours of argument, the Court takes a half-hour out for lunch, finally adjourning for the day at 4:30 P.M.

In general, there are three main categories of cases that come before this most celebrated court in the world. In the cases involving citizens or companies of different states, the Supreme Court is concerned to see that the federal courts have applied the state laws fairly. These decisions rarely reach the headlines. The cases that make the Court famous—or infamous —are those involving interpretation of a federal law and those concerning a question of constitutional power.

To perform this work the justices are in session from the first Monday in October through June. In its gleaming Corinthian palace, the Court listens to oral arguments for two weeks and then adjourns for two weeks to consider the cases and write their opinions. Six justices must participate in each decision, and cases are decided by a majority. In the event of a tie vote the decision of the lower court is sustained, although the case may be reargued.

Each Saturday the justices meet in conference. During the week they have heard the oral arguments, read and studied the briefs, and examined the petitions. Before the conference, each justice receives a list of the cases that will be discussed in the conference. Each brings to the meeting a red leather book (carefully locked) to record the cases and the votes of the justices. The conferences are highly secret affairs; what goes on in these meetings has to be gleaned from the infrequent comments of members of the Court. The Chief Justice presides; it is in the Saturday meetings that he has the greatest opportunity to exert his influence over his brethren. Chief Justice Hughes ran these conferences like a stern taskmaster, keeping the justices talking to the point, moving the discussion along, and doing his best to work out compromises. He frowned upon too many dissents and preferred to mass the Court in order to give greater weight to its decisions. Chief Justice Stone, on the other hand, perhaps influenced by his New England town-meeting background, encouraged each justice to state his own point of view, and let the discussion wander wherever the members wanted to go.

Although the procedure varies, it is marked by informality and vigorous give and take. The Chief Justice usually opens the discussion by making a brief statement of the facts, summarizing the questions of law, and making suggestions for the case's disposition. He then asks each member of the Court, in order of seniority, to give his views and conclusions. After full discussion a vote is taken, the least senior justice voting first.

The decision is of vital interest to the parties concerned, but the grounds for the decision are apt to be more important to the public. Except for routine cases that can be disposed of by well-settled principles of law, the High Court always announces the reasons for the decision. If the Chief Justice is not among the majority, the senior justice is responsible for either writing himself or for assigning to one of his colleagues the writing of the *Opinion for the Court*. This opinion is then circulated for comments and suggestions. Often an individual justice agrees with the majority on the decision, but he differs on the reasoning. He is then likely to write his own opinion, which is known as a *concurring opinion*. Justices who are among the minority normally select one of their number to write a *dissenting opinion,* although each dissenter is free to write his own opinion. While dissenting opinions have no force in disposing of the case nor as precedents, they are not futile gestures. "A dissent in a court of last resort," wrote Chief Justice Hughes, "is an appeal to the brooding spirit of the law, to the intelligence of a future day when a later decision may possibly correct the error into which the dissenting judge believes the court to have been betrayed. . . . Nor is this appeal always in vain. In a number of cases dissenting opinions have in time become the law."[5]

Supreme Court opinions usually state the facts, present the issues, give the reasoning, and announce the decision. The Court's opinion stating the ruling of law is binding on all lower federal courts and, when pertinent, all state courts. Sometimes the justices wander off in their opinions and talk about issues not involved in the case before them. Chief Justice John Marshall, for example, in the case of *McCulloch* v. *Maryland* (see Chapter 4) stated that he thought the national government could tax instrumentalities of the states. Since the question before the Court was whether the

---

[5] Charles Evans Hughes, "The Supreme Court of the United States: Its Foundation, Methods and Achievements," *American Bar Association Journal,* April 1930.

states could tax an instrumentality of the federal government, Marshall's opinion about federal taxation of the states was *obiter dictum,* reasoning and ruling on an issue not before the Court. *Obiter dicta* often give valuable clues as to the justices' views, but they are not controlling on other courts.

THE JUDGES—GUARDIANS OF THE CONSTITUTION

Judicial review is an American contribution to the art of government, though an independent judiciary is a means of enforcing constitutional limitations in all free governments. If an Englishman or an American is thrown into prison without cause, either can appeal to the courts of his respective country for protection. When Parliament passes a law, however, no English judge has the authority to declare it null and void because *he believes* it to violate the English constitution. Not the judge but Parliament is the guardian of the English constitution. But in the United States the courts, ultimately the Supreme Court, are the keepers of the constitutional conscience—not Congress and not the President. How did the judges get this tremendous responsibility?

Origins of judicial review

The Constitution itself does not say who should be the final arbiter of disputes that might arise over its meaning. It does not specifically grant such power to the Supreme Court. Whether the members of the Convention of 1787 intended to secure to the courts the power of judicial review is a question that has long been debated. There is little doubt that the framers intended the Supreme Court to have the power to declare *state* legislation unconstitutional, but the evidence as to review of the actions of the other two branches of the *national* government is inconclusive. Professor Edward S. Corwin, perhaps the outstanding authority on the American Constitution, concluded that unquestionably "the framers anticipated some sort of judicial review. . . . But it is equally without question that the ideas generally current in 1787 were far from presaging the present vast role of the Court."[6] Why, then, did the framers not specifically provide for judicial review? Probably because they believed the power rested upon certain general provisions that made specific statement unnecessary.

Certainly Alexander Hamilton intended the Supreme Court to have the power to set aside congressional legislation. He favored, as he said in *Federalist No. 78,* a strong and independent judiciary as a check upon the majority, as an "excellent barrier to the encroachments and oppressions of the representative body." He wanted judges appointed for life to protect private rights against "the occasional ill humors in society" that

[6] Edward S. Corwin, "The Constitution as Instrument and as Symbol," *American Political Science Review,* Vol. 30 (1936), p. 1078.

might lead the Congress to pass laws interfering with the propertied minority.

Not all people looked so kindly upon the courts. During the conflict with England the patriots invoked the doctrine that the courts should refuse to enforce the laws of Parliament that were against "natural equity" and the constitution. But after the Revolution, when some state judges dared to void acts of the state legislatures because of conflict with a "higher law," there was popular protest. Only a few persons thought of the courts as instruments to enforce constitutional limitations in behalf of the liberties of the people. Most of those who favored judicial review hoped to check the power of popular majorities.

The First Congress adopted—without much debate—the Judiciary Act of 1789 in which it was assumed that the Supreme Court had the power to refuse to enforce congressional legislation that the justices believed to be unconstitutional. Early in its history the Supreme Court did in several cases review acts of Congress, and in 1794 it apparently even declared an act of Congress invalid, but little attention was paid to this incident.

The Federalists—the men who wrote the Constitution and controlled the national government until 1801—generally supported the courts and favored judicial review, but their opponents, the Jeffersonian Republicans, were less enthusiastic. In 1798 and 1799 Jefferson and Madison (the latter had by this time left the Federalist party) came very close in the Virginia and Kentucky Resolutions to arguing that the state legislatures and not the Supreme Court had the ultimate power to interpret the Constitution. This would seem to imply that the Supreme Court did not even have the final authority to review *state* legislation, something about which there had been little doubt.

When the Jeffersonians defeated the Federalists in the elections of 1800, it was still an undecided issue whether the Supreme Court would actually exercise the power of judicial review. "The idea was in the air, the ingredients to support a doctrine of judicial review were at hand, and a few precedents could even be cited"; nevertheless, it was not an established power. Then in 1803 came the case of *Marbury* v. *Madison,* a case intimately related to the political struggles between the Federalists and the Jeffersonians.

The case of *Marbury* v. *Madison*

The elections of 1800 marked the rise to power of those who were ultimately to extend political control of the government to the great body of the citizenry. President John Adams and his fellow Federalists did not take their defeats easily. On the contrary, they were greatly alarmed at what they considered to be the "enthronement of the rabble." There was not much they could do about it—or was there? The Constitution gives the President, with the consent of the Senate, the power to appoint federal judges to hold office during "good behavior"—virtually for life. If the judiciary should be manned by good Federalists, thought Adams and his party followers, they could stave off the worst consequences of Jefferson's victory. These Federalists were not motivated solely by partisan purposes; for some time they had contemplated reform of the judicial structure. But between their defeat in November 1800 and the expiration of their terms on March 4, 1801, they worked with renewed zeal.

By the end of February 1801 the Federalist lame-duck Congress had created sixteen new circuit judgeships and forty-two justiceships of the peace for the District of Columbia. By March 3, Adams had appointed, and the Senate had confirmed, deserving Federalists to all these new positions. Adams signed the commissions and turned them over to John Marshall, the Secretary of State, to be sealed and delivered. Marshall had just received his own commission as Chief Justice of the United States, but he was continuing to serve as Secretary of State until Adams' term expired. Working right up until nine o'clock on the evening of March 3, Marshall sealed but was unable to deliver all the commissions. The important ones were taken care of, only those for the justices of the peace for the District of Columbia being undelivered. It was late and the Chief Justice had a big day ahead: he was going to administer the presidential oath of office to his distant cousin and political enemy Thomas Jefferson. He retired to his lodgings and left delivery of the commissions to his successors.

Jefferson had been highly aroused by this packing of the judiciary. When he discovered that some of the commissions had not been delivered, he told the new Secretary of State, James Madison, to hold up seventeen of those still in his possession. Jefferson could see no reason why the District needed so many J.P.'s, especially Federalist J.P.'s.

Among those commissions not delivered was one for William Marbury. After waiting in vain, Marbury decided to seek action from the courts. Searching through the statute books, he came across Section 13 of the Judiciary Act of 1789, which authorized the Supreme Court "to issue writs of mandamus, in cases warranted by the principles and usages of law, to . . . persons holding office, under the authority of the United States." *A writ of mandamus* is a court order directing an official to perform a nondiscretionary or ministerial act. Delivering a commission is a ministerial act; the Secretary of State is a person holding office under the authority of the United States; so why not, thought Marbury, ask the Supreme Court to issue a writ of mandamus to force Madison to deliver the commission? He and his companions went directly to the Supreme Court and, citing Section 13, they so asked.

What could Marshall do? If the Court issued the mandamus, Madison and Jefferson would probably ignore it. The Court would be powerless and its prestige, already low, might suffer a fatal blow. On the other hand, by refusing to issue the mandamus, the judges would appear to vindicate the Republican party's claim that the Court had no authority to interfere with the executive. Would Marshall issue the mandamus? Most people thought so; angry Republicans talked of impeachment.

On February 24, 1803, five dignified gentlemen in judicial robes took their seats in a small, dingy room in the basement of the Capitol.

John Marshall's decision

The first part of the opinion was what had been predicted. Marbury was entitled to his commission, said Marshall, and Madison should have delivered it to him; a writ of mandamus could be issued by the proper court against even such an august officer as the Secretary of State.

Then came the surprise. Although Section 13 of the Judiciary Act purports to give the Supreme Court original jurisdiction in just such cases, this section, said Marshall, *is contrary to Article III of the Constitution.* This article gives the Supreme Court original jurisdiction in *only* those cases in which an ambassador or other foreign minister is affected or in which a state is a party. This is a case of original jurisdiction, but Marbury is neither a state nor a foreign minister. If we follow Section 13, wrote Marshall, we have jurisdiction; if we follow the Constitution we have no jurisdiction.

Then in characteristic fashion, Marshall stated the question in such a way that the answer was obvious, namely, should the Supreme Court enforce an unconstitutional law? Of course not, he concluded; the Constitution is the supreme and binding law, and the courts cannot enforce any action of Congress that conflicts with it.

The real question remained unanswered. Congress, in passing the law, and the President, in signing it, had also read the Constitution, and according to *their* interpretation (which was also reasonable), Section 13 was compatible with Article III. Where does the *Supreme Court* get the right to say they were wrong? Why should the *Supreme Court's* interpretation of the Constitution be preferred to that of the Congress and the President?

Marshall, paralleling Hamilton's argument in *Federalist No. 78,* reasoned that the Constitution is law, that judges—not legislators or executives—interpret law; therefore as a normal incidence of their judicial function, the judges should interpret the Constitution. "If two laws conflict with each other, the courts must decide on the operation of each," he said. Obviously the Constitution is to be preferred to any ordinary act of Congress.

Case dismissed.

Jefferson fumed; he fumed primarily because Marshall had said that a court with the proper jurisdiction could mandamus even the Secretary of

State, the President's right-hand man. But there was little Jefferson could do about it. There was no court order to refuse to obey. Thus in a single stroke Marshall had given the Republicans a lecture for failing to perform their duties, and had gone a long way toward acquiring for the Supreme Court the power of judicial review—all in a manner that made it difficult for the Republicans to retaliate.

Marbury v. *Madison* is a masterpiece of judicial strategy. Marshall, contrary to modern canons of judicial interpretation, had to go out of his way to declare Section 13 unconstitutional. He could have interpreted the section to mean that the Supreme Court could issue writs of mandamus in those cases in which it did have jurisdiction. He could have interpreted Article III to mean that Congress could add to the original jurisdiction of the Supreme Court. He could have dismissed the case for want of jurisdiction without discussing Marbury's right to his commission. But none of these would have suited his purpose. Jefferson and his fellow Republicans had been threatening to use the impeachment powers to remove Federalist partisans from the federal bench. Marshall was fearful for the Supreme Court's future, and he felt unless the Court spoke out it would become subordinate to the President and the Congress.

Marshall's decision, important as it was, did not by itself establish for the Supreme Court the power to review and declare unconstitutional acts of the Congress. *Marbury* v. *Madison* could have meant simply that the Supreme Court had the right to interpret the scope of *its own* powers under Article III, but that Congress and the President had the authority to interpret their own powers under Articles I and II, respectively. Marshall's decision was not interpreted in this way (though it was not until the Dred Scott case in 1857 that another act of Congress was declared unconstitutional). Had Marshall not spoken when he did, the Court might not have been able to assume the power of judicial review. The vital precedent had been created. Here we have a classic example of constitutional development through judicial interpretation. There is no specific authorization in the Constitution for the Supreme Court's power to declare congressional enactments null and void; yet it is today a cardinal part of our constitutional system.

THE SUPREME COURT IN AMERICAN HISTORY

The importance of the Supreme Court in shaping the contours and policy of the American Republic has been hardly less than that of the Congress and the President. A story of over 170 years cannot be told briefly without distortion. Yet we can see the rhythm of the law by highlighting the general attitudes of the most prominent of the more than eighty men who have served on the High Bench.

The formative period: John Marshall and Roger B. Taney

Until John Marshall became Chief Justice in 1801, the Supreme Court was a minor branch of the federal government. During the first ten years of its history, three Chief Justices came and departed without finding the position of sufficient importance to challenge their talents. Then came Marshall, a leading Federalist lawyer. During his 34 years as Chief Justice, he elevated the judiciary to a position of coordinate importance with the Congress and the President.

After 1811 a majority of his fellow justices were nominally Jeffersonians, but Marshall's strong personality and intellect, combined with the fundamentally conservative character of the men appointed to serve with him, enabled the Chief Justice to dominate the Supreme Court to an extent never since equaled. Under his leadership the Court "struck blow after blow in support of the doctrine that the United States was a sovereign nation and not a mere confederacy of sovereign states."[7]

Although Marshall represented a political party whose views were less popular with the passage of each year, the Court continued to uphold the authority of the national government and to protect the rights of property. Marshall's classic opinions for the Court in *Marbury* v. *Madison, McCulloch* v. *Maryland, Gibbons* v. *Ogden,* and *Cohens* v. *Virginia* remain among the most influential opinions ever handed down by any court.

Roger B. Taney (pronounced Tawney), Marshall's successor, also started his political life as a Federalist, but he became an ardent supporter of Jackson, whom he served as Attorney General and as Secretary of the Treasury. When Jackson appointed Taney to the High Bench in 1835 only two men remained from the great days of the Marshall Court, and under Taney the ideas of Jacksonian democracy began to work their way into the Court's opinions. The break between the Marshall and Taney Courts is often exaggerated. Taney and his brethren were just as devoted to the protection of property as was the Marshall Court. The Taney Court was concerned especially with property rights in land and slavery. And Taney did not differ with Marshall on the supremacy of the national government. Nevertheless, there were important differences between the dominant spirit of the Taney Court and that of its predecessor. The Supreme Court began a limited retreat from Marshall's nationalism to stress the power of the states. The Taney Court was more inclined than its predecessor to recognize the rights of legislative majorities to regulate the uses of private property, especially property that was given exclusive privilege by the states.

It is unfortunate that Taney's *Dred Scott* decision toward the end of his 29 years as Chief Justice has obscured his many earlier constructive opinions. The *Dred Scott* case is now generally recognized as a misguided

[7] Alfred H. Kelley and Winfred A. Harbison, *The American Constitution* (New York: W. W. Norton & Company, 1948), p. 272.

attempt by the Supreme Court to interfere in a political controversy in order to resolve the issue of slavery. The majority opinion that the national government did not have the power to exclude slavery from the territories merely aggravated the conflict. The Court dealt itself a serious injury.

Civil War and Reconstruction

During the period that Salmon P. Chase presided over the Supreme Court, 1864-1874, the Court tried to keep out of the cross fire in the struggle between President Johnson and the Radical Republicans in Congress. The Radical Republicans were in control, and they rode roughshod over those who got in their way. Nevertheless, the Chase Court declared ten acts of Congress unconstitutional, as contrasted with the two acts held void in the previous eighty-four years. It was during this period that the Court asserted the modern doctrine of judicial review and acquired the exclusive official right to interpret the Constitution.

The High Court could not insulate itself from the rough and tumble of postwar party politics. The *Legal Tender Cases* made this clear. To pay for the Civil War, Congress authorized the Treasury to issue greenbacks (paper currency), and to drive notes of state banks out of existence by a 10 per cent tax. The right of Congress to authorize paper currency not redeemable in gold or silver was vigorously challenged, and in 1870 a bare plurality of Supreme Court justices declared the Legal Tender Act unconstitutional. President Grant, however, had the opportunity to appoint two new justices. Soon after these appointments the Supreme Court in 1871 reversed its decision of the previous year and upheld the Legal Tender Act.[8] President Grant's appointees "voted the right way."

The primary concern of the Supreme Court during the Chief Justiceship of Morrison R. Waite, 1874-1888, was to re-establish the equilibrium between the states and the national government that had been upset by the Civil War and Reconstruction. In the name of the federal system, the Court nullified the Fourteenth Amendment as a constitutional prop for a positive national program of protection for civil rights. At the same time the Court, despite bitter dissent of a minority, refused to expand its own powers by using the due process clause to judge the reasonableness of state regulation of business enterprise. The Supreme Court should not become, said the Court, "a perpetual censor upon all legislation of the States."[9]

The Supreme Court becomes a superlegislature

Between the Civil War and the New Deal, Republicans were in the White House for all but sixteen years. Regardless of party affiliation, most of the Presidents and the influential senators believed in unalterable eco-

[8] *Hepburn v. Griswold* (1870) and *Legal Tender Cases* (1871).
[9] *Slaughter-House Cases* (1873).

nomic laws beyond the sphere of governmental control. They looked with suspicion on any proposal that interfered with the rights of men to invest their capital or to hire workers, deeming it dangerous, socialistic, populistic, and anarchistic. These were the men who selected most of the members of the Supreme Court.

The appointment of Melville Fuller as Chief Justice in 1888 marked the beginning of a new period in the Court's history. Between 1888 and 1937 the Supreme Court became "an aristocracy of the robe and twisted the due process clause into a moat around all forms of private property." The Supreme Court became a censor of legislation which, in the justices' opinions, unreasonably interfered with the use of private property. The Court also gave such a restrictive interpretation of congressional power over interstate commerce that effective federal regulation of the economy was forestalled. The Court, by interpretation, took the teeth out of the Sherman Antitrust and Interstate Commerce Commission laws, and vetoed all attempts by Congress to outlaw child labor.

In 1895 the Supreme Court demonstrated, perhaps too clearly, its concept of itself as the protector of property against the "revolutionaries." By a five-to-four decision, the Court, reversing an old and theretofore unquestioned precedent, made it impossible for the federal government to levy an income tax. Justice Field, in a concurring opinion, brought to the surface the majority's feelings about such dangerous experiments. The income tax was an assault on capital, he wrote, "it will be but the stepping stone to others, larger and more sweeping, till our political contests will become a war of the poor against the rich; a war constantly growing in intensity and bitterness."[10] The Sixteenth Amendment was passed to reverse this decision.

The Supreme Court's assumption of power as a superlegislature was always contested by a minority of the Supreme Court justices. Justice Oliver Wendell Holmes spent much of his thirty years on the Court, 1902-1932, protesting against his colleagues' habit of writing their own economic predilections into the Constitution. Although he was not Chief Justice and was often in dissent, Holmes became the most famous member of the Court. He was a conservative with little faith in social reform by legislation. But with Olympian detachment, he refused to let his own social views become the measure of the constitutionality of legislation. In 1916 Louis D. Brandeis, appointed by President Wilson, joined with Holmes in protesting the major direction of the Supreme Court's opinions and exposing the reasons behind the reasons of the Court majority. Brandeis's constitutional and social philosophy was radically different from that of Holmes, but it often produced the same results. When Harlan Fiske Stone became a member of the Court in 1925, he joined with the two dissenters, and "Holmes,

[10] *Pollock* v. *Farmers' Loan and Trust Co.*

Brandeis, and Stone dissenting" became a familiar phrase in the law reports.

The New Deal and after

Charles Evans Hughes was a majestic-looking man, a stereotype of a Chief Justice. He was a liberal-conservative who used his great talents to guide the Supreme Court during the stormy period (1930-1941) when it collided with the New Deal (see page 547). The Hughes Court was split into fairly consistent conservative and liberal blocks. Four of the Justices— Sutherland, Van Devanter, Butler, and McReynolds—held views that reflected the conservative political attitudes dominant in the times when they were appointed. They were not reluctant to veto legislation that ran counter to their own economic and social attitudes, and they looked upon the New Deal as an unconstitutional and dangerous interference with the rights of property and the constitutional system. On the other hand, Justices Brandeis, Stone, and Cardozo (the distinguished jurist who replaced Holmes in 1932), though they found constitutional objections to some New Deal legislation, could find nothing in the Constitution that prevented the national government from doing what was necessary and proper to fight the depression. Chief Justice Hughes and Justice Owen Roberts, both Hoover appointees, held the balance of power. They wavered, then joined the conservatives to rule that much of the New Deal was unconstitutional.

President Roosevelt counterattacked his judicial foes, and after the battle Justice Roberts and the Chief Justice altered their positions. Then the conservatives—who had been holding on all during Roosevelt's first term—began to leave the Court. By 1939 a liberal majority controlled the Supreme Court, and by 1941 all the old guard had been replaced by Roosevelt appointees. The "New Court," as it was called after 1937, soon knocked down the barriers that its predecessors had erected against social and economic reform. The Holmes, Brandeis, and Stone dissents became the ruling doctrine of the Court. The "New Court" returned to Marshall's broad construction of Congress' power over interstate commerce, and to the doctrine that the Fourteenth Amendment was not intended to give the Supreme Court justices "carte blanche to embody [their] economic or moral beliefs in its prohibitions."

Although tolerant of governmental regulation of business enterprise, the New Court became increasingly intolerant of any attempt to restrict civil liberties, especially attempts by the state governments. Between 1937 and 1950 the Supreme Court handed down many important decisions protecting the civil liberties of individuals.

Harlan Fiske Stone's elevation to the chief justiceship by President Roosevelt in 1941 did not mark any basic change in the Court's doctrines. By that date eight of the nine members of the Court were Roosevelt appointees. Many critics of the New Deal accused the President of creating a rubber-stamp court. To be sure, all his appointees shared the general political position symbolized by the New Deal, and none of them agreed with the constitutional doctrines of Sutherland or McReynolds. But they were far from united. There were more dissenting opinions penned after 1940 than at any previous time in the Court's history. In many cases as many as five justices felt impelled to write separate opinions, often sharply attacking one another's views. The dissents reflected divergent constitutional attitudes among the men who were rapidly tailoring constitutional construction to the facts of the twentieth century, an adjustment that had been opposed by the old Court. The justices, most of whom had previously been active in politics, discussed the philosophical and political premises of their decisions to a much greater extent than had any of their predecessors.

Civil rights to the fore

By the early 1950's, the Roosevelt Court gave way to the Truman Court, as the four Truman appointees frequently held the balance of power. Under the leadership of Chief Justice Fred M. Vinson, the Truman Court retreated in case after case from the strong civil *liberties* position it had espoused prior to 1950. At the same time, the Court began to construe the Constitution in a fashion more favorable to the cause of civil *rights* for minority groups. No longer were the "constitutional cards being stacked" in favor of those who wished to use governmental power to segregate or unduly restrict Negroes (see pages 176-177). But no significant change took place in other areas, and the justices continued to permit governmental programs regulating and promoting business, agricultural, and labor activities.

In 1953, with the death of Chief Justice Vinson, President Eisenhower had his first opportunity to select a man to reflect the views of the victorious 1952 political majority. He chose the governor of California, Earl Warren, whose brand of Republicanism is much like that of the President. When Justice Jackson died, President Eisenhower chose to fill the vacancy with John Marshal Harlan, the grandson of the only justice to dissent in *Plessy* v. *Ferguson* (see page 175). The Supreme Court under Warren continues to support civil rights. It has moved slightly back to the Court's earlier strong civil liberties position and has become somewhat less tolerant of governmental regulation of speech activities than it was in the early 1950's. With the Roosevelt appointees on the Court reaching retirement, an "Eisenhower Court" might be in the offing. Constitutional doctrine will, as always, continue to be remolded—in what direction remains to be seen.

JUDGES AS TECHNICIANS

The Constitution does not require a judge to be a lawyer. Yet all Supreme Court justices, as well as all other federal judges, have been members of the bar. No businessman, farmer, or labor leader has ever served on any federal court. The reason is not hard to uncover. Although ignorance of the law is no excuse for the wrongdoer, knowledge of the law is a professional mystery of the lawyers. The law is a technical subject that can be mastered only after long study.

What kind of law do federal judges apply? Where do they find it?[11]

The Law

Sometimes judges apply *constitutional law*. Since the Constitution contains only 7000 words and can be read in a half hour or so, it might be assumed that any person could know constitutional law. But even the Constitution has become a possession of the specialists, and to read it sheds little light on constitutional law. Indeed, Professor T. R. Powell, one of Harvard's most distinguished teachers, is reported to have warned his students in constitutional law not to read the Constitution because it would "confuse their minds." Constitutional law is full of phrases like "the clear and present danger rule" and "separate but equal doctrine," that are not to be found in the written words of the Constitution. They come from the decisions of the Supreme Court. Constitutional law is, in other words, those statements about the interpretation of the Constitution that have been given Supreme Court sanction.

Constitutional law is applied in a relatively small number of cases. In many instances it is *statutory law* that controls the judge's decision. This is law formulated by the legislature, although it also includes treaties and executive orders; it is law that comes from authoritative and specific lawmaking sources. The legislature perforce must state the rules in general terms and cannot anticipate all the questions that will arise as to their meaning. Even the most specific law must be applied to an infinite variety of concrete situations. The initial interpretation is often made by an administrator, but the final interpretation, short of a change in the law, is made by the judges.

Again, intelligence alone is not enough to interpret even the simplest of laws. The law must be interpreted according to *The Law,* by the application of legal principles. In general, judges try to discover legislative intent—what the legislators intended to do. When possible this is done from the words of the statute. Sometimes judges must look to legislative journals, legislative debates, and committee hearings to get clues as to the intention of the legislators. A layman might try to consult the men who drafted, introduced, or considered the bill in committee, for they might seem to be the most informative and reliable source of legislative intent. But according to the judges' rules, which in large part they make themselves, *The Law* does not permit this.

What happens if there is no statutory law governing the case? What if

[11] See Appendix to find out where the lay citizen can look up the law.

the legislature has not formalized any rule to apply to the dispute? Then the judges must apply the *common law*. Common law is judge-made law. It has an ancient lineage and can be found by reading through the reports of judicial decisions. It originated in England in the twelfth century when royal judges began traveling around the country settling disputes in each locality according to prevailing custom. Gradually these principles became the same for the entire nation. The common law develops according to the rule of *stare decisis,* meaning, "let the decision stand." *Stare decisis* requires that once a rule has been established by a court, it shall be followed in all similar cases. It makes the decisions of judges of superior courts binding not only on all subordinate courts in the same judicial system, but also on their own successors.

The American common law began to branch off from the English system in the seventeenth century. Today we have 47 separate common-law systems, or 48, counting the federal interpretation of law. (In Louisiana the legal system is based on the other great western legal tradition, the *civil law*. The civil law gives more emphasis to codes of lawgivers and less to past judicial decisions. In Louisiana the civil law has been greatly influenced by and intermingled with the common law.) There is no federal common law. Whenever federal judges have to decide disputes between citizens of two states, they apply the common law as interpreted by the state courts. But when there is no state interpretation, federal judges strike out for themselves. In many fields the common law is the only law. Even where it has been superseded by statute, the statutory law is usually a modification and codification of the old common-law rules and is normally interpreted according to the common-law tradition.

Federal judges also apply *equity*. Like common law, equity is a system of judge-made law, and had its origins in England. Early in the development of the common law, it was discovered that in certain circumstances the common law did not provide justice. Under the common law, for example, a person whose property rights are about to be injured has no choice but to wait until the injury has taken place and then to seek money damages. But the injury may do irreparable harm for which money damages cannot provide adequate compensation. Accordingly another set of rules was worked out to be used where the law is inadequate. A person may go to a judge, show why the common-law remedy is inadequate, and ask for equitable relief, an injunction, for example, to prevent an act which threatens irreparable harm. If the wrongdoer persists, he is punishable for contempt of court.

Other types of law

Admiralty and maritime law is also applied by federal judges. It is a highly complex and technical body of rules applicable to cases arising in connection with shipping and water-borne commerce on the high seas and, by decision of the Supreme Court,[12] on the navigable waters of the United States.

A relatively new kind of law that has become increasingly prominent in the work of federal judges is *administrative law*. Congress has, within the last several decades, delegated to administrators and administrative agencies so much rule-making authority that today there is, in volume, more administrative than statutory law. Administrative laws are the rules and regulations issued by administrative agencies that deal with the operations of the government or that determine private rights. An example is the Federal Trade Commission regulation that interstate advertisers shall not use the word "free" in such a way as to mislead the reader. The rules and decisions of administrators are reviewable by federal judges, as noted above, and judges are often called upon to determine whether the administrators have acted properly and within their authority.

Law can also be classified as *criminal* or *civil*. Criminal law, almost entirely statutory, defines crimes against the public order and provides for punishment. The government has the primary responsibility for enforcing this type of law. The great body of criminal law is administered by the state and not the federal courts, but the criminal business of federal judges is by no means negligible, and it is growing. The Constitution insists upon certain minimum procedures in the trial of criminal cases (see Chapter 8) and these procedures have been supplemented by law. The Supreme Court, as supervisor of the administration of justice in the federal courts, has adopted other rules that federal judges must follow.

Civil law governs the relations between individuals and defines their legal rights. For example: Jones has a trademark for "Atomic Pills," and he finds that Smith is advertising "Atomic Tablets" in national magazines. If Jones wishes to protect his trademark, he may proceed against Smith before a federal judge. But the government can also be a party to a civil action. During World War II the federal courts did a brisk business hearing cases started by the Office of Price Administration to enforce price control regulations. Under the Sherman Antitrust Act, the federal government may initiate civil as well as criminal action to prevent violations of the law.

The Constitution has little to say about procedure to be followed in civil cases, though it does require that suits at common law involving $20 or more be tried before a jury. This pertains, however, only to suits under the common law, and even in those arising under the common law parties may, and frequently do, waive the right to trial before a jury. Congress has given to the federal courts authority to determine their own rules of civil procedure.

The scope of judicial power

Some people seem to think that judges have a roving commission to ferret out injustice. Perhaps they visualize a judge reading through the

[12] *The Genesee Chief* (1852).

morning paper, looking for evidence of violations of the laws or for laws passed by Congress that he should declare unconstitutional. This is not the way judges operate. They have only *judicial power* and that is the power "to decide and pronounce a judgment and carry it into effect between persons . . . who bring a case before [them] for decision."[13] The Supreme Court has steadfastly refused to permit the constitutional courts to exercise any nonjudicial functions. These courts cannot make any decisions "not binding on the parties or subject to later . . . alteration by administrative action." Hence, the Supreme Court will not give any advisory opinions to Congress or the President; it will act, and permits other constitutional courts to act, only when presented with a controversy over which it has jurisdiction.

Not all disputes are within the scope of judicial power. Judges decide only *justiciable* disputes, those that grow out of actual cases and that are capable of settlement by legal methods. A rabid Dodger fan might engage in a violent dispute with a booster of the Cardinals, but no judge will use his judicial authority to determine which is the better team. Not even all governmental questions or constitutional problems are justiciable. For example, judges will not determine which government of a foreign state should be recognized by the United States. The Constitution gives this authority to the President, and judges will not question his decision. Similarly, the Supreme Court has ruled that some claims of unconstitutionality raise political and not justiciable questions. What does the Court mean by "political"? They mean one which requires knowledge of a nonlegal character, which requires the use of techniques not suitable for a court, or which the Constitution addresses to the political branch of government. Examples of political questions are: Which of two competing state governments is the proper one? What is a republican form of state government? Has a constitutional amendment been ratified within a reasonable time after it was proposed? Are congressional districts properly drawn?[14]

Judges will not use their power unless the controversy is a real one. Two people cannot trump up a suit merely to contest the actions of the legislature. For example, in 1889 one Wellman tried to purchase a railway ticket the day after the Michigan legislature fixed the rates. The ticket agent refused to sell a ticket at the new rate and Wellman brought suit. During the trial Wellman made no attempt to contest the railway company's testimony. It became clear that Wellman wanted the railway company to win; he had no adverse interest and made no attempt to present fully the facts in the case. The Supreme Court said, however, "It was never thought that, by means of a friendly suit, a party beaten in the legislature could transfer to the courts an inquiry as to the constitutionality of a legislative act."[15] (This, of course,

[13] Justice Miller, *Constitution* 314, quoted by Justice Day for Supreme Court in *Muskrat* v. *United States* (1911).

[14] *Luther* v. *Borden* (1849); *Coleman* v. *Miller* (1939); and *Colegrove* v. *Green* (1946).

[15] *Chicago & Grand Trunk Railway Co.* v. *Wellman* (1892).

is exactly what is done in a nonfriendly suit. In such cases, however, the two parties have an interest in getting the full facts before the Court.)

Can anybody challenge a law? Not unless he has "sustained or is immediately in danger of sustaining a direct injury. It is not sufficient that he has merely a general interest common to all members of the public."[16] Furthermore, the injury must be substantial. In 1921 Congress passed a law providing for federal grants to the states for the purpose of reducing maternal and infant mortality. When a Miss Frothingham heard about the law she was indignant. It was, she thought, clearly unconstitutional, as the subject was one reserved to the states and beyond the power of the national government. She instructed her attorneys to seek an injunction to prevent Secretary of the Treasury Mellon from disbursing money in accordance with the law. Did she have the right to maintain the suit? Yes, her lawyers argued, because if the unconstitutional appropriations were made it would increase the burden of future taxes and thereby take her property without due process of the law. The Supreme Court decided, however, that Miss Frothingham's interest in the money in the Federal Treasury was too minute, and the effects of appropriation on future taxation too remote and uncertain to give her any standing to contest the act.[17]

Judges are careful to decide only what is necessary to dispose of the case before them, especially when the constitutionality of an act of Congress is in question. The Supreme Court has frequently shown extreme reluctance to rule on such matters. As Mr. Justice Brandeis wrote: "It is not the habit of the court to decide questions of a constitutional nature unless absolutely necessary to a decision of the case. . . . The Court will not 'formulate a rule of constitutional law broader than is required by the precise facts to which it is applied. . . .' The Court will not pass upon a constitutional question although properly presented by the record, if there is also present some other ground upon which the case may be disposed of. . . . [I]t is a cardinal principle that this Court will first ascertain whether a construction of the statute is fairly possible by which the question [of constitutionality] may be avoided."[18]

Judges do not always observe the restrictions and confine themselves to their judicial functions. At times the Supreme Court justices, despite their professed reluctance to do so, have had little hesitancy about striking down laws of Congress. Disputes have been trumped up entirely for the purpose of getting a Court decision; the *Dred Scott* case, for example, appears to have been a dispute of this kind. Other cases have been presented in which it is questionable whether the parties actually stood in an adverse relationship, for example, the case in which the Guffey Coal Act was declared un-

[16] *Ex parte Levitt* (1937).
[17] *Frothingham* v. *Mellon* (1923).
[18] Concurring opinion in *Ashwander* v. *T.V.A.* (1936).

constitutional. Despite these breaches, the judges generally are careful to stay within their proper field of operations.

Laymen are often impatient with what they consider to be technicalities. But judges are not free agents with the power to right any and all wrongs according to their own sense of justice. "We do not sit," wrote Justice Frankfurter in the *Terminiello* case, "like a kadi under a tree dispensing justice according to considerations of individual expediency. . . ." In the long run, violation of the settled rules of judicial procedure seems to lead to more uncertainty, to more abuse of judicial power, and to more delay than does the slow but inexorable movement of justice. "Some of these rules," Justice Frankfurter has admitted, ". . . may well appear over-refined or evasive to the laity. But they have the support not only of the profoundest wisdom. They have been vindicated, in conspicuous instances of disregard, by the painful lessons of our constitutional history." The rules restricting judges are designed to prevent them from interfering in matters beyond their competence and to confine them to the functions for which they were established.

JUDGES AS POLITICIANS

"Do judges make law? 'Course they do. Made some myself," remarked Jeremiah Smith, former judge of the New Hampshire Supreme Court.[19] Today such statements raise few judicial eyebrows. But just a few generations ago, such frankness would have shocked many of the leading gentlemen of the bench and bar. In some quarters, criticism of judges, especially of Supreme Court justices, was considered to be poor taste. Despite glaring evidence to the contrary and the realistic statements of some outstanding judges and lawyers, the orthodox position was that judges *discovered* but never made laws. According to this orthodoxy, the judges' own views of public policy were irrelevant, since their only function was to apply the rule or principle applicable to the case before them. Judging, it was insisted, was solely a matter of knowledge and reasoned judgment, and the will of the judges did not enter into the picture. According to the "discovery" theory of the law, a judge is bound by the rule of *stare decisis*. A judge merely *discovers* the right precedents; and when there are no precedents, he extends the old principles.

How judges make law

In deciding most cases, however, it is easy to find precedents to support a preconceived decision. There are competing lines of principles, each of

---

[19] Quoted in Paul H. Freund, *On Understanding the Supreme Court* (Boston: Little, Brown & Company, 1950), p. 3.

which might appropriately support a decision. In choosing between them the judge acts very much like a legislator. The judge also has an area of choice when he interprets statutory law, for many statutes are so hastily and poorly drawn that there is no clear guide to legislative intent. But even carefully drafted legislation does not seriously restrict the judge. Although judges profess to search for legislative intent, how is one to discover the intention of all the congressmen and the President who make the law? Legislative intention is, as Professor Max Radin has written, "a transparent and absurd fiction."[20] Even where legislative history affords clear guides to the intent of the legislators, James M. Landis has pointed out, "strong judges prefer to override the intent of the legislature in order to make law according to their own views."[21] According to Judge Learned Hand, one of America's great jurists, the words of a statute that a judge must construe are "empty vessels into which he can pour nearly anything he will."

Judicial legislation is well illustrated by an example that is extreme but not unique. In 1890, when Congress passed the Sherman Antitrust Law and declared, "Every contract in restraint of trade and commerce among the several States is illegal," the legislators inevitably left to the judges the determination of the concrete meaning of this law. In order to discover, for example, whether the law outlaws contracts pertaining to *manufacturing* that ultimately will restrain interstate commerce, one looks not to the words of the law or even to legislative history, but to the decisions of the Supreme Court. This was the question in *United States* v. *E. C. Knight Co.* (1895), the first case under the Sherman Act that came before the High Tribunal. The government had asked the Court to set aside a contract among a group of companies that gave them control over refining 98 per cent of the sugar in the United States. But a majority of the Supreme Court justices declared that the act did not outlaw such a contract. The sugar companies, they said, had restrained manufacturing—not commerce—and the restraint of commerce that might result was indirect. By this interpretation the Supreme Court took the heart out of the Sherman Antitrust Law, though the rationale of the *Knight* case was undercut by the Supreme Court a few years later. In 1911 the Court further "amended" the Sherman Act by ruling that, despite the words of the statute, Congress had intended to make illegal only "unreasonable contracts."[22]

The Supreme Court is even more legislative in interpreting the Constitution than it is in interpreting statutes. Yet the old orthodoxy insisted that the power of judicial review was merely the power to follow the obvious

[20] Max Radin, "Statutory Interpretation," *Harvard Law Review,* Vol. 43, (April 1930), pp. 863-885.

[21] James M. Landis, "Statutory Interpretation," *Harvard Law Review,* Vol. 43, (April 1930), pp. 886-893.

[22] *United States* v. *American Tobacco Co.*

intent of the Constitution. As recently as 1936, Mr. Justice Roberts, speaking for the Court, wrote in *United States* v. *Butler:*

> It is sometimes said that the court assumes a power to overrule or control the action of the people's representatives. This is a misconception. . . . When an act of Congress is appropriately challenged in the courts as not conforming to the constitutional mandate the judicial branch of the Government has only one duty,—to lay the article of the Constitution which is involved beside the statute which is challenged and to decide whether the latter squares with the former. All the court does, or can do, is to announce its considered judgment upon the question. The only power it has, if such it may be called, is the power of judgment. This court neither approves nor condemns any legislative policy. Its delicate and difficult office is to ascertain and declare whether the legislation is in accordance with, or in contravention of, the provisions of the Constitution; and, having done that, its duty ends.

Professor Roscoe Pound has called this "the slot machine theory" of judicial review. It is true that the meaning of many parts of the Constitution is obvious and can be interpreted by a mechanical process. If Congress passed a law extending the term of United States senators beyond six years, its unconstitutionality would be apparent to everyone. If constitutional interpretation amounted only to this, judges would have no special claim as guardians of the Constitution. But it is not the specifically worded clauses of the Constitution that present any questions of interpretation. Rather it is those open-ended clauses, those few words whose meaning cannot be interpreted solely with a dictionary. Judges have few external guides, for example, in trying to determine the meaning of due process or the First Amendment.

In giving content to constitutional ambiguities, Supreme Court justices are not seriously restricted by the doctrine of *stare decisis*.[23] The doctrine is even less controlling in the field of constitutional than in the field of statutory interpretation. The legislature can correct judicial errors of statutory interpretation, but only the Supreme Court or a constitutional amendment can alter the Court's "erroneous" construction of the Constitution. Justices are, therefore, less hesitant to overrule decisions on constitutional matters. Even when they do not wish to repudiate openly an earlier doctrine, it is easy to "distinguish" each new case from the old ones and thus permit a new ruling. Justice Harlan told a group of students, "I want to say to you young gentlemen that if we [the Supreme Court] don't like an act of Congress, we don't have much trouble to find grounds for declaring it unconstitutional."[24]

[23] Justice William O. Douglas, *"Stare Decisis," Columbia Law Review,* Vol. 49, No. 6, June 1949, pp. 735-758.

[24] Quoted by E. S. Corwin, *Constitutional Revolution, Ltd.* (Claremont: Claremont and Associated Colleges, 1941), p. 38. For a recent and fresh treatment of the extent and limitations of judicial power, see John P. Roche, "Judicial Self-Restraint," *The American Political Science Review,* Vol. XLIX, No. 3 (Sept. 1955), pp. 762-772.

To recognize the facts of judicial life—that the judges often write their own views into law, that, in the words of Max Lerner, "judicial decisions are not babies brought by constitutional storks"—is not to criticize the judges. Nor is it to be thought that there are no limits to the judges' discretion. They are restricted, as we have seen, by precedent, by legal principles and procedures, by the severe discipline of the law itself, and by other techniques designed to offset their own political opinions. Those who insist that the law is only a reflection of the personal biases of the judges are as extreme as those who insist that these biases have no effect on the law.

Activists versus self-restrainers

Not all judges are convinced of the possibility or of the desirability of achieving objectivity, and of withdrawing from the field of policymaking. These judges, roughly characterized as "judicial activists," insist that political choice is inevitable and inherent in judging, and that judges should make no false pretense of objectivity. Rather, they feel, they should recognize that they are making policy, and they should consciously exercise their judicial power to achieve social justice.

The judicial self-restrainers take another view. They recognize the judge's difficulty in rising above his own biases, but they insist that objectivity is the goal that he should aim for. As the people's *political* representatives, the legislators and executives, they argue, have the chief responsibility for working out the accommodation of interests that is the essence of legislation. The self-restrainers insist that judges must be very careful to avoid injecting their own wishes into the judicial process, since it is not their responsibility to determine public policy. Judges should be especially hesitant to check the full play of the democratic process. As Justice Stone wrote in his dissenting opinion in the *Butler* case, "Courts are not the only agency of government that must be assumed to have the capacity to govern," and "The only check upon our own exercise of power is our own sense of self-restraint. For removal of unwise laws from the statute books appeal lies not to the courts but to the ballot and to the process of democratic government."

Some people take a position midway between activists and self-restrainers. They believe that the judges should not invalidate economic and social laws affecting property rights, but should have full authority to void laws restricting civil liberties, such as free speech. Their argument for this compromise position goes like this: The majority should not be stopped from experimenting with social and economic arrangements. If mistakes are made, new majorities will arise to correct them. But majorities should not be permitted to tamper with basic liberties. For if they go too far, the very instruments for publicizing and correcting the mistakes—such as free speech and free press—will not be able to operate effectively. This argument in part underlies the doctrine of presuming economic and social legislation to be valid, but restrictions on civil liberties to be invalid.

These divergent views about the proper role of the judiciary have been formulated more explicitly in the recent opinions of the Supreme Court than they were when the discovery theory was prevalent. Yet judges cannot be fitted into neat categories; accusations that the judges are being influenced by their own political beliefs often stem from a dislike of the Court's opinions rather than from disagreement over its proper scope. Prior to 1937, when the Supreme Court majority was announcing constitutional doctrines that protected the business community, supporters of these doctrines insisted that the justices were merely applying the clear dictates of the Constitution. On the other hand, those who disliked the conservative tenor of the doctrines accused the justices of usurping the legislative function, of making their own partisan views the measure of constitutionality. From 1937 to the present, the shoe has been on the other foot. Those who dislike the decisions sustaining government regulation of the economy and striking down laws supporting racial segregation have accused the justices of being "New Dealers," "partisan politicians," and "incompetent judges." Those who like the decisions and approve of the new doctrines insist that the justices have merely returned to the true meaning of the Constitution.

Judges must make choices among conflicting values. By the very nature of their duties, judges—especially those on the Supreme Court—are forced into the storm center of politics and policy making. What problems does this raise for democratic government?

JUDGES AND DEMOCRATIC GOVERNMENT

Judges are at one and the same time legal technicians and, in the broad sense, politicians. As legal technicians, it is their legal competence that controls their decisions; as policy makers it is their political attitude that counts. As impartial dispensers of equal justice under the law, judges should not be dependent on the pleasure of the executive, the legislature, or the parties to a case. As determiners of basic public policy, judges should be politically responsible and publicly accountable. As legal experts applying legal principles to the solution of justiciable controversies, judges should be above politics. As policy makers, judges should be—and inevitably are—in politics.

The Constitution takes into account the confusion occasioned by the blending of these dual and inextricably related functions in the person of a judge. In some of its provisions it looks to the independence of the judiciary; judges are appointed by the President with the consent of the Senate to serve for life terms; Congress is forbidden to decrease their salaries during their term of service. On the other hand, judges depend on Congress for the money they need to operate, and for their jurisdiction to hear cases. Congress creates the inferior courts, determines the size of all courts, and may remove judges by impeachment and conviction.

Should the Constitution be what the judges say it is?

This is the familiar pattern of separation of powers and checks and balances. The principle of separation of powers, however, is more pertinent to the independence of the judiciary than it is to the other branches. Many who urge the consolidation of legislative and executive powers in the same agency still insist upon an independent judiciary. In the first place, it is an ancient and seldom questioned maxim of justice that no man be trusted as both prosecutor and judge. The active enforcement of the law, the investigation of crimes, and the prosecution of wrongdoers are executive functions. If judges depended on the pleasure of the executive, then two incompatible functions would be consolidated in the same agency. Secondly, "a government of laws and not of men" is one in which public officials as well as private individuals operate under and in accordance with the law. To check the illegal actions of these officials requires an appeal to an independent judiciary.

Judges must also be free to apply the law impartially, even against the most popular person in a community or in favor of the most hated. Sometimes justice requires a judge to favor a person who has aroused the active hostility of his neighbors or to rule against one who has a strong popular following. He must have the independence to apply the law fearlessly— especially when the community has been swept by emotions that make it intolerant of restrained action. Independence is always a matter of degree, and even if the judges' sole duty were to serve as legal experts, complete isolation from the community and lack of all popular control would not be desirable. Yet few would question the value of an independent judiciary when judges are thought of as legal technicians.

What about the *legislative* activities of judges? Even if deprived of the authority to declare laws unconstitutional, judges in carrying out their ordinary functions of interpreting the law would of necessity continue to make choices among policy alternatives. Should they be independent of the majority?

Few people have ever seriously questioned the arrangements that give national judges great independence, but many, including Presidents Jefferson, Jackson, Lincoln, and both Roosevelts, have tilted with the defenders of judicial review. Although most people admit the necessity of having independent judges, some have questioned the need to give these independent judges the power to veto the desires of the majority as expressed through their elected representatives. All agree that an unconstitutional law should not be enforced. The question remains, *is the Supreme Court's interpretation to be preferred to that of Congress or the President?*

The most important parts of the Constitution, as we have noted, are vague and leave room for difference of opinion. Of the three branches of government, it is argued, the Supreme Court is the least responsive to the public will. If the Constitution is supreme because it is an expression of the people's ideas, then those agents who most directly represent those ideas have the best right to interpret the Constitution. Why should five men (i.e., a majority of the Court) holding office for life have the power to tell Congress and the President, elected by the people, what they may or may not do?

Other opponents of judicial review have pointed out that John Marshall's logic in *Marbury* v. *Madison* could be turned against him. Confronted with a Supreme Court decision that he considered unconstitutional, a President might reason that his duty would be to follow the Constitution and to refuse to enforce the Court's decision.

But despite the persistent attacks on judicial review, most Americans continue to hold it as a desirable feature of our governmental system. Generally speaking Americans have never been willing to put full trust in the majority. An independent judiciary with the power of judicial review has been the major institutional sign of this fear of unchecked legislative and popular majorities. The belief in judicial review reflects and rests on the belief that the Constitution, like the higher law, contains certain fundamental principles that no majority should tamper with. It is argued that the independence of judges from temporary majorities is their strength in protecting these rights, not their weakness. Justice Jackson phrased it, in a somewhat different context, "One's right to life, liberty, and property, to free speech, a free press, freedom of worship and assembly, and other fundamental rights may not be submitted to vote; they depend on the outcome of no election."[25]

But just how independent in fact are the judges? Are they so independent with their power of interpreting the Constitution and the laws that they are the masters of the majority? For the moment, yes; in the long—and not so very long—run, no.

"The Constitution is what most of us say it is"

The most important way in which political majorities have brought their weight to bear on the judiciary is through the selection of the judges by the popularly elected President and senators. Political considerations have been of crucial significance in the selection of federal judges. Party political considerations have been of particular importance in choosing judges of the lower federal courts. By the rule of senatorial courtesy, as noted above, the senators of the state in which the district court is located, provided they are of the same party as the President, have a veto over all judicial appointments. In practice, the senators often send the President a list from which he is requested to nominate one for Senate confirmation, and this list seldom includes a member of the opposing political party.

[25] *West Virginia State Board of Education* v. *Barnette* (1943).

Party considerations have not been ignored in selecting members of the Supreme Court. Only Presidents Taft and Franklin D. Roosevelt selected a member of the opposition to serve as Chief Justice. But party considerations are much less important in the choosing of associate justices. Here the determining factors are the basic social, economic, and judicial attitudes of the individual. Every President since Washington has felt that his responsibilities demanded that he nominate to the Supreme Court men who could be depended on to make the "right" decisions, meaning decisions compatible with the views of the popularly elected President. President Theodore Roosevelt gave voice to this attitude in a letter to Senator Lodge about Judge Holmes of the Massachusetts Supreme Judicial Court, whom he was considering for the United States Supreme Court. He wrote:

In the ordinary and low sense which we attach to the words "partisan" and "politician," a judge of the Supreme Court should be neither. But in the higher sense, in the proper sense, he is not in my judgment fitted for the position unless he is a party man, a constructive statesman, constantly keeping in mind his adherence to the principles and policies under which this nation has been built up. . . . Now I should like to know that Judge Holmes was in entire sympathy with our views, that is with your views and mine. . . . I should hold myself guilty of an irreparable wrong to the nation if I should [appoint] any man who was not absolutely sane and sound on the great national policies for which we stand in public life.[26]

Presidents have occasionally been disappointed. Once on the bench, some justices have departed from the "sound policies" that the Presidents expected them to support. But by and large, through their selection of the personnel of the federal judiciary, Presidents and Senates have *eventually* been able to bring the Court's decisions into line with the general attitudes of contemporary political majorities.

The difficulty, however, is that the judge's life tenure often keeps him in office long after the political climate has changed, and he continues to represent views of the era in which he was appointed. Some justices have even stayed on the Court to prevent incumbent Presidents from appointing their successors. Chief Justice Taft, for example, feared to resign lest the "radical" Hoover be allowed to appoint someone in his place. In 1929 he wrote, "I am older and slower and less acute and more confused. However, as long as things continue as they are, and I am able to answer in my place, I must stay on the court in order to prevent the Bolsheviki from getting control. . . ."[27]

[26] Henry Cabot Lodge, *Selections from the Correspondence of Theodore Roosevelt and Henry Cabot Lodge* (New York: Charles Scribner's Sons, 1925), I, 518-519.
[27] Letter to Horace Taft, November 14, 1929, quoted by H. F. Pringle, *The Life and Times of William Howard Taft* (New York: Farrar & Rinehart, Inc., 1939), Vol. II, p. 967.

In most cases, however, the tardiness of the Supreme Court in adjusting to changing political climates is the normal result of the long tenure of the justices. Jefferson, for instance, became President only to discover that the judiciary was entirely manned by Federalists who represented the doctrines Jefferson had just defeated in the election. Many of these Federalist judges had no scruples against using their power to attack Jefferson's political doctrines.

Faced with this opposition, Jefferson and his followers tried to use the impeachment power to modernize the judiciary. Although judges hold office during good behavior, they may be impeached for "treason, other high crimes and misdemeanors." Despite his avowed attachment to the doctrine of strict construction, Jefferson wished to interpret liberally the impeachment clause and to develop it as a device for keeping the judiciary in line with current views. The Federalist judges had not committed treason, high crimes, or misdemeanors, though some of them were guilty of conduct unbecoming a judge and of using their positions for frankly partisan purposes. Yet Jefferson felt that judges who held political views not in harmony with those of the political majority should not be permitted to thwart the wishes of the people and should be subject to some kind of political control. As a result, his supporters in the House of Representatives impeached Justice Chase. Chief Justice Marshall was apparently next on the list. Although Chase had been an intemperate Federalist partisan, he had committed no crimes, and the Senate refused to sustain the impeachment charge. Since that date impeachment has never been used to remove judges except, in a very few cases, for criminal or patently unethical practices.

Congressional control over the structure and jurisdiction of the federal courts has been used more successfully to influence the course of judicial decision. Although thwarted in their attempts to impeach the judges, the Jeffersonians abolished the circuit courts that the Federalist Congress had created just prior to leaving office. In 1869 the Radical Republicans in Congress altered the Supreme Court's appellate jurisdiction to snatch from the Court a case it was about to review that involved legislation of dubious constitutionality (*Ex parte McCardle*).

They also negatively packed the Court by reducing its size to prevent President Johnson from filling two vacancies. After Johnson left the White House, Congress increased the size of the Court to permit Grant to select two justices. As noted above, Grant selected men who made it possible to reverse the Supreme Court invalidation of the Legal Tender Act. Historians are still debating whether Grant packed the Court. Certainly he was not unaware that his two appointees shared his sentiments about the desirability of reversing the earlier decision.

F.D.R. versus the "Nine Old Men"

President Franklin D. Roosevelt's battle with the Supreme Court is a more recent and more dramatic attempt by a political leader to influence the course of judicial decisions. President Roosevelt took office on March 4, 1933, in the midst of the Great Depression. Under his leadership, Congress passed in quick succession a series of important laws designed to give Americans a "New Deal." By 1935 these measures began to come before the Supreme Court. In the next sixteen months the Supreme Court invalidated eight out of the ten measures that came before it. Despite the Supreme Court's judgment that the New Deal was unconstitutional, in 1936 Franklin D. Roosevelt won an overwhelming victory at the polls. An irresistible force seemed to be moving toward an immovable object. One or the other would have to give way.

Early in 1937, as the conflict between the President and the Supreme Court was moving toward its climax, a variety of proposals were put forward to limit the judges' power. One suggested amendment would require a two-thirds vote of the justices before the Supreme Court could declare acts of Congress unconstitutional; another would permit Congress to override Supreme Court decisions by a two-thirds vote. But President Roosevelt decided that it would be impossible to secure ratification of such a constitutional amendment or, at any rate, that it would take too long. On February 5, 1937, he presented to Congress his own program to reorganize the federal judiciary. The most significant recommendation was to give the President the right to appoint an additional justice for each member of the Court over the age of seventy who chose not to retire after ten years' service. The maximum size of the Supreme Court was to be set at fifteen. The ostensible purpose of the recommendation was to make the Supreme Court more efficient so that it could keep up with its work. The real purpose was obvious. The President wished to modernize the Supreme Court by "packing" it.

Clearly the Supreme Court, dominated by very conservative justices, was blocking the program endorsed by a majority of the voters. But the electorate that had given that program an overwhelming vote of confidence was less enthusiastic about the President's attack on the Supreme Court. Opponents of the New Deal were able to mobilize opinion against the President by manipulating the symbol of the Supreme Court as the inviolable guardian of the Constitution standing above the noisome sea of politics. The President was accused of wanting to be a dictator and, like Hitler and Mussolini, to subjugate the judiciary to his own will. Many persons who agreed with the President that something should be done to restrict the power of the Supreme Court could not accept the method he suggested. Others believed that while the President's proposal would be an expedient solution to the immediate problem, its ultimate result would be to weaken an important instrument for protecting individual liberties.

Yet the President was not without resources. Although many could not agree as to the corrective, they could not deny that Supreme Court justices were writing their own doctrines into the Constitution and blocking social progress endorsed by the electorate. The President had the support of powerful groups, but the Supreme Court itself dealt the final blow to the President's program. It simply reversed its direction. Between March and June 1937, in the midst of the debate over the President's proposal, the High Court upheld a state minimum wage law, the Farm Mortgage Act, the amended Railway Labor Act, the Wagner Act, and the Social Security Act. Justice Roberts and Chief Justice Hughes, who theretofore had voted with the conservatives, switched their support to the liberals.[28] Here was the famous "switch in time that saved nine." No longer did the Supreme Court stand in the way of social and economic legislation. The President's proposal was rendered superfluous, as far as the immediate crisis was concerned, and it was defeated in Congress.

Did the Supreme Court follow the election returns? There is no way of knowing why Justice Roberts and the Chief Justice changed their position. But they could hardly have been blind to the 1936 election returns. They might well have interpreted these returns to mean that if the Supreme Court persisted in denying to the national and state governments the power that a majority of the people wanted them to exercise, it might be the Supreme Court and not the New Deal that would have been destroyed.

The Constitution is what the judges say it is. True, but ultimately the Constitution is what the people want it to be. The American democratic system has reached a pragmatic compromise between the desire for the independence of the judges and the desire to provide political checks on their policy-making activities. Judges have no armies or police to execute their laws. They have no authority to levy taxes to support their activities. In the long run they must adapt themselves to the nature and demands of government by the people. Ultimately the power they enjoy rests upon their retention of public support. No better criterion for determining the power of a government official has ever been invented.

[28] Merlo J. Pusey in his biography, *Charles Evans Hughes,* 2 vols. (New York: The Macmillan Company, 1951), chapters 69-71, argues that Hughes did not change his position, but see E. S. Corwin's review of this book for contrary position, *American Political Science Review,* Vol. XLVI, No. 4, December 1952, pp. 1167-1175.

FOR THE LAST SIX CHAPTERS WE HAVE BEEN TALK-
ing about "those guys in Washington," the ones that many people blame
for "the mess"—whatever "mess" may exist at the moment. These are
the men who rule us. But we in turn rule them. This reciprocal relationship
between the people and their leaders is both the glory and the perplexity
of democratic government. There is more to government, however, than
this simple two-way relation between the governors and the governed. Self-
government is also a cluster of crisscrossing and interacting connections
among all the groups that make up the people and all the leaders who
represent the groups.

Sometimes we forget that the men in Washington—President, congressmen, judges, administrators—are *representatives.* They are leaders of
groups (see Chapter 10), some small, some large, some very noisy, some
hardly visible. We say that "the President wants the immigration laws
revised but Senator So-and-So opposes." This is just a shorthand way of
saying that "some Americans including the President want the immigration laws revised; but other Americans, including Senator X, are opposed."
It is not simply a private fight between the President and a senator. Politics is not solely a series of struggles among leaders in Washington, but
battles directly or indirectly among all of us.

What our leaders do, in short, depends in large part on the attitudes
and activities of people throughout the country. It works the other way,
too. The attitudes and activities
of leaders help shape those of
private citizens. This is as it
should be in a "government by
the people."

By this time we have some
idea of how self-government
works. In our discussion we
have noted how the several
parts operate—how congressmen, presidents, bureaucrats,
judges, party leaders, interest
group spokesmen, and most of
the rest of the people take part
in the political process. Now let
us try to put these together
and see what happens when the
country is suddenly faced with
an urgent political problem—a
serious strike in 1952. The parenthetical comments refer back

21 ★

How can

we control

our leaders?

549

to some of the aspects of the process described in preceding pages.

THE STEEL STRIKE OF 1952

A political event has no beginning and no end. It is a maze of action and reaction that only occasionally breaks out into headlines. On November 1, 1951, the United Steel Workers of America, C.I.O., notified the steel industry that they wished to discuss wage increases and other benefits to go into effect when the contract expired at the end of the year.

For six weeks labor and management bargained. The union asked for wage increases, fringe benefits, a guaranteed annual wage, and a union shop. Management offered a small wage increase and refused to consider a union shop. It became obvious that no agreement would be reached. On December 17, 1951, President Philip Murray of the Steel Workers called a strike for the last day of the month.

A steel strike is damaging at any time. During the winter of 1952 it would have been perilous. American troops in Korea were fighting with weapons made largely out of steel. America was supplying munitions for most of the rest of the United Nations forces there. The nation was rearming as the "cold war" intensified, and had adopted wage and price controls to forestall inflation. Now a serious strike loomed. What should be done? Who should do it?

On December 22 the President of the United States referred the dispute to the Wage Stabilization Board. Composed of representatives of labor, management, and the public, this board had the responsibility for passing on wage increases to insure that they did not jeopardize the nation's anti-inflation program. It also could make recommendations for wage settlements. The union agreed to postpone the strike until the board could hold a hearing and make its recommendations. (The *threat* of a strike is often as effective as a strike itself.)

The board held hearings and deliberated for two months. Representatives of union and management argued their cases. Charge and countercharge flew. Each side accused the other of distorting the facts and attempting to mislead the public. On March 20, 1952, the board recommended immediate benefits that came to around twenty cents an hour, with increases to a total of about twenty-six cents an hour by the end of the year. It also recommended a union shop (see p. 674). Industry members of the board violently dissented. So did many congressmen and most newspapers. The public members had failed to represent the public and had sold out to labor, it was charged. (Note the characteristic tendency of each group to identify its idea of the public interest as the only good one and to accuse the opposition of looking out only for its own special interest. Defining the "public interest" was of course the point of the dispute.)

The steel executives rejected the recommendations. They would agree only to the 13.7 cent "package" that had been recommended by industry members of the board. Labor, on the other hand, was willing to accept the board's recommendations. But wages were only one side of the problem. What about the price of steel? The Office of Price Stabilization had authority to bar or permit a price increase. Steel spokesmen said that they would need a price increase of twelve dollars a ton to pay for the recommended wage increase. Labor maintained that steel profits were so high that the industry could pay the wage increase with only a slight increase in price— no more than the $2.86 that the price stabilization law automatically permitted. Price officials took the latter stand. It was clear that the workers would readily get their whole wage increase if management could get its price increase. But labor officials refused to back up the steel heads' demands for higher steel prices.

The national nominating conventions were approaching and the presidential election would take place a few months after that. Industry heads charged the Truman Administration with selling the public out in order to buy labor's votes. Labor and administration leaders accused the steel companies of seeking big profits at the expense of the workers and the public. Management argued that wage increases would cause inflation; labor contended that price increases would cause inflation. A fight for public support was under way. (Elections come so frequently in the United States that any important and protracted dispute among major groups becomes an election issue.)

By April no agreement was in sight. Labor prepared to use its classic weapon to enforce its demands. A strike was called for April 8. (It would be interesting to discover how this decision was made within the union— the division, if any, among union officials on the advisability of calling a strike—how concerned they were as to the reaction of various nonlabor groups to the strike. In times of crisis interest group organizations keep their affairs to themselves. Chances are that the crisis produced great unity in the union and a willingness to follow the leaders' advice.)

In the White House the President was seeking advice. The Secretary of Defense warned that "a work stoppage in the steel industry will result immediately in serious curtailment of production of essential weapons and munitions of all kinds." Atomic Energy Commission officials stressed the urgency of the situation. Political and labor advisers went over the implications of various lines of action. Memos and other reports were channeled to the President's desk. Some advised the President to use the Taft-Hartley Act and seek a court injunction preventing the union from striking for another eighty days. (In an election year a Democratic President would fear the effect of using an act that was anathema to most labor leaders.) Some argued that the President should order price stabilization officials to grant steel price increases and thus settle the whole issue. Others in the Administration held that this would wreck the economy and help industry at the expense of the "public." (Advice from all the experts—but the *President* had to make the decision. He alone was the elected representative and ultimately it was his responsibility. Failure to act would have been just as significant a decision as action itself.)

On April 8 the President by executive order instructed the Secretary of Commerce to take possession of the steel companies. The steel workers would not strike against the government. (The steel heads were still actually managing the industry, but the *symbolic* situation had changed.) At the same time the President went to Congress and the country. To the Congress he sent a message explaining why he had felt compelled to act, and he asked for congressional guidance. He defended his authority to act on the grounds that as chief executive and commander in chief he had the inherent power to act in an emergency and then to report to Congress on his action. (Note the President's use of several of his constitutional and extraconstitutional powers; the President was acting here as chief of state.) The President received little support in Congress.

That night President Truman made a nationwide radio address. He reviewed the steps in the dispute and placed blame on the steel industry for failing to abide by recommendations of the Wage Stabilization Board. The steel executives, he said, had made "outrageous" demands for price increases and were "recklessly forcing a shutdown of the steel mills." His opponents were quick to reply. The next night a steel executive speaking for all the companies made a nationwide radio and television address. "Happily," he said, "we still live in a country where a private citizen may look the President in the eye and tell him that he was wrong." He charged that the President was playing election politics, that the Wage Stabilization Board was partisan, that the President "takes at least two thirds" of steel profits in taxes. "Is your boy making $1.70 an hour in Korea?" he asked. (Note the use by both sides of propaganda techniques such as name calling and transfer, and the ingenious *personalization* of the issues —that is, *Mr. Truman* takes the taxes.)

The country—or the informed part of it—began to debate constitutional issues. (Political controversy often becomes clothed in legal terminology, and judges are called on to place immediate controversy in more long-range terms.) Both sides cited their authorities. Industry spokesmen, lawyers, Republican leaders, most editorial writers and radio commentators held that the President had exceeded his authority. Defenders of the President cited historical examples. The Supreme Court had never addressed itself directly to the inherent powers of the President; so there were few clues in the law books. (One of the important aspects of the whole debate was that both sides assumed without arguing that if *Congress* had authorized the seizure there would be no doubt of its constitutionality. The idea that *any* branch of the national government could authorize such a seizure would have been hotly denied by many only fifteen years before.)

The steel companies turned to the courts as well as to the people. They went into the United States District Court to seek an injunction against the Secretary of Commerce to prevent the government from continuing to control steel. On April 29 Federal Judge Pine granted the injunction requested by the steel companies. He accepted the arguments that they were suffering irreparable damage and that the President had no authority to take over steel in an emergency. But before the strike could be resumed by the workers, the Court of Appeals stayed Judge Pine's order until the Supreme Court had an opportunity to rule on the case.

Now the Supreme Court became the focus of attention. Newspapers reported the give-and-take between the attorneys and the justices during oral argument. Prominent among the steel companies' attorneys was the distinguished John W. Davis, onetime Democratic nominee for President. (Could the government's $12,000-a-year attorneys compete successfully with $50,000-a-year corporation lawyers?) All the nine justices had been appointed by Democratic Presidents, four by President Truman. Those who were critical of the Roosevelt-Truman appointees thought that they never could be counted on to stand up against the President. But on June 2 the Court ruled, six to three, against the presidential action. (Appointing members of the Court obviously does not give the President a group of "yes-men.") This notable case is *Youngstown Co.* v. *Sawyer.*

Six of the justices agreed that the injunction should be issued, but they could not agree why. Justice Black asserted that the President had no inherent authority to seize private property even during an emergency— at least this particular emergency. Justices Frankfurter and Burton stressed the fact that Congress had withheld from the President the power of seizure when it passed the Taft-Hartley Act. Justice Clark held that Congress had laid down specific procedures and that the President must follow these procedures. Many questions remained unanswered, but the Court had given its official support to the steel companies and to all those who felt that the President had gone too far. (Only a minority of congressmen had supported the President; the majority believed that he should have used the Taft-Hartley Act. Thus both a majority of Congress and the Supreme Court majority represented groups different from those represented by the President.)

On June 2 the plants were returned to their private owners. Immediately the workers struck. The nations' steel furnaces were banked out. Collective bargaining was resumed, while each side jockeyed for public support. Discussion of the steel strike quickly merged into talk about the approaching party conventions. The Republicans nominated General Eisenhower and adopted a platform endorsing the principle of the union shop. (Republican leaders, seeking majority support in the coming election, knew that they could not risk antagonizing broad segments of labor.) On July 22 the Army's largest shell-making plant closed. Now the Democrats were assembling in their convention in Chicago. Before leaving for Chicago, President Truman called both sides to the White House. He took a firm line. The situation was desperate, he said, and a settlement must be reached. (Whatever his legal authority, a President can wield tremendous moral authority as leader of the nation.)

A new contract was announced on July 24. The workers received a raise of sixteen cents an hour, fringe benefits worth another 5.4 cents, and a modified union shop contract. Steel received a price increase of $5.20 per ton for carbon steel. On signing the contract, the president of United States Steel called Murray "a great leader, an honest man and a great American," and Murray said equally nice things about the president of United States Steel. (After a crisis, rival groups "shake hands" in the manner of boxers after a championship bout.)

The strike was over, but its consequences were felt in many ways—in the election in the fall, in the economic situation, in war production, in constitutional doctrine, in popular attitudes. The political process has no real ending.

RULE BY CONCURRENT MAJORITY

The story of the steel strike, as the parenthetical comments suggest, illustrates many of the processes of democratic government in the United States—the role of President, congressmen, and judges, of parties and interest groups, of opinion leaders and followers, of economic power and military crisis, of old constitutional powers and new social legislation. The story suggests, too, the interrelationship of these forces; the events of the strike, like most events in a large and complex democratic system, made up a tangle of individuals, interests, institutions, and ideas. But perhaps the most important lesson for us as students of American politics is the further proof the story affords that the *checks and balances* built into our system by the framers of the Constitution are still a vital part of our system despite all the changes of the past 170 years.

This system was described in Chapter 3. It may be useful, following our excursion through the highways and byways of American government and politics, to review it here. The framers sought to limit the powers of the national government to prevent the kind of arbitrary rule that they hated. They did so first by dividing up power among the different branches of government, and then by making the different branches of government responsible to different groups of people. "Ambition" was to "counteract ambition."[1] A popular majority could take control of the

---

[1] *Federalist, No. 51.*

whole government only with great difficulty, if at all. Power was inextricably mingled and blended throughout the various branches of government.

As we have seen, the framers planned well. The system of intermingled powers and conflicting loyalties that they set up is still very much alive today. To be sure, some things have been changed. Senators are directly elected by the voters, and Presidents virtually so. But the basic arrangement endures. President, senators, representatives, and judges are chosen by different electorates. Their terms of office vary. Their responsibilities and loyalties differ. And as almost every newspaper tells us, their interests and ambitions often clash.

Consider the practical effects of this arrangement. Straight majority rule is impossible. If, for example, a majority of the voters should elect a President, he would face powerful minorities entrenched in Congress, the Supreme Court, even the bureaucracy. If a majority of the voters should elect a President *and* a Congress, the opposition would still remain. Witness what happened to Franklin D. Roosevelt's programs after he was re-elected in 1936 with 62 per cent of the two-party vote, and the Democratic party held 76 of the 96 seats in the Senate, and 333 of the 435 seats in the House. As we have seen, Mr. Roosevelt tried to pack the Supreme Court, but his court reform bill was beaten in the Senate. He tried to assert control of the executive branch, but Congress balked at his administrative reorganization bill. He tried to purge anti-New Deal Democrats in Congress, and in most cases he failed.

How, then, can government govern? How do we get things done? If the majority does not rule, who does? The answer is that we are governed by *shifting coalitions of minorities* rather than by *simple majorities*. Under this system government *can act only with the consent of the several major interests in society*. What are these interests? Most of them are economic, such as the big farm, labor, and business interests. Some are sectional, such as the West or the South. Some are religious, such as Catholics or Protestants. Some are national-origin, such as the Irish or the Italians. Each of these major interests has a voice in government actions. Each has some kind of modified veto over those actions.

The doctrine of *concurrent majority rule* has long been part of American political theory. A century ago John C. Calhoun stated the theory in extreme form. Calhoun wanted to safeguard the diversity of the American nation. He wanted to protect minority rights against the unchecked rule of numerical majorities. Calhoun, of course, had good reason to support such a theory. He was desperately anxious to prevent the North from oppressing the planter interests in the South. But the fact that he represented a minority interest made the theory no less impressive.

Broker rule today

Our system of concurrent majority rule today is not so extreme as Calhoun would have wanted. Very few single interests, if any, hold a complete and final veto over the rest of the community. But the main features of the system are with us. As previous chapters indicate, this system shows itself in every one of our major governmental and political institutions. The majority party in Congress runs afoul of minority blocs that exploit their control of committees, the filibuster in the Senate, and other devices for obstruction. Business is done by trading votes (logrolling) among the main interest groups involved. Powerful minorities show their hand also in the Supreme Court, in the bureaucracy, and even in the Cabinet. Even a candidate for President, under the tradition of "availability," cannot be nominated if he has antagonized some minority group, such as Negroes, Catholics, or farmers.

Above all, our system of concurrent majority rule reveals itself in our *party system*. Neither major party stands for a definite ideology or program. Both major parties follow shifting courses, straddling important issues, as they seek to pick up votes from this group and that. Both parties appeal to every major interest. Both parties attract all types of people —labor, businessmen, farmers, old people, young people, reformers, standpatters, rich, poor, upper class, middle class, working class, Negro, Irish, and so on. Whatever issue becomes popular, whatever group becomes powerful, both parties adapt their principles and move in to catch what votes they can. Unlike the ideological parties of Europe, American parties are mainly concerned not with expounding programs but with winning majorities.

Government by concurrent majority rule, in short, is a sort of "broker rule." Brokers act essentially as go-betweens; likewise broker rule is a system of government that mediates between interest groups, veering now right, now left, as political pressures rise and fall. Instead of acting for a firm, united majority with a fairly set program, the government tries to satisfy virtually all minority groups by giving them a voice in decisions and a veto over action. In the pushing and hauling of political groups, the government does a sort of delicate balancing act. Its condition is always one of unstable equilibrium.

The system defended

Broker rule has its supporters. Many thoughtful Americans believe that government by concurrent majorities is the price we pay—and not a very large price—for the maintenance of unity in a great, sprawling diverse nation such as ours. Their arguments go something like this:

1. The system protects minorities. Broker rule will not hurt interest groups of any size because by definition it acts only with their support—

or at least acquiescence. At the same time the system defends individual rights, which often find expression in minority action.[2]

2. Broker rule safeguards our diversity. Our varied nationality, religious, economic, and ideological groups are both the pride and strength of America. Our system of government should reflect the rich diversity of our group life. "The very multiplicity of interests," Merle Fainsod has said, "their freedom to maneuver and combine, and the open character of the society in which newly felt demands may always find organizational expression insure against the possibility of a frozen society and the rise of centers of intransigence within it." In short, our society is *pluralistic;* should our government not be pluralistic in nature too?

3. Broker rule tames down the extremists on both sides. It does this by giving them a stake in government—and some favors from government. By thus absorbing groups on the right and left, the system minimizes conflict and hardship. "A modern adaptation of Calhoun's plan, giving to the major economic interests and functional groups in our society the concurring power which Calhoun would give to the States," Herbert Agar has said, "might go a long way toward removing both class and sectional oppression."[3]

4. Broker rule permits a dynamic, flexible political system just as laissez faire encourages a competitive, dynamic economy. Power is not concentrated at the top, but is distributed throughout society, and as one student of the problem has said, "if there are economic checks and balances to parallel the political checks and balances, then society will be democratic."[4]

5. For all these reasons broker rule is the price of unity. It results in a party system that cannot become hopelessly divided on ideological grounds, because each party embraces a diversity of interests stretching across the political spectrum. Such parties serve as unifying agents. When they fail to do so, the nation is likely to become involved in civil war, as in 1861. "A federal nation," says one historian, "is safe so long as the parties are undogmatic and contain members with many contradictory views. But when the people begin to divide according to reason, with all the voters in one party who believe one way, the federal structure is strained."[5]

Supporters of broker rule, then, answer in this way the question—"How shall we control our leaders?"—posed in this chapter: Give our leaders limited power under the Constitution. Give them the means to check

[2] Pendleton Herring, *The Politics of Democracy* (New York: W. W. Norton & Company, 1940), pp. 92-94.

[3] Herbert Agar, *Pursuit of Happiness* (Boston: Houghton Mifflin Company, 1938), p. 198.

[4] John Chamberlain, *The American Stakes* (New York: Carrick & Evans, 1940), p. 31.

[5] Herbert Agar, *The Price of Union* (Boston: Houghton Mifflin Company, 1950), pp. 689-690.

one another. Give them the ambition to check one another. Make these rulers responsible to different combinations of voters—especially to shifting combinations of minority groups. Make it difficult for them to represent a simple majority of the people, at least for any length of time. Above all, prevent the rulers from governing through a strong party representing an organized majority.

Broker rule criticized

Many Americans dislike certain features of concurrent majority rule. They say:

1. Broker rule is unrepresentative. True, it tends to give every major interest a voice in decisions. But leaders of organized interests are often not truly representative of the members of those groups. And what about the millions of Americans not organized in vocal, self-seeking groups? Does not broker rule mean government at their expense? Moreover, studies have shown wide differences on some issues between public opinion and congressional action.

2. Broker rule results in parties that do not stand for much of anything. The choice between them is often one between Tweedledum and Tweedledee. This is dangerous. If people think that parties will not take honest and definite positions on major issues, the feeling may grow that democratic government evades problems instead of solving them. Such a feeling may cause people to turn to extremist leaders and parties, especially in time of social conflict and economic depression.

3. Broker rule may be all very well for a laissez-faire economy and a loose social organization, such as we had to some extent in the nineteenth century. But the world today is putting heavy demands on government, and these demands cannot be met by a polity of pressure groups. According to some observers, "the expanding responsibilities of modern government have brought about so extensive an interlacing of governmental action with the country's economic and social life that the need for coordinated and coherent programs, legislative as well as administrative, has become paramount."[6] The shifting, unstable alliances of minority interests cannot do the job of translating nationwide policy issues into firm decisions and action.

4. The view that broker rule tends to protect diversity is wrong. Heterogeneity, minority interests, and individual rights thrive best in a society that is productive, stable, and secure. A depression-ridden, frightened society cannot afford—or at least does not tolerate—diversity. Only positive action can keep the nation productive and strong. If democratic government cannot act, frustrated people may turn to more drastic ways out. In short,

[6] "Toward a More Responsible Two-Party System," A Report of the Committee on Political Parties of the American Political Science Association, *The American Political Science Review*, Vol. XLIV (1950), Pt. 2, p. 31.

strong—not weak—government is necessary to safeguard democracy which in turn protects diversity.[7]

5. Nor does broker rule lead to unity in the long run. On the contrary, by responding to pressures it sets group against group, section against section. Broker rule does not achieve genuine unity, but only temporary agreements and fleeting coalitions. By responding to minority pressures so readily, it fails to achieve a basic consensus in the attitude of a majority of the people, and such a consensus can be the only basis of real unity.

Naturally enough, most supporters of broker rule do not seek major changes in the American system. Some of them might want improvements here and there to gain more efficiency in normal times and more stability during crisis times, but on the whole they are glad to stand pat.

Not so the opponents of broker rule. Some of them urge the type of *constitutional* reform designed to bring President and Congress into closer collaboration (see Chapter 18). By allowing the Chief Executive to dissolve the legislature and appeal to the country, the two branches would be compelled to work together. Other opponents of broker rule take a different tack. Constitutional reform in the direction of cabinet government, they fear, might bring instability instead. Even if it united President and Congress, it might not gain governmental teamwork from the other two sets of national leaders, namely bureaucrats and judges. The only hope, according to this argument, is party reform.

PARTY REFORM: PROS AND CONS

Those who wish to improve our governmental system by working through our political party system believe that the essential structure of our national *government* cannot—and need not—be changed, but that our *political organization* must—and can—be improved.

Their reasoning runs as follows: The framers devised not only *governmental* checks and balances. They planned (as we have seen) for *political* checks and balances, also. Consequently any real attempt to unify and brace our governmental system must attack the problem in the political area, not merely the governmental. All the structural and mechanical reforms in the world are futile if our rulers continue to respond to shifting and conflicting groups of voters. Reorganizing the government—whether it involves mere tinkering or basic constitutional changes—will do no good unless it is accompanied by political reorganization reaching deep down into the political grass roots. Given such reorganization, our eighteenth century government could effectively face the problems of the twentieth.

[7] See Max Lerner, *It Is Later Than You Think* (New York: The Viking Press, 1938).

Wanted: responsible parties

The crux of the problem, according to this argument, lies in the make-up of our parties.[8] They are, as we saw in Chapter 13, loose associations of state and local groups, lacking in effective national machinery or real national cohesion. National and state party organizations are virtually independent of each other. Leadership is diffused. At the same time, the parties have a tremendous potential contribution to make. They can be whatever the people want them to be; no constitutional amendments need be passed, no basic governmental institutions changed. And this is the time that the party potential must be realized. For today, governments must draw up and enact a broad range of social, economic, and military policy. Strong parties are needed to help formulate, coordinate, and develop popular support for the vital work plans of government.

To party reformers the issue is *responsibility*. They maintain that parties must be more responsible to the general public and to their own members. Parties should be less responsive to pressures from organized minority groups and local politicos. The emphasis within parties must be on developing positive party policies reflecting a broad national consensus of the membership. The party in power must be responsible for enacting the policies on the basis of which it waged the campaign. It must be willing to discipline its members in office—especially those in Congress—if they desert the party platform. All this goes for the opposition party, too. It must act as the critic of the party in power, constantly developing and presenting alternative policies that it would fully back up whenever it took power. It must serve as a strong and united loyal opposition.

The specific proposals for party responsibility may be summarized as follows:

1. *Build up and improve the national party organization.* The national convention should continue as the party's main organ, but it should be more representative and more active. It should meet every year or two instead of only quadrennially, as at present. A new party council of about fifty members should serve as the full-time governing organ of the party. It would plan party strategy, interpret the platform, and run the organization. Above all—in the case of the party in power—it should take responsibility for pushing through the party platform—a task that involves coordinating the whole party, national, regional, state, and local.

2. *Make the party platform mean something.* Today platforms are hardly taken seriously. They are collections of pious hopes and vague promises. A newly nominated presidential candidate may interpret the platform as freely as he wishes during the campaign and later. Party platforms, it is proposed,

[8] The arguments for party government described here are taken largely from "Toward a More Responsible Two-Party System," A Report of the Committee on Political Parties (E. E. Schattschneider, ed.) of the American Political Science Association, *American Political Science Review*, Vol. XLIV (1950), No. 3, Pt. 2.

should be drawn up at least every other year so that they will keep abreast of the times. State and local platforms should be consistent with the national. A broad range of groups within the party, including congressmen, should take part in platform making, and the adopted platform should be binding on all members.

3. *Strengthen the party in Congress.* Advocates of responsible parties see Congress as the graveyard of party hopes and party pledges. Congressional party organization, they suggest, should be tightened up. The various leadership groups in both the Senate and the House should be merged into one responsible leadership committee for each party in each chamber. These four committees would submit proposed policies to the party members and would direct the legislative program. The caucus should meet more often, and its decisions should carry greater weight. The seniority rule should not enable party rebels to become chairmen of important committees. At any rate, the power of individual chairmen, of the House Rules Committee, and of senatorial filibusters should be curbed.

4. *Develop party activity at the grass roots.* Supporters of stronger national parties believe that the problem turns largely on the factor of political participation. They know, for example, that the only way to make congressmen more responsible to the party is to make the party mean more to the congressmen. The local party, fully backed up by the national party leaders, must build a strong democratic organization that could carry much of the burden of the congressional campaigns. Local party groups should meet more frequently to discuss and initiate policy. Party membership should mean something. Members should have certain obligations to their parties, such as paying dues and taking part in party activities. In return they should expect to see party policies that reflect their views and party leaders who act on those views. Thus democracy within the parties would be invigorated not merely in a formal sense, but on the basis of greater popular participation in party debate and action.

5. *Reform our electoral machinery.* The electoral college method of electing the President allots all the electoral votes of a state to the candidate who wins the most votes, no matter how small his margin may be. Such a system fosters one-party monopoly in certain sections of the country, especially in the South. The electoral college should be modified to give all sections a real voice in presidential elections. Nominating procedures that weaken party cohesiveness, such as the open primary and cross-filing, should be abandoned. Barriers to voting should be lifted. Voting should be made as easy as possible through such means as permanent registration and the short ballot (see Chapter 14).

The price of party responsibility

So much for the specific proposals for party responsibility. We still must face the question: Would party responsibility lead to a more democratic system of government? Would it help us better control our leaders?

The party reformers answer "yes." They believe that an invigorated party system would forge a firmer link between the people and the government. The men in power would be the leaders of the majority party. They would be bound by the wishes of the party rank and file, as embodied in the platform. To ignore the basic party policy would be dangerous; it would mean the risk of losing the support of sections of the party, and perhaps of losing the next election. Thus the millions of party members would not only *sustain* the government, they would also *constrain* it, forcing it to abide by its mandate at the previous election. The opposition party would serve as another check on the rulers. By holding out alternative policies and by continuously criticizing the government, the opposition would strive to win over a majority of the voters at the next election. The opposition party, like the party in power, would act as a responsible organization.

Not all political scientists agree with this diagnosis or with the proposed cure. It has been argued that these proposals underestimate the present extent of party responsibility. Examples are cited in which the parties have presented clear alternatives to the voters. It is feared, too, that more discipline in the parties would cut down party competition in certain areas, for the national leaders of a party might enforce doctrine unpopular in certain localities (for example, racial equality in the South).[9] Not party discipline but *party competition* is the great need, according to this view. "Our parties are big and clumsy and loosely hung together," says Professor Ruth C. Silva, "because our country is big and clumsy and loosely hung together." Nevertheless, virtually all students of the problem agree that in a democracy responsibility is an important goal, however it may be achieved.

Notice the difference between the party-reform approach and the idea of broker rule based on the doctrine of the concurrent majority. Party reorganization stresses responsibility and accountability to the *popular majority* that won the election. It involves *strict majority rule*—the idea that when a majority of the people vote a set of party leaders into power, the new government represents that majority and is largely responsible to it. Its job is to enact the majority's wishes into law. It has no obligation to the platform of the minority. Broker rule, on the other hand, shuns strict majority action. It stresses representation of people with diverse views. Under broker rule various minorities or combinations of minorities use governmental machinery to achieve their aims. They work through now one branch of government, now another. Both parties and all major interest groups have a voice in every major governmental action. The government acts not for a relatively solid and identifiable group of voters generally ranged on one side of the fence, but allots its favors to all sorts of groups and to both parties.

[9] Julius Turner, "Responsible Parties: A Dissent from the Floor," *American Political Science Review,* March 1951, pp. 143-152.

It is on this crucial point that many part company with the party reformers. Americans tend to fear majority rule. They believe that the majority holds in it the seeds of tyranny. They feel that a realignment of parties (which would be necessary under a system of majority rule) would end up with all the conservatives in one party, all the liberals and radicals in the other. The result would be extremism, whatever party was in power. Broker rule, they suggest, minimizes conflict by absorbing forces on the right or left. Majority rule would result in violent wrenches in the whole society as first one party, then the other, comes to power. And neither party would be really representative of the people as a whole. Far better, they say, for each party to be a cross section of all major viewpoints, interests, and sections. This is the price of unity.

The party reformers deny all this. They maintain that majority rule must be safe because the majority, by definition, must embrace a tremendous variety of attitudes and interests. A simple, nationwide, popular majority is the safest kind of backing for a ruling group, they say. It forces the leaders to act in the interests of a tremendous diversity of voters. Thus a popular majority—and hence a government based on the majority party—furnishes its own checks and balances.[10] Minorities—not majorities—tend to be extremist. Majority rule, the party reformers add, is not prone to violate minority rights. They point to Great Britain as an example of a system of party government and majority rule that has fully protected the rights of minorities.

Opponents of majority rule fear that the majority, acting rashly, may make fatal mistakes. The present governmental system, with all its checks and delays, forces the rulers to think twice before acting. Government based on a party majority, they say, would command such strength in the White House and Congress that it could move ahead precipitately. Party reformers answer that the great need of the day is *action*. It is better, they say, to run the risk of making a few mistakes than to make the fatal error of not acting at all. Broker rule means that government can do little until all major interests in both parties are appeased by compromises and concessions. Majority rule allows government to move ahead once a consensus has been achieved among a majority of the people. And a strong and responsible party, they conclude, is the vital agent both in achieving that consensus and in organizing our divided government for rapid and effective action.

NEEDED: RESPONSIBLE LEADERS

This matter of the urgency of action deserves a few more words. But first a summary of the chapter so far:

1. The steel strike of 1952 illustrated how our national leaders in Wash-

[10] H. S. Commager, *Majority Rule and Minority Rights* (New York: Oxford University Press, 1943), pp. 57 ff.

ington hold differing beliefs and loyalties and respond to conflicting alignments of voters.

2. The conflicts in Washington did not happen by chance, but were simply
another example of our political system at work. The framers carefully
planned a system of checks and balances with *different officials* responding
to *different political forces.*

3. Our system is not one of strict majority rule but one of *concurrent majority rule* or "broker rule" that allows *combinations of minorities* to govern.

4. Broker rule is defended on the grounds that it produces flexible government, prevents extremism, protects diversity. It is attacked on the grounds
that it results in weak government, disunity, inefficiency, and irresponsibility.

5. The chief alternative to broker rule is *majority rule;* supporters of the
latter system, stressing the need for *responsible* government, feel that the
only way to strengthen our system is by uniting it through the machinery of
a more *centralized* and *responsible party system.*

6. Critics of majority rule combined with a stronger party system fear that
these would enable the party in power to tyrannize over the minority and
would end up in rash, extremist government.

Each proposal, as this chapter has shown, has much to recommend it. But
can we let the matter drop here? Is there no choice among the different paths?
The answer depends largely on one's diagnosis of the main ills of the American system of government. The chief question one can raise about that system is: *In a time of deep and drawn-out crisis, can it act boldly and positively
and persistently over a long period of time, commanding a reliable source of
popular support and a steady flow of governmental power?* In short, can our
government *govern?*

What kind of leadership?

Arnold J. Toynbee, the famous English historian, has concluded from his
study of history that "the ultimate criterion and the fundamental cause of the
breakdowns which precede disintegrations is an outbreak of *internal discords*
through which societies forfeit their faculty of self-determination."[11] When
groups in a community fail to resolve their differences, the community may
disintegrate. Such a result has been called *stasis.* The threat of *stasis* may be
especially grave in the United States, for our governmental system, as we have
seen, is particularly subject to deadlock. During prolonged military or economic emergency, hostility among persons and groups might be reflected in
a government ridden by warring blocs unable to agree on a program of
action.

If, then, the great weakness of American government seems to be its failure to overcome internal divisions and face the challenge of threats at home
or abroad, what can be done? The answer seems to be: *"Provide for effective*

[11] Arnold J. Tonybee, *A Study of History,* Abridgement by D. C. Somervell (New
York: Oxford University Press, 1947), p. 365. Italics supplied.

and responsible leadership." Effective leadership can do several important things. First, it can rise above the disputes dividing men and find areas of *agreement.* Second, effective leadership involves the capacity to *educate* and *persuade* people. And third, because effective leadership means both these things, it can spur men and governments to action.

But leadership must be *responsible,* too. In a democracy men have a deep, almost instinctive fear of the man on horseback. And quite rightly. "One-man rule" and democracy are obviously incompatible. On the other hand, democracy not only can afford leadership—it *needs* leadership. "Without leadership alert and sensitive to change," Franklin D. Roosevelt said, "we are all bogged up or lose our way." By the same token, however, leadership must meet the tests of responsibility. These tests are crude but clear. Does the leader keep in touch with the rank and file even when he is ahead of his followers in his thinking and planning? Does he observe the basic rules of the game such as the maintenance of civil liberties and free elections? Is he working, ultimately, for the interests of his nation or party as a whole, or merely for the interests of himself and his immediate coterie?

The American system of government makes effective and responsible leadership very difficult. Because of the factors discussed in Chapter 18, it is to the Presidency that we turn for such leadership, for only this office has the necessary constitutional, political, and administrative resources to lead the nation. Yet the President, as we have seen, is constantly hamstrung by minority groups operating through key places in Congress, the courts, and the bureaucracy. Some Presidents have been overcome by these groups. Others have exerted leadership despite them. But the danger, as we have seen, is that the President may violate constitutional provisions or political understandings. Lincoln's early conduct of the war without Congress and Franklin D. Roosevelt's blunt threats to enact legislation on his own are cases in point.

The art of being governed

How, then, can we gain responsible yet effective leadership? Surely not by standing still. Our present system seems to hobble our leaders without effectively controlling and channeling the flow of needed power. What about the two basic courses outlined in this chapter and in Chapter 18?

The first basic course—constitutional or governmental reform—might strengthen responsible leadership, but we cannot be sure of this. The minor governmental changes, such as a question hour, might improve communication and understanding between Capitol and White House, but it is hard to see how they would allow more presidential leadership or hold it more responsible. The more sweeping proposals, involving constitutional changes, might make the President more responsible to Congress, but they might sap presidential leadership by tying him too closely to the legislative apron strings.

There remains the second alternative: stronger parties. The preceding discussion of party reform centered largely on the possibilities of such reform achieving more coordination and responsibility in our national government. These are important goals, but another role that a rejuvenated party system might play is to allow the President the power and discretion he must have as a leader, and yet to set some limits to his power. For a stronger majority party would play a more important part in electing the President, in furnishing popular support to him in office, and in compelling the different governmental agencies and political factions in Washington to pull together as a team. In doing so, the majority party (the one that polled the most electoral votes at the previous presidential election) would become more indispensable to the President and thus might be in a position to erect a "go slow" sign when the President seemed to go too fast for his followers. More particularly, the party might surround the President with other nationally minded party leaders, much as the British Prime Minister is surrounded by powerful party leaders in his cabinet.

In essence, this approach calls for more emphasis on *majority rule*. It means tying the President more tightly to the majority that elected him or sustains him, and freeing him from the fetters that minority groups fasten on him in Congress and elsewhere. Under a real system of majority rule the President must heed the party rank and file and consult its leaders before taking important steps. But he need not gain the support of *every* important minority before acting. In this sense presidential leadership and presidential responsibility to the majority party represent a sort of golden mean between Calhoun's concurrent majority rule on the one hand and caesaristic, irresponsible leadership on the other. The President may still need to educate his popular majority, to render articulate their indistinct feelings, but he must abide by the majority program, however broadly conceived. The majority, in short, must be not only the basis of presidential *power* but also the source of presidential *containment*.

Whichever of these two courses one may choose, the problem of responsible leadership puts the basic question of this chapter—"How Can We Control Our Leaders?"—in a different light. That question cannot be solved by loading down our leaders with all kinds of checks and shackles. Such a procedure is self-defeating, for it renders leadership powerless to meet the economic, political, social, and military challenges of our time. We can rule our rulers best by making vigorous use of our civil liberties and free elections, by insisting that our leaders consult with the rank and file, and by holding our leaders ultimately responsible for their actions—and also by allowing our leaders to *act*. Democracy involves both the art of governing and the art of being governed.

Big government in action

PART SIX ~ A PROBLEM GUIDE

Part Six deals with the policies and functions of our national government, with a tremendous number and variety of activities ranging from crucial foreign policy decisions to routine domestic activities such as regulating interstate commerce. Part Six is related to the first of our five basic problems (see pp. 1-2): how a democratic, representative government can administer thousands of activities in an efficient, orderly, and progressive manner. These chapters raise the question ultimately as to whether, as some people fear, big government puts too great a strain on the democratic process and results in an overbureaucratic and even dictatorial system.

We shall probe into specific problems of efficient government, for example, (1) recruiting able and devoted officials, but doing so in a fair and democratic manner (pp. 602-603); (2) the impact of our type of legislative process on the shaping of fiscal policy (pp. 739-741); and (3) a resources policy (water, soil, power, etc.) that will achieve the most efficiency and economy over the long run (pp. 715-721).

But the problems in Part Six go beyond the matter of efficient and progressive gov-

PART SIX

ernment. They involve several of our other basic problems. The functions of the national government are pictured in the following pages as part of the political *process—that is, as affected by the pushing and hauling of interest groups, by political parties, by public opinion, as described above in Part Four. All these political factors directly affect, for example, the shaping of foreign policy (pp. 581-590), even though we like to talk about "taking politics out of foreign policy." Federal promotional activities (Chapter 26) are particularly subject to the demands of organized groups who want to protect and expand the favors they receive from Washington (pp. 715-717).*

This situation takes us back to the third and fourth of our basic questions, the problem of representation and of responsibility. Do these vast activities of the federal government clearly reflect the needs of the great majority of Americans, or are they the result of pressures exerted by strong interest groups? In the case of military policy (Chapter 24), do the people as a whole, operating through their elected and appointed civilian officials, have enough control of the military leaders, bureaucrats, and technicians (pp. 647-649)? If we want our officials to be responsible to the people, especially in regard to foreign and military policy, should that responsibility be to the people as a whole through bipartisanship (pp. 590-594), or to the party in power (pp. 586-588), or should we allow them to respond more to the play of minority pressures (pp. 594-595)?

Finally, the scope of government functions, the efficiency with which they are conducted, and the people on behalf of whom they are carried out—all relate to our fifth basic problem, the vigor and indispensability of American democratic government, to which we will return in the Epilogue of this book.

ONE MOMENTOUS FACT DOMINATES FOREIGN policy making in the United States. This is the fact that the United States exists in a world of sovereign and independent nations. Above these nations there is no world government that can guarantee to each of them that it shall be secure in its life, liberty, or property. There is little formal machinery for settling differences. In contrast to the ordered relations of people *within* nations, the relations *among* nations are in a state of semi-anarchy. World order rests on a precarious balance-of-power system and on a meager set of international rules and customs.

Some day the present system of separate state sovereignties may come to an end. A single nation may conquer the world and impose, as Hitler tried to do, a "new order" directed from one capital. Or perhaps the peoples of the world some day may join hands and establish a world government capable of making and enforcing law for all individuals everywhere. But these are future possibilities, not present-day realities. For good or for ill, the present system of sovereign independent states sets the framework of the international politics in which the United States must strive to achieve its objectives.

What are these objectives? Have they changed significantly over the eighteen decades of our national existence? Who determines the objectives and the general means of reaching them? What role is played by organized interests, political parties, public opinion as a whole? What is the role of the United Nations in our foreign policy making? How democratic is the procedure of making foreign policy in the United States?

THE UNITED STATES IN A CHANGING WORLD

The chief objective of American foreign policy has been to safeguard the security—in the broadest sense—of the United States. Given the nature of the world we live in, our objective could be none other than this. For if there is no world order to protect the interests of individual nations, each national government must take care of its own interests. To be sure,

22 ★

Foreign

policy:

politics and

problems

it has not always been clear that this was our major objective. For American politicians have often preferred to speak in high moral terms about "safeguarding world peace" and "helping our little brown brothers" rather than to talk the blunt language of power politics. But beneath the high-flown rhetoric the central purpose has been fairly consistent.

We have not always achieved this objective. In a complex and turbulent world, the means of achieving maximum national security without war have sometimes been beyond the capabilities of our rulers and diplomats. To make things more difficult, the world about us, and the United States itself, have been in a process of constant change. A brief review may indicate some of the major forces at work.

Security in the nineteenth century

In his famous *Farewell Address* George Washington said: "Europe has a set of primary interests, which to us have none, or a very remote relation. Hence she must be engaged in frequent controversies, the causes of which are essentially foreign to our concerns. Hence, therefore, it must be unwise in us to implicate ourselves, by artificial ties, in the ordinary vicissitudes of her politics, or the ordinary combinations or collisions of her friendships or enmities." Quoted over the years by thousands of politicians, these words for decades keynoted American foreign policy making.

During much of the nineteenth century this formula of "minding our own business" worked. It worked not because American officials had some special knack of "keeping out of foreign entanglements." It worked because Americans "were the beneficiaries of a world balance of power which was unique and temporary but was confused in most American minds (when they were aware of it at all) with the unchanging pattern of the cosmos."[1] The factors in that balance were threefold: British naval supremacy over most of the seas, a fairly stable balance of power in Europe, and the inability of foreign powers to conquer this hemisphere.

In the nineteenth century Britain was mistress of the seas. Her navy controlled strategic sea lanes from Gibraltar to Hong Kong. It stood between our virtually undefended shores and the other major powers. Any threat by a continental power to the United States was a threat to Britain. At the same time the European powers could neither permit Britain to regain control over its former colonies, nor allow any nation to threaten South America, because such action would upset the balance of power. That balance of power rested on a diffusion of military strength and on an elaborate network of treaties and understandings. Shaky though the structure was, it endured for a century.

This is not to say that the United States was insulated from international power politics. Americans fought a war with Britain at the beginning of the

[1] F. L. Schuman, *International Politics*, 4th ed. (New York: McGraw-Hill Book Company, Inc., 1948), p. 769.

nineteenth century and a war with Spain at the end of it. We had frequent brushes with other great powers. We fought a war with Mexico. President Lincoln and Secretary of State Seward had their hands full trying to prevent foreign intervention during the Civil War. There were disputes with England over fisheries and boundaries, with France over intervention in Mexico, with Germany and England over Venezuela. But the world situation was such that the essential security of the United States was not seriously threatened in the hundred years after 1815.

Then, in the chaotic years after 1914, the balance of power wavered violently and the nineteenth-century world came tumbling down around us.

Security in the mid-twentieth century

It is impossible to review here the past eventful forty years. It is important, however, to see the changed world American foreign policy makers now look out on.

Europe is no longer the pivot of world politics. World Wars I and II shattered the old balance-of-power system. Britain, France, Italy, and Germany are still important powers, but highly vulnerable to both economic and military stress. Dominating world politics are two super-powers, the United States of America and the Union of Soviet Socialist Republics. This polarization of power tends to pull the other nations into the orbits of the giants.

This sharp division between immense power blocks is perilous enough in itself. But along with it—and greatly intensifying it—is an ideological split. The new religion of communism confronts believers in democracy and the values democracy stands for. Russian propaganda asserts that democracy in the West stands actually for rule by imperialistic, warmongering militarists and profiteers who would drown the world in blood for their own selfish ends. The Voice of America proclaims that communism in practice brings rule by a self-elected elite, tyranny over the many, slave labor camps, secret trials, mass purges, and ultimately war. The conflict between the Soviet Union and the noncommunist nations is more than a traditional power struggle between nations; it is also a battle for the minds of men.

Another fact of international politics may be more significant in the long run than the changed balance of power. This is the "awakening" of the peoples of Asia, the Middle East, and Africa. Nearly two billion people live in these lands. For centuries they have for the most part accepted squalor, hunger, and sickness as inevitable conditions of life. In the nineteenth century many of them were introduced to western ideas of liberty, equality, and progress, and western technical and scientific methods. Today that introduction is bearing fruit in national movements, reforms, and revolutions. India, Burma, and other countries have won their independence. Communists rule China. Japan is once again a sovereign nation. Other countries in Asia and the Middle East are convulsed by social ferments, rebellion, and strife.

The super-powers have not ignored the explosive potentialities of these movements. The Soviet Union has usually been quick to take advantage of mass unrest and social revolution, and communism has a powerful appeal for those people who feel they have nothing to lose but their chains. The democracies have been slower in sensing the profound consequences of the changes at work. But for defensive reasons, if no other, the United States and its allies have been forced to give economic and military aid to the governments in these areas and to step up their propaganda against Soviet communism. All this is a far cry from the day when American activities in these areas took place in sleepy consulates and embassies handling trivial duties that brought Americans into contact with a tiny fraction of the native population.

Finally, the world has seen immense technological changes in the past fifty years. While ideologies have been dividing it, technology has tended to make it one. The techniques of communications, transportation, and war have brought the continents of the world closer together than were the thirteen states of the Union in 1790. War especially has gone through revolutionary change. Russian rockets located on the northern shore of Europe can lay waste the industrial areas of southern England. Giant American airplanes can take off from Texas, drop hydrogen bombs deep in the heart of Europe, and land at British bases. Our geographical isolation, which, along with our powerful friends, in past years gave us a "cushion of time and distance," has lost much if its importance. Even the Arctic has become a strategic frontier.

New times, new problems

Such is the world that our foreign policy makers look out on. A world sharply split geographically and ideologically but closely knit technologically. A world in which added tens of millions of people are demanding a larger role. A world in which the decisive events of our times are those affecting our relations with other nations.

Has our thinking kept pace with these vast changes? In the nineteenth century a policy of isolationism worked. It worked not because of the policy itself but because the external circumstances discussed above kept the United States safe. Twentieth-century America inherited a deep popular belief in "no foreign entanglements" as the best means of safeguarding our national security. But the objective world situation had changed. National security now seemed to demand that the United States play a positive and active part on the world stage. Slowly, grudgingly, almost belatedly, Americans, led by such men at Woodrow Wilson, Henry Stimson, Franklin D. Roosevelt, Cordell Hull, Wendell Willkie, Arthur Vandenberg, Dwight D. Eisenhower, and many others, made this shift. Doubtless the objective world situation will continue to change. New conditions will demand new thinking and new techniques.

Our foreign policies have become increasingly linked with domestic policies. The issue of federal protection of civil rights, for example, is sometimes discussed simply as a question of domestic politics or states' rights. But in the perspective of world politics the problem takes on a new dimension. The United States spends billions of dollars trying to win the friendship of the colored peoples in Africa and Asia. At the same time every denial of civil rights to Negroes is seized upon by our enemies to create ill will against the United States in these areas. Or take "domestic" economic matters. A high level of production not only supplies Americans with goods, it helps sustain our economic and military power abroad. A depression in this country dislocates the economies of other nations, vindicates communist predictions of "capitalist doom," causes political turmoil abroad as well as at home.

The makers of foreign policy in the United States must face all these facts of international politics today. As if these were not difficult enough, they must also face the uncertainties and complexities of American politics at home. For example, in planning some new policy toward a foreign nation, American officials must consider not only the political situation in that nation, the attitude of our allies, the reaction of Soviet Russia and her satellites, and the effect on western military strength; they must also consider the attitude of the opposition party in this country and of the interest groups concerned (including the national-origin groups) and the state of public opinion. No wonder that foreign policy making is the most challenging and critical job facing Americans and their rulers today.

WHO MAKES FOREIGN POLICY?

Foreign policy involves determining the basic objectives that are vital to American national interests, formulating policies and programs to achieve them, and administering these policies and programs. The broad objective is to use American power and influence to create conditions that make us more secure. Foreign policy in a sense is our first line of defense. The most important instruments of foreign policy are *force, economic power, propaganda,* and *negotiation.* When we face a crop failure in India, revolt of the Polish and Hungarian peoples against Communist control from Moscow, revolutions in Latin America, strikes in France, Communist agitation in the Middle East, these instruments can be brought into play in one form or another to further American national interests.

Foreign policy making includes everything from the decision not to send troops into Indo-China to the decision to grant a visa to John Schmidt. But these two kinds of decisions are different in nature. The first is "high-level policy." The second is made in accordance with previously established policy. The distinction is of course arbitrary, for high and low policy are an interrelated and continuous process. For purposes of convenience alone this chapter deals with the problems and politics of over-all policy; Chapter 23 takes up the management of foreign relations.

Who makes "high-level" policy? Who determines the basic objectives and formulates the broad policies and programs? The answer, of course, is the elected representatives of the people, namely Congress and the President. Earlier chapters of this book discussed their roles in foreign policy making. We will return to the chief executive and the legislators—and the problem of the relations among them—in later pages. First we must look at the other officials who help the President make foreign policy.

The President's right-hand man

While the Constitution scatters responsibility for foreign policy making among President, Senate, and the House of Representatives, the initiative, as noted above, rests with the President. The President's role depends not only on his great constitutional powers, but also on his political influence, the attitudes of congressmen, and the very nature of foreign policy making. Obviously the job is too big for the President to perform without help.

The President's chief adviser is the *Secretary of State,* the most important member of the President's Cabinet and chief of the Department of State. The Secretary of State is politically important too. Many people who cannot identify any other member of the Cabinet know his name. The influence of the Secretary of State is suggested by the naming of many famous American foreign policies or actions—the Hay Open Door Policy, the Kellogg Pact, the Stimson Doctrine, the Hull Reciprocal Trade Program, the Marshall Plan.

Officially the Secretary of State helps the President in making decisions. In actual practice the Secretary himself formulates much foreign policy and secures the President's backing. According to Secretary of State Cordell Hull, "with the present immense network and mass of details involved in conducting our foreign relations, the President finds it impossible to keep familiar with more than the principal acts of the State Department. The Secretary of State must do the rest." But the extent of the Secretary's influence may depend largely on the wishes of the President. Presidents Harding, Coolidge, and Hoover turned over to their Secretaries almost full responsibility for making important policy decisions. Other Presidents have taken a more active part; indeed, at times they have been their own Secretaries of State. Wilson and both Roosevelts are examples. Even so, important decisions in this area are so numerous that both President and Secretary of State can play important roles.

The Secretary has a large and many-sided department to administer. He receives many visits in Washington from foreign diplomats. He attends important international conferences and usually heads our delegation in the General Assembly of the United Nations. He makes key statements on foreign policy, sometimes speaking directly to the people. He visits other nations to confer with chiefs of state and foreign ministers. He deals directly with our ambassadors and ministers in other countries. As a leading member of the Cabinet, he may have a hand in shaping general Administration policy.

In all these activities the Secretary of State serves as the President's "right-hand man." But in a very real sense the Secretary depends on support in Congress. Unless he keeps some measure of congressional confidence, the policies proposed by the President may have rough going on Capitol Hill. For this reason one of the Secretary's top assistants has the assignment of keeping congressmen in touch with the Secretary's policies and of serving as a channel of communication between the legislators and the Secretary. Broadly speaking, however, the Secretary is at the mercy of power relationships in Washington—the relations between President and Congress, the political strength of the President, the attitudes of key congressmen, all reflecting the temper of the country.

The President's left-hand men

There may once have been a time when the President needed only to call on the Secretary of State for advice in determining foreign policy aims and formulating programs and policies. But today foreign policy covers every phase of governmental activity—financial policy, transportation, agriculture, commerce, and of course military activity. Suppose, for example, the President needed to make a decision on a matter of international trade. The specialized knowledge and expert help he would need are scattered throughout the executive structure, in the Departments of the Treasury, Commerce, Labor, and Agriculture, in the Federal Trade Commission, and in the United States Tariff Commission. The first Hoover Commission Task Force on Foreign Affairs points out that if the President wished to reconsider the policies of the United States in relation to Brazil, he would find the financial data in the Treasury, trade and commerce data in the State and Commerce departments and in the Tariff Commission, agricultural information in the Department of Agriculture, and military data in the Department of Defense.

At least 46 federal agencies are concerned in one way or another with foreign policy, and virtually all of them are called upon to furnish advice and make decisions. Sometimes these decisions may be of great importance. It was the Secretary of the Treasury and not the Secretary of State, for example, who played the leading role in negotiating the Bretton Woods agreement to establish the International Bank for Reconstruction and Development and The International Monetary Fund. The Greek-Turkish aid program was developed with the advice of the heads of the Departments of Agriculture, State, Treasury, Labor, and Defense, the public health agencies, and others. In one sense the entire executive structure serves as the President's left hand in making foreign policy.

Next to the State Department, however, the Defense Department is the chief source of advice on foreign policy. Since the main goal of American foreign policy is the largest possible security for the United States, military factors are involved in almost every major foreign policy decision. It is not surprising that military men and the military agencies play a leading part in shaping that policy. Moreover, the line between military and foreign policy is often hard to draw. The relationship is so close that foreign policy makes little sense unless coordinated with military policy. The military were in direct control of occupied areas such as Japan, and have had the guiding hand in the development of the Atlantic Pact military organization. Generals have been assigned to important diplomatic positions, have been given command of international military forces, and have been called upon to testify before Congress and to speak to the people on controversial foreign policies. The influence of a MacArthur, a Marshall, a Ridgeway, or a Radford on foreign policy is incalculable.

Linking right hand and left—the National Security Council

At ten every Thursday morning, about fifteen men file into the Cabinet Room in the West Wing of the White House. They carry papers marked "top secret." It is time for the meeting of the *National Security Council,* one of the most powerful and most secret of all governmental agencies, an agency that has become a primary foreign policy developing source.[2]

The President presides at council meetings, since it is he who must make the decisions. The council merely recommends. The other statutory members are the Vice-President, Secretary of State, Secretary of Defense, and Director of the Office of War Mobilization. The Chairman of the Joint Chiefs of Staff and the Director of Central Intelligence are always there as advisers, and in recent years the President has asked the Secretary of the Treasury and Director of the Bureau of the Budget to serve. In addition, the President frequently requests others such as the Attorney General or Director of United States Information Agency to sit in on some meetings. The Special Assistant to the President for National Security Affairs is there, as is the Executive Secretary of the council staff.

The council has the awesome responsibility of helping the President integrate foreign, military, economic, fiscal, internal security, and psychological policies that affect national security. Members of the council are expected to act not merely as representatives of their departments "but as a collegiate body seeking over-all policies rather than compromises of agencies' positions." Only as directors of the Central Intelligence Agency, however, does

[2] The National Security Council's operations have been described by two who have served as Special Assistant to the President for National Security Affairs. See Dillon Anderson, "The President and National Security," *Atlantic,* Vol. 197, No. 1, January 1956, pp. 42-46 and Robert Cutler, "The Development of the National Security Council," *Foreign Affairs,* Vol. 34, No. 3, April 1956, pp. 440-458.

the council have any formal legal duty as a unit. Its main job is to assist the President in weighing our foreign risks and commitments against our domestic and military strength and to bring them into balance.

The Planning Board insures that the busy men who make up the council are prepared for the weekly meetings. This board meets at least three times a week with the Special Assistant to the President for National Security Affairs presiding, and consists of representatives at the assistant secretary level of each of the agencies represented on the council. Members of this central staff agency prepare the policy papers to be discussed at council meetings. They are nominated by the departments concerned but hold their appointments from the President.

To integrate security policy is one thing; to carry out this policy in an integrated manner is another. Council decisions, when initialed by the President, become official policies that the State Department is supposed to translate into foreign policy, the Joint Chiefs of Staff into strategic plans, and the Office of Defense Mobilization into production programs. To insure that the detailed operational programs of each agency are so coordinated that council policies will be carried out is the task of the *Operations Coordinating Board*. This board consists of the Under Secretary of State as chairman, the Deputy Secretary of Defense, the Director of Central Intelligence, the Director of the United States Information Agency, the Director of the International Cooperation Administration, and several special assistants to the President. Periodically, the Operations Coordinating Board reports to the National Security Council. If it discovers that council decisions are too obscure to achieve coordinated administration, it may request the council to clarify and further refine policy. The Operations Coordinating Board gives special attention to the overseas activities of the departments and through over forty subcommittees, "watchdogs" the various programs.

Membership of the Vice-President on the council is an interesting feature of this agency. The council gains from the Vice-President's knowledge of attitudes on Capitol Hill; the Vice-President keeps in touch with day-to-day developments in top policy making—a matter of the utmost importance if he should suddenly succeed to the Presidency. How well the plan is working out cannot easily be estimated. Vice-President Nixon has had an active role in this respect; on the other hand, as we have seen, our political system makes it likely that the President and Vice-President will have major differences over policy. If the President should meet difficulty in working with the Security Council, he might lean more heavily on the Bureau of the Budget, the head of which is his personal choice.

The intermeshing of the executive departments at the top level for foreign policy is only one step in unifying the executive structure. The telephone, the lunch table, the cocktail bar are still useful instruments of coordination. Of the formal methods, one of the most important is the interdepartmental committee, of which there are about 30 with over 140 subcommittees. Most of these interdepartmental committees have been established by simple agreement among the departments, without action by Congress. As an example, the Committee on Trade Agreements was established under the chairmanship of the State Department, to be composed of representatives from Commerce, Agriculture, Labor, Treasury, Tariff Commission, and the military departments. Subcommittees for each country assemble data and prepare analyses on the basis of which the whole committee recommends to the Secretary of State what trade agreements he might negotiate with other nations.

Intelligence and foreign policy

What is the significance of an election in Istanbul? How many trained infantrymen are there in Hungary? What is the morale of the Romanian peasants? What instrument for achieving a particular objective should be used? Should it be a diplomatic note, a resolution in the United Nations, the use of military power, propaganda, or something else? Before decisions can be made, the policy makers must know a great deal about other countries—how they may react to a particular policy, what their strengths and weaknesses may be, and—if possible—their strategic plans and intentions. To answer such questions it is necessary to know about their geographical and physical structure; about the people—their numbers, skills, age distributions; about the status of their arts, technology, engineering, and sciences; and about their political and social systems.

Moreover, the policy makers must have the information they need to anticipate problems. They must be able to counter the moves of other nations, and have some idea of what instrumentalities of policy these nations are likely to use and in what direction they are going to move. They need, in other words, "high-level foreign policy intelligence." Those who gather and analyze this material are among the most important assistants to the policy leaders. The term "intelligence work" conjures up visions of spies and undercover agents, but at least 95 per cent of the information comes from open sources. Yet secret intelligence often supplies the crucial data.

Intelligence work involves two operations, surveillance and research. Surveillance is the bringing of the world into close and systematic observation. Research is the "attempt to establish meaningful patterns out of what was observed in the past and attempts to get meaning out of what appears to be going on now."[3]

Many agencies of the government are engaged in intelligence work. The State Department gathers materials through its missions abroad and interprets it in its intelligence divisions; the military branches have their own intelligence services, as do the Foreign Agricultural Service, the Bureau of Foreign Commerce (Commerce), the Office of International Finance (Treas-

[3] Sherman Kent, *Strategic Intelligence* (Princeton: Princeton University Press, 1949), especially p. 4.

ury), the Atomic Energy Commission, and others. But each of these agencies is primarily interested in gathering information within its own particular field of activity. The divisions between the various kinds of intelligence—military and diplomatic, political and economic—are arbitrary and fictitious. In many cases information held by the military is required by the civilian policy makers. When all the bits of information gathered by the many agencies are pieced together, they often reveal what is not evident when viewed separately.

In the past American intelligence work has often been inadequate. Each department has gathered and analyzed its own information, often duplicating work done elsewhere and not taking advantage of materials available in other places. On occasion American policy makers have been caught by surprise and forced to improvise policies to meet situations for which they could have been forewarned by proper intelligence. Even when good intelligence work has been done, and when it has been evaluated by experienced intelligence men, it has not always been disseminated to those responsible for making the decisions.

To correct these deficiencies the Central Intelligence Agency was established to serve directly under the National Security Council. This highly secret agency is exempt from laws and regulations requiring reporting to Congress and the public, and its appropriations are secretly split up throughout the budget so that not even congressmen know how much it spends. The agency makes recommendations to the Security Council for improving the government's intelligence services, correlates and evaluates intelligence, provides for its distribution, supplements the work of the other intelligence agencies when necessary, and collects secret intelligence abroad. It is not a police agency; it does not catch spies or do "counter-intelligence" work. These are the responsibility of the FBI, the Armed Forces Security Agency, and others.

The various interdepartmental committees, the National Security Council, Central Intelligence, are all organizational attempts to improve the executive machinery for the formulation of foreign policy. The problem is tremendous. All the information and all the ramifications must be considered so that the influence and power of the United States can be effectively directed to secure its objectives. The final solution is still to be found. Policy makers are constantly forced to meet problems as they arise and are so immersed in everyday affairs that they hardly have time to think ahead to meet tomorrow's contingencies. Decisions often have to be made so fast that the elaborate machinery is sometimes short-circuited. But the executive structure is probably better organized than ever to meet its responsibilities.

In summary, the President is the star performer in the making of foreign policy. But everybody in the executive department gets into the act. The co-star is Congress, and like all co-stars, Congress and the President vie with each other for top billing.

President and Congress—friends or foes?

The problems of the American system of checks and balances are no-where more obvious or potentially disastrous than in the field of foreign relations.[4] The President and his advisers often lack faith in the capacity of Congress to act wisely and responsibly. Congressmen suspect the President and Secretary of State of siding with foreigners and ignoring American interests. The State Department has no powerful interest group to help it win friends and influence congressmen, in contrast to the Agriculture Department, for example. The State Department symbolizes relations with foreigners; it supports programs that cost money and require sacrifices for what seems, superficially at least, only to benefit other nations. The result is that the President and Congress are often at odds with each other. The delay, confusion, and disunity that result are dangerous in a time of international tension.

Who speaks for the United States? What are our intentions? Will we meet our obligations? Our friends, it is said, hesitate to depend upon our pledges. They fear that they will be forgotten in the midst of congressional-executive infighting. Our enemies overlook our warnings. They are encouraged to believe that congressional-executive conflict will make American action too little and too late. Negotiations with other nations are difficult because no one can speak with assurance. Neither the legislators nor the President and his advisers have enough power to make policies for themselves, but each side has enough authority to thwart the policies proposed by the other. Periods of presidential domination alternate with periods of congressional rebellion. One close student of foreign affairs has said, "The constitutional separation of powers . . . together with the stalemate in Russo-American diplomatic relations, have brought about the paradox that the traditional diplomatic techniques of persuasion, pressure, and bargaining are applied by the executive branch of the American Government in its relations with Congress rather than with foreign powers."[5]

Recognizing the urgency of the problem, some would take the bull by the horns and give the President a free hand in shaping foreign policy. Partnership is manifestly impossible, it is pointed out, and Congress lacks the necessary speed, flexibility, secrecy, information, and expertness. Since the President has all these advantages he should be given the job. Furthermore, he is responsible to a nationwide electorate; he is not so much at the mercy of local and sectional feeling as are most congressmen.

Constitutional aspects aside, this argument overlooks a crucial difficulty. Foreign policy is so closely related to domestic policy that to free the Presi-

---

[4] Daniel S. Cheever and H. Field Haviland, Jr., *American Foreign Policy and the Separation of Powers* (Cambridge: Harvard University Press, 1952).

[5] Hans J. Morgenthau, "Conduct of American Foreign Policy," *Parliamentary Affairs*. Winter, 1949, Vol. III (1949), No. 1, p. 155.

dent's hand in directing the former would be to give him tremendous power over the latter. Foreign policy demands money, organization, and man power. It may exact the commitment of American lives. If the President were able to make these commitments unchecked, his policies, both domestic and foreign, might be more sensible, but they might not be more responsible. Americans would hesitate to place such wide powers in one elected official and a few other officials appointed by him.

Few will deny, however, that the chief executive must have the initiative. What should be the role of Congress? There is much that Congress can do. It can provide the arena for the discussion of basic policies. It can educate both the people and the officials, and perhaps create wider understanding. It can mediate between the people and the experts, introducing the experts to the people's preferences and the people to the experts' knowledge.

Nevertheless, such advantages will not outweigh the cardinal defects of present presidential-congressional conflict. For that conflict is not a result of "bad" people in Congress or White House, or of simple misunderstanding, or of failure to experiment with new mechanical arrangements. It results from both the constitutional checks and balances and the political disunities of the American people (see Chapter 21). A glance at the politics of foreign policy making will perhaps make this clear.

THE POLITICS OF FOREIGN POLICY MAKING

Under government by the people, foreign policy making cannot be divorced from public opinions, from the pressures of interest groups, from the operations of political parties. Those who attack the idea of democratic government in general find particular reason to decry popular control of foreign relations. The people, they say, are especially ignorant, selfish, fickle, narrow-minded, and impetuous when they come to deal with foreign nations. They can find evidence to support their position. But government by the people assumes that the people can make the ultimate decisions, that ultimately they can choose the "right" course of action, that at the very least they can tell "when the shoe pinches."

Public opinion and foreign policy

Even in government by the people, however, public opinion ordinarily is less concerned with foreign than with domestic policy. Despite the seeming concern of most Americans with international affairs, it would appear, according to one study, that "a third of the people live in a world that psychologically does not include foreign affairs. As for the other two-thirds . . . 'only a minority of the people can be considered actively conversant with contemporary world problems.' "[6] The "hard core of chronic know-noth-

[6] Leonard S. Cottrell, Jr. and Sylvia Eberhart, *American Opinion on World Affairs in the Atomic Age* (Princeton: Princeton University Press, 1948), p. 14.

ings" that we noted in Chapter 11 is even larger in respect to foreign affairs. Public opinion polls show that about 30 per cent of the voters have never heard or read about the important issues in American foreign policy. Approximately 45 per cent have heard or read about the issues, but they have only an elementary knowledge of them. Only 25 per cent of the electorate consistently has any knowledge about foreign policy. And of this 25 per cent not many showed any real understanding. Even at the height of the discussion about the Greek-Turkish aid program, for example, only 37 per cent of the people, according to the public opinion polls, knew something about the program. The less than 25 per cent of the public considered informed about international affairs compares with about 30 per cent considered informed on domestic affairs.[7]

Why are so many people indifferent or uninformed? The hundred years of effortless security have left their mark on American attitudes. The feeling still persists that what happens outside the boundaries of the United States is of less importance than what happens here. We still tend to exaggerate the importance of our geographic isolation. Most Americans learn their geography from American-centered Mercator projection maps whose distortions confirm their feeling that the United States lives in a world of its own. Some people still consider diplomacy and foreign affairs to be concerned only with the squabbles of far-off Europeans.

Foreign affairs are more remote than domestic problems. People have more first-hand information about inflation than about Chinese communism. The worker in the factory and the boss in the front office know what labor-management relations are about, and they have strong opinions on the subject. They are less concerned about the consequences of revolt in Algeria. Not only are the issues of foreign policy more remote, they are complex.

Many people, lacking information and interest, tend to react to foreign policy issues on the basis of moods that have no intellectual structure or factual content.[8] These mood reactions are unstable; optimism gives way to pessimism, idealism to cynicism. As long as there is no glaring threat to American interests the public mood is one of withdrawal from international affairs, but the moment danger appears, the mood is one demanding full-scale intervention. Then as the danger *appears* to subside, the mood shifts back to withdrawal. The ordinary voter oversimplifies the problems of foreign politics. He tends to reduce all issues of world politics to the issue that at any given time presses for solution. He thinks of the issues in terms of heroes and villains. He favors oversimplified remedies—remove the Secretary of State, lower trade barriers, get rid of Krushchev, and all will be well.

---

[7] Martin Kriesberg, "Dark Areas of Ignorance," Chapter 2 in Lester Markel and others, *Public Opinion and Foreign Policy* (New York: Harper & Brothers for the Council on Foreign Relations, 1949).

[8] This material is drawn from Gabriel A. Almond, *The American People and Foreign Policy* (New York: Harcourt, Brace and Company, 1950).

The "expert" and the "informed citizen" are also subject to mood responses and oversimplification, but as the level of interest and information rises, the degree of sophistication increases.

Popular indifference toward international politics means that the official policy makers often have to make the issues dramatic in order to arouse public support for their programs. On the other hand, in periods of public excitement, fear of rash public opinion causes policy makers to be over-cautious. In order to secure American participation in the United Nations, for example, the State Department carried on an intensive publicity campaign, and in so doing many people got the impression that the United Nations would insure peace and order in the world. To arouse public support for the Truman Doctrine, people were told of the "crisis." But then officials had to spend their energies gentling down public opinion to avoid demands for hasty action. This overselling of policies may lead to a "giddy-ap and whoa" conduct of foreign relations.

Even if these generalizations are overdrawn, it does seem that the instability of public moods makes it difficult for the official policy makers to plan ahead, to take the long view after full consideration of the military, political, diplomatic, psychological, and other subtle factors involved in any major decision. The unorganized general public does not, of course, make foreign policy. Yet public opinion determines the broad limits within which others make the decisions. Public attitudes—the political climate, in general—determine the political possibilities open to the policy makers. The President and the congressional leaders know that, at a minimum, they must not arouse public hostility to their proposals. At times they have to secure active public support for programs that call for large expenditures of money or for commitments that involve risk of grave danger. Even when the public plays a negative role in the making of foreign policy, that role may still be important. The people do not lack means of making their attitudes felt both at elections and between elections.

Congressmen have their own ways of gauging popular feeling. The Department of State makes a systematic effort to uncover public attitudes and to discover what groups are concerned with particular issues. Experts in the Division of Public Studies read public opinion polls, resolutions and publications of organized groups, ninety or more newspapers, and sixty or more magazines. Each noon the Secretary of State and his hundred top advisers receive a summary of opinions expressed in these media during the preceding 24 hours. The Division also publishes weekly and monthly summaries of the state of public opinion. The Division of Public Services sends representatives to conventions of various organizations in order to sound out public opinion, receives and answers several hundred letters a day, and publishes an analysis of the mail on foreign policy. These activities are, however, more likely to tell the State Department what the opinion and interest group leaders are thinking than what the so-called "average citizen" has on his mind.

The State Department also does its best to inform the public of the policies of the United States and the reasons behind them. The Assistant Secretary for Public Affairs supervises an extensive program designed to keep the American public informed. The Secretary himself frequently holds press conferences. The Public Service Division issues a long list of pamphlets, periodicals, and books. Speakers are sent from the department to clubs and organizations. On important issues the President himself takes a hand, and through radio and TV addresses, messages to Congress, and public speeches, tries to "educate" the public. Despite all these efforts, however, evidence indicates that their message does not get through, at least directly, to those people who are indifferent and uninformed about international politics. Rather the materials are read and the speeches are heard by those who are already interested. But these interested groups are important in the process of opinion formation.

The way in which public opinion conditions the making of our foreign policy, and conversely the way in which the officials mold public opinion, are dramatically illustrated by the events of the late 1930's. By 1937 President Roosevelt and his advisers became convinced that Germany, Italy, and Japan threatened American security. They believed that the power of the United States had to be thrown behind England and France if the aggressors were to be prevented from controlling the Eurasian Continent. They hoped that a strong stand by the United States would swing the balance of power in favor of the democracies and deter the aggressors. In October 1937, President Roosevelt made his famous "quarantine the aggressor" speech in which he cautiously stated his position. But the public response, both inside and outside congressional chambers, seemed to be hostile. Most Americans still seemed to cling to the doctrines of nonintervention, neutrality, and freedom from entangling alliances. The people insisted upon neutrality laws that tied the executive's hands in the hope that if war came in Europe, we could stay out. So the President proceeded to move cautiously. Aided by the unfolding of events in Europe, he began to "educate" the public to support a more vigorous program. As public opinion became more favorable, the President gradually used the powers of his office to give as much aid and comfort to the democracies as public opinion would tolerate. But even as late as 1941, just prior to Pearl Harbor, public opinion was sharply divided. A large and vocal part of the population opposed the President's program. He had to move without the vigor and dispatch that many observers thought the crisis called for. The division of public opinion also obscured the intentions of the United States. Japanese and German leaders misjudged its significance. They thought it meant that the United States would be so divided that we would not have the unity needed to fight the war.

In Chapter 11 we noted that the American public is composed of many hundreds of smaller publics, and that what we call public opinion is the complex interrelation and interaction of hundreds of interests, organized and unorganized. If the unorganized American public is indifferent to foreign politics, the same cannot be said of the organized publics and their spokesmen.

Organized interests and foreign policy

General public indifference gives an opportunity to the specially interested publics to increase their influence over foreign policy. The general public is not organized to support the broad public interest, nor are political parties able to do so. The result is that special publics have little opposition except from a strong President. The special publics have the greatest influence on Congress. By the use of all the familiar devices—letter-writing campaigns, advice to congressmen, testimony before committees, and publicity and public relations, the special-interest groups are highly effective in molding the direction of foreign policy.

The staff members of the organized groups and the opinion leaders sprinkled through society—the priests and preachers, newspaper, radio, and TV commentators, teachers and public speakers—form an elite, an attentive public whose support is actively sought by the official policy makers. State Department officials and the officials of the major interest groups often work together. The Department of State maintains relations with over four hundred national citizens' organizations, consulting with them and sending them materials and background information.

What groups are most interested in foreign affairs? First of all there is a small, but very influential, group of citizens' organizations that is concerned about increasing public knowledge and understanding of international politics. These groups do not bring pressure for particular programs, but provide information and discussion of issues. Many of them have their own publications, and in their meetings they bring together influential citizens and public officials. The Council on Foreign Relations, the Foreign Policy Association, and the Foundation for Foreign Affairs are examples of organizations that have assumed a leadership responsibility. Other citizen organizations operate in much the same manner, although they are not exclusively concerned with foreign affairs. The League of Women Voters, for example, takes stands on particular issues and carries on campaigns to improve the level of citizen understanding. These groups, representing no particular social class or occupation, are in a sense trying to balance foreign policy against the demands of those who look at the problems from the point of view of a special interest.

Foreign policies so affect the domestic scene that inevitably the major interest groups of agriculture, labor, and business are closely involved. The big interest groups may represent such a wide cross section of the public, however, that they speak for broad national interests. Pacifist, patriotic, and veterans' organizations are also closely concerned with foreign policy. The patriotic and veterans' groups, for example, support large military appropriations whereas the pacifists oppose them. Farm, labor, and business interests have heavy economic stakes in foreign policy. Developments abroad affect businessmen's profits, farmers' markets, workers' jobs and wages.

Religious and national-origin publics are particularly interested in certain phases of foreign policy. These groups have intense feelings about some issues, and they are often strategically located to affect the outcome of elections.[9] Policy makers are highly conscious of the wishes of these articulate groups. Many Americans of Irish origin, reflecting feelings aroused by English-Irish relations, are hostile toward Anglo-American cooperation. Many Americans of German origin voted against Roosevelt in 1940 because of his strong stand against Germany.[10] The attitude of Roman Catholics has been a significant factor in shaping American policy toward Spain both during the Spanish Civil War and after World War II. American policy toward Israel has been intimately affected by the pressures of American Zionists.

Parties and foreign policy

Parties, as such, do not play a major role in shaping foreign policy. The reasons are twofold. Many Americans would prefer to keep foreign policy out of politics; party politics, it is said, should "stop at the water's edge." In the second place, parties take even less clear and candid stands on foreign policy than they do on domestic policy. All the party weaknesses discussed earlier in this book operate in full measure in foreign policy-making. Party platforms often obscure the issues instead of highlighting them; many congressmen fail to follow even the very general party "line" that may exist; and the parties fail to discipline even the most outspoken rebels.

On the other hand, congressional voting during recent years does indicate that on some issues significant differences exist between the major parties. Speaking very generally, congressional Democrats are more likely to support commitment of American troops and resources to back up our European allies, American participation in international organization, proposals for foreign aid, and large military appropriations; and they give first priority to European rather than to Asiatic defense against communism. Republicans, on the other hand, tend to look with suspicion on foreign aid programs, oppose tariff reductions, regard more skeptically American participation in international organization, view our European allies more criti-

[9] Thomas A. Bailey, *The Man in the Street* (New York: The Macmillan Company, 1948).

[10] Samuel Lubell, "Who Votes Isolationist and Why," *Harper's Magazine*, April 1951.

cally, are more reluctant to support large military appropriations except during "all-out" war, and favor exertion of American power in Asia.[11] Of course striking exceptions can be found to these tendencies; certain Republicans are far more internationally minded than some Democrats.

Sectional and economic interests, however, easily disrupt these rough party lines.[12] A case in point is the action of a Democratic senator from a midwestern border state in connection with appropriations for the European Recovery Program. In this case the Democratic President and the Democratic party platform both stood behind large-scale help to Europe. The senator, however, moved to amend the measure to require that $1½ billion of the appropriation be devoted to the purchase of agricultural products. Although this amendment might have aided the American farmer, impartial observers agreed that it would reduce the effectiveness of the aid to Europe. Three major farm lobbies opposed the amendment because they objected to mixing farm and foreign policy, but 32 senators—all from predominantly farm states—supported it.

Should parties be concerned with foreign policy? Toward the end of World War II sentiment grew markedly in favor of a "bipartisan approach" to foreign policy. An ambiguous term, bipartisanship seems to mean (1) collaboration between the executive and the congressional foreign policy leaders of both parties; (2) support of the policies by both parties in Congress; (3) withdrawal of the issues from debate in political campaigns. In general bipartisanship is an attempt to remove the issues of foreign policy from partisan politics. In its defense, it is argued that despite the differences that divide Americans among themselves, they share a common interest with respect to other nations. During times of national danger we readily unite behind policies necessary to preserve the national well-being, and such unity is needed to support our foreign policies. American foreign policy, it is asserted, was ineffective following World War I because of its involvement in the partisan struggle between Democrats and Republicans.

Between 1942 and 1950, the leaders of the two parties, both in and outside of Congress, worked closely together on foreign policy. Once policies were agreed upon, they received broad support from both parties in Congress and were not seriously debated in the political campaigns. Democrats supported the policies largely out of loyalty to the Democratic Administration, and the Republicans at least partly because of their respect for Senator Vandenberg, the Republican foreign policy spokesman. For the most part, the bipartisan policy was limited to those programs calling for American

---

[11] See R. A. Dahl, *Congress and Foreign Policy* (New York: Harcourt, Brace and Company, 1950), pp. 229, 284-287. See also, Ralph H. Smuckler, "The Region of Isolationism," *The American Political Science Review* (Vol. XLVII), June 1953, pp. 386-401.

[12] See H. Bradford Westerfield, *Foreign Policy and Party Politics* (New Haven: Yale University Press, 1955), pp. 32-52 for discussion of sectional differences within parties.

participation in the United Nations and to policies of economic and military support for our European friends. Policy with respect to the Far East, however, won little bipartisan support. After 1950 bipartisanship began to break down. The problems of the Far East came to the front of public attention, and Senator Vandenberg died. Under the accident of seniority, his leadership did not pass to a man of comparable influence in the Senate. With the election of President Eisenhower, the bipartisan approach made its reappearance. The party division within the Congress was so close that the President needed the support of Democrats as well as Republicans to gain the needed legislation and appropriations.

The Bricker Amendment: a case study

Senator John Bricker, with the backing of a large number of other members of the upper chamber, has proposed a constitutional amendment of major importance. Involving both the division of power between the national and state governments and the checks and balances between President and Congress, the so-called Bricker Amendment is an excellent example of the close involvement with one another of foreign policy, the decision-making process, and political attitudes, groups, and parties. The most important sections are:

1. A provision of a treaty which conflicts with this Constitution shall not be of any force or effect.
2. A treaty shall become effective as internal law in the United States only through legislation which would be valid in the absence of a treaty.
3. Congress shall have power to regulate all executive and other agreements with any foreign power or international organization. All such agreements shall be subject to the limitations imposed on treaties by this article.

On first glance these provisions would seem to be of little importance; indeed, they would seem to describe existing practice. Actually they are of great significance and they have stirred up vigorous controversy. Why?

The first section in particular seems to state present law. Its supporters, however, argue that the treaty power can now be used to override the Constitution. They grant, perhaps, that the treaty power has never been so used, but they want to insure that such an overriding will never take place. Opponents of the provision respond that if it is intended to assert the supremacy of the Constitution over treaties it is unnecessary since no responsible person has ever denied that supremacy. They fear that the provision will simply invite endless arguments over its meaning as disputes over particular treaty provisions arise.

The second section contains two important changes. The first part—the clause through the word "legislation"—would prevent any treaty from being self-executing and would require not merely the present two-thirds vote in the Senate but also concurrence of both House and Senate by majority vote. The advantage of this proposal is that it would bring the lower house, which is the more directly representative of the two, into the treaty-making picture; the disadvantage is that the process of treaty-making would be greatly slowed and treaties might be harder to ratify. The second part of this second provision—the last nine words—is "filled with dynamite," as one observer put it. Under this clause the only treaties that would be the supreme law of the land would be those that Congress could put into effect under its regular lawmaking authority. Reversing the holding in *Missouri* v. *Holland* (see pp. 94-95), it would restrict the treaty power to matters that may be dealt with only by the use of the *delegated powers* of the national government. Supporters of this provision argue that it is needed to prevent the national government from using treaties to increase its control over states and to jeopardize our federal system. Opponents see it as a crippling limitation on the power of the national government to conduct foreign relations effectively.

The third section of the Bricker Amendment cuts squarely across the field of presidential-congressional relations. It is aimed at the power of the President to make executive agreements with foreign nations—agreements that, as we have seen, do not require action by the Senate or House. Actually most such agreements have been backed up by majority votes in both chambers of Congress. The proposed change would give Congress power to *require* that the President get congressional backing for his agreements with other nations; even more, it would permit Congress to control both the negotiation and implementation of such agreements. Debate over this provision has been somewhat akin to that over the others: proponents want to limit the President's discretion in making foreign agreements; opponents want him to keep whatever freedom he has traditionally had.

The Bricker Amendment can be understood best not in terms of constitutional "pros and cons" but in terms of the ideas and interests that lie behind its support and its opposition. Who wants the amendment? Those who are convinced that present arrangements enable and encourage the national government in general and the President in particular to involve the nation in international agreements that may be harmful to our national interest. In short, they favor a more "nationalistic" and less "internationalistic" course for the United States, and feel that they can achieve the former by giving the Senate more control over the conduct of foreign relations and extending control to the House of Representatives and even to the states. They are especially fearful that international organizations such as the United Nations may interfere with our internal politics and deprive American citizens of some of their freedoms.

Opponents of the Bricker Amendment—who include both President Eisenhower and former President Truman—advance many objections: that it is merely a concealed attack on the United Nations, that it is unnecessary since a treaty cannot now be used to abridge constitutional rights, that the President and two-thirds of the Senate can be trusted not to sell the United States out, that passage of the amendment would so burden and clog foreign policy making as to weaken the United States in its leadership of the free world. Most of the opponents are, in short, "internationalists." They want to keep some discretion in the hands of the President not because they believe in presidential power as such, but because they believe that historically the President has been more internationally minded than Congress, while the legislature has tended to reflect the interests and attitudes less hospitable to closer working relationships with foreign nations.

Thus the issue, while involving grave constitutional matters, is essentially political. It involves less matters of procedure than of attitudes and interests. Whether the Bricker proposal or some amended version of it becomes part of the Constitution turns less on abstract constitutional questions than on how the American people feel about our foreign policies—at least to the extent that their feeling is reflected in Congress and in the legislatures of three-fourths of the states.

IS A DEMOCRATIC FOREIGN POLICY POSSIBLE?

Over a century ago, de Tocqueville wrote that democracies were decidedly inferior to other types of governments in the conduct of their foreign relations. "Foreign politics," he observed, "demand scarcely any of these qualities which are peculiar to a democracy; they require, on the contrary, the perfect use of almost all those in which it is deficient. . . . [A] democracy can only with great difficulty regulate the details of an important undertaking, persevere in a fixed design, and work out its execution in spite of serious obstacles. It cannot combine its measures with secrecy or await their consequences with patience."[13] Others have expressed somewhat similar misgivings over the handling of foreign relations in the American democracy. Hans Morgenthau, for example, has observed that policy makers "either . . . must sacrifice what they consider good policy upon the altar of public opinion, or they must by devious means gain support for policies whose true nature is concealed from the public."[14] How serious is this situation? What is the role of the general electorate?

How much popular control?

Democratic foreign policy making does not require that a general election be held before every decision is made. Everyone cannot be an expert; the people as a whole cannot actively take part in drawing up policy. "In

---

[13] Alexis de Tocqueville, *Democracy in America*, The Henry Reeve text (New York: Alfred A. Knopf, 1946), Vol. 1, pp. 234-235.

[14] Morgenthau, *op. cit.*, p. 147.

the case of foreign affairs," it has been said, "where the given elements in a situation consist largely of the attitudes and intentions of foreign communities, to expect a very high level of information on the part of the electorate is utopian."[15] But it is equally unrealistic to conclude that the policy makers can or should ignore the electorate. Foreign policies that commit American manpower and resources will have little success if Americans, through ignorance, apathy, or downright opposition, refuse to back up those policies. The electorate cannot fashion policy, but the voters can set limits to the policies they are willing to support.

The people, too, have a more positive responsibility. No matter how able the top officials, a twentieth-century foreign policy cannot be produced over the long run without the support of an informed electorate. Undoubtedly we need better ways of spreading information, of enlarging the opportunities for discussion.

Granting all this, however, the basic trouble in the United States is perhaps not so much democracy or democrats but our particular set of institutional arrangements. Weak parties, strongly organized interests, halting legislative procedures—these difficulties disrupt democratic control of foreign policies in the same way that they threaten effective control by the people of domestic policies. Indeed, some thoughtful observers believe that our governmental and political weaknesses in the foreign policy area are far more serious than in the domestic. We do not enjoy the margin for error, the time, and the chance to improvise in fast-moving international crises, they argue, that we do in internal affairs.

In the face of these difficulties Americans have evolved two methods of achieving effective national action in foreign affairs. One is to vest wide powers in the President. The framers of the Constitution gave the chief executive a paramount role in foreign relations, as we have seen, and with the passage of time he has taken on new powers, such as frequent resort to executive agreements. This situation has advantages. The President can act swiftly and decisively. He can see the more general interest above the clamor of the crowd and the tugging of special interests. He must face the people in elections, but not so often that he feels the need to follow public opinion instead of leading it. But there are disadvantages too. The President may bear responsibilities that are a tremendous load for one man. In a time of crisis—a time when he may see factors that most of the people do not see—the President may have to withhold information, or at least his own true opinions, from the people. Many of those who approved President Roosevelt's course in the year or two before Pearl Harbor would agree that the President "when confronted by an apathetic public and a critical foreign menace, felt compelled to deceive the people into an awareness of their peril."

[15] Max Beloff, *Foreign Policy and the Democratic Process* (Baltimore: The Johns Hopkins Press, 1955), p. 58.

HIGHLIGHTS OF

CONSTITUTIONAL

TREATIES TO BE RATIFIED BY MAJORITY OF BOTH HOUSES INSTEAD OF 2/3 VOTE OF THE SENATE.

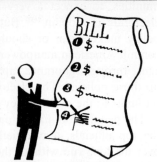

PRESIDENT EMPOWERED TO VETO ITEMS OF BILL WITHOUT REJECTING IT ENTIRELY.

DIVIDE ELECTORAL VOTES IN PROPORTION TO TOTAL NUMBER OF VOTES CAST.

EXECUTIVE

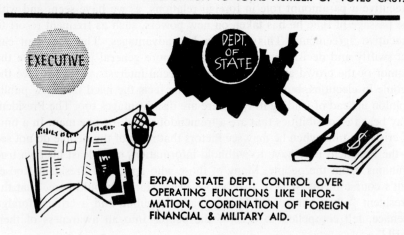

EXPAND STATE DEPT. CONTROL OVER OPERATING FUNCTIONS LIKE INFORMATION, COORDINATION OF FOREIGN FINANCIAL & MILITARY AID.

SUGGESTED REFORMS

FOREIGN POLICY PROGRAM SHOULD BE
PRESENTED IN GENERAL PACKAGE
BILLS AS FAR AS POSSIBLE.

SECRETARY OF STATE MIGHT
APPEAR PERSONALLY BE-
FORE BOTH HOUSES AND
ANSWER QUESTIONS.

MORE INFORMAL CONFERENCES
BETWEEN PRESIDENT, SECRETARY
OF STATE AND CONGRESSMEN.

STRONG PARTY DIS-
CIPLINE TO MAINTAIN
AND SUPPORT CONTINUITY OF
FOREIGN POLICY.

Illustrations by Graphics Institute

From "Suggested Reforms to Improve U.S. Foreign Policy Machinery," STRENGTHENING OUR
FOREIGN POLICY, *Public Affairs Pamphlet No. 189, pp. 14-15. A report by a study group of the
Woodrow Wilson Foundation. Reproduced by permission of Public Affairs Committee, Inc, New
York, N.Y.*

To what extent should the President be a leader in shaping our foreign policy? To what extent a follower? These questions go to the heart of democratic government. One answer, as we have noted in Chapter 21, is that the President should act as leader of the majority party and should be responsible to that party. But again, institutional arrangements for party rule are lacking in this country. This brings us to the second method of evading the weaknesses of the American system of government.

Bipartisanship and responsibility

The second method of evading the weaknesses of our government in foreign policy making is *bipartisanship*. Although bipartisanship, as noted above, means different things to different people, it is essentially an arrangement by which Administration leaders consult with minority party leaders before making important decisions, *and by which both parties share responsibility for those decisions and their consequences.*

Bipartisanship has enormous appeal. In this era of chronic crisis, it seems to symbolize a people standing shoulder to shoulder as they face their enemies abroad. It provides more continuity of policy, and it insures that a wider variety of leaders and interests are consulted in foreign policy making. Psychologically, it helps to satisfy the instinct of people to turn to one another for reassurance as they shrink from the dark and disjointed world outside. Its motto—"Partisan politics stops at the water's edge"—is comforting to the many Americans worried about disunity at home.

But the idea of bipartisanship has been under sharp attack. Critics charge that bipartisanship denies a basic tenet of democracy—the right of a people to choose between alternative lines of action. According to this argument, in a free society men should be allowed and even encouraged to differ. The need in a democracy is not to stifle differences, or to ignore them, or to elude them. The need is to express the differences in a meaningful way, to find the will of the majority, to permit the government to act and the opposition to oppose. This is where parties come in. They present alternatives. Because they want to win as many votes as possible, parties find common denominators in the views of millions of people. Because we have a two-party system, each party distills the essence of agreement from a medley of conflicting opinions. The party that wins a majority takes office. The losing party has the equally important job of furnishing opposition.

Thus parties—and partisanship—are vital to democracy. "Why should we abandon them at the water's edge?" ask the opponents of bipartisanship. Certainly not because Americans are agreed on foreign policy. The nation abounds with differences, as recent crises have made clear. Surely not because we hope to show a united front to our enemies. We cannot deceive them with a pretense of agreement. With their trained observers stationed in Washington and throughout the country, they know our differences as well as we do. Besides, our party divisions should be something to flaunt with pride—not something to be slammed into the closet whenever foreigners seem to be looking at us.

Even more serious, the critics conclude, bipartisanship erodes responsibility. A great virtue of partisan government is that the men in office can be held to account simply because these men have held authority. But when the leaders of both parties have had their hands on the tiller, responsibility fades. After things go badly politicians begin the grand game of passing the buck. The leaders of each party maintain that it was the other gang that really steered the ship onto the rocks. Instead of a sober consideration of alternative courses of action, there is a frantic hunt for scapegoats.

Despite these criticisms, Americans will probably continue to resort to bipartisan arrangements in foreign policy making. The reason is clear. Our constitutional system encourages bipartisanship. The two-thirds requirement for ratification of treaties forces the President to rely upon the minority party. Moreover, in a time of international tension and crisis, democracies must *act*. Any device that will permit action without violating constitutional forms is indispensable. Bipartisanship permits action. So does broad presidential power. These methods may flout democratic ideals of responsibility and popular control, but they seem to be part of the price we must pay for living in a chaotic world of sovereign nations.

T HE HIGH-LEVEL FOREIGN POLICY LEADERS ARE concerned mainly with the key issues of state. They work at the top of a governmental iceberg, and the organization below them is wide and deep. The day-by-day administration, the handling of routine problems, and the decisions that do not immediately involve great discretion are in the hands of others. These thousands of men and women, by gathering and evaluating data and by making the scores of little decisions out of which the big ones are often compounded, greatly influence the making of big policies. The President, Congress, the Secretary of State, and the people depend on these officials for information and advice, and for the execution of policy once it has been determined. What finally emerges as a policy decision is the product of many minds.

THE ROLE OF THE STATE DEPARTMENT

Who handles the day-by-day routine? The key agency is of course the State Department. This department has six traditional duties. (1) It must provide the President with the *information* he needs to conduct international relations. The department, through its missions abroad, collects data on political and economic events, sorts and analyzes it, sends some to other interested departments, and some to Central Intelligence. (2) The department assists the President in the *formulation and implementation of policy.* It evaluates the information, makes recommendations to the President, the National Security Council, and others, or it makes the decisions in the President's name. (3) The department has the primary responsibility for *representing* the United States in our dealings with other nations and international organizations. Messages to and from other nations are routed through the department. (4) The department has the primary but not exclusive responsibility for carrying on *negotiations* with other nations and international organi-

★ 23

Conducting

foreign

relations

zations. Recently, only 25 per cent of the United States representatives in 390 international meetings were from the Department of State, but in most cases the heads of the delegations were State Department men. (5) The department has the *operating responsibility for technical and economic assistance* programs administered by the International Cooperation Administration (now part of the department). (6) A final function of the department is to *coordinate* the activities of the many groups, agencies, and interdepartmental committees that participate in the formulation and execution of foreign policy.

Organization

The general organization of the Department of State is determined by its two major activities: one to advise on the formulation of policy; the other to handle the day-by-day relations of the United States with other nations and international organizations. For many years the department was able to handle its duties with a small staff. As new activities were added, the organization became unwieldy. In an attempt to improve its organization, the department has been reorganized seven times since January 1944. Though many critics still insist that the more it changes the more it stays the same, the department is now probably better organized to handle the problems of a major world power.

The policy making and advisory activities of the department are centered in a team of high-ranking officers. At the top is, of course, the Secretary. Second in command is the Under Secretary who serves as Acting Secretary during the Secretary's frequent absences. Three Deputy Under Secretaries assist in the running of the department and giving advice, as does the Counselor who serves as a senior adviser and assists in negotiations. The Assistant Secretary for Policy Planning represents the department on the Planning Staff of the National Security Council and assists the Secretary in the formulation of long-range policy. The existence of an Assistant Secretary for Public Affairs and an Assistant Secretary for Congressional Relations points up the department's concern with internal politics.

The actual operations are centered in the department's bureaus. Four bureaus are organized along functional lines: one for international organizations, one for economic affairs, one for security and consular affairs, and one for personnel and housekeeping matters. The International Cooperation Administration functions as a semi-autonomous unit within the department; its director reports directly to the Secretary, and it maintains its own staff. This administration handles economic and technical assistance and coordinates military aid programs. It works on the assumption that we can use our productive power to help build the strength of nations whose security and stability are vital to our own and who share our determination to stop aggression.

The *geographic* offices have become the pivot of the department's operations. Each embraces a varying number of country desks. The "desk man," a specialist on a particular country, receives copies of all communications from our representatives in that country, and through him instructions are sent to these representatives. The desk man is expected to have a thorough understanding of his country. The geographic offices have their own staffs of economists, geographers, and other specialists.

What should be the function of the Department of State? Should it limit its activities to the *making* of policy but leave its *execution* to others? This is more or less the official view of the State Department. Except for the traditional agencies of diplomacy and the recently designated task of economic and technical assistance, the *instruments* of policy are operated by others—for example, military force and military assistance by the Department of Defense, and information programs by the United States Information Agency. A first Hoover Commission Task Force recommended that the department, in addition to representation, reporting, and negotiation, should "concentrate on the task of obtaining definition of proposed objectives, of formulating proposed policies, . . . and of recommending the choice and timing of the use of various instruments to carry out foreign policies. . . ."[1] As far as *operations* are concerned, however, the first Hoover Commission suggested that the department merely assist and supervise other departments to assure that they were using their respective instruments to achieve approved policy objectives. Not all students agree with the commission[2] and the second Hoover Commission hedged on this point.[3] It is doubtful if any clean-cut division of responsibility can be established. Whatever the State Department's role, foreign affairs touch so many interests and activities that inevitably some of them will be handled outside the State Department.

The State Department's partners

To list the other agencies that manage some phase of our foreign policy would be a long task. A brief description of the activities of a few of the chief agencies will give some idea of the complexity and scope of our relations with other nations. Since military power is one of the chief instruments of foreign policy, some of the most important programs are

---

[1] Commission on Organization of the Executive Branch of the Government, *Task Force Report on Foreign Affairs* (Washington: Government Printing Office, 1949), p. 15.

[2] For example, The Brookings Institution, *The Administration of Foreign Affairs and Overseas Operations* (Washington, D.C.: 1951), p. xix. Also Arthur W. Macmahon, *Administration in Foreign Affairs* (University, Alabama: University of Alabama Press, 1953), pp. 94 ff.

[3] Commission on Organization of the Executive Branch of the Government, *Overseas Economic Operations, A Report to the Congress* (Washington, D.C.: Government Printing Office, 1955), p. 42.

administered in the *Defense Department.* An Assistant Secretary of Defense for International Security Affairs coordinates within the department all politico-military matters. He administers the military assistance programs, supervises the Department of Defense activities in the National Security Council, and helps the Secretary develop military policy that relates to foreign relations.

The United States Information Agency was established in 1953 to take over from the State Department the operating responsibility for managing an important instrument of foreign policy—propaganda. The agency under the guidance of the Secretary of State and the National Security Council has control over all facets of our informational programs. The Voice of America broadcasts are well-known, but they are only a part of an elaborate program of explaining American foreign policies to the people abroad. During the war the United States for the first time seriously began to use propaganda as an instrument of policy. Under the Office of War Information, an independent agency, propaganda was used in order to soften the enemy and gain the support of neutral countries. All kinds of propaganda, "white" (objective and balanced), "black" (slanted), and "gray" (mixed) were used. Today the emphasis is on the use of *white* propaganda. In addition to radio broadcasts, the United States maintains libraries in foreign countries containing books and magazines about this country and its culture and has an elaborate program to help foreign students come to the United States to secure their education. Democracies in general and the United States in particular have been reluctant to establish propaganda bureaus, but the success of the Soviet Union in painting the United States as a country dominated by capitalist warmongers has forced us to engage in "campaigns of truth." The propaganda instrument is especially important in gaining the support of peoples in colonial areas where programs must be designed in terms of the idea-systems of those peoples. The American effort has been criticized for failure to provide materials that are meaningful to peoples of different cultures.

The *Department of the Treasury* has become increasingly important in the international relations of the United States because of the key role of fiscal activities in world affairs. It has chief responsibility for all foreign financial, monetary, and exchange activities of the government. The Office of International Finance makes reports and recommendations on the economic and financial aspects of international treaties and agreements. It also administers the frozen funds of other nations in this country and the laws prohibiting certain transactions with communist countries.

At least eight separate bureaus in the *Department of Commerce* are concerned with foreign activities. The most important is the Bureau of Foreign Commerce, which promotes American interests in connection with exports and imports, works to reduce barriers in international trade, and represents the department in economic negotiations with other countries. The Commerce Department has a major role in United States foreign economic activities and is represented on many interdepartmental economic committees. It has primary responsibility for the administration of export and import controls on all except agricultural commodities.

The *Department of Agriculture* in addition to furnishing advice on top policy has certain operational responsibilities. The Foreign Agricultural Service assists in agricultural phases of foreign assistance programs.

AMERICANS OVERSEAS

American diplomacy is older than the United States. Even before the Revolution, Benjamin Franklin was sent as our representative to France by the Continental Congress. Today the United States maintains 67 embassies, 9 legations, and approximately 200 consular posts in more than 70 nations.

During our early years as a nation the caliber of our representation was high. Men like John Adams, Thomas Jefferson, and James Monroe served American interests in foreign capitals. But following the War of 1812 diplomatic posts were in the main used to reward persons for political activities. High diplomatic assignments were given to wealthy men who had contributed to the campaigns of victorious presidents. Salaries of diplomats were small and the expenses large, with the result that only men of independent means could afford to take posts in the more important nations. The *consular* offices were in much demand because of "the fees that went into the consul's pocket; at big ports such as Hamburg and London, the yearly plunder often exceeded the salary of the President of the United States."[4] Various minor reforms were made, but it was not until 1924 that the modern career service was established. In that year the Rogers Act consolidated the diplomatic and consular service and provided for a Foreign Service of the United States established on a career basis. The service was further modernized and reorganized in 1946, 1949, and 1954.

The elaborate protocol surrounding diplomacy gives an unwarranted impression of daintiness and mystery to the profession. Historical and popular novelists make out that diplomacy is the work of adroit and gallant heroes, voluptuous heroines, and scheming diplomats. Of course some diplomats are handsome and adept at making pretty compliments to beautiful ladies, but diplomacy is, as an experienced diplomat has written, a "grim business . . . a laborious business, singularly free from glamour and mystery."

[4] J. Rives Childs, *American Foreign Service* (New York: Henry Holt and Company, Inc., 1948), p. 6.

The American Foreign Service

The American Foreign Service is the eyes and ears of the United States. Although a part of the State Department, the service represents the entire government and performs jobs for many other agencies. Almost 90 per cent of its reports go to departments other than State. Its main duties are to carry out foreign policy as expressed in the directives of the Secretary of State, gather data for American policy makers, protect Americans and American interests in foreign countries, and cultivate friendly relations with foreign peoples. Although theoretically the service is only an instrument to assist policy leaders, its influence on policy is reflected in the quip, "foreign policy is made on the cables."

The Foreign Service is composed of officers, reserve officers, and staff.[5] At the core of the service are the Foreign Service officers, comparable to the officers of the regular Army in the military services. It is a select, specially-trained body of men and women who are expected to take an assignment at any place in the world on short notice. There are approximately 3900 such officers, over 250 junior officers being appointed each year. They have their own training school, the Foreign Service Institute, where new officers and their wives are briefed and where mature officers receive advanced instruction. Officers have either diplomatic or consular duties and provide the general direction of our missions abroad. As a small elite group, the Foreign Service has a high *esprit de corps*.

The Foreign Service is one of the most respected and most criticized branches of the national government. Recently the criticism seemed to outweigh the respect, and the service's morale suffered. Henry M. Wriston, chairman of a distinguished committee appointed in 1954 by the Secretary of State to study the service, stated that it "was dying at the bottom, they were resigning in the middle, and it was withering away at the top."[6] In loyalty-security hearings officers were being asked to justify remarks sometimes taken out of context from confidential reports made years ago to their superiors. Often the recommendations of yesterday were evaluated by the hindsight of today. Critics were accusing the service of being infiltrated by Communist sympathizers, and at the same time others were charging that it was dominated by a high society elite who were still under the impression that diplomacy was the business of "gentlemen." But the trouble is, said the critics, it is more important that our diplomats understand the social and economic problems of the Chinese peasant, for example, than to know how to behave at a fashionable cocktail party. The charges about Communist infiltration were undoubtedly overdrawn, as were

[5] See Epilogue for discussion of method of appointment and preparation for entering the Foreign Service.

[6] Quoted by Dorothy Fosdick, "For the Foreign Service—Help Wanted," *The New York Times Magazine,* November 20, 1955, p. 13.

those of the service's preoccupation with manners. The latter charges probably stemmed in part from the conventional stereotype of a diplomat. Still, the personnel of the service came from the same general social background—a fact that cut down on the effectiveness of their reporting, for every reporter, no matter how objective he tries to be, selects and evaluates what he sees on the basis of his own attitudes and "picture of the world."

Prior to 1954 most stateside positions within the Department of State were held by civil service employees whose salary and retirement systems were less favorable than those of the Foreign Service but who had no obligation to serve outside the United States. Since the Foreign Service was small, there was little opportunity to bring officers back for a tour of duty in Washington. Because of this situation it was charged that they had lost contact with American domestic conditions. At the same time, the civil service employees with little or no service abroad often failed to understand other nations, appreciate foreign conditions, or sympathize with the job of the men working abroad. Friction occurred between the two groups: the Foreign Service officers felt that their system of selection and obligation to serve abroad made them an elite corps, the civil service employees felt that the Foreign Service officers were limited in viewpoint and got excessively high salaries, sometimes for doing the same kind of jobs assigned to civil service people.[7]

Between 1949 and 1954 five commissions or special committees studied the Foreign Service. All recommended that there should be a single service to staff both overseas and Washington positions, all persons being obliged to serve where needed. The most recent group to endorse this proposal was the Secretary of State's Public Committee on Personnel, popularly known after the name of its chairman as the Wriston Committee, which was appointed after the attacks on the loyalty of the Foreign Service had led to a decline in morale and to loss of public confidence in it. The committee also recommended that the service broaden its representative character, more actively and imaginatively recruit young men, and improve its training programs.[8]

Finally in 1954 Congress authorized an expansion of the service and the bringing within it of most of the State Department's policy positions. Holders of these positions wherever qualified were given a chance to accept a Foreign Service commission, getting both the higher salary and the obligation to serve abroad. With this expansion of the Foreign Service

[7] The Commission on Organization of the Executive Branch of the Government, *Foreign Affairs* (Washington: Government Printing Office, 1949), p. 62.

[8] Report of the Secretary of State's Public Committee on Personnel, *Toward A Stronger Foreign Service,* Department of State Publication 5458 (Washington, D.C.: Government Printing Office, 1954).

it is hoped that Foreign Service officers will have a stateside assignment at least after every six-year tour abroad.[9]

Except for clerical, custodial, and administrative jobs, key positions in the State Department are now held by members of the Foreign Service. The Foreign Service Reserve, really misnamed, permits the Secretary to appoint a few specialists to serve for a temporary period. Foreign Service Staff now consists of technical, clerical, and custodial personnel lower than officer rank. Steps are also being taken to comply with other recommendations of the Wriston Committee to recruit more men and women from the colleges, to make the examinations less costly, and to place less emphasis on "personality" and "foreign service characteristics."

Operations overseas

The United States has diplomatic missions in the capital cities of almost all nations with whom we maintain relations. In addition, we maintain permanent missions at the North Atlantic Treaty Organization, European regional organizations, and the United Nations. The heads of these missions, designated by the President with the consent of the Senate, hold the ranks of ambassador, minister, or chargé d'affaires. Historically ambassadors were sent to the larger and more important countries, but now we maintain embassies (each headed by an ambassador) in many smaller countries. Over 60 per cent of the chiefs of missions are now foreign service officers.

Diplomatic missions located in capital cities are chiefly concerned with political and important economic relations between governments. Consular offices, though part of the Foreign Service, are largely concerned with the activities of individuals. Consuls are not official representatives of one government to another, but are in the nature of public agents to promote the commercial interest and protect the citizens of the sending state. Their powers and privileges are determined by arrangement with the countries concerned. The ranks of the consular officers are in descending order: consul general, consul, vice-consul, and consular agents. The latter are not members of the Foreign Service, and operate in the less important places.

Some idea of the many duties of the Foreign Service can be gained by looking at the activities of a typical American mission.

Americans in Paris

Right off the Place de la Concorde stands an imposing building with the stars and stripes flying from the top of the portico overlooking the

[9] For a recent treatment of personnel in the service, see James L. McCamy and Alessandro Corradini, "The People of the State Department and Foreign Service," *The American Political Science Review*, Vol. XLVIII, No. 4, December 1954, pp 1067-1082.

circular driveway. This is the American Embassy in Paris, the largest American mission in the world. This mission operates out of seven office buildings, spends over $15 million a year, and employs 2485 people. (Only part of these people make up the mission to France; the others make up the mission to NATO.) In addition, fifteen departments and agencies have smaller American missions attached to the embassy. The ambassador is the ranking American representative in France and is responsible for the coordination of all American officials in Paris.

The work of the embassy is divided into four major sections: political, administrative, economic, and consular. The political section, presided over by Foreign Service officers, keeps the Department of State informed regarding developments in the internal and foreign politics of the French government. It reports and analyzes, for example, debates in the French Assembly, election results, French public opinion, and decisions of the French Cabinet. These officers usually handle routine negotiations with the French government and transmit notes received from the French Ministry of Foreign Affairs to the Department of State. The political section reviews all messages from the Department of State and makes the necessary inquiries or gathers the information requested by the department.

The economic section, directed by an economic counselor, keeps the ambassador and the department informed of important economic developments in France. This section reviews all messages touching upon matters of economic policy, represents the mission in negotiations dealing with economic matters, keeps close contact with the French finance minister, the minister of national economy, the Bank of France, and other French officials responsible for economic policy. Liaison is also maintained with French businessmen and labor leaders. Some idea of the scope of the economic section's work can be seen by the names of the units within the division: wartime and emergency economic problems, civil aviation, telecommunications, commercial finance and statistics, agriculture, petroleum, commercial policy.

Since Paris is the economic as well as the political capital of France, there is no separate consular office; the consular section is part of the embassy. This section coordinates the activities of the various consular offices throughout France and serves for Americans in France the same functions as secretaries of chambers of commerce, justices of the peace, notaries public, commissioners of immigration and naturalization, and Veterans Administration officials. It examines applicants for admission to the United States, issues permits to exporters of goods destined for the United States, enforces maritime and health laws, administers customs laws, takes care of estates of American citizens who die abroad, and collects information for American business and agriculture.

Attached to the embassy are various kinds of specialists. Information and cultural relations specialists of the United States Information Agency issue a magazine known as *U.S.A.* that contains materials not available through commercial press agencies. This publication is distributed to every newspaper in France, to leading officials, libraries, schools, and universities. A weekly bulletin is published containing materials of general background information on the United States, such as *Political Parties in the United States, American Views on Economic Reconstruction.* A financial bulletin is issued weekly for distribution to French financial newspapers. Radio broadcasts are arranged, speakers' tours organized, a reference library operated, and information and cultural centers maintained throughout France. The cultural relations attaché tries to stimulate interest in American education, literature, the arts, and to encourage an exchange between French and American teachers, artists, and cultural leaders.

Military and naval attachés send reports direct to the Defense Department; indeed, about half of the Americans attached to the embassy are either military men or civilian officials of the Defense Department. Other departments send representatives to the mission to gather special materials or perform particular tasks. Just under a third of the Americans are actually employees of the State Department. In short, the American Embassy in Paris mirrors the diversity of interests and jobs found in the executive branch in Washington. The embassy is a miniature duplicate of the federal executive structure.

The Foreign Service has competitors. Of the over 30,000 Americans employed abroad, exclusive of the armed services, only about one-fifth are Foreign Service personnel. Prior to 1939 the Departments of Commerce, Agriculture, Treasury, and others had their own overseas staff service. In that year, however, the principle was established that there should be but one foreign service, and that all American employees in a foreign country should be responsible to the chief of mission. Services of the Commerce and Agriculture Departments were merged with those of the Foreign Service. During the war, however, many agencies set up their own offices. The diplomatic missions in many cases were overshadowed, and friction and lack of coordination resulted. The American ambassador in England was not even kept informed of various Anglo-American relations, and was all but superseded by the American lend-lease expediter.

After World War II many of these agencies were abolished and some of their duties and personnel were assigned to diplomatic and consular missions. But as postwar programs developed, the principle that the United States should have but one overseas arm was again violated and separate overseas missions were frequently established; for example the United States Information Agency has its own staff, as do the economic assistance agencies (most of whom are classified as Foreign Service Staff). Again friction and waste of effort developed. For example, a simmering conflict took place between the American ambassador in Greece and the head of the economic aid mission.

An Executive Order of the President makes the chief of the diplomatic mission the ranking American in each foreign country and makes him the coordinator of the overseas programs. His control is often nominal, however, as overseas personnel continue to deal directly with their superiors in Washington. Despite the contrary recommendations of the first Hoover Commission, the overseas representation of the United States was further splintered when agricultural attachés were in effect detached from diplomatic missions. Other agencies are also pressing for greater control over their attachés.

The second Hoover Commission reported that as a result of these independent overseas personnel systems, "The United States frequently speaks with numerous, often conflicting voices; its representatives can be played off one against the other by foreign officials, and its manifold policies and programs can be misconstrued."[10] The Commission urged "remedial measures . . . to strengthen the position of our Chief of Diplomatic Mission in each country" through assignment of overseas personnel of all United States agencies (except the military) under a single unified foreign service system, and for the integration of all separate field missions and overseas personnel of these agencies into the regular organizational units of the embassy, subject to the authority and control of the Ambassador or Minister.

The incorporation of the International Cooperation Administration as a semi-autonomous unit of the State Department is a step in the direction of the Hoover Commissions' recommendations. Still, the expansion of the Foreign Service by its integration with key personnel of the State Department will probably be all the integration that the Foreign Service can undertake for several years. And the pressure for separate establishments continues. It is likely that the United States Information Agency, for example, will establish its own overseas career service.[11]

CONDUCTING FOREIGN RELATIONS: THREE CASE STUDIES

Foreign policy is not made in any one way. Much depends upon the nature of the issues, the speed with which the problem is presented, the personality of the President, the political situation, and the accidents of history. Sometimes Congress initiates the policy; more often it is the President, the Secretary of State, the Joint Chiefs of Staff, or an ambassador. Each problem calls for new decisions; each decision makes for new problems. The initiative is sometimes in the hands of our government, unfortunately more often in the hands of other governments. To search for the origins of any

[10] Commission on Organization of the Executive Branch of the Government, *Overseas Economic Operations* (Washington, D.C.: Government Printing Office, 1955), p. 46.

[11] Robert E. Elder, "A Career Service for U.S.A.?" *Foreign Service Journal*, Vol. 33, No. 2, February 1956, pp. 26 ff.

particular policy, to isolate the critical areas, to focus on the alternatives is not the purpose here. But the following cases may suggest the way in which the machinery works.

The Truman Doctrine

On February 26, 1947, the British ambassador in Washington sent a note to the Secretary of State. The note advised the Secretary that after March 31 the United Kingdom would no longer be able to provide economic, financial, and advisory assistance to Greece. The Greek government was in a precarious position. It was not a government to inspire confidence, and had never been accepted by certain groups in that country. In the northern part of Greece, communist guerrillas, aided and abetted by the Soviet Union, were threatening to overthrow the government. This would have given the Soviet Union control over a strategically located state athwart the Mediterranean and in a position to exert even more pressure on Turkey, which also was being threatened by the communists. The domination of these two countries by the communists would be a serious blow to American national interests.

Should the United States take action? What kind of action? Should we operate through the United Nations? Could the Greek government be saved? Why had not the British been successful? What groups within Greece supported the existing government? What groups opposed it? What would the Soviet Union do if we assisted Greece with economic and military supplies? What would we do if the Soviet Union backed up the communist forces with military assistance? Should we extend aid to Turkey? How would the other nations in the world react to American intervention?

These were only a few of the problems, and they had to be met in a hurry. Already ground had been lost. Our intelligence work had been faulty, for the situation in Greece was one that could have been anticipated if we had had proper information and contacts with the United Kingdom. To be sure, there were some who had anticipated the issue, and many of the problems had been studied, but the President was forced to act without full consultation with his principal advisers on the military, economic, and political aspects. On March 3, the Greek government formally appealed to the United States for assistance. On March 12, the President spoke before a joint session of the Congress, a speech that was broadcast throughout the world.

The President told Congress of the urgency of the situation. He said: "The foreign policy and the national security of this country are involved. . . . It must be the policy of the United States to support free peoples who are resisting attempted subjugation by armed minorities or by outside pressures." The United Nations could not provide the assistance, he stated, because immediate action was required, and that organization was not in a position to extend the help needed. Moreover, the action by the United States would support the principles of the Charter through helping free and independent nations to maintain their freedom and through preventing their conquest by subterfuge and political infiltration. He asked the Congress to authorize a program of military and economic aid for Greece and Turkey, and to appropriate $400 million.

That evening the State Department, in order to avoid any appearance of secret diplomacy, translated the President's speech into eight languages and broadcast it to Latin America, Europe, the Soviet Union, and the Far East. Summaries of the address were broadcast in 25 languages over the Voice of America programs. Even before the President spoke to Congress, the State Department was establishing committees of representatives of the Departments of Treasury, Agriculture, Commerce, Army, Navy, Air Force, Labor, and others, to work out legislation to put into effect the policy announced by the President. The proposals were introduced in Congress by Administration congressmen.

The President urged Congress to act immediately, at least by the end of March. But Congress was not to be hurried. The President was asking for a major commitment, to back up with economic and military assistance nations in danger of communist conquest. Before it approved such a program, Congress wanted all the information. From March until May 22, the measure was thoroughly discussed. The Senate Foreign Relations and the House Foreign Affairs Committees held long hearings. Administration spokesmen and representatives of private organizations testified.

One of the major objections, both inside and outside Congress and inside and outside the United States, was that the President's program would by-pass and thereby weaken the United Nations. The President in his message had attempted to answer such criticism, but apparently the President and his advisers had misjudged the intensity of the criticism. Steps were taken to remedy the situation. On March 28, Warren Austin, United States representative to the United Nations, explained the proposed action to the Security Council and stated that any agreements entered into would be registered with the United Nations for publication by the Secretary General. The Senate Foreign Relations Committee, at the urging of Senator Vandenberg, amended the legislation to tie the program more closely in with the United Nations. The United Nations Security Council and the General Assembly were given the power to end the assistance if they found that its continuance was unnecessary or undesirable.

While the bill was still being debated in Congress, the State Department, on April 7, established an Interdepartmental Committee for Aid to Greece and Turkey. This committee, composed of representatives from the White House, the interested departments, the Public Roads Administration, Federal Security Agency, and the Army Corps of Engineers, began work on operating policies and plans. Basic policies were agreed upon so that it would be possible to show the congressional appropriations committees how the funds would be spent.

On May 22, the enabling act was passed. The President issued an executive order making the State Department responsible for administration of the program, but the other departments were to be used in its execution. Hearings were then held by congressional appropriations committees, and eventually the money was authorized. On June 26, 1947, the State Department created a Coordinator for Aid to Greece and Turkey, a small Washington staff was established, and missions were opened in Greece and Turkey. The military aspects of the program were handled by the military departments; the Greek agricultural rehabilitation program was the responsibility of the Department of Agriculture; the Commerce Department was in charge of development of trade; the Public Health Service worked out the program for public health; the Bureau of the Budget attended to the reorganization of Greek administration.

The Marshall Plan

The Greek-Turkish aid program took care of an urgent situation. Yet it was becoming clear from overwhelming evidence that all Europe was in dire need of assistance. Much was already being done by the United States through the various branches of the government. It seemed likely that unless a greater and broader program was adopted, European economies would be subject to such stresses and strains that the situation would become highly unstable. On March 8, 1947, Undersecretaries Acheson and Clayton discussed the emergency with the President. On May 8, Acheson in a speech at Cleveland, Mississippi, outlined the situation. This was the Administration's trial balloon to sound out public and congressional opinion. The department, meanwhile, consulted Senator Vandenberg, who warned that a carefully prepared long-range program had to be worked out. The State Department's policy planning staff advised that European nations should take the initiative and work out the plan. Secretary of State Marshall approved, but insisted that all Europe, including Russia, be included in the program. Meanwhile the State Department experts published a study on *The Development of the Foreign Reconstruction Policy of the United States.*

On June 5, the Secretary gave a speech at Harvard University. It was the commencement address. Instead of an "as I look at your bright and shining faces" speech, Secretary Marshall took advantage of the opportunity to make a major policy statement. He described the serious situation in Europe, and the need for American help. But the initiative, he said, must come from Europe. The United States should aid in the drafting of a European recovery program and later support such a program.

The U.S.S.R. and her satellites refused to participate but the other European nations "seized the proposal with both hands." Soon sixteen nations met in Paris and formed the Committee of European Economic Cooperation. Within the United States, groups of specialists, calling upon consultants and experts from outside the government, made reports covering every phase of European recovery. The State Department studied these reports, and advised the President. The Congress was not in session, but on November 10, Secretary Marshall appeared before a joint session of the Senate Foreign Relations Committee and the House Committee on Foreign Affairs. He outlined the program, calling for an appropriation of over $6 billion for the first fifteen months of the program, which was to run for four years.

President Truman then called a special session of Congress. The legislators were presented with a proposed bill by the State Department, and Administration officials made numerous appearances before committees and addresses to the public. Three special committees, composed of over 350 State Department employees, were set up in the department to work out the details of the program.

Congressmen had their own ideas. Many of them were unconvinced that such vast expenditures were needed to protect American national interests. Then the Communist coup in Czechoslovakia startled the world. Congress quickly approved the legislation, but not without amendments. The House included Franco Spain in the program, contrary to the wishes of the President or the Department of State, but aid to Spain was defeated in conference committee.

The Foreign Assistance Act of 1948 was passed on April 3. The next step was to secure the appropriations. The chairman of the House Committee on Appropriations was interested in saving money, and despite the fact that the House had previously approved the program, he recommended and the House approved a billion dollar reduction in the program. Senator Vandenberg used his great prestige to have the amount restored, and except for the fact that the money was authorized for only a year instead of fifteen months, the program was substantially as requested. The administration of the program was vested, however, not in the Department of State, but in a separate Economic Cooperation Administration.

Both the Truman Doctrine and the Marshall Plan had been initiated by the President and the State Department, but they had been approved by the Congress, both houses of which were controlled by the opposite party to that of the chief executive. In both of these programs, the leaders of the State Department and of Congress worked closely together, consulting on the details and collaborating in securing approval. Not all decisions, however, require congressional approval or permit public discussion.

Trieste and the Italian elections[12]

On April 18, 1948, the Italian people were scheduled to go to the polls to choose their government. One of the strongest contenders was the Italian Communist party. Victory for that party would turn Italy over to the Communists, would affect favorably the fortunes of communism elsewhere in Europe, especially in France, and might upset the whole political and military balance of power in Europe.

During the first week in March, Central Intelligence placed a top-secret report on the President's desk. From absolutely reliable sources it had been learned that Moscow had promised Togliatti, leader of the Italian Communists, that one week before the elections the Soviet Union would officially come out in favor of the return of Trieste to Italy. Trieste for many years had been the object of bitter disputes between Yugoslavia and Italy. In 1948 it was occupied by Allied troops and served as a toe hold of the noncommunist nations in that region of Europe. Under the terms of the Italian Peace Treaty, Trieste was to be a neutralized area. But Italians were not reconciled to this loss. The Soviet Union's support for its return to Italy would have a tremendous appeal; such a move might very well insure a Communist victory at the election.

For some time experts in the lower echelons of the State Department had been saying that the Italian-Yugoslav arrangements for the neutralization of Trieste were unworkable and that the city should be returned to Italy. Now the problem became urgent. On March 5, the executive secretary of the National Security Council told his staff to drop everything and to get to work on a preliminary policy paper on Trieste.

The job of making the first draft was given the two members of the National Security Council staff on assignment from the State Department. They immediately consulted with the State Department experts. Should Anglo-American troops be withdrawn from Trieste? What would be the effect on the Italian people of American support for return of Trieste? Would England and France support our position? What would be the effect of such an announcement on the people of Yugoslavia? Calling upon the knowledge of the various officials in the department, and on the basis of reports already prepared in the department, a working paper was drawn up, but limited in its attention to the political aspects of the matter.

The working paper was then turned over to two members of the National Security staff who were on assignment from the military departments. They took the paper and consulted with military officials. The working paper was then redrafted. The next step was to clear with the consultants of the National Security Council—top-drawer officials from State, Army, Navy,

[12] Materials in this section are based on Joseph and Stewart Alsop, "How Our Foreign Policy Is Made," *The Saturday Evening Post*, April 30, 1949.

and Air Force who were called together to discuss the matter. The paper was then redrafted and returned to the executive secretary.

This had taken three days. It was now March 8. By this time it had been agreed at the level below the Secretaries that a communist Italy would be a strategic catastrophe, and that the need to prevent Italy from being controlled by the communists should outweigh all other considerations. It had been agreed that France, Great Britain, and the United States should propose the return of Trieste to Italy, and to do this before the Soviet Union had a chance to act. The preliminary policy paper was quickly circulated among the members of the council, who were notified that it would be discussed at a special emergency meeting on March 11, at 2:30 P.M. in the Cabinet Room of the White House. At the appointed hour, the members assembled. The President, in order to encourage discussion, did not attend, and the Secretary of State took the chair. The Secretary opened the discussion. He had some reservations. He disliked descending to the level of the Russians; he was disturbed by the handling of the problem under so much pressure. But as it became clear that all the other men were convinced that the move was essential, the Secretary dropped his objections and the paper was unanimously approved.

Not until the President approved, however, would it become official American policy. So far it was but advice to the President. The next morning at 9:30 A.M. the executive secretary made his regular visit to the President. In his briefcase he had the policy paper; stamped on the top in lavender ink were the words TOP SECRET. The paper was divided into three parts, the problem, the analysis, conclusions. The President read the paper, he asked a few questions, and then on the lower right corner of the first page he wrote, "O.K., H.S.T." The decision now became official policy.

The executive secretary called the State Department, "O.K., you can go ahead." Immediately coded cables were sent to the American embassies in London, Paris, and Rome. Our ambassadors in England and France were instructed to get in touch immediately with the foreign offices. The British and the French agreed. On March 20, the French foreign minister conferred with the Italian foreign minister. After the conference it was announced, "France, the United States, and Britain favor the incorporation of Trieste as part of Italy." Just what influence this action had on the election we do not know. But on April 18, the Communists were defeated at the polls.

THE UNITED STATES AND THE UNITED NATIONS

The United States is an international joiner. Today it belongs to all the most important world organizations, and attends all major international conferences. The story of how the United States failed to join the League of Nations but took the leading role in the formation of the United Nations is well known. But not so many people realize that the international organization, and the international conference, are major weapons of American diplomacy. In addition to the United Nations and its related agencies, the United States is a member of well over two hundred international organizations of various types. The United States joins with the other nations to take care of functions that can be best handled on an international basis. Slowly but inevitably certain functions are being transferred from the national to the international level.

In its own hemisphere the United States is a member of the *Organization of American States,* a regional organization of the nations of North and South America. Under its auspices Inter-American Conferences meet about once every five years, and special conferences meet more frequently to consider special problems. Foreign ministers' meetings convene whenever necessary to consider urgent questions and to consult in cases of threats to the security of the Western Hemisphere. A council forms a continuing group between meetings of conferences and foreign ministers. The famous Pan-American Union serves as a central administrative unit, along with several specialized organizations, including the Inter-American Economic and Social Council and the Inter-American Cultural Council.

The United Nations

The most important international organization is of course the United Nations. It is so important that the United States maintains a permanent diplomatic mission at the United Nations headquarters, headed by a chief of the mission holding the rank of ambassador, and including three other leading diplomats. These diplomats are appointed by the President with the advice and consent of the Senate. In addition, the President with the consent of the Senate appoints five representatives to the General Assembly, who serve for the duration of a particular session. The United States is also represented on the many scores of other parts and divisions of the United Nations. The chief of the mission is responsible for coordinating the actions of our many delegates. Within the Department of State, a separate Bureau of International Organization Affairs coordinates American policies and activities with other federal agencies, helps to prepare instructions to our representatives, serves as technical advisers to them, spreads information to the public and the department regarding the United Nations, and assumes a general responsibility for American participation.

Major United Nations agencies

The United Nations is an organization of *nations* established in order to bring people together to maintain international peace and security, to develop friendly relations, to achieve international cooperation in solving world problems, to promote and encourage respect for human rights, and to be a center for harmonizing the actions of nations in the attainment of these common goals. Although basically an association of nations, the United Nations is an international legal personality with the power to make treaties and competence to claim reparations for injury to its agents. It maintains its own legal staff, operates its own headquarters, and has its own flag. The major United Nations organs are the Security Council, the General Assembly, the Social and Economic Council, the Trusteeship Council, the Secretariat, and the International Court of Justice.

The *Security Council* consists of five permanent members—China, the Soviet Union, France, Great Britain, and the United States—plus six non-permanent members elected by the General Assembly for two-year terms and ineligible for immediate re-election. Its chief function is to preserve and maintain international peace, and it has wide authority to take steps necessary to maintain world security. All the members of the United Nations are pledged by its charter to accept the decisions of the Security Council and to resolve their disputes by peaceful methods.

The Security Council acting in behalf of all member nations carries on discussions, makes investigations and recommendations, and even has enforcement authority. It may call upon nations to apply sanctions including military force. It was originally intended that the several nations would make available in advance stipulated armed forces that the Security Council could use whenever in its judgment they were needed. Disputes between the Soviet bloc and the free nations have made it impossible to carry out these provisions. Nevertheless, nations are pledged to supply the military power that the Security Council requires to secure the peace. The council has, of course, only as much power to enforce its decisions as the nations composing the United Nations are willing to supply.

Each member of the Security Council appoints a representative whose full-time job it is to serve on the Council, which meets in continuous session. Council sessions are dramatic events. The representatives, behind the placards bearing the names of their countries, sit around the now famous curved table. Behind the representatives are their advisers. Under the kleig lights the delegates carry on their debates in five languages. Each month the chairmanship of the Council rotates among the national representatives.

Each member of the Council has one vote. Decisions on *procedural* matters require the approval of *any* seven members. Decisions on *substantive* issues must have the approval of seven nations, but any one of the five permanent members can *veto* the decision. A substantive issue has been defined to include any contemplated action, even as small as calling for a report or hearing a witness. And the veto applies to a vote on the question of whether an issue involves a procedural or a substantive question. When a permanent member *abstains* from voting, however, it is not counted as a veto.

This big-power veto has hit the headlines because of its frequent use by the Soviet Union. Many students of world affairs believe that the veto is only a reflection of the realities of the situation. In the present world of sovereign nations no great power can be induced except by armed might to act contrary to its own wishes on matters it considers essential. With or without the formal power of veto, the Security Council can maintain peace and security only if the big powers cooperate. The veto does, nevertheless, permit a nation to block collective action without expending its resources. The Soviet Union has been able by a veto to stop activities that would not have been worth preventing by force or other diplomatic measures. It was only the Soviet Union's absence from the Security Council that enabled that body to organize United Nations armed forces readily in the face of aggression against the Republic of Korea. At the same time it was the determination of the United States to act that gave substance to the Security Council's decision.

Although the United States originally insisted upon the veto so that we would not be forced to accept decisions that we thought contrary to our national interest, the Soviet use of the veto has caused our government to "re-think" its position. In general, the view of the American government today is that the veto should be retained to prevent the use of force by the council against the wishes of a permanent member, but that it should be abolished as applied to the *procedures* for the settlement of disputes not involving military force.

Despite the Soviet Union's obstreperous tactics, the Council has in its short period of existence demonstrated its usefulness as a diplomatic force. It has had a part in mitigating disputes between Russia and Iran, India and Pakistan, the Netherlands and Indonesia, Israel and the Arab world. The most spectacular move was the decision to use force to stop the aggression of the Communists of North Korea and China. On June 24, 1950, North Korean armies attacked the Republic of Korea, a regime established under United Nations auspices. The United States promptly responded by sending in air and naval forces. On June 25 the Security Council (the Soviet Union was absent) called on the North Koreans to withdraw their invasion forces. On July 7 the Council—the Soviet Union still being absent—made the United States its agent in support of the charter and in directing and organizing United Nations forces in the area. Although the United States furnished the bulk of the troops, over thirty nations supplied men and munitions. For the first time, an international army had been organized under the command of an international organization to maintain the peace and security of the world. The independence of the Korean Republic was maintained and aggression was stopped. Again in 1956-1957, the United Nations furnished a military force to police the Suez Canal.

The *General Assembly* is composed of all the 80 member nations of the United Nations. Each nation has one vote, and not more than five repre-

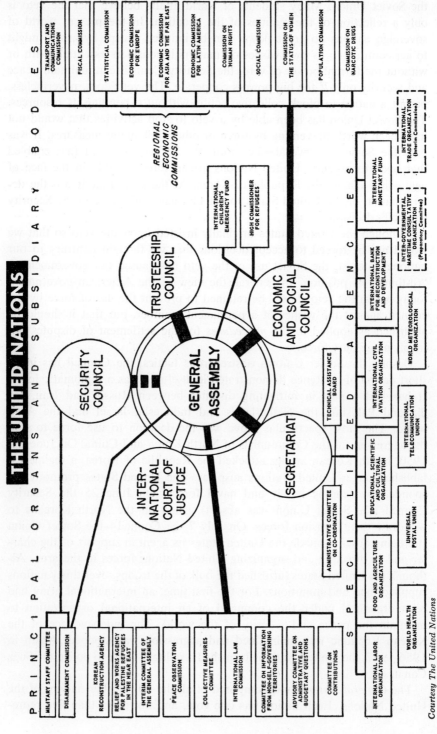

Courtesy The United Nations

sentatives. The Assembly can make investigations and recommendations on any questions except those currently before the Council or matters that are "essentially within the domestic jurisdiction of any state." The latter limitation is easier to state than to define, for the distinction between domestic and foreign affairs is elusive. The Assembly's decisions are only recommendations since enforcement action is a responsibility of the Security Council. But a nation that votes in favor of a General Assembly decision is likely to heed its own recommendation.

Decisions of the Assembly require only a two-thirds vote even on important questions. The conflict between the Soviet Union and the other big powers and the Soviet's use of the veto have forced many issues that the Council has failed to act on to be referred to the General Assembly. The Assembly has taken over some of the Council's functions of maintaining peace and security.

In addition to these deliberative, investigating, and recommending activities, the Assembly has supervisory responsibilities over other organs of the United Nations except for the Security Council and the International Court of Justice. Both the Council and Secretary General make annual reports to the Assembly; the Economic and Social Council and the Trusteeship Council operate under its authority.

The Assembly draws up the budget and apportions United Nations expenses among the members. It elects new member nations and the Secretary General on the recommendations of the Security Council, and shares with the Council the election of judges to the International Court of Justice. By itself it elects the nonpermanent members of the Security Council, all members of the Economic and Social Council, and some of the members of the Trusteeship Council. The Assembly shares with the Council responsibility for proposing amendments to the charter and the authority to call a general conference to review the charter.

The General Assembly meets in regular annual sessions on the third Tuesday in September and such special sessions as are called by the Security Council or by a majority of the members of the United Nations. Each session a president is chosen, generally from the small or middle powers, along with seven vice-presidents. Much of the business is carried on in committees. English, French, Spanish, Chinese, and Russian are the official languages; the first three are "working languages."

The General Assembly, the "town meeting of the world," has, among other things, adopted and presented for national signatures a convention outlawing genocide—"the destruction of national, ethnic, racial, or religious groups"—adopted The Universal Declaration of Human Rights, established a system of relief for Palestinian refugees, provided for the feeding and medical care of nearly five million children, administered a large-scale anti-tuberculosis project, established a program to provide technical assistance to backward nations, and assisted in the settlement of disputes and resistance to aggression. An example of the latter is the General Assembly's action in recommending sanctions against communist China because of its intervention and aggression against the Republic of Korea. The Assembly has also appointed a committee to report in 1957 with recommendations for the time, place, and organization of a conference (which the charter calls for) to review the United Nations Charter and to make recommendations for its alteration in light of the experience of the last decade.

More specialized agencies

The Economic and Social Council is less spectacular than either the Security Council or the General Assembly, but in many ways its work offers the most promise for developing an orderly and peaceful world community. This council consists of eighteen nations elected by the General Assembly. Its job is to promote and coordinate activities designed to provide higher standards of living; solve international economic, social, and health programs; promote international cultural and educational cooperation; and encourage universal respect for and observance of human rights. The council has established fact-finding and consulting commissions through which international conferences are held, draft conventions are prepared, and recommendations are made to the General Assembly.

The Economic and Social Council is the United Nations' point of contact with the specialized agencies that have been established by agreements among most governments. Some of these agencies were established many years before the United Nations was organized, a great many have been created since that time. They include such agencies as the Universal Postal Union, International Labor Organization, Food and Agricultural Organization, World Health Organization, United Nations Educational, Scientific and Cultural Organization. Each of these specialized agencies has its own charter, budget, staff, and the like. In some cases the specialized agencies include representatives from private organizations as well as governmental representatives.

The United Nations Educational, Scientific and Cultural Organization, more generally known as UNESCO, is one of the more active specialized agencies. Composed of 80 member nations, it has the responsibility of promoting peace and security through educational, scientific, and cultural cooperation. "Since wars begin in the minds of men," its preamble states, "it is in the minds of men that the defences of peace must be constructed." UNESCO functions in member nations through national commissions. The United States National Commission for UNESCO consists of one hundred members representing various types of private organizations, local, state, and federal officials. The National Commission advises our delegation to the UNESCO General Conference and sponsors projects designed to advance mutual knowledge, diffuse information, and increase popular education.

UNESCO and the other specialized agencies of the United Nations are getting people of various nations together in order to do needed jobs and in so doing are helping to build a sense of community among the peoples of the world. As more and more functions are taken over by the international community, the people of the world will have concrete evidence that it is one world, that economic prosperity of one nation is tied to the prosperity of other nations, and that the health and security of the people of the world cannot be adequately protected by any single nation but require international cooperation.

The *Trusteeship Council* of the United Nations supervises the administration of territories held by nations in trust for the people who live in the territories until they "become of age" and can govern themselves. The council, composed of six trustee and six nontrustee nations, is responsible to the General Assembly for general supervision of colonial powers to insure that they meet their charter obligations to the 200 million people living in territories that are not fully self-governing.

The *Secretariat,* administered by the Secretary General, provides an international civil service to staff and operate the United Nations agencies. The Secretary General, however, is more than the director of this civil service; as the chief administrative officer of the United Nations, he is the only person who stands for the United Nations as a whole, and he has certain political responsibilities. Authorized to bring to the Security Council's attention any matter that in his opinion may threaten peace, he can direct world attention to world issues. The Security Council, meeting in private session, recommends the candidate for the Secretary-Generalship to the General Assembly. The appointment of a candidate requires only a majority vote of the nations present in the Assembly. The charter itself specifies no term of office, but the General Assembly has made five years the normal term. The Secretary General appoints the staff under regulations prescribed by the Assembly. Members of the staff retain their citizenship, but they are prohibited from seeking instructions from any government since they function as an international civil service.

The *International Court of Justice* is the United Nations' judicial branch. It provides a judicial forum for the settlement of disputes between *nations.* It has jurisdiction over disputes only when the parties to the case give their consent. Some 34 states have signed the optional clause, and have thus agreed in advance to submit to the court certain types of legal disputes. The court (unlike the United States Supreme Court) also renders advisory opinions when so requested by the General Assembly or the Security Council. The court is composed of fifteen judges who have a term of nine years, no more than two of the judges being of the same state.

The United Nations' failure to solve each and every dispute among the nations of the world and its inability to resolve the conflict between the East and West, have caused some Americans to become disillusioned. Part of their disillusionment stems from their failure to understand the nature of the organization. The United Nations is essentially the collective name of some 80 nations that have organized themselves in order to facilitate co-operation. It is a diplomatic technique that simplifies the problem of multi-lateral consultation. The United Nations, unlike the United States of America, is not an entity separate and above its member states. Its power is the power of the nations of the world. What the United Nations can do is what the member nations want to do.

The United Nations is a useful organization for diplomatic consultation. It provides techniques and machinery for discussion, for working out joint plans of action, and for establishing international organizations to perform functions. As such it has been a useful device by which the United States has been able to carry on its relations with the other nations of the world. But the United Nations, like every other agency of international politics, is affected by the fact that the world is divided into separate national sovereignties.

AT 8:15 ON THE MORNING OF AUGUST 6, 1945, A bomb fell on the city of Hiroshima. At this moment there were 340,000 people living there. One minute later only 280,000 were left alive; and of these 31,000 more were to die because of the bomb. A total of 91,000 men, women, and children were killed by this single bomb; tens of thousands more were injured and maimed. This was a small bomb. Two days later an "improved model" was dropped on Nagasaki.

Seven years later in the Central Pacific, a deserted island was destroyed by a fusion type—the hydrogen—bomb. Spectacular as the reports were, seven years of living with atomic weapons had exhausted the supply of superlatives, and many thought that the fusion bomb introduced nothing new except a larger area of death. But as one expert on military policy and new weapons reports, "That unfortunately is not the case."[1] The hydrogen bomb with its associated fallout and radiation added a dimension of destruction to atomic weapons as great as these weapons had added to more conventional techniques. Moreover, intercontinental bombers to carry these fusion bombs are an actuality, and intercontinental missiles are an immediate probability.

We live in a world in which literally hundreds of millions could be killed in a single night.[2] Winston Churchill has warned that it may no longer be possible "for nations to fight each other and survive as nations, or even for armies to fight a battle and have at the end of it enough men on either side to fight another."[3] The age of absolute weapons has arrived.

To some, the fact that men are able to destroy their fellow-men by the millions brings hope that they will be wise enough to forego such a foolish venture. To others, it means

24 ★

To provide for

the common

defense

[1] Bernard Brodie, "Strategy Hits a Dead End," *Harpers,* Vol. 211, No. 1265, October 1955, p. 34.

[2] See testimony of Lt. Gen. James M. Gavin, Chief of Research and Development, Department of the Army, before Subcommittee on Air Force of Senate Committee on Military Affairs, May 25, 1956 reported in *The New York Times,* June 29, 1956.

[3] Paraphrase of Churchill by Roger Hilsman, *Military Policy and National Security,* ed. William W. Kaufman (Princeton: Princeton University Press, 1956), p. 44.

that modern civilization is doomed. But whether we are optimistic or not, all agree that the United States must pay a high price to maintain its security in the days of absolute weapons.

War and peace are no longer separate and exclusive categories. The United States must maintain powerful combat forces in peace as well as in war. We are vulnerable to attack; our traditional allies have declined in strength; the European balance-of-power system has been destroyed; our cushion of distance and time has been reduced; and powerful and resourceful nations threaten our vital interests. If an all-out thermonuclear war should come, it would be too late to begin to build up military strength. Ten years ago Dwight D. Eisenhower said, "What we are able or not able to do within the first sixty days of another war will be decisive in its determination of our ability to carry the war to a successful conclusion."[4] Developments of the last decade make it likely that a full-scale war would not last even sixty days.

Not only is a powerful United States essential if we are to win a war; it is essential to avoid such a war. As John Jay wrote in *Federalist No. 4,* the best possible state of defense "instead of inviting war, will tend to repress and discourage it." Americans were slow to learn this lesson. During the 1930's the United States and other democracies disarmed while the aggressor grew powerful. Even after World War II the United States and its friends began to disband the powerful military forces that had been slowly and laboriously organized to fight the fascist aggressors.

Within a short time, however, the hostile intentions of the Soviet Union became clear. By our weakness we encouraged aggression. Gradually the free nations began to realize that under conditions of international anarchy, only by remaining strong and being prepared for war could they hope to maintain peace. Although the leaders of the Soviet Union have used every method—propaganda, economic coercion, military pressure—to expand their powers, they have shown no disposition to commit suicide. By making it clear that they have nothing to gain and everything to lose by starting a war, we hope to avoid that war.

Military power includes more than combat forces. The armed services are, in both peace and war, but the striking edge of the nation's military strength. Behind the soldier stands a complex organization of men, materials, tools, and knowledge. American power includes both its armed forces and its industrial, scientific, agricultural, and organizational resources. But security for the United States cannot be conceived solely in military terms. "The best defense we can have is not to have any war at all." To defend American interests without war is the task of the makers of foreign policy. Even in strictly defense terms, the security program must include many activities outside the sphere of the soldier's competence. The maintenance of

---

[4] *Final Report of the Chief of Staff, United States Army, to the Secretary of the Army,* February 7, 1948.

a strong stable economy, the stockpiling of essential materials, preparation of civilian defense, accurate intelligence services—these are all civilian-directed defense programs.

What are the minimum elements of a defense program? First, foreign policies that will make war as unlikely as possible. Second, military power of the United States and its friends, built to such proportions that any potential aggressor will think, not twice, but many times before attacking the United States or its allies. This military power must be *in being,* with forces that at a moment's notice can strike a retaliatory knock-out blow at the enemy's homeland. But we also require forces equipped to achieve limited objectives in situations where it would be suicidal to use major nuclear weapons and start a holocaust. Finally, we must make preparations for the increased mobilization of our resources if it becomes necessary.

The national government has ample constitutional authority to provide for the common defense. It is limited by the Constitution in war, cold or hot, as well as in peace; but there is little, if anything, that the government cannot do if necessary to protect the country against external danger. The problem of security is not one of constitutional power. It is one of foresight, resources, and organization.

FRIENDS AND NEIGHBORS

The power that the United States can bring to bear includes that of other nations whose security is inextricably interwoven with its own. During World Wars I and II France and England were powerful enough to give the United States two to three years to build up its own strength. The situation is now reversed. American aid is needed to build up the defenses of western Europe.

Over 300 million intelligent and well-trained people make up our western European allies. They produce over 65 million tons of steel, they operate the second strongest navy in the world; they have bases, plants, airports, and a great military and industrial potential. Unless defended, however, this great potential could in the early stages of the next war fall under the control of the communist world. Moreover, the United States would lose military bases needed to carry the fighting to the enemy.

One of the most important links in the American defense effort is the North Atlantic Treaty among the United States, Canada, United Kingdom, France, Italy, Belgium, Denmark, Iceland, Luxembourg, Netherlands, Norway, Portugal, Greece, Turkey, and West Germany. Under the terms of this treaty these nations have agreed "by means of continuous and effective self-help and mutual aid" to develop their own capacities to resist armed attack. Each nation has pledged itself to regard an attack upon one or more of them

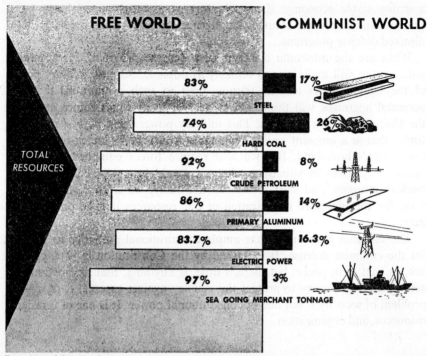

From *Mutual Security Agency*

as an attack upon all, and to take such action as may be considered necessary to maintain the security of the North Atlantic area.

The North Atlantic Treaty is more than a scrap of paper.[5] A permanent
defense organization has been established to give it real meaning. A North
Atlantic Council composed of top cabinet officers—foreign, defense, and
financial ministers—meets intermittently, and a board of permanent representatives works continuously in Paris on long-range strategical matters.
There is also an International Staff under the direction of a Secretary-Gen-
eral who serves as vice-chairman of the council. The staff provides technical
services, prepares reports, and insures that the council's decisions are carried
out. A Military Committee of the top military leaders meets frequently, and
there is a permanent group of military men, the Standing Group, located
in Washington, in which France, the United Kingdom, and the United
States are represented, as well as regional military committees. Financial,
economic, and military production committees round out the North Atlantic
Treaty Organization, popularly known as NATO.

NATO has at its disposal several military commands, of which the best
known is The Supreme Headquarters, Allied Powers, Europe (SHAPE)
under the direction of an American commander. Although the United States

[5] Department of State Publication 4630, *North Atlantic Treaty Organization, Its
Development and Significance,* 1952.

is not required by the terms of the treaty to provide military assistance, it has taken the lead in supplying troops and munitions for NATO forces. In addition, the United States furnishes machines, tools, and technical assistance to its allies in order to increase their ability to contribute to mutual defense.

The Southeast Asia Treaty Organization, popularly known as SEATO, forms another link in the American defense system. The United States, France, United Kingdom, Australia, New Zealand, Philippines, Pakistan, and Thailand have pledged to consider as a threat to their own security communist aggression against any of these nations or against Cambodia, Laos, or South Viet Nam and to meet the common danger in accord with their own constitutional processes. In case of nonmilitary aggression or attacks by noncommunist nations, these nations have agreed to consult about common action. Bangkok, Thailand is the permanent headquarters of SEATO where each nation maintains a permanent representative. The council, composed of foreign ministers, is the governing body and meets from time to time. SEATO has largely absorbed the ANZUS treaty among Australia, New Zealand, and the United States.

The United States also is joined with its southern neighbors through the Rio Pact (The Inter-American Treaty of Reciprocal Assistance) in a multilateral treaty of mutual help. To the north, the United States has a defensive alliance with Canada that predates World War II and recognizes that the two countries are a strategic entity. We also have bilateral agreements of mutual defense and assistance with Nationalist China, Korea, Japan, and the Philippines.

POLITICIANS, BUREAUCRATS, AND SOLDIERS— ORGANIZATION FOR NATIONAL SECURITY

President and Congress both have powers and duties to provide for the common defense. Congress appropriates the money and makes the rules and regulations for the governance of the armed forces. Congress determines the general organizational structure of our defense establishment as well as the size and organization of the fighting forces. It does this chiefly through its military affairs and appropriations committees where the plans and programs of the soldiers and their civilian superiors are scrutinized.[6] Congress controls the purse; the President directs the sword. As chief executive, commander in chief of the armed services, and director of our foreign relations, he joins with Congress in determining the basic security policy and he supervises its execution. Congress declares war; the President directs it.

Every branch of the government has defense responsibilities, but those with special security duties are the Department of State, the Department of

[6] Elias Huzar, *The Purse and the Sword* (Ithaca: Cornell University Press, 1950).

Defense, the Joint Chiefs of Staff, the Office of Defense Mobilization, the Atomic Energy Commission, Federal Civil Defense Administration, Selective Service System, and the National Security Council. With the help of these advisers, the President and Congress must decide some tough questions. What portion of our resources should be allocated for security purposes? How should these resources be divided between military and non-military security programs? How much of the military portion should be divided between combat power in being and combat power for tomorrow? How large should the armed forces be, where and when shall they be used, how shall they be organized?

All the plans and activities of the various departments must be brought together to produce unified policies. Strategic plans must be integrated with political policy and scientific developments. Plans and programs for industrial mobilization must be unified with military policies. This is the re-

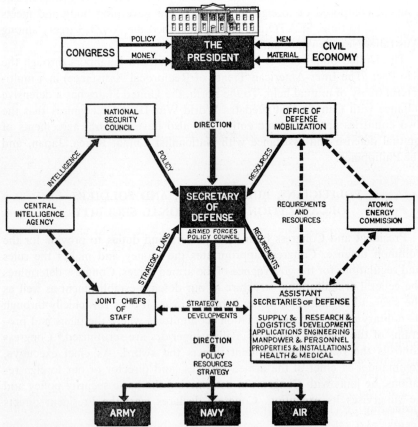

Source: Department of Defense.

Based on chart from Dixon and Plischke, American Government—Basic Documents and Materials (New York: D. Van Nostrand Co., Inc., 1950)

Relations among national security agencies.

sponsibility of the National Security Council. It is here that the military get the architectural plans of our foreign policy, and that the military tell the architects how much it is going to cost. But the day-by-day work of developing and executing our military policy is the job of the Department of Defense.

Pentagonia

The world's largest office building, the famed Pentagon, is the head-quarters of the United States Defense Department, a holding company for the Departments of Army, Navy, and Air Force. At work here are 21,000 civilians and 10,000 soldiers. Over 170 security officers prowl the corridors to guard the restricted areas in which the nation's war plans are made. In the vast building is the communications center where constant communication is maintained with armed forces throughout the world.

Prior to 1947 there were two military executive departments, War and Navy. Lack of coordination between the Army and Navy had disastrous consequences at Pearl Harbor and elsewhere. During World War II the Army and Navy combat forces were united under single field commanders, but they were separately administered from Washington. The War Department and the Navy Department procured their own materials. They often built duplicating facilities and competed with each other for manpower and materials.

At the end of the war, attempts were made to unify the two departments. Navy men held out, however, because of the fear that if combined with the Army they would come under the control of generals who would not give the Navy due consideration. In 1947 a compromise was negotiated between the two departments. The Air Force, already an autonomous unit within the War Department, was made an independent branch, and the three military departments—Army, Navy, Air Force—were placed under the "general supervision" of a Defense Secretary, the President's agent. Each department, however, retained most of its authority.

Soon it became obvious that though the organization charts indicated one department, in reality there were three. The Defense Secretary had neither the authority nor the assistance to direct the three military departments. The Hoover Commission and other groups assigned to study the problem recommended that the position of the Defense Secretary be strengthened. Important changes were made in 1949 by legislation and in 1953 by executive order. The Defense Secretary was given direct supervision over the three services. Integrating research and development, coordinating procurement, translating strategic plans into industrial requirements, and other over-all departmental activities were transferred from boards within the department to the Secretary of Defense. In addition he was given a number of special assistants and assistant secretaries to help him carry out his responsibilities.

Each of the three military departments still exists as a separate organization with its own civilian secretary, undersecretary, assistant secretaries, and military chief of staff. Although only the Defense Secretary has cabinet rank and only he alone normally sits with the Cabinet and National Security Council, the civilian secretary and military heads of each service have access to congressional ears. The extent to which the Defense Secretary can control the three departments still depends in large part upon his influence with the President and Congress.

Key military agencies

The *Armed Forces Policy Council* is the department's "little cabinet." It is composed of the Secretary, Deputy Secretary, the three civilian secretaries of the military departments, the Chairman of the Joint Chiefs of Staff, and the chief of staff of each of the services. It advises the Secretary on matters of broad policy. The *Joint Secretaries* is another advisory group composed of the civilian heads of the military departments.

The *Joint Chiefs of Staff* serve as the principal military advisers to the President, the National Security Council, and the Secretary of Defense. They comprise the military heads of the three armed services, the Commandant of the Marine Corps—whenever a matter comes up directly concerning the Marine Corps—and a Chairman, all appointed by the President with consent of the Senate for a two-year term eligible in peacetime for only one reappointment. Behind double steel doors in the Pentagon the Joint Chiefs shape strategic plans, prepare joint supply programs, review major supply and personnel requirements, formulate programs for joint training, make recommendations to the Secretary of Defense with respect to the establishment of unified commands in strategic areas, and provide American representation on the military commissions of the United Nations and on the North Atlantic and South East Asia Treaty Organizations.

The Chairman of the Joint Chiefs takes precedence over all other military officers. He presides over the meetings but does not have a vote. He prepares the agenda, directs the Joint Staff, and informs the Secretary of Defense and the President of the issues on which the Joint Chiefs have been unable to reach agreement.

The Joint Chiefs of Staff are the pivot on which unification turns. Although progress has been made, a first Hoover Commission Task Force charged that the individual chiefs were "influenced far too much by considerations of service particularism and aggrandizement" and had "failed sufficiently to recognize and accept their responsibilities as an integrating agency of national policy."[7] And Defense Secretary Lovett wrote to the President upon his resignation that it was difficult for the Joint Chiefs to

[7] Commission on the Executive Branch of the Government, *Task Force Report on National Security Organization* (Washington, D.C.: Government Printing Office, 1949), p. 66.

achieve a nonservice point of view because "they wear two hats—one as chief of an armed service and the other as a member of the Joint Chiefs. It was difficult," he continued, "for them to detach themselves from the hopes and ambitions of their own service without having their own staff feel that they were being let down by the chief."

There is more to the disputes among the military services than mere personality clashes or jealousy. Basic differences exist over military policy (see pages 630-633). There are differences growing out of the rapid technological developments that have rendered obsolete existing concepts of the role of the several services. For example, the Army believes that guided missiles are an extension of artillery, the Air Force considers them a new kind of airplane. And both question the need for "super" aircraft carriers—which the Navy thinks indispensable.

Conflicts among the military men have raised problems about the relations between soliders and their civilian superiors, the White House and Congress. The President is commander in chief, but Congress provides the men and the money. Most Presidents have taken the view that after policy has received presidential approval, it is the duty of all military men to support it before Congress and the country, irrespective of their own judgment. But Congressmen want to know what the professionals think, and it has been difficult for military commanders who are worried about the nation's safety to remain silent. The disagreements are usually brought before the nation, sometimes indirectly by the prevalent Washington practice of "leaking" the information to reporters.[8]

Conflicts among the Joint Chiefs have led some to advocate their replacement by a single Chief of Staff to initiate and terminate discussion and make over-all strategic plans. This suggestion has been advocated, for example, by Army spokesmen, the strongest supporters of unification. The first Hoover Commission studied the question, and though there were strong dissents, a majority of the commissioners rejected the idea of a single chief on the grounds that "in the broad field of grand strategy a meeting of several minds is far safer—and in the end more sound—than the dictates of one."[9] The commission merely recommended the creation of a chairman, and this recommendation was adopted. The chairman's authority has gradually been increased, but interservice disputes have not stopped or been silenced, and support for the single chief of staff idea has been growing.

Other war agencies

Outside the Defense Department, other agencies are also concerned with military matters. One of the most important is the *Atomic Energy Commission*. The implications of atomic energy are so far-reaching that Congress

[8] See summary of various views by Edward L. Katzenbach, "Should Our Military Leaders Speak Up?" *The New York Times Magazine*, April 15, 1956.

[9] See *Task Force Report*, p. 58.

decided it would be unwise to place control over atomic weapons in the hands of a military department. Instead authority was given to this commission, composed of five men appointed by the President with the consent of the Senate. The commission builds atomic and hydrogen bombs, stockpiles them, and turns them over to the armed services on orders from the President. The military aspect of the commission's work is coordinated with the Defense Department by a Military Liaison Committee, normally presided over by an Assistant to the Secretary of Defense.

Another agency with important security obligations is the *Office of Defense Mobilization*. This agency, located in the Executive Office of the President, is responsible for mobilization efforts including both current defense activities and preparations for any further emergencies. Its Director has been made a member of the National Security Council so that industrial mobilization plans may be integrated with military and foreign policies. The Office of Defense Mobilization makes recommendations for the coordination of military and civilian resources for war, for programs to keep in balance the relationship between potential requirements for manpower, resources, and facilities and potential supplies of these commodities, for stabilizing the economy, and for policies insuring adequate reserves of strategic materials. It coordinates the work of the other departments that have defense production responsibilities. The Director is advised by a Defense Mobilization Board, consisting of heads of executive departments who have mobilization responsibilities.

These agencies along with the *Federal Civil Defense Administration* (see page 646) and the *Selective Service System* (see page 634) form the basic organization for national defense. But the organizational structure is only the bare skeleton of a national defense program. To provide for the common defense requires action on many fronts and involves many areas.

MILITARY POLICY IN THE NUCLEAR AGE

Supersonic aircraft, guided missiles, nuclear weapons, and the other new weapons systems have poured out of scientists' laboratories and the

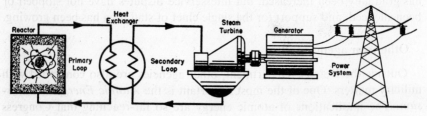

Courtesy Westinghouse

How an atomic power plant works: hot, radioactive water from reactor heats nonradioactive water into steam for the turbine.

engineers' workshops during the past decade. These weapons have forced the military men and the nation to reconsider our military policy. More is involved, of course, than military policy itself. The kind of fighting forces we have conditions foreign policy—and vice versa.

During the first years of the Atomic Age no basic changes in traditional military programs seemed to be called for. The United States had an atomic monopoly that seemed to reinforce our traditional policy of not having large standing armies. American superiority in atomic weapons and airpower appeared to deter the Soviet Union. Even after the Soviet Union exploded its first atomic bomb, the situation was not seriously altered. Our technological superiority, it was believed, would keep us ahead, and our overseas bases could rain down hundreds of bombs on the Soviets in the event of attack. At the same time, our defense system would reduce the enemy's ability to deliver these expensive weapons to American targets. Although wars would be terribly costly, it was then still possible to talk about "winning" such wars.

Then came the development of the hydrogen bomb, the intercontinental bomber, and the realization that Soviet technology could give the Russians a generous supply of nuclear weapons. The result was the "evaporation of the myth of scarcity." Since the enemy had sufficient power to destroy us, superior power to obliterate him provided little comfort to Americans. It has gradually become clear that air-atomic power provides weapons that cannot be used except under extreme provocation and—we hope—the rarest circumstances.

What military strategy for America?

These conditions have given rise to serious and important problems of military policy. All agree that a strong air-atomic arm capable of delivering a knock-out punch is central to our policy of deterring the Soviets from starting a major war. It would be dangerous to relax even after massing sufficient power to destroy the enemy, for he might achieve a technological breakthrough that would give him a temporary advantage, such as a system to stop intercontinental missiles or to reduce the dangers of radiation. But should we continue to devote the lion's share of our resources to air-nuclear weapons of mass destruction? Or should we allocate more materials to development and maintenance of conventional and selective-nuclear weapons? Do we need to maintain large standing armies, or can we achieve our objectives with primary reliance on airpower?

Army spokesmen, as well as others, have been critical of the tendency to place so much emphasis on air-atomic power. They contend that the desire to balance the national government's budget by reducing the Army and relying on relatively less expensive airpower has left us dangerously exposed to localized aggressions. Neither the United States nor the Soviet Union, they argue, is likely to start a thermonuclear war of mass destruction, since such a war would lead to their own destruction. Such a war is "morally, politically and practically unjustifiable."[10] At the same time, it is said, to rely only on nuclear weapons might even increase the chances of such a war. If the Soviet Union is led to believe that these are our only weapons and that we will use them, the Russians may be tempted to shoot first. Even more likely, leaders of the Soviet Union know that the United States will not let loose a catastrophic conflict merely to prevent localized aggressions such as Korea, Indo-China, or the Middle East. The risk of unleashing an all-out war would be too great, and it would bring down on the United States the disapproval of the entire world. Nor, according to this view, is air-atomic power suitable to stop Soviet conquest of Western Europe because its use would also destroy our allies. Hence, the Army and others argue, we must divide our resources and spend more on forces that can be used restrictively in order to prevent the Communists from nibbling at the edges of the free world.

Air Force spokesmen and some Navy men, on the other hand, argue that at the present time it would be dangerous to slow down the build-up of our air-atomic weapons. They argue that we have not as yet achieved decisive superiority; and unless we do, the Soviet Union will be tempted, despite the risks, to take advantage of any superiority it might gain. Some spokesmen for airpower—but not necessarily for the Air Force—argue that mass armies are obsolete, that airpower can be used for limited conflicts, and that by concentrating on airpower we will be able to get more defense for less money—"More bang for the buck," as this policy is sometimes popularly known. They believe it is foolish to commit our forces to peripheral small scale wars—"brushfires"—and that we need have only the ability to retaliate massively if the enemy starts trouble. Here is a good example of how military and foreign policy are interrelated. Dependence on a policy of massive retaliation, for example, places less emphasis on allies than if we have standing armies able to resist invasion of friendly nations without resorting to mass destruction.

Differences among military leaders are not, it should be stressed, of the "either-or" kind, but differences of emphasis and priorities. However they are resolved, the nation has to be prepared to fight all kinds of wars—limited, middle-size attrition, and all-out nuclear-mass destruction. Our combat forces have three missions for which they must be immediately ready: (1) to deliver massive power on the enemy home, primarily to deter him from starting such a war, but to "win" it if possible; (2) to serve as an instrument of foreign policy to resist local aggression such as in Korea,

[10] Army Staff Paper, *The New York Times*, June 24, 1956, Section 1, p. 46. See also Army Staff Paper discussed in *The New York Times*, July 15, 1956, Section 1, pp. 1, 22, and General Matthew B. Ridgeway, *Soldier* (New York: Harper & Brothers, 1956), pp. 295-361.

Berlin, and Formosa; (3) to serve as the first line of defense to give the nation time, if needed, to mobilize more of its resources and manpower.

The first line of defense

A large force ready for action is the first element in a security program. But the standing force can be too large as well as too small. There is no such thing as complete military security. Resources of materials and manpower are limited; to support a combat force of eleven or twelve million men for a long time might create such a drain on our resources that the whole economy would be weakened. It would interfere with other programs also essential to security. Furthermore, it would be politically difficult to secure public support for such a program. The problem is to maintain a first line of defense for an indefinite period at a steady level and "guard against the tendency to let defenses sink or rise depending upon each breeze that blows from the Kremlin." As General Marshall said, "We must keep a durable layer of military protection that would survive the alternate moods of public alarm or complacency."

The first line of defense consists of the Regular Army, the United States Navy, the Marine Corps, the United States Air Force, and the Coast Guard.

The United States Air Force, like the other services, has both offensive and defensive responsibilities. Its primary strategic mission is to be ready on a few hours' notice to strike a retaliatory blow at the enemy. This is the job of the Strategic Air Command which recently has received the most financial support. The Air Defense Command is charged with providing the air defense of the United States. The Air Force, through the Tactical Air Command, also provides tactical air support to our ground and naval forces.

The Army has to be prepared to defend the United States and our overseas allies, seize and hold bases, and invade enemy territory. It has the primary responsibility for all land operations, including airborne attack and antiaircraft activity. Army divisions are now deployed in Germany, Japan, and the Philippines as well as in the United States.

The Navy's mission is to be instantly ready to seek out and destroy enemy naval forces and to gain control of the seas, including the air above and water below. The Coast Guard, which during time of peace is under the jurisdiction of the Treasury Department, becomes part of the Navy in an emergency. Also a part of the Navy, but a complete unit in itself, is the Marine Corps, which holds itself in its traditional state of readiness to be deployed where needed from the "halls of Montezuma to the shores of Tripoli."

The core of these services consists largely of career soldiers. The officers are drawn from several sources, including the military academies. In addition some honor graduates of the Reserve Officer Training Corps programs are given regular commissions. Until recently most of the enlisted

personnel were secured through voluntary enlistments. Pay and other benefits have been made more attractive, and the number of enlistments has
increased, but the demand for soldiers and sailors has grown even more.
Reluctantly the United States has turned to the drafting of men to fill out
the ranks. Draftees are not career soldiers, but during their period of service they become part of our first line of defense and are trained and
equipped to be ready for battle.

Congress establishes the top limits to the size of the armed forces, authorizes the drafting of men, and sets the broad standards to be used in
selecting those for military duty. The actual administration of the selective
service program is a joint function of federal, state, and local governments.
The *Director of the Selective Service System,* operating directly under the
President, sets broad policies. In each state the President appoints, upon
the recommendation of the governor, a director of selective service, who
coordinates the activities of the local draft boards, of which there is with
few exceptions at least one for each county. The local draft boards consist
of three or more civilian residents of the county, and they are responsible
for registration, examination, classification, selection, and delivery of men
to the armed forces for induction. The local boards' decisions are subject
to review by appeal boards established at the state and national level.

The Selective Service System, in addition to providing men for the
peacetime fighting forces, stands by, ready in an emergency to step up the
pace. It classifies registrants, keeps records, and maintains the machinery
so that precious time will not be lost in the event of war.

Second line of defense

In the event of full-scale hostilities or a national emergency, larger military forces would be needed than could be furnished by the regulars. In
the past, primary reliance was placed on a small standing force that would
be joined in an emergency by all able-bodied men. A century and a half ago
the sturdy farmer could be called to take his musket from above the fire-
place and rush to the battlefield. Today, however, the armed forces are a
complex organization of trained specialists. It takes many months, even
years, to train a man to serve with the modern fighting machine. A stout
heart and a straight-shooting gun are not enough. The time lag between the
decision to create a large military organization and its actual existence as
a fighting unit can be fatal.

Today, standing behind the combat forces is a second line of defense, the
Ready Reserves, consisting of the National Guard—Air Force and Army—
and the Army, Navy, Air Force, and Coast Guard Reserves. During the
next several years, the Ready Reserves are to be built up to a force of
2,900,000 men, one million of whom the President is authorized to call
into active duty in the event of an emergency. And it would not take Congress long to authorize the calling of the others. These men engage in

weekly drills and attend summer camp so that they will be ready with a minimum of additional training.

In the immediate future, all able-bodied men between 18 and 26 (in some cases 35) will be required to serve some time in the Reserves in addition to their active service. Draftees who serve two years on active service, for example, are now obligated to spend four more years in the Ready Reserves. The President is also authorized to permit direct enlistments in the Reserves, and men between 17 and 18½ may enlist in the Reserve, spend only six months on active duty, and complete the enlistment during evenings and summers. The Reserve Officer Training Corps programs of the land grant colleges and other participating universities furnish many of the Reserves' officers. Graduates of these programs receive commissions and, after a period of active duty, keep themselves prepared by weekly and summer duty.

How does a young man today meet his military obligations? At 18 he must register with his local draft board; from 18½ to 26 he is liable for military service; and from age 26 to 35 he is liable if previously deferred for any reason. For example, a person granted deferment as a college student extends his draft liability to age 35. Ways of fulfilling the military obligation are listed in terms of age brackets at the bottom of page 636.

An important component of the Ready Reserves is the National Guard, composed of the organized militias of the several states. Except when called into federal service the Guard is under the command of the governors of the respective states. The governors commission the officers, and through their adjutant generals supervise the training of the militias. The national government, however, provides most of the money for their training and equipment, and has established minimum standards.

A state-controlled militia is an established tradition. In fact, in 1787 it was considered so necessary that the states insisted upon the adoption of the Second Amendment that prohibits the national government from depriving the states of the right to maintain their own militias. During the War of 1812 some states would not even let their militias be used outside their own boundaries. Today, however, the national government exercises far-reaching supervision over the Guard. Congress has the authority to call the National Guard of any or all states into federal service, and it has given the President power to call the Guard into immediate federal service. Once this is done, the Guard becomes an integral part of the national fighting forces subject only to such limitations as Congress may impose.

The chief purpose of the Guard today is to provide a trained reserve for the national military forces. Its service to the states is less important. The state police have taken over many of its duties. For this reason and because the states have not always done a good job in training the Guard, it has been suggested that it be "federalized" and combined with the organized reserves to provide one reserve unit as an integral part of the federal defense establishment. Such a proposal was tentatively put forth by the Defense Department, but it drew little support and much opposition.

Behind the Ready Reserves are the Standby Reserves. The Standby Reserves, however, are merely a pool of men who have completed their military duty—active and reserve—and who are not liable for any further service except during time of war or an emergency of such proportions that it cannot be handled by the Regulars and Ready Reserves.

Such, then, are the fighting forces of the United States. A large combat force, a second line of defense of trained reserves, and finally a backlog of all able-bodied men to be called in case of war. But no matter how large our armed forces, they are useless unless equipped. And it is the equipment of these men that makes the United States the strongest military nation in the world. For in terms of numbers of fighting men, the United States can

---

FROM AGE 17 to 18½

• Enlist in Reserve for 8 years; serve 6 months on active duty for training, then be deferred from the draft, assuming you satisfactorily complete 7½ years in the Reserve. [Weekly drills, 15-day maneuvers annually.] Or —

• Enlist in the National Guard; be deferred from the draft as long as you drill in an organized unit, with draft liability ending at age 28. Period of liability can be reduced to 8 years if you take at least 3 consecutive months of active duty for training.

FROM AGE 17 to 26

• Volunteer for induction for 2 years of active duty followed by 4 years in Reserve. [Apply to your draft board in this case.] Or —

• Enlist in the Army or Marine Corps for 3 or more years, or in the Navy, Coast Guard, or Air Force for 4 or more years, serving remainder of 6 years' liability in Reserve. Or —

• Enlist in Reserve for 6 years, including 2 years of active duty.

FROM AGE 18 to 28

• Get a commission, by successfully completing a college officers' training program such as ROTC; then, after college, enter on active duty as an officer for 2 or more years, and serve the remainder of a 6-year obligation in Reserve; if not needed on active duty, undergo 6 months of active duty for training and serve the remainder of an 8-year obligation in Reserve.

FROM AGE 18½ to 26 (or to age 35 if once deferred)

• Enlist [before age 26] in Army for 2 years of active duty, then serve 4 years in Reserve. Or —

• Wait for the draft; if inducted, serve 2 years on active duty followed by 4 years in Reserve. Men inducted after age 26 have no Reserve obligation. Or —

• Enlist in Reserve for 8 years, if approved by Selective Service as critically skilled and employed in defense-supporting industry or research; then serve 6 months on active duty and 7½ years in Reserve. [Apply to your draft board for this—a mathematics teacher might qualify, for example.]

---

never compete with the Soviet Union. Our policy is to match quality against quantity by equipping our fighting forces with the most modern weapons of war. For these weapons, the United States depends upon its vast resources, industrial and scientific.

FOUNDATIONS OF MILITARY POWER

To support a large standing force and to be prepared to expand it enormously takes manpower, resources, facilities, knowledge, and organiza-

---

★ THESE CHOICES ARE OPEN TO DRAFT-AGE YOUTHS ★

★ **DRAFT —**
2 years' active duty, 4 years' Reserve

★ **ENLISTMENT —**
6-year obligation, active and Reserve
Army: 2 to 5 years' active duty, remainder Reserve
Navy and Air Force: 6 years on active duty, no Reserve; or 4 years on active duty, 2 years in Reserve
Marines: 3 or 4 years on active duty, remainder in Reserve
Coast Guard: 4 years on active duty, 2 years in Reserve

★ **NATIONAL GUARD, ARMY AND AIR —**
6 consecutive months on active duty, 7 1/2 years in National Guard; or no active duty, remain in National Guard to age 28

★ **OFFICER CANDIDATE PROGRAM, NAVAL AVIATION —**
3 years' active duty, 3 years' Reserve

★ **SIX-MONTH DUTY PLAN, ARMY AND MARINES —**
6 months' active duty, 7 1/2 years' Reserve

★ **ROTC, ARMY —**
2 years on active duty, 4 years in Reserve; or, 6 months on active duty, 7 1/2 years in Reserve

★ **ROTC, AIR FORCE AND NAVY (REGULAR) —**
3 years' active duty, 3 years' Reserve

★ **ROTC, NAVY (CONTRACT) —**
2 years' active duty, 4 years' Reserve

★ **ENLISTED RESERVE, ARMY, NAVY, AIR FORCE, MARINES AND COAST GUARD —**
2 years' active duty, 4 years' Reserve

★ **RESERVE OFFICER CANDIDATE PROGRAM, NAVY —**
2 years' active duty, 4 years' Reserve

★ **AVIATION CADET PROGRAMS —**
Navy: 4 years of active duty, 2 years in Reserve
Air Force: 3 years of active duty, 3 years in Reserve

★ **MARINE CORPS PLATOON LEADERS CLASS —**
2 years' active duty, 4 years' Reserve

★ **OFFICER CANDIDATE SCHOOL (FOR SELECTED ENLISTED MEN) —**
Army: 2 years of active duty, 4 years in Reserve
Navy and Marine Corps: 2 years of active duty, 4 years in Reserve; or, no active duty, continue Reserve training to age 35
Coast Guard: 3 years of active duty, 3 years in Reserve

★ **ACADEMIES (SERVICE AFTER GRADUATION) —**
Military (West Point): 3 years of active duty, 3 years in Reserve
Naval (Annapolis): 4 years of active duty, 2 years in Reserve
Air Force (Colorado Springs): 3 years of active duty, 3 years in Reserve
Coast Guard (New London): 4 years of active duty, 2 years in Reserve

NOTE: Choices given here are stated in general terms. Eligibility varies according to the individual's age, qualifications and previous military service, active and Reserve. Full details can be obtained from the armed services.

Reprinted from U.S. NEWS & WORLD REPORT, *an independent weekly news magazine published at Washington. Copyright 1956 U.S. News Publishing Corporation*

tion. It is the great industrial power of the United States that supplies the broad base of our defense program. Today, our power potential is less important than it was when we had time to mobilize and to bring power into being. Nevertheless, to keep a military machine in a state of constant readiness still requires the exploitation of our full industrial strength. Moreover, an allout thermonuclear war would be so devastating that even if it required only limited accompanying military power, it would still be of an extent to tax our industrial might. The United States still has to be prepared to mobilize its reserve industrial potential both for an emergency and for maintaining existing forces.

Manpower

Quantitatively our manpower resources are not so great as those of many nations. The number of men and women between the ages of sixteen and sixty-four in the United States is approximately one-half that of the Soviet Union. From this group must come the bulk of the manpower for the fighting forces and for producing the vast array of items needed to fight a modern war. For every man in the armed forces many other men and women must provide facilities for feeding, sheltering, transporting, arming, and clothing him. In addition, the workers must assume the additional burden of doing what was formerly done by the men taken from the labor force and placed in the army. In times of emergency the labor force can be expanded by drawing upon the young, the retired, the handicapped, and by more extensive employment of women. Hours of labor can be lengthened (but too much will decrease productivity), and other expedients can be adopted to increase production. In assessing manpower resources, however, numbers alone do not give the true picture. The skills, the education, the health, and the morale of that manpower are also important.

Preparedness plans must include programs to allocate manpower among the armed services, industry, and agriculture. The skills and location of labor must be catalogued, and organizational techniques for determining the best utilization of manpower must be developed. Workers are not interchangeable. Steelworkers drafted into the armed forces cannot be replaced by women and the aged. The limited supply of trained medical men has to be divided between the armed forces and the civilian population. Decisions have to be made whether to draft into the armed forces students whose education is a national asset. During World War II, the government adopted many devices to provide the right kind of labor at the right time and in the right places, but the United States, unlike the other major belligerents, did not adopt compulsory manpower controls.

The assessment of a nation's manpower resources must take into account the intangible factors of morale and cohesion. Prejudice and discrimination, for example, are dangerous liabilities. When people are denied

PLANNING FOR MILITARY SECURITY

STRATEGIC ESTIMATE OF THE SITUATION
based on
Military, Political, Technical
Psychological and Economic Estimates

when combined with

NATIONAL OBJECTIVES
and
Reasoned Assumptions Concerning
UNKNOWNS

leads to

A GENERAL STATEMENT OF OVER-ALL MILITARY STRATEGY
and
Determination of the Tasks which Must be
Accomplished during the First Months of
Hostilities if We are to Survive in a War

and to

AN OUTLINE WAR PLAN
Extending over at least First Two Years
of Hostilities

Estimate Time-Phased
NATIONAL MOBILIZATION CAPABILITIES
Including those of Allies

Outline
TIME-PHASED SCHEDULES OF REQUIREMENTS
Including Support of Allies

Prepare
**DETAILED PLANS FOR MILITARY OPERATIONS,
CIVIL DEFENSE, ECONOMIC WARFARE, etc.**

Develop
DETAILED MOBILIZATION SCHEDULES:
Manpower, Finished Items, Industrial
Facilities, Raw Materials

INTEGRATE REQUIREMENTS AND CAPABILITIES
Revise and adjust plans, schedules and estimates of
capabilities

MOBILIZATION PROGRAM
Civilian Economy,
Industry and
Armed Forces

**PEACETIME PREPAREDNESS MEASURES
TO MAINTAIN MOBILIZATION POTENTIAL**
e.g., Stockpiling and Organized
Reserves

**MILITARY
READINESS**
Forces in Being
in Peacetime

Based on chart in Lincoln, ECONOMICS OF NATIONAL SECURITY, 2nd ed. (Englewood Cliffs, N.J.: Prentice-Hall, Inc., 1954), p. 36

the chance to advance, to study medicine, to go to graduate school to study history, or to get a job as a mechanic, because of their race or religion, the nation is deprived of the advantages of the skills and brain power of many of its citizens. Moreover, divisions among people along religious or racial lines make it more difficult for them to work together.

Raw materials and production

Raw materials are basic for national welfare and for national defense. War consumes vast quantities of goods. The development of new weapons adds to the variety of raw materials necessary for the common defense. Rich in raw materials, the United States has been slow to husband them. Periodically there are public demands for the development of more sensible programs for the use of the materials from which we fashion our high standard of living and on which our military strength depends. But only feeble beginnings have been made to attack the problem. Yet it now appears that where considerations of national welfare have not been sufficient to arouse concern about our prodigal use of raw materials, considerations of national security are forcing us to act.

The United States has already used up its best grades of iron ore. Though the experts differ as to the exact date, they agree that continuation of the high level of consumption of oil will lead to the depletion of our oil reserves within a few decades. Other basic materials are in short supply. Moreover, the United States is not self-sufficient. During peacetime we get many materials that we need from foreign sources. During war these sources are not always available, or if available, only at large cost in much-needed manpower, materials, and facilities. To be secure we must conserve what we have, stockpile the materials we need, develop new substitutes and synthetics for materials in short supply, and expand our facilities for developing and processing strategic materials.

Mobilization plans must also include programs for allocating raw materials among various competing demands. Although American production of steel, aluminum, copper, coal, and electricity is by far the largest of any nation in the world, in wartime these materials must be rationed. During World War II, for example, "steel was needed to build steel plants that would make steel needed to make plants that would produce tanks that would use steel." Machinery had to be established to distribute scarce steel among the various programs. Iron ore production was increased, and greater quantities of hard-to-get manganese were sought.

Food is also one of the most important raw materials. The United States has to produce food and foodstuffs not only for its own population and armed services, but for its allies. Bacteriological weapons make it possible that in future wars food will be short. Rationing and severe conservation of some food must also be considered by war mobilizers.

Men without tools and productive plants cannot make effective use of raw materials. It is the capital equipment available per worker that accounts for our high standard of living. We make tools that make tools that make parts that are joined by other tools with other parts to make finished usable products.

The government itself builds and operates a few arsenals to make some of the direct items of war, such as rifles and ammunition. Much more important in our defense program are the facilities owned by private individuals and corporations. The government encourages private owners of capital to expand their facilities to produce munitions through tax concessions and other devices. In times of emergency, peacetime facilities can be converted to war production. Automobile factories produce tanks and trucks, lipstick manufacturers make ammunition, railroads and trucks carry the materials and weapons of war. Yet these changes cannot be accomplished overnight. Elaborate advance planning is required for rapid conversion. Facilities have to be assessed, manpower indexed, and machines catalogued so that in an emergency, conversion and expansion of facilities can be undertaken with great speed.

The constant increase in our capital equipment and its modernization are important assets in our security program. The building of new and better machines, the development of our power resources, the expansion of our steel mills, the increase in the production of automobiles—all those things that help us to produce better products at lower costs also add to our military strength.

Science and security

When the atomic bomb was dropped on Hiroshima, few could any longer doubt that science had become a decisive element in a defense program. Science is not merely a side show that produces fancy military gadgets. Wars are fought and won in large measure in a nation's scientific laboratories.

The nature of war has been altered by the invention of the proximity fuse, the snorkel submarine, radar, sonar, the guided missile and many other inventions. The scientist's contribution to the war effort during World War II is well-known. But what is not so well known is that the scientists drew "heavily on the accumulated stockpile of fundamental scientific knowledge that was all but exhausted when fighting stopped."[11] Further advance will depend upon the extension of fundamental scientific knowledge, on what is sometimes called pure science. Such science is not preoccupied with finding more powerful explosives or better devices to guide missiles, but is interested in finding keys to the mysteries of the world in which we live.

It is essential, therefore, to create the conditions under which scientific inquiry can best operate. Hitler's misunderstanding of the importance of

[11] Vannevar Bush, *Modern Arms and Free Men* (New York: Simon & Schuster, Inc., 1949), p. 27.

this factor led him to expel from Germany those who did not conform to the "New Order." The Communists' insistence upon a science that follows a party line has given to the free world a priceless advantage. In this country preoccupation with *applied* science and with only those applications that have military significance risks using up the store of knowledge without replenishing it. For this reason the government has established a National Science Foundation, which through scholarships and other forms of assistance helps to train all scientists without respect to immediate military value.

The military departments themselves have tapped the knowledge and skill of scientists in commercial laboratories and universities. This problem of integrating scientific and military knowledge is an essential but difficult task. Soldiers, like those in other professions, tend to be cautious in the adoption of new techniques. In the past almost every new weapon of war —gunpowder, submarine, tank, airplane, proximity fuse—had to be pushed on the military by civilians.

Because of the military importance of scientific knowledge a great deal of organizational effort and thought has been devoted to the question of science and secrecy. Some scientific knowledge must be kept secret. Yet to restrict all knowledge can do more harm than good, for scientific progress depends on the wide sharing of information. Many scientists—men whose patriotism is beyond doubt—have questioned whether we are not losing more than we gain by our excessive concern over secrecy.[12] Moreover, the withholding of information sometimes deprives the policy planners of essential knowledge. One atomic scientist has written, "The most fateful step, which has permitted the Soviet Union to achieve its present atomic strength, was not the betrayal of our secrets by May, Fuchs, and Greenglass, but the decision of American political and military leaders in 1945 to give to the Soviet Union control over the parts of Czechoslovakia and Germany in which important uranium ore deposits were known to exist. . . . Perhaps, if the atomic bomb development in the United States had not been surrounded with such extreme secrecy, those responsible for the drawing of the demarcation line would have known better what they were giving away. . . ."[13]

PROTECTING THE HOME FRONT

The home front is the basis upon which our military power depends. It must be protected. There are two major threats: one is economic instability, the other is enemy attacks.

[12] Walter Gellhorn, *Security, Loyalty, and Science* (Ithaca: Cornell University Press, 1950), chapters 2, 4.
[13] Eugene Rabinowitch, "Atomic Spy Trials: Heretical Afterthoughts," *Bulletin of the Atomic Scientists,* May 1951, p. 140.

The economy is a delicate instrument. When the government buys large quantities of materials, it increases the demands for labor, materials, and facilities. At the same time, fewer items are available for civilians to buy. People have more money as the result of the defense expenditures, and they begin to compete for scarce items. Prices go up, and those with enough money get the items that are in short supply. If inflation is permitted to go unchecked, the maladjustments in the price structure will greatly damage the nation's ability to produce, and there may be dangerous political consequences. The cost of defense items will go up and the government will have to spend more money, adding to the inflationary spiral.

The danger of inflation is less when the war munitions program is added to an economy that is not producing at full steam, as was the case in 1939. Unused facilities, manpower, and materials can be used. In such a situation the government's expansion of credit will cause prices to rise, but the condition is not critical. On the other hand, when the munitions program is imposed on an economy that is already using all its resources, the dangers of inflation become acute.

Stabilizing the economy

It is for these reasons that defense programs sometimes call for government programs to stabilize the economy. Taxes must be increased not only to finance the war production but to curb inflation. The government has to borrow money. If the money is borrowed from banks, it increases the amount of money in circulation at the very time when fewer items are available for civilian consumption. This is why the government makes such an effort to sell war bonds to private individuals, for such purchases do not have the same inflationary consequences. Depending upon the size of the mobilization program and the state of the economy, other controls may be necessary. In the event of a large demand for defense production,

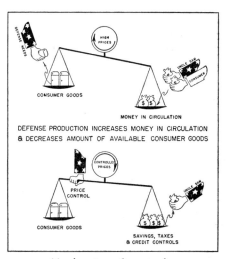

Mechanics of controls.

price and wage controls and rationing are essential. Rationing insures that scarce commodities are passed around according to need rather than according to ability to buy. It also counterattacks inflation; no matter how many dollars a man has, if he wishes to get a pair of shoes he needs a ration coupon. The government controls the number of ration coupons in circulation and can keep them in balance with the supply of goods.

If war should come and require more guns, civilians will of course have less butter. If our productivity continues to increase in the future as it has in the immediate past, however, the United States during "normal" times will be able to support a large military establishment, furnish military assistance to our allies, and at the same time improve our standard of living. But to provide both guns and butter will tax our productive power and political maturity.

Civil defense

It is doubtful if the United States will be as lucky in the next war as it has been in the past. An attack on the American mainland is now technically possible; and in case of a full-scale war, our factories, transportation centers, atomic plants, and other vital installations, will be prime targets. The defense circle cannot be closed without an adequate program to defend the home base. Until 1953, when the Soviet Union exploded their H-bomb, the military tended to neglect defensive power on the theory that the best defense is a good offense. More attention is now paid, however, to strengthening the Continental Air Command and developing an early warning system. The Continental Air Command operates on a 24-hour alert, instantly ready to send planes into the air. A "crash" program is underway to develop three radar lines across Canada. Warning of an enemy attack is vital both to defend the home base and to unleash our retaliatory power. The radar lines are supplemented by 13,000 Ground Observer Corps stations manned by civilian volunteers who watch for enemy bombers sneaking under the radar signals.

Even the best warning systems cannot guarantee more than six hours notice at most and, with the development of intercontinental missiles, perhaps no more than a few minutes. Even the finest defense will not be able to prevent some of the enemy bombers and missiles from getting through. The most optimistic estimate is that 30 per cent of the bombers approaching the United States could be stopped. A more realistic figure is perhaps half that.

Civil defense means "the protection of the home front by civilians acting under civilian authority to minimize casualties and war damage and preserve maximum civilian support of the war effort." The functions of civil defense can be grouped under four general categories: "(1) measures designed to prevent enemy attack; (2) measures designed to reduce the effects of an an enemy attack; (3) services that will alleviate the damage of an enemy attack; and (4) general measures pertaining to the over-all program."[14] Civilian activity designed to prevent enemy attack is limited

[14] Carey Brewer, "Civil Defense in the United States: Federal, State and Local," *Public Affairs Bulletin 92* (Washington, D.C.: The Library of Congress, Legislative Reference Service), p. 4.

to camouflage programs, black-out measures, and aircraft observation. The main task is to be prepared with plans and organizations to keep community life going if an attack comes. Air-raid warning; dispersion of vital facilities; evacuation; emergency medical, health, rescue, salvage, fire-fighting, and decontamination services; education; and intelligence are some of the key jobs.

The industrial power of the United States is concentrated in the area north of the Ohio and east of the Mississippi and along the west coast. Many of our basic industries are in the coastal cities, those most vulnerable to attack. The decentralization of industry and the creation of duplicate facilities dispersed throughout the United States are to be encouraged. But large-scale decentralization is not feasible. There is strong political opposition. Decentralization itself would require the expenditures of enormous quantities of manpower, resources, and facilities. In some cases, it would result in lower productivity. While gradually there will be, not only for security but for welfare purposes, greater decentralization, this in itself is not sufficient for civil defense. Accordingly, air-raid shelters must be built, millions of citizens must be trained to fight fires and to aid in the evacuation of wounded persons, medical supplies must be stockpiled, emergency communications networks created. Until the development of hydrogen bombs, most civil defense preparations were based on "duck and cover" tactics, but recently more attention has been paid to a "run for the hills" strategy and plans have been made to keep roads open and to evacuate areas without panic.

Americans have been reluctant to face up to the necessity for civil defense. Not until the Korean conflict was any progress made, and organization and training are still in their infancy. As late as June 1955 a *New York Times* survey of our major cities, the primary targets of the enemy, showed that Chicago is "helpless," Bostonians have "almost no chance of survival," Cleveland is a "sitting duck," Seattle "is not ready," Fort Worth "woefully unprepared."[15]

Civil defense has been retarded by an attitude of "It can't happen here," and perhaps even more by an attitude that if it does happen, advance preparation will do little good since millions will be killed anyway. Although the Federal Civil Defense Administrator has reported, "There is no certainty that any nation can survive an all-out nuclear attack,"[16] he has also pointed out that with an effective defense, millions of Americans can be saved who otherwise would die. Furthermore, a strong defense may discourage attack and along with our offensive power must be considered part of our policy of deterrence.[17]

[15] *The New York Times,* June 12, 1955.
[16] *The New York Times,* April 18, 1956.
[17] See Klaus Knorr, "Passive Air Defense for the United States," *Military Policy and National Security,* ed. William W. Kaufman (Princeton: Princeton University Press, 1956), pp. 75-101.

Administration of civil defense

The responsibility for civil defense programs is shared by federal, state, and local governments. The Federal Civil Defense Administrator—with the advice of a twelve-member advisory council of national, state, and local officials and an eighteen-man coordinating board of national officials—controls the federal effort and also administers disaster relief. The Federal Civil Defense Administration provides some of the money, coordinates plans of state and local governments, trains and provides educational materials, and prepares national programs. Most of the states have adopted civil defense programs, although many of them are inadequate and guided by considerations applicable during World War II, but now out-dated. Local governments have the job of providing on-the-spot services.

The basic principles behind the civil defense program are to use existing agencies and levels of government and to encourage self-help at every level of society. These principles have come in for increasing criticism. The overlapping and duplication of American governmental units causes real problems. In some metropolitan areas, for example, fire-fighting equipment is under the jurisdiction of twenty to fifty separate municipalities. Many state governments, the Commission on Intergovernmental Regulations, and a special citizens commission on civil defense have all recommended that the national government should assume the primary responsibility for civil defense, and they have criticized the self-help principle as inadequate.[18] Some congressmen have argued that the Federal Civil Defense Administrator should be raised to cabinet level and a crash program be adopted to strengthen this weakest link in our defense program.

SECURITY AND LIBERTY

So long as the United States exists in a world of sovereign independent nations it must look to its defenses. As we have seen, this means large standing military forces, adequately trained reserves, the application of scientific and other knowledge to military problems, a strong and stable economy able to convert quickly to war production, an alert and trained citizen body, and powerful allies.

Not by power alone

To fail to do what is necessary to provide for the common defense would be disastrous. Equally dangerous is to depend solely on military power to provide security. Power alone will not solve problems. Not even the United States has sufficient resources, even if the people had the stomach for it, to control the destinies of the international community. Politics is conflict, but

[18] *The New York Times,* January 4, 1956, Part 4, p. 1.

it is also cooperation, and power must be used to help build the kind of world community in which eventually armies and tanks may become archaic.

What should be the role of the military in a democratic society? A fear of the military is deeply rooted in American traditions. The framers of the Constitution, recognizing the incompatibility between free government and military domination, wove into the Constitution several precautions. The President, an elected officer, is commander in chief of the armed forces. With the Senate's consent, he commissions all officers, Congress makes the rules for the governance of the military services, and appropriations for the Army are limited to a two-year period. Congress has supplemented these provisions by statutes requiring that the Secretary of Defense and the heads of the military departments be civilians, and by elaborate provisions to prevent the military from controlling the selection of men for West Point, Annapolis, and the Air Force Academy.

In the past, the soldiers were largely ignored. During time of peace, their suggestions as to the need for building strong defenses were shrugged off, or the generals were accused of wanting war. A career in the armed services was not attractive. The military mind was stereotyped as conservative, stodgy, and concerned mainly with protocol. Failure to heed the words of our professional soldiers, sailors, and airmen has cost us much. Certain it is that in the future what they have to say will be given serious consideration. At the other extreme there is the danger of elevating them into positions where what they have to say is accepted uncritically. This would be disastrous both for the preservation of liberty and for the promotion of security.

War and defense today, more than ever, are too important and too complex to leave to the generals. As we have seen, security programs require the talents of the bureaucrat, social scientist, natural scientist, labor leader, engineer, industrialist, and all other skills. What the soldier knows must be meshed with what others know. But the soldier may not know enough to be trusted with the running of our defense program.

Militarism versus democracy

Maintaining civilian supremacy today is harder than ever. Modern warfare has so expanded the scope of military affairs that there is no longer a clear separation between military and civilian spheres of activity. All aspects of society—labor relations, science, the press, entertainment—affect the nation's military power. As military aspects of problems are brought to the fore, the generals, often reluctantly, are called upon to pass judgment on issues that in the past have not been thought to be within the scope of their competence. At the same time, their civilian superiors find it more difficult to secure the information that they need to exercise control. In many cases it is the military who decide what information must remain top secret. Congressmen and the general public are at a disadvantage in exercising effective supremacy over the military.

The dangers to liberty arising from the garrison state—one that is constantly prepared for total war and that is organized to exert its military might—were recognized by Alexander Hamilton when he wrote: "Safety from external danger is the most powerful director of national conduct. Even the ardent love of liberty will after a time give way to its dictates. The violent destruction of life and property incident to war, the continual effort and alarm attendant on a state of continual danger, will compel nations the most attached to liberty to resort for repose and security to institutions which have a tendency to destroy their civil and political rights. To be more safe, they at length become willing to run the risk of being less free."[19]

Professor Harold D. Lasswell has summarized the impact of militarization upon individual freedom as follows: "To militarize is to governmentalize. It is also to centralize. To centralize is to enhance the effective control of the executive over decisions, and thereby to reduce the control exercised by courts and legislatures. To centralize is to enhance the role of the military in the allocation of national resources. Continuing fear of external attack sustains an atmosphere of distrust that finds expression in spy hunts directed against fellow officials and fellow citizens. Outspoken criticism of official measures launched for the national defense is more and more resented as unpatriotic and subversive of the common good. The community at large, therefore, acquiesces in denials of freedom that go beyond the technical requirements of military security."[20] There is nothing inevitable about this trend. The choice is not between arming and becoming militarized or not arming and becoming conquered.

The threat of militarization comes not only from soldiers. As John McCloy wrote in dissent to one of the recommendations of the Hoover Commission's task force on security organization, "I doubt whether we need fear the men in uniform in this regard [seeking unfettered power] any more than the man or men in civil clothes to whom we have given far greater authority. Indeed, as many examples as there are of authority usurped by generals or admirals, I believe history records as many instances of usurpation on the part of civilians with at least as many disastrous results."[21]

[19] Federalist No. 8, The Modern Library edition (New York: Random House, 1937), p. 42. For a recent thoughtful treatment of the problem, see Samuel P. Huntington, "Civilian Control and the Constitution," The American Political Science Review, Vol. L, No. 3, September 1956, pp. 676-699.

[20] Harold D. Lasswell, "Does the Garrison State Threaten Civil Rights?" Civil Rights in America, The Annals of the American Academy of Political and Social Science, May 1951, p. 111.

[21] Task Force Report on National Security Organization, p. 59.

The threat, however, is not essentially one of usurpation of power, but the gradual abandonment of control over decisions to men who are not responsible to the electorate. The dangers of militarization stem from the assumption of authority by civilian and soldier who justify any and all actions because of overriding considerations of safety.

The United States has been fortunate. It has never developed a military caste. Its generals and admirals have demonstrated statesmanlike qualities, including respect for civilian authority. American soldiers have been imbued with democratic principles of civilian supremacy. Now that the skills required of military men are so varied, it becomes all the more necessary to educate them not only to be good soldiers but also to be good democrats. For it is by "civilizing" the military that much can be done to prevent militarizing the civilians.

I T IS IMPOSSIBLE TO DRAW A SHARP LINE BETWEEN
the activities of the national government in waging war and peace on the
one hand and its so-called domestic functions on the other. The two are
inextricably intertwined. The foreign policies administered by the State
Department have a direct impact on American businessmen and farmers.
Fighting a war mobilizes both the nation's economy and the whole peacetime bureaucracy. Our foreign economic policies directly affect employment, wages, prices, and taxes at home. This book discusses domestic activities separately from foreign affairs only for purposes of convenience.

There is, however, a significant difference between the national government's overseas activities and its domestic ones. However critical people may be of our particular foreign and war policies, they do not question the idea that the *government* must make the policy. No one has
been heard to argue that because of governmental inefficiency foreign
policy should be turned over to businessmen, or that because of the huge
military bureaucracy the job of defending the country should be reserved
to the state governments. All agree that the national government must
manage the relations of Americans with other peoples. But relations of
Americans with *one another*—that is a different matter. On domestic
questions people differ not only as to *what* policies should be adopted.
They also argue hotly as to *whether* government should act at all, and
if so, what government. And if they agree that government should act, a
host of new questions imme-
diately arises. How far should
government go? What kinds of
controls or procedures should
it use? Should it act as the
partner of such major interests
as business, labor, or farmers
—or as their boss? These and
other questions continue to
provoke fierce disputes in editorial pages, over the air, in
legislative chambers, and on
the platform.

★ 25

Government

as regulator

It would seem rather pointless to describe the functions
of our national government
without considering some of
the answers given to such
questions as those raised
above. Consequently this chapter and the next two will each

describe federal functions *that illustrate a major technique of governmental control or intervention.* The present chapter will show the national government's major *regulatory* functions—regulatory in the narrow sense as meaning its attempts to set limits to the activities of private groups, to prevent "bad" practices, to restrict one interest from interfering with the rights of others (as defined, of course, by the politicians in power). This is government in a somewhat negative or restrictive sense. The next chapter will describe some of the newer welfare functions of government. Chapter 27 will take up the role in America of the so-called positive state—that is, a government that *actively intervenes in the economy* at strategic points to strengthen it, stabilize it, and reform it.

A traditional type of governmental regulation is of course the regulation of human behavior to *prevent crime.* In the United States such regulation has been largely the job of state and local governments. The national government has been concerned with crime prevention mainly in connection with such functions as delivering mail or collecting taxes. Increasingly in recent years, however, fighting crime has become an important national function. The Department of Justice, employing the services of the highly efficient Federal Bureau of Investigation and other agencies, has the main responsibility for investigating crime and prosecuting criminals. The Secret Service in the Treasury Department has special functions, such as investigating counterfeiting. Other members of the "federal police" are postal inspectors, narcotics agents, treasury inspectors, border patrols, and many others. Under the kind of cooperative federalism described in Chapter 5, these federal officials work closely with state and local police. Paradoxically, this kind of law enforcement is one of the most ancient functions of government, but it is a relatively new responsibility of the national government. However, since crime has become a big interstate business, the national government will probably become more and more involved in policing the country. For example, after the Kefauver committee in 1951 publicized the power of huge crime syndicates, it recommended a number of measures such as enlarging the rackets squad in the Justice Department and the fraud squad in the Bureau of Internal Revenue, and barring interstate transportation of punch-boards and roulette wheels.

The main regulatory task of the national government, however, is policing the practices and relations of interest groups, such as business and labor. Here we are concerned with the role of the government as regulator of, and mediator among, such major economic interests. Two words of caution are necessary. First, government is not the only regulating agency. People are regulated by their families, friends, church, and over-all social environment, as we saw in earlier chapters. Second, the type of activity described in this chapter is only one type of regulation. Government acts as a regulating agency also in some of its newer functions, as we shall see later.

REGULATING BUSINESS

Businessmen today operate amid a complex web of national, state, and local laws. It was not always thus. Business has never been free of restrictive legislation, of course, but during much of the latter part of the nineteenth century our national policy was to leave business alone. Most of the nation's leaders believed broadly in laissez faire—or hands off—and they reflected the prevailing economic ideas of our society. Given their head, businessmen set about developing a nation enormously rich in natural resources. The heroes of the 1870's and 1880's were not politicians but business magnates—Rockefellers, Morgans, Carnegies, Fricks, and the rest. "From rags to riches" become the nation's motto.

Toward the end of the century a reaction set in. Sharp depressions rocked the nation's economy and threw men out of jobs. Large numbers of people, including many workers and farmers, labored long hours in factory and field for little money. "Muckrakers" revealed that some of the most famous business leaders had indulged in shoddy practices and corrupt deals, with a "public-be-damned" attitude. A demand for regulation developed. The series of national and state laws that ensued did not follow any methodical plan or philosophy. One after another they were adopted to meet specific abuses on the pragmatic assumption that problems could be handled as they arose. One of the major efforts was to curb the evils that seemed to flow from sheer bigness.

Antitrust policy: background

Americans tend to have a mixed attitude toward big business. On the one hand we are easily impressed by bigness—the tallest skyscraper, the largest football stadium, the biggest corporation—and the efficiency and power that seem to go with bigness. On the other hand, we like to believe that our economic system functions best under conditions of fair competition among small businessmen. We hear much praise of the "little man." This mixed attitude has affected our attempts to prevent monopoly and restraint of trade.

Much of the popular unrest late in the nineteenth century culminated in attacks on monopoly. The trust busters argued that little business was being squeezed out by huge trusts in oil, sugar, whisky, steel, and other commodities. In 1890 Congress responded to this sentiment by passing the famous Sherman Act. Designed to foster real competition and to stop the growth of private monopolies, this act in its preamble made clear its intention "to protect trade and commerce against unlawful restraints and monopolies." Henceforth, persons making contracts, combinations, or conspiracies in restraint of trade in interstate and foreign commerce could be sued for damages, required to stop their illegal practices, and subjected to criminal penalties.

Cleveland and McKinley showed little interest in enforcing the Sherman Act. Indeed, a Supreme Court decision in the Sugar Trust case considerably limited the scope of the act by ruling that a sugar refining company that produced 98 per cent of the sugar used in the United States was primarily engaged in *manufacturing* rather than *commerce,* and hence could not be regulated by the national government.[1] But in 1901 Theodore Roosevelt became President. Wielding a "big stick," he responded to the growing sentiment against the "giant octopus" of monopoly. Yet even Roosevelt talked more than he acted. Like most Americans he had conflicting attitudes toward bigness. Mr. Dooley, the Chicago bartender-philosopher, poked fun at Roosevelt's vacillation by pretending to quote him as saying: "Th' trusts are heejoous monsthers built up be th'enlightened intherprise iv th'men that have done so much to advance progress in our beloved country. On wan hand I wud stamp thim undher fut; on th'other hand not so fast." During the Taft and Wilson Administrations the trusts were prosecuted with some vigor. As a result of rulings by the courts, the rather vague provisions of the act took on more definite meaning. Certain consolidations were permitted unless a clear intent to monopolize was proved. Voting trusts, pools, and some collusive practices were sharply curbed.

"THIS HURTS ME MORE THAN IT DOES YOU."

A typical cartoon of a half century ago against the "trusts."

The Clayton Act in 1914 further clarified antitrust policy. It outlawed specific abuses affecting interstate commerce, such as charging different prices to different buyers, the granting of rebates, and the making of false statements about competitors in order to take business away from them. Corporations were prohibited from acquiring stock (amended in 1950 to include assets) in competing concerns if such acquisitions substantially lessened interstate competition, and interlocking directorates in large corporations were banned. Labor had been enraged by a Supreme Court ruling

[1] *United States* v. *E. C. Knight Co.* See Chapter 20.

that applied the Sherman Act to a union boycott against the products of a nonunion manufacturer; the new act exempted labor from the 1890 act and was greeted by unions as their Magna Carta. Later legislation exempted various business activities from the Sherman Act.

Antitrust activity languished in the 1920's. Times were prosperous; the Republican administrations were actively probusiness; and the Department of Justice, charged with enforcing the Sherman Act, paid little attention to it. During the Depression popular resentment mounted against big business as abuses were revealed. At first the Roosevelt Administration tried a new method of industrial self-policing under the National Industrial Recovery Act of 1933, which tried to promote cooperation among businessmen by allowing them to work out codes of fair competition. This was virtually a suspension of antitrust policy. The N.I.R.A., however, was invalidated by the Supreme Court in 1935.

Recent years have seen a revival of trust busting. In the late 1930's a well-publicized committee of congressmen and New Deal experts, the Temporary National Economic Committee, made an elaborate investigation of economic concentration and monopoly. It unanimously urged that enforcement be strengthened "to cope with the gigantic aggregations of capital which have become so dominant in our economic life."[2] Under the leadership of Thurman Arnold, a former Yale professor, the antitrust division of the Justice Department was given a larger staff to commence trust busting in earnest. In one year, 1940, the government instituted 345 suits; of the 280 suits that were terminated, the government won 265. Antitrust activity flagged during World War II but was revived during the postwar years.

Bigness—curse or blessing?

The attitude of the government during the Roosevelt-Truman years has been well expressed by Justice William O. Douglas in a Supreme Court dissenting opinion: "Size is the measure of the power of a handful of men over our economy. That power can be utilized with lightning speed. It can be benign or it can be dangerous. The philosophy of the Sherman Act is that it should not exist. For all power tends to develop into a government in itself. Power that controls the economy should be in the hands of elected representatives of the people, not in the hands of an industrial oligarchy. Industrial power should be decentralized. It should be scattered into many hands so that the fortunes of the people will not be dependent on the whim or caprice, the political prejudices, the emotional stability, of a few self-appointed men."[3]

[2] Temporary National Economic Committee, *Investigation of Concentration of Economic Power, Final Report and Recommendations, Senate Document 35,* Seventy-seventh Congress, first session (Washington, D.C.: Government Printing Office, 1941), p. 35.

[3] *United States* v. *Columbia Steel Co.* (1948).

What success have we had with our antitrust policies? After a half century of experience observers are still divided. Some believe that antitrust laws have curbed monopolistic tendencies and have forced business to keep its own house in order. It has become difficult, for example, for rival manufacturers to agree to restrict output in order to maintain prices. Other students of monopoly believe that antitrust action has had little effect on monopoly. There are other questions. Have the antitrust laws been successful in preventing concentration? Economists, business, and government officials argue at length over the answer. A few years ago the Federal Trade Commission reported that a recent increase in mergers by large concerns constituted a menace to competition. It is held by others that the economy is more competitive today than in the past.

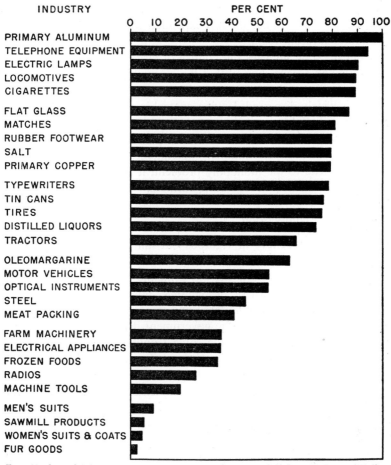

From Nordin and Salera, ELEMENTARY ECONOMICS (Englewood Cliffs, N.J.: Prentice-Hall, Inc., 1950)

Industrial concentration in 1947, selected industries.

Should bigness as such be outlawed? Yes, say some Americans, taking the view of Justice Douglas. Others, like David E. Lilienthal, former Director of the Tennessee Valley Authority and Chairman of the Atomic Energy Commission, say no. Lilienthal believes that "in Big Business we have more than an efficient way to produce and distribute basic commodities, and to strengthen the Nation's security; we have a social institution that promotes human freedom and individualism."[4] Rather than outlaw bigness, Lilienthal would encourage it, since he believes that big businesses stimulate competition between ideas, products, and services; develop through research more and better products; strengthen constructive labor-management relations; produce greater stability of employment; increase industrial output; promote conservation of natural resources, and create new opportunities for independent and small businessmen. Any danger from big business abusing its power has been reduced to manageable proportions, argues Lilienthal, by the expanded role of government in economic affairs in recent years.

Another question involves the control of large corporations. In a classic study, Berle and Means showed that the ownership of the modern corporation has been divorced from control.[5] The ownership of stock in large corporations is widely dispersed, leaving control in the hands of a small group of managers. To whom are these managers responsible? If they are not truly responsible to the owners, should they be made more responsible to all the people through the national government? While this problem does not directly relate to the monopoly problem, it involves the whole role of the national government in regulating business.

Traffic cop for competition

Most Americans believe in vigorous but fair and open competition. In a simple economy competition virtually enforces itself; buyers and sellers know one another and follow the old principle of *caveat emptor*—let the buyer beware. By the turn of the century, however, the American business economy was becoming so large and impersonal that a demand arose for policing of competition by the government. Big business was especially suspect for its trade practices; the same Congress that passed the Clayton Act in 1914 also enacted the Federal Trade Commission Act. As a candidate for President, Wilson had said that one vice of the trusts was their tendency to stop men of ability and enterprise but of little capital from making their way under the competitive system. The new act was a

[4] D. E. Lilienthal, *Big Business: a New Era* (New York: Harper & Brothers, 1952), ix.

[5] A. A. Berle, Jr. and Gardiner C. Means, *The Modern Corporation and Private Property* (New York: The Macmillan Company, 1932). For an interesting picture of the "checks and balances" in the American economy that, in the author's opinion, tend to prevent excessive concentration of power, see J. K. Galbraith, *American Capitalism, The Concept of Countervailing Power* (Boston: Houghton Mifflin, 1952).

sort of "Magna Carta" for businessmen opposed to unfair and injurious methods of competition.

Because our industrial life is so diverse, Congress put enforcement of the law in the hands of a five-member Federal Trade Commission, an independent regulatory board, whose job is to apply the act to specific practices. As its membership slowly changed (the term of office is seven years), the F.T.C.'s conception of its job changed too. In the 1920's the commission exercised its powers rather mildly, but more recently it has taken a stricter view toward business practices, and has been given new responsibilities by Congress. Today the F.T.C. exercises a wide range of powers. For example, it can outlaw:

1. *Misrepresentation.* A businessman who sells in interstate commerce must not sell rebuilt or second-hand products as new. Watches cannot be branded "Made in U.S.A." if the movements come from Switzerland. An attempt to issue a 1917 film, "The Love Pirate," in 1919 as "The She Tiger" was branded unfair.

2. *Tying contracts.* The Radio Corporation of America, doing most of the business in radio tubes, was forbidden to require radio manufacturers to buy from R.C.A. all vacuum tubes needed for first use in the sets. On the other hand, when the General Motors Corporation required its Buick and Chevrolet agents to use only G.M. replacement parts in repair work, an F.T.C. ban on this practice was overturned by the Supreme Court.

3. *Misbranding.* Putting misleading names on products sold in interstate commerce, and using deceptive containers, is illegal. A coat made of cheap fur cannot be described as made of beaver. A physical culture outfit that advertised its courses as starting "new inches of massive power pushing out your chest" and as banishing constipation, skin blotches, etc., etc., was ordered to desist. More recently, the maker of Gosewich's Odorless Garlic Tablets was ordered to drop the word "Garlic" because the F.T.C. found the pills contain no substantial amount of garlic.

4. *Price discrimination.* It is unfair to sell below cost in order to destroy weaker competitors and thus secure a monopoly position. This practice had been a favorite one with the "robber barons" of old.

5. *Monopolistic practices.* There are a host of these, such as buying up supplies in order to stifle competition, conspiring to set uniform selling prices and conditions, harassing competitors (such as by bribing their employees or bringing vexatious law suits), and selling below cost in order to hinder competition. The F.T.C. works closely with the Justice Department in trying to curb practices in restraint of trade among the states.

Some of the F.T.C.'s decisions affect deeply the whole system of trade. Take the case of "Pittsburgh plus." For years steel producers had a friendly arrangement whereby the same prices were charged to all steel fabricators throughout the country no matter where they were located and where their steel came from. For example, if you were a Chicago fabricator buying steel from a Chicago mill, you would have to pay a Pittsburgh base price plus transportation charges from Pittsburgh even though no transportation was involved. For years the F.T.C. watched with interest this collusive arrangement in steel and other industries such as cement. For three years commission officials held hearings. On the basis of almost 100,000 pages of oral testimony and exhibits, the F.T.C. in 1943 issued a cease and desist order against the basing point system in the cement industry. The case went to the Supreme Court, which in 1948—eleven years after the F.T.C. investigation got under way—upheld the commission's action. Even this decision did not end the story. Supporters of the basing point system carried the battle to Congress, where bills were introduced to legalize the system. Pressures have been exerted on the Federal Trade Commission to modify its stand. Presidential appointments to the commission have been made amid the pulling and hauling of interests trying to secure the "right" men.

Another trade problem that affects us all is *re-sale price maintenance.* You may have noticed that the makers of nationally advertised brand-name products often set the prices you pay at the drugstore or corner grocery. Manufacturers of such products sometimes require by contract that retailers maintain these prices. What if some retailers do not wish to sign such a contract? To simplify their operation, manufacturers in recent decades have induced most of the states to pass "Fair Trade Acts" legalizing re-sale price maintenance—that is, requiring (in most cases) that when such a contract has gone into effect in a certain state it becomes binding on all retailers of the product, including signers of the contract and *nonsigners.*

These laws were state laws applying only to *intra*state commerce. In 1937 business groups persuaded Congress to pass the Miller-Tydings amendment as a rider to an appropriation act. President Roosevelt denounced the rider method (see page 426) but signed the bill. The Miller-Tydings amendment legalized re-sale price maintenance for *inter*state commerce where states approved it for intrastate commerce. In 1950, however, the Supreme Court ruled that Congress had not intended the amendment to apply to nonsigners engaged in interstate commerce who hence could not be compelled to charge the required prices. For a time "cut-rate" establishments—that is, highly competitive ones—had a field day; but other business groups, alarmed by the decision, induced Congress to pass a law (the McGuire Act) permitting the control of nonsigners' prices.

Policing the money markets

The American economy rests on a vast system of investment and credit. Our resources could not have been developed unless people were willing to invest money in factories and machinery. The credit system—the "economic promises men live by"—has helped make possible enormous investments and the development of the economy. Before World War I there were hardly half a million investors in this country, but during the war and the 1920's millions of little people began to buy securities. Investment trusts and brokerage houses mushroomed.

For many years individual states had tried to deal with some of the abuses of the money markets, such as outright swindling. It took the stock market crash of 1929 and the collapse of the rosy hopes of millions of investors, however, to bring vigorous national action. Investigation during the Depression revealed that abuses had been many and varied. Worthless or questionable securities had been unloaded on the public through various kinds of fraud. Insiders had used confidential information to arrange deals for themselves at the expense of thousands of fleeced lambs. Investment bankers had sponsored stock issues that created unsound corporate structures. An enormous amount of speculating on margin (buying stocks on credit) had helped precipitate the 1929 crash. Pools, rigging the market, and preferred lists were other means of manipulating the money markets. More specifically, there was the wash sale, whereby one speculator agrees to sell a stock, and another agrees to buy it, at a point higher than it normally would command, in order to give the impression of a stronger market for the stock. There was the matched order, whereby two innocent brokers are hired, one to sell a stock and another to buy, to give the appearance of an active market for the stock.

The Federal Securities Act in 1933 and the Securities Exchange Act in 1934 were passed in response to wide bitterness and disillusionment over "Wall Street" practices. The 1933 act required the registration of all issues of stocks, bonds or other securities offered in interstate commerce or by mail, along with a registration statement providing full information for potential investors. The 1934 act regulated the buying and selling of securities on exchanges throughout the country. To administer both acts Congress established the Securities and Exchange Commission, an independent regulatory board of five men with five-year terms. All firms having securities listed must file regular reports with the S.E.C. and with the exchanges. The main objective is full publicity for stock market transactions, but manipulation and other unsavory practices of the past are outlawed. The S.E.C. has even the power to impose new trading rules on exchanges.

The commission has special powers over *public utility* holding companies—corporations controlling networks of operating companies. Holding companies could escape regulation by incorporating in one state to take control of operating companies in another. Many abuses developed, such as siphoning funds from operating utilities into holding companies. There was also a problem of concentration. An investigation revealed that thirteen large holding company groups controlled three-fourths of the entire privately owned electric utility industry, and over 40 per cent was concentrated in the hands of the three largest groups. To meet the problem, Congress in 1935 passed the Public Utility Holding Act. Not only must holding companies register full information with the S.E.C., but many of their transactions, such as issuing and buying securities, can be made only with the commission's consent. Congress also gave the holding companies a few years to get rid of their extraneous operating companies and to confine themselves each to a single integrated system.

TRANSPORTATION AND COMMUNICATION

In August 1787, the framers of the Constitution were debating the question of how much power they should give the new national government to regulate commerce. One day, as relief from their labors, they junketed to the banks of the Delaware River to watch John Fitch demonstrate his sensational steamboat. "As we look back," Professor Fairman has written, "it seems that Fitch and the Founding Fathers were working at different parts of one unfolding problem. His experiment was an episode in the application of steam to transportation. The Founders, purposing that American commerce should develop under the authority of an adequate national government, framed the grant that 'The Congress shall have Power . . . To regulate commerce with foreign Nations, and among the several States. . . .' "[6] Today Congress has virtually complete power to regulate interstate commerce.

National power over interstate commerce is a far more powerful weapon today than the framers could have expected. For today that power extends to hundreds of thousands of miles of railways, to waterborne commerce, to motor and air transportation. Congress controls not only the movement of persons, things, and words from state to state; it also has broad powers over the conduct of industries that *affect* interstate commerce.

Railroad politics

It is hard for us today to realize how deeply the railroads were involved in the politics of the late nineteenth century. To many Americans of that time the railroads were ogres intent on ruining the little man. Farmers especially had grievances. They charged that railroads extorted outrageously high rates, conspired with one another to prevent competition, discriminated against certain localities and individuals, corrupted state officials, evaded taxes, watered their capital, and stole the money that the farmer had invested in railroads to aid in their building. Angry and desperate, the farmers turned to political action. The powerful Granger movement, which swept the West in the 1870's and 1880's, was a response to the tactics of railroads as well as to monopoly, middlemen, and the money power.

[6] Charles Fairman, *American Constitutional Decisions* (New York: Henry Holt and Company, Inc., 1948), p. 173.

The Granger movement helped secure a number of state laws regulating the railroads. The railroads fought the new laws with appeals to the courts, evasion, and propaganda. For a time the Supreme Court allowed the states to regulate, within their boundaries, the rates of carriers engaged in interstate commerce. But in 1886 the Court in the *Wabash* decision held that states could not regulate transportation within their areas that constituted a part of commerce among the states. A void was created that only the national government could fill. Not only farmers but shippers and small businessmen demanded that Congress do something.

The result was the Interstate Commerce Act of 1887. Under this measure carriers were ordered to publicize their rates and to give advance notices of proposed increases. Special rates, rebates, and other methods of discrimination were illegalized. In order to enforce competition, pooling was forbidden, as was the old trick of charging more for a short haul over a line than for a long haul (where there might be competition). The act also set up the Interstate Commerce Commission, the first independent regulatory commission established by Congress and a landmark in the development of systematic national regulation of business. Composed initially of five men holding six-year terms, this body was given limited power to enforce the new law.

The act of 1887 was only a modest beginning. For its first two decades of life the I.C.C. had little weight. While the act had given the commis-

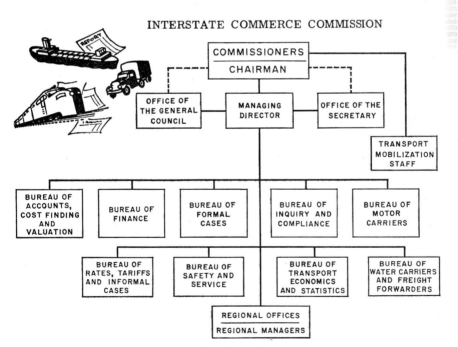

INTERSTATE COMMERCE COMMISSION

U.S. GOVERNMENT ORGANIZATION MANUAL, *1956-57, p. 619.*

sion no power to set blanket rates, supposedly the agency did have authority to find individual rates to be unreasonable and to modify them. A series of Supreme Court decisions stripped I.C.C. of its authority over these rates, however, as well as control of the long and short haul and of pooling. By 1897 the I.C.C. was formally complaining that it was powerless to protect the people. As a result of popular pressure during Theodore Roosevelt's Administration, however, Congress in 1906 passed the Hepburn Act, which explicitly granted rate-making power to the commission and broadened its jurisdiction to include express companies, sleeping-car companies, and other railroad facilities. In the following years a steady stream of laws bolstered the power and scope of the commission.

As a result of these extensions of its authority the commission today regulates not only railroads but also motor carriers, certain domestic water carriers, and pipe lines. Its functions are varied. The I.C.C. has wide powers to fix rates for the various types of carriers, to prevent undue discrimination in rates, to require carriers to provide adequate facilities and reasonable service, such as through routes. Carriers must obtain from the commission permits or certificates of convenience and necessity in order to engage in transportation. The I.C.C. has control over mergers among railroads and among motor carriers, and over the issuance of securities by these carriers. It regulates safety standards and methods. In exercising these powers the commission has considerable discretion. It has filled out the general terms of congressional statutes by hundreds of decisions over the years—enough cases to fill over 300 printed volumes.

Today the I.C.C. is a large agency composed of eleven commissioners (now holding seven-year terms) and a staff of almost 2000. It is organized into fifteen bureaus, including the important Bureaus of Motor Carriers, Traffic, Transport Economics and Statistics, Valuation, Law, Formal Cases, Informal Cases, and into numerous field offices. The eleven members are divided into five divisions, each usually composed of three members, for deciding most classes of cases coming before the agency. Each division specializes in certain types of cases. When the parties consent, individual commissioners will handle cases. As in other independent commissions, trial examiners do the great bulk of the hearing work, research, and initial writing of reports. Many disputes are disposed of informally.

The I.C.C.'s most difficult and important job is *rate making*. In the Transportation Act of 1920, Congress established a rule under which the commission was to set such rates that carriers in general would earn, assuming "honest, efficient and economical management," an aggregate net income equal to a fair return on the railway property. The commission's job was thus twofold: to determine the value of the railways and to decide what would be a fair return. Neither task is an easy one. Many factors enter into the valuation of property, and the railroads and the consumers naturally differ on the question of what is a fair return. Alternating periods of depression and prosperity put a heavy strain on rate structures; wars, whether hot or cold, mean heavier traffic but also higher costs. Finally, rate making is greatly complicated by the fact that over the last three decades railroads have faced increasing competition from bus lines, truck lines, air lines, and even pipe lines and ship lines.

Who shall haul what?

For decades the railroads had little inland competition except for boats plying lakes, rivers, and canals. The railroad was transportation king. In the 1920's, however, the picture changed. Buses and trucks began to handle passengers and freight on a tremendous scale. And the infant air industry showed positive signs of growing out of its swaddling clothes.

Thus transportation was becoming a more complex industry than ever, and so were transportation problems. One of the most pressing questions was that of *coordination*. It was clear that left to themselves the different carriers, railroads, motor, and air, might bring about an inefficient and poorly planned transportation system. This was one area where free competition seemed undesirable. In 1933 an act of Congress established for three years a Federal Coordinator of Transportation, whose main job was to study the industry as a unit and to draw up plans for greater efficiency. Following studies by the coordinator and others, Congress made some progress toward a unified transportation policy. Since the states had had little success in regulating interstate motor transportation, Congress in 1935 gave the I.C.C. power to regulate motor carriers operating between states. Today the commission regulates motor carriers in much the same way as it regulates railroads; it can, for example, require certain standards of service, establish systems of records and reports, and set safety requirements. The I.C.C.'s transportation authority was further broadened by the Transportation Act of 1940, which extended its regulatory power to water carriers in domestic service (such as carriers operating on canals or rivers).

Congress has not, however, established an integrated system of transportation regulation. While it has, as noted, concentrated regulation of railroads, buses, trucks, and some water carriers in the I.C.C., it has put the regulation of two vital segments of transportation—air and trans-oceanic —into the hands of other agencies.

In 1936 Congress established the United States Maritime Commission and gave it wide regulatory powers over *ocean carriers* as well as important operating and promotional functions (see Chapter 26). A five-man independent board, the commission had power to consider complaints of shippers or passengers alleging discrimination by ocean carriers in forwarding freight or furnishing docks or other facilities in ports. It could approve, disapprove, or modify cooperative working agreements among shipping companies. In some respects this commission's problems were even more difficult than those of the I.C.C., for our ships must compete with foreign lines that often can operate at lower cost. In 1949 the first Hoover Commission recommended that the managerial responsibilities of the Maritime Commission be vested in a line department. The following year President Truman abolished the commission and distributed its functions between two new agencies, the Federal Maritime Board and a Maritime Administration. While both these agencies are located in the Department of Commerce under an undersecretary, the Maritime Board retains its status of an independent agency because of the unfettered judicial decisions it must make in regulating ocean carriers.

Regulation of *air transportation* was put into the hands of still another agency. This was the Civil Aeronautics Authority. The Civil Aeronautics Act of 1938 was passed to foster aviation and a system of air transportation adaptable both to the needs of foreign and domestic commerce and to the requirements of national defense. Under the act air carriers must obtain a certificate from the agency in order to engage in domestic or foreign air transportation. Applicants for new routes must prove public convenience and necessity for the service and their fitness as operators. The agency may modify or suspend certificates; it may authorize the suspension of services and the abandonment of routes. Under the law carriers must charge fair rates, file public tariffs, and provide safe and adequate services. The board may prescribe rates except for foreign air transportation.

As in the case of the Maritime Commission the functions of the new aeronautics agency were promotional and managerial as well as regulatory. And as in the case of the Maritime Commission, vesting these three different types of powers in one agency proved awkward and unsatisfactory. At first the Civil Aeronautics Authority was composed of an independent commission of five members, an administrator responsible to the President, and an independent Air Safety Board charged with investigating air accidents. In 1940, President Roosevelt placed the administrator in the Department of Commerce, abolished the Air Safety Board, and transferred its functions to the Civil Aeronautics Board. Today the board hears and decides cases, enforces its decisions, and regulates and sets safety standards as an independent agency, while the much larger Civil Aeronautics Administration conducts its operating and promotional functions (see Chapter 26) as a unit in the Commerce Department.

Through all this elaborate machinery the federal government has a good deal of influence over the question of "who shall haul what?" Yet there is little basic plan. For one thing, Congress has never declared a broad and definite transportation policy. It has preferred to deal with policies in a piecemeal, pragmatic fashion as they arose. In the second place—and partly as a result of the lack of basic policy—the administrative machinery for direction of transportation is broken up. As agencies largely independent of a central directing force such as the President, the regulatory boards and commissions can often go their own way. There is some virtue in this. Our transportation system is still in a somewhat changing and fluid situation, and rigid controls might restrict initiative and progress. Some believe, however, that a unified transportation policy is vitally needed, especially in the present era of international crisis, and that the first step must be a single, over-all transportation agency. Two members of the first Hoover Commission, for example, called for the integration of the various forms of transportation into an efficient, economical, and progressive national system so that the government could follow a "consistent and balanced policy among competing forms of transportation."[7] Such a policy will be hard to achieve, however, as long as government must both regulate transportation and promote it, and must do so both for war needs and peace needs.

Patrolling the air waves

Nowhere is regulation more necessary than in the field of radio and television. Without a strong umpire, broadcasters would quickly become involved in a tussle for wave lengths on the limited broadcasting spectrum. Yet nowhere is regulation more difficult. Not only are there the ordinary problems of regulation of areas affected with a public interest—problems of concentration of control, licensing and withholding of licenses, technical standards, and the like, but regulation also touches on the delicate problem of censorship versus freedom of the air. Moreover, such regulation means not merely adjusting the claims of rival broadcasters, but also mediating between commercial broadcasting and alternative uses, such as ship-to-shore radio services, amateur broadcasting, police and aviation communication, and educational broadcasting.

The need for regulation of radio was well demonstrated in 1926. For several years the Secretary of Commerce had been allocating radio frequencies under an old law. Dissatisfied with its assigned frequency a Chicago station in 1926 jumped its wave length. When the Secretary of Commerce tried to penalize the company for this action, the company appealed to the courts and won its case. As soon as it appeared that the Secretary lacked authority, a wild scramble took place for favorable wave lengths and greater power. The chaos that resulted led to a wide demand for congressional action. The Radio Act of 1927 gave authority to a new Federal Radio Commission to police the industry.

Today the act is administered by the Federal Communications Commission, an independent regulatory board of seven men holding staggered seven-year terms. Aside from regulating the radio and television industry, the F.C.C. licenses operators and prescribes their qualifications, inspects radio and television installations, and monitors the radio and television spectrum, among other services. The commission's main job, of course, is

[7] Commission on Organization of the Executive Branch of the Government, *Regulatory Commissions* (Washington, D.C.: Government Printing Office, 1949), pp. 19-22.

allocating frequencies and licensing broadcasting stations. The allocation of frequencies calls for a just and expert sense of the needs of the various services. In handling applications for licenses the commission must decide whether a license to a particular applicant would be consistent with the public convenience, interest, or necessity. It must make its grants in such a way as to provide services throughout the nation. Licenses are good for three years and can be renewed; this provision enables the F.C.C. to keep a periodic check on the activities of broadcasting stations.

The F.C.C. has the ticklish task of *policing* the broadcasters without *censoring* them. On the one hand the Communications Act of 1934 specifies that nothing therein shall be understood to give the commission the power to interfere with the right of free speech by radio and television. The commission has stated that it has no power to make regulations governing the content of programs. On the other hand, in considering applications for the renewal of licenses it takes into account the content and character of their past programs. It also has power to suspend the license of any operator who is proved to have transmitted profane or obscene words on the air. Despite these ambiguities the F.C.C. has a good record of guarding the freedom of the air. It tries to enforce the statutory requirement that if a station's facilities are made available to one candidate for a public office they must be opened to all candidates for that office on the same terms. It has been suggested that the commission has guarded freedom of the air more zealously than have individual broadcasters.

The advent of television has re-emphasized all the problems facing the F.C.C. One of these is the place of education in the broadcasting system. The central question has involved the division of facilities for commercial and educational purposes. Quite naturally, the commercial broadcasters want to emphasize programs that bring revenue rather than educational programs that might not have the drawing power of a Steve Allen. Television, with its enormous powers both to inform and misinform, has greatly underlined the problem. The F.C.C. has made some headway in encouraging educational features, but progress has been slow. There has been some discussion of other methods of furthering radio and television education, such as requiring radio and television companies to devote a certain portion of their facilities to education, or setting up either a privately endowed or government-owned and operated network. The problem is a vital one; it involves not only the maintenance of free speech but its vigor and scope (see chapters 6, 11).

The F.C.C. also regulates interstate telephone and telegraph. It has power to fix reasonable rates, prescribe standards of service, control mergers and expansion or curtailment of service, and to undertake other activities typical of the modern independent commissions that regulate transportation and communication agencies. The F.C.C. does not face such difficult problems in this area as in radio and television, but the problem of mergers has been a challenging one. For example, it was only with the permission of the F.C.C. that two competing telegraph companies, Western Union and Postal Telegraph, combined into one company in 1943.

LABOR

As we have seen, governmental regulation of business has been essentially *restrictive*. Most of the laws and rules have involved curbing certain business practices and channeling the dynamic force of private enterprise into socially useful channels. But regulation cuts two ways. In the case of American workers, most laws in recent decades have tended not to *restrict* labor but to *confer rights* and *opportunities* on it. Actually, many labor laws do not touch labor directly, but regulate its relations with employers, including contract provisions.

Most business leaders in general would prefer a hands-off policy from government (with exceptions noted in the next chapter). But not labor leaders. For in the absence of governmental regulation they fear that business would impose far more strict regulations on labor. They see, for example, the likelihood of longer working hours if government did not regulate the length of the workday. This difference in the attitudes of labor and business toward governmental regulation is a significant factor in American politics.

Labor and the government

Of course, labor did not always look on government with a friendly eye. Traditionally the workers have viewed federal and state judges with particular suspicion. Steeped in the common law, judges tended to follow the *conspiracy doctrine*—the idea that men must not combine to injure others. Since organized labor's traditional weapon has been the strike, this doctrine could be used by antiunion judges to prevent workers from acting effectively. Employing the conspiracy doctrine and other maxims, some judges freely issued injunctions against strikes, boycotts, and other kinds of union activities. Moreover, the courts *interpreted* laws in such a way as to hurt labor. As we have seen earlier in this chapter, the Supreme Court turned against labor the Sherman Antitrust Act, which the workers thought had been passed to curb business combinations, not their own unions. Finally, the courts held unconstitutional a number of acts designed to improve the worker's lot. Perhaps the most famous example was the Supreme Court's invalidation of the New York law limiting employment in bakeries to sixty hours a week and ten hours a day, on the grounds that the law interfered with freedom of contract and therefore violated the due process clause of the Fourteenth Amendment.[8]

[8] *Lochner* v. *New York* (1905).

Today the situation is different. The first half of this century has seen the extension of governmental protection and promotion over the whole range of labor activity and organization. The change did not come by chance. It was a result of two basic political developments—labor's growing political power, and the awareness of millions of Americans in all walks of life that a healthy and secure nation depends in large measure on a healthy and secure labor force. Both these factors were reflected in the election of prolabor Presidents, such as Wilson and the two Roosevelts, and of friendly legislators in Senate and House and the state capitols.

Labor's basic struggle was for the *right to organize*. For many decades trade unions had been held to be lawful by acts of state legislatures, but here again the courts had chipped away at this right by legalizing certain antiunion devices. The most notorious of these devices was the yellow-dog contract, by which antiunion employers in hiring workers extracted promises from them not to join a labor organization. If labor organizers later tried to unionize such workers, the employer, on the basis of yellow-dog contracts, could apply for injunctions from the courts to stop the organizers. This was a great stumbling block in the path of American unions.[9] Chafing under this restriction, labor in 1932 secured the passage of the Norris-La Guardia Act, which made yellow-dog contracts unenforceable in federal courts. Acknowledging the right of labor to organize, the act also drastically limited the issuance of labor injunctions in other respects.

By 1932 labor had won other kinds of protection from the federal government. Almost a century before, in 1840, the government had established the ten-hour day in its navy yards, and later the working day of governmental employees was shortened to eight hours. Earlier in the present century Congress voted the eight-hour day for railroad employees and for seamen. In 1931 the government moved to maintain wage standards for employees of private contractors on public works. Nevertheless, progress was slow, and limited to only a few fields. In 1918 the Supreme Court had invalidated a national law prohibiting the interstate transportation of goods produced by child labor, and a constitutional amendment to give Congress this power had not got very far. By 1932 the United States still lagged far behind several European countries in the protection afforded to labor.

A New Deal for labor

On the eve of the Roosevelt Administration the A.F.L. was down to barely two million members—partly a result of unemployment during the Great Depression. Its political influence was small. But the new Administration was sympathetic toward labor. During the next decade organized

[9] H. A. Millis and R. E. Montgomery, *Organized Labor* (New York: McGraw-Hill Book Company, Inc., 1945), p. 513.

labor rose to a position of tremendous economic and political power. From the New Deal, labor achieved both an array of protective legislation and governmental help in its campaign to organize the unorganized. Not only did the C.I.O. split off from the A.F.L. and unionize a number of vital industries, such as steel, automobiles, and rubber, but the A.F.L. itself re-formed its ranks and became larger and stronger than ever.

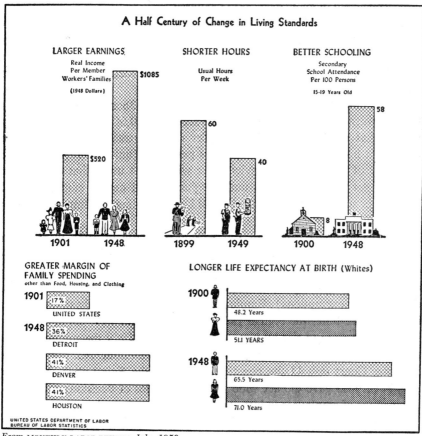

A Half Century of Change in Living Standards

LARGER EARNINGS
Real Income Per Member Workers' Families
(1948 Dollars)

$1085
$520
1901   1948

SHORTER HOURS
Usual Hours Per Week

60
40
1899   1949

BETTER SCHOOLING
Secondary School Attendance Per 100 Persons
15-19 Years Old

58
8
1900   1948

GREATER MARGIN OF FAMILY SPENDING
other than Food, Housing, and Clothing

1901   17%   UNITED STATES
1948   36%   DETROIT
41%   DENVER
41%   HOUSTON

LONGER LIFE EXPECTANCY AT BIRTH (Whites)

1900   48.2 Years
51.1 YEARS
1948   65.5 Years
71.0 Years

UNITED STATES DEPARTMENT OF LABOR
BUREAU OF LABOR STATISTICS

From MONTHLY LABOR REVIEW, *July, 1950*

The city worker during the last fifty years.

The National Industrial Recovery Act of 1933 laid the stage for the New Deal's labor policies. This act was essentially a means of giving business a shot in the arm by allowing industries to work out codes of fair competition. Such codes, however, involved labor standards, such as wages, hours, and child labor, and the unions were given a part in the code-making process. Moreover, Section 7a of the act contained the famous provision that "employees shall have the right to organize and bargain collectively through representatives of their own choosing, and shall be free from the interference, restraint, or coercion of employers of labor, or their agents, in the designation of such representatives or in self-organization or in other concerted activities for the purpose of collective bargaining or other mutual aid or protection." Under the stimulus of this act and the up-turn in business, the unions blossomed. As Blue Eagle placards appeared in store windows, new members flocked into unions, and violent organizational strikes occurred in many parts of the country.

The N.R.A. was short-lived. The Supreme Court declared the act unconstitutional in 1935. But a New Deal Congress was determined to maintain national protection and encouragement of labor. In the next few years it passed a series of acts that amounted to a sort of N.R.A. for labor. These acts involved:

Public contracts. The Walsh-Healey Act of 1936 requires that all national government supply contracts in excess of $10,000 must contain provisions that no worker employed under such contracts shall work more than eight hours per day or forty hours per week (unless permitted by the Secretary of Labor); that convict labor will not be used; that child labor (boys under sixteen and girls under eighteen) will not be employed; and that all persons employed will be paid a prevailing minimum wage as determined by the Secretary of Labor.

Wages and hours. The Fair Labor Standards Act of 1938 went much further. It set a maximum work week of 44 hours, to be successively reduced to 42 and then to 40 hours, for all employees engaged in interstate commerce, or in the production of goods for interstate commerce (with certain major exemptions). Employees could work beyond these limits only if paid at 1½ times the regular rate. Minimum wages were set at 25 cents an hour, but were to rise by jumps to 40 cents. In 1949 the minimum was raised to 75 cents an hour, and in 1956 to $1.00 an hour. Not only did the Supreme Court uphold the constitutionality of the Fair Labor Standards Act, but it also gave the act wide scope in a series of decisions relating to its coverage of employees in interstate commerce.

Today about 24 million workers are protected, including most of the workers in factories and mining, transportation and communications. But millions are not covered. In addition to those who do not come under the interstate commerce coverage, Congress has also exempted agricultural workers, most employees in the retail and service trades, immediate processors of agricultural commodities, outside salesmen, seamen, and others.

The Fair Labor Standards and Walsh-Healey Acts are administered by the Wage and Hour and Public Contracts Divisions of the Department of Labor; the two divisions are jointly administered by a head appointed by the President (with the consent of the Senate). The divisions have a crew of inspectors who check business firms to insure compliance with the law, but their administrator has frequently asked Congress for more funds in order to make the inspections necessary for full enforcement.

Child labor. The Fair Labor Standards Act prohibited child labor (under sixteen years of age or under eighteen in hazardous occupations) in industries that are in or that produce goods for interstate commerce. These provisions are enforced by the Wage and Hour Division and the Bureau of Labor Standards (in the Labor Department), which sets standards of employment.

Labor relations. Section 7a of the N.I.R.A. was resurrected in the National Labor Relations Act, passed in 1935 only two months after the Supreme Court struck down the former act. In the preamble, the Wagner Act (so called after its chief sponsor, Senator Robert Wagner of New York) declared that workers in industries affecting interstate commerce (with certain exceptions) should have the right to organize and bargain collectively, and that inequality in bargaining power between employers and workers led to industrial strife and economic instability. The act set forth five types of action that were unfair for employers to practice: (1) interfering with workers in their attempts to organize unions or bargain collectively; (2) supporting company unions (unions set up and dominated by the employer); (3) discriminating against membership in unions; (4) firing or

Children in the Labor Force

14 AND 15 YEARS OLD

Number Per 1000 In Population

309

1900   Mar. 1950

U.S. Bureau of the Census

otherwise victimizing an employee for having taken action under the act; (5) refusing to bargain with union representatives. The act was intended to end the practices of open-shop employers who had used violence, espionage, propaganda, and community pressure to resist unionization of their plants.

The Wagner Act also set up machinery to decide contests over what union should represent a given group of employers. Such conflicts—which became numerous and bitter when the C.I.O. broke away from the A.F.L.—were to be settled by secret ballot and majority rule. To administer the act a board of three members, holding overlapping terms of five years each, was set up. The National Labor Relations Board, an independent regulatory commission, has the ticklish job of determining the appropriate bargaining unit—that is, whether the employees should vote by employer unit, plant unit, craft unit, or on some other basis. The board operates largely through regional officers, who investigate charges of unfair labor practices and may issue formal complaints, and through trial examiners, who hold hearings and submit reports to the board in Washington.

Striking a balance

Of these measures the Wagner Act was by far the most important and controversial. The Fair Labor Standards Act, in its efforts to put a floor under wages and a ceiling over hours, tended to lag behind the tremendous rise in wages during the 1940's. The child labor and public contracts measures affected limited sections of the public. The Wagner Act, however, strengthened unions everywhere and aided them in seizing greater economic and political power.

UNITED STATES DEPARTMENT OF LABOR
BUREAU OF LABOR STATISTICS

Based on Union Reports

From MONTHLY LABOR REVIEW, *July, 1950*

From the start the Wagner Act was a center of controversy. In 1936 a committee of eminent attorneys declared that the measure was unconstitutional. Taking heart from this "opinion," many corporations simply ignored the board. Unions, unwilling to wait for the slow-moving procedures of the law, organized a series of violent strikes, including the much criticized sit-down strikes. In April 1937, during President Roosevelt's campaign to pack the Supreme Court, the Court by a six-to-three vote upheld the constitutionality of the Wagner Act.[10] The fight then shifted to Congress, where senators and representatives attacked the board by denunciation, by investigations, and by slashing appropriations.

What was behind all this uproar? The causes were threefold. From the outset the board applied vigorously the prolabor provisions of the act. For example, the act prohibited the employer from interfering with employee unionization; the board interpreted this to mean that employers could not make public statements advising workers not to join unions. Such rulings

[10] *National Labor Relations Board* v. *Jones & Laughlin Steel Corp.*

raised a storm of protest from employers. In the second place, the board soon ran into the widening split between the A.F.L. and C.I.O. Whichever way it decided certain representation cases, it was bound to antagonize one labor faction. Some of these cases, moreover, were highly consequential; in one decision the board designated the C.I.O. Longshoremen's Union as the bargaining agent for all west coast ports, although the A.F.L. claimed majority support of employees in particular companies. Finally, there was much misunderstanding of the simple purpose of the act. Employers and editorial writers solemnly charged the measure and the board with being one-sided, when the very aim of the act had been to improve the workers' bargaining power.

A number of union practices stimulated criticism. These were not new, but now that labor was achieving greater power these abuses came in for more public attention. One was featherbedding. Faced with labor-saving devices that seemed to cut down on the number of workers needed to do a given job, some unions demanded that the original number of workers be paid, even if they had nothing to do and merely stood around. For example, James C. Petrillo, head of the A.F.L. Musicians' Union, barred his members from making records, taking part in television broadcasts, or making transcriptions that could be played over the radio. Then there was the charge of union dictatorship. Some union leaders seemed to stay in office for years, even decades; some received exorbitant salaries (for example, Petrillo, $46,000 a year). To be sure, many union leaders had no more dictatorial control over their unions than did many business executives over their enterprises, but as we saw in Chapter 10, the stereotype of organized labor tends to be hostile. And unions are supposed to be run in a democratic manner. Moreover, protected by the *closed shop* (an establishment where only union members can be hired), some union heads seemed to have as much power to discipline members as had the more ruthless employers of old. And a few unions were simple rackets. Investigations revealed intimate connections between certain union leaders and the underworld.

Most unions continued to be run honestly and democratically. Nevertheless, public opinion, fed by antiunion propaganda, seemed to swing against labor after World War II. Not only labor excesses but a wave of great industry-wide strikes intensified demands in Congress for a law that would equalize the obligations of labor and management. In 1946 the Republicans won majorities in House and Senate, paving the way for modification of the Wagner Act.

The Taft-Hartley Act

The upshot was the Labor-Management Relations Act of 1947, commonly called the Taft-Hartley Act after its sponsors. The Act, which applies with certain exceptions to industries affecting interstate commerce:

Outlawed the closed shop.

Permitted the *union shop* (under which newly employed workers must join the union within a stated time period) only under certain conditions.

Required unions to file affidavits that their officers are not Communists, if such unions wished to secure federal action on complaints against employers.

Outlawed jurisdictional strikes (strikes arising from disputes between unions as to which had the right to do a job), secondary boycotts, political expenditures by unions in connection with federal elections, excessive union dues or fees, strikes by federal employees.

Made it an unfair labor practice for unions to refuse to bargain with employers.

Permitted employers and unions to sue each other for violation of contracts in federal courts.

Allowed the use of the labor injunction on a limited scale, reversing the policy under the Norris-La Guardia Act.

Revamped the Labor Board, increasing its membership to five and strengthening the semi-independent position of the board's general counsel.

Organized labor greeted the new measure as a "slave-labor" act. It vowed that it would use its political power to wipe the act from the statute books. Senator Taft saw the bill as "an extraordinary reversal along the right lines toward equalizing the power of labor unions and employers." Most observers saw the measure as neither a slave-labor act nor as a cure-all. While acknowledging the seriousness of some labor practices, they have expressed fears that the Taft-Hartley Act may have put the government too far into the hitherto voluntary area of collective bargaining.

At any rate, the Taft-Hartley Act may be here to stay for some time. Although President Truman during his successful 1948 campaign promised to seek the act's repeal, a majority in Congress stoutly refused to repeal or amend it drastically. The act has continued, however, to be a major political issue. As his first Secretary of Labor, President Eisenhower appointed a union leader named Martin P. Durkin, who had long opposed the measure —an appointment that Senator Taft labeled "incredible." Knowing that the President favored some changes in the Taft-Hartley law, Secretary of Labor Durkin proceeded to work out nineteen specific amendments that he understood the White House would accept. It developed, however, that the President did not favor Durkin's amendments, and the latter resigned with a statement that the President had broken his word. Mr. Eisenhower continued to ask Congress for minor modifications of the Taft-Hartley Act, but both Senate and House have been so divided internally over the kind of changes to be made that no action has been taken. The 1956 Republican platform promised to "revise and improve, the Taft-Hartley Act so as to protect more effectively the rights of labor unions, management, the individual worker, and the public." President Eisenhower's re-election in 1956 along with a Democratic Congress made it unlikely that the act would be repealed or changed in any major fashion.

Keeping labor-management peace

The Federal Mediation and Conciliation Service, headed by a director and with mediators located in twelve regional offices, offers its facilities in labor-management disputes in any industry affecting interstate commerce (except railroads and airlines which are covered by the Railway Labor Act), either on request of one of the parties to the dispute or whenever in the judgment of the service the dispute threatens to cause a substantial interruption of interstate commerce. Under the terms of the Taft-Hartley Act, which also placed the service outside the Labor Department, the service avoids mediation of disputes which would have only a minor effect on interstate commerce if state or other conciliation services are available. Employers and unions are required to notify the service of every dispute affecting interstate commerce not settled within 30 days after either party has notified the other that it wishes to terminate or modify an existing labor contract. Through tact and persuasion the trouble shooters of the Federal Mediation and Conciliation Service induce unions to call off strikes and employers to make concessions. The service has no power to dictate terms; the parties to the dispute can ignore the conciliators and their suggestions. If mediation fails the parties may ask the service to assist in the selection of an arbitrator; under this arrangement the parties agree in advance to accept the arbitrator's decision.

The Taft-Hartley Act also set up new machinery for handling disputes affecting an entire industry, or a major part of it, where a stoppage would threaten the national health or safety. In the event of such a strike, the following procedure may take place:

1. The President appoints a special board to investigate and report the facts.

2. The President may then instruct the Attorney General to seek an injunction against the strike.

3. The (federal) court grants this injunction if it agrees that the national health or safety is endangered.

4. If the parties have not settled the strike within eighty days, the board reports to the President on the nature of the employer's last offer of settlement.

5. The N.L.R.B. takes a secret vote among the employees to see if they will accept the employer's last offer.

6. If no settlement is reached, the injunction expires, and the President reports to Congress with such recommendations as he may wish to make.

It is too early to evaluate the effectiveness of the Taft-Hartley Act in keeping labor peace. It has been invoked several times against strikes in vital sectors of the economy, such as atomic energy, coal, shipping, and telephone service, sometimes successfully, sometimes not. On one occasion an injunction was issued ordering John L. Lewis to send his coal miners back to work. Lewis sent out the orders, but the miners stayed out. The government asked the court for a contempt of court citation against the miners' leader, but the court held that Lewis had done his best. Neither President Truman nor Eisenhower made use of the act in the 1952 or 1956 steel strikes but the latter invoked its provisions in waterfront disputes in the fall of 1953.

RESOURCES

The period after the Civil War was one of feverish development of the nation's enormous resources. The General Land Office of the federal government handed our western riches—lands, forests, minerals—to thousands

WHAT FEDERAL LANDS ARE USED FOR

Principal use	Number of acres	Principal use	Number of acres
Forests and wildlife	186.3 million	Reclamation and irrigation	8.8 million
Grazing	169.6 million	Flood control and navigation	3.2 million
Military (except airfields)	15.2 million	Industrial uses, including atomic energy	1.8 million
Airfields	2.0 million	Power development	1.5 million
Parks and historic sites	15.0 million	Sites for hospitals, offices, storage, housing, other purposes	1.7 million

 TOTAL LAND OWNED BY THE GOVERNMENT IN THE U.S.— 405.1 million acres OR 21.3% of entire country

Reprinted from U.S. NEWS & WORLD REPORT, an independent weekly news magazine published at Washington. Copyright 1955 U.S. News Publishing Corporation

of individuals and corporations. At the time our resources seemed inexhaustible. But as the years passed, people began to demand that the government act to protect the public interest and to curb some of the worst abuses of exploitation. Well before the end of the century Yellowstone National Park had been created and many million acres of forest reservation had been set aside.

The conservation movement came to a head in Theodore Roosevelt's administration. The rough rider had lived in the West as a young man and had come to cherish its scenic beauties and its wild life. On assuming office he told Congress that "forest and water problems are perhaps the most vital internal problems of the United States." With the help of Gifford Pinchot, another conservation zealot and chief of the Forestry Bureau, Roosevelt drew national attention to conservation problems and greatly enlarged the nation's public coal, oil, phosphate, and forest reserves. In the years since the Square Deal the federal government not only has continued to protect and enlarge public reserves of forest land and other resources: it also has extended regulation over *private* exploitation of the nation's riches.

Coal

Federal intervention in conservation has been largely conducted through the method of promotion and subsidy, as we shall see in the next chapter. Two important resources, however, have been largely left in private hands under governmental regulation. These are coal and oil.

The bituminous coal industry has a vital place in our economy, for it provides almost half the nation's supply of energy. Earlier in this century bituminous coal came to be regarded as a sick industry. The main trouble was overcapacity. Production had grown sharply in the nineteenth century, but later coal began to meet the competition of fuel oil, natural gas, and electric power. Labor relations were bitter and sometimes violent. The depression beginning in 1929 further weakened an already unstable industry. Profits and wages fell drastically. By 1932 both employers and labor were turning to the federal government for help. The N.R.A., which lessened the pressures of competition and raised labor standards, gave temporary relief. When the N.R.A. was invalidated, the industry sought more permanent help.

The result was the Bituminous Coal Conservation Act of 1935. This measure was only in part a conservation act. It set up a commission of five members who, along with a number of district boards, were empowered to set coal prices for the industry by region and district. Labor was guaranteed the right to organize and bargain collectively and was granted other concessions. Maximum hours, agreed upon by producers' and workers' representatives, were to be binding on the industry. Within a year of passage the Supreme Court held the act invalid, declaring that the labor provisions were beyond the scope of federal authority under the commerce clause.[11] A new law was promptly enacted that omitted the labor provisions. The emphasis was largely on price stabilization. The new commission promulgated a code that was endorsed by 95 per cent of the industry. On the basis of exhaustive studies and of proposals from producers throughout the industry, an elaborate schedule of thousands of prices was drawn up. Ample opportunity was afforded parties to protest proposed prices. The schedules finally adopted were compromises among many conflicting interests in the industry.

[11] *Carter* v. *Carter Coal Co.*

Undoubtedly the Bituminous Coal Commission provided a good deal of temporary relief and stability to the industry. But it had no opportunity to show a more lasting effect. The commission itself was abolished by President Roosevelt and its functions transferred to a Bituminous Coal Division under the Secretary of the Interior. In 1943 the basic act expired, and Congress failed to renew it. This failure was partly a recognition of the improved position of the industry during World War II.

Oil

Regulation of petroleum resources has been based on the need for *conservation* to a greater extent than our coal policy. Oil can easily be wasted. It can be produced in such a way as to give quick profits to a few operators, while leaving underground millions of barrels that can be recovered only by costly processes. Moreover, oil can be wasted by burning, running off into the ground, or by uncontrolled blowing off of gas. Our reserves are still vast but by no means limitless. Since oil is a vitally urgent mineral in war as well as peace, the federal government has been involved in the problem.

During the depression, hundreds of new wells were opened up, and prices dropped to less than 25 cents a barrel. Individual states attempted to stabilize the industry and conserve oil by restricting production, but they had little success. The National Industrial Recovery Act gave the President power to regulate the industry, including authority to prohibit the interstate transportation of oil produced in excess of quotas set by state law. In 1935, however, the Supreme Court invalidated the oil control section of N.I.R.A. on the grounds that the President's power to stop the shipment

GOVERNMENT OWNS NEARLY HALF OF ALL LAND IN THE WEST

LEGEND
Per cent of land owned by Government

Per cent of total acreage owned by the Federal Government

Washington	30.3%	Arizona	41.6%
Oregon	51.8%	Montana	30.0%
California	46.2%	Wyoming	47.7%
Idaho	65.3%	Colorado	36.2%
Nevada	87.4%	New Mexico	32.6%
Utah	64.6%		

Government holdings in 11 Western States
359,100,000 acres, or 47.7% of total

of hot oil (oil produced above the quota) was an unconstitutional delegation of legislative power.[12] Congress then passed a new measure directly forbidding the shipment in interstate commerce of oil produced in excess of state quotas. The President had authority to suspend this embargo on oil if he found a lack of balance between supply and demand. Congress also authorized an interstate compact among the big producing states, and this was soon drawn up and ratified by Texas, Oklahoma, and other states.

Some conservationists believe that the federal government has not done enough to conserve oil. Proposals have been made for tougher federal laws requiring and enforcing rigid standards of conservation. Representatives of the oil states, however, have resisted further federal control. As our oil resources become more depleted, the political disputes between conservationists and producers may become more bitter. Consumers of oil and gasoline may also become more directly involved in oil politics.

In recent years a political struggle has taken place over ownership of the rich oil deposits off the shore of the United States between low-water mark and the three-mile limit. The Supreme Court has ruled that the national government has a paramount interest in the offshore oil. In 1946 President Truman vetoed an act of Congress handing over ownership of the oil to the states. In 1952, however, offshore oil became an election issue, and the following year Congress passed and President Eisenhower signed a bill vesting in the states involved title to submerged lands and resources within their "historic" boundaries while confirming federal ownership of submerged lands of the continental shelf beyond state boundaries. Democrats denounced the Act as a "give-away"; Republicans replied that it was merely part of their program of "restoring more power to the states." The issues are complex, involving the views of states' righters and conservationists and the struggles of oil companies and state governments for control of the oil. Since the oil off the coasts of Texas and Louisiana alone has been valued at $27 billion, the controversy is likely to continue for some time.

Other resources

Water is both a vital resource in itself (see Chapter 26) and also a source of electric power. In 1920 Congress passed the Federal Water Power Act to regulate the use of water power on public lands and navigable streams. A Federal Power Commission, composed of the Secretaries of Agriculture, Interior, and War, was set up. Ten years later the F.P.C. was converted into a new independent regulatory commission, with five full-time members holding five-year terms, and its powers were broadened. The major job of the commission is to protect the rights of the American people in the water power potential of navigable streams. Private companies can build dams and other hydroelectric facilities only after receiving a license from the F.P.C. Such licenses are granted only if the project is adapted to a comprehensive

[12] *Panama Refining Co. v. Ryan.*

plan for developing the waterway for use of water power, development of navigation, recreation, and other beneficial purposes.

The commission regulates rates, services, and securities issued by companies so licensed (where a state commission does not do so). Furthermore, under the Federal Power Act of 1935, the commission has jurisdiction over all public utilities engaged in selling or sending electricity across state boundaries. Here, too, the F.P.C. has power to fix just and reasonable rates, and its approval is required for selling or merging facilities and buying or selling securities. The F.P.C. is a sort of I.C.C. for electricity. It also has some voice in the development of power facilities by other federal agencies, such as the Army.

Natural gas, an increasingly important commodity in recent years, has also been subject to regulation by the Federal Power Commission. The Natural Gas Act of 1938 requires that natural-gas companies selling in interstate commerce must obtain certificates of convenience and necessity from the commission. The F.P.C. also has power to fix reasonable rates. Since natural gas is a relatively young industry, the commission was involved in the scramble of private companies for authorization to build new pipe lines to urban areas in the North and East. It has sought to protect the welfare of the consumer and to prevent the overbuilding of pipe lines to one community.

In recent years, independent natural gas producers have tried to gain exemption from federal regulation. Arguing that such regulation was unnecessary and discriminatory, they persuaded Congress to pass an exemption measure in 1956. President Eisenhower had been expected to sign the bill; but during debate in the upper chamber, a senator announced that he could not vote for the bill because a lawyer working for its passage had given $2500 to the senator's campaign manager. The President vetoed the bill because of what he called the "arrogant tactics" of gas-and-oil lobbyists. Supporters of exemption indicated, however, that they would again introduce the bill in a subsequent session of Congress.

THE POLITICS OF REGULATION

Karl Marx, the theorist of "capitalist decay," maintained that in the long run the interests of all the capitalists were the same. He argued that the proletariat had a similar unity of interest, and that eventually the exploiting class would give way to the government of the workers. Relations among the new proletarian rulers would be so harmonious that eventually the state would just wither away.

A look at the American economy today is enough to dispel the idea of a united group of businessmen facing a united group of workers. To be sure, there is conflict between businessmen and workers. But such conflict is obscured by a vast complex of antagonistic interests operating *within* economic groups. The American political scene, as this book has tried to show, reflects not only the struggle of employer against worker, but also the struggles of consumer against producer, of businessmen against businessmen, of labor against labor, of section against section. And all these interests are intertwined and interlocked in such a way as to make the whole picture very complex indeed.

The clash of interests

Earlier (see Chapter 10) we noted some of the characteristics and weapons of the larger economic interests. Here it might be well to look closer at the competition among interest groups in the light of the problem of governmental regulation.

Some of the sharpest contests take place within the world of business. Consider, for example, the railroad interests. The early attempts to regulate the railroads involved chiefly a struggle between the railroads and consumers. But other interests were concerned too—for example, financial control groups, railroad investors, railroad equipment and supply industries. Later, the railroads began to meet intense competition from other forms of transportation, and railroad politics became more intricate than ever.

Today a political battle constantly simmers between railroad carriers and the trucking business, and occasionally this battle erupts in full-page advertisements in leading newspapers. The railroads argue that the trucking business offers unfair competition. Motor transportation, they protest, receives subsidies by virtue of the fact that government builds and maintains highways, while the railroads must provide their own. The truckers reply that they contribute heavily to highway maintenance through gasoline and other taxes—and so the battle rages. The railroads also complain of the subsidies granted air lines and water shippers.

The internal rivalries of labor are another factor in the politics of regulation. Labor, as we have seen in Chapter 10, is by no means a unified, monolithic body; it is a cluster of unions of all kinds, sizes, and interests, along with many unorganized workers. The cleavages that can develop within the ranks of organized labor were dramatically revealed in the 1930's when the C.I.O. broke away from the A.F.L. But less conspicuous rivalries are also important. One of these is between workers employed in rival industries. For example, the Railroad Brotherhoods and the Teamsters' Union (mainly truck drivers) often clash on national transportation policy simply because industrially these two groups stand in a competitive relationship with one another. Sometimes, of course, unions largely ignore such competitive situations. Ford, General Motors, and Chrysler may compete in selling cars, but there is little indication that this rivalry has much effect on the solidarity of the United Auto Workers Union, which embraces workers from all these corporations.

Two other cleavages are worth noting. One is between small business and big. Much of the popular sentiment for trust busting arose from little businessmen who felt that they were being squeezed economically by the mammoth corporations. Today associations of little businessmen give some support to federal antitrust activities and to the regulation of the money markets. The other type of cleavage is *geographical*. Perhaps the most important of these is the competition between northern and southern industry, especially in textiles, but there is also intense rivalry between West and East. Such cleavages are especially important because of the fact that Congress is organized on a geographical basis.

Washington battleground

Indeed, Congress more than any other branch of government mirrors the efforts of interest groups to gain or evade federal regulation. Many members of Congress, as we have seen, represent states or districts dominated by one or two economic interests. The "silver" senators and the "cotton" representatives are only two cases in point. Other members of Congress—especially those from heavily populated areas—may be concerned more with the interests of consumers. When the consumer feels that he is pinched by excessive rates, when a transportation industry believes that it cannot make a fair profit on present charges, when little businessmen think that they are being squeezed out by the big fellows, their complaints are quickly followed—indeed, sometimes aroused by—outcries in the halls of Congress.

Congress has delegated to the regulatory agencies the big job of mediating the claims of affected interests. It is significant that most of these regulatory agencies are *independent regulatory boards*. Thus this chapter has dealt mainly with such boards as the I.C.C., F.T.C., F.C.C., S.E.C., N.L.R.B., and others. This is not accidental. For a variety of reasons Congress has seen fit to put the regulatory function in the hands of agencies somewhat independent of elected officials, and especially independent of the President (see Chapter 19). As a practical matter this procedure was not necessary. Regulatory functions can be—and are—effectively and fairly handled by line agencies in regular federal departments. For example, the Packers and Stockyards Act of 1921, which seeks to protect farmers against arbitrary charges and other unfair practices, is administered by the Bureau of Animal Industry in the Department of Agriculture. Too, wages and hours are administered by a line agency headed by an administrator and lodged in the Labor Department. Nevertheless Congress has generally preferred the independent agency. It has given board members long, staggered terms; it has limited the President's power to remove members; and it has usually required that members must be selected from both parties.

The result is that the commissions have been somewhat insulated from partisan politics and partisan control. But they have not been kept out of politics; no agency making important decisions can be. A commission ultimately reflects prevailing sentiment, as did the F.T.C. in its probusiness decisions during the 1920's. A commission is inevitably influenced by new members; if a President appoints a series of consumer-conscious commissioners, the decisions of the agency will respect consumer interests. And, as we have seen, the regulatory agencies are influenced by Congress, which allots them funds, investigates them, and shares in the making of appointments.

The lake cargo coal rate controversy in the 1920's is an example of the exposure of regulatory agencies to political rough and tumble. In this case the I.C.C. was caught in the cross fire between coal operators in the northern coal fields and those in the southern. Each group wanted to supply lake cargo coal and to gain preferential freight rates to Lake Erie ports. The fight became so "intense as to lead to direct political interference with the rate-making process. Appointments were made and rejected with a view to swaying the decision of the Commission."[13] The commission was divided; finally the railroads themselves worked out a compromise.

The conflict between the A.F.L. and C.I.O. closely affected regulatory politics. The passage of the Wages and Hours Act was gravely imperiled by the fear of the Federation that it was essentially a C.I.O. bill and might upset craft union arrangements. More important, the N.L.R.B. ran head on into A.F.L.-C.I.O. jurisdictional rivalry in attempting to determine the appropriate bargaining unit. When the President nominated new board appointees, they were carefully scrutinized by each labor organization to see if they had leanings to the other side. During its early years the N.L.R.B. was greatly handicapped by the need to follow a cautious policy of neutrality between the two labor groups. The reunion of A.F.L. and C.I.O. more recently may mean that government labor agencies will not be caught so much in the struggles between those two organizations, but the rivalries among individual unions will certainly be reflected in the Washington battleground.

To be sure, some regulatory agencies have protected themselves from political cross currents better than others have. The I.C.C. in recent years is an example. This agency is often cited as one of the most judicial and independent agencies in Washington. Yet such an agency may become highly political in another sense—namely, of being overly protective of the industry it is designed to regulate. The I.C.C., which is rarely charged with favoritism as between one railroad and another, is often accused of being prorailroad as compared with other forms of transportation. Whether this particular charge is true or not, the capture of a regulatory agency by the regulated interests is not unknown in Washington.

[13] Merle Fainsod and Lincoln Gordon, *Government and the American Economy* (New York: W. W. Norton & Co., Inc., 1941), p. 272. See H. C. Mansfield, *The Lake Cargo Coal Rate Controversy* (New York: Columbia University Press, 1932) for the full account.

I

N RECENT YEARS WE HAVE HEARD MUCH OF THE welfare state or service state. Politicians have charged that spendthrifts in Washington have been trying to buy the votes or blocs of voters through give-away programs. Supporters of promotional activities have denounced their opponents as heartless skinflints who would put dollars before human lives. Amid these arguments certain facts are sometimes ignored.

In the first place, governmental promotion in the United States is by no means a recent development. In his first annual address to Congress, President Washington called for a tariff to protect business. In his famous *Report on the Subject of Manufactures* in 1791, Secretary of the Treasury Alexander Hamilton proposed that government help in the development of business through such means as giving bounties to new enterprises. Henry Clay's American System was a plan for federally subsidized internal improvements, a strengthened banking system, and tariff protection. Parts of these ambitious programs were carried out during the first half of the nineteenth century, and after the Civil War the Republican party followed a considered program of giving subsidies to businessmen, farmers, veterans, and others.

In the second place, almost all groups have at one time or another benefited directly from government aid. During much of the nation's history, business was the main recipient of help from Washington; today the farmers and veterans seem to have first preference. Governmental promotion is neutral; it can be used to help any group. The main questions of policy are: Who shall be aided? In what way? And to what extent? The politics of promotion revolve around these questions.

★ 26

Government

as promoter

As treated here, *promotion* is something different from *regulation,* but *no sharp distinction is possible.* Regulation means setting restraints on individuals and groups, directly compelling them to take, or not to take, certain actions. Promotional activity involves the use of government to encourage, strengthen, safeguard, or advance the interests of particular persons, groups, industries, or sectors of the economy. In

684

the case of either regulation or promotion the aim may be the benefit of one group or of the whole nation. Similarly, promotion can be used to *regulate* interests as well as help them, as the following pages will show. Promotion savors a little more of the carrot, regulation of the stick, but often either one, or a combination, can be used to carry out a purpose of government.

Federal promotion is an expensive operation. It was estimated on the basis of government reports that in one recent year the national government gave veterans $4.7 billion, farmers $1.7 billion, newspapers and magazines (through mail charges far below actual cost) over $250 million, road users almost $750 million, and needy people over $1.5 billion, aside from grants to foreign countries of over $4 billion. Let us see just where this money goes, and why.

HELPING BUSINESSMEN

In the broadest sense, government assists business by maintaining an orderly legal and economic system. When government helps promote a prosperous economy, business enjoys a large volume of sales and good profits. When government protects private property and enforces contracts, businessmen can operate in a stable situation where agreements can be enforced. A high or low tariff can have considerable effect on the profits of individual concerns. The kind of monetary system established by government is of direct interest to businessmen (see Chapter 27).

Aside from such obvious aids to business, the national government supplies a number of specific services, and assists individual sectors of business.

The Department of Commerce

Occupying one of the largest office buildings in the world, the Department of Commerce in Washington is the nation's "service center for business." The Secretary of Commerce is usually a person of business background who is also prominent in the party in power. Under his direction the department assists business in many ways. One of these is furnishing business with a vast amount of information on a variety of matters. For example, the Bureau of Foreign Commerce and the Office of Business Economics report on business activities and prospects at home and abroad. The National Bureau of Standards makes scientific investigations and tries to standardize units of weight and measurement.

One of the most important of such services is the *Census Bureau*, which has been called the greatest fact-finding and figure-counting agency in the world. The Constitution requires that a national census be taken every ten years. This census serves as a basis for congressional apportionment. Between the periods of taking the decennial census the bureau keeps busy with other important projects. It collects information on business and agricultural activity, incomes, occupations, employment, housing, home ownership, governmental finances, crime, and many other matters. Its findings are presented in bulky volumes published by the Government Printing Office. Perhaps the most valuable of these, especially for businessmen, is the annual *Statistical Abstract of the United States.* The Census Bureau is a large agency, employing over 10,000 permanent people and 100,000 during census taking.

Another historic bureau now in the Commerce Department is the *Patent Office.* The granting of patent rights is a major method of promoting business, and the first article of the Constitution authorizes Congress to secure to authors and inventors for a limited period "the exclusive right to their respective writings and discoveries." A patent, conferring the right of exclusive use of an invention for seventeen years, is a valuable property right that may influence the course of a business and the profits of businessmen. Upon the receipt of an application for a patent right the office must study its records to see if any prior patent is infringed and if the invention is sufficiently original and useful to be patentable; meanwhile the applicant marks his product "Patent Pending." Since decisions of the Patent Office directly involve legal rights, its rulings may be appealed to a board of appeals in the Patent Office and then to the Court of Customs and Patent Appeals or to a federal district court. Some cases go even to the Supreme Court. While most patent problems are technical, patent policy basically involves such broad problems as the stimulation of invention and the threat of monopoly and economic concentration.

Two other promotional services in the Department of Commerce are:

The Weather Bureau. We still like to quote Mark Twain, who is reported to have said that "Everybody talks about the weather but nobody does anything about it." Such a remark today overlooks the United States Weather Bureau, which tries not only to forecast the weather, but with private agencies also attempts to do something about the weather. Staffed with over 8000 employees by the latest count, this agency makes forecasts on the basis of data from its 400 field stations in this country and overseas. Formerly the bureau was mainly the farmers' service agency, but today it is used by air lines, the resort business, and by other industries. Such experiments as seeding clouds to make rain suggest that the Weather Bureau may have an even greater role for both civilian and military activities in days to come.

The Coast and Geodetic Survey. This bureau provides important services to mariners. It charts the nation's coastlines, lake and river beds, and the ocean tides and currents along routes of commerce. Its maps and charts are used by air and sea navigators, engineers, fishermen, and others.

Aids to transportation

Of all the government aid given to business, the *transportation industry* probably has had the lion's share. Part of this has been historic circumstance;

DEPARTMENT OF COMMERCE

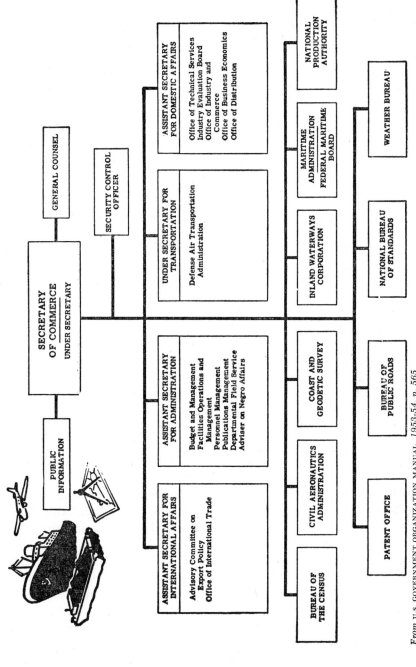

SECRETARY OF COMMERCE
UNDER SECRETARY

GENERAL COUNSEL

PUBLIC INFORMATION

SECURITY CONTROL OFFICER

ASSISTANT SECRETARY FOR INTERNATIONAL AFFAIRS

Advisory Committee on Export Policy
Office of International Trade

ASSISTANT SECRETARY FOR ADMINISTRATION

Budget and Management
Facilities Operations and Management
Personnel Management
Publications Management
Departmental Field Service
Adviser on Negro Affairs

UNDER SECRETARY FOR TRANSPORTATION

Defense Air Transportation Administration

ASSISTANT SECRETARY FOR DOMESTIC AFFAIRS

Office of Technical Services
Industry Evaluation Board
Office of Industry and Commerce
Office of Business Economics
Office of Distribution

BUREAU OF THE CENSUS

CIVIL AERONAUTICS ADMINISTRATION

COAST AND GEODETIC SURVEY

INLAND WATERWAYS CORPORATION

MARITIME ADMINISTRATION
FEDERAL MARITIME BOARD

NATIONAL PRODUCTION AUTHORITY

PATENT OFFICE

BUREAU OF PUBLIC ROADS

NATIONAL BUREAU OF STANDARDS

WEATHER BUREAU

From U.S. GOVERNMENT ORGANIZATION MANUAL, 1953-54, p. 565

part the role of transportation politics; part the result of deliberate national policy.

Railroads led the way. During the second half of the nineteenth century the national government gave huge land grants to the railroads, which were by that time spanning the continent. During the years 1862-1866 alone over 100 million acres of land were given away by Congress to the railroad builders. Later, as we have seen (see Chapter 25), public opinion turned against the railway magnates, and promotion was followed by regulation. In the 1930's, however, the government made loans to railroads weakened by depression, for the purpose of meeting costs and maintaining equipment. It has been estimated that the grand total of all types of aid (including loans) given railroads by national, state, and local governments amounts to almost a billion and a half dollars.[1]

Shipping also has a lengthy history of government aid. In its very first session in 1789 Congress provided that only ships built in the United States and belonging to American citizens could register under the American flag, and such shipping was favored through discriminatory tonnage taxes and customs duties. In effect the important coastal trade was fenced off for American-owned ships. At times during the nineteenth century the national government followed a policy of subsidizing steamship companies by means of grants to carry mail. But these mail subsidies invariably brought inefficiency and corruption and provoked long arguments as to the propriety of giving public money to private businessmen. World War I, however, caught us with a severe shortage of shipping. This put the problem in a different light. Between the two world wars Congress passed a series of acts designed to aid and strengthen the shipping industry. In 1936 it abandoned the mail subsidy system, which had led to more scandals, in favor of direct subsidies.

In the present time of recurrent international tension the federal government is responsible for keeping alive a merchant marine that could quickly convert to a wartime footing. The Federal Maritime Administration in the Department of Commerce administers a subsidy program designed to enable American shipbuilders and shipping companies to compete with those of foreign nations. This agency subsidizes both the building and operating of ships. It finances the construction of vessels in American shipyards, and sells these vessels for an amount equal to the estimated cost of building the ships in foreign yards. It pays shipping companies the amounts by which certain items of expense, such as wages, exceed those of foreign competitors. The administration's other promotional functions include acquiring obsolete vessels in exchange for credit on the purchase of new ones, administering a federal ship mortgage insurance fund, and operating construction re-

---

[1] *Public Aids to Transportation* (Washington, D.C.: Federal Coordinator of Transportation, 1940), I, 13.

serve funds for American shipowners. The Maritime Administration also has sizable regulatory functions, as noted in Chapter 25.

Another vital concern is *air transportation*. To back up its military air arm, the United States government encourages civil aviation by large subsidies. The chief method of helping air carriers financially is through fixing rates for carrying air mail. In setting these rates the Civil Aeronautics Board considers the need of each air carrier for enough revenues from mail and other sources to enable it to maintain air transportation as needed for commerce, the postal service, and national defense. The board also has regulatory functions (see Chapter 25). Most of the promotional activity is conducted by the Civil Aeronautic Administration in the Department of Commerce. The C.A.A, operating through a large staff in the field, administers the Federal Airport Act of 1946, which provides for the construction of a nationwide system of civil airports by federal aid to states and municipalities. It also operates an extensive system of federal airways, and conducts research projects designed to benefit civil aviation in general.

By far the largest federal transportation promotional activity has to do with *highways*. Ever since 1916 the national government has given financial support to the states; but by the Federal Highway Act of 1956, the national government has increased its aid manyfold. The states do the planning, estimate the costs, and get the construction done. In order to receive federal support, however, states must submit their plans and have their work inspected by the Department of Commerce's Bureau of Public Roads so that federal standards will be met. These standards apply to engineering conditions of the road, employment conditions for construction workers, and weight and load conditions for trucks using the roads.

The federal government participates in three road building programs. Most important is the National System of Interstate and Defense Highways, known as the Interstate System, which is to be built during the next thirteen years. When finished it will consist of 41,000 miles of superhighways linking every state capital and all major cities. All but 7000 miles will be of at least four lanes, grades are to be no more than a three-foot rise per 100 feet, there will be a limited number of entry roads, and no signs, roadside stands, or filling stations will be allowed on the right of way. Although some of these superhighways will use existing roads, most will be built along new rights of way. The federal government will pay 90 per cent of the costs, securing most of the money from user taxes—gasoline, tires, trucks—which are to be placed in a specially earmarked trust fund. Funds will be distributed among the states according to a formula that gives greater weight to population than has been given in other federal-aid highway programs. No federal moneys can be used for toll roads, bridges, or tunnels, although these may be part of the Interstate System. And the national government will not give the money to the states until the roads are completed, at which time it will reimburse the states for the federal share.

Besides this new Interstate System, the national government has stepped up its traditional aid for the construction and rebuilding of existing primary, secondary, and urban roads. For this program, the federal government continues to match state appropriations on a fifty-fifty basis. These roads provide access to the Interstate Highways, permit farmers to get their products to the market, and help reduce traffic congestion in cities.

Finally, the national government is stepping up its own construction of roads that give access to federally owned lands and public domains such as national parks and military reservations.

All told, national and state governments are expected to spend $50 billion to rebuild or construct about 750,000 miles of highways and streets during the next thirteen years, making it the largest nondefense public construction program in our history.

Uncle Sam, moneylender

The second Hoover Commission reported, "There are 104 agencies, instrumentalities, or entities of the Federal Government engaged in lending, guaranteeing, or insuring activities. They employ about 40,000 people. The Government has an investment of about $16.9 billion in these entities and they are authorized to call on the Treasury for about $14.1 billion of additional funds."[2]

Courtesy THE CHICAGO TRIBUNE and Parrish

The big hearted donor—a critical view

The national government's first ventures in moneylending date from the establishment of the Federal Reserve System in 1913. Following World War I federal credit was used to strengthen rural banks facing the postwar agricultural depression. In 1932, during the Great Depression, Congress carried government lending much further by setting up the Reconstruction Finance Corporation in response to President Hoover's recommendation. Starting only as an emergency agency, the R.F.C. proved so successful that it survived to help meet the recession of 1939 and the defense needs of World War II. As a result of many extensions of its authority, it lent not only to banks and other financial institutions but also to business firms in general, mining companies,

[2] Citizens Committee for the Hoover Report, *Digest and Analyses of The Nineteen Hoover Commission Reports* (New York and Washington, D.C.: Citizens Committee for the Hoover Report, 1955), p. 38.

and reclamation projects. Its loans were used for expanding plant capacity, paying teachers' salaries, and other rather specialized purposes.

In 1953 Congress abolished the R.F.C. but created a Small Business Administration to replace it. The new agency has a narrower scope than the R.F.C. Its small revolving fund of $275 million can be used mainly for loans for small business, but only if the latter cannot receive private credit. No more than $150,000 may be lent to any one business. Funds are also made available to help small concerns secure government contracts, and for disaster loans.

The national government also lends, guarantees, or insures in order to promote public housing and slum clearance, keep the costs of home mortgages down, support farm insurance programs, aid veterans get started in business, keep farm prices up, help build ships, and it makes its credit available in other ways to accomplish those tasks that Congress considers to be in the general welfare.

AIDING FARMERS

Nowhere is the diversity of American life more apparent than in agriculture. American farmers grow an amazing variety of crops. There are big farmers employing scores of workers on hundreds of acres of land; there are "family-sized" farmers operating farms of 100 to 200 acres with the help of one or two hired hands; there are tenant farmers working other men's farms for a share of the produce and profits; there are, finally, millions of farm laborers, many of whom move on from farm to farm.

Other important facts:

American farming is highly mechanized. The average farmer in this country is not "the man with the hoe." He uses a complex array of equipment—sixteen-ton rice combines, air-driven hoes, tractor-towed self-tying hay balers, to name but a few. Some farms, however, have very little machinery.

American farming is enormously productive. Mainly because of climate, geography, machinery, increased demand for food in recent years, and know-how, our farmers have met both a large part of our huge domestic needs and a heavy foreign demand.

American farming is highly sensitive to developments in the world outside. A war in Europe, a depression at home, even changes in the supply-and-demand situation in Canada or Australia or Latin America, have an immediate effect on agricultural stability in this country.

At home farmers find that the *prices* they *get* for their *products* tend to be highly *flexible,* rising and falling in a competitive market, while the *prices* they *pay* for *goods*—prices administered by corporations and influenced by union demands—tend to be *rigid.*

All these facts closely affect the relation of government and agriculture.

The growth of federal aid

The historical background of farm policy covers three important periods: the development of a farm program during the last century; World War I and postwar problems; early New Deal farm policy.

The main agricultural role of the federal government during much of the nineteenth century was disposing of the broad stretches of land that it owned. The government practically gave away this land, charging a dollar or two an acre, but giving away land was not as simple as it might seem. For one thing, speculators bought up large tracts and sold them at a high profit. For another, many Americans were opposed to a free-and-easy land policy. In 1862, however, Congress passed the Homestead Act, which was designed to encourage the family farm and discourage the speculator by giving 160 acres of public land to each settler willing to occupy the land for at least five years. In the same year Congress granted large tracts of land for the establishment of colleges in the states, and also set up a Department of Agriculture (which, however, did not become a full-fledged department with Cabinet rank until 1889).

Other promotional activities were launched during the latter part of the century. The federal government set up agricultural experiment stations, encouraged the development of farm cooperatives, fought the spread of animal diseases and insect pests. It undertook conservation and reclamation activity. In 1916 Congress passed a Federal Farm Loan Act to provide credit for agricultural purposes.

Thus even before World War I the government was directly involved in agriculture, and the war and postwar years speeded up the trend. World War I created a boom for the farmers. Prices of food, cotton, and farm land skyrocketed. Farmers borrowed money, bought land and machinery, and produced more meat and crops. In 1920 the bubble burst. Prices dropped abruptly, and millions of farmers were left with surplus land, machinery not paid for, higher taxes, and debts. Inevitably they turned to Washington for help. In response to a bipartisan demand Congress passed measures to *police* the *trading* in contracts for future delivery (an activity open to many abuses), to *encourage agricultural cooperatives,* and to *ease credit facilities.* But these steps did little to lighten what was becoming an agricultural depression. The farm bloc in Congress pressed for an equalization fee plan, under which the government would buy up farm products for sale abroad and raise prices at home over the world level by the amount of the tariff on products, but this plan, as embodied in the McNary-Haugen bill, was twice vetoed by President Coolidge. The government did, however, provide loans to enable farmers to hold surpluses off the market.

The Great Depression simply intensified agricultural stagnation. Demand fell off, and so did prices. Once again, farmers began to "raise less corn and more hell," as Populist leaders had urged them to do decades before. They organized protest demonstrations, burned or dumped their products, defied the courts that ordered mortgaged farms to be foreclosed and sold. It was this situation that faced the Roosevelt Administration on taking office in March 1933. The new President and Congress acted fast. In two months an almost revolutionary new farm measure—the Agricultural Adjustment Act —was drawn up and passed.

The new act was a complicated piece of legislation, but its chief objective was simple—to raise farm prices so that the farmer would have a higher standard of living for himself, and to stimulate the whole economy. Experience had clearly shown that the more the farmer produced, the greater were the surpluses and the lower the prices. The central method of the act was to induce farmers to *cut down production* to a level low enough to force prices to rise. But how to induce the farmers to decrease production? The answer was: pay him to do it. So in return for cash bounties several million farmers voluntarily cut down production, plowed under part of their crops, and killed sows and pigs. Results were quickly forthcoming. Farm production went down, prices rose, and farm income increased by over a third.

To pay for the cash benefits the 1933 act levied a tax on processors of farm commodities, such as millers and meat packers. This provision proved to be the act's Achilles' heel, for in 1936 the Supreme Court found the measure unconstitutional on the grounds that the taxes were not levies to finance government but levies on one group to give benefits to another, and that Congress had entered a field reserved for state action under the Tenth Amendment.[3]

Recent farm policy

Stunned by this decision, the Administration soon set about formulating a new farm program. The new strategy was to tie a control plan to *soil conservation*. Drought and dust storms had dramatized the need for soil conservation, and it was reasoned that the Supreme Court would not veto an act involving this purpose provided no processing tax was involved. Furthermore, the government could build on experience, for a soil erosion act in 1935 had authorized paying farmers out of general Treasury funds for taking land out of production in order to conserve soil. Accordingly, Congress in 1936 enacted the Soil Conservation and Domestic Allotment Act. Half a billion dollars was appropriated to pay farmers for adopting good conservation methods, such as cutting down on soil-depleting crops like wheat, corn, and cotton, and growing more grasses and legumes that replenish the soil.

This act helped stabilize prices and production, but it did not meet the immensity of the problem. Faced with continuing surpluses and low prices— and with increased political agitation in farm regions—Congress passed a

[3] *United States* v. *Butler.*

new Agricultural Adjustment Act in 1938. The new measure was somewhat similar to the ill-fated 1933 act, except that it carefully avoided the processing tax. Control of production was achieved by these steps: First, if in any year forecasts indicated a heavy production of basic farm commodities and a possible price break, producers of the crop involved would be asked in a referendum if they favored setting limits on production. Second, if two-thirds of the voting farmers supported limitations, each county was to be allotted a certain number of acres for the crop; in turn, each farmer was allotted a maximum acreage for growing crops under the plan. Third, if the farmer wished to grow more than his allotment allowed, he could do so, but he would be subject to a fine if he marketed his excess production during a time of surplus conditions. Fourth, on controlled crops the farmer would receive government loans; the government would then store the surplus crops until a time of scarcity arrived, at which point the farmer might sell them at stable prices and pay back his loan. The essential idea was an ever-normal granary plan that would store surplus crops in time of high production and release them in years of shortage. This approach is still one of the pillars of our agricultural policy.

World War II brought an abrupt change in farm policy. The problem in the years 1942-1945 was not to restrict production but to meet the immense needs of our armed forces, our allies, and our civilian population. Following the war the old problem of surpluses developed, and the government continued its stabilization program. The Agricultural Acts of 1949 and 1956, establishing a more flexible system of price supports, defined various types of commodities that called for different types of action by the Secretary of Agriculture.

The Eisenhower Administration ran into thorny farm problems as soon as it took office in 1953. Huge surpluses of wheat, cotton, and other farm commodities were piling up, and farmers felt caught in a squeeze between rising production and falling commodity prices. On the one hand, the Administration wanted to reduce federal control of agriculture and to cut down the cost to taxpayers of buying up and storing farm produce. On the other hand the Republicans feared to take any action that jeopardized farm income for fear of alienating millions of farmers who might have a balance-of-power role in the 1954 and 1956 elections. Agriculture officials hoped to establish a system of farm supports that would be more flexibly related to production, but many farmers were more interested in firm price support than in flexibility.

In 1954, following a study by farm representatives and Agriculture Department experts, the Eisenhower Administration proposed a somewhat new farm program. The key item in the ensuing act passed that year involved the old question of parity. A system of *flexible* price supports was set up for the basic or staple commodities at a sliding scale of 82½ to 90 per cent of parity. Huge quantities of wheat, cotton, milk solids, and other products were set aside for donations to disaster relief or school aid and for such other purposes not likely to undermine the home market for farm goods. Democrats denounced the new program as inadequate and resolved to substitute their own plan after they won control of Congress in 1954.

After the farm economy weakened in 1954 and 1955, the battle over farm policy came to a head in the 1956 session of Congress. First the Democrats passed a bill to return to the *rigid* price supports of 90 per cent that President Eisenhower had persuaded the legislators to drop in the previous Congress. The President vetoed this bill, and the Democrats, holding only a small majority in the House, were unable to override his veto. The Democrats in the Senate failed in their attempt to put through the upper house a long-term extension of the 90 per cent formula. With the 1956 campaigns rapidly approaching, leaders of both parties decided that some sort of compromise was the safest policy. An act was passed embodying an old conservation idea in the new form of a "soil bank." Under this plan the government, through the soil bank, pays farmers for taking certain types of land out of production. Although Democratic proposals for high-support prices were well watered down in the measure, Mr. Eisenhower by executive action raised supports above levels set by the supply situation under his sliding scale support program.

As a result of these and other additions and changes, governmental control of farm production and marketing today involves essentially these elements:

Acreage allotments. Government experts estimate probable demand for staple commodities like cotton, wheat, and rice. The national acreage allotments are broken down ultimately to individual allotments by an elaborate system that takes into account past and present characteristics of each farm.

Acreage reserves. This is a temporary program, authorized in 1956 and due to expire in 1959, designed to get the soil bank underway. Farmers may voluntarily reduce their acreage of basic commodities beyond their allotment and take the acres out of production in return for payments. Producers of corn must participate in this program in order to be eligible for support loans.

Conservation reserves. This is the long-term phase of the soil bank in which lands are taken out of production for three to fifteen years. The farmers who agree to plant their lands in grass or trees receive from the government most of the costs of planting and a "reasonable annual return." No grazing on this land is to be permitted. It is estimated that expenditures for the soil bank will reach $2 billion a year.

Benefit payments. As mentioned above, these are grants to farmers to secure their cooperation in acreage reserves and conservation programs, in order to induce them to plan production in the light of the national and international situation and the needs of soil conservation.

Commodity loans. The average farmer must sell his crops as soon as they are harvested, for he probably needs the cash to meet out-of-pocket expenses. The basic purpose of commodity loans is to enable the farmer to store his crops until such time as he can sell them at a good price. These loans prevent sudden flooding of the markets with farm commodities; hence they encourage orderly marketing and discourage sharp price changes.

Marketing quotas. These supplement the acreage allotments. When production becomes high and a price collapse threatens, farmers by a two-thirds vote may approve the establishment of marketing quotas. Each producer is alloted his share; he pays a penalty if he markets more than his share.

Price support. The government buys up commodities when it appears that excess production may cause prices to fall below a certain minimum. This policy does for farmers what the Wages and Hours Act does for labor—it puts a floor under income.

Farm policy: pros and cons

These farm policies have led to wide differences of opinion. The defenders of the policies point to three outstanding and undeniable facts: that American farmers as a group are better off today than ever in history; that working and living conditions on the farm have been vastly improved; that farm production is high and yet relatively stable. These facts are important, they say, not only for the farmers but also for the economic and military security of all Americans. Admitting that the machinery of administration is somewhat cumbersome, they stress the democratic nature of the program —for example, the way farmers can vote on production quotas, and the way decisions are made at the grass roots level. Finally they point out that while the program has been expensive in terms of dollars, the cost has been low considering the tremendous benefits to the farmers.

Herblock in THE WASHINGTON POST AND TIMES HERALD

"We interrupt this farm program for a brief recess."

Opponents of the farm program believe that it involves a tragic paradox. On the one hand, they point out, the government under its price support program has been buying up farm products, storing them, and then selling them for fertilizer and even destroying them or allowing them to rot. On the other hand, millions of Americans—not to mention tens of millions of foreigners—need more potatoes or eggs than they now consume. Artificial price supports may help the farmer, but they certainly pinch the consumer. The present policies, these critics say, have created a sort of Frankenstein's monster in the form of surpluses that the government hardly knows what to do with. So far, at least, production-control measures have not been sufficient to prevent large surpluses. And present policy, it is said, tends to freeze existing agricultural activity and render it less adaptable to changing conditions.

Long-term farm problems

The key issue in the struggle over farm policy is the extent to which the federal government should subsidize the farmers, and in what manner. This issue is summed up in the word *parity*. Farmers demand that their income should be roughly equal to the income of other sections of the population. Parity, they argue, means that the products the farmer sells should bring him a return roughly equal to the things he buys. But what should parity amount to? This is the nub of the problem. Farmers feel that the 1920's were a time when they were not receiving a fair income, for their costs were high while farm prices were low. The fairest ratio between farm and other prices, they say, was achieved in the period 1909 to 1914. One of the main efforts of farmers' organizations has been to induce Congress to use the 1909-1914 yardstick in establishing price supports and other controls.

Quotas, allotments, benefit payments, price supports—these and other devices have given the farmer a large measure of stability and even prosperity. But basic long-term problems remain. One of these is the constant increase in agricultural technology and productivity, with the possibility of long-term farm surpluses. Another problem is rural poverty. Half of the nation's farms produce only 10 per cent of the farm products. Many farmers till substandard land, lack equipment and expertness, and live in deplorable conditions. At the opposite pole are farm operators who own thousands of acres and make a good deal of money, and at the same time are receiving federal subsidies. A special problem is the lack of housing, medical, and educational facilities for the families of migratory workers.[4] But the basic problem is: "How can we give farmers—influenced as they are by faraway events—a measure of security in an unstable economy and an unstable world?"

It is important to remember that farming is more than an occupation or a livelihood; it is a way of life. Despite the significant movement of people from the country to the city, many people still cling to farming even when the economic returns may hardly justify it. Partly because of his wish to stay close to the soil, partly because of the nature of agriculture, the farmer is in a vulnerable position. Consider for a moment his difficulties as con-

[4] See Carey McWilliams, *Ill Fares the Land* (Boston: Little, Brown & Company, 1942).

trasted with those of a businessman. When demand for his products falls, the businessman can retrench. He lets some of his workers off, cuts down on his orders for materials, decreases his output, and thus can cut back on his expenses. But the farmer has little he can cut back; most of his expenses go on. So when the price of wheat drops, for example, from $1 a bushel to 50 cents, the farmer's answer is to try to grow more wheat to make the same income. Result: next year, if conditions remain the same, wheat may be down to 25 cents a bushel. Nor can farmers get together to agree to reduce production—they are too numerous and widely scattered.

Essentially what the first New Deal agricultural program tried to do for farmers was what businessmen have done without governmental aid. Although plowing under corn and killing little pigs was good newspaper copy, the same thing was done throughout the country by private businessmen. Millions of automobiles, washing machines, houses, radios were not plowed under but simply not produced. The second New Deal farm program differed from the first not only in constitutional underpinnings but also in essential philosophy. The first A.A.A. was an attempt to fight agricultural depression by reducing production. Since then we have been moving generally, although in a halting manner, in the direction of meeting the farm problem by increasing consumption, by creating new demand, by changing the pattern of farm production toward commodities for which there is a good market.

From a strictly economic viewpoint, farm prices could be allowed to drop and the market allowed to force out of farming those who cannot make a go of it at prevailing prices. But farming is a *political* as well as an economic matter; it well illustrates the inseparability of economics and politics. As we have seen earlier, farmers are politically potent in Washington and the state capitals. And the people as a whole, however they may grumble about the cost of farm produce, wish to protect the farmer's economic position and way of life.

The Department of Agriculture

Administering the complex set of controls described above is the job of the Department of Agriculture, one of the largest and most influential civilian agencies in Washington. This is the farmers' agency; the department makes no bones about protecting the farmer's interest and promoting his welfare. The Secretary of Agriculture is usually a man from a farming state who has the respect of the leading farm organizations (see Chapter 10). Indeed, the political influence of the department in Washington cannot be understood apart from the close connections that exist between the department and farm interests. The department also works closely with the farm bloc and the agricultural committees in Congress.[5]

[5] See J. M. Gaus and L. O. Wolcott, *Public Administration and the United States Department of Agriculture* (Chicago: Public Administration Service, 1940).

Aside from price and production controls, the Department of Agriculture is responsible for many other activities:

Research. The department is one of the world's great research agencies. Its Agricultural Research Service employs about 18,000 people, among them internationally known scientists. The department's laboratories have helped to develop remarkable methods for combating animal and plant diseases, overcoming the scourges of insects, improving the yield and quality of crops, making soils more productive, improving the breeding of hogs, cattle, and other domestic animals.

Education and information. For over ninety years the federal government has helped sponsor and finance state agricultural colleges, and some of the most significant educational and research activities are conducted at these institutions. The Department of Agriculture has an extensive information program in Washington and in the field. For example, it employs several thousand county demonstration agents to improve home and community living. Its experts in nutrition and home economics seek to induce farm people to use more nourishing types of food, and to buy more wisely for home and farm.

Soil conservation. Aside from the conservation aspect of the benefit-payment program, the department engages directly in soil conservation activities. Its Soil Conservation Service, employing over 14,000 people, teaches farmers how to maintain the value of the soil, demonstrates erosion control methods, develops water facilities, and buys and develops land worn out by wind, rain, and bad farming or grazing practices. This service works closely with the Forest Service and with the Interior Department's Reclamation Bureau as well as state agencies and local soil conservation districts.

Rural rehabilitation. The department also tries to help tenant farmers, sharecroppers, and farm workers, many of whom live in rural slums. The Farmers Home Administration—once the Farm Security Administration, a New Deal agency of the 1930's—makes easy, forty-year loans to grubstake such farmers in the purchase of farms and equipment of their own. In some cases outright grants are provided. The Farmers Home Administration has helped to improve the lot of the marginal farm, but the only hope for lasting improvement may involve resettlement programs or moving people off substandard farms.

Rural electrification. Twenty years ago most farmers lacked many of the conveniences enjoyed by their city brethren. Many were without adequate telephone facilities and few had electricity. In 1935 the Rural Electrification Administration, now in the Department of Agriculture, started making low interest loans to public bodies and cooperatives for the construction of electric generation and transmission facilities and for financing the purchase of electrical appliances. By January 1956, there were 1026 REA-financed power systems covering 1,360,960 miles of line and serving 4,236,724 consumers. Since 1950 REA has been making loans to extend rural telephone facilities and by March, 1956 money had been allocated to bring new or improved service to 629,707 rural families. Other farm families have been indirectly benefited by the availability of REA credit since it has stimulated private utilities to expand their facilities.

Farm credit. Most farmers have an acute need for loans at reasonable interest rates. Federal land banks in leading farm centers make loans through local farm associations to individual members for farm improvements. Intermediate credit banks lend to livestock companies, credit associations, and similar institutions. Production credit services provide short-term loans secured on the farmer's products. These and other credit activities are coordinated by the Farm Credit Administration. Not part of the Department of Agriculture, this independent agency is governed by a board of thirteen members, twelve of whom are appointed for a six-year term by the President with the advice and consent of the Senate on the basis of nominations by the various organizations especially concerned with farm credit. The thirteenth member serves at the pleasure of the Secretary of Agriculture. The board appoints a governor (until all government capital is retired from the various institutions supervised by the Farm Credit Administration, the President's approval of the board's choice is necessary) who is the chief administrative officer of the agency. The purpose of this rather elaborate organization is to give farmers more of a voice in the agricultural credit system and with the ultimate hope that all government capital can be withdrawn so that the borrowers will own the institutions of farm credit.

SOCIAL WELFARE

There is nothing new—as the foregoing pages show—in the idea of governmental aid to certain sectors of the economy or to certain groups of people. For at least 160 years we have had the "welfare state," to some degree. This is true of social services too. As far back as Colonial times parishes and counties undertook poor relief, and later on the states maintained hospitals, asylums, and other institutions. Nevertheless, until recent years American government—and especially the national government— lagged far behind other countries in furnishing social services. The situation was paradoxical. On the one hand the federal government gave huge bounties to railroads, farmers, veterans, and other groups. On the other, Washington shrugged its shoulders in the face of dire need on the part of millions of "ill-housed, ill-clad, ill-nourished."

How explain this paradox? Part of the answer is the fact that America has been the land of opportunity. The millions of acres of free land, the enormous resources, the technical advances—all helped absorb the people who otherwise might not have made a go of it. Closely linked with this was the wide support of the philosophy of rugged individualism and devil

AMERICA'S LOWER-INCOME FAMILIES

OUT OF 39.200,000 FAMILIES IN THE U.S. THERE ARE
9,700,000 WITH INCOME OF LESS THAN $2,000 A YEAR

OF THOSE FAMILIES
6,300,000 ARE IN CITY AREAS

3,400,000 ARE ON FARMS

2,900,000 ARE HEADED BY PERSONS WITH ONLY GRADE SCHOOLING

2,800,000 ARE HEADED BY PERSONS IN UNSKILLED OCCUPATIONS

2,400,000 ARE HEADED BY PERSONS 65 YEARS OR OLDER

1,400,000 ARE HEADED BY WOMEN

1,200,000 ARE HEADED BY NONWHITES

ESTIMATES BASED ON 1950 POPULATION AND INCOME PROJECTIONS, FROM
OFFICIAL DATA FOR 1948.
From U.S. NEWS & WORLD REPORT. *Copyright 1950 by United States News
Publishing Corporation, January 20, 1950*

take the hindmost. If a man didn't get ahead, people said, it was his own fault. Rather grudgingly the state governments—mainly during the early twentieth century—extended relief to needy groups, especially old people, blind persons, and orphans. But government aid was limited. Much reliance was placed on private charity.

The Great Depression and the New Deal drastically changed this situation. Unemployment mounted to unprecedented heights; in the early 1930's the number averaged between ten and fifteen million. Bread lines, soup kitchens, private charity, the meager state and local programs—these were pitifully inadequate. In 1932 the federal government began making loans to states and localities for public relief. As state and local funds dried up, the federal government assumed more and more responsibility. The Roosevelt Administration established a series of relief programs designed to give the country a shot in the arm by increasing purchasing power. Directed by

Harry Hopkins, the famous W.P.A.—Works Progress Administration—spent billions of dollars on local projects. The Public Works Administration, under Secretary of the Interior Harold Ickes, built more permanent projects such as dams and roads.

Before long a reaction set in to the makeshift nature of much of the relief program. People grew critical of useless leaf-raking projects—popularly called "boondoggles"—and of the cost and waste of the relief program. Some wanted to go back to the dole—simple handouts of food or cash by the government. But there was much sentiment in favor of a well planned, long-term program that would foster both the security and self-respect of the people aided. Progress was slow. The first federal attempt at an extensive security program—the Railroad Retirement Act of 1934—was declared unconstitutional by the Supreme Court.[6] Insurance companies and even some labor groups were hostile to any extensive action. But over the last decade and a half the national government has built a social security program that has come to be widely accepted by the American people.

Broadly speaking, the program is based on the assumption that society must take care of old people, the unemployed, the helpless and others needing some protection. For such people are in any event a cost charged against the rest of the community. Old people are a good example. In the past, when large families were common, much of the cost of social security for the aged was borne by the family itself. The family was often large enough to bear this burden without too much difficulty, for a century ago it might be composed of father and mother, six to ten children, a grandmother, Aunt Susie, and Uncle George. Today the typical family in an urban society will consist of mother and father and two children. It is impossible to let relatives move in. Some primitive societies kill off excess and helpless people, or let them starve. Some communities today put them in poorhouses at the expense of the rest of the citizens. Most modern democratic societies have governmental social security systems that try to plan ahead and make provision for needy people in a fair and orderly fashion.

Social Security

The foundation of the present system in the United States is the Social Security Act, passed by Congress in 1935 after elaborate study, and since then frequently amended and supplemented. Today the national government's social security activities involve two different kinds of programs—financial grants to the states for *assistance* to some needy persons, and social *insurance*. There are two separate insurance programs, one to help meet the risks of unemployment, the other to cover the needs of old age.

The *unemployment insurance system* is a joint enterprise of the national and state governments. The essential idea of unemployment insurance is

[6] *Railroad Retirement Board* v. *Alton Railroad Company* (1935).

HOW THE SOCIAL SECURITY SYSTEM FUNCTIONS

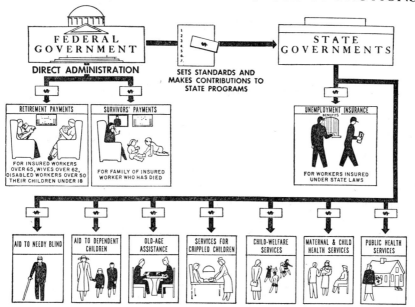

CHART BY GRAPHICS INSTITUTE, N.Y.C.

simple—to save for a rainy day. Until Congress acted, however, many states were reluctant to establish their own unemployment insurance programs. They were afraid that the cost of such insurance would place their businessmen at a competitive disadvantage with industries in states which had no such systems. In order to deprive the reluctant states of such an advantage—in fact, to place them at a disadvantage—in 1935 Congress levied on all employers of eight (since amended to four) persons or more a 3 per cent payroll tax on the first $3000 paid each year to each employee. If an employer, however, contributes to a state unemployment program that meets federal standards, he may deduct from his federal payroll tax all that he pays to the state fund, provided it is no more than 90 per cent of his federal tax. A state could stay out of the program, but none has done so because the national government levies the payroll tax in any event, and the money cannot be used by the state's unemployed unless the state adopts a plan satisfactory to Washington.

The national government helps defray administrative costs of running the programs, but the states administer the system. Programs vary in eligibility requirements, the amount paid, the period of payment, and in other ways. All states levy a tax upon employers; Alabama and New Jersey also collect from employees. Almost half of the states cover firms with fewer than four workers, and since 1954 Congress has extended unemployment benefits to federal civilian employees. These employees receive the same amounts and are governed by the same conditions as if their employment had been subject to a state law. Payments are made through the state employment security agencies, but the federal government reimburses the states for payments made to federal employees. The national government also supplements the program to insure that unemployed veterans receive at least $26 per week of total unemployment up to $676, but veterans must otherwise comply with requirements of state laws. Altogether about 50 million workers earn some credits toward unemployment payments, the major groups not covered being self-employed workers, agricultural employees, domestics, and—in half the states—employees of firms that have less than four workers. Railway workers are covered under a separate system administered by the Federal Railroad Retirement Board.

Money collected by each state is deposited to that state's account in the United States Treasury. From this fund each state pays benefits to workers who report to state public employment agencies and are willing and *able* to work, but for whom there are no jobs. Each state sets its own scale of benefits and determines who is eligible to receive them. In most states, to be eligible a person must be able to work. Indeed, if a worker is drawing benefits and becomes ill, he is no longer entitled to payments. Although states have *workmen's compensation* programs that pay disability benefits to some workers for industrial accidents or occupational diseases, these programs give no protection to those who are unable to work because of illness or accidents suffered off the job. Only four states—Rhode Island, California, New Jersey and New York—pay unemployment compensation or workmen's compensation to workers who are unemployed because of nonoccupational illness or injury. The recent amendment to old-age insurance (see below) giving benefits to permanently disabled workers over fifty will provide help to some of these workers.

Federal-state cooperation meets local demands and keeps the program flexible. It also has disadvantages. Benefits vary considerably. In 1954 the average weekly benefit ranged from $32.27 in Alaska to $17.06 in North Carolina (the *average* national weekly benefit was $25.05). The number of weeks for which benefits were paid varied between 26 and 12 (the national average was 13.6 weeks). Administrative services in some states have been inefficient and expensive. In some states "chiselers" are able to collect payments where jobs are available, and even while holding jobs. In other states the test of unemployment is so stiff that unemployed persons find it difficult to get benefits. Because of the state-federal arrangement, there has not always been full success in locating jobs and steering workers to them. However, the Bureau of Employment Security in the Department of Labor, which administers the federal part of the program, does attempt to coordinate the states' efforts to place jobless workers.

Old-age and survivors insurance, unlike unemployment insurance, is run solely by the national government. In 1935 it was recognized that old age was becoming a problem requiring national action. For some time the percentage of old people in the population had been steadily increasing. Persons over sixty-five now number twelve million; their percentage in the whole population has quadrupled in the last 100 years. This is a social and economic problem; it is also a political problem. By 1935 the Townsend movement, clamoring for "thirty dollars every Thursday" for the aged, had reached formidable proportions. The Social Security Act was in part a move to head off this political force.

The act of 1935 established a nationwide contributory retirement system under which payments to workers when they retire are made out of a fund built up from money collected equally from employers and employees through payroll taxes. Payments vary according to the earnings of the employee and the length of time his salary was taxed. Since this is an *insurance* program, the plan pays for itself, except for the cost of administration, which the federal government assumes.

In 1939, old-age insurance was broadened to *old-age* and *survivors insurance,* so that not only the wage earner but the whole family benefits. Under present rates, employers and employees each pay 2¼ per cent on the employee's income up to $4200 a year and a self-employed person pays 3⅜ per cent on his income up to $4200. The rate is scheduled to rise gradually so that by 1975 it will be 4 per cent for each employer and employee and 6 per cent for self-employed persons.

Today the system, as amended in 1956, pays men sixty-five or over and women sixty-two or over monthly retirement benefits which vary from $30 to $217, in accordance with the worker's contributions and the number of persons in his family entitled to secondary benefits. (If the insured has a wife sixty-two or over or a dependent husband sixty-five or over, dependent children under eighteen, or disabled children whatever their age, the family receives additional benefits.) Permanently disabled workers may retire and draw their benefits as early as age 50. Full benefits are paid to men between sixty-five and seventy-two and women between sixty-two and seventy-two only if they are not earning more than $1200 a year from services covered by social security. Income from dividends, interests, rents, and annuities is not counted, but by a complicated formula a worker loses part or all of his retirement benefits, depending upon his earnings, if he continues to work. After age seventy-two, however, a person is entitled to his retirement benefits regardless of his wages. Survivors' benefits for wives, dependent parents, children under eighteen, and disabled children include a lump sum of money and monthly payments. Benefits are subject to change by Congress, which has been liberalizing them since the system was started in 1939.

The old-age and survivors insurance program now covers almost all workers, either on a mandatory or permissive basis. The only major professions not now covered are the doctors, whose spokesmen have opposed participation, and those public employees who have their own special retirement systems. Approximately 70 million workers participate, with over 15 million now drawing benefits. The fact that social security has been broadened extensively under both the Truman and Eisenhower administrations suggests that the basic system is now outside the arena of party battle.

Public assistance

Eventually, it is hoped, social insurance will reduce the need for public assistance. But even with such insurance programs there will always be people who cannot support themselves. Some are not eligible for payments under the insurance programs. Even with monthly benefits, some lack sufficient income to maintain themselves. Some are physically handicapped.

The states have the primary responsibility for public assistance to needy persons. They initiate and administer the programs, but the national government helps. It makes yearly grants to the states to help maintain the income of four groups—needy aged, needy blind, needy persons who are permanently and totally disabled, and children in need because of loss of parental support by reason of death, abandonment, or physical or mental incapacity of a parent. These assistance programs are, unlike the insurance schemes, essentially a charity service since recipients of benefits make no contributions.

Federal assistance is given to the states on certain conditions. The states must contribute some of the money, they must establish a single state agency to administer or supervise the program, and other details must meet federal minimum standards. In the case of certain programs, Washington contributes from 60 to 75 per cent of the money. The average individual old-age assistance monthly payment varies from state to state, depending on local standards, but the average is just a little over $50.

In addition to these four programs which are basically designed to maintain the income of non-institutionalized needy persons, federal grants are also available to enable states to extend their services to crippled children, health services to mothers and children, and child welfare services especially in the rural regions. The Children's Bureau of the Social Security Administration approves state programs and distributes federal money in accordance with each state's contribution, its number of live births, its need for help, and its rural child population.

The people's health

Security also involves the health of the population. No one is more insecure than a worker facing months in the hospital or years of chronic illness. Not only is sickness a personal discomfort or tragedy; it is a drain on the nation's strength and efficiency. The main cause of absenteeism from work is illness; every year the nation loses over four million man years of work through ill health alone. If one can measure such things by dollars, we lose over $25 billion a year from this cause. Finally, bad health saps our military strength. During World War II five million men were found to be physically or mentally unfit for military service. The Women's Army Corps rejected over one-third of the young women who volunteered for service. Fifteen per cent of the draftees examined between July 1950 and June 1951 were rejected for solely medical reasons.

For many years the federal government has been concerned with aspects of the nation's health. According to the second Hoover Commission, twenty-six federal departments and agencies administer one or more health activities. The national government gives some kind of direct medical care to thirty million people (most of them veterans) and employs about 10 per cent of the doctors, 9 per cent of the dentists, and 6 per cent of the nurses. Thirteen per cent of all hospital beds are in institutions operated by the national government, and 7 per cent of the total number of patients admitted each year to hospitals are admitted to these hospitals.[7] In addition, the national government makes grants to the states to construct hospitals and research facilities and to maintain medical programs, including maternal and child welfare services. The national government also directly supports research in its own and private facilities and has special programs to meet problems such as cancer, venereal diseases, tuberculosis, mental illness, and heart disease.

Much of the responsibility for these programs rests with the Public Health Service, headed by a surgeon general and lodged in the Department of Health, Education, and Welfare. The Health Service operates several dozen general hospitals, quarantine stations, outpatient clinics and dispensaries. The Service licenses the manufacture and interstate sale of serums, toxins, vaccines, and analogous products. Perhaps most important for the long run, it carries on research through its national institutes of health. Scientists in these institutes, working closely with experts in nongovernmental laboratories, study the cause and cure of a number of serious diseases. Fellowships for research are given to scientists and physicians. The service administers grants to the states and local communities to support their research programs.

Another agency that protects the nation's health makes use of the method of *regulation* rather than subsidy. This is the *Food and Drug Administration,* also located in the Health, Education, and Welfare Department. Intense popular concern over pure food and drugs dates from early in the century, when Upton Sinclair and other muckrakers exposed the filthy practices in slaughterhouses and the evil effects of adulterated foods. Congress passed the Pure Food and Drug Act in 1906, has strengthened it in later amendments, and passed others covering tea, milk, and caustic poisons.

[7] *Digests and Analyses of the Nineteen Hoover Commission Reports* (New York and Washington, D.C.: Citizens Committee for the Hoover Report, 1955), p. 22.

The Food and Drug Administration polices the misbranding, false labeling, and adulteration of foods, drugs, cosmetics, and therapeutic devices destined for interstate shipment. Its agents inspect sanitary conditions in factories and the processing, packaging, and labeling of products covered by the law. They keep drugstores under surveillance to prevent the dispensation of dangerous drugs without prescriptions, engage in research to evaluate safety of goods, drugs, and cosmetics, and make studies in order to formulate definitions and standards that will promote honest and accurate labeling of foods. Before new drugs may be placed on sale for the interstate market, the Food and Drug Administration must give its approval and be assured that the drug is safe, effective, and fairly labeled.

One of the most heatedly debated subjects in recent years is the national government's role in helping to pay for the costs of hospital and medical services. Some have proposed—the Truman Administration, for example— that the social security system be expanded to provide for a *national system of medical care insurance*. The heart of such proposals is a scheme for *compulsory prepaid* federal insurance. The national government would match, out of its general funds, money raised by states through payroll taxes on employers and employees. People would choose their own doctors, but doctors' bills would be paid out of the insurance fund.

The proposals for federally imposed medical insurance have stirred up a hornet's nest. Leading the opposition is the American Medical Association, representing most of the nation's doctors, which calls these proposals "socialized medicine." The A.M.A. argues that (1) tremendous strides have been made in improving the nation's health under the present system; (2) the plan would bring politics into the traditionally private doctor-patient relationship; (3) standards might be lowered; (4) the program would be expensive and wasteful; and (5) private plans such as Blue Cross and Blue Shield are covering more and more people.

The 1952 Republican Party Platform expressly opposed compulsory federal health insurance. President Eisenhower suggested that the national government should help private insurance companies lower their rates by insuring them against major losses, much as is done in the case of housing loans. This proposal, too, is opposed by the American Medical Association. Recently, agitation for governmental action to help finance cost of illness has, for the moment at least, died down, but it remains as a potential political issue.

Department of Labor

The Labor Department was set up in 1913 (after having been a part of the Department of Commerce and Labor for ten years) as a frankly pro-labor agency. Its purpose, according to the act establishing it, is "to foster, promote, and develop the welfare of the wage earners of the United States . . . ." The Secretary of Labor and leading officials have traditionally been chosen either from the ranks of labor, or from groups friendly to labor. This may be one reason that the Labor Department is one of the smallest and weakest departments. It has seemed inappropriate to put general welfare functions under such a special service type of department. Moreover, the former split between A.F.L. and C.I.O. weakened the clientele group which, if united, would be a powerful force for strengthening the department.

The Hoover Commission in 1949 concluded that the Labor Department had "lost much of its significance." The commission recommended that the Bureau of Employment Security, the Selective Service System, and several other agencies be transferred to it.[8] At the same time the commission advised that a new department, headed by a Cabinet officer, take over the main welfare functions.[9] The first proposal, however, did not get far. The Bureau of Employment Security, however, was transferred to the Labor Department.

Today this department is still not as strong as the commission wished, but some of its bureaus play a notable role in government. One of these is the *Bureau of Labor Statistics,* set up in 1885 to collect information on hours, wages, jobs, living costs, strikes, accidents, and other labor matters. Today the bureau does a remarkably comprehensive job, and its findings are used throughout the government. Its reports on prices, based on checks of literally thousands of stores, are essential to price control programs. It makes up the complex cost of living index, which is economically and politically important today because under many union contracts wages are tied to this index. The *Women's Bureau* makes studies of such problems as hours and wages of women workers, equal pay, and conditions. The *Office of International Labor Affairs* assists in the participation of the United States in the International Labor Organization and other world agencies and it helps handle the administration of international training and technical programs.

OTHER SERVICES

The Departments of Commerce, Agriculture, Labor, and Health, Education and Welfare are obviously *clientele* agencies catering to special groups, large and small. A two-way relationship exists between such agencies and their clients. The bureaucrats serve certain of the needs of the groups; the groups give popular support to the programs. When Congress is considering annual appropriations for these services, representatives of interested groups often appear before House or Senate committees to defend the agency concerned and the work performed. It is not surprising that

[8] Commission on Organization of the Executive Branch of the Government, *Department of Labor* (Washington, D.C.: Government Printing Office, 1949), pp. 4, 9.
[9] Commission on Organization of the Executive Branch of the Government, *Social Security and Education* (Washington, D.C.: Government Printing Office, 1949), pp. 7-12.

in the pushing and hauling of national politics other groups besides business-men, farmers, and workers would enlist the aid of the federal government.

When Johnny comes marching home

Caring for veterans is one of the oldest federal activities. Ever since the Revolution the voters have seen an obligation to reward the returning soldiers with money, land, and other benefits. And for much of this time power-ful veterans' groups (see Chapter 10) have backed up ex-servicemen's claims by mobilizing political support. Moreover, many ex-servicemen have been disabled during their war service and have needed special attention.

There are over 22 million American veterans, and caring for them is one of the biggest federal activities. The Veterans Administration, an independ-ent agency operating directly under the President, spends more money than any other federal civilian agency. It employs more persons (by latest count about 178,000) than any civilian agency except the Post Office Department.

Here are the major benefits that the V.A. administers:

Medical and hospital benefits. It operates 173 hospitals and uses other facilities for 110,000 or more patients per day, about half of whom are being treated for mental illness. Any veteran of any war who is suffering from a service-connected disability or one made worse by service is entitled to free medical care. If beds are available, veterans with nonservice disabilities may receive treatment if they will state under oath that they are unable to pay for private treatment.

Educational benefits. Generally considered to be one of the most con-structive programs, this system was inaugurated by the Servicemen's Read-justment Act of 1944—the G.I. Bill of Rights—which provided generous grants to veterans for education or training. By the time this program ex-pired on July 25, 1956, more than 7,800,000 veterans had enrolled for some kind of training, 2,300,000 of whom attended college. The success of this program as an investment in the veteran's welfare and as a general en-richment of the nation's human resources, led to the continuation of the program for Korean veterans, who are entitled to one and one-half days of education or training for each day in service during the Korean war, with maximum training limited to 36 months. The government grants the vet-eran a monthly allowance from which he pays for tuition, fees, books, and living costs, with benefits going up to $160 a month for those with more than one dependent. The V.A. also provides vocational training for veterans dis-abled as a result of World War II or the Korean conflict, to help these men overcome their handicaps and become self-sufficient.

G.I. loans. Veterans of both World War II and Korea are assisted by the V.A. in borrowing money to build homes, buy farms, or go into business. The V.A. guarantees the lender that the loan will be repaid if the veteran defaults. Because of this guarantee, veterans can borrow more money and at lower rates than they could otherwise. Over a million of these loans, most for homes, have been made, and the veterans have an excellent record of paying up.

Compensation and pensions. Veterans with service-connected disabilities from war or peacetime service are entitled to monthly compensation. The wartime rates—including Korea—range from $17 to $181 a month, depending on the degree of disability. Additional payments are made for certain serious disabilities such as blindness or loss of limbs. *Needy* veterans of World War I and II or Korea receive pensions if they are permanently and totally disabled for nonservice connected reasons. Almost three million veterans are now receiving compensation or pensions.

Insurance. The V.A. administers several insurance programs for veterans and also for those presently on active duty. These insurance programs enable veterans to get coverage for considerably less than they could through regular sources. The program is huge. Veterans life insurance serves about seven million men; insurance outstanding amounts to over $44 billion.

In addition to the above programs, which are the major ones handled by the V.A., veterans are entitled to special privileges in securing government employment, to help in getting readjusted to civilian employment, to mustering-out allowances, and other benefits.

Behind the V.A. stand the American Legion, Veterans of Foreign Wars, and other ex-servicemen's groups. "The pressures of veterans' groups on this agency are virtually continuous," McKean has said.[10] It is often hard to tell whether a proposal of the V.A. to expand veterans' services originates with the agency or with some veterans' organization. It is certain that veterans' groups defend the V.A. against any attempt to slash its appropriations or to trim its offices. Actually, the huge medical program for veterans and their families is an example of "socialized medicine," for the doctors are employed by the national government, and the services are provided free. Yet the veterans are so powerful politically, and the idea of helping veterans is so popular generally, that few politicians are heard denouncing this particular form of socialism!

Housing programs

The problem of bad housing is an old one, but the federal government's entrance into this field is of relatively recent date. For a long time housing was considered a strictly private concern; and for a long time after that it was considered a matter only for state and local action, if any. Local government, however, was unable to cope with slums (both city and rural), crowded conditions, and poor sanitation. The depression beginning in 1929 intensified a housing situation that was already bad. Here, too, social trends have had a major impact. The housing problem has been intensified

[10] D. D. McKean, *Party and Pressure Politics* (Boston: Houghton Mifflin Company, 1949), p. 519.

by the growing population and the even faster growth of family units. Smaller families mean that the same population requires a greater number of separate housing units.

At first the federal government's interest in housing stemmed mainly from the need to bail out impoverished homeowners during the early 1930's. Under government auspices, home loan banks were set up to furnish credit to local banks engaged in financing homes, and a Home Owners' Loan Corporation was established to make long-term loans to hard-up homeowners. A Federal Housing Administration was created to insure loans made by lending institutions in order to promote the building of low-rent dwellings. Even more important, in 1937 the United States Housing Authority (now called Public Housing Administration) was set up to lend money to state or local housing authorities for building low-rent housing and clearing slums.

So far the government had not directly engaged in building; it had simply stimulated construction or demolition through financial incentives. During World War II housing agencies did build several hundred thousand war-housing units but these were undertaken to meet conditions near military posts and war plants, and after the war the housing situation was worse than ever. Civilian construction had all but lapsed during the war; returning veterans looked vainly for homes; young married people had to live with their in-laws. The government renewed its program of financial aids to private enterprise by lending to home buyers, builders, and others. But a strong demand developed for more direct and positive action. Following the war, legislation was proposed for governmental construction of low-cost housing for low and middle-income groups.

There followed a long and bitter legislative battle. Real estate and building interests, declaring that the legislation was socialistic and wasteful, mobilized their lobbies in Washington. Supporters of the bill were also active. Legislation quickly passed the Senate, but was held up in the House for four years. Following the Democratic victory in 1948— gained partly on the basis of its support of social services—a law was passed in the summer of 1949 providing for 810,000 new housing units. Under the legislation the national government itself is not to build dwellings; its chief role is to lend money to local housing authorities and to contribute yearly a sum of money so that low-income families can rent adequate housing at a rate they could afford (estimated at not over $30 a month), but less than actual cost. Construction and operation is undertaken by local housing authorities, but Congress has tied several conditions to receipt of federal subsidy. Among other restrictions, the units are available only to American citizens (except for families of some servicemen).

The 1949 Housing Act was but a temporary victory for proponents of low-cost public housing. Congress has appropriated money for only a fraction of the 810,000 authorized units. For the fiscal year 1954, for example, Congress stipulated that no more than 20,000 dwelling units should be started. Two years later, however, Congress authorized 70,000 low-rent public housing units over the ensuing two years and liberalized loan terms on federally guaranteed mortgages for financing home improvements, single-family home purchases, and rental housing. It seems likely that future political battles will revolve around *how much* the federal government will help subsidize housing, rather than *whether* it will at all.

In 1937 President Roosevelt declared that one-third of the nation was "ill-housed, ill-clad, ill-nourished." Has the housing problem improved? During the last decade and a half millions of new houses have been produced, but millions of dwellings have become obsolete, too. In this area, as in so many others, the worst problem is the condition of certain groups. Housing conditions are generally better in the case of white families than of Negro, of city people than of country, of northerners than of southerners. As late as 1947 only one-fifth of the nation's farm houses had both bath and toilet facilities, and over half lacked running water. Housing for some people, such as migratory workers, was atrocious. Private building was at a peak during the early 1950's. Almost a million new houses a year were built, but housing remains one of our major social problems.

Education

The same problem of unequal facilities is found in the vital area of education. The amount of money spent on school children varies from well over $100 per pupil per year in some states to well under $50 in others. Compared to a national average of 5 per cent, 5 states count 12 to 18 per cent of their 25- to 34-year-old population as functionally illiterate, people with less than 5 years of schooling. In these 5 states Korean war draft rejections caused by failure to pass the Armed Forces Qualifications Test ran about 48 per cent. The over-all national average was approximately 19 per cent.[11] In 1950, more than 33 per cent of the white adult Americans, but only 13 per cent of the nonwhites, had at least 4 years of high school. There has been a vast improvement in the scope, at least, of public education in the last half century. Yet 9½ million adult Americans, according to the 1950 census, had received less than 5 years of elementary schooling. To add to the challenge, the school-age population is on the edge of a tremendous expansion. "Every 10 minutes a new classroom of children reaches school age, and a new room and another teacher are *needed*. This goes on day and night, 7 days a week."[12]

Education is essentially a state and local governmental function; but as we have seen, the federal government has long been indirectly involved in education through such activities as its aid to land-grant colleges, its re-

[11] *Annual Report of the U.S. Department of Health, Education, and Welfare, 1954* (Washington, D.C.: Government Printing Office, 1954), p. 176.
[12] *Ibid.,* p. 10.

search activities, and its rehabilitation programs for veterans. In recent years federal participation has involved the expenditure of over $2.5 billion annually, most of it for veterans. The range of activities is remarkably broad and varied. At the elementary and secondary level the federal government aids the school lunch program (by giving perishable foods acquired under farm price support operations), works on problems of curriculum, and educates Indians and others. The federal government helps local school districts construct and operate schools where many new pupils have been brought in by military installations or other federal activities. At the level of higher education it provides research grants to colleges and universities, operates special educational projects (such as the famed Howard University, the extension service of the Department of Agriculture, and the military academies), gives annual grants for agricultural and mechanical arts education at land-grant colleges, and offers special education and training for the public services. Other activities include on-farm training and education in nonmilitary subjects for members of the armed services. Obviously these activities are administered by a variety of agencies; but many functions, including vocational education and assistance to land-grant colleges, are centralized in the Office of Education in the Department of Health, Education, and Welfare.

Is the federal government doing enough for education? Many proposals have urged Washington to make large grants-in-aid to the states to help hard-pressed local districts build and operate the many schools needed to educate our growing population. These proposals, however, have run into heavy opposition stemming mainly from three sources: fear that the federal government might eventually control educational subject matter; a dispute among supporters of federal aid over the question of allowing parochial schools to receive benefits; and wide differences about whether federal money should be given to school districts that practice racial segregation.

Although the Eisenhower Administration at first minimized the part that the national government should play in providing educational services, the President told Congress: "Youth—our greatest resource—is being seriously neglected in a vital respect. The Nation as a whole is not preparing teachers or building schools fast enough to keep up with the increase in our population." The President asked, and Congress authorized, a study of the problem. In each state conferences of educators, parents, and representatives of organizations were held to study resources and make recommendations. In 1955 these state conferences sent representatives to the White House Conference on Education, the first such to be held. Late in 1955 the conference recommended a plan providing federal aid to the states for building schools.

On the basis of the conference's recommendations, President Eisenhower submitted to Congress a plan authorizing $1.6 billion in federal school grants, spread over four years, in order to build 23,000 new classrooms annually. In the House a number of representatives argued that federal funds would lead to federal control of schools, including, ultimately, thought control of the children. They joined with others to vote an amendment to the bill banning help to school districts that continued to defy the Supreme Court's *School Segregation* decision. This amendment so inflamed southern congressmen that, together with many who opposed any kind of federal aid, they mustered a majority to defeat the measure.

School aid was dead—but it was certain that it would continue as a pressing political problem, for the current national shortage of classrooms will be aggravated by an expected 37 per cent increase in our school-age population by 1965. In view of the tremendous financial resources of the federal government and the dire need of more and better education, a nationwide system of federal grants seems a likely possibility for the future. An even bolder proposal, urged by the President's Commission on Higher Education in 1947, was in favor of federal subsidization of two years of college training for all worthy students.

THE POLITICS OF PROMOTION: A CASE STUDY

"Everybody who comes to this town," a Washington official once complained, "seems to want his own group subsidized and every other group regulated." There is a good deal of truth to this remark. Big government, with its power to disburse billions of dollars, is the object of pressure from any group that needs help and that can think up some reason to get in on the gravy. Once a group receives federal help it fights to keep it. At the same time, there is pressure for regulation of other groups. Even those who most dislike interference from Washington are often in favor of new acts of Congress that will restrict other people's activities.

This tendency is not surprising; on the contrary it is inevitable and desirable. As long as we have a responsible government and a free society, people will agitate for governmental help. The important question is not whether people demand help; it is whether government is organized in such a way that it can sift out and give priority to those demands that have some relation to the general welfare. As an example of the politics of government promotion in just one area, federal administration of water resources is worth a brief glance.

Water resources

Water is a vital resource. Not only does it supply power, as noted above, but it provides transportation lines for lake and river craft, irrigates the land for farming, and offers recreational opportunities such as boating, bathing, and fishing. Water can also be a menace; it erodes land and floods cities and farms. People with special water needs have long turned to the federal government for help. Today the government spends over a billion yearly in managing water resources. The Army Corps of Engineers, one of the oldest federal agencies, is responsible for navigation improvements in rivers and harbors. The Bureau of Reclamation in the Department of the Interior was established in 1902 to promote irrigation in the dry states of the West. The Federal Power Commission, the Department of Agriculture, the Fish and Wildlife Service (Interior Department), the Public Health Service, and several other federal agencies have a keen interest in rivers and their uses.

Ed Fisher in THE SATURDAY REVIEW

"Well, Clambertson, a fine botch you've made of the Department of Rivers and Highways!"

If each of these agencies supervised different rivers, things might be simpler. But this of course is impossible. "The same river can provide irrigation, supply a constant flow for navigation, cause floods, generate electrical energy, provide a habitat for fish and wildlife, and at the same time absorb the pollution of factories and mines."[13] Rivers, in short, have many purposes. It is this *multiple-purpose* nature of rivers that lies at the heart of the problem of federal promotion.

Located in the river valleys are groups that maintain lobbies in Washington and the state capitals to press for their interests. Often these interests compete fiercely with one another for governmental favors. One of the most powerful of these is the National Rivers and Harbors Congress, a sort of holding company of lobbies, which is mainly interested in navigation, harbor development, and flood control. Composed of contractors, state and local officials, and representatives of groups benefiting from river and harbor improvements, the congress works closely with other groups, such as intercoastal canal associations and flood control organizations. The farmers and

[13] Robert de Roos and A. A. Maass, "The Lobby that Can't Be Licked," *Harper's Magazine,* August 1949, p. 22.

livestock producers interested in irrigation and reclamation have their organizations, too. The National Reclamation Association has connections
with farmers' groups and livestock marketing associations. Both the supporters and opponents of using new dams to generate public power have
organized for political action. Associations of lumbermen, fish and game
clubs, bird lovers—even dude ranchers—are interested in the development of water resources. And each association is quite likely to put its own
interest first.

Virtually all these groups maintain lobbies in Washington. Some do even
better than that. The chairman of the flood control committee of the House
of Representatives has served also as vice-president of both the National
Rivers and Harbors Congress and of the Mississippi Valley Flood Control
Association. Other members of the so-called rivers and harbors bloc have
high seniority on congressional committees handling navigation, flood control, and harbor improvement. Reclamation interests are not so well entrenched as their down-river neighbors, but congressional committees
handling irrigation and reclamation have been dominated by representatives of arid and semiarid areas.

Perhaps even more important, strong connections exist between the interested groups and federal officials both in Washington and in the field. As
clientele agencies, the Reclamation Bureau, the Corps of Engineers, and
other water resource agencies naturally wish to keep the good will of their
"clients." Actually a triangular relationship links bureau, clients, and interested congressmen. In the case of the Corps of Engineers, this relationship
is strengthened by the fact that the corps has power to pass on the desirability of hundreds of projects in congressional districts throughout the
nation.

This situation is not unique with water resources. Similar triangles existed
among labor agencies, trade unions, and the labor bloc in Congress, among
farm agencies, farm organizations, and the farm bloc in Congress, and so on.
But again, the problem is to distill the national interest out of the special-
interest demands mirrored—and magnified—in the national government.
The President, as a national leader, is in a position to give priority to the
general welfare. But can he do it? The Missouri Valley is a case in point.

Missouri Valley Development

In this broad valley, covering about one-sixth of the nation's area, a sharp
cleavage exists between people in the semiarid regions of the upper valley
and those of the more populated areas in the lower part. The former wish
to exploit the river's water for irrigation, the latter want it for navigation—
and each group fears that there is not enough water for all. Navigation interests, railroads, public power supporters, public power opponents, farmers—all these and many other groups are involved in the fight. And the same

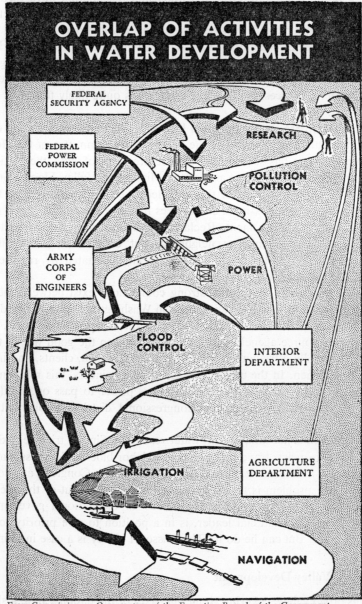

OVERLAP OF ACTIVITIES
IN WATER DEVELOPMENT

From Commission on Organization of the Executive Branch of the Government,
CONCLUDING REPORT, 1949, p. 28

splits reveal themselves in Washington—the Reclamation Bureau, the Fish
and Wildlife Service, and other agencies of the Interior Department lining
up on one side, and the Corps of Engineers on the other. However, as a result of the threat that a Missouri Valley Authority might be established (see

Chapter 27) the agencies arranged a shotgun marriage and divided the river among them.

Obviously the problem is not simply one of squabbling agencies or rival congressional blocs. It is a problem of recognizing the *multiple-purpose* nature of water resource development and of coordinating the several agencies involved in carrying out a comprehensive program. Experts who have studied our water resources have emphasized again and again the importance of planning for a river basin as a whole instead of having a patchwork of plans by separate agencies for separate purposes. Such a procedure, said the President's Water Resources Policy Commission in 1950, "will assure the most harmonious development of the water resources of the basin, enabling them to make their greatest contribution to the welfare of the people."[14] Since a river basin is an integrated, nondivisible unit, the committee recommended the motto, "one river, one plan."

Recognizing the need for better coordination and more protection of the national interest, the Hoover Commission recommended that water development work be consolidated in a new Water Development and Use Service in the Department of the Interior. Under this proposal army engineers who could be spared from military duties would be detailed to the Interior Department.[15] Actually, only a few army officers would have been involved, because over 90 per cent of the army staff for river projects are civilian engineers. But the proposals ran head on into opposition from local interests, congressmen, and the Corps of Engineers. There seemed to be little likelihood of their adoption.

Again we must see the problem in broad perspective. Promotional politics in water resource development is comparable to promotional politics in other areas. The triangular relationship among businessmen receiving subsidies, agencies handing out subsidies, and interested congressmen raises the same problems. It is pointless to denounce selfish interests or kept congressmen or entrenched bureaucrats. The individuals and groups concerned will protect what they consider are their interests as long as this is a free country. The real questions are: How can we plan our federal promotional activities so that the public interest is safeguarded? To what extent should local interests be promoted? In short, how can we maintain a balance between the national good and local rights?

The Eisenhower Administration and Hell's Canyon Development

The Eisenhower Administration, with new leadership in the Interior Department, brought a fresh approach to these questions. The new policy in

[14] President's Water Resources Policy Commission, *A Water Policy for the American People* (Washington, D.C.: Government Printing Office, 1950), Vol. I, p. 9.

[15] Commission on Organization of the Executive Branch of the Government, *Reorganization of the Department of the Interior* (Washington, D.C.: Government Printing Office, 1949), p. 35.

electric power development from the nation's rivers, it was announced, was to increase the part of state and local committees and private citizens in the encouragement of resource development. This approach was dubbed by the Administration as a "partnership policy." Many Americans hailed the idea of putting more control in local hands. But the basic questions remained. Would this move reconcile the real interests of the groups concerned? Would it establish the proper balance between the "national," more general interest and the local, more special interest? Or would it simply help local groups who might—through charging high power rates, for example—promote their interests at the expense of the rest of the nation's consumers and taxpayers?

The dispute over Hell's Canyon illustrates the nature of the new Administration's shift in policy. Hell's Canyon, a deeply eroded reach of the Snake River on the Idaho-Oregon border, is one of the greatest unexploited sources of power and water in the country. How can we best use these resources? The issue was whether the development and operation of Hell's Canyon was to be carried out by the federal government in line with the comprehensive, multipurpose plan for the whole Columbia River or by a privately owned electric utility company with a less ambitious development plan. The Truman Administration favored the federal program. The local utility, the Idaho Power Company, applied to the Federal Power Commission for permission to go ahead with its own development program, against opposition from the Department of the Interior.[16]

So matters stood when the Eisenhower Administration came to office in January 1953. The Interior Department, now under Republican leadership, soon withdrew its opposition to private development. The Idaho Power Company renewed its application to the F.P.C., whose examiner, after hearing the parties to the case, recommended granting the company its requested license, although he found the federal plan superior to the company's plan in a number of respects. The commission then found the company's proposal acceptable on several economic, financial, and engineering grounds, and in July 1955 issued the company a license.

Meantime, however, widespread opposition to the company's plan had developed. Labor groups, public power associations, fish and wildlife associations, Rural Electrification Administration cooperatives, farm organizations, and Democratic leaders in the area and in Congress complained that the company's plan was too limited, that the power would cost too much, that comprehensive development of the Columbia valley would be stunted, and that above all the plan was a simple "give-away." The company presented answers to each of these points. The upshot was a petition to the federal courts contesting the validity of the F.P.C.'s grant of the license to the company.

[16] This case study is based chiefly on Roy F. Bessey, "The Political Issues of the Hell's Canyon Controversy," *The Western Political Quarterly*, Vol. IX, No. 3, September 1956, pp. 676-690.

President Eisenhower's re-election in 1956 came while the case was still tied up in the courts. His victory seemed to some a national endorsement of the "partnership policy," but others disagreed. Many Democratic candidates in the area, including most notably Senator Wayne Morse of Oregon, defeated their opponents partly on the Hell's Canyon issue. In any event, it was clear that the problem involved much more than the simple question of "partnership" between the government and private businessmen. Other vital issues were the best means of effective resource development from an engineering and economic standpoint, the overlapping role of federal and state agencies, the dependence of political leaders on experts who had conflicting views on technical matters, the representation or misrepresentation of the variety of local and regional interests cutting across state boundaries, and ultimately the question of who was responsible—federal, state, or private officials, or some combination of these—for intelligent action. In short, the situation brings us back to our basic question: how do we distill a general interest out of the medley of local, regional, and national interests involved?

THE LAST TWO CHAPTERS HAVE DESCRIBED TWO major methods of governmental influence over society—*regulation* and *promotion*. Under the former method, government directly lays down rules as to what men may and may not do. Under the latter, government directly or indirectly helps certain groups mainly through financial grants. It has been stressed that regulation and promotion are not separate approaches. Promotion can be used for regulatory purposes, regulation for promotional. The same government agency—indeed the same law—can embody both approaches. Many promotional laws, as we have seen, have strings attached in the form of regulations that must be followed if grants are awarded.

A third major method of governmental influence is that of *direct management* or *control*. The term is used here in two ways. One is the *direct operation* or *management* of *enterprise*. The Post Office is a good example. Presumably the government could allow a private company to handle mail, and it could regulate that company in the public interest, or subsidize it, or do both. Instead, the government long ago directly assumed the job. The second sense in which the term manager is used involves *control of the economy*. Government has come to intervene in the economy in so many ways, with such broad powers and effective instruments of control, that our political rulers are to a real extent our economic rulers as well.

Regulation and promotion by government, as preceding pages suggest, are by no means new. Nor is direct management. For many decades state and local authorities have run the schools; the national government runs the mails. What is new is the tremendous increase in governmental management during the last decade or two. All over the world, in both democratic and totalitarian countries, governments have come to direct national economies and to take over operating areas hitherto reserved for private enterprise. The trend has not gone so far in the United States as in Britain, Soviet Russia, Sweden, or Australia, but the trend has clearly shown up here too.

Some call this socialism.

★ 27

Government

as manager

Others call it the "welfare state." It is well here to ignore the name-calling —at least for the moment—and examine just what is happening. What enterprises does our federal government directly operate? With what success? To what extent does government manage the economy as a whole? What methods does it use? What political and governmental problems does this kind of management raise?

MANAGING ENTERPRISES

Americans have a curiously mixed attitude toward governmental operation of certain services. On the one hand, almost all of us stolidly and unquestioningly accept the fact that the federal government fights wars, runs some hospitals and public utilities, operates parks, delivers mail, manages a huge insurance system, and during emergencies takes over private enterprises such as coal mines and railroads. On the other hand, most of us oppose governmental operation of enterprise, and we can think up pretty good reasons to support our views. We dislike socialism—but we seem willing to take socialism if it comes in little chunks.

Despite the dogmatic positions of some, most Americans seem to approach the question of governmental ownership on a practical, matter-of-fact basis. Nobody seriously objects to governmental management of the

A MORE COMPLEX LIFE MEANS MORE "GOVERNMENT IN BUSINESS"

From Maxwell S. Stewart, "The American Way," PUBLIC AFFAIRS PAMPHLET NO. 90

armed forces. Few would want the government to take over the retail stores on Main Street. Disagreements arise over governmental control of activities in the vast area between these extremes. In general, we feel that most enterprises should be owned and managed privately, and that the burden of proof is on those who wish to extend governmental control. Even so, the national government has assumed direct control of important economic activities.

The types of enterprises operated are highly varied, ranging from the Forest Service to the Government Printing Office to the Hoover Dam. The national government, according to the Director of the Budget, owns 19,771 business enterprises with assets of $11.86 billion, employing 258,425 people. And this report does not include the Post Office.[1] A review of all these activities is impossible here. Case studies of the Post Office, the Tennessee Valley Authority, and The Atomic Energy Commission will suggest some of the major problems involved.

World's biggest business

The United States Post Office likes to call itself the biggest single business in the world. It is the largest nonmilitary department of the national government, and its 500,000 employees account for almost one-quarter of the entire federal civil service. It handles over 40 billion pieces of mail every year; supervises over 38,000 post offices; operates more than 10,000 trucks; and spends over $2 billion annually. Aside from delivering mail, it operates a postal savings system and a money-order service. It contracts for ship, rail, air, and truck transportation at a cost of many million dollars per year.

At the head of the postal service is the Postmaster General. His is a historic office; Benjamin Franklin served for twenty years as British postmaster general for the colonies, and for two years during the Revolution ran the system for the independent states.[2] The Post Office achieved Cabinet rank in 1829. For many years, however, the "PMG" has been more important politically than administratively, for it was long traditional for the President to appoint to the post the national chairman of his own party. The reason for putting a politician in this post was obvious: the PMG had thousands of patronage jobs to parcel out to the loyal party workers. Over the years, however, postal employees have gradually been brought under civil service. While perhaps 20,000 jobs are still political appointments (including some top officials and first-, second-, and third-class postmasters), postal patronage is not what it used to be. In 1948 President Truman broke tradition by appointing a career postal official as Postmaster General.

The postal service, a business agency, has only its headquarters in Washington. All but a tiny fraction of the employees work in the field. Assisting

---

[1] *U.S. Code Congressional and Administrative News* (St. Paul: West Publishing Company, 1956), No. 9, p. i, June 1956.

[2] See R. L. Butler, *Doctor Franklin: Postmaster General* (New York: Doubleday Doran & Company, Inc., 1928).

the Postmaster General are a deputy and four assistant postmasters general, and underneath them are a host of officials supervising operations in the field. Local post offices come in all sizes. Some are enormous, like that in New York with its 100 sub-stations. The smallest are branch offices run in their stores by small merchants who contract with the government. In between are the stations run by fourth-class postmasters—almost half the whole number—who are appointed by the PMG partly on a civil service, partly on a political basis. First-, second-, and third-class postmasters are appointed by the President with Senate approval; these are prize patronage plums; but appointees now have to pass competitive examinations and, if given permanent appointments, are not subject to dismissal for political reasons.

Here is a gigantic experiment in socialism. How well has the experiment worked? In 1949 the Hoover Commission had some severe criticisms to make of the Post Office. The administrative structure, it said, was obsolete and overcentralized. A maze of old-fashioned practices had stifled progress. Although a business-type establishment, the Post Office lacked the flexibility essential to good business operation. Rate-making machinery was inadequate and concealed subsidies to carriers. There were still too many political appointments. Most important, the service was losing money—up to $500 million a year.[3] Ludicrous situations resulted from the failure to decentralize. In one reported case, when the bough of a tree dropped through a post office roof, the postmaster had to write to Washington for authorization to fix the roof; he could not act on his own. In another case, a postmaster was not allowed to buy a badly needed tow truck from army surplus even though he offered to do so at his own expense.

The Hoover Commission report was a damaging indictment, but the Post Office had some answers, especially on the financial side. One reason that it loses money is that it provides services below cost. Government officials, including congressmen, have the franking privilege under which they send official mail free. More important, a huge volume of printed matter is carried at a very low rate. The air lines are in effect subsidized at rates fixed by the C.A.B. (see Chapter 26); rail shipping rates are not set by the Post Office but by the I.C.C. Postal authorities figured that of a deficit in a recent year, one-sixth was lost in carrying free mail, one-half in carrying second-class mail, one-sixth in subsidizing the air lines.

This situation illustrates the difficulties in applying ordinary dollars-and-cents profits standards to a government enterprise. If an efficient business firm took over the job, it might make a profit—but at what cost to certain sections of the public? The farmer on a remote hillside would no longer, perhaps, have rural free delivery. Newspapers and magazines would cost much more to distribute, and some might go out of existence. A cut in the air subsidy might impair the nation's military strength.

Nevertheless, many of the Hoover Commission's criticisms could not be

[3] Commission on Organization of the Executive Branch of the Government, *The Post Office* (Washington, D.C.; Government Printing Office, 1949).

refuted, and attempts have been made to improve operations. A reorganization plan for the Post Office has been under consideration that would give it more departmental autonomy. An advisory board, representing interested groups of the public, has been created to serve the agency. Certain postal rates have been increased. There is little immediate prospect, however, that the Post Office will get out of the red. Attempts to run services at cost invariably arouse the opposition of groups who benefit from present below-cost services.

Harnessing a river: the T.V.A.

During World War I the federal government bought a good deal of land, a dam, a powerhouse, and other facilities at Muscle Shoals, on the Tennessee River, for the production of nitrogen for explosives. After the war the question arose as to what should be done with this property. Some wanted to sell it to private interests. Others had a different plan. Led by a man of great vision and integrity, Senator George W. Norris, a Republican from Nebraska, they urged that the federal government assume responsibility for developing the whole Tennessee Valley.[4] After years of controversy, Congress in May 1933 passed a comprehensive act to improve the navigability of the Tennessee, to provide for flood control, reforestation, agricultural and industrial development, and the national defense. A *government corporation*, called the Tennessee Valley Authority and headed by a board of three men, was set up. The T.V.A. was given a big job: the physical, social, and economic development of the Tennessee Valley, covering more than 40,000 square miles.

The T.V.A.'s physical achievements have been remarkable. Today it operates over a score of dams on the Tennessee and its tributaries. It produces a vast quantity of electricity, much of which has been used for defense activities such as making atomic energy, explosives, and aluminum. It manufactures and sells fertilizers for the soil. The Tennessee is now navigable for 630 miles, and there have been no damaging floods since the elaborate storage system was completed. Water pollution has been reduced, malaria all but wiped out, hillsides reforested, fish and wildlife fostered, recreation areas developed. But T.V.A.'s main impact has been on the people of the valley. Not only have they benefited directly from the low electricity rates, cheap fertilizer, flood control, and construction jobs. T.V.A. experts have taught them how to conserve soil, make use of machinery, diversify their farming, improve their education and health.

All this would suggest that the T.V.A. experiment has turned out well. Much of the early criticism of valley socialism has disappeared. Nevertheless, controversial questions remain. One of these concerns the T.V.A.'s financial policies. Originally the agency was viewed as a yardstick against

[4] See *Fighting Liberal, The Autobiography of George W. Norris* (New York: The Macmillan Company, 1945), especially pp. 245-267.

which private utilities would be measured. As things have turned out, the average kilowatt hour price of T.V.A. electricity is 1.5 cents, about one-half of that for the whole country. But critics of T.V.A. charge that this is not a fair yardstick because T.V.A.'s rates do not include all the costs that a comparable private utility would have to pay. They argue, for example, that T.V.A. pays far less in taxation than private utilities (T.V.A. does make some payments to local governments in lieu of taxes) and can pay a lower rate of interest on borrowed money. Furthermore, they declare, too small a portion of the original investment was assessed to electric power, and the T.V.A. has not returned from its sale of electricity enough funds to repay the original investment.

The real truth has been shrouded in a confusion of charges, counter-charges, and fancy figure juggling, but it does seem clear that the yardstick idea has not worked out very well. Here again we see the difficulty of judging public enterprise in terms of standards applicable to private. On the other hand, there seem to be wide agreements on the following:

1. The Tennessee Valley Authority has been run efficiently and honestly, al-though management by a three-man board has raised serious problems.
2. Politics in the narrow sense of party patronage and spoils has been kept out of the agency.
3. The people in the valley have benefited enormously from T.V.A.'s work. (Average per capita income rose from $148 in 1933 to $797 in 1947 as compared with an increase in the same period from $368 to $1,323 for the whole country.)
4. The Tennessee Valley Authority has cost a good deal of money, and much of this has come from the national treasury, but T.V.A. has strengthened the national defense and the whole economy.

It has also made a major contribution to the science of government, and has developed interesting new methods of cooperating with state and local officials. It has shown how the federal government can decentralize and still do its job. Above all, it has shown the enormous possibilities of *unified regional development*. It has proved the truth of the first Hoover Commission's judgment that "A plan for the development of a river basin can-not be devised by adding together the special studies and the separate recommendations of unifunctional agencies concerned, respectively, with navigation, flood control, irrigation, land drainage, pollution abatement, power development, domestic and industrial water supply, fishing, and rec-reation. These varied and sometimes conflicting purposes must be put to-gether and integrated in a single plan of development."[5]

Will there be more T.V.A.'s? No one can say, but two obstacles may prevent further unified valley authorities. One is the opposition of interests

[5] Commission on Organization of the Executive Branch of the Government, *Reorganization of the Department of the Interior* (Washington, D.C.: Government Printing Office, 1949), p. 28.

in the valleys and key officials in Washington, as related in the previous chapter. The other is the fear that if further regional authorities are created, a problem will arise of coordinating the different authorities. It is possible that future authorities—if any are created—might operate under the general supervision of the Department of the Interior.

Atomic energy for peace

The Atomic Energy Commission, as noted in Chapter 24, is busy mainly with building and stockpiling atomic bombs. This is a supremely important job; yet the peacetime aspects of atomic energy may in the long run be even more significant. The Atomic Energy Act of 1946, which established the commission, has been called "perhaps the most radical law ever enacted in the United States"—one that virtually set up "an island of socialism in the midst of a free enterprise economy."[6] How did it happen that a conservative Congress could pass such a measure?

The answer lies in the nature of the problem. Congress in 1945 found itself in the remarkable position of being able to provide in advance for the rational control of a gigantic new resource—atomic energy. Some voices were raised in favor of private control. But most congressmen decided that the orderly development of atomic resources demanded control by the federal government. Scientists testified that the use of fissionable and radioactive materials would lead to further significant discoveries, which in time would create numberless and unpredictable problems. Without some kind of central control and planning there would be chaos. So certain was Congress of the need for government development that, in the end, it socialized atomic energy with virtually no discussion at all.

Legislative battles did take place, however, over several provisions of the bill. Civilian versus military control was the most controversial issue. As first introduced, the atomic energy bill explicitly provided that members of the proposed Atomic Energy Commission might be officers of the Army or Navy. Shortly a new type of pressure group sprang into action—atomic scientists. Many of them had chafed under military control during the war, and they feared that such control might be authoritarian, militaristic, and harmful to the spirit of free, scientific inquiry. The scientists organized citizens' committees, testified before Congress, made speeches, put out propaganda, and lobbied on Capitol Hill. Partly as a result of this skillful political action, the bill was changed. The commission would be entirely civilian, but it would be advised on military matters by a military liaison committee. This compromise was part of the final measure.

Another battle took place over patents. In handing over atomic energy to governmental control the bill also gave the commission unprecedented

[6] J. R. Newman, "America's Most Radical Law," *Harper's Magazine*, May 1947, p. 436.

NATIONAL ATOMIC ENERGY COMMISSION

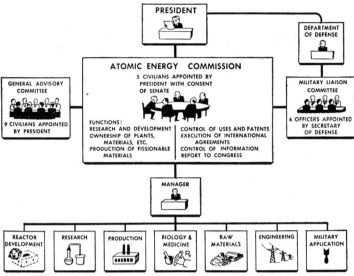

Based on *Foreign Policy Association*, HEADLINE SERIES NO. 63

power over patents. The agency might, for example, abrogate existing patent rights in areas apparently remote from the field of atomic energy. Business organizations attacked this provision as interfering with the traditional patent system, but to no avail. Other issues involved secrecy of information and research. While the act put restrictive controls around the dissemination of data, it did allow broad freedom of research. The commission was given the job of stimulating, promoting, and coordinating scientific research in atomic energy and all its applications.

Since passage of the act in the summer of 1946 the main purpose of the measure—"assuring the common defense and security"—has been decidedly the first concern of the Atomic Energy Commission. Its operations are largely shrouded in secrecy, but we do know that it owns huge installations at Hanford, Washington, and Oak Ridge, Tennessee, and elsewhere, that larger atomic bombs and hydrogen bombs are being made and at a faster rate, that the A.E.C. contracts out research and operations to private companies and universities, and that basic work is going ahead on peacetime uses for atomic energy.

Obviously it will be a long time before we can evaluate the success of this experiment in governmental management of all fissionable material. For the long-range test is not making bigger and better bombs, but, in the words of Congress in the act, "improving the public welfare, increasing the standard of living, strengthening free competition in private enterprise, and promoting world peace." The A.E.C. is conducting vast research operations through its research centers, such as Argonne and Brookhaven National Laboratories, and in its proving and testing grounds at Los Alamos, Las Vegas, and in the Pacific.

As industry makes increasing use of atomic energy, the question of the relation between government and industry in this area becomes sharper. Atomic energy is fraught with a heavy public interest. Even aside from our common stake in its successful development and exploitation, there are such problems as conflict stemming from overlapping federal and state safety codes, the extent of permissible competition among private atomic enterprises, the impact of atomic energy on other sources of power, and the effects on the economy of the location of atomic facilities. As an example of the last problem, the A.E.C.'s decision to concentrate the bulk of its atomic installations in the Ohio Valley stimulated the whole economy in that region and caused a major shift of population. In 1954 Congress modified security provisions of the basic act to make possible wider understanding of the nature of nuclear energy, and it gave more encouragement to private industry to enter the field by such means as liberalizing the patent provisions described above. The extent to which atomic energy should be made part of the normal pattern of American enterprise is bound to be an increasingly sharp political problem during coming years.

So much for three case studies in direct public management of enterprises. Now we turn to an even more important role of the federal government—the indirect *fiscal* management of the whole economy through taxing, spending, investment, and other economic methods.

RAISING THE MONEY

Big government is expensive. In 1955 federal, state, and local governments spent $109.7 billion. This is between one-fourth and one-third of the income of all Americans; in short our government spends about 30 cents of every dollar we earn. Of this the national government spends by far the most. In recent years Washington has expended about three times as much as all state and local governments combined.

Where does the money come from? The federal government gets most of its money from taxes of various kinds. Other sources are loans, commercial revenues from governmental enterprises, income from special fees and fines, and grants and gifts.

Levying taxes

"In this world," Benjamin Franklin once said, "nothing is certain but death and taxes." Levying taxes is one of the oldest activities of government. Indeed, one of the few contacts many people had with government in earlier societies was through the tax collector. He was the dread figure who represented the demands and the authority of some far-off ruler. Putting power over taxation into the hands of the people was a landmark in the rise of self-government. "No taxation without representation" has been the war cry not only of early Americans but, in effect, of people in many other countries.

The new Constitution in 1787 clearly provided that Congress "shall have power to lay and collect taxes, duties, imposts, and excises." But duties and excise taxes had to be levied uniformly throughout the United States; direct taxes had to be apportioned among the states according to population; and no tax could be levied on articles exported from any state. Except during the Civil War, the federal government relied for a century mainly on revenue from the tariff. This hidden tax—which many people falsely thought to be a tax on foreigners—fluctuated with the rise and fall of trade and tariff levels. Congress supplemented these taxes with *excise taxes* on the manufacture or sale of certain goods. In 1894 an *income tax* law was enacted (such a tax had been used during the Civil War, but given up shortly afterwards). The 1894 tax was not very drastic—only 2 per cent on all incomes over $4000—but it seemed a portent of worse things to come. The next year, as noted in Chapter 20, the Supreme Court in *Pollock* v. *Farmers Loan and Trust Co.,* held the tax measure unconstitutional on the ground that it was a direct tax and therefore had to be apportioned among the states according to population. Twenty years later the Sixteenth Amendment was adopted authorizing Congress "to lay and collect taxes on incomes, from

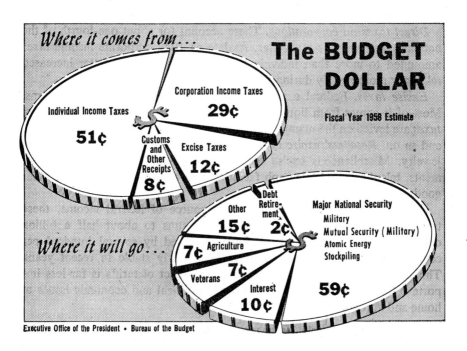

Where it comes from... The **BUDGET DOLLAR**

Corporation Income Taxes **29¢**

Individual Income Taxes **51¢**

Fiscal Year 1958 Estimate

Customs and Other Receipts **8¢**

Excise Taxes **12¢**

Where it will go...

Other **15¢**

Debt Retirement **2¢**

Major National Security
Military
Mutual Security (Military)
Atomic Energy
Stockpiling
59¢

Agriculture **7¢**

Veterans **7¢**

Interest **10¢**

Executive Office of the President • Bureau of the Budget

whatever source derived, without apportionment among the several States, and without regard to any census or enumeration."

Raising money is only one objective of taxation; *regulation* is almost as important. In a broad sense, all taxation regulates human behavior; for example, a graduated income tax has a leveling influence on incomes, and a tariff act affects foreign trade. More specifically, Congress has used its taxing power to prevent or regulate certain practices. Years ago Congress laid a 10 per cent tax on the circulation of notes by state banks, immediately putting an end to such issues. Certain kinds of professional gamblers are now required to secure a federal license and pay a tax of 10 per cent on their receipts. Congress maintains a prohibitively heavy tax on sawed-off shotguns. The Supreme Court has in the past invalidated regulation by taxation when the regulation itself was held to be unconstitutional.[7] Today, however, the Court is likely to sustain taxation for regulatory purposes, especially if it can be tied to the other great constitutional power, control over interstate commerce.

Today the federal tax cake looks something like this:

Direct taxes on individuals. Levies on the income of individuals account for about two-fifths of the federal government's tax revenue. Originally a low rate, the tax was greatly increased during World War I and went to new heights during World War II and the Korean war. One advantage of income taxes is their flexibility. Rates can be raised and lowered, exemptions can be permitted, and the individual's ability to pay can be taken into account. The federal government—and most of the states—also levy *estate, inheritance,* and *gift* taxes.

Direct taxes on corporations. These account for about one-fourth of the national government's tax dollar. As late as 1942 corporate income taxes amounted to more than individual, but returns from the latter increased relatively more rapidly during World War II.

Excise taxes. Federal excise taxes yield about one-fifth of tax returns. Most of it comes from liquor, with tobacco second. *Manufacturers' excise taxes* are levied on the manufacture of automobiles, gasoline, electric power, and so on. *Retailers' excise taxes* hit mainly luxury items such as furs and jewelry. Miscellaneous excise taxes include those on tickets to amusements, telephone and telegraph facilities, and a surprising variety of other goods.

Customs duties. No longer the main source of federal income, these taxes are not negligible. The annual yield runs to about half a billion dollars. While other tax returns have increased by several hundred per cent, however, customs returns have been fairly stable in recent years. The reason, of course, is that the revenue aspect of tariffs is far less important today than their relation to broad political and economic issues at home and abroad.

[7] See, for example, the child labor tax case, *Bailey* v. *Drexel Furniture Co.* (1922).

Taxation politics and machinery

When a young law assistant once commiserated with Justice Holmes on the taxes he had to pay, the old man replied, "With taxes I buy civilization." Most people do not have this philosophical view toward taxes. Most of us, in fact, complain that our tax load is too heavy and that someone else is not carrying his fair share. People with high incomes naturally grumble under income taxes as high as 70 per cent or even more. Low-income people point out that even a low tax on them may mean their having less of the necessities of life. People in the middle-income brackets feel that their plight is worst of all: their incomes are not high but their taxes are.

Courtesy MINNEAPOLIS STAR and Justus

Under our form of federalism the taxpayer supports three levels of government.

People differ widely over the best type of tax to be used. The graduated *income* tax is held by some to be the best type of tax because it is relatively easy to collect, it hits hardest those who are most able to pay taxes, and it hardly touches those at the bottom of the income ladder. Others argue that *excise* taxes are the fairest tax because they are paid by people who are actually spending money for goods— especially luxury goods—and thus obviously have money to spare. Furthermore, it is said, excise taxes have a desirable deflationary effect in time of rising prices because they discourage buying of expensive goods, such as jewelry. On the other hand, excise taxes are more expensive to collect than income taxes, and in some cases, such as the tax on tobacco, they may hit the poor man hardest. Most controversial of all types of taxes, perhaps, is the *general* sales tax, which resembles the excise tax except that it is levied against the sales of all goods. Labor and liberal organizations denounce this form of tax as regressive— that is, it would hurt the poor man more than the rich man, because the former uses all his earnings to buy goods, while the latter may devote more of his income to buying personal services or to savings. Proponents of the sales tax stress its anti-inflationary effect and point to its successful use in a number of states.

A recent tax bill illustrated the wide impact of taxes on a variety of individuals and groups. Testifying on proposed tax changes before a congressional committee, 138 witnesses expressed their views and scores of briefs were submitted, all covering more than 1600 pages of printed testimony. Business representatives opposed new taxes on corporations. Small businessmen complained that existing taxes favored big business. Spokesmen for tobacco growers, transportation interests, the wine and spirits industry, movies, the legitimate theater, candy makers, telephone companies, bowling alley proprietors, and other groups came to argue that the proposed tax would discriminate against them. Labor demanded a lighter burden for low-income groups, higher taxes on business. Unorganized workers and consumers, however, were not represented.

Although the Constitution provides that all revenue bills must be initiated in the House of Representatives, the originator of tax legislation is usually the *President*. With the help of tax experts on his staff and in the Treasury Department he draws up a program for tax changes designed to meet the government's revenue needs for the coming fiscal year. Often the representatives of interest groups are consulted during the stage of executive formulation of the bill. Following this phase the President submits his tax program to Congress, often in conjunction with his budget message. The powerful House Ways and Means Committee then holds hearings on the bill; Administration spokesmen, headed by the Secretary of the Treasury, usually lead off the parade of witnesses, followed by representatives of interested groups, taxation experts, and others. Following committee consideration, tax measures go through Congress in much the same manner as other bills. While the Senate cannot initiate tax legislation, it refuses to take a back seat on tax matters. It often differs with the House, and forces extensive changes of bills coming from the lower chamber. Sometimes Congress refuses to follow the President's recommendations, and works out a tax measure largely on its own.

The Treasury Department has the job of collecting the taxes levied by Congress. One of the original departments set up in 1789 and headed by the second highest-ranking Secretary, this department today is a large agency employing about 80,000 people. The actual tax-collecting job falls mainly to the huge Internal Revenue Service. Sixty-four district directors are located throughout the country, and taxes are paid into district offices rather than directly to Washington. The Bureau takes in $40 to $50 billion a year at a cost of less than 50 cents for each $100 in returns. Customs are collected by the Treasury Department's Bureau of Customs, which maintains ports of entry, inspects the discharge of cargo, assesses the value of merchandise, and, through the services of the United States Coast Guard, prevents smuggling.

Uncle Sam, borrower

When a person is suddenly faced with heavy expenses, such as hospital bills, his regular income may not be enough and he may have to borrow money. The same thing is true of government. During military and economic crises the federal government has gone heavily in debt. It borrowed $23 billion during World War I, about $13 billion more during the 1930's, and over $200 billion more during World War II. During other periods the government has tried to pay off its debts, but progress has been slow. By the end of 1956 the national debt was about $275 billion.

Borrowing costs money. The federal government can borrow at a low rate—recently about 3 per cent—because no security is any safer than a government bond. Nevertheless the public federal debt is so huge today that the interest alone is costing approximately $7 billion a year. The size of the debt and of the interest alarm many Americans. How long can we continue to allow the debt to go on at these staggering proportions? Two considerations must be kept in mind. In the first place, the government owes most of the money to its own people (rather than to foreign governments or persons); or, in another sense, we all owe the money to one another. Second, the most important consideration is not the size of the public debt but the economic strength and resources of the country. As we shall see later in this chapter, more borrowing may actually improve the country's economic position. The most discouraging aspect of the situation has been our failure to pay off the debt during years between wars and depressions. The debt was reduced by about $25 billion after World War II, but then it began to go up again.

How is money borrowed? Under the Constitution Congress may "borrow money on the credit of the United States," and there is no constitutional limit on either the extent or the method of borrowing. Under congressional authorization the Treasury Department sells securities to banks, corporations, and individuals. Usually these securities take the form of long-term bonds or short-term treasury notes. Some bonds may be cashed in any time; others not until their maturity dates. Because the United States government backs up these bonds they are in great demand, especially by banks and investment companies. However, the government, particularly in time of war, likes to induce as many individual persons as possible to buy bonds, because individuals who buy bonds have that much less money to purchase goods, and thus will contribute less to inflationary pressures. To this end famous athletes and movie stars are enlisted to help out in well-publicized bond drives. If voluntary methods fail, the government may require purchases under compulsory deductions from wages and salaries.

Besides taxing and borrowing, a third source of federal funds consists of *administrative* and *commercial revenues*. The fee paid to the State Department for a passport, the fine paid by a criminal, are administrative revenues that account for a portion—though a very small portion—of federal income. More important are the funds paid to the federal government in exchange for direct services. Payments to the Post Office for stamps, to the Park Service for recreation, to the Government Printing Office for pamphlets, are examples of this kind of revenue.

Finally, some public-spirited people actually *give* money or property to the government! Mr. Justice Holmes, who didn't mind taxes, left the government almost his entire estate on his death. But gifts, needless to say, are an almost infinitesimal source of federal revenue.

SPENDING THE MONEY

All these billions are funneled into the Treasury and then rapidly move out through hundreds of channels to points throughout the nation and, indeed, throughout the world. Nothing shows the rise of big government more clearly than the change in the amount and methods of its spending. As recently as 1932 the federal government spent only $4 billion, about $30 per capita. In 1955 the respective figures were $72 billion and $438. The machinery for spending has changed, too. Spending at one time was loosely administered. Records show, for example, that in an early year of the Republic one Nicholas Johnson, a Navy agent of Newburyport, Massachusetts, was handed several thousand dollars to supply "Capt. Brown for recruiting his Crew."[8] Today that machinery is highly organized.

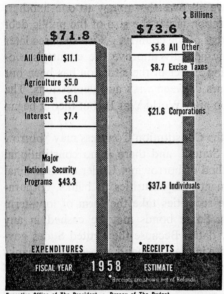

The FEDERAL BUDGET

$ Billions

$71.8

All Other $11.1

Agriculture $5.0

Veterans $5.0

Interest $7.4

Major National Security Programs $43.3

EXPENDITURES

$73.6

$5.8 All Other

$8.7 Excise Taxes

$21.6 Corporations

$37.5 Individuals

*RECEIPTS

FISCAL YEAR 1958 ESTIMATE

*Receipts are shown net of Refunds

Executive Office of The President • Bureau of The Budget

Where does the money go? Most of it, of course, for national defense. The 71.8 billion dollars estimated budget for the fiscal year 1958 allots about 59 per cent to the military services; 3⅓ per cent goes to international activities, 2½ per cent for interest on the national debt, 7 per cent to veterans, and 28 per cent for all other services. Interesting changes have taken place even in the last two decades. In 1939 total expenditures of the federal government amounted to $9 billion. Of this national defense took about $1 billion, interest less than $1 billion, and veterans about $600 million. It is hard to realize today that as recently as 1939 most federal expenses were for domestic relief and welfare functions. Significantly, in 1939 we spent about 0.5 per cent

[8] L. D. White, *The Federalists* (New York: The Macmillan Company, 1948), p. 341.

of our outlays on international activities. That proportion has risen many-fold as we have faced up to our global responsibilities.

The sheer fact of spending $72 billions a year is most significant of all. Years ago federal revenues and outlays were so small compared to the national income that Washington's taxing and spending had little impact on the over-all economy. But today the federal government cannot drain all those billions from certain areas in the economy and pump them back into other areas without making Washington's fiscal decisions of vital importance for both the national and world economic situation. This problem will be considered later in the chapter. First we must see how the federal budget is drawn up and made into law.

Formulating the budget

The power to spend is one of the basic powers granted to Congress in the Constitution. The Supreme Court has put very few limitations on that authority—so few, indeed, that some observers predict that Congress might use its vast spending powers to bribe the states into following its lead by grants-in-aid, thus undermining the federal system.[9] Today, while Congress must authorize the spending of funds, the *initiation* of appropriations has come to be essentially an executive function. Indeed, under the Budget and Accounting Act of 1921, the President is formally responsible for preparing an executive budget; the act was designed to focus responsibility in the chief executive and to put an end to a situation where budget making had become highly disorganized and decentralized throughout the executive establishment.

The first step is budgetary planning in the various departments and agencies. This process starts very early; while Congress is debating the consolidated budget for the fiscal year immediately ahead, the agencies are making budget estimates for the year following. (The fiscal year runs half a year ahead of the calendar year, from July 1 through the subsequent June 30. Thus fiscal year 1958 starts July 1, 1957, and ends June 30, 1958). The job in the agencies is handled largely by budget officers at all levels working under the direction of the agency chief and heads of subordinate units. The agency officials must figure on the basis not only of their needs as they see them, but also the over-all presidential program and the probable reactions of Congress.[10] Departmental budgets are highly detailed, for they include estimates on expected needs for personnel, supplies, office space, and the like.

The Budget Bureau is the scene of the next phase of budget making. As a staff agency of the President, the bureau scrutinizes each agency budget

[9] See, for example, E. S. Corwin, *The Twilight of the Supreme Court* (New Haven: Yale University Press, 1934).

[10] See Chapter 19 for an example of the kind of considerations that may enter at this stage.

carefully to see if it is in accord with the President's budget plans. This job is done by experienced budget examiners who usually have a long acquaintance with a particular agency, and can look over its requests with a sharp eye for accuracy, economy, and good program planning. Hearings are then held at which agency spokesmen can clarify and defend their esti-

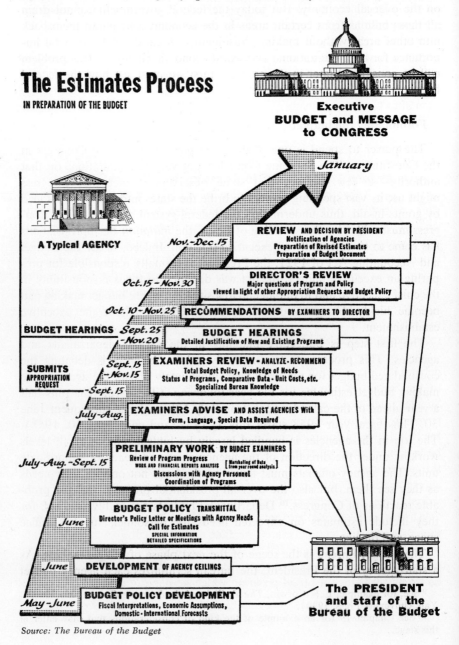

The Estimates Process
IN PREPARATION OF THE BUDGET

Executive
BUDGET and MESSAGE
to CONGRESS

January

A Typical AGENCY

Nov.–Dec. 15
REVIEW AND DECISION BY PRESIDENT
Notification of Agencies
Preparation of Revised Estimates
Preparation of Budget Document

Oct. 15 – Nov. 30
DIRECTOR'S REVIEW
Major questions of Program and Policy
viewed in light of other Appropriation Requests and Budget Policy

Oct. 10 – Nov. 25   **RECOMMENDATIONS** BY EXAMINERS TO DIRECTOR

BUDGET HEARINGS *Sept. 25 – Nov. 20*
BUDGET HEARINGS
Detailed Justification of New and Existing Programs

SUBMITS APPROPRIATION REQUEST
Sept. 15 – Nov. 15
EXAMINERS REVIEW – ANALYZE – RECOMMEND
Total Budget Policy, Knowledge of Needs
Status of Programs, Comparative Data - Unit Costs, etc.
Specialized Bureau Knowledge

– Sept. 15

July–Aug.
EXAMINERS ADVISE AND ASSIST AGENCIES With
Form, Language, Special Data Required

July–Aug. – Sept. 15
PRELIMINARY WORK BY BUDGET EXAMINERS
Review of Program Progress
WORK AND FINANCIAL REPORTS ANALYSIS [Marshaling of Data from year round analysis]
Discussions with Agency Personnel
Coordination of Programs

June
BUDGET POLICY TRANSMITTAL
Director's Policy Letter or Meetings with Agency Heads
Call for Estimates
SPECIAL INFORMATION
DETAILED SPECIFICATIONS

June   **DEVELOPMENT** OF AGENCY CEILINGS

May–June
BUDGET POLICY DEVELOPMENT
Fiscal Interpretations, Economic Assumptions,
Domestic - International Forecasts

The PRESIDENT
and staff of the
Bureau of the Budget

Source: The Bureau of the Budget

mates. The director of the budget and his aides make the final decisions; sometimes they prune agencies' requests rather severely.

The third step is at the presidential level. For months the budget director has conferred periodically with the chief executive and has attempted to keep the agencies within budget ceilings set by the President. Finally—it is probably December by now—the director arrives at the White House with a single consolidated set of estimates of both revenue and expenditures, the product of perhaps a year's work. The President has reserved a day or two for a final review of the budget, and the two men check final estimates. The budget director also assists the President on a budget message that will stress key aspects of the budget and tie it in with broad national plans. By January, soon after Congress convenes, the budget and the message are ready for the legislature and the people.

The legislative gantlet

After its formal presentation to Congress, the President's budget goes first to the Appropriations Committee of the House of Representatives. This committee operates through nine subcommittees, each of which considers appropriations for a particular department or group of agencies. Agency representatives are invited before the subcommittees to defend their requests in formal hearings. The subcommittees have their own staff assistants who help in examining the budgets. Following the hearings, the subcommittee and its staff work out legislative schedules embodying the agency budgets as modified by the legislators. The full Appropriations Committee goes over the subcommittee reports and schedules and incorporates them, perhaps with further changes, into appropriation bills.

The Appropriations Committee submits each bill to the House, which debates it for two or three days, amends it, and passes it. The bill then goes to the Senate, which refers it to the Senate Appropriations Committee. Smaller than its counterpart in the House, this committee usually concentrates on controversial items and even allows agency spokesmen to appeal for restoration of funds slashed in the House.[11] Debate in the Senate may be freer and more general than in the lower chamber. Differences between the two houses are resolved in conference committee. The President must accept the whole appropriations measure, or veto it; he cannot veto individual items. So he almost always signs the measure.

All this is the formal procedure, and it looks like a sensible, efficient—though somewhat cumbersome—arrangement. Actually, the whole treatment of an appropriations bill is inevitably dominated by the conflicting positions of President, bureaucrats, and congressmen. The President may be trying to finance a broad program which he has promised to carry out.

[11] See A. W. Macmahon, "Congressional Oversight Over Administration: The Power of the Purse," *Political Science Quarterly,* June, September 1943, pp. 161-190, 380-414.

The bureaucrats are of course committed to their own projects, and they are supported by the groups that benefit from their agencies. The congressmen have all kinds of interests. They may be eager to push through a project of benefit to their constituents, to hamstring an agency that they oppose, to prove themselves watchdogs of the Treasury, or to ingratiate themselves with the President, with an influential Cabinet member, or with a powerful interest group.

Politics is, of course, both desirable and inevitable in the handling of any legislation, including appropriations measures. Unfortunately, such bills are subjected to a type of political pulling and hauling that raises hob with orderly responsible fiscal policy. The reasons are twofold. First, despite improvement in recent years, the appropriations are *highly detailed*. This condition both helps and hurts the legislator: it helps him to accomplish specific objectives, but it also immerses him in such a flood of detail that he is often unable to look at the appropriations situation in broad perspective. (If a congressman were to spend an hour studying each million dollars of expenditures, it would take him over twenty years to go over the annual budget.) Second, the committees and subcommittees handling appropriations are often manned largely by legislators who may be out of touch with general needs of the country. These legislators enjoy long seniority, and because of the seniority rule they rise to positions of great influence on the committees. To be sure, the committee and subcommittee chairmen are members of the majority party in Congress. But the majority, as we have seen, has little internal cohesion or discipline. And when the President and the congressional majority are of different parties, the problem of confusion, irresponsibility, and delay is compounded.

What can be done? Both the first and second Hoover Commissions made recommendations to improve budget procedure in both the executive and lesislative branches. The first Hoover Commission recommended that the "whole budgetary concept of the Federal Government should be refashioned by the adoption of a budget based upon functions, activities, and projects."[12] This is called a *performance* or *program budget*. The idea is simple. Instead of concentrating on things to be acquired, such as personnel and supplies, the commission said, the budget should focus attention on the *general character and relative importance of the work to be done, or service to be rendered*. For example, the commission noted that a naval hospital was receiving allotments from twelve different Navy appropriations titles, such as Bureau of Ships, Bureau of Ordnance; under a performance budget all the costs of this hospital would be compared with those for previous years and those of other hospitals. Since fiscal year 1951 some budg-

---

[12] Commission on Organization of the Executive Branch of the Government, *Budgeting and Accounting* (Washington, D.C.: Government Printing Office, 1949), pp. 8-12.

etary statements from the executive branch have been couched in performance terms.

Despite legislative criticism of performance budgeting, the second Hoover Commission also recommended its use, but suggested "a review of performance by organizational units where these do not coincide with performance budget classifications."[13] This commission also recommended that agencies should formulate their budget requests in terms of estimated costs of goods and services actually to be received during a year instead of in terms of estimated obligations to be incurred. Perhaps the most drastic recommendation was that Congress make appropriations on an annual accrued expenditure basis. For example, instead of authorizing the Navy to spend $150 million for a ship over a four-year period, each year Congress should appropriate only the amount the Navy would need for actual goods and services to be received during the year. The commission argued that under the existing system Congress does not have a clear picture of how much money an agency is actually going to spend. Many agencies actually have money left over from previous years' appropriations.

Some of the Hoover Commissioners dissented, holding that the recommended procedures might be suitable for a business where profits are the main concern but would be harmful to many government agencies whose main job is service. Congress refused to make its own appropriations on an annual accrued costs basis, but in 1956 it did enact legislation adopting other of the Hoover Commission recommendations, including the requirement that executive budget requests be stated in performance terms, that they be formulated on the basis of costs, and that agencies show how much they will need for the goods and services actually to be received during the year. It will take four or five years for these reforms to be put into effect and whether they will be effective remains to be seen.

Some congressmen have shown interest in improving their own procedures. The Legislative Reorganization Act of 1946 provided for a *legislative budget* which was designed to emphasize the budgetary forest instead of the trees. The act authorized the members of the appropriations and revenue committees of House and Senate to meet jointly early each calendar year in order to map out a broad budgetary program and to set appropriations ceilings for the coming year in relation to expected income. The plan, in short, was to set an over-all framework in the light of which executive requests might be studied. This laudable plan has been tried but it has not worked, partly because the four committees have been too busy with their regular tasks, and partly because individual congressmen are prone to go their own way on individual budgetary items.

[13] Commission on Organization of the Executive Branch of the Government, *Budget and Accounting* (Washington, D.C.: Government Printing Office, 1955), p. 13.

Checking up on expenditures

It is a traditional legislative prerogative not only to appropriate money but to scrutinize the spending of that money. In this way the legislators know whether the money is spent properly and for the purposes they authorized. Under the Budget and Accounting Act of 1921 the *General Accounting Office* does the national government's accounting job. The G.A.O. is headed by a Comptroller General, who is appointed by the President with the approval of the Senate, but who has a measure of independence by virtue of the fact that his term of office is fifteen years, he is ineligible for reappointment, and he can be removed only for specific cause by a joint resolution of Congress.

The Comptroller General was set up to operate as an independent auditor serving as an arm of Congress to guard against improper and unauthorized expenditures. In fact, however, for many years he was involved in a gigantic *accounting* job that forced him to handle administrative matters in the executive branch without being responsible to the chief executive. At the same time, over-all management in the executive branch suffered, because day-to-day accounting, an important instrument of administrative control, had been placed in a separate agency. Prior to 1949 the G.A.O. imposed rigid requirements on the agencies, maintained detailed accounting records that frequently duplicated agency records, and brought tons of papers to Washington to check laboriously for irregularities.

In recent years, partly in response to recommendations of the Hoover Commissions, improvements have been made. The G.A.O. uses spot sampling methods to check vouchers, and makes its audits in the field rather than in Washington. Although the Comptroller General still has the authority to disallow expenditures, his approval is no longer needed prior to the disbursement of funds. Being relieved of personal responsibility for payments that may subsequently be disallowed (provided they have acted in good faith and with reasonable diligence), disbursing officers have been encouraged to make their own decisions about the legality of expenditures. Moreover, in 1950 Congress gave the departments and agencies, subject to supervision of the G.A.O., the responsibility and authority to set up their own internal accounting operations. Both the first and second Hoover Commissions have urged legislation to give the executive departments even greater authority.[14] These new procedures presumably will allow the Comptroller General to spend more time carrying out the vital legislative function of scrutinizing administrative fiscal practices, of making sure that laws governing appropriations were being correctly interpreted,

[14] Commission on Organization of the Executive Branch of the Government, *Budgeting and Accounting* (Washington: Government Printing Office, 1949), pp. 39, 47 ff; see also Commission on Organization of the Executive Branch of the Government, *Budgeting and Accounting* (Washington, D.C.: Government Printing Office, 1955), pp. 29 ff.

of checking the efficiency of accounting and other administrative practices —and reporting on all these to Congress.

It might seem that accounting is a technical matter that could be settled without much argument. On the contrary, accounting is a political problem, too, for it reflects two struggles that go on in Washington. One is the attempt of Congress as a whole to maintain as much control as possible over the still mushrooming bureaucratic machine. The other is the struggle of individual legislators in Washington to keep a system that checks individual administrative payments.

MANAGING MONEY

Today's economy is essentially a money economy. Instead of using a system of barter—such as that of South Sea islanders who swap fruit for beads—"civilized" peoples base the exchange of commodities on a vast system of money and credit. We have seen the tremendous role the federal government has in this system simply because it gets and spends $60 or $70 billion a year. But aside from its role as the biggest buyer and seller of goods and services, the federal government has a more direct impact on our money economy. First, it manufactures money. Second, it regulates the value of money. Third, it controls the nation's credit system.

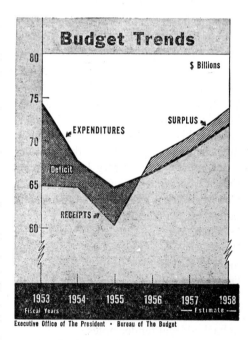

Making money is the easiest of these functions. The Bureau of Engraving and Printing in the Treasury Department, using carefully designed plates and special types of paper, turns out millions of dollars of bills, bonds, and postage stamps every week. This "folding-money" is fed into general circulation through the Treasury and the Federal Reserve banks. The Bureau of the Mint in Philadelphia, Denver, and San Francisco (also under the Treasury) coins the silver dollars, half dollars, quarters, and dimes, the nickel-copper nickels, and the copper and iron pennies that together make up about one-twentieth of the country's cash.

This money is only so much paper and metal in itself. How does government maintain its value?

The currency system

One reason that the federal government manages the money system is that it has the constitutional right to do so. The framers were unhappy about the situation under the Articles of Confederation, when the national currency consisted mainly of almost worthless paper money and the states maintained separate currencies. The Constitution of 1787 carefully vested in Congress authority to coin money and to regulate its value, and it carefully withheld this power from the states. Thanks partly to Secretary of the Treasury Hamilton, the early Americans did not keep the confusing British system of guineas, pounds, shillings, and pence, but adopted a decimal system.

The government gave value to its money by manufacturing coins from two precious metals, gold and silver, which had intrinsic values of their own. Fifteen ounces of coined silver were exchangeable for one ounce of coined gold. This was a *bimetallic* monetary standard, then quite common among commercial nations. The trouble with this system was that gold and silver, having market values of their own (for wedding rings, gold teeth, silverware, and so on) fluctuated in relative value as both supply and demand rose and fell. For example, the discovery of gold in California made gold much cheaper and drove silver out of circulation. After striving for many years to keep both gold and silver coin in circulation, Congress in 1900 established the gold dollar of 23.22 grains of pure gold as the standard unit of value. This was the famous gold standard, under which all money was maintained on a parity with the yellow metal.

Of course, the country had not been using only metal currency all this time. Coin is hard to handle and expensive to ship in big quantities. In 1791 Congress chartered a national bank with power to issue bank notes. These notes were not legal tender—that is, no person was forced to accept them in payment of a debt—they were simply a convenience. During the Civil War, however, the federal government needed unprecedented sums of money, and it had trouble borrowing enough funds. So Congress issued "greenbacks," with no metal to back them up, and these were made legal tender. After a long and bitter battle in the courts, the Supreme Court in the *Legal Tender Cases* in 1884 held that Congress had the right to issue unbacked legal tender notes.

The Great Depression beginning in 1929 affected our monetary arrangements just as it did other sectors of the economy. Under the gold standard any lawful money could be redeemed in gold, individuals could freely trade in that metal, and gold reserves backed up all other money. But the depression forced many depositors to withdraw their gold from the banks. The decline in bank reserves imperiled the whole banking and credit system. In 1933 the gold standard was abandoned. In a series of rapid moves, private possession of gold was outlawed, coinage of gold was ended, holders of gold were compelled to turn it in to the government in exchange for other currency, and the value of the gold dollar was reduced to about 59 cents.

Today the United States is on the "gold standard" in the limited sense that the money and credit supply is backed up in part with a huge store of gold at Fort Knox, Kentucky, and the unit of monetary value is defined in terms of gold. But all the currency of the United States—Federal Reserve notes, Silver Certificates, silver dollars, and subsidiary coins—are legal tender and cannot be freely exchanged for gold. (A few United States notes, Treasury notes, Federal bank notes, and national bank notes are still outstanding but they are in the process of retirement.) The money of the United States is freely redeemable only for other money of the United States.

Money makes up only a part of the circulating medium and is less important to our economy than *credit*. In the expansion and contraction of credit the most important institutions are the nation's banks and the Federal Reserve System.

Banks and lending institutions

Banking is a private business but subject to close governmental supervision. There are over 14,000 banks in the United States, 5000 chartered by the national government, the others by the states. The national banks, however, have almost 50 per cent of all bank deposits in their custody. The Comptroller of the Currency in the Department of Treasury supervises their operations. At least three times a year each national bank must file reports on its financial conditions and bank examiners inspect their books at least twice a year—at unannounced times.

Although state authorities have the primary responsibility to supervise state-chartered banks, most of these banks are also subject to federal regulation, since their deposits are insured by the Federal Deposit Insurance Corporation. All national banks must participate in this program, and state banks that meet approved standards are permitted to do so. All but a few hundred of the 13,756 commercial bank and trust companies in the United States have their deposits insured by the F.D.I.C. as do some of the 529 mutual savings banks. The F.D.I.C. routinely examines banks not members of the Federal Reserve System (see below) and establishes rules designed to keep them solvent. In case of an insolvent member bank, the F.D.I.C. takes over its management and pays off each depositor up to $10,000.

The Federal Savings and Loan Insurance Corporation, operating under the supervision of the Federal Home Loan Bank Board, protects investors in federal savings and loan associations and those state chartered institutions approved for participation. Like the F.D.I.C. it guarantees savings up to $10,000 for each account.

The national government has also been active in promoting the establishment of *credit unions,* associations of persons having a common bond of occupation or residence who may secure a federal charter and receive assistance from the Bureau of Federal Credit Unions in the Department of Health, Education, and Welfare. These unions, which now number over 7500, encourage members to deposit excess funds and make loans to members at relatively low interest rates.

Credit and politics

In many nations a central bank owned and operated by the national government determines general monetary policies. The Constitution does not specifically authorize the national government to create such a bank—indeed, it says nothing about the subject of banking. But Alexander Hamilton believed some such institution was necessary; and in 1791, on his initiative, the United States Bank was incorporated by the national government and given a twenty-year charter. The United States Bank was partly private and partly public, as the national government owned only a minority of the shares and had only a minority voice in its management. Jefferson and his supporters opposed the bank on monetary, political, and constitutional grounds. Nevertheless, President Madison found it necessary to have the bank rechartered for another twenty years in 1816, after the Jeffersonians first refused to do so in 1811.

In 1819 the Supreme Court in *McCulloch* v. *Maryland* (see Chapter 4) upheld the constitutionality of the bank as a necessary and proper way for the national government to establish a uniform national currency and to care for the property of the United States. During Jackson's administration the bank issue was reopened again and dominated the political scene. Headed by the formidable Nicholas Biddle, the Second United States Bank became extremely unpopular in the rural West after wholesale foreclosures of mortgaged farm land. The bank came to symbolize the financial and political power of vested interests. Jackson seized on this issue. After vetoing Senator Henry Clay's bill to recharter the bank, he won re-election despite the efforts of Biddle and other of the bank's friends. After his re-election he decided to withdraw government funds from the bank and thus destroy it even before its old charter expired. When his Secretary of the Treasury refused to withdraw the funds, Jackson fired him and hired another Secretary who would. And when Clay put a resolution of censure through the Senate, Jackson mobilized his supporters and had the resolution expunged.

After the bank closed its doors in 1836, state banks, which had previously been restrained by the Second United States Bank, embarked on an orgy of issuing notes that often could not be redeemed. A military crisis forced a housecleaning. To stabilize an economy beset with war demands and to support the desires of the "dear money" groups, Congress in 1863 authorized the chartering of national banks, privately owned corporations not to be confused with a central bank or an institution like the United States Bank.

State banks were permitted to continue in business, but a 10 per cent federal tax on their notes quickly drove state bank notes out of existence.

The struggle over bank policy was in part a struggle over cheap versus dear money. Those who possess money and who are creditors naturally want to maintain, and if possible increase, its value. Those who do not have much money and especially those who owe money often want to cheapen it. This struggle reached bitter proportions during the decades following the Civil War. Faced with low farm prices and entangled in debt, farmers campaigned for printing more paper money and thus cheapening the dollar. William Jennings Bryan waged a long fight to restore free coinage of silver at the rate of sixteen ounces of silver to one ounce of gold. As a candidate for President, however, he was beaten by both McKinley and Taft.

The national bank system created during the Civil War was stable—indeed, so stable that it was inflexible. Financial crises during the late nineteenth century and in 1907 revealed unhappy tendencies: banks restricted their loans, and national banks contracted their issuance of notes just at the times when an *expansion* of money was needed. In order to furnish an elastic currency, and for other reasons, Congress established the Federal Reserve System in 1913.

The Federal Reserve System

The Act of 1913 was a compromise. Some wanted a strong central bank, but many feared, just as did the Jacksonians eighty years before, that this would centralize control over currency in too few hands. So a system was established that gives us a modified central banking program with considerable decentralization.

The country is divided into twelve Federal Reserve Districts, in each of which there is a Federal Reserve Bank (most Federal Reserve Banks have branches). Each Federal Reserve Bank is owned by member banks. All national banks must join the system, and state banks that meet standards are permitted to do so. Today approximately 6500 of the more than 14,000 banks are members of the Federal Reserve System, and these consist of the largest banks with around 75 per cent of total deposits.

Each Federal Reserve Bank is headed by a board of directors, six elected by the member banks, and three appointed by the Board of Governors (see immediately below) in Washington. Three of the directors elected by the member banks must be bankers, and three must be active in business and industry. The three directors appointed by the Board of Governors cannot have any financial interest in, or work for, any bank. The Board of Governors designates one of its appointees to be chairman of the Board of Directors and this board in turn selects a president to serve as its chief executive officer.

A seven-man Board of Governors sitting in Washington supervises the entire system. These men are selected by the President with the consent of

HIGHLIGHTS OF THE FEDERAL RESERVE SYSTEM

From "A Visual History of the United States," by Harold U. Faulkner & Graphics Institute; Abelard-Schuman.

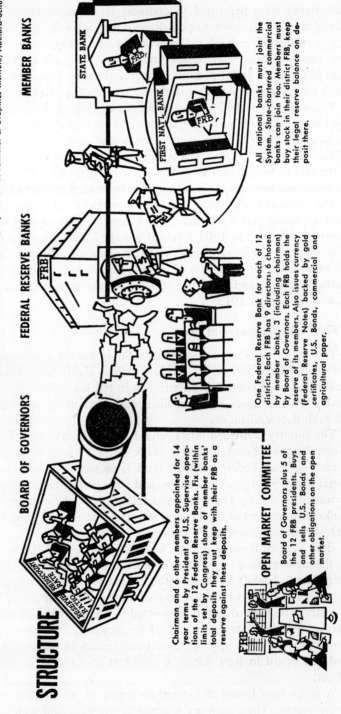

STRUCTURE

BOARD OF GOVERNORS

Chairman and 6 other members appointed for 14 year terms by President of U.S. Supervise operations of the 12 Federal Reserve Banks. Fix (within limits set by Congress) share of member banks' total deposits they must keep with their FRB as a reserve against these deposits.

OPEN MARKET COMMITTEE

Board of Governors plus 5 of the 12 FRB presidents. Buys and sells U.S. Bonds and other obligations on the open market.

FEDERAL RESERVE BANKS

One Federal Reserve Bank for each of 12 districts. Each FRB has 9 directors: 6 chosen by member banks, 3 (including chairman) by Board of Governors. Each FRB holds the reserve of its members. Also issues currency (Federal Reserve Notes) backed by gold certificates, U.S. Bonds, commercial and agricultural paper.

MEMBER BANKS

All national banks must join the System. State-chartered commercial banks can join too. Members must buy stock in their district FRB, keep their legal reserve balance on deposit there.

FUNCTIONS

A. Influences the Supply of Money and Credit

To INCREASE supply	To DECREASE supply

1. Lowers the % of cash (reserve) the members must put up against their deposits. Members can then use excess funds to extend credit.

1. Increases the reserve requirement. Member banks put up additional money by calling loans, selling investments.

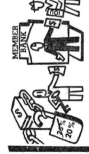

2. Buys U.S. Govt. securities in open market. This provides member banks with additional reserve funds.

2. Sells U.S. Govt. securities, draining deposits from member banks.

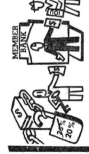

3. Lowers discount rate it charges members for loans. Makes it profitable for members, in turn, to make more loans.

3. Raises discount rate. This causes banks to be reluctant to lend additional amounts of money.

B. Provides special services for the Federal Government

1. Maintains an orderly market in Federal securities.

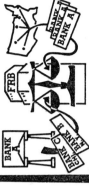

2. Acts as Treasury's banker, and helps issue and redeem its bonds.

3. Sets amount of down payment that must be made by buyers of stock market securities.

C. Provides services for Member Banks and the Public

1. Furnishes elastic supply of currency for circulation.

2. Safeguards, keeps track of members' reserve balances.

3. Settles up for checks drawn on members or received by them.

4. Supplies credit by discounts, loans, security purchases.

the Senate for fourteen-year terms, and the President designates the chairman. The Board of Governors, advised by the Federal Advisory Council composed of a member from each Federal Reserve district that meets in Washington at least four times a year, determines general monetary and credit policies. It has four major weapons to tighten or loosen the financial activities of the nation's banks and, in turn, of the whole economy. They are as follows:

1. Increase or decrease within legal limits the reserves that member banks must maintain against their deposits in the Federal Reserve Bank.

2. Raise or lower the rediscount rate charged by Federal Reserve banks to member banks. The rediscount rate is the price member banks must pay to get cash from the Federal Reserve Banks for acceptable commercial notes that the banks hold.

3. Through the Open Market Committee (composed of all members of the Board of Governors and five representatives of the Reserve Banks) sell or buy government securities and certain other bills of exchanges, bank acceptances, and so on.

4. Exercise direct control over the credit that may be extended in order to purchase securities (called "margin requirements"). From time to time Congress has given the Board of Governors temporary authority to fix terms of consumer credit.

Through these and other devices, the Board of Governors may affect the flow of circulating medium by tightening or loosening credit. For example, if inflation is threatening, the board can dampen down the economy by raising member bank reserve requirements (thus cutting down on the cash they have available for lending), by raising rediscount rates (thus forcing member banks to raise the rates for which they will lend money), by selling government securities in the open market (thus absorbing funds from the economy), and by raising margin requirements (thus reducing credit available to bid up the prices of securities).

The Federal Reserve Banks also serve as depository institutions for government funds, operate a system of clearing checks and transferring funds among member banks, and may in case of economic emergency even lend money directly to businesses.

The Board of Governors is intentionally isolated from the direct influence of the executive and is supposed to make its monetary decisions in accord with its own judgment. However, the Treasury Department also has important techniques for influencing the flow of credit, and at times Treasury officials and the Board of Governors have worked at cross-purposes. The Treasury may wish to pay a low interest on government securities, in order to borrow money as cheaply as possible at a time when the Board of Governors is moving to raise interest rates in order to dampen inflation. Despite the Board's organizational independence, the President's influence and prestige are at times difficult for the Board to withstand.

It is not surprising to discover that money and credit policies are still in politics. Groups struggle over these policies and have conflicting ideas of what they should be. One of the most influential groups in Washington, for example, has been the silver lobby, working hand in hand with the silver bloc in Congress. Yet the situation has changed in at least one important respect from the past. Money and banking in today's battles figure less as isolated policies and more as parts of over-all economic strategy. Monetary policy has become but one phase, one weapon, used to combat depression, control inflation, foster full employment and high national income. The crucial political issue today, in short, is what should the government do to keep the economy sound?

MANAGING THE ECONOMY

This chapter has described how the federal government directly manages certain economic activities, as in the case of the post office, T.V.A., and others. It has shown how the government raises and spends billions of dollars a year, how it largely controls currency, banking, and credit (although the banks themselves are legally under private control). It has described the political and governmental processes that shape the way in which government operates these controls.

Now it may be argued that government does not manage the economy in the way that it directly operates the post office or national forests. This, of course, is true. Only if we had a socialized economy administered from Washington would we have a managed economy in that sense. Actually we have—and, one hopes, will always have—an economy in which there is a great deal of power left with a broad range of private individuals and enterprises. The point is, however, that government, occupying the pilot house of the economy, has its hands on gears and levers that together give the government far-reaching control over the general functioning and direction of the economy. These gears and levers are marked taxes, spending, credit, and the like.

Operated independently of one another, these levers might not have much effect on the economy, or the effect might be unpredictable or even catastrophic, as in the case of a battleship commander ordering full speed ahead and then a sharp turn to starboard. Operated jointly, they have a significant role. It is only rather recently that Americans have seen the part that government *could* play in stabilizing and invigorating the economy. (There are still differences of opinion over the part that it *should* play.) The slow development of our understanding, the political struggle over the question of whether the federal government should take responsibility for full employment, the enactment of the Employment Act of 1946—these are fascinating episodes in the trend toward over-all control of the economy by the federal government.

Economic groping

Austerity is a hard teacher. The depression beginning in 1929 had a tremendous impact on American thinking about the role of government in economic matters. We had had long, severe depressions before—for example, in the 1870's and 1890's. But the Great Depression came after the United States had become a rich and powerful nation, and when prosperity seemed here to stay. And the Great Depression hit hard, long, and deep. Millions of unemployed, falling prices and income, the drop in production—all added up to misery on a mass scale. "One vivid, gruesome moment of those dark days we shall never forget," wrote one observer. "We saw a crowd of some fifty men fighting over a barrel of garbage which had been set outside the back door of a restaurant. American citizens fighting for scraps of food like animals!"[15]

During the "dismal thirties" many ideas were put forward to end the depression. There were schemes for printing paper money, for huge public works, for "hot money" that would decline in value if not spent, for sharing the work or sharing the profits, for wholesale changes in the banking and credit system, to name a few.[16] Some of the proposals were nostrums; others had real merit. As we have seen in the last chapter, the Hoover Administration, after waiting for some time for the economy to recover by itself, attempted to stimulate the economy through such devices as the R.F.C. The New Deal intensified and widened the attack on depression through the N.R.A., A.A.A., P.W.A., W.P.A., social security, wages and hours legislation, and many other measures.

Despite all these efforts, however, the depression hung on. New Deal spending and other factors brought some recovery in the mid-1930's, but the recession of 1937-1938 indicated that we were by no means out of the woods. Eight or nine million people were jobless in 1939. Then war came, and unemployment was cured—for a while. Millions of people had more income, more security, a higher standard of living—and this during war. Lord Beveridge in England posed a question that bothered many thoughtful Americans: "Unemployment has been practically abolished twice in the lives of most of us—in the last war and in this war. Why does war solve the problem of unemployment which is so insoluble in peace?"[17] Worried that the economy might collapse after the war, literally thousands of people came up with plans to insure jobs for all.

These plans were infinitely varied, but two approaches to the problem of mass unemployment were most important. Many businessmen and news-

[15] Quoted in F. L. Allen, *Since Yesterday* (New York: Harper & Brothers, 1940), p. 64.

[16] The remainder of this chapter is drawn largely from S. K. Bailey, *Congress Makes a Law* (New York: Columbia University Press, 1950).

[17] W. H. Beveridge, *The Pillars of Security* (New York: The Macmillan Co., 1943), p. 51.

paper editors and some economists believed that the depression of the 1930's had gone on so long mainly because of New Deal policies hostile to business. If only the government had left the economy alone, they argued, recovery would have come much sooner. They urged the government to cut down on spending, lower taxes, reduce the national debt, curb the power of labor, and generally to leave business alone except for traditional regulation and aids to certain businesses. Give private enterprise a chance, they urged, and the problem of economic stagnation and unemployment would be solved in short order.

Another large group, made up of economists, labor representatives, government officials, and others, took a very different tack. They said that the trouble with the New Deal was not that it had done too much, but that it had done too little. The thinking of this group was much influenced by the work of John Maynard Keynes, a world-famous English economist who had also advised the British government on economic matters and had run a large insurance company in England. In visits to the United States during the 1930's, Keynes warned that if people do not consume enough or invest enough, national income will fall. The way to increase national income is either to spend money on consumption goods (such as clothes or food or automobiles) or on investment goods (steel mills and dock facilities) or do both. Finally—and this was the dynamite in the proposition—*government must do the spending and investing if private enterprise by itself would not or could not.* The Keynesian approach was tied in with related concepts involving governmental influence on public works, wages, prices, credit, taxation, and the like.

These two approaches dominated the efforts of Congress to grapple with the problem of unemployment after World War II. The story of the Full Employment bill of 1946 is the story of how the national government came to assume a large measure of responsibility for maintaining employment. It suggests that full employment is a political as well as an economic problem.

The Employment Act of 1946

The story of the Employment Act of 1946 is amazingly complex; we can review it only in broad outline.[18] Supporting the idea of full employment legislation were a group of government officials, the head of the National Farmers Union (which, it will be recalled, represents smaller farmers), some economists who were more or less Keynesian in their thinking, a number of United States senators, representatives of organized labor, and members of several Senate committee staffs. During the war, members of this group had been impressed by two things: the powerful impact on employment of heavy government spending, and the possibility that the bottom might drop out of the economy when federal spending decreased after the war. A bill was drafted that began, "It is the policy of the United States to foster free com-

[18] For the full history of the bill see Bailey, *Congress Makes a Law.*

petitive enterprise. . . . All Americans able to work and seeking work have the right to a useful and remunerative job in the industries or shops or offices or farms or mines of the nation." To enlist as much support as possible, the bill was introduced not by one Democratic senator but by four, representing the states of New York, Utah, Wyoming, and Montana. Supporters of the bill, mainly representatives of liberal and labor organizations, proceeded to line up congressional backing, arouse public interest, win over members of business, farm, and veterans' groups.

The bill had relatively easy going in the Senate. The four Democratic senators were joined by four Republicans, thus providing bipartisan support for the bill. Of sixty-seven witnesses who testified before the committee considering the bill, only four were strongly opposed to the measure. In the Senate debate, supporters of the measure argued that it was not left wing or radical but would strengthen the free enterprise system. Liberals in both parties combined to defeat hostile amendments, although some changes were made in the bill to appease the opposition. The bill passed the Senate, 71-10.

But the opposition was mobilizing outside the Senate. This bill, it was argued by its opponents, would not work. It might kill initiative. Government spending would undermine business confidence. It would lead to inflation. It might bring socialism or even communism. The National Association of Manufacturers circulated criticism of the bill to its 16,000 members and to a much wider mailing list. Chambers of Commerce in states and localities were active. The American Farm Bureau Federation put heavy pressure on key members of Congress.

Partly as a result of these activities, the bill had a hard time in the House. First of all, it was sent to an unfriendly committee. President Truman agreed to talk with leading members of the committee on the basis of party loyalty, but he made little progress. The Administration itself was divided. The House committee submitted to the lower chamber a weak bill that was hardly more than a pious indication of government interest in employment. Composed largely of conservative-minded members, the Rules Committee provided a rule that made certain that either this weak bill would be passed, or no bill. The House was divided three ways among those who wanted no bill, those who wanted a strong bill, and those who wanted a weak bill. The weak bill won out in the lower chamber.

The measure had been kept alive, however, and a final compromise was reached in conference committee behind a measure that had some teeth to it. Finally passed in February 1946, the bill declared:

It is the continuing policy and responsibility of the Federal Government to use all practicable means consistent with its needs and obligations and other essential considerations of national policy, with the assistance and cooperation of industry, agriculture, labor, and State and local governments, to coordinate and utilize all its plans, functions, and resources for the purpose of creating and maintaining, in a manner calculated to foster and promote free competitive enterprise and the general welfare, conditions under which there will be afforded useful employment, for those able, willing, and seeking to work, and to promote maximum employment, production, and purchasing power.

If this declaration sounds like gobbledygook or double talk, the reason lies in the many compromises necessary to produce the bill. In effect, it placed responsibility on the federal government to act in the face of rising unemployment instead of relying wholly on nongovernmental forces. Equally important, the act established machinery to carry out that responsibility. It created:

The Council of Economic Advisers. Part of the President's staff organization, the council studies and tries to forecast economic trends, assesses federal programs in terms of their contribution to maximum employment, and recommends to the President "national economic policies to foster and promote free competition, to avoid economic fluctuations or to diminish the effects thereof, and to maintain employment, production, and purchasing power."

The Economic Report of the President. The President must submit to Congress every January an economic report based on the data and forecasts

MECHANICS OF THE EMPLOYMENT ACT OF 1946

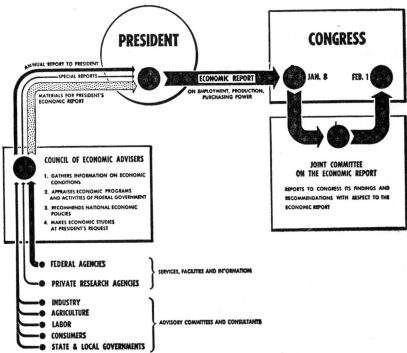

From REPORT OF COUNCIL OF ECONOMIC ADVISERS, *December, 1947*

of the council. The report must include a program for carrying out the policy of the act, together with recommendations for legislation if the President sees fit.

Joint Committee on the Economic Report. This is a committee of Congress authorized by the act. Composed of seven senators and seven representatives, it must report early in each year its findings and proposals in respect to presidential recommendations.

How has the act worked out in practice? So far, of course, it has faced no stern test, because employment and income have generally been high since 1946. The chief problem has been inflation, not depression. The economic reports of the council and of the President have received a good deal of publicity and probably have had considerable educational value. The council itself has operated in a somewhat different manner from that originally contemplated by some. Instead of being an independent agency acting entirely objectively and nonpolitically, the council has tended to become subordinate to the President. Indeed, the chairman of the council has been a sort of personal economic adviser to the chief executive. On the other hand, the council has not, as some feared, propagandized for radical philosophies. It has frequently consulted with businessmen and has stressed the role of private enterprise in maintaining employment.

The difficulties lie much more in the legislative and political parts of the act. The Joint Committee on the Economic Report has not played a major role. It has had little time to act, and its members have usually been busy with more pressing legislative duties. The committee has little influence over the really important committees, such as those handling taxing or spending. The council itself has said:[19]

Early experience under the Employment Act of 1946 has brought into sharp focus the practical difficulties which lie between the initiation of a national economic policy and the adoption of that policy by the Congress. Our American democracy will yield only slowly to the need for the deliberate formulation and integration of national policies in the interest of sustained prosperity.

The problem, in short, is not one of economic know-how. Hard experience and the work of both economists and men of affairs have taught us a lot about the workings and management of the national economy. The problem is not unwillingness to accept governmental responsibility for maintaining employment. The Act of 1946 specifically recognizes that responsibility. The problem is whether a governmental system such as ours can act effectively when action is needed. The true test would come in the unhappy event that our economy took a serious turn downward after the high level of prosperity we have enjoyed for almost two decades.

[19] Council of Economic Advisers, *Third Annual Report to the President* (Washington, D.C.: Government Printing Office, 1948), p. 12.

State and local government

PART SEVEN ~ A PROBLEM GUIDE

Since Part Seven deals with entire systems of government at the state and local levels, it raises all five basic problems listed on pages 1-2. State and local governments face the same problems as the national government—problems of maintaining stable, efficient, and progressive government; of maintaining a balance between liberty and order; of achieving democratic representation for all interests, including the majority; of keeping state and local leaders responsible to the people; and of proving that democratic government is not a luxury but a vital and indispensable way of ruling the people.

State and local government, however, puts some of these problems in sharper focus than others. One of the most acute problems of state and local government is simple efficiency, getting the most from money and manpower available. This involves matters such as adequate executive power for administrative direction (pp. 789-792, 794-798), recruitment of state and local officials (pp. 869-872), and raising and spending money (pp. 872-886). More broadly, these matters raise the problem of federalism—if state and local officials cannot govern effectively, more and more powers and functions will doubtless be shifted to the national government.

Our state and local governments also pose the problems of representation and responsibility. Many state legislatures are not properly representative of the people because of gerrymandering and other aspects of districting (pp. 782-786). Genuine political responsibility is lacking in some states, as the result of dividing up executive power (pp. 792-793) and the weakness of most party systems at the state and local level (pp. 889-893). This latter problem receives special emphasis in Chapter 35, which shows that party responsibility and even party influence are sharply limited in the executive (pp. 897-898) and legislature (pp. 895-897). To a lesser extent these problems are found at the local level (chapters 31 and 32).

Whether more party responsibility is desirable is an important value question, both sides of which are presented back in Chapter 21.

S TATES, TOO, ARE BIG GOVERNMENT. SAND-
wiched between the more dramatic national and the more close-at-hand
local governments, the states seem to be a kind of hidden layer. The important part they play is sometimes minimized. But throughout this book
(especially in chapters 4 and 5) we have seen that state politicians and
officials play a vital part in running our federal system—for example, in
amending the Constitution and in ruling who shall have the right to vote.

States are more than important cogs in the federal system. They have big
jobs to do. Theirs is the major responsibility for providing education, policing
our morals, protecting our safety, building our roads, regulating intrastate
labor and industry. In Part Two, we saw that the framers of the Constitution granted blocks of power to the national government and left "reserved"
powers to the states. Though expansion at the national level receives most
publicity, state governments also have gained in power and expanded their
functions tremendously. Indeed, in recent years the activities of state and local
governments have been increasing faster than the nondefense activities of the
national government.[1]

Each of the 48 states is unique. Moreover, the government of the state
is only a part of a much larger picture. To understand the government of
New York, for example, one must know something about the people of New
York—how they make their living, where they came from, what they believe
in, into what groups they are organized, and how they are related to groups
elsewhere in the United States
and throughout the world. To
discuss the government of
Mississippi without mentioning
the dominance of one party,
the government of Massachusetts without mentioning relations between Yankee Protestants and Irish Catholics, the
government of Texas without
mentioning cattle and oil, the
government of Illinois without
mentioning the *Chicago Tribune,* would be to ignore the
dynamics of the political process. State governments, just

28 ★

Constitutions

and

constitutional

change

[1] The Commission on Intergovernmental Relations, *A Report to
the President,* (Washington, D.C.:
Government Printing Office, June
1955), p. 36.

like the national government, cannot be described meaningfully as structure or laws divorced from the people.

We have seen how the national government can be understood only as part of a vast and tangled web of interests, individuals, institutions, and ideas. The same political processes operate at the state and local level. The groups that are active on the national scale—groups such as farmers, workers, doctors, taxpayers—are concerned with state and local governmental policies too. But there are differences. Some states tend to be dominated by interests that are strong in the area—coal miners in West Virginia, corn and hog growers in Iowa, cotton farmers in Mississippi, automobile manufacturers and workers in Michigan. Yet the politicians in every state, as in the nation, must mediate among competing interest groups and between organized groups and potentially organized ones.

Parties at the state and local level resemble the national organizations —but again with variations. Some state parties, such as the Republicans in Pennsylvania and New York, and the Democrats in Illinois and Rhode Island, are relatively well organized and centrally led. Others, especially in the South, are loose confederations of local leaders and groups shifting from faction to faction within the party. Some states are "one-party" states; the "opposition" party has almost no chance to win power and may be dominated by the party in power. Organizationally, our national parties are a mean between the extremes of cohesion and slackness found in the states.

But whatever the differences, our main problems remain the same. Through what institutions do people govern themselves? How do they resolve conflicts? How well do the state governments meet the tests of exercising power democratically, efficiently, and responsibly?

STATE CONSTITUTIONS—CHARTERS OR STRAIT JACKETS?

"The state constitutions are the oldest things in the political history of America."[2] The early state constitutions, themselves an outgrowth of the colonial charters, were models for the national Constitution. The 48 states have had over 200 constitutions, although some states have had more than their share while others have had only one or two.

The people of each state, subject only to the broad limitations of the national Constitution, are free to create whatever kind of republican government they wish. Despite the opportunities for experimentation, the general outlines of all state constitutions are similar. No state has established a parliamentary system; none has deprived its judges of the power of judicial review. As people moved westward across the United States, they copied the constitutions of the older states and—sometimes without much question —adopted the system to which they had been accustomed. The usual pattern

[2] James Bryce, *The American Commonwealth* (New York: The Macmillan Company, 1911), Vol. I, p. 427.

is a preamble, a bill of rights, articles providing for the separation of powers, a bicameral legislature, an executive department, an independent judiciary with power of judicial review, the form and powers of local units of government, an amendment article, and miscellaneous provisions dealing with corporations, railroads, finances, and numerous other topics.

Constitutional detail

How do the state constitutions differ from the federal Constitution? Most of them contain more *detail* and are thus *longer, less flexible,* require *more frequent formal amendment,* and *do not last so long.*

California's much-amended constitution (over 370 amendments since 1879) goes into great detail regarding such things as the breeding of crustaceans and mollusks, the length of wrestling matches, and the internal organization of several major departments. Article XX, Section 2, of Oklahoma's constitution proclaims, "Until changed by the Legislature, the flash test . . . for all kerosene oil for illuminating purposes shall be 115 degrees Fahrenheit; and the specific gravity test of all such oil shall be 40 degrees." Minnesota's constitution has a route-by-route description of its highway system. Mississippi's basic charter announces, "Human life shall not be imperiled by the practice of dueling." Oregon's constitution stipulates that "the governor shall receive an annual salary of $1,500." New Hampshire's sets the wages of its legislators at a figure that amounts to a little over $3 a day. State constitutions vary in length from approximately 9000 words of Vermont, Indiana, Connecticut, and Iowa through the 57,000 of Alabama, 85,000 of California, to the 184,000 of Louisiana.[3]

Although many of these detailed provisions deal with trivial subjects, others are concerned with important matters. As we noted, the national Constitution grants powers in broad and sweeping terms, letting future generations write in the details and adapt the basic charter of government to ever-changing conditions. Not so the state constitutions. They are written in restrictive terms. Whereas the national Constitution requires only a clause to authorize Congress to spend money, state constitutions require dozens of pages to specify the purposes for which the money can be spent, how much can be spent, and in what manner.

Constitutional autocracy

A written constitution, as we saw in Chapter 3, is *an instrument of government that sets forth, among other things, the terms upon which public officials are authorized to act in behalf of the sovereign voters.* The more detailed the constitution, the smaller the discretion the public officials enjoy.

[3] Karl A. Bosworth, "Law-making in State Governments," in *The Forty-Eight States: Their Tasks as Policy Makers and Administrators* (New York: The American Assembly, 1955), p. 88.

In fact, this limiting of governmental power was the very purpose of those who wrote the state constitutions. It will be remembered that the early constitutions gave large amounts of authority to the legislatures without much restriction on how they should use that power. Difficulties soon arose. Various groups began to use this legislative power to promote activities that a majority of the citizens came to think were against the public interest. Many people grew distrustful of the state legislature—often with good reason. They counterattacked and secured constitutional limitations. As abuses were uncovered, the constitutions were amended to narrow and confine legislative power.

As new constitutions were adopted, the constitution-makers took away more and more legislative discretion. Various groups turned to constitutional amendment rather than legislation to get their favorite measures adopted. All this cut down the authority of future political majorities. The result? Many public officials believe that the state constitutions have become *strait jackets* rather than *charters* of government.

To be sure, such constitutions may prevent unwise changes dictated by sudden shifts in a fickle public opinion. But at least on the state level, the effect is more often to put roadblocks in the path of effective government. With public officials lacking scope and discretion, political majorities find it difficult to get the kind of state services they desire. The Delaware Bridge, linking Philadelphia with Camden, New Jersey, was delayed for five years because restrictive clauses in the Pennsylvania Constitution prevented the necessary financing. The Oregon Legislature could not create a state college in Portland, "the only large city in the West without a state university nearby because Article XIV, Section 3, of the Constitution forbids the founding of any new public institution outside Marion County."[4]

Detailed enumeration of powers soon dates constitutions. The fixing of salaries by constitutional provision, for example, makes it difficult to keep them in line with the fluctuating economic situation. Constitutional provisions for administrative organization hinder attempts to keep the government adjusted to ever changing needs. Detailed constitutional provisions, moreover, breed the need for more detail, producing the vicious circle of long constitutions requiring hosts of amendments. Voters have the chore of voting on scores of proposals about which they can know very little. On the 1948 California ballot, for example, were fifteen proposed constitutional amendments, along with a dozen other measures. Some of the amendments simply involved technicalities—for example, an amendment to Section 25½ of Article IV having to do with the succession of members of the Fish and Game Commission. Important issues like legislative reapportionment were sandwiched between these details, and all the amendments were explained in such technical language that they almost guaranteed voter confusion. In

[4] Richard L. Neuberger, "States in Strait Jackets," *The American Magazine,* April 1951, p. 34.

1954 the Louisiana legislature asked the voters to vote on 31 proposed amendments. The New Orleans Bureau of Governmental Research estimated it would take five hours to read the texts of these proposals—and the Bureau ". . . did not guarantee that reading would make them intelligible." No wonder the Bureau termed the situation "Biennial bingo or 31 more in '54."[5]

Does all this mean that state constitutions can prevent *forever* the kind of activity demanded by the majority or impede indefinitely the functions of state governments? Not necessarily. The constitutions of our states, like that of the national government, include more than the formal written document. The unwritten rules, the practices, the basic statutes, the political parties, the interest groups must also be considered. The state constitution does not stand apart from the political process and does not determine alone the course of events. When large groups of people want their officials to act, they usually find that they can overcome constitutional barriers. Sometimes the situation calls for some delicate tightrope walking. As former Illinois Governor Adlai E. Stevenson explained, "For years the machinery of our state government has been kept in motion only by continued violations of plain and positive provisions in the Illinois constitution."[6] Despite their constitution, the people of Oregon pay their chief executive $15,000 a year. Besides simply ignoring them, constitutional barriers can be overcome by securing formal amendment or interpreting the written words so that support will be given to the activity as the effective majority desires. Nevertheless, rigid state constitutions create a "constitutional autocracy" by making it more difficult for new majorities to achieve their aims.

Perhaps one of the most significant consequences of the detailed state constitution is that it enhances the authority of the state judiciary. The more complex the constitution, the easier it is for the judges to veto legislation. In fact, one of the reasons for the growing length of some state constitutions is that formal amendments are often required to reverse judicial interpretations opposed by those strong enough to secure formal amendment.

Because these constitutions cannot readily be adapted, the procedures for formal change are especially important. How then are the state constitutions amended?

AMENDING THE CONSTITUTION

Constitutional amendments must be first *proposed* (initiated), then *ratified*. There are three ways to *propose* amendments: (1) by the legislature; (2) by initiative petition; and (3) by constitutional convention. The third method is discussed in the next section.

---

[5] Cited in and quoted by Karl A. Bosworth, "Law-making in State Governments," in *The Forty-eight States: Their Tasks as Policy Makers and Administrators* (New York: The American Assembly, 1955), p. 90.

[6] Quoted by Neuberger, *op. cit.*

Proposing and ratifying amendments

Proposal of constitutional amendments by initiative petition (see pp. 786-787) is permitted in approximately one-fourth of the states. Initiation by the legislature, the most common method, is permitted in all states except New Hampshire. Although the requirement varies among the states, the most general practice is to require approval of two-thirds of the members elected in each chamber of the legislature (except in Nebraska, with its unicameral legislature) in order to initiate an amendment. Some states require only a simple majority but the approval of two successive legislatures.

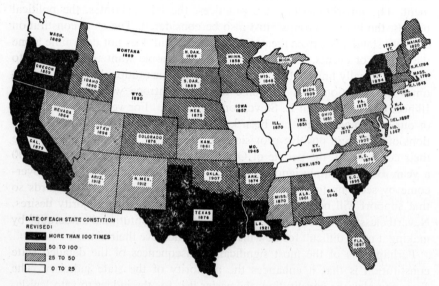

Constitutional rigidity and change.

After an amendment has been proposed by one of the above three methods it must be *ratified*. In all states except Delaware (where the legislature can ratify as well as propose amendments), ratification is by the voters. In most states if a majority of those voting on the amendment approve it, the amendment becomes part of the constitution. In a few states, however, approval of a majority of *all* the voters *voting in the election* is required. Such a provision is a real obstacle. Since amendments are submitted at the time of a general election, and since many people who vote for candidates fail to vote at all on constitutional amendments, ratification is difficult to achieve with such a requirement.

Initiation of the amendment by the state legislature and ratification by a majority of the voters voting on the amendment is the most common method of constitutional change. But in some states, requirements for adoption are so stringent that it is practically impossible to get an amendment adopted, and a relatively small minority can veto desires of the majority. In

Tennessee, for example, amending the constitution was so difficult that the 1870 constitution was not amended until 1953, when eight amendments were finally approved. One of these slightly liberalized the amending process. Constitutional change in Tennessee has had to come by methods other than formal amendment.

The requirements for amendment, of course, do not tell the whole story. In some states where the formal requirements for amendment are relatively liberal, there have been few amendments. Paradoxically, in others where the limits on the amendatory power are more stringent, frequent amendments have been made. And some of the excessive constitutional detail results from *ease* of amendment.

Amendments usually involve piecemeal change. Many people believe, however, that most state constitutions are so bad that they cannot be sufficiently improved by such amendment. Rather than repairing the old model, they advocate trading in the constitutions for new ones. The officials of the National Municipal League—an organization devoted to the cause of governmental reform—have said "most state constitutions are serious obstacles to responsible and effective state and local government." How can the people get a new constitution if they want one?

Constitutional conventions

The United States is the country *par excellence of* constitutional conventions. We have had over 200. The constitutional convention was born of our insistence upon written constitutions and our distinction between fundamental and statutory law. Since the constitution is an expression of popular will, since it is fundamental law controlling public officals and unchangeable by ordinary methods, people felt that constitution-making required some agency more immediately expressive of popular sentiment than the legislature.

Thirty-three state constitutions specifically authorize the legislature to submit to the voters the question of calling a convention, and in the other states it is generally considered that the legislature has the inherent power to do so. In eight states, the constitution requires the legislature to submit the question to the voters at fixed intervals.

If the voters approve the calling of a convention, the next step is to elect delegates. Some constitutions contain elaborate procedures as to the number, composition, method of election, time, and place of the convention. In others, the details are left up to the legislature. After the delegates are chosen for this specific job of considering a new constitution, they assemble to perform their work. The more recent conventions have profited by professional research assistants.

When the convention has prepared a draft, the constitution is now normally submitted to the voters of the state. The convention has to make a difficult choice. Shall the new constitution be submitted as a unit or should it be divided and the voters permitted to vote on separate parts of it as amendments to the old constitution? The advantage of the former is that one provision of a constitution ties in with another; and in order to secure all the advantages of constitutional revision, it is desirable that the entire constitution be adopted. The disadvantage is that all the groups who take issue with any particular provision may vote against the entire constitution in order to defeat the offending provision. Especially when there is much opposition to particular articles, conventions often choose to submit the controversial provision separately. But regardless of the method of ratification, the proponents of constitutional change need to look to their political fences in order to get their handiwork approved. Those states most successful in securing new constitutions have made elaborate arrangements to educate—or propagandize—the voters.

Instead of calling a constitutional convention, the legislature may appoint a small *commission* to make recommendations. If the legislature approves the recommendations, it can then submit them to the voters by the regular procedures for proposing amendment. Constitutional revision by commission has been used successfully in several states. Its major weakness is that the commission is not representative of all the interests, and the necessary compromises and bargainings may not be made. The commission's work is often rejected either by the legislature or by the voters.

Although many students believe that a number of states need new constitutions, and although demand has been growing for conventions in some states, only a few states have drawn up new constitutions in the last couple of decades. The various groups supporting existing constitutional arrangements have been strong enough to prevent the calling of conventions. This is not just a question of good government versus bad government. It is also a situation where there are too few people in most states who think the existing constitutions are good and not enough people who think they are too bad—and the difficulty of change helps the former. The struggle over calling a convention is also but part of the greater struggle among the various interests that make up the American political society. The constitutional convention is merely one of several techniques available to groups who are working to bring about certain changes.

The political struggle does not cease when the convention has assembled. In many cases, the groups who are strongest in the state legislatures are also the strongest in the conventions, so that the proposed changes reflect the desires of these groups. But service in conventions usually has greater prestige than sitting in the legislature, and many men are willing to interrupt their normal activities in order to spend some time at constitution-writing. Moreover, conventions sometimes attract greater popular attention than regular legislative sessions. Because of these and other factors, the interests represented at the convention in some cases do vary from those reflected by the legislature. Battles between the legislature and the assembled convention often result from such a situation. At times, the legislature has tried to restrict the authority of the convention and to limit the subjects it can discuss. Some conventions, on the other hand, have gone so far as to try to govern the state by taking over the legislative as well as the constitution-writing function.

CONSTITUTION MAKING IN THE EMPIRE STATE

In the summer of 1938, the Eighth Constitutional Convention of New York assembled in Albany. Two years before, the citizens of New York had given a favorable response to the question that is presented to them every twenty years, "Should a constitutional convention be held?" They had given their response at the same time they voted for President of the United States and for a full slate of state officers. The presidential and gubernatorial elections had aroused much excitement, but there had been little public discussion about the convention. Less than half of those who went to the polls even bothered to vote on this issue. Up-state New Yorkers were satisfied with the existing constitution which gave them a dominant voice in the state legislature, and they generally voted against disturbing the status quo. But the favorable votes of those who lived in New York City outweighed the negative up-state vote.

The next task was to select delegates. Three were to be chosen from each of the state's 51 senatorial districts plus 15 elected from the state at large. Under the slogan of "nonpartisanship" and "keeping politics out of the convention," Democratic and Republican leaders carried on a strenuous campaign. Party organizations controlled the nomination of candidates, although there were serious struggles within both major parties. The Republicans were divided between up-state conservatives and an urban-based liberal faction. Democrats were divided among New Dealers, Tammany men, and Anti-New Dealers, the latter two factions frequently uniting against the former. The Republicans outmaneuvered the Democrats in the elections, with the result that they elected 91 delegates to the Democrats' 76. There was one Fusion-American Labor Party man.

Two-thirds of the delegates were lawyers, over three-fourths were active party workers, and two-thirds had held elective public office. They stayed in active session for about four months, received a salary of $2500 and expenses for one round-trip from their homes to the convention. The delegates had the aid of studies prepared by a fact finding committee that Governor Lehman had appointed. This was an unofficial group, since the legislature had refused to sanction an official organization. The convention adopted the rules of procedure of the lower house of the New York legislature, organized itself into committees, all controlled by the Republicans, and started to consider the proposals—about 700 of them—that were introduced by the delegates.

Reapportionment was a major issue, although the victory of the Republicans in controlling the convention made the outcome more or less a foregone conclusion. The state had not been redistricted since 1917, with the result that New York City with roughly 55 per cent of the population elected only 41 per cent of the assemblymen and 43 per cent of the senators. Republican up-state delegates, ably aided by Republicans from the city, pushed through a reapportionment provision that not only retained the advantages for the rural communities, but also, most observers believed, would aggravate the disparity.

Considerable controversy arose between Republicans and Democrats over a proposal to ban the use in criminal prosecutions of evidence seized illegally. The Republicans opposed such a move as a repudiation of the activities of Thomas E. Dewey in prosecuting the racketeering of certain New York Tammany leaders. Such a measure would also seriously hamper Dewey's exposés and might hurt his chances as Republican candidate for governor in the coming election. On the other hand, if the Republicans opposed the provision, they would provide the Democrats with campaign material against the party that had been denouncing the New Deal for violating constitutional guarantees. After a bitter debate, the Republicans put through a measure that forbade unreasonable searches and seizures but said nothing about the use of illegally obtained evidence in courts.

There were debates on all other phases of governmental activities—powers of the governor, judicial review, public development of power, social legislation, especially housing and slum clearance. Interest groups were active, even more active than at a legislative session since "the stakes were higher than those played for when the legislature meets. More could be won; more could be lost."[7] As one delegate reported: "I came up on the train and there were droves and hordes of them . . . buttonholing you as you went along, and you find them in the lobbies, in the hotels, all coming up here to get special grants, a special favor, a special exemption for a specific group."[8]

During much of the convention delegates debated issues that opponents charged were really "legislative." The delegates to the constitutional convention, it was argued, should be concerned only with fundamental matters leaving to the legislators the authority to enact detailed laws and to work out statutory measures. The difficulty was that the delegates could not agree on what was "fundamental."

Finally, the convention finished its work and submitted to the voters nine

---

[7] Vernon A. O'Rourke and Douglas W. Campbell, *Constitution-Making in a Democracy* (Baltimore: The Johns Hopkins Press, 1943), p. 162. The materials in this section are taken from this careful analysis of the New York convention of 1938.
  [8] *Ibid.*, p. 175.

GOVERNMENT UNDER THE MODEL STATE CONSTITUTION*

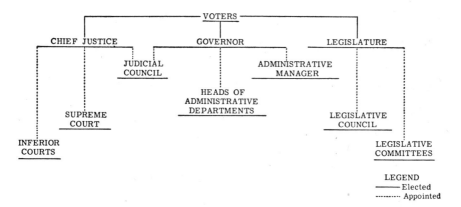

GOVERNMENT UNDER A TYPICAL STATE CONSTITUTION*

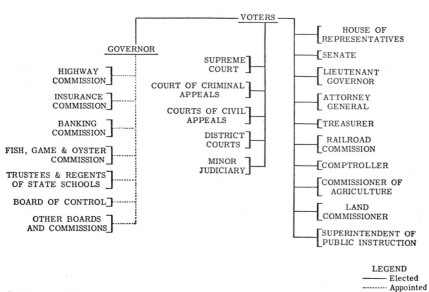

Courtesy National Municipal League

Government under a model state constitution. Government under a typical state constitution.

* Charts prepared for the Committee on State Government of the National Municipal League by Robert S. Bourn, University of Texas. Although the chart for "Government under a Typical State Constitution" is based upon the Texas Constitution, the set-up is typical of those states whose constitutions provide for a considerable number of popularly elected commissions and heads of departments.

amendments. The first amendment was an omnibus amendment containing fifty separate so-called "non-controversial items," such as increasing the measure of home rule for cities over 5000, prohibiting racial or religious discrimination, limiting the passage of special laws affecting counties, increasing traveling expenses of legislators, permitting the legislature to provide for the transportation of children to schools, and so on. The other eight amendments dealt with more explosive matters, such as reapportionment, expansion of judicial review of administrative tribunals, forbidding the use of proportional representation by any city, and authorizing slum clearance and low-rent housing programs.

The amendments were submitted during the election of state-wide officers. Again the question of constitutional revision was overshadowed by the election campaign. The vote for governor was twice that of the vote on the amendments. The voters approved six amendments and rejected those dealing with reapportionment, judicial review, and the ban on proportional representation.

What lessons can be learned from this convention? Obviously one cannot generalize about all the conventions on the basis of a study of just one. Each of the over 200 constitutional conventions has had its own peculiarities. Other states' conventions, for example, have been less openly subject to party influences than the New York convention. Nevertheless, the New York experience does draw into question the validity of certain common assumptions such as 1) the quality of delegates is higher than that of legislators, 2) public attention greater, and 3) consideration more deliberate. O'Rourke and Campbell concluded after a careful investigation of the New York convention that "in form, substance, and spirit, the convention could easily have passed for its technically inferior sister, the legislature."[9] Obviously, politics—the adjustment of differences—cannot be taken out of constitution-making in a free society.

[9] *Ibid.*, p. 192.

Ontml O NE OF THE MOST SIGNIFICANT TRENDS IN OUR political history has been the rise and fall of the state legislatures. During the struggle for independence, the state legislatures played a central role and came out of the fray with much power and great prestige. But almost from the day that royal authority was vanquished, this prestige began to diminish. The adoption of the Constitution was, as we have seen, a victory for those who wished to curtail the authority of the state legislatures.

In recent times state legislatures have come under heavy criticism. They have been described as unrepresentative, inefficient, badly organized, and composed of too many mediocre members.

Do the legislators deserve the criticism that is often heaped upon them? What are the defects of our state legislatures? What could be done to improve their performance? Before we turn to these problems, let us glance at the characteristic organization and procedure of our state assemblies.

ORGANIZATION, POWER, MEMBERSHIP

In all states except Nebraska, the legislature is bicameral. The lower and more numerous chamber is generally called the House of Representatives. Its size varies from a low of 35 in Delaware (Alaska has only 24 and Hawaii only 30) to a high of 399 in New Hampshire. The typical number is around 100. In most states a two-year term prevails, and members are most commonly elected by counties (except in New England, where they represent the town). The upper chamber, known in all of the states as the Senate, is composed of about 40 members elected by various kinds of districts, but usually on the basis of population. Senators have a four-year term in most states.

In all but 14 states and three territories, the legislature meets in regular session once every 2 years (biennial sessions), the most common time being in January of odd-numbered years. In about two-thirds of the states, the constitution limits the legislature to a regular session of a fixed number of days, usually 60

29 ★

Under the

capitol dome:

the legislature

days. This restriction reflects the old distrust of government, the feeling that "the faster we get it over with the better." The governor has the power to call the legislature into special session, a power which is frequently used because of constitutional time limitation on regular sessions. In over half the states, however, the legislature can discuss during special sessions only those matters stipulated by the governor.

The organization and procedure of the state legislatures are similar to those of Congress. A speaker, chosen by the majority party, presides over the lower house. In some states, the speaker has more power to control proceedings than his national counterpart, having, for example, in addition to all the powers of the Speaker of the national House of Representatives, the right to appoint committees and considerable influence in determining the rules. In three-fourths of the states, a lieutenant governor presides over the senate. In the others, the presiding officer is chosen by the majority party in the senate.

The committee system prevails, and the committees have great power over the bills that are assigned to them. In some states, notably Massachusetts, joint committees are used regularly, a procedure favored by most students of legislation.

Although the structure and procedure of the legislatures are similar from state to state, this is not true of their actual operation. Some states, like New York, have strong political parties that take an active part in policy formation. Here and in perhaps a dozen other states, the party caucus is an important part of the legislative machinery. In others, the parties assume no responsibility for the actions of their legislative members. In some states, the governor leads the legislative way; in others, he is relatively unimportant. The type of competitive two-party system found in Congress exists in not more than one-third of the states[1] while in others representatives of interest groups directly guide the legislators. In order to describe with any accuracy the actual functioning of a particular state legislature, one must be acquainted with the entire social and political environment in which it operates.

What can—and cannot—state legislatures do?

What do the 7500 state legislators do? A former prominent state legislator replies, "We enact the laws that set speed limits on the highways; we specify minimum salaries for classroom teachers; we fix the content of butterfat in Grade-A milk; we draw up the rules governing the purity of drinking water; and we determine whether a citizen convicted of murder in the

[1] Belle Zeller, ed., *American State Legislatures* (New York: Thomas Y. Crowell Co., 1954), p. 192. This is the excellent report of the Committee on American Legislatures of the American Political Science Association.

first degree shall be gassed, hanged, shot, electrocuted, or merely clapped behind iron bars."[2]

The state legislatures have all governmental powers that are not given to some other governmental agency. The Tenth Amendment makes it clear that the governmental power not given to the national government nor denied to the states lies with the states or with the people. The *state* constitutions in turn give some of this reserved power exclusively to nonlegislative agencies and specifically deny some to the legislature. All that is left is inherited by the state legislatures. To be sure, some state courts have developed the doctrine of *implied limitations* on the legislatures by ruling that when the constitution authorizes the legislature to do a particular thing, by implication it denies the legislature the power to do other things.

Subject to the national and to their own constitutions, the legislature levies the state taxes, appropriates the moneys, creates the agencies to carry out the tasks of government, allots functions among these agencies, and investigates them to make sure that they are doing what the lawmakers intend them to do. These legislators, like their national counterpart, also participate in amending their constitutions, have authority to impeach and try public officials, and share to some degree in the appointive power.

Despite their great reservoir of power, legislatures are often closely controlled by constitutional limitations. Quite commonly, the constitution prescribes the *procedures* they must follow in order to legislate. The power to tax, appropriate, and borrow money is hedged by numerous limitations. The rate of taxation, the kinds of taxes, the subjects that may be taxed, and the purposes of taxation are often detailed in the constitution. *Special legislation*—laws dealing with particular persons or localities—is usually prohibited. Many constitutions state that special laws are to be avoided wherever possible, and in addition they list particular subjects—divorce, chartering of corporations, licensing banks, affairs of local units of government—which the legislature is forbidden to deal with by special legislation. Such restrictions do not, however, prevent classifications, and by refined classifications (a law for cities of over 14,350 and under 15,600 population when only one city in the state fits into this category, for example) the legislatures are able to overcome these limits—the state courts willing.

Who are the state legislators?

A United States senator or congressman has a full-time job for which he receives full-time pay. But a state legislator is only a part-time legislator and in most cases receives but a part-time salary. The latter goes to the capital for a short time every two years. In some states, he is paid so little that only if he were independently wealthy could he afford to spend full time

[2] Richard L. Neuberger, "Tribulations of a State Legislator," *The Reporter,* January 31, 1950, p. 31.

LEGISLATIVE SESSIONS

State	Years in which sessions are held	Sessions convene		Limitations on lengths of sessions		Length of last regular session (a)	Special sessions		
		Month	Day	Regular	Special		Legislature may call	Petition	Legislature may determine subject
Alabama	Odd	May	1st Tues.(b)	36 L	36 L	36 L	No	Petition 2/3 members	2/3 vote those present
Arizona	Annual	Jan.	2nd Mon.	60 C(c)	20 C(c)	84 C	2/3 members		Yes
Arkansas	Odd	Jan.	2nd Mon.	60 C	15 C(d)	60 C	No		(d)
California	Annual (e)	Mar.	Odd-Mon. after Jan. 1 / Even-1st. Mon.	120 C / 30 C	None	120 C	No		No
Colorado	Annual (e)	Jan.	Wed. after 1st Tues.	120 C(c)	None	92 C	No		No
Connecticut	Odd	Jan.	Wed. after 1st Mon.	150 C(f)	30(c)	145 C	Yes		Yes
Delaware	Odd	Jan.	1st Tues.	None	None	(z)	No		No
Florida	Odd	Apr.	Tues. after 1st Mon.	60 C(g)	20 C(h)	60 C	No		2/3 vote
Georgia	Annual	Jan.	2nd Mon.	40 C	(i)	40 C	No	Petition 3/5 members (j)	Yes
Idaho	Odd	Jan.	Mon. after Jan. 1	60 C(c)	20 C	60 C	No		No
Illinois	Odd	Jan.	Wed. after 1st Mon.	None (k)	None	175 C	No		No
Indiana	Odd	Jan.	Thurs. after 1st Mon.	61 C	40 C	61 C	No		Yes
Iowa	Odd	Jan.	2nd Mon.	None (l)	None	115 C	No		Yes
Kansas	Annual (e)	Jan.	Odd-2nd Tues. / Even-2nd Tues.	60 L(c) / 30 C(c)	30 L(c)	86 C	No		Yes
Kentucky	Even	Jan.	Tues. after 1st Mon.	60 L	None	60 L	No		No
Louisiana	Annual (e)	May / May	Even-2nd Mon. / Odd-2nd Mon.	60 C / 30 C	30 C	60 C	No	Petition 2/3 members	No(m)
Maine	Odd	Jan.	1st Wed.	None	None	70 L	No		Yes
Maryland	Annual (e)	Jan.	Odd-1st Wed. / Even-1st Wed.	90 C / 30 C	30 C	90 C	No		Yes
Massachusetts	Annual	Jan.	1st Wed.	None	None	255 C	Yes		Yes
Michigan	Annual	Jan.	2nd Wed.	None	None	185 C	No		No
Minnesota	Odd	Jan.	Tues. after 1st Mon.	90 L	None	H-79 L / S-78 L	No		Yes
Mississippi	Even	Jan.	Tues. after 1st Mon.	150 C(f,n)	None	122 C	No		No
Missouri	Odd (m)	Jan.	Wed. after Jan. 1	60 C	60 C(c)	147 C	No		No
Montana	Odd	Jan.	1st Mon.	None	60 C(c)	60 C	No		No
Nebraska	Odd	Jan.	1st Tues.	None	None	114 L	No	Petition 2/3 members	No
Nevada	Odd	Jan.	3rd Mon.	60 C	20 C	60 C	No		No
New Hampshire	Odd	Jan.	1st Wed.	None	15 C(c)	213 C	Yes		Yes
New Jersey	Annual	Jan.	2nd Tues.	None	None	(z)	(o)		Yes
New Mexico	Odd	Jan.	2nd Tues.	60 C	30 C(p)	60 C	Yes(p)		Yes(p)
New York	Annual	Jan.	Wed. after 1st Mon.	None	None	88 C	No		No
North Carolina	Odd	Jan. (q)	Wed. after 1st Mon.	90 C(c)	25 C(c)	142 C	No		Yes
North Dakota	Odd	Jan.	Tues. after 1st Mon.	60 L	None	60 C	No		Yes
Ohio	Odd	Jan.	1st Mon.	None	None	103 L	No		No
Oklahoma	Odd	Jan.	Tues. after 1st Mon.	None	None	81 L	No(r)		No
Oregon	Odd	Jan.	2nd Mon.	None	None	115 C	No		Yes
Pennsylvania	Odd (s)	Jan.	1st Tues.	None	None	(z)	No		No

State	Session	Month	Day					
Rhode Island	Annual	Jan.	1st Tues.	60 L(c)	None	65 L	Yes	Yes
South Carolina	Annual	Jan.	2nd Tues.	None	None	137 C	Yes	Yes
South Dakota	Odd	Jan.	Tues. after 1st Mon.	60 C	None	60 C	Yes	No
Tennessee	Odd	Jan.	1st Mon.	75 C(c)	20 C(c)	75 C	No	No
Texas	Odd	Jan.	2nd Tues.	120 C(c)	30 C	148 C	No	No
Utah	Odd	Jan.	2nd Mon.	60 C	30 C	60 C	No	No
Vermont	Odd	Jan.	Wed. after 1st Mon.	None	None	158 L	No	Yes
Virginia	Even	Jan.	2nd Wed.	60 C(c,t)	30 C(c,t)	60 C	Petition 2/3 members	Yes
Washington	Odd	Jan.	2nd Mon.	60 C	None	60 C	No	No
West Virginia	Annual (e)	Jan.	Odd-2nd Wed. Even-2nd Wed.	60 C(u) 30 C(u)	None	62 C	Petition 2/3 members	Yes
Wisconsin	Odd	Jan.	2nd Wed.	None	None	(z)	No	No
Wyoming	Odd	Jan.	2nd Tues.	40 C	40 C	40 C	No	Yes
Alaska	Odd	Jan.	4th Mon.	30 C	30 C	60 C	No	No
Guam	Annual	Jan.	2nd Mon.	60 C(v)	14 C	60 C	No	No
Hawaii	Odd	Feb.	3rd Wed.	60 L(w)	None	60 L(x)	Yes	Yes
Puerto Rico	Annual	Jan.	2nd Mon.	111 C(f,aa)	20 C	142 C	No	No
Virgin Islands	Annual	Apr.	2nd Mon.	60	15(y)	60	No	No

Abbreviations: L—Legislative days; C—Calendar days.

(a) 1955 session, except for Kentucky, Louisiana, Mississippi and Virginia, where last general session was held in 1954.

(b) Legislature meets quadrennially on second Tuesday in January after election for purpose of organizing.

(c) Indirect restriction on session length. Legislators' pay ceases but session may continue.

(d) Governor may convene General Assembly for specified purpose. After specific business is transacted, a 2/3 vote of members of both houses may extend sessions up to 15 days.

(e) Alternate year budget sessions are held, all except the Louisiana session meeting in the even-numbered years.

(f) Approximate length of session. Connecticut session must adjourn by first Wednesday after first Monday in June, Missouri by May 31, and Puerto Rico by April 30.

(g) Length of session may be extended by 30 days, but not beyond Sept. 1, by 3/5 vote of both houses.

(h) Proposed constitutional amendment referred for vote in 1956 would permit the legislature to call 30-day special session by 3/5 vote of the legislature in a poll conducted by the Secretary of State.

(i) Seventy-day session limit except for impeachment proceedings if Governor calls session; 30-day limit if legislature convenes itself.

(j) Thirty-day limit.

(k) By custom legislature adjourns by July 1, since all bills passed after that day are not effective until July 1 of following year.

(l) Custom and pay limit session to 100 calendar days.

(m) Unless legislature petitions for session.

(n) Proposed constitutional amendment referred for vote in 1956 would provide for annual sessions, odd-year sessions to be six months long, even-year budgetary sessions to be two months long, and, in addition, a 15-day session to be scheduled three months after each session for consideration of vetoes.

(o) Petition by majority members of each house to Governor, who then "shall" call special session.

(p) Limitation does not apply if impeachment trial is pending or in process. Legislature may call 30-day "extraordinary" session if Governor refuses to call session when requested by 3/5 of legislature.

(q) Proposed constitutional amendment referred for vote in 1956 would change convening date to first Wednesday after first Monday in February.

(r) Governor may convene Senate alone in special session.

(s) Legislature in 1953 adopted a proposal calling for annual sessions with even-year budgetary sessions which, if re-enacted in 1955, will be submitted for vote as a proposed constitutional amendment.

(t) May be extended up to 30 days by 3/5 vote of each house, but without pay.

(u) Must be extended by Governor until general appropriation passed; may be extended by 2/3 vote of legislature.

(v) Organic Act specifies legislature may meet for 60 days during each year, statutes specify legislature shall meet for 30 days twice each year.

(w) Governor may extend session up to 30 days, with no additional legislative pay.

(x) Sixtieth legislative day lasted from April 29 to May 27.

(y) No special session may continue longer than 15 calendar days and the aggregate for the year may not exceed 30.

(z) 1955 legislature was in session when table was compiled.

(aa) Session may be extended by adoption of joint resolution.

From BOOK OF THE STATES, 1956-1957. Courtesy of the Council of State Governments.

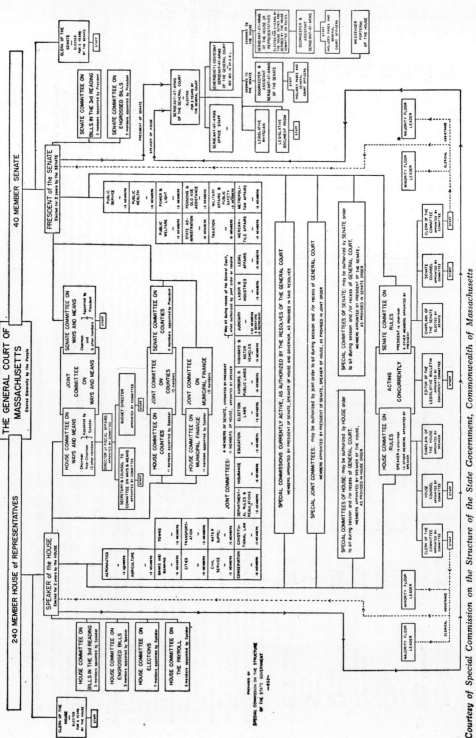

Organization chart of the General Court of Massachusetts showing its complexity

Courtesy of Special Commission on the Structure of the State Government, Commonwealth of Massachusetts

as a legislator. The legislative salaries paid vary from $7500 a year in New York to $200 a year in New Hampshire, with the median salaries around $1300.

James Bryce argued that legislative salaries should be abolished since they served only to attract men who had no interest in the job except the money. However, most observers today favor payment of much higher salaries because inadequate compensation disqualifies a large number of people. Only those with independent sources of income or who have jobs that can be combined with legislative service may be legislators under present conditions. Few businessmen, teachers, or salaried workers, for example, can interrupt their activities to attend to legislative duties, and they cannot afford to give up their jobs and live on the salary the state will pay. Some states do not have a pressing need for full-time legislators, but larger salaries in all states would help to make the legislators more representative.

The lawyers are the largest single occupational group in state assemblies, as they are in Congress. Many young attorneys who have not developed large practices enter the legislature in order to perform a public service, secure a reputation, and build up a practice. Farmers are the next largest group. Farming can be adjusted—at least more so than many professions —to fit legislative schedules. Furthermore, rural areas are often given more representation in legislatures than are urban ones. Merchants, insurance, real estate, and other types of salesmen are also found in significant numbers. "Professional politicians," too, are found among the ranks, although they usually have a business on the side.

What kind of men and women (there are over 200 of the latter) are the legislators? Bryce, writing at the end of the nineteenth century, stated that the average state legislature had "fewer able and high-minded men among its members" than did the Congress. The reason, he believed, was that the state legislature "is surrounded by temptations relatively greater. It is guarded by a less watchful and less interested public opinion," which is probably true, although Richard Neuberger, author and former member of the Oregon legislature, argues that the "voters are looking right down your throat." But as Neuberger also points out, it is primarily the organized interest group that is heard at the state capitols, since the unorganized public probably pays even less attention to its state legislature than to Congress in far away Washington. When Neuberger introduced a measure to limit the number of billboards on the highways, a few men, "stung on the pocket nerve," were able to make it appear that the entire state was up in arms against the bill, although the billboard owners themselves never once appeared during the entire operation. The head of the Signpainters' Union called Neuberger an enemy of labor anxious to put men out of work. The omnipresent widows and orphans came to the capitol and argued that they could not live without the rent they received from their roadside property. A delegation from the state advertising club charged that the Bill of Rights and

Courtesy THE NEW YORK TIMES MAGAZINE
and Tom Little

"The State Legislatures have traditionally been the training ground for future Governors, Congressmen and Presidents."

freedom of speech were being jeopardized. The measure was stigmatized as Communist in origin. (Actually it had been suggested by a wealthy old woman who loved scenery.) Under these pressures, the bill was defeated. There are many other stories of legislators yielding to interests other than that of the majority. But this weakness —if it be such—is not peculiar to the state legislators.

Unquestionably, much less prestige accrues to the position of state legislator than to the job of national congressman. Especially in states with large chambers, the individual member may cut a small figure. With small salaries and little influence, many men serve a term or two and then voluntarily retire. The turnover is so large that continuity of leadership is interrupted. "Over half of the state legislators are new at each session."[3]

Despite all this and despite the abuse heaped upon him, there is much to be said for the state legislator. He is usually a hard-working, public-spirited citizen. Of course, those who dislike the legislation that is passed, or who like legislation that is defeated, often claim that the fault lies with the intelligence of the legislators. Quite naturally the state legislatures have their share of ignorant and dishonest men, but there is no evidence to support many of the more extreme charges directed against them. On the contrary, the general level of intelligence and devotion to the public interest displayed by the state legislators is probably a fairly accurate reflection of the people who elect them.

HOW CAN WE IMPROVE OUR STATE LEGISLATURES?

The weaknesses of some of our state legislatures are much like those of Congress. Legislative business is not conducted efficiently. Committee work is not carefully planned. Records are not always well kept. Expert information is sometimes lacking. Introducing special and private legislation is too easy. Parliamentary rules impede rather than expedite action and play into the hands of minorities. Other weaknesses are peculiar to the states. Legislatures are unnecessarily restricted as to length of session. Salaries are too low. Some legislatures starve themselves financially and lack necessary services.

[3] Zeller, *op. cit.*, p. 65. See also Charles S. Hyneman, "Tenure and Turnover of Legislative Personnel," *The Annals,* Vol. 195, January 1938, pp. 21-31.

Some specific recommendations

Here are the recommendations of a group of experts to improve legislative performance in the states:

1. *Remove the restrictions upon the length of regular sessions.* Constitutional provisions that give the legislators a set number of days to do their work should be abolished. These restrictions have resulted in jamming up the legislative business so that during the last days of the legislature hundreds of bills are passed in a bedlam of activity. Some authorities would go even further and provide for annual sessions such as are already used in some states.

2. *Raise legislators' salaries so that competent persons can serve without financial sacrifice.*

3. *Increase the length of the term in order to provide continuity of membership.* Perhaps staggered terms should be used, as in the case of some state senates.

4. *Appoint skilled legislative employees on the basis of merit.*

5. *Reduce the number of legislative committees, equalize their work, schedule their meetings, and keep permanent and public records of their action.* Other students encourage the greater use of *joint committees* composed of members from both houses to avoid duplication of hearings and wasted effort. The joint committee has been adopted in Massachusetts, Maine, and Connecticut with great success.

6. *Provide for public hearings on all major bills.*

7. *Establish legislative councils or interim committees with adequate clerical and research facilities.* The legislative council idea, first attempted in Kansas and now found in over two-thirds of the states, calls for a small group of legislators to meet between sessions. The council prepares the legislative agenda and, with the aid of a research staff, makes investigations and circulates reports so that the legislators who meet for a short session can still have the best available information to work on a planned legislative schedule.

8. *Improve legislative reference, research, bill drafting, and statutory revision services wherever necessary.* Most states have some kind of legislative reference service, but in too many of them the service is primarily a bookkeeping and report-classifying operation. There are others, however, which are first-rate research organizations providing the legislators with complete information on current issues.

9. *Limit the period during which new bills may be introduced and provide for the drafting, filing, and printing of bills before the opening of the sessions.* To avoid the last-minute rush, a few states, notably California, have tried the "split session." During the first period, bills can be introduced. The legislature then recesses for a short period, and, upon reconvening, no new bills are ordinarily permitted. The split session has not

worked as well as many hoped. To preserve their freedom of action, legislators during the second session merely amend everything except the number and title of bills. Pre-session filing and enforcement of time limit on introduction of bills serve the same purpose and do it better.

10. *Establish permanent committees on organization, rules, and procedure to review and revise the regulations.*

11. *Provide an adequate budget for legislative operations.*

12. *Delegate settlement of claims against the state to judicial or administrative agencies and give local governments greater authority to make their own laws and determine their own governmental structures.*

13. *Install electrical voting.* This device, a great timesaver,[4] has now been installed in thirty states.

Other suggestions include those for smaller legislatures. Some legislatures are so large that conducting business is awkward, and placing responsibility for action or inaction where it belongs is difficult. There is of course no "right" size, and the legislature should be large enough so that all the major interests will be represented. It is doubtful, however, that the large bodies now prevalent are needed. Half as many men, paid twice as much, would probably give the public more for its money.

But will the above changes be enough? Many think not. Some advocate more basic alteration such as unicameralism.

Two houses or one?

Bicameralism became the established pattern in the United States early in our history (see Chapter 2). During Colonial days, the two chambers represented distinct interests—the upper house, royal authority; the lower house, the colonial cause. The desire to balance the aristocratic against the popular interest and the belief in a government of checks and balances were later reasons for maintaining two-house legislatures. In the eighteenth and early nineteenth centuries, the suffrage requirements for voting for senators and the qualifications to run for senator were more stringent than those for the lower house. But by the middle of the nineteenth century, the same electorate was choosing the members of both houses. In many states, the two houses today represent the same people (although usually in different districts). Why then do we retain the bicameral system?

Defenders of bicameralism insist that the two chambers provide essential checks against hasty and ill-considered legislation. The record of the legis-

---

[4] Council of State Governments, *Our State Legislatures*, 1948. These recommendations were endorsed by the American Political Science Association's Committee on State Legislatures; see Zeller, *op. cit.*, pp. 26-162. For a useful survey of legislative councils, see "The Legislative Council Movement in the United States, 1933-1953," *The American Political Science Review*, Vol. XLVII, No. 3, September 1953, pp. 785-797.

latures, however, often does not support this conclusion. In some states, legislation is rushed through the two houses, especially in the closing days, with little consideration by either chamber. Of course, some bills proposed by one chamber are defeated by the other, but it is difficult to determine whether the legislation so defeated was "ill-considered." Most observers conclude that the governor's veto, the courts, and the electorate are better checks on hasty action. They believe that too many road-blocks impede legislation, with the result that minority groups find it easy to prevent desirable legislation.

Bicameralism is also supported as a means of balancing the interests of the city groups and rural groups. In many states, metropolitan city interests are lined up against the country people on some issues. By enabling each group to have one chamber to represent its interests, it is argued, bicameralism provides proper balance. Under such circumstances the two chambers would not represent the same interests, and bicameralism would not be superfluous.

Defenders of unicameralism answer that such reasoning would lead to a multi-chamber legislature with a separate chamber to represent each interest—one for the farmers, one for the businessmen, one for the workers, one for people living in large cities, one for people living in small towns, and so on. The interests of all groups can be fairly represented in one chamber, they insist. Moreover, bicameralism encourages buck-passing and secret legislation in conference committees, and requires elaborate committee systems. Unicameralism, on the other hand, concentrates responsibility, encourages abler men to run for office, avoids the need of conference committees, and is less expensive.

Despite the impressive arguments in behalf of unicameralism, only Nebraska operates under such a system. Under the leadership of the late Senator George Norris, Nebraska created a unicameral legislature of 43 men who are elected on a nonpartisan ballot. Most observers have concluded that the Nebraska unicameral system has proved its value. The Nebraska one-house legislature, according to two experts, "has improved and simplified legislative procedure, has provided for adequate committee hearings and publicity, has kept lobbyists under control, and has worked well with the governor."[5] Nevertheless, the single chamber legislature has not won much support in other states, and there is, indeed, some dissatisfaction with it in Nebraska.

Regardless of whether the legislature is composed of one house or two, a perplexing problem facing all the states is that of determining the basis on which the members of the legislature shall be elected.

[5] William Anderson and Edward W. Weidner, *State and Local Government* (New York: Henry Holt & Company, 1951), p. 331.

REPRESENTATION IN STATE LEGISLATURES

In most state legislatures, representation shows a "rural bias." People who live in large cities and metropolitan suburbs elect proportionately fewer legislators than do their farm and small-town neighbors. Chicago, for example, has 42 per cent of the state's population and its citizens pay almost half the state taxes, but they elect only 31 per cent of the membership of the state Senate and 39 per cent of the state lower chamber. Los Angeles county has more than 40 per cent of California's population but elects only one out of forty senators. The six largest urban counties of Georgia select only 9 per cent of the lower house and 7 per cent of the state Senate. And so it goes in most states.[6]

Country hicks vs. city slickers

How does this discrimination against city people come about? It is due in part to constitutional restrictions and in part to the failure of the state legislatures to reapportion representatives or to redistrict the state as most of them are supposed to do every ten years. Some legislatures have done nothing in this respect for the last thirty or more years. Vermont last reapportioned its lower house in 1793, Connecticut in 1876; Delaware last realigned its legislative districts in 1897, Alabama in 1901, Minnesota in 1913, Mississippi in 1916, Indiana in 1921.

Even when the legislators comply with their state constitutions, city people are still frequently under-represented. The constitutions themselves provide for this. Sometimes the constitution forbids any county or town to be given more than a certain number or certain percentage of seats regardless of its population. Sometimes the constitution requires that each county or town be given at least one member. When this requirement is combined with a limit upon the total membership of a chamber, it leads to disproportionate representation, since there are insufficient seats left to afford adequate representation for the more populous areas after the required number have been allotted to the rural areas. Sometimes the constitution calls for equal representation in one chamber for counties or towns regardless of population.

These constitutional provisions did not result in glaringly disproportionate representation when population was more evenly spread out. But the concentration of people in large cities has created "rotten boroughs" in the rural areas where few people have excessive voting power. The failure of the legislatures to redraw election districts or to reapportion delegates in

[6] For other examples see Gordon E. Baker, *Rural versus Urban Political Power* (Garden City, New York: Doubleday & Company, Inc., 1955), pp. 16-17. For an index of "unrepresentation" of all state legislatures, see Manning J. Dauer and Robert G. Kelsay, "Unrepresentative States," *National Municipal Review*, Vol. XLIV, No. 11 (December 1955), pp. 571-575.

accordance with population movements exaggerates the disparity in voting strength between the city man and his country cousin.

The battle over reapportionment—and it is a hot political issue in many states—is more complex than a split just between rural and city groups. Some groups with their headquarters in the city find it to their advantage to maintain rural supremacy in the legislature. Professor Dean E. McHenry discovered that in California, "Privately owned utilities, banks, insurance companies, and others . . . have discovered some 'cow county' legislators more responsive to their demands and less committed to contrary points of view on key social and economic questions than are urban representatives. The urban legislator is more likely to be influenced by organized labor and by the many popular movements that ebb and flow *through* California politics."[7]

Ridiculous, Isn't It?

From: GOVERNMENT OF THE PEOPLE, BY THE PEOPLE, FOR THE PEOPLE, *published by The United States Conference of Mayors, Washington 6, D.C.*

The legislators from smaller towns and farmlands, who now dominate these assemblies, and their city allies naturally do not wish to reapportion themselves out of a job or lose their control of the legislature. Urban groups pressing for reapportionment have found the courts unwilling to use judicial power to force the legislators to comply with constitutional mandates. Con-

[7] "Urban vs. Rural in California," *National Municipal Review,* XXXV, No. 7 (July 1946), p. 350.

stitutional amendment has been successful in some states, especially those
that provide for proposing of amendments through the initiative procedure.
Where action of the legislature is required to propose an amendment or
call a convention, however, this tactic has been less successful. Even when
constitutional conventions have been called, in many cases the convention
delegates are chosen on the same basis of representation as the legislators, so
the convention is not likely to propose changes which alter drastically the
basis of representation. But in some states, groups desiring to insure periodic reapportionment have been able to assign the task to agencies other
than legislatures; for example, in Maryland the governor reapportions the
lower house. In Texas, if the legislature fails to act, the job is assigned to
an ex officio board and the state supreme court is specifically authorized to
compel the board to act.

What are the consequences of urban under-representation? In the first
place, the rural areas are, on the whole, more conservative in their politics
than are the more cosmopolitan urban centers. Outside of the South, rural
America tends to be more Republican, and the large cities tend to be more
Democratic. Hence, rural over-representation tends to give the Republicans
and conservative groups a louder voice in the legislature than would otherwise be the case.

The legislatures have much to say about the form and power of local
governments (see page 809), and the conflict between city and state is
often a conflict between rural groups who run the legislature and city
people who are trying to run their city. City officials often are bitter against
the legislators who, they feel, are not sympathetic toward city problems
and who try to enforce rural standards of right and wrong upon their city
brethren. Some observers believe that the failure to reapportion explains
why cities have, during recent years, by-passed the states and taken their
problems directly to Washington.

Rural dominance of state legislatures affects the scheme of representation
in the national House of Representatives. As we have noted, the state legislatures, subject only to the most minor congressional restrictions, establish
congressional districts. "State lawmakers," writes Professor Baker, "have
been almost as cavalier about periodic equalization of congressional districts as they have been about reapportioning their own seats."[8] The disproportionate representation of rural areas in state legislatures is thus often
transmitted to the states' congressional representation.

George Washington Plunkitt, the Tammany Hall patriot, was one of
those who felt strongly about the control of the New York legislature by
rural Republicans. The hayseeds, as he called them, "think we are like the
Indians to the National Government—that is, sort of wards of the State,
who don't know how to look after ourselves and have to be taken care of
by the Republicans of St. Lawrence, Ontario, and other backwoods

[8] Baker, *op. cit.,* p. 42.

counties. . . . Say, you hear a lot about the downtrodden people," continued Plunkitt, "of Ireland. . . . Now, let me tell you that they have more real freedom and home rule than the people of this grand and imperial city. . . . In this State the Republican government makes no pretense at all. It says right out in the open: 'New York City is a nice big fat Goose. Come along with your carvin' knives and have a slice.' "[9]

Plunkitt accused the Republican-controlled state government of levying all the taxes on liquor, corporations, banks, insurance companies, and then spending the money for the country people. One of his fondest dreams was to see New York City withdraw from the state. But what would happen to the people up-state? "These hayseeds," he said, "have been so used to livin' off of New York City that they would be helpless. . . . It wouldn't do to let them starve. We might make some sort of an appropriation for them for a few years." Plunkitt even wanted to pass a law to require up-state politicians to get a passport in order to come below the Bronx. He admitted that such a law might be difficult to draw, but as he said, "With a Tammany Constitution, Governor, Legislature, and Mayor, there would be no trouble in settlin' a little matter of that sort."[10]

It is not merely the Plunkitts who have protested against what they consider to be an injustice. More respectable opposition has been voiced by the U. S. Conference of Mayors and the National Municipal League. In 1949 at a crowded meeting of the Conference of Mayors, the cry of "Taxation without representation is tyranny!" was frequently raised. And it is reported that a president of this conference once stated that unless the cities received a fairer share of representation that "there will be a tea party which will make a bigger smash than the original one in Boston." The mayors summarized their views by declaring, "Equal representation is not a mere theory or doctrine. It is a fundamental feature of democracy; and the failure of any legislative body to enforce the principle should be met with instant and vigorous protest on the part of the people affected."[11]

How do the rural legislators and those who oppose reapportionment defend their position? They point out that representation on the basis of population has never been consistently followed in the United States, that area too has been a basis of representation. The United States Senate is organized to represent states, not population. If representation were on the basis of population, they argue, the city legislators would dominate, and this would be even worse than country rule. A Michigan state senator from a town of 719 people, opposed to giving Detroit full representation on a population basis, has quoted approvingly from Roger W. Babson that "large cities are the main sources of poverty, gangsters, and immorality.

[9] W. L. Riordon, *Plunkitt of Tammany Hall* (New York: McClure, Phillips, 1905), pp. 38-39.

[10] *Ibid.*, pp. 125-126.

[11] United States Conference of Mayors, *Government of the people, by the people, for the people?* 1948.

. . . Rural people have much better character and more time to think and read than do large city people . . . the votes of people in small *cities* and rural communities should count more than the vote of the ordinary city man."[12]

In the struggle over reapportionment, the farmer has the advantage of the "rural bias" that has existed in the United States at least since the days of Jefferson. Although a majority of the people now live in cities (see Chapter 1), the United States originated as a rural nation, and the belief in the superior virtues of country life and country people is still strongly held. Even among city people themselves, the city is often thought of as a den of iniquity and a center of un-American and radical thought. It seems certain, however, as the urbanization of the nation continues, that the struggle of urban majorities to secure more equal representation in their state legislatures will continue.

DIRECT DEMOCRACY

In some of our states, the legislature and the governor are not the only agencies vested with law-making powers. The voters themselves act on laws. Around the turn of the twentieth century, one of the battle cries of the Populists, Progressives, and reformers in general was to "return the government to the people" through the initiative, referendum, and recall. Give the voters the power to make or veto laws and to recall officials, they asserted, and the political machines will be destroyed and the special interests routed. Opponents of these measures vehemently replied that their adoption would destroy representative government and open the way for crackpot and radical legislation.

During the first two decades of this century, about a third of the states, mostly in the West, adopted the initiative and referendum, and so did hundreds of cities, especially those with commission and city manager forms of government (see Chapter 32). A smaller number of states and cities also adopted the recall.

The details of these procedures vary, but their purpose is everywhere the same. The initiative allows the voters to enact legislation or constitutional amendments when the legislature fails to act, the referendum permits the majority of the voters to veto legislation or reject constitutional amendments, and the recall allows the electorate to separate an elected public official from his job before the end of his term.

The *referendum* is simply the method of allowing the people to vote on proposed measures. The referendum is required in every state except Delaware for ratification of constitutional amendments. As applied to legislation, there are two general types of referenda, *mandatory* and *optional*. If

[12] Roger W. Babson, "Babson Discusses Small Cities," Publishers Financial Bureau, December 23, 1949.

the state constitution provides for mandatory referendum, there is a waiting period, usually sixty to ninety days, before legislation goes into effect. If during this period a prescribed number of voters sign a referendum petition requesting that the act be referred to the voters, the law does not go into effect unless a majority of the voters give their approval at the next election. (The legislature may avoid the possibility of a referendum election by declaring the law to be "emergency legislation" to go into immediate effect.) The *optional* legislative referendum permits the legislature, at its discretion, to provide that a measure shall not become law until it shall have been approved by the voters at an election.

The *direct initiative* applies in some states to constitutional amendments and to legislation. In other states, the initiative can be used for only one or the other. In a state that permits the use of the initiative, an individual or group of voters may, on their own initiative, draft a proposed law. After the supporters have secured a certain number of signatures (often 5 to 10 per cent of the total electorate), the measure is placed before the voters at the next election.

In some states, the *indirect initiative* is used, and the legislature is given an opportunity to act on the measure before it is referred to the voters. If the legislature does not approve, the proposed legislation is then placed on the ballot, although in some states additional signatures are required.

Only twelve states provide for *recall* of state officers, but many others permit the recall of local officials. The recall provision involves the familiar petition, but the requirement for signatures is normally larger than in the case of the initiative and referendum. There are various kinds of recall elections. In some, the official must stand on the single issue of his removal; in others, candidates are permitted to file and run against him.

The recall has not been widely used, and it seems doubtful that it has much effect on the course of government. It provides a shotgun which the voters can use if necessary. The impeachment technique is not too effective, for it requires proof of violations of the law or serious misbehavior. The recall carries none of these overtones, since it is permissible to recall an official merely because a majority of the voters do not like him.

What have been the consequences of the devices for direct democracy? Professor C. F. Snider, an outstanding authority, has concluded, "They have neither been the boon to democracy contemplated by their friends nor produced the dire consequences predicted by their enemies. Actually, it seems doubtful that they have exerted any profound influence upon the course of legislation."[13]

[13] C. F. Snider, *American State and Local Government* (New York: Appleton-Century-Crofts, 1950), p. 155.

LIKE THE NATIONAL GOVERNMENT, EACH STATE government is organized into three branches of government: legislative, executive, and judicial. As in Washington, power is divided among these three branches, and then divided again between upper and lower chambers (except in Nebraska). Hence, every state is a test tube for the American experiment in government, the experiment of mingling powers among the several branches of government and of making different leaders responsible to different electorates. Each state, to a greater or less degree, makes it difficult for a simple majority of the voters to win power; each requires, to some extent, rule by concurrent majorities (see Chapter 21).

This is not to say, however, that the governmental and political systems of the states as a whole are much alike. Constitutional structure may be roughly the same, but other vital aspects of government and politics—local idea-systems, interest groups, voting, parties, public attitudes, administrative arrangements, for example—differ widely. Indeed, the state governments are interesting examples of how constitutional *form* is only one element of government. Almost as many differences can be found between one state with a fully developed two-party system, a strong chief executive, and centralized administration and another state with a diffused one-party system, weak governor, and decentralized administration as can be found between our national government and that of Great Britain or France.

★ 30

Governors

and

judges

HIS EXCELLENCY—THE GOVERNOR

"A strong executive is an engine of tyranny." This ancient suspicion is reflected in the state constitutions. At the outset, the governor was subordinated to the legislature. Then during the period of Jacksonian Democracy, the idea spread that the people should directly elect the major officials of government. Of course, the governor became only one of several elected executive officials. Nevertheless, beginning slowly and picking up speed during the last fifty years, the governor has grown from "figure-head to leader."

In over half the states, the governor is elected for a four-year term; in the others for two years. The trend is toward the longer period. In about half the states where he has a four-year term (mostly southern and border states) the governor is ineligible for a second consecutive term. His salary varies from a high of $50,000 in New York to a low of $9000 in South Dakota, with most governors receiving between $12,000 and $25,000.

Because of the average governor's relatively small salary, short tenure, and limited powers, one might expect difficulty in getting able men to run for the office. But this is not so. The governor has a position of great prestige in his state. Governors of the larger states are national figures. They often control powerful political machines. The office can be an important step toward national office—the Senate or even the Presidency.

POWERS AND PROBLEMS OF THE GOVERNOR

"The executive power," says the Constitution, "shall be vested in the President of the United States." Compare this flat statement with its counterpart in a typical state constitution which declares, "The executive department shall consist of a Governor, Lieutenant Governor, Secretary of State, Auditor, Treasurer, Superintendent of Public Instruction, Attorney General, and perhaps other officials." In the states, the governor shares the executive power with numerous other *elected* officers. Most state constitutions, nevertheless, go on to say that "the Supreme executive power shall be vested in the Governor, who shall take care that the laws be faithfully executed." And it is the governor to whom the public looks for law enforcement and supervision of administrative agencies.

Governor Samuel W. Pennypacker, Pennsylvania's chief executive in 1903-1907, told how he came into office aware of his high duty to see that the laws of the state were faithfully executed. He looked around to see what instruments he had to carry out this responsibility. He discovered that the only persons he could look to for help were his secretary, the janitor, and his chauffeur. The prosecutors and police, locally elected and locally controlled, were subject to little or no gubernatorial supervision. The attorney general was elected by the voters and not responsible to the governor. Of course, the governor could call out the National Guard, but this is a clumsy way to enforce the law. "So," said Governor Pennypacker, "I created the state police." Today the governors of about three-fourths of the states have a state police force which they may use when the local police fail to perform. Furthermore, in some states the governor has been given authority over local prosecutors so that he can supervise their activities. Even so, most governors have little power to see that the laws are enforced by the police and prosecutors.

How does the governor supervise the administrative structure? During the nineteenth century, as the states took on new functions, new agencies

APPOINTING POWER OF THE GOVERNOR

	Sec. of State	Treasurer	Auditor (b)	Attorney General	Tax Commissr.	Finance (a)	Budget Officer	Comptroller (c)	Education	Agriculture	Labor	Health	Welfare	Insurance	Highways	Conservation
Alabama	E	E	E	E	G	G	O	O	E	E	G	B	R	G	G	G
Arizona	E	E	E	E	G	GS	O	O	E	G	GS	B	BG	E	GS	GS
Arkansas	E	E	L(v)	E	GS	O	DG	O	R	O	G	BG	GS	GS	B	G
California	E	E	GS	E	E	G	O	E	E	G	G	G	GS	GS	G	G
Colorado	E	E	L	E	CS	O	CS	CS	B	CS	CS	CS	CS	CS	CS	CS
Connecticut	E	E	L	E	GE	GE	GS	E(d)	B	GE	GE	GE	GS	GE	GE	O
Delaware	GS	E	E	E	GS	O	B(e)	B(e)	B	B	B	BG	B	E	B	B
Florida	E	E	GS	E	E(f)	O	O	E(f)	B	E	G	R	G	E	G	G
Georgia	E	E	L	E	GS	O	C(g)	E	E	E	E	GS	GS	E	L	O
Idaho	E	E	E(d)	E	GS	O	G	E(d)	B	G	GS	GS	GS	GS	GS	GS
Illinois	E	E	E(d)	E	GS	GS	G	O	B	GS	GS	GS	G	GS	GS	GS
Indiana	E	E	E	E	G	GS	O	O	E	E	GS	GS	G	GS	B(j)	GS
Iowa	E	L	E	E	GS	GS	O	G	B	E	GS	CS	GS	GS	GS	GS
Kansas	E	E	E	E	GS	G	DG	DG	B	B	GS	GS	R	E	GS	O
Kentucky	E	E	E	E	GS	G	DG	DG	E	B	GS	B	G	GC	GS	GS
Louisiana	GS	E	E	E	GS	G	C(h)	O	E	E	GS	GS	B(j)	(i)	B(j)	GS
Maine	L	L	L	L	(k)	GC	O	(k)	B	L	GC	GC	GC	GC	GC	GC
Maryland	GS	E	G	E	GC	O	G	E	B	GS	GC	GC	GC	GC	GC	GC
Massachusetts	E	E	E	E	GC	GC	O	O	B	GC	GS	GC	GC	GC	GC	GC
Michigan	E	E	E	E	G	O	O	O	E	GS	GS	GS	GS	E	E	E
Minnesota	E	E	E(d)	E	GS	GS	GS	O	B	GS	GS	B	GS	GS	GS	GS
Mississippi	E	E	E	E	GS	O	G(e)	G(e)	B	E	GS	GS	GS	E	E	E
Missouri	E	E	E	E	GS	GS	GS	GS	E	GS	GS	GS	GS	GS	GS	GS
Montana	E	E	E	E	GS	GS	O	O	E	GS	GS	GS	GS	GS	GS	GS
Nebraska	E	E	E(d)	E	GS(l)	O	(l)	E(d)	B	GS	GS	B	GS	GS	GS	O
Nevada	L	E	L	E	SC	GC	O	O	E	GC	GC	G	B	GC	E	O
New Hampshire	GS	L	O	GC	GS	GS	O	O	B	BG	GC	B	B	GC	GC	GS
New Jersey	GS	E	L	GS	GS	GS	O	O	GS	BG	GC	G	B	GC	GC	O
New Mexico	E	E	E	E	G	O	G	G	E	O	GS	GS	GS	E	GS	GS
New York	GS	GS	O	E	GS	O	G	E	B	GS	GS	GS	B	GS	GS	GS
North Carolina	E	E	E	E	E	GC	B	(m)	B	GC	GC	G	B	GC	GS	O
North Dakota	E	E	E(d)	E	E	O	B	E(d)	E	E(n)	E(n)	G	B	E	G	O

State											
Ohio	E	E	E	GS	GS	GS	O	GS	B	GS	GS
Oklahoma	E	E	E(p)	GS	G	(o)	O	(o)	E	E	(o)
Oregon	E(p)	E(p)	E(p)	E	O	O	O	GS	E(w)	GS	(o)
Pennsylvania	GS	E	E(u)	GS	GS	E(u)	E(u)	GS	GS	GS	GS
Rhode Island	E	E	O	DG	DG	DG	DG	GS	BG	GS	GS
South Carolina	E	E	B(q)	E	B(q)	O	E	L	GS	E	GC
South Dakota	E	E	E	GS	GS	O	L	L	GS	GS	GS
Tennessee	L	L	O	G	O	L	L	G	G	G	G
Texas	GS	L	E	(r)	(t)	E	E	B	B	B	GS
Utah	E	E	E	GS	O	GS	B	GS	GS	GS	(o)
Vermont	E	E(d)	E(d)	O	GS	GS	B	GS	GS	GS	GS
Virginia	GSH	L	GSH	GSH	GSH	GSH	B(t)	GS	GSH	GSH	B(t)
Washington	E	E(d)	E(d)	GS	O	GS	E	GS	GS	GS	GS
West Virginia	E	GS	E(u)	GS	GS	E	B	B	GS	B	(o)
Wisconsin	E	E(d)	GS	GS	O	GS	GS	R	GS	GS	B
Wyoming	E	E(d)	E	GS	O	G	E	GS	GS	GS	GS

Legend: E—Elected. G—Appointed by Governor alone. GS—Appointed by Governor and approved by Senate. O—Office or equivalent does not exist. [See footnote (a) below.] B—Appointed by appropriate departmental board. GE—Appointed by Governor and approved by either House. L—Chosen by Legislature. GC—Appointed by Governor and Council. SC—Appointed by Judges of Supreme Court. DG—Director with approval of the Governor. GSH—Appointed by Governor and approved by appropriate departmental board with approval of Governor. CS—Civil service appointment by competitive examination.

(a) The term finance refers to a department, variously designated a finance, revenue, administration, treasury, or executive department, in which fiscal and related operations have been grouped together. The department is ordinarily distinguished by the inclusion of a division of the budget and a division of accounts and control. In a few cases, either budget preparation or accounting control may be performed by another agency; yet the department is included under finance because the department head is the chief fiscal advisor of the Governor. Where it is indicated that a state has a finance department and it includes divisions of taxation, budget, or accounting, the columns with these headings will be marked with an "O" to indicate that there are no separate agencies for these functions.

(b) The auditor does not have post-audit functions in every state. See table on page 167.

(c) See table on page 167 for performance of pre-audit functions.
(d) Audit and accounting control are responsibilities of the same person.
(e) Budget preparation and accounting control are the responsibilities of the same person.
(f) The Comptroller collects most of Florida's taxes.

(g) Governor ex-officio budget officer assisted by auditor.
(h) Governor is Director of Budget; Assistant Director appointed by Governor.
(i) Secretary of State is ex-officio Insurance Commissioner.
(j) Board of eight appointed by Governor from recommendations. Governor is ex-officio member of board.
(k) Appointed by Commissioner of Finance; approved by Governor and Council.
(l) The office of Tax Commissioner is responsible for budget preparation as well as revenue collection.
(m) Appointed by Auditor.
(n) There is a combined Department of Agriculture and Labor in North Dakota headed by a single elective official.
(o) Governor appoints board with consent of Senate, board appoints Executive Director except in Agriculture where board elects a member as President.
(p) Secretary of State is ex-officio auditor.
(q) State Auditor, appointed by Budget and Control Board, is head of Finance Division.
(r) The Tax Commission in Texas is an ex-officio body which fixes the tax rate. The Comptroller is Tax Administrator.
(s) Legislative Budget Board separate. In Texas this agency and Governor's budget officer work in the same budget field.
(t) Appointed by State Corporation Commission.
(u) Treasurer also serves as comptroller.
(v) Auditor General is appointed by Joint Legislative Audit Committee; authority of Auditor General confined to examining and reporting.
(w) Attorney General serves ex-officio as Industrial Commissioner.

From BOOK OF THE STATES, 1956-1957. Courtesy Council of State Governments.

were added more or less haphazardly. Boards and commissions were established, power was parcelled out among numerous officials, the *long ballot* with its many elective offices was created, and lines of authority and responsibility became confused. The ship of state went in several directions, and the governor had little power to control the administration. In some states, the diffuse structure was integrated by bosses who took control behind the facade of numerous elective officials.

Such was the general state of affairs until the reorganization movement was born. Beginning with Illinois in 1917, many commonwealths moved to rationalize their administrative structures. The universal recommendation of the reorganizers was to integrate the executive structure, centralize its direction under the governor, and make him the manager of the administration. The reorganizers argued that it is better to make the governor the manager of the executive branch than to leave the integrating job to behind-the-scenes bosses. Make the governor accountable to the people, they urged, shorten the ballot, and give the governor the authority he needs.

The trend toward *integrated administration* is still strong, but integration is by no means an accomplished fact. Many a governor is still one executive among many, with only limited authority over his subordinates. He has practically no authority over the other elected officials. He does not appoint them, and he cannot dismiss them. If they are his political enemies, they will not accept his leadership. The governor has greater but still limited power over other executive officials. In most states he shares the appointive power with the senate and may remove subordinates only by bringing charges that they have violated the law or failed in their legal duties.

The most important weapon in the governor's arsenal, however, is his control over the *budget*. In those states in which he prepares and presents the budget to the legislature and in which he has the item veto, he can control to a considerable extent the flow of funds to the executive departments and hence affect their activities—always assuming, of course, that he has sufficient political power to make his budget and his veto stick. Purchasing, fiscal, and personnel matters, moreover, are frequently centralized under the governor. When assisted by a strong staff, and backed by strong political power, the governor has an important role in directing the course of administration.

Governors' helpers—or enemies?

In many states the other executive officials elected by the people include the Lieutenant Governor, Secretary of State, Attorney General, Treasurer, and Auditor. What do they do?

The *Lieutenant Governor* does very little. He presides over the senate and, in most states, in case of the death, disability, or absence of the governor from the state, he becomes acting governor. The states lacking a lieutenant governor do not seem to miss him. The lieutenant governor is often a leader of a faction in the party opposed to the governor and becomes a thorn in the side of the chief executive. There is a tendency, though not a marked one, to enlarge the duties of the lieutenant governor.

The *Secretary of State* is custodian of the state records and keeper of the state seal. He publishes the laws, supervises elections, issues certificates of incorporation. In some states, he issues automobile licenses and registers corporate securities. His office is often the "dumping ground" for jobs that do not seem to belong to any existing office and are not important enough to justify a new agency. Classification of his duties is difficult.

The *Attorney General* is the governor's lawyer. His office gives advice to the state officials, represents the state before the courts, and supervises prosecutions by local prosecutors. Some attorney generals have real authority over local prosecutors and may prosecute cases on their own initiative. The attorney generalship is often a stepping stone to the governorship and occasionally attorney generals have made political capital out of investigating the state administration.

The *Treasurer* is custodian of state funds. Although in some states he has tax collection duties, in most states his job is largely ministerial.

The *Auditor* has two major jobs: to authorize disbursements from the treasury, and to make periodic audits of those officials who handle state moneys. Before money can be spent, the auditor must sign a warrant indicating that he is convinced that the appropriation is authorized by law and that money is available in the treasury. This is the *pre-audit,* which many students believe should be given to a comptroller appointed by and responsible to the governor. The auditing *after* the money has been spent, however, is a job which most students believe should be vested in an officer responsible to the legislature. The auditor is the one official who, even in the opinion of some of the most extreme advocates of centralized administration, should not be responsible to the governor.

The reorganization movement and its critics

The wave of state reorganizations that followed World War I was repeated again after World War II under the stimulus of the national Hoover Commission. Today most of the states have appointed their own "Little Hoover Commissions" to make recommendations for improving the efficiency of the state governmental structure. Not all of the states have participated, and it is much too early to judge the work of these groups.

Attempts to reorganize the state structures have not received universal praise. In many states, the commissions assemble, make studies, and submit reports—which are soon filed and forgotten. One student of the problem discovered that by the end of 1952, the legislative response was "pronouncedly positive" in only two of the 24 states in which the legislature had a chance to consider commission recommendations.[1] Groups that profit by existing structure, as for example those who have a pet bureau over which they exert much influence, can be counted upon to resist changes. Opposition comes from public officials who fear loss of job or prestige. Legislators who suspect that the recommendations will make the governor too powerful are often reluctant to approve recommendations. And the politicians who have lived with the existing structure and know how to operate it do not like to change the environment in which they feel so much at home.

Another group of critics opposes not so much the idea of reorganization but the basic principle that has dominated the movement. This is the principle of *executive power* and *responsibility*. During the last several decades, the reorganizers have given their almost unanimous assent to the proposition that the governor should be made the manager of the executive branch. They have developed the following canons of reorganization:

1. All agencies should be consolidated and integrated into as few departments as possible, so that similar functions will be grouped together and the governor's span of control will be manageable.

2. Lines of responsibility should be fixed and definite.

3. Single-head executives are to be preferred over boards and commissions.

4. The governor should have power to appoint and remove subordinates, including officers who are now elected, with the possible exception of the auditor.

5. The governor should have control over budgeting, accounting, reporting, purchasing, personnel, and planning, and should have the necessary staff that will enable him to do these jobs.

These standard administrative principles have been challenged. Some critics, although accepting the desirability of centralized budgeting, purchasing, and the like, are skeptical of the basic assumptions of reorganization. They argue that conditions differ in each state and no cookie-cutter pattern of administration fits all conditions. There is little demonstrable evidence, they argue, to support the proposed reforms other than the arguments of the reorganizers themselves and their mutual citation of each other as authorities. What is the evidence, they ask, that the people will hold the governor accountable and that the governor will devote his time and energy to administrative matters? Most governors are chiefly interested in legislative problems, are not concerned with administrative detail, and are seldom judged on their executive talent. Furthermore, the critics decry the emphasis upon efficiency and economy. There is a real danger, they argue, that the reorganizers are overlooking basic values by their concern

[1] Karl A. Bosworth, "The Politics of Management Improvement in the States," *The American Political Science Review,* Vol. XLVII, No. 1, March 1953, pp. 84 ff.

with saving money. The threat of executive tyranny, they fear, is dismissed too cavalierly. As one critic phrased it, "Men invited to recommend a program which promises efficiency and economy for a state . . . have not only mistaken supposition for fact and hypothesis for principle; they have failed to warn their clients . . . of the enormous risk involved in creating a powerful chief executive in a state which has no responsible legislature and in many instances no effective opposition party."[2]

The reorganizers respond as follows: Of course it is ridiculous to make changes without regard to local conditions and particular problems. But the basic idea—the integration of authority, centralized direction, simplification of structure—is sound. There is little danger of creating dictators. In fact, it is much more likely that men not responsible to the electorate will run government when the administrative structure is cumbersome, confusing, and diffused. The legislature retains its essential powers and can more effectively supervise an integrated administration than it can when responsibility is diffused. In actual practice in states where the governor's formal authority is slight, some governors have become as powerful as those in states where gubernatorial authority is strong.

Effects of reorganization

What have been the results of thirty years of reorganization? Again there is controversy. Some observers say that reorganization has not given us more efficient or democratic government, others say it has, and still others say there is little evidence one way or another. Professor W. H. Edwards made a careful study of results of reorganization in 1938. He concluded that in many cases the reorganizations were made on paper only, and that no significant changes in actual operations were effected. He discovered that the largest savings came as a result of centralized purchasing and adoption of modern fiscal practices rather than the consolidation of departments or the strengthening of the governor's control over the executive branch.[3]

At the same time, it can be said that in general the best governed states are those in which the administrative structure has been most closely integrated under the governor. Whether this integration has caused good government in those states is another, though closely related, question.

The basic idea of reorganization is to apply knowledge to improve what we have. But to make reorganization pay the biggest dividends, it must be a continuous process of adjustment. There is a danger of overemphasizing the importance of efficiency and of reducing the tax rate. Few would deny the importance of saving money, but the costs of operating our state

[2] C. S. Hyneman, "Administrative Reorganization—an Adventure into Science and Theology," *The Journal of Politics*, February 1939, Vol. I, No. 26, pp. 74-75.
[3] W. H. Edwards, "Has State Reorganization Succeeded?" *State Government*, October 1938, Vol. II, pp. 184-185.

THE EXECUTIVE VETO

State	Days after which bill becomes law (before adjournment) unless vetoed (Sundays excepted)	Fate of bill after adjournment — Days after which bill is law unless vetoed (Sundays excepted)	Fate of bill after adjournment — Days after which bill dies unless signed (Sundays excepted)	Item veto on appropriation bills	Vetoes required in House and Senate to pass bills or items over veto(a)	Constitution prohibits Governor from vetoing — Initiated measures	Constitution prohibits Governor from vetoing — Referred measures
Alabama	6	10	10	★	Majority elected	(b)	(b)
Arizona	5	20(d)		★	Two-thirds elected(c)	★	★
Arkansas	5		30	★	Majority elected	★	★
California	10			★	Two-thirds elected	★	★
Colorado	10(d)	30(d)		★	Two-thirds elected	(b)	(b)
Connecticut	5(e)	15(d)		★	Majority present	(b)	(b)
Delaware	10	20(d)		★	Three-fifths elected	(b)	(b)
Florida	5		(g)	★	Two-thirds present	(h)	
Georgia (f)	30	10		★	Two-thirds elected	(b)	(b)
Idaho	5	10		★	Two-thirds elected	(b)	(b)
Illinois	10	5(d,i)		★	Majority elected	(b)	(b)
Indiana	3				Two-thirds elected	(b)	
Iowa	3	(j)	30	★	Two-thirds elected	(b)	(b)
Kansas	3	(k)		★	Majority elected	(b)	(b)
Kentucky	10	10		★	Two-thirds elected	(n)	★
Louisiana	10(d,l)	20(d,l)		★	Two-thirds elected	★	★
Maine	5		6(q)		Two-thirds present	★	★
Maryland (o)	6	6(p)			Three-fifths elected	(b)	(b)
Massachusetts	5(e)	5(e)		★	Two-thirds present	(b)	(b)
Michigan	10		3	★	Two-thirds elected	(b)	★
Minnesota	3	3		★	Two-thirds elected	(b)	(b)
Mississippi	5	(m)		★	Two-thirds elected	(b)	(b)
Missouri	(r)5	15(d,s)		★(t)	Two-thirds present	★	★
Montana	5	5		★	Two-thirds elected	★	★
Nebraska	5	5		★	Three-fifths elected	★	★
Nevada	5	10	(g)	★	Two-thirds elected	(b)	(b)
New Hampshire	5	45			Two-thirds elected	(b)	(b)
New Jersey	10(u)	(g)		★	Two-thirds elected	(b)	(b)
New Mexico	3	20(s)		★	Two-thirds present	(h)	
New York	10	30(d)		★	Two-thirds elected	(h)	
North Carolina	(v)	(v)		(v)		(h)	
North Dakota	3	15(d)		★	Two-thirds elected	★	★

State	Days (in session)	Days (after adjournment)	Days to become law	Vote required to pass over veto	Item veto	Initiative/referendum
Ohio	10	10		Three-fifths elected	★★	★★
Oklahoma	5	20	15	Two-thirds elected	★★★(w)	★★
Oregon	5	30(d)		Two-thirds present	★★	(b)
Pennsylvania	10(d)			Three-fifths present		(b)
Rhode Island	6	10(d)		Two-thirds elected	★★	(b)
South Carolina	3	(m)		Two-thirds present	★★(x)	★ (b)
South Dakota	5	10(d)		Majority elected	★★	(b)
Tennessee		10		Two-thirds present		(h)
Texas	10	10		Two-thirds elected	★★	(b)
Utah	5	20(j)		Two-thirds present		★ (b)
Vermont	5	10		Two-thirds present(y)		(b)
Virginia			(g) / 10(j)	Two-thirds elected	★(z)	★ (b)
Washington	5	10		Two-thirds elected	★★	(b)
West Virginia	5(aa)	5(d)		Majority elected	★★	(b)
Wisconsin	6(i)	15(d)	6(l)	Two-thirds present	★★★★	(b)
Wyoming	3			Two-thirds elected	★	(b)
Alaska	3		3	Two-thirds elected		
Guam			30(g)	Two-thirds elected		(b)
Hawaii	10		10(p)	Two-thirds elected		(b)
Puerto Rico	10		30(ab)	Two-thirds elected		
Virgin Islands	10		30	Two-thirds elected		

(a) Bill returned to house of origin with objections, except in Georgia, where Governor need not state objections, and in Kansas, where all bills are returned to House.

(b) No provision for initiative or referendum in state.

(c) Three-fourths in case of an emergency measure.

(d) Sundays not excepted unless last day is Sunday.

(e) Sundays and legal holidays excepted.

(f) New constitution, passed by General Assembly, withholds right to veto constitutional amendments.

(h) No provision for initiative in state.

(i) Bill becomes law if not filed with objections with Secretary of State within five days after adjournment.

(k) Sundays not excepted.

(l) In practice, the legislature closes consideration of bills three days before adjournment sine die.

(l) Governor has 10 days (in Wisconsin 6 days) from time bill was presented to him in which to approve or disapprove.

(m) Bill passed in one session becomes law if not returned within 2 days (Maine and Mississippi 3) after reconvening.

(n) Constitution provides that Governor may veto initiated measures and if legislature sustains veto, measure is referred to vote of people at next general election.

(o) 1950 constitutional amendment requires any bill vetoed after adjournment, or dying because of pocket veto after adjournment, to be returned to the legislature when it next convenes, for a vote on overriding the veto.

(p) Within 6 days (in Hawaii 10 days) after presentation to the Governor, regardless of how long after adjournment.

(q) Within 5 days of receipt by Governor. In practice General Court not prorogued until Governor has acted on all bills.

(r) If Governor does not return bill in 15 days, a joint resolution is necessary for bill to become law.

(s) Governor must file bills with Secretary of State.

(t) Governor may not veto items in budget submitted by himself after it has passed legislature with three-fifths vote.

(u) If house of origin is in temporary adjournment on 10th day, becomes law on day house of origin reconvenes unless returned by Governor on that day. Governor has power of veto after repassage of bills in amended form with condition bill must be approved in 10 days or pocket veto.

(v) No veto; bill becomes law 30 days after adjournment of session unless otherwise expressly directed.

(w) Also may veto items in new bills declaring an emergency.

(x) Governor may reduce or eliminate items but must give written notice of item veto either 3 days before adjournment or one day after bill is presented for signature.

(y) Including majority elected.

(z) May veto items in any bill containing items or sections.

(aa) Budget (appropriation) bill not submitted to Governor after passage.

(ab) Sundays are not excepted.

From BOOK OF THE STATES, *1956-1957. Courtesy of the Council of State Governments*

governments cannot be seriously reduced except by reducing their functions. Moreover, in many fields, effective state government requires larger,
not smaller, expenditures of money. The question must always be: reorganization for what? Not merely to save money but to strengthen self-
government—government by the people.

The governor as chief legislator

Just as the role of the President in determining national policy has
grown over the last several decades, so has the governor become a more
active participant in the making of state policy. In fact, some governors
dominate their legislatures to an extent that surpasses the influence that even
the strongest of our Presidents have had. The governor has the constitutional
power to call the legislature into special session and in some states to restrict
the subjects that the legislators can discuss in such sessions. He is authorized
to address the legislature and send messages to it. He has the responsibility
in over forty of the states to submit the budget to the legislature. Moreover,
in all states except North Carolina, he has strong veto powers, usually much
stronger than those of the President.

In all but a handful of states, the governor, in addition to the regular
qualified veto, has the power to strike out—that is, *veto*—individual items
in appropriation measures while approving the rest of the measures. In a
few states, the governor can even reduce a particular appropriation. The
item veto, like all vetoes, can be overridden by the legislature (normally a
two-thirds vote in both chambers is required), but in many states most new
laws are sent to the governor after the legislature has adjourned. Thus when
he vetoes bills or items of appropriations, in many cases there is no chance
for the legislature to override the veto.

How much legislative influence do governors have? Although their constitutional authority varies a good deal, their actual ability to influence
legislative policy varies even more widely from state to state and from
time to time than a reading of the constitutions might suggest. Much depends upon the governor's ability, his personal popularity, the political
situation in which he operates. Some states have a long tradition calling
for executive leadership; when the governor has the support of powerful
political organizations, he can guide policy. The governors of New York
and Illinois, for example, have strong constitutional positions, and they
are also apt to have strong party organizations behind them and close ties
with their party followers in the legislature. Furthermore, governors of
these large states, and others like Ohio, Pennsylvania, and California with
active two-party systems, are potential presidential candidates. These governors—men like Averell Harriman of New York, Mennen Williams of
Michigan, Goodwin J. Knight of California—attract the national spotlight.
Many of them look forward to national political careers, and they speak

with the authority of men who might someday be President of the United States. In these states the governorship attracts able men and gives them much prestige and power. But even in states where the governor is less likely to be a national figure, the governor has influence whenever he can build a large popular following or depend upon strong party organizations.

Emergency powers

Emergencies enhance the authority of the executive, since they call for swift and decisive measures. The governor is commander in chief of the state's National Guard when it is not in federal service. He is responsible for using this force when the ordinary civil authorities are inadequate—in case of riots, floods, and other catastrophes. During the depression of the 1930's, many governors used the Guard, not always too wisely, to handle various kinds of social disturbances. And hardly a year goes by without the Guard of some state seeing emergency duty. In about three-fourths of the states, the governor has a state police force at his command (see p. 849) which can be used wherever needed.

The national government has the major responsibility for providing for the national defense, but the states also have vital jobs. During World War II, when the National Guard was called into federal service, most states created State Guards operating under the governor's direction. Moreover, the governor was authorized to act in emergencies by doing whatever was necessary to provide for the public safety—for example, to regulate supplies of fuel and electric power, or to issue orders for air-raid protection. The present civil defense program, as we noted in Chapter 24, places the major responsibility on the states, and in almost all cases, the states have turned the job over to the governor. He is normally advised by a civil defense council which helps him supervise and coordinate civil defense activities of the local governments and to be prepared for emergency action.

A judicial function

The governor in half the states has the *pardoning power,* and in the others he has some share in this onerous duty. Persons who have violated the *state* law look to the governor "to temper justice with mercy." The governor may, except in cases of certain specified crimes such as treason or in cases of impeachment, pardon the offender or commute his sentence by reducing its severity, or grant a reprieve by delaying the punishment. The governor is normally assisted by pardon attorneys or pardon boards who hold hearings and sift the evidence to determine where there are extenuating circumstances. But it is the governor who usually is faced with the responsibility of the decision. Many are the stories of governors maintaining all night vigils in their offices when men are destined to die as punishment for their crimes. The governor as the last earthly judge has an unenviable task.

THE STATE JUDICIARY

The judges of our state courts do most of the judicial business in the United States (see Chapter 20). These are the judges who preside over most criminal trials, settle most disputes between individuals, and administer most of the estates. They are the ones who interpret their state constitutions and apply the state laws. Of course, they are required by the national Constitution to follow the national Constitution, federal laws and treaties, "anything in the constitution or laws of any state to the contrary notwithstanding."

Except for the practicing members of the bar, many people know little about their judges, not even the name of the chief judge of their own supreme court. But these judges—perhaps even more than those of our federal courts—are important policy makers. The legislature passes the law, but the judges interpret it. The state judges who determine the "reasonableness" of legislative classifications decide whether a state regulation of business is "arbitrary," force county officials to comply with the law, rule whether the city council has exceeded its authority, decide whether the governor has the power to remove a local district attorney, and generally have an equal role with the other branches of government in determining who gets what, when, where, and how.

Because of their important position in the political process and their key role in the administration of justice, our understanding of the American process of government is incomplete unless we know how these judges operate, what is their relation to the legislature, the executive, and the interest groups, what procedures they use, how they are chosen, and what groups have the greatest voice in selecting them. Our answers must be very tentative. Only recently have the state courts come in for the serious study of those interested in the judicial processes. In the past, they tended to be obscured by the federal court system or by the other branches of the state government. Moreover, each state has its own unique court system. There is a tremendous variety in their procedures and structural arrangements. It is difficult even to generalize about these matters. But for convenience, we can classify state courts into three groups: minor courts of limited jurisdiction, general trial courts, and appellate courts.

Minor and trial courts

D. W. Brogan, the celebrated English student of American politics, has written of one of his adventures in America:

I had often heard of the "Jeddart justice" doled out by rural magistrates to motorists, of the iniquities of paying magistrates on a commission basis, of the insult to the law and its majesty which these methods involved. My host, whose car was moving rapidly down the great highway to the warm sun and true spring of Central Illinois after the rain, fog, and cold of the shores of Lake Michigan, had written on the subject. He had been the pupil and the collaborator of one of the greatest of American constitutional lawyers. His opinion was worth having. A car was backed off the road and a policeman signalled us in. I innocently assumed that there had been an accident, that we were being asked to take someone to hospital. How wrong I was! We were pinched for speeding. The traffic cop's not very smart uniform bore the words "Special Police." He had cartridges on his belt; they were of different colours and may have been dummies, but he was in complete command of the situation. He demanded the licence which was fortunately available. He gave instructions. "Turn round and stop at the grocery store." "Can I make a U-turn?" asked my host ironically. "Sure." We entered the grocery store, and there was American justice at the receipt of custom.

The magistrate was a bronzed jurist in a shabby shirt. He had one arm and no badge of office. This was not the Old Bailey. The representative of the "Senatus Populusque Illinoisensis" required no fasces, no mace to impress his customers. He duly pointed out that the accused could claim a jury trial, but that if he didn't, and pleaded guilty, the whole thing could be expedited. The policeman's complaint-sheet was produced; a conviction for speeding was duly entered in it; a receipt (a flimsy piece of paper) was issued. Ten dollars fine, $4 costs (which we believed went to the jurist). In two minutes it was all over. After all, there were other customers. My friend had "a record"; for the first time in his life he had been in an American police court.

In a famous opinion Mr. Justice Frankfurter had laid it down that a court of the American system was not to be compared to the court of a Cadi sitting down under a tree. There was no tree, simply a third-rate village store. I recalled Mr. Frankfurter's dictum to my friend. He was not consoled. He thought of various points he might have made. The "esprit d'escalier" worked overtime. He recalled what he had written on this aspect of the American judicial system. I tried to console him by pointing out that he had got down from his ivory tower as the song suggested. He was not amused. He had got out of the ivory tower all right, but as another song puts it, "Baby, it's cold outside." There will be a footnote in the next edition. . . .[4]

Unfortunately, this story is too typical of the way in which justice is administered in our *minor courts*. These minor courts handle summary offenses or misdemeanors and civil suits involving relatively small amounts of money. They are minor only in the sense that they provide accessible forums for the settlement of small suits and for the trial of petty offenses. But it is in these courts that most disputes are settled. A fifty-dollar judg-

[4] D. W. Brogan, "Down from the Ivory Tower," *The Manchester Guardian Weekly,* May 31, 1956.

ment is small potatoes as these things go; but to the parties involved, it is no small matter. Although decisions of these courts can be appealed and tried *de novo*—that is, they are tried all over again without reference to what happened before the minor court—few people bother.

Of course, there is another side to the story. The defendant in the above case was evidently guilty of speeding. A basic canon of justice—the separation of the prosecuting from the judicial functions—was observed. The fine was not out of proportion to the offense. Appeal to a jury was allowed if desired. To be sure, the whole prosecuting and judicial function was informal and undignified, but greater dignity and formality would have meant a more expensive court and probably higher costs for the defendant.

The most general kind of minor court is that presided over by the *justice of the peace*. The J.P., as he is popularly known, is usually elected for a two- or four-year term by the people of each township, but his jurisdiction extends throughout the county. In addition to solemnizing marriages and notarizing papers, he is the man, especially in small towns and rural places, who fines traffic violators, decides who should go to the workhouse for thirty days, and settles disputes between neighbors about who hit whom first. He usually has power to determine who should be "held over" for possible indictment by the grand jury. He sets bail and handles the preliminaries in more serious criminal matters.

The J.P. does not need to be trained in the law, and few of them are. Their lack of legal training has aroused much criticism, but a more glaring weakness of the J.P. system stems from the fact that they are commonly paid out of the fees they collect. Plaintiffs have their choice among several justices of the peace; and in order to get as much business as possible, the J.P.'s have been known to advertise quietly to plaintiffs that they should bring their cases to them to be assured that "justice will be done." Several studies have confirmed the validity of the saying that J.P. stands for "Judgment for the Plaintiff." Even worse, despite the fact that the Supreme Court has condemned the practice, some J.P.'s get their fee in criminal matters only when the defendant is held to be guilty and costs assessed against him. Even where there is no abuse, the fee system leads to distrust and suspicion. Because of dissatisfaction with the justices of the peace, some states have replaced them by magistrates who are paid a standard salary and who are required to have some knowledge of the law.

In cities, there are other minor courts, some of which have more jurisdiction than the justice of the peace and handle more serious matters. Municipal courts are frequently divided into traffic courts, police courts, juvenile and domestic relations courts. A small claims court with informal procedures, including the exclusion of lawyers, is provided by some cities to handle cases for a small set fee.

Trial courts with complete original jurisdiction are variously called county courts, circuit courts, superior courts, district courts, and common pleas courts. They administer equity, criminal, common, and statutory law (see Chapter 20). In some states, there are separate courts, however, for criminal and civil matters. More commonly, there are special probate courts to administer estates and to handle related matters. Although decisions of the general trial courts can be reviewed by appellate courts, in practice the trial court has final say in approximately 90 per cent of cases.

Appellate courts

In most states, appeals from the trial courts are carried to the state supreme court, but about a dozen states have set up intermediate appeals courts that fit into the court structure in much the same way that the United States courts of appeals fit into the federal structure.

The final court of resort is usually called the Supreme Court. (In New York, the Supreme Court is a trial court, and the court of last resort is called the Court of Appeals.) Unless a federal question is involved, the state supreme courts are the highest to which a case can be carried.

The appellate courts vary in size from three to nine in membership, with seven being the most common number. State judges have the power of judicial review and may refuse to enforce state laws on the grounds that they violate the state or national constitution. They may also declare federal laws unconstitutional, although of course their decisions on this are subject to review by the United States Supreme Court. All state judges take an oath to uphold the supremacy of the national Constitution, laws, and treaties, despite anything in their own constitutions or laws.

In contrast to federal judges, ten states allow the supreme court to give *advisory opinions* to the legislature or the governor upon request. These advisory opinions are not binding precedents except in Colorado and are opinions of the judges rather than court decisions.

How should judges be chosen?

Judges are selected in several ways. *Popular election* is used in about three-fourths of the states. In the others—primarily eastern states—the judges are *appointed by the governor* (with the consent of the Senate or executive council) or *elected by the legislature*. Recent years have seen growing dissatisfaction with the method of popular election among the members of the bar. They argue that the voters are not competent to judge legal learning and judicial abilities. Popular election, they assert, puts a premium on a pleasing personality and political popularity, requires judges to enter into the political arena, and discourages many able lawyers from running for the office. Furthermore, they insist, judges are often in effect appointed by party machines despite the elective apparatus.

Some states have turned to the nonpartisan primary as a technique for nominating judges or have held the election of judges on a separate day

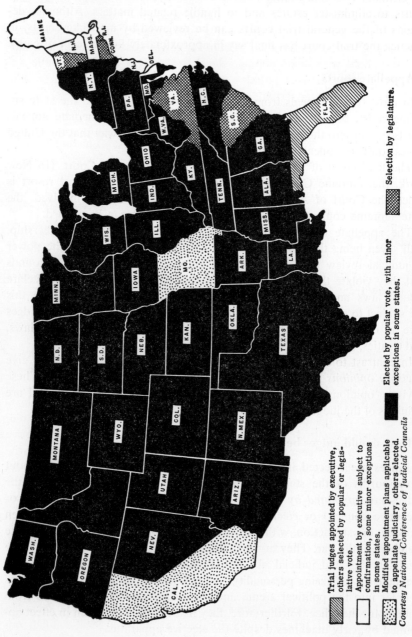

Trial judges appointed by executive, others selected by popular or legislative vote.

Appointment by executive subject to confirmation, some minor exceptions in some states.

Modified appointment plans applicable to appellate judiciary, others elected.

Elected by popular vote, with minor exceptions in some states.

Selection by legislature.

Selection of judges—principal modes.

Courtesy National Conference of Judicial Councils

from the election of other officers. But these devices have not met the issue, argue those who oppose the elective system. The problem is not one of party but of *politics*. Should judges be accountable directly to the people? Should they not be *indirectly* responsible so that they can serve better as a check on popular majorities acting through governor and legislature? The basic question involves the role of judges in a democracy (see Chapter 20). Those who favor popular election of judges believe that the appointive system removes popular control, divorces the judges from the electorate, gives the governor too much power over the judiciary, and requires judges to support those who are in a position to secure their appointment.

Is there any alternative method? California and Missouri have developed ways of selecting judges that many people believe eliminate the defects of popular election but still retain popular control. In Missouri, whenever a vacancy occurs in a court to which the plan applies, a special nominating commission, composed of three lawyers elected by the bar, three laymen appointed by the governor, and the chief justice, nominate three candidates. The governor selects one who serves as a judge for at least one year. The voters at the next general election are asked, "Shall Judge ——— be retained in office?" If a majority of the voters answer yes, the judge gets a full new term; if not, another person is selected by the same procedure. At the expiration of his term, the judge does not have to be renominated and reappointed but merely certifies his wish to have his name placed on the ballot, and the voters are asked whether they desire to retain him in office.[5] The California Plan differs only in that the governor initially nominates the judge, and a commission on qualifications confirms his appointment.

Although the argument concerning the relative merits of appointive and elective judiciary has been raging for over 150 years, there is little clearcut evidence of the desirability of selecting judges by one method rather than another. About all that one can conclude is that courts in *appointive* states seem to have generally, but not always, a higher standing among the members of the bar than those in elective states. In any event, the leaders of lawyers' groups favor the appointive method.

It seems likely that the *length of term,* which varies from two years to life, and with six years the most common, has at least as much to do with the kind of decisions that courts produce as does the method of selecting the judges.

Judicial reform

In 1906, a young lawyer from Nebraska, Roscoe Pound, who later became dean of the Harvard Law School and a renowned legal scholar, ad-

[5] Robert F. Karsch, *Essentials of Missouri Government,* 3rd ed. (Columbia, Missouri, Lucas Bros., 1953), pp. 113-115.

dressed the American Bar Association on "The Causes of Popular Dissatisfaction with the Administration of Justice." The judicial system, he charged, involved

. . waste of judicial power; waste of time and money of litigants and public time and money because of hard and fast jurisdiction lines ill-defined and frequently changed before judicial decision could draw clear bounds; hard and fast statutory terms of court raising unnecessary technical questions and wasting the time of courts; piecemeal handling of what were in reality single controversies by simultaneous proceedings in different courts; and general want of cooperation between court and court and between judge and judge in the same court for want of any real administrative head.[6]

Legal procedures were so complex and the overlap of court jurisdictions so confusing that persons might spend years trying simply to discover which court had jurisdiction to hear their complaint. The judicial structure had been allowed to grow without any attention to the relations among the various parts. Some judges had so much business that litigants often had to wait years to have their cases disposed of. Other judges did not have enough to keep them busy.

Pound's speech touched off a wave of judicial reform. During the last fifty years, bar associations and lay groups have been working to improve our system for the administration of justice. "The concepts of unification, flexibility, conservation of judicial manpower, and responsibility proposed by Pound have set the standards of improvement for an entire generation."[7] The trend is toward the same centralization of judicial structure that has taken place in the executive branch. The guidelines were set down by the Committee on the Administration of the State Judicial System submitted to the 1954 Conference of Chief Justices, which recommended:

1. The office of the Chief Justice . . . of each state should be a permanent one, and the Chief Justice should be responsible for the administration of the state judicial system. He should be empowered to assign and reassign judges . . . , establish an administrative office, require reports from judges on the status of their dockets, be responsible for preparing financial budgets for the courts, and publish reports on the work of the courts.
2. Each state should adopt an act . . . to provide for a court administrator to assist the Chief Justice in carrying out his administrative responsibilities.
3. Provision should be made in each state for the holding of regular meetings of state judicial conferences with membership composed of judges, legislative leaders, law officers, deans of law schools, representatives of state and city bar associations and laymen . . . to discuss judicial administration and procedure.

[6] Roscoe Pound, quoted in, "The Council of State Governments," *The Courts of Last Resort in the Forty-Eight States,* 1950, pp. 1-2.
[7] *Ibid.*

Provision also should be made for a smaller body, a representative judicial council, to study the judicial administration . . . and to assist in formulating and activating programs to improve the state's judicial system.

4. The granting of rule making power to the courts of the state is essential . . . and should be adopted by every state. . . .[8]

These reforms along with adequate compensation, retirement programs, improved clerical and professional assistance, and better trial procedures have all received considerable attention. The unified court system has been strongly pressed by judicial reform groups. Under this system all the major courts would be organized into a single court. All the judges would be members of this court and could be assigned to the various divisions according to the needs of the system. Only New Jersey has a really unified court system, but a vital step toward it has been taken in other states by giving the highest court rule-making and assignment authority.

Judicial councils exist in about three-fourths of the states. These councils, composed of judges, lawyers, and laymen, compile statistics, conduct research, and recommend to the legislature improvements in judicial administration. Some councils, usually those consisting only of judges, have the authority to make rules of procedure and to assign judges to various courts.

Despite a generation of reform, there still remains much room for improvement, and few states have reorganized their judiciary to the same extent that they have improved their administrative structure. Perhaps the desire to achieve "efficiency and economy" is stronger than the desire to "improve the administration of justice."

THE PUBLIC DEFENDER AND THE RIGHT TO COUNSEL

In all states prosecutors have the job of bringing law breakers to justice. But who *defends* persons accused of crime? As we have noted in the case of federal courts, the assistance of counsel is required by the Sixth Amendment. But *state* constitutions do not go that far—more exactly, they have not been interpreted by the state courts to go that far. In most states the accused can have the help of a lawyer if he desires and can afford one, and the trial judge is required to inform the accused that he has such a right.

What of the person who cannot afford to hire a lawyer? The complexities of the law place such a person at a serious disadvantage, so serious that some people believe that they cannot secure a fair trial. The United States Supreme Court has, however, refused to make the assistance of counsel a constitutional necessity in state courts except in cases involving *capital punishment.*[9]

[8] Quoted in "The Council of State Governments," *The Book of the States 1956-1957* (Chicago: The Council of State Governments, 1956), Vol. XI, p. 193.

[9] *Betts* v. *Brady* (1942).

In other cases, as far as the national Constitution is concerned, whether assistance of counsel is required depends upon circumstances. If an ignorant youth is charged with a serious crime, the Fourteenth Amendment would require the state to be sure that an attorney was appointed. But unless there is some such special circumstance, the matter is left up to each state.

In most states it is the practice of the judge to appoint a member of the bar—frequently a young and unexperienced lawyer—to defend persons unable to secure counsel if the case involves possibility of serious punishment. Sometimes the state pays a small fee, often not. Such a system has serious defects. Criminal law is a specialized field, and many lawyers have little knowledge of its operation. Frequently, counsel has no opportunity to consult with the accused. Lawyers are often unable to devote the time to prepare the case or undertake the expense of digging up evidence. Finally, state judges, in contrast to federal practice, seldom appoint counsel except for the trial of important cases. It is, however, during the preliminary proceeding, the fixing of sentence, and the handling of ordinary minor offenders where help of a professionally trained person is most needed.

In order to remedy some of the defects of the assigned-counsel system, voluntary defender committees have been formed in many cities, and the bar has taken an active role in securing private contributions for these agencies. In some cities legal aid bureaus, which furnish advice on civil matters for a small fee, also provide counsel in criminal cases. In about thirty jurisdictions, *public defenders* have been created. Public defenders are paid a set salary out of tax funds, and they have the duty to defend persons unable to afford counsel. The details vary from place to place. In most areas, the public defender is elected in the same manner as the prosecutor and paid the same salary. In other places, he is appointed by the judge. In some jurisdictions, the defender is given the help of several assistants and can furnish aid from the time of arrest through the final appeal, but in other counties or cities he is unable to enter a case until trial and unable to stay with it through final appeal.

Although most observers believe that the defender system is sound, it has been criticized, primarily on the ground that the defender as a public servant cannot serve the interests of the accused with the same diligence and singlemindedness that can be exercised by an assigned attorney. But whatever method is used, our goal of justice for all cannot be reached until all persons have the assistance of counsel.

T HERE ARE ABOUT 115,000 UNITS OF LOCAL GOV-
ernment in the United States (about 100,000 too many, some people feel).
Illinois alone has over 6500. Even Rhode Island, which enjoys fewer than
any other state, has almost ninety. Cities, counties, school districts, townships, water control districts, park districts are crowded together and piled
on top of one another. The average citizen lives under five or six layers of
government. He pays taxes to all of them—federal, state, county, municipal,
and others—and is supposed to select the persons in charge of most of them.

Why do we have such a patchwork of governments? The basic pattern
is an importation from England, like so many of our governmental forms.
As the years passed, new governments were created to take on new jobs.
The existing units were too small or were not up to the job. The present
pattern took shape as a result of compromise and struggle among various
groups with their conflicting interests and values. The system creaks and
groans. It costs a lot of money. It is not particularly efficient. It makes
self-government somewhat difficult.

The several kinds of local governments vary in structure, size, power, and
relations to each other. But, at least in a limited constitutional sense, they
live on power "borrowed" from states. The states of our union are basically
unitary governments (see Chapter 4), and local units of government are
agents of the state—in fact they are the state.

"LITTLE FEDERALISM": STATE-LOCAL RELATIONS

How does the *unitary* nature
of state-local relations contrast
with the *federal* nature of nation-state relations? The slicing
up of governmental power
among the various local units
and the state government leads
to many of the same problems
that we noted in the chapters
on federalism. There is the
same conflict between groups
who want the state to do something and those who fear invasions of local rights. There is
the same difficulty of constantly
adjusting functions among the
various units of government as
economic and social conditions

31 ★

Government

at the

grass roots

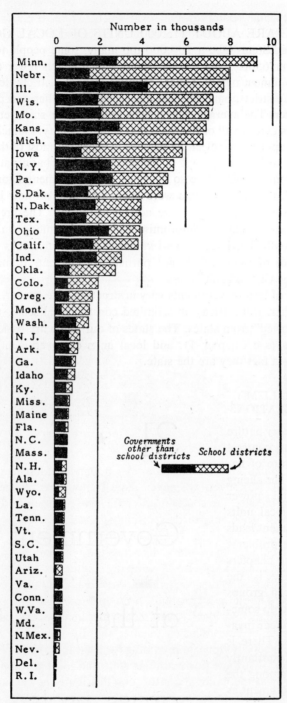

Number of governments by state— 1952.

From Bureau of the Census

alter. There are the same vexing disputes over whether a local majority is to have its way or whether it is to be controlled by a state-wide majority. And just as the assignment of jobs between the national and state governments is determined largely by the relative strength of the conflicting groups, so it is between the state and the local units of government.

Since subdivisional governments, however, are created by the state legislatures and have no inherent powers of local government, fewer constitutional obstacles and weaker pressures operate against state interference in local matters than in the case of national interference in state affairs. State officers par-

NUMBER OF LOCAL GOVERNMENTS IN THE UNITED STATES, BY TYPE: 1942 AND 1952

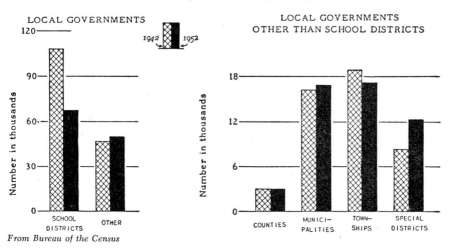

From Bureau of the Census

ticipate in local governments to a much greater extent than federal officers enter into state politics. Moreover, whenever there is doubt as to the authority of local governments, the courts in the past have generally resolved the issue against them. In other words, *powers of local units have been strictly construed.*

But the difference between the unitary state-local and the federal nation-state relations can be exaggerated. As in so many matters of politics, the difference is one of degree rather than kind. Moreover, during the last several decades, the federal principle has been incorporated into some state constitutions authorizing local governments to run their own affairs and limiting the power of state officials to alter the distribution of functions. Thus these state constitutions, in providing for what is known as "constitutional home rule," distribute power among state and local governments in much the same way as the national constitution distributes power among national government and the states.

At the outset of our history, the state legislatures had almost unlimited

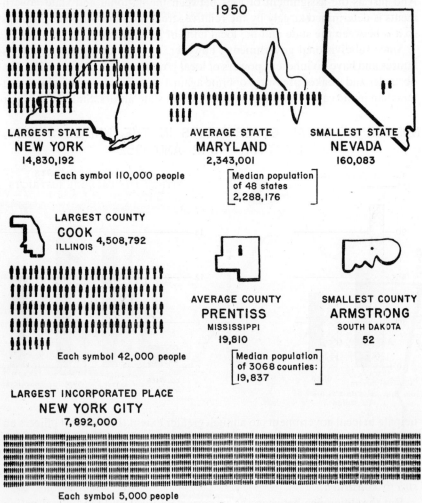

COMPARISON OF POPULATIONS OF LARGEST, AVERAGE, AND SMALLEST STATES, COUNTIES, AND INCORPORATED PLACES

1950

LARGEST STATE
NEW YORK
14,830,192

Each symbol 110,000 people

AVERAGE STATE
MARYLAND
2,343,001

[Median population of 48 states 2,288,176]

SMALLEST STATE
NEVADA
160,083

LARGEST COUNTY
COOK
ILLINOIS 4,508,792

Each symbol 42,000 people

AVERAGE COUNTY
PRENTISS
MISSISSIPPI
19,810

[Median population of 3068 counties: 19,837]

SMALLEST COUNTY
ARMSTRONG
SOUTH DAKOTA
52

LARGEST INCORPORATED PLACE
NEW YORK CITY
7,892,000

Each symbol 5,000 people

SMALLEST INCORPORATED PLACE
DOUGLAS
ARKANSAS
1

Reprinted from William Anderson, THE UNITS OF GOVERNMENT IN THE UNITED STATES *(Chicago: Public Administration Service, 1949), pp. 22, 30*

constitutional authority over local governments and ran them pretty much as they wished. They granted charters to cities, amended and rescinded these charters, established counties, determined city and county structure, set their debt limits, and passed ordinances for them. But by the end of the nineteenth century, the constitutions were often amended to forbid the

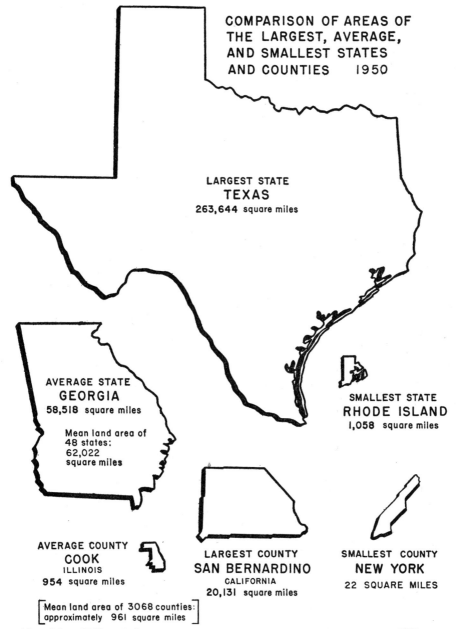

COMPARISON OF AREAS OF
THE LARGEST, AVERAGE,
AND SMALLEST STATES
AND COUNTIES   1950

LARGEST STATE
TEXAS
263,644 square miles

AVERAGE STATE
GEORGIA
58,518 square miles

Mean land area of
48 states:
62,022
square miles

SMALLEST STATE
RHODE ISLAND
1,058 square miles

AVERAGE COUNTY
COOK
ILLINOIS
954 square miles

LARGEST COUNTY
SAN BERNARDINO
CALIFORNIA
20,131 square miles

SMALLEST COUNTY
NEW YORK
22 SQUARE MILES

[Mean land area of 3068 counties:
approximately 961 square miles]

Adapted from William Anderson, THE UNITS OF GOVERNMENT IN THE UNITED STATES *(Chicago:
Public Administration Service, 1949), pp. 22, 30*

legislature to pass laws dealing with particular local governments, and the
structures—in some cases, even the powers—of local governments were
determined by constitutional provisions.

The hedging in of legislative power did not mean, however, the end to state domination of local government. At the same time that the legislature's authority was being curtailed, the power of *state administrative officials* was being expanded. Problems once thought to be local came to be viewed as state-wide. Many local governments lacked the money to do some jobs. They could not afford to hire the specialists. Their administrative standards were notoriously low. In the face of rising social and economic problems, states began to enter new fields. Sometimes the state just took over the job previously handled by local people. In other cases the state offered local governments financial assistance with strings attached. Gradually, state officials were given more and more authority to supervise local officials. This tendency has been especially evident in the fields of law enforcement, finance, health, highways, social security, and police (see Chapter 33).

Professor Dale Pontius has listed types of state supervision ranked on a scale from the slightest degree of control to complete replacement. They are as follows: *Reports:* frequently required, making "the local official aware that other professional people . . . will review his efforts . . . the form of reports often effects a certain standardization of methods. . . ." *Advice and information:* state officials often give advice to local officials in the form of bulletins, conferences, and so on. *Technical aid:* often provided in the form of laboratories and equipment that individual communities cannot provide. *Inspection:* state inspectors often review work of local officials in order to be sure that state statutes are observed or in order to stimulate higher efficiency. *Cooperative administration:* in some fields both state and locality may have jurisdiction, and administration is intermeshed. *Rules and Regulations:* issued by state officials for local administration. *Orders:* issued by state departments when authorized by law. *Grants-in-aid and subsidies:* grants-in-aid are normally given to localities provided they accept certain administrative controls, while subsidies are given unconditionally. *Loans: like grants-in-aid,* often have conditions attached. *Appellate reviews:* frequently state officials can be appealed to in order to review decisions of local officials; tax appeals and license proceedings are examples. *Prior permission:* in some areas, the local officials must have plans approved by state officials before they may act—plans for school buildings, nominations of certain technical officers, for example. *Appointments and removal:* often state civil service systems are made applicable to some local officials such as police and firemen; in some states local officials may be removed by state officers for misconduct. *Assumption of activities— partial or total:* highway construction in some states is an example, so is welfare work.[1]

The amount of local autonomy and degree of state control vary among

[1] Dale Pontius, *Supervision of Local Government: Its Development in Massachusetts* (Washington, D.C.: Public Affairs Press, 1942), pp. 1-9.

the different kinds of subdivisional governments and from state to state. Out of the welter of local governments, two stand out: the *city* for people living in densely populated regions and the *county* (the town in New England) for people living in rural regions.

GOVERNMENT BY THE PEOPLE, COUNTY STYLE

For those who live outside the city, the county and township (in New England the town) are the most important kinds of local government. In most places, counties are not alternatives to city government but merely additional layers. Most city people look to both the city hall and, to a lesser extent, the county court house as the places where community affairs are managed. Where there is no city hall, the county court house has no serious rival as the center of politics.

All states are divided into counties (in Louisiana they are called parishes). A few areas have no organized county government. Twenty-nine Virginia cities exercise county functions, and some cities have taken over county functions (or there is some form of city-county consolidation). Denver, Baltimore, San Francisco, St. Louis are examples. And the five counties of Rhode Island have no powers of local self-government. With these exceptions, county governments exist for all the territory of the United States. The 3000-plus counties vary in size, population, and importance. Some are densely populated, others are inhabited by a few men and lots of desert. Approximately 2400 of them are predominantly rural in nature.

Counties are most important in southern and middle western states and least important in New England. In New England, the county is essentially a judicial district; county officials do a little road building but not much else. Elsewhere the traditional functions of counties are law enforcement, highway construction and maintenance, tax collection and property assessment, recording of legal papers, and welfare. Despite predictions in the past that the counties were dying governments, they have within recent years taken over more jobs than they have lost. Although counties in some states have given up major responsibility for relief or highway construction, they have taken on planning, zoning, licensing of businesses, airport building and operation, ambulance service, health services, and other kinds of new functions.

County government and governors

How are counties organized to do their jobs? Counties, even more than municipalities, exist to enforce state laws and to serve as units for administration of state government. In general, most counties have little legislative power, but the typical county has a group of officials who are in some fashion the governing body. These agencies have a variety of titles—board of commissioners, supervisors of roads, county court, commissioners' court, and so on. They vary in size from one to more than fifty members. They administer state laws, levy taxes, appropriate money, issue bonds, sign contracts in behalf of the county, and handle whatever jobs the state laws and constitution assign to them.

County boards, as we shall call these agencies, are of two types. The larger boards are usually composed of township supervisors or other township officials, the smaller boards of representatives are elected from the county at large. The rural county board is the one "legislative" body in the United States in which the lawyers are outnumbered by the farmers. County fathers are often key political leaders and in some states control local affairs through their power over state patronage. Consequently, they are much more important than a mere enumeration of their formal pow-ers might suggest. Road problems and the granting of contracts to road contractors are frequently the major topics at board meetings.

The county board shares its powers with a number of other officials, most commonly the sheriff, the prosecutor, the county clerk, the coroner, and the auditor. These are generally elected officials. Often, county treas-urers, health officers, surveyors are also found on the ballot. There is sel-dom a single administrative head or chief executive responsible for coor-dinating the activities of the many officials—unless they are all integrated into a unit by a party organization.

What do county officials do?

Sheriff. Except in Rhode Island, where he is appointed by the governor, the sheriff is elected by the people of the county, usually for a two- or four-year term. He is charged with enforcing the law and keeping the county jail and is an officer of the county's court of record. A few sheriffs are active as law enforcement officers, but many let the city police do the job within the cities, and the state police (where existing) bear the burden of rural law enforcement. In some rural places, however, the sheriff and his deputies are the only ones to keep law and order. If the sheriff meets seri-ous trouble, he can summon all able-bodied men to come to his assistance.

Law enforcement is dangerous, and it does not pay very much. Espe-cially in those counties in which the sheriff is paid on a fee basis, he is apt to spend his time on the more profitable jobs of acting as court official and keeping the jail. The sheriff serves legal processes issued by the court, summons jurors, subpoenas witnesses, and sells property to satisfy judg-ments. In many states he receives a fixed sum for the custody and feeding of prisoners. Some sheriffs have been known to make a substantial profit from this operation.

Prosecutor. The prosecuting attorney—also known as county attorney, state's attorney, or district attorney—is commonly elected by voters of the county. He aids the grand jury in preparing indictments, and in some states he may on his own authority bring persons to trial by what is known as "information." He prosecutes state law violators and represents the state and county in civil suits. His discretion is wide, and decision whether or not to prosecute is often made by him alone. The job is especially attractive to young graduates from the law schools, and it often serves as a stepping stone to higher political posts.

Coroner. This is another ancient office found in most counties, generally elected for a short term. His main job is to hold inquests to determine

AVERAGE NUMBER OF GOVERNMENTAL UNITS PER COUNTY, BY STATE, 1952

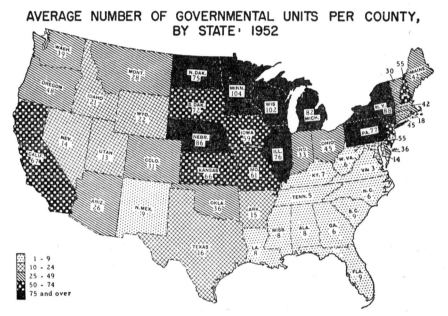

1 - 9
10 - 24
25 - 49
50 - 74
75 and over

From Bureau of the Census

the cause of accidental or suspicious deaths. In many states he selects a jury of about six men to help conduct the inquest. If the coroner or his jury believe that a crime has been committed, they turn their report over to the police and prosecutor. The coroner and his jury may actually name the person they suspect of foul play and issue warrants for his arrest.

The office has been severely criticized. One student of government in rural America, Lane Lancaster, has written: "The office nearly everywhere is held in something approaching contempt. . . . In many counties it goes by default; in many others it ranks simply as a wizened and wormy fruit from the political plum tree, being held by a dreary succession of down-at-the-heel party waterboys. . . . If the coroner is wide-awake . . . he may add to his income by discreet connections with local funeral directors. Indeed it is a lugubrious fact that in a good many counties the office is held by an undertaker who thus is in a strategic position to add to his business."[2] Many authorities favor the substitution of an appointed medical examiner, a qualified physician with training in pathology, to be paid a set salary. The legal aspects of the work, they feel, should be turned over to the prosecutor. This is the system now used in at least five states. Some counties are too small or too poor to support a full-time trained examiner, and it has been suggested that several counties join together to provide for a qualified official.

County Clerk. The clerk is found in about half the states. In other states, the *clerk of the court* often performs his jobs. He is secretary to the county board and has miscellaneous other duties such as supervision of elections, issuance of hunting, fishing, and marriage licenses, and the granting of permits for operation of amusement establishments outside city limits. In some states he is also clerk of the courts of record.

County Treasurer. The treasurer, also elected by the people, receives, keeps, and distributes county funds in accordance with the law. In some counties he collects taxes for the townships and those due the state and then remits the proper shares to these governments. Some counties have abolished the office and transferred functions to other officials or designated banks to assume his task.

County Assessor. The assessor is responsible for locating property and determining its value for tax purposes (see Chapter 34). Frequently, he is assisted by a rather large staff. In most places, the county assessor does the job for city, township, and state tax purposes.

The *"Courthouse Gang."* County governments are not always as headless as it might appear. "It is safe to say," according to Lancaster, "that, in nine-tenths of the counties in the United States, public affairs are in the hands of what the irreverent call the 'courthouse gang.' This 'gang' may be described as a more or less permanent group of elective and appointive officeholders together with private individuals whose business normally brings them into contact with public officials."[3] Here will be found road contractors, printers, purveyors of supplies, lawyers in criminal and probate work, and "ex-officials who have grown old in party service and who have become masters of the lower sorts of intrigue and so habituated to playing politics as to make residence at the county seat a psychological necessity."[4] Lancaster also points out that the county is also an electoral district and that members of the state legislature "are normally graduates of the school of courthouse politics."[5]

Frequently one member of the courthouse gang is recognized as the

[2] Lane W. Lancaster, *Government in Rural America,* 2nd ed. (New York: D. Van Nostrand Company, Inc., 1952), p. 171.

[3] *Ibid.,* p. 57.

[4] *Ibid.,* p. 58.

[5] *Ibid.,* p. 59.

boss. It may be the editor of the local newspaper, the president of the local bank, the chairman of the county farm bureau, the head of the oldest family, or the leader of a local party or party faction. Particular county officials are also recognized as having general, if informal, supervisory powers. Sometimes it is the chairman of the governing body. In Indiana, Ohio, Minnesota, and South Dakota it is often the county auditor, in Illinois the chairman of the board of county commissioners or supervisors, in Missouri the judge of the county court, in Tennessee, Kentucky, and Alabama, the county or probate judge.

County reorganization

How well do the counties do their job? Their rating is not very high. In the first place, there are too many of them. When counties were first organized, the idea was to provide a county seat within a day's journey for any person. The farmer could pile the family into the wagon and head for the courthouse. While he was attending to his business the family could shop and pick up the local gossip. They could all get home in time to do the evening chores.

Today farmers with high-speed automobiles and modern highways can travel through ten or eleven average-sized counties in a single day. The small area and population of many counties often means that they are inefficient units for the performance of their functions. Study after study has shown that money could be saved and services improved by *consolidating* counties. Some state constitutions have been amended to permit such consolidations, but in the last fifty years only two Tennessee and three Georgia counties have united.

County residents take pride in their county and do not like to see it lose its identity. Office-holders, their families, and their friends do not want the jobs to disappear. Businessmen at the county seat depend upon these officers, employees, and persons drawn to the city by county business for much of their patronage. In view of the practical obstacles to county consolidation, Professor C. F. Snider has concluded, "Those interested in the improvement of county government would . . . seem well advised to waste little time or effort in the support of consolidation but to concentrate on more practicable means, such as internal reorganization and the consolidation of functions."[6]

Internal reorganization and consolidation of functions have already demonstrated both their value and their practicality. Counties have joined together to provide health officers, to share equipment, to purchase materials, and for numerous other purposes. There is still great opportunity

[6] C. F. Snider, "American County Government: a Mid-Century Review," *American Political Science Review,* Vol. XLVI, No. 1, March 1952, p. 68.

for better services through greater cooperation and consolidation of functions.

What progress has been made in reorganizing county structure? Just a little. The headless character of county administration has long been lamented. The same arguments that are used to support integration of national and state administration have been put forth to support county reorganization. Counties are even worse off than the states. At least, each state has a governor who in some fashion or other is the chief executive.

A few counties have made formal attempts to provide executive leadership. This is especially true in the urban or suburban counties such as Nassau and Westchester in New York, Cook County in Illinois, and others where an elected executive has been given general supervisory powers. About twenty counties have some kind of county-manager plan in effect. But among the rural counties the traditional pattern still dominates.

For the most part, county governments still lack merit systems or modern fiscal and purchasing methods, and auditing practices often leave much to be desired. Even an obvious money-saving program such as centralized purchasing has not been widely adopted. But progress is being made, slow as it is.

Townships

North of the Ohio River, from the Dakotas and Kansas eastward, and outside of New England, the general practice is to subdivide the county into *townships*. The township is gradually losing many of its functions either to the counties or to the cities.[7] Oklahoma, after whittling township functions to almost nothing, recently abolished them altogether. In Iowa, townships still exist formally, but they have lost so many of their functions that the Census Bureau has stopped counting them! Where they exist, townships often handle outdoor relief, build and maintain roads, and sometimes serve as districts for school purposes. In some states, all the voters of the townships are entitled to attend an annual meeting to elect officers and to levy taxes and make appropriations. These town meetings are usually poorly attended.

A board of supervisors, justice of the peace, and a constable are the typical township officials, all elected. The constable is to the township and the justice of the peace what the sheriff is to the county and the county courts of record. Since constables make their fees from court work, they do little law enforcement except for catching traffic violators.

The middle western and middle Atlantic townships are often confused with the New England towns. But they are essentially different breeds of government.

[7] James W. Drury, "Townships Lose Ground," *National Municipal Review,* Vol. XLIV, No. 1, January 1955, pp. 10-13.

THE NEW ENGLAND TOWN—DIRECT DEMOCRACY

The town is the principal kind of rural government in New England. It is sometimes difficult for "outsiders" to understand that a New England town is an area of government that includes whatever villages there may be, plus the open country. Except where a municipality has been incorporated, the town does most of the things that a county does elsewhere.

Each town holds an annual meeting open to all voters. In the United States, this town meeting is the outstanding example of a *direct democracy* where all the voters participate directly in making the rules, passing new laws, levying taxes, and appropriating money. Before each meeting the selectmen issue a warrant designating the time and place of the meeting and setting forth the agenda. At the appointed time, a moderator is chosen to preside. The items on the agenda are then taken up and the floor is open to any citizen who wishes to have his say. Before or during the meeting, the polls are open for the voters to choose the town officers.

The meeting may select a board of selectmen, usually three or five members. Between meetings they carry on the business of the town, have charge of town property, grant licenses, supervise other town officials, and call special town meetings. A town clerk, treasurer, assessor, overseer of the poor, constable, school board, and numerous other persons are elected by the voters or appointed by the selectmen. The town meeting often elects a finance committee to prepare the town budget.

The New England town meeting has long been celebrated. The picture of the sturdy and independent citizens coming together to talk over public affairs and speak their minds is a stirring one. The New England town has often been pointed to as the one place in the United States where no political bosses exist. In fact, however, a recognized group of town leaders often provide leadership. Politics is inevitable—even at town meeting. This is not to disparage the New England town but to recognize that under conditions of freedom and diversity, groups will be formed and leaders emerge.

Over a hundred towns, especially the more populous ones, have created the position of *town manager*. Like the city manager (see page 828), he is the one who appoints the principal administrative officials and is responsible to the voters through the selectmen. In spite of such innovations, the traditional New England town government still flourishes. Some larger towns have adopted a limited town meeting. Under this system, the town is divided into precincts, the voters in each precinct elect a number of delegates, and the delegates in turn form the town meeting. Any voter can speak at the town meeting, but only the delegates can vote. In some larger towns, city governments would appear to be more appropriate, but the people still cling to their traditional town government.

Mention the word "city." What does it call to mind? Bright lights, crowded streets, museums, slums, skyscrapers, and lots of people. Or to some of us, the city may be Main Street, Courthouse Square, the old cannon, and farm families shopping and talking on Saturday night. For a city is not merely improved real estate. It is also people, a live exciting conglomerate of men and women living and working together.

This exciting thing, the city, is made to sound like a dull bit of lawyers' talk by our state statutes. For in law a city is a *municipal corporation;* there are over 16,500 of them in the United States. Some have millions of people, others a couple of hundred people. Sometimes the smaller ones are called villages, boroughs, or towns. And not all densely populated places are governed as a municipality. But the city is the major kind of local government for the urban dweller.

Each city has two major functions. One, to provide government by the people within its boundaries in order that the citizenry may maintain law and order, keep their streets clean, educate their children, dispose of their garbage, purify their water, create parks, and in other ways by community action make their city a good place in which to live. But the city has a second function—it is an instrumentality of the *state* to carry out *state* functions. It is distinguished from a county, a quasi-corporation, in the greater amount of discretion given to the local officials and by the greater emphasis upon their local functions. A county, on the other hand, is supposed to operate primarily as an administrative unit of the state. The distinction is of course one of emphasis.

★ 32

Our

fair

cities

Each city has its own charter. This may not be a single document; in some states one has to read through the state statutes to discover the organization, powers, and functions of cities. The charter is to the city what a constitution is to the national or state government. It outlines the structure of government, determines the authority of the various officials, provides for their selection, and includes such other matters as are considered desirable. Where do the charters come from? Who draws them up?

In about ten states the legislature writes a *special* charter for each city and may amend the charter as it wishes, although in a few of these states the charter must be submitted to the local voters for their approval. In practice, local groups often draft the charter in consultation with their legislative representatives, and other members of the legislature usually defer to the legislative delegation from the city. Since the representatives need local support to get elected, in practice the groups that dominate local politics also write their own charters, even though the state legislature has the constitutional authority. Sometimes there is a major battle when the legislature is controlled by groups hostile to those in control of the city.

In most states, however, the constitution requires the legislature to classify cities and provide charters for cities by classes. If the legislature makes refined enough classifications, it can, in effect, write special charters. And in many states the constitution specifically permits special legislation for the largest city. Many legislatures list several kinds of charters and permit the local citizenry to choose the particular kind they wish. This is known as the *optional charter plan.*

Home rule

In most states the legislatures still exercise a great deal of control over city affairs. In addition to drawing up charters for the cities, the legislature allots functions to local officials and withdraws them at will. In case of conflict between a state law and a local ordinance, the *state* law is enforced. In some states, every time a city wants to put a stop light on the corner of Broadway and High, the city fathers have to get the permission of either the legislature or the appropriate state officials.

In about one-half of the states, however, the constitutions give to citizens of certain sized cities authority that they may exercise regardless of the wishes of the state legislature. A few of these other states extend this power to all municipalities. These are the *home rule* states. Where the constitution so permits, the people of the city may elect a group of citizens who draw up a charter. After the charter has been approved by local voters (in some states it must also be approved either by the legislature or the governor, or both, to insure no conflict with the constitution), it becomes the city's basic instrument of government and may be amended by local citizens. Furthermore, home rule cities have the general power to dispose of matters of local concern without special authorization from the legislature.

Constitutional home rule thus introduces the *federal* principle. But who is to decide in case of a conflict whether a given measure is within the authority of the city? Is a health regulation, for example, a matter of local or statewide concern? To avoid conflict, some constitutions, besides giving

JUDICIAL WHITTLING OF HOME RULE IN OHIO

These court decisions have undermined home rule in Ohio:

1913 City cannot obtain home rule powers by amending its old charter—it is forced to adopt an entire new one.

1916 City cannot prohibit showing of a motion picture which was passed by the state censor.

1921 City is required to pay expenses of health districts the state creates.

1924 City cannot require a building permit for a school.

1925 City cannot license automobiles owned by its residents.

1929 City is required to pay expenses of courts the state creates for it.

1931 City cannot require a license to operate a gas station.

1941 City cannot prescribe qualifications for its policemen.

1944 City cannot provide for earlier closing of taverns than is permitted by State Board of Liquor Control.

1946 City cannot levy a tax on utility bills.

1947 City cannot provide for a check-off of union dues.

Source: Rodney L. Mott, *Home Rule for America's Cities* (Chicago: American Municipal Association, 1949), p. 29.

cities general grants of power, also specify certain subjects as being within the province of local officials. But no listing avoids all the disputes. And it is the *state* judges who umpire the system in much the same manner as Supreme Court justices umpire the larger federal system.

In addition to constitutional home rule, some state legislatures on their own responsibility have permitted certain cities to draw up their own charters and have delegated to these cities general authority over local matters. This kind of home rule differs from that established by the constitution because the legislature is supreme in all fields, and any state law that comes into conflict with a local ordinance supersedes it. And the legislature may withdraw power at will.

Although constitutional home rule introduces an element of rigidity into state-local relations and enhances the authority of judges, most observers favor its adoption. It frees the legislature from the necessity of dealing with local matters. More important, it gives the people of a particular locality more opportunity to decide for themselves how they wish to be governed.

Regardless of who draws up the charter, Americans have shown a much greater tendency to experiment with the forms of their city governments than with those of any other kind. The 16,500 cities in the United States seem to have 16,500 different kinds of government. Generalizations are hazardous,

HOME RULE POWERS IN TEXAS

Texas cities enjoy a wide range of home rule powers, among which are the following:

Require a street railway to pave its right of way.

Prohibit the operation of slaughter houses in the city.

Prescribe district within which liquor may be sold.

Establish a Board of City Development.

License taxicabs.

Annex additional territory by charter amendment without consent of inhabitants of area annexed.

Establish a public market.

Fix rates charged by utilities.

Monopolize the gathering of garbage.

Regulate pawnbrokers.

Limit the weight of trucks operating on the streets.

Increase the liability of property owners for paving in front of their property above the liability prescribed by statutes.

Source: Mott, *Home Rule for America's Cities*, p. 39.

but city *charters* can be classified into three general groups: mayor-council, commission, and council-manager.

The mayor-council charter

The mayor-council charter is the oldest and still the most popular charter. It predominates in the very smallest and in the very largest cities. The council is usually a single chamber, although the bicameral form still lingers on in a few cities. The size varies—some are as small as two and some as large as fifty. Seven is the median in cities over 5000. Many methods are used to select the councilmen—nonpartisan elections, by wards, from the city at large, proportional representation, and so on. In most cities the council members receive little or no salary, but in some large cities they are paid substantial sums and are expected to devote a good deal of time to city business. The council passes city ordinances, approves the budget, and supervises the administration of city affairs. Meetings are often informal, and citizens are allowed to speak and present their petitions in person. As in the state and national legislatures, the committee system prevails.

The powers of the mayor vary from charter to charter (and even more widely from city to city and mayor to mayor). The mayor is elected by the people, but in some cases the charter assigns little more than ceremonial powers to him. He welcomes "visiting firemen" and gives them the key to the city. In some cities his appointive power is limited, and he shares administrative authority with other elected officials and numerous boards and commissions. This is known as the *weak mayor-council* system.

Tracing the office of mayor through various charters, one finds the familiar trend in the direction of increasing the authority of executive officials. Like the presidency and the governorship, the office of mayor over the

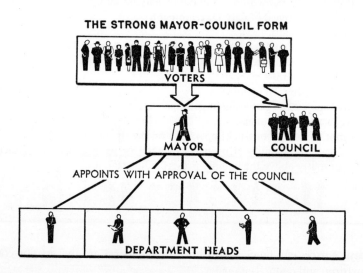

THE STRONG MAYOR-COUNCIL FORM

VOTERS

MAYOR   COUNCIL

APPOINTS WITH APPROVAL OF THE COUNCIL

DEPARTMENT HEADS

years has grown in importance. Many cities have altered their charters in order to give him the power to appoint and remove heads of departments and investigate their activities, to send messages to the city council, to prepare the budget, and to veto council ordinances. In other words, he has been given a share in policy making, and city administration has been centralized under his direction. A recent development is the creation of a chief administrative officer, appointed by the mayor to assist him in directing city administration.

Is the *strong mayor-council* the best charter for the large cities? Many people believe so. This charter, they argue, gives the city a strong political leader, makes efficient administration possible, and by centering authority in the hands of a few individuals makes less likely the growth of "invisible government" by men who have power but who are not publicly accountable for its use.

The commission charter

In the year 1900, the stock of the Galveston city fathers was low. Then the city was inundated by a tidal wave. Over 6000 people lost their lives, and public and private property worth millions was destroyed. The mayor and the twelve aldermen floundered. In the emergency, power began to fall into the hands of a group of businessmen who had been discussing methods of improving the harbor. They decided to act. After studying the charters of several cities, they went to the legislature with what was then almost a novel proposal for a new charter. They asked that control of the city be vested in five commissioners. The legislature approved.

THE COMMISSION FORM

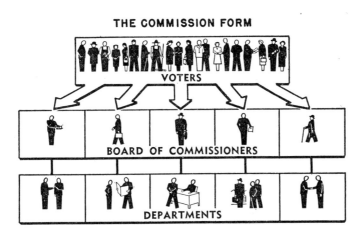

About five years later, the attorney for the city of Des Moines, Iowa, took a business trip to Galveston. He was so impressed with the commission government that he returned to Iowa with the proposal that the Iowa legislature let cities adopt commission charters.

The placing of all governmental powers in the hands of five men flew in the face of the traditional doctrines of separation of powers. Many felt that it was too dangerous to give a small group of men control over both administration and legislation. For this reason the Des Moines plan, as it was known, included the initiative, referendum, recall, and nonpartisan ballots for primaries and elections in addition to the ideas of the Galveston businessmen. The plan became very popular, and by 1917 over 500 cities were so governed. Since that time the number has declined, although Jersey City, St. Paul, Memphis, and a few other cities, still have this kind of charter.

The commissioners, usually five, are collectively the city council; individually they are the heads of the departments of city administration. Most commissioners devote full time to their jobs and actively administer the affairs of their particular department. One of the commissioners is designated as mayor, but he normally has little more power than the other commissioners.

The commission charter was widely heralded as the introduction of safe and sane business methods to city affairs. But after a brief wave of popularity, the new idea lost some of its glamor. The party bosses were suspicious, and the city reformers were disappointed. Although providing for more integrated control than the old mayor-council system, the city was still left without a single responsible administrative head. In fact, a commission city has five mayors. Moreover, commissioners chosen because they represent major groups within the city often leave something to be desired as administrators of departments of public welfare, public safety, and so on. By 1917, reformers had discovered a new kind of charter which they believed had greater merit.

Council-manager charter

The city manager plan was warmly acclaimed by James Bryce as "the latest word in municipal reform." Certainly it is one of our most significant innovations in governmental form. In 1908 the little city of Staunton, Virginia, appointed a general manager to direct the city's work. Little note was taken of this step, but Richard Childs, an advertising man active in the short-ballot movement, became very much interested.

Childs was enthusiastic about the commission plan because it applied two basic ideas, *unification of power* and a *short ballot,* to city affairs. But it did not go far enough. Add to this a chief administrative officer, he reasoned, and the results should be even better. So, as he said, he became "the minister who performed the ceremony that united" the commission plan with the idea of a general manager.

The city manager plan was adopted by a few small cities but it did not receive much publicity. Then in 1913, Dayton, Ohio, had a flood. (City charters owe much to tidal waves and floods.) The flood came in the midst of a campaign to select members for a charter commission. The existing city officials, like their predecessors in Galveston, demonstrated their inability to meet the emergency. The disaster added to the strength of those who were advocating the city manager charter. These reformers argued that the city is a corporation and should be run like any other corporation. The voters, as "stockholders," should elect a board of directors, and these directors should select a professional administrator. This is the essence of the council-manager plan, and its adoption by Dayton attracted national attention.

Today the council-manager charter is used in 42 states and by more than 1400 cities. Each year new municipalities adopt the council-manager plan. Although it does not exist in any of the largest cities, over half the cities in the 50,000 to 100,000 class have adopted it.

Under the council-manager charter, the council is usually elected in nonpartisan primaries and elections, either on a citywide basis or by election districts much larger than the wards used in mayor-council cities. The size of the councils varies, but they run smaller than those in cities with mayor-council charters. The council appoints a city manager, supervises his activities, and fires him when he is unsatisfactory. It makes the laws, approves the budget, and—although it is not supposed to interfere in administration—it does supervise operation of city government through the manager. A mayor is usually provided for the purpose of presiding over the council and representing the city on ceremonial occasions.

The city manager advises the council on policy and supervises the administration of city business. The council-manager charter permits selection of the best available person; for this reason, most charters do not require the council to appoint a local citizen, nor do the charters prescribe detailed qualifications. Twenty universities now have special courses for the training of city managers. The International City Manager's Association has its own code of ethics and works to develop higher standards among its members. City managers receive substantial salaries; and as more and more cities adopt this form of government, the opportunities for promotion and advancement continue to increase.

How has the city manager charter worked out? Although some skeptics remain, the idea has now won the approval of most students of city government. Cities that adopted this kind of charter have generally enjoyed an improvement in standards of public employment, reduction in unit costs, better services, and the cities have become institutions "with a broader and more vital function in the community."[1]

Adoption of a city manager charter usually reflects an awakened interest among civic groups. No doubt this awakened interest and its organization into effective political power accounts in part for the general improvement in government. Forms of government, of course, are merely patterns for organizing the activities of human beings. A lot depends on who those human beings are.

COUNCIL ELECTIONS

Many who have successfully urged adoption of the council-manager form have much less successfully backed proportional representation. Most councilmen are selected to represent a district of the city, commonly called "wards." This system of single-member districts has been sharply criticized for not giving enough representation to minority groups. Under the workings of this arrangement, a substantial minority may lose out in district after district because it cannot garner quite enough votes. A minority group or party might poll 40 per cent of the total popular vote, but if the vote were distributed uniformly throughout the city, that group or party might not win any seats at all.

[1] Harold A. Stone, Don K. Price, and Kathy H. Stone, *City Manager Government in the United States* (Chicago: Public Administration Service, 1940), p. 260.

Proportional representation

The first step in establishing "PR" is to abolish single-member districts and form large new districts, each of which elects several representatives. In smaller cities, no subdivisions of the city would be needed at all. The mechanics of PR are more complex than the basic idea. The single transferable vote or Hare system has been advocated for local elections and is often used by private groups. From a list of perhaps a dozen candidates (assuming, say, five persons to be elected) each voter chooses five candidates, listing them in order of his preference. As soon as any candidate receives a quota of votes (established by dividing the number of votes cast by the number of persons to be elected plus one and adding one to the result), he is elected, and his excess votes are transferred to the candidates given second place on his ballots. The process is repeated until the weakest candidates are eliminated and the highest five are elected.

Whatever the type of PR—over 200 different schemes have been contrived—the result is the same: to give more representation to minorities than they can secure under the single-member, single vote system. PR also overcomes gerrymandering and eliminates the need of primaries. Those who favor PR feel that since any community is made up of minorities, PR is best suited to select a council that will accurately reflect the strength and views of the people of the city.

Opponents of PR, on the other hand, argue that perfect representation is not the major goal. They insist that PR splinters the local party system into a host of minority groups who are likely to be dogmatic advocates for their own group of voters pursuing narrow goals. Instead of trying to work out moderate, workable programs, they pursue balance-of-power tactics. PR, in short, weakens government, divides the people, and postpones the process of compromise until after elections, hence making it difficult to pin responsibility on any group.

PR has been adopted in a few small cities. It was tried for a while in New York City and then abandoned, partly because of the confusion it caused, partly because the mathematics worked out so exactly that the small Communist minority in the city was able to elect a Communist to the Council. The dominant party in the city also can be expected to oppose PR because without it they can win most election districts.

Nonpartisan elections

Although PR has not been widely adopted, a large number of cities have moved to nonpartisan elections for the selection of city officials. Under this system there is a nonpartisan primary in which the voters narrow down the choice to two men who are running without party designation for a particular office. Then in a final election the voters select their representatives, again on a ballot carrying no party labels. Defenders of nonpartisan elections argue that the issues of city governments are different from those of national and state politics and that party labels tend to direct the voter's attention away from the candidates' merits and local issues. Opponents of the nonpartisan system respond that political parties are an indispensable instrument for the operation of free government and that to deprive them of an active role in city affairs undercuts the parties and weakens them as organizations for state and national affairs. Moreover, they argue, the same reasons that make party government desirable at national level make it desirable at local level.

This much seems clear: merely to take the candidate's party designation off an election ballot does not make elections nonpartisan. In Boston, for example, the adoption of nonpartisan ballots had little impact upon the role of the Democratic party, and few did not know that James Michael Curley, long mayor of that city, was an active Democrat.

CAMBRIDGE ADOPTS A NEW CHARTER: A CASE STUDY

City charters and other forms of city government are only a part of the story. As we saw in earlier chapters, the ways in which people behave and respond to one another do not always correspond with legal institutions. In some cities, the charter gives the mayor only small amounts of power; but in reality the mayor, backed by powerful political groups, runs the city. In some cities the manager is strong and the council is weak; in others the councilmen run things and the manager serves as their handyman. Some city managers are active in local affairs, have larger popular followings, and a great deal of political influence. In short, a city charter is but a starting place for investigation; by itself it tells us little about the form of city government.

The story of how one city adopted a new charter, and of its early experiences under it, may suggest some of the political dynamics that operate at the local level.

Trouble in Cambridge[2]

In 1936 the city of Cambridge, Massachusetts, was in difficulties. The tax rate was high, the city was deep in debt, and city administration was poor. The city was controlled by a Democratic organization that governed without inspiration through a charter providing for a weak mayor and a fifteen-man council. The worst aspect of the situation was that seemingly not much could be done about it. Only a few of the 100,000 citizens of the city seemed actively dissatisfied with things.

---

[2] This section is drawn from F. C. Libretto, "The Cambridge City Manager," *Public Administration and Policy Development*, ed. Harold Stein (New York: Harcourt, Brace and Company, 1952), pp. 573-619.

Moreover, the people of Cambridge are of diverse backgrounds. The Irish, the largest ethnic group, live side by side with Yankees, French Canadians, Italians, and other national-origin groups. Although known for its great universities, Cambridge also is an industrial area, part of the Greater Metropolitan Boston region. The older residents of Yankee stock have been standoffish toward immigrant and minority groups, and there are wide extremes in wealth, housing conditions, and education. The strength of the Democratic organization was built on the grievances of the less privileged elements and on their resentment against the "aristocrats" and Yankees.

Any real improvement seemed a distant hope. Nevertheless, there was some open dissatisfaction, and soon a group of citizens was meeting to see whether something could be done. They became particularly interested in the city-manager idea. Under Massachusetts laws at this time, cities could choose from among four types of optional charters, but these laws did not provide for the city-manager type of charter. The Cambridge reformers, however, were able to induce the Massachusetts legislature to provide for a fifth charter—the city manager form—called "Plan E."

As soon as the legislature acted, officers of the Cambridge Taxpayers Association decided to call a meeting of other people known to be dissatisfied with existing civic affairs. To this meeting came representatives of the Taxpayers Association, the Chamber of Commerce, and the League of Women Voters. After much discussion, the group decided to go ahead and make an attempt in the coming 1938 election to secure adoption of the Plan E Charter in Cambridge.

What should be the strategy? Obviously the group had to be made more representative in character. It would not do to have only Republicans, businessmen, and Yankees behind the new charter. So a Plan E Committee was created. Who should be chairman? The name of Dean James M. Landis of the Harvard Law School was suggested. "He is too liberal," said some; "he is a New Dealer." "His Harvard connection," said others, "will play into the hands of the opposition, who will insist that this is merely an attempt on the part of the Harvard aristocrats to take control of the city." But after long discussion it was decided that Dean Landis's great prestige and Democratic party affiliations would outweigh any liabilities that he might bring to the chairmanship. At least it would take the sting out of the charge that Plan E was a device inspired by wealthy Republican businessmen.

Dean Landis was a vigorous leader. He saw to it that the other positions of leadership were filled by persons of all religious, political, and ethnic affiliations. With the active help of the League of Women Voters, the necessary signatures for the referendum petition were filed with the city council.

Political rough-and-tumble

Under the law, the city council was to forward the petition to the Secretary of State by a certain day. As the deadline approached, the city council refused to act. The deadline was Saturday. A big football game was sched-

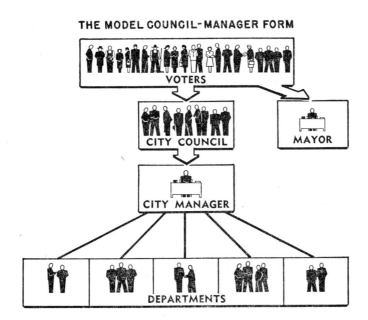

THE MODEL COUNCIL-MANAGER FORM

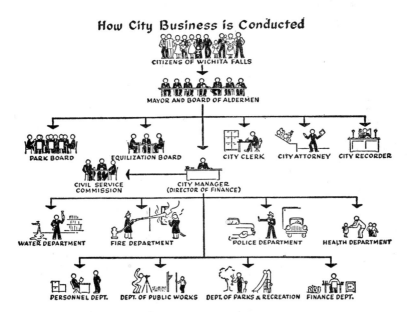

How City Business is Conducted

uled for that afternoon, and the members of the city council were on their way to the game to occupy the special seats reserved for them by Harvard. Unless they met on the resolution that day, it would be too late. At the last minute, the Plan E group found a judge of the Superior Court who was willing to act. He issued a mandamus to compel the council to meet and take the necessary action. As the council members filed into their stadium seats expecting to forget the problems created by the reformers and to enjoy an afternoon of football, they had a rude shock. By each of their seats stood a court deputy with a warrant from the judge requiring the council to meet immediately and transmit the petitions to the Secretary of State as the law required them to do.

The campaign for city manager then began in earnest, and the going became rough. The opponents charged that the council-manager form of government was dictatorial and communistic. Moreover, they said, it was

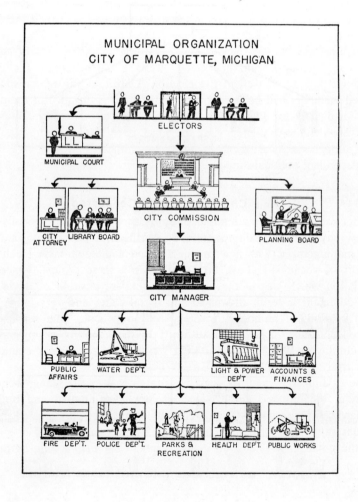

a plot to place control of the city in the hands of the "Harvard-Brattle Street-Money-Taxpayer-Republican forces." The result of the election was defeat for Plan E, but by a narrow margin.

Despite their narrow victory, those who continued to run city affairs were not chastised. They took little action to improve things. In fact, their ineptitude brought them to further public attention by the failure of the mayor and council to comply with the law in preparing the city budget. The financial plight became desperate. And then the District Attorney began to investigate city services.

The reform groups returned to battle. In the 1940 elections, Plan E was again before the voters. And this time the Plan carried. But the battle was not over. Everything depended now on the election of the new council members under the system of proportional representation that was part of Plan E. The new city council would choose the manager and execute the new charter. If the anti-city manager forces controlled the city council, there was little chance that the new form of government would be any improvement over the old.

Despite the fact that the old mayor was convicted of bribery and that stories of corruption and inefficiency were in the headlines, the Plan E group did not do so well in the election. Only four out of the nine new council members had been endorsed by the Plan E group. But the opposition, fortunately for Plan E, was split. Of the five other councilmen, only two were definitely aligned with the local party organization. The other three, though skeptical of city-manager government, had their own sources of independent political support.

A city manager takes over

After sorting through a number of applications, the council finally chose as new city manager Colonel John B. Atkinson, a prominent Cambridge shoe manufacturer. The new manager faced a difficult task. He had the support of vocal and active civic groups, but these groups "represented population which was in the unenviable political position of having long been dominant in terms of wealth and social status and very much dominated in terms of numbers of voters."[3] Many people were suspicious of the concentration of so much authority in the hands of a single person. City employees were fearful for their positions. And the city council was not friendly.

The city manager went to work. He straightened out the tangled financial situation, rehabilitated and cleaned up public equipment and buildings, standardized pay schedules, and generally improved operations of the city. Popular support for the new government began to increase. The manager and the council tangled over many issues. They had a long battle over

[3] *Ibid.*, p. 590.

pay for firemen and policemen. The city manager went to the courts, and found that the judges were on his side. Opponents of the city manager plan went to the legislature in an effort to cripple Plan E by legislative amendment.

The reformers who had introduced Plan E came to realize that they would need a permanent political organization. In 1945 they formed the Cambridge Civic Association and an affiliated Research Association. At first, the board of directors was composed of upper-class Republicans. Again the opposition charged that these people were interested only in keeping their own taxes down and in depriving the people of the "lower wards" of needed services. Finally, the Cambridge Civic Association broadened its directorship. The program was changed from the essentially negative emphasis upon economy to a positive program of civic betterment. In the ensuing years, the battle has continued. City manager government still has to fight for its existence in Cambridge.

METROPOLITAN GOVERNMENT AND ITS PROBLEMS

There are many "Philadelphians"—that is, people who work in Philadelphia, shop in Philadelphia, sell goods in Philadelphia, hire men in Philadelphia, read Philadelphia newspapers—who do not *live* in Philadelphia. Only about half the "St. Louisians" live in St. Louis, and so it is with most of the larger American cities. The large cities and their environs suffer from the disease of "suburbanitis." The commuter who lives in Sunnyside or Kirkwood or Westchester but who earns his living in the central city is well known in fact and fiction. Surrounding the central city are a host of smaller "bedroom" communities, places where people live but do not work.

This is the natural history of a city: As population increases and the means of rapid transportation improve, people who can afford to do so leave the crowded and dirty business areas and move out into more desirable living quarters. They go in search for cheaper land, lower taxes, more room, better air, a larger share in community life. New shopping centers develop in these communities. Interesting political trends develop. In many places the population pushes out into the country where there is no form of city government whatsoever. Industries move across city boundaries for cheaper land, lower taxes, and to escape more stringent regulations of the city building and health codes. The "core" city's expenses remain high, but its revenue shrinks. As noted above, most of the nation's population now lives in a metropolitan area, and about one-fourth of the people now live in suburbs, the most rapidly growing areas in the country. Between 1950 and 1955 over 97 per cent of the total population increase occurred in the 168 standard metropolitan areas listed in the 1950 census.

"Suburbanitis"

The people of a metropolitan region form one natural and interdependent unit. Yet they may have forty to fifty separate city governments. When the other kinds of government are added, the figure becomes startling. Cook County, Illinois—metropolitan Chicago—contains over 400 independent tax-collecting agencies. The New York metropolis covers 17 counties, 3 major cities, a population of 13 million—and at least 1000 separate governments. Detroit covers 3 counties, part of another, 59 townships, 37 cities, and 29 villages.[4]

Each suburban city has its own city government, its own fire and police department, its own school system, its own library, street removal equipment, its own building code, its own health code, and all the other apparatus of city government. What are the results? Consider police protection. In the Chicago area, some 300 different agencies have police powers. The central city usually maintains an elaborate police department with detective bureaus, crime-detection laboratories, and an involved communications network. But its jurisdiction stops at the city line. Suburban police are fewer, often untrained in combating criminals. Some suburban police forces are well run, others are lax and offer protection to the mobsters. Or take water supply. The costs are greatly increased when each city maintains its own reservoirs, plants, pumping stations. In matters of health, there is often a wide difference in the health standards of the various cities. And the people living outside the limits of any city often dump their raw sewage into water courses that supply the people of the city with their water. The same problem is encountered in fire protection. The people of a wealthy suburb may have the finest equipment to protect their homes and businesses, but the equipment is idle much of the time because it is used only in the suburbs. At the same time, those in less wealthy cities often have inadequate equipment. Such arrangements are clearly inefficient and wasteful.

The well-to-do suburbanite, however, is often not convinced by such arguments. He knows that his taxes are lower, his schools are better, his surroundings healthier, and his control over his officials greater than those of the people in the central city. Professor Charles R. Cherington describes the situation as it pertains to Greater Boston:

"He who moves from Boston to Concord or Acton, or to Weston or Needham, leaves a considerable part of his municipal burdens behind him. He leaves tremendous problems of public health and public welfare back in the central urban core, or back in the industrial soot of Cambridge or Somerville or Chelsea. He leaves Boston to solve its own street problem while he drives to work on a state supported, federally aided highway, or

[4] Lyle C. Fitch, "Fiscal and Political Problems of Increasing Urbanization," *Political Science Quarterly,* Vol. LXXI, No. 1, March 1956, p. 75.

he may park his car at the end of the rapid transit line and ride into State Street on the Metropolitan Transit Authority's deficit. He knows that his suburban government is cheaper and in terms of his own mythology it is 'better.' He draws a State Street salary but pays a farmer's taxes. We can scarcely find a better example of having your cake and eating it too."[5]

In the central city, there are pressing problems. Many cities are faced with large interest payments on debts they incurred to build streets, lay sewers, and generally provide for the larger population which has now moved outside the city. More money is needed to build schools, provide social services, clean up slums. Although the region as a unit has adequate wealth to meet its problems, that wealth is not equally distributed. The people in suburbia accept no responsibility for supporting the central city either through their votes or their tax money.

But there are signs that even the suburbanites are feeling the bite of suburbanitis. Many of them have discovered that the lower price for land and the lower taxes are deceptive. Fire insurance rates are often higher, they have to pay more for garbage collection, they often have to build and maintain their own septic tanks, and other costs are higher. Moreover, as suburban real estate becomes improved and as the suburb grows in size, new waterworks and other facilities are needed. The schools become crowded, the parks are inadequate, and the part-time village government is unsatisfactory. The suburbs, too, are beginning to look around for some solution.

Proposals to alleviate the pressing governmental problems of our metropolitan regions are not lacking. As one distinguished student of the subject has pointed out, "So far we have accomplished little more than a world's record for words used in proportion to cures effected."[6] But as the disease bites deeper, there is greater hope for action. What can be done?

Several palliative remedies are now being used. *Cooperation* among the several governmental units takes many forms. Two governments sometimes get together to perform a particular function. One government may agree to provide services for another in return for a fee. For example, 33 suburban communities buy water from Chicago. Such an arrangement can have curious results. Not too long ago, Chicago was selling water to the city of Harvey for 6.8 cents a thousand gallons. Harvey then sold it to the city of Markham for 19 cents. Markham then sold the water to the Cook County Infirmary for 25 cents. The taxpayers of Chicago are the chief supporters of the Infirmary. They were buying back their own water at 3½ times its original selling price.[7] But other examples of more success-

[5] Charles R. Cherington, "Pattern for Greater Boston," *National Municipal Review,* Vol. XXXVIII, February 1949, p. 70.

[6] T. H. Reed, "Hope for 'Suburbanitis,'" *National Municipal Review,* Vol. XXXIX, December 1950.

[7] Frederick G. Brownell, *The American Magazine,* May 1947.

ful cooperation can be noted. Dozens of independent police forces often work out arrangements for sharing of information and for the tying in of communications systems. Planning boards of the several governments have pooled their efforts.

There are many examples of *functional consolidation*. Special single-purpose metropolitan agencies have been created to handle a particular function. The Cook County Sanitary District and the Metropolitan [Park] District Commission for Boston are two well-known agencies. Although such agencies provide better service for less cost, they add one more unit to an already complex situation, make the problem of coordination even more difficult, and often remove control from the hands of local people.

Another type of functional consolidation is the transferring of jobs to the county. Where the county covers the entire metropolitan region, real integration can be achieved in this manner. Erie County in New York, for example, has taken over health, hospitals, libraries, and welfare which formerly were handled by many cities. Los Angeles County has assumed many functions for all the hundreds of communities in the sprawling Los Angeles metropolitan region.

Some believe that the problem can best be solved by these palliative reforms. Others, however, argue that major surgery is called for. Among the more drastic proposals is the *annexation* by the central city of all the surrounding territory. In 1955, 526 cities took in 348 square miles of fringe population. During the last four years cities have annexed more than 1200 square miles, "an area equivalent to the whole state of Rhode Island."[8] Nevertheless, annexation has not kept up with the movement outside the city limits. To succeed, annexation must be a continuing process. Matters become especially difficult when the fringe population creates its own incorporated suburbs, for then annexation is likely to be stoutly opposed by the city officials of the small surrounding cities, by suburban taxpayers, and by those with strong feelings of local pride.

The "Federal City" idea has its champions. Proponents of this plan suggest that the local city governments retain their identity and remain in charge of certain functions, but that a federal city be established to take over metropolitan problems. Toronto, London, and Berlin are such cities. No American metropolitan region as yet has taken to the idea. However, the governments of metropolitan Miami are considering for Dade County a federated program that has been recommended by the Department of Government of Miami University and the Public Administration Service.[9] New York has some aspects of a federal city, since each borough has its own president who administers functions such as street repairs and maintenance

[8] "Why People Move Out of Cities," *U.S. News & World Report,* August 10, 1956, p. 72.
[9] *The Government of Metropolitan Miami* (Chicago: Public Administration Service, 1954).

of public buildings. But the central city government of all the five boroughs really governs the entire city.

The Federated City offers real advantages for the 22 large metropolitan regions that are now cut into pieces by state boundary lines. Yet it may be too drastic a change to win wide acceptance.[10] Unhappily, it may take a flood or some other catastrophe to serve as a catalyst for metropolitan reform.

City and county

The duplication and lack of coordination among the central city and its satellites is further complicated by the fact that the county also duplicates functions. Many people pay taxes to support a city superintendent of schools and a county superintendent of schools, a city police department and a sheriff, a city street department and a county highway department, city welfare and county relief. At best, this is an inefficient way to handle single problems.

Various kinds of city-county consolidations or city-county separations have been suggested, although not widely adopted, for city areas. In Virginia, however, all cities over 10,000 are separated from the county, and St. Louis, Baltimore, and several other cities have withdrawn from their counties. This avoids duplication of effort within the city, but it sometimes leaves the people in the county out in the cold. Moving in the other direction but toward the same objective is the trend in some metropolitan regions, previously mentioned, to make the county the basic unit of metropolitan government. Of course, in many places the county is not large enough to encompass the region, or its boundaries make it inappropriate.

Although progress toward order and sanity among the governments of metropolitan regions has been discouragingly slow, there is still hope. The demands of civil defense have re-enforced the pressures for action. Fifty independent fire and police departments do not provide the most desirable organization to defend a metropolitan region against enemy attack. Will the Sunnyside Fire Department move into a bombed out area in Jonesville? Who is to pay for the defense expenditures? How are plans to be coordinated? Perhaps in answering these problems, plans for metropolitan governments will be taken off the professors' shelves and given serious consideration.

City beautiful

Are American cities good places to live and work? Crowded shopping areas, dented fenders, shattered nerves, slums and blighted regions, factories next to schools, baseball diamonds in the middle of the streets, checkerboard street pattern. Are these things necessary?

[10] Daniel R. Grant, "The Development of Interstate Metropolitan Areas," *The Western Political Quarterly*, Vol. VIII, No. 1, March 1955.

Many city people have asked these questions. City manager charters, consolidated cities and counties, and the like—these are fine things, they argue, and so is saving money and making government more efficient. But the problem, they argue, is much larger than this. Structural changes are not enough. Intelligent planning could have avoided many of the costly problems that now confront us.

Until several decades ago, cities were allowed to grow in a haphazard fashion. There was little interest in trying to apply systematic knowledge to building better cities. Men were permitted to erect factories wherever they wanted. As buildings became higher, sunlight was shut off from the streets below. Traffic conditions became such that a man could hardly cross the city without suffering a traumatic experience. Schools were built where land could be bought cheap or where the political organization could make a profit.

To make cities better places to live in and to plan city growth in orderly fashion, most cities over 25,000 today have some kind of *planning agency.* There are also 400 county planning commissions, usually in the urban counties. The national government adds grants-in-aid to help support planning work of state, county, city, and regional planning agencies. Most cities, moreover, have some kind of zoning regulations.

Zoning ordinances are one phase of the planning process. They are an attempt to bring some order out of the chaos of present city living. The most common kind of city zoning regulation is to divide up into areas the city and limit the uses to which buildings may be devoted in each area. Thus, the city may be divided into areas for single family dwellings, two-family dwellings, multi-family dwellings, commercial purposes, and light and heavy industry. Other regulations often restrict the height of buildings and require that buildings be located certain distances apart and certain distances back from the front of the lot.

Cities use zoning to stop junk yards from being located next to residential areas, to stabilize land values, to plan more intelligently the development of city services in accordance with uses of land in various places. The major weakness of many zoning regulations is that they have been imposed too late. Sometimes they even perpetuate past mistakes. Existing buildings are usually allowed to remain in use without conforming to zoning requirements. But some zoning laws attempt to correct past mistakes. Boston, for example, has provided that nonconforming use of any buildings shall not be permitted after April 1, 1961.

Some counties also are zoned. During World War II, many counties in which war industries were located suddenly discovered that they were flooded with thousands of new residents. As people spill over into the counties from the cities, new slums and blighted regions may result when no zoning regulations exist.

A zoning ordinance is no better than its enforcement. This is usually the responsibility of a building inspector who grants permits after buildings have been approved as consistent with building, zoning, fire, and sanitary regulations. In most cases, a zoning or planning commission or the city council can amend the zoning ordinances and make exceptions to the regulations. These officials are often under tremendous pressures to grant exceptions. Where too many exceptions are granted, the whole purpose of zoning is defeated.

Zoning is, however, only one phase of city planning. Until recently, city planners were primarily concerned with streets and buildings. Today, many city planners are concerned with broader matters, and planning covers virtually all the activities of people. The basic job of the planners is to collect all the information they can about the city, and then prepare long-range plans. What sections of the city are growing? Where should new schools be built? Where should main highways be constructed to meet future needs? Will water supply be adequate in ten years? Are the parks accessible enough to all the people?

The importance of the planning program varies from city to city. In some cities, planning is a small operation and those who make the decisions pay little attention to it. Other cities have elaborate organizations, full-time planners, large staffs; and the plan is taken seriously by city councils and other public officials. Obviously, planning must be built upon public support since no plan, however it looks on paper, will be followed unless it recognizes the interests and values of major groups within the community.

Reformers and bosses

The fifty years following the Civil War marked the height of municipal corruption and inefficiency. In 1890 Andrew D. White, professor and politician, wrote: "Without the slightest exaggeration we may assert that, with very few exceptions, the city governments of the United States are the worst in Christendom—the most expensive, the most inefficient, and the most corrupt. No one who has any considerable knowledge of our own country and of other countries can deny this."

These observations were backed up by Lincoln Steffens who, after touring the United States, reported, "St. Louis exemplified boodle; Minneapolis, police graft; Pittsburgh, a political and industrial machine; and Philadelphia, general *civic* corruption."[11] The other cities were not much better.

Toward the end of the nineteenth century, various good government groups were formed in various cities throughout the United States. In 1894 the National Municipal League, composed of associations and indi-

[11] Lincoln Steffens, *The Shame of the Cities* (New York: Peter Smith, republished, 1948, original edition, 1904), p. 16.

viduals interested in improving municipal government, was organized. During the next fifty or sixty years, the League was active in sponsoring studies and publicizing programs for municipal reform. Many of the reformers leveled their heaviest charges against the bosses.

Fifty years ago the boss was the typical ruler of many of our larger cities, and some of our smaller ones. Why were American cities boss-ridden? There were almost as many diagnoses of the illness as there were doctors. Some argued that the low state of municipal affairs resulted chiefly from the lack of public interest and the refusal of the businessmen to take part in public affairs. The latter were too busy attending to profits, it was charged, so civic affairs fell into the hands of unsavory people. But others asserted that the businessmen themselves were behind the political bosses, that they had used the political organization to secure favorable franchises and immunities from regulations. Still others attributed the boss system to the influx of new immigrants who found that the ward leaders and precinct men were their friends and that politics offered opportunities for economic and social advancement. Still others argued that the bosses resulted from the faulty structural organization of city government.

Whatever the cause, people were aware of the conditions. For the last half century, reform groups have been at work. City manager plans have been adopted; some progress has been made toward establishing merit systems, and modern accounting and purchasing practices have been installed. Periodically reform organizations have defeated the boss at the polls and have taken over control of the city. Within a few years, however, the bosses often get back into the saddle. Only in relatively few cities— Cincinnati, Ohio; Grand Rapids, Michigan; and Cambridge, Massachusetts —have civic associations continued as effective organizatons.

How much better are cities today than fifty years ago? Some argue that city government today shows great improvement, others maintain that the situation has not been basically changed. A group of journalists recently surveyed our cities and concluded "it is the same bedraggled and malodorous story that Lincoln Steffens unfolded in 1904. . . . It is the same shame, and just as widespread, degrading, and entrenched."[12] A veteran crime fighter reported, "In virtually every section of the country the underworld has become part and parcel of political organizations that rule over cities and sometimes states."[13] On the other hand, Luther Gulick, a close student of municipal affairs, believes that the last fifty years has resulted in improvement. He writes: "There is now less mugging, kidnapping, and political murder. . . . There is less direct vote fraud. . . . There is now less franchise boodling and sale of rights to use city streets. . . . There is less raw sweeping patronage. . . . We have fewer sudden, hidden, crooked

[12] Robert S. Allen, ed. *Our Fair Cities* (New York: Vanguard Press, 1947), p. 4.
[13] Virgil W. Peterson, *Barbarians in Our Midst* (Boston: Little, Brown and Company, 1952), p. 322.

deals now. . . . There is less municipal jobbery in the state legislature by men who have no local responsibility. . . . Our city voters are vastly better educated. . . . A man is disgraced today for acts that were 'smart politics'

in Steffen's time."[14] But Gulick does not believe that all is well. "Graft and corruption," he writes, "and the dominance of bosses are not the shame of the cities today as they were forty years ago. . . . Our shame is urban

[14] Luther Gulick, "The Shame of the Cities—1946," *National Municipal Review*, XXXVI, No. 1, January 1947, pp. 18-25.

mediocrity without revolt; filth, slums, decay, and traffic snarls without action; private preoccupation and lazy contentment without compelling civic loyalties or great civic dreams."

Some believe that the reformers, despite their good intentions, have overlooked the basic problem. They argue that the reformers have emphasized efficiency and saving of taxes, that they have often been middle and upper class people whose major objection to the political organization and the people who control city government is that they are unlettered. Often it is claimed that the reformers are strong enough to defeat a boss at an election, but then they take no action to correct the underlying causes of bossism or to strike at the roots of his power. They are not interested, it is argued, in the "lower wards," in slum clearance, better housing, park development—in short, in improving the environment of those who now turn to the boss.

Wherever the merit lies, it is certainly true that structural reforms are not the whole story—and the reformers have never so argued. It is also true that despite the real progress that has been made, much remains to be done to make city government a democratic instrument and a vital force in community life.

The city, county, township, and New England town do not exhaust the kinds of local governments. Among the others, perhaps the school districts are the most important; they are discussed in Chapter 33; the functioning of state and various kinds of local government is taken up in the chapter that follows.

T HE ROADS WE RIDE ON, THE SCHOOLS WE GO TO, the teachers we listen to, the electric light bills we pay, the purity of the water we drink, the safety of the elevators we ride in, the persons we can get married to—all these matters and many others are affected by what state and local officials do. Merely to list the activities of state and local officials would take a large book, and probably a rather dull one.

Dull as such a list might be, these activities are part and parcel of the exciting business of politics. Listen to the debates in the state legislature, attend the meetings of the city council, watch the candidates on the stump, and you come face to face with the problems of law enforcement, education, welfare, highways. Should the city build another school building? Where should it be located? Will the voters approve a bond issue to construct a new hospital? Should the state superintendent of schools be given authority to establish minimum standards for teachers? Are the gambling syndicates being protected by the police? What can be done about the traffic jam on Main Street? Everybody—mayors, legislators, judges, ward bosses, civil commissions, unions, Chambers of Commerce—participates in the process of determining what the officials shall do, which ones of them shall do it, and how they shall do it.

It is obviously impracticable to discuss each activity of our states and our cities, counties, school districts, townships, and so on. Rather the approach must be selective. Only a few of the highlights of a few of the programs can be touched on here.

★ 33

State

and local

government

in action

"THE PUBLIC SAFETY IS A PUBLIC TRUST"

Everything that government does is supposed to protect the public safety. But the term has a more narrow meaning—the protection of people and their property against law breakers, fires, floods, riots, and the like. Civil defense, fire protection, disaster relief, and police protection are examples of public safety functions. Probably the most important of these is police protection.

One of government's oldest and most accepted functions is to maintain law and order, but organized city police departments are of relatively recent origin. Until the middle of the nineteenth century, the sheriff, the constable, and the town marshal made up the police force of rural areas. In the smaller cities, citizens took turns serving on the night watch. In the larger ones, men were paid a small fee to patrol the streets during the night.

It was in the larger cities that the need for better police protection first became acute. The city with its opportunity for great anonymity offered more temptation to law breakers and made detection difficult. Furthermore, the informal methods of social control—neighborhood pressure, social ostracism, family authority—that are often effective in smaller communities had less importance in large urban centers. The early night watchmen in some of our large cities were ineffective. They were not organized into a disciplined force, and in some places the only difference between the night watchmen and the criminals was that the night watchmen were paid a small salary.

Day shifts were organized around the middle part of the nineteenth century, but nothing resembling a modern police department developed until the two shifts were consolidated and brought under central city control. By the third quarter of the nineteenth century, most of the large cities had police departments. At first, these departments were the haven of spoilsmen. The police force is still ridden by patronage in some cities, but in most a merit system has been adopted. The force is normally headed by a "civilian" commissioner and by an experienced chief of police appointed by the mayor or manager.

The policeman's lot

Many students of police science believe that proper administration requires merit systems specially tailored to the needs of police work. In some cities, civil service regulations so restrict the chief's authority that he cannot maintain discipline. Sometimes he cannot penalize or even reprimand his men except by bringing formal charges before a civil service commission. The result is that minor infractions of the rules go unpunished, discipline is lax, and morale suffers.

In many cities the police officer, who risks his life daily, is paid a small salary. Protection for his family in the event he is killed or disabled in line of duty is often inadequate. The public is indifferent, even hostile, to making the policeman's lot a happier one. Under the circumstances, policemen find it difficult to resist the many temptations that come their way. Many a police officer can readily supplement his income by merely looking the other way while a cigar store operates a policy game, by overlooking violations of the fire code, by permitting Mrs. Jones to double-park. Under such circumstances, stories of graft and corruption among police departments should not surprise us. Other cities, however, have established first-rate departments. Salaries have been raised, entrance standards increased, training programs introduced, and methods of scientific detection adopted. As the caliber of the force has improved, the public has usually responded with greater respect and greater support.

City police and county sheriffs enforce the great body of law. These officials are officers of the state as well as of the locality and are supposed to enforce all the laws of the commonwealth in addition to local ordinances en-

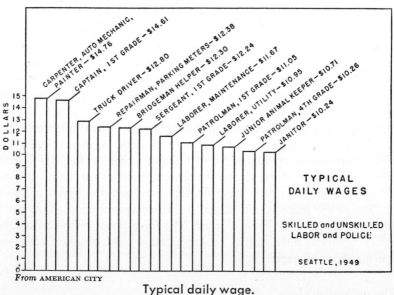

From AMERICAN CITY

Typical daily wage.

acted by their own city councils or county governing bodies. They serve two masters—the state and the local community to which they owe their job. In case of conflict, it is obvious that the latter will win out.

Americans have been reluctant to permit control over police to pass out of the hands of the local community. They know that centralization of all the police agencies is one of the characteristics of totalitarian states and that safety, if nothing else, requires decentralization of police authority. But does this mean that we must have a complex pattern of vertical and horizontal duplication? Over 40,000 separate public law enforcement agencies, composed of 250,000 men and women (including single constables in small townships) and costing about a billion dollars a year, operate at the different levels of government. Yet our crime bill in 1954 was 2¼ million major felonies, 36,000 traffic deaths, and property damages estimated at many millions.

People fear centralized police, but at the same time they demand better service. Gradually the national and state governments have assumed a greater share of the responsibility for law enforcement. The role of the

Federal Bureau of Investigation and of other law enforcement agencies has been noted in previous chapters. Today the states also are active in the business of law enforcement.

The state police

The famous Texas Rangers, a small border patrol at the beginning, were organized in 1835. In 1865 Massachusetts appointed a few state constables to suppress commercialized vice, a job that local police had been unwilling and unable to do. But it was not until 1905 when the Pennsylvania State Constabulary was formed that a real state police system came into being. This system was so successful that other states followed suit. At the present time, 36 states have police forces with substantially full law enforcement authority, although less than half of these make any real effort to enforce all the laws. Twelve states restrict their police to the enforcement of traffic laws on the rural highways and to prevention of crime committed on the highways.

The state police have been established for a variety of reasons varying in importance from state to state. The breakdown of rural law enforcement, the invention of the automobile requiring greater police protection on the highways and demanding a mobile force to ferret out criminals in rural regions, the need to give the governor a force so that he might execute his responsibilities, and the desire to have a force to use during emergencies such as strikes, fires, floods—all these have contributed to establishment of state police forces.

The use of the state police during the early days to break strikes won them the hostility of organized labor, which dubbed them the "American Cossacks." State police have not served as strike breakers for many years, but the fear lingers on. For this reason, the state police's jurisdiction in many states is restricted to make it more difficult to use them as strike-breaking agencies. For example, in some states the police cannot be moved into a region where there is a strike until actual violence has occurred and only then with specific authorization of the governor.

When the Pennsylvania State Constabulary was established, a sharp break was made with traditional police methods. The force was a mounted and uniformed body organized on a military basis, with centralized control being vested in a superintendent who, in turn, was directly responsible to the governor. This pattern has been followed by other states—New York, Michigan, Massachusetts, to mention just a few. These forces are now among the most respected police organizations in the world. They are equipped with automobiles and airplanes, modern systems of communication, and elaborate crime detection laboratories. They maintain high standards and rigid discipline.

The military organization of these forces shields them from some pressures, builds morale, and helps to develop a pride in one's outfit that contrasts sharply with the cynical attitude of some urban police. Because of their mobile nature and professional character, the state police are often less accessible to "the smaller fry of urban and rural politics." Moreover, these organizations have established rigorous systems of recruitment and training, and provide for close supervision.

Other state police have developed out of the highway patrol movement. During the 1930's, highway traffic control in rural regions became an acute problem, and state after state organized highway patrols. These patrols were usually organized as subordinate units of the highway or motor vehicle department. The tendency has been to extend their authority from enforcing the rules of the road to general police powers. Generally speaking, the state police which have grown out of highway patrols do not have as rigid training programs or as high standards as do those created after the Pennsylvania pattern. Even when they have statewide jurisdiction, most state police do not go into cities unless ordered to by the governor or at the request of local officials. Local police are often resentful of this intrusion and consider it to be a reflection upon their own abilities—which it often is.

State police are not the only law enforcement agencies maintained by state governments. Liquor law enforcement officials, fish and game wardens, fire wardens, independent detective bureaus, special motor vehicle law police, and other specialized forces abound. This fragmentization of function has been much criticized, but each department insists that it needs its own law enforcement group in order to handle its own special problems. So far, the forces working toward fragmentization have been stronger than those working toward centralization.

GOVERNMENT AS EDUCATOR

Long ago, Plato and Aristotle stressed the importance of education as a vital job for government. Indeed, to them government itself was essentially an educational institution. Thomas Jefferson emphasized the importance of an educated citizenry in a government operating on a democratic basis. But it has been only during the last century that the idea has become generally accepted that government should provide tax-supported schools.

Many groups opposed "free" education. They argued that it would lead to social unrest, that it would undermine the family, that it would give government the opportunity to control the minds of the young, that it would require an extensive bureaucracy, and that it would result in a fatal mixture of education and politics. Was it fair, they asked, to tax people who could afford to educate their own children in private schools in order to educate others?

Today, however, *compulsory* education through the public primary and secondary schools is an established fact (although parents may, if they choose, send their children to approved private schools). A strong movement has developed to extend public education downward to kindergarten and nursery school, upward through college and adult education, outward to cover more subjects, and deeper to cover them better. State and local governments spend more money for education than for any other function.

The organization of education

The city, the county, the township, or the school district has the chief responsibility for providing public education. The school district, of which there are about 60,000, is the most common basic unit. In each district the voters commonly elect a board of education. This board levies taxes, in most cases independently of the city or county. It appoints a superintendent of schools and other supervisory personnel, hires the teachers, and runs the schools from grade one through twelve.

Each state has a superintendent of public instruction or a commissioner of education. In a little over half of the states he is popularly elected, and in most states he shares some authority with a board of education. Although immediate operation of the public schools is the responsibility of the local community, state officers have important supervisory powers. For one thing, they distribute financial assistance. State money is passed out according to many formulas, but growing stress is being placed on equalization of resources among the local communities. The states give more money to the poorer communities.

State officials often certify competence of teachers and set minimum salaries. They are sometimes consulted by local authorities who wish to build new school buildings to insure that the buildings meet state minimum specifications. Some state officials have the authority (subject to the state constitution and laws) to prescribe the course of study and to determine what must be taught and what may not be taught. Twenty-four southern and western state authorities determine what books will be used in the schools.

The national government, too, plays a role (see Chapter 26). It makes yearly grants of money for agricultural and vocational education, supports research programs, and through the Office of Education collects statistics, conducts surveys, and advises state and local officials.

The number and popularity of books, articles, and newspaper accounts entitled "Education at the Crossroads," "Educational Crisis," and so on attest to the large educational problems that the people of this nation face. Many school districts are so small that they cannot meet the demands. School buildings are overcrowded. The number of competent teachers is insufficient.

Population shifts require expansion of capital equipment. In five states, school-board members outnumber teachers. There are still thousands of one-room-one-teacher schools in the United States. But the trend is toward unification of school districts and pooling of resources. The little red school-house is slowly disappearing.

"Higher learning"

Most communities provide only for public elementary and secondary education. But over 250 of them, and the number grows each year, also operate junior colleges. In addition to the locally supported and operated junior colleges, some of the nation's outstanding universities and colleges are supported by cities. States spend large sums of money to support higher education. More than forty states run universities, every state has one or more land-grant colleges, some states provide technical schools, and there are over forty state-supported junior colleges. The methods of administration used to operate these schools and the 162 state teachers' colleges defy classification. Today, about half of the students attending college go to publicly supported institutions.

The Children's Hour

Copyright 1949, NEW YORK HERALD TRIBUNE, INC.

Educational politics

One of the chief characteristics of elementary and secondary educational administration is the control over the school by groups who are relatively insulated from the rest of the government. Each school board has a tenuous connection with the city council or mayor or with the governor or state legislature. The professional educators have been successful in separating education from the other functions of government.

The desire for functional independence is characteristic of specialists. Each group believes that its duties are so important that it should be able to determine its policies without too much dependence upon other branches of government. The educators have been the most successful in this respect. In many states, they have even their own independent sources of money. Certain taxes are earmarked for educational uses, and school boards determine their own tax rates.

Publicly supported higher education, however, is more closely tied into the governmental machinery. State universities and colleges depend upon the legislature for their appropriations. Boards of trustees are often appointed by the governor with the consent of the senate. The amount of financial and public support that the institution gets depends upon the number of supporters it has among the legislators and those who elect the legislators.

The isolation of elementary and secondary education from the rest of government has strong organized group support. Parent-Teachers Associations, the National Education Association, and the various state teachers' groups wield considerable political power. Furthermore, many groups of citizens are convinced that education is of supreme importance and that it must be kept out of the hands of the "politicians."

Education and educational policy are, of course, part of the democratic political process. What kinds of schools, what shall be taught, who shall teach, and so on, are hotly contested issues. Schools are target spots for all groups who are eager that the students be taught the "right" things. Patriotic groups are concerned about "un-American" doctrines sneaking into textbooks or classrooms. Labor leaders are anxious that students receive the right impression about labor and its role in society. Business leaders want the children to see the free enterprise system in the correct light. Educators advocate that schools should be as isolated as possible from demands of various groups. They argue that censors, whether public or private, must be prevented from determining what the people learn.

Some believe that the professional educators have too much authority over the schools. Others assert that only these people should determine teacher competence and school curriculum. And so the debate goes on. Controversies also rage around the place of religious education and around the virtues of "progressive" education.

Schools are important molders of opinion. It is not surprising to discover that the differences among groups are reflected in their attitudes toward the schools. The resolution of these differences is a matter for democratic politics. Educational policy, like that in agriculture, law enforcement, or any other field, is determined in our free government by the political processes available to a free people.

Despite public education, private schools still flourish. Public education has by no means replaced private education, especially at the college and university level. The same disputes revolve around private educational systems as around public schools. There is the same struggle among groups in the making of educational policy. It is this rich mixture of public and private institutions, and of the groups involved with them, that provides one of our best guarantees that no one group can dominate the educational system of the United States. The diversity in kinds of schools, the variety of patterns of administration, and their dependence upon numerous sources for funds and support help prevent totalitarian control by any one party, class, religion, or section.[1]

[1] James B. Conant, *Education and Liberty* (Cambridge: Harvard University Press, 1953).

SOCIAL SERVICE

The poor, the blind, the sick, the handicapped, the homeless children, the old—what happens to these people? How are they taken care of? Prior to the Great Depression these unfortunate groups were helped for the most part by privately operated social agencies, charities, and small haphazard systems of public relief. Today all our governments have extensive welfare programs, and the costs for these services loom large in state budgets. Public activity has neither replaced private social services and charity nor lessened their importance. But public welfare is not merely a depression activity. In 1955, a year of prosperity and full employment, there were more than five million people, not counting veterans, receiving some kind of public assistance. State and local spending for welfare amounted to about $4.5 billion.

It was not too many years ago that poverty was considered by many to be a disgrace, mental illness a moral weakness, and public assistance a waste. The state maintained a few institutions for the poor, often run by political appointees who were untrained and unconcerned about those under their care. But most of the needy were taken care of by the county in its poorhouse. In the poorhouse were placed unfortunates of all kinds—the infirm, the handicapped, the drug addicts, alcoholics, mentally ill, and those who just did not have any place to live. Each county or township supplemented this *indoor* relief by a program of *outdoor* relief. Those unable to make their own living but not requiring institutional care were given money or goods.

This was the basic public welfare arrangement when the economy went down the toboggan slide in the early 1930's. The local communities were swamped by persons in distress. With their facilities overtaxed, they put in a call for help. The state governments in turn were unable to handle the problem. In 1932, the national government entered the field on a large-scale basis. The dole, work relief programs, and then a long-range program of social security were instituted.

The national government's social security program, as we noted in Chapter 26, is designed only to assist the states, but to leave to the state and local community the job of administering welfare programs and determining the details of welfare policies. The national government has concentrated its attention on *categorized* relief, as the professional social workers call it, for example, aid for special groups, especially the needy aged, the needy blind, dependent children, and the permanently and totally disabled. It will be remembered that in order to get federal money, each state must put up some of its own money, establish a central state agency to deal with the federal government, submit programs to federal officials for their approval, and hire only qualified persons to administer federally supported programs.

State programs

All states now have some kind of department of welfare. This agency directly administers categorical welfare programs or, as in most states, supervises local officials, usually county officials, who actually administer the programs. The county welfare departments, which in order to be qualified for federal help must also be manned by persons selected on the basis of merit, determine what individuals are entitled to assistance (appeals can be taken to state welfare departments), and deal with clients. State and county welfare departments often provide assistance beyond that established

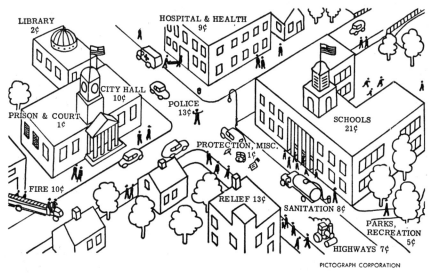

Your tax dollar pays for many services.

by the national social security program. And even within the limits of the federal program, each state is free to determine the size and details of its own welfare assistance.

Groups other than the aged, blind, disabled, and dependent children have not been so successful in securing their own relief programs. General relief programs are not ordinarily as well administered or as strongly supported as categorized relief. General relief is almost entirely a state and local governmental activity. General outdoor, noninstitutionalized relief, is essentially a county responsibility. Some townships have this job but most welfare workers believe that townships are too small to support adequate welfare departments. A properly administered department requires trained case workers to process applications, make home visits, and act to rehabilitate individuals and to maintain families.

Relief administration presents the familiar pictures—overlap and duplication. In one midwestern county, 65 separate public agencies administer

some kind of general relief, and in the average New York county, 22 welfare agencies operate under 21 governments. Recently the trend has been
to centralize welfare activities in a county or city welfare department. Some
city departments are among the best in the country.

The county poorhouse is still the basic institution for general indoor,
institutionalized relief. Development of outdoor programs of assistance has
lessened to a slight extent the need to put some kinds of people into institutions, but there are still many who have no home of their own, who are ill,
and who require care. County poorhouses, often renamed county homes, of
today are more attractive places than they were yesterday. The physical
plant of these usually dreary and depressing institutions is being improved.
Children have special homes, and the mentally ill are being placed in state
hospitals. Some counties have joined together to maintain one adequate
rather than two or more inadequate homes for the chronically ill and persons of advanced age.[2]

Most states have assumed the responsibility for the insane, feeble-minded,
or emotionally disturbed people, and have set up reformatories for juvenile
delinquents. In some states, institutions for youthful law breakers have
been placed under the jurisdiction of welfare rather than penal authorities.
Although many of these institutions are still run by incompetents, in recent
years there has been encouraging progress toward trained staffs. Most of
these distressed persons are not politically organized, and their needs are
apt to be overlooked unless other citizens champion their cause.

Public health

During a summer in the 1780's, the streets of Philadelphia were deserted. Those who could afford to do so had taken their families and fled
into the country. Every night the mournful sounds of the death cart could
be heard. The city was striken by a yellow fever epidemic. Only when cool
weather arrived did the disease abate and the city return to normal activity.
There were few families that did not grieve the loss of a child, father, or
mother.

Yellow fever, dysentery, malaria, and other dreaded scourges periodically have swept through American cities. These catastrophes were one of
the hazards of city life. As late as 1878-1879 yellow fever swept through the
South; Memphis was nearly depopulated. Drastic action seemed imperative.
State after state followed the lead of Louisiana and Massachusetts and
established boards of health. Spurred by the medical discoveries of Pasteur
and other scientists, authorities inaugurated programs for the protection of
public health. Open city sewers were covered and other hygienic measures
instituted. In fact, it was not until contagious diseases were brought under
control that the large city became a safe place to live.

[2] See Clyde F. Snider, "The Fading Almshouse," *National Municipal Review,* Vol.
XLV, No. 2, February 1956, pp. 60-65.

Today city people live without constant fear of the plague. Over 18,000 local governments—counties, cities, townships, special health districts—have some kind of public health program. Every state has an agency, usually called a department of health, that administers the state program and supervises local officials. The United States Public Health Service conducts research, assists state and local authorities, and administers federal grants to encourage them to expand their programs.

Despite the supposed virtues of country life and the supposed threats to health caused by city living, today it is the city people who have the best health records and the most public health protection. The bigger cities have a full-time health officer who is assisted by a large well-staffed department. The counties have lagged behind. About forty million Americans, most of them living in rural places, are protected either by a part-time agency or none at all. The American Public Health Association, the professional society of the public health workers, recommends that counties and cities join with one another to establish health districts with at least 50,000 people, the number they believe necessary in order to maintain a minimum program. Again, the trend toward larger units is apparent.

Prevention and control of communicable disease is still one of the major parts of public health activities. Doctors are required to report cases of communicable disease. Health department officials then investigate to discover the source of the infection, isolate the afflicted persons, and take whatever action seems to be called for. Most state health departments give doctors free vaccine and serum, and many local departments give free vaccinations to those who cannot afford to go to private physicians—in some cases this service is open to everybody.

Since more public support can be obtained for particular programs than for general disease control, some diseases come in for special attention. The national government provides financial assistance for such activities as tuberculosis and venereal disease control. Mobile x-ray machines provide free x-rays to school children, teachers, and the general public. Venereal disease clinics are open, and premarital examinations are required in many states for persons who apply for marriage licenses. Chronic ailments, such as cardiac and rheumatic diseases, are receiving more attention.

Public health officials protect water supplies and see to it that waste and sewage are safely disposed of. They protect the community's food supply by inspecting hotels, restaurants, and food markets. Many cities now require domestic servants, waiters, cooks, and other food handlers to secure a special license and undergo a health department medical examination.

Meat and milk are of special concern. Meat products shipped in interstate commerce are inspected by federal officials, but it is the job of state and local authorities to safeguard the public against dangers from the large amount of meat slaughtered locally. Some cities do this by maintaining a municipal slaughterhouse (known as an *abattoir*) and require all meat sold within the city and not inspected elsewhere to be slaughtered there. Milk is especially dangerous and requires extreme precautions. Most large cities insist that milk be pasteurized. But this alone is not enough to insure its purity. Licensing, inspecting, and testing of milk, cows, and dairies are also required.

In 1948 the dense "smog" that descended on Donora, Pennsylvania and killed some residents demonstrated dramatically the dangers to public health from air pollution. In many cities, staffs of inspectors visit industrial establishments to enforce laws that require certain equipment and fuel to be used to avoid sending noxious waste into the air.

One of the most important persons in the public health agency is the public health nurse. To many people, she *is* public health. Traveling throughout the community, she advises on prenatal and postnatal care, assists mothers in childbirth and in caring for their children, and nurses the sick. Public health education among school children, periodic inspections of teeth, lungs, hearing, eyes and so on, and general health lectures are carried on by health and educational officials. Vital statistics, recording of births, deaths, and causes of illness is another important job. Maintenance of laboraties for diagnosis of disease and service to all private physicians, for testing of purity of goods, and the like are other functions of most public health departments.

Even this brief description of public health activities indicates that they are among the most significant functions of our government. They require experienced people, doctors and nurses with special training, and a staff of efficient inspectors to enforce health regulations. In too many places, these jobs, especially those of inspectors, are still handed out according to favor and influence rather than merit.

Hospitals

Most of the hospitals in the United States are owned and operated by private organizations, but there are many public hospitals and more are being built each year. These hospitals are run by cities, counties, and states and are administered in all kinds of ways—some by their own separate boards, some by departments of welfare, some by departments of health, some by departments of mental health, some by departments of state institutions.

Most municipal hospitals are general hospitals. They care for those who cannot afford private hospitals, but they also have paying patients. State hospitals are usually special hospitals—tuberculosis hospitals, mental hospitals—and are available to all, but those who can afford it usually are required to pay part of the costs. Mental diseases and tuberculosis require long, expensive care, which is beyond the means of most people. So the states, cities, and counties have assumed the major responsibility for building and operating such hospitals.

Congress has authorized federal aid to states and localities in order to encourage them to build nonprofit hospitals and health centers. To date, over 2000 hospitals have been completed and more are being built. The program, slated to expire at the end of 1957, will eventually cost the states one and a third billion dollars and the national government another two-thirds billion.

Mental health—still the "Snake Pit"?

Over half the hospital beds in the United States are occupied by persons suffering from mental illness; more than half a million such persons are now in state mental hospitals; and they are increasing at a rate of 10,000 a year. There are another 134,000 mentally deficient in other public institutions. The problem is a serious and challenging one.

One of the first steps in developing a more humane attitude toward the insane, the feeble-minded, and persons with emotional disturbances was to place them in separate institutions where they could be properly cared for. Advances in medicine and psychology have taught that these people are to be treated as patients and not as criminals. But during the last several years, novels, motion pictures, and newspapers have focused public attention on the scandalous conditions that exist in many mental hospitals. The people discovered that patients were being maltreated, that hospitals were woefully undermanned, and that patients were crowded into filthy quarters.

Various groups began to demand action. In state after state, the legislature has appropriated larger sums of money and reorganized the operation of mental hospitals. In a few short years, great improvement has been noted. But much still remains. Shortage of qualified doctors, crowded quarters and lack of proper facilities are still normal in many states. Persons suffering from senility, who need to be cared for in homes for the old, are placed in hospitals where the already hard-pressed doctors find little time to treat those who can profit from help. The solution of this social problem is still high on the agenda of state governments. Although the national government helps, in fiscal 1955 the total amount of money spent on mental illness research by national, state and voluntary agencies equalled merely the cost of a single B-52 bomber.[3]

Homes, houses, and slums

In the 1930's, President Roosevelt pointed out that one-third of the nation was "ill-housed, ill-clad, ill-nourished." We have made tremendous strides since then. Today there are relatively few individuals who are ill-clothed and ill-fed, but as we noted in Chapter 26, many ill-housed remain with us. According to the United States Public Housing Administra-

[3] Mike Gorman, *Every Other Bed* (Cleveland and New York: The World Publishing Company, 1956), p. 32.

tion, some seven million of our forty-six million dwellings do not measure up to proper standards. The national government has supplied credit and built some defense housing, but local officials are the most active public authorities in the housing field.

Cities have a direct financial interest in improving housing conditions and getting rid of slums, for the costs of education, police and fire protection, and public welfare are considerably greater in slums than in the areas of better housing. Juvenile delinquency, unemployment, disease, and other social problems flourish in blighted regions. Slum areas account for 45 per cent of major crimes, 50 per cent of arrests, 55 per cent of juvenile delinquency, 50 per cent of all diseases, and 35 per cent of fires. In Atlanta it was discovered that 53 per cent of all city services were consumed by slum regions that payed only 6 per cent of the real estate taxes. In Baltimore each acre of slums produced a $25,000 yearly deficit for the city.[4] The people of Newark were informed by one group of experts that their slums were costing them about $14 million a year. Proper housing, it was estimated, would save $700,000 a year by reducing fire losses and communicable disease.

Cities, in addition to zoning ordinances, have building codes. These codes are designed to avoid structural breakdowns, prevent fires, stop overcrowding, and protect health. More stringent restrictions are provided for public buildings such as theatres, schools, office buildings, and stores than for private dwellings. Building codes vary widely from city to city. Some cities have no comprehensive code but a mass of detailed and separate regulations dealing with construction, electrical wiring, plumbing, ventilation, heating, and safety requirements. Enforcement of the code is sometimes lax. Confusion results from vesting authority to enforce particular parts of the code in several agencies—for example, the health department enforces plumbing and sanitation regulations, the building inspector is responsible for the structural regulations, the fire department for the fire regulations. In too many cities inspectors lack any preparation or power to enforce the regulations. Often it is not until a building collapses or a fire starts in a building with blocked exits that the lack of adequate building codes and proper enforcement comes to public attention.

Cities also have slum clearance programs. Since 1937, the national government has encouraged them to act by lending money to local public housing agencies and by helping with annual subsidies. Over three-fourths of the states have legislation authorizing cities or counties to set up local housing authorities. These authorities are usually composed of five men appointed by the mayor or county board. They have the power to borrow money, condemn land and buildings, and build and operate public housing projects to replace slums. Cities have also encouraged private builders to

[4] Donald Robinson, "Slum Clearance Pays Off," *National Municipal Review*, Vol. XLIV, No. 9, October 1955, p. 461.

invest money in slum clearance by granting tax exemptions and other concessions. Although action in this field is quickening, public housing is still a
peripheral function of our governments. Most people prefer to leave the job
to private builders.

Government as builder

State and local governments build things. They build highways, public
buildings, airports, parks, and recreational facilities. But by far the major
program is *building roads*. State and local governments spend more money
on the roads than they do for any other thing except education.

Until mass production of the automobile, the canals and the railroads
were the major method of long distance travel. Local roads, such as they
were, were built and repaired under the direction of city, township, and
county officials. Able-bodied male citizens were required either to put in a
certain number of days working on the public roads or to pay taxes for that
purpose.

By the 1890's, safety brakes and the pneumatic tire had been invented;
and in the Gay Nineties, those who could not afford a carriage began to use
the bicycle. Bicycle clubs began to push for the building of hard-surfaced
roads. But it was not until the 1900's and the Age of the Automobile that
road building became a major industry. It is not surprising that the function
of road building gradually was transferred from the township to larger units
of government—the county and the state. But counties and townships still
have important road building and maintenance problems. Nearly four-fifths
of the rural road mileage is under their control. The other one-fifth, which
includes almost all the main highways and most of the hard-surfaced roads,
is built and maintained by the states. Cities are responsible for urban streets.
The national government contributes billions each year for road improvements.

Today our network of main roads touches almost every city with a population of 5000 or more. A 41,000-mile highway system has been designated
for national defense and is coming in for special attention. This system
when finished will reach all state capitals and 90 larger cities. Although
many of the major highways are marked with the familiar "U.S." shield,
they are actually state and local highways partly financed by a grant-in-
aid program but not owned by the national government. Since the end of
World War II, the states have been spending large sums of money to modernize their systems. In spite of progress, they have barely kept up with the growing needs arising out of increasing numbers of cars on the highways, their
greater speed, and more truck traffic. Four-lane limited access roads, cut-
offs to avoid business traffic, and better engineered roads are continuing
needs. The Federal-Aid Highway Construction Act of 1956 described on
pages 862-863 will support a vigorous state road building program for the
next thirteen years.

Few aspects of government are more mixed up in patronage politics than highway building. The large sums of money spent and the larger number of workers involved offer many opportunities for graft and favoritism. In some states the highway department is the chief agency used to support the political organization in power. Contractors are rewarded for their support and loyal party members are given jobs.

An array of potent interest groups support highway development. Automobile manufacturers, tire makers, oil companies, motel and restaurant associations, automobile and tourist clubs, trucking associations, and others join hands to protect their common cause. In most states they have been strong enough to persuade legislatures to earmark gasoline taxes, automobile drivers' license fees, trucking fees, and other "user-taxes" for road purposes. But there is always conflict over how the money should be spent. Farmers want secondary roads developed, but truckers and tourists favor improvement of the main highways. Merchants want the roads to come their way, and their representatives try to get top priority for roads in their districts.

The 1956 Highway Act, although sending large sums of money to the states, will also add to state officials' troubles. Because present routes are so crowded by commercial establishments, most of these new superhighways will be in new locations. It would be too costly to buy out the service stations, eating places, garages, and souvenir shops in order to get the land needed to add three or more lanes with a strip of land down the middle. Already congressmen report that they are being asked by constituents to tell them where the new roads will be, so that speculators can buy land for roadside services before the prices go shooting up. State highway departments will feel pressures from all sides. Farmers will object to having their lands cut in two, especially since they will not be able to go across these highways except at the nearest exchange or grade separation, perhaps miles away. Roadside business on present routes will fight loss of business. Some cities will want the expressways to go through them; others will not.

Another problem grows out of the procedures for taking land. Most of the states have "quick take" procedures, enabling the government to use its eminent domain to take land, pay the owner what the state appraisers consider a fair price, and go ahead and build roads on the land while the courts finally determine the exact price. But in 21 states the courts have interpreted the state constitution to deny the state government such a power and have required the condemnation proceedings to be finished—sometimes at the cost of a delay of several years—before the officials can actually enter on the property and start the roads. The national law authorizes the Secretary of Commerce to use national eminent domain powers if he determines that a state is unable to handle it or to buy with sufficient promptness, and it is probable that several states will be only too glad to turn this task over to him.

The coming of the rural highway has added to many of the states' problems. Law enforcement, as we have noted, and demands for safety patrols have raised costs. In order to cut down on the appalling death rate many states have enacted drivers' licensing laws and motor vehicle inspection. Most states now require drivers of automobiles to provide some kind of bond or insurance to cover any damages they may cause. The Three E's of highway safety—engineering, enforcement, and education—are important jobs for government.

REGULATION AT THE GRASS ROOTS

Corporations receive their charters from the state. Banks, insurance companies, securities dealers, doctors, lawyers, barbers, and various other kinds of business and professions are licensed, and their activities supervised by state officials. These regulations vary from stringent protection of the public to mere window dressing. Both farmers and workers—especially union labor—are regulated. But of all the businesses, those that we designate as "public utilities" are the most closely restricted.

Public utility regulation

Public utilities have been variously defined. They are usually given certain privileges such as power of eminent domain, the right to use streets and other public properties, and some protection from the competition of other companies. In return for this, they are required to give the public adequate services at reasonable rates without discrimination among customers. These utilities render essential services in a field in which competition cannot be depended upon to protect the interest of all the customers.

In the United States, regulation rather than public ownership has been the favored method of social control. Nevertheless, in some fields there is a tendency toward public ownership. More than two-thirds of our cities, for example, own their own water works. Approximately 2000 of them run their own electric systems, and less than 100 operate their own gas utilities. Over fifty—and the number here is increasing—operate their own transit systems. But the other services—intercity transportation, railroads, airplanes, telephone, and telegraph—are almost everywhere provided by private enterprises subject to governmental regulation and some subsidization.

Every state has a utility commission with jurisdiction over some or all phases of utility operation. In most states the utility commissioners are appointed by the governor with the consent of the senate for overlapping terms. The size of the commissions varies, the most common number of commissioners being three. In some states, mostly in the South and West, commissioners are elected by the voters. States with "strong regulation" make the commissions responsible for supervising management of utilities in a wide variety of matters. The extent of commission regulation varies with the type of business, but commissioners have authority to set rates, require uniform systems of accounts, approve security issues, pass on re-organization plans, approve mergers, permit services to be abandoned, and to require a certificate of convenience and necessity before a company is permitted to enter new territory. Many commissions also license drivers of trucks and busses, inspect equipment of railroads and others to insure that they are safe, investigate all accidents, and so on. Unlike the national government, most states have only one utility commission, which combines for the state the duties performed at the national level by the Interstate Commerce Commission, the Federal Communications Commission, the Federal Power Commission, the Civil Aeronautics Board, and (in some states) the Securities and Exchange Commission.

These commissions are charged with the responsibility of protecting interests of customers and investors and managers of the utilities. Although the commissions have considerable legal power, the managers of the utilities are not as restricted as the legal powers might suggest. Utilities have the right to appeal to courts and there are many restraints upon commissioners' authority—restraints imposed by courts and by political checks.

The state utility commissions operate under so many handicaps that a great number of students of the subject have concluded that they are not doing the job they should. Utility managers, on the other hand, are just as convinced that the commissioners are doing a good job—perhaps too good a job—of regulation. Here are some of the problems.

1. The requirements for a good utility commissioner are staggering. The commissions are supposed to do everything from inspect gas and locomotives, set rates in a variety of fields, and assess valuations of complex properties to protect vigorously the public interest and judicially listen to company grievances. Hence, a commission should have the ability to use the technical knowledge of the accountant, the lawyer, the engineer, the economist, and the political scientist. Not many states provide either the salary or the challenge to attract the kind of men needed.

2. The judges have made the work of the commissions difficult. Until recently, federal judges often set aside rulings of state utility commissions, listened to the arguments all over again, and came to their own independent conclusions as to what constituted a fair return on the fair value of the property. In 1898 the Supreme Court decided (in *Smyth* v. *Ames*), that the Constitution required utility commissioners to make their rate regulation orders so that they would allow a "reasonable return" on "the fair value of the property being used by it for the convenience of the public." In the view of James Bonbright, a noted utility specialist, this formula made it impossible for commissioners to develop adequate standards of regulation. Instead, it fastened upon them a formula that is fatal to administration, since the heavy expenses, time-wasting efforts, and controversial nature

of any valuation of a complex utility is so difficult. And as he wrote, "These difficulties are multiplied when the results of the appraisal that is reached by a commission are then appealed by a dissatisfied company—first to a lower court, then to an appellate court, and finally perhaps to the Supreme Court of the United States."[5] Often it took ten years or more to settle the controversy, and by that time conditions had so changed that the settlement was obsolete. Moreover, this form of regulation "encourages" mediocrity and invites inefficiency on the part of private management. Knowing that their rates are likely to be reduced if their profits seem excessive, companies are under no adequate incentive to practice economies and to make voluntary rate reductions in the hope of increasing the demands for their services.

For many years consumer groups, utility commissioners, and utility managers have been debating how the "fair value" of the utilities should be estimated. Since the over-all trend for the last fifty years has been one of increasing prices, the utility managers have argued that the *reproduction cost* of the companies' facilities should serve as the rate base, while consuming groups have championed the *original cost*. Since both these figures are difficult to compile, the process has in many cases amounted to a guessing game. Today the federal courts are more tolerant of state regulatory commissions. The Supreme Court no longer interprets the national Constitution as requiring utility commissions to follow any particular rate-making formula. But many state courts still have a voice in the matter. They still set aside commissioners' regulations, rehear the evidence, and make their own independent rulings as to what are reasonable returns.

3. The small size of utility commission staffs makes it difficult for the commissions to do their job. In most states, these staffs comprise less than half a dozen professional men—lawyers, engineers, accountants. These men are expected to process the accounts, make rate-valuations, do studies of managerial efficiency, and so on. There are so few of them that they often do not have time to make studies of comparative costs or gather independent data, for example. They may have to rely on data furnished by outside groups—including utilities themselves.

These then are some of the reasons commonly listed to account for lack of aggressive protection of consumer interest. It is interesting to note that in all the states some attempt is made to isolate the utility commissions from the rest of the executive structure. James Fesler, after close study of state utility commissions, came to the conclusion, however, that to free these regulatory commissions from direct control of the governor in some cases merely drives the commission into the hands of other groups. As he said, to call a utility commission "independent" does not free it from "this necessity of winning friends—so as to influence legislators. The method of

[5] James C. Bonbright, *Public Utilities and The National Power Policies* (New York: Columbia University Press, 1940), pp. 16-17.

winning these friends varies with each state and with different periods in each state's political history."[6] Sometimes it includes a "reasonable" attitude toward the groups it is supposed to regulate.

Regulation of employers and employees

Despite the expanded role of the national government, state and local officials have much to say about working conditions. Here are some of the kinds of laws they enforce:

Health and safety legislation. In the opening years of this century dramatic episodes like the disastrous garment workers' fire and the revelations about "sweatshop" conditions led to laws for improving conditions of work. States now require proper heating, lighting, ventilation, fire escapes, and sanitary facilities. Machinery must be equipped with safety guards, and standards have been established to cut down occupational diseases. Health, building, and labor inspectors make tours of industrial plants to insure compliance with the laws.

Workmen's compensation. Although the common law made an employer liable for injuries or deaths of his workers resulting from his failure to provide reasonably safe conditions of work, the common law also gave him three defenses that made it almost impossible for an employee or his family to win a case. The employer was not liable if he could show: (1) the employee contributed to the accident by his own negligence, (2) a "fellow-servant" caused the accident, (3) the employee had assumed the risk of injury that flowed from dangers ordinarily associated with the job.

Today all states have abolished these common law defenses and have created workmen's compensation programs based on the belief that employees should not have to assume the costs of accidents. As with depreciation of machinery and other items, the costs of accidents are borne by the employer and, like other costs, are part of the price that the consumer of the product must ultimately pay. No longer does the employee have to sue and prove that his employer was at fault. If he is injured or suffers from a disease in the ordinary course of his employment, he is entitled to compensation set by a prearranged schedule.

Workmen's compensation programs vary from state to state. Most commonly, a board determines the awards. Employers either take out insurance or furnish proof that they are financially able to make payments when called upon to do so. In most states the insurance is sold by private companies, but about one-fourth of the states operate their own insurance programs. Although all states have workmen's compensation laws, their coverage varies. Agricultural, domestic, and temporary workers are not commonly covered, nor are those who work for a company employing only one or two workers. About half of the working force is presently protected.

[6] James W. Fesler, *The Independence of State Regulatory Agencies* (Chicago: Public Administration Service, 1942), Chapter 5, p. 61.

Child labor. All states forbid child labor, but laws vary widely in their coverage and in their definition of child labor. A good many states set the minimum age at just fourteen. Higher age requirements are normal for employment in hazardous occupations and during school hours.

Hours and wages. Women and young people are protected by maximum hours laws in most states. Men are covered only in certain especially dangerous occupations, or where the public safety is directly involved; operators of buses and trucks are an example. Sunday closing laws, and those requiring that employees be allowed at least one day of rest in seven, generally apply to men as well as women and children.

About half the states have minimum-wage laws, but only four of these apply to men. Since standards set by these laws have not kept up with inflation and rising wages and prices, they currently have little effect.

Regulation of Unions and Collective Bargaining. National regulation of collective bargaining applies only to industries in, or affecting, *inter*state commerce. Furthermore, in recent years the National Labor Relations Board has tended to leave to state laws and agencies regulation of industries whose effect on interstate commerce is slight. Although national law takes precedence over state enactments, in some important areas states are left to impose their own regulations. The Taft-Hartley Act, for example, permits states to outlaw the union shop (i.e., agreements that all employees must eventually join the union).

During the 1930's state laws were patterned after the Wagner Act and aimed mainly at protecting the workers' right to form unions and engage in collective bargaining. Since World War II state laws have been more restrictive of union activities. Over a third of the states, mostly in the South and West, do not permit union or closed shop contracts. State courts have also shown a trend in postwar years to supervise closely picketing practices and to ban those activities that are either contrary to statute or in the opinion of the judges contrary to public policy.

"SAY, DID YOU HEAR ABOUT THAT CIVIL SERVICE reform association kickin' because the tax commissioners want to put their fifty-five deputies on the exempt list and fire the outfit left to them by Low [previous reform mayor]? That's civil service for you. Just think! Fifty-five Republicans and mugwumps holdin' $3000 and $4000 and $5000 jobs in the tax department when 1555 good Tammany men are ready and willin' to take their places! It's an outrage! What did the people mean when they voted for Tammany? What is representative government, anyhow? Is it all a fake that this is a government of the people, by the people, and for the people? If it isn't a fake, then why isn't the people's voice obeyed and Tammany men put in all the offices?"

This is our old friend Boss Plunkitt talking. Once again we would doubtless disagree with the views of the Sage of Tammany Hall. But once again we must admire his flair for seeing into the essence of matters political. For Plunkitt was not interested in the tax department merely because of the patronage involved. As a realist he saw the importance of Tammany control of the agency that collected the taxes and turned the dollars over to the city officials.

To Plunkitt, government was a matter essentially of men and money. So it is today. Men must be elected and hired. Salaries must be paid and materials purchased. Moreover, the two are closely related. The cost of government depends partly on the ability of the men, and their ability to do a good job depends in part on how much money they have to spend.

★ 34

Men

and

money

WHERE DO THE MEN COME FROM?

When we talk about the "state," the "city," or the "county," we are using shorthand symbols that can be misleading. These are nothing more than terms for groups of people. Although we say that "the government" builds the roads or runs the schools, what we really mean is that a group of men whom we call public officials or public employees build the roads or run the schools. Over 4½ million people—engineers, clerks, governors, teachers, and the like—work for our state and local governments. In a sense they *are* state and local governments. How are these people chosen?

A few of them are elected, but only a very few. As to the rest, it is probably a safe guess to say that well over half of them are chosen because they know the right person and belong to the right political factions. Many of these persons are qualified, and some are among the best public officials in the nation. Nevertheless, they were chosen for patronage or party reasons, and no systematic attempt was made to bring people into governmental service on the basis of merit.

State and local merit systems

Approximately 25 states—most of them the larger and more populous states—have general merit systems. In all the states, however, the welfare workers who administer grants under the national Social Security law are selected on the basis of merit, since this is a condition attached to receiving federal money. The most general method of administering the merit system is by a civil service commission, usually composed of three members appointed by the governor with the consent of the senate, for six-year overlapping terms. The commission prepares and administers examinations, provides "eligible" registers for various jobs from which appointments may be made, establishes job classifications and prepares salary schedules, administers a system of efficiency ratings, makes and gives promotional examinations, administers regulations having to do with sick leaves, vacations, and so on, and serves as a board of appeal for persons who are discharged by their bosses. Commissions are becoming increasingly active in providing for in-service training and other programs to improve the morale of public servants.

How well do the commissions do their jobs? Their critics are many. Some argue that the commissions are too slow and wrapped up in red tape and cumbersome rules. Eligible lists are not kept up to date; it takes days to fill vacancies, they say. But a more serious charge is that civil service commissions have deprived responsible officials of the authority they need over their subordinates. There is too much emphasis, it is argued, on keeping the rascals out. The tendency is to give the employees so much job security in order to avoid any political coercion that administrators cannot get rid of incompetents. Cases have been cited where it has taken months and several elaborate hearings to get rid of secretaries who cannot type or librarians who cannot read.

In order to invigorate merit system administration and to get a more positive program, it has been suggested that commissions should be replaced by a director of personnel who in turn should be responsible to the governor, and that administrators be given greater discretion in choosing and disciplining their subordinates. Today there are some states—for example, Maryland, Connecticut, Virginia, Michigan, Wisconsin, Minnesota —that have what amounts to a single head personnel director.

One point needs to be emphasized. The mere passage of civil service legislation does not create a merit system. In many states the laws have been placed on the books and civil service commissions appointed, but the commissions are window dressing, and the patronage system still operates. Legislatures cripple the commissions by reducing their budgets and limiting their staffs. Payrolls are crowded with "temporary" or "provisional" employees. "Friendly" civil service commissioners are appointed. Employees with friends in the legislature get amendments to civil service laws in order to exempt their jobs from the regulations. In some states, some incumbents have been able to get technical amendments that result in their having what is tantamount to life tenure.

All the larger American cities have a merit system, and so do many of the smaller cities. In addition, some state laws require that certain kinds of employees such as policemen and firemen be chosen by merit. Most counties have no merit system, although there are exceptions. School teachers are almost always chosen today by school boards, but only after they have earned the appropriate certificates.

Salaries vary tremendously from state to state, city to city, and county to county. Most jobs, however, do not pay as much as is given for corresponding work by business and industry. Many able people are thus discouraged from entering state or local government service. Perhaps even more damaging is the lack of integrated systems. Each state, if it has a merit or career system at all, has its own program, each city has its own career service, and so on. A young man entering the service of a city cannot look forward to advancement up through the ranks with possibility of transferring as jobs open up to other cities or to the state service. If he leaves one service to enter another, he often loses retirement benefits and other privileges.

"Fallacies about Public Servants"

A Commission of Inquiry on Public Service Personnel published a famous and influential report in 1935 entitled "Better Government Personnel."[1] The Commission stated: "It is apparent that the weakest link in American democracy, the point at which we fall most conspicuously behind the other self-governing peoples, is in the appointive services where the great bulk of the work of modern government is carried on." The Commission concluded that the reason why our governments had failed to attract to public service their share of able men grew out of certain "fallacies." What are these fallacies?

[1] *Better Government Personnel* (New York: Whittlesey House, 1935).

1. "The false notion that 'to the victor belong the spoils.'

2. "The mistaken idea that duties of governmental employees are, as President Jackson said, 'so plain and simple that men of intelligence can readily qualify themselves for their performance.'

3. "The false idea that charity begins on the public payroll." As previously noted, too many people are elected or appointed to office because they need a job or have suffered some misfortune. The cost is poor service and lowered morale of other employees.

4. "The erroneous assumption that 'patronage is the price of democracy,' that the parties which we need for self-government cannot exist without spoils." Perhaps the Commission had in mind George Washington Plunkitt's famous "sillygism." Said Plunkitt: "First, this great and glorious country was built up by political parties; Second, parties can't hold together if their workers don't get offices when they win; Third, if the parties go to pieces, the government they built up must go to pieces, too; Fourth, then there'll be hell to pay. Say, honest, now; can you answer that argument?" But said the Commission, "There are, it is true, large cities, certain states, and other areas where political parties . . . are *at present* sustained by patronage. But in great sections of the United States, and in other democracies of the world, democracy exists, . . . parties thrive, without the spoliation of the appointive administrative services. The truth is, as Theodore Roosevelt once observed, that patronage is the curse of politics."

5. "The idea that 'the best public servant is the worst one. . . .'" The Commission pointed out that groups who have selfish reasons for desiring bad government indulge in the vilification of public employees. "Indiscriminate vilification lessens the morale of all public officials, dissuades capable persons from entering the public service, and discredits the authority of government."

6. "The erroneous thought that 'tenure is the cure of spoils.'

7. "The superficial thought that the way to eradicate spoils and favoritism is to begin at the bottom. . . ." In many states and cities the top administrative positions are exempt from the merit system, but these are the very positions where spoilsmen can demoralize the entire service.

8. "The belief in 'home town jobs for home town boys.'" "Residence qualifications," reports the Commission, "are a benefit only to incompetent applicants and petty politicians."

9. "The notion that 'the public service is always less capable and efficient than private enterprise.'" The Commission came to the conclusion that businesses and governments are about on a par, "what business gains through the profit motive and elasticity being apparently lost in many instances through hereditary management, labor difficulties, and outside control." Governments as a rule have not taken over a job except after

private agencies have demonstrated their inability or unwillingness to provide the service.

10. "The erroneous idea that the spoils system, the eleemosynary system and the other corrosive influences can be driven out of the public service through the prohibition of specific abuses. . . . What is clearly required is not negative laws, but the positive and militant handling of the problem of personnel with the active backing of the public and the press."[2]

The slow progress that has been made in the more than fifteen years since the Commission made its report indicates that these fallacies, if that they be, are still widely held. But slow as progress has been, it has been progress. Gradually people are coming to realize that "government is only as good as the men in it." But government needs more than able men. It needs financial resources, too.

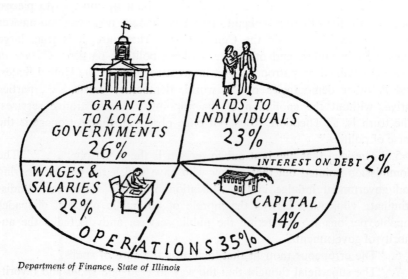

Department of Finance, State of Illinois

Illinois expenditures, 1950.

WHERE DOES THE MONEY COME FROM?

State and local governments, like the national government, get most of their money through taxation. But the states and local governments definitely play second fiddle to the national government. In recent years the demands of depression, wars, and defense have caused national taxes to surpass those collected by states and local communities. National officials have been forced to search for new sources of revenue; and as they have

[2] *Ibid.*, pp. 16-22.

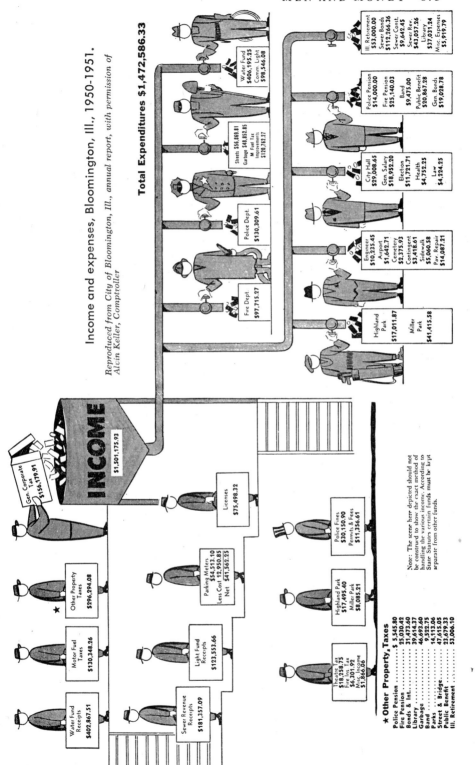

Income and expenses, Bloomington, Ill., 1950-1951.

Reproduced from City of Bloomington, Ill., annual report, with permission of Alvin Keller, Comptroller

Total Expenditures $1,472,586.33

done so, they have pushed into fields heretofore reserved for the other governments.[3]

The duplication—or virtually quadruplication—of governments by which the people of the United States govern themselves complicates the tax picture. Tax policies often conflict with one another. When the national government is reducing taxes to encourage spending by the public, states may be raising taxes. When the national government increases taxes in order to reduce inflation, the states often lower taxes. Indeed, state and local governments normally spend most money during periods of inflation and spend less money during periods of deflation. But whatever policies are pursued, each level of government pays little attention to the tax policy of the other.

The number of taxing authorities also makes tax-gathering an expensive operation. National officials collect taxes on gasoline, state officials collect taxes on gasoline, and so do some local officials. Each often maintains its own tax-gathering organization. Duplication of taxes is common. Naturally, the taxpayer is often confused. He is allowed to deduct certain business expenses from his federal income tax, but the same expenses are not deductible from his state income tax. The problem is complicated in another way in that changes in state laws often change the amount of federal tax. For example, the national government permits taxpayers to deduct state taxes in making their federal income tax return. Thus if a state increases its taxes, the national government gets less money.

No matter who collects the taxes, however, the money comes out of a single national economy. Each of the governments has a different tax base, and each of the taxes hits particular groups; but all government services, just as all our national wealth, rest on the productivity of the American people. At the same time, we must remember that these people, through their governments, add to that productivity. With their taxes they buy police protection, school buildings, highways, and other things that they— or at least many of them—think desirable. Who pays for these services?

Who shall pay the taxes?

A good tax might be defined as one that the other fella has to pay, a bad tax, one that I have to pay. Who shall bear the cost of state and local government is decided in the United States by the pushing and tugging of the political process. The people of any state are free to collect whatever taxes they wish from whomever (in that state) they wish, subject only to the restrictions imposed by the people of the United States through the national Constitution.

The Constitution, as we have noted, forbids states to tax exports or imports, or to levy tonnage duties without the consent of Congress; to use their

[3] H. M. Groves, *Financing Government*, 3d ed. (New York: Holt and Co., 1950).

taxing power to interfere with federal operations; to discriminate against interstate commerce, unduly burden it, or directly tax it; or to use their taxing power to deprive persons of equal protection of the law or deprive them of their property without due process and just compensation. Constitutional lawyers and judges spend much of their time trying to give concrete application to these constitutional generalities. Out of hundreds of disputes, they have decided, among other things, that states may not tax

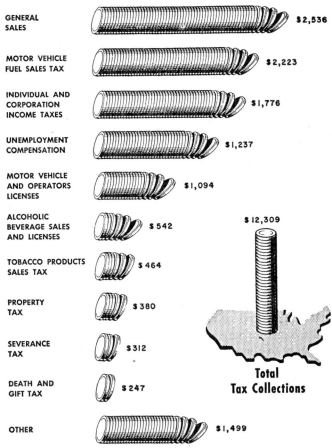

GENERAL SALES — $2,536

MOTOR VEHICLE FUEL SALES TAX — $2,223

INDIVIDUAL AND CORPORATION INCOME TAXES — $1,776

UNEMPLOYMENT COMPENSATION — $1,237

MOTOR VEHICLE AND OPERATORS LICENSES — $1,094

ALCOHOLIC BEVERAGE SALES AND LICENSES — $542

TOBACCO PRODUCTS SALES TAX — $464

PROPERTY TAX — $380

SEVERANCE TAX — $312

DEATH AND GIFT TAX — $247

OTHER — $1,499

$12,309

Total Tax Collections

Adapted from FACTS AND FIGURES ON GOVERNMENT FINANCE, *publication of The Tax Foundation*

State tax collections by source, fiscal year 1954 (millions).

tangible property located outside the state but may tax intangible property located outside the state but owned by their own citizens, may collect sales taxes from interstate sales, may collect income taxes from persons and corporations within the state even though the income was earned from interstate businesses, but may not tax the privilege of engaging in interstate commerce or the unapportioned gross receipts from interstate transactions.

State constitutions also restrict state taxing power. Certain kinds of property are exempt from taxation—property used for educational, charitable, or religious purposes, for example. State constitutions frequently list the kind of taxes that may be collected, forbidding those not mentioned. The amount of taxes that may be collected from various sources is also often stipulated.

The people of a city, county, or other local unit are hedged in even more by restrictions on their ability to tax themselves. Local governments have no inherent power of taxation. Their officials can levy only those taxes, in the amount, by the procedures, and for the purposes which the state constitution or the state legislature authorizes. What kind of taxes can they collect?

General property tax

Universally lambasted and considered by many to be "one of the worst taxes known to the civilized world," the *general property tax* is still the chief revenue source for local governments. It used to be the major state tax too, but in most states it is now of minor importance. The tax is cumbersome to administer, conducive to favoritism and inequities, and takes insufficient account of ability to pay.

A hundred years ago, wealth was primarily *real* property—land and buildings. And this real property was relatively easy to value. Without too much difficulty, assessors could guess the value of the property a man owned, and this was a good test of his ability to help pay for government. Today wealth takes on many forms. People own large amounts of *personal* property—both *tangible,* such as furniture, jewels, washing machines, expensive rugs, high-priced paintings, and *intangible,* such as stocks, bonds, money in the bank. A man can place a large amount of wealth, difficult to value and easy to conceal, into a small rented apartment. Real property too has altered. It no longer takes the form mainly of barns, houses, and land, but of large industrial plants, great retail stores, and office buildings the value of which is hard to measure.

Furthermore, ownership of property is less likely these days to correspond to ability to pay. The old couple with a large house valued at $15,000 are living from a small allowance provided by their children. They have to pay larger local taxes than does the young couple living in a rented apartment, both of whom work and have sizable incomes. Or compare the case of the man who borrows $7000 to buy a $10,000 house and who is paying off the mortgage out of his $4000 a year job, and the case of the man who owns a $10,000 house debt free and has a $5000 a year job. They both pay the same tax on their homes.

Although in many communities the lawbooks stipulate that the tax should be collected from all property, the tax falls in fact upon limited amounts of real property. Over 20 per cent of property in cities is exempt. Intangible personal property is seldom taxed. Some communities place a lower rate on intangible property in order to induce owners to announce their ownership. Tangible personal property, such as watches, rings, and so on, often escape taxation or are grossly undervalued. In most cities an unwritten general understanding develops as to what kind of property the honest taxpayer should list. The good citizen who attempts to follow the written word of the law is kindly advised by the assessor that it is not necessary.

Certain kinds of property are traditionally undervalued. Generally speaking, the more valuable the house and personal possessions, the greater the undervaluation. This is true of industrial properties as well. These valuations often require more technical training than most assessors possess. Considering these technical problems and the fact that assessors, locally elected, are under pressures from friends and political supporters, it is not surprising that assessments are sometimes inequitable. This same inequality often appears as between various units of the county or state. The assessor is under pressure to undervalue property so that the people who elect him will have to pay less taxes than those in other townships or counties.

In most states, *review and equalization boards* are established for each county and one for the entire state. Persons dissatisfied with the assessment on their property may appeal to these boards. Since only those who believe that their assessments are too high are likely to appeal, the boards do not correct undervaluations. They do, however, equalize total assessments among the various townships within the county and among the counties within the state. If, for example, property in one township is assessed at 80 per cent of value but only at 60 per cent of value in another township, the board for the county makes the necessary adjustment. The state review and equalization board often has responsibility for making assessment of utilities, railroads, and other selected kinds of properties. The boards in most counties and even at state level are often part-time jobs. Members receive small salaries and are not much more versed in arts of assessments than their local counterparts. The errors of one group sometimes merely compound those of the other.

The general property tax is also inflexible. During times of rising prices, assessed values move up much more slowly than the general price level. Thus when governments need more money, the tax basis does not move up fast enough. Conversely, when prices are deflated, valuations do not adjust downward as fast as the price level. When persons cannot pay taxes, much property is thrown onto the market for tax delinquency. During the 1930's, for example, the general property tax added to the miseries of many home owners and to the problems of state and local officials.

The complications of the general property tax make it difficult to compare tax rates among several communities. The rate in one city may be only $10 per thousand as compared with another city with a rate of $40 per thousand. But in the second city, valuation may be computed only at a tenth of "real" value. Claims of local politicians that they have kept down the tax rate must be scrutinized with care.

Despite its weaknesses, the general property tax will probably remain an important source of revenue for local governments. It is especially well suited, of all the levels of government, to local government because real property rather than personal property is the chief beneficiary of many local services, such as fire protection. Alternative taxes are few, and they have their own disadvantages. Moreover, some of the bad features of the general property tax can be and are being avoided by more sensible administration.

In the first place, duplicate assessments of the same property can be avoided. Rather than have the township assessor, city assessor, county assessor each make an independent valuation of the same property, the better practice, and the more frequent practice today, is to have one assessor do the job for all the governments.

Courtesy NATION'S BUSINESS

Politically speaking, the property tax raises the loudest squawks.

Secondly, the job of assessor can be given to a qualified person who is paid a decent salary. He should be appointed by larger governments, the county instead of township, which have the resources to support full time assessors. Boards of review and equalization should be established in districts large enough to support a small board of competent and highly paid individuals. Some progress has been made. In Kentucky, assessors are still elected, but they must pass an examination. In Iowa, county assessors are now selected on an examination basis. Other states have also moved in this direction.

Thirdly, systematic methods of appraising property can be adopted and modern property records maintained. In many cities, and all of the larger ones, city tax maps and modern techniques of appraisal are used. Fourthly, state governments should abandon the general property tax. A number of the states have already done this, and in most of them the state takes little from this source. Finally, after property has been assessed and the tax rate for each unit (township, county, school district) determined, one agency can collect the taxes for all local units and then remit a share to each. This is the general practice, although some duplication still exists.

Other reforms have been suggested. But even with improved tax administration the general property tax will not supply states or the localities with all the money they need to render the services their citizens want. What other taxes do they use?

Other taxes

Sales taxes. This depression-born tax is now one of the most important sources of money for many of the states. Almost three-fourths of the states impose some kind of general sales tax, normally applied to retail sales. City sales taxes are less common, although nearly 1000 cities collect them. City sales taxes are readily evaded; people simply do their shopping outside the city limits. Sales taxes are often unpopular with local merchants, who fear that such levies drive trade away. Most cities and states try to prevent evasion by imposing also a *use tax* payable by persons who purchase items outside the city or state for use within the city or state. Most use taxes are, however, difficult to collect.

Sales taxes, especially those levied by the state, are relatively easy to administer and produce large amounts of revenue. Despite their regressive nature (that is, their tendency to bear hardest on the lower-income groups), their popularity is increasing. They seem relatively painless since the consumer puts out the few cents on each item rather than paying a large tax bill at one time. Labor groups and persons with small incomes who pay a larger percentage of their income for the sales tax than do those with higher incomes are generally opposed to the sales tax. They would favor more use of the progressive income tax. They argue that persons with small incomes spend a larger part of their budget for food and clothing than do the wealthy, and sales taxes fall on those least able to pay. In some states, food has been exempted from the sales tax. In others these groups have been strong enough either to block passage of sales taxes or to push through an income tax along with it.

Income taxes. Personal income taxes are now collected in 31 states, but in most states the income tax is a less important source of money than the sales tax. Income taxes are generally progressive or graduated—that is, the rate goes up with the size of the income. State income tax rates, however,

What you SPENT largely determined your Illinois STATE tax bill

What you OWNED largely determined your LOCAL tax bill

What you EARNED largely determined your FEDERAL tax bill

Department of Finance, State of Illinois.

The tax bill of Illinois.

do not rise as sharply as the federal tax and rarely go over 10 per cent. Exemption policies vary, but in most states they are generous enough to exclude large numbers of people. Corporation incomes are frequently taxed at a flat rate. Because of the importance and burden of the federal income tax there is a strong feeling that states should go slow.

Some cities have followed the lead of Philadelphia and Toledo and collect a payroll tax. Philadelphia imposes a relatively small flat tax on salaries of all persons and net profits of unincorporated businesses and professions. The Toledo tax applies also to corporate profits. These taxes are attractive to hard-pressed cities and enable them to collect money from those "daytime" citizens who use city facilities but reside in the suburbs.

Special excise taxes. All states tax gasoline and alcohol, and most of them tax tobacco. Since many cities also tax these items, the local, state, and federal levies often double the cost of these "luxury" items to the consumer. Gasoline taxes are sometimes combined with the funds collected from automobile and drivers' licenses and earmarked for highway purposes. Liquor taxes often come in the form of licenses to manufacture or sell alcoholic beverages and of levies on the sale or consumption of the beverage. Some states maintain state-owned liquor dispensaries and receive revenues in this manner in addition to taxation. High taxation of liquor is justified on the grounds that it reduces the amount consumed, falls on an item that is not generally considered a necessity of life, and through licensing, eases the job of law enforcement. If the tax is raised too high, however, liquor tends to be diverted into illegal channels, and tax revenues from this source fall off.

This list does not begin to exhaust the kinds of taxes collected by states and their subdivisional governments. Admissions taxes, stock transfer taxes, inheritance taxes, parimutuel taxes, corporate franchise taxes, and others are quite common. The severance tax on the privilege of "severing" natural resources such as coal, oil, and timber is important in some states. In Texas and Oklahoma, for example, the severance tax on oil and natural gas is a major source of state revenue.

Nontax revenues

In addition to taxation, states get some money from fees and special service charges. In fact, about 8 per cent of the money collected by the states and 10 per cent of local government revenue come from these sources. Fees are charged for building inspection, for recording of titles, for court costs, for licensing of professions, for garbage disposal, and other special services. Parking meters have become an important revenue source for many cities. Special assessments against property owners whose property is benefited by public improvements, such as streets or sewers, are a general practice.

Some cities run business enterprises from which they make money (sometimes they lose money, too). Municipally owned waterworks or gas and light companies often contribute to the city treasury. In some cases, utility profits are large enough so that no other city taxes are collected. State owned liquor dispensaries are good sources of money.

Grants from one level of government to another have become increasingly important during the last several decades. As we have noted, the national government through grants-in-aid allots large sums to the states. The states are giving more and more money to the local governments, in the form of state grants to support particular programs or in the form of shared taxes. In the latter case, state officials return to local governments revenues collected from certain taxes. States allot money to their various local governments on the basis of many factors. Increasingly, they are giving them sums of money without specifying the purposes for which the money shall be used.

When all the taxes and fees are added together, states and local governments collect large sums. But often they are still not enough to build the highways or provide the amount of public assistance to the elderly or perform the other functions that the voters have insisted upon. What then? Even as you and I, our governments often have to borrow money.

BORROWING MONEY

During the early years of the nineteenth century, states and cities often gave money to railroads and canal builders. Or they issued bonds to finance public improvements. Frequently, the standards were not high, and bribery and favoritism were common. Provision for payment of debts was inadequate. At times, the people were stuck with the paying off of old debts for improvements long after the improvements had lost their value. As a result, default on obligations frequently occurred, and city and state credit fell off.

Aroused by legislative abuse of powers, voters insisted on constitutional amendments to reduce legislative discretion. Today most state constitutions contain elaborate restrictions on the power of state and local legislatures to borrow money or to pledge the credit of the state. In large measure the power to borrow money for a long term has been transferred from the legislatures and city councils to the voters, since most constitutions require that the question be presented to the voters for their approval.

The amount of short-term borrowing has been reduced by improved fiscal planning so that taxes are collected in time to be used for necessary operating expenses. Even so, officials sometimes need to borrow money for a short term. This "floating debt" consists of bank loans, tax-anticipation warrants, and other notes and is paid off out of current revenues.

States and localities, especially cities, sometimes need to borrow money for longer periods—fifteen or twenty years. During the depression, money was needed for relief. Since the end of World War II many states have gone into debt in order to pay bonuses to veterans. Expenditures for highway construction, school buildings, slum clearance, and so on are so large that it is not feasible to pay for these capital improvements out of current revenue. Moreover, these improvements have a long life and add to the wealth of the community, so it is desirable to pay for them by spreading the cost. For this purpose, governments issue bonds. The best practice, and one now required by many constitutions, is to issue *serial bonds,* a portion of which come due each year and are retired out of current revenues.

State and local bonds are especially attractive to wealthy investors since interest received from them is at the present time exempt from federal income tax. For this reason, these governments can borrow money at a lower interest rate than can private businesses. The credit of most cities and states is good, and they readily find buyers for their bonds. Some bonds are *general obligation bonds* and are backed by the credit of the issuing governments. Other bonds, *revenue bonds,* have the backing of only the income of the particular project in which the money is invested. Governments are often permitted to issue revenue bonds beyond the limitations upon their general indebtedness, and this type is used wherever possible.

During World War II, with incomes high and tax collections good, many states were able to retire much of their indebtedness. Building was restricted and public improvements curtailed. Since the end of the war, state and municipal borrowing has increased in order to pay veterans' bonuses and to finance improvements that had been postponed by the emergency. Debts of state governments have mounted sharply in recent years, climbing from $2.4 billion in 1946 to $11.3 billion in 1955.

SPENDING THE MONEY

The states and local governments are spending more money for more things than they did fifty years ago. Spending by state governments has almost tripled since World War II, rising from $7.1 billion in 1946 to $20.5 billion in 1955. But it is interesting to note that the percentage of the national income taken by these governments has not materially increased. Their expenditures in terms of real and not inflated dollars are not relatively much greater than they were twenty years ago, despite the fact that they have more duties than they ever had before. Even with their weaknesses—and there are many—state and local governments are giving better services than they did in the past without taking any appreciably larger part of the national income. Most citizens are probably getting their money's worth. Of course, there remains much room for improvement.

Who controls the purse strings? City councils, town meetings, school boards—the legislature—as might be expected, at any level of American government, all share in deciding how much and what kinds of taxes shall be collected and how much and for what purpose the money shall be spent, subject to constitutional limitations. But the preparation of the budget and the responsibility for planning the state or city's program is becoming more and more the job of the chief executive. In at least forty states the governor prepares the budget; his staff reviews estimates coming from the various departments, correlates the program, and transmits it to the legislature. The mayor or manager has the same job in many municipalities. In other places, either the legislature or a group of officials prepares the budget.

The *executive budget* is preferred because the governor or mayor who manages the administration can review programs from the point of view of the over-all needs of the government. Each department head is always convinced that his department needs more money. but the chief executive has to balance the needs of all the departments. The budget is prepared in much the same way as the national budget. In fact, the practice of the national government was adapted from the experiences of the states. The legislative body, normally through its committees, holds hearings and acts upon the executive's budget recommendations. In some states and in a few cities, however, the legislature cannot increase or add to the executive's recommendations. Whether or not the governor has the political

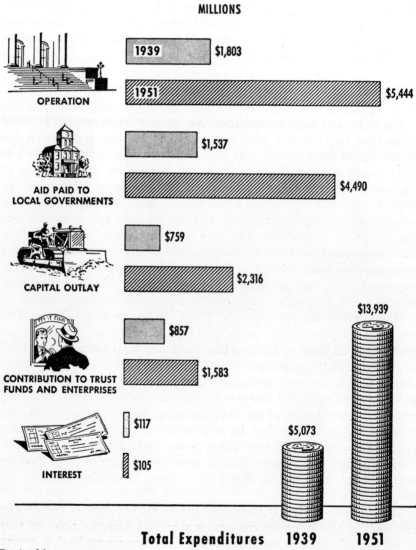

MILLIONS

1939 — $1,803
1951 — $5,444
OPERATION

$1,537
$4,490
AID PAID TO LOCAL GOVERNMENTS

$759
$2,316
CAPITAL OUTLAY

$857
$1,583
CONTRIBUTION TO TRUST FUNDS AND ENTERPRISES

$117
$105
INTEREST

$13,939
$5,073

Total Expenditures   1939   1951

Reprinted from FACTS & FIGURES ON GOVERNMENT FINANCE, *publication of the Tax Foundation*

General expenditures of state governments by character.

power to make his control effective, most of them probably have greater control over state expenditures than does the President over national. In addition to the item veto, governors often have control over allotment of funds to departments even after appropriations have been approved by the legislature. This power over the budget, as we have noted, makes it possible for the executive to control departmental operations, to prevent duplication and overlapping, and to require efficient operations.

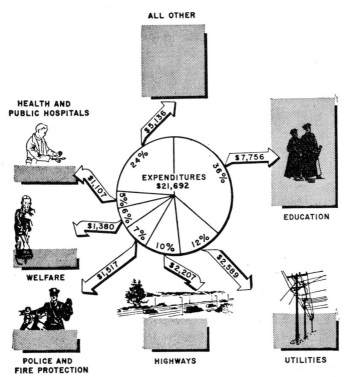

ALL OTHER

HEALTH AND PUBLIC HOSPITALS

EXPENDITURES $21,692

24%

36%

$5,136

$7,756

EDUCATION

$1,107

$1,380

7%

10%

12%

WELFARE

$1,517

$2,207

$2,589

POLICE AND FIRE PROTECTION

HIGHWAYS

UTILITIES

Reprinted from FACTS AND FIGURES ON GOVERNMENT FINANCE, *publication of the Tax Foundation*

Total local government expenditures, fiscal year 1953
(in millions).

Centralized purchasing

The recent budget for a large city provided, among other things, for $10 for two sapphire phonograph needles for use by the municipal radio station; $96,500 to heat a museum; $4.80 for canned coal for the Mayor's fireplace; $30 for a pair of electric clippers to shear mice, rats, and rabbits used by the Department of Health; $250,000 for bread and $1,735,000 for meat to feed persons in city prisons and hospitals.

How should supplies be purchased? In the past each department went out into the market and bought its own supplies. Favoritism and inefficiency were the inevitable result. Today most states and most larger cities have some kind of centralized purchasing. One agency buys supplies for all the departments. Sometimes departments are permitted to purchase certain kinds of special equipment for themselves, while the purchasing agency handles items used by several departments. Central purchasing makes it easier to curb favoritism. It permits large purchases and thus better discounts. It allows for laboratories so that materials can be tested for quality and performance. It means that the government is more likely to get the best for its money. Specialists who know the market and who have contacts with suppliers do the buying instead of some clerk in a department. Small cities and counties have not generally been as quick as states and large cities in adopting modern purchasing methods. Many of them are too small to support a central purchasing agency. In some regions several counties and smaller cities have pooled their resources to employ a purchasing agent who serves them all.

NEW YORK CITY ADOPTS A BUDGET

New York City spends more than any other government in the United States except the national government. Its yearly expenses run over a billion dollars. How does it go about making up its budget?

New York's fiscal year begins on July 1st. During the previous fall, the Director of the Budget, after consulting the Mayor, sends out a letter and a folder of instructions to the heads of the city's 109 departments, asking for requests. In the meantime, the Comptroller makes his estimates of how much money the city can expect to get in taxes, grants from the federal and state governments, and from various licenses and fees.

The fifty examiners in the city's Budget Bureau, who have been checking up on where the money from last year's budget is going, begin to get to work on the various departmental estimates. They have to have their work finished by early March, at which time the Mayor goes into a two-week-long session with the department heads, who appear before him to try to convince him that they need more money than the budget examiners and the Budget Director are recommending. Although department heads who disagree with the budget examiners often complain to the Budget Director, he usually can be expected to back up the examiners. At the end of the two weeks, after having gone over each item in the budget, deciding disputes between department heads and the Budget Bureau, the Mayor gives the revised budget his approval.

In 1947, for example, the biggest item in the budget was debt service on the city's $2,857,230,990.47 debt. Much of this debt was the result of earlier mismanagement, but it was still saddled on the people of New York. Some of the trouble goes back to 1870 when the city issued $278,-000 worth of 7 per cent non-callable bonds in order to lay some wooden planks on a street in the Bronx. The last of those bonds will not mature until March 1st, 2147! In 1947, $198,000 worth of them were still outstanding, costing the city over $14,000 in interest in that year.

Practically all of the bonds the city has ever issued have been non-callable, because these are the only sort the banks seem willing to accept. In 1940, when the city took over the subways, it issued more than 300 million dollars' worth of 3 per cent bonds with a maturity date of 1980. In 1947 that money could have been borrowed for 2 per cent or less, but it was impossible to call in the formerly issued bonds. By that time most of the subway equipment the city had bought with that money already had been discarded. The city was paying $10,200,000 a year interest on non-callable bonds for equipment that was already worn out.

The laws of the state did not permit the city to tax real estate more than 2 per cent of the average assessed value for the prior five years, except what was needed to service the debt. For this reason the city had to keep its budget down, since there were few places it could go for additional revenue. It did have a sales tax and a hotel-room tax, but rates were fixed by state law.

By April 1st, 1947, the budget had been approved by the Mayor, and the 21½ pound volume containing it was printed. The next step was its consideration by the Board of Estimates. This board is composed of the Mayor (three votes), the Comptroller (three votes), the President of the City Council (three votes), and the five Borough Presidents (two votes each for Manhattan and Brooklyn, and one vote each for the other three boroughs). The Board has the authority to raise or lower the budget.

During the second week in April, the Board, sitting at a horseshoe-shaped mahogany table on a dais, held public hearings to listen to the 167 citizens who had something to say about the budget. Most of those who appeared were city employees who came to ask for higher wages. But a couple of dozen private citizens came to ask the Board to cut the budget. Others were there with suggestions as to how the city could raise more money.

Three days after the public hearings, the Board met in a closed session. The Comptroller reported the happy news that he had underestimated the city's revenues by about $2,000,000. In a short time, the Board boosted the budget by $2,841,440 adding to appropriations for schools, child-care centers, hospitals, and charitable institutions.

Within a week the budget was presented to the City Council. The Council has no authority to raise the budget—it can only accept or lower it. The Mayor has power to veto any changes the Council might make, and it takes a three-fourths vote of the Council to over-rule him. The Council turned the budget over to a Finance Committee for study. The Finance Committee also held public hearings, but these hearings lasted less than an hour.

On May 6, the City Council met to consider the Finance Committee's report. Twenty-three of the twenty-seven council members were present. The Chairman of the Finance Committee reported that the Committee had no changes to recommend and advocated that the Council adopt the budget. An hour-long debate followed. Then the budget was adopted, 23-0. Two days later, the Mayor signed a statement certifying that the city could spend $1,031,961,754.73 during the next fiscal year.

T HE SUBJECTS OF THE PRECEDING SEVEN CHAP-
ters—state constitutions and lawmakers, governors and judges, local forms
of government, state and local officials and services—can be understood
only as part and parcel of a stream of political forces that operate in every
state. Forms of government and political patterns intermesh. How the state
lawmakers carry on their proceedings in a particular state, or the relation
between governor and legislature, or the functions of state government
cannot be explained without considering the nature of the party system
and the pattern of politics in that state.

In a country as diversified as the United States, it is not surprising that
the nature of the political forces and party relationships varies widely from
state to state. There are the politics of California with its fluid electoral
arrangements, such as cross-filing; the well-organized party politics of New
York; the one-party states of the South and the North, with their endless
factional struggles within the single dominant party. This variety is too great
to be encompassed here. All we can seek to do is to discuss some of the
political patterns common to many of the states and indicate in a general
way the significance of party arrangements in the operation of our state and
local governments.

Variety is not the only problem in describing state politics. Precise information is often lacking. Only recently has there been much systematic
study of state politics. Comments about state politics, therefore, must be
unusually tentative, and the
generalizations must be accepted with more than normal
skepticism.

35 ★

INTERDEPENDENCE OF
NATIONAL AND STATE
POLITICS

It is difficult to separate national from state and local
politics. As we have already
noted, national parties are intermeshed with, and in large
part are made up of, state and
local parties. The very structure of the national party organizations, as noted in Chapter 13, grows out of the state
parties. The issues that divide
the nation are issues having

Patterns of

state and

local politics

roots in the state and local communities.

National issues are today dominant. The voters have not only little concern with state politics, but as Professor Dayton D. McKean has written, "It is probably safe to assume that the level of information is very low. Probably not one per cent of the voters have read their state constitutions or know the name of any state official except the governor."[1] Moreover, partisan affiliations are more likely to grow out of and to be changed by national issues than by state or local divisions. Here are some of the ways national politics are related to state politics.

One important relation between national and state politics is reflected in the manner in which swings in party fortunes at the national level are associated with swings at the state level. Whenever the Democratic party's fortunes, for example, are on the upswing in presidential and congressional races, an increase in the number of Democratic governors, state legislators, mayors, and local councilmen can also be expected. The same is true for the Republicans (although a Republican national victory seldom has a decisive impact on Democratic control of southern state governments). Moreover, the relationship is a constant one—the greater the national party sweep, the greater the local party victories. As votes for the two parties at the national level even off, the number of states that split the presidential and gubernatorial results also increases.[2] The famous coattails effect (see p. 304) is a factor here, but the situation is not necessarily a one-way cause and effect relationship. Strong candidates at the state level help the national candidates, and strong national candidates help those running for state and local office. All that we know is that victories of the party at one level are normally associated with victories at the other.

The almost unprecedented 1956 election, in which the presidency went Republican and Congress Democratic, did not belie this basic tendency. It seems clear that the strong presidential vote for Eisenhower produced many state and local victories for Republican candidates who, without Eisenhower's "coattails," would not have won.

Impact of national politics in the one-party states

Party systems of our states can and have been classified according to many different criteria. One useful classification has been made by Professors Ranney and Kendall who divided the states into three categories: the *two-party* type in which the two parties share the bulk of the votes and public offices between them, the winning party gains a majority of the votes and offices, and the two dominant parties alternate in winning majorities; the

---

[1] Dayton D. McKean, "The Politics of the States," *The Forty-eight States: Their Tasks as Policy Makers and Administrators,* ed. James W. Fesler (New York: The American Assembly, 1955), p. 66.

[2] V. O. Key, Jr., *American State Politics* (New York: Alfred A. Knopf, 1956), pp. 29-33. Many of the materials in this chapter come from this fruitful volume.

modified one-party type in which one party wins all or almost all the offices, but the second party normally receives a substantial percentage of the votes; and the *one-party* type in which one party wins all or nearly all the offices and the second party usually receives only a small percentage of the popular votes.[3] The map below shows how the state party systems are classified by this procedure.

The impact of national politics varies with the kind of party system in the states. In the one-party and modified one-party states, the second party

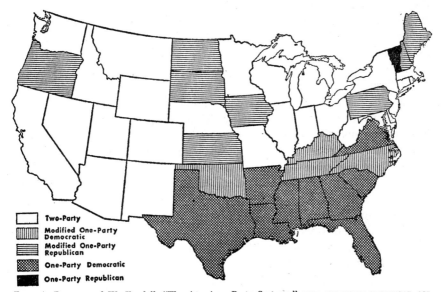

Two-Party

Modified One-Party
Democratic

Modified One-Party
Republican

One-Party Democratic

One-Party Republican

From A. Ranney and W. Kendall, "The American Party Systems," THE AMERICAN POLITICAL SCI-
ENCE REVIEW, *Vol. XLVIII, No. 2, June, 1954, p. 485, with permission of the authors and of the*
REVIEW

The state party systems.

organization often has little interest in state and local politics. Although in some of the modified one-party states the second party may occasionally win the presidential race, the dominant party controls the machinery of state and local affairs. The second party organization is apt to be concerned only with national politics and with the patronage that its national party leaders can pass out if they capture the White House. Within the state, however, that party's leaders make only nominal efforts to gain control of state affairs. Often they do not even bother to nominate candidates or maintain local party organizations. Indeed, some members of these second-party organizations have a vested interest in keeping their party in the minority. For if their little party should become a serious contender within the state, these leaders would have to share their patronage and influence in national politics with other political leaders in their state.

[3] A. Ranney and W. Kendall, "The American Party Systems," *The American Political Science Review*, Vol. XLVIII, No. 2, June 1954, pp. 477-485.

National politics sometimes tends to solidify sectional differences and strengthen one-partyism. The Deep South offers the classic example. In the one-party states of the Deep South the race issue dominates all other matters. It has led the state politicians to smother their other differences and has blurred conflict on state issues in the face of the southern whites' felt need to maintain unity against the rest of the nation.

On the other hand, there are signs that industrialization and urbanization are having an impact on both the rural Republican-dominated states and the rural Democratic ones. In the border and upper southern states, the race issue has become somewhat less prominent. Industry brings to these regions the same issues that it brought earlier to the rest of the country—management versus labor, large industry versus small, railroads versus trucks, and so on. These issues appear to create the same pattern of political differences that can be found in other regions and tend to move the states in the direction of two-party, or at least modified one-party, systems.

While national issues are usually the major concern of the state and local politicians of the second party in the one-party and modified one-party states, the reverse is often the case with the party professionals in the stronger party in one-party states as well as those of both parties in the two-party states. These professionals, though concerned with the party's national fortunes, depend on success at home for their political lives and influence. They tend to view national leaders in terms of the latter's ability to help the state organization to victory and have little sense of obligation to the party in other states, or nationally. We will return to this when we discuss the *independence* of state politics.

Impact of national politics on city politics

At one time the classical big city party organization existed almost exclusively by handing out a generous quantity of favors and patronage and receiving in return support at the polls. The boss and his lieutenants were always ready to help a voter. The city political organization was an expensive but fairly efficiently organized welfare agency. Issues were not discussed, but Mrs. Jones voted for the men who had helped her get coal in the winter and who ran a social club for her boys.

Today, trade unions, civic clubs, and national party leaders instruct, educate, and cajole the voters. The boss has competitors for the voters' favors. Mrs. Jones is no longer so willing to give her votes for small favors; rather, she may want to know how the candidates stand on aid to Israel, partition of Ireland, and the current presidential candidates.

The party organization is no longer the only organization trying to pull out the voters. Many interest groups are also active. And as the government has extended its social services, the voters have less need for help from the party organization. Moreover, national candidates are no longer so dependent on the local party in order to get their messages to the voters and to get out the vote. National candidates can speak to the voters by radio and television without the intermediation of local party officials. Local organizations are still with us, but national politics has had an impact on the nature of their operations and their functions.

THE INDEPENDENCE OF STATE POLITICS

Despite the interrelations between national and state politics as just described, American federalism plays up some aspects of state politics and tends to separate them out of the national picture. Our federal system gives to the state parties a large measure of independence. Moreover, state politicians have much to do with the structure and shape of national parties.

Each state regulates its own political parties. Save for a few national laws dealing with timing of national elections, expenditures of candidates for national offices, and activities of federal employees and those state employees receiving federal assistance, it is the states who regulate party affairs.

Each state has the power to establish the schedule of state elections. Subject to constitutional limitations, each state establishes qualifications for voters and for participation in party affairs. Each state exercises control over its own nominating procedures. The states, not the national party officials, decide which candidates shall carry the party label. For example, in 1948 despite the fact that President Truman was nominated by the Democratic National Convention as the Democratic candidate for President, his name was kept completely off the ballot in Alabama, and he was not the official Democratic candidate for President in Louisiana, Mississippi, and South Carolina. Likewise the states determine how other candidates are to be nominated and the role of party officials in this process.

The independent character of state parties is further illustrated by the fact that state parties secure their own financial support and receive little or no help from the national parties. Each state party is also free to adopt its own party platform. Despite the fact that there is seldom much interest in these platforms—sometimes they are not even printed—at times they differ with, and even flatly contradict, the national platform.

Exercising their authority, about twenty states have attempted to isolate state from national politics by scheduling state elections in years when no presidential election is being held. This is not done solely or even mainly because of some desire to concentrate the voters' attention on state issues; rather it is part of the tactics of party warfare. In some states the smaller of the two parties can hope to win state offices only in those years when it can tie in the fortunes of its state candidates with those of a popular presidential candidate. Such was the case with some weak Republican state parties in 1956. For states where the parties are more evenly matched, the separate scheduling of gubernatorial and presidential elections deprives the state candidates of the wide appeal and coattails effect of the party with the winning presidential candidate. For example, when Franklin D. Roosevelt was winning presidential elections, it was to the Democrats' advantage that gubernatorial elections in states such as Ohio, Connecticut, or Massachusetts coincided with the presidential elections. On the other hand, Republicans in 1952 and 1956 benefited from the support that President Eisenhower brought to their ticket by running for President at the same time.

STATE PARTIES AND SEPARATION OF POWERS

It is often supposed that one of the functions of political parties is to moderate the constitutionally imposed separation of powers, especially between the governor and the state legislature. The voters are supposed to select one of the parties which then brings executive and legislative leaders together in the management of state affairs. Do the parties perform this function?

Aside from the one-party and the modified one-party states, the legislature and governorship are often controlled by different parties. This is especially true of states with more evenly matched parties. In states where the Democratic party is stronger, the Republicans may capture the governorship, but often the Democrats will still control the legislature. But in the North, as both V. O. Key and Dayton D. McKean have pointed out, a much more frequent pattern is for Democratic governors to face Republican legislative majorities.[4]

In many northern states, Democratic majorities can elect a governor but only a minority of the legislators. The legislative over-representation of small towns and rural areas, the centers of Republican strength, give to that party an advantage in securing control of the state legislatures. In some states this amounts to almost a permanent monopoly. In Massachusetts, for example, in eight out of nineteen elections between 1920 and 1956, the Democrats won the governorship, but in no case did they gain a majority in both houses of the concurrently chosen state legislature.[5] In New Jersey, New York, Connecticut, California, and Wisconsin the story is much the same.

The staggering of elections over different years also contributes to party division between the legislature and the executive. Some state constitutions stagger senate terms; others give the governor a term different from that of one of the legislative chambers. In short, constitutional provisions added to political obstacles are largely the reasons that in many states voters cannot take control of state government away from a party and hand it to the other. Party responsibility in such circumstances is impossible. Rather, all that

[4] McKean, *op. cit.*, p. 72, and Key, *op. cit.*, p. 58.
[5] Key, *op. cit.*, p. 65.

voters can do to chastise one party is to give control of the governorship to the other party.

Whether such conditions are desirable is a complex question that was discussed at length in Chapter 21. In any event, the result is often a stalemate between governor and legislature. To get action the chief executive has to depend on dramatic appeals to the electorate or handing out patronage. Even when the governor and legislature are of the same party a deadlock may ensue because the gerrymandering of the legislature causes it to represent a constituency different from the governor's. To quote McKean, when the late Governor Hoffman of New Jersey was presented with a deadlock, "in one session [he] appointed so many state senators to jobs that the senate lost its constitutional quorum. The separation of powers often presents, therefore, the choice between no action and unethical action."[6]

Parties and the judiciary

Party control over the selection of judicial personnel is difficult to describe. First, the conditions are greatly varied. Second, so little detailed study has been made that our generalizations, always tentative in talking about state politics, must be even more tentative when describing relations between party and state judiciaries.

In those states where judges are appointed, the men selected usually belong to the same party as the appointing authority, usually the governor. Judges who are elected, as most of them are, are often affected by the same national trends as the other state officials. Many states attempt to isolate judicial elections from party politics by holding them at times different from other elections or by establishing nonpartisan nominations and elections. But a judicial post is a much sought after position, and the party faithful are often rewarded by the support of the party organization in securing the nomination and the election.

Judicial and legal canons attempt to minimize the partisan activities of judicial candidates. But voters frequently know little about these men except their party labels. By and large, the party that dominates the legislative and executive branches dominates the judicial as well.

Parties in the state legislatures

Except for Minnesota and Nebraska, all candidates for the state legislature are nominated by political parties and elected as party members. There is a great variety within the several state legislatures, however, as to the role of the parties in the actual management of the legislature and in policymaking.

The American Political Science Association's Committee on State Legis-

[6] Dayton D. McKean, "The Politics of the States," *The Forty-eight States: Their Tasks as Policy Makers and Administrators*, p. 71.

latures discovered a strong degree of party spirit and cohesion in seventeen state legislatures; within these states members of the same political party tend to vote alike.[7] Eleven states reported that parties are only occasionally or moderately strong, and twenty indicated weak or nonexistent party control within the state legislatures. In the states lacking strong party cohesion, differences within the legislature follow other than party lines. In some states, for example, the control of the legislature reflects the rural-versus-urban split; in others legislators cluster around conservative or liberal coalitions; and in still others there appear to be no stable alignments, but shifting combinations of factions. The committee also reported fairly even divisions in nineteen states between the two parties in the legislature; in nine states one of the parties dominated, but the other had a sizable number of seats in the legislature; and in eighteen states one party overwhelmingly dominated the legislature.

Party cohesion and party spirit are most likely to be found in the two-party legislatures. It is also in these legislative assemblies that party caucuses are most likely to function. In some of these party meetings, policy is made that party members are expected to support in the legislative sessions. Some of the two-party legislatures, however, exhibit little party cohesion, and even where party cohesion exists, its role may be exaggerated.

In states where one party dominates the legislature, but the minority party has a sizable number of seats, a greater variety is found in the role of the party. For example, in New Jersey, where the Republicans dominate but the Democrats have a significant voice, both the political parties are highly organized; but in Iowa and Maryland only the majority party has cohesion, and the minority party is weak.[8] But the most prevalent pattern in these states is for both parties to be weak.

In legislatures where a single party has overwhelming control (the Democrats held every seat in both houses in six southern states), parties have little role in legislative business. In these states, however, factions within the dominant party are sometimes very active. For example, in North Dakota, where the Republicans hold most of the seats, there have been two factions within the party: the Republican Organizing Committee, which has been more or less conservative, and the Non-Partisan League, which represented the more progressive forces. Sometimes in these states, factions organize

[7] Belle Zeller, ed., *American State Legislatures* (New York: Thomas Y. Crowell Company, 1954), pp. 192 ff.

[8] Zeller, *op. cit.*, p. 206. For other studies of role of party in state legislature see Malcolm E. Jewell, "Party Voting in American State Legislatures," *American Political Science Review,* Vol. XLIX (September 1955), pp. 773-791, and for studies of particular states, see William J. Keefe, "Parties, Partisanship, and Public Policy in the Pennsylvania Legislature," *The American Political Science Review,* Vol. XLVIII, No. 2, June 1954, pp. 450-464, and, on a more general aspect, Leon D. Epstein, "A Two-Party Wisconsin," *The Journal of Politics,* Vol. 18, No. 3, August 1956, pp. 427-458.

around dominant personalities—the Long and Anti-Long factions in Louisiana, for example.

In summary, parties are more likely to be strong in the two-party legislatures, weakest in the one-party legislatures, and in the middle in the
modified one-party legislatures. In a few state legislatures, parties seem to
play a more prominent role than they do in Congress, but they are considerably weaker in most state legislatures. Party control of legislation, in
short, is far weaker in most states than it is even in Congress.

Parties and the executive department

In the states, as we have seen in Chapter 30, the governor is only one
of several elected executives. Do political parties help to integrate these
many different executives into a cooperating team? In the one-party states,
the same party wins all the executive offices and all or most of the elections.
But it is precisely in these one-party states, where the dominant party
faces the weakest opposition, that the parties are least likely to be cohesive
and have the "least capacity to tie together the work of the scattered agencies
of government." To quote again from V. O. Key, "whatever order and coherence develops within the administration in one-party situations must rest
on some factor other than the tie of party. When one party holds both
governorship and minor offices without effective challenge, the incentives
for collaboration among fellow partisans are not apt to be strong."[9]

What of the role of party in those states where the political parties are
more evenly matched? In such states one party frequently fails to carry the
whole slate. Where the Republican party tends to be the stronger—as is
the case in most states outside the South and the border states—the Democrats encounter difficulty in getting a full slate elected. Although, as the
lesser of the two parties, the Democrats may gather enough strength to
elevate one of their men to the gubernatorial office, it takes an unusually
sizable victory for them to gain control of the entire executive slate. The
Republicans have the same difficulty in border and other states where the
Democrats are normally the larger party.

The division of party control of executive departments creates obvious
difficulties in developing any sense of party responsibility for the conduct
of administration. In addition, administrative difficulties arise to face a governor who has to work with officials who are likely to be his partisan
enemies. Executive teamwork is difficult under such circumstances. In those
states where party competition is keenest and where party control of the
executives is divided, we are most likely to find party discipline. Key has
well summed up the dilemma: In those states where a party has unchal-
lenged control of all executive positions, the party is apt to be too weak
to impose order over the several offices. But the states where party bonds

9 Key, *op. cit.,* pp. 200-201.

are strong enough to impose the discipline are the states where a single party is often unable to place all its men into all the offices.[10]

PARTIES AND NOMINATIONS

One of the central duties of parties is to nominate candidates for office. For most state and local offices nomination is made by the direct party primary, as previously described. Voters stay away from the primaries in droves, even when candidates for governor and other important offices are selected. Even in areas where the primary winner of the dominant party is likely or certain to be elected, the primary attracts a relatively small proportion of the potential voters.

What are some of the consequences of the small turnout in party primaries? The most strongly partisan areas often cast a disproportionate number of the votes in the primary.[11] The candidate chosen often represents only one faction of the party, and he may not have very wide appeal in the general election. This tendency for one segment of a party to dominate the nominations is illustrated by recent party history in Massachusetts. Despite the views of some Democratic party leaders that their party should present a balanced ticket in the general elections, the Boston Irish, who have been the most active in the primary elections, almost always chose Boston Irish—"the Green Ticket" for major positions. In the same fashion, the Yankee Republicans were most active in their primary and were able to select a straight Yankee ticket, again to the anguish of the other Republican leaders who would have preferred a ticket more likely to appeal to a wide variety of groups in the coming election. In an attempt to correct this tendency of one faction of the party to dominate primaries, Massachusetts and some other states have adopted the pre-primary convention (see below).

The direct primary and two-party competition

One reason for the adoption of the direct primary was to escape from some of the evils of one-partyism. If a single party wins all the elections, the only chance that the ordinary voter has to participate in the selection of his public officials is in the primary of the dominant party. Hence it is within the *primary* that the struggle among groups for control of the state government takes place.

Although the direct primary is an obvious device to introduce an element of choice in the one-party states, the primary itself may have a tendency to intensify one-partyism and to help maintain it where it exists.[12] In the South, the Republicans find it difficult to build up a strong party

[10] Key, *op. cit.*, p. 201.
[11] Key, *op. cit.*, pp. 145 ff.
[12] Key, *op. cit.*, pp. 169 ff.

organization, since most voters and potential leaders are unwilling to participate in the affairs of a party that never wins elections. If such Republicans want to have a voice in government, they feel compelled to vote in the Democratic primary.

Even in states with two competing parties, the primary may decrease interparty competition. Members of the lesser of the two parties may come to feel that their best chance at influence is in voting in the majority party primary. Hopeful office seekers may decide that it is easier to join the larger party and gain office under its auspices than to attempt the long and arduous task of building up the second party. If this happens, the smaller party may disintegrate. In many areas of the United States the second party often fails even to nominate candidates; or if candidates are chosen, they make only a half-hearted attempt to get elected. Although the increase in the number of noncompetitive election districts (i.e., those in which one of the parties fails to nominate candidates) cannot be solely attributed to the use of the direct primary, the primary is probably one of the factors.

Revival of state party organizations

The direct primary nominating system appears to be firmly planted in the United States. There is little evidence to indicate much support for a return to the earlier convention system which, whatever its defects, did give the party leaders more of a voice in selecting candidates and did give the party organization greater reason for existence. But a system that has won the favor both of the academic political scientists and of practicing politicians is the *pre-primary convention* now used in six states. Party delegates in these conventions designate official party candidates to run in the primaries, but anti-organization candidates can still get on the primary ballots by petition and thus oppose the party choice. Endorsement by the party leaders gives the rank and file voters some guidance in the primary, but these voters are always free to reject their leadership.

In states and cities that have no provision for a formal pre-primary convention, party leaders often get together unofficially before the primary to draw up the party slate. Slate-making by the party organization is most effective in areas where the parties are highly organized and disciplined, since endorsement by a strong organization gives the organization candidate a decided advantage in the primary.

Cohesive parties are most likely in places where the two major parties are most evenly matched. Where one party usually wins, political differences are more apt to be organized around factions, dominant personalities, coalitions of interest groups. These generalizations, however, are not true of all states. In Virginia, for example, where the Democratic party is overwhelmingly strong there is also strong organization within the party, where the followers of Senator Byrd maintain a firm grip over nominations and party affairs.

SOCIAL BASIS OF STATE PARTIES

Party affiliations tend to change slowly and then only under severe shock. The basic strength of our two parties remains fairly stable and can be traced back at least as far as the Civil War. Here is a short outline of the kinds of state party systems and their social basis.

Rural states

It is in rural America that one-partyism is most prevalent, the rural North and Midwest being predominantly Republican and the rural South being Democratic. In the rural regions, community integration and the pressures to conform to local sentiments are strongest. Young lawyers, merchants, clergymen, and newspaper editors discover that their elders at the Rotary Club, church meetings, around the Court House, at the Grange Hall, all belong to the same party. Naturally, those who have political ambitions join the leading party, since membership in the lesser parties probably means little influence and perhaps even social ostracism. Here political contests tend to take place *within* the major party, and the issues are those of personality and local administration rather than of the state or nation.

The strength of these rural political affiliations can be traced in the westward migration. In the places originally settled by southerners—southern Ohio, southern Indiana, southern Oklahoma, for example—the Democrats are still strong. Similarly, the Republican strongholds of the Dakotas, Kansas, northern Illinois, Indiana, and Ohio were originally settled by New Englanders. In these rural regions, political affiliations change slowly.

Urban states

Two-party politics are most likely to be found in states containing large cities. Although the clash between city and country dweller is often exaggerated, the two-party politics of many of our states can be conveniently, and for the most part accurately, described in terms of a metropolitan versus nonmetropolitan clash.

First consider states with a single large metropolitan city—New York, Illinois, Michigan, for example, where New York City, Chicago, and Detroit contain almost half of the state's population.[13] In these states the center of gravity of the Democratic party is in the metropolitan regions, while the center of gravity of the Republicans is "upstate" (as it is called

[13] These and the following examples are drawn from Key, *op. cit.*, pp. 230 ff.

in New York), "downstate" (as it is called in Illinois), and "outstate" (as it is called in Michigan). These metropolitan versus nonmetropolitan cleavages appear in the legislature as well as in the elections for governor and other statewide offices. As we noted in Chapter 12, the pattern of politics in these regions changes more rapidly than it does in rural states, and the movement of people from the central city to the suburbs is altering the social basis of American politics. It needs be repeated, however, that the description of state politics as merely a division between big city and the rural areas is over-simplified, for many other factors cut across this division.

Second, we find states with two large metropolitan centers: Pennsylvania, California, and Missouri. Here two-party politics exists, and again the center of gravity of Democratic strength tends to be in the metropolitan regions. But the rivalry between the political organizations both *within* the city and *between* the cities complicates the picture. In the past, for example, Pittsburgh was Democratic, but Philadelphia was Republican and, combined with the rest of the state, gave control of Pennsylvania state politics to the Republicans. In recent years, the Democrats have secured control of Philadelphia and have been more successful at the state level.

The metropolitan states such as Ohio, with a number of large cities, provide still another pattern of politics. Here we find two-party politics with the Democrats having the center of their strength in the cities, but the Democratic organizations are more diffuse and their legislative representation less cohesive than in those states where a single, large metropolitan center exists. Although they win the governorship occasionally, the Democrats are seldom able to put into office any of the other elected executives or to control the state legislatures.

PARTY REFORM?

What questions does this brief description of state politics raise? What is the general condition of political parties in the operation of our state and local governments? Here is a paraphrase of how V. O. Key has summarized the situation:

1. State politics combined with constitutional arrangements, especially the nature of state legislative representation, contributes to centralization of power in the national government by incapacitating the states for action.

2. The rapid growth of state responsibilities makes it even more important to modernize the organization of political forces within the states which at the present time may be characterized as erratic and atomized.

3. The political system places serious obstacles in the path of popular government, making it impossible for broad popular mandates to be expressed in some situations and at some times.

4. Over the last half century, party organization has seriously deteriorated. This decay in party organization has been associated with the rise of the direct primary, which makes it important to consider lines of action necessary to strengthen party government.[14]

The problems presented by lack of party government are the same ones and involve essentially the same considerations that we discussed in connection with the role of parties in the national government (see Chapter 21). Although the role of parties at the national level has received much attention, primarily from the academics, it is only recently that much thought has been given to party reform within our states. Many have concerned themselves with changes in administrative and constitutional arrangements of the states, but the organization and operation of the parties has been given much less attention. Perhaps neglect is due to the difficulty in changing party structure to effect any significant impact on the nature of politics. No amount of tinkering with party structure can do much about the fact that most of the people in Vermont are Republicans and most of those in the South are Democrats. As long as strong personal factions continue within a party, preaching about the desirability of party cohesion will have little effect. Attitudes and political behavior change slowly and grow out of basic social, economic, and psychological conditions that reorganization and reform committees can little alter.

However, to recognize that political forces and factors are relatively stable is not to conclude that they do not change or that they are not affected by institutional arrangements, especially in our dynamic society. Changes in legislative representation, for example, or alterations in procedures for nominating candidates have an impact upon party structure. Much will depend on those who take part in party activity and seek to translate their democratic principles into political reality. To those who believe that political parties should have a stronger role in state leadership and policy making, the difficulties are many but the challenge is great.

[14] Key, *op. cit.,* pp. 266-267.

Epilogue—Challenge and Opportunity

TOWARD THE END OF THE FIRST CHAPTER, THE authors presented the totalitarian challenge to democracy. They invited the reader to formulate his answer to the challenge as he read this volume, and they reserved the opportunity to meet that challenge in this last chapter. The authors' answer to the case against democratic government (to which the reader may wish to compare his own) is as follows:

Is democratic government unrealistic? The antidemocrats charge that man is irrational and selfish, hence incapable of governing himself. But because men are not always rational, it does not follow that they are never rational. The use of reason is still the best method for arriving at the truth, and the truth is still the best basis for action. And if men are selfish, if human nature is so bad, that is all the more reason for not trusting any man or single group of men with irresponsible power. It is all the more reason for having *democratic* government, which prevents any narrow clique from monopolizing power. "Sometimes it is said that man cannot be trusted with the government of himself," Jefferson once said. "Can he, then, be trusted with the government of others?" Or to quote one of the world's great contemporary theologians, Reinhold Niebuhr, "Man's capacity for justice makes democracy possible; but man's inclination to injustice makes democracy necessary."

Democratic government, moreover, is best designed to bring out the rational and the good that is in man. If men are denied any voice in directing their own affairs, they are deprived of the one experience that is most likely to make them social, rational, and responsible persons.

Nor are the authors impressed by the charge that the average man is too poorly informed to make intelligent judgments on governmental matters, and for that reason democratic government means mediocre government. Democratic theory does not require that the voters as a whole make *all* the decisions. It does require that those who make the decisions must, over the long run, please the majority of the people. And the great number of people are fully capable of making over-all judgments on the general course of the na-

Epilogue —

challenge

and

opportunity

tion. They are capable, as A. D. Lindsay has said so well, to tell when their shoes are pinching. "No doubt," Lindsay concedes, "the ordinary voter has the vaguest ideas as to what legislative or administrative reform will stop the pinching of his shoes. . . . But for all that, only he, the ordinary man, can tell whether the shoe pinches and where; and without that knowledge the wisest statesman cannot make good laws."

Indeed, this idea of leaving government in the hands of "the best" is a self-defeating one. Who are the best? Authoritarians talk about government by the best, the supermen, the party elite. Of course, the authoritarians themselves disagree as to who are the best—the Politburo, or Nordics, or the upper class, or the working class, or Anglo-Saxon whites, or the intellectuals, or businessmen. The fact is that good government requires many talents, and talents are not concentrated in any one individual or group. A brilliant physicist may be an innocent about politics; an All-American football player is the best in his business, but by himself he might make a botch of foreign policy. Even if we limited political power to the most highly educated groups, those who should most clearly see the good, what assurance do we have that they will *seek* the general good? None whatsoever. Where power is restricted to the few, those few define the good in terms of their own narrow interests. In the long run, the best can be found in equal measure among all groups. By giving political power to all people, we allow men and women of real talents, regardless of group or origin, the best opportunity of rising to the top of the political ladder and governing intelligently in behalf of the great number of people.

To defend democratic government in general, the authors grant, is easier than defending a particular democratic government. Certainly this is true of the American governmental system. Throughout this book the authors have raised sharp questions as to the caliber of our government measured in terms of the first four basic questions listed toward the close of Chapter 1. But none of these problems is insuperable, and perhaps not even critical; indeed, other students of government might express somewhat less concern over them than have the authors of this book. Consider, for example, the problems of representation and responsibility. The authors believe that fairer representation in the nation's legislatures and more clear-cut party responsibility would bring about a stronger democratic system and also a more efficient and effective government. But there is another whole side to the problem, as Chapter 21 suggests. In any case, there are no failings in the American system that cannot be resolved through traditional processes of constitutional and political change.

Democratic government is not perfect, in America or anywhere else. But defense of democratic government does not require proof of its perfection. Sir Winston Churchill, British prime minister and a member of the rich and wellborn, summed it all up when he said, "Democracy is the worst form of government except for any other that has ever been tried."

It is well to keep in mind, though, that government by the people needs thinkers and doers, leaders who can heed the famous injunction, "Think as men of action, act as men of thought." So the remainder of this last chapter takes up some of the ways that the student can put his knowledge and his belief in democratic government to good use.

NEEDED: 100,000,000 POLITICIANS

College men and women do not need to be told the importance of their taking part in politics. Since grade school, they have had this sermon dinned into their ears. Nor do they agree with Boss Plunkitt that "if you have been to college, so much the worse for you" in the rough-and-tumble of American politics. They do not feel the need to "unlearn" all they learned in college. The question is, have they learned enough?

The fact is that playing an effective part in politics depends on more than good will and interest in community affairs. It demands a good deal of political know-how. It would be pleasant to be able to say about political activity that "there's nothing to it—just learn as you go." But this would not be true. American political mechanics are a complex affair—far more complex, for example, than those in Great Britain.

Many of the procedures of American politics discussed above may seem dull and difficult. So they are, until you suddenly come face to face with them in a real situation. Registration requirements, for example, seem dull matters, until someone publicly challenges your right to vote. Getting out the vote on election day seems an overrated problem—until you find yourself in campaign headquarters at 2 A.M. waiting tensely for the last wards to report in. Spending limitations seem unimportant—until the opposition accuses your candidate of trying to buy the election.

Plunging in

The first step is to find out who is the local chairman of your party. Someone will know at city hall or at the court house. Calling on the chairman to tell him that you would like to help out in the campaign is the next step. Chances are that he will give you a warm welcome.

Voting lists must be checked, letters stamped, leaflets distributed, meetings arranged, publicity sent out, posters put up. Special skills will come in handy. Anyone in the advertising business can help on radio or newspaper publicity. Amateur sign painters will have ample occasion to make use of their talents. A good money-raiser can help meet the problems of campaign expenses—usually the worst headache of all. Typists, from the hunt-and-peck variety on up, are needed (with their typewriters). Good organizers are required to direct doorbell ringing, which is an art and a science in itself. Cars and drivers are wanted for the countless errands that must be run.

One of the most important jobs in a political campaign is to get people registered to vote. Registration, it will be recalled (Chapter 14), falls into two types: permanent and periodic. The chart which follows indicates the qualifications for voting in every state. How does one go about getting people registered? At best, it is a chore. First, one must find names and addresses of those not registered. One way to do this is to check city directories or police lists against registration lists. Another, and more common practice, is to check the membership lists of organizations such as the American Legion or a labor union for names not on the voting lists. Then the unregistered person must be approached by mail, over the phone, or, best of all, in his home.

The unregistered voter is often an apathetic citizen. He may not see much point in voting. He will probably not know when the registration period comes. He may ask questions: Will they ask me how old I am? Will they make me take a reading test? Do I have to pay anything? How long do I have to live in the area? Answers to these questions—almost always they can be reassuring ones—will be expected of anyone taking part in a registration drive. In many cases, transportation and baby sitters also must be provided.

Another highly important job in political campaigning is to get people to vote on election day. The most effective work here is usually done by party committees and candidates. Workers are stationed at every polling booth to check off the names of persons as they vote. Then "checkers" send hourly reports to people at party headquarters, who begin telephoning voters who have not shown up. Other party workers drive voters to the polls. The success of the whole operation depends on good timing, carefully checked lists, and efficient communication and transportation.

The heart of registration and voting drives lies in approaching the individual voter in person, but the approach is much more effective if it comes as part of a general drive. This is especially true of registration drives. A nonpartisan, community-wide program is often the most fruitful procedure. The drive is carried on through the press, radio, television, posters, civic groups, trade unions, veterans' organizations, window displays, churches, schools, door-to-door canvassing, rallies—even sky-writing! In some communities police cars have carried "get-out-the-vote" signs, "vote-mobiles" have toured the area with sample voting machines or sample ballots, and "REGISTER TO VOTE" has been stenciled on the sidewalks.

Much of this work would be simple drudgery under any other circumstances. In the heat of a campaign, however, it takes on an aura of the dramatic. Volunteers are part of a team that is engaged in a keen struggle. Party headquarters is always crowded; the phone seems always to be ringing. Crisis follows crisis. Candidates dash in to make arrangements for coming meetings, rush out to speak at the Odd Fellows' barbecue. Rumors flow thick and fast. A few of them are even true.

Taking part in party politics is a rewarding business. Perhaps the biggest satisfaction comes on election day. The blinders have been taken off; the names on the ballot are those of flesh-and-blood persons. Politics has taken on a new dimension. At this stage you can feel that you are no longer an outsider, but an insider in party affairs. You have learned something of the rules and gimmicks of the political game.

After the election, what then? We will be told on all sides that "politics is now adjourned." But politics is not adjourned. It is a year-round business —at least for the professionals. The only question is whether they will have the game all to themselves.

Keeping at it

Vitally important decisions will be made between elections. New members will be added to local party committees, precinct captains will be appointed, perhaps new chairmen will be elected. Members of state committees and delegates to conventions will be chosen. Plans will be made for registration drives, election of candidates to national conventions, future campaigns. These activities will determine the shape of politics in the elections ahead. Obviously, running a party, like running a war, is too important to be left to the professionals. The period between elections is the ideal time for public-spirited citizens to make their influence felt in the party councils—an influence that will be all the greater because important party decisions are made by relatively few persons.

In most cases party workers will have no trouble gaining a foothold in the party organization. Occasionally, the old-line leaders may try to close out newcomers to keep the organization as their private preserve. They should not be allowed to succeed without a struggle. If necessary, one can often work with another part of the organization, or join or form auxiliary groups like the Young Democrats or Young Republicans.

Our mental picture of a local party leader is usually one of a ruthless boss, complete with cigar, jowls, and a taste for "honest graft." In real life the party leader usually turns out to be an amiable and honest individual who holds his position as a result of working hard and doing countless favors. Of course, unscrupulous bosses are to be found. But one should not be discouraged from taking part in politics because the local party organization seems to be controlled by a disreputable group. It is far easier to clean the organization from within than from without. Party bosses often can ignore the criticism of outsiders, but they cannot long resist those who outwork and outvote them within their own domain.

Let there be fair warning. Anyone going into party politics with illusions as to the way the parties operate is likely to be in for a shock. On the local level, organization is often stagnant, if not moribund. Committees rarely meet and attendance is poor. Where the local organization is energetic and influential, it is usually because a leader has infused some life

REGISTRATION REQUIREMENTS

(*Check your state*)

State	Registration Type — Permanent		Registration Type — Periodic			Coverage	
	All areas	Some areas	All areas	Some areas	Frequency	All elections	Some elections
Alabama	(a)	....	....	....	....	★	....
Arizona	(b)	....	....	....	....	(f)	....
Arkansas							
California	★	....	....	....	....	★	....
Colorado	★	....	....	....	....	....	(i)
Connecticut	★	....	....	....	....	★	....
Delaware	★	....	....	....	....	★	....
Florida	★	....	....	....	....	★	....
Georgia	★	....	....	....	....	★	....
Idaho	★	....	....	....	....	★	....
Illinois	★	....	....	....	....	....	(j)
Indiana	★	....	....	....	....	....	(h)(i)
Iowa	....	....	★	★	4 years	....	(h)(i)
Kansas	....	....	....	....	....	★	....
Kentucky	★	....	....	....	....	★	....
Louisiana	....	....	★	★	4 years	★	....
Maine	★	....	....	....	....	★	....
Maryland	....	★	....	★	....	★	....
Massachusetts	★	....	....	....	....	★	....
Michigan	★	....	....	....	....	★	....
Minnesota	....	....	★	★	....	★	....
Mississippi	(a)	....	....	....	....	....	(k)
Missouri	....	....	★	★	4 years	★	....
Montana	★	....	....	....	....	....	(h)(i)
Nebraska	....	....	★	★	6 years	....	(i)
Nevada	★	....	....	....	....	★	....
New Hampshire	★	....	....	....	....	★	....
New Jersey	★	....	....	....	....	★	....
New Mexico	★	....	....	....	....	★	....
New York	....	★	....	★	Annual	....	★
North Carolina	★	....	....	....	....	★	....
North Dakota	....	....	★	★	....	....	★
Ohio	....	....	★	★	....	★	....
Oklahoma	★	....	....	....	....	(g)	....
Oregon	(c)	....	....	....	....	★	....
Pennsylvania	★	....	....	....	....	★	....
Rhode Island	★	....	....	....	....	★	....
South Carolina	....	....	....	★	Decennial	★	....
South Dakota	★	....	....	....	....	★	....
Tennessee	★	....	....	....	....	★	....
Texas	(d)	(d)	(d)	(d)	Annual	....	....
Utah	★	....	....	....	....	....	(i)
Vermont	(e)	....	....	....	....	....	★
Virginia	★	....	....	....	....	★	....
Washington	(b)	....	....	....	....	(f)	....
West Virginia	★	....	....	....	....	(h)	....
Wisconsin	....	....	★	★	....	★	....
Wyoming	....	....	★	....	Every gen. elec.	....	★

(a) Registration is permanent unless removed for cause.
(b) Conditioned upon voting and continued residence.
(c) Re-register in two years if not voting within that time.
(d) Constitutional provisions for registration in cities over 10,000 but no system exists. Poll tax receipts determine eligibility of voters aged 21 to 60; exemption certificates for those over 60 in cities over 10,000, and certain others.
(e) Except in some cities.
(f) Except irrigation district elections.
(g) Except school district elections.
(h) All elections except special elections.
(i) All except certain minor elections.
(j) For all state and federal elections.
(k) Registration is for all elections of state and county, but voters must be registered in municipality also to vote in municipal elections.

From THE BOOK OF THE STATES, *1956-1957. Courtesy Council of State Government.*

into it. His reward is to be called the local "boss"—whether or not he is serving private rather than public needs.

The South is spoken of slightingly as a one-party area, but in many parts of the North only one effective party organization can be found. A rival party may exist in name, but not in fact. Often, especially in the cities, one party organization is the "captive" of the other. It exists on crumbs of patronage handed out by the dominant organization which is willing to pay for token opposition in order to prevent real competition. Real party rivalry cannot be expected in a situation like this.

Most disillusioning of all is the inglorious nature of local party operations. Any hope that men have banded together for the sake of grand principles may quickly evaporate. The main reason for party activity often turns out to be the "cohesive power of public plunder." Doubtless local politics has been purified a bit since the days of the "muckrakers," but in all too many cases, city and county organizations still are occupied with personalities and petty business rather than with the real needs of the community.

This is disconcerting to the good citizen who has gone to party headquarters to stay. The local problems worrying him concern schools for his children, lower taxes, better roads, faster snow removal in winter, a new library building. He has only one consolation, but it is a big one. The greater the need for improving the character of local politics, the larger the opportunity for him and his fellows to pitch in and do something.

"You're the boss," Mr. Edward J. Flynn of the Bronx told us reassuringly. But he added an important proviso. We're the boss only if we are willing to dirty our hands a bit at the grass roots of party politics. Never was the need greater than today.

RUNNING FOR OFFICE

For those interested in making a career of politics there are few set rules. Generalizations about the road to election day victories are risky; the exceptions to the rules are legion. But before entering politics the individual would be wise to reflect on his assets and liabilities. If he is sensitive to criticism, excessively shy, if he dislikes "good fellowship" and wants to lead a quiet and peaceful life, the chances are against his being successful—or at least happy—in politics. On the other hand, if one enjoys working with others, likes to speak, and can look forward without fear to countless dinners of cold peas and roast beef, then politics offers an exciting and rewarding career.

Some hints from an expert

Hugh D. Scott, Jr., a congressman, former chairman of the Republican National Committee, and an experienced politician, believes that the following traits are helpful to politically active men and women:

1. Be politically informed.

2. Integrity is the most valuable tool of the trade. Despite cynicism about politics, a dishonest politician is almost always exposed sooner or later.

3. "Patience is a prime political virtue," says Representative Scott after observing that he had spent "twenty years or so of being stopped several times a day by people with something on their mind, of having my lapels seized firmly or my sleeve tugged by someone who wants something done that he feels I may be able to do, of long interviews with people with a grievance, a petition, a plan, an invention, or just a two-way ball-bearing tongue."

4. Courtesy—"on Ballot Boulevard there's no market at all for the sour stuff."

5. Gregariousness.

6. Hard work. "To know your neighborhood and to help your neighbors is a 365-day-a-year job."

7. A sense of humor. Freshman members of Congress are warned by their elders "Don't violate Rule Six." And what is Rule Six? "Don't take yourself too seriously." And Rules One to Five? "Don't take yourself too seriously." A sense of proportion, a sense of humor.

8. Courage.[1]

Politics does not offer much in the way of job security. It is, therefore, helpful if the aspiring politician has some other source of income. In American politics this has often been the case. Lawyers have more of an opportunity to combine politics and business than do doctors, teachers, workers, and others. The young graduate from law school is forbidden by the ethics of his profession to advertise, but he can run for office. If he wins, he will make valuable contacts. If he loses, he can return to the practice of law with a name that is better known to the public.

Insurance and farming are other professions that are often readily combined with politics. But one need not be a lawyer, insurance man, or farmer to enter politics. The avenues to public office are many, and the halls of Congress and the offices of the executive departments are filled with men and women who came into politics from every conceivable background.

Do's and don't's

Here are some of the do's and don't's of politics.

1. Be a joiner. Try to join as great a variety of organizations as possible. By working for the Community Chest, becoming active in the union, the chamber of commerce, the service club, the lodges, and in church work, the candidate makes his name familiar, wins friends, and learns the skills of his trade.

---

[1] From Hugh D. Scott, Jr., *How to Go into Politics* (New York: The John Day Company, 1949), pp. 26 ff.

2. Be one of the boys and avoid snobbish mannerisms, but be colorful.

3. Learn to remember names and faces, but don't be overeffusive.

4. Ignore unfriendly attacks. "Never get into an argument with a newspaper or a preacher; the newspaper always has the last word with its readers, and the preacher always calls on Heaven as witness that he is right."[2]

5. Know your facts.

6. "Don't overestimate the people's knowledge or underestimate their intelligence."

7. Remember that a nice personality and a mastery of all the do's and don't's of politics are no substitute for intelligence, integrity, and conviction.

A CAREER IN THE CIVIL SERVICE

Political work often leads to appointive as well as elective public positions. Lawyers who have come to the aid of their party are sometimes in line for judgeships, and others may be appointed to places in state or local government. But today more and more of the positions in the federal administrative structure are open to qualified nonpoliticians. These positions offer much to those individuals who have a desire for public service—but little liking for politics—or for people who have administrative talents. The government needs all kinds of people with all kinds of skills. These positions offer reasonable compensation, considerable security, and an exciting challenge. How does one become a bureaucrat?

Men and women may apply for commissions as officers in the armed forces. Young men between the ages of 17 and 22 can apply for admission to West Point, Annapolis, or the Air Force Academy, and on graduation will receive commissions in the Regular Army, Navy, or Air Force. Candidates for these positions must pass stiff physical and mental examinations. Congressmen, senators, the President, and the Vice-President have the authority to appoint candidates, if they meet the qualifications. Information on entrance can be obtained from any congressman. The Secretaries of Army, Navy, and Air Force can also select some cadets from among honor graduates of military schools. Sons of men and women killed in the armed services of the United States military forces are given some preferential treatment.

How to get into government

How does one go about getting a position in one of the civilian agencies of government? There are now approximately $2\frac{1}{3}$ million civilian positions

---

[2] *Ibid.,* p. 32. See also Harold Gauer, *How To Win in Politics* (Boston: Bruce Humphries, Inc., 1946), and E. E. Schattschneider, Victor Jones, Stephen K. Bailey, *A Guide to the Study of Public Affairs* (New York: William Sloane Associates, Inc., 1952), a citizens' manual.

in the federal government. Only 533 of these are filled by election, namely, 435 representatives, 96 senators, the President, and the Vice-President. To secure one of these positions it is necessary to go into politics. The same is generally true of an appointment to the Supreme Court or an inferior federal court, district attorneyship, or appointment as a first-, second-, or third-class postmaster, or a Cabinet member. These and other such positions are filled by presidential appointment with the consent of the Senate.

But well over 80 per cent of the positions in the executive branch are open to qualified citizens regardless of their politics, except to the extent that they must be loyal to the United States and not be fascists or Communists. Most of these positions are filled through civil service examinations. Veterans receive preference on these examinations, which are held throughout the United States at the various regional headquarters of the Civil Service Commission. If one does not live in a city with a Civil Service Regional Headquarters, information can be secured from the Civil Service Secretary at the local post office.

Only about 10 per cent of these positions are in Washington. The rest are in places throughout the entire world. Unlike English practice, American civil service examinations are for particular kinds of jobs. Positions calling for professional training are filled through unassembled examinations. Such examinations are not examinations in the usual sense, but questionnaires that enable the Civil Service Commission and the appointing agencies to know the competence and experience of the individual.

Civil service jobs are now graded in a general schedule of 18 grades with salaries going up in steps from $2690 to $14,800, and a crafts, protective, and custodial schedule of 10 grades with compensation ranging from $1945 to $5715. The work normally involves a 5-day, 40-hour week with vacations of from 13 to 26 days and with generous sick leave arrangements. Low-cost life insurance is available, employees are entitled to unemployment compensation, and there is an attractive retirement system. The Hatch Act protects civil servants from being obligated to contribute to political funds, but it also bars them from participating in any partisan political activity.

Types of jobs

The positions open are so many and varied that only a few can be mentioned here. Engineers, physicists, chemists, and other technical personnel are recruited through specially designed unassembled examinations. The *Federal Service Entrance Examination* is of special interest to college graduates who wish to enter the career civil service and work up to high-level assignments. This new examination is designed to recruit upwards of 5000 college-caliber people each year, and its purpose is not just to fill particular jobs, but to secure talented persons who have the ability to mature on the jobs. It is a move in the direction of English civil service recruitment concepts.

The Federal Service Entrance Examination is open continuously. Following are examples of the types of fields in which positions are filled: general administration, economics and other social sciences, communications, library science, information and records management, statistics, personnel management. Appointments are made for college graduates at a minimum beginning salary of $3670 (Grade GS-5). Those with a year's graduate study are eligible for Grade GS-7 positions, with starting salaries of $4525.

To qualify for the Federal Service Entrance Examination a person (1) must have completed a four-year college course, or have three years experience in responsible work, or have a combination of education and experience; (2) must pass a written test of general abilities; (3) must be rated satisfactory in an oral interview; (4) must submit satisfactory references; (5) must be a United States citizen of undoubted loyalty; (6) must be physically able to perform the duties of the position. College seniors may take the examination and may receive provisional appointments which permit them to enter on duty after graduation. To apply for these positions, obtain Card Form 5000-AB from any post office, civil service office, or college placement office. The examinations are given every few months at cities throughout the nation.

Of special interest to persons of unusual ability are the management internships (formerly known as Junior Management Assistant) that are offered by some of the agencies. These agencies have specially planned programs that give varied work assignments and training designed to develop persons of unusual promise. In order to obtain one of these internships, in addition to passing the Federal Service Entrance Examination the candidate must also pass a more comprehensive written test of general abilities and a special written test on either administrative problems or public affairs, and must demonstrate in an oral interview that he has the personal qualities required for higher managerial positions.

There is always room in the civil service for persons with secretarial skills. Men and women with college training or comparable experience and secretarial skills often get into the service as secretaries and then quickly move up to administrative positions. Persons who wish to go from agency to agency to look for civil service positions should secure Form 57 from the Civil Service Commission and fill it out before going job hunting. Completing this form is required procedure, and to fill it out before seeing appointing officers will save much time. Several federal agencies have their own personnel systems and are not covered by regular civil service rules. The T.V.A., the F.B.I., the Armed Forces Security Agency, and the Central Intelligence Agency, for example, recruit and hire their own employees. The F.B.I. appoints its special agents from among physically and mentally eligible lawyers (those who have graduated from an accredited law school) and accountants (of at least three years experience). G-men receive a starting salary of $5915 and after a probationary period are given raises and permanent appointments.

In addition to opportunities in the federal service, many attractive positions are open in state and municipal public service. Since each year the states and cities improve the conditions of their public service, opportunities are becoming more attractive for able people.

Although positions with the United Nations are difficult to secure because the American quota is usually filled, the effort may be worthwhile, for service with the United Nations offers many advantages in pay and other benefits, in addition to the satisfaction of working for the community of mankind.

ENTERING THE FOREIGN SERVICE

The Foreign Service has attractions for many people. In some ways it is the glamor service of the federal government, but as noted in Chapter 23, much of the work is routine, and life can be dull and even unpleasant in some posts. Yet the Service has many advantages.

In order to be eligible to take the Foreign Service Officer examinations 'one must: (1) be at least 20 and under 31 years of age; (2) be a citizen of the United States for at least 10 years; (3) not be married to an alien. Examinations for these positions are written, oral, and physical. The written examination is usually held in June and December in approximately fifty cities within the United States, and at any American diplomatic or consulate post that candidates residing abroad may designate. The oral examinations are held in Washington, at certain regional centers in the United States, and certain posts abroad. Persons who wish to take the examinations may receive applications from the Board of Examiners for the Foreign Service, Department of State, Washington 25, D.C., and these applications should be completed at least six weeks before the date set for the examination.

Foreign Service examinations

Taking a full day to complete, the written examination is composed of three parts. The first part is an English Expression test (90 minutes) intended to examine the candidate's ability to apply the basic principles of rhetoric and usage; ability to organize ideas in logical order; and "sensitivity to the appropriateness of a piece of writing for a particular situation and a particular audience."[3] The second part is a General Ability test (90

[3] "Analysis of the Written Examination for Foreign Service Officer Candidates," *Foreign Service News Letter,* No. 113, July 15, 1956, p. 4.

minutes) designed to measure the candidate's basic learning skills—ability to read, to analyze, and to interpret data present in a variety of forms, and to make simple mathematical deductions. The third part (2 hours) is a General Background test consisting of 50 per cent social studies, 25 per cent humanities, and 25 per cent science questions.

The oral examination is designed to test qualities such as appearance, manner, diction, personality, and the like. The Service uses the oral interview to eliminate candidates who are "shy, aggressive, boorish, unable to defend their views, who give evidence of low standards of conduct, and who show a lack of knowledge of the United States." To test this last quality, natives of one section of the country are often questioned on the other sections. Factual knowledge is given less weight than "ability to form thoughtful opinions based on the facts at the candidates disposal, to organize his views logically, and to speak clearly and understandably." While the examinations are exacting, they are less so than formerly, and the number of positions open has recently been increased.

Service abroad

The President, with the consent of the Senate, appoints successful candidates as Foreign Service officers (since 1956 most of them at Class 8). The salaries in this class range from $4300 to $5350; moreover, officers may work themselves up the scale until they get to the top class, where the salaries are $20,000. In addition, career officers may be appointed as ambassadors and ministers at higher salaries, up to $27,500. While abroad, salaries are supplemented by quarters allowances; officers receive from 13 to 26 days of annual leave; and after two years abroad they are entitled to home leave in the United States with pay and travel expenses for their families. Unless an officer is promoted within a maximum period in each class, except for the top two classes, he must retire.

Before foreign assignment, Foreign Service officers are trained at the Foreign Service Institute, and throughout their careers they continue special studies. There is no one method of preparation for the Foreign Service, but persons interested in taking the examination should, while in college, learn to write clear and correct English, master a foreign language, and take enough social science, humanities, and science courses to be able to pass the examinations.

A LAST WORD

Some of you may have no interest in learning about political or administrative jobs. Your future lies elsewhere. Even so, you can and should have a political career—in the party of your choice. As we have seen, our parties badly need strengthening at every level. The country needs more *party* politicians who hunt out good candidates and help elect them, drive workers to the polls on election day, spread the party gospel, and remind the officeholders of their responsibilities to the people.

Every individual in a democracy contributes to its success or failure. Those who, because of ignorance or indifference, try to stay on the side lines, nevertheless influence the course of events, negative and destructive though that influence may be. If the 170 million Americans are to keep their free government, it will be mainly because of the activities of the people as a whole. Leaders dedicated to the principles of free government, and leaders with vision and courage are essential, but it is from the private citizens that the leaders are recruited. The standards and values of the people determine broadly the type of leadership they get.

"Fourscore and seven years ago," said Abraham Lincoln in the midst of a crucial struggle, "our fathers brought forth on this continent a new nation, conceived in liberty, and dedicated to the proposition that all men are created equal." Lincoln saw that struggle as a test of whether government of the *people,* by the *people,* for the *people* could endure. Eighty years later another President, Franklin D. Roosevelt, could report in the midst of another great war that "the state of this Nation is good—the heart of this Nation is sound—the spirit of this Nation is strong—the faith of this Nation is eternal." Government by the people has met and mastered many crises. How well will it meet the tests to come?

$\mathbf{N}$EWSPAPERS, RADIO, AND TELEVISION ARE IM-
portant, but the person who depends solely on these sources will not understand all the world around him, for they give a disconnected picture of the
sensational—the newsworthy—events. They tell little of the whys and
wherefores. The successful negotiation of a hundred collective bargaining
contracts during a day will go unnoticed while public attention is focused
on the one case in which negotiations break down.

To some extent magazines supplement the news. Some give background
information; others digest the weekly events for those too busy to read the
daily papers. *Time* and *Newsweek* with their clipped and dramatic reporting of the week's events are major sources of information for many citizens. *United States News and World Report,* though smaller in circulation,
presents the news in attractive form, and is especially aimed toward influential members of the business community. While *Time, Newsweek,* and *The
United States News and World Report* are "right of center," *The Nation,
The New Leader,* and *The New Republic* are militantly liberal journals of
opinion which report the week's events from left of center; the *National Review* discusses events from the conservative point of view. Though these last
four have, compared to the others, only a relatively small circulation, their
audience includes many opinion leaders, clergymen, teachers, lawyers, public officials, and the like. *The Reporter,* also liberal in tone, gives less attention to the news of the week and more to extended discussion of issues
of contemporary significance.

Among the monthly maga-
zines, *Harper's Magazine, The
Atlantic Monthly,* and *Fortune,* have relatively small audiences but great influence
since they are read by strategically placed individuals. The
first two are more "liberal" in
tone than *Fortune,* but all
three attempt to present a balanced diet. *Fortune* features
materials of interest to businessmen, but it covers all
phases of American society.
By far the largest-circulation
monthly is *The Reader's Digest,* read each month by millions of persons. In addition to
features written by its own staff
members, *The Reader's Digest*

Keeping

informed:

bibliography

selects and abridges articles that appear in other magazines.

Magazines of general circulation contain useful material, but they do not go deeply into particular questions. Where do you find a law? How do you look up a court decision? Where can one find information on the United Nations? How do you find out how your congressman has voted? What are some good books on the U.S.S.R.? Many aids and services have been designed to make such information readily available.

Important information-dispensing centers are the over 7500 public libraries as well as the many hundreds of private libraries that are open to the public. In the periodical room can be found, in addition to magazines of general interest, many specialized journals such as the *American Political Science Review*. The articles in these and many other periodicals are indexed by subject and author in the *Reader's Guide to Periodical Literature*. Another useful index for persons looking for materials on public affairs is the *Bulletin of the Public Affairs Information Service*. This *Bulletin* is published monthly and indexed cumulatively at the end of the year; it contains references not only to articles, but books, government documents, and pamphlets on economic and public affairs. By the use of these indexes, materials on most subjects can be located quickly. The card catalogue in the library will reveal the books that are available there, and something of the author's credentials and the opinion of informed persons about the volume can be obtained in *The Book Review Digest*.

In the reference room one of the most useful volumes is the *United States Government Organization Manual,* an annual publication. The *Manual,* which can be obtained from the Superintendent of Documents, Government Printing Office, covers the authority, organization, and functions of all branches of the government. It has up-to-date organization charts, tells which individuals hold the higher executive positions, and gives a brief description of the work of each unit of government. If one wishes to know, for example, who is the head of the Bureau of Mines, Department of Interior and what that bureau does, the *Manual* is the place to look. The *Congressional Directory,* published each year, has some of the materials found in the *Manual,* and it includes autobiographical sketches of members of Congress, lists of congressional committees and committee assignments, election statistics for the last several congressional elections, and maps of congressional districts. The *Directory* is the place to find out the name of your congressman, a short autobiographical sketch of his life, what committees he is on, and the boundaries of the district he represents.

The general reference volumes are useful, of course, but of special interest to persons concerned with public affairs is *The Encyclopedia of Social Sciences.* Though in some respects bearing the mark of the 1930's, this *Encyclopedia* contains articles on various topics—political parties, sovereignty, representation, John Locke, for example—that remain among the best short treatments to be found. In *Current Biography* one can find materials and background information on men in the news, and *Facts on File* provides a quick reference to current events.

Those who are interested in statistical information will find valuable the *Statistical Abstract of the United States,* which is published yearly by the Commerce Department. Many arguments could be readily settled by resorting to this volume. The reference librarian will be able to point out other useful tools for getting information.

Where does one find a *law?* We often hear people talk about some statute without having seen it. Where can the actual text be found?

The laws of the United States as passed by Congress are first printed individually and are known as *slip laws.* Each law has a number; the Taft-Hartley Act, for example, is known as Public Law 101, Eightieth Congress, First Session. At the end of each year the laws are collected and published by the Government Printing Office under the title of *United States Statutes at Large.* Each year's collection is separately numbered, though there are two separate parts for each number. Part One contains *public* laws, that is, laws affecting the people generally or having to do with governmental organization. Part Two comprises *private* laws, those having to do with particular groups or individuals. The laws in the *Statutes at Large* are listed chronologically, each law being a separate chapter. The Taft-Hartley Act, for example, is Chapter 120 of Volume 61, on page 136. (It is cited as follows: 61 Stat. 136.)

The *Statutes at Large* are useful for research, but they include many laws only of specialized interest, such as rivers and harbors appropriations. Furthermore, many of the measures modify earlier legislation and are themselves modified by later legislation. To find *current* laws on a topic it is best to use the *United States Code,* which contains the public laws of the United States that are in force at the present time. The last codification was in 1946, but each year the *Code* is supplemented by a volume that brings the subject up to date. The laws are arranged according to fifty titles, each title is divided into sections, and each section into paragraphs that are numbered consecutively for each title. The fifty titles cover such subjects as Congress, Title 2; Army, Title 10; Bankruptcy, Title 11; Labor, Title 29, and so on. The *Code* is cited by title and paragraph. The citation of the Taft-Hartley Act, for example, is 29 U. S. C. 141 ff.

The *Code,* like the *Statutes at Large,* is printed by the Government Printing Office, but there are also commercially published editions known as *United States Code Annotated* (U. S. C. A.) and the *Federal Code Annotated* (F. C. A.). These annotated editions include notes on judicial interpretations of the law as well as the law itself. If available, they are more useful than the *Code* itself.

Where to find the rules and regulations issued by the President and the executive agencies? Every day except Sunday and Monday the government publishes *The Federal Register,* which contains executive orders, regulations, and proclamations issued by the President, as well as the orders and regulations promulgated by the executive agencies (including the independent regulatory commissions). These administrative rules and regulations are collected, codified, and kept up-to-date in the *Code of Federal Regulations,* organized on the same plan as the *United States Code.*

The laws as they finally appear on the statute books give, however, only part of the story. Where does one find out what went on before the laws were passed or why certain laws were not passed? This information can, in part, be found in one of the most edifying and interesting items of American letters—the *Congressional Record.* The *Record* is issued every day Congress is in session, and is bound and indexed at the end of each session. It contains everything that is said on the floors of the two chambers, plus a lot that is not said. Congress freely gives its consent to requests of its members "to revise and extend their ramarks," which is a polite way of saying that congressmen are permitted to include in the *Record* statements that they did not make before the Congress. These speeches are then reprinted and distributed to the folks back home. Congressmen, with the unanimous consent of their colleagues, also place in the *Record* poems, articles, letters, editorials, and other materials they find interesting. Each day's *Record* is now accompanied by a *Daily Digest* that highlights the events on both the floor of Congress and in committees.

Action on specific items can be traced by searching through the index. An easier method is to use the *Digest of Public General Bills* published by the Legislative Reference Service, which gives a brief summary of all public bills and their progress in the legislative mills.

There are several commercial services that provide convenient references to congressional activities. *The Congressional Quarterly News Reports: Weekly Log* contains voting records, legislative action, reports on lobbying, and other materials about Congress in action. This is the best source for materials on lobbying activity. The materials are indexed and collected in an *Annual Almanac.* The *United States Code: Congressional and Administrative News,* and the *Congressional Index* also provide ready reference to congressional activity.

Since most of the real work of Congress is done in committees, the reports of these committees and the printed records of hearings are important sources of information. The hearings and reports can be found in any of the over 500 depository libraries in the United States (libraries that receive most publications issued by the Government Printing Office) and the more important ones are in most libraries.

Congress is not the only branch of the federal government that keeps a record of its work. All the other agencies have their own publications, describing their work and supplying the citizen with general and specialized information. These can be obtained from the Superintendent of Documents, Government Printing Office, Washington 25, D.C., for a nominal price. They are indexed in the *Monthly Catalogue of United States Government Publications*. W. P. Leidy, *A Popular Guide to Government Publications* (1953) is an annotated bibliography of 2500 of the most popular Government Printing Office titles.

Where does one find the reports of the federal judiciary? Legal bibliography is a complex subject, but the law is too important to leave to lawyers. The decisions of the Supreme Court are published by the government in numbered volumes known as the *United States Reports*. Cases are cited by volume and page number, e.g., *Illinois ex rel McCollum* v. *Board of Education,* 333 U. S. 203 (1948) means that this case can be found in the 333rd volume of the *United States Reports* on page 203 and that the opinion was handed down in 1948. Decisions of the Court prior to 1875 are cited by the name of the Supreme Court reporter. Thus, *Marbury* v. *Madison,* 1 Cranch 137 (1803) can be found in the first volume of Cranch's Supreme Court reports on page 137 and the opinion was announced in 1803. Two other editions of the Supreme Court opinions are commercially published and each has its own form of citation. Some of the federal district court rulings are now commercially published in volumes known as the *Federal Supplement.* Those of the federal courts of appeals are now also published by the same commercial publisher in volumes known as the *Federal Reporter.* These reports are not available in many general libraries, but in almost every town a special law library, usually located in the court house, contains the reports of the cases plus other materials needed by lawyers in their professional work.

SELECTED BIBLIOGRAPHY

This bibliography makes no pretense of including even all the good books pertinent to the American experiment in government by the people. Its purpose is to provide an *initial* guide to the literature. With few exceptions the rich periodical literature is not mentioned. Twenty books which in the opinion of the authors are of special importance to the general reader have been starred.

Part One: 170,000,000 AMERICANS

GENERAL SOURCES

* R. M. MacIver, *The Web of Government,* 1947, analysis of government.

H. Finer, *Theory and Practice of Modern Government,* abr. ed., 1954, description of political institutions of modern governments.

R. C. Snyder and H. H. Wilson, *Roots of Political Behavior,* 1949, readings that show the interrelations among the many forces that influence political action.

Of special interest to professionals and those interested in the development of a systematic political science are the following:

C. E. Merriam, *Systematic Politics,* 1945.

A. F. Bentley, *The Process of Govern-*

ment, 1908, reprinted 1949, a seminal study in methodology and systematic treatment of the role of interest groups in the political process.

* D. B. Truman, *The Governmental Process,* 1951, builds on Bentley's work, analysis of political interests and public opinion.

D. Easton, *The Political System,* 1953, analysis of theoretical structure of political science, need to develop systematic causal theory.

E. Voegelin, *The New Science of Politics,* 1952, attack on positivism and liberalism and defense of thesis that political science must rest on Greek and Christian philosophy.

GENERAL TREATMENTS OF AMERICAN GOVERNMENT AND SOCIETY

A. de Tocqueville, *Democracy in America,* Phillips Bradley edition, 1946, 2 vols., first published in 1835; classic study of American government.

J. Bryce, *The American Commonwealth,* 1888, 2 vols., ranks with de Tocqueville, more descriptive and less analytical.

D. W. Brogan, *Politics in America,* 1954, special emphasis on party system.

H. J. Laski, *The American Democracy,* 1948, provocative interpretation by another English political scientist.

* C. A. Beard, *The Republic,* 1943, comments by distinguished scholar presented in the form of dialogues between Beard and his friends.

* G. Myrdal, *The American Dilemma,* 1944, monumental study of American society with special attention to the problems of Negro-white relationships.

R. M. Williams, *American Society,* 1951, sociological interpretation.

J. F. Dewhurst and Associates, *America's Needs and Resources: A New Survey,* 1955, survey of basic trends—for example, capital requirements, income—in the decade 1950-1960.

S. H. Slichter, *The American Economy,* 1948, analysis by outstanding American economist.

AMERICAN POLITICAL THOUGHT

C. E. Merriam, *A History of American Political Theories,* 1903 (reissued, 1928), standard classic.

V. L. Parrington, *Main Currents in American Thought,* 1927-1930, interpretation of American literature including the writings of the major political theorists and practitioners.

R. H. Gabriel, *The Course of American Democratic Thought,* 2nd ed., 1955, interpretation of democratic thought from 1815 to present.

A. Heckscher, *The Pattern of Politics,* 1947, exposition of the major "schools" of American political theory.

R. Hofstadter, *The American Political Tradition and the Men Who Made It,* 1948, study of the ideology of American statesmen, emphasizing the basic agreement underlying their political conflicts.

A. T. Mason, *Security Through Freedom,* 1955, "American Political Thought and Practice."

L. Hartz, *The Liberal Tradition in America: An Interpretation of American Political Thought since the Revolution,* 1955, emphasizes uniqueness of American liberal tradition.

F. G. Wilson, *The American Political Mind,* 1949, traces the development of American thought.

H. S. Commager, *The American Mind,* 1950, an interpretation of American thought and character since the 1880's.

A. T. Mason, *Free Government in the Making,* rev. ed., 1956, a selection of readings with introductory essays.

C. L. Rossiter, *Seedtime of the Republic,* 1952, political ideas of those who founded the Republic.

W. F. Craven, *The Legend of the Founding Fathers,* 1956, emphasizes contributions of Puritans.

DEMOCRACY

J. S. Mill, *Representative Government,* 1882, one of the most important books on foundations and problems of democracy.

C. L. Becker, *Modern Democracy,* 1941, study accenting the economic basis of democracy and the discrepancy between the ideal and the actual.

R. A. Dahl, *A Preface to Democratic Theory,* 1956, constructs model of democracy and analyzes Madisonian and populistic models as inadequate.

C. J. Friedrich, *The New Image of the Common Man*, enl. ed., 1950, defense of the belief that the common man is better able to govern than the uncommon man.

R. B. Perry, *Puritanism and Democracy*, 1944, study of two American ideals; has been called a "Thesaurus of democratic thought and an arsenal of democratic defense."

R. Niebuhr, *The Children of Light and the Children of Darkness*, 1944, short defense of democracy by one of America's leading theologians.

* A. D. Lindsay, *The Modern Democratic State*, 1947, statement of the nature of democracy, its development, its essence, and defense of it, by an English scholar.

L. Stapleton, *The Design of Democracy*, 1949, analysis of the basis of democracy, with special attention to conditions necessary to develop a democratic world order.

W. Lippmann, *Essays in the Public Philosophy*, 1955, antimajoritarian, Burkean defense of democracy.

J. H. Hallowell, *The Moral Foundation of Democracy*, 1954, statement that democracy depends upon Hebraic-Greek-Christian tradition.

D. Spitz, *Patterns of Anti-democratic Thought*, 1949, refutation of the major critics of democracy from the "Right."

J. R. Pennock, *Liberal Democracy*, 1950, defense of democracy, major threats to it, and the limitations on the majority in democratic government.

Y. R. Simon, *Philosophy of Democratic Government*, 1951, special attention to authority and role of persuasion.

E. Mims, Jr., *The Majority of the People*, 1941, defense of majority rule and attack upon the theorists who would restrict its application.

W. Kendall, *John Locke and the Doctrine of Majority Rule*, 1941, written by an exponent of the absolute majority rule principle.

H. S. Commager, *Majority Rule and Minority Rights*, 1943, defense of majority rule principle and attack upon the limitations of judicial review.

CONSTITUTIONALISM

W. H. Hamilton, "Constitutionalism," *Encyclopedia of the Social Sciences*, vol. 9.

C. H. McIlwain, *Constitutionalism: Ancient and Modern*, rev. ed., 1947, papers and essays by distinguished scholar showing the evolution of the concept of limited government.

F. D. Wormuth, *The Origins of Modern Constitutionalism*, 1949, examination of the origins and development of constitutional limitations—separation of powers, checks and balances, judicial review, and so on.

F. M. Watkins, *The Political Tradition of the West*, 1948, traces development of modern liberalism.

C. J. Friedrich, *Constitutional Government and Democracy*, rev. ed., 1950, analysis of relations between democracy and constitutionalism, covers all major contemporary constitutional governments.

Part Two: THE RULES AND HOW THEY GREW

REVOLUTION AND CONFEDERATION

C. M. Andrews, *The Colonial Period of American History*, 1934-1938, 4 vols., comprehensive history of the colonial period.

J. C. Miller, *Origins of the American Revolution*, 1943.

J. F. Jameson, *The American Revolution Considered as a Social Movement*, 1926.

C. L. Becker, *The Declaration of Independence*, new ed., 1942.

E. Dumbauld, *The Declaration of Independence and What It Means Today*, 1950, a phrase-by-phrase explanation of the Declaration placing it in the context of the days in which it was written.

M. Jensen, *The Articles of Confederation*, 1940, the most comprehensive volume on the making and adoption of the Articles of Confederation.

A. C. McLaughlin, *The Confederation and the Constitution, 1783-1789*, 1905, standard work.

M. Jensen, *The New Nation*, 1950, study of the Confederation, contains sharp criticism of the "chaos and patriots-to-the-rescue" interpretation.

E. P. Douglas, *Rebels and Democrats*, 1955, a study of the democratic forces at work during the Revolution.

THE CONSTITUTIONAL CONVENTION

Primary sources of basic records are:

M. Farrand, *The Records of the Federal Convention of 1787*, 4 vols., rev. ed., 1937.

A. T. Prescott, *Drafting the Federal Constitution*, 1941, rearrangement of the debates in the Constitutional Convention according to topics.

J. Elliot, *The Debates in the Several Conventions on the Adoption of the Federal Constitution*, 1835-1846, 2nd ed., 5 vols., source for the debates in the state ratifying conventions.

J. A. Smith, *The Spirit of American Government*, 1911, spirited statement of the thesis that the Constitution is the platform of an antidemocratic movement.

C. A. Beard, *An Economic Interpretation of the Constitution of the United States*, 1913, caused a popular furor and has had a strong influence on historians and political scientists.

R. E. Brown, *Charles Beard and the Constitution*, 1956, "A Critical Analysis of 'An Economic Interpretation of the Constitution.' "

B. C. Rodick, *American Constitutional Custom*, 1953, European backgrounds of our political system.

C. Warren, *The Making of the Constitution*, 1937, disputes the Beard thesis, contains day-by-day account of the activities of the delegates.

R. L. Schuyler, *The Constitution of the United States*, 1923, shows that the delegates to the Convention were in substantial agreement on major issues.

C. Van Doren, *The Great Rehearsal*, 1948, popularly written account of the Constitutional Convention.

W. W. Crosskey, *Politics and the Constitution*, 2 vols., 1953, argument that framers intended to create a unitary system.

J. Jay, J. Madison, and A. Hamilton, *The Federalist*, 1788-1789, basic source material, classic exposition of Constitution.

The following general histories contain chapters on the background, formation, and adoption of the Constitution:

A. C. McLaughlin, *A Constitutional History of the United States*, 1935.

C. B. Swisher, *American Constitutional Development*, 2nd ed., 1954.

A. H. Kelly and W. A. Harbison, *The American Constitution*, 1948.

THE LIVING CONSTITUTION

B. Schwartz, *American Constitutional Law*, 1955, written for British audience, provides handy summary of recent developments.

B. F. Wright, *The Growth of American Constitutional Law*, 1942, concise discussion of the development of constitutional system.

C. B. Swisher, *The Growth of Constitutional Power in the United States*, 1946, the Constitution as symbol, as limitation, and as grant of power.

A. N. Holcombe, *Our More Perfect Union*, 1950, defense of American constitutional principles as expounded by Madison and other Founding Fathers.

* E. S. Corwin, *The Constitution and What It Means Today*, 11th ed., 1955, phrase-by-phrase explanation.

E. S. Corwin and J. W. Peltason, *Understanding the Constitution*, 1949, more elementary phrase-by-phrase explanation.

L. B. Orfield, *Amending the Federal Constitution*, 1942, the leading book on the subject.

C. E. Merriam, *The Written Constitution and the Unwritten Attitude*, 1931, emphasizes the impact of urbanism and political parties on constitutional system.

H. L. McBain, *The Living Constitution*, 1927, reprinted 1942, discussion of basic principles and their growth.

W. B. Munro, *The Makers of the Unwritten Constitution*, 1930, biographical essays on some of the persons who have shaped our constitutional tradition.

C. Read, ed., *The Constitution Recon-*

sidered, 1938, essays on the Constitution, its background and development.

E. S. Corwin, ed., *The Constitution of the United States of America: Analysis and Interpretation, Revised and Annotated 1952,* Senate Doc. 170, 82 Cong. 2 Sess., 1953.

W. O. Douglas, *We the Judges,* 1955, comparison of Indian and American law with surveys of the American developments.

FEDERALISM

K. C. Wheare, *Federal Government,* London, 2nd ed., 1951, comparative analysis of federal systems, has a critical bibliography.

A. W. Macmahon, ed., *Federalism: Mature and Emergent,* 1955, symposium by participants at Columbia University Bicentennial Conference dealing with federalism throughout the world.

R. Pound, C. H. McIlwain, R. F. Nichols, *Federalism as a Democratic Process,* 1942, essays.

M. McHendry, *Treaties and Federal Constitutions,* 1955, problems of federal states in international relations with emphasis on U.S., Canada, Australia, and Switzerland.

J. P. Clark, *The Rise of a New Federalism,* 1938, pioneering discussion of the several varieties of federal-state cooperation.

G. C. S. Benson, *The New Centralization,* 1941, interpretation of the changing nature of federal-state relations.

W. Anderson, *The Units of Government in the United States,* 2nd ed., 1942, survey with recommendations for decreasing the number of governmental units.

Commission on Intergovernmental Relations, *A Report to the President for Transmittal to Congress,* 1955, findings, recommendations, and survey of national-state relations with emphasis on financial aspects.

——— *Reports of Study Committees,* 1955, fifteen publications of reports of staff and subcommittees.

W. Anderson, *The Nation and the States, Rivals or Partners?* 1955, history and present status by senior political scientist and member of Commission on Intergovernmental Relations.

L. D. White, *The States and the Nation,* 1953, another distinguished political scientist's interpretation with somewhat different emphasis from Anderson's, especially in connection with dangers of growth of national functions.

J. W. Fesler, *Area and Administration,* 1949, lectures on problems arising from functional and regional administration.

V. V. Thursby, *Interstate Cooperation,* 1952, "A Study of the Interstate Compact."

Council of State Governments, *Federal Grants-in-Aid,* 1949, most recent survey; presents point of view of state officials.

V. O. Key, Jr., *The Administration of Federal Grants to States,* 1937, administration of the grant system.

J. A. Maxwell, *The Fiscal Impact of Federalism in the United States,* 1946.

J. E. Kallenbach, *Federal Co-operation with the States under the Commerce Clause,* 1942.

Senate Special Committee to Investigate Organized Crime in Interstate Commerce, *Hearings,* 81 Cong., 2 Sess., 1950; 82 Cong., 1 Sess., 1951, and *Third Interim Report,* Senate Report 307, 82 Cong., 1 Sess., 1951, hearings of the much televised Kefauver Committee and Report containing conclusions, survey of local conditions, and recommendations for federal action.

Council of State Governments, *Federal-State Relations,* Sen. Doc. No. 81, 81 Cong., 1 Sess., 1949, report to the Hoover Commission.

TERRITORIES AND THE DISTRICT OF COLUMBIA

Senate Committee on Interior and Insular Affairs, *Report, Providing for the Admission of Alaska into the Union,* Senate Report No. 1929, 81 Cong., 2 Sess., 1950.

——— *Hearings, Alaska Statehood,* 81 Cong., 2 Sess., 1950.

T. B. Clark, *Hawaii, the Forty-ninth State,* 1947.

Senate Committee on Interior and Insular Affairs, *Report, Statehood for Hawaii,* Senate Report No. 1928, 81 Cong., 2 Sess., 1950.

——— *Hearings, Statehood for Hawaii,* 81 Cong., 2 Sess., 1950.

R. G. Tugwell, *The Stricken Land: The Story of Puerto Rico,* 1946.

WORLD FEDERALISM

G. Clark, *Plan for Peace,* 1950, pleas for world government.

E. A. Mowrer, *Challenge and Decision,* 1950, analysis of world conditions, and argument for world federal government.

C. Meyer, Jr., *Peace or Anarchy,* 1947, by one of the leaders of the world federalist movement.

C. Brinton, *From Many, One,* 1948, criticism of world federalist theories as unrealistic and fallacious.

R. Niebuhr, "The Illusion of World Government," *Foreign Affairs,* April 1949, attack on world federalist position.

F. L. Schuman, *The Commonwealth of Man,* 1952, wide-ranging study of relation of world government and power politics.

Part Three: CIVIL LIBERTIES AND CITIZENSHIP

FREEDOM OF RELIGION

A. W. Johnson and F. H. Yost, *Separation of Church and State in the United States,* rev. ed., 1948, theory and development of American law.

J. M. O'Neill, *Religion and Education under the Constitution,* 1949.

J. M. Dawson, *Separate Church and State Now,* 1948.

A. P. Stokes, *Church and State in the United States,* 1950, 3 vols., encyclopedic source material.

FREEDOM OF SPEECH

L. Whipple, *The Story of Civil Liberty in the United States,* 1927, a history.

J. M. Smith, *Freedom's Fetters,* 1956, intensive study of Alien and Sedition Laws.

R. E. Cushman, *Civil Liberties in the United States,* 1956, summary of laws and court rulings.

A. H. Kelley, *Where Constitutional Liberty Came From,* 1954, pamphlet dealing with origins of Bill of Rights.

R. K. Carr, ed., "Civil Rights in America," *The Annals,* May 1951, articles covering all phases of civil liberties.

* J. S. Mill, *Essay on Liberty,* 1859, many editions, famous defense of free speech.

Z. Chafee, *Free Speech in the United States,* rev. ed., 1941, most comprehensive study of restrictions on speech during and after World War I; discussion of dangers inherent in sedition laws.

———, *Freedom of Speech and Press,* 1954, pamphlet describing problems in American history.

A. Meiklejohn, *Free Speech and Its Relation to Self-government,* 1948, attack upon "clear and present danger doctrine" and defense of the absolute right of political speech.

J. E. Gerald, *The Press and the Constitution, 1931-1947,* 1948, survey of cases, development of concept of freedom of the press in constitutional law, application of labor laws to newspaper industry.

Commission on the Freedom of the Press, *A Free and Responsible Press,* 1947, critical report of media of mass communication, emphasizes dangers of irresponsible economic control.

W. E. Hocking, *Freedom of the Press,* 1947, by leading American philosopher.

M. L. Ernst, *The First Freedom,* 1946, discussion of problem of concentration of control over media of communication.

H. Brucker, *Freedom of Information,* 1949, discussion of problems; dissent from some of criticisms and recommendations of Commission on the Freedom of the Press.

W. L. Chenery, *Freedom of the Press,* 1955, by an editor.

THE BATTLE AGAINST SUBVERSIVE CONDUCT AND SEDITIOUS SPEECH

S. Stouffer, *Communism, Conformity and*

Civil Liberties, 1955, survey of American attitudes.

H. D. Lasswell, *National Security and Individual Freedom*, 1950, pressures during cold war, with recommendations.

H. W. Chase, *Security and Liberty*, 1955, legislative and judicial handling of native Communists, 1947-1955.

W. Gellhorn, *The States and Subversion*, 1952, symposium dealing with activities of six states.

M. Grodzins, *The Loyal and the Disloyal*, 1956, discussion of factors that make men loyal.

E. Bontecou, *The Federal Loyalty-Security Program*, 1953, coverage through 1952.

A. Westin, *The Constitution and Loyalty Programs*, 1954, pamphlet describing programs and commenting on the constitutional problems involved.

W. Gellhorn, *Security, Loyalty, and Science*, 1950, critical discussion of important phase of security program.

T. Sellin, ed., "Internal Security and Civil Rights," July 1955, *The Annals*.

"Problems of American Democracy, Security in a Free Society," *Current History*, October 1955.

J. L. O'Brian, *National Security and Individual Freedom*, 1955, critical evaluation of our security programs.

T. I. Cook, *Democratic Rights versus Communist Activity*, 1954, defends view that it is consistent with democratic principles and practices to make Communist political activity illegal.

J. Peltason, *Constitutional Liberty and Seditious Activity*, 1954, pamphlet describing laws aimed at seditious speech and constitutional problems involved.

Subcommittee on Constitutional Rights of Senate Judiciary Committee, *Hearings, Security and Constitutional Rights*, 84 Cong., 2 Sess., 1955, testimony of officials who administer programs and of witness critical of the programs.

Senate Judiciary Committee, *The Communist Party of the United States*, 84 Cong., 2 Sess., Senate Doc. No. 117, 1956, "A Handbook on Operations of Communist Party."

Internal Security Subcommittee of Senate Judiciary Committee, *Interlocking Subversion in Government Departments*, Report, 83 Cong., 1 Sess., July 30, 1953 (Committee print). Report on communist penetration in government.

—— *Subversive Influence in the Educational Process*, Report, 82 Cong., 1 Sess., Jan. 2, 1953 (Committee print).

A. Yarmolinsky, *Case Studies in Personnel Security*, 1955, series of security-loyalty cases.

Association of the Bar of the City of New York, Special Committee on Federal Loyalty-Security Program, *The Federal Loyalty-Security Program*, 1956, critical report by this influential body.

Subcommittee Senate Committee on Post Office and Civil Service, Preliminary Report on *Administration of Federal Employees' Security Program*, 84 Cong. 2 Sess., Senate Report No. 1760, 1956.

EQUALITY UNDER THE LAW

C. Vann Woodward, *The Strange Career of Jim Crow*, 1955, account of growth of segregation laws.

Southern School News, periodic reports on desegregation in public schools.

Race Relations Law Reporter, periodic presentation of court cases, legislation, orders, regulations.

U.S. President's Committee on Civil Rights, *To Secure These Rights*, 1947.

M. R. Konvitz, *The Constitution and Civil Rights*, 1947, study of civil rights in employment and accommodation in public places.

R. K. Carr, *Federal Protection of Civil Rights*, 1947, study of activities of Civil Rights Section of Department of Justice.

R. L. Hale, *Freedom through Law*, 1952, public control of private power.

M. R. Konvitz, ed., *Law and Social Action*, 1951, essays on infringement of civil rights by private groups.

H. S. Ashmore, *The Negro and The Schools*, 2d ed., 1954, legal and socioeconomic information.

P. Lewinson, *Race, Class, and Party*, 1932, detailed study of Negro voting and problems of Negro suffrage.

C. Abrams, *Forbidden Neighbors*, 1955, "A Study of Prejudice in Housing."

J. ten Broek, *et al.*, *Prejudice, War, and the Constitution*, 1954, origins, politics, and legality of Japanese American evacuations in World War II.

M. Berger, *Equality by Statute*, 1952, review of case law and analysis of work of the New York Commission against Discrimination, set in a broad social science framework.

P. Murray, ed., *States' Laws on Race and Color and Appendices Containing International Documents, Federal Laws and Regulations, Local Ordinances and Charts*, 1950, published by Woman's Division of Christian Service of The Methodist Church.

M. Grodzins, *Americans Betrayed: Politics and the Japanese Evacuation*, 1949, treats what many considered a violation of civil liberties during World War II.

RIGHTS TO LIFE, LIBERTY, AND PROPERTY

E. S. Corwin, *Liberty against Government*, 1948, essays on the growth and decline of substantive due process.

B. F. Wright, *The Contract Clause of the Constitution*, 1938, standard source.

L. B. Orfield, *Criminal Procedure from Arrest to Appeal*, 1947, detailed study.

R. Pound, *Criminal Justice in America*, 1930, by noted legal scholar.

H. Mannheim, *Criminal Justice and Social Reconstruction*, 1946, survey of recent developments, suggestions for practical reform.

J. Frank, *Courts on Trial*, 1950, by federal circuit judge, criticism of court procedures, especially jury trials.

F. H. Heller, *The Sixth Amendment*, 1951, origin and contemporary application of procedural guarantees of this amendment.

A. R. Beisel, *Control over Illegal Enforcement of the Criminal Law*, 1955.

W. B. Beaney, *Right to Counsel in American Courts*, 1955, survey of law and decisions.

E. N. Griswold, *The Fifth Amendment Today*, 1955, Dean of the Harvard Law School writes about self-incrimination clause.

R. E. Edwards, *The Fourteenth Amendment and Civil Liberty*, 1955, pamphlet describing application of some civil rights as restrictions on states via Fourteenth Amendment.

IMMIGRATION AND CITIZENSHIP

President's Commission on Immigration and Naturalization, *Whom Shall We Welcome*, 1952, report of commission appointed by President Truman, critical of Immigration and Nationality Act of 1952.

M. R. Konvitz, *Civil Rights in Immigration*, 1953, critical study of legislation relating to admission, exclusion, deportation, and naturalization of immigrants.

O. Handlin, *The Uprooted*, 1952, moving history of immigration from the perspective of the immigrants.

M. L. Hanse, *The Immigrant in American History*, 1940.

Part Four: THE PEOPLE IN POLITICS

INTEREST GROUPS

C. E. Merriam, *Public and Private Government*, 1944.

C. A. Beard, *The Economic Basis of Politics*, 1922, the importance of economic interests in the political process.

K. Schriftgiesser, *The Lobbyists*, 1951, history of lobbying, discussion of lobbyists of 1946, case studies of lobbyists at work; contains excellent bibliography.

Select Committee on Lobbying Activities of the House, *Hearings*, 81 Cong., 2

Sess., 1950, important congressional investigation; materials on some major organizations.

———, *General Interim Report*, House Report 3138; *Report and Recommendations on Federal Lobbying Act*, House Report 3239, 81 Cong. 2 Sess., 1950, recommendations for national legislation to control the lobbyists more effectively.

D. C. Blaisdell, *Economic Power and Political Pressures*, 1941, TNEC Monograph 26.

S. Chase, *Democracy under Pressure*, 1945, a critical analysis of the role of interest groups.

H. L. Childs, *Labor and Capital in National Politics*, 1930, study of the American Federation of Labor and the Chamber of Commerce.

P. H. Odegard, *Pressure Politics: The Study of the Anti-saloon League*, 1928, standard source.

R. A. Brady, *Business as a System of Power*, 1943, operation of business interest groups.

Senate Committee on Education and Labor, *Report No. 6, 76 Cong., 1 Sess.*, 1939, materials on the N.A.M. and other employer associations.

E. Gruening, *The Public Pays*, 1931, critical study of propaganda activities of the electric power industry.

Federal Trade Commission, *Summary Report . . . on Efforts by Associations . . . of Electric and Gas Utilities to Influence Public Opinion*, Senate Doc. 92, 70 Cong., 1 Sess., 1934, efforts of industry to defeat Public Utility Holding Company Act.

J. G. Shott, *The Railroad Monopoly*, 1950, study of the railroad lobby.

M. Starr, *Labour Politics in U.S.A.*, London, 1949.

J. Gaer, *The First Round: The Story of the C.I.O. Political Action Committee*, 1944, contains facsimile examples of C.I.O. pamphlets.

F. Calkins, *The C.I.O. and the Democratic Party*, 1952, five case studies in 1950 elections by research assistant of C.I.O.-P.A.C.

W. McCune, *The Farm Bloc*, 1943, balanced account of activities of American Farm Bureau Federation and other farm organizations.

O. M. Kile, *The Farm Bureau through Three Decades*, 1948, the official history.

R. Baker, *The American Legion and American Foreign Policy*, 1954, recent analysis.

J. Gray and V. H. Bernstein, *The Inside Story of the Legion*, 1948, critical of the American Legion.

R. S. Jones, *A History of the American Legion*, 1946, the "official" history.

D. Wecter, *When Johnny Comes Marching Home*, 1944, study of return of soldiers after Revolutionary, Civil, and First World War.

O. Garceau, *The Political Life of the American Medical Association*, 1941, pioneering study of the political activities of America's doctors.

M. L. Rutherford, *The Influence of the American Bar Association on Public Opinion and Legislation*, 1937, story of a politically active profession.

B. R. Twiss, *Lawyers and the Constitution*, 1942, "how laissez faire came to the Supreme Court."

C. E. Jacobus, *Law Writers and the Courts*, 1954.

L. C. Kesselman, *The Social Politics of FEPC*, 1948, "A Study in Reform Pressure Movements."

L. E. Ebersole, *Church Lobbying in the Nation's Capital*, 1951, the religious lobbies—the causes for which they work, and the methods they use.

D. D. McKean, *Pressures on the Legislature of New Jersey*, 1938, by political scientist and former member of New Jersey legislature.

B. Zeller, *Pressure Politics in New York*, 1937.

E. P. Herring, *Group Representation before Congress*, 1929, the relations between interest groups and formal institutions of government.

E. E. Schattschneider, *Politics, Pressures, and the Tariff*, 1935, case study based on mass of evidence from hearings on the Smoot-Hawley tariff bill.

E. Latham, *The Group Basis of Politics*, 1952, interplay of group pressures in basing-point legislation.

F. W. Riggs, *Pressures on Congress: A Study of the Repeal of Chinese Exclusion*, 1950, informing case study.

E. P. Herring, *Public Administration and the Public Interest*, 1936, the interaction between interest groups and the administrative machinery.

J. Frank, *If Men Were Angels*, 1942, social, economic, and psychological factors in the working of administrative agencies.

A. Leiserson, *Administrative Regulation*, 1942, analysis of interest groups and regulatory agencies.

A. Maass, *Muddy Waters*, 1951, indictment of the Army Corps of Engineers as "The Lobby That Can't Be Licked."

VOTING AND VOTING BEHAVIOR

H. F. Gosnell, *Democracy, the Threshold of Freedom*, 1948, contains discussion of several theories of citizenship, and of the theoretical premises of the right to vote.

K. H. Porter, *A History of Suffrage in the United States*, 1918, single-volume history.

D. O. McGovney, *American Suffrage Medley*, 1949, survey of voting requirements, argument for constitutional amendment to secure national suffrage standards.

E. C. Stanton, and Others, *History of Woman Suffrage*, 6 vols., 1881-1921, by leading suffragettes.

J. Higham, *Strangers in the Land*, 1955, antiforeignism in the United States.

C. E. Merriam and H. F. Gosnell, *Nonvoting*, 1924, pioneering study.

G. M. Connelly and H. H. Field, "The Non-Voter—Who He Is, What He Thinks," *Public Opinion Quarterly*, 1944, two excellent articles.

S. Lubell, *The Future of American Politics*, 1951, basic party and voting trends, interestingly presented.

———, *The Revolt of the Moderates*, 1956, a more recent study by one who has spent much time talking with all kinds of voters in all kinds of places.

L. Harris, *Is There a Republican Majority?* 1954, study of 1952 election by associate in the Roper polling organization.

E. Roper and L. Harris, "Crime, Reform and the Voter," *The Saturday Review of Literature*, April 7, 1951.

H. F. Gosnell, *Grass Roots Politics*, 1942, voting behavior in several key states.

C. H. Titus, *Voting Behavior in the United States*, 1935.

J. K. Pollock, *Voting Behavior, a Case Study*, 1939, data drawn from Ann Arbor, Michigan.

E. H. Litchfield, *Voting Behavior in a Metropolitan Area* [Detroit], 1941.

D. Anderson and P. E. Davidson, *Ballots and the Democratic Class Struggle*, 1943, class and voting behavior.

L. H. Bean, *How to Predict Elections*, 1948, demonstration of use of statistics to project election trends and to study voting behavior.

P. F. Lazarsfeld, B. Berelson, and H. Gaudet, *The People's Choice*, 1948, demonstrates the technique of panel interviewing on "How the Voter Makes Up His Mind in a Presidential Campaign."

A. Campbell, G. Gurin, and W. E. Miller, *The Voter Decides*, 1954, most comprehensive report on 1952 elections based on data gathered by sampling.

B. R. Berelson, P. F. Lazarsfeld, and W. N. McPhee, *Voting*, 1954, 1948 voting in a New York community, with useful summary of findings of other voting studies.

A. Campbell and H. C. Cooper, *Group Differences in Attitudes and Votes*, 1956, study of 1954 election based on nationwide survey.

H. L. Moon, *Balance of Power*, 1948, the Negroes' use of political power.

*V. O. Key, *Southern Politics in State and Nation*, 1949, the impact of the "Negro problem" on Southern politics.

E. L. Tatum, *The Changed Political Thought of the Negro, 1915-1940*, 1952, causes and consequences of changing political allegiances of Negroes.

H. J. Abraham, *Compulsory Voting*, 1955, an evaluation.

PUBLIC OPINION

Two journals of special interest are:

Public Opinion Quarterly.
International Journal of Opinion and Attitude Research.

Three pioneer students have compiled annotated bibliographies:

H. D. Lasswell, R. D. Casey, and B. L. Smith, *Propaganda and Promotional Activities—an Annotated Bibliography*, 1935; and *Propaganda, Communication, and Public Opinion, a Reference Guide*, 1946.

Five classic volumes:

A. C. Dicey, *Law and Public Opinion in England*, 1905.

G. Wallas, *Human Nature in Politics*, 1919, first published in 1908, this book marked a reaction from earlier over-rationalistic interpretation of politics and public opinion.

A. L. Lowell, *Public Opinion and Popular Government,* 1913.

W. Lippmann, *Public Opinion,* 1922.

J. Dewey, *The Public and Its Problems,* 1927.

Some more recent books providing general coverage are:

N. J. Powell, *Anatomy of Public Opinion,* 1951, by a political scientist.

F. C. Irion, *Public Opinion and Propaganda,* 1950, by a political scientist; summaries of views of classical writers in the field.

M. B. Ogle, Jr., *Public Opinion and Political Dynamics,* 1950, emphasizes theory.

C. D. MacDougall, *Understanding Public Opinion,* 1951, sociological explanation of how public opinion is formed.

H. L. Childs, *An Introduction to Public Opinion,* 1940, essays on the nature and fundamental problems of public opinion and public relations.

C. W. Smith, *Public Opinion in a Democracy,* 1939.

S. Kelley, Jr., *Professional Public Relations and Political Power,* 1956, role of "Madison Avenue" in American politics.

J. A. R. Pimlott, *Public Relations and American Democracy,* 1951, informational and propaganda activities of the federal government.

B. Berelson and M. Janowitz, eds., *Reader in Public Opinion and Communication,* 1951, readings on all major phases of subject.

PUBLIC OPINION POLLS

G. Gallup, *A Guide to Public Opinion Polls,* 1944, by leading practitioners of scientific sampling; general accounts of the workings of the polls, defense of their functions in a democracy.

M. B. Parten, *Surveys, Polls, and Samples,* 1950, comprehensive description of polling procedures.

F. Mosteller, *et al., The Pre-Election Polls of 1948,* 1949, essays by experts who investigated the reasons for the 1948 polling fiasco.

L. Rogers, *The Pollsters,* 1949, criticism of procedures, and attack upon contribution of public opinion polls.

H. Cantril, ed., *Public Opinion: Directory of Polls, 1935-1946,* 1951, most comprehensive collection of poll data.

L. S. Cottrell, Jr. and S. Eberhart, *American Opinion on World Affairs in the Atomic Age,* 1948, summary of American attitudes toward foreign affairs, materials based primarily on special surveys.

Public Opinion Quarterly and *International Journal of Opinion and Attitude Research* publish results of the several polls.

MEDIA OF COMMUNICATION

P. F. Lazarsfeld, *Radio and the Printed Page,* 1940, role of radio by outstanding authorities.

W. Schramm, *Mass Communications,* readings, 1949.

Z. Chafee, *Government and Mass Communications,* 1947, published under auspices of the Commission on Freedom of the Press.

F. L. Mott, *American Journalism,* 1941, standard history.

W. Lippmann, *Liberty and the News,* 1920, critical essay by one of America's famous journalists.

A. M. Lee, *The Daily Newspaper in America,* 1937, traces the growth and influence of newspapers on American life.

L. C. Rosten, *The Washington Correspondents,* 1937, study of the men who cover the nation's capital and the influences brought to bear upon them.

C. A. H. Thomson, *Television and Presidential Politics,* 1956.

L. C. Ferguson and R. H. Smuckler, *Politics in the Press: An Analysis of Press Content in 1952 Senatorial Campaigns,* 1954.

C. A. Siepmann, *Radio, Television and Society,* 1950, analysis of the problems of the role of radio and television in a free society.

———, *Radio's Second Chance,* 1946, critical discussion of radio's contributions.

L. White, *The American Radio,* 1947, comprehensive study that formed one of the reports of the Commission on Freedom of the Press.

Federal Communications Commission, *Public Service Responsibility of Broadcast Licenses,* March 7, 1946.

National Association of Broadcasters, ed., *Broadcasting and the Bill of Rights,* 1947, radio industry's response to F.C.C. regulations.

L. C. Rosten, *Hollywood,* 1941, an interpretation of social and political pressures.

R. A. Inglis, *Freedom of the Movies,* 1947, under the auspices of the Commission on Freedom of the Press.

M. D. Huettig, *Economic Control of the Motion Picture Industry,* 1944.

P. Wood, *Magazines in the United States,* 1949, one of the few books on the subject.

POLITICAL PARTIES

R. Michels, *Political Parties,* reprinted in 1949, important sociological study of the oligarchical tendencies of European democratic political parties.

M. Ostrogorski, *Democracy and the Organization of Political Parties,* 2 vols., 1908, early, classic interpretation of development of parties in the United States and England.

F. J. Turner, *The Significance of Sections in American History,* 1937, the importance of sectionalism in American politics was first projected by Turner at the beginning of the twentieth century.

H. D. Lasswell, *Politics: Who Gets What, When, How,* 1946, reissued 1950, one of Lasswell's more popular treatments.

*E. E. Schattschneider, *Party Government,* 1942; *The Struggle for Party Government,* 1948, in these books a strong case is made for more centralized and disciplined parties by an outstanding scholar who has virtually developed a "school of thought" about American politics.

Committee on Political Parties of the American Political Science Association, *Toward a More Responsible Two Party System,* 1950, by committee of sixteen authorities under chairmanship of Professor Schattschneider; recommendations for strengthening the American party system.

*E. P. Herring, *The Politics of Democracy,* 1940, interpretation and defense of present system; interpretations somewhat contrary to those of Schattschneider and the committee report mentioned above.

A. N. Holcombe, *The Political Parties of Today,* 1924; *The New Party Politics,* 1933; *The Middle Classes in American Politics,* 1940, interpretation of American politics as moving from sectional to urban or "class" politics with the middle class holding the balance and preserving free government.

W. E. Binkley, *American Political Parties,* 1943, history stressing the role of parties as coalitions of interest groups.

H. Agar, *The Price of Union,* 1950, history stressing the thesis that loosely organized and undisciplined parties are essential to the preservation of the Union.

D. Acheson, *A Democrat Looks at His Party,* 1955.

A. Larson, *A Republican Looks At His Party,* 1956, by Director of United States Information Agency and member of the "liberal" wing of the Republican Party.

M. Moos, *Republicans: A History of Their Party,* 1956, thoughtful and readable treatment.

W. B. Hesseltine, *The Rise and Fall of Third Parties,* 1948, short history.

M. Stedman and S. Stedman, *Discontent at the Polls,* 1950, incisive account of legal, political, and other aspects of third parties.

S. Forthal, *Cogwheels of Democracy,* 1946, "A Study of the Precinct Captain."

K. H. Porter and D. B. Johnson, *National Party Platforms 1840-1956,* 1956.

LEADERSHIP

C. E. Merriam, *Four American Party Leaders,* 1926.

H. Lasswell, *Psychopathology and Politics,* 1930; and *Power and Personality,* 1948, through use of interviews, observations, and psychological techniques Lasswell has developed a typology of political leaders and related their public careers to their psychological characters.

H. H. Gerth and C. W. Mills, tr. and ed., *From Max Weber: Essays in Sociology,* 1946, essays by famous German sociologist, pioneering student of leadership.

W. F. Whyte, *Street Corner Society,* 1943, close study of informal leadership.

A. W. Gouldner, ed., *Studies in Leadership,* 1950, essays on apathy, and various kinds of leadership.

J. M. Burns, *Roosevelt: The Lion and the Fox,* 1956, problems and practices of FDR as a democratic leader.

ELECTIONS

J. P. Harris, *Election Administration in the United States,* 1934, standard work.

S. D. Albright, *The American Ballot,* 1942, discussion of the various kinds of ballots.

C. A. M. Ewing, *Primary Elections in the South,* 1953, statistical study.

G. Gallup, *et al., The Political Almanac,* 1952, collection of election statistics.

C. E. Merriam and L. Overacker, *Primary Elections,* 1928, standard source.

J. B. Johnson, *Registration for Voting in the United States,* rev. ed., 1946, survey of methods used.

E. M. Kirkpatrick and J. J. Kirkpatrick, *Elections—U.S.A.,* 1956, selection of articles from The *New York Times Magazine* covering many phases of electoral process.

R. M. Scammon, *America Votes,* 1956, most comprehensive collection of recent election statistics, to be kept up to date with additional volumes every two years.

Subcommittee of the Senate Committee on the Judiciary, *Hearings, Nomination and Election of President and Vice-President,* 84 Cong., 1 Sess., testimony on several proposals to alter electoral college.

P. T. David *et al., Presidential Nominating Politics in 1952,* 1954, five-vol. report undertaken by over 150 political scientists.

W. J. Bryan, *A Tale of Two Conventions,* 1912, by perennial candidate for President.

H. L. Mencken, *Making a President,* 1932, the 1932 conventions by leading satirist.

H. L. Stoddard, *Presidential Sweepstakes,* 1948, story of many campaigns by one who actively participated in them.

R. V. Peel and T. C. Donnelly, *The 1928 Campaign,* 1931; *The 1932 Campaign,* 1935; accounts of two campaigns from nomination to election.

J. A. Farley, *Behind the Ballots,* 1938, contains account of the 1932 Democratic Convention and campaign.

C. Michelson, *The Ghost Talks,* 1944, account of party propaganda by former publicity director for Democratic National Committee.

L. Overacker, *Money in Elections,* 1932, standard source, supplemented by numerous articles in the *American Political Science Review.*

——, *Presidential Campaign Funds,* 1946.

M. Moos, *Politics, Presidents, and Coattails,* 1953, study of congressional elections, emphasizing interaction of presidential and congressional elections.

Part Five: POLICY MAKERS FOR THE PEOPLE

THE LEGISLATIVE PROCESS

R. Luce, *Legislative Procedure,* 1922; *Legislative Assemblies,* 1924; *Legislative Principles,* 1930; *Legislative Problems,* 1935; by a scholar in politics.

T. V. Smith, *The Legislative Way of Life,* 1940, defense of the legislature by an ex-congressman, ex-state legislator, philosopher, and political scientist.

H. Walker, *The Legislative Process,* 1948, latest text on organization, procedure, and theory of lawmaking.

H. F. Gosnell, *Democracy, the Threshold of Freedom,* 1948, contains discussion of the functions of representatives and representative assemblies.

A. de Grazia, *Public and Republic,* 1951, history of who represents what and how.

CONGRESS

W. Wilson, *Congressional Government,* 1885, a classic interpretation.

F. M. Riddick, *The United States Congress,* 1949, comprehensive discussion of organizational and procedural aspects.

G. B. Galloway, *The Legislative Process in Congress,* 1953, organization, procedures, and problems by political scientist who played leading role in reorganization of Congress in 1946; sequel to his earlier *Congress at the Crossroads.*

Joint Committee on Organization of the Congress, *Organization of Congress,* Senate Report 1011, 79 Cong., 2 Sess., 1946, favorable report on Reorganization Act.

R. A. Young, *This Is Congress,* 1943, a general description and interpretation.

———, *Congressional Politics in the Second World War,* 1956, analysis of congressional behavior reflecting the pattern of politics during the war years.

E. S. Griffith, *Congress: Its Contemporary Role,* 1951, favorable assessment of operation of Congress by Director of its Legislative Reference Service.

L. H. Chamberlain, *The President, Congress, and Legislation,* 1946, study of roles of the President and Congress in lawmaking; conclusion that Congress is more capable of thinking in national terms than is sometimes thought; a different view is given in the following book.

J. M. Burns, *Congress on Trial,* 1949, description of the politics of lawmaking; presentation of view that the fundamental defect arises from the nature of the party system.

S. K. Bailey, *Congress Makes a Law,* 1950, detailed account of the enactment of the Employment Act of 1946 and analysis of the forces interacting in, on, and through Congress.

S. K. Bailey and H. Samuel, *Congress at Work,* 1952, series of brief case studies exploring all aspects of Congress at work.

*B. M. Gross, *The Legislative Struggle,* 1953, probing analysis of Congress as the battleground of interest struggles.

H. B. Westerfield, *Foreign Policy and Party Politics,* 1955, analysis of congressional voting and role of parties.

G. L. Grassmuck, *Sectional Biases in Congress on Foreign Policy,* 1951, statistical study of congressional behavior.

M. E. Ridgeway, *The Missouri Basin's Pick-Sloan Plan,* 1955, "A Case Study in Congressional Policy Determination."

J. Turner, *Party and Constituency,* 1952, measurement of relative impact of parties and constituencies upon congressional voting behavior.

R. A. Dahl, *Congress and Foreign Policy,* 1950, evaluation of Congress's role in the making of foreign policy; suggestions for improving its functioning.

H. H. Wilson, *Congress: Corruption and Compromise,* 1951, comparison of English and American records, recommendations for improvement, and analysis of general problem of corruption in politics.

G. H. Haynes, *The Senate of the United States,* 2 vols., 1938.

J. P. Harris, *The Advice and Consent of the Senate,* 1953, "A Study of the Confirmation of Appointments by the United States Senate."

F. L. Burdette, *Filibustering in the Senate,* 1940, standard source.

R. J. Dangerfield, *In Defense of the Senate: A Study in Treaty-Making,* 1933, evidence that Senate's obstruction is less serious than usually thought.

K. Colegrove, *The American Senate and World Peace,* 1944, criticism of two-thirds treaty requirement.

W. A. Robinson, *Thomas B. Reed, Parliamentarian,* 1930, biography of one of the most powerful Speakers.

E. B. Bolles, *The Tyrant from Illinois,* 1951, biography of "Uncle Joe" Cannon, the man who ruled the House for many years as Speaker.

COMMITTEES

E. E. Dennison, *The Senate Foreign Relations Committee,* 1942.

A. C. F. Westphal, *The House Committee on Foreign Affairs,* 1942.

G. Y. Steiner, *The Congressional Conference Committee: Seventieth to Eightieth Congress,* 1951, case study of the operations of this important committee.

Congressional investigations are covered in four major books:

M. E. Dimock, *Congressional Investigating Committees*, 1929.

E. J. Eberling, *Congressional Investigations*, 1928.

M. N. McGeary, *The Development of Congressional Investigative Power*, 1940, builds on the earlier volumes.

R. K. Carr, *The House Un-American Activities Committee*, 1952, scholarly and balanced discussion.

————, *The Constitution and Congressional Investigating Committees*, 1955, pamphlet covering constitutional limits.

T. Taylor, *Grand Inquest*, 1955, critical study of congressional investigations.

A. Barth, *Government by Investigation*, 1955, also critical.

THE PRESIDENT

S. Lorant, *The Presidency*, 1951, picture history of the Presidency and presidential elections.

R. J. Donovan, *The Inside Story*, 1956, taken from notes on the Eisenhower Cabinet meetings, gives picture of this and other aspects of Eisenhower Administration.

E. S. Corwin, *The President: Office and Powers*, rev. ed., 1948, comprehensive discussion of the historical and constitutional development.

———— and L. W. Koenig, *The Presidency Today*, 1956.

S. Hyman, *The American President*, 1954, interpretative study.

*C. Rossiter, *The American Presidency*, 1956, description and analysis of growth and uses of Presidency.

H. J. Laski, *The American Presidency*, 1940, interpretation of the dynamics of the Presidency.

P. Herring, *Presidential Leadership*, 1940, analysis of the interrelations among President, party, and Congress; defense of the presidential system.

C. P. Patterson, *Presidential Government in the United States*, 1947, presentation of thesis that ours is now "irresponsible presidential government" and

plan for creation of cabinet government.

S. Hyman, ed., "The Office of the American Presidency," symposium in September, 1956, *The Annals*.

R. S. Rankin, and others, *The Presidency in Transition*, 1949, essays by experts on various facets of the office.

L. Brownlow, *The President and the Presidency*, 1949, discussion of the adequacy of the office to meet the many demands upon it.

J. Hart, *The American Presidency in Action 1789*, 1948, study of the formative years.

L. D. White, *The Federalists*, 1948; *The Jeffersonians*, 1951; and *The Jacksonians*, 1955, cover the early years and emphasize the administrative organization of the Executive.

W. E. Binkley, *President and Congress*, 1947, history of the Presidency and its relation to Congress.

W. Wilson, *Constitutional Government in the United States*, reprint 1921; written before he became President; indicates Wilson's concept of the role and responsibility of the office.

W. H. Taft, *Our Chief Magistrate and His Powers*, 1916, presents a much more limited concept of the Presidency.

N. J. Small, *Some Presidential Interpretations of the Presidency*, 1932, rounds out the picture.

C. A. Berdahl, *War Powers of the Executive in the United States*, 1921, standard source for the story before the events of World War II.

C. L. Rossiter, *The Supreme Court and the Commander in Chief*, 1951, how the Supreme Court has interpreted the President's status and authority as commander in chief.

L. W. Koenig, *The Presidency and the Crisis*, 1944, scope of presidential emergency powers.

C. L. Rossiter, *Constitutional Dictatorship*, 1948, analysis of crisis government in several nations including the United States.

I. G. Williams, *The American Vice-Presidency: New Look*, 1955, analyzes facets of the vice-presidential role.

———, *The Rise of the Vice-Presidency,* 1956, more comprehensive report.

L. C. Hatch, *A History of the Vice-Presidency of the United States,* 1934, standard source.

R. C. Silva, *Presidential Succession,* 1951, study of "history, interpretation, statutory development, and practical application of the provisions . . . for presidential succession."

PRESIDENT AS ADMINISTRATOR

E. H. Hobbs, *Behind the President,* 1954, study of the agencies working directly under the President.

Senate Committee on Government Operations, *Hearings, Administrative Vice President,* 84 Cong., 2 Sess., also *Report,* Senate Report No. 1960.

H. D. Smith, *The Management of Your Government,* 1945, by Director of the Bureau of the Budget during the important years 1939-1946.

The President's Committee on Administrative Management, *Reports . . . with Studies of Administrative Management in the Federal Government,* 1937, influential studies; primary source for understanding the problems of "high-level" governmental administration.

The Commission on the Organization of the Executive Branch of the Government, *General Management of the Executive Branch;* and *Concluding Report,* 1949 and 1955, attempt to strengthen Presidency as central agency of administration.

H. M. Somers, *Presidential Agency: OWMR,* 1950, problems of coordinating administrative agencies; suggestions for strengthening the Presidency.

PUBLIC ADMINISTRATION

C. Seckler-Hudson, *Bibliography on Public Administration,* 4th ed., 1953, annotated bibliography.

W. Wilson, "The Study of Administration," *Political Science Quarterly,* June 1887, classic essay marking the beginning of the modern study of administration.

F. J. Goodnow, *Politics and Administration,* 1900, another pioneering volume; attempt to isolate administration from politics as separate branch of study.

These works of the early pioneers contrast with those of modern writers mentioned below. The early students tended to divide policy and administration into separable categories.

*C. S. Hyneman, *Bureaucracy in a Democracy,* 1950, study of the control and role of the bureaucracy with special attention to the question of legislative and executive responsibilities.

P. H. Appleby, *Big Democracy,* 1945; and *Policy and Administration,* 1949, interpretations of the dynamic aspects of administration; the interrelations between policy and administration.

———, *Morality and Administration in Democratic Government,* 1952, how to promote "public interest" against demands of "special interests."

J. C. Charlesworth, ed., "Bureaucracy and Democratic Government," March, 1954, *The Annals,* collection of articles.

H. A. Simon, *Administrative Behavior,* 1950, "A Study of Decision-Making Processes in Administrative Organization."

P. M. Blau, *The Dynamics of Bureaucracy,* 1955, interpersonal relationships of civil servants.

D. Waldo, *The Administrative State,* 1948, the theory of American public administration; survey of the various "schools" of thought.

H. Stein, *Public Administration and Policy Development,* 1952, series of case studies with interesting essay by editor.

R. K. Merton, and others, *Reader in Bureaucracy,* 1951, collection of articles by authorities in sociology and political science.

FEDERAL ADMINISTRATIVE STRUCTURE

D. C. Tompkins, *Materials for the Study of the Federal Government,* 1948, annotated bibliographical aids; arranged primarily on a functional basis.

General Services Administration, *United States Government Organization Manual,* published annually; contains descriptions of legislative, judicial, and executive branches—their organization and functions, organization charts of the major agencies, select lists of government publications, and other information.

L. M. Short, *The Development of National Administrative Organization in the United States,* 1923, standard history.

S. C. Wallace, *Federal Departmentalization,* 1941, critical analysis of the theories of federal departmentalization.

W. S. Sayre, ed., *The Federal Government Service: Its Character, Prestige, and Problems,* 1955, an American Assembly Symposium.

In addition to the Reports and Studies of the Committee on Administrative Management other reorganization literature includes:

Brookings Institution, *Report to the Special Senate Committee to Investigate the Executive Agencies,* Senate Report 1275, 70 Cong., 1 Sess., 1937.

L. Meriam and L. K. Schmeckebier, *Reorganization of the National Government,* 1939, critical discussion of the Reports of the President's Committee on Administrative Management.

Commission on Organization of the Executive Branch of the Government (the Hoover Commission), *Reports and Task Force Reports,* 1949 and 1954, especially those on personnel and civil service.

B. D. Nash and C. Lynde, *A Hook in Leviathan,* 1950, interpretative analysis of the work of the Hoover Commission.

L. W. Koenig, ed., "The Hoover Commission: A Symposium," *American Political Science Review,* October 1949, critical review.

H. Emmerich, *Essays on Federal Reorganization,* 1950, discussion of reorganization stressing theme that it is a continuous process.

REGULATORY ADMINISTRATION

G. A. Graham and H. Reining, Jr., ed., *Regulatory Administration,* 1943, general discussion of several important areas.

E. Freund, *Administrative Powers over Persons and Property,* 1928, investigation that brought to light the extent to which "policy-power" had been conferred upon administrators.

J. R. Pennock, *Administration and the Rule of Law,* 1941, regulatory agencies and their relations to the courts.

J. M. Landis, *The Administrative Process,* 1938, brief, cogent analysis.

Attorney General's Committee on Administrative Procedure, *Administrative Procedure in Government Agencies,* Senate Doc. 8, 77 Cong., 1 Sess., 1941, survey and recommendations, many of which were incorporated in the Administrative Procedure Act of 1946.

G. Warren, ed., *The Federal Administrative Procedure Act and the Administrative Agencies,* 1947, essays pro and con the Administrative Procedure Act of 1946.

R. E. Cushman, *The Independent Regulatory Commissions,* 1941, most comprehensive general discussion of the independent regulatory commissions.

M. H. Bernstein, *Regulating Business by Independent Commissions,* 1955, critical study of politics of regulation.

PUBLIC PERSONNEL MANAGEMENT

O. G. Stahl, *Public Personnel Administration,* 4th ed., 1956, general discussion.

Commission of Inquiry on Public Service Personnel, *Better Government Personnel,* 1935, influential report accompanied by important monographs by outstanding authorities.

J. J. Corson, *Executives for the Federal Service,* 1952, difficulties of recruiting executives for top-level jobs.

W. S. Carpenter, *The Unfinished Business of Civil Service Reform,* 1952, discussion of failure "to reconcile the merit system with a method of positive administrative control by the responsible executive."

A. W. Macmahon and J. D. Millett, *Federal Administrators,* 1939, bureaucrats —their background and method of selection.

J. Rosow, ed., *American Man in Government,* 1949, biographical encyclopedia.

G. A. Graham, *Education for Public Administration,* 1941, description of practices and recommendations for improvement.

THE JUDGES

See also books mentioned under "The Living Constitution."

B. N. Cardozo, *The Nature of the Judicial Process*, 1921, one of the American classics in legal theory.

J. Frank, *Law and the Modern Mind*, 1930, discussion of the various factors, especially psychological, that affect men, including judges.

F. Frankfurter, *Law and Politics*, 1939, articles, book reviews, occasional papers written before the author became a Justice.

S. P. Simpson and J. Stone, *Case and Readings on Law and Society*, 1948, selection of materials ranging from the Code of Hammurabi to United Nations Commission on Atomic Energy.

J. W. Peltason, *Federal Courts in the Political Process*, 1955.

J. W. Hurst, *The Growth of American Law*, 1950, discussion of the role of legislatures, courts, constitution makers, the Bar, and the executives in development of American law.

L. Mayers, *The American Legal System*, 1955, comprehensive description of legal machinery.

THE SUPREME COURT

G. G. Haines, *The Role of the Supreme Court in American Government and Politics, 1789-1835*, 1944, detailed history of the formative years.

T. R. Powell, *Vagaries and Varieties in Constitutional Interpretation*, 1955, survey of Supreme Court behavior in "deed and work."

R. K. Carr, *Democracy and the Supreme Court*, 1936.

C. E. Hughes, *The Supreme Court of the United States*, 1928, essays.

W. Hurst, ed., *Supreme Court and Supreme Law*, 1954, symposium by distinguished scholars.

* C. P. Curtis, *Lions under the Throne*, 1947, interpretation of role of courts in the American system.

P. A. Freund, *On Understanding the Supreme Court*, 1950, interpretive lectures with comments on the Supreme Court and Supreme Court commentators.

R. H. Jackson, *The Supreme Court in the American System of Government*, 1955, brief essays, unfinished because of the Justice's death.

O. J. Roberts, *The Court and the Constitution*, 1951, critical discussion of recent Court decisions by former member of the Court.

F. Rodell, *Nine Men*, 1955, brief popular history.

C. M. Ewing, *The Judges of the Supreme Court, 1789-1937*, 1938, information about the men who have served on the High Court.

C. H. Pritchett, *The Roosevelt Court*, 1948, survey of the Court from 1937 to 1947 with statistical charts on each Justice's "batting average" on particular issues.

———, *Civil Liberties and the Vinson Court*, 1954, continuation of earlier volume during period 1946-1953.

J. Alsop and T. Catledge, *The 168 Days*, 1938, account of the "Supreme Court Battle of 1937."

F. V. Cahill, Jr., *Judicial Legislation*, 1952, analytical survey of modern American jurisprudence, stressing the problem of right of the judiciary to review acts of other levels of government.

Senate Committee on Judiciary, *Hearings, Reorganization of the Federal Judiciary*, 79 Cong., 2 Sess., 1937, verbatim testimony of the many people who appeared for and against President Roosevelt's Court Plan.

V. G. Rosenblum, *Law as a Political Instrument*, 1955, exploration of the Supreme Court's policy-making role.

JUDICIAL BIOGRAPHY

A. J. Beveridge, *The Life of John Marshall*, 1916-1919, 4 vol. history; has become the prototype of judicial biography.

W. M. Jones, ed., *Chief Justice John Marshall: A Reappraisal*, 1956, symposium on the occasion of Marshall's bicentennial.

C. P. Smith, *James Wilson, Founding Father*, 1956.

D. G. Morgan, *Justice William Johnson, the First Dissenter*, 1954.

C. B. Swisher, *Roger B. Taney*, 1935.

B. R. Trimble, *Chief Justice Waite*, 1938.

J. E. McLean, *William Rufus Day*, 1947.

C. Fairman, *Mr. Justice Miller and the Supreme Court*, 1939, contains account of the Court's work and Reconstruction politics during the critical years, 1860-1890.

C. B. Swisher, *Stephen J. Field, Craftsman of the Law,* 1930, biography of a Justice who had much to do with the development of substantive due process.

W. L. King, *Melville Weston Fuller, Chief Justice of the United States,* 1950, study of a moderately able Justice and outstanding Chief Justice; informing on the internal working of the Court.

Max Lerner, ed., *The Mind and Faith of Justice Holmes,* 1943, collection of Justice Holmes's speeches, essays, letters, and judicial opinions with introduction and notes by the editor.

A. T. Mason, *Brandeis, a Free Man's Life,* 1946.

S. Hendel, *Charles Evans Hughes and the Supreme Court,* 1951.

M. J. Pusey, *Charles Evans Hughes,* 1951, 2 vol. biography.

H. F. Pringle, *The Life and Times of William Howard Taft,* 1939, 2 vol. biography of former President and Chief Justice.

F. J. Paschal, *Mr. Justice Sutherland,* 1951.

G. S. Hellman, *Benjamin N. Cardozo,* 1940.

A. T. Mason, *Harlan Fiske Stone,* 1956.

S. J. Konefsky, *The Constitutional World of Mr. Justice Frankfurter,* 1949, collection of opinions with introductory notes by editor.

C. Williams, *Hugo L. Black,* 1950.

JUDICIAL REVIEW

C. Warren, *The Supreme Court in United States History,* rev. ed., 1932, 2 vols., standard history, sympathetic to the Court's use of judicial review.

L. B. Boudin, *Government by Judiciary,* 1932, 2 vols., critical of the judiciary and of judicial review.

C. G. Haines, *The American Doctrine of Judicial Supremacy,* 2nd ed., 1932, balanced investigation of the role of the Supreme Court and its use of judicial review.

R. K. Carr, *The Supreme Court and Judicial Review,* 1942, among other things discusses *Marbury* v. *Madison, McCullough* v. *Maryland.*

E. S. Corwin, *The Doctrine of Judicial Review,* 1914, essays including famous article on Marbury v. Madison.

————, *Court over Constitution,* 2nd ed., 1942, in terms of its subtitle, "A Study of Judicial Review as an Instrument of Government."

R. H. Jackson, *The Struggle for Judicial Supremacy,* 1941, critical discussion of Supreme Court, especially its activities during the New Deal period.

THE AMERICAN SYSTEM AND PROPOSALS FOR REFORM

Many of the books previously mentioned discuss plans and programs for improving the operation of the governmental system. They are not mentioned again here.

H. Hazlitt, *A New Constitution Now,* 1942, argument in favor of cabinet government and charge that presidential government is irresponsible.

G. A. Graham, *Morality in American Politics,* 1952, study of subject in particular relation to the three branches of government.

Part Six: BIG GOVERNMENT IN ACTION

JOURNALS AND ANNUALS

World Politics, published quarterly by the Institute of International Affairs, approaches the subject more in the framework of social science and less in terms of history and current policy than do some of the other journals.

Foreign Affairs, published quarterly by the Council of Foreign Affairs, contains articles by scholars and practicing diplomats, and emphasizes the substantive aspect of current policy and diplomatic history.

World Organization published quarterly by the World Peace Foundation; survey of the activities of the several international organizations; articles by various authorities on world politics.

The American Journal of International Law is published quarterly by The American Society of International Law, the professional journal for those interested in legal aspects of international affairs.

Foreign Policy Reports published twice a month by the Foreign Policy Association; extended treatment of particular topics of current significance.

Foreign Policy Bulletins published weekly by the Foreign Policy Association; shorter and more popularly written than the Reports mentioned above.

The United Nations Bulletin, published every two weeks by the United Nations Department of Public Information.

The Department of State Bulletin, issued weekly; articles explaining United States policy, speeches by officials, and documents such as treaties and executive agreements.

Foreign Policy Briefs, biweekly news sheet issued by State Department giving reports on current affairs.

Foreign Service Journal, unofficial "house organ" containing articles and reports of Foreign Service published by The American Foreign Service Institute.

Current Developments in U.S. Foreign Policy, published monthly by The Brookings Institution and supplemented by a yearly survey entitled Major Problems of U.S. Foreign Policy.

The United States in World Affairs, annual survey edited by R. P. Stebbins and the Research Staff of the Council on Foreign Relations.

Documents on American Foreign Relations, annual collection published by World Peace Foundation presented under editorship of R. Dennett and R. K. Turner.

Yearbook of the United Nations, annual survey published by the United Nations.

C. Eagleton and R. V. Swift, eds., Annual Review of United Nations Affairs.

INTERNATIONAL POLITICS

Here are just a few of the many general studies of international politics that provide necessary framework for understanding American foreign policy.

H. J. Mackinder, Democratic Ideals and Reality, 1919, republished, 1942, semi-

nal study of what is too narrowly called "geopolitics."

* E. H. Carr, The Twenty Years' Crisis 1919-1939, London, 1940, discussion of trends and forces in world politics, has had important impact on students of international politics.

W. F. Ogburn, ed., Technology and International Relations, 1949, analysis of airplane, steel, gasoline engine, and other technological developments in international relations.

H. Sprout and M. Sprout, eds., Foundations of National Power, rev. ed., 1951, readings on major factors that determine power and policy; notes by the editors.

G. Kirk, et al., The Changing Environment of International Relations, 1956, lectures by experts.

AMERICAN FOREIGN POLICY

N. J. Spykman, America's Strategy in World Politics, 1942, geopolitical analysis of American policy.

G. F. Kennan, American Diplomacy: 1900-1950, 1951, by former Director of State Department's Policy Planning Staff; important as background of American policy of containment, has famous article, "The Sources of Soviet Conduct."

W. Lippmann, The Cold War, 1947, articles attacking Kennan's basic thesis.

G. F. Kennan, Realities of American Foreign Policy, 1954.

F. Tannenbaum, The American Tradition in Foreign Policy, 1955, opposes "realpolitik" basis of interpretation.

L. B. Pearson, Democracy in World Politics, 1955, by Canadian Secretary of State.

C. B. Marshall, The Limits of Foreign Policy, 1954.

T. I. Cook and M. Moos, Power through Purpose, 1954, "The Realism of Idealism as a Basis for Foreign Policy."

L. J. Halle, Civilization and Foreign Policy, 1955, by former State Department official.

T. K. Finletter, Power and Policy: U.S. Foreign Policy and Military Power in the Hydrogen Age, 1954.

D. Perkins, The American Approach to Foreign Policy, 1952, topical historical analysis of principles and parties in American foreign policy.

W. R. Sharp, *International Technical Assistance*, 1952, analysis of U.S. and U.N. programs.

International Development Advisory Board, *Partners in Progress*, 1951, Rockefeller Report on Point Four Program to aid underdeveloped regions.

H. J. Morgenthau, *In Defense of the National Interest*, 1951, critical evaluation of American foreign policy since end of War.

J. W. Pratt, *A History of United States Foreign Policy*, 1955.

S. F. Bemis, *A Diplomatic History of the United States*, 3rd ed., 1950, most comprehensive single-volume history.

T. A. Bailey, *A Diplomatic History of the American People*, 4th ed., 1950, lively account emphasizing the role of public opinion and interest groups.

HOW FOREIGN POLICY IS MADE

K. London and K. Ives, *How Foreign Policy Is Made*, 1949, machinery for making foreign policy in the major democratic nations.

M. Beloff, *Foreign Policy and the Democratic Process*, 1955, by noted English scholar.

E. Plischke, *Conduct of American Diplomacy*, 1950, forms, procedure, and machinery of American diplomacy.

L. Markel, *et al., Public Opinion and Foreign Policy*, 1949, readings.

S. Huddleston, *Popular Diplomacy and War*, 1954, critical comments about the impact of mass opinion on diplomacy.

H. B. Westerfield, *Foreign Policy and Party Politics*, 1955, role of parties and bipartisanship in Congress.

* G. A. Almond, *The American People and Foreign Policy*, 1950, analysis of the effect of public, interest groups, and opinion leaders in shaping foreign policy.

A. W. Macmahon, *Administration in Foreign Affairs*, 1953.

J. L. McCamy, *The Administration of American Foreign Affairs*, 1950, critical evaluation of the machinery for the making and administering of foreign policy.

W. Y. Elliott, *United States Foreign Policy*, 1953, report of a distinguished study group with recommendations for improving organizational procedures.

J. J. McCloy, *The Challenge to American Foreign Policy*, 1953, brief discussion of problems of making and executing foreign policy, special attention to problem of civil-military relations, by former U.S. High Commissioner for Germany.

T. V. Kalijarvi and C. E. Merrow, eds., "Congress and Foreign Relations," September 1953, *The Annals*, a symposium.

D. S. Cheever and H. F. Haviland, Jr., *American Foreign Policy and the Separation of Powers*, 1952, survey of constitutional arrangements, case studies, and recommendations for improving machinery of government.

L. H. Chamberlain and R. C. Snyder, eds., *American Foreign Policy*, 1948, readings with comments by the editors.

W. J. Parks, *U.S. Administration of International Economic Affairs*, 1951.

W. Y. Elliott *et al., The Political Economy of American Foreign Policy*, 1955, policy recommendations.

U.S. Department of Commerce, *Foreign Aid by the United States Government, 1940-1951*, 1952, comprehensive report with facts and figures.

H. B. Price, *The Marshall Plan and Its Meaning*, 1955, evaluation and history.

W. L. Thorp, *Trade, Aid, or What?* 1954, "A Report on International Economic Policy."

G. H. Stuart, *The Department of State*, 1949, comprehensive history.

J. R. Childs, *American Foreign Service*, 1948, by veteran Foreign Service officer.

Foreign Service, *American Foreign Service Journal*, monthly professional journal.

Report of the Secretary of State's Public Committee on Personnel, *Toward A Stronger Foreign Service*, 1954, the important Wriston Report which resulted in major organizational changes in Foreign Service.

Commission on Organization of the Executive Branch of the Government,

Report on Overseas Economic Operations and *Task Force Report*, 1955.

V. M. Barnett, Jr., ed., *The Representation of the U.S. Abroad*, 1956, study papers for a meeting of the American Assembly.

Commission on the Organization of the Government, *Task Force Report on the Organization of the Government for the Conduct of Foreign Affairs*, 1949, prepared under direction of H. H. Bundy and J. G. Rogers; generally considered one of the better Task Force Reports.

C. A. H. Thomson, *Overseas Information Service of the United States Government*, 1948, survey and evaluation of U.S. program; contains comprehensive bibliography.

E. W. Barrett, *Truth Is Our Weapon*, 1953, defense of American information programs.

S. Kent, *Strategic Intelligence for American World Policy*, 1949, analysis of American programs and discussion of needed program.

THE U.N. AND WORLD ORGANIZATION

N. Hill, *International Organization*, 1952.

F. S. C. Northrup, *The Taming of the Nations*, 1953, "A Study of the Cultural Basis of International Policy."

A. Vandenbush and W. N. Hogan, *The United Nations*, 1952, processes and practices of the U.N.

E. P. Chase, *The United Nations in Action*, 1950, nontechnical general survey of activities of U.N. and its related agencies.

C. M. Eichelberger, *UN: The First Ten Years*, 1955, by one who helped prepare first American draft and believes U.N. to be a success.

C. Manly, *The UN Record*, 1955, by severe critic who believes U.N. to be a failure and an instrument of subversion.

L. M. Goodrich and A. P. Simons, *The United Nations and the Maintenance of International Peace and Security*, 1955, appraisal of activity.

J. MacLaurin, *The United Nations and Power Politics*, 1951, why U.N. promises have not been fulfilled.

F. S. Dunn, *War and the Minds of Men*, 1950, centered around activities of UNESCO, an interpretation of the scope and limitations of communicational activities in reaching and influencing the "minds of men."

T. Besterman, *UNESCO*, 1951, aims, achievements, and failures.

United Nations, *Everyman's United Nations*, 1953, a handbook on the U.N. and its related agencies.

D. Sterling, *United Nations, N.Y.*, 1953, story of the work of the U.N. Secretariat.

L. W. Holborn, *The International Refugee Organization*, 1956, comprehensive report.

C. G. Fenwick, *The Inter-American Regional System*, 1949.

WAR AND NATIONAL DEFENSE

E. S. Corwin, *Total War and the Constitution*, 1947, impact of war and defense requirements upon constitutional system.

E. Huzar, *The Purse and the Sword*, 1950, study of "the control of the Army by Congress through military appropriations."

J. G. Rogers, *World Policing and the Constitution*, 1945, the war power in 9 wars and 100 military campaigns from 1789 to 1945.

H. and M. Sprout, *The Rise of American Naval Power, 1776-1918*, 1939; and *Toward a New Order of Sea Power, 1918-1922*, 1940, the relations among naval policy, domestic politics, and foreign policy.

D. O. Smith, *U.S. Military Doctrine*, 1955, by Air Force general.

R. Strausz-Hupé and S. T. Possony, eds., "Air Power and National Security," March 1955, *The Annals*.

The politics and high strategy of democracies at war are revealed in the memoirs of statesmen who guided the U.N. during World War II; among these are:

R. E. Sherwood, *Roosevelt and Hopkins*, 1948.

H. L. Stimson and McG. Bundy, *On Active Service in Peace and War*, 1948.

ECONOMIC MOBILIZATION

D. M. Nelson, *Arsenal of Democracy*,

1946, recollections of the Chairman of the War Production Board.

Bureau of the Budget, *The United States at War,* 1946, covers the entire history of the administration of the war mobilization program.

E. Janeway, *The Struggle for Survival,* 1951, history of World War II economic mobilization program, stressing role of politics.

H. M. Somers, *Presidential Agency: The Office of War Mobilization and Reconversion,* 1950, story of the office with over-all responsibility for the war economy.

C. Brewer, *Civil Defense in the United States,* Public Affairs Bulletin 92, Legislative Reference Service, 1951, summary of the problem and the program of federal, state, and local governments.

R. A. Walker, ed., *America's Manpower Crisis,* 1952, findings and recommendations of seminars held by scholars and public officials.

S. A. Devan, *Planning National Defense, 1950 to 1970,* Public Affairs Bulletin 75, Legislative Reference Service, 1949, discussion of long-range defense program.

G. A. Lincoln, *et al., Economics of National Security,* 2nd ed., 1954, the economic bases of national defense, considerable attention to the experiences of World War II.

B. Brodie, *National Security Policy and Economic Stability,* 1950.

D. L. Gordon and R. J. Dangerfield, *The Hidden Weapon—The Story of Economic Warfare,* 1947, history of World War II experiences.

E. Davis and B. Price, *War Information and Censorship,* 1943, two experienced newsmen and officials who played major roles during World War II.

SCIENCE, SCIENTISTS, AND NATIONAL SECURITY

V. Bush, *Modern Arms and Free Men,* 1949, head of Office of Scientific Research and Development during World War II, discusses the relations between new weapons and modern warfare and the conditions under which science can make its best contribution to national security.

W. Gellhorn, *Security, Loyalty, and Science,* 1950, presents the view that national security and scientific development are being jeopardized by overzealous concern for security and secrecy.

Bulletin of Atomic Scientists, published monthly; articles on science and international security.

H. D. Smyth, *Atomic Energy for Military Purposes,* 1946, first official report.

J. R. Newman and B. S. Miller, *The Control of Atomic Energy,* 1948, discussion of political control.

W. L. Laurence, *The Hell Bomb,* 1951, the Hydrogen Bomb—its implications, and recommendations for American policy toward its use; by *The New York Times'* science editor.

R. E. Lapp, *Atoms and People,* 1956, the atomic world of the future, by a physicist.

WARS, MILITARY, AND CIVILIANS

J. G. Kerwin, ed., *Civil-Military Relations in American Life,* 1948, essays.

H. D. Lasswell, *National Security and Individual Freedom,* 1950, recommendations as to how to avoid the "garrison state."

Senate Committee on Armed Services and Committee on Foreign Relations, *Hearings, Military Situation in Far East,* 82 Cong., 1 Sess., 1951, MacArthur hearings contain materials on how decisions are made, the relations among the President, his military, and his civilian advisers.

L. Smith, *American Democracy and Military Power,* 1951, survey of democratic theory, constitutional law, and administrative practices and evaluation of their adequacy to preserve civilian control of the armed forces.

A. A. Ekirch, Jr., *The Civilian and the Military,* 1956, survey of American tradition and discussion of contemporary application.

GOVERNMENT AND THE ECONOMY

N. J. Ware, *Wealth and Welfare,* 1949, brief history of the evolution of our economic system.

H. K. Girvetz, *From Wealth to Welfare,*

1950, interpretation of the forces that have led to the welfare state.

J. K. Galbraith, *American Capitalism,* 1952, role of government, business and labor in modern American competitive economy, "the concept of counter-vailing power."

R. A. Dahl and C. E. Lindblom, *Politics, Economics and Welfare,* 1953, an important book that analyzes patterns of economic and political power and suggests new theoretical approaches.

Although the several writers vary considerably in their beliefs, the following are just a few of the many books that in general support the thesis "the less government the better."

H. Spencer, *The Man versus the State,* T. Beale edition, 1916, classic statement of belief in limited government by one of the most influential men of the late nineteenth century.

F. A. Hayek, *The Road to Serfdom,* 1944, attack upon governmental planning.

F. H. Knight, *Freedom and Reform,* 1947, by outstanding economists.

* H. C. Simons, *Economic Policy for a Free Society,* 1947, devoted to the thesis that capital and labor monopolies must be destroyed so that free enterprise can be re-established.

J. A. Schumpeter, *Capitalism, Socialism, and Democracy,* 1950, defense of the entrepreneur.

Disagreeing with views in above volumes, the following authors believe that government should perform certain welfare functions, regulate the economy for full employment, and act positively to preserve a free society.

H. Finer, *Road to Reaction,* 1945, vigorous answer to Hayek.

* J. M. Clark, *Alternative to Serfdom,* 1948, comments upon the role of government; less faith in planning than the above author.

C. E. Ayres, *The Divine Right of Capital,* 1946, analysis of the causes and cures for depression.

A. M. Schlesinger, Jr., *The Vital Center,* 1949, diagnosis of liberal tradition and statement of program to secure freedom.

K. Mannheim, *Freedom, Power, and Democratic Planning,* 1950, by famous sociologist.

T. Arnold, *et al., The Future of Democratic Capitalism,* 1951, essays by leading public men.

GOVERNMENT AS PROMOTER OF BUSINESS

F. W. Taussig, *The Tariff History of the United States,* 8th ed., 1937, standard history.

Board of Investigation and Research, *Public Aids to Domestic Transportation,* House Document 159, 79 Cong., 1 Sess., 1945.

D. R. Fuller, *Government Financing of Private Enterprise,* 1948.

The Commission on Organization of the Executive Branch of the Government, *Department of Commerce,* 1949.

B. N. Behling, *Subsidies to Transportation,* Public Affairs Bulletin 86, Legislative Reference Service, 1950.

GOVERNMENT AS PROMOTER OF AGRICULTURE

M. R. Benedict, *Farm Policies of the United States, 1790-1950,* 1953, comprehensive study of origins and development of governmental policy.

Department of Agriculture, *Farmers in a Changing World,* Year Book of Agriculture, 1940, farmers' economic position and changing governmental policy.

T. W. Schultz, *Agriculture in an Unstable Economy,* 1945, discussion of governmental policy.

R. L. Mighell, *American Agriculture,* 1955, "Its Structure and Place in the Economy."

M. Hardin, *The Politics of Agriculture,* 1952, taking field of soil conservation author makes penetrating contribution to development of methods to describe the political process.

American Farm Economic Association, *Readings in Agricultural Policy,* 1949.

M. R. Benedict, *Can We Solve the Farm Problem? An Analysis of Federal Aid to Agriculture,* 1955.

W. W. Wilcox, *Alternative Policies for American Agriculture,* Public Affairs Bulletin 67, Legislative Reference Service, 1949, summary.

D. C. Blaisdell, *Government and Agriculture*, 1940.

Commission on Organization of the Executive Branch of the Government, *Department of Agriculture;* and *Task Force Report on Agricultural Activities,* 1949.

G. L. Baker, *The County Agent,* 1939, traces the work of this link between government and the farmer from 1911 to 1939.

C. McWilliams, *Factories in the Field,* 1939, story of migratory farm workers in California.

President's Commission on Migratory Labor, *Report, Migratory Labor in American Agriculture,* 1951, latest study of this social problem.

CONSERVATION

Popular discussions that deal with general problems are:

M. W. Straus, *Why Not Survive?* 1955.

F. Osborn, *Our Plundered Planet,* 1948.

W. Vogt, *Road to Survival,* 1948.

G. Pinchot, *Breaking New Ground,* 1947, autobiography of a crusader for conservation.

Important works:

President's Materials Policy Commission, *Resources for Freedom,* 1952, and five supporting volumes, one of the most significant studies of resources and public policy in recent years.

N. Wengert, *Natural Resources and the Political Struggle,* 1955, history and politics of conservation.

C. McKinley, *Uncle Sam in the Pacific Northwest,* 1952, detailed study of federal government's program for management of natural resources in the area.

C. N. Elliott, *Conservation of American Resources,* rev. ed., 1951.

L. S. Greene and R. de Williamson, eds., *Resources and Policy,* 1951, symposium reprinted from *Journal of Politics,* Vol. 13, No. 3, August 1951.

R. M. Robbins, *Our Landed Heritage,* 1942, history of public land policies.

F. Tilden, *The National Parks,* 1951, description of each park, and its contributions to national life.

L. H. Gulick, *American Forest Policy,* 1951, survey of current policy and description of administrative techniques.

W. B. Greeley, *Forests and Men,* 1951, former Chief of the Forest Service discusses problems and programs.

President's Water Resources Policy Commission, *A Water Policy for the American People; Ten Rivers in America's Future; Water Resources Law,* 1950, primary source of information, presentation of program with supporting data.

J. W. Fesler, ed., "Government and Water Resources," *American Political Science Review,* September 1950, symposium.

Commission on Organization of the Executive Branch of the Government, *Reorganization of the Department of Interior;* and *Task Force Report on Natural Resources,* 1949; also 1954 reports on water resources and power.

THE LABOR MOVEMENT

P. Taft, *The Structure and Government of Labor Unions,* 1954.

S. Perlman, *A Theory of the Labor Movement,* 1928.

F. Tannenbaum, *A Philosophy of Labor,* 1951, presents interpretation that unions are the great conservative force in modern capitalistic society.

C. E. Lindblom, *Unions and Capitalism,* 1949, questions compatibility of unions and capitalism.

C. S. Golden and H. J. Ruttenberg, *The Dynamics of Industrial Democracy,* 1942, by two experienced leaders of the United Steelworkers of America, C.I.O.

C. W. Mills, *The New Men of Power,* 1948, study of the leaders of organized labor by a sociologist.

J. R. Commons, *et al., History of Labor in the United States,* 4 vols., 1935, one of the best labor histories covering period before New Deal.

H. Millis and R. Montgomery, *Organized Labor,* 1945, another outstanding labor history.

L. Lorwin, *The American Federation of Labor,* 1933, standard history written before development of C.I.O. and events of 1930's and 1940's.

GOVERNMENT LABOR POLICY

U.S. Department of Labor, *Federal Labor Laws and Agencies,* Bulletin No. 123, August 1950, periodically revised, provides quick reference to laws and regulations.

H. A. Millis and E. C. Brown, *From the Wagner Act to Taft-Hartley,* 1950, labor policy from the New Deal to Taft-Hartley.

J. H. Leek, *Government and Labor in the United States,* 1952, "survey of legislation, administration, and major court decisions."

C. O. Gregory, *Labor and the Law,* 1946, labor law from the common law through the Wagner Act.

F. A. Hartley, *Our New National Labor Policy,* 1948, defense of Taft-Hartley by one of its principal authors.

E. E. Witte, *The Government in Labor Disputes,* 1932.

F. Frankfurter and N. Greene, *The Labor Injunction,* 1930, closely documented standard source.

J. Lombardi, *Labor's Voice in the Cabinet,* 1942, history and background of the Department of Labor up to 1921.

V. I. Breen, *The United States Conciliation Service,* 1943.

R. N. Baldwin and C. B. Randall, *Civil Liberties and Industrial Conflict,* 1938.

H. David, *The History of the Haymarket Affair,* 1936, story of one of the great *causes célèbres.*

SOCIAL SECURITY

E. M. Burns, *Social Security and Public Policy,* 1956, general survey emphasizing problems.

A. Larson, *Know Your Social Security,* 1955, by former Under Secretary of Department of Health, Education and Welfare.

K. De Schweinitz, *People and Process in Social Security,* 1948.

L. Meriam, K. T. Schotterbeck, and M. Maroney, *The Cost and Financing of Social Security,* 1950.

House of Representatives, *Public Social Security Programs in the United States,* House Document 545, 81 Cong., 2 Sess, 1950, summary of programs.

HEALTH INSURANCE

H. E. Livingston, *National Health Insurance,* Public Affairs Bulletin 85, Legislative Reference Service, 1950.

O. R. Ewing, *The Nation's Health—A Ten Year Program,* 1948, former administrator of Federal Security Agency presents summary of existing conditions, program for compulsory health insurance, federal aid to build hospitals and to educate doctors.

G. W. Bachman and L. Meriam, *The Issue of Compulsory Health Insurance,* 1948.

L. S. Reed, *Health Insurance, the Next Step in Social Security,* 1937.

The President's Commission on the Health Needs of the Nation, *Building America's Health,* 5 vols., 1953, findings of fact and recommendations of action needed to meet the nation's health requirements.

J. S. Simmons, ed., *Public Health in the World Today,* 1949, essays by 24 experts on all aspects of public health.

H. S. Mustard, *An Introduction to Public Health,* 1953.

EDUCATION

H. P. Allen, *The Federal Government and Education,* 1950, study made for the Hoover Commission of federal activities in field of education.

Legislative Reference Service, *Highlights in the Development of Federal Policies and Activities in Education,* Public Affairs Bulletin 30, 1944, summary of the educational activities of the federal government.

S. E. Harris, *How Shall We Pay for Education?* 1948.

The growing interest of the federal government in education is indicated by the creation of two presidential commissions in recent years, both of which published five-volume studies containing recommendations for future action.

President's Commission on Higher Education, *Higher Education for American Democracy,* 1947.

President's Scientific Research Board, *Science and Public Policy,* 1947.

HOUSING

Joint (Congressional) Committee on Housing, *Final Majority Report, Hous-*

ing Study and Investigation, House Report 1564, 80 Cong., 2 Sess., 1949.

House and Home Finance Agency, *The Housing Situation,* 1949, factual background of housing conditions in various parts of the U.S.

Housing and House Finance Agency, *A Handbook of Information on Provisions of the Housing Act of 1949 and Operations under the Various Programs,* 1949, explanation of housing legislation.

Senate Committee on Banking and Currency, *Summary of Housing Act of 1950,* Senate Document 165, 81 Cong., 2 Sess., 1950.

N. Straus, *The Seven Myths of Housing,* 2nd ed., 1945, former administrator of U.S. Housing Authority makes brief for public housing and slum clearance.

FEDERAL POLICEMEN

B. Smith, *Police Systems in the United States,* rev. ed., 1949, general discussion of all police systems; special chapters on federal agencies.

M. Lowenthal, *The Federal Bureau of Investigation,* 1951, criticism of the FBI.

D. Whitehead, *The F.B.I. Story,* 1956, readable, sympathetic, and wide-ranging account.

A. C. Millspaugh, *Crime Control by the National Government,* 1937.

GOVERNMENT AND THE REGULATION OF BUSINESS

E. S. Redford, *Administration of National Economic Controls,* 1952, analysis of process by which policy is made and instruments through which it is executed.

* A. A. Berle, Jr. and G. C. Means, *The Modern Corporation and Private Property,* 1933, analysis of the growth of large industry, the separation between ownership and control, and problems of social control.

W. Adams and H. M. Gray, *Monopoly in America,* 1956, evidence to support argument that governmental policy in recent years tends to promote monopoly.

R. E. Lane, *The Regulation of Businessmen,* 1954, responses of businessmen to regulation.

T. W. Arnold, *The Folklore of Capitalism,* 1937, mythology of business and trust-busting with emphasis on its futility by man who subsequently became an active trust-buster.

D. Lynch, *The Concentration of Economic Power,* 1946, summary of the hearings and reports of the Temporary National Economic Committee (TNEC).

A. D. H. Kaplan, *Big Enterprise in a Competitive System,* 1954.

J. Scoville and N. Sargent, *Fact and Fancy in the T.N.E.C. Monographs,* 1942, critical review of TNEC reports prepared under auspices of NAM.

Federal Trade Commission, *The Concentration of Productive Facilities,* 1949.

H. A. Wells, *Monopoly and Social Control,* 1952, thesis that there is conflict between government policy and economic forces.

D. E. Lilienthal, *Big Business: A New Era,* 1952, argues for an affirmative program to help develop big business and discussion of its contributions.

C. D. Edwards, *Maintaining Competition,* 1949, recommendations for a governmental policy.

E. Latham, *The Group Basis of Politics,* 1952.

House Select Committee on Small Business, *Congress and the Monopoly Problem,* 1950, summary of congressional action, 1900-1950.

House Committee on the Judiciary, Subcommittee on Study of Monopoly Power, *Hearings,* 81 Cong., 1 and 2 Sess., 1949-1950, most recent congressional investigation.

I. L. Sharfman, *The Interstate Commerce Commission,* 4 vols., 1931-1937, comprehensive study of the oldest federal regulatory agency.

C. L. Dearing and W. Owen, *National Transportation Policy,* 1949, argument for one national agency to regulate all forms of transportation.

J. M. Edelman, *The Licensing of Radio Services in the U.S., 1927 to 1947,* 1950, study in administrative formulation of policy.

H. Coon, *American Tel and Tel,* 1939, the Federal Communications Commission and the telephone empire.

R. D. Baum, *Federal Power Commission and State Utility Regulation,* 1943.

J. Bauer, *Transforming Public Utility Regulations,* 1950, recommendations for improving regulatory activities.

E. T. McCormick, *Understanding the Securities Act and the S.E.C.,* 1948, comprehensive discussion by a key S.E.C. official.

GOVERNMENT AS MANAGER

D. K. Price, *Government and Science,* 1954, shows major role of government in scientific activity.

Commission on Organization of the Executive Branch of the Government, *Report on Federal Business Enterprises; and Report on the Post Office,* 1949 and 1955.

J. McDiarmid, *Government Corporations and Federal Funds,* 1938.

J. R. Newman and B. S. Miller, *The Control of Atomic Energy,* 1948.

L. C. Merritt, *United States Government as Publisher,* 1943.

G. R. Clapp, *The TVA: An Approach to the Development of a Region,* 1955, by former chairman.

D. E. Lilienthal, *TVA: Democracy on the March,* rev. ed., 1953, defense by former director of TVA as major instrument of grass roots democracy.

C. H. Pritchett, *The Tennessee Valley Authority: A Study in Public Administration,* 1943, standard study of TVA administration.

P. Selznick, *TVA and the Grass Roots,* 1949, sociological interpretation.

BIG GOVERNMENT, ITS PROBLEMS, AND ITS LIMITS

Commission on the Organization of the Executive Department, *Report on Budgeting and Accounting; and Task Force Report on Fiscal, Budgeting, and Accounting Activities,* 1949 and 1955, contains discussion of organizational problems.

V. J. Browne, *The Control of the Public Budget,* 1949.

P. H. Douglas, *Economy in the National Government,* 1952, by U.S. senator, includes critical comments on budget and appropriation process.

A. Smithies, *The Budgetary Process in the United States,* 1955, surveys role of federal budget.

A. E. Buck, *The Budget in Governments of Today,* 1934, standard source; contains information on state as well as federal budgetary programs.

Bureau of the Budget, *The Federal Budget in Brief;* published annually, summary of budget; many illustrations.

H. C. Mansfield, *The Comptroller General,* 1939, standard work on little known but major government official.

J. M. Keynes, *The General Theory of Employment, Interest, and Money,* 1936, one of the most influential books of modern times; interpretation of economics that calls for governmental fiscal and monetary policy and public works to offset unemployment.

A. H. Hansen, *Monetary Theory and Fiscal Policy,* 1949, by leading American Keynesian; how to avoid booms and busts.

W. E. Upjohn Institute for Community Research, *Public Works and Employment,* 1956, impact of public works on local unemployment.

A. Hart, *The Economics of Illusion,* 1949, criticism of Keynesian economics.

B. Blough, *The Federal Taxing Process,* 1952, the forces at work and institutions involved in the taxing process.

A Conference of the Universities-National Bureau Committee for Economic Research, *Policies to Combat Depression,* 1956, a symposium.

R. E. Paul, *Taxation in the United States,* 1954, by former high Treasury official.

E. G. Nourse, *The 1950's Come First,* discussion of governmental economic policy by former chairman, Council of Economic Advisers.

H. C. Simons, *Federal Tax Reform,* 1950, by distinguished anti-Keynesian economist.

L. Kimmel, *Taxes and Economic Incentives,* 1950.

S. Ratner, *American Taxation,* 1942, "Its History as a Social Force in Democracy."

C. C. Abbott, *Management of the Federal Debt,* 1946.

G. L. Bach, *Federal Reserve Policy-Making,* 1950.

Federal Reserve System, *The Federal Reserve System: Its Purposes and Functions,* 2nd ed., 1947, popular description.

E. W. and D. L. Kemmerer, *The ABC of the Federal Reserve System,* rev. ed., 1950.

The several reports resulting from the Employment Act of 1946 are primary sources for the whole problem of governmental fiscal and monetary policy. These reports include the *President's Economic Report to the Congress, Report of the Council of Economic Advisers,* and *Reports and Hearings of the Joint Congressional Committee on Economic Report.*

Part Seven: STATE AND LOCAL GOVERNMENTS

Many of the books mentioned in the other sections of this bibliography, especially those noted in connection with federalism, also pertain to government of the states and their subdivisions. Except in a few cases they will not be again listed here; nor will the standard texts be noted. Furthermore, the wealth of materials—some produced by individual scholars and some by the many research organizations connected with universities, cities, state organizations and associations of officials—dealing with the government of a particular state, city, county or region, are not mentioned, but only the more general works.

ANNUALS, MANUALS, AND PERIODICALS

W. B. Graves, N. J. Small, and E. F. Dowell, *American State Government and Administration,* 1949, "A state by state bibliography of significant general and special works."

D. C. Tompkins, *State Government and Administration,* 1954, selected bibliography arranged by topic with primary emphasis on legislature.

Council of State Governments, *The Book of the States,* published biennially with semi-annual supplements, a basic source, contains selected bibliography of state government, short articles on current developments, charts and lists of personnel.

———, *State Government,* published monthly, articles by state officials and scholars and reports on programs of state governments.

State Manuals, published by most states yearly, usually contain directories of public officials, election statistics, descriptions of activities of various government agencies, and so on.

Library of Congress, *Monthly Checklist of State Publications,* a state by state list of publications.

International City Managers' Association, *The Municipal Year Book,* published yearly, contains up-to-date information on every aspect of municipal activity.

National Municipal League, *National Municipal Review,* published monthly, the trade journal of city officials, articles dealing with problems of those who run our cities.

American City Magazine Corporation, *The American City,* published monthly, another trade journal of city officials.

U. S. Conference of Mayors, *The U.S. Municipal News,* biweekly newsletter of current events, suggests political pressures operating on mayors.

National Association of County Officials, *The County Officer,* monthly trade journal of county officials.

American Judicature Society, *Journal of the American Judicature Society,* monthly publication devoted to the cause of judicial reform and improvement in the administration of justice.

OUR SOVEREIGN STATES: CONSTITUTIONS AND LAWMAKERS

J. W. Fesler, ed., *The Forty-eight States: Their Tasks as Policy Makers and Administrators,* 1955, symposium prepared for American Assembly conference evaluating how well the states are doing their jobs.

R. V. Peel, *State Government Today,* 1948, sprightly analysis of the ability of state governments to do their jobs.

R. S. Allen, ed., *Our Sovereign States,*

1949, journalistic essays on the politics of some of the states.

New York State Constitutional Convention Committee, *Constitutions of the States and the United States,* Vol. III, 1938, most comprehensive and recent collection.

National Municipal League, *Model State Constitution,* 5th ed., 1948, recommendations of the League with explanatory comments.

C. N. Callender, ed., "The State Constitution of the Future," *The Annals* of the American Academy of Political and Social Science, September, 1935, collection of articles.

A. L. Sturm, *Methods of State Constitutional Reform,* 1954, monograph covering background and methods for change.

V. A. O'Rourke and D. W. Campbell, *Constitution-Making in a Democracy,* 1943, case study of a New York constitutional convention.

C. B. Swisher, *Motivations and Political Techniques in the California Constitutional Convention, 1878-1879,* 1930, study of the constitutional convention as part of the process of government.

UNDER THE CAPITOL DOME

B. Zeller, ed., *American State Legislatures,* 1954, report of the American Political Science Association's Committee on American Legislatures.

Council of State Governments, *Our State Legislatures,* rev. ed. 1949, compilation of materials and recommendations for reform.

A. W. Johnson, *The Unicameral Legislature,* 1938, historic arguments and discussion of movement toward unicameralism in Nebraska.

R. F. Still, *The Gilmer-Aikin Bills,* 1950, "A Study in the Legislative Process" in Texas legislature by a member of the legislature and political scientist.

G. E. Baker, *Rural Versus Urban Political Power,* 1955, problems and consequences.

G. Y. Steiner, *Legislation by Collective Bargaining,* 1951, a case study of legislative process used in state legislatures.

GOVERNORS AND JUDGES

L. Lipson, *American Governor from Figurehead to Leader,* 1939, basic source of the development of governor's office, special attention to reorganization period and experiences of Virginia, Massachusetts, New York, and Illinois.

A. E. Buck, *Reorganization of State Governments in the United States,* 1938, comprehensive discussion of 1917-1938 reorganization movement, state by state survey.

J. C. Bollens, *Administrative Reorganization in the States Since 1939,* 1947, brings Buck's work down to date of publication.

C. S. Hyneman, "Administrative Reorganization: An Adventure into Science and Theology," *Journal of Politics,* Vol. 1, February, 1939, one of better known "broadsides" against reorganization principles.

Council of State Governments, *Reorganizing State Government,* 1950, examination of "the current situation of administrative management in the states" and a review of "the important recommendations . . . of recent . . . reorganization studies."

There are a number of excellent biographies and memoirs of American governors.

THE STATE JUDICIARY

R. Pound, *Organization of the Courts,* 1940, by leader in judicial reform movement and famous legal scholar.

A. T. Vanderbilt, ed., *Minimum Standards of Judicial Administration,* 1949, survey by Chief Justice of New Jersey Supreme Court of the extent to which standards of the American Bar Association have been accepted by the states, discussion of such problems as jury selection, judicial selection, pretrial practice, and so on.

Council of State Governments, *The Courts of Last Resort of the Forty-Eight States,* 1950, comparative study of major aspects of organization and operation of the highest state courts.

——, *Trial Courts of General Jurisdiction in the Forty-Eight States,* 1951, companion report.

E. Haynes, *The Selection and Tenure of Judges,* 1944, the standard history, a basic source.

J. W. Peltason, *Missouri Plan for Selection of Judges,* 1945, description of the Missouri system and of the activities of a judicial reform interest group.

GOVERNMENT AT THE GRASS ROOTS

W. Anderson, *Units of Government in the United States,* 1942, with appendix in 1945 and 1949, primary source of numbers and kinds of governmental units.

W. Anderson and E. W. Weidner, eds., *Research in Intergovernmental Relations,* 1950-1952, series of ten monographs on various phases of state-local relations.

Council of State Governments, *State-Local Relations,* 1946, study of existing practices in the 48 states.

GOVERNMENT BY THE PEOPLE—COUNTRY STYLE

J. A. Fairlie and C. M. Kneier, *County Government and Administration,* 1930, a basic work.

L. W. Lancaster, *Government in Rural America,* 1952, broad study of all forms of rural government.

P. W. Wager, ed., *County Government across the Nation,* 1950, case studies of county and township government in all the 48 states.

E. W. Weidner, *The American County, Patchwork of Boards,* 1946, comments on trends and suggestions for improvement.

C. F. Snider and N. F. Garvey published annual articles summarizing developments in field of county and township government from 1937 to 1949 in the *American Political Science Review.*

OUR FAIR CITIES

C. M. Kneier and G. Fox, *Readings in Municipal Government and Administration,* 1953, a collection of readings in all phases of municipal government.

R. S. Allen, ed., *Our Fair City,* 1947, critical sketches of political manipulation in some major American cities.

R. L. Mott, *Home Rule for American Cities,* 1949, how home rule works and

why it is desirable, published by American Municipal Association.

W. C. Hallenbeck, *American Urban Communities,* 1951, comprehensive and sociologically oriented discussion.

L. Mumford, *The Culture of Cities,* 1938, learned discussion of problems and roles of cities throughout the ages by influential person in the city planning movement.

J. C. Bollens, director, *The States and the Metropolitan Problem,* 1956, problems and proposed solutions.

F. K. Vigman, *Crisis of the Cities,* 1955, highlights problems in terms of social-historical trends.

A. H. Hawley, *The Changing Shape of Metropolitan America,* 1956, analysis of trend to suburbs.

R. M. Fisher, ed., *The Metropolis in Modern Life,* 1955, symposium.

H. A. Stone, D. K. Price, and K. H. Stone, *City Manager Government in the United States,* 1940, review of results of city manager government in 48 cities.

F. M. Steward, *A Half Century of Municipal Reform,* 1950, "The History of the National Municipal League."

R. S. Childs, *Civic Victories,* veteran fighter for civic reform surveys progress made during last forty years and sets forth his recipe for future progress.

National Municipal League, *Model City Charter,* 1941.

V. M. Jones, *Metropolitan Government,* 1942, standard source, discussion of basic problems.

B. Tableman, *Governmental Organization in Metropolitan Areas,* 1951, special attention to problems of Detroit area, but contains detailed information on 140 metropolitan districts.

The International City Managers' Association has published eight specialized training manuals on municipal finance, police, fire, public works, and personnel administration, municipal recreation, local planning, and "technique of municipal administration."

STATE AND LOCAL GOVERNMENT IN ACTION

See also pages 946-951.

B. Smith, *Police Systems in the United*

States, rev. ed., 1949, standard source by outstanding authority in police administration.

A. C. Millspaugh, *Local Democracy and Crime Control,* 1936, survey of activities, recommendations for improvement, and analysis of role of local communities.

GOVERNMENT AS EDUCATOR

Council of State Governments, *The Forty-Eight State School Systems,* 1949, survey of school administration, finances and other aspects of public elementary and secondary education.

H. A. Dawson, F. W. Reeves, and others, *Your School District,* 1948, survey of existing pattern of organization and recommendations for reorganization sponsored by National Education Association's National Commission on School District Reorganization.

N. Edwards and H. G. Richey, *The School in the American Social Order,* 1947, history of education and discussion of relation between educational policy and social change.

R. L. Morlan, *Intergovernmental Relations in Education,* 1950, one of the Minnesota Monographs edited by Anderson and Weidner.

H. K. Allen and R. G. Axt, *State Public Finance and State Institutions of Higher Education in the United States,* 1952, a volume in series produced by commission to study all phases of education sponsored by Association of American Universities.

SERVICES

A. P. Miles, *An Introduction to Public Welfare,* 1949, recent comprehensive text.

B. Y. Landis, *Rural Welfare Services,* 1949.

H. E. Martz, *Participation in Government,* 1948, "A Study of County Welfare Boards."

J. W. Mountain and E. Flook, *Guide to Health Organization in the United States,* 1947, survey published by U.S. Public Health Service.

G. W. Bachman and Associates, *Health Resources in the United States,* 1952, Brookings study of personnel, facilities, and services now available.

W. G. Smillie, *Public Health Administration in the United States,* 3rd ed., 1947, useful text.

L. Wyatt, *Intergovernmental Relations in Public Health,* 1951, monograph, emphasizing Minnesota experiences.

Council of State Governments, *The Mental Health Programs of the Forty-Eight States,* wealth of factual data.

A. Deutsch, *The Shame of the States,* 1948, eyewitness report of conditions in state hospitals.

F. I. Wright, Jr., *Out of Sight Out of Mind,* 1947, "shock treatment" for the complacent citizens about life in certain mental hospitals.

M. Meyerson and E. C. Banfield, *Politics, Planning and the Public Interest,* 1955, a case study of public housing in Chicago that emphasizes the policy-making process.

U.S. Public Roads Administration, *Highway Practice in the United States of America,* 1949.

C. L. Dearing, *American Highway Policy,* 1942.

R. A. Gomez, *Intergovernmental Relations in Highways,* 1950, another of the Minnesota monographs.

P. N. Ylvisaker, "The Natural Cement Issue," Herbert Kaufman, "Gotham in the Air Age," in H. Stein, ed., *Public Administration and Policy Development,* case studies of highway and airport politics, respectively.

H. M. Somers and A. R. Somers, *Workmen's Compensation,* 1954, covers all aspects of oldest social insurance program.

REGULATION AT THE GRASS ROOTS

J. W. Fesler, *The Independence of State Regulatory Agencies,* 1942, discussion of existing practices, problems, weaknesses, and solutions.

Council of State Governments, *Securities Regulation in the 48 States,* 1942, survey.

Federal Power Commission and National Association of Railroad and Utilities Commissioners, *State Commission Jurisdiction and Regulation of Electric and Gas Utilities,* 1948, survey of powers, organizations, and practices.

Council of State Governments, *Occupa-*

tional Licensing Legislation in the States, 1952, state by state data.

MONEY AND MEN

H. M. Groves, *Financing Government*, 3rd ed., 1950, standard text.

A. H. Hansen and H. S. Perloff, *State and Local Finance in the National Economy*, 1944, problems of integrated national fiscal policy as complicated by federal system.

J. R. McKinley, *Local Revenue Problems and Trends*, 1949.

L. H. Kimmel, *Governmental Costs and Tax Levels*, 1948, appraisal of fiscal situation, conclusion that demands for larger expenditures and lower taxes presage troubled times.

Federation of Tax Administrators, *Recent Trends in State Finance*, 1948.

Tax Foundation, Tax Institute, and Tax Policy League, among other organizations, publish numerous monographs dealing with problems of state and local taxation, expenditure and debt.

U.S. Bureau of Census, numerous reports dealing with state and local finances.

Municipal Finance Officers Association, *Municipal Finance*, quarterly report on current developments.

International City Managers Association, *Municipal Finance Administration*, 1949, a textbook for practitioners.

A. M. Hillhouse and M. Magelssen, *Where Cities Get Their Money*, 1945, a *1947 Supplement* by A. M. Hillhouse and a *1949 Supplement* by M. B. Phillips, surveys published by Municipal Finance Officers Association.

Council of State Governments, *Purchasing by the States*, 1947, survey of state practices.

WHERE THE MEN COME FROM

U.S. Civil Service Commission, *Personnel Administration*, 1949, excellent bibliography.

Civil Service Assembly of the United States and Canada, *A Digest of State Civil Service Laws*.

Civil Service Assembly, *Public Personnel Review*, quarterly journal, articles, and reports on developments.

National Civil Service League, Civil Service Assembly, and National Municipal League, *A Model State Civil Service Law*, 1946, each section is accompanied by explanatory comments.

International City Managers' Association, *Municipal Personnel Administration*, 1947, day to day problems of city administrators.

PATTERNS OF STATE AND SOCIAL POLITICS

W. Moscow, *Politics in the Empire State*, 1948, a veteran journalist's account of the pattern of politics in this key state.

J. K. Howard, *Montana: High, Wide, and Handsome*, 1944, the story of copper and politics in a lusty state.

D. G. Farrelly and I. Hinderacker, eds., *The Politics of California*, 1951.

V. O. Key and A. Heard, *Southern Politics*, 1949, one of the most comprehensive studies of regional politics.

M. E. Garnsey, *America's New Frontier*, 1950, politics and economics of the Mountain West from Montana to New Mexico and from Colorado to Nevada.

G. Hutton, *Midwest at Noon*, 1946.

R. B. Nye, *Midwestern Progressive Politics*, 1951, a historical interpretation.

V. O. Key, Jr., *American State Politics*, 1956, important study, one of the few dealing with politics within the states.

Epilogue: CHALLENGE AND OPPORTUNITY

POLITICS AND YOU

P. P. Van Riper, *Handbook of Practical Politics*, 1952, materials drawn from many sources "to familiarize citizens with concrete ways . . . of carrying on effective political activity on the local and state levels."

E. E. Schattschneider, V. Jones, and S. Bailey, *A Guide to the Study of Public Affairs*, 1952, practical guides to gathering political information.

R. E. Baldwin, *Let's Go into Politics*, 1952, former state legislator, governor, U.S. senator, and now judge relates his experiences.

J. E. McLean, *Politics Is What You Make It*, 1952, pamphlet with information and suggestions on how to be an effective citizen-politician.

M. Tallman, *Dictionary of Civics and Government*, 1953.

H. D. Scott, Jr., *How to Go into Politics*, 1949, by former chairman of Republican National Committee and member of Congress.

H. Gauer, *How to Win in Politics*, 1946.

National Municipal League, *The Citizen Association: How to Organize and Run It*, 1953, and *The Citizen Association: How to Win Civic Campaigns*, 1953.

CONSTITUTION OF THE UNITED STATES

We the People of the United States, in Order to form a more perfect Union, establish Justice, insure domestic Tranquility, provide for the common defence, promote the general Welfare, and secure the Blessings of Liberty to ourselves and our Posterity, do ordain and establish this Constitution for the United States of America.

Section. 1. All legislative Powers herein granted shall be vested in a Congress of the United States, which shall consist of a Senate and House of Representatives.

Section. 2. The House of Representatives shall be composed of Members chosen every second Year by the People of the several States, and the Electors in each State shall have the Qualifications requisite for Electors of the most numerous Branch of the State Legislature.

No Person shall be a Representative who shall not have attained to the age of twenty five Years, and been seven Years a Citizen of the United States, and who shall not, when elected, be an Inhabitant of that State in which he shall be chosen.

Representatives and direct Taxes shall be apportioned among the several States which may be included within this Union, according to their respective Numbers, which shall be determined by adding to the whole Number of free Persons, including those bound to Service for a Term of Years, and excluding Indians not taxed, three fifths of all other Persons.[1] The actual Enumeration shall be made within three Years after the first Meeting of the Congress of the United States, and within every subsequent Term of ten Years, in such Manner as they shall by Law direct. The Number of Representatives shall not exceed one for every thirty Thousand, but each State shall have at Least one Representative; and until such enumeration shall be made, the State of New Hampshire shall be entitled to chuse three, Massachusetts eight, Rhode-Island and Providence Plantations one, Connecticut five, New-York six, New Jersey four, Pennsylvania eight, Delaware one, Maryland six, Virginia ten, North Carolina five, South Carolina five, and Georgia three.

When vacancies happen in the Representation from any State, the Executive Authority thereof shall issue Writs of Election to fill such Vacancies.

The House of Representatives shall chuse their Speaker and other Officers; and shall have the sole Power of Impeachment.

[1] See 14th Amendment.

Section. 3. The Senate of the United States shall be composed of two Senators from each State, chosen by the Legislature thereof,[2] for six Years; and each Senator shall have one Vote.

Immediately after they shall be assembled in Consequence of the first Election, they shall be divided as equally as may be into three Classes. The Seats of the Senators of the first Class shall be vacated at the Expiration of the second Year, of the second Class at the Expiration of the fourth Year, and of the third Class at the Expiration of the sixth Year, so that one third may be chosen every second Year; and if Vacancies happen by Resignation, or otherwise, during the Recess of the Legislature of any State, the Executive thereof may make temporary Appointments until the next Meeting of the Legislature, which shall then fill such Vacancies.[3]

No Person shall be a Senator who shall not have attained to the Age of thirty Years, and been nine Years a Citizen of the United States, and who shall not, when elected, be an Inhabitant of that State for which he shall be chosen.

The Vice President of the United States shall be President of the Senate, but shall have no Vote, unless they be equally divided.

The Senate shall chuse their other Officers, and also a President pro tempore, in the Absence of the Vice President, or when he shall exercise the Office of President of the United States.

The Senate shall have the sole Power to try all Impeachments. When sitting for that Purpose, they shall be on Oath or Affirmation. When the President of the United States is tried, the Chief Justice shall preside: And no Person shall be convicted without the Concurrence of two thirds of the Members present.

Judgment in Cases of Impeachment shall not extend further than to removal from Office, and disqualification to hold and enjoy any Office of honor, Trust or Profit under the United States: but the Party convicted shall nevertheless be liable and subject to Indictment, Trial, Judgment and Punishment, according to Law.

Section. 4. The Times, Places and Manner of holding Elections for Senators and Representatives, shall be prescribed in each State by the Legislature thereof; but the Congress may at any time by Law make or alter such Regulations, except as to the Places of chusing Senators.

The Congress shall assemble at least once in every Year, and such Meeting shall be on the first Monday in December, unless they shall by Law appoint a different Day.[4]

Section. 5. Each House shall be the Judge of the Elections, Returns and Qualifications of its own Members, and a Majority of each shall constitute a Quorum to do Business; but a smaller Number may adjourn from day to day, and may be authorized to compel the Attendance of absent Members, in such Manner, and under such Penalties as each House may provide.

[2] See 17th Amendment.
[3] *Ibid.*
[4] See 20th Amendment.

Each House may determine the Rules of its Proceedings, punish its Members for disorderly Behaviour, and, with the Concurrence of two thirds, expel a Member.

Each House shall keep a Journal of its Proceedings, and from time to time publish the same, excepting such Parts as may in their Judgment require Secrecy; and the Yeas and Nays of the Members of either House on any question shall, at the Desire of one fifth of those Present, be entered on the Journal.

Neither House, during the Session of Congress, shall, without the Consent of the other, adjourn for more than three days, nor to any other Place than that in which the two Houses shall be sitting.

Section. 6. The Senators and Representatives shall receive a Compensation for their Services, to be ascertained by Law, and paid out of the Treasury of the United States. They shall in all Cases, except Treason, Felony and Breach of the Peace, be privileged from Arrest during their Attendance at the Session of their respective Houses, and in going to and returning from the same; and for any Speech or Debate in either House, they shall not be questioned in any other Place.

No Senator or Representative shall, during the Time for which he was elected, be appointed to any civil Office under the Authority of the United States, which shall have been created, or the Emoluments whereof shall have been encreased during such time; and no Person holding any Office under the United States, shall be a Member of either House during his Continuance in Office.

Section. 7. All Bills for raising Revenue shall originate in the House of Representatives; but the Senate may propose or concur with Amendments as on other Bills.

Every Bill which shall have passed the House of Representatives and the Senate, shall, before it become a Law, be presented to the President of the United States; if he approve he shall sign it, but if not he shall return it, with his Objections to that House in which it shall have originated, who shall enter the Objections at large on their Journal, and proceed to reconsider it. If after such Reconsideration two thirds of that House shall agree to pass the Bill, it shall be sent, together with the Objections, to the other House, by which it shall likewise be reconsidered, and if approved by two thirds of that House, it shall become a Law. But in all such Cases the Votes of both Houses shall be determined by yeas and Nays, and the Names of the Persons voting for and against the Bill shall be entered on the Journal of each House respectively. If any Bill shall not be returned by the President within ten Days (Sundays excepted) after it shall have been presented to him, the Same shall be a Law, in like Manner as if he had signed it, unless Congress by their Adjournment prevent its Return, in which Case it shall not be a Law.

Every Order, Resolution, or Vote to which the Concurrence of the Senate and House of Representatives may be necessary (except on a question of Adjournment) shall be presented to the President of the United States; and before the Same shall take Effect, shall be approved by him, or

being disapproved by him, shall be repassed by two thirds of the Senate and House of Representatives, according to the Rules and Limitations prescribed in the Case of a Bill.

Section. 8. The Congress shall have Power To lay and collect Taxes, Duties, Imposts and Excises, to pay the Debts and provide for the common Defence and general Welfare of the United States; but all Duties, Imposts and Excises shall be uniform throughout the United States;

To borrow Money on the credit of the United States;

To regulate Commerce with foreign Nations, and among the several States, and with the Indian Tribes;

To establish an uniform Rule of Naturalization, and uniform Laws on the subject of Bankruptcies throughout the United States;

To coin Money, regulate the Value thereof, and of foreign Coin, and fix the Standard of Weights and Measures;

To provide for the Punishment of counterfeiting the Securities and current Coin of the United States;

To establish Post Offices and post Roads;

To promote the Progress of Science and useful Arts, by securing for limited Times to Authors and Inventors the exclusive Right to their respective Writings and Discoveries;

To constitute Tribunals inferior to the Supreme Court;

To define and punish Piracies and Felonies committed on the high Seas, and Offences against the Law of Nations;

To declare War, grant Letters of Marque and Reprisal, and make Rules concerning Captures on Land and Water;

To raise and support Armies, but no Appropriation of Money to that Use shall be for a longer Term than two Years;

To provide and maintain a Navy;

To make Rules for the Government and Regulation of the land and naval Forces;

To provide for calling forth the Militia to execute the Laws of the Union, suppress Insurrections and repel Invasions;

To provide for organizing, arming, and disciplining, the Militia, and for governing such Part of them as may be employed in the Service of the United States, reserving to the States respectively, the Appointment of the Officers, and the Authority of training the Militia according to the discipline prescribed by Congress;

To exercise exclusive Legislation in all Cases whatsoever, over such District (not exceeding ten Miles square) as may, by Cession of particular States, and the Acceptance of Congress, become the Seat of the Government of the United States, and to exercise like Authority over all Places purchased by the Consent of the Legislature of the State in which the Same shall be, for the Erection of Forts, Magazines, Arsenals, dock-Yards, and other needful Buildings;—And

To make all Laws which shall be necessary and proper for carrying into Execution the foregoing Powers, and all other Powers vested by this Constitution in the Government of the United States, or in any Department or Officer thereof.

Section. 9. The Migration or Importation of such Persons as any of the States now existing shall think proper to admit, shall not be prohibited by the Congress prior to the Year one thousand eight hundred and eight, but a Tax or duty may be imposed on such Importation, not exceeding ten dollars for each Person.

The Privilege of the Writ of Habeas Corpus shall not be suspended, unless when in Cases of Rebellion or Invasion the public Safety may require it.

No Bill of Attainder or ex post facto Law shall be passed.

No Capitation, or other direct, Tax shall be laid, unless in Proportion to the Census or Enumeration herein before directed to be taken.

No Tax or Duty shall be laid on Articles exported from any State.

No Preference shall be given by any Regulation of Commerce or Revenue to the Ports of one State over those of another: nor shall Vessels bound to, or from, one State, be obliged to enter, clear or pay Duties in another.

No Money shall be drawn from the Treasury, but in Consequence of Appropriations made by Law; and a regular Statement and Account of the Receipts and Expenditures of all public Money shall be published from time to time.

No Title of Nobility shall be granted by the United States: And no Person holding any Office of Profit or Trust under them, shall, without the Consent of the Congress, accept of any present, Emolument, Office, or Title, of any kind whatever, from any King, Prince, or foreign State.

Section. 10. No State shall enter into any Treaty, Alliance, or Confederation; grant Letters of Marque and Reprisal; coin Money; emit Bills of Credit; make any Thing but gold and silver Coin a Tender in Payment of Debts; pass any Bill of Attainder, ex post facto Law, or Law impairing the Obligation of Contracts, or Grant any Title of Nobility.

No State shall, without the Consent of the Congress, lay any Imposts or Duties on Imports or Exports, except what may be absolutely necessary for executing its inspection Laws: and the net Produce of all Duties and Imposts, laid by any State on Imports or Exports, shall be for the Use of the Treasury of the United States; and all such Laws shall be subject to the Revision and Controul of the Congress.

No State shall, without the Consent of Congress, lay any Duty of Tonnage, keep Troops, or Ships of War in time of Peace, enter into any Agreement or Compact with another State, or with a foreign Power, or engage in War, unless actually invaded, or in such imminent Danger as will not admit of delay.

ARTICLE. II.

Section. 1. The executive Power shall be vested in a President of the United States of America. He shall hold his Office during the Term of four Years, and, together with the Vice President, chosen for the same Term, be elected, as follows

Each State shall appoint, in such Manner as the Legislature thereof may direct, a Number of Electors, equal to the whole Number of Senators and

Representatives to which the State may be entitled in the Congress: but no Senator or Representative, or Person holding an Office of Trust or Profit under the United States, shall be appointed an Elector.

The Electors shall meet in their respective States, and vote by Ballot for two Persons, of whom one at least shall not be an Inhabitant of the same State with themselves. And they shall make a List of all the Persons voted for, and of the Number of Votes for each; which List they shall sign and certify, and transmit sealed to the Seat of the Government of the United States, directed to the President of the Senate. The President of the Senate shall, in the Presence of the Senate and House of Representatives, open all the Certificates, and the Votes shall then be counted. The Person having the greatest Number of Votes shall be the President, if such Number be a Majority of the whole Number of Electors appointed; and if there be more than one who have such Majority, and have an equal Number of Votes, then the House of Representatives shall immediately chuse by Ballot one of them for President; and if no Person have a Majority, then from the five highest on the List the said House shall in like Manner chuse the President. But in chusing the President, the Votes shall be taken by States, the Representation from each State having one Vote; A quorum for this purpose shall consist of a Member or Members from two thirds of the States, and a Majority of all the States shall be necessary to a Choice. In every Case, after the Choice of the President, the Person having the greatest Number of Votes of the Electors shall be the Vice President. But if there should remain two or more who have equal Votes, the Senate shall chuse from them by Ballot the Vice President.[5]

The Congress may determine the Time of chusing the Electors, and the Day on which they shall give their Votes; which Day shall be the same throughout the United States.

No Person except a natural born Citizen, or a Citizen of the United States, at the time of the Adoption of this Constitution, shall be eligible to the Office of President; neither shall any Person be eligible to that Office who shall not have attained to the Age of thirty five Years, and been fourteen Years a Resident within the United States.

In Case of the Removal of the President from Office, or of his Death, Resignation, or Inability to discharge the Powers and Duties of the said Office, the Same shall devolve on the Vice President, and the Congress may by Law provide for the Case of Removal, Death, Resignation or Inability, both of the President and Vice President, declaring what Officer shall then act as President, and such Officer shall act accordingly, until the Disability be removed, or a President shall be elected.

The President shall, at stated Times, receive for his Services, a Compensation which shall neither be increased nor diminished during the Period for

[5] Superseded by the 12th Amendment.

which he shall have been elected, and he shall not receive within that Period any other Emolument from the United States, or any of them.

Before he enter on the Execution of his Office, he shall take the following Oath or Affirmation:—"I do solemnly swear (or affirm) that I will faithfully execute the Office of President of the United States, and will to the best of my Ability, preserve, protect and defend the Constitution of the United States."

Section. 2. The President shall be Commander in Chief of the Army and Navy of the United States, and of the Militia of the several States, when called into the actual Service of the United States; he may require the Opinion, in writing, of the principal Officer in each of the executive Departments, upon any Subject relating to the Duties of their respective Offices, and he shall have Power to grant Reprieves and Pardons for Offences against the United States, except in Cases of Impeachment.

He shall have Power, by and with the Advice and Consent of the Senate, to make Treaties, provided two thirds of the Senators present concur; and he shall nominate, and by and with the Advice and Consent of the Senate, shall appoint Ambassadors, other public Ministers and Consuls, Judges of the supreme Court, and all other Officers of the United States, whose Appointments are not herein otherwise provided for, and which shall be established by Law: but the Congress may by Law vest the Appointment of such inferior Officers, as they think proper, in the President alone, in the Courts of Law, or in the Heads of Departments.

The President shall have Power to fill up all Vacancies that may happen during the Recess of the Senate, by granting Commissions which shall expire at the End of their next Session.

Section. 3. He shall from time to time give to the Congress Information of the State of the Union, and recommend to their Consideration such Measures as he shall judge necessary and expedient; he may, on extraordinary Occasions, convene both Houses, or either of them, and in Case of Disagreement between them, with Respect to the Time of Adjournment, he may adjourn them to such Time as he shall think proper; he shall receive Ambassadors and other public Ministers; he shall take Care that the Laws be faithfully executed, and shall Commission all the Officers of the United States.

Section. 4. The President, Vice President and all civil Officers of the United States, shall be removed from Office on Impeachment for, and Conviction of, Treason, Bribery, or other high Crimes and Misdemeanors.

ARTICLE. III.

Section. 1. The judicial Power of the United States, shall be vested in one supreme Court, and in such inferior Courts as the Congress may from time to time ordain and establish. The Judges, both of the supreme and inferior Courts, shall hold their Offices during good Behaviour, and shall, at stated Times, receive for their Services, a Compensation, which shall not be diminished during their Continuance in Office.

Section. 2. The judicial Power shall extend to all Cases, in Law and Equity, arising under this Constitution, the Laws of the United States, and Treaties made, or which shall be made, under their Authority;—to all Cases affecting Ambassadors, other public Ministers and Consuls;—to all Cases of admiralty and maritime Jurisdiction;—to Controversies to which the United States shall be a Party;—to Controversies between two or more States;—between a State and Citizens of another State;[6]—between Citizens of different States;—between Citizens of the same State claiming Lands under Grants of different States, and between a State, or the Citizens thereof, and foreign States, Citizens or Subjects.[7]

In all cases affecting Ambassadors, other public Ministers and Consuls, and those in which a State shall be Party, the supreme Court shall have original Jurisdiction. In all the other Cases before mentioned, the supreme Court shall have appellate Jurisdiction, both as to Law and Fact, with such Exceptions, and under such Regulations as the Congress shall make.

The Trial of all Crimes, except in Cases of Impeachment, shall be by Jury; and such Trial shall be held in the State where the said Crimes shall have been committed; but when not committed within any State, the Trial shall be at such Place or Places as the Congress may by Law have directed.

Section. 3. Treason against the United States, shall consist only in levying War against them, or in adhering to their Enemies, giving them Aid and Comfort. No Person shall be convicted of Treason unless on the Testimony of two Witnesses to the same overt Act, or on Confession in open Court.

The Congress shall have Power to declare the Punishment of Treason, but no Attainder of Treason shall work Corruption of Blood, or Forfeiture except during the Life of the Person attainted.

ARTICLE. IV.

Section. 1. Full Faith and Credit shall be given in each State to the public Acts, Records, and judicial Proceedings of every other State. And the Congress may by general Laws prescribe the Manner in which such Acts, Records and Proceedings shall be proved, and the Effect thereof.

Section. 2. The Citizens of each State shall be entitled to all Privileges and Immunities of Citizens in the several States.

A Person charged in any State with Treason, Felony, or other Crime, who shall flee from Justice, and be found in another State, shall on Demand of the executive Authority of the State from which he fled, be delivered up, to be removed to the State having Jurisdiction of the Crime.

No Person held to Service or Labour in one State, under the Laws thereof, escaping into another, shall, in Consequence of any Law or Regulation therein, be discharged from such Service or Labour, but shall be delivered up on Claim of the Party to whom such Service or Labour may be due.[8]

[6] See the 11th Amendment.
[7] *Ibid.*
[8] See 13th Amendment.

Section. 3. New States may be admitted by the Congress into this Union; but no new State shall be formed or erected within the Jurisdiction of any other State; nor any State be formed by the Junction of two or more States, or Parts of States, without the Consent of the Legislatures of the States concerned as well as of the Congress.

The Congress shall have Power to dispose of and make all needful Rules and Regulations respecting the Territory or other Property belonging to the United States; and nothing in this Constitution shall be so construed as to Prejudice any Claims of the United States, or of any particular State.

Section. 4. The United States shall guarantee to every State in this Union a Republican Form of Government, and shall protect each of them against Invasion; and on Application of the Legislature, or of the Executive (when the Legislature cannot be convened) against domestic Violence.

ARTICLE. V.

The Congress, whenever two thirds of both Houses shall deem it necessary, shall propose Amendments to this Constitution, or, on the Application of the Legislatures of two thirds of the several States, shall call a Convention for proposing Amendments, which, in either Case, shall be valid to all Intents and Purposes, as Part of this Constitution, when ratified by the Legislatures of three fourths of the several States, or by Conventions in three fourths thereof, as the one or the other Mode of Ratification may be proposed by the Congress; Provided that no Amendment which may be made prior to the Year One thousand eight hundred and eight shall in any Manner affect the first and fourth Clauses in the Ninth Section of the first Article; and that no State, without its Consent, shall be deprived of its equal Suffrage in the Senate.

ARTICLE. VI.

All Debts contracted and Engagements entered into, before the Adoption of this Constitution, shall be as valid against the United States under this Constitution, as under the Confederation.

This Constitution, and the Laws of the United States which shall be made in Pursuance thereof; and all Treaties made, or which shall be made, under the Authority of the United States, shall be the supreme Law of the Land; and the Judges in every State shall be bound thereby, any Thing in the Constitution or Laws of any State to the Contrary notwithstanding.

The Senators and Representatives before mentioned, and the Members of the several State Legislatures, and all executive and judicial Officers, both of the United States and of the several States, shall be bound by Oath or Affirmation, to support this Constitution; but no religious Test shall ever be required as a Qualification to any Office or public Trust under the United States.

ARTICLE. VII.

The Ratification of the Conventions of nine States, shall be sufficient for the Establishment of this Constitution between the States so ratifying the Same.

DONE in Convention by the Unanimous Consent of the States present the Seventeenth Day of September in the Year of our Lord one thousand seven hundred and Eighty seven and of the Independence of the United States of America the Twelfth In witness whereof We have hereunto subscribed our Names,

G° Washington—Presidt.
and deputy from Virginia

New Hampshire	{ John Langdon Nicholas Gilman
Massachusetts	{ Nathaniel Gorham Rufus King
Connecticut	{ Wm. Saml. Johnson Roger Sherman
New York . . .	Alexander Hamilton
New Jersey	{ Wil: Livingston David Brearley. Wm. Paterson. Jona: Dayton
Pennsylvania	{ B Franklin Thomas Mifflin Robt Morris Geo. Clymer Thos. FitzSimons Jared Ingersoll James Wilson Gouv Morris
Delaware	{ Geo: Read Gunning Bedford jun John Dickinson Richard Bassett Jaco: Broom
Maryland	{ James McHenry Dan of St. Thos. Jenifer Danl Carroll
Virginia	{ John Blair— James Madison Jr.

North Carolina
{ Wm. Blount
Richd. Dobbs Spaight.
Hu Williamson }

South Carolina
{ J. Rutledge
Charles Cotesworth Pinckney
Charles Pinckney
Pierce Butler }

Georgia
{ William Few
Abr Baldwin }

ARTICLES IN ADDITION TO, AND AMENDMENT OF, THE CONSTITUTION OF THE UNITED STATES OF AMERICA, PROPOSED BY CONGRESS, AND RATIFIED BY THE SEVERAL STATES, PURSUANT TO THE FIFTH ARTICLE OF THE ORIGINAL CONSTITUTION.

AMENDMENT I.

[Ratification of the first ten amendments was completed December 15, 1791]

Congress shall make no law respecting an establishment of religion, or prohibiting the free exercise thereof; or abridging the freedom of speech, or of the press; or the right of the people peaceably to assemble, and to petition the Government for a redress of grievances.

AMENDMENT II.

A well regulated Militia, being necessary to the security of a free State, the right of the people to keep and bear Arms, shall not be infringed.

AMENDMENT III.

No Soldier shall, in time of peace be quartered in any house, without the consent of the Owner, nor in time of war, but in a manner to be prescribed by law.

AMENDMENT IV.

The right of the people to be secure in their persons, houses, papers, and effects, against unreasonable searches and seizures, shall not be violated, and no Warrants shall issue, but upon probable cause, supported by Oath or affirmation, and particularly describing the place to be searched, and the persons or things to be seized.

AMENDMENT V.

No person shall be held to answer for a capital, or otherwise infamous crime, unless on a presentment or indictment of a Grand Jury, except in cases arising in the land or naval forces, or in the Militia, when in actual service in time of War or public danger; nor shall any person be subject for the same offence to be twice put in jeopardy of life or limb; nor shall be compelled in any criminal case to be a witness against himself, nor be deprived of life, liberty, or property, without due process of law; nor shall private property be taken for public use, without just compensation.

AMENDMENT VI.

In all criminal prosecutions, the accused shall enjoy the right to a speedy and public trial, by an impartial jury of the State and district wherein the crime shall have been committed, which district shall have been previously ascertained by law, and to be informed of the nature and cause of the accusation; to be confronted with the witness against him; to have compulsory process for obtaining witness in his favor, and to have the Assistance of Counsel for his defence.

AMENDMENT VII.

In Suits at common law, where the value in controversy shall exceed twenty dollars, the right of trial by jury shall be preserved, and no fact tried by a jury, shall be otherwise re-examined in any Court of the United States, than according to the rules of the common law.

AMENDMENT VIII.

Excessive bail shall not be required, nor excessive fines imposed, nor cruel and unusual punishments inflicted.

AMENDMENT IX.

The enumeration in the Constitution, of certain rights, shall not be construed to deny or disparage others retained by the people.

AMENDMENT X.

The powers not delegated to the United States by the Constitution, nor prohibited by it to the States, are reserved to the States respectively, or to the people.

AMENDMENT XI.
[January 8, 1798]

The Judicial power of the United States shall not be construed to extend to any suit in law or equity, commenced or prosecuted against one of the United States by Citizens of another State, or by Citizens or Subjects of any Foreign State.

AMENDMENT XII.

[September 25, 1804]

The Electors shall meet in their respective states and vote by ballot for President and Vice-President, one of whom, at least, shall not be an inhabit- ant of the same state with themselves; they shall name in their ballots the person voted for as President, and in distinct ballots the person voted for as Vice-President, and they shall make distinct lists of all persons voted for as President, and of all persons voted for as Vice-President, and of the number of votes for each, which lists they shall sign and certify, and transmit sealed to the seat of the government of the United States, directed to the President of the Senate;—The President of the Senate shall, in the presence of Senate and House of Representatives, open all the certificates and the votes shall then be counted;—The person having the greatest number of votes for President, shall be the President, if such number be a majority of the whole number of Electors appointed; and if no person have such majority, then from the persons having the highest numbers not exceeding three on the list of those voted for as President, the House of Representatives shall choose immediately, by ballot, the President. But in choosing the President, the votes shall be taken by states, the representation from each state having one vote; a quorum for this purpose shall consist of a member or members from two-thirds of the states, and a majority of all the states shall be necessary to a choice. And if the House of Representatives shall not choose a President whenever the right of choice shall devolve upon them, before the fourth day of March next following,[9] then the Vice-President shall act as President, as in the case of the death or other constitutional disability of the President.— The person having the greatest number of votes as Vice-President, shall be the Vice-President, if such number be a majority of the whole number of Electors appointed, and if no person have a majority, then from the two highest numbers on the list, the Senate shall choose the Vice-President; a quorum for the purpose shall consist of two-thirds of the whole number of Senators, and a majority of the whole number shall be necessary to a choice. But no person constitutionally ineligible to the office of President shall be eligible to that of Vice-President of the United States.

AMENDMENT XIII.

[December 18, 1865]

Section 1. Neither slavery nor involuntary servitude, except as a punish- ment for crime whereof the party shall have been duly convicted, shall exist within the United States, or any place subject to their jurisdiction.

Section 2. Congress shall have power to enforce this article by appropri- ate legislation.

[9] Altered by the 20th Amendment.

AMENDMENT XIV.

[July 28, 1868]

Section 1. All persons born or naturalized in the United States, and subject to the jurisdiction thereof, are citizens of the United States and of the State wherein they reside. No State shall make or enforce any law which shall abridge the privileges or immunities of citizens of the United States; nor shall any state deprive any person of life, liberty, or property, without due process of law; nor deny to any person within its jurisdiction the equal protection of the laws.

Section 2. Representatives shall be apportioned among the several States according to their respective numbers, counting the whole number of persons in each State, excluding Indians not taxed. But when the right to vote at any election for the choice of electors for President and Vice President of the United States, Representatives in Congress, the Executive and Judicial officers of a State, or the members of the Legislature thereof, is denied to any of the male inhabitants of such State, being twenty-one years of age, and citizens of the United States, or in any way abridged, except for participation in rebellion, or other crime, the basis of representation therein shall be reduced in the proportion which the number of such male citizens shall bear to the whole number of male citizens twenty-one years of age in such State.

Section 3. No person shall be a Senator or Representative in Congress, or elector of President and Vice President, or hold any office, civil or military, under the United States, or under any State, who, having previously taken an oath, as a member of Congress, or as an officer of the United States, or as a member of any State legislature, or as an executive or judicial officer of any State, to support the Constitution of the United States, shall have engaged in insurrection or rebellion against the same, or given aid or comfort to the enemies thereof. But Congress may by a vote of two-thirds of each House, remove such disability.

Section 4. The validity of the public debt of the United States, authorized by law, including debts incurred for payment of pensions and bounties for services in suppressing insurrection or rebellion, shall not be questioned. But neither the United States nor any State shall assume or pay any debt or obligation incurred in aid of insurrection or rebellion against the United States, or any claim for the loss or emancipation of any slave; but all such debts, obligations and claims shall be held illegal and void.

Section 5. The Congress shall have power to enforce, by appropriate legislation, the provisions of this article.

AMENDMENT XV.

[March 30, 1870]

Section 1. The right of citizens of the United States to vote shall not be denied or abridged by the United States or by any State on account of race, color, or previous condition of servitude.

Section 2. The Congress shall have power to enforce this article by appropriate legislation.

AMENDMENT XVI.

[February 25, 1913]

The Congress shall have power to lay and collect taxes on incomes, from whatever source derived, without apportionment among the several States, and without regard to any census or enumeration.

AMENDMENT XVII.

[May 31, 1913]

The Senate of the United States shall be composed of two Senators from each State, elected by the people thereof, for six years; and each Senator shall have one vote. The electors in each State shall have the qualifications requisite for electors of the most numerous branch of the State legislatures.

When vacancies happen in the representation of any State in the Senate, the executive authority of such State shall issue writs of election to fill such vacancies: *Provided,* That the legislature of any State may empower the executive thereof to make temporary appointments until the people fill the vacancies by election as the legislature may direct.

This amendment shall not be so construed as to affect the election or term of any Senator chosen before it becomes valid as part of the Constitution.

AMENDMENT XVIII.

[January 29, 1919]

Section 1. After one year from the ratification of this article the manufacture, sale, or transportation of intoxicating liquors within, the importation thereof into, or the exportation thereof from the United States and all territory subject to the jurisdiction thereof for beverage purposes is hereby prohibited.

Sec. 2. The Congress and the several States shall have concurrent power to enforce this article by appropriate legislation.

Sec. 3. This article shall be inoperative unless it shall have been ratified as an amendment to the Constitution by the legislatures of the several States, as provided in the Constitution, within seven years from the date of the submission hereof to the States by the Congress.[10]

AMENDMENT XIX.

[August 26, 1920]

The right of citizens of the United States to vote shall not be denied or abridged by the United States or by any State on account of sex.

Congress shall have power to enforce this article by appropriate legislation.

[10] Repealed by the 21st Amendment.

AMENDMENT XX.

[February 6, 1933]

Section 1. The terms of the President and Vice President shall end at noon on the 20th day of January, and the terms of Senators and Representatives at noon on the 3d day of January, of the years in which such terms would have ended if this article had not been ratified; and the terms of their successors shall then begin.

Sec. 2. The Congress shall assemble at least once in every year, and such meeting shall begin at noon on the 3d day of January, unless they shall by law appoint a different day.

Sec. 3. If, at the time fixed for the beginning of the term of the President, the President elect shall have died, the Vice President elect shall become President. If a President shall not have been chosen before the time fixed for the beginning of his term, or if the President elect shall have failed to qualify, then the Vice President elect shall act as President until a President shall have qualified; and the Congress may by law provide for the case wherein neither a President elect nor a Vice President elect shall have qualified, declaring who shall then act as President, or the manner in which one who is to act shall be selected, and such person shall act accordingly until a President or Vice President shall have qualified.

Sec. 4. The Congress may by law provide for the case of the death of any of the persons from whom the House of Representatives may choose a President whenever the right of choice shall have devolved upon them, and for the case of the death of any of the persons from whom the Senate may choose a Vice President whenever the right of choice shall have devolved upon them.

Sec. 5. Sections 1 and 2 shall take effect on the 15th day of October following the ratification of this article.

Sec. 6. This article shall be inoperative unless it shall have been ratified as an amendment to the Constitution by the legislatures of three-fourths of the several States within seven years from the date of its submission.

AMENDMENT XXI.

[December 5, 1933]

Section 1. The eighteenth article of amendment to the Constitution of the United States is hereby repealed.

Sec. 2. The transportation or importation into any State, Territory, or possession of the United States for delivery or use therein of intoxicating liquors, in violation of the laws thereof, is hereby prohibited.

Sec. 3. This article shall be inoperative unless it shall have been ratified as an amendment to the Constitution by conventions in the several States, as provided in the Constitution, within seven years from the date of the submission hereof to the States by the Congress.

AMENDMENT XXII.

[February 26, 1951]

Section 1. No person shall be elected to the office of the President more than twice, and no person who has held the office of President, or acted as President, for more than two years of a term to which some other person was elected President shall be elected to the office of President more than once. But this Article shall not apply to any person holding the office of President when this Article was proposed by the Congress, and shall not prevent any person who may be holding the office of President, or acting as President, during the term within which this Article becomes operative from holding the office of President or acting as President during the remainder of such term.

Sec. 2. This article shall be inoperative unless it shall have been ratified as an amendment to the Constitution by the legislatures of three-fourths of the several States within seven years from the date of its submission to the States by the Congress.

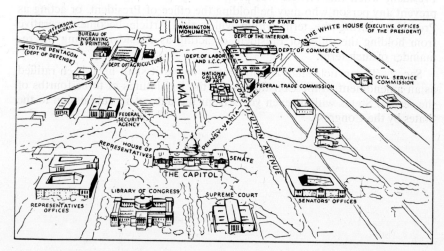

Key to aerial photograph of Washington, D.C., on title page.

Index

2930

LEGISLATIVE

THE CONGRESS

Senate House

{ Architect of the Capitol

General Accounting Office

Government Printing Office

Library of Congress

United States Botanic Garden

THE CONSTITUTION

EXECUTIVE

THE PRESIDENT

{ Executive Office of the President

The White House Office

Bureau of the Budget

Council of Economic Advisers

National Security Council

Office of Defense Mobilization

JUDICIAL

THE SUPREME COURT
of the United States

{ United States Courts of Appeals

District Courts of the United States

United States Court of Claims

United States Court of Customs and
Patent Appeal

United States Customs Court

Territorial Courts

Note: This chart, adapted from U.S. Government Organization Manual,
seeks to show only the more important agencies of the Federal Government.